20th Century
Literary Criticism

A READER

Edited by David Lodge

LONGMAN

LONGMAN GROUP LIMITED
London
Associated companies, branches and representatives throughout the world

© David Lodge 1972

First published 1972
ISBN 0 582 48422 7

Manufactured in the United States of America

Contents

[Note: titles in square brackets are the editor's]

A *Contents arranged in chronological order of first publication*

Contents

iv

Contents

B *Contents arranged according to the literary form or topic principally discussed*

Contents

Contents

Contents

C Contents arranged according to the critical method or approach exhibited or discussed

Contents

Contents

Contents

Acknowledgements

We are grateful to the following for permission to reproduce copyright material: Calder & Boyars Ltd for 'A Future for the Novel' from *For a New Novel* by Alain Robbe-Grillet, translated by Richard Howard (1965); Cambridge University Press for 'Regulated Hatred: an aspect of the work of Jane Austen' by Denys Harding from *Scrutiny*; Charles Scribner's Sons for the Preface to *The Ambassadors* by Henry James (Copyright 1909 Charles Scribner's Sons; renewal copyright 1937 Henry James) is reprinted with the permission of Charles Scribner's Sons from *The Art of the Novel* by Henry James; Chatto & Windus Ltd for extracts from 'Realism and the Contemporary Novel' from *The Long Revolution* by Raymond Williams, for 'Restoration Comedy: the reality and the myth' from *Explorations* by L. C. Knights, an extract from *Seven Types of Ambiguity* by William Empson, and an extract of 'Illustrations from Popular Art—Peg's Paper', Chapter 4 Section 'C' from *The Uses of Literacy* by Richard Hoggart; The University of Chicago Press for 'General Rules, II: All Authors Should Be Objective' from Chapter iii of *The Rhetoric of Fiction* by Wayne Booth; Dennis Dobson Publishers for 'The Language of Paradox' from *The Well-Wrought Urn* by Cleanth Brooks; Edward Arnold (Publishers) Ltd for Chapter 4 of *Aspects of the Novel* by E. M. Forster; Encounter Ltd for 'The Middle Against Both Ends' by Leslie Fiedler from *Encounter*, v (1955); Essays in Criticism for 'The First Paragraph of *The Ambassadors*: an explication' by Ian Watt from *Essays in Criticism*, x (July 1960); Faber & Faber Ltd for an extract of 'Writing' from *The Dyer's Hand* by W. H. Auden, for 'Tradition and the Individual Talent' and 'The Function of Criticism' from *Selected Essays* by T. S. Eliot, for an extract of 'A Retrospect' from *Literary Essays of Ezra Pound* by Ezra Pound edited by T. S. Eliot, and 'F. R. Leavis' from *Language and Silence* by George Steiner; Farrar, Straus & Giraux Inc. Book Publishers for 'Technique as Discovery' by Mark Schorer from *The Hudson Review*, i (1948); Geoffrey Bles Ltd for *De Descriptione Temporum* by C. S. Lewis from *They Asked for a Paper*; Harcourt Brace Jovanovich Inc. for 'The Archetypes of Literature' and 'Literature as Context: Milton's *Lycidas*' from *Fables of Identity* by Northrop Frye; A. M. Heath & Co. Ltd for 'Politics and the English Language' from *Collected Essays* by George Orwell; The Hogarth Press Ltd, Quentin Bell and Angelica Garnett for an extract from *The Common Reader* by Virginia Woolf; Sigmund Freud Copyrights Ltd. The Institute of Psycho-Analysis and The Hogarth Press Ltd for 'Creative Writers and Day-Dreaming' from Vol. IX of the Standard Edition of the *Complete Psychological Works* of Sigmund Freud, revised and edited by James Strachey; Jonathan Cape Ltd for an extract from *The Scope of Anthropology* by Claude Lévi-Strauss, translated by Sherry Ortner Paul and Robert A. Paul; Macmillan & Co. Ltd for 'A Dialectic of

Aural and Objective Correlatives' from *The Barbarian Within* by Walter J. Ong, and for extracts from 'English Poets II. The Industrial Revolution' from *Illusion and Reality: a study of the sources of poetry* by Christopher Caudwell; Martin Secker & Warburg Ltd for 'Freud and Literature' from *The Liberal Imagination* by Lionel Trilling; Merlin Press Ltd for extracts from 'The Ideology of Modernism' from *The Meaning of Contemporary Realism* by Georg Lukács, translated by John and Necke Mander; Methuen & Co. Ltd for 'The Intentional Fallacy' and 'The Affective Fallacy' from *The Verbal Icon* by W. K. Wimsatt Jnr. and Monroe C. Beardsley, 'Macbeth and the Metaphysic of Evil', Ch. viii, from *The Wheel of Fire* by G. Wilson Knight, and Ch. 11 'Why Write?' from *What is Literature* by Jean-Paul Sartre translated by Bernard Frechtman; Oxford University Press for extracts from *Archetypal Patterns in Poetry* by Maud Bodkin and 'Orientation of Critical Theories', Introduction to *The Mirror and the Lamp* by M. H. Abrams (1953); Laurence Pollinger Ltd for the title essay from *Against Interpretation* by Susan Sontag, and 'Morality and the Novel', 'Why the Novel Matters' and 'The Spirit of Place' from *Selected Literary Criticism* by D. H. Lawrence, edited by Anthony Beale; Princeton University Press for 'Odysseus' Scar' Chapter 1 of *Mimesis* by Erich Auerbach, translated by Willard Trask (1953), and for 'Oedipus Rex: the Tragic Rhythm of Action' (minus the last section), from *The Idea of a Theater* by Francis Fergusson; Routledge & Kegan Paul Ltd for an extract from Chapter 13, 'The Experimental Vision' from *Life Against Death* by Norman O. Brown (1959), 'Romanticism and Classicism' from *Speculations* by T. E. Hulme, 'The Four Kinds of Meaning' from *Practical Criticism* by I. A. Richards, extracts from 'The Two Uses of Language' Chapter xxiv of *Principles of Literary Criticism* by I. A. Richards, 'Communication and the Artist' Chapter IV of *Principles of Literary Criticism* by I. A. Richards, 'Psychology and Literature', Chapter VIII of *Modern Man in Search of a Soul* by C. G. Jung. translated by W. S. Dell and Cary F. Baynes, extract of 'Poetry and Abstract Thought' from *The Art of Poetry*, translated by Denise Folliot (vol. VII of the *Collected Works* of Paul Valéry), for 'Preliminary Problems' from *In Defence of Reason* by Yvor Winters, for extracts from *The Gütenberg Galaxy* by Marshall McLuhan, for 'Objects, Jokes, and Art' Part ii of 'The Modern' from *Continuities* by Frank Kermode, and for 'The Houyhnhnms, the Yahoos, and The History of Ideas' from *The Idea of the Humanities and other essays*, Vol. II by R. S. Crane; Charles Scribner's Sons for 'Criticism Inc.' (Copyright 1937 University of Virginia; renewal copyright © 1964 John Crowe Ransom) is reprinted by permission of Charles Scribner's Sons from *The World's Body* by John Crowe Ransom; The *Sewanee Review* as first publisher (Copyright © 1960 by The University of the South) for 'Literary Theory, Criticism, and History' from *Concepts of Criticism* by René Wellek; *The Times* for 'Criticism as Language' from *The Critical Moment* by Roland Barthes, which first appeared in *The Times Literary Supplement* in 1963; A. P. Watt & Son, Macmillan & Co. Ltd and Mr M. B. Yeats for 'The Symbolism of Poetry' by W. B. Yeats, from *Selected Criticism*, edited by Norman Jeffares; Wesleyan University Press, for Copyright © 1959 by Wesleyan University, 'The Exremental Vision' is Chapter 13 of *Life Against Death* by Norman O. Brown, reprinted by permission of Wesleyan University Press; and Mr Edmund Wilson for an extract of 'Marxism and Literature' from *The Triple Thinkers* by Edmund Wilson.

Acknowledgements

We are grateful to the following for permission to reproduce copyright material in the U.S.A.: Atheneum Publishers Inc. for an extract of 'F. R. Leavis' from *Language and Silence* by G. Steiner 1962, 1976 © G. Steiner, repr. by permission of the publishers; Basic Books Inc. for 'The Relation of the Poet to Day-dreaming' in *Collected Papers*, IV/9 by S. Freud, ed. E. Jones M.D., authorised transl. supervised by J. Riviere, pubd by Basic Books Inc. New York, by arrangement with The Hogarth Press Ltd., and The Institute of Psycho-analysis, London; Cambridge Univ. Press for 'Regulated Hatred: an Aspect of the Work of Jane Austen' by D. Harding from *Scrutiny*, VIII; Jonathan Cape Ltd., for an extract from *The Scope of Anthropology*, transl. S. O. and R. A. Paul, dist. in the U.S.A. by Grossman Publishers Inc; Chatto & Windus Ltd., for extracts from 'Realism and the Contemporary Novel' from *The Long Revolution* by R. Wilson and 'Restoration Comedy: the Reality and the Myth' from *Explorations* by L. C. Knight; The Univ. of Chicago Press for 'General Rules II: All Authors Should Be Objective' from *The Rhetoric of Fiction* by W. Booth; Columbia Univ. Press for 'The Houyhnhnms, The Yahoos and the History of Ideas' by R. S. Crane in *Reason and the Imagination: Studies in the History of Ideas*, I, ed. J. A. Mazzeo; Curtis Brown Ltd. for 'De Descriptione Temporum' from *The World's Last Night* (American title) by C. S. Lewis © 1960, pubd by Harcourt Brace Jovanovich Inc., repr. by permission of Curtis Brown Ltd; Encounter Ltd. and the author L. Fiedler for 'The Middle against Both Ends' from *Encounter* V (1955); *Essays in Criticism* for the first paragraph of 'The Ambassadors: an Explication', by I. Watt from *Essays in Criticism*, X (July 196); Farrer, Straus & Giroux Inc., for title essay from *Against Interpretation* by S. Sontag and 'Technique as Discovery' from *The World We Imagine: Selected Essays* by M. Schorer © 1948, 1949, 1953, 1956, 1957, 1959, 1962, 1963, 1968, repr. by permission of the publishers; Grove Press Inc., for 'A Future for the Novel' from *For A New Novel* by A. Robbe-Grillet, transl. R. Howard, © 1965 by Grove Press Inc.; Harcourt Brace Jovanovich Inc., for 'The Arche-types of Literature' and 'Literature as Context: Milton's Lycidas' from *Fables of Identity* by N. Frye, for an extract from *The Common Reader* by V. Woolf, © 1925 by Harcourt Brace Jovanovich Inc., © 1953 by L. Woolf, for 'Tradition and the Individual Talent' and 'The Function of Criticism' from *Selected Essays* of T. S. Eliot, © 1932, 1936, 1950 by Harcourt Jovanovich Inc., renewed 1960, 1964 by T. S. Eliot, for 'The Language of Paradox' from *The Well Wrought Urn* © 1947 renewed by Cleanth Brooks, for *Aspects of the Novel*, Ch. 4, by E. M. Forster © 1927 by Harcourt Brace Jovanovich Inc., renewed 1955 by E. M. Forster, for 'Politics and the English Language' from *Shooting an Elephant and Other Essays* by G. Orwell © 1946, 1947, 1949, 1950 by S. B. Orwell © 1973, 1974 by S. Orwell, for 'The Four Kinds of Meaning' from *Practical Criticism* by I. A. Richards, for extracts from 'The Two Uses of Language' Ch. 24 and 'Communication and the Artist' Ch. 4 of *Principles of Literary Criticism* by I. A. Richards and for 'Psychology and Literature' Ch. 8 from *Modern Man in Search of a Soul* by C. G. Jung, transl. W. S. Dell and C. F. Baynes, all repr. by permission of the publishers; Harper & Row Publishers Inc., for 'Why Write' Ch. 2 from *What is Literature?* by J.-P. Sartre © 1965, copyright 1949 by Philosophical Library Inc., repr. by permission of the publishers; The Univ. Press of Kentucky for 'The Intentional Fallacy' and 'The Affective Fallacy' from *The Verbal Icon* by W. K. Wimsatt Jnr. and M. C. Beardsley; the author's agent and author F. Kermode for 'Objects, Jokes and Art' Part ii of 'The Modern' from *Continuities* pubd by Random House, repr. by permission of A. D. Peters & Co. Ltd.; Macmillan Publishing Co. for extracts from 'English Poets II: The Industrial Revolution' from *Illusion and Reality: A Study of Sources of Poetry* by C. Caudwell, repr. by permission of Macmillan London & Basingstoke; Macmillan Publishing Co. Inc. for 'A Dialectic of Aural and Objective Correlatives' from *The Barbarian Within* by W. J. Ong and Macmillan Publishing Co. Inc., and M. B. Yeats for 'The Sym-bolism of Poetry' from *Essays and Introductions* by W. B. Yeats; Merlin Press Ltd., for extracts from 'The Ideology of Modernism' from *The Meaning of Contemporary Realism* by G. Lukács, transl. J. and N. Mander; Methuen & Co. Ltd., for 'Macbeth and the Metaphysics of Evil' from *The Wheel of Fire* by G. Wilson-Knight; New Directions

Publishing Corp. for an extract from *Seven Types of Ambiguity* by W. Empson (All Rights Reserved) and for an extract of 'A Retrospect' from *Literary Essays* by E. Pound © 1918, 1920, 1935 by E. Pound, repr. by permission of the publishers; Oxford Univ. Press for extracts from *Archetypal Patterns in Poetry* by M. Bodkin; Oxford Univ. Press (New York) for 'Orientation of Critical Theories' an introduction to *The Mirror and the Lamp: Romantic Theory and the Critical Tradition* by M. H. Abrams © 1953 by Oxford Univ. Press Inc. and for 'Illustrations from Popular Art—Peg's Paper' from *The Uses of Literacy*, Ch. 4/C by R. Hoggart, repr. by permission of the publishers; Princeton Univ. Press for extract 'Poetry and Abstract Thought' from *The Collected Works of Paul Valéry*, ed. J. Mathews, Bollingen Series 25/VII, *The Art of Poetry* transl. D. Folliot © 1958 by Bollingen Foundation, for 'Odysseus's Scar' from *Mimesis: The Representation of Reality in Western Literature* by E. Auerbach, transl. W. R. Trask © 1953 by Princeton Univ. Press, Princeton Paperback 1968 and for selections from 'Oedipus Rex: The Tragic Rhythm of Action' in *The Idea of a Theater: A Study of Ten Plays, The Art of Drama in Changing Perspective* by F. Fergusson © 1949 Princeton Paperback, rev. edn. 1968, all repr. by permission of the publisher; Random House Inc., for an extract of 'Writing' repr. from *The Dyer's Hand and Other Essays* by W. H. Auden © 1962; Charles Scribner's Sons for 'Freud and Literature' from *The Liberal Imagination* © 1940, 1947 by L. Trilling, for the preface to *The Ambassadors* by H. James © 1909 by Charles Scribner's Sons, renewal copyright 1937 H. James, reprinted with permission of Charles Scribner's Sons from *The Art of the Novel* by H. James and for 'Criticism Inc.' (copyright 1937 Univ. of Virginia: renewal © 1964 J. C. Ransom) repr. by permission of Charles Scribner's Sons from *The World's Body* by J. C. Ransom; The *Sewanee Review* as first publisher (copyright 1960 by the Univ. of the South) for 'Literary Theory, Criticism and History' from *Concepts of Criticism* by R. Wellek; The Swallow Press Inc. for an extract from 'Preliminary Problems' from *In Defense of Reason* © 1937, 1947 by Y. Winters repr. by permission of the publishers; *The Times* for 'Criticism as Language' from *The Critical Moment* by R. Barthes from the *Times Literary Supplement* in 1963; Univ. of Toronto Press for an extract from *The Gutenberg Galaxy* by M. McLuhan by permission of Univ. of Toronto Press © 1962; The Viking Press Inc., for 'The Spirit of Place' from *Studies in Classic American Literature* by D. H. Lawrence, copyright 1923, 1951 by F. Lawrence, copyright 1961 by the Estate of the late Mrs F. Lawrence, and for 'Morality and the Novel' and 'Why the Novel Matters' from *Phoenix*, I by D. H. Lawrence copyright 1936 by F. Lawrence, © 1964 by the Estate of the late Frieda Lawrence Ravagli (All Rights Reserved) repr. by permission of the publishers; Wesleyan Univ. Press for Ch. 13 'The Excremental Vision' from *Life Against Death* by N. O. Brown copyright 1959 repr. by permission; and E. Wilson for an extract of 'Marxism and Literature' from *The Triple Thinkers* by E. Wilson.

Foreword

The uses of this book

The compilation of this Reader has grown out of the editor's experience of teaching a course in the history, theory, and practice of literary criticism at Birmingham University, and it has been designed, in the first instance, for use as a textbook in such courses in colleges and universities. The arrangement of contents and the apparatus of introductory and explanatory notes will also enable the individual student who is not pursuing a formal course in the subject to acquaint himself with the basic map of modern literary criticism and to pursue more detailed investigation into authors and topics of particular interest to him. Finally, by referring to the index, the student may use the Reader as an anthology of critical comment by the most distinguished critics of this century upon a good deal of the world's great literature, past and present. Although it is intended primarily for students of English and American literature, the Reader should also be of interest and value to students of other literatures, since the problems discussed and the methods displayed in most of the pieces collected here are relevant to literature in general.

There are, of course, teachers of literature who believe that students should be discouraged from reading criticism, on the grounds that such reading blunts their capacity for independent response and judgment. While respecting the educational motives behind this argument, I do not think it will survive scrutiny. A moment's reflection will reveal that there is no such thing as a completely independent, unconditioned response to a literary text. Works of literature have their meaning, and their very existence, in a continual stream of human conversation *about* them, which at its most formalized and articulate we call literary criticism. The main point of studying literature in an academic context is to get into this conversation at its highest levels, to listen and to participate; and it is a conversation, one should remember, not only about individual works and individual authors, but also about larger blocks of literary materials, and about theoretical problems of intellectual method, aesthetics, communication, and epistemology. To offer students instruction and guidance in this regard seems self-evidently useful and desirable. In this way they will learn discrimination in the use of secondary materials and extend their own critical potentialities. They will learn, too, that no single method or approach can answer all the questions that may legitimately be asked about a work of literature, nor exhaust the sources of possible interest within it.

It is something of a commonplace that the modern era is particularly rich in literary criticism—that, indeed, many men who in other periods might have distinguished themselves as creative writers, or as moralists, philosophers, and men of affairs, have in our century communicated their ideas or expressed themselves in one form or another of literary criticism. We are often told that most of the scientists in the history of the world are living at this moment; very nearly the same ratio probably obtains in the field of criticism. This seems to be partly the consequence of the spectacular expansion of university education in this century, which has made academe the natural habitat of the literary intellectual; and partly a more mysterious manifestation of the *Zeitgeist*, implying some widespread distrust or disablement of the fictive imagination, and a corresponding tendency to fall back upon the creative monuments of the past, suitably reinterpreted to fit our needs and preoccupations. Such an emphasis on criticism can certainly be invoked easily enough as evidence of cultural decadence, but whether it is welcomed or deplored, it is a fact that must be faced by students and teachers of literature. In our era, criticism is not merely a library of secondary aids to the understanding and appreciation of literary texts, but also a rapidly increasing body of knowledge in its own right, and a primary vehicle for the values and ideas of the literary imagination. The sheer quantity and diversity of modern criticism, however, makes it a daunting area for exploration. Where does one begin? What are the main landmarks, the useful trails, the crucial difficulties and dangers? It is hoped that this Reader will serve as a useful map or guide to this difficult, problematical territory.

Scope and criteria of selection

The chronological span of the Reader is the twentieth century. The aim has been to represent the varieties, achievements, and developments of literary criticism in this period as fully as possible in the space available. Since the Reader is designed in the first place for students of literature in English, the selection is heavily biased towards English and American criticism, but European writers whose work has entered into the mainstream of Anglo-American critical debate, or significantly impinged on it, have also been included. Some of these writers—e.g. Freud and Jung—are not, strictly speaking, literary critics, but thinkers whose ideas have profoundly affected literary critics. Inevitably the selection reflects the editor's own conscious and unconscious preferences, but I have tried as far as possible to include all the critics of universally recognized originality and distinction who come within the above terms of reference. I very much regret that Dr F. R. Leavis was unwilling to allow any of his criticism to be included: fortunately, it is widely available, and the appraisal by George Steiner reprinted below (see pp. 622-35) provides a basis for studying and discussing it.

In no other case was the editor prevented from including an author of his choice. Individual distinction of the critic was not, however, the only criterion.

The aim of the Reader is also to display as fully as possible the varieties of method and approach exhibited by modern literary criticism. This desideratum has conditioned the selection of authors and in many cases the choice of a particular item from a writer's *oeuvre*. I have also tried to keep a reasonable balance between the following categories: English and American criticism; academic criticism and the criticism of practising writers; descriptive and theoretical criticism; criticism that has already acquired a kind of classical status, and criticism that is still the subject of lively interest and controversy. Finally, I have, where possible, selected items that naturally invite comparison and cross reference in pairs, or in larger groups, because they are concerned with the same texts, or similar issues, or directly refer to each other.

Arrangement of contents, apparatus, and editorial conventions

The essays and extracts are arranged in chronological order of first publication. Where two or more items by any one critic are included, they are grouped together and placed according to the first publication of the earliest item. The text of any item is not, however, necessarily that of the first published version. For example, in the case of periodical essays subsequently collected in book form, the text has usually been taken from the book. In every case, the source of the text is given in the introductory notes.

There is one exception to the chronological arrangement of contents: M. H. Abrams's 'Orientation of critical theories', first published as the opening chapter of *The Mirror and the Lamp* (1953), is placed at the beginning of the Reader to serve as a general introduction. It surveys the historical development of literary criticism up to the modern period and provides a useful conceptual scheme for distinguishing between different kinds of critical principles and practice.

Read through in the order presented (A), the contents of the Reader should convey a sense of the historical development of modern literary criticism (allowing for the fact that individual critics may be represented by their early, middle, or late work). There are, however, other and equally useful ways of studying the same materials, and to this end two alternative lists of contents have been provided which group the essays and extracts (B) according to the subject matter discussed and (C) according to the approach or orientation of the critic. Furthermore, at the end of each introductory note, under the heading 'Cross reference', the student's attention is directed to other closely related items in the Reader for comparison and contrast. Finally, by using the index, the student may compare all the comments which occur in the Reader on any particular text or writer.

The introductory note on each critic gives essential biographical and bibliographical information, and attempts to place the selected specimen of his work in its immediate and wider contexts. In addition to the cross references mentioned above, the editor has, where appropriate, listed, under the heading 'Commentary', one or two books or articles in which the critic concerned is discussed. In these ways the student is helped to extend and deepen his knowledge of the critics represented in the Reader by further independent study.

Authors' notes and references are keyed by numerals and are in all cases gathered at the end of the relevant essay or extract. Footnotes keyed by letters of the alphabet are the editor's. In writing these explanatory notes I have borne in mind that references and allusions which are familiar to professional scholars and critics may be puzzling to students, and I have tried to clarify any ambiguities or obscurities caused by extracting a piece of criticism from its original context. In those cases where only a few words seemed required (for example, when translating a foreign phrase) I have interpolated them in the text in square brackets. All matter within square brackets is editorial, including titles, when the latter have been supplied or amended for the purposes of this Reader.

The dates given for books mentioned in the editorial matter are dates of first publication, and the place of publication is London unless otherwise indicated.

In compiling this book I have gratefully received advice and information from sources too numerous to name; but I should like to acknowledge a special indebtedness to two friends with whom it has been my pleasure and privilege to collaborate in teaching courses in criticism : Malcolm Bradbury and Michael Green.

D.L.

1   M. H. Abrams

The orientation of critical theories' is the first chapter of *The Mirror and the Lamp: romantic theory and the critical tradition* (1953). In his Preface, Professor Abrams explains: 'The title of the book identifies two common and antithetical metaphors of mind, one comparing the mind to a reflector of external objects, the other to a radiant projector which makes a contribution to the objects it perceives. The first of these was characteristic of much of the thinking from Plato to the eighteenth century; the second typifies the prevailing Romantic conception of the poetic mind.' The principal subject of Professor Abrams's brilliant study is the supersession of the first attitude by the second, and the ramifications of the latter in aesthetics, poetics, and practical criticism. But his introductory chapter also provides a concise history of criticism and a simple diagrammatic scheme for discriminating various kinds of critical theory and practice. It thus constitutes the best possible introduction to the study of modern criticism, and for this reason has been placed, out of chronological order, at the beginning of this Reader.

M. H. Abrams (b. 1912) was educated at Harvard and is Whiton Professor of English at Cornell University. In addition to *The Mirror and the Lamp*, which was awarded the Christian Gauss Prize in 1954, his publications include A *Glossary of Literary Terms* (New York, 1957) and the Norton *Anthology of English Literature* (New York, 1962).

Orientation of critical theories

BOSWELL. 'Then, Sir, what is poetry?'

JOHNSON. 'Why, Sir, it is much easier to say what it is not. We all *know* what light is; but it is not easy to *tell* what it is.'

It is the mark of an educated man to look for precision in each class of things just so far as the nature of the subject admits.

ARISTOTLE, *Nicomachean Ethics*

To pose and answer aesthetic questions in terms of the relation of art to the artist, rather than to external nature, or to the audience, or to the internal requirements of the work itself, was the characteristic tendency of modern criticism up to a few decades ago, and it continues to be the propensity of a great many—perhaps the majority—of critics today. This point of view is very young measured against the twenty-five-hundred-year history of the Western theory of art, for its emergence as a comprehensive approach to art, shared by a large number of critics, dates back not much more than a century and a half. The intention of this book is to chronicle the evolution and (in the early nineteenth century) the triumph, in its diverse forms, of this radical shift to the artist in the alignment of aesthetic thinking, and to describe the principal alternate theories against which this approach had to compete. In particular, I shall be concerned with the momentous consequences of these new bearings in criticism for the identification, the analysis, the evaluation, and the writing of poetry.

The field of aesthetics presents an especially difficult problem to the historian. Recent theorists of art have been quick to profess that much, if not all, that has been said by their predecessors is wavering, chaotic, phantasmal. 'What has gone by the name of the philosophy of art' seemed to Santayana 'sheer verbiage'. D. W. Prall, who himself wrote two excellent books on the subject, commented that traditional aesthetics 'is in fact only a pseudo-science or pseudo-philosophy'.

> Its subject matter is such wavering and deceptive stuff as dreams are made of; its method is neither logical nor scientific, nor quite whole-heartedly and empirically matter of fact ... without application in practice to test it and without an orthodox terminology to make it into an honest superstition or a thorough-going, soul satisfying cult. It is neither useful to creative artists nor a help to amateurs in appreciation.[1]

And I. A. Richards, in his *Principles of Literary Criticism*, labelled his first chapter 'The Chaos of Critical Theories', and justified the pejorative attribute by quoting, as 'the apices of critical theory', more than a score of isolated and violently discrepant utterances about art, from Aristotle to the present time.[2] With the optimism of his youth, Richards himself went on to attempt a solid grounding of literary evaluation in the science of psychology.

It is true that the course of aesthetic theory displays its full measure of the rhetoric and logomachy which seem an inseparable part of man's discourse about all things that really matter. But a good deal of our impatience with the diversity and seeming chaos in philosophies of art is rooted in a demand from criticism for something it cannot do, at the cost of overlooking many of its genuine powers. We still need to face up to the full consequences of the realization that criticism is not a physical, nor even a psychological, science. By setting out from and terminating in an appeal to the facts, any good aesthetic theory is, indeed, empirical in method. Its aim, however, is not to establish correlations between facts which will enable us to predict the future by reference to the past, but to establish principles enabling us to justify, order, and clarify our interpretation and appraisal of the aesthetic facts themselves. And as we shall see, these facts turn out to have the curious and scientifically reprehensible property of being conspicuously altered by the nature of the very principles which appeal to them for their support. Because many critical statements of fact are thus partially relative to the perspective of the theory within which they occur, they are not 'true', in the strict scientific sense that they approach the ideal of being verifiable by any intelligent human being, no matter what his point of view. Any hope, therefore, for the kind of basic agreement in criticism that we have learned to expect in the exact sciences is doomed to disappointment.

A good critical theory, nevertheless, has its own kind of validity. The criterion is not the scientific verifiability of its single propositions, but the scope, precision, and coherence of the insights that it yields into the properties of single works of art and the adequacy with which it accounts for diverse kinds of art. Such a criterion will, of course, justify not one, but a number of valid theories, all in their several ways self-consistent, applicable, and relatively adequate to the range of aesthetic phenomena; but this diversity is not to be deplored. One lesson we gain from a survey of the history of criticism, in fact, is the great debt we owe to the variety of the criticism of the past. Contrary to Prall's pessimistic appraisal, these theories have not been futile, but as working conceptions of the matter, end, and ordonnance of art, have been greatly effective in shaping the activities of creative artists. Even an aesthetic philosophy so abstract and seemingly academic as that of Kant can be shown to have modified the work of poets. In modern times, new departures in literature almost invariably have been accompanied by novel critical pronouncements, whose very inadequacies sometimes help to form the characteristic qualities of the correlated literary achievements, so that if our critics had not disagreed so violently, our artistic inheritance would doubtless have been less rich and various. Also, the very fact that any well-grounded critical theory in some degree alters the aesthetic perceptions it purports to discover is a source of its value to the amateur of art, for it may open his senses to aspects of a work which other theories, with a different focus and different categories of discrimination, have on principle overlooked, underestimated, or obscured.

The diversity of aesthetic theories, however, makes the task of the historian a very difficult one. It is not only that answers to such questions as 'What is art?' or 'What is poetry?' disagree. The fact is that many theories of art cannot readily be compared at all, because they lack a common ground on which to meet and clash. They seem incommensurable because stated in diverse terms, or in identical terms with diverse signification, or because they are an integral part of larger systems of thought which differ in assumptions and procedure. As a result it is hard to find where they agree, where disagree, or even, what the points at issue are.

Our first need, then, is to find a frame of reference simple enough to be readily manageable, yet flexible enough so that, without undue violence to any one set of statements about art, it will translate as many sets as possible onto a single plane of discourse. Most writers bold enough to undertake the history of aesthetic theory have achieved this end by silently translating the basic terms of all theories into their own favourite philosophical vocabulary,

3

but this procedure unduly distorts its subject matter, and merely multiplies the complications to be unravelled. The more promising method is to adopt an analytic scheme which avoids imposing its own philosophy, by utilizing those key distinctions which are already common to the largest possible number of the theories to be compared, and then to apply the scheme warily, in constant readiness to introduce such further distinctions as seem to be needed for the purpose in hand.

I Some coordinates of art criticism

Four elements in the total situation of a work of art are discriminated and made salient, by one or another synonym, in almost all theories which aim to be comprehensive. First, there is the *work*, the artistic product itself. And since this is a human product, an artifact, the second common element is the artificer, the *artist*. Third, the work is taken to have a subject which, directly or deviously, is derived from existing things—to be about, or signify, or reflect something which either is, or bears some relation to, an objective state of affairs. This third element, whether held to consist of people and actions, ideas and feelings, material things and events, or super-sensible essences, has frequently been denoted by that word-of-all-work, 'nature'; but let us use the more neutral and comprehensive term, *universe*, instead. For the final element we have the *audience*: the listeners, spectators, or readers to whom the work is addressed, or to whose attention, at any rate, it becomes available.

On this framework of artist, work, universe, and audience I wish to spread out various theories for comparison. To emphasize the artificiality of the device, and at the same time make it easier to visualize the analyses, let us arrange the four coordinates in a convenient pattern. A triangle will do, with the work of art, the thing to be explained, in the centre.

UNIVERSE

↑

WORK

↙   ↘

ARTIST   AUDIENCE

Although any reasonably adequate theory takes some account of all four elements, almost all theories, as we shall see, exhibit a discernible orientation towards one only. That is, a critic tends to derive from one of these terms his principal categories for defining, classifying, and analysing a work of art, as well as the major criteria by which he judges its value. Application of this analytic scheme, therefore, will sort attempts to explain the nature and worth of a work of art into four broad classes. Three will explain the work of art principally by relating it to another thing: the universe, the audience, or the artist. The fourth will explain the work by considering it in isolation, as an autonomous whole, whose significance and value are determined without any reference beyond itself.

4

To find the major orientation of a critical theory, however, is only the beginning of an adequate analysis. For one thing, these four coordinates are not constants, but variables; they differ in significance according to the theory in which they occur. Take what I have called the *universe* as an example. In any one theory, the aspects of nature which an artist is said to imitate, or is exhorted to imitate, may be either particulars or types, and they may be only the beautiful or the moral aspects of the world, or else any aspect without discrimination. It may be maintained that the artist's world is that of imaginative intuition, or of common sense, or of natural science; and this world may be held to include, or not to include, gods, witches, chimeras, and Platonic Ideas. Consequently, theories which agree in assigning to the represented universe the primary control over a legitimate work of art may vary from recommending the most uncompromising realism to the most remote idealism. Each of our other terms, as we shall see, also varies, both in meaning and functioning, according to the critical theory in which it occurs, the method of reasoning which the theorist characteristically uses, and the explicit or implicit 'world view' of which these theories are an integral part.

It would be possible, of course, to devise more complex methods of analysis which, even in a preliminary classification, would make more subtle distinctions.[3] By multiplying differentiae, however, we sharpen our capacity to discriminate at the expense both of easy manageability and the ability to make broad initial generalizations. For our historical purpose, the scheme I have proposed has this important virtue, that it will enable us to bring out the one essential attribute which most early nineteenth-century theories had in common: the persistent recourse to the poet to explain the nature and criteria of poetry. Historians have recently been instructed to speak only of 'romanticisms', in the plural, but from our point of vantage there turns out to be one distinctively romantic criticism, although this remains a unity amid variety.

II   Mimetic theories

The mimetic orientation—the explanation of art as essentially an imitation of aspects of the universe—was probably the most primitive aesthetic theory, but mimesis is no simple concept by the time it makes its first recorded appearance in the dialogues of Plato. The arts of painting, poetry, music, dancing, and sculpture, Socrates says, are all imitations.[4] 'Imitation' is a relational term, signifying two items and some correspondence between them. But although in many later mimetic theories everything is comprehended in two categories, the imitable and the imitation, the philosopher in the Platonic dialogues characteristically operates with three categories. The first category is that of the eternal and unchanging Ideas; the second, reflecting this, is the world of sense, natural or artificial; and the third category, in turn reflecting the second, comprises such things as shadows, images in water and mirrors, and the fine arts.

Around this three-stage regress—complicated still further by various supplementary distinctions, as well as by his exploitation of the polysemism of his key terms—Plato weaves his dazzling dialectic.[5] But from the shifting arguments emerges a recurrent pattern, exemplified in the famous passage in the tenth book of the *Republic*. In discussing the nature of art, Socrates makes the point that there are three beds: the Idea which 'is the essence of the bed' and is made by God, the bed made by the carpenter, and the bed found in a painting. How shall we describe the painter of this third bed?

> I think, he said, that we may fairly designate him as the imitator of that which the others make.
> Good, I said; then you call him who is third in the descent from nature an imitator?
> Certainly, he said.
> And the tragic poet is an imitator, and therefore, like all other imitators, he is thrice removed from the king and from the truth?
> That appears to be so.[6]

From the initial position that art imitates the world of appearance and not of Essence, it follows that works of art have a lowly status in the order of existing things. Furthermore, since the realm of Ideas is the ultimate locus not only of reality but of value, the determination that art is at second remove from the truth automatically establishes its equal remoteness from the beautiful and good. Despite the elaborate dialectic—or more accurately, by means of it— Plato's remains a philosophy of a single standard; for all things, including art, are ultimately judged by the one criterion of their relation to the same Ideas. On these grounds, the poet is inescapably the competitor of the artisan, the lawmaker, and the moralist; indeed, any one of these can be regarded as himself the truer poet, successfully achieving that imitation of the Ideas which the traditional poet attempts under conditions dooming him to failure. Thus the lawmaker is able to reply to the poets seeking admission to his city,

> Best of strangers—we also according to our ability are tragic poets, and our tragedy is the best and noblest; for our whole state is an imitation of the best and noblest life, which we affirm to be indeed the very truth of tragedy. You are poets and we are poets ... rivals and antagonists in the noblest of dramas ...[7]

And the poor opinion of ordinary poetry to which we are committed on the basis of its mimetic character, is merely confirmed when Plato points out that its effects on its auditors are bad because it represents appearance rather than truth, and nourishes their feelings rather than their reason; or by demonstrating that the poet in composing (as Socrates jockeys poor obtuse Ion into admitting) cannot depend on his art and knowledge, but must wait upon the divine afflatus and the loss of his right mind.[8]

The Socratic dialogues, then, contain no aesthetics proper, for neither the structure of Plato's cosmos nor the pattern of his dialectic permits us to consider poetry as poetry—as a special kind of product having its own criteria and reason for being. In the dialogues there is only one direction possible, and one issue, that is, the perfecting of the social state and the state of man; so that the question of art can never be separated from questions of truth, justice, and virtue. 'For great is the issue at stake,' Socrates says in concluding his discussion of poetry in the *Republic*, 'greater than appears, whether a man is to be good or bad.'[9]

Aristotle in the *Poetics* also defines poetry as imitation. 'Epic poetry and Tragedy, as also Comedy, Dithyrambic poetry, and most flute-playing and lyre-playing, are all, viewed as a whole, modes of imitation'; and 'the objects the imitator represents are actions ...'[10] But the difference between the way the term 'imitation' functions in Aristotle and in Plato distinguishes radically their consideration of art. In the *Poetics*, as in the Platonic dialogues, the term implies that a work of art is constructed according to prior models in the nature of things, but since Aristotle has shorn away the other world of criterion-Ideas, there is no longer anything invidious in that fact. Imitation is also made a term specific to the arts, distinguishing these from everything else in the universe, and thereby freeing them from rivalry with other human activities. Furthermore, in his analysis of the fine arts, Aristotle at once introduces supplementary distinctions according to the objects imitated, the medium of imitation, and the manner—dramatic, narrative, or mixed, for example— in which the imitation is accomplished. By successive exploitation of these distinctions in object, means, and manner, he is able first to distinguish poetry from other kinds of art, and then to differentiate the various poetic genres, such as epic and drama, tragedy and comedy. When he focuses on the genre of tragedy, the same analytic instrument is applied to the discrimination of the parts constituting the individual whole: plot, character, thought, and so on. Aristotle's criticism, therefore, is not only criticism of art as art, independent of statesmanship, being, and morality, but also of poetry as poetry, and of each kind of poem by the criteria appropriate to its particular nature. As a result of this procedure, Aristotle bequeathed an arsenal of instruments for technical analysis of poetic forms and their elements which have proved indispensable to critics ever since, however diverse the uses to which these instruments have been put.

A salient quality of the *Poetics* is the way it considers a work of art in various of its external relations, affording each its due function as one of the 'causes' of the work. This procedure results in a scope and flexibility that makes the treatise resist a ready classification into any one kind of orientation. Tragedy cannot be fully defined, for example, nor can the total determinants of its construction be understood, without taking into account its proper effect on the audience: the achievement of the specifically 'tragic pleasure', which is 'that of pity and fear'.[11] It is apparent, however, that the mimetic concept—the reference of a work to the subject matter which it imitates— is primary in Aristotle's critical system, even if it is *primus inter pares*. Their character as an imitation of human actions is what defines the arts in general, and the kind of action imitated serves as one important differentia of an artistic species. The historical genesis of art is traced to the natural human instinct for imitating, and to the natural tendency to find pleasure in seeing imitations. Even the unity essential to any work of art is mimetically grounded, since 'one imitation is always of one thing', and in poetry 'the story, as an imitation of action, must represent one action, a complete whole ...'[12] And the 'form' of a work, the presiding principle determining the choice and order and internal adjustments of all the parts, is derived from the form of the object that is imitated. It is the fable or plot 'that is the end and purpose of tragedy', its 'life and soul, so to speak', and this because 'tragedy is essentially an imitation not of persons but of action and life ... We maintain that Tragedy is primarily an imitation of action, and that it is mainly for the sake of the action that it imitates the personal agents.'[13]

If we refer again to our analytic diagram, one other general aspect of the *Poetics* presses on our attention, particularly when we have the distinctive orientation of romantic criticism in mind. While Aristotle makes a distribution (though an unequal one) among the objects imitated, the necessary emotional effects on an audience, and the internal demands of the product itself, as determinants of this or that aspect of a poem, he does not assign a determinative function to the poet himself. The poet is the indispensable efficient cause, the agent who, by his skill, extracts the form from natural things and imposes it upon an artificial medium; but his personal faculties, feelings, or desires are not called on to explain the subject matter or form of a poem. In the *Poetics*, the poet is invoked only to explain the historical divergence of comic from serious forms, and to be advised of certain aids towards the construction of plot and the choice of diction.[14] In Plato, the poet is considered from the point of view of politics, not of art. When the poets make a personal appearance all the major ones are dismissed, with extravagant courtesy, from the ideal Republic; upon later application, a somewhat greater number are admitted to the second-best state of the *Laws*, but with a radically diminished repertory.[15]

'Imitation' continued to be a prominent item in the critical vocabulary for a long time after Aristotle—all the way through the eighteenth century, in fact. The systematic importance given to the term differed greatly from critic to critic; those objects in the universe that art imitates, or should imitate, were variously conceived as either actual or in some sense ideal; and from the first, there was a tendency to replace Aristotle's 'action' as the principal object of imitation with such elements as human character, or thought, or even inanimate things. But particularly after the recovery of the *Poetics* and the great burst of aesthetic theory in sixteenth-century Italy, whenever a critic was moved to get down to fundamentals and frame a comprehensive definition of art, the predicate usually included the word 'imitation', or else one of those parallel terms which, whatever differences they might imply, all faced in the same direction: 'reflection', 'representation', 'counterfeiting', 'feigning', 'copy', or 'image'.

Through most of the eighteenth century, the tenet that art is an imitation seemed almost too obvious to need iteration or proof. As Richard Hurd said in his 'Discourse on Poetical Imitation', published in 1751, 'All *Poetry*, to speak with Aristotle and the Greek critics (if for so plain a point authorities be thought wanting) is, properly, *imitation*. It is, indeed, the noblest and most extensive of the mimetic arts; having all creation for its object, and ranging the entire circuit of universal being.' [16] Even the reputedly radical proponents of 'original genius' in the second half of the century commonly found that a work of genius was no less an imitation for being an original. '*Imitations*,' Young wrote in his *Conjectures on Original Composition*, 'are of two kinds: one of nature, one of authors. The first we call *Originals* ...' The original genius in fact turns out to be a kind of scientific investigator: 'The wide field of nature lies open before it, where it may range unconfined, make what discoveries it can ... as far as visible nature extends ...'[17] Later the Reverend J. Moir, an extremist in his demand for originality in poetry, conceived genius to lie in the ability to discover 'a thousand new variations, distinctions, and resemblances' in the 'familiar phenomena of nature', and declared that original genius always gives 'the identical impression it receives'.[18] In this identification of the poet's task as novelty of discovery and particularity of description we have moved a long way from Aristotle's conception of mimesis, except in this respect, that criticism still looks to one or other aspect of the given world for the essential source and subject matter of poetry.

Instead of heaping up quotations, it will be better to cite a few eighteenth-century discussions of imitation that are of special interest. My first example is the French critic, Charles Batteux, whose *Les Beaux Arts réduits à un même principe* [*The Arts Reduced to a Single Principle*] (1747) found some favour in England and had immense influence in Germany, as well as in his native country. The rules of art, Batteux thought, which are now so numerous, must surely be reducible to a single principle. 'Let us,' he cries, 'imitate the true physicists, who assemble experiments and then on these found a system which reduces them to a principle.'

That Batteux proposes for his procedure 'to begin with a clear and distinct idea'—a principle 'simple enough to be grasped instantly, and extensive enough to absorb all the little detailed rules'—is sufficient clue that he will follow in method not Newton, the physicist, but rather Euclid and Descartes. In pursuance of his clear and distinct idea, he burrowed industriously through the standard French critics until, he says ingenuously, 'it occurred to me to open Aristotle, whose *Poetics* I had heard praised'. Then came the revelation; details fell neatly into place. The source of illumination?—none other than 'the principle of imitation which the Greek philosopher established for the fine arts'.[19] This imitation, however, is not of crude everyday reality, but of 'la belle nature'; that is, 'le vrai-semblable', formed by assembling traits taken from individual things to compose a model possessing 'all the perfections it is able to receive'.[20] From this principle Batteux goes on, lengthily and with great show of rigour, to extract one by one the rules of taste—both the general rules for poetry and painting and the detailed rules for the special genres. For 'the majority of known rules refer back to imitation, and form a sort of chain, by which the mind seizes at the same instant consequences and principles, as a whole perfectly joined, in which all the parts are mutually sustained'.[21]

Next to this classic instance of *a priori* and deductive aesthetics I shall set a German document, Lessing's *Laokoon*, published in 1776. Lessing undertook to undo the confusion in theory and practice between poetry and the graphic and plastic arts which, he believed, resulted from an uninquisitive acceptance of Simonides' maxim that 'painting is dumb poetry and poetry a speaking painting'. His own procedure, he promises, will be continually to test abstract theory against 'the individual instance'. Repeatedly he derides German critics for their reliance on deduction. 'We Germans have no lack of systematic books. We are the most expert of any nation in the world at deducing, from a few given verbal explanations, and in the most beautiful order, anything whatever that we wish.' 'How many things would prove incontestable in theory, had not genius succeeded in proving the contrary in fact!' [22] Lessing's intention, then, is to establish aesthetic principles by an inductive logic which is deliberately opposed to the procedure of Batteux. Nevertheless, like Batteux, Lessing concludes that poetry, no less than painting, is imitation. The diversity between these arts follows from their difference in medium, which imposes necessary differences in the objects each is competent to imitate. But although poetry consists of a sequence of articulate sounds in time rather than of forms and colours fixed in space, and although, instead of being limited, like painting, to a static but pregnant moment, its special power is the reproduction of progressive action, Lessing reiterates for it the standard formula: 'Nachahmung' [Imitation] is still for the poet the attribute 'which constitutes the essence of his art.' [23]

As the century drew on, various English critics began to scrutinize the concept of imitation very closely, and they ended by finding (Aristotle to the contrary) that differences in medium between the arts were such as to disqualify all but a limited number from being classed as mimetic, in any strict sense. The trend may be indicated by a few examples. In 1744 James Harris still maintained, in 'A Discourse on Music, Painting, and Poetry', that imitation was common to all three arts. 'They agree by being all mimetic or imitative. They differ, as they imitate by different media ...' [24] In 1762 Kames declared that 'of all the fine arts, painting only and sculpture are in their nature imitative'; music, like architecture, 'is productive of originals, and copies not from nature'; while language copies from nature only in those instances in which it 'is imitative of sound or motion'.[25] And by 1789, in two closely reasoned dissertations prefixed to his translation of the *Poetics*, Thomas Twining confirmed this distinction between arts whose media are 'iconic' (in the later terminology of the Chicago semiotician, Charles Morris), in that they resemble what they denote, and those which are significant only by convention. Only works in which the resemblance between copy and object is both immediate' and 'obvious', Twining says, can be described as imitative in a strict sense. Dramatic poetry, therefore, in which we mimic speech by speech, is the only kind of poetry which is properly imitation; music must be struck from the list of imitative arts; and he concludes by saying that painting, sculpture, and the arts of design in general are 'the only arts that are *obviously* and *essentially* imitative'.[26]

The concept that art is imitation, then, played an important part in neoclassic aesthetics; but closer inspection shows that it did not, in most theories, play the dominant part. Art, it was commonly said, is an imitation—but an imitation which is only instrumental towards producing effects upon an audience. In fact, the near-unanimity with which post-Renaissance critics lauded and echoed Aristotle's *Poetics* is deceptive. The focus of interest had shifted, and, on our diagram, this later criticism is primarily oriented, not from work to universe, but from work to audience. The nature and consequences of this change of direction is clearly indicated by the first classic of English criticism, written sometime in the early 1580s, Sir Philip Sidney's *The Apologie for Poetry*.

III   Pragmatic theories

> Poesy therefore [said Sidney] is an arte of imitation, for so Aristotle termeth it in the word *Mimesis*, that is to say, a representing, counterfetting, or figuring foorth—to speake metaphorically, a speaking picture: with this end, to teach and delight.[27]

In spite of the appeal to Aristotle, this is not an Aristotelian formulation. To Sidney, poetry, by definition, has a purpose—to achieve certain effects in an audience. It imitates only as a means to the proximate end of pleasing, and pleases, it turns out, only as a means to the ultimate end of teaching; for 'right poets' are those who 'imitate both to delight and teach, and delight to move men to take that goodnes in hande, which without delight they would flye as from a stranger ...'[28] As a result, throughout this essay the needs of the audience become the fertile grounds for critical distinctions and standards. In order 'to teach and delight', poets imitate not 'what is, hath been, or shall be', but only 'what may be, and should be', so that the very objects of imitation become such as to guarantee the moral purpose. The poet is distinguished from, and elevated above, the moral philosopher and the historian by his capacity to move his auditors more forcefully to virtue, since he couples 'the general notion' of the philosopher with 'the particular example' of the historian; while by disguising his doctrine in a tale, he entices even 'harde harted evill men', unaware, into the love of goodness, 'as if they tooke a medicine of Cherries'. The genres of poetry are discussed and ranked from the point of view of the moral and social effect each is suited to achieve: the epic poem thus demonstrates itself to be the king of poetry because it 'most inflameth the mind with desire to be worthy', and even the lowly love lyric is conceived as an instrument for persuading a mistress of the genuineness of her lover's passion.[29] A history of criticism could be written solely on the basis of successive interpretations of salient passages from Aristotle's *Poetics*. In this instance, with no sense of strain, Sidney follows his Italian guides (who in turn had read Aristotle through the spectacles of Horace, Cicero, and the Church fathers) in bending one after another of the key statements of the *Poetics* to fit his own theoretical frame.[30]

For convenience we may name criticism that, like Sidney's, is ordered towards the audience, a 'pragmatic theory', since it looks at the work of art chiefly as a means to an end, an instrument for getting something done, and tends to judge its value according to its success in achieving that aim. There is, of course, the greatest variance in emphasis and detail, but the central tendency of the pragmatic critic is to conceive a poem as something made in order to effect requisite responses in its readers; to consider the author from the point of view of the powers and training he must have in order to achieve this end; to ground the classification and anatomy of poems in large part on the special effects each kind and component is most competent to achieve; and to derive the norms of the poetic art and canons of critical appraisal from the needs and legitimate demands of the audience to whom the poetry is addressed.

The perspective, much of the basic vocabulary, and many of the characteristic topics of pragmatic criticism originated in the classical theory of rhetoric. For rhetoric had been universally regarded as an instrument for achieving persuasion in an audience, and most theorists agreed with Cicero that in order to persuade, the orator must conciliate, inform, and move the minds of his auditors.[31] The great classical exemplar of the application of the rhetorical point of view to poetry was, of course, the *Ars Poetica* of Horace. As Richard McKeon points out, 'Horace's criticism is directed in the main to instruct the poet how to keep his audience in their seats until the end, how to induce cheers and applause, how to please a Roman audience, and by the same token, how to please all audiences and win immortality'.[32]

In what became for later critics the focal passage of the *Ars Poetica*, Horace advised that 'the poet's aim is either to profit or to please, or to blend in one the delightful and the useful'. The context shows that Horace held pleasure to be the chief purpose of poetry, for he recommends the profitable merely as a means to give pleasure to the elders, who, in contrast to the young aristocrats, 'rail at what contains no serviceable lesson'.[33] But *prodesse* and *delectare*, to teach and to please, together with another term introduced from rhetoric, *movere*, to move, served for centuries to collect under three heads the sum of aesthetic effects on the reader. The balance between these terms altered in the course of time. To the overwhelming majority of Renaissance critics, as to Sir Philip Sidney, the moral effect was the terminal aim, to which delight and emotion were auxiliary. From the time of the critical essays of Dryden through the eighteenth century, pleasure tended to become the ultimate end, although poetry without profit was often held to be trivial, and the optimistic moralist believed with James Beattie that if poetry instructs, it only pleases the more effectually.[34]

Looking upon a poem as a 'making', a contrivance for affecting an audience, the typical pragmatic critic is engrossed with formulating the methods—the 'skill, or Crafte of making' as Ben Jonson called it—for achieving the effects desired. These methods, traditionally comprehended under the term *poesis*, or 'art' (in phrases such as 'the art of poetry'), are formulated as precepts and rules whose warrant consists either in their being derived from the qualities of works whose success and long survival have proved their adaptation to human nature, or else in their being grounded directly on the psychological laws governing the responses of men in general. The rules, therefore, are inherent in the qualities of each excellent work of art, and when excerpted and codified these rules serve equally to guide the artist in making and the critics in judging any future product. 'Dryden,' said Dr Johnson, 'may be properly considered as the father of English criticism, as the writer who first taught us to determine upon principles the merit of composition.' [35] Dryden's method of establishing those principles was to point out that poetry, like painting, has an end, which is to please; that imitation of nature is the general means for attaining this end; and that rules serve to specify the means for accomplishing this end in detail:

> Having thus shewn that imitation pleases, and why it pleases in both these arts, it follows, that some rules of imitation are necessary to obtain the end; for without rules there can be no art, any more than there can be a house without a door to conduct you into it.[36]

Emphasis on the rules and maxims of an art is native to all criticism that grounds itself in the demands of an audience, and it survives today in the magazines and manuals devoted to teaching fledgling authors 'how to write stories that sell'. But rulebooks based on the lowest common denominator of the modern buying public are only gross caricatures of the complex and subtly rationalized neoclassic ideals of literary craftsmanship. Through the early part of the eighteenth century, the poet could rely confidently on the trained taste and expert connoisseurship of a limited circle of readers, whether these were Horace's Roman contemporaries under Emperor Augustus, or Vida's at the papal court of Leo X, or Sidney's fellow-courtiers under Elizabeth, or the London audience of Dryden and Pope; while, in theory, the voices even of the best contemporary judges were subordinated to the voice of the ages. Some neoclassic critics were also certain that the rules of art, though empirically derived, were ultimately validated by conforming to that objective structure of norms whose existence guaranteed the rational order and harmony of the universe. In a strict sense, as John Dennis made explicit what was often implied, Nature 'is nothing but that Rule and Order, and Harmony, which we find in the visible Creation'; so 'Poetry, which is an imitation of Nature', must demonstrate the same properties. The renowned masters among the ancients wrote not

> to please a tumultuous transitory Assembly, or a Handful of Men, who were call'd their Countrymen; They wrote to their Fellow-Citizens of the Universe, to all Countries, and to all Ages.... They were clearly convinc'd, that nothing could transmit their Immortal Works to Posterity, but something like that harmonious Order which maintains the Universe...[37]

Although they disagreed concerning specific rules, and although many English critics repudiated such formal French requisites as the unity of time and place, and the purity of comedy and tragedy, all but a few eccentrics among eighteenth-century critics believed in the validity of some set of universal rules. At about mid-century, it became popular to demonstrate and expound all the major rules for poetry, or even for art in general, in a single inclusive critical system. The pattern of the pragmatic reasoning usually employed may conveniently be studied in such a compendious treatment as James Beattie's *Essay*

13

on *Poetry and Music as they affect the Mind* (1762), or more succinctly still, in Richard Hurd's 'Dissertation of the Idea of Universal Poetry' (1766). Universal poetry, no matter what the genre, Hurd says, is an art whose end is the maximum possible pleasure. 'When we speak of poetry, as an *art*, we mean *such a way or method of treating a subject, as is found most pleasing and delightful to us.*' And this idea 'if kept steadily in view, will unfold to us all the mysteries of the poetic art. There needs but to evolve the philosopher's idea, and to apply it, as occasion serves.' From this major premise Hurd evolves three properties, essential to all poetry if it is to effect the greatest possible delight: figurative language, 'fiction' (that is to say, a departure from what is actual, or empirically possible), and versification. The mode and degree in which these three universal qualities are to be combined in any one species of poetry, however, will depend on its peculiar end, because each poetic kind must exploit that special pleasure which it is generically adapted to achieve. 'For the art of every *kind* of poetry is only this general art so modified as the *nature* of each, that is, its more immediate and subordinate end, may respectively require.'

> For the name of poem will belong to every composition, whose primary end is to *please*, provided it be so constructed as to afford *all* the pleasure, which its kind or *sort* will permit.[38]

On the basis of isolated passages from his *Letters on Chivalry and Romance*, Hurd is commonly treated as a 'pre-romantic' critic. But in the summation of his poetic creed in the 'Idea of Universal Poetry', the rigidly deductive logic which Hurd employs to 'unfold' the rules of poetry from a primitive definition, permitting 'the reason of the thing' to override the evidence of the actual practice of poets, brings him as close as anyone in England to the geometric method of Charles Batteux, though without that critic's Cartesian apparatus. The difference is that Batteux evolves his rules from the definition of poetry as the imitation of *la belle nature*, and Hurd, from its definition as the art of treating a subject so as to afford the reader a maximum pleasure; and this involves his assuming that he possesses an empirical knowledge of the psychology of the reader. For if the end of poetry is to gratify the mind of the reader, Hurd says, knowledge of the laws of mind is necessary to establish its rules, which are 'but so many MEANS, which experience finds most conducive to that end'.[39] Since Batteux and Hurd, however, are both intent on rationalizing what is mainly a common body of poetic lore, it need not surprise us that, though they set out from different points of the compass, their paths often coincide.[40]

But to appreciate the power and illumination of which a refined and flexible pragmatic criticism is capable, we must turn from these abstract systematizers of current methods and maxims to such a practical critic as Samuel Johnson. Johnson's literary criticism assumes approximately the frame of critical reference I have described, but Johnson, who distrusts rigid and abstract theorizing, applies the method with a constant appeal to specific literary examples, deference to the opinions of other readers, but ultimately, reliance on his own expert responses to the text. As a result Johnson's comments on poets and poems have persistently afforded a jumping-off point for later critics whose frame of reference and particular judgments differ radically from his own. For an instance of Johnson's procedure which is especially interesting because it shows how the notion of the imitation of nature is coordinated with the judgment of poetry in terms of its end and effects, consider that monument of neoclassic criticism, Johnson's *Preface to Shakespeare*.

Johnson undertakes in his *Preface* to establish Shakespeare's rank among poets, and to do so, he is led to rate Shakespeare's native abilities against the general level of taste and achievement in the Elizabethan age, and to measure these abilities in turn 'by their proportion to the general and collective ability of man'.[41] Since the powers and excellence of an author, however, can only be inferred from the nature and excellence of the works he achieves, Johnson addresses himself to a general examination of Shakespeare's dramas. In this systematic appraisal of the works themselves, we find that mimesis retains for Johnson a measure of authority as criterion. Repeatedly Johnson maintains that 'this therefore is the praise of *Shakespeare*, that his drama is the mirror of life', and of inanimate nature as well: 'He was an exact surveyor of the inanimate world.... *Shakespeare*, whether life or nature be his subject, shews plainly, that he has seen with his own eyes....'[42] But, Johnson also claims, 'The end of writing is to instruct; the end of poetry is to instruct by pleasing.'[43] It is to this function of poetry, and to the demonstrated effect of a poem upon its audience, that Johnson awards priority as aesthetic criterion. If a poem fails to please, whatever its character otherwise, it is, as a work of art, nothing; though Johnson insists, with a strenuous moralism that must already have seemed old-fashioned to contemporary readers, it must please without violating the standards of truth and virtue. Accordingly, Johnson discriminates those elements in Shakespeare's plays which were introduced to appeal to the local and passing tastes of the rather barbarous audience of his own time ('He knew,' said Johnson, 'how he should most please'),[44] from those elements which are proportioned to the tastes of the common readers of all time. And since in works 'appealing wholly to observation and experience, no other test can be applied than length of duration and continuance of esteem', Shakespeare's long survival as a poet 'read without any other reason than the desire for pleasure' is the best evidence on the subsidiary principle that 'nothing can please many, and please long, but just representations of general nature'. Shakespeare exhibits the eternal 'species' of human character, moved by 'those general passions and principles by which all minds are agitated'.[45] Thus Shakespeare's excellence in holding up the mirror to general nature turns out, in the long run, to be justified by the superior criterion of the appeal this achievement holds for the enduring tastes of the general literary public.

A number of Johnson's individual observations and judgments exhibit a play of the argument between the two principles of the nature of the world the poet must reflect, and the nature and legitimate requirements of the poet's audience. For the most part the two principles co-operate towards a single conclusion. For example, both the empirical nature of the universe and of the universal reader demonstrate the fallacy of those who censure Shakespeare for mixing his comic and tragic scenes. Shakespeare's plays, Johnson says, exhibit 'the real state of sublunary nature, which partakes of good and evil, joy and sorrow, mingled with endless variety'. In addition, 'the mingled drama may convey all the instruction of tragedy or comedy' by approaching nearer 'to the appearance of life'; while the objection that the change of scene 'wants at last the power to move' is a specious reasoning 'received as true even by those who in daily experience feel it to be false'.[46] But when the actual state of sublunary affairs conflicts with the poet's obligation to his audience, the latter is the court of final appeal. It is Shakespeare's defect, says Johnson,

> that he seems to write without any moral purpose.... He makes no just distribution of good or evil, nor is always careful to shew in the virtuous a disapprobation of the wicked.... It is always a writer's duty to make the world better, and justice is a virtue independent of time or place.[47]

The pragmatic orientation, ordering the aim of the artist and the character of the work to the nature, the needs, and the springs of pleasure in the audience, characterized by far the greatest part of criticism from the time of Horace through the eighteenth century. Measured either by its duration or the number of its adherents, therefore, the pragmatic view, broadly conceived, has been the principal aesthetic attitude of the Western world. But inherent in this system were the elements of its dissolution. Ancient rhetoric had bequeathed to criticism not only its stress on affecting the audience but also (since its main concern was with educating the orator) its detailed attention to the powers and activities of the speaker himself—his 'nature', or innate powers and genius, as distinguished from his culture and art, and also the process of invention, disposition, and expression involved in his discourse.[48] In the course of time, and particularly after the psychological contributions of Hobbes and Locke in the seventeenth century, increasing attention was given to the mental constitution of the poet, the quality and degree of his 'genius', and the play of his faculties in the act of composition. Through most of the eighteenth century, the poet's invention and imagination were made thoroughly dependent for their materials —their ideas and 'images'—on the external universe and the literary models the poet had to imitate; while the persistent stress laid on his need for judgment and art—the mental surrogates, in effect, of the requirements of a cultivated audience—held the poet strictly responsible to the audience for whose pleasure he exerted his creative ability. Gradually, however, the stress was shifted more and more to the poet's natural genius, creative imagination, and emotional spontaneity, at the expense of the opposing attributes of judgment, learning, and artful restraints. As a result the audience gradually receded into the background, giving place to the poet himself, and his own mental powers and emotional needs, as the predominant cause and even the end and test of art. By this time other developments, which we shall have occasion to talk about later, were also helping to shift the focus of critical interest from audience to artist and thus to introduce a new orientation into the theory of art.

IV   Expressive theories

'Poetry', Wordsworth announced in his Preface to the *Lyrical Ballads* of 1800, 'is the spontaneous overflow of powerful feelings.' He thought well enough of this formulation to use it twice in the same essay, and on this, as the ground-idea, he founded his theory of the proper subjects, language, effects, and value of poetry. Almost all the major critics of the English romantic generation phrased definitions or key statements showing a parallel alignment from work to poet. Poetry is the overflow, utterance, or projection of the thought and feelings of the poet; or else (in the chief variant formulation) poetry is defined in terms of the imaginative process which modifies and synthesizes the images, thoughts, and feelings of the poet. This way of thinking, in which the artist himself becomes the major element generating both the artistic product and the criteria by which it is to be judged, I shall call the expressive theory of art.

Setting the date at which this point of view became predominant in critical theory, like marking the point at which orange becomes yellow in the colour spectrum, must be a somewhat arbitrary procedure. As we shall see, an approach to the expressive orientation, though isolated in history and partial in scope, is to be found as early as Longinus' discussion of the sublime style as having its main sources in the thought and emotions of the speaker; and it recurs in a variant form in Bacon's brief analysis of poetry as pertaining to the imagination and 'accommodating the shows of things to the desires of the mind'. Even Wordsworth's theory, it will appear, is much more embedded in a traditional matrix of interests and emphases, and is, therefore, less radical than are the theories of his followers of the 1830s. The year 1800 is a good round number, however, and Wordsworth's Preface a convenient document, by which to signalize the displacement of the mimetic and pragmatic by the expressive view of art in English criticism.

In general terms, the central tendency of the expressive theory may be summarized in this way: A work of art is essentially the internal made external, resulting from a creative process operating under the impulse of feeling, and embodying the combined product of the poet's perceptions, thoughts, and feelings. The primary source and subject matter of a poem, therefore, are the attributes and actions of the poet's own mind; or if aspects of the external world, then these only as they are converted from fact to poetry by the feelings and operations of the poet's mind. ('Thus the Poetry...' Wordsworth wrote, 'proceeds whence it ought to do, from the soul of Man, communicating its creative energies to the images of the external world.')[49] The paramount cause of poetry is not, as in Aristotle, a formal cause, determined primarily by the human actions and qualities imitated; nor, as in neoclassic criticism a final cause, the effect intended upon the audience; but instead an efficient cause—the impulse within the poet of feelings and desires seeking expression, or the compulsion of the 'creative' imagination which, like God the creator, has its internal source of motion. The propensity is to grade the arts by the extent to which their media are amenable to the undistorted expression of the feelings or mental powers of the artist, and to classify the species of an art, and evaluate their instances, by the qualities or states of mind of which they are a sign. Of the elements constituting a poem, the element of diction, especially figures of speech, becomes primary; and the burning question is, whether these are the natural utterance of emotion and imagination or the deliberate aping of poetic conventions. The first test any poem must pass is no longer, 'Is it true to nature?' or 'Is it appropriate to the requirements either of the best judges or the generality of mankind?' but a criterion looking in a different direction; namely, 'Is it sincere? Is it genuine? Does it match the intehtion, the feeling, and the actual state of mind of the poet while composing?' The work ceases then to be regarded as primarily a reflection of nature, actual or improved; the mirror held up to nature becomes transparent and yields the reader insights into the mind and heart of the poet himself. The exploitation of literature as an index to personality first manifests itself in the early nineteenth century; it is the inevitable consequence of the expressive point of view.

The sources, details, and historical results of this reorientation of criticism, in its various forms, will be a principal concern of the rest of this book. Now, while we have some of the earlier facts fresh in mind, let me indicate what happened to salient elements of traditional criticism in the essays 'What is Poetry?' and 'The Two Kinds of Poetry', written by John Stuart Mill in 1833. Mill relied in large part on Wordsworth's Preface to the *Lyrical Ballads*, but in the intervening thirty years the expressive theory had emerged from the network of qualifications in which Wordsworth had carefully placed it, and had worked out its own destiny unhindered. Mill's logic in answering the question, 'What is poetry?' is not *more geometrico*, like that of Batteux, nor stiffly formal, like Richard Hurd's; nonetheless, his theory turns out to be as tightly dependent upon a central principle as theirs. For whatever Mill's empirical pretensions, his initial assumption about the essential nature of poetry remains continuously though silently effective in selecting, interpreting, and ordering the facts to be explained.

The primitive proposition of Mill's theory is: Poetry is 'the expression or uttering forth of feeling'.[50] Exploration of the data of aesthetics from this starting point leads, among other things, to the following drastic alterations in the great commonplaces of the critical tradition:

1. *The poetic kinds.* Mill reinterprets and inverts the neoclassic ranking of the poetic kinds. As the purest expression of feeling, lyric poetry is 'more eminently and peculiarly poetry than any other...' Other forms are all alloyed by non-poetic elements, whether descriptive, didactic, or narrative, which serve merely as convenient occasions for the poetic utterances of feeling either by the poet or by one of his invented characters. To Aristotle, tragedy had been the highest form of poetry, and the plot, representing the action being imitated, had been its 'soul'; while most neoclassic critics had agreed that, whether judged by greatness of subject matter or of effects, epic and tragedy are the king and queen of poetic forms. It serves as an index to the revolution in critical norms to notice that to Mill, plot becomes a kind of necessary evil. An epic poem 'in so far as it is epic (i.e. narrative) ... is not poetry at all', but only a suitable

frame for the greatest diversity of genuinely poetic passages; while the interest in plot and story 'merely as a story' characterizes rude stages of society, children, and the 'shallowest and emptiest' of civilized adults.[51] Similarly with the other arts; in music, painting, sculpture, and architecture Mill distinguishes between that which is 'simple imitation or description' and that which 'expresses human feeling' and is, therefore, poetry.[52]

2. *Spontaneity as criterion.* Mill accepts the venerable assumption that a man's emotional susceptibility is innate, but his knowledge and skill—his art—are acquired. On this basis, he distinguishes poets into two classes: poets who are born and poets who are made, or those who are poets 'by nature', and those who are poets 'by culture'. Natural poetry is identifiable because it 'is Feeling itself, employing Thought only as the medium of its utterance'; on the other hand, the poetry of 'a cultivated but not naturally poetic mind', is written with 'a distinct aim', and in it the thought remains the conspicuous object, however surrounded by 'a halo of feeling'. Natural poetry, it turns out, is 'poetry in a far higher sense, than any other; since ... that which constitutes poetry, human feeling, enters far more largely into this than into the poetry of culture'. Among the moderns, Shelley represents the poet born and Wordsworth the poet made; and with unconscious irony Mill turns Wordsworth's own criterion, 'the spontaneous overflow of feeling', against its sponsor. Wordsworth's poetry 'has little even of the appearance of spontaneousness: the well is never so full that it overflows'.[53]

3. *The external world.* In so far as a literary product simply imitates objects, it is not poetry at all. As a result, reference of poetry to the external universe disappears from Mill's theory, except to the extent that sensible objects may serve as a stimulus or 'occasion for the generation of poetry', and then, 'the poetry is not in the object itself', but 'in the state of mind' in which it is contemplated. When a poet describes a lion he 'is describing the lion professedly, but the state of excitement of the spectator really', and the poetry must be true not to the object, but to 'the human emotion'.[54] Thus severed from the external world, the objects signified by a poem tend to be regarded as no more than a projected equivalent—an extended and articulated symbol—for the poet's inner state of mind. Poetry, said Mill, in a phrasing which anticipates T. E. Hulme[a] and lays the theoretical groundwork for the practice of symbolists from Baudelaire through T. S. Eliot, embodies 'itself in symbols, which are the nearest possible representations of the feeling in the exact shape in which it exists in the poet's mind'.[55] Tennyson, Mill wrote in a review of that poet's early poems, excels in 'scene-painting, in the highest sense of the term'; and this is

> not the mere power of producing that rather vapid species of composition usually termed descriptive poetry ... but the power of *creating* scenery, in keeping with some state of human feeling; so fitted to it as to be the embodied symbol of it, and to summon up the state of feeling itself, with a force not to be surpassed by anything but reality.[56]

[a] See below pp. 92–104.

And as an indication of the degree to which the innovations of the romantics persist as the commonplaces of modern critics—even of those who purport to found their theory on anti-romantic principles—notice how striking is the parallel between the passage above and a famous comment by T. S. Eliot:

> The only way of expressing emotion in the form of art is by finding an 'objective correlative'; in other words, a set of objects, a situation, a chain of events which shall be the formula of that *particular* emotion; such that when the external facts, which must terminate in sensory experience, are given, the emotion is immediately evoked.[57]

4. *The audience.*   No less drastic is the fate of the audience. According to Mill, 'Poetry is feeling, confessing itself to itself in moments of solitude...' The poet's audience is reduced to a single member, consisting of the poet himself. 'All poetry,' as Mill puts it, 'is of the nature of soliloquy.' The purpose of producing effects upon other men, which for centuries had been the defining character of the art of poetry, now serves precisely the opposite function: it disqualifies a poem by proving it to be rhetoric instead. When the poet's

> act of utterance is not itself the end, but the means to an end—viz. by the feelings he himself expresses, to work upon the feelings, or upon the belief, or the will, of another—when the expression of his emotions ... is tinged also by that purpose, by that desire of making an impression upon another mind, then it ceases to be poetry, and becomes eloquence.[58]

There is, in fact, something singularly fatal to the audience in the romantic point of view. Or, in terms of historical causes, it might be conjectured that the disappearance of a homogeneous and discriminating reading public fostered a criticism which on principle diminished the importance of the audience as a determinant of poetry and poetic value. Wordsworth still insisted that 'Poets do not write for Poets alone, but for Men', and that each of his poems 'has a worthy purpose'; even though it turns out that the pleasure and profit of the audience is an automatic consequence of the poet's *spontaneous* overflow of feeling, provided that the appropriate associations between thoughts and feelings have been established by the poet in advance.[59] Keats, however, affirmed roundly that 'I never wrote one single line of Poetry with the least Shadow of public thought'.[60] 'A poet is a nightingale,' according to Shelley, 'who sits in darkness and sings to cheer its own solitude with sweet sounds; his auditors are as men entranced by the melody of an unseen musician...'[61] For Carlyle, the poet utterly replaces the audience as the generator of aesthetic norms.

> On the whole, Genius has privileges of its own; it selects an orbit for itself; and be this never so eccentric, if it is indeed a celestial orbit, we mere star-gazers must at last compose ourselves; must cease to cavil at it, and begin to observe it, and calculate its laws.[62]

The evolution is complete, from the mimetic poet, assigned the minimal role of holding a mirror up to nature, through the pragmatic poet who, whatever his natural gifts, is ultimately measured by his capacity to satisfy the public taste, to Carlyle's Poet as Hero, the chosen one who, because he is 'a Force of

Nature', writes as he must, and through the degree of homage he evokes, serves as the measure of his reader's piety and taste.[63]

V Objective theories

All types of theory described so far, in their practical applications, get down to dealing with the work of art itself, in its parts and their mutual relations, whether the premises on which these elements are discriminated and evaluated relate them primarily to the spectator, the artist, or the world without. But there is also a fourth procedure, the 'objective orientation', which on principle regards the work of art in isolation from all these external points of reference, analyses it as a self-sufficient entity constituted by its parts in their internal relations, and sets out to judge it solely by criteria intrinsic to its own mode of being.

This point of view has been comparatively rare in literary criticism. The one early attempt at the analysis of an art form which is both objective and comprehensive occurs in the central portion of Aristotle's *Poetics*. I have chosen to discuss Aristotle's theory of art under the heading of mimetic theories, because it sets out from, and makes frequent reference back to the concept of imitation. Such is the flexibility of Aristotle's procedure, however, that after he has isolated the species 'tragedy', and established its relation to the universe as an imitation of a certain kind of action, and to the audience through its observed effect of purging pity and fear, his method becomes centripetal, and assimilates these external elements into attributes of the work proper. In this second consideration of tragedy as an object in itself, the actions and agents that are imitated re-enter the discussion as the plot, character, and thought which, together with diction, melody, and spectacle, make up the six elements of a tragedy; and even pity and fear are reconsidered as that pleasurable quality proper to tragedy, to be distinguished from the pleasures characteristic of comedy and other forms.[64] The tragic work itself can now be analysed formally as a self-determining whole made up of parts, all organized around the controlling part, the tragic plot— itself a unity in which the component incidents are integrated by the internal relations of 'necessity or probability'.

As an all-inclusive approach to poetry, the objective orientation was just beginning to emerge in the late eighteenth and early nineteenth centuries. We shall see later on that some critics were undertaking to explore the concept of the poem as a heterocosm, a world of its own, independent of the world into which we are born, whose end is not to instruct or please but simply to exist. Certain critics, particularly in Germany, were expanding upon Kant's formula that a work of art exhibits *Zweckmässigkeit ohne Zweck* (purposiveness without purpose), together with his concept that the contemplation of beauty is disinterested and without regard to utility, while neglecting Kant's characteristic reference of an aesthetic product to the mental faculties of its creator and receptor. The aim to consider a poem, as Poe expressed it, as a 'poem *per se* ... written solely for the poem's sake',[65] in isolation from external causes and ulterior ends, came to constitute one element of the diverse doctrines usually huddled together by historians under the heading 'Art for Art's Sake'. And with differing emphases and adequacy, and in a great variety of theoretical contexts, the objective approach to poetry has become one of the most prominent elements in the innovative criticism of the last two or three decades. T. S. Eliot's dictum of 1928, that 'when we are considering poetry we must consider it primarily as poetry and not another thing' is widely approved, however far Eliot's own criticism sometimes departs from this ideal; and it is often joined with Mac-Leish's verse aphorism, 'A poem should not mean But be.' The subtle and incisive criticism of criticism by the Chicago Neo-Aristotelians[a] and their advocacy of an instrument adapted to dealing with poetry as such have been largely effective towards a similar end. In his 'ontological criticism', John Crowe Ransom[b] has been calling for recognition of 'the autonomy of the work itself as existing for its own sake';[66] campaigns have been organized against 'the personal heresy',[c] 'the intentional fallacy', and 'the affective fallacy';[d] the widely influential handbook, *The Theory of Literature*, written by René Wellek and Austin Warren, proposes that criticism deal with a poem *qua* poem, independently of 'extrinsic' factors; and similar views are being expressed, with increasing frequency, not only in our literary but in our scholarly journals. In America, at least, some form of the objective point of view has already gone far to displace its rivals as the reigning mode of literary criticism.

According to our scheme of analysis, then, there have been four major orientations, each one of which has seemed to various acute minds adequate for a satisfactory criticism of art in general. And by and large the historic progression, from the beginning through the early nineteenth century, has been from the mimetic theory of Plato and (in a qualified fashion) Aristotle, through the pragmatic theory, lasting from the conflation of rhetoric with poetic in the Hellenistic and Roman era almost through the eighteenth century, to the expressive theory of English (and somewhat earlier, German) romantic criticism.

Of course romantic criticism, like that of any period, was not uniform in its outlook. As late as 1831 Macaulay (whose thinking usually followed traditional patterns) still insists, as an eternal rule 'founded in reason and in the nature of things', that 'poetry is, as was said more than two thousand years ago, imitation', and differentiates between the arts on the basis of their diverse media and objects of imitation. Then, in an essay packed with eighteenth-century catchlines, he ungratefully employs the mimetic principle to justify his elevation of Scott, Wordsworth, and Coleridge over the eighteenth-century poets because they imitate nature more accurately, and attacks the neoclassic rules of correctness on the ground that they 'tend to make ... imitations less perfect than they otherwise would be...'[67] The mode of criticism which subjects art and the artist to the audience also continued to flourish, usually in a vulgarized form, among influential journalists such as Francis Jeffrey, who deliberately set them-

[a] See introductory note on R. S. Crane, p. 592 below.
[b] See below, pp. 227–39.
[c] *The Personal Heresy: a controversy*, by E. M. W. Tillyard and C. S. Lewis (1939).
[d] See the essays by W. K. Wimsatt and Monroe C. Beardsley, pp. 333–58 below.

selves to voice the literary standards of the middle class and to preserve unsullied what Jeffrey called 'the purity of the female character'.[68]

But these are not the innovative critical writings which contributed to the predominant temper of what Shelley, in his 'Defence of Poetry', called 'the spirit of the age'; and the radical difference between the characteristic points of view of neoclassic and romantic criticism remains unmistakable. Take such representative productions of the 1760s and '70s as Johnson's *Preface to Shakespeare*, Kames's *Elements of Criticism*, Richard Hurd's 'On the Idea of Universal Poetry', *The Art of Poetry on a New Plan* (of dubious authorship), Beattie's *Essays on Poetry and Music*, and the first eight *Discourses* of Sir Joshua Reynolds. Place these next to the major inquiries into poetry and art of the romantic generation: Wordsworth's Prefaces and collateral essays, Coleridge's *Biographia Literaria* and Shakespearean lectures, Hazlitt's 'On Poetry in General' and other essays, even Shelley's Platonistic 'Defence of Poetry'; then add to this group such later documents as Carlyle's 'Characteristics' and early literary reviews, J. S. Mill's two essays on poetry, John Keble's *Lectures on Poetry*, and Leigh Hunt's 'What is Poetry?'. Whatever the continuity of certain terms and topics between individual members of the two eras, and however important the methodological and doctrinal differences which divide the members within a single group, one decisive change marks off the criticism in the Age of Wordsworth from that in the Age of Johnson. The poet has moved into the centre of the critical system and taken over many of the prerogatives which had once been exercised by his readers, the nature of the world in which he found himself, and the inherited precepts and examples of his poetic art.

Notes

1. Foreword to *Philosophies of Beauty*, ed. E. F. Carritt (Oxford, 1931), p. ix.
2. (5th edn, London, 1934), pp. 6–7. Richards's later change of emphasis is indicated by his recent statement that ' "Semantics" which began by finding nonsense everywhere may well end up as a technique for widening understanding' (*Modern Language Notes*, lx, 1945, p. 350).
3. For a subtle and elaborate analysis of diverse critical theories, see Richard McKeon, 'Philosophic bases of art and criticism', *Critics and Criticism, Ancient and Modern*, ed. R. S. Crane (The University of Chicago Press, 1952).
4. *Republic* (trans. Jowett) x. 596–7; *Laws* ii. 667–8, vii. 814–16.
5. See Richard McKeon, 'Literary criticism and the concept of imitation in antiquity', *Critics and Criticism*, ed. Crane, pp. 147–9. The article exhibits those multiple shifts in Plato's use of the term 'imitation' which have trapped many later commentators as successfully as they once did the rash spirits who engaged Socrates in controversy.
6. *Republic* x. 597.
7. *Laws* vii. 817.
8. *Republic* x. 603–5; *Ion* 536–6; cf. *Apology* 22.
9. *Republic* x. 608.
10. *Poetics* (trans. Ingram Bywater) 1. 1447^a, 1448^a. On imitation in Aristotle's criticism see McKeon, 'The Concept of Imitation', op. cit. pp. 160–8.
11. *Poetics* 6. 1449^b, 14. 1453^b
12. Ibid., 8. 1451^a.
13. Ibid., 6. 1450^a–1450^b.
14. Ibid., 4. 1448^b, 17. 1455^a–1455^b.

15. *Republic* iii. 398, x. 606–8; *Laws* vii. 817.

16. *The Works of Richard Hurd* (London, 1811), ii, 111–12.

17. Edward Young, *Conjectures on Original Composition*, ed. Edith Morley (Manchester, 1918), pp. 6, 18. See also William Duff, *Essay on Original Genius* (London, 1767), p. 192n. John Ogilvie reconciles creative genius and original invention with 'the great principle of poetic imitation' (*Philosophical and Critical Observations on the Nature, Characters, and Various Species of Composition*, London, 1774, i, 105–7). Joseph Warton, familiar proponent of a 'boundless imagination', enthusiasm, and 'the romantic, the wonderful, and the wild', still agrees with Richard Hurd that poetry is 'an art, whose essence is imitation', and whose objects are 'material or animate, extraneous or internal' (*Essay on the Writings and Genius of Pope*, London, 1756, i, 89–90). Cf. Robert Wood, *Essay on the Original Genius and Writings of Homer* (1769), London, 1824, pp. 6–7, 178.

18. 'Originality', *Gleanings* (London, 1785), i, 107, 109.

19. Charles Batteux, *Les Beaux Arts réduits à un même principe* (Paris, 1747), pp. i–viii.

20. Ibid., pp. 9–27.

21. Ibid., p. xiii. For the important place of imitation in earlier French neoclassic theories, see René Bray, *La Formation de la doctrine classique en France* (Lausanne, 1931), pp. 140 ff.

22. Lessing, *Laokoon*, ed. W. G. Howard (New York, 1910), pp. 23–5, 42.

23. Ibid., pp. 99–102, 64.

24. *Three Treatises*, in *The Works of James Harris* (London, 1803), i, 58. Cf. Adam Smith, 'Of the nature of that imitation which takes place in what are called the imitative arts', *Essays Philosophical and Literary* (London, n.d.), pp. 405 ff.

25. Henry Home, Lord Kames, *Elements of Criticism* (Boston, 1796), ii, 1 (chap. xviii).

26. Thomas Twining, ed., *Aristotle's Treatise on Poetry* (London, 1789), pp. 4, 21–2, 60–1.

27. Sir Philip Sidney, 'An Apology for Poetry', *Elizabethan Critical Essays*, ed G. Gregory Smith (London, 1904), i, 158.

28. Ibid., i, 159.

29. Ibid., i, 159, 161–4, 171–80, 201.

30. See, e.g., his use of Aristotle's statement that poetry is more philosophical than history (i, 167–8), and that painful things can be made pleasant by imitations (p. 171); and his wrenching of Aristotle's central term, *praxis*—the actions which are imitated by poetry—to signify the moral action which a poem moves the spectator to practise (p. 171).

31. Cicero, *De oratore* ii, xxviii.

32. 'The Concept of Imitation,' op. cit. p. 173.

33. Horace, *Ars Poetica*, trans. E. H. Blakeney, in *Literary Criticism, Plato to Dryden*, ed. Allan H. Gilbert (New York, 1940), p. 139.

34. *Essays on Poetry and Music* (3rd edn, London, 1779), p. 10.

35. 'Dryden', *Lives of the English Poets*, ed. Birkbeck Hill (Oxford, 1905), i, 410.

36. 'Parallel of poetry and painting' (1695), *Essays*, ed. W. P. Ker (Oxford, 1926), ii, 138. See Hoyt Trowbridge, 'The place of rules in Dryden's criticism', *Modern Philology*, xliv (1946), 84 ff.

37. *The Advancement and Reformation of Modern Poetry* (1701), in *The Critical Works of John Dennis*, ed. E. N. Hooker (Baltimore, 1939), i, 202–3. For Dennis's derivation of specific rules from the end of art, which is 'to delight and reform the mind', see *The Grounds of Criticism in Poetry* (1704), ibid., pp. 336 ff

38. 'Dissertation on the Idea of Universal Poetry', *Works*, ii, 3–4, 25–6, 7. For a parallel argument see Alexander Gerard, *An Essay on Taste* (London, 1759), p. 40.

39. 'Idea of Universal Poetry', *Works*, ii, 3–4. On the rationale underlying the body of Hurd's criticism, see the article by Hoyt Trowbridge, 'Bishop Hurd: A Reinterpretation', *PMLA*, lviii (1943), 450 ff.

40. e.g. Batteux 'deduces' from the idea that poetry is the imitation, not of unadorned reality, but of *la belle nature*, that its end can only be 'to please, to move, to touch, in a word, pleasure' (*Les Beaux Arts*, pp. 81, 151). Conversely, Hurd infers from the fact that the end of poetry is pleasure that the poet's duty is 'to illustrate and adorn' reality, and to delineate it 'in the most taking forms' ('Idea of Universal Poetry', *Works*, ii, 8). For purposes of a specialized investigation into the evidences for plagiarism among poets, Hurd himself, in another essay, shifts his ground, and like Batteux, sets out from a definition of poetry as an imitation, specifically, of 'the fairest forms of things' ('Discourse on Poetic Imitation', *Works*, ii, 111).

41. *Johnson on Shakespeare*, ed. Walter Raleigh (Oxford, 1908), pp. 10, 30–1.

42. Ibid., pp. 14, 39. Cf. pp. 11, 31, 33, 37, etc.

43. Ibid., p. 16.

44. Ibid., pp. 31–33, 41.

45. Ibid., pp. 9–12.

46. Ibid., pp. 15–17. See also Johnson's defence of Shakespeare for violating the decorum of character-types, by the appeal to 'nature' as against 'accident'; and for breaking the unities of time and place, by the appeal both to the actual experience of dramatic auditors, and to the principle that 'the greatest graces of a play, are to copy nature and instruct life' (ibid. pp. 14–15, 25 30). Cf. *Rambler* No. 156.

47. Ibid., 20–1. The logic appears even more clearly in Johnson's early paper on 'works of fiction', in *Rambler* No. 4, 1750 (*The Works of Samuel Johnson*, ed. Arthur Murphy, London, 1824, iv, 23): 'It is justly considered as the greatest excellency of art, to imitate nature; but it is necessary to distinguish those parts of nature which are most proper for imitation', etc. For a detailed analysis of Johnson's critical methods, see W. R. Keast, 'The theoretical foundations of Johnson's criticism', *Critics and Criticism*, ed. R. S. Crane, pp. 389–407.

48. See the masterly précis of the complex movements within English neo-classic criticism by R. S. Crane, 'English neoclassical criticism', *Critics and Criticism*, pp. 372–88.

49. *Letters of William and Dorothy Wordsworth: The Middle Years*, ed. E. de Selincourt (Oxford, 1937), ii, 705; 18 January 1816.

50. *Early Essays by John Stuart Mill*, ed. J. W. M. Gibbs (London, 1897), p. 208.

51. Ibid., pp. 228, 205–6, 213, 203–4.

52. Ibid., pp. 211–17.

53. Ibid., pp. 222–31.

54. Ibid., pp. 206–7.

55. Ibid., pp. 208–9. Cf. Hulme, 'If it is sincere in the accurate sense ... the whole of the analogy is necessary to get out the exact curve of the feeling or thing you want to express ...' ('Romanticism and classicism', *Speculations*, London, 1936, p. 138).

56. Review, written in 1835, of Tennyson's *Poems Chiefly Lyrical* (1830) and *Poems* (1833), in *Early Essays*, p. 242.

57. 'Hamlet', *Selected Essays 1917–32* (London 1932), p. 145.

58. *Early Essays*, pp. 208–9. Cf. John Keble, *Lectures on Poetry* (1832–41), trans. E. K. Francis (Oxford, 1912), i, 48–9: 'Cicero is always the orator' because 'he always has in mind the theatre, the benches, the audience'; whereas Plato is 'more poetical than Homer himself' because 'he writes to please himself, not to win over others'.

59. Preface to the *Lyrical Ballads*, *Wordsworth's Literary Criticism*, ed. N. C. Smith (London, 1905), pp. 30, 15–16.

60. *Letters*, ed. Maurice Buxton Forman (3rd edn, New York, 1948), p. 131 (to Reynolds, 9 April 1818).

61. 'Defence of Poetry', *Shelley's Literary and Philosophical Criticism*, ed. John Shawcross (London, 1909), p. 129.

62. 'Jean Paul Friedrich Richter' (1827), *Works*, ed. H. D. Traill (London, 1905), xxvi, 20.

63. See *Heroes, Hero-Worship, and the Heroine in History*, in *Works*, v, esp. pp. 80–5, 108–12. Cf. Jones Very's indignant denial of the inference that because the general ear takes delight in Shakespeare, 'his motive was to please.... We degrade those whom the world has pronounced poets, when we assume any other cause of their song than the divine and original action of the soul in humble obedience to the Holy Spirit upon whom they call' ['Shakespeare' (1838), *Poems and Essays*, Boston and New York, 1886, pp. 45–6].

64. 'Not every kind of pleasure should be required of a tragedy, but only its own proper pleasure. The tragic pleasure is that of pity and fear ...' (*Poetics* 14, 1453^b).

65. 'The poetic principle', *Representative Selections*, ed. Margaret Alterton and Hardin Craig (New York, 1935), pp. 382–3.

66. See John Crowe Ransom, *The World's Body* (New York, 1938), esp. pp. 327 ff., and 'Criticism as pure speculation', *The Intent of the Critic*, ed. Donald Stauffer (Princeton, 1941).

67. 'Moore's *Life of Lord Byron*', in *Critical and Historical Essays* (Everyman's Library; London, 1907), ii, 622–8.

68. *Edinburgh Review*, viii (1806), 459–60. On Jeffrey's use of an elaborate associationist aesthetics in order to justify the demand that an author or artist have as his aim 'to give as much [pleasure] and to as many persons as possible', and that he 'fashion his productions according to the rules of taste which may be deduced' from an investigation of the most widespread public preferences, see his *Contributions to the Edinburgh Review* (London, 1844), i, 76–8, 128; iii, 53–4. For contemporary justifications, on sociological and moral grounds, for instituting a petticoat government over the republic of letters, see, e.g., John Bowring's review of Tennyson's *Poems*, in *Westminster Review*, xiv (1831), 223; *Lockhart's Literary Criticism*, ed. M. C. Hildyard (Oxford, 1931), p. 66; Christopher North (John Wilson), *Works*, ed. Ferrier (Edinburgh and London, 1857), ix, 194–5, 228.

W. B. Yeats

William Butler Yeats (1865-1939) was, in the opinion of many judges, the greatest modern poet of the English language. He was born, the son of the artist John Butler Yeats, in Dublin, but spent most of his childhood in County Sligo in the West of Ireland, where his grandfather had been a rector in the protestant Church of Ireland. After studying for a while in Dublin, where he was exposed to the influence of the Irish nationalist movement and the associated revival of interest in Irish folklore, Yeats migrated to London. Here he formed many friendships with the poets and artists of the Decadence, took a leading role in the founding of the Rhymers' Club, and dabbled enthusiastically in theosophy, magic, spiritualism, and other exotic and esoteric traditions.

Yeats's first volume of poems, *The Wanderings of Oisin and other poems* was published in 1889. In the following decade he began to write plays, and his meeting with Lady Gregory and John Synge in 1896 led to the opening of the Abbey Theatre in Dublin, dedicated to the encouragement of native Irish drama. Meanwhile Yeats continued to publish books of verse which showed an amazing capacity for technical development at the same time as they reflected changes in his personal and public life: greater involvement in politics and cultural affairs, the bitter experience of World War I and the nationalist rising in Dublin of 1916, the subsequent 'Troubles' and the achievement of Irish independence, his marriage in 1917 and his construction of an elaborate occult 'System' for interpreting history and individual destiny, which provided a reservoir of symbolism for his mature poetry. In 1922 Yeats was made a Senator of the Irish Free State, and in the following year he was awarded the Nobel Prize for Literature. He died in 1939, and his *Last Poems* were published in the same year.

W. B. Yeats is chiefly celebrated as a poet and playwright—*Collected Poems* (1950) and *Collected Plays* (1952) being the standard texts. But he also wrote a great deal of prose, particularly in the early part of his career. Most, though not all, of these prose writings have been collected in *Autobiographies* (1955), *Mythologies* (1959), *Essays and Introductions* (1961), and *Explorations* (1962). A useful selection of Yeats's literary criticism has been compiled by A. Norman Jeffares, *Selected Criticism* (1964).

'The Symbolism of Poetry' was first published in 1900 and collected in *Ideas of Good and Evil* (1903). It shows very clearly how the Decadence was, as far as England was concerned, a period of transition between Victorian and modern ideas about art. Beneath the Shelleyan rhetoric, the aesthete's posturing, of Yeats's prose, one may discern ideas which link together

27

the theory and practice of the English Romantics, the French Symbolists (Mallarmé, Verlaine, Rimbaud, etc.), the English poets of the 1890s and the experiments of Pound and Eliot early in the twentieth century. Like Pound and Eliot, Yeats was seeking to recover, or to create, a meaningful tradition on which to base his vocation as a poet, and like them he saw this as, in one essential respect, a critical enterprise.

CROSS REFERENCES :   5. Ezra Pound
6. T. S. Eliot ('Tradition and the Individual Talent')
15. Maud Bodkin
20. Paul Valéry
47. W. H. Auden

COMMENTARY :   Richard Ellmann, *Yeats, the Man and the Masks* (New York, 1948)

The symbolism of poetry

I

Symbolism, as seen in the writers of our day, would have no value if it were not seen, also, under one 'disguise or another, in every great imaginative writer', writes Mr Arthur Symons in *The Symbolist Movement in Literature,[a]* a subtle book which I cannot praise as I would, because it has been dedicated to me; and he goes on to show how many profound writers have in the last few years sought for a philosophy of poetry in the doctrine of symbolism, and how even in countries where it is almost scandalous to seek for any philosophy of poetry, new writers are following them in their search. We do not know what the writers of ancient times talked of among themselves, and one bull[b] is all that remains of Shakespeare's talk, who was on the edge of modern times; and the journalist is convinced, it seems, that they talked of wine and women and politics, but never about their art, or never quite seriously about their art. He is certain that no one who had a philosophy of his art, or a theory of how he should write, has ever made a work of art, that

[a] First published in 1899, Arthur Symons's study of the French Symbolist poets had considerable influence on many English poets besides Yeats.

[b] 'Bull' in the sense of 'ludicrous jest'. Yeats is probably alluding to the anecdote recorded by John Manningham in his journal, 13 March 1602: 'Upon a time when Burbage played Richard III there was a citizen grew so far in liking with him that before she went from the play she appointed him to come that night unto her by name of "Richard the Third". Shakespeare, overhearing their conclusion, went before, was entertained, and at his game ere Burbage came. Then, message being brought that Richard the Third was at the door, Shakespeare caused return to be made that William the Conqueror was before Richard the Third.'

people have no imagination who do not write without forethought and after-thought as he writes his own articles. He says this with enthusiasm, because he has heard it at so many comfortable dinner-tables, where someone had mentioned through carelessness, or foolish zeal, a book whose difficulty had offended indolence, or a man who had not forgotten that beauty is an accusation. Those formulas and generalizations, in which a hidden sergeant has drilled the ideas of journalists and through them the ideas of all but all the modern world, have created in their turn a forgetfulness like that of soldiers in battle, so that journalists and their readers have forgotten, among many like events, that Wagner spent seven years arranging and explaining his ideas before he began his most characteristic music; that opera, and with it modern music, arose from certain talks at the house of one Giovanni Bardi*a* of Florence; and that the Pléiade*b* laid the foundations of modern French literature with a pamphlet. Goethe has said, 'a poet needs all philosophy, but he must keep it out of his work', though that is not always necessary; and almost certainly no great art, outside England, where journalists are more powerful and ideas less plentiful than elsewhere, has arisen without a great criticism, for its herald or its interpreter and protector, and it may be for this reason that great art, now that vulgarity has armed itself and multiplied itself, is perhaps dead in England.

All writers, all artists of any kind, in so far as they have had any philosophical or critical power, perhaps just in so far as they have been delicate artists at all, have had some philosophy, some criticism of their art; and it has often been this philosophy, or this criticism, that has evoked their most startling inspiration, calling into outer life some portion of the divine life, or of the buried reality, which could alone extinguish in the emotions what their philosophy or their criticism would extinguish in the intellect. They had sought for no new thing it may be, but only to understand and to copy the pure inspiration of early times, but because the divine life wars upon our outer life, and must needs change its weapons and its movements as we change ours, inspiration has come to them in beautiful startling shapes. The scientific movement brought with it a literature which was always tending to lose itself in externalities of all kinds, in opinion, in declamation, in picturesque writing, in word-painting, or in what Mr Symons has called an attempt 'to build in brick and mortar inside the covers of a book'; and now writers have begun to dwell upon the element of evocation, of suggestion, upon what we call the symbolism in great writers.

II

In 'Symbolism in painting', I tried to describe the element of symbolism that

a The Conte del Vernio (1534?–1612), Italian aristocrat and scholar who has been credited with the invention of opera.

b A group of French poets in the sixteenth century, of whom Pierre de Ronsard and Joachim du Bellay were the most celebrated. The pamphlet alluded to by Yeats was du Bellay's *Deffence et illustration de la langue francoyse* (1549).

is in pictures and sculpture, and described a little the symbolism in poetry, but did not describe at all the continuous indefinable symbolism which is the substance of all style.

There are no lines with more melancholy beauty than these by Burns:

> The white moon is setting behind the white wave,[a]
> And Time is setting with me, O!

and these lines are perfectly symbolical. Take from them the whiteness of the moon and of the wave, whose relation to the setting of Time is too subtle for the intellect, and you take from them their beauty. But, when all are together, moon and wave and whiteness and setting Time and the last melancholy cry, they evoke an emotion which cannot be evoked by any other arrangement of colours and sounds and forms. We may call this metaphorical writing, but it is better to call it symbolical writing, because metaphors are not profound enough to be moving, when they are not symbols, and when they are symbols they are the most perfect of all, because the most subtle, outside of pure sound, and through them one can best find out what symbols are. If one begins the reverie with any beautiful lines that one can remember, one finds they are like those by Burns. Begin with this line by Blake:

The gay fishes on the wave when the moon sucks up the dew;

or these lines by Nash:

> Brightness falls from the air,
> Queens have died young and fair,
> Dust hath closed Helen's eye;

or these lines by Shakespeare:

> Timon hath made his everlasting mansion
> Upon the beached verge of the salt flood;
> Who once a day with his embossed froth
> The turbulent surge shall cover;

or take some line that is quite simple, that gets its beauty from its place in a story, and see how it flickers with the light of the many symbols that have given the story its beauty, as a sword-blade may flicker with the light of burning towers.

All sounds, all colours, all forms, either because of their preordained energies or because of long association, evoke indefinable and yet precise emotions, or, as I prefer to think, call down among us certain disembodied powers, whose footsteps over our hearts we call emotions; and when sound, and colour, and form are in a musical relation, a beautiful relation to one another, they become, as it were, one sound, one colour, one form, and evoke an emotion that is made out of their distinct evocations and yet is one emotion. The same relation exists between all portions of every work of art, whether it be an epic or a song, and the more perfect it is, and the more various and numerous the elements that have flowed into its perfection, the more powerful will be the

[a] Burns actually wrote: 'The wan moon is setting ayont the white wave.' 'Ayont' is a Scottish dialect word meaning 'beyond'.

emotion, the power, the god it calls among us. Because an emotion does not exist, or does not become perceptible and active among us, till it has found its expression, in colour or in sound or in form, or in all of these, and because no two modulations or arrangements of these evoke the same emotion, poets and painters and musicians, and in a less degree because their effects are momentary, day and night and cloud and shadow, are continually making and unmaking mankind. It is indeed only those things which seem useless or very feeble that have any power, and all those things that seem useful or strong, armies, moving wheels, modes of architecture, modes of government, speculations of the reason, would have been a little different if some mind long ago had not given itself to some emotion, as a woman gives herself to her lover, and shaped sounds or colours or forms, or all of these, into a musical relation, that their emotion might live in other minds. A little lyric evokes an emotion, and this emotion gathers others about it and melts into their being in the making of some great epic; and at last, needing an always less delicate body, or symbol, as it grows more powerful, it flows out, with all it has gathered, among the blind instincts of daily life, where it moves a power within powers, as one sees ring within ring in the stem of an old tree. This is maybe what Arthur O'Shaughnessy[a] meant when he made his poets say they had built Nineveh with their sighing; and I am certainly never sure, when I hear of some war, or of some religious excitement, or of some new manufacture, or of anything else that fills the ear of the world, that it has not all happened because of something that a boy piped in Thessaly. I remember once telling a seeress to ask one among the gods who, as she believed, were standing about her in their symbolic bodies, what would come of a charming but seeming trivial labour of a friend, and the form answering, 'the devastation of peoples and the overwhelming of cities'. I doubt indeed if the crude circumstance of the world, which seems to create all our emotions, does more than reflect, as in multiplying mirrors, the emotions that have come to solitary men in moments of poetical contemplation; or that love itself would be more than an animal hunger but for the poet and his shadow the priest, for unless we believe that outer things are the reality, we must believe that the gross is the shadow of the subtle, that things are wise before they become foolish, and secret before they cry out in the market-place. Solitary men in moments of contemplation receive, as I think, the creative impulse from the lowest of the Nine Hierarchies[b], and so make and unmake mankind, and even the world itself, for does not 'the eye altering alter all'?

> Our towns are copied fragments from our breast;
> And all man's Babylons strive but to impart
> The grandeurs of his Babylonian heart.

[a] Arthur O'Shaughnessy (1844–81), Irish poet and playwright.
[b] This seems to be an allusion to angels, who were traditionally divided into three hierarchies, each containing three choirs, in the following order of precedence: Seraphim, Cherubim and Thrones; Dominations, Virtues, and Powers; Principalities, Archangels, and Angels. Of these only the last two had an immediate mission to men.

31

III

The purpose of rhythm, it has always seemed to me, is to prolong the moment of contemplation, the moment when we are both asleep and awake, which is the one moment of creation, by hushing us with an alluring monotony, while it holds us waking by variety, to keep us in that state of perhaps real trance, in which the mind liberated from the pressure of the will is unfolded in symbols. If certain sensitive persons listen persistently to the ticking of a watch, or gaze persistently on the monotonous flashing of a light, they fall into the hypnotic trance; and rhythm is but the ticking of a watch made softer, that one must needs listen, and various, that one may not be swept beyond memory or grow weary of listening; while the patterns of the artist are but the monotonous flash woven to take the eyes in a subtler enchantment. I have heard in meditation voices that were forgotten the moment they had spoken; and I have been swept, when in more profound meditation, beyond all memory but of those things that came from beyond the threshold of waking life. I was writing once at a very symbolical and abstract poem, when my pen fell on the ground; and as I stooped to pick it up, I remembered some fantastic adventure that yet did not seem fantastic, and then another like adventure, and when I asked myself when these things had happened, I found that I was remembering my dreams for many nights. I tried to remember what I had done the day before, and then what I had done that morning; but all my waking life had perished from me, and it was only after a struggle that I came to remember it again, and as I did so that more powerful and startling life perished in its turn. Had my pen not fallen on the ground and so made me turn from the images that I was weaving into verse, I would never have known that meditation had become trance, for I would have been like one who does not know that he is passing through a wood because his eyes are on the pathway. So I think that in the making and in the understanding of a work of art, and the more easily if it is full of patterns and symbols and music, we are lured to the threshold of sleep, and it may be far beyond it, without knowing that we have ever set our feet upon the steps of horn or of ivory.

IV

Besides emotional symbols, symbols that evoke emotions alone—and in this sense all alluring or hateful things are symbols, although their relations with one another are too subtle to delight us fully, away from rhythm and pattern —there are intellectual symbols, symbols that evoke ideas alone, or ideas mingled with emotions; and outside the very definite traditions of mysticism and the less definite criticism of certain modern poets, these alone are called symbols. Most things belong to one or another kind, according to the way we speak of them and the companions we give them, for symbols, associated with ideas that are more than fragments of the shadows thrown upon the intellect by the emotions they evoke, are the playthings of the allegorist or the pedant, and soon pass away. If I say 'white' or 'purple' in an ordinary line of poetry, they evoke emotions so exclusively that I cannot say why they move me; but if I bring them into the same sentence with such obvious intellectual symbols as a cross or a crown of thorns, I think of purity and sovereignty. Furthermore, innumerable meanings, which are held to 'white' or to 'purple' by bonds of subtle suggestion, and alike in the emotions and in the intellect, move visibly through my mind, and move invisibly beyond the threshold of sleep, casting lights and shadows of an indefinable wisdom on what had seemed before, it may be, but sterility and noisy violence. It is the intellect that decides where the reader shall ponder over the procession of the symbols, and if the symbols are merely emotional, he gazes from amid the accidents and destinies of the world; but if the symbols are intellectual too, he becomes himself a part of pure intellect, and he is himself mingled with the procession. If I watch a rushy pool in the moonlight, my emotion at its beauty is mixed with memories of the man that I have seen ploughing by its margin, or of the lovers I saw there a night ago; but if I look at the moon herself and remember any of her ancient names and meanings, I move among divine people, and things that have shaken off our mortality, the tower of ivory, the queen of waters, the shining stag among enchanted woods, the white hare sitting upon the hilltop, the fool of Faery with his shining cup full of dreams, and it may be 'make a friend of one of these images of wonder', and 'meet the Lord in the air'. So, too, if one is moved by Shakespeare, who is content with emotional symbols that he may come the nearer to our sympathy, one is mixed with the whole spectacle of the world; while if one is moved by Dante, or by the myth of Demeter[a], one is mixed into the shadow of God or of a goddess. So, too, one is furthest from symbols when one is busy doing this or that, but the soul moves among symbols and unfolds in symbols when trance, or madness, or deep meditation has withdrawn it from every impulse but its own. 'I then saw,' wrote Gérard de Nerval[b] of his madness, 'vaguely drifting into form, plastic images of antiquity, which outlined themselves, became definite, and seemed to represent symbols of which I only seized the idea with difficulty.' In an earlier time he would have been of that multitude whose souls austerity withdrew, even more perfectly than madness could withdraw his soul, from hope and memory, from desire and regret, that they might reveal those processions of symbols that men bow to before altars, and woo with incense and offerings. But being of our time, he has been like Maeterlinck[c], like Villiers de l'Isle-Adam[d] in Axël, like all who are preoccupied with intel-

[a] Demeter: Greek goddess of the fruits of the earth (known as Ceres to the Romans), mother of Persephone (Proserpine), who was carried off by Aidoneus (Pluto) to the Underworld, but was subsequently allowed to return to earth for six months in each year.

[b] Gérard de Nerval, pseudonym of Gérard Labrunie (1808–55), was a French Romantic writer who took his own life.

[c] Maurice Maeterlinck (1862–1949), Belgian dramatist.

[d] Auguste, Comte de Villiers de l'Isle Adam (1838–89) was one of the earliest figures in the French Symbolist movement. His Axel, published in 1890, has been called 'the "Faust" of the later nineteenth century'. It is vividly described and discussed in Edmund Wilson's Axel's Castle (1931).

lectual symbols in our time, a foreshadower of the new sacred book, of which all the arts, as somebody has said, are beginning to dream. How can the arts overcome the slow dying of men's hearts that we call the progress of the world, and lay their hands upon men's heartstrings again, without becoming the garment of religion as in old times?

V

If people were to accept the theory that poetry moves us because of its symbolism, what change should one look for in the manner of our poetry? A return to the way of our fathers, a casting out of descriptions of nature for the sake of nature, of the moral law for the sake of the moral law, a casting out of all anecdotes and of that brooding over scientific opinion that so often extinguished the central flame in Tennyson, and of that vehemence that would make us do or not do certain things; or, in other words, we should come to understand that the beryl stone was enchanted by our fathers that it might unfold the pictures in its heart, and not to mirror our own excited faces, or the boughs waving outside the window. With this change of substance, this return to imagination, this understanding that the laws of art, which are the hidden laws of the world, can alone bind the imagination, would come a change of style, and we would cast out of serious poetry those energetic rhythms, as of a man running, which are the invention of the will with its eyes always on something to be done or undone; and we would seek out those wavering, meditative, organic rhythms, which are the embodiment of the imagination, that neither desires nor hates, because it has done with time, and only wishes to gaze upon some reality, some beauty; nor would it be any longer possible for anybody to deny the importance of form, in all its kinds, for although you can expound an opinion, or describe a thing, when your words are not quite well chosen, you cannot give a body to something that moves beyond the senses, unless your words are as subtle, as complex, as full of mysterious life, as the body of a flower or of a woman. The form of sincere poetry, unlike the form of the 'popular poetry', may indeed be sometimes obscure, or ungrammatical as in some of the best of the *Songs of Innocence and Experience*, but it must have the perfections that escape analysis, the subtleties that have a new meaning every day, and it must have all this whether it be but a little song made out of a moment of dreamy indolence, or some great epic made out of the dreams of one poet and of a hundred generations whose hands were never weary of the sword.

3   Sigmund Freud

Sigmund Freud (1856-1939) was one of the seminal minds of the modern era, whose influence has extended far beyond the boundaries of psychoanalysis, of which he is the recognized founder. In a long series of publications, based partly on his clinical experience of treating neurotic patients, Freud developed a theory of and descriptive terminology for the workings of the human mind which has permeated the whole of modern culture in the West. Perhaps the most significant emphasis in his work was the idea that most human mental activity is unconscious, and that the primary source of psychic energy, libido, is sexual. Freud divided the human mind schematically into three zones, the Id (or unconscious), the Ego (conscious personality), and Super-ego (conscience), and explained dreams and neurotic symptoms as the result of drives rising from the Id, being repressed by the Ego and Super-ego, and finding expression in 'displaced' forms.

In the essay of 1908 reprinted here, Freud applies this model to the creative writing in a way that is not altogether flattering to the literary imagination; and he and his followers have often been accused of a demeaning, reductive attitude to art. Yet Freud was deeply interested in literature, and the theory of human behaviour for which he is most famous (or notorious)—the 'Oedipus complex'—is significantly named after a Greek myth. 'The poets and philosophers before me discovered the unconscious,' he said. 'What I discovered was the scientific method by which the unconscious can be studied.' There is the further paradox that the 'scientific' validity of Freud's method has been seriously questioned, and that his thought has been kept alive and developed by literary rather than by scientific intellectuals. For a subtle and understanding discussion of this complex topic, the reader is directed to Lionel Trilling's essay in this volume.

CROSS REFERENCES: 14. C. G. Jung
                     21. D. W. Harding
                     22. Lionel Trilling
                     38. Norman O. Brown

COMMENTARY: F. T. Hoffman, *Freudianism and the Literary Mind*
               (Baton Rouge, 1945)
               Claudia C. Morrison, *Freud and the Critic: the early use
               of depth psychology in literary criticism*
               (Chapel Hill, 1968)

Creative writers and day-dreaming

We laymen have always been intensely curious to know—like the Cardinal who put a similar question to Ariosto[1]—from what sources that strange being, the creative writer, draws his material, and how he manages to make such an impression on us with it and to arouse in us emotions of which, perhaps, we had not even thought ourselves capable. Our interest is only heightened the more by the fact that, if we ask him, the writer himself gives us no explanation, or none that is satisfactory; and it is not at all weakened by our knowledge that not even the clearest insight into the determinants of his choice of material and into the nature of the art of creating imaginative form will ever help to make creative writers of *us*.

If we could at least discover in ourselves or in people like ourselves an activity which was in some way akin to creative writing! An examination of it would then give us a hope of obtaining the beginnings of an explanation of the creative work of writers. And, indeed, there is some prospect of this being possible. After all, creative writers themselves like to lessen the distance between their kind and the common run of humanity; they so often assure us that every man is a poet at heart and that the last poet will not perish till the last man does.

Should we not look for the first traces of imaginative activity as early as in childhood? The child's best-loved and most intense occupation is with his play or games. Might we not say that every child at play behaves like a creative writer, in that he creates a world of his own, or, rather, rearranges the things of his world in a new way which pleases him? It would be wrong to think he does not take that world seriously; on the contrary, he takes his play very seriously and he expends large amounts of emotion on it. The opposite of play is not what is serious but what is real. In spite of all the emotion with which he cathects his world of play, the child distinguishes it quite well from reality; and he likes to link his imagined objects and situations to the tangible and visible things of the real world. This linking is all that differentiates the child's 'play' from 'fantasying'.

The creative writer does the same as the child at play. He creates a world of fantasy which he takes very seriously—that is, which he invests with large amounts of emotion—while separating it sharply from reality. Language has preserved this relationship between children's play and poetic creation. It gives (in German) the name of '*Spiel*' ('play') to those forms of imaginative writing which require to be linked to tangible objects and which are capable of representation. It speaks of a '*Lustspiel*' or '*Trauerspiel*' ('comedy' or 'tragedy': literally, 'pleasure play' or 'mourning play') and describes those who carry out the representation as '*Schauspieler*' ('players': literally 'show-players'). The unreality of the writer's imaginative world, however, has very important consequences for the technique of his art; for many things which, if they were real, could give no enjoyment, can do so in the play of fantasy, and many excitements which, in themselves, are actually distressing, can become a source of pleasure for the hearers and spectators at the performance of a writer's work.

There is another consideration for the sake of which we will dwell a moment longer on this contrast between reality and play. When the child has grown up and has ceased to play, and after he has been labouring for decades to envisage the realities of life with proper seriousness, he may one day find himself in a mental situation which once more undoes the contrast between play and reality. As an adult he can look back on the intense seriousness with which he once carried on his games in childhood; and, by equating his ostensibly serious occupations of today with his childhood games, he can throw off the too heavy burden imposed on him by life and win the high yield of pleasure afforded by *humour*.[2]

As people grow up, then, they cease to play, and they seem to give up the yield of pleasure which they gained from playing. But whoever understands the human mind knows that hardly anything is harder for a man than to give up a pleasure which he has once experienced. Actually, we can never give anything up; we only exchange one thing for another. What appears to be a renunciation is really the formation of a substitute or surrogate. In the same way, the growing child, when he stops playing, gives up nothing but the link with real objects; instead of *playing*, he now fantasies. He builds castles in the air and creates what are called *day-dreams*. I believe that most people construct fantasies at times in their lives. This is a fact which has long been overlooked and whose importance has therefore not been sufficiently appreciated.

People's fantasies are less easy to observe than the play of children. The child, it is true, plays by himself or forms a closed psychical system with other children for the purposes of a game; but even though he may not play his game in front of the grown-ups, he does not, on the other hand, conceal it from them. The adult, on the contrary, is ashamed of his fantasies and hides them from other people. He cherishes his fantasies as his most intimate possessions, and as a rule he would rather confess his misdeeds than tell anyone his fantasies. It may come about that for that reason he believes he is the only person who invents such fantasies and has no idea that creations of this kind are widespread among other people. This difference in the behaviour of a person who plays and a person who fantasies is accounted for by the motives of these two activities, which are nevertheless adjuncts to each other.

A child's play is determined by wishes: in point of fact by a single wish— one that helps in his upbringing—the wish to be big and grown up. He is always playing at being 'grown up', and in his games he imitates what he knows about the lives of his elders. He has no reason to conceal this wish. With the adult, the case is different. On the one hand, he knows that he is expected not to go on playing or fantasying any longer, but to act in the real world; on the other hand, some of the wishes which give rise to his fantasies are of a kind which it is essential to conceal. Thus he is ashamed of his fantasies as being childish and as being unpermissible.

But, you will ask, if people make such a mystery of their fantasying, how is it that we know such a lot about it? Well, there is a class of human beings upon whom, not a god, indeed, but a stern goddess—Necessity—has allotted the task of telling what they suffer and what things give them happiness. These are the victims of nervous illness, who are obliged to tell their fantasies, among other things, to the doctor by whom they expect to be cured by mental treatment. This is our best source of knowledge, and we have since found good reason to suppose that our patients tell us nothing that we might not also hear from healthy people.

Let us make ourselves acquainted with a few of the characteristics of fantasying. We may lay it down that a happy person never fantasies, only an unsatisfied one. The motive forces of fantasies are unsatisfied wishes, and every single fantasy is the fulfilment of a wish, a correction of unsatisfying reality. These motivating wishes vary according to the sex, character, and circumstances of the person who is having the fantasy; but they fall naturally into two main groups. They are either ambitious wishes, which serve to elevate the subject's personality; or they are erotic ones. In young women the erotic wishes predominate almost exclusively, for their ambition is as a rule absorbed by erotic trends. In young men egoistic and ambitious wishes come to the fore clearly enough alongside of erotic ones. But we will not lay stress on the opposition between the two trends; we would rather emphasize the fact that they are often united. Just as, in many altar-pieces, the portrait of the donor is to be seen in a corner of the picture, so, in the majority of ambitious fantasies, we can discover in some corner or other the lady for whom the creator of the fantasy performs all his heroic deeds and at whose feet all his triumphs are laid. Here, as you see, there are strong enough motives for concealment; the well-brought-up young woman is only allowed a minimum of erotic desire, and the young man has to learn to suppress the excess of self-regard which he brings with him from the spoilt days of his childhood, so that he may find his place in a society which is full of other individuals making equally strong demands.

We must not suppose that the products of this imaginative activity—the various fantasies, castles in the air and day-dreams—are stereotyped or unalterable. On the contrary, they fit themselves in to the subject's shifting impressions of life, change with every change in his situation, and receive from every fresh active impression what might be called a 'datemark'. The relation of a fantasy to time is in general very important. We may say that it hovers, as it were, between three times—the three moments of time which our ideation involves. Mental work is linked to some current impression, some provoking occasion in the present which has been able to arouse one of the subject's major wishes. From there it harks back to a memory of an earlier experience (usually an infantile one) in which this wish was fulfilled; and it now creates a situation relating to the future which represents a fulfilment of the wish. What it thus creates is a day-dream or fantasy, which carries about it traces of its origin from the occasion which provoked it and from the memory. Thus past, present, and future are strung together, as it were, on the thread of the wish that runs through them.

A very ordinary example may serve to make what I have said clear. Let us take the case of a poor orphan boy to whom you have given the address of some employer where he may perhaps find a job. On his way there he may indulge in a day-dream appropriate to the situation from which it arises. The content of his fantasy will perhaps be something like this. He is given a job, finds favour with his new employer, makes himself indispensable in the business, is taken into his employer's family, marries the charming young daughter of the house, and then himself becomes a director of the business, first as his employer's partner and then as his successor. In this fantasy, the dreamer has regained what he possessed in his happy childhood—the protecting house, the loving parents, and the first objects of his affectionate feelings. You will see from this example the way in which the wish makes use of an occasion in the present to construct, on the pattern of the past, a picture of the future.

There is a great deal more that could be said about fantasies; but I will only allude as briefly as possible to certain points. If fantasies become overluxuriant and overpowerful, the conditions are laid for an onset of neurosis or psychosis. Fantasies, moreover, are the immediate mental precursors of the distressing symptoms complained of by our patients. Here a broad bypath branches off into pathology.

I cannot pass over the relation of fantasies to dreams. Our dreams at night are nothing else than fantasies like these, as we can demonstrate from the interpretation of dreams. Language, in its unrivalled wisdom, long ago decided the question of the essential nature of dreams by giving the name of 'day-dreams' to the airy creations of fantasy. If the meaning of our dreams usually remains obscure to us in spite of this pointer, it is because of the circumstance that at night there also arise in us wishes of which we are ashamed; these we must conceal from ourselves, and they have consequently been repressed, pushed into the unconscious. Repressed wishes of this sort and their derivatives are only allowed to come to expression in a very distorted form. When scientific work had succeeded in elucidating this factor of *dream-distortion*, it was no longer difficult to recognize that night-dreams are wish-fulfilments in just the same way as day-dreams—the fantasies which we all know so well.

So much for fantasies. And now for the creative writer. May we really attempt to compare the imaginative writer with the 'dreamer in broad daylight', and his creations with day-dreams? Here we must begin by making an initial distinction. We must separate writers who, like the ancient authors of epics and tragedies, take over their material ready-made, from writers who seem to originate their own material. We will keep to the latter kind, and, for the purposes of our comparison, we will choose not the writers most highly esteemed by the critics, but the less pretentious authors of novels, romances, and short stories, who nevertheless have the widest and most eager circle of readers of both sexes. One feature above all cannot fail to strike us about the creations of these story-writers: each of them has a hero who is the centre of interest, for whom the writer tries to win our sympathy by every possible means and whom he seems to place under the protection of a special Providence. If, at the end of one chapter of my story, I leave the hero unconscious and bleeding from severe wounds, I am sure to find him at the beginning of the next being carefully nursed and on the way to recovery; and if the first volume closes with the ship he is in going down in a storm at sea, I am certain, at the opening of the second volume, to read of his miraculous rescue—a rescue without which the story could not proceed. The feeling of security with which I follow the hero through his perilous adventures is the same as the feeling with which a hero in real life throws himself into the water to save a drowning man or exposes himself to the enemy's fire in order to storm a battery. It is the true heroic feeling, which one of our best writers has expressed in an inimitable phrase: 'Nothing can happen to *me*!' It seems to me, however, that through this revealing characteristic of invulnerability we can immediately recognize His Majesty the Ego, the hero alike of every day-dream and every story.

Other typical features of these egocentric stories point to the same kinship. The fact that all the women in the novel invariably fall in love with the hero can hardly be looked on as a portrayal of reality, but it is easily understood as a necessary constituent of a day-dream. The same is true of the fact that the other characters in the story are sharply divided into good and bad, in defiance of the variety of human characters that are to be observed in real life. The 'good' ones are the helpers, while the 'bad' ones are the enemies and rivals, of the ego which has become the hero of the story.

We are perfectly aware that very many imaginative writings are far removed from the model of the naïve day-dream; and yet I cannot suppress the suspicion that even the most extreme deviations from that model could be linked with it through an uninterrupted series of transitional cases. It has struck me that in many of what are known as 'psychological' novels only one person—once again the hero—is described from within. The author sits inside his mind, as it were, and looks at the other characters from outside. The psychological novel in general no doubt owes its special nature to the inclination of the modern writer to split up his ego, by self-observation, into many part-egos, and, in consequence, to personify the conflicting currents of his own mental life in several heroes. Certain novels, which might be described as 'eccentric', seem to stand in quite special contrast to the types of the day-dream. In these, the person who is introduced as the hero plays only a very small active part; he sees the actions and sufferings of other people pass before him like a spectator. Many of Zola's later works belong to this category. But I must point out that the psychological analysis of individuals who are not creative writers, and who diverge in some respects from the so-called norm, has shown us analogous variations of the day-dream, in which the ego contents itself with the role of spectator.

If our comparison of the imaginative writer with the day-dreamer, and of poetical creation with the day-dream, is to be of any value, it must, above all, show itself in some way or other fruitful. Let us, for instance, try to apply to these authors' works the thesis we laid down earlier concerning the relation between fantasy and the three periods of time and the wish which runs through them; and, with its help, let us try to study the connections that exist between the life of the writer and his works. No one has known, as a rule, what expectations to frame in approaching this problem; and often the connection has been thought of in much too simple terms. In the light of the insight we have gained from fantasies, we ought to expect the following state of affairs. A strong experience in the present awakens in the creative writer a memory of an earlier experience (usually belonging to his childhood) from which there now proceeds a wish which finds its fulfilment in the creative work. The work itself exhibits elements of the recent provoking occasion as well as of the old memory.

Do not be alarmed at the complexity of this formula. I suspect that in fact it will prove to be too exiguous a pattern. Nevertheless, it may contain a first approach to the true state of affairs; and, from some experiments I have made, I am inclined to think that this way of looking at creative writings may turn out not unfruitful. You will not forget that the stress it lays on childhood memories in the writer's life—a stress which may perhaps seem puzzling—is ultimately derived from the assumption that a piece of creative writing, like a day-dream, is a continuation of, and a substitute for, what was once the play of childhood.

We must not neglect, however, to go back to the kind of imaginative works which we have to recognize, not as original creations, but as the refashioning of ready-made and familiar material. Even here, the writer keeps a certain amount of independence, which can express itself in the choice of material and in changes in it which are often quite extensive. In so far as the material is already at hand, however, it is derived from the popular treasure-house of myths, legends, and fairy tales. The study of constructions of folk psychology such as these is far from being complete, but it is extremely probable that myths, for instance, are distorted vestiges of the wishful fantasies of whole nations, the *secular dreams* of youthful humanity.

You will say that, although I have put the creative writer first in the title of my paper, I have told you far less about him than about fantasies. I am aware of that, and I must try to excuse it by pointing to the present state of our knowledge. All I have been able to do is to throw out some encouragements and suggestions which, starting from the study of fantasies, lead on to the problem of the writer's choice of his literary material. As for the other problem— by what means the creative writer achieves the emotional effects in us that are aroused by his creations—we have as yet not touched on it at all. But I should like at least to point out to you the path that leads from our discussion of fantasies to the problems of poetical effects.

You will remember how I have said that the day-dreamer carefully conceals his fantasies from other people because he feels he has reasons for being ashamed of them. I should now add that even if he were to communicate them to us he could give us no pleasure by his disclosures. Such fantasies, when we learn them, repel us or at least leave us cold. But when a creative writer presents his plays to us or tells us what we are inclined to take to be his personal day-dreams, we experience a great pleasure, and one which probably arises from the confluence of many sources. How the writer accomplishes this is his innermost secret; the essential *ars poetica* lies in the technique of overcoming the feeling of repulsion in us which is undoubtedly connected with the barriers that rise between each single ego and the others. We can guess two of the methods used by this technique. The writer softens the character of his egoistic day-dreams by altering and disguising it, and he bribes us by the purely formal —that is, aesthetic—yield of pleasure which he offers us in the presentation of his fantasies. We give the name of an *incentive bonus*, or a *forepleasure*, to a yield of pleasure such as this, which is offered to us so as to make possible the release of still greater pleasure arising from deeper psychical sources. In my opinion, all the aesthetic pleasure which a creative writer affords us has the character of a forepleasure of this kind, and our actual enjoyment of an imaginative work proceeds from a liberation of tensions in our minds. It may even be that not a little of this effect is due to the writer's enabling us thenceforward to enjoy our own day-dreams without self-reproach or shame. This brings us to the threshold of new, interesting, and complicated inquiries; but also, at least for the moment, to the end of our discussion.

Notes

1. Cardinal Ippolito d'Este was Ariosto's first patron, to whom he dedicated the *Orlando Furioso*. The poet's only reward was the question: 'Where did you find so many stories, Lodovico?'
2. See [Freud's] *Wit and Its Relation to the Unconscious*, vii, 7.

4 Henry James

Henry James (1843-1916) was born in New York, but much of his early life was spent in the major cities of Europe. He finally settled in England in 1875, making his home first in London and later at Rye, Kent. He became a naturalized British citizen in 1915. James had a long and prolific career as a novelist and short-story writer, extending from 'Watch and Ward' (1871) to the unfinished *Ivory Tower* (1917). His early novels, like *Roderick Hudson* (1875) and *Portrait of a Lady* (1881), were characteristically concerned with the interaction of American and European characters and cultures, and he returned to this theme in the three major novels of his later life, *The Wings of the Dove* (1902), *The Ambassadors* (1903), and *The Golden Bowl* (1904).

More than any other single writer, James may be said to have presided over the transformation of the Victorian novel into the modern novel, and at the same time to have laid the foundations of modern criticism of the novel. The two enterprises were necessarily related for James, who fervently believed that 'Art lives upon discussion, upon experiment, upon curiosity, upon variety of attempt, upon the exchange of views and the comparison of standpoints'. The quotation is from his famous essay 'The Art of Fiction' (1884), in which he analysed the aesthetic and moral implications of his subject with a subtlety and eloquence unprecedented in English letters.

Between 1907 and 1909, Charles Scribner's Sons reissued most of James's fiction in a uniform edition, generally known as the New York edition, for which James not only revised the texts but wrote a series of Prefaces in which he discussed the genesis and composition of the novels and stories and expounded an aesthetic of the novel based on his own practice. These prefaces have been collected together by R. P. Blackmur under the title *The Art of the Novel* (New York, 1934), and constitute one of the classics of modern criticism. Some of James's occasional essays and reviews on other novelists are collected in *The House of Fiction* (1957) edited by Leon Edel.

James is represented here by his Preface to *The Ambassadors*, which he considered 'quite the best, "all round", of all my productions'. This is the story of Lambert Strether, a middle-aged American bachelor who is sent to Europe by Mrs Newsome, a wealthy widow to whom Strether is engaged. His mission is to bring home Mrs Newsome's son, Chad, who is neglecting the family business and reportedly having a sordid affair with a French woman. Strether, however, finds Chad much improved, and when he finally identifies the woman as the charming and gracious Madame de Vionnet, he cannot believe that there is anything evil—or even carnal—in the liaison.

Thus, all the assumptions and values Strether had brought with him from America are overturned, and he becomes convinced that Chad should stay in Paris, not to lose the chance—as Strether feels he himself lost it—to 'live'. In due course, the sublimity of Chad's relationship with Mme de Vionnet proves to be an illusion—a discovery which qualifies, but does not entirely erase, Strether's moral revolution. In the first part of the Preface, James describes the 'germ' or original inspiration for the novel: an anecdote about 'a man of distinction' (actually William Dean Howells, a friend of James's) who in a Paris garden delivered a poignant and rueful exhortation to a younger companion to 'Live all you can'.

One of James's principal contributions to criticism of the novel was to make writers and critics fully conscious of the significance of narrative method—of the 'point of view' from which the story is told. *The Ambassadors* exemplifies the method James himself usually preferred and perfected—the rendering of experience through the consciousness of a created character, maintaining the control and flexibility of third-person narration, but observing the limitations of ordinary human perception, so that we share the character's doubts and confusions. James's comments on this aspect of his novel—'the refinements and ecstasies of method'—are particularly fascinating. His precept and practice were subsequently used as the basis for a more systematic theory of the novel by his friend, Percy Lubbock, in *The Craft of Fiction* (1921).

CROSS REFERENCES : 7. Virginia Woolf
                      11. E. M. Forster
                      39. Ian Watt

COMMENTARY : R. P. Blackmur :
                  Introduction to *The Art of the Novel: Critical Prefaces by Henry James* (New York, 1934)
                  F. O. Matthiesen, 'The Ambassadors' in *Henry James: the major phase* (New York, 1944)

Preface to *The Ambassadors*

Nothing is more easy than to state the subject of *The Ambassadors*, which first appeared in twelve numbers of *The North American Review* (1903) and was published as a whole the same year. The situation involved is gathered up betimes, that is in the second chapter of Book Fifth, for the reader's benefit, into as few words as possible—planted or 'sunk', stiffly and saliently, in the centre of the current, almost perhaps to the obstruction of traffic. Never can a composition of this sort have sprung straighter from a dropped grain of suggestion, and never can that grain, developed, overgrown and smothered, have yet lurked more in the mass as an independent particle. The whole case, in fine, is in Lambert Strether's irrepressible outbreak to little Bilham on the Sunday afternoon in Gloriani's garden, the candour with which he yields, for his young friend's enlightenment, to the charming admonition of that crisis. The idea of the tale resides indeed in the very fact that an hour of such unprecedented ease should have been felt by him *as* a crisis, and he is at pains to express it for us as neatly as we could desire. The remarks to which he thus gives utterance contain the essence of *The Ambassadors*, his fingers close, before he has done, round the stem of the full-blown flower; which, after that fashion, he continues officiously to present to us. 'Live all you can; it's a mistake not to. It doesn't so much matter what you do in particular so long as you have your life. If you haven't had that what *have* you had? I'm too old—too old at any rate for what I see. What one loses one loses; make no mistake about that. Still, we have the illusion of freedom; therefore don't, like me today, be without the memory of that illusion. I was either, at the right time, too stupid or too intelligent to have it, and now I'm a case of reaction against the mistake. Do what you like so long as you don't make it. For it *was* a mistake. Live, live!' Such is the gist of Strether's appeal to the impressed youth, whom he likes and whom he desires to befriend; the word 'mistake' occurs several times, it will be seen, in the course of his remarks—which gives the measure of the signal warning he feels attached to his case. He has accordingly missed too much, though perhaps after all constitutionally qualified for a better part, and he wakes up to it in conditions that press the spring of a terrible question. *Would* there yet perhaps be time for reparation?—reparation, that is, for the injury done his character; for the affront, he is quite ready to say, so stupidly put upon it and in which he has even himself had so clumsy a hand? The answer to which is that he now at all events *sees*; so that the business of my tale and the march of my action, not to say the precious moral of everything, is just my demonstration of this process of vision.

Nothing can exceed the closeness with which the whole fits again into its germ. That had been given me bodily, as usual, by the spoken word, for I was to take the image over exactly as I happened to have met it. A friend had repeated to me, with great appreciation, a thing or two said to him by a man of distinction, much his senior, and to which a sense akin to that of Strether's melancholy eloquence might be imputed—said as chance would have, and so easily might, in Paris, and in a charming old garden attached to a house of art, and on a Sunday afternoon of summer, many persons of great interest being present. The observation there listened to and gathered up had contained part of the 'note' that I was to recognize on the spot as to my purpose—had contained in fact the greater part; the rest was in the place and the time and the scene they sketched: these constituents clustered and combined to give me further support, to give me what I may call the note absolute. There it stands, accordingly, full in the tideway; driven in, with hard taps, like some strong stake for the noose of a cable, the swirl of the current round about it. What amplified the hint to more than the bulk of hints in general was the gift with it of the old Paris garden, for in that token were sealed up values infinitely precious. There was of course the seal to break and each item of the packet to count over and handle and estimate; but somehow, in the light of the hint, all the elements of a situation of the sort most to my taste were there. I could even remember no occasion on which, so confronted, I had found it of a livelier interest to take stock, in this fashion, of suggested wealth. For I think, verily, that there are degrees of merit in subjects—in spite of the fact that to treat even one of the most ambiguous with due decency we must for the time, for the feverish and prejudiced hour, at least figure its merit and its dignity as *possibly* absolute. What it comes to, doubtless, is that even among the supremely good— since with such alone is it one's theory of one's honour to be concerned—there is an ideal *beauty* of goodness the invoked action of which is to raise the artistic faith to its maximum. Then truly, I hold, one's theme may be said to shine, and that of *The Ambassadors*, I confess, wore this glow for me from beginning to end. Fortunately thus I am able to estimate this as, frankly, quite the best, 'all round', of all my productions; any failure of that justification would have made such an extreme of complacency publicly fatuous.

I recall then in this connection no moment of subjective intermittence, never one of those alarms as for a suspected hollow beneath one's feet, a felt ingrati- tude in the scheme adopted, under which confidence fails and opportunity seems but to mock. If the motive of *The Wings of the Dove,* as I have noted, was to worry me at moments by a sealing-up of its face—though without prejudice to its again, of a sudden, fairly grimacing with expression—so in this other busi- ness I had absolute conviction and constant clearness to deal with; it had been a frank proposition, the whole bunch of data, installed on my premises like a monotony of fine weather. (The order of composition, in these things, I may mention, was reversed by the order of publication; the earlier written of the two books having appeared as the later.) Even under the weight of my hero's years I could feel my postulate firm; even under the strain of the difference between those of Madame de Vionnet and those of Chad Newsome, a difference liable to be denounced as shocking, I could still feel it serene. Nothing resisted, nothing betrayed, I seem to make out, in this full and sound sense of the matter; it shed from any side I could turn it to the same golden glow. I rejoiced in the promise of a hero so mature, who would give me thereby the more to bite into— since it's only into thickened motive and accumulated character, I think, that the painter of life bites more than a little. My poor friend should have accum- ulated character, certainly; or rather would be quite naturally and handsomely possessed of it, in the sense that he would have, and would always have felt he had, imagination galore, and that this yet wouldn't have wrecked him. It was immeasurable, the opportunity to 'do' a man of imagination, for if *there* mightn't be a chance to 'bite', where in the world might it be? This personage of course, so enriched, wouldn't give me, for his type, imagination in *predomin- ance* or as his prime faculty, nor should I, in view of other matters, have found that convenient. So particular a luxury—some occasion, that is, for study of the high gift in *supreme* command of a case or of a career—would still doubtless come on the day I should be ready to pay for it; and till then might, as from far back, remain hung up well in view and just out of reach. The comparative case meanwhile would serve—it was only on the minor scale that I had treated myself even to comparative cases.

I was to hasten to add however that, happy stopgaps as the minor scale had thus yielded, the instance in hand should enjoy the advantage of the full range of the major; since most immediately to the point was the question of that *supplement* of situation logically involved in our gentleman's impulse to deliver himself in the Paris garden on the Sunday afternoon—or if not involved by strict logic then all ideally and enchantingly implied in it. (I say 'ideally', because I need scarce mention that for development, for expression of its maximum, my glimmering story was, at the earliest stage, to have nipped the thread of connection with the possibilities of the actual reported speaker. He remains but the happiest of accidents; his actualities, all too definite, precluded any range of possibilities; it had only been his charming office to project upon that wide field of the artist's vision—which hangs there ever in place like the white sheet suspended for the figures of a child's magic-lantern—a more fantastic and more movable shadow.) No privilege of the teller of tales and the handler of puppets is more delightful, or has more of the suspense and the thrill of a game of difficulty breathlessly played, than just this business of looking for the un-seen and the occult, in a scheme half-grasped, by the light or, so to speak, by the clinging scent, of the gage already in hand. No dreadful old pursuit of the hidden slave with bloodhounds and the rag of association can ever, for 'excite-ment', I judge, have bettered it at its best. For the dramatist[a] always, by the very law of his genius, believes not only in a possible right issue from the rightly-conceived tight place; he does much more than this—he believes, irresist-ibly, in the necessary, the precious 'tightness' of the place (whatever the issue) on the strength of any respectable hint. It being thus the respectable hint that I had with such avidity picked up, what would be the story to which it would most inevitably form the centre? It is part of the charm attendant on such ques-tions that the 'story', with the omens true, as I say, puts on from this stage the authenticity of concrete existence. It then *is*, essentially—it begins to be, though it may more or less obscurely lurk; so that the point is not in the least what to make of it, but only, very delightfully and very damnably, where to put one's hand on it.

In which truth resides surely much of the interest of that admirable mixture for salutary application which we know as art. Art deals with what we see, it must first contribute full-handed that ingredient; it plucks its material, other-wise expressed, in the garden of life—which material elsewhere grown is stale and uneatable. But it has no sooner done this than it has to take account of a *process*—from which only when it's the basest of the servants of man, incurring ignominious dismissal with no 'character', does it, and whether under some muddled pretext of morality or on any other, pusillanimously edge away. The process, that of the expression, the literal squeezing-out, of value is another affair—with which the happy luck of mere finding has little to do. The joys of finding, at this stage, are pretty well over; that quest of the subject as a whole

[a] James's narrative method, especially in his later fiction, tended towards a 'dramatic' rendering of experience. Hence he often uses the word 'dramatist' to mean 'novelist'.

by 'matching', as the ladies say at the shops, the big piece with the snippet, having ended, we assume, with a capture. The subject is found, and if the problem is then transferred to the ground of what to do with it the field opens out for any amount of doing. This is precisely the infusion that, as I submit, completes the strong mixture. It is on the other hand the part of the business that can least be likened to the chase with horn and hound. It's all a sedentary part —involves as much ciphering, of sorts, as would merit the highest salary paid to a chief accountant. Not, however, that the chief accountant hasn't *his* gleams of bliss; for the felicity, or at least the equilibrium, of the artist's state dwells less, surely, in the further delightful complications he can smuggle in than in those he succeeds in keeping out. He sows his seed at the risk of too thick a crop; wherefore yet again, like the gentlemen who audit ledgers, he must keep his head at any price. In consequence of all which, for the interest of the matter, I might seem here to have my choice of narrating my 'hunt' for Lambert Strether, of describing the capture of the shadow projected by my friend's anecdote, or of reporting on the occurrences subsequent to that triumph. But I had probably best attempt a little to glance in each direction; since it comes to me again and again, over this licentious record, that one's bag of adventures, conceived or conceivable, has been only half-emptied by the mere telling of one's story. It depends so on what one means by that equivocal quantity. There is the story of one's hero, and then, thanks to the intimate connection of things, the story of one's story itself. I blush to confess it, but if one's a dramatist one's a dramatist, and the latter imbroglio is liable on occasion to strike me as really the more objective of the two.

The philosophy imputed to him in that beautiful outbreak, the hour there, amid such happy provision, striking for him, would have been then, on behalf of my man of imagination, to be logically and, as the artless craft of comedy has it, 'led up' to; the probable course to such a goal, the goal of so conscious a predicament, would have in short to be finely calculated. Where has he come from and why has he come, what is he doing (as we Anglo-Saxons, and we only, say, in our foredoomed clutch of exotic aids to expression) in that *galère* [difficult place]? To answer these questions plausibly, to answer them as under cross-examination in the witness-box by counsel for the prosecution, in other words satisfactorily to account for Strether and for his 'peculiar tone', was to possess myself of the entire fabric. At the same time the clue to its whereabouts would lie in a certain *principle* of probability: he wouldn't have indulged in his peculiar tone without a reason; it would take a felt predicament or a false position to give him so ironic an accent. One hadn't been noting 'tones' all one's life without recognizing when one heard it the voice of the false position. The dear man in the Paris garden was then admirably and unmistakably *in* one —which was no small point gained; what next accordingly concerned us was the determination of *this* identity. One could only go by probabilities, but there was the advantage that the most general of the probabilities were virtual certainties. Possessed of our friend's nationality, to start with, there was a general probability in his narrower localism; which, for that matter, one had really but to keep under the lens for an hour to see it give up its secrets. He

would have issued, our rueful worthy, from the very heart of New England—
at the heels of which matter of course a perfect train of secrets tumbled for me
into the light. They had to be sifted and sorted, and I shall not reproduce the
detail of that process; but unmistakably they were all there, and it was but a
question, auspiciously, of picking among them. What the 'position' would
infallibly be, and why, on his hands, it had turned 'false'—these inductive steps
could only be as rapid as they were distinct. I accounted for everything—and
'everything' had by this time become the most promising quantity—by the
view that he had come to Paris in some state of mind which was literally under-
going, as a result of new and unexpected assaults and infusions, a change
almost from hour to hour. He had come with a view that might have been
figured by a clear green liquid, say, in a neat glass phial; and the liquid, once
poured into the open cup of *application*, once exposed to the action of another
air, had begun to turn from green to red, or whatever, and might, for all he
knew, be on its way to purple, to black, to yellow. At the still wilder extremes
represented perhaps, for all he could say to the contrary, by a variability so
violent, he would at first, naturally, but have gazed in surprise and alarm;
whereby the *situation* clearly would spring from the play of wildness and the
development of extremes. I saw in a moment that, should this development
proceed both with force and logic, my 'story' would leave nothing to be desired.
There is always, of course, for the story-teller, the irresistible determinant and
the incalculable advantage of his interest in the story *as such*; it is ever,
obviously, overwhelmingly, the prime and precious thing (as other than this
I have never been able to see it); as to which what makes for it, with whatever
headlong energy, may be said to pale before the energy with which it simply
makes for itself. It rejoices, none the less, at its best, to seem to offer itself in a
light, to seem to know, and with the very last knowledge, what it's about—
liable as it yet is at moments to be caught by us with its tongue in its cheek
and absolutely no warrant but its splendid impudence. Let us grant then that
the impudence is always there—there, so to speak, for grace and effect and
allure; there, above all, because the Story is just the spoiled child of art, and
because as we are always disappointed when the pampered don't 'play up', we
like it, to that extent, to look all its character. It probably does so, in truth,
even when we most flatter ourselves that we negotiate with it by treaty.

All of which, again, is but to say that the *steps*, for my fable, placed themselves with a prompt and, as it were, functional assurance—an air quite as of
readiness to have dispensed with logic had I been in fact too stupid for my
clue. Never, positively, none the less, as the links multiplied, had I felt less
stupid than for the determination of poor Strether's errand and for the apprehension of his issue. These things continued to fall together, as by the neat
action of their own weight and form, even while their commentator scratched
his head about them; he easily sees now that they were always well in advance
of him. As the case completed itself he had in fact, from a good way behind, to
catch up with them, breathless and a little flurried, as he best could. The false
position, for our belated man of the world—belated because he had endeavoured
so long to escape being one, and now at last had really to face his doom—the

false position for him, I say, was obviously to have presented himself at the gate of that boundless menagerie primed with a moral scheme of the most approved pattern which was yet framed to break down on any approach to vivid facts; that is to any at all liberal appreciation of them. There would have been of course the case of the Strether prepared, wherever presenting himself, only to judge and to feel meanly; but *he* would have moved for me, I confess, enveloped in no legend whatever. The actual man's note, from the first of our seeing it struck, is the note of discrimination, just as his drama is to become, under stress, the drama of discrimination. It would have been his blest imagination, we have seen, that had already helped him to discriminate; the element that was for so much of the pleasure of my cutting thick, as I have intimated, into his intellectual, into his moral substance. Yet here it was, at the same time, just here, that a shade for a moment fell across the scene.

There was the dreadful little old tradition, one of the platitudes of the human comedy, that people's moral scheme *does* break down in Paris; that nothing is more frequently observed; that hundreds of thousands of more or less hypocritical or more or less cynical persons annually visit the place for the sake of the probable catastrophe, and that I came late in the day to work myself up about it. There was in fine the *trivial* association, one of the vulgarest in the world; but which give me pause no longer, I think, simply because its vulgarity is so advertised. The revolution performed by Strether under the influence of the most interesting of great cities was to have nothing to do with any *bêtise* [foolishness] of the imputably 'tempted' state; he was to be thrown forward, rather, thrown quite with violence, upon his lifelong trick of intense reflection : which friendly test indeed was to bring him out, through winding passages, through alternations of darkness and light, very much *in* Paris, but with the surrounding scene itself a minor matter, a mere symbol for more things than had been dreamt of in the philosophy of Woollett. Another surrounding scene would have done as well for our show could it have represented a place in which Strether's errand was likely to lie and his crisis to await him. The *likely* place had the great merit of sparing me preparations; there would have been too many involved—not at all impossibilities, only rather worrying and delaying difficulties—in positing elsewhere Chad Newsome's interesting relation, his so interesting complexity of relations. Strether's appointed stage, in fine, could be but Chad's most luckily selected one. The young man had gone in, as they say, for circumjacent charm; and where he would have found it, by the turn of his mind, most 'authentic', was where his earnest friend's analysis would most find *him*; as well as where, for that matter, the former's whole analytic faculty would be led such a wonderful dance.

The Ambassadors had been, all conveniently, 'arranged for', its first appearance was from month to month, in the *North American Review* during 1903, and I had been open from far back to any pleasant provocation for ingenuity that might reside in one's actively adopting—so as to make it, in its way, a small compositional law—recurrent breaks and resumptions. I had made up my mind here regularly to exploit and enjoy these often rather rude jolts—having found, as I believed, an admirable way to it; yet every question of form and pressure, I easily remember, paled in the light of the major propriety, recognized as soon as really weighed; that of employing but one centre and keeping it all within my hero's compass. The thing was to be so much this worthy's intimate adventure that even the projection of his consciousness upon it from beginning to end without intermission or deviation would probably still leave a part of its value for him, and *a fortiori* [all the more] for ourselves, unexpressed. I might, however, express every grain of it that there would be room for —on condition of contriving a splendid particular economy. Other persons in no small number were to people the scene, and each with his or her axe to grind, his or her situation to treat, his or her coherency not to fail of, his or her relation to my leading motive, in a word, to establish and carry on. But Strether's sense of these things, and Strether's only, should avail me for showing them; I should know them but through his more or less groping knowledge of them, since his very gropings would figure among his most interesting motions, and a full observance of the rich rigour I speak of would give me more of the effect I should be most 'after' than all other possible observances together. It would give me a large unity, and that in turn would crown me with the grace to which the enlightened story-teller will at any time, for his interest, sacrifice if need be all other graces whatever. I refer of course to the grace of intensity, which there are ways of signally achieving and ways of signally missing—as we see it, all round us, helplessly and woefully missed. Not that it isn't, on the other hand, a virtue eminently subject to appreciation—there being no strict, no absolute measure of it; so that one may hear it acclaimed where it has quite escaped one's perception, and see it unnoticed where one has gratefully hailed it. After all of which I am not sure, either, that the immense amusement of the whole cluster of difficulties so arrayed may not operate, for the fond fabulist, when judicious not less than fond, as his best of determinants. That charming principle is always there, at all events, to keep interest fresh : it is a principle, we remember, essentially ravenous, without scruple and without mercy, appeased with no cheap nor easy nourishment. It enjoys the costly sacrifice and rejoices thereby in the very odour of difficulty— even as ogres, with their 'Fee-faw-fum !' rejoice in the smell of the blood of Englishmen.

Thus it was, at all events, that the ultimate, though after all so speedy, definition of my gentleman's job—his coming out, all solemnly appointed and deputed, to 'save' Chad, and his then finding the young man so disobligingly and, at first, so bewilderingly not lost that a new issue altogether, in the connection, prodigiously faces them, which has to be dealt with in a new light— promised as many calls on ingenuity and on the higher branches of the compositional art as one could possibly desire. Again and yet again, as, from book to book, I proceed with my survey, I find no source of interest equal to this verification after the fact, as I may call it, and the more in detail the better, of the scheme of consistency 'gone in' for. As always—since the charm never fails —the retracing of the process from point to point brings back the old illusion. The old intentions bloom again and flower—in spite of all the blossoms they were to have dropped by the way. This is the charm, as I say, of adventure *transposed*—the thrilling ups and downs, the intricate ins and outs of the compositional problem, made after such a fashion admirably objective, becoming the question at issue and keeping the author's heart in his mouth. Such an element, for instance, as his intention that Mrs Newsome, away off with her finger on the pulse of Massachusetts, should yet be no less intensely than circuitously present through the whole thing, should be no less felt as to be reckoned with than the most direct exhibition, the finest portrayal at first hand could make her, such a sign of artistic good faith, I say, once it's unmistakably there, takes on again an actuality not too much impaired by the comparative dimness of the particular success. Cherished intention too inevitably acts and operates, in the book, about fifty times as little as I had fondly dreamt it might; but that scarce spoils for me the pleasure of recognizing the fifty ways in which I had sought to provide for it. The mere charm of seeing such an idea constituent, in its degree; the fineness of the measures taken—a real extension, if successful, of the very terms and possibilities of representation and figuration—such things alone were, after this fashion, inspiring, such things alone were a gage of the probable success of that dissimulated calculation with which the whole effort was to square. But oh the cares begotten, none the less, of that same 'judicious' sacrifice to a particular form of interest! One's work should have composition, because composition alone is positive beauty; but all the while—apart from one's inevitable consciousness too of the dire paucity of readers ever recognizing or ever missing positive beauty—how, as to the cheap and easy, at every turn, how, as to immediacy and facility, and even as to the commoner vivacity, positive beauty might have to be sweated for and paid for! Once achieved and installed it may always be trusted to make the poor seeker feel he would have blushed to the roots of his hair for failing of it; yet, how, as its virtue can be essentially but the virtue of the whole, the wayside traps set in the interest of muddlement and pleading but the cause of the moment, of the particular bit in itself, have to be kicked out of the path! All the sophistications in life, for example, might have appeared to muster on behalf of the menace—the menace to a bright variety—involved in Strether's having all the subjective 'say', as it were, to himself.

Had I, meanwhile, made him at once hero and historian, endowed him with the romantic privilege of the 'first person'—the darkest abyss of romance this, inveterately, when enjoyed on the grand scale—variety, and many other queer matters as well, might have been smuggled in by a back door. Suffice it, to be brief, that the first person, in the long piece, is a form foredoomed to looseness, and that looseness, never much my affair, had never been so little so as on this particular occasion. All of which reflections flocked to the standard from the moment—a very early one—the question of how to keep my form amusing while sticking so close to my central figure and constantly taking its pattern from him had to be faced. He arrives (arrives at Chester) as for the dreadful purpose of giving his creator 'no end' to tell about him—before which rigorous mission the serenest of creators might well have quailed. I was far from the serenest; I was more than agitated enough to reflect that, grimly deprived of one alternative or one substitute for 'telling', I must address myself tooth and nail to another. I couldn't, save by implication, make other persons tell *each other* about him—blest resource, blest necessity, of the drama, which reaches its effects of unity, all remarkably, by paths absolutely opposite to the paths of the novel: with other persons, save as they were primarily *his* persons (not he primarily but one of theirs), I had simply nothing to do. I had relations for him none the less, by the mercy of Providence, quite as much as if my exhibition *was* to be a muddle; if I could only by implication and a show of consequence make other persons tell each other about him, I could at least make him tell *them* whatever in the world he must; and could so, by the same token —which was a further luxury thrown in—see straight into the deep differences between what that could do for me, or at all events for *him*, and the large ease of 'autobiography'. It may be asked why, if one so keeps to one's hero, one shouldn't make a single mouthful of 'method', shouldn't throw the reins on his neck and, letting them flap there as free as in *Gil Blas* or in *David Copperfield,[a]* equip him with the double privilege of subject and object—a course that has at least the merit of brushing away questions at a sweep. The answer to which is, I think, that one makes that surrender only if one is prepared *not* to make certain precious discriminations.

The 'first person' then, so employed, is addressed by the author directly to ourselves, his possible readers, whom he has to reckon with, at the best, by our English tradition, so loosely and vaguely after all, so little respectfully, on so scant a presumption of exposure to criticism. Strether, on the other hand, encaged and provided for as *The Ambassadors* encages and provides, has to keep in view proprieties much stiffer and more salutary than any our straight and credulous gape are likely to bring home to him, has exhibitional conditions to meet, in a word, that forbid the terrible *fluidity* of self-revelation. I may seem not to better the case for my discrimination if I say that, for my first care, I had thus inevitably to set him up a confidant or two, to wave away with energy the custom of the seated mass of explanation after the fact, the inserted block of merely referential narrative, which flourishes so, to the shame of the modern impatience, on the serried page of Balzac, but which seems simply to appal our actual, our in general weaker, digestion. 'Harking back to make up' took at any rate more doing, as the phrase is, not only than the reader of today demands, but than he will tolerate at any price any call upon him either to understand or remotely to measure; and for the beauty of the thing when done the current editorial mind in particular appears wholly without sense. It is not, however, primarily for either of these reasons, whatever their weight, that Strether's friend Waymarsh is so keenly clutched at, on the threshold of the book, or that no less a pounce is made on Maria Gostrey—without even the pretext, either, of *her* being, in essence, Strether's friend. She is the reader's friend much rather—in consequence of dispositions that make him so eminently require one; and she acts in that capacity, and *really* in that capacity alone, with exemplary devotion, from beginning to end of the book. She is an enrolled, a direct, aid to lucidity; she is in fine, to tear off her mask, the most

[a] Like Charles Dickens's *David Copperfield*, René Lesage's picaresque novel *Gil Blas* (1715–35) is narrated by the central character.

unmitigated and abandoned of *ficelles* [devices]. Half the dramatist's art, as we well know—since if we don't it's not the fault of the proofs that lie scattered about us—is in the use of *ficelles*; by which I mean in a deep dissimulation of his dependence on them. Waymarsh only to a slighter degree belongs, in the whole business, less to my subject than to my treatment of it; the interesting proof, in these connections, being that one has but to take one's subject for the stuff of drama to interweave with enthusiasm as many Gostreys as need be.

The material of *The Ambassadors*, conforming in this respect exactly to that of *The Wings of the Dove*, published just before it, is taken absolutely for the stuff of drama; so that, availing myself of the opportunity given me by this edition for some prefatory remarks on the latter work, I had mainly to make on its behalf the point of its scenic consistency. It disguises that virtue, in the oddest way in the world, by just *looking*, as we turn its pages, as little scenic as possible; but it sharply divides itself, just as the composition before us does, into the parts that prepare, that tend in fact to over-prepare, for scenes, and the parts, or otherwise into the scenes, that justify and crown the preparation. It may definitely be said, I think, that everything in it that is not scene (not, I of course mean, complete and functional scene, treating *all* the submitted matter, as by logical start, logical turn, and logical finish) is discriminated preparation, is the fusion and synthesis of picture. These alternations propose themselves all recognizably, I think, from an early stage, as the very form and figure of *The Ambassadors*; so that, to repeat, such an agent as Miss Gostrey, pre-engaged at a high salary, but waits in the draughty wing with her shawl and her smelling-salts. Her function speaks at once for itself, and by the time she has dined with Strether in London and gone to a play with him her intervention as a *ficelle* is, I hold, expertly justified. Thanks to it we have treated scenically, and scenically alone, the whole lumpish question of Strether's 'past', which has seen us more happily on the way than anything else could have done; we have strained to a high lucidity and vivacity (or at least we hope we have) certain indispensable facts; we have seen our two or three immediate friends all conveniently and profitably in 'action'; to say nothing of our beginning to descry others, of a remoter intensity, getting into motion, even if a bit vaguely as yet, for our further enrichment. Let my first point be here that the scene in question, that in which the whole situation at Woollett and the complex forces that have propelled my hero to where this lively extractor of his value and distiller of his essence awaits him, is normal and entire, is really an excellent *standard* scene; copious, comprehensive, and accordingly never short, but with its office as definite as that of the hammer on the gong of the clock, the office of expressing *all that is* in the hour.

The 'ficelle' character of the subordinate party is as artfully dissimulated, throughout, as may be, and to that extent that, with the seams or joints of Maria Gostrey's ostensible connectedness taken particular care of, duly smoothed over, that is, and anxiously kept from showing as 'pieced on', this figure doubtless achieves, after a fashion, something of the dignity of a prime idea: which circumstance but shows us afresh how many quite incalculable but none the less clear sources of enjoyment for the infatuated artist, how many copious springs of our never-to-be-slighted 'fun' for the reader and critic susceptible of contagion, may sound their incidental plash as soon as an artistic process begins to enjoy free development. Exquisite—in illustration of this—the mere interest and amusement of such at once 'creative' and critical questions as how and where and why to make Miss Gostrey's false connection carry itself, under a due high polish, as a real one. Nowhere is it more of an artful expedient for mere consistency of form, to mention a case, than in the last 'scene' of the book, where its function is to give or to add nothing whatever, but only to express as vividly as possible certain things quite other than itself and that are of the already fixed and appointed measure. Since, however, all art is *expression*, and is thereby vividness, one was to find the door open here to any amount of delightful dissimulation. These verily are the refinements and ecstasies of method—amid which, or certainly under the influence of any exhilarated demonstration of which, one must keep one's head and not lose one's way. To cultivate an adequate intelligence for them and to make that sense operative is positively to find a charm in any produced ambiguity of appearance that is not by the same stroke, and all helplessly, an ambiguity of sense. To project imaginatively, for my hero, a relation that has nothing to do with the matter (the matter of my subject) but has everything to do with the manner (the manner of my presentation of the same) and yet to treat it, at close quarters and for fully economic expression's possible sake, as if it were important and essential—to do that sort of thing and yet muddle nothing may easily become, as one goes, a signally attaching proposition; even though it all remains but part and parcel, I hasten to recognize, of the merely general and related question of expressional curiosity and expressional decency.

I am moved to add after so much insistence on the scenic side of my labour that I have found the steps of re-perusal almost as much waylaid here by quite another style of effort in the same signal interest—or have in other words not failed to note how, even so associated and so discriminated, the finest proprieties and charms of the non-scenic may, under the right hand for them, still keep their intelligibility and assert their office. Infinitely suggestive such an observation as this last on the whole delightful head, where representation is concerned, of possible variety, of effective expressional change and contrast. One would like, at such an hour as this, for critical licence, to go into the matter of the noted inevitable deviation (from too fond an original vision) that the exquisite treachery even of the straightest execution may ever be trusted to inflict even on the most mature plan—the case being that, though one's last reconsidered production always seems to bristle with that particular evidence, *The Ambassadors* would place a flood of such light at my service. I must attach to my final remark here a different import; noting in the other connection I just glanced at that such passages as that of my hero's first encounter with Chad Newsome, absolute attestations of the non-scenic form though they be, yet lay the firmest hand too—so far at least as intention goes—on representational effect. To report at all closely and completely of what 'passes' on a given occasion is inevitably to become more or less scenic; and yet in the instance I allude to, with the conveyance, expressional curiosity, and expressional decency are sought and arrived at under quite another law. The true inwardness of this may be at bottom but that one of the suffered treacheries has consisted precisely, for Chad's whole figure and presence, of a direct presentability diminished and compromised—despoiled, that is, of its *proportional* advantage; so that, in a word, the whole economy of his author's relation to him has at important points to be redetermined. The book, however, critically viewed, is touchingly full of these disguised and repaired losses, these insidious recoveries, these intensely redemptive consistencies. The pages in which Mamie Pocock gives her appointed and, I can't but think, duly felt lift to the whole action by the so inscrutably-applied side-stroke or short-cut of our just watching, and as quite at an angle of vision as yet untried, her single hour of suspense in the hotel salon, in our partaking of her concentrated study of the sense of matters bearing on her own case, all the bright warm Paris afternoon, from the balcony that overlooks the Tuileries garden—these are as marked an example of the representational virtue that insists here and there on being, for the charm of opposition and renewal, other than the scenic. It wouldn't take much to make me further argue that from an equal play of such oppositions the book gathers an intensity that fairly adds to the dramatic—though the latter is supposed to be the sum of all intensities; or that has at any rate nothing to fear from juxtaposition with it. I consciously fail to shrink in fact from that extravagance—I risk it, rather, for the sake of the moral involved; which is not that the particular production before us exhausts the interesting questions it raises, but that the Novel remains still, under the right persuasion, the most independent, most elastic, most prodigious of literary forms.[a]

[a] This paragraph is complicated to a degree unusual even in the late James. Essentially, he is talking about two modes of 'representation' in fiction: the 'scenic' (i.e., corresponding to action in drama) and the 'non-scenic' (i.e., descriptive or discursive writing). Though he gives priority to the scenic method, he takes pleasure, here, in the way the non-scenic passages in *The Ambassadors* contribute to the overall effectiveness of the novel. Strether's first meeting with Chad occurs in a theatre box, with no possibility of conversation, and most of the writing at this point consists of Strether's retrospective brooding on the little that 'passes'. James explains that this treatment was dictated by a change of his original plan (or 'treachery' to it), entailing a more oblique and diminished presentation of Chad.

5   Ezra Pound

Ezra Pound (b. 1885) is one of the most colourful and controversial figures
in modern literature. Born in Idaho, America, he studied at Hamilton
College and the State University of Pennsylvania before making his way to
Europe. In 1908 he published his first book of poems, A Lume Spento, in
Venice, and he came to England in the same year. Until 1921 Pound lived
in London actively involved not only in writing his own verse and prose,
but also in editing, criticizing, publishing, and encouraging the work of
others in the literary and artistic avant-garde of the time. 'Make it new' was
Pound's slogan, and perhaps he, more than any other single man, was
responsible for the emergence of an authentically modernist literature in
England at this time.

From his association with T. E. Hulme (see below, pp. 92-104), F. S. Flint
and others around 1910, and their interest in the Japanese haiku and tanka,
came the poetic style known as Imagism. A little later, Pound befriended
Wyndham Lewis, and contributed to the latter's Vorticist magazine Blast.
In 1912-13 Pound acted as a kind of secretary-companion to W. B. Yeats,
and this association undoubtedly influenced Yeats's poetic development.
James Joyce was another writer who owed a great deal to Pound for moral
and financial support. But Pound's most important literary friendship was
with T. S. Eliot, whom he met in 1915. Pound immediately perceived Eliot's
great gifts and worked tirelessly to get them generally recognized. As is
well known, he significantly contributed to the form of The Waste Land
(1922) by recommending drastic cuts in Eliot's original version. During this
period Pound was also writing and publishing poetry of his own, much of
it translation or 'imitation' of poetry in various languages—Chinese,
Provençal, Anglo-Saxon and several others—in which Pound was not always
competent by normal linguistic criteria. Probably his most successful
volume of this period was Hugh Selwyn Mauberley (1920). In the following
year, Pound moved to Paris, befriending fellow-expatriates like Gertrude
Stein and Ernest Hemingway; and in 1925 he settled in the Italian coastal
resort of Rapallo.

Italy was at this time in the early stages of Mussolini's fascist régime,
the achievements of which Pound greatly admired. He was not the only
literary figure of his time to be dazzled by right-wing political radicalism,
but Pound, unfortunately, failed to see the evil in fascism even after the
outbreak of World War II. During the war he made radio broadcasts which

57

were deemed sufficiently treasonable by the American authorities to warrant his arrest at the end of the war. He was however considered mentally unfit to stand trial, and after a long sequestration in mental hospitals, Pound was finally allowed to live out his last years in Italy. During all this time—since 1921—he had been writing and publishing parts of a long, encyclopaedic poem in *vers libre* known as the *Cantos*, the value and significance of which is as problematic as everything else connected with this writer.

'A Retrospect' conveys the flavour of Pound's thought and personality in his role as pundit and patron of modern poetry in the second decade of the century. His style is aphoristic, informal, provocative; his stance professional, committed, anti-academic. He describes his own approach perfectly as treating the reader 'as if he were a new friend come into the room, intent on ransacking my bookshelf'. Yet the disarming casualness should not blind us to the fact that many seminal ideas are to be found in Pound's early criticism. Eliot's reverence was no affectation. When, for example, Pound says, 'An "Image" is that which presents an intellectual and emotional complex in an instant of time', we can recognize the seed of Eliot's poetic method in *The Waste Land* and of the poetic theory expounded in 'Tradition and the Individual Talent'. 'A Retrospect' is reprinted here from *The Literary Essays of Ezra Pound* (1954), edited by T. S. Eliot, who has added the notes indicating the original dates of composition for the various pieces.

CROSS REFERENCES : 2. W. B. Yeats
6. T. S. Eliot
8. T. E. Hulme
47. W. H. Auden

COMMENTARY : G. S. Fraser, *Ezra Pound* (1960)
Hugh Kenner, *The Poetry of Ezra Pound* (1951)

A retrospect[1]

There has been so much scribbling about a new fashion in poetry, that I may perhaps be pardoned this brief recapitulation and retrospect.

In the spring or early summer of 1912, 'H. D.' [Hilda Doolittle], Richard Aldington and myself decided that we were agreed upon the three principles following:

1. Direct treatment of the 'thing' whether subjective or objective.
2. To use absolutely no word that does not contribute to the presentation.
3. As regarding rhythm: to compose in the sequence of the musical phrase, not in sequence of a metronome.

Upon many points of taste and of predilection we differed, but agreeing upon these three positions we thought we had as much right to a group name, at least as much right, as a number of French 'schools' proclaimed by Mr [F. S.] Flint in the August number of Harold Monro's magazine [*Poetry Review*] for 1911.

This school has since been 'joined' or 'followed' by numerous people who, whatever their merits, do not show any signs of agreeing with the second specification. Indeed *vers libre* has become as prolix and as verbose as any of the flaccid varieties that preceded it. It has brought faults of its own. The actual language and phrasing is often as bad as that of our elders without even the excuse that the words are shovelled in to fill a metric pattern or to complete the noise of a rhyme-sound. Whether or no the phrases followed by the followers are musical must be left to the reader's decision. At times I can find a marked metre in 'vers libres', as stale and hackneyed as any pseudo-Swinburnian, at times the writers seem to follow no musical structure whatever. But it is, on the whole, good that the field should be ploughed. Perhaps a few good poems have come from the new method, and if so it is justified.

Criticism is not a circumscription or a set of prohibitions. It provides fixed points of departure. It may startle a dull reader into alertness. That little of it which is good is mostly in stray phrases; or if it be an older artist helping a younger it is in great measure but rules of thumb, cautions gained by experience.

I set together a few phrases on practical working about the time the first remarks on imagisme were published. The first use of the word 'Imagiste' was in my note to T. E. Hulme's five poems, printed at the end of my 'Ripostes' in the autumn of 1912. I reprint my cautions from *Poetry* for March 1913.

A few don'ts

An 'Image' is that which presents an intellectual and emotional complex in an instant of time. I use the term 'complex' rather in the technical sense employed by the newer psychologists, such as [Bernard] Hart, though we might not agree absolutely in our application.

It is the presentation of such a 'complex' instantaneously which gives that sense of sudden liberation; that sense of freedom from time limits and space limits; that sense of sudden growth, which we experience in the presence of the greatest works of art.

It is better to present one Image in a lifetime than to produce voluminous works.

All this, however, some may consider open to debate. The immediate necessity is to tabulate A LIST OF DON'TS for those beginning to write verses. I can not put all of them into Mosaic negative.

To begin with, consider the three propositions (demanding direct treatment, economy of words, and the sequence of the musical phrase), not as dogma—never consider anything as dogma—but as the result of long contemplation, which, even if it is someone else's contemplation, may be worth consideration.

Pay no attention to the criticism of men who have never themselves written a notable work. Consider the discrepancies between the actual writing of the Greek poets and dramatists, and the theories of the Graeco-Roman grammarians, concocted to explain their metres.

Language

Use no superfluous word, no adjective which does not reveal something.

Don't use such an expression as 'dim lands *of peace*'. It dulls the image. It mixes an abstraction with the concrete. It comes from the writer's not realizing that the natural object is always the *adequate* symbol.

Go in fear of abstractions. Do not retell in mediocre verse what has already been done in good prose. Don't think any intelligent person is going to be deceived when you try to shirk all the difficulties of the unspeakably difficult art of good prose by chopping your composition into line lengths.

What the expert is tired of today the public will be tired of tomorrow.

Don't imagine that the art of poetry is any simpler than the art of music, or that you can please the expert before you have spent at least as much effort on the art of verse as the average piano teacher spends on the art of music.

Be influenced by as many great artists as you can, but have the decency either to acknowledge the debt outright, or to try to conceal it.

Don't allow 'influence' to mean merely that you mop up the particular decorative vocabulary of some one or two poets whom you happen to admire. A Turkish war correspondent was recently caught red-handed babbling in his despatches of 'dove-grey' hills, or else it was 'pearl-pale', I can not remember.

Use either no ornament or good ornament.

Rhythm and rhyme

Let the candidate fill his mind with the finest cadences he can discover, preferably in a foreign language,[2] so that the meaning of the words may be less likely to divert his attention from the movement; e.g. Saxon charms, Hebridean Folk Songs, the verse of Dante, and the lyrics of Shakespeare—if he can dissociate the vocabulary from the cadence. Let him dissect the lyrics of Goethe coldly into their component sound values, syllables long and short, stressed and unstressed, into vowels and consonants.

It is not necessary that a poem should rely on its music, but if it does rely on its music that music must be such as will delight the expert.

Let the neophyte know assonance and alliteration, rhyme immediate and delayed, simple and polyphonic, as a musician would expect to know harmony and counterpoint and all the minutiae of his craft. No time is too great to give to these matters or to any one of them, even if the artist seldom has need of them.

Don't imagine that a thing will 'go' in verse just because it's too dull to go in prose.

Don't be 'viewy'—leave that to the writers of pretty little philosophic essays. Don't be descriptive; remember that the painter can describe a landscape much better than you can, and that he has to know a deal more about it.

When Shakespeare talks of the 'Dawn in russet mantle clad' he presents something which the painter does not present. There is in this line of his nothing that one can call description; he presents.

Consider the way of the scientists rather than the way of an advertising agent for a new soap.

The scientist does not expect to be acclaimed as a great scientist until he has *discovered* something. He begins by learning what has been discovered already. He goes from that point onward. He does not bank on being a charming fellow personally. He does not expect his friends to applaud the results of his freshman class work. Freshmen in poetry are unfortunately not confined to a definite and recognizable class room. They are 'all over the shop'. Is it any wonder 'the public is indifferent to poetry'?

Don't chop your stuff into separate *iambs*. Don't make each line stop dead at the end, and then begin every next line with a heave. Let the beginning of the next line catch the rise of the rhythm wave, unless you want a definite longish pause.

In short, behave as a musician, a good musician, when dealing with that phase of your art which has exact parallels in music. The same laws govern, and you are bound by no others.

Naturally, your rhythmic structure should not destroy the shape of your words, or their natural sound, or their meaning. It is improbable that, at the start, you will be able to get a rhythm-structure strong enough to affect them very much, though you may fall a victim to all sorts of false stopping due to line ends and caesurae.

The musician can rely on pitch and the volume of the orchestra. You can not. The term harmony is misapplied in poetry; it refers to simultaneous sounds of different pitch. There is, however, in the best verse a sort of residue of sound which remains in the ear of the hearer and acts more or less as an organ-base.

A rhyme must have in it some slight element of surprise if it is to give pleasure; it need not be bizarre or curious, but it must be well used if used at all.

Vide further Vildrac and Duhamel's[a] notes on rhyme in *Technique Poétique*.

That part of your poetry which strikes upon the imaginative *eye* of the reader will lose nothing by translation into a foreign tongue; that which appeals to the ear can reach only those who take it in the original.

Consider the definiteness of Dante's presentation, as compared with Milton's rhetoric. Read as much of Wordsworth as does not seem too unutterably dull.

If you want the gist of the matter go to Sappho, Catullus, Villon, Heine when he is in the vein, Gautier when he is not too frigid; or, if you have not the tongues, seek out the leisurely Chaucer. Good prose will do you no harm,

---

[a] Charles Messager Vildrac and Georges Duhamel were founder-members of the 'Abbaye' writers' community near Paris, 1906–7.

and there is good discipline to be had by trying to write it.

Translation is likewise good training, if you find that your original matter 'wobbles' when you try to rewrite it. The meaning of the poem to be translated cannot 'wobble'.

If you are using a symmetrical form, don't put in what you want to say and then fill up the remaining vacuums with slush.

Don't mess up the perception of one sense by trying to define it in terms of another. This is usually only the result of being too lazy to find the exact word. To this clause there are possibly exceptions.

The first three simple prescriptions will throw out nine-tenths of all the bad poetry now accepted as standard and classic; and will prevent you from many a crime of production.

'... *Mais d'abord il faut être un poète*' ['But first one must be a poet'], as MM Duhamel and Vildrac have said at the end of their little book, *Notes sur la Technique Poétique.*

Since March 1913, Ford Madox Hueffer has pointed out that Wordsworth was so intent on the ordinary or plain word that he never thought of hunting for *le mot juste.*

John Butler Yeats has handled or man-handled Wordsworth and the Victorians, and his criticism, contained in letters to his son, is now printed and available.

I do not like writing *about* art, my first, at least I think it was my first essay on the subject, was a protest against it.

Prolegomena[3]

Time was when the poet lay in a green field with his head against a tree and played his diversion on a ha'penny whistle, and Caesar's predecessors conquered the earth, and the predecessors of golden Crassus[a] embezzled, and fashions had their say, and let him alone. And presumably he was fairly content in this circumstance, for I have small doubt that the occasional passerby, being attracted by curiosity to know why anyone should lie under a tree and blow diversion on a ha'penny whistle, came and conversed with him, and that among these passers-by there was on occasion a person of charm or a young lady who had not read *Man and Superman;*[b] and looking back upon this naïve state of affairs we call it the age of gold.

Metastasio,[c] and he should know if anyone, assures us that this age endures —even though the modern poet is expected to holloa his verses down a speak-

---

[a] Licinius Crassus, surnamed Dives, a Roman consul of the first century BC, notorious for his love of money.

[b] G. B. Shaw's play, first published in England in 1908, portrayed a woman taking the initiative in courtship.

[c] Metastasio was the pseudonym of Pietro Trapassi (1698–1782), Italian poet and dramatist.

ing tube to the editors of cheap magazines—S. S. McClure,[a] or someone of that sort—even though hordes of authors meet in dreariness and drink healths to the 'Copyright Bill'; even though these things be, the age of gold pertains. Imperceivably, if you like, but pertains. You meet unkempt Amyclas[b] in a Soho restaurant and chant together of dead and forgotten things—it is a manner of speech among poets to chant of dead, half-forgotten things, there seems no special harm in it; it has always been done—and it's rather better to be a clerk in the Post Office than to look after a lot of stinking, verminous sheep—and at another hour of the day one substitutes the drawing-room for the restaurant and tea is probably more palatable than mead and mare's milk, and little cakes than honey. And in this fashion one survives the resignation of Mr Balfour, and the iniquities of the American customs-house, *e quel bufera infernal* [and that infernal disaster], the periodical press. And then in the middle of it, there being apparently no other person at once capable and available one is stopped and asked to explain oneself.

I begin on the chord thus querulous, for I would much rather lie on what is left of Catullus's parlour floor and speculate the azure beneath it and the hills off to Salo and Riva with their forgotten gods moving unhindered among them, than discuss any processes and theories of art whatsoever. I would rather play tennis. I shall not argue.

Credo

Rhythm I believe in an 'absolute rhythm'; a rhythm, that is, in poetry which corresponds exactly to the emotion or shade of emotion to be expressed. A man's rhythm must be interpretative, it will be, therefore, in the end, his own, uncounterfeiting, uncounterfeitable.

Symbols I believe that the proper and perfect symbol is the natural object, that if a man use 'symbols' he must so use them that their symbolic function does not obtrude; so that *a* sense, and the poetic quality of the passage, is not lost to those who do not understand the symbol as such, to whom, for instance, a hawk is a hawk.

Technique I believe in technique as the test of a man's sincerity; in law when it is ascertainable; in the trampling down of every convention that impedes or obscures the determination of the law, or the precise rendering of the impulse.

Form I think there is a 'fluid' as well as a 'solid' content, that some poems may have form as a tree has form, some as water poured into a vase. That most symmetrical forms have certain uses. That a vast number of subjects cannot be precisely, and therefore not properly rendered in symmetrical forms.

'Thinking that alone worthy wherein the whole art is employed.'[4] I think the artist should master all known forms and systems of metric, and I have

---

[a] S. S. McClure (1857–1949) founded the first newspaper syndicate in the United States, and edited his own *McClure's Magazine*.

[b] Amyclas is a place-name. It occurs in the Latin poem *Pervigilium Veneris*, where Pound may have seen it and misconstrued it as the name of a poet.

with some persistence set about doing this, searching particularly into those periods wherein the systems came to birth or attained their maturity. It has been complained, with some justice, that I dump my note-books on the public. I think that only after a long struggle will poetry attain such a degree of development, or, if you will, modernity, that it will vitally concern people who are accustomed, in prose, to Henry James and Anatole France, in music to Debussy. I am constantly contending that it took two centuries of Provence and one of Tuscany to develop the media of Dante's masterwork, that it took the latinists of the Renaissance, and the Pleiade,[a] and his own age of painted speech to prepare Shakespeare his tools. It is tremendously important that great poetry be written, it makes no jot of difference who writes it. The experimental demonstrations of one man may save the time of many—hence my furore over Arnaut Daniel[b]—if a man's experiments try out one new rime, or dispense conclusively with one iota of currently accepted nonsense, he is merely playing fair with his colleagues when he chalks up his result.

No man ever writes very much poetry that 'matters'. In bulk, that is, no one produces much that is final, and when a man is not doing this highest thing, this saying the thing once for all and perfectly; when he is not matching, Ποικιλόθρον', ἀθάνατ' Ἀφρόιδτα,[c] or 'Hist—said Kate the Queen',[d] he had much better be making the sorts of experiment which may be of use to him in his later work, or to his successors.

'The lyf so short, the craft so long to lerne.'[e] It is a foolish thing for a man to begin his work on a too narrow foundation, it is a disgraceful thing for a man's work not to show steady growth and increasing fineness from first to last.

As for 'adaptations'; one finds that all the old masters of painting recommend to their pupils that they begin by copying masterwork, and proceed to their own composition.

As for 'Every man his own poet', the more every man knows about poetry the better. I believe in every one writing poetry who wants to; most do. I believe in every man knowing enough of music to play 'God bless our home' on the harmonium, but I do not believe in every man giving concerts and printing his sin.

The mastery of any art is the work of a lifetime. I should not discriminate between the 'amateur' and the 'professional'. Or rather I should discriminate quite often in favour of the amateur, but I should discriminate between the amateur and the expert. It is certain that the present chaos will endure until the Art of poetry has been preached down the amateur gullet, until there is such a general understanding of the fact that poetry is an art and not a pastime; such a knowledge of technique; of technique of surface and technique of content, that the amateurs will cease to try to drown out the masters.

[a] See note on p. 29 above.
[b] One of the most famous of the Provençal troubadours, highly praised by Dante and Petrarch.
[c] 'Richly enthroned, immortal Aphrodite' (Sappho, Ode to Aphrodite).
[d] Robert Browning, Pippa Passes, II (Noon).
[e] Geoffrey Chaucer's translation of Hippocrates' aphorism, Ars longa, vita brevis.

64

If a certain thing was said once for all in Atlantis or Arcadia, in 450 Before Christ or in 1290 after, it is not for us moderns to go saying it over, or to go obscuring the memory of the dead by saying the same thing with less skill and less conviction.

My pawing over the ancients and semi-ancients has been one struggle to find out what has been done, once for all, better than it can ever be done again, and to find out what remains for us to do, and plenty does remain, for if we still feel the same emotions as those which launched the thousand ships, it is quite certain that we come on these feelings differently, through different nuances, by different intellectual gradations. Each age has its own abounding gifts yet only some ages transmute them into matter of duration. No good poetry is ever written in a manner twenty years old, for to write in such a manner shows conclusively that the writer thinks from books, convention and *cliché*, and not from life, yet a man feeling the divorce of life and his art may naturally try to resurrect a forgotten mode if he finds in that mode some leaven, or if he thinks he sees in it some element lacking in contemporary art which might unite that art again to its sustenance, life.

In the art of Daniel and Cavalcanti,[a] I have seen that precision which I miss in the Victorians, that explicit rendering, be it of external nature, or of emotion. Their testimony is of the eyewitness, their symptoms are first hand.

As for the nineteenth century, with all respect to its achievements, I think we shall look back upon it as a rather blurry, messy sort of a period, a rather sentimentalistic, mannerish sort of a period. I say this without any self-righteousness, with no self-satisfaction.

As for there being a 'movement' or my being of it, the conception of poetry as a 'pure art' in the sense in which I use the term, revived with Swinburne. From the puritanical revolt to Swinburne, poetry had been merely the vehicle —yes, definitely, Arthur Symons's scruples and feelings about the word not withholding—the ox-cart and post-chaise for transmitting thoughts poetic or otherwise. And perhaps the 'great Victorians', though it is doubtful, and assuredly the 'nineties' continued the development of the art, confining their improvements, however, chiefly to sound and to refinements of manner.

Mr Yeats has once and for all stripped English poetry of its perdamnable rhetoric. He has boiled away all that is not poetic—and a good deal that is. He has become a classic in his own lifetime and *nel mezzo del cammin* [in the middle of his life]. He has made our poetic idiom a thing pliable, a speech without inversions.

Robert Bridges, Maurice Hewlett, and Frederic Manning are[5] in their different ways seriously concerned with overhauling the metric, in testing the language and its adaptability to certain modes. Ford Hueffer is making some sort of experiments in modernity. The Provost of Oriel[b] continues his translation of the *Divina Commedia*.

As to twentieth-century poetry, and the poetry which I expect to see written

[a] Guido Cavalcanti (1250–1300), Italian philosopher and poet, friend of Dante.
[b] Charles Lancelot Shadwell (1840–1919), Provost of Oriel 1905–14, published translations of the *Purgatorio* and *Paradiso* in 1892, 1899 and 1915.

65

during the next decade or so, it will, I think, move against poppy-cock, it will be harder and saner, it will be what Mr Hewlett calls 'nearer the bone'. It will be as much like granite as it can be, its force will lie in its truth, its interpretative power (of course, poetic force does always rest there); I mean it will not try to seem forcible by rhetorical din, and luxurious riot. We will have fewer painted adjectives impeding the shock and stroke of it. At least for myself, I want it so, austere, direct, free from emotional slither.

What is there now, in 1917, to be added?

Re vers libre

I think the desire for vers libre is due to the sense of quantity reasserting itself after years of starvation. But I doubt if we can take over, for English, the rules of quantity laid down for Greek and Latin, mostly by Latin grammarians.

I think one should write vers libre only when one 'must', that is to say, only when the 'thing' builds up a rhythm more beautiful than that of set metres, or more real, more a part of the emotion of the 'thing', more germane, intimate, interpretative than the measure of regular accentual verse; a rhythm which discontents one with set iambic or set anapaestic.

Eliot has said the thing very well when he said, 'No *vers* is *libre* for the man who wants to do a good job.'

As a matter of detail, there is vers libre with accent heavily marked as a drum-beat (as par example my 'Dance Figure'), and on the other hand I think I have gone as far as can profitably be gone in the other direction (and perhaps too far). I mean I do not think one can use to any advantage rhythms much more tenuous and imperceptible than some I have used. I think progress lies rather in an attempt to approximate classical quantitative metres (NOT to copy them) than in a carelessness regarding such things.[6]

I agree with John Yeats on the relation of beauty to certitude. I prefer satire, which is due to emotion, to any sham of emotion.

I have had to write, or at least I have written a good deal about art, sculpture, painting, and poetry. I have seen what seemed to me the best contemporary work reviled and obstructed. Can anyone write prose of permanent or durable interest when he is merely saying for one year what nearly every one will say at the end of three or four years? I have been battistrada for a sculptor, a painter, a novelist, several poets. I wrote also of certain French writers in *The New Age* in nineteen twelve or eleven.

I would much rather that people would look at Brzeska's sculpture and Lewis's drawings, and that they would read Joyce, Jules Romains, Eliot, than that they should read what I have said of these men, or that I should be asked to republish argumentative essays and reviews.

All that the critic can do for the reader or audience or spectator is to focus his gaze or audition. Rightly or wrongly I think my blasts and essays have done their work, and that more people are now likely to go to the sources than are likely to read this book.

Jammes's[a] 'Existences' in '*La Triomphe de la Vie*' is available. So are his early poems. I think we need a convenient anthology rather than descriptive criticism. Carl Sandburg wrote me from Chicago, 'It's hell when poets can't afford to buy each other's books.' Half the people who care, only borrow. In America so few people know each other that the difficulty lies more than half in distribution. Perhaps one should make an anthology: Romains's 'Un Etre en Marche' and 'Prières', Vildrac's 'Visite'. Retrospectively the fine wrought work of Laforgue, the flashes of Rimbaud, the hard-bit lines of Tristan Corbière, Tailhade's sketches in 'Poèmes Aristophanesques', the 'Litanies' of De Gourmont.

It is difficult at all times to write of the fine arts, it is almost impossible unless one can accompany one's prose with many reproductions. Still I would seize this chance or any chance to reaffirm my belief in Wyndham Lewis's genius, both in his drawings and his writings. And I would name an out of the way prose book, the '*Scenes and Portraits*' of Frederic Manning, as well as James Joyce's short stories and novel, *Dubliners* and the now well known *Portrait of the Artist* as well as Lewis's *Tarr*, if, that is, I may treat my strange reader as if he were a new friend come into the room, intent on ransacking my bookshelf.

Only emotion endures

'Only emotion endures.' Surely it is better for me to name over the few beautiful poems that still ring in my head than for me to search my flat for back numbers of periodicals and rearrange all that I have said about friendly and hostile writers.

The first twelve lines of Padraic Colum's 'Drover'; his 'O Woman shapely as a swan, on your account I shall not die'; Joyce's 'I hear an army'; the lines of Yeats that ring in my head and in the heads of all young men of my time who care for poetry: Braseal and the Fisherman, 'The fire that stirs about her when she stirs'; the later lines of 'The Scholars', the faces of the Magi; William Carlos Williams's 'Postlude', Aldington's version of 'Atthis', and H. D.'s waves like pine tops, and her verse in 'Des Imagistes' the first anthology; Hueffer's 'How red your lips are' in his translation from Von der Vogelweide, his 'Three Ten', the general effect of his 'On Heaven'; his sense of the prose values or prose qualities in poetry; his ability to write poems that half-chant and are spoiled by a musician's additions; beyond these a poem by Alice Corbin, 'One City Only', and another ending 'But sliding water over a stone'. These things have worn smooth in my head and I am not through with them, nor with Aldington's 'In Via Sestina' nor his other poems in 'Des Imagistes', though people have told me their flaws. It may be that their content is too much embedded in me for me to look back at the words.

[a] Francis Jammes (1868–1938), French poet and novelist.

I am almost a different person when I come to take up the argument for Eliot's poems.

Notes

1. A group of early essays and notes which appeared under this title in *Pavannes and Divisions* (1918). 'A Few Dont's' was first printed in *Poetry*, I, 6 (March, 1913).
2. This is for rhythm, his vocabulary must of course be found in his native tongue.
3. *Poetry and Drama* (then the *Poetry Review*, edited by Harold Monro), February 1912.
4. Dante, *De Volgari Eloquio*.
5. December 1911.
6. Let me date this statement 20 August 1917.

T. S. Eliot

Thomas Stearns Eliot (1888-1965) was one of the greatest poets and most influential critics of our time. Born in St Louis, Missouri, he was educated at Harvard and Oxford universities, and also studied for short periods in France and Germany. In 1914 he settled permanently in England, and became a naturalized citizen in 1927. His first major poem, *The Love Song of J. Alfred Prufrock* appeared in 1915. *The Waste Land*, which made Eliot the poetic spokesman of his generation, was published in 1922. In the meantime Eliot had become the friend and protégé of Ezra Pound (see above, pp. 57-68) and had begun to publish the essays and reviews that were collected in *The Sacred Wood* (1920). In 1922 Eliot founded his own journal, *The Criterion*, which he edited until 1939. After earning his living as a banker for some years, Eliot joined the publishing firm of Faber and Faber, of which he eventually became a director. In the Preface to a volume of essays, *For Lancelot Andrewes* (1928), Eliot described his beliefs as 'classical in literature, royalist in politics, anglo-catholic in religion', and these attitudes became more marked in his prose and verse through the subsequent decade. *The Collected Poems 1909-35* (1936) and *Four Quartets* (1944) comprise the essential canon of his poetry. In 1935 he produced a verse drama, *Murder in the Cathedral*, and subsequently wrote several more verse plays of which the most successful was *The Cocktail Party* (1950). In 1948 T. S. Eliot's career was crowned with the award of the Nobel Prize for Literature and the Order of Merit.

Eliot's critical output was copious, and much of it is uncollected or out of print. *Selected Essays* (3rd edition, 1951) is the basic text, a substantial collection of representative work. It is usefully supplemented by *Selected Prose* (1953), edited by John Hayward. Eliot's was a mind cultured and cosmopolitan, that ranged widely and confidently over European literature, ancient and modern. Like many critics his interests, focused intently on literature at the beginning of his career, broadened out gradually to encompass 'culture' as a whole—popular art, religion, education, and social institutions (see particularly *Notes Towards the Definition of Culture*, 1948). Almost everything he wrote gave food for thought, but as far as the development of modern literary criticism is concerned, it was the early essays that had the decisive influence. They created, at least for a time, a powerful alliance between the literary avant-garde and the more progressive critics and teachers of literature in the universities. Here, English was rapidly emerging after World War I as the central humanities subject, but it lacked intellectual discipline and a concept of literary tradition that made sense in the twentieth century. Eliot's early essays seemed to offer both these things—or at least hints towards achieving them which were quickly taken up by academic critics like I. A. Richards, F. R. Leavis, and the American New Critics. In the area of literary taste, Eliot focused enthusiastic attention upon Elizabethan and Jacobean drama and the Metaphysical poets of the seventeenth century, while casting doubts upon the achievement of Milton and the major Romantic and Victorian poets. This redefinition of the English poetic tradition had the double effect of stimulating a good deal of healthy controversy in the groves of academe, and of educating public taste in understanding and appreciation of the kind of poetry Eliot himself was writing. The connection is clearly made in the essay 'The Metaphysical Poets' (1921):

> It appears likely that poets in our civilization, as it exists at present, must be difficult.... The poet must become more and more comprehensive, more allusive, more indirect, in order to force, to dislocate if necessary, language into his meaning.... Hence we get something which looks very much like the conceit—we get, in fact, a method curiously similar to that of the 'metaphysical poets'.

The theoretical basis for making this kind of connection between contemporary and past poetry is formulated in 'Tradition and the Individual Talent' (1919), probably the most celebrated critical essay in English of the twentieth century. 'The Function of Criticism' (1923) is less well known, but the essays are complementary, and it is not by chance that they are paired together at the beginning of *Selected Essays*.

The main dynamic of Anglo-American criticism from the 'twenties to the 'fifties might be described as the pursuit of objectivity in criticism, by eliminating as far as possible all evidence extraneous to the text, the 'words on the page'. The essays on the intentional and affective fallacies by W. K. Wimsatt and Monroe C. Beardsley (see below, pp. 333-58) are late and sophisticated expositions of this critical doctrine. 'Tradition and the Individual Talent' is essentially anti-intentionalist, and 'The Function of Criticism' essentially anti-affective: when this is recognized, the seminal significance of Eliot's early essays becomes vividly apparent.

CROSS REFERENCES: 2. W. B. Yeats
5. Ezra Pound
8. T. E. Hulme
26. W. K. Wimsatt and Monroe C. Beardsley

COMMENTARY: Northrop Frye, *T. S. Eliot* (1963)
John Crowe Ransom, 'T. S. Eliot' in *The New Criticism* (Norfolk, Conn., 1941)
John Casey, 'Art and Feeling—T. S. Eliot', in *The Language of Criticism* (1966)

Tradition and the individual talent

I

In English writing we seldom speak of tradition, though we occasionally apply its name in deploring its absence. We cannot refer to 'the tradition' or to 'a tradition'; at most, we employ the adjective in saying that the poetry of So-and-so is 'traditional' or even 'too traditional'. Seldom, perhaps, does the word appear except in a phrase of censure. If otherwise, it is vaguely approbative, with the implication, as to the work approved, of some pleasing archaeological reconstruction. You can hardly make the word agreeable to English ears without this comfortable reference to the reassuring science of archaeology.

Certainly the word is not likely to appear in our appreciations of living or dead writers. Every nation, every race, has not only its own creative, but its own critical turn of mind; and is even more oblivious of the shortcomings and limitations of its critical habits than of those of its creative genius. We know, or think we know, from the enormous mass of critical writing that has appeared in the French language the critical method or habit of the French; we only conclude (we are such unconscious people) that the French are 'more critical' than we, and sometimes even plume ourselves a little with the fact, as if the French were the less spontaneous. Perhaps they are; but we might remind ourselves that criticism is as inevitable as breathing, and that we should be none the worse for articulating what passes in our minds when we read a book and feel an emotion about it, for criticizing our own minds in their work of criticism. One of the facts that might come to light in this process is our tendency to insist, when we praise a poet, upon those aspects of his work in which he least resembles anyone else. In these aspects or parts of his work we pretend to find what is individual, what is the peculiar essence of the man. We dwell with satisfaction upon the poet's difference from his predecessors, especially his immediate predecessors; we endeavour to find something that can be isolated in order to be enjoyed. Whereas if we approach a poet without this prejudice we shall often find that not only the best, but the most individual parts of his work may be those in which the dead poets, his ancestors, assert their immortality most vigorously. And I do not mean the impressionable period of adolescence, but the period of full maturity.

Yet if the only form of tradition, of handing down, consisted in following the ways of the immediate generation before us in a blind or timid adherence to its successes, 'tradition' should positively be discouraged. We have seen many such simple currents soon lost in the sand; and novelty is better than repetition. Tradition is a matter of much wider significance. It cannot be inherited, and if you want it you must obtain it by great labour. It involves, in the first place, the historical sense, which we may call nearly indispensable to anyone who

71

would continue to be a poet beyond his twenty-fifth year; and the historical sense involves a perception, not only of the pastness of the past, but of its presence; the historical sense compels a man to write not merely with his own generation in his bones, but with a feeling that the whole of the literature of Europe from Homer and within it the whole of the literature of his own country has a simultaneous existence and composes a simultaneous order. This historical sense, which is a sense of the timeless as well as of the temporal and of the timeless and of the temporal together, is what makes a writer traditional. And it is at the same time what makes a writer most acutely conscious of his place in time, of his own contemporaneity.

No poet, no artist of any art, has his complete meaning alone. His significance, his appreciation is the appreciation of his relation to the dead poets and artists. You cannot value him alone; you must set him, for contrast and comparison, among the dead. I mean this as a principle of aesthetic, not merely historical, criticism. The necessity that he shall conform, that he shall cohere, is not one-sided; what happens when a new work of art is created is something that happens simultaneously to all the works of art which preceded it. The existing monuments form an ideal order among themselves, which is modified by the introduction of the new (the really new) work of art among them. The existing order is complete before the new work arrives; for order to persist after the supervention of novelty, the whole existing order must be, if ever so slightly, altered; and so the relations, proportions, values of each work of art towards the whole are readjusted; and this is conformity between the old and the new. Whoever has approved this idea of order, of the form of European, of English literature will not find it preposterous that the past should be altered by the present as much as the present is directed by the past. And the poet who is aware of this will be aware of great difficulties and responsibilities.

In a peculiar sense he will be aware also that he must inevitably be judged by the standards of the past. I say judged, not amputated, by them; not judged to be as good as, or worse or better than, the dead; and certainly not judged by the canons of dead critics. It is a judgment, a comparison, in which two things are measured by each other. To conform merely would be for the new work not really to conform at all; it would not be new, and would therefore not be a work of art. And we do not quite say that the new is more valuable because it fits in; but its fitting in is a test of its value—a test, it is true, which can only be slowly and cautiously applied, for we are none of us infallible judges of conformity. We say: it appears to conform, and is perhaps individual, or it appears individual, and may conform; but we are hardly likely to find that it is one and not the other.

To proceed to a more intelligible exposition of the relation of the poet to the past: he can neither take the past as a lump, an indiscriminate bolus, nor can he form himself wholly on one or two private admirations, nor can he form himself wholly upon one preferred period. The first course is inadmissible, the second is an important experience of youth, and the third is a pleasant and highly desirable supplement. The poet must be very conscious of the main current, which does not at all flow invariably through the most distinguished reputations. He must be quite aware of the obvious fact that art never improves, but that the material of art is never quite the same. He must be aware that the mind of Europe—the mind of his own country—a mind which he learns in time to be much more important than his own private mind—is a mind which changes, and that this change is a development which abandons nothing *en route*, which does not superannuate either Shakespeare, or Homer, or the rock drawing of the Magdalenian draughtsmen. That this development, refinement perhaps, complication certainly, is not, from the point of view of the artist, any improvement. Perhaps not even an improvement from the point of view of the psychologist or not to the extent which we imagine; perhaps only in the end based upon a complication in economics and machinery. But the difference between the present and the past is that the conscious present is an awareness of the past in a way and to an extent which the past's awareness of itself cannot show.

Someone said: 'The dead writers are remote from us because we *know* so much more than they did.' Precisely, and they are that which we know.

I am alive to a usual objection to what is clearly part of my programme for the *métier* of poetry. The objection is that the doctrine requires a ridiculous amount of erudition (pedantry), a claim which can be rejected by appeal to the lives of poets in any pantheon. It will even be affirmed that much learning deadens or perverts poetic sensibility. While, however, we persist in believing that a poet ought to know as much as will not encroach upon his necessary receptivity and necessary laziness, it is not desirable to confine knowledge to whatever can be put into a useful shape for examinations, drawing-rooms, or the still more pretentious modes of publicity. Some can absorb knowledge, the more tardy must sweat for it. Shakespeare acquired more essential history from Plutarch than most men could from the whole British Museum. What is to be insisted upon is that the poet must develop or procure the consciousness of the past and that he should continue to develop this consciousness throughout his career.

What happens is a continual surrender of himself as he is at the moment to something which is more valuable. The progress of an artist is a continual self-sacrifice, a continual extinction of personality.

There remains to define this process of depersonalization and its relation to the sense of tradition. It is in this depersonalization that art may be said to approach the condition of science. I therefore invite you to consider, as a suggestive analogy, the action which takes place when a bit of finely filiated platinum is introduced into a chamber containing oxygen and sulphur dioxide.

II

Honest criticism and sensitive appreciation are directed not upon the poet but upon the poetry. If we attend to the confused cries of the newspaper critics and the susurrus of popular repetition that follows, we shall hear the names of poets in great numbers; if we seek not Blue-book knowledge but the enjoyment of poetry, and ask for a poem, we shall seldom find it. I have tried to point out the importance of the relation of the poem to other poems by other authors, and suggested the conception of poetry as a living whole of all the poetry that has ever been written. The other aspect of this Impersonal theory of poetry is the relation of the poem to its author. And I hinted, by an analogy, that the mind of the mature poet differs from that of the immature one not precisely in any valuation of 'personality', not being necessarily more interesting, or having 'more to say', but rather by being a more finely perfected medium in which special, or varied, feelings are at liberty to enter into new combinations.

The analogy was that of the catalyst. When the two gases previously mentioned are mixed in the presence of a filament of platinum, they form sulphurous acid. This combination takes place only if the platinum is present; nevertheless the newly formed acid contains no trace of platinum, and the platinum itself is apparently unaffected: has remained inert, neutral, and unchanged. The mind of the poet is the shred of platinum. It may partly or exclusively operate upon the experience of the man himself; but, the more perfect the artist, the more completely separate in him will be the man who suffers and the mind which creates; the more perfectly will the mind digest and transmute the passions which are its material.

The experience, you will notice, the elements which enter the presence of the transforming catalyst, are of two kinds: emotions and feelings. The effect of a work of art upon the person who enjoys it is an experience different in kind from any experience not of art. It may be formed out of one emotion, or may be a combination of several; and various feelings, inhering for the writer in particular words or phrases or images, may be added to compose the final result. Or great poetry may be made without the direct use of any emotion whatever: composed out of feelings solely. Canto XV of the *Inferno* (Brunetto Latini) is a working up of the emotion evident in the situation; but the effect, though single as that of any work of art, is obtained by considerable complexity of detail. The last quatrain[a] gives an image, a feeling attaching to an image, which 'came', which did not develop simply out of what precedes, but which was probably in suspension in the poet's mind until the proper combination arrived for it to add itself to. The poet's mind is in fact a receptacle for seizing and storing up numberless feelings, phrases, images, which remain there until all the particles which can unite to form a new compound are present together.

If you compare several representative passages of the greatest poetry you see how great is the variety of types of combination, and also how completely any semi-ethical criterion of 'sublimity' misses the mark. For it is not the 'greatness', the intensity, of the emotions, the components, but the intensity of the artistic process, the pressure, so to speak, under which the fusion takes place, that

[a] In the translation of Dorothy L. Sayers:

> Then he turned round,
> And seemed like one of those who over the flat
> And open course in the fields beside Verona
> Run for the green cloth; and he seemed, at that,
> Not like a loser, but the winning runner.

74

counts. The episode of Paolo and Francesca employs a definite emotion, but the intensity of the poetry is something quite different from whatever intensity in the supposed experience it may give the impression of. It is no more intense, furthermore, than Canto XXVI, the voyage of Ulysses, which has not the direct dependence upon an emotion. Great variety is possible in the process of transmutation of emotion: the murder of Agamemnon, or the agony of Othello, gives an artistic effect apparently closer to a possible original than the scenes from Dante. In the *Agamemnon*, the artistic emotion approximates to the emotion of an actual spectator; in *Othello* to the emotion of the protagonist himself. But the difference between art and the event is always absolute; the combination which is the murder of Agamemnon is probably as complex as that which is the voyage of Ulysses. In either case there has been a fusion of elements. The ode of Keats contains a number of feelings which have nothing particular to do with the nightingale, but which the nightingale, partly perhaps because of its attractive name, and partly because of its reputation, served to bring together.

The point of view which I am struggling to attack is perhaps related to the metaphysical theory of the substantial unity of the soul: for my meaning is, that the poet has, not a 'personality' to express, but a particular medium, which is only a medium and not a personality, in which impressions and experiences combine in peculiar and unexpected ways. Impressions and experiences which are important for the man may take no place in the poetry, and those which become important in the poetry may play quite a negligible part in the man, the personality.

I will quote a passage which is unfamiliar enough to be regarded with fresh attention in the light—or darkness—of these observations:

> And now methinks I could e'en chide myself
> For doating on her beauty, though her death
> Shall be revenged after no common action.
> Does the silkworm expend her yellow labours
> For thee? For thee does she undo herself?
> Are lordships sold to maintain ladyships
> For the poor benefit of a bewildering minute?
> Why does yon fellow falsify highways,
> And put his life between the judge's lips,
> To refine such a thing—keeps horse and men
> To beat their valours for her?...[a]

In this passage (as is evident if it is taken in its context) there is a combination of positive and negative emotions: an intensely strong attraction towards beauty and an equally intense fascination by the ugliness which is contrasted with it and which destroys it. This balance of contrasted emotion is in the dramatic situation to which the speech is pertinent, but that situation alone is inadequate to it. This is, so to speak, the structural emotion, provided by the drama. But the whole effect, the dominant tone, is due to the fact that a number of floating feelings, having an affinity to this emotion by no means

---

[a] Cyril Tourneur, *The Revenger's Tragedy* (1607), III, iv.

superficially evident, have combined with it to give us a new art emotion.

It is not in his personal emotions, the emotions provoked by particular events in his life, that the poet is in any way remarkable or interesting. His particular emotions may be simple, or crude, or flat. The emotion in his poetry will be a very complex thing, but not with the complexity of the emotions of people who have very complex or unusual emotions in life. One error, in fact, of eccentricity in poetry is to seek for new human emotions to express; and in this search for novelty in the wrong place it discovers the perverse. The business of the poet is not to find new emotions, but to use the ordinary ones and, in working them up into poetry, to express feelings which are not in actual emotions at all. And emotions which he has never experienced will serve his turn as well as those familiar to him. Consequently, we must believe that 'emotion recollected in tranquility'[a] is an inexact formula. For it is neither emotion, nor recollection, nor, without distortion of meaning, tranquillity. It is a concentration, and a new thing resulting from the concentration, of a very great number of experiences which to the practical and active person would not seem to be experiences at all; it is a concentration which does not happen consciously or of deliberation. These experiences are not 'recollected', and they finally unite in an atmosphere which is 'tranquil' only in that it is a passive attending upon the event. Of course this is not quite the whole story. There is a great deal, in the writing of poetry, which must be conscious and deliberate. In fact, the bad poet is usually unconscious where he ought to be conscious, and conscious where he ought to be unconscious. Both errors tend to make him 'personal'. Poetry is not a turning loose of emotion, but an escape from emotion; it is not the expression of personality, but an escape from personality. But, of course, only those who have personality and emotions know what it means to want to escape from these things.

III

ὁ δὲ νοῦς ἴσως θειότερόν τι καὶ ἀπαθές ἐστιν.[b]

This essay proposes to halt at the frontier of metaphysics or mysticism, and confine itself to such practical conclusions as can be applied by the responsible person interested in poetry. To divert interest from the poet to the poetry is a laudable aim: for it would conduce to a juster estimation of actual poetry, good and bad. There are many people who appreciate the expression of sincere emotion in verse, and there is a smaller number of people who can appreciate technical excellence. But very few know when there is an expression of *significant* emotion, emotion which has its life in the poem and not in the history of the poet. The emotion of art is impersonal. And the poet cannot reach this impersonality without surrendering himself wholly to the work to be done. And he is not likely to know what is to be done unless he believes in what is not

[a] 'Poetry is the spontaneous overflow of powerful feelings: it takes its origins from emotion recollected in tranquillity.' Wordsworth, Preface to *Lyrical Ballads* (1800).

[b] 'While the intellect is doubtless a thing more divine and is impassive.' Aristotle, *De Anima.*

merely the present, but the present moment of the past, unless he is conscious, not of what is dead, but of what is already living.

The function of criticism

I

Writing several years ago on the subject of the relation of the new to the old in art, I formulated a view to which I still adhere, in sentences which I take the liberty of quoting, because the present paper is an application of the principle they express:

> The existing monuments form an ideal order among themselves, which is modified by the introduction of the new (the really new) work of art among them. The existing order is complete before the new work arrives; for order to persist after the supervention of novelty, the *whole* existing order must be, if ever so slightly, altered; and so the relations, proportions, values of each work of art towards the whole are readjusted; and this is conformity between the old and the new. Whoever has approved this idea of order, of the form of European, of English literature, will not find it preposterous that the past should be altered by the present as much as the present is directed by the past.

I was dealing then with the artist, and the sense of tradition which, it seemed to me, the artist should have; but it was generally a problem of order; and the function of criticism seems to be essentially a problem of order too. I thought of literature then, as I think of it now, of the literature of the world, of the literature of Europe, of the literature of a single country, not as a collection of the writings of individuals, but as 'organic wholes', as systems in relation to which, and only in relation to which, individual works of literary art, and the works of individual artists, have their significance. There is accordingly something outside of the artist to which he owes allegiance, a devotion to which he must surrender and sacrifice himself in order to earn and to obtain his unique position. A common inheritance and a common cause unite artists consciously or unconsciously: it must be admitted that the union is mostly unconscious. Between the true artists of any time there is, I believe, an unconscious community. And, as our instincts of tidiness imperatively command us not to leave to the haphazard of unconsciousness what we can attempt to do consciously, we are forced to conclude that what happens unconsciously we could bring about, and form into a purpose, if we made a conscious attempt. The second-rate artist, of course, cannot afford to surrender himself to any common action; for his chief task is the assertion of all the trifling differences which are his distinction: only the man who has so much to give that he can forget himself in his work can afford to collaborate, to exchange, to contribute.

If such views are held about art, it follows that *a fortiori* whoever holds them must hold similar views about criticism. When I say criticism, I mean of course in this place the commentation and exposition of works of art by means of written words; for of the general use of the word 'criticism' to mean such writings, as Matthew Arnold uses it in his essay[a], I shall presently make several qualifications. No exponent of criticism (in this limited sense) has, I presume, ever made the preposterous assumption that criticism is an autotelic[b] activity. I do not deny that art may be affirmed to serve ends beyond itself; but art is not required to be aware of these ends, and indeed performs its function, whatever that may be, according to various theories of value, much better by indifference to them. Criticism, on the other hand, must always profess an end in view, which, roughly speaking, appears to be the elucidation of works of art and the correction of taste. The critic's task, therefore, appears to be quite clearly cut out for him; and it ought to be comparatively easy to decide whether he performs it satisfactorily, and in general, what kinds of criticism are useful and what are otiose. But on giving the matter a little attention, we perceive that criticism, far from being a simple and orderly field of beneficent activity, from which impostors can be readily ejected, is no better than a Sunday park of contending and contentious orators, who have not even arrived at the articulation of their differences. Here, one would suppose, was a place for quiet co-operative labour. The critic, one would suppose, if he is to justify his existence, should endeavour to discipline his personal prejudices and cranks—tares to which we are all subject—and compose his differences with as many of his fellows as possible, in the common pursuit of true judgment. When we find that quite the contrary prevails, we begin to suspect that the critic owes his livelihood to the violence and extremity of his opposition to other critics, or else to some trifling oddities of his own with which he contrives to season the opinions which men already hold, and which out of vanity or sloth they prefer to maintain. We are tempted to expel the lot.

Immediately after such an eviction, or as soon as relief has abated our rage, we are compelled to admit that there remain certain books, certain essays, certain sentences, certain men, who have been 'useful' to us. And our next step is to attempt to classify these, and find out whether we establish any principles for deciding what kinds of book should be preserved, and what aims and methods of criticism should be followed.

II

The view of the relation of the work of art to art, of the work of literature to literature, of 'criticism' to criticism, which I have outlined above, seemed to me natural and self-evident. I owe to Mr Middleton Murry[c] my perception of the contentious character of the problem; or rather, my perception that there is a

[a] 'The Function of Criticism at the Present Time' (1864).
[b] Containing within itself its end or purpose.
[c] Middleton Murry (1889–1957) literary critic and (at this time) editor of the *Adelphi*, which he founded.

definite and final choice involved. To Mr Murry I feel an increasing debt of gratitude. Most of our critics are occupied in labour of obnubilation; in reconciling, in hushing up, in patting down, in squeezing in, in glozing over, in concocting pleasant sedatives, in pretending that the only difference between themselves and others is that they are nice men and the others of very doubtful repute. Mr Murry is not one of these. He is aware that there are definite positions to be taken, and that now and then one must actually reject something and select something else. He is not the anonymous writer who in a literary paper several years ago asserted that Romanticism and Classicism are much the same thing, and that the true Classical Age in France was the Age which produced the Gothic cathedrals and—Jeanne d'Arc. With Mr Murry's formulation of Classicism and Romanticism I cannot agree; the difference seems to me rather the difference between the complete and the fragmentary, the adult and the immature, the orderly and the chaotic. But what Mr Murry does show is that there are at least two attitudes towards literature and towards everything, and that you cannot hold both. And the attitude which he professes appears to imply that the other has no standing in England whatever. For it is made a national, a racial issue.

Mr Murry makes his issue perfectly clear. 'Catholicism,' he says, 'stands for the principle of unquestioned spiritual authority outside the individual; that is also the principle of Classicism in literature.' Within the orbit within which Mr Murry's discussion moves, this seems to me an unimpeachable definition, though it is of course not all that there is to be said about either Catholicism or Classicism. Those of us who find ourselves supporting what Mr Murry calls Classicism believe that men cannot get on without giving allegiance to something outside themselves. I am aware that 'outside' and 'inside' are terms which provide unlimited opportunity for quibbling, and that no psychologist would tolerate a discussion which shuffled such base coinage; but I will presume that Mr Murry and myself can agree that for our purpose these counters are adequate, and concur in disregarding the admonitions of our psychological friends. If you find that you have to imagine it as outside, then it is outside. If, then, a man's interest is political, he must, I presume, profess an allegiance to principles, or to a form of government, or to a monarch; and if he is interested in religion, and has one, to a Church; and if he happens to be interested in literature, he must acknowledge, it seems to me, just that sort of allegiance which I endeavoured to put forth in the preceding section. There is, nevertheless, an alternative, which Mr Murry has expressed. 'The English writer, the English divine, the English statesman, inherit no rules from their forebears; they inherit only this: a sense that in the last resort they must depend upon the inner voice.' This statement does, I admit, appear to cover certain cases; it throws a flood of light upon Mr Lloyd George. But why 'in the last resort'? Do they, then, avoid the dictates of the inner voice up to the last extremity? My belief is that those who possess this inner voice are ready enough to hearken to it, and will hear no other. The inner voice, in fact, sounds remarkably like an old principle which has been formulated by an elder critic[a] in the now familiar phrase of 'doing as

[a] Matthew Arnold, in *Culture and Anarchy* (1869).

one likes'. The possessors of the inner voice ride ten in a compartment to a football match at Swansea, listening to the inner voice, which breathes the eternal message of vanity, fear, and lust.

Mr Murry will say, with some show of justice, that this is a wilful misrepresentation. He says: 'If they (the English writer, divine, statesman) dig *deep enough* in their pursuit of self-knowledge—a piece of mining done not with the intellect alone, but with the whole man—they will come upon a self that is universal'—an exercise far beyond the strength of our football enthusiasts. It is an exercise, however, which I believe was of enough interest to Catholicism for several handbooks to be written on its practice. But the Catholic practitioners were, I believe, with the possible exception of certain heretics, not palpitating Narcissi; the Catholic did not believe that God and himself were identical. 'The man who truly interrogates himself will ultimately hear the voice of God,' Mr Murry says. In theory, this leads to a form of pantheism which I maintain is not European—just as Mr Murry maintains that 'Classicism' is not English. For its practical results, one may refer to the verses of *Hudibras.a*

I did not realize that Mr Murry was the spokesman for a considerable sect, until I read in the editorial columns of a dignified daily that 'magnificent as the representatives of the classical genius have been in England, they are not the sole expressions of the English character, which remains at bottom obstinately "humorous" and nonconformist'. This writer is moderate in using the qualification *sole*, and brutally frank in attributing this 'humorousness' to 'the unreclaimed Teutonic element in us'. But it strikes me that Mr Murry, and this other voice, are either too obstinate or too tolerant. The question is, the first question, *not* what comes natural or what comes *easy* to us, but what is right? Either one attitude is better than the other, or else it is indifferent. But how can such a choice be indifferent? Surely the reference to racial origins, or the mere statement that the French are thus, and the English otherwise, is not expected to settle the question: which, of two antithetical views, is *right*? And I cannot understand why the opposition between Classicism and Romanticism should be profound enough in Latin countries (Mr Murry says it is) and yet of no significance among ourselves. For if the French are *naturally* classical, why should there be any 'opposition' in France, any more than there is here? And if Classicism is not natural to them, but something acquired, why not acquire it here? Were the French in the year 1600 classical, and the English in the same year romantic? A more important difference, to my mind, is that the French in the year 1600 *had already a more mature prose*.

III

This discussion may seem to have led us a long way from the subject of this paper. But it was worth my while to follow Mr Murry's comparison of Outside Authority with the Inner Voice. For to those who obey the inner voice (perhaps 'obey' is not the word) nothing that I can say about criticism will have the

---

a A long poem by Samuel Butler (1612–80) satirizing puritan dissenting sects.

slightest value. For they will not be interested in the attempt to find any common principles for the pursuit of criticism. Why have principles, when one has the inner voice? If I like a thing, that is all I want; and if enough of us, shouting all together, like it, that should be all that *you* (who don't like it) ought to want. The law of art, said Mr Clutton Brock[a], is all case law. And we can not only like whatever we like to like but we can like it for any reason we choose. We are not, in fact, concerned with literary *perfection* at all—the search for perfection is a sign of pettiness, for it shows that the writer has admitted the existence of an unquestioned spiritual authority outside himself, to which he has attempted to *conform*. We are not in fact interested in art. We will not worship Baal. 'The principle of classical leadership is that obeisance is made to the office or to the tradition, never to the man.' And we want, not principles, but men.

Thus speaks the Inner Voice. It is a voice to which, for convenience, we may give a name: and the name I suggest is Whiggery.

IV

Leaving, then, those whose calling and election are sure[b] and returning to those who shamefully depend upon tradition and the accumulated wisdom of time, and restricting the discussion to those who sympathize with each other in this frailty, we may comment for a moment upon the use of the terms 'critical' and 'creative' by one whose place, on the whole, is with the weaker brethren. Matthew Arnold distinguishes far too bluntly, it seems to me, between the two activities: he overlooks the capital importance of criticism in the work of creation itself. Probably, indeed, the larger part of the labour of an author in composing his work is critical labour; the labour of sifting, combining, constructing, expunging, correcting, testing: this frightful toil is as much critical as creative. I maintain even that the criticism employed by a trained and skilled writer on his own work is the most vital, the highest kind of criticism; and (as I think I have said before) that some creative writers are superior to others solely because their critical faculty is superior. There is a tendency, and I think it is a whiggery tendency, to decry this critical toil of the artist; to propound the thesis that the great artist is an unconscious artist, unconsciously inscribing on his banner the words Muddle Through. Those of us who are Inner Deaf Mutes are, however, sometimes compensated by a humble conscience, which, though without oracular expertness, counsels us to do the best we can, reminds us that our compositions ought to be as free from defects as possible (to atone for their lack of inspiration), and, in short, makes us waste a good deal of time. We are aware, too, that the critical discrimination which comes so hardly to us has in more fortunate men flashed in the very heat of creation; and we do not assume that because works have been composed without apparent critical labour, no critical labour has been done. We do not know what previous labours

[a] Arthur Clutton-Brock (1868–1924), English critic.
[b] An ironical allusion to the Calvinistic doctrine of salvation.

have prepared, or what goes on, in the way of criticism, all the time in the minds of the creators.

But this affirmation recoils upon us. If so large a part of creation is really criticism, is not a large part of what is called 'critical writing' really creative? If so, is there not creative criticism in the ordinary sense? The answer seems to be, that there is no equation. I have assumed as axiomatic that a creation, a work of art, is autotelic; and that criticism, by definition, is *about* something other than itself. Hence you cannot fuse creation with criticism as you can fuse criticism with creation. The critical activity finds its highest, its true fulfilment in a kind of union with creation in the labour of the artist.

But no writer is completely self-sufficient, and many creative writers have a critical activity which is not all discharged into their work. Some seem to require to keep their critical powers in condition for the real work by exercising them miscellaneously; others, on completing a work, need to continue the critical activity by commenting on it. There is no general rule. And as men can learn from each other, so some of these treatises have been useful to other writers. And some of them have been useful to those who were not writers.

At one time I was inclined to take the extreme position that the *only* critics worth reading were the critics who practised, and practised well, the art of which they wrote. But I had to stretch this frame to make some important inclusions; and I have since been in search of a formula which should cover everything I wished to include, even if it included more than I wanted. And the most important qualification which I have been able to find, which accounts for the peculiar importance of the criticism of practitioners, is that a critic must have a very highly developed sense of fact. This is by no means a trifling or frequent gift. And it is not one which easily wins popular commendations. The sense of fact is something very slow to develop, and its complete development means perhaps the very pinnacle of civilization. For there are so many spheres of fact to be mastered, and our outermost sphere of fact, of knowledge, of control, will be ringed with narcotic fancies in the sphere beyond. To the member of the Browning Study Circle, the discussion of poets about poetry may seem arid, technical, and limited. It is merely that the practitioners have clarified and reduced to a state of fact all the feelings that the member can only enjoy in the most nebulous form; the dry technique implies, for those who have mastered it, all that the member thrills to; only that has been made into something precise, tractable, under control. That, at all events, is one reason for the value of the practitioner's criticism—he is dealing with his facts, and he can help us to do the same.

And at every level of criticism I find the same necessity regnant. There is a large part of critical writing which consists in 'interpreting' an author, a work. This is not on the level of the Study Circle either; it occasionally happens that one person obtains an understanding of another, or a creative writer, which he can partially communicate, and which we feel to be true and illuminating. It is difficult to confirm the 'interpretation' by external evidence. To anyone who is skilled in fact on this level there will be evidence enough. But who is to prove his own skill? And for every success in this type of writing there are thousands of impostures. Instead of insight, you get a fiction. Your test is to apply it again and again to the original, with your view of the original to guide you. But there is no one to guarantee your competence, and once again we find ourselves in a dilemma.

We must ourselves decide what is useful to us and what is not; and it is quite likely that we are not competent to decide. But it is fairly certain that 'interpretation' (I am not touching upon the acrostic element in literature) is only legitimate when it is not interpretation at all, but merely putting the reader in possession of facts which he would otherwise have missed. I have had some experience of Extension lecturing*a*, and I have found only two ways of leading any pupils to like anything with the right liking: to present them with a selection of the simpler kind of facts about a work—its conditions, its setting, its genesis—or else to spring the work on them in such a way that they were not prepared to be prejudiced against it. There were many facts to help them with Elizabethan drama: the poems of T. E. Hulme*b* only needed to be read aloud to have immediate effect.

Comparison and analysis, I have said before, and Remy de Gourmont has said before me (a real master of fact—sometimes, I am afraid, when he moved outside of literature, a master illusionist of fact), are the chief tools of the critic. It is obvious indeed that they *are* tools, to be handled with care, and not employed in an inquiry into the number of times giraffes are mentioned in the English novel. They are not used with conspicuous success by many contemporary writers. You must know what to compare and what to analyse. The late Professor [W. P.] Ker had skill in the use of these tools. Comparison and analysis need only the cadavers on the table; but interpretation is always producing parts of the body from its pockets, and fixing them in place. And any book, any essay, any note in *Notes and Queries*, which produces a fact even of the lowest order about a work of art is a better piece of work than nine-tenths of the most pretentious critical journalism, in journals or in books. We assume, of course, that we are masters and not servants of facts, and that we know that the discovery of Shakespeare's laundry bills would not be of much use to us; but we must always reserve final judgment as to the futility of the research which has discovered them, in the possibility that some genius will appear who will know of a use to which to put them. Scholarship, even in its humblest forms, has its rights; we assume that we know how to use it, and how to neglect it. Of course the multiplication of critical books and essays may create, and I have seen it create, a vicious taste for reading about works of art instead of reading the works themselves, it may supply opinion instead of educating taste. But *fact* cannot corrupt taste; it can at worst gratify one taste—a taste for history, let us say, or antiquities, or biography—under the illusion that it is assisting another. The real corrupters are those who supply opinion or fancy; and Goethe and Coleridge are not guiltless—for what is Coleridge's *Hamlet*: is it an honest inquiry as far as the data permit, or is it an attempt to present Coleridge in an attractive costume?

a Adult evening classes organized by a university.
b See below, pp. 92–104.

We have not succeeded in finding such a test as anyone can apply; we have been forced to allow ingress to innumerable dull and tedious books; but we have, I think, found a test which, for those who are able to apply it, will dispose of the really vicious ones. And with this test we may return to the preliminary statement of the policy of literature and of criticism. For the kinds of critical work which we have admitted, there is the possibility of cooperative activity, with the further possibility of arriving at something outside of ourselves, which may provisionally be called truth. But if anyone complains that I have not defined truth, or fact, or reality, I can only say apologetically that it was no part of my purpose to do so, but only to find a scheme into which, whatever they are, they will fit, if they exist.

7 Virginia Woolf

Virginia Woolf (1882-1941) was born Adeline Virginia Stephen, the daughter of Leslie Stephen, man-of-letters and first editor of the *Dictionary of National Biography*. After his death in 1904, Virginia, with her two brothers and her sister Vanessa (a painter who married the art critic Clive Bell), moved to a house in the Bloomsbury area of London and thus formed the nucleus of what was to become famous as the Bloomsbury Group. The biographer and critic Lytton Strachey, the economist Maynard Keynes, and the novelist E. M. Forster were among the luminaries of this circle, which exerted considerable (some would say excessive) influence over English literary and intellectual life between the wars.

Virginia Woolf (she married Leonard Woolf in 1912) began her literary career as a reviewer and essayist; and she continued to write occasional criticism after she had achieved fame as a novelist. 'Modern Fiction', first published in 1919, appears in retrospect as a kind of manifesto, attempting to do for the novel what T. S. Eliot's 'Tradition and the Individual Talent' (published in the same year) did for poetry. The date is significant, both for Virginia Woolf herself, and for modern literature generally. As references in the essay indicate, James Joyce's *Ulysses* (1922), the most enduring masterpiece of modernist fiction in English, was at that time appearing in serial form in the *Little Review*; and despite what now appear rather prim and grudging qualifications, Virginia Woolf clearly recognized the power and originality of Joyce's techniques, and the possibilities they suggested for replacing the conventional (and, it seemed to Virginia Woolf, obsolete) 'realism' of the most popular novelists of the preceding generation— Bennett, Wells, and Galsworthy. Virginia Woolf's own first two novels, *The Voyage Out* (1915) and *Night and Day* (1919) had been conventional enough in form. 'Modern Fiction' therefore seems to herald her formal experimentation, especially in rendering the 'stream of consciousness', which began with *Jacob's Room* (1922) and reached its mature expression in *Mrs Dalloway* (1925), *To the Lighthouse* (1927), and *The Waves* (1931). 'Modern Fiction' is reprinted here from Virginia Woolf's *Collected Essays*, vol. ii (1966).

CROSS REFERENCES: 4. Henry James
10. D. H. Lawrence ('Why the Novel Matters')
11. E. M. Forster
29. Mark Schorer
35. Georg Lukács

COMMENTARY: J. K. Johnston, *The Bloomsbury Group: a study of E. M. Forster, Lytton Strachey, Virginia Woolf and their circle* (1954)

Modern fiction

In making any survey, even the freest and loosest, of modern fiction, it is difficult not to take it for granted that the modern practice of the art is somehow an improvement upon the old. With their simple tools and primitive materials, it might be said, Fielding did well and Jane Austen even better, but compare their opportunities with ours! Their masterpieces certainly have a strange air of simplicity. And yet the analogy between literature and the process, to choose an example, of making motor cars scarcely holds good beyond the first glance. It is doubtful whether in the course of the centuries, though we have learnt much about making machines, we have learnt anything about making literature. We do not come to write better; all that we can be said to do is to keep moving, now a little in this direction, now in that, but with a circular tendency should the whole course of the track be viewed from a sufficiently lofty pinnacle. It need scarcely be said that we make no claim to stand, even momentarily, upon that vantage-ground. On the flat, in the crowd, half blind with dust, we look back with envy to those happier warriors, whose battle is won and whose achievements wear so serene an air of accomplishment that we can scarcely refrain from whispering that the fight was not so fierce for them as for us. It is for the historian of literature to decide; for him to say if we are now beginning or ending or standing in the middle of a great period of prose fiction, for down in the plain little is visible. We only know that certain gratitudes and hostilities inspire us; that certain paths seem to lead to fertile land, others to the dust and the desert; and of this perhaps it may be worth while to attempt some account.

Our quarrel, then, is not with the classics, and if we speak of quarrelling with Mr Wells, Mr Bennett, and Mr Galsworthy, it is partly that by the mere fact of their existence in the flesh their work has a living, breathing, everyday imperfection which bids us take what liberties with it we choose. But it is also true, that, while we thank them for a thousand gifts, we reserve our unconditional gratitude for Mr Hardy, for Mr Conrad, and in much lesser degree for the Mr Hudson[a] of *The Purple Land*, *Green Mansions*, and *Far Away and Long Ago*. Mr Wells, Mr Bennett, and Mr Galsworthy have excited so many hopes and disappointed them so persistently that our gratitude largely takes

[a] William Henry Hudson (1841–1922), was born of American parents near Buenos Aires, came to England in 1869, and took British citizenship in 1900. *Green Mansions* (1904), probably his best known work, is a romance of the South American forest.

the form of thanking them for having shown us what they might have done but have not done; what we certainly could not do, but as certainly, perhaps, do not wish to do. No single phrase will sum up the charge or grievance which we have to bring against a mass of work so large in its volume and embodying so many qualities, both admirable and the reverse. If we tried to formulate our meaning in one word we should say that these three writers are materialists. It is because they are concerned not with the spirit but with the body that they have disappointed us, and left us with the feeling that the sooner English fiction turns its back upon them, as politely as may be, and marches, if only into the desert, the better for its soul. Naturally, no single word reaches the centre of three separate targets. In the case of Mr Wells it falls notably wide of the mark. And yet even with him it indicates to our thinking the fatal alloy in his genius, the great clod of clay that has got itself mixed up with the purity of his inspiration. But Mr Bennett is perhaps the worst culprit of the three, inasmuch as he is by far the best workman. He can make a book so well constructed and solid in its craftsmanship that it is difficult for the most exacting of critics to see through what chink or crevice decay can creep in. There is not so much as a draught between the frames of the windows, or a crack in the boards. And yet—if life should refuse to live there? That is a risk which the creator of *The Old Wives' Tale*, George Cannon, Edwin Clayhanger, and hosts of other figures, may well claim to have surmounted. His characters live abundantly, even unexpectedly, but it remains to ask how do they live, and what do they live for? More and more they seem to us, deserting even the well-built villa in the Five Towns*a* to spend their time in some softly padded first-class railway carriage, pressing bells and buttons innumerable; and the destiny to which they travel so luxuriously becomes more and more unquestionably an eternity of bliss spent in the very best hotel in Brighton. It can scarcely be said of Mr Wells that he is a materialist in the sense that he takes too much delight in the solidity of his fabric. His mind is too generous in its sympathies to allow him to spend much time in making things shipshape and substantial. He is a materialist from sheer goodness of heart, taking upon his shoulders the work that ought to have been discharged by Government officials, and in the plethora of his ideas and facts scarcely having leisure to realize, or forgetting to think important, the crudity and coarseness of his human beings. Yet what more damaging criticism can there be both of his earth and of his Heaven than that they are to be inhabited here and hereafter by his Joans and his Peters?*b* Does not the inferiority of their natures tarnish whatever institutions and ideals may be provided for them by the generosity of their creator? Nor, profoundly though we respect the integrity and humanity of Mr Galsworthy, shall we find what we seek in his pages.

If we fasten, then, one label on all these books, on which is one word, materialists, we mean by it that they write of unimportant things; that they

---

a The Pottery towns of Tunstall, Burslem, Hanley, Stoke-on-Trent and Longton which, under altered names, provide the setting for many of Bennett's novels and stories.
b H. G. Wells's novel *Joan and Peter* was published in 1918.

spend immense skill and immense industry making the trivial and the transitory appear the true and the enduring.

We have to admit that we are exacting, and, further, that we find it difficult to justify our discontent by explaining what it is that we exact. We frame our question differently at different times. But it reappears most persistently as we drop the finished novel on the crest of a sigh—Is it worth while? What is the point of it all? Can it be that, owing to one of those little deviations which the human spirit seems to make from time to time, Mr Bennett has come down with his magnificent apparatus for catching life just an inch or two on the wrong side? Life escapes: and perhaps without life nothing else is worth while. It is a confession of vagueness to have to make use of such a figure as this, but we scarcely better the matter by speaking, as critics are prone to do, of reality. Admitting the vagueness which afflicts all criticism of novels, let us hazard the opinion that for us at this moment the form of fiction most in vogue more often misses than secures the thing we seek. Whether we call it life or spirit, truth or reality, this, the essential thing, has moved off, or on, and refuses to be contained any longer in such ill-fitting vestments as we provide. Nevertheless, we go on persevering, conscientiously, constructing our two and thirty chapters after a design which more and more ceases to resemble the vision in our minds. So much of the enormous labour of proving the solidity, the likeness to life, of the story is not merely labour thrown away but labour misplaced to the extent of obscuring and blotting out the light of the conception. The writer seems constrained, not by his own free will but by some powerful and unscrupulous tyrant who has him in thrall, to provide a plot, to provide comedy, tragedy, love interest, and an air of probability embalming the whole so impeccably that if all his figures were to come to life they would find themselves dressed down to the last button of their coats in the fashion of the hour. The tyrant is obeyed; the novel is done to a turn. But sometimes, more and more often as time goes by, we suspect a momentary doubt, a spasm of rebellion, as the pages fill themselves in the customary way. Is life like this? Must novels be like this?

Look within and life, it seems, is very far from being 'like this'. Examine for a moment an ordinary mind on an ordinary day. The mind receives a myriad impressions—trivial, fantastic, evanescent, or engraved with the sharpness of steel. From all sides they come, an incessant shower of innumerable atoms; and as they fall, as they shape themselves into the life of Monday or Tuesday, the accent falls differently from of old; the moment of importance came not here but there; so that, if a writer were a free man and not a slave, if he could write what he chose, not what he must, if he could base his work upon his own feeling and not upon convention, there would be no plot, no comedy, no tragedy, no love interest or catastrophe in the accepted style, and perhaps not a single button sewn on as the Bond Street tailors would have it. Life is not a series of gig-lamps symmetrically arranged; life is a luminous halo, a semi-transparent envelope surrounding us from the beginning of consciousness to the end. Is it not the task of the novelist to convey this varying, this unknown and uncircumscribed spirit, whatever aberration or complexity it may display, with as little mixture of the alien and external as possible? We are not pleading merely for courage and sincerity; we are suggesting that the proper stuff of fiction is a little other than custom would have us believe it.

It is, at any rate, in some such fashion as this that we seek to define the quality which distinguishes the work of several young writers, among whom Mr James Joyce is the most notable, from that of their predecessors. They attempt to come closer to life, and to preserve more sincerely and exactly what interests and moves them, even if to do so they must discard most of the conventions which are commonly observed by the novelist. Let us record the atoms as they fall upon the mind in the order in which they fall, let us trace the pattern, however disconnected and incoherent in appearance, which each sight or incident scores upon the consciousness. Let us not take it for granted that life exists more fully in what is commonly thought big than in what is commonly thought small. Anyone who has read *The Portrait of the Artist as a Young Man* or, what promises to be a far more interesting work, *Ulysses*, now appearing in the *Little Review*, will have hazarded some theory of this nature as to Mr Joyce's intention. On our part, with such a fragment before us, it is hazarded rather than affirmed; but whatever the intention of the whole, there can be no question but that it is of the utmost sincerity and that the result, difficult or unpleasant as we may judge it, is undeniably important. In contrast with those whom we have called materialists, Mr Joyce is spiritual; he is concerned at all costs to reveal the flickerings of that innermost flame which flashes its messages through the brain, and in order to preserve it he disregards with complete courage whatever seems to him adventitious, whether it be probability, or coherence, or any other of these signposts which for generations have served to support the imagination of a reader when called upon to imagine what he can neither touch nor see. The scene in the cemetery, for instance, with its brilliancy, its sordidity, its incoherence, its sudden lightning flashes of significance, does undoubtedly come so close to the quick of the mind that, on a first reading at any rate, it is difficult not to acclaim a masterpiece. If we want life itself, here surely we have it. Indeed, we find ourselves fumbling rather awkwardly if we try to say what else we wish, and for what reason a work of such originality yet fails to compare, for we must take high examples, with [Conrad's] *Youth* or [Hardy's] *The Mayor of Casterbridge*. It fails because of the comparative poverty of the writer's mind, we might say simply and have done with it. But it is possible to press a little further and wonder whether we may not refer our sense of being in a bright yet narrow room, confined and shut in, rather than enlarged and set free, to some limitation imposed by the method as well as by the mind. Is it the method that inhibits the creative power? Is it due to the method that we feel neither jovial nor magnanimous, but centred in a self which, in spite of its tremor of susceptibility, never embraces or creates what is outside itself and beyond? Does the emphasis laid, perhaps didactically, upon indecency contribute to the effect of something angular and isolated? Or is it merely that in any effort of such originality it is much easier, for contemporaries especially, to feel what it lacks than to name what it gives? In any case it is a mistake to stand outside examining 'methods'. Any method is right, every method is right, that expresses what we wish to express, if we are writers; that brings us closer to the novelist's intention if we are readers. This method has the merit of bringing us closer to what we were prepared to call life itself; did not the reading of *Ulysses* suggest how much of life is excluded or ignored, and did it not come with a shock to open *Tristram Shandy* or even *Pendennis* and be by them convinced that there are not only other aspects of life, but more important ones into the bargain.

However this may be, the problem before the novelist at present, as we suppose it to have been in the past, is to contrive means of being free to set down what he chooses. He has to have the courage to say that what interests him is no longer 'this' but 'that': out of 'that' alone must he construct his work. For the moderns 'that', the point of interest, lies very likely in the dark places of psychology. At once, therefore, the accent falls a little differently; the emphasis is upon something hitherto ignored; at once a different outline of form becomes necessary, difficult for us to grasp, incomprehensible to our predecessors. No one but a modern, no one perhaps but a Russian, would have felt the interest of the situation which Tchekov has made into the short story which he calls 'Gusev'. Some Russian soldiers lie ill on board a ship which is taking them back to Russia. We are given a few scraps of their talk and some of their thoughts; then one of them dies and is carried away; the talk goes on among the others for a time, until Gusev himself dies, and looking 'like a carrot or a radish' is thrown overboard. The emphasis is laid upon such unexpected places that at first it seems as if there were no emphasis at all; and then, as the eyes accustom themselves to twilight and discern the shapes of things in a room we see how complete the story is, how profound, and how truly in obedience to his vision Tchekov has chosen this, that, and the other, and placed them together to compose something new. But it is impossible to say 'this is comic', or 'that is tragic', nor are we certain, since short stories, we have been taught, should be brief and conclusive, whether this, which is vague and inconclusive, should be called a short story at all.

The most elementary remarks upon modern English fiction can hardly avoid some mention of the Russian influence, and if the Russians are mentioned one runs the risk of feeling that to write of any fiction save theirs is waste of time. If we want understanding of the soul and heart where else shall we find it of comparable profundity? If we are sick of our own materialism the least considerable of their novelists has by right of birth a natural reverence for the human spirit. 'Learn to make yourself akin to people.... But let this sympathy be not with the mind—for it is easy with the mind—but with the heart, with love towards them.' In every great Russian writer we seem to discern the features of a saint, if sympathy for the sufferings of others, love towards them, endeavour to reach some goal worthy of the most exacting demands of the spirit constitute saintliness. It is the saint in them which confounds us with a feeling of our own irreligious triviality, and turns so many of our famous novels to tinsel and trickery. The conclusions of the Russian mind, thus comprehensive and compassionate, are inevitably, perhaps, of the utmost sadness. More accurately indeed we might speak of the inconclusiveness of the Russian mind.

It is the sense that there is no answer, that if honestly examined life presents question after question which must be left to sound on and on after the story is over in hopeless interrogation that fills us with a deep, and finally it may be with a resentful, despair. They are right perhaps; unquestionably they see further than we do and without our gross impediments of vision. But perhaps we see something that escapes them, or why should this voice of protest mix itself with our gloom? The voice of protest is the voice of another and an ancient civilization which seems to have bred in us the instinct to enjoy and fight rather than to suffer and understand. English fiction from Sterne to Meredith bears witness to our natural delight in humour and comedy, in the beauty of earth, in the activities of the intellect, and in the splendour of the body. But any deductions that we may draw from the comparison of two fictions so immeasurably far apart are futile save indeed as they flood us with a view of the infinite possibilities of the art and remind us that there is no limit to the horizon, and that nothing—no 'method', no experiment, even of the wildest—is forbidden, but only falsity and pretence. 'The proper stuff of fiction' does not exist; everything is the proper stuff of fiction, every feeling, every thought; every quality of brain and spirit is drawn upon; no perception comes amiss. And if we can imagine the art of fiction come alive and standing in our midst, she would undoubtedly bid us break her and bully her, as well as honour and love her, for so her youth is renewed and her sovereignty assured.

8 T. E. Hulme

Thomas Ernest Hulme (1883-1917) attended the University of Cambridge without taking a degree, and it was mainly through private study in Europe and later in London that he trained himself as a philosopher and aesthetician. He was particularly interested in the work of the French philosopher Henri Bergson, and published a translation of the latter's *Introduction to Metaphysics* in 1913. On the outbreak of World War I, Hulme volunteered for military service. He was killed in France in 1917. From his unpublished papers Herbert Read edited a volume of critical essays entitled *Speculations* (1924) from which 'Romanticism and Classicism' (probably written in 1913 or 1914) is taken.

T. E. Hulme acquired an almost legendary posthumous reputation as the key thinker behind the Pound–Eliot revolution in English poetry in the second decade of the century. He was a close acquaintance of Pound (who printed five short poems as *The Collected Poetical Works of T. E. Hulme* in 1915) and he was a member of the 'Imagist' group. 'Romanticism and Classicism' may indeed be read as in part a manifesto for Imagism, especially in its recommendation of a 'dry, hard' poetic style (cf. Ezra Pound, pp. 58-60 above). Although it is not certain that the two men ever actually met, the influence of Hulme's thought has been discerned in the poetry and criticism of T. S. Eliot. Certainly the combination we find in 'Romanticism and Classicism', of a modernist poetics based on a preference for classical over romantic values, with a dogmatic Christian pessimism about the perfectibility of man, is one that would have been congenial to Eliot. It should be borne in mind, however, that 'romantic' and 'classical' are pliable terms, which Hulme and Eliot shaped for their own purposes.

CROSS REFERENCES: 5. Ezra Pound
                              6. T. S. Eliot

    COMMENTARY: Michael Roberts, *T. E. Hulme* (1938)
                         Alun Richard Jones, *The Life and Opinions of T. E. Hulme* (1960)

Romanticism and classicism

I want to maintain that after a hundred years of romanticism, we are in for a classical revival, and that the particular weapon of this new classical spirit, when it works in verse, will be fancy. And in this I imply the superiority of fancy—not superior generally or absolutely, for that would be obvious nonsense, but superior in the sense that we use the word good in empirical ethics—good for something, superior for something. I shall have to prove then two things, first that a classical revival is coming, and, secondly, for its particular purposes, fancy will be superior to imagination.

So banal have the terms Imagination and Fancy become that we imagine they must have always been in the language. Their history as two differing terms in the vocabulary of criticism is comparatively short. Originally, of course, they both meant the same thing; they first began to be differentiated by the German writers on aesthetics in the eighteenth century.

I know that in using the words 'classic' and 'romantic' I am doing a danger-ous thing. They represent five or six different kinds of antitheses, and while I may be using them in one sense you may be interpreting them in another. In this present connection I am using them in a perfectly precise and limited sense. I ought really to have coined a couple of new words, but I prefer to use the ones I have used, as I then conform to the practice of the group of polemical writers who make the most use of them at the present day, and have almost succeeded in making them political catchwords. I mean Maurras, Lasserre, and all the group connected with *L'Action Française.*[a]

At the present time this is the particular group with which the distinction is most vital. Because it has become a party symbol. If you asked a man of a certain set whether he preferred the classics or the romantics, you could deduce from that what his politics were.

The best way of gliding into a proper definition of my terms would be to start with a set of people who are prepared to fight about it—for in them you will have no vagueness. (Other people take the infamous attitude of the person with catholic tastes who says he likes both.)

About a year ago, a man whose name I think was Fauchois gave a lecture at the Odéon on Racine, in the course of which he made some disparaging remarks about his dullness, lack of invention and the rest of it. This caused an immediate riot: fights took place all over the house; several people were arrested and imprisoned, and the rest of the series of lectures took place with hundreds of gendarmes and detectives scattered all over the place. These people

---

[a] *L'Action Française* was the chief organ of a group of French intellectuals of the extreme right, active from 1899 till World War II. Though the movement was essentially fascist, Charles Maurras, at least, was a considerable intellectual force and influenced T. S. Eliot among others.

interrupted because the classical ideal is a living thing to them and Racine is the great classic. That is what I call a real vital interest in literature. They regard romanticism as an awful disease from which France had just recovered.

The thing is complicated in their case by the fact that it was romanticism that made the revolution. They hate the revolution, so they hate romanticism.

I make no apology for dragging in politics here; romanticism both in England and France is associated with certain political views, and it is in taking a concrete example of the working out of a principle in action that you can get its best definition.

What was the positive principle behind all the other principles of '89? I am talking here of the revolution in as far as it was an idea; I leave out material causes—they only produce the forces. The barriers which could easily have resisted or guided these forces had been previously rotted away by ideas. This always seems to be the case in successful changes; the privileged class is beaten only when it has lost faith in itself, when it has itself been penetrated with the ideas which are working against it.

It was not the rights of man—that was a good solid practical war-cry. The thing which created enthusiasm, which made the revolution practically a new religion, was something more positive than that. People of all classes, people who stood to lose by it, were in a positive ferment about the idea of liberty. There must have been some idea which enabled them to think that something positive could come out of so essentially negative a thing. There was, and here I get my definition of romanticism. They had been taught by Rousseau that man was by nature good, that it was only bad laws and customs that had suppressed him. Remove all these and the infinite possibilities of man would have a chance. This is what made them think that something positive could come out of disorder, this is what created the religious enthusiasm. Here is the root of all romanticism: that man, the individual, is an infinite reservoir of possibilities; and if you can so rearrange society by the destruction of oppressive order then these possibilities will have a chance and you will get Progress.

One can define the classical quite clearly as the exact opposite to this. Man is an extraordinarily fixed and limited animal whose nature is absolutely constant. It is only by tradition and organization that anything decent can be got out of him.

This view was a little shaken at the time of Darwin. You remember his particular hypothesis, that new species came into existence by the cumulative effect of small variations—this seems to admit the possibility of future progress. But at the present day the contrary hypothesis makes headway in the shape of De Vries's mutation theory, that each new species comes into existence, not gradually by the accumulation of small steps, but suddenly in a jump, a kind of sport, and that once in existence it remains absolutely fixed. This enables me to keep the classical view with an appearance of scientific backing.

Put shortly, these are the two views, then. One, that man is intrinsically good, spoilt by circumstance; and the other that he is intrinsically limited, but disciplined by order and tradition to something fairly decent. To the one party man's nature is like a well, to the other like a bucket. The view which regards man as a well, a reservoir full of possibilities, I call the romantic; the one which regards him as a very finite and fixed creature, I call the classical.

One may note here that the Church has always taken the classical view since the defeat of the Pelagian[a] heresy and the adoption of the sane classical dogma of original sin.

It would be a mistake to identify the classical view with that of materialism. On the contrary it is absolutely identical with the normal religious attitude. I should put it in this way: That part of the fixed nature of man is the belief in the Deity. This should be as fixed and true for every man as belief in the existence of matter and in the objective world. It is parallel to appetite, the instinct of sex, and all the other fixed qualities. Now at certain times, by the use of either force or rhetoric, these instincts have been suppressed—in Florence under Savonarola, in Geneva under Calvin, and here under the Roundheads. The inevitable result of such a process is that the repressed instinct bursts out in some abnormal direction. So with religion. By the perverted rhetoric of Rationalism, your natural instincts are suppressed and you are converted into an agnostic. Just as in the case of the other instincts, Nature has her revenge. The instincts that find their right and proper outlet in religion must come out in some other way. You don't believe in God, so you begin to believe that man is a god. You don't believe in Heaven, so you begin to believe in a heaven on earth. In other words, you get romanticism. The concepts that are right and proper in their own sphere are spread over, and so mess up, falsify and blur the clear outlines of human experience. It is like pouring a pot of treacle over the dinner table. Romanticism then, and this is the best definition I can give of it, is spilt religion.

I must now shirk the difficulty of saying exactly what I mean by romantic and classical in verse. I can only say that it means the result of these two attitudes towards the cosmos, towards man, in so far as it gets reflected in verse. The romantic, because he thinks man infinite, must always be talking about the infinite; and as there is always the bitter contrast between what you think you ought to be able to do and what man actually can, it always tends, in its later stages at any rate, to be gloomy. I really can't go any further than to say it is the reflection of these two temperaments, and point out examples of the different spirits. On the one hand I would take such diverse people as Horace, most of the Elizabethans and the writers of the Augustan age, and on the other side Lamartine, Hugo, parts of Keats, Coleridge, Byron, Shelley, and Swinburne.

I know quite well that when people think of classical and romantic in verse, the contrast at once comes into their mind between, say, Racine and Shakespeare. I don't mean this; the dividing line that I intend is here misplaced a little from the true middle. That Racine is on the extreme classical side I agree, but if you call Shakespeare romantic, you are using a different definition to the one I give. You are thinking of the difference between classic and romantic as being merely one between restraint and exuberance. I should say

[a] Pelagius was an early Christian heretic who denied the doctrine of original sin. His teaching was condemned by the Council of Ephesus (431).

with Nietzsche that there are two kinds of classicism, the static and the dynamic. Shakespeare is the classic of motion.

What I mean by classical in verse, then, is this. That even in the most imaginative flights there is always a holding back, a reservation. The classical poet never forgets this finiteness, this limit of man. He remembers always that he is mixed up with earth. He may jump, but he always returns back; he never flies away into the circumambient gas.

You might say if you wished that the whole of the romantic attitude seems to crystallize in verse round metaphors of flight. Hugo is always flying, flying over abysses, flying up into the eternal gases. The word infinite in every other line.

In the classical attitude you never seem to swing right along to the infinite nothing. If you say an extravagant thing which does exceed the limits inside which you know man to be fastened, yet there is always conveyed in some way at the end an impression of yourself standing outside it, and not quite believing it, or consciously putting it forward as a flourish. You never go blindly into an atmosphere more than the truth, an atmosphere too rarefied for man to breathe for long. You are always faithful to the conception of a limit. It is a question of pitch; in romantic verse you move at a certain pitch of rhetoric which you know, man being what he is, to be a little high-falutin. The kind of thing you get in Hugo or Swinburne. In the coming classical reaction that will feel just wrong. For an example of the opposite thing, a verse written in the proper classical spirit, I can take the song from *Cymbeline* beginning with 'Fear no more the heat of the sun'. I am just using this as a parable. I don't quite mean what I say here. Take the last two lines:

> Golden lads and girls all must,
> Like chimney sweepers come to dust.

Now, no romantic would have ever written that. Indeed, so ingrained is romanticism, so objectionable is this to it, that people have asserted that these were not part of the original song.

Apart from the pun, the thing that I think quite classical is the word lad. Your modern romantic could never write that. He would have to write golden youth, and take up the thing at least a couple of notes in pitch.

I want now to give the reasons which make me think that we are nearing the end of the romantic movement.

The first lies in the nature of any convention or tradition in art. A particular convention or attitude in art has a strict analogy to the phenomena of organic life. It grows old and decays. It has a definite period of life and must die. All the possible tunes get played on it and then it is exhausted; moveover its best period is its youngest. Take the case of the extraordinary efflorescence of verse in the Elizabethan period. All kinds of reasons have been given for this—the discovery of the new world and all the rest of it. There is a much simpler one. A new medium had been given them to play with—namely, blank verse. It was new and so it was easy to play new tunes on it.

The same law holds in other arts. All the masters of painting are born into the world at a time when the particular tradition from which they start is imperfect. The Florentine tradition was just short of full ripeness when Raphael came to Florence, the Bellinesque was still young when Titian was born in Venice. Landscape was still a toy or an appanage of figure-painting when Turner and Constable arose to reveal its independent power. When Turner and Constable had done with landscape they left little or nothing for their successors to do on the same lines. Each field of artistic activity is exhausted by the first great artist who gathers a full harvest from it.

This period of exhaustion seems to me to have been reached in romanticism. We shall not get any new efflorescence of verse until we get a new technique, a new convention, to turn ourselves loose in.

Objection might be taken to this. It might be said that a century as an organic unity doesn't exist, that I am being deluded by a wrong metaphor, that I am treating a collection of literary people as if they were an organism or state department. Whatever we may be in other things, an objector might urge, in literature in as far as we are anything at all—in as far as we are worth considering—we are individuals, we are persons, and as distinct persons we cannot be subordinated to any general treatment. At any period at any time, an individual poet may be a classic or a romantic just as he feels like it. You at any particular moment may think that you can stand outside a movement. You may think that as an individual you observe both the classic and the romantic spirit and decide from a purely detached point of view that one is superior to the other.

The answer to this is that no one, in a matter of judgment of beauty, can take a detached standpoint in this way. Just as physically you are not born that abstract entity, man, but the child of particular parents, so you are in matters of literary judgment. Your opinion is almost entirely of the literary history that came just before you, and you are governed by that whatever you may think. Take Spinoza's example of a stone falling to the ground. If it had a conscious mind it would, he said, think it was going to the ground because it wanted to. So you with your pretended free judgment about what is and what is not beautiful. The amount of freedom in man is much exaggerated. That we are free on certain rare occasions, both my religion and the views I get from metaphysics convince me. But many acts which we habitually label free are in reality automatic. It is quite possible for a man to write a book almost automatically. I have read several such products. Some observations were recorded more than twenty years ago by Robertson on reflex speech, and he found that in certain cases of dementia, where the people were quite unconscious so far as the exercise of reasoning went, very intelligent answers were given to a succession of questions on politics and such matters. The meaning of these questions could not possibly have been understood. Language here acted after the manner of a reflex. So that certain extremely complex mechanisms, subtle enough to imitate beauty, can work by themselves—I certainly think that this is the case with judgments about beauty.

I can put the same thing in slightly different form. Here is a question of a conflict of two attitudes, as it might be of two techniques. The critic, while he has to admit that changes from one to the other occur, persists in regarding them as mere variations to a certain fixed normal, just as a pendulum might swing. I admit the analogy of the pendulum as far as movement, but I deny the further consequence of the analogy, the existence of the point of rest, the normal point.

When I say that I dislike the romantics, I dissociate two things: the part of them in which they resemble all the great poets, and the part in which they differ and which gives them their character as romantics. It is this minor element which constitutes the particular note of a century, and which, while it excites contemporaries, annoys the next generation. It was precisely that quality in Pope which pleased his friends, which we detest. Now, anyone just before the romantics who felt that, could have predicted that a change was coming. It seems to me that we stand just in the same position now. I think that there is an increasing proportion of people who simply can't stand Swinburne.

When I say that there will be another classical revival I don't necessarily anticipate a return to Pope. I say merely that now is the time for such a revival. Given people of the necessary capacity, it may be a vital thing; without them we may get a formalism something like Pope. When it does come we may not even recognize it as classical. Although it will be classical it will be different because it has passed through a romantic period. To take a parallel example: I remember being very surprised, after seeing the Post Impressionists, to find in Maurice Denis's account of the matter that they consider themselves classical in the sense that they were trying to impose the same order on the mere flux of new material provided by the impressionist movement, that existed in the more limited materials of the painting before.

There is something now to be cleared away before I get on with my argument, which is that while romanticism is dead in reality, yet the critical attitude appropriate to it still continues to exist. To make this a little clearer: For every kind of verse, there is a corresponding receptive attitude. In a romantic period we demand from verse certain qualities. In a classical period we demand others. At the present time I should say that this receptive attitude has outlasted the thing from which it was formed. But while the romantic tradition has run dry, yet the critical attitude of mind, which demands romantic qualities from verse, still survives. So that if good classical verse were to be written tomorrow very few people would be able to stand it.

I object even to the best of the romantics. I object still more to the receptive attitude. I object to the sloppiness which doesn't consider that a poem is a poem unless it is moaning or whining about something or other. I always think in this connection of the last line of a poem of John Webster's which ends with a request I cordially endorse:

End your moan and come away.

The thing has got so bad now that a poem which is all dry and hard, a properly classical poem, would not be considered poetry at all. How many people now can lay their hands on their hearts and say they like either Horace or Pope? They feel a kind of chill when they read them.

The dry hardness which you get in the classics is absolutely repugnant to them. Poetry that isn't damp isn't poetry at all. They cannot see that accurate description is a legitimate object of verse. Verse to them always means a bringing in of some of the emotions that are grouped round the word infinite.

The essence of poetry to most people is that it must lead them to a beyond of some kind. Verse strictly confined to the earthly and the definite (Keats is full of it) might seem to them to be excellent writing, excellent craftsmanship, but not poetry. So much has romanticism debauched us, that, without some form of vagueness, we deny the highest.

In the classic it is always the light of ordinary day, never the light that never was on land or sea. It is always perfectly human and never exaggerated: man is always man and never a god.

But the awful result of romanticism is that, accustomed to this strange light, you can never live without it. Its effect on you is that of a drug.

There is a general tendency to think that verse means little else than the expression of unsatisfied emotion. People say: 'But how can you have verse without sentiment?' You see what it is: the prospect alarms them. A classical revival to them would mean the prospect of an arid desert and the death of poetry as they understand it, and could only come to fill the gap caused by that death. Exactly why this dry classical spirit should have a positive and legitimate necessity to express itself in poetry is utterly inconceivable to them. What this positive need is, I shall show later. It follows from the fact that there is another quality, not the emotion produced, which is at the root of excellence in verse. Before I get to this I am concerned with a negative thing, a theoretical point, a prejudice that stands in the way and is really at the bottom of this reluctance to understand classical verse.

It is an objection which ultimately I believe comes from a bad metaphysic of art. You are unable to admit the existence of beauty without the infinite being in some way or another dragged in.

I may quote for purposes of argument, as a typical example of this kind of attitude made vocal, the famous chapters in Ruskin's *Modern Painters*, vol. II, on the imagination. I must say here, parenthetically, that I use this word without prejudice to the other discussion with which I shall end the paper. I only use the word here because it is Ruskin's word. All that I am concerned with just now is the attitude behind it, which I take to be the romantic.

> Imagination cannot but be serious; she sees too far, too darkly, too solemnly, too earnestly, ever to smile. There is something in the heart of everything, if we can reach it, that we shall not be inclined to laugh at.... Those who have so pierced and seen the melancholy deeps of things, are filled with intense passion and gentleness of sympathy. (Part III, chap. iii, § 9.)

> There is in every word set down by the imaginative mind an awful undercurrent of meaning, and evidence and shadow upon it of the deep places out of which it has come. It is often obscure, often half-told; for he who wrote it, in his clear seeing of the things beneath, may have been impatient of

detailed interpretation; for if we choose to dwell upon it and trace it, it will lead us always securely back to that metropolis of the soul's dominion from which we may follow out all the ways and tracks to its farthest coasts. (Part III, chap. iii, § 5.)

Really in all these matters the act of judgment is an instinct, an absolutely unstatable thing akin to the art of the tea taster. But you must talk, and the only language you can use in this matter is that of analogy. I have no material clay to mould to the given shape; the only thing which one has for the purpose, and which acts as a substitute for it, a kind of mental clay, are certain metaphors modified into theories of aesthetic and rhetoric. A combination of these, while it cannot state the essentially unstatable intuition, can yet give you a sufficient analogy to enable you to see what it was and to recognize it on condition that you yourself have been in a similar state. Now these phrases of Ruskin's convey quite clearly to me his taste in the matter.

I see quite clearly that he thinks the best verse must be serious. That is a natural attitude for a man in the romantic period. But he is not content with saying that he prefers this kind of verse. He wants to deduce his opinion like his master, Coleridge, from some fixed principle which can be found by metaphysic.

Here is the last refuge of this romantic attitude. It proves itself to be not an attitude but a deduction from a fixed principle of the cosmos.

One of the main reasons for the existence of philosophy is not that it enables you to find truth (it can never do that) but that it does provide you a refuge for definitions. The usual idea of the thing is that it provides you with a fixed basis from which you can deduce the things you want in aesthetics. The process is the exact contrary. You start in the confusion of the fighting line, you retire from that just a little to the rear to recover, to get your weapons right. Quite plainly, without metaphor this—it provides you with an elaborate and precise language in which you really can explain definitely what you mean, but what you want to say is decided by other things. The ultimate reality is the hurly-burly, the struggle; the metaphysic is an adjunct to clear-headedness in it.

To get back to Ruskin and his objection to all that is not serious. It seems to me that involved in this is a bad metaphysical aesthetic. You have the metaphysic which in defining beauty or the nature of art always drags in the infinite. Particularly in Germany, the land where theories of aesthetics were first created, the romantic aesthetics collated all beauty to an impression of the infinite involved in the identification of our being in absolute spirit. In the least element of beauty we have a total intuition of the whole world. Every artist is a kind of pantheist.

Now it is quite obvious to anyone who holds this kind of theory that any poetry which confines itself to the finite can never be of the highest kind. It seems a contradiction in terms to them. And as in metaphysics you get the last refuge of a prejudice, so it is now necessary for me to refute this.

Here follows a tedious piece of dialectic, but it is necessary for my purpose. I must avoid two pitfalls in discussing the idea of beauty. On the one hand there is the old classical view which is supposed to define it as lying in conformity to certain standard fixed forms; and on the other hand there is the romantic view which drags in the infinite. I have got to find a metaphysic between these two which will enable me to hold consistently that a neoclassic verse of the type I have indicated involves no contradiction in terms. It is essential to prove that beauty may be in small, dry things.

The great aim is accurate, precise and definite description. The first thing is to recognize how extraordinarily difficult this is. It is no mere matter of carefulness; you have to use language, and language is by its very nature a communal thing; that is, it expresses never the exact thing but a compromise—that which is common to you, me and everybody. But each man sees a little differently, and to get out clearly and exactly what he does see, he must have a terrific struggle with language, whether it be with words or the technique of other arts. Language has its own special nature, its own conventions and communal ideas. It is only by a concentrated effort of the mind that you can hold it fixed to your own purpose. I always think that the fundamental process at the back of all the arts might be represented by the following metaphor. You know what I call architect's curves—flat pieces of wood with all different kinds of curvature. By a suitable selection from these you can draw approximately any curve you like. The artist I take to be the man who simply can't bear the idea of that 'approximately'. He will get the exact curve of what he sees whether it be an object or an idea in the mind. I shall here have to change my metaphor a little to get the process in his mind. Suppose that instead of your curved pieces of wood you have a springy piece of steel of the same types of curvature as the wood. Now the state of tension or concentration of mind, if he is doing anything really good in this struggle against the ingrained habit of the technique, may be represented by a man employing all his fingers to bend the steel out of its own curve and into the exact curve which you want. Something different to what it would assume naturally.

There are then two things to distinguish, first the particular faculty of mind to see things as they really are, and apart from the conventional ways in which you have been trained to see them. This is itself rare enough in all consciousness. Second, the concentrated state of mind, the grip over oneself which is necessary in the actual expression of what one sees. To prevent one falling into the conventional curves of ingrained technique, to hold on through infinite detail and trouble to the exact curve you want. Wherever you get this sincerity, you get the fundamental quality of good art without dragging in infinite or serious.

I can now get at that positive fundamental quality of verse which constitutes excellence, which has nothing to do with infinity, with mystery or with emotions.

This is the point I aim at, then, in my argument. I prophesy that a period of dry, hard, classical verse is coming. I have met the preliminary objection founded on the bad romantic aesthetic that in such verse, from which the infinite is excluded, you cannot have the essence of poetry at all.

After attempting to sketch out what this positive quality is, I can get on to the end of my paper in this way: That where you get this quality exhibited in the realm of the emotions you get imagination, and that where you get this quality exhibited in the contemplation of finite things you get fancy.

In prose as in algebra concrete things are embodied in signs or counters which are moved about according to rules, without being visualized at all in the process. There are in prose certain type situations and arrangements of words, which move as automatically into certain other arrangements as do functions in algebra. One only changes the X's and the Y's back into physical things at the end of the process. Poetry, in one aspect at any rate, may be considered as an effort to avoid this characteristic of prose. It is not a counter language, but a visual concrete one. It is a compromise for a language of intuition which would hand over sensations bodily. It always endeavours to arrest you, and to make you continuously see a physical thing, to prevent you gliding through an abstract process. It chooses fresh epithets and fresh metaphors, not so much because they are new, and we are tired of the old, but because the old cease to convey a physical thing and become abstract counters. A poet says a ship 'coursed the seas' to get a physical image, instead of the counter word 'sailed'. Visual meanings can only be transferred by the new bowl of metaphor; prose is an old pot that lets them leak out. Images in verse are not mere decoration, but the very essence of an intuitive language. Verse is a pedestrian taking you over the ground, prose—a train which delivers you at a destination.

I can now get on to a discussion of two words often used in this connection, 'fresh' and 'unexpected'. You praise a thing for being 'fresh'. I understand what you mean, but the word besides conveying the truth conveys a secondary something which is certainly false. When you say a poem or drawing is fresh, and so good, the impression is somehow conveyed that the essential element of goodness is freshness, that it is good because it is fresh. Now this is certainly wrong, there is nothing particularly desirable about freshness *per se*. Works of art aren't eggs. Rather the contrary. It is simply an unfortunate necessity due to the nature of language and technique that the only way the element which does constitute goodness, the only way in which its presence can be detected externally, is by freshness. Freshness convinces you, you feel at once that the artist was in an actual physical state. You feel that for a minute. Real communication is so very rare, for plain speech is unconvincing. It is in this rare fact of communication that you get the root of aesthetic pleasure.

I shall maintain that wherever you get an extraordinary interest in a thing, a great zest in its contemplation which carries on the contemplator to accurate description in the sense of the word accurate I have just analysed, there you have sufficient justification for poetry. It must be an intense zest which heightens a thing out of the level of prose. I am using contemplation here just in the same way that Plato used it, only applied to a different subject; it is a detached interest. 'The object of aesthetic contemplation is something framed apart by itself and regarded without memory or expectation, simply as being itself, as end not means, as individual not universal.'

To take a concrete example. I am taking an extreme case. If you are walking behind a woman in the street, you notice the curious way in which the skirt rebounds from her heels. If that peculiar kind of motion becomes of such interest to you that you will search about until you can get the exact epithet which hits it off, there you have a properly aesthetic emotion. But it is the zest with which you look at the thing which decides you to make the effort. In this sense the feeling that was in Herrick's mind when he wrote 'the tempestuous petticoat' was exactly the same as that which in bigger and vaguer matters makes the best romantic verse. It doesn't matter an atom that the emotion produced is not of dignified vagueness, but on the contrary amusing; the point is that exactly the same activity is at work as in the highest verse. That is the avoidance of conventional language in order to get the exact curve of the thing.

I have still to show that in the verse which is to come, fancy will be the necessary weapon of the classical school. The positive quality I have talked about can be manifested in ballad verse by extreme directness and simplicity, such as you get in 'On Fair Kirkconnel Lea'. But the particular verse we are going to get will be cheerful, dry, and sophisticated, and here the necessary weapon of the positive quality must be fancy.

Subject doesn't matter; the quality in it is the same as you get in the more romantic people.

It isn't the scale or kind of emotion produced that decides, but this one fact: Is there any real zest in it? Did the poet have an actually realized visual object before him in which he delighted? It doesn't matter if it were a lady's shoe or the starry heavens.

Fancy is not mere decoration added on to plain speech. Plain speech is essentially inaccurate. It is only by new metaphors, that is, by fancy, that it can be made precise.

When the analogy has not enough connection with the thing described to be quite parallel with it, where it overlays the thing it describes and there is a certain excess, there you have the play of fancy—that I grant is inferior to imagination.

But where the analogy is every bit of it necessary for accurate description in the sense of the word accurate I have previously described, and your only objection to this kind of fancy is that it is not serious in the effect it produces, then I think the objection to be entirely invalid. If it is sincere in the accurate sense, when the whole of the analogy is necessary to get out the exact curve of the feeling or thing you want to express—there you seem to me to have the highest verse, even though the subject be trivial and the emotions of the infinite far away.

It is very difficult to use any terminology at all for this kind of thing. For whatever word you use is at once sentimentalized. Take Coleridge's word 'vital'. It is used loosely by all kinds of people who talk about art, to mean something vaguely and mysteriously significant. In fact, vital and mechanical is to them exactly the same antithesis as between good and bad.

Nothing of the kind; Coleridge uses it in a perfectly definite and what I call dry sense. It is just this: A mechanical complexity is the sum of its parts. Put them side by side and you get the whole. Now vital or organic is merely a convenient metaphor for a complexity of a different kind, that in which the parts cannot be said to be elements as each one is modified by the other's presence, and each one to a certain extent is the whole. The leg of a chair by itself is still a leg. My leg by itself wouldn't be.

Now the characteristic of the intellect is that it can only represent complexities of the mechanical kind. It can only make diagrams, and diagrams are essentially things whose parts are separate one from another. The intellect always analyses—when there is a synthesis it is baffled. That is why the artist's work seems mysterious. The intellect can't represent it. This is a necessary consequence of the particular nature of the intellect and the purposes for which it is formed. It doesn't mean that your synthesis is ineffable, simply that it can't be definitely stated.

Now this is all worked out in Bergson, the central feature of his whole philosophy. It is all based on the clear conception of these vital complexities which he calls 'intensive' as opposed to the other kind which he calls 'extensive', and the recognition of the fact that the intellect can only deal with the extensive multiplicity. To deal with the intensive you must use intuition.

Now, as I said before, Ruskin was perfectly aware of all this, but he had no such metaphysical background which would enable him to state definitely what he meant. The result is that he has to flounder about in a series of metaphors. A powerfully imaginative mind seizes and combines at the same instant all the important ideas of its poem or picture, and while it works with one of them, it is at the same instant working with and modifying all in their relation to it and never losing sight of their bearings on each other—as the motion of a snake's body goes through all parts at once and its volition acts at the same instant in coils which go contrary ways.

A romantic movement must have an end of the very nature of the thing. It may be deplored, but it can't be helped—wonder must cease to be wonder.

I guard myself here from all the consequences of the analogy, but it expresses at any rate the inevitableness of the process. A literature of wonder must have an end as inevitably as a strange land loses its strangeness when one lives in it. Think of the lost ecstasy of the Elizabethans. 'Oh my America, my new found land'[a], think of what it meant to them and of what it means to us. Wonder can only be the attitude of a man passing from one stage to another, it can never be a permanently fixed thing.

[a] John Donne, 'To His Mistress Going to Bed'.

9   I. A. Richards

Ivor Armstrong Richards (b. 1893) was one of the first teachers of English at the University of Cambridge, where the English School was founded in 1917, and certainly one of the most important. Richards's own academic training had been in philosophy, and he brought to English studies a (then) unusual interest in aesthetics, psychology, and semantics. His first book was *The Foundation of Aesthetics* (1922) written in collaboration with C. G. Ogden and James Wood, and his second (again with Ogden) *The Meaning of Meaning* (1923). *The Principles of Literary Criticism* (1924) was a bold and enormously influential attempt to provide literary criticism with a firm and logical base in theory. In Richards's view, criticism should emulate the precision of the exact sciences, though literature itself was important precisely because it was *not* concerned with verifiable facts, but with attitudes and values. Fundamental to Richards's thinking is the distinction between the 'referential' language of science and the 'emotive' language of poetry. A good deal of subsequent Anglo-American criticism, especially that called 'New', started from this position and attempted to find alternative, or more refined ways of describing the special character of literary language (cf. William Empson's 'ambiguity' (pp. 146-57 below) and Cleanth Brooks's 'paradox' (pp. 291-314 below).)

Richards maintained that 'the best life is that in which as much as possible of our possible personality is engaged ... without confusion', and that literature helps us to organize and evaluate experience to this end. This theory of value— and the cultural role it assigns to literature and literary education—is essentially Arnoldian, as *Science and Poetry* (1926), with its epigraph from Arnold, makes clear. In *Principles* it is formulated in terms and concepts borrowed from psychology, though Richards had no interest in Freudian criticism of the speculative, biographical kind. The focus of his attention is upon the nature of literary works and their effects upon readers. As a teacher at Cambridge in the 1920s he regularly distributed copies of various short, unidentified poems, and invited his students to comment freely on them; he would then lecture on the poems and the written responses, which he called 'protocols'. In the first part of *Practical Criticism* (1929) he documented this experiment, which suggested to Richards that even intelligent students experienced grave difficulties in understanding and evaluating what they read. In the second part of the book he tried to identify some characteristic obstacles to good reading, and to provide a basic terminology for the analysis of poetry. Though sometimes attacked as an artificial and anti-historical exercise, Practical Criticism in one form or another has since become a staple method of teaching students of literature to read attentively and with discrimination.

In 1929 Richards left Cambridge for Peking, and later Harvard, finally settling at the latter university in 1939. His later publications include *Coleridge and the Imagination* (1934) and *Interpretation in Teaching* (New York, 1938). He has also published volumes of poetry. His influence on Anglo-American literary criticism and education—the extent of which would be difficult to exaggerate—derives largely from his early work. He is represented here by Chapter 4, 'Communication and the Artist', and part of Chapter 34, 'The Two Uses of Language' from *Principles*; and the chapter on 'The Four Kinds of Meaning' with which Part III of *Practical Criticism* begins.

CROSS REFERENCES : 12. William Empson
18. John Crowe Ransom
23. Cleanth Brooks
26. W. K. Wimsatt and Monroe C. Beardsley ('The Affective Fallacy')

COMMENTARY : John Crowe Ransom, 'I. A. Richards. The psychological critic', in *The New Criticism* (Norfolk, Conn., 1941)
W. K. Wimsatt and Cleanth Brooks, 'I. A. Richards: A Poetics of Tension', in *Literary Criticism: A Short History* (New York, 1957)

Communication and the artist

Poetry is the record of the best and happiest moments of the happiest and best minds.

[SHELLEY :] *The Defence of Poetry.*

The two pillars upon which a theory of criticism must rest are an account of value and an account of communication. We do not sufficiently realize how great a part of our experience takes the form it does, because we are social beings and accustomed to communication from infancy. That we acquire many of our ways of thinking and feeling from parents and others is, of course, a commonplace. But the effects of communication go much deeper than this. The very structure of our minds is largely determined by the fact that man has been engaged in communicating for so many hundreds of thousands of years, throughout the course of his human development and beyond even that. A large part of the distinctive features of the mind are due to its being an instrument for communication. An experience has to be formed, no doubt, before it is communicated, but it takes the form it does largely because it may have to be communicated. The emphasis which natural selection has put upon communicative ability is overwhelming.

106

There are very many problems of psychology, from those with which some of the exponents of *Gestalttheorie*[a] are grappling to those by which psychoanalysts are bewildered, for which this neglected, this almost overlooked aspect of the mind may provide a key, but it is pre-eminently in regard to the arts that it is of service. For the arts are the supreme form of the communicative activity. As we shall see, most of the difficult and obscure points about the structures of the arts, for example the priority of formal elements to content, or the impersonality and detachment so much stressed by aestheticians, become easily intelligible as soon as we consider them from this angle. But a possible misunderstanding must be guarded against. Although it is as a communicator that it is most profitable to consider the artist, it is by no means true that he commonly looks upon himself in this light. In the course of his work he is not as a rule deliberately and consciously engaged in a communicative endeavour. When asked, he is more likely than not to reply that communication is an irrelevant or at best a minor issue, and that what he is making is something which is beautiful in itself, or satisfying to him personally, or something expressive, in a more or less vague sense, of his emotions, or of himself, something personal and individual. That other people are going to study it, and to receive experiences from it may seem to him a merely accidental, inessential circumstance. More modestly still, he may say that when he works he is merely amusing himself.

That the artist is not as a rule consciously concerned with communication, but with getting the work, the poem or play or statue or painting or whatever it is, 'right', apparently regardless of its communicative efficacy, is easily explained. To make the work 'embody', accord with, and represent the precise experience upon which its value depends is his major preoccupation, in difficult cases an overmastering preoccupation, and the dissipation of attention which would be involved if he considered the communicative side as a separate issue would be fatal in most serious work. He cannot stop to consider how the public or even how especially well qualified sections of the public may like it or respond to it. He is wise, therefore, to keep all such considerations out of mind altogether. Those artists and poets who can be suspected of close separate attention to the communicative aspect tend (there are exceptions to this, of which Shakespeare might be one) to fall into a subordinate rank.

But this conscious neglect of communication does not in the least diminish the importance of the communicative aspect. It would only do so if we were prepared to admit that only our conscious activities matter. The very process of getting the work 'right' has itself, so far as the artist is normal, immense communicative consequences. Apart from certain special cases, to be discussed later, it will, when 'right', have much greater communicative power than it would have had if 'wrong'. The degree to which it accords with the relevant experience of the artist is a measure of the degree to which it will arouse similar experiences in others.

But more narrowly the reluctance of the artist to consider communication as

[a] A school of psychology, originating in Germany, which interprets phenomena as organized wholes rather than as aggregates of distinct parts.

one of his main aims, and his denial that he is at all influenced in his work by a desire to affect other people, is no evidence that communication is not actually his principal object. On a simple view of psychology, which overlooked unconscious motives, it would be, but not on any view of human behaviour which is in the least adequate. When we find the artist constantly struggling towards impersonality, towards a structure for his work which excludes his private, eccentric, momentary idiosyncrasies, and using always as its basis those elements which are most uniform in their effects upon impulses; when we find private works of art, works which satisfy the artist,[1] but are incomprehensible to everybody else, so rare, and the publicity of the work so constantly and so intimately bound up with its appeal to the artist himself, it is difficult to believe that efficacy for communication is not a main part of the 'rightness'[2] which the artist may suppose to be something quite different.

How far desire actually to communicate, as distinguished from desire to produce something with communicative efficacy (however disguised), is an 'unconscious motive' in the artist is a question to which we need not hazard an answer. Doubtless individual artists vary enormously. To some the lure of 'immortality' of enduring fame, of a permanent place in the influences which govern the human mind, appears to be very strong. To others it is often negligible. The degree to which such notions are avowed certainly varies with current social and intellectual fashions. At present the appeal to posterity, the 'nurslings of immortality' attitude to works of art appears to be much out of favour. 'How do we know what posterity will be like? They may be awful people!' a contemporary is likely to remark, thus confusing the issue. For the appeal is not to posterity merely as living at a certain date, but as especially qualified to judge, a qualification most posterities have lacked.

What concerns criticism is not the avowed or unavowed motives of the artist, however interesting these may be to psychology, but the fact that his procedure does, in the majority of instances, make the communicative efficacy of his work correspond with his own satisfaction and sense of its rightness. This may be due merely to his normality, or it may be due to unavowed motives. The first suggestion is the more plausible. In any case it is certain that no mere careful study of communicative possibilities, together with any desire to communicate, however intense, is ever sufficient without close natural correspondence between the poet's impulses and possible impulses in his reader. All supremely successful communication involves this correspondence, and no planning can take its place. Nor is the deliberate conscious attempt directed to communication so successful as the unconscious indirect method.

Thus the artist is entirely justified in his apparent neglect of the main purpose of his work. And when in what follows he is alluded to without qualification as being primarily concerned with communication, the reservations here made should be recalled.

Since the poet's unconscious motives have been alluded to, it may be well at this point to make a few additional remarks. Whatever psychoanalysts may aver, the mental processes of the poet are not a very profitable field for investi-

gation. They offer far too happy a hunting-ground for uncontrollable conjecture. Much that goes to produce a poem is, of course, unconscious. Very likely
the unconscious processes are more important than the conscious, but even if
we knew far more than we do about how the mind works, the attempt to display
the inner working of the artist's mind by the evidence of his work alone must
be subject to the gravest dangers. And to judge by the published work of Freud
upon Leonardo da Vinci or of Jung upon Goethe (e.g. *The Psychology of the
Unconscious*, p. 305), psychoanalysts tend to be particularly inept as critics.

The difficulty is that nearly all speculations as to what went on in the artist's
mind are unverifiable, even more unverifiable than the similar speculations as
to the dreamer's mind. The most plausible explanations are apt to depend upon
features whose actual causation is otherwise. I do not know whether anyone
but Mr Graves has attempted to analyse *Kubla Khan*, a poem which by its
mode of composition and by its subject suggests itself as well fitted for analysis.
The reader acquainted with current methods of analysis can imagine the results
of a thoroughgoing Freudian onslaught.

If he will then open *Paradise Lost*, Book IV, at line 223, and read onwards for
sixty lines, he will encounter the actual sources of not a few of the images and
phrases of the poem. In spite of—

> Southward through *Eden* went a River large,
> Nor changed his course, but through the shaggie hill
> Pass'd underneath ingulft...

in spite of—

> Rose a fresh Fountain, and with many a rill
> Water'd the Garden; thence united fell
> Down the steep glade, and met the neather Flood...

in spite of—

> Rowling on Orient Pearl and sands of Gold
> With mazie error under pendant shades
> Ran Nectar...

in spite of—

> Meanwhile murmuring waters fall
> Down the slope hills, disperst...

his doubts may still linger until he reaches

> Nor where *Abassin* Kings thir issue Guard,
> Mount Amara.

and one of the most cryptic points in Coleridge's poem, the Abyssinian maid,
singing of Mount Abora, finds its simple explanation. The closing line of the
poem perhaps hardly needs this kind of derivation.

From one source or another almost all the matter of *Kubla Khan* came to
Coleridge in a similar fashion. I do not know whether this particular indebtedness has been remarked before, but *Purchas his Pilgrimage*, Bartram's *Travels*

in North and South Carolina, and Maurice's *History of Hindostan* are well-known sources, some of them indicated by Coleridge himself.

This very representative instance of the unconscious working of a poet's mind may serve as a not inapposite warning against one kind at least of possible applications of psychology in criticism.

The extent to which the arts and their place in the whole scheme of human affairs have been misunderstood, by Critics, Moralists, Educators, Aestheticians ... is somewhat difficult to explain. Often those who most misunderstood have been perfect in their taste and ability to respond, Ruskin for example. Those who both knew what to do with a work of art and also understood what they were doing, have been for the most part artists and little inclined for, or capable of, the rather special task of explaining. It may have seemed to them too obvious to need explanation. Those who have tried have as a rule been foiled by language. For the difficulty which has always prevented the arts from being explained as well as 'enjoyed' (to use an inadequate word in default of an adequate) is language.

> 'Happy who can
> Appease this virtuous enemy of man!' *a*

It was perhaps never so necessary as now that we should know why the arts are important and avoid inadequate answers. It will probably become increasingly more important in the future. Remarks such as these, it is true, are often uttered by enthusiastic persons, and are apt to be greeted with the same smile as the assertion that the future of England is bound up with Hunting. Yet their full substantiation will be found to involve issues which are nowhere lightly regarded.

The arts are our storehouse of recorded values. They spring from and perpetuate hours in the lives of exceptional people, when their control and command of experience is at its highest, hours when the varying possibilities of existence are most clearly seen and the different activities which may arise are most exquisitely reconciled, hours when habitual narrowness of interests or confused bewilderment are replaced by an intricately wrought composure. Both in the genesis of a work of art, in the creative moment, and in its aspect as a vehicle of communication, reasons can be found for giving to the arts a very important place in the theory of Value. They record the most important judgments we possess as to the values of experience. They form a body of evidence which, for lack of a serviceable psychology by which to interpret it, and through the desiccating influence of abstract Ethics, has been left almost untouched by professed students of value. An odd omission, for without the assistance of the arts we could compare very few of our experiences, and without such comparison we could hardly hope to agree as to which are to be preferred. Very simple experiences—a cold bath in an enamelled tin, or running for a train—may to some extent be compared without elaborate vehicles; and friends exceptionally well acquainted with one another may manage some rough com-

a Marvell, 'The Picture of little T.C. in a Prospect of Flowers'.

110

parisons in ordinary conversation. But subtle or recondite experiences are for most men incommunicable and indescribable, though social conventions or terror of the loneliness of the human situation may make us pretend the contrary. In the arts we find the record in the only form in which these things can be recorded of the experiences which have seemed worth having to the most sensitive and discriminating persons. Through the obscure perception of this fact the poet has been regarded as a seer and the artist as a priest, suffering from usurpations. The arts, if rightly approached, supply the best data available for deciding what experiences are more valuable than others. The qualifying clause is all-important however. Happily there is no lack of glaring examples to remind us of the difficulty of approaching them rightly.

Notes

1. Again the normality of the artist has to be considered.
2. As will be seen, I am not going to identify 'beauty' with 'communicative efficacy'. This is a trap which is easy to fall into. A number of the exoteric followers of Croce may be found in it, though not Croce himself.

The two uses of language

To declare Science autonomous is very different from subordinating all our activities to it. It is merely to assert that so far as any body of references is undistorted it belongs to Science. It is not in the least to assert that no references may be distorted if advantage can thereby be gained. And just as there are innumerable human activities which require undistorted references if they are to be satisfied, so there are innumerable other human activities not less important which equally require distorted references or, more plainly, *fictions*.

The use of fictions, the imaginative use of them rather, is not a way of hoodwinking ourselves. It is not a process of pretending to ourselves that things are not as they are. It is perfectly compatible with the fullest and grimmest recognition of the exact state of affairs on all occasions. It is no make-believe. But so awkwardly have our references and our attitudes become entangled that such pathetic spectacles as Mr Yeats trying desperately to believe in fairies or Mr Lawrence impugning the validity of solar physics, are all too common. To be forced by desire into any unwarrantable belief is a calamity. The state which ensues is often extraordinarily damaging to the mind. But this common misuse of fictions should not blind us to their immense services provided we do not take them for what they are not, degrading the chief means by which our attitudes to actual life may be adjusted into the material of a long drawn delirium.[1]

If we knew enough it might be possible that all necessary attitudes could be obtained through scientific references alone. Since we do not know very much yet, we can leave this very remote possibility, once recognized, alone.

Fictions whether aroused by statements or by analogous things in other arts may be used in many ways. They may be used, for example, to deceive. But this is not a characteristic use of poetry. The distinction which needs to be kept clear does not set up fictions in opposition to verifiable truths in the scientific sense. A statement may be used for the sake of the *reference*, true or false, which it causes. This is the *scientific* use of language. But it may also be used for the sake of the effects in emotion and attitude produced by the reference it occasions. This is the *emotive* use of language. The distinction once clearly grasped is simple. We may either use words for the sake of the references they promote, or we may use them for the sake of the attitudes and emotions which ensue. Many arrangements of words evoke attitudes without any reference being required *en route*. They operate like musical phrases. But usually references are involved *as conditions* for, or *stages in*, the ensuing development of attitudes, yet it is still the attitudes not the references which are important. It matters not at all in such cases whether the references are true or false. Their sole function is to bring about and support the attitudes which are the further response. The questioning, verificatory way of handling them is irrelevant, and in a competent reader it is not allowed to interfere. 'Better a plausible impossibility than an improbable possibility', said Aristotle very wisely; there is less danger of an inappropriate reaction.

The differences between the mental processes involved in the two cases are very great, though easily overlooked. Consider what failure for each use amounts to. For scientific language a difference in the references is itself failure: the end has not been attained. But for emotive language the widest differences in references are of no importance if the further effects in attitude and emotion are of the required kind.

Further, in the scientific use of language not only must the references be correct for success, but the connections and relations of references to one another must be of the kind which we call logical. They must not get in one another's way, and must be so organized as not to impede further reference. But for emotive purposes logical arrangement is not necessary. It may be and often is an obstacle. For what matters is that the series of attitudes due to the references should have their own proper organization, their own emotional interconnection, and this often has no dependence upon the logical relations of such references as may be concerned in bringing the attitudes into being.

A few notes of the chief uses of the word 'Truth' in Criticism may help to prevent misunderstanding:

1. The scientific sense—that, namely, in which references, and derivatively statements symbolizing references, are true, need not delay us. A reference is true when the things to which it refers are actually together in the way in which it refers to them. Otherwise it is false. This sense is one very little involved by any of the arts. For the avoidance of confusions it would be well if the term

'true' could be reserved for this use. In purely scientific discourse it could and should be, but such discourse is uncommon. In point of fact the emotive power which attaches to the word is far too great for it to be abandoned in general discussion; the temptation to a speaker who needs to stir certain emotions and evoke certain attitudes of approval and acceptance is overwhelming. No matter how various the senses in which it may be used, and even when it is being used in no sense whatever, its effects in promoting attitudes will still make it indispensable; people will still continue to use the word with the same promiscuity as ever.

2. The most usual other sense is that of acceptability. The 'Truth' of *Robinson Crusoe* is the acceptability of the things we are told, their acceptability in the interests of the effects of the narrative, not their correspondence with any actual facts involving Alexander Selkirk or another. Similarly the falsity of happy endings to *Lear* or to *Don Quixote*, is their failure to be acceptable to those who have fully responded to the rest of the work. It is in this sense that 'Truth' is equivalent to 'internal necessity' or rightness. That is 'true' or 'internally necessary' which completes or accords with the rest of the experience, which co-operates to arouse our ordered response, whether the response of Beauty or another. 'What the Imagination seizes as Beauty must be Truth', said Keats, using this sense of 'Truth', though not without confusion. Sometimes it is held that whatever is redundant or otiose, whatever is not required, although not obstructive or disruptive, is also false. 'Surplusage!' said Pater, 'the artist will dread that, as the runner on his muscles[2]' himself perhaps in this instance sweating his sentence down too finely. But this is to make excessive demands upon the artist. It is to apply the axe of retrenchment in the wrong place. Superabundance is a common characteristic of great art, much less dangerous than the preciousness that too contrived an economy tends to produce. The essential point is whether what is unnecessary interferes or not with the rest of the response. If it does not, the whole thing is all the better probably for the extra solidity which it thereby gains.

This internal acceptability or 'convincingness' needs to be contrasted with other acceptabilities. Thomas Rymer, for example, refused to accept Iago for external reasons:

> To entertain the audience with something new and surprising against common sense and nature, he would pass upon us a close, dissembling rascal, instead of an open-hearted, frank, plain-dealing Souldier, a character constantly born by them for some thousands of years in the World.

'The truth is' he observes 'this author's head was full of villainous, unnatural images.'[3]

He is remembering no doubt Aristotle's remark that 'the artist must preserve the type and yet ennoble it', but interpreting it in his own way. For him the type is fixed simply by convention and his acceptances take no note of internal necessities but are governed merely by accordance with external canons. His is an extreme case, but to avoid his error in subtler matters is in fact sometimes the hardest part of the critic's undertaking. But whether our conception of the type is derived in some such absurd way, or taken, for example, as from a handbook of zoology, is of slight consequence. It is the taking of any *external* canon which is critically dangerous. When in the same connection Rymer objects that there never was a Moorish General in the service of the Venetian Republic, he is applying another external canon, that of historic fact. This mistake is less insidious, but Ruskin used to be particularly fond of the analogous mistake in connection with the 'truth' of drawing.

3. Truth may be equivalent to Sincerity. This character of the artist's work we have already touched upon briefly in connection with Tolstoy's theory of communication. It may perhaps be most easily defined from the critic's point of view negatively, as the absence of any apparent attempt on the part of the artist to work effects upon the reader which do not work for himself. Too simple definitions must be avoided. It is well known that Burns in writing 'Ae fond kiss' was only too anxious to escape *Nancy's* (Mrs Maclehose's) attentions, and similar instances could be multiplied indefinitely. Absurdly naïve views upon the matter[4] exemplified by the opinion that Bottomley[a] must have believed himself to be inspired or he would not have moved his audiences, are far too common. At the level at which Bottomley harangued any kind of exaltation in the orator, whether due to pride or to champagne, would make his stuff effective. But at Burns's level a very different situation arises. Here his probity and sincerity *as an artist* are involved; external circumstances are irrelevant, but there is perhaps internal evidence in the poem of a flaw in its creating impulse. Compare as a closely similar poem in which there is no flaw, Byron's 'When we two parted.'

[a] Horatio Bottomley (1860–1933) was a demagogic politician, journalist and financier who enjoyed a huge popular following in Britain, especially during World War I. He was eventually convicted of fraud.

Notes

1. Revelation Doctrines when once given a foothold tend to interfere everywhere. They serve as a kind of omnipotent major premise justifying any and every conclusion. A specimen: 'Since the function of Art is to pierce through to the Real World, then it follows that the artist cannot be too definite in his outlines, and that good drawing is the foundation of all good art.' Charles Gardner, *Vision and Vesture*, p. 54.
2. *Essay on Style*.
3. *A Short View of Tragedy*.
4. Cf. A. Clutton-Brock, *The Times*, 11 July 1922, p. 13.

The four kinds of meaning

From whence it happens, that they which trust to books, do as they that cast up many little summs into a greater, without considering whether those little summes were rightly cast up or not; and at last finding the errour visible, and not mistrusting their first grounds, know not which way to cleere themselves; but spend time in fluttering over their bookes; as birds that entring by the chimney, and finding themselves inclosed in a chamber, flutter at the false light of a glasse window, for want of wit to consider which way they came in.

[Hobbes] *Leviathan.*

After so much documentation the reader will be in a mood to welcome an attempt to point some morals, to set up some guiding threads by which the labyrinth we have perambulated may be made less bewildering. Otherwise we might be left with a mere defeatist acquiescence in *quot homines tot sententiae* [opinions are as numerous as men] as the sovereign critical principle, a hundred verdicts from a hundred readers as the sole fruit of our endeavours—a result at the very opposite pole from my hope and intention. But before it can be pointed, the moral has first to be disengaged, and the guiding threads cannot be set up without some preliminary engineering. The analyses and distinctions that follow are only those that are indispensable if the conclusions to which they lead are to be understood with reasonable precision or recommended with confidence.

The proper procedure will be to inquire more closely—now that the material has passed before us—into the ten difficulties listed towards the end of Part I[a], taking them one by one in the order there adopted. Reasons for this order will make themselves plain as we proceed, for these difficulties depend one upon another like a cluster of monkeys. Yet in spite of this complicated interdependence it is not very difficult to see where we must begin. The *original* difficulty of all reading, the problem of *making out the meaning*, is our obvious starting-point. The answers to those apparently simple questions: 'What is a meaning?' 'What are we doing when we endeavour to make it out?' 'What is it we are making out?' are the master-keys to all the problems of criticism. If we can make use of them the locked chambers and corridors of the theory of poetry open to us,

[a] These ten difficulties, or obstacles to good criticism, are as follows: 1. 'the difficulty of *making out the plain sense of poetry*'; (2) 'difficulties of *sensuous apprehension*'; 3. 'difficulties connected with the place of *imagery*'; 4. '*mnemonic irrelevances*' [i.e. irrelevant personal associations]; 5. '*Stock responses*'; 6. '*Sentimentality*'; 7. '*Inhibition*'; 8. '*Doctrinal adhesions*' [i.e. the occurrence in poetry of statements that in other contexts would be judged as either true or false]; 9. '*technical presuppositions*' [i.e. readers' preconceptions of what conventions are acceptable and likely to be effective]; 10. '*general critical preconceptions*'.

and a new and impressive order, is discovered even in the most erratic twists of the protocols.[a] Doubtless there are some who, by a natural dispensation, acquire the 'Open Sesame!' to poetry without labour, but, for the rest of us, certain general reflections we are not often encouraged to undertake can spare us time and fruitless trouble.

The all-important fact for the study of literature—or any other mode of communication—is that there are several kinds of meaning. Whether we know and intend it or not, we are all jugglers when we converse, keeping the billiard-balls in the air while we balance the cue on our nose. Whether we are active, as in speech or writing, or passive,[1] as readers or listeners, the Total Meaning we are engaged with is, almost always, a blend, a combination of several contributory meanings of different types. Language—and pre-eminently language as it is used in poetry—has not one but several tasks to perform simultaneously, and we shall misconceive most of the difficulties of criticism unless we understand this point and take note of the differences between these functions. For our purposes here a division into four types of function, four kinds of meaning, will suffice.

It is plain that most human utterances and nearly all articulate speech can be profitably regarded from four points of view. Four aspects can be easily distinguished. Let us call them *Sense*, *Feeling*, *Tone*, and *Intention*.

1. *Sense* We speak *to say something*, and when we listen we expect something to be said. We use words to direct our hearers' attention upon some state of affairs, to present to them some items for consideration and to excite in them some thoughts about these items.

2. *Feeling*[2] But we also, as a rule, have some feelings *about these items*, about the state of affairs we are referring to. We have an attitude towards it, some special direction, bias, or accentuation of interest towards it, some personal flavour or colouring of feeling; and we use language to *express* these feelings, this nuance of interest. Equally, when we listen we pick it up, rightly or wrongly; it seems inextricably part of what we receive; and this whether the speaker be conscious himself of his feelings towards what he is talking about or not. I am, of course, here describing the normal situation, my reader will be able without difficulty to think of exceptional cases (mathematics, for example) where no feeling enters.

3. *Tone* Furthermore, the speaker has ordinarily *an attitude to his listener*. He chooses or arranges his words differently as his audience varies, in automatic or deliberate *recognition of his relation to them*. The tone of his utterance reflects his awareness of this relation, his sense of how he stands towards those he is addressing. Again the exceptional case of dissimulation, or instances in which the speaker unwittingly reveals an attitude he is not consciously desirous of expressing, will come to mind.

4. *Intention*[3] Finally, apart from what he says (Sense), his attitude to what he is talking about (Feeling), and his attitude to his listener (Tone), there is the speaker's intention, his aim, *conscious or unconscious*, the effect he is endeavour-

[a] See introductory note.

ing to promote. Ordinarily he speaks for a purpose, and his purpose modifies his speech. The understanding of it is part of the whole business of apprehending his meaning. Unless we know what he is trying to do, we can hardly estimate the measure of his success. Yet the number of readers who omit such considerations might make a faint-hearted writer despair. Sometimes, of course, he will purpose no more than to state his thoughts (1), or to express his feelings about what he is thinking of, e.g. Hurrah! Damn! (2), or to express his attitude to his listener (3). With this last case we pass into the realm of endearments and abuse.

Frequently his intention operates through and satisfies itself in a combination of the other functions. Yet it has effects not reducible to their effects. It may govern the stress laid upon points in an argument for example, shape the arrangement, and even call attention to itself in such phrases as 'for contrast's sake' or 'lest it be supposed'. It controls the 'plot' in the largest sense of the word, and is at work whenever the author is 'hiding his hand'. And it has especial importance in dramatic and semi-dramatic literature. Thus the influence of his intention upon the language he uses is additional to, and separable from, the other three influences, and its effects can profitably be considered apart.

We shall find in the protocols instances, in plenty, of failure on the part of one or other of these functions. Sometimes all four fail together; a reader garbles the sense, distorts the feeling, mistakes the tone and disregards the intention; and often a partial collapse of one function entails aberrations in the others. The possibilities of human misunderstanding make up indeed a formidable subject for study, but something more can be done to elucidate it than has yet been attempted. Whatever else we may do by the light of nature it would be folly to maintain that we should read by it. But before turning back to scrutinize our protocols some further explanation of these functions will be in place.

If we survey our uses of language as a whole, it is clear that, at times, now one now another of the functions may become predominant. It will make the possible situations clearer if we briefly review certain typical forms of composition. A man writing a scientific treatise, for example, will put the *Sense* of what he has to say first, he will subordinate his *Feelings* about his subject or about other views upon it and be careful not to let them interfere to distort his argument or to suggest bias. His *Tone* will be settled for him by academic convention; he will, if he is wise, indicate respect for his readers and a moderate anxiety to be understood accurately and to win acceptance for his remarks. It will be well if his *Intention*, as it shows itself in the work, be on the whole confined to the clearest and most adequate statement of what he has to say (Function 1, Sense). But, if the circumstances warrant it, further relevant aims—an intention to reorientate opinion, to direct attention to new aspects, or to encourage or discourage certain methods of work or ways of approach—are obviously fitting. Irrelevant aims—the acceptance of the work as a thesis for a Ph.D., for example—come in a different category.

Consider now a writer engaged upon popularizing some of the results and hypotheses of science. The principles governing his language are not nearly so simple, for the furtherance of his intention will properly and inevitably inter-fere with the other functions.

In the first place, precise and adequate statement of the sense may have to be sacrificed, to some degree, in the interests of general intelligibility. Simplifica-tions and distortions may be necessary if the reader is to 'follow'. Secondly, a much more lively exhibition of feelings on the part of the author towards his subject-matter is usually appropriate and desirable, in order to awaken and encourage the reader's interest. Thirdly, more variety of tone will be called for; jokes and humorous illustrations, for example, are admissible, and perhaps a certain amount of cajolery. With this increased liberty, tact, the subjective counterpart of tone, will be urgently required. A human relation between the expert and his lay audience must be created, and the task, as many specialists have discovered, is not easy. These other functions will interfere still more with strict accuracy of statement; and if the subject has a 'tendency', if political, ethical, or theological implications are at all prominent, the intention of the work will have further opportunities to intervene.

This leads us to the obvious instance of political speeches. What rank and precedence shall we assign to the four language functions if we analyse public utterances made in the midst of a general election? Function 4, the furtherance of intentions (of all grades of worthiness) is unmistakably predominant. Its instruments are Function 2, the expression of feelings about causes, policies, leaders, and opponents, and Function 3, the establishment of favourable rela-tions with the audience ('the great heart of the people'). Recognizing this, ought we to be pained or surprised that Function 1, the presentation of facts (or of objects of thought to be regarded as facts are regarded), is equally subordin-ated?[4] But further consideration of this situation would lead us into a topic that must be examined later, that of Sincerity, a word with several important meanings.

In conversation, perhaps, we get the clearest examples of these shifts of func-tion, the normal verbal apparatus of one function being taken over by another. Intention, we have seen, may completely subjugate the others; so, on occasion, may Feeling or Tone express themselves through Sense, translating themselves into explicit statements about feelings and attitudes towards things and people —statements sometimes belied by their very form and manner. Diplomatic formulae are often good examples, together with much of the social language (Malinowski's 'phatic communion'),[5] the 'Thank you so very much' es and 'Pleased to meet you' s, that help us to live amicably with one another.

Under this head, too, may be put the psychological analyses, the introspective expatiations that have recently flourished so much in fiction as well as in sophisticated conversation. Does it indicate a confusion or a tenuousness in our feelings that we should now find ourselves so ready to make statements about them, to translate them into disquisitions, instead of expressing them in more direct and natural ways? Or is this phenomenon simply another result of the increased study of psychology? It would be rash to decide as yet. Certainly some psychologists lay themselves open to a charge of emptiness, of having so dealt with themselves that they have little left within them to talk about.

'Putting it into words', if the words are those of a psychological textbook, is a process which may well be damaging to the feelings. I shall be lucky if my reader does not murmur *de te fabula* [the story is about you] at this point.

But Feeling (and sometimes Tone) may take charge of and operate through Sense in another fashion, one more constantly relevant in poetry. (If indeed the shift just dealt with above might not be better described as Sense interfering with and dominating Feeling and Tone.)

When this happens, the statements which appear in the poetry are there for the sake of their effects upon feelings, not for their own sake. Hence to challenge their truth or to question whether they deserve serious attention *as statements claiming truth*, is to mistake their function. The point is that many, if not most, of the statements in poetry are there *as a means* to the manipulation[6] and expression of feelings and attitudes, not as contributions to any body of doctrine of any type whatever. With narrative poetry there is little danger of any mistake arising, but with 'philosophical' or meditative poetry there is great danger of a confusion which may have two sets of consequences.

On the one hand there are very many people who, if they read any poetry at all, try to take all its statements seriously—and find them silly. 'My soul is a ship in full sail', for example, seems to them a very profitless kind of contribution to psychology. This may seem an absurd mistake but, alas! it is none the less common. On the other hand there are those who succeed too well, who swallow 'Beauty is truth, truth beauty...', as the quintessence of an aesthetic philosophy, not as the expression of a certain blend of feelings, and proceed into a complete stalemate of muddle-mindedness as a result of their linguistic naïvety. It is easy to see what those in the first group miss; the losses of the second group, though the accountancy is more complicated, are equally lamentable.

A temptation to discuss here some further intricacies of this shift of function must be resisted.... It will be enough here to note that this subjugation of statement to emotive purposes has innumerable modes. A poet may distort his statements; he may make statements which have logically nothing to do with the subject under treatment; he may, by metaphor and otherwise, present objects for thought which are logically quite irrelevant; he may perpetrate logical nonsense, be as trivial or as silly, logically, as it is possible to be; all in the interests of the other functions of his language—to express feeling or adjust tone or further his other intentions. If his success in these other aims justify him, no reader (of the kind at least to take his meaning as it should be taken) can validly say anything against him.

But these indirect devices for expressing feeling through logical irrelevance and nonsense, through statements not to be taken strictly, literally or seriously though pre-eminently apparent in poetry, are not peculiar to it. A great part of what passes for criticism comes under this head. It is much harder to obtain statements about poetry, than expressions of feelings towards it and towards the author. Very many apparent statements turn out on examination to be only these disguised forms, indirect expressions, of Feeling, Tone, and Intention. Dr Bradley's remark that *Poetry is a spirit*, and Dr Mackail's that it is *a continuous substance or energy whose progress is immortal* are eminent examples

119

that I have made use of elsewhere, so curious that I need no apology for referring to them again. Remembering them, we may be more ready to apply to the protocols every instrument of interpretation we possess. May we avoid if possible in our own reading of the protocols those errors of misunderstanding which we are about to watch being committed towards the poems.

Notes

1. Relatively, or technically, 'passive' only; a fact that our protocols will help us not to forget. The reception (or interpretation) of a meaning is an activity, which may go astray; in fact, there is always some degree of loss and distortion in transmission.

2. Under 'Feeling' I group for convenience the whole conative-affective aspect of life—emotions, emotional attitudes, the will, desire, pleasure-unpleasure, and the rest. 'Feeling' is shorthand for any or all of this.

3. This function plainly is not on all fours with the others.

4. The ticklish point is, of course, the implication that the speaker believes in the 'facts'—not only as powerful arguments but *as facts*. 'Belief' here has to do with Function 2, and, as such examples suggest, is also a word with several senses, at least as many as attach to the somewhat analogous word 'love'.

5. See *The Meaning of Meaning*, Supplement I, § iv.

6. I am not assuming that the poet is conscious of any distinction between his means and his ends.

10   D. H. Lawrence

David Herbert Lawrence (1885-1930) was born in Eastwood, Nottinghamshire, the fourth son of a miner. His childhood and youth, and the environment in which he grew up, are vividly evoked in his autobiographical third novel *Sons and Lovers* (1913). On the publication of his first novel *The White Peacock* (1911) Lawrence gave up school-teaching to become a full-time writer. In 1914 he married Frieda von Richthofen. Until his death from tuberculosis in 1930, he travelled extensively in Europe, Australia, and America, writing continually.

Lawrence's present reputation as one of the great creative geniuses of the twentieth century rests principally on his novels, especially *Sons and Lovers*, *The Rainbow* (1915), and *Women in Love* (1920), and his short stories. But he was also a free-verse poet of considerable gifts, and prolific writer of non-fictional prose on all kinds of subjects, including literature. As a literary critic, Lawrence was an extreme and unashamed perpetrator of what has been called the 'affective fallacy' (see below, pp. 345-58). His principles are set out, with a characteristic acceleration from argument to polemic, in the opening paragraph of his essay on John Galsworthy:

> Literary criticism can be no more than a reasoned account of the feeling pro-
> duced upon the critic by the book he is criticizing. Criticism can never be a
> science: it is, in the first place much too personal, and in the second, it is
> concerned with values which science ignores. The touchstone is emotion, not
> reason. We judge a work by its effect on our sincere and vital emotion, and
> nothing else. All the critical twiddle-twaddle about style and form, all this
> pseudo-scientific classifying and analysing of books in imitation-botanical
> fashion, is mere impertinence and usually dull jargon.

Despite Lawrence's anti-academic temper, his criticism has inspired many academic critics. His insistence, against the grain of modernist orthodoxy, on the direct action of literature upon life, and his critique of industrial society, had a strong influence on the literary and cultural criticism associated with Dr F. R. Leavis and the journal *Scrutiny*. His brilliantly unconventional and opinionated *Studies in Classic American Literature* (1924), largely ignored in Lawrence's lifetime, provided a starting-point for critics like Richard Chase (*The American Novel and its Tradition*, Garden City, N.Y., 1957) and Leslie Fiedler (*Love and Death in the American Novel*, New York, 1960) who have been concerned with the distinctive and often oblique and deeply buried meanings peculiar to American literature. 'The Spirit of Place' is the opening chapter of *Studies*. 'Morality and the Novel' first appeared in the *Calendar of*

Modern Letters, 1925, and 'Why the Novel Matters' was first published
posthumously in *Phoenix* (1936), which with *Phoenix II* (1968) contains most
of Lawrence's occasional prose. *Selected Literary Criticism*, ed. Anthony Beale
(1956), is a useful selection which includes substantial extracts from *Studies in
Classic American Literature* and from the interesting, eccentric *Study of
Thomas Hardy*, written during World War I, but not published in full until
after Lawrence's death.

CROSS REFERENCES: 7. Virginia Woolf
11. E. M. Forster
14. C. G. Jung
33. Leslie Fiedler

COMMENTARY: Harry T. Moore, *The Intelligent Heart: the story of
D. H. Lawrence* (1955)
Graham Hough, *The Dark Sun: a study of D. H.
Lawrence* (1956)

The spirit of place

We like to think of the old fashioned American classics as children's books.
Just childishness, on our part. The old American art-speech contains an alien
quality, which belongs to the American continent and to nowhere else. But, of
course, so long as we insist on reading the books as children's tales, we miss all
that.

One wonders what the proper highbrow Romans of the third and fourth or
later centuries read into the strange utterances of Lucretius or Apuleius or
Tertullian, Augustine or Athanasius. The uncanny voice of Iberian Spain, the
weirdness of old Carthage, the passion of Libya and North Africa; you may bet
the proper old Romans never heard these at all. They read old Latin inference
over the top of it, as we read old European inference over the top of Poe or
Hawthorne.

It is hard to hear a new voice, as hard as it is to listen to an unknown
language. We just don't listen. There is a new voice in the old American classics.
The world has declined to hear it, and has babbled about children's stories.

Why?—Out of fear. The world fears a new experience more than it fears
anything. Because a new experience displaces so many old experiences. And it
is like trying to use muscles that have perhaps never been used, or that have
been going stiff for ages. It hurts horribly.

The world doesn't fear a new idea. It can pigeon-hole any idea. But it can't
pigeon-hole a real new experience. It can only dodge. The world is a great
dodger, and the Americans the greatest. Because they dodge their own very
selves.

There is a new feeling in the old American books, far more than there is in the modern American books, which are pretty empty of any feeling, and proud of it. There is a 'different' feeling in the old American classics. It is the shifting over from the old psyche to something new, a displacement. And displacements hurt. This hurts. So we try to tie it up, like a cut finger. Put a rag round it.

It is a cut too. Cutting away the old emotions and consciousness. Don't ask what is left.

Art-speech is the only truth. An artist is usually a damned liar, but his art, if it be art, will tell you the truth of his day. And that is all that matters. Away with eternal truth. Truth lives from day to day, and the marvellous Plato of yesterday is chiefly bosh today.

The old American artists were hopeless liars. But they were artists, in spite of themselves. Which is more than you can say of most living practitioners.

And you can please yourself, when you read *The Scarlet Letter*, whether you accept what that sugary, blue-eyed little darling of a Hawthorne has to say for himself, false as all darlings are, or whether you read the impeccable truth of his art-speech.

The curious thing about art-speech is that it prevaricates so terribly, I mean it tells such lies. I suppose because we always all the time tell ourselves lies. And out of a pattern of lies art weaves the truth. Like Dostoievsky posing as a sort of Jesus, but most truthfully revealing himself all the while as a little horror.

Truly art is a sort of subterfuge. But thank God for it, we can see through the subterfuge if we choose. Art has two great functions. First, it provides an emotional experience. And then, if we have the courage of our own feelings, it becomes a mine of practical truth. We have had the feelings *ad nauseam*. But we've never dared dig the actual truth out of them, the truth that concerns us, whether it concerns our grandchildren or not.

The artist usually sets out—or used to—to point a moral and adorn a tale.[a] The tale, however, points the other way, as a rule. Two blankly opposing morals, the artist's and the tale's. Never trust the artist. Trust the tale. The proper function of a critic is to save the tale from the artist who created it.

Now we know our business in these studies; saving the American tale from the American artist.

Let us look at this American artist first. How did he ever get to America, to start with? Why isn't he a European still, like his father before him?

Now listen to me, don't listen to him. He'll tell you the lie you expect. Which is partly your fault for expecting it.

He didn't come in search of freedom of worship. England had more freedom of worship in the year 1700 than America had. Won by Englishmen who wanted freedom, and so stopped at home and fought for it. And got it. Freedom of worship? Read the history of New England during the first century of its existence.

a 'He left the name, at which the world grew pale,
   To point a moral, or adorn a tale.'
   —Samuel Johnson, *The Vanity of Human Wishes.*

Freedom anyhow? The land of the free! This the land of the free! Why, if I say anything that displeases them, the free mob will lynch me, and that's my freedom. Free? Why I have never been in any country where the individual has such an abject fear of his fellow-countrymen. Because, as I say, they are free to lynch him the moment he shows he is not one of them.

No, no, if you're so fond of the truth about Queen Victoria, try a little about yourself.

Those Pilgrim Fathers and their successors never came here for freedom of worship. What did they set up when they got here? Freedom, would you call it?

They didn't come for freedom. Or if they did, they sadly went back on themselves.

All right then, what did they come for? For lots of reasons. Perhaps least of all in search of freedom of any sort: positive freedom, that is.

They came largely to get *away*—that most simple of motives. To get away. Away from what? In the long run, away from themselves. Away from everything. That's why most people have come to America, and still do come. To get away from everything they are and have been.

Which is all very well, but it isn't freedom. Rather the reverse. A hopeless sort of constraint. It is never freedom till you find something you really *positively want to be*. And people in America have always been shouting about the things they are *not*. Unless, of course, they are millionaires, made or in the making.

And after all there is a positive side to the movement. All that vast flood of human life that has flowed over the Atlantic in ships from Europe to America has not flowed over simply on a tide of revulsion from Europe and from the confinements of the European ways of life. This revulsion was, and still is, I believe, the prime motive in emigration. But there was some cause, even for the revulsion.

It seems as if at times man had a frenzy for getting away from any control of any sort. In Europe the old Christianity was the real master. The Church and the true aristocracy bore the responsibility for the working out of the Christian ideals: a little irregularly, maybe, but responsible nevertheless.

Mastery, kingship, fatherhood had their power destroyed at the time of the Renaissance.

And it was precisely at this moment that the great drift over the Atlantic started. What were men drifting away from? The old authority of Europe? Were they breaking the bonds of authority, and escaping to a new more absolute unrestrainedness? Maybe. But there was more to it.

Liberty is all very well, but men cannot live without masters. There is always a master. And men either live in glad obedience to the master they believe in, or they live in a frictional opposition to the master they wish to undermine. In America this frictional opposition has been the vital factor. It has given the Yankee his kick. Only the continual influx of more servile Europeans has provided America with an obedient labouring class. The true obedience never outlasting the first generation.

But there sits the old master, over in Europe. Like a parent. Somewhere deep in every American heart lies a rebellion against the old parenthood of Europe. Yet no American feels he has completely escaped its mastery. Hence the slow, smouldering patience of American opposition. The slow, smouldering, corrosive obedience to the old master Europe, the unwilling subject, the unremitting opposition.

Whatever else you are, be masterless.

> Ca Ca Caliban
> Get a new master, be a new man.
>
> [*The Tempest*, II, 2]

Escaped slaves, we might say, people the republics of Liberia or Haiti. Liberia enough! Are we to look at America in the same way? A vast republic of escaped slaves. When you consider the hordes from eastern Europe, you might well say it: a vast republic of escaped slaves. But one dare not say this of the Pilgrim Fathers, and the great old body of idealist Americans, the modern Americans tortured with thought. A vast republic of escaped slaves. Look out, America! And a minority of earnest, self-tortured people.

The masterless.

> Ca Ca Caliban
> Get a new master, be a new man.

What did the Pilgrim Fathers come for, then, when they came so gruesomely over the black sea? Oh, it was in a black spirit. A black revulsion from Europe, from the old authority of Europe, from kings and bishops and popes. And more. When you look into it, more. They were black, masterful men, they wanted something else. No kings, no bishops maybe. Even no God Almighty. But also, no more of this new 'humanity' which followed the Renaissance. None of this new liberty which was to be so pretty in Europe. Something grimmer, by no means free-and-easy.

America has never been easy, and is not easy today. Americans have always been at a certain tension. Their liberty is a thing of sheer will, sheer tension: a liberty of THOU SHALT NOT. And it has been so from the first. The land of THOU SHALT NOT. Only the first commandment is: THOU SHALT NOT PRESUME TO BE A MASTER. Hence democracy.

'We are the masterless.' That is what the American Eagle shrieks. It's a Hen-Eagle.

The Spaniards refused the post-Renaissance liberty of Europe. And the Spaniards filled most of America. The Yankees, too, refused, refused the post-Renaissance humanism of Europe. First and foremost, they hated masters. But under that, they hated the flowing ease of humour in Europe. At the bottom of the American soul was always a dark suspense, at the bottom of the Spanish-American soul the same. And this dark suspense hated and hates the old European spontaneity, watches it collapse with satisfaction.

Every continent has its own great spirit of place. Every people is polarized in some particular locality, which is home, the homeland. Different places on the face of the earth have different vital effluence, different vibration, different chemical exhalation, different polarity with different stars: call it what you like. But the spirit of place is a great reality. The Nile valley produced not only the corn, but the terrific religions of Egypt. China produces the Chinese, and will go on doing so. The Chinese in San Francisco will in time cease to be Chinese, for America is a great melting-pot.

There was a tremendous polarity in Italy, in the city of Rome. And this seems to have died. For even places die. The Island of Great Britain had a wonderful terrestrial magnetism or polarity of its own, which made the British people. For the moment, this polarity seems to be breaking. Can England die? And what if England dies?

Men are less free than they imagine; ah, far less free. The freest are perhaps least free.

Men are free when they are in a living homeland, not when they are straying and breaking away. Men are free when they are obeying some deep, inward voice of religious belief. Obeying from within. Men are free when they belong to a living, organic, *believing* community, active in fulfilling some unfulfilled, perhaps unrealized, purpose. Not when they are escaping to some wild west. The most unfree souls go west, and shout of freedom. Men are freest when they are most unconscious of freedom. The shout is a rattling of chains, always was.

Men are not free when they are doing just what they like. The moment you can do just what you like, there is nothing you care about doing. Men are only free when they are doing what the deepest self likes.

And there is getting down to the deepest self! It takes some diving.

Because the deepest self is way down, and the conscious self is an obstinate monkey. But of one thing we may be sure. If one wants to be free, one has to give up the illusion of doing what one likes, and seek what IT wishes done.

But before you can do what IT likes, you must first break the spell of the old mastery, the old IT.

Perhaps at the Renaissance, when kingship and fatherhood fell, Europe drifted into a very dangerous half-truth: of liberty and equality. Perhaps the men who went to America felt this, and so repudiated the old world altogether. Went one better than Europe. Liberty in America has meant so far the breaking away from *all* dominion. The true liberty will only begin when Americans discover IT, and proceed possibly to fulfil IT. IT being the deepest *whole* self of man, the self in its wholeness, not idealistic halfness.

That's why the Pilgrim Fathers came to America, then; and that's why we come. Driven by IT. We cannot see that invisible winds carry us, as they carry swarms of locusts, that invisible magnetism brings us as it brings the migrating birds to their unforeknown goal. But it is so. We are not the marvellous choosers and deciders we think we are. IT chooses for us, and decides for us. Unless, of course, we are just escaped slaves, vulgarly cocksure of our ready-made destiny. But if we are living people, in touch with the source, IT drives us and decides us. We are free only so long as we obey. When we run counter, and think we will do as we like, we just flee around like Orestes pursued by the Eumenides.

And still, when the great day begins, when Americans have at last discovered America and their own wholeness, still there will be the vast number of escaped

126

slaves to reckon with, those who have no cocksure, ready-made destinies.

Which will win in America, the escaped slaves, or the new whole men?

The real American day hasn't begun yet. Or at least, not yet sunrise. So far it has been the false dawn. That is, in the progressive American consciousness there has been the one dominant desire, to do away with the old thing. Do away with masters, exalt the will of the people. The will of the people being nothing but a figment, the exalting doesn't count for much. So, in the name of the will of the people, get rid of masters. When you have got rid of masters, you are left with this mere phrase of the will of the people. Then you pause and bethink yourself, and try to recover your own wholeness.

So much for the conscious American motive, and for democracy over here. Democracy in America is just the tool with which the old master of Europe, the European spirit, is undermined. Europe destroyed, potentially, American democracy will evaporate. America will begin.

American consciousness has so far been a false dawn. The negative ideal of democracy. But underneath, and contrary to this open ideal, the first hints and revelations of IT. IT, the American whole soul.

You have got to pull the democratic and idealistic clothes off American utterance, and see what you can of the dusky body of IT underneath.

'Henceforth be masterless.'

Henceforth be mastered.

Morality and the novel

The business of art is to reveal the relation between man and his circumambient universe, at the living moment. As mankind is always struggling in the toils of old relationships, art is always ahead of the 'times', which themselves are always far in the rear of the living moment.

When Van Gogh paints sunflowers, he reveals, or achieves, the vivid relation between himself, as man, and the sunflower, as sunflower, at that quick moment of time. His painting does not represent the sunflower itself. We shall never know what the sunflower itself is. And the camera will *visualize* the sunflower far more perfectly than Van Gogh can.

The vision on the canvas is a third thing, utterly intangible and inexplicable, the offspring of the sunflower itself and Van Gogh himself. The vision on the canvas is for ever incommensurable with the canvas, or the paint, or Van Gogh as a human organism, or the sunflower as a botanical organism. You cannot weigh nor measure nor even describe the vision on the canvas. It exists, to tell the truth, only in the much-debated fourth dimension. In dimensional space it has no existence.

It is a revelation of the perfected relation, at a certain moment, between a man and a sunflower. It is neither man-in-the-mirror nor flower-in-the-mirror,

127

neither is it above or below or across anything. It is between everything, in the fourth dimension.

And this perfected relation between man and his circumambient universe is life itself, for mankind. It has the fourth-dimensional quality of eternity and perfection. Yet it is momentaneous.

Man and the sunflower both pass away from the moment, in the process of forming a new relationship. The relation between all things changes from day to day, in a subtle stealth of change. Hence art, which reveals or attains to another perfect relationship, will be for ever new.

At the same time, that which exists in the non-dimensional space of pure relationship is deathless, lifeless, and eternal. That is, it gives us the *feeling* of being beyond life or death. We say an Assyrian lion or an Egyptian hawk's head 'lives'. What we really mean is that it is beyond life, and therefore beyond death. It gives us that feeling. And there is something inside us which must also be beyond life and beyond death, since that 'feeling' which we get from an Assyrian lion or an Egyptian hawk's head is so infinitely precious to us. As the evening star, that spark of pure relation between night and day, has been precious to man since time began.

If we think about it, we find that our life *consists in* this achieving of a pure relationship between ourselves and the living universe about us. This is how I 'save my soul' by accomplishing a pure relationship between me and another person, me and other people, me and a nation, me and a race of men, me and the animals, me and the trees or flowers, me and the earth, me and the skies and sun and stars, me and the moon: an infinity of pure relations, big and little, like the stars of the sky: that makes our eternity, for each one of us, me and the timber I am sawing, the lines of force I follow; me and the dough I knead for bread, me and the very motion with which I write, me and the bit of gold I have got. This, if we knew it, is our life and our eternity: the subtle, perfected relation between me and my whole circumambient universe.

And morality is that delicate, for ever trembling and changing *balance* between me and my circumambient universe, which precedes and accompanies a true relatedness.

Now here we see the beauty and the great value of the novel. Philosophy, religion, science, they are all of them busy nailing things down, to get a stable equilibrium. Religion, with its nailed-down One God, who says *Thou shalt, Thou shan't*, and hammers home every time; philosophy, with its fixed ideas; science with its 'laws': they, all of them, all the time, want to nail us on to some tree or other.

But the novel, no. The novel is the highest example of subtle inter-relatedness that man has discovered. Everything is true in its own time, place, circumstance, and untrue outside of its own place, time, circumstance. If you try to nail anything down, in the novel, either it kills the novel, or the novel gets up and walks away with the nail.

Morality in the novel is the trembling instability of the balance. When the novelist puts his thumb in the scale, to pull down the balance to his own predilection, that is immorality.

The modern novel tends to become more and more immoral, as the novelist tends to press his thumb heavier and heavier in the pan: either on the side of love, pure love: or on the side of licentious 'freedom'.

The novel is not, as a rule, immoral because the novelist has any dominant *idea*, or *purpose*. The immorality lies in the novelist's helpless, unconscious predilection. Love is a great emotion. But if you set out to write a novel, and you yourself are in the throes of the great predilection for love, love as the supreme, the only emotion worth living for, then you will write an immoral novel.

Because *no* emotion is supreme, or exclusively worth living for. All emotions go to the achieving of a living relationship between a human being and the other human being or creature or thing he becomes purely related to. All emotions, including love and hate, and rage and tenderness, go to the adjusting of the oscillating, unestablished balance between two people who amount to anything. If the novelist puts his thumb in the pan, for love, tenderness, sweetness, peace, then he commits an immoral act: he *prevents* the possibility of a pure relationship, a pure relatedness, the only thing that matters: and he makes inevitable the horrible reaction, when he lets his thumb go, towards hate and brutality, cruelty and destruction.

Life is so made that opposites sway about a trembling centre of balance. The sins of the fathers are visited on the children. If the fathers drag down the balance on the side of love, peace, and production, then in the third or fourth generation the balance will swing back violently to hate, rage, and destruction. We must balance as we go.

And of all the art forms, the novel most of all demands the trembling and oscillating of the balance. The 'sweet' novel is more falsified, and therefore more immoral, than the blood-and-thunder novel.

The same with the smart and smudgily cynical novel, which says it doesn't matter what you do, because one thing is as good as another, anyhow, and prostitution is just as much 'life' as anything else.

This misses the point entirely. A thing isn't life just because somebody does it. This the artist ought to know perfectly well. The ordinary bank clerk buying himself a new straw hat isn't 'life' at all: it is just existence, quite all right, like everyday dinners: but not 'life'.

By life, we mean something that gleams, that has the fourth-dimensional quality. If the bank clerk feels really piquant about his hat, if he establishes a lively relation with it, and goes out of the shop with the new straw hat on his head, a changed man, be-aureoled, then that is life.

The same with the prostitute. If a man establishes a living relation to her, if only for one moment, then it is life. But if it *doesn't*: if it is just money and function, then it is not life, but sordidness, and a betrayal of living.

If a novel reveals true and vivid relationships, it is a moral work, no matter what the relationships may consist in. If the novelist *honours* the relationship in itself, it will be a great novel.

But there are so many relationships which are not real. When the man in *Crime and Punishment* murders the old woman for sixpence, although it *is* *actual* enough, it is never quite real. The balance between the murderer and the old woman is gone entirely; it is only a mess. It is actuality, but it is not 'life', in the living sense.

The popular novel, on the other hand, dishes up a *réchauffé* [re-heated dish] of old relationships: *If Winter Comes.a* And old relationships dished up are likewise immoral. Even a magnificent painter like Raphael does nothing more than dress up in gorgeous new dresses relationships which have already been experienced. And this gives a gluttonous kind of pleasure of the mass: a voluptuousness, a wallowing. For centuries, men say of the voluptuously ideal woman: 'She is a Raphael Madonna.' And women are only just learning to take it as an insult.

A new relation, a new relatedness hurts somewhat in the attaining; and will always hurt. So life will always hurt. Because real voluptuousness lies in re-acting old relationships, and at the best, getting an alcoholic sort of pleasure out of it, slightly depraving.

Each time we strive to a new relation, with anyone or anything, it is bound to hurt somewhat. Because it means the struggle with and the displacing of old connections, and this is never pleasant. And moreover, between living things at least, an adjustment means also a fight, for each party, inevitably, must 'seek its own' in the other, and be denied. When, in the parties, each of them seeks his own, her own, absolutely, then it is a fight to the death. And this is true of the thing called 'passion'. On the other hand, when, of the two parties, one yields utterly to the other, this is called sacrifice, and it also means death. So the Constant Nymph*b* died of her eighteen months of constancy.

It isn't the nature of nymphs to be constant. She should have been constant in her nymph-hood. And it is unmanly to accept sacrifices. He should have abided by his own manhood.

There is, however, the third thing, which is neither sacrifice nor fight to the death: when each seeks only the true relatedness to the other. Each must be true to himself, herself, his own manhood, her own womanhood, and let the relationship work out of itself. This means courage above all things: and then discipline. Courage to accept the life-thrust from within oneself, and from the other person. Discipline, not to exceed oneself any more than one can help. Courage, when one has exceeded oneself, to accept the fact and not whine about it.

Obviously, to read a really new novel will *always* hurt, to some extent. There will always be resistance. The same with new pictures, new music. You may judge of their reality by the fact that they do arouse a certain resistance, and compel, at length, a certain acquiescence.

The great relationship, for humanity, will always be the relation between man and woman. The relation between man and man, woman and woman, parent and child, will always be subsidiary.

And the relation between man and woman will change for ever, and will for ever be the new central clue to human life. It is the *relation itself* which is the

a By A. S. M. Hutchinson (1921).
b Title of a popular romantic novel by Margaret Kennedy.

quick and the central clue to life, not the man, nor the woman, nor the children that result from the relationship, as a contingency.

It is no use thinking you can put a stamp on the relation between man and woman, to keep it in the *status quo*. You can't. You might as well try to put a stamp on the rainbow or the rain.

As for the bond of love, better put it off when it galls. It is an absurdity, to say that men and women *must love*. Men and women will be for ever subtly and changingly related to one another; no need to yoke them with any 'bond' at all. The only morality is to have man true to his manhood, woman to her womanhood, and let the relationship form of itself, in all honour. For it is, to each, *life itself*.

If we are going to be moral, let us refrain from driving pegs through anything, either through each other or through the third thing, the relationship, which is for ever the ghost of both of us. Every sacrificial crucifixion needs five pegs, four short ones and a long one, each one an abomination. But when you try to nail down the relationship itself, and write over it *Love* instead of *This is the King of the Jews*, then you can go on putting in nails for ever. Even Jesus called it the Holy Ghost, to show you that you can't lay salt on its tail.

The novel is a perfect medium for revealing to us the changing rainbow of our living relationships. The novel can help us to live, as nothing else can: no didactic Scripture, anyhow. If the novelist keeps his thumb out of the pan.

But when the novelist *has* his thumb in the pan, the novel becomes an unparalleled perverter of men and women. To be compared only, perhaps, to that great mischief of sentimental hymns, like 'Lead, Kindly Light', which have helped to rot the marrow in the bones of the present generation.

Why the novel matters

We have curious ideas of ourselves. We think of ourselves as a body with a spirit in it, or a body with a soul in it, or a body with a mind in it. *Mens sana in corpore sano*. The years drink up the wine, and at last throw the bottle away, the body, of course, being the bottle.

It is a funny sort of superstition. Why should I look at my hand, as it so cleverly writes these words, and decide that it is a mere nothing compared to the mind that directs it? Is there really any huge difference between my hand and my brain? Or my mind? My hand is alive, it flickers with a life of its own. It meets all the strange universe in touch, and learns a vast number of things, and knows a vast number of things. My hand, as it writes these words, slips gaily along, jumps like a grasshopper to dot an *i*, feels the table rather cold, gets a little bored if I write too long, has its own rudiments of thought, and is just as much *me* as is my brain, my mind, or my soul. Why should I imagine that there is a *me* which is more *me* than my hand is? Since my hand is absolutely alive, me alive.

Whereas, of course, as far as I am concerned, my pen isn't alive at all. My pen *isn't me* alive. Me alive ends at my finger-tips.

Whatever is me alive is me. Every tiny bit of my hands is alive, every little freckle and hair and fold of skin. And whatever is me alive is me. Only my finger-nails, those ten little weapons between me and an inanimate universe, they cross the mysterious Rubicon between me alive and things like my pen, which are not alive, in my own sense.

So, seeing my hand is all alive, and me alive, wherein is it just a bottle, or a jug, or a tin can, or a vessel of clay, or any of the rest of that nonsense? True, if I cut it it will bleed, like a can of cherries. But then the skin that is cut, and the veins that bleed, and the bones that should never be seen, they are all just as alive as the blood that flows. So the tin can business, or vessel of clay, is just bunk.

And that's what you learn, when you're a novelist. And that's what you are very liable *not* to know, if you're a parson, or a philosopher, or a scientist, or a stupid person. If you're a parson, you talk about souls in heaven. If you're a novelist, you know that paradise is in the palm of your hand, and on the end of your nose, because both are alive; and alive, and man alive, which is more than you can say, for certain, of paradise. Paradise is after-life, and I for one am not keen on anything that is *after*-life. If you are a philosopher, you talk about infinity, and the pure spirit which knows all things. But if you pick up a novel, you realize immediately that infinity is just a handle to this self-same jug of a body of mine; while as for knowing, if I find my finger in the fire, I know that fire burns, with a knowledge so emphatic and vital, it leaves Nirvana merely a conjecture. Oh, yes, my body, me alive, *knows*, and knows intensely. And as for the sum of all knowledge, it can't be anything more than an accumulation of all the things I know in the body, and you, dear reader, know in the body.

These damned philosophers, they talk as if they suddenly went off in steam, and were then much more important than they are when they're in their shirts. It is nonsense. Every man, philosopher included, ends in his own finger-tips. That's the end of his man alive. As for the words and thoughts and sighs and aspirations that fly from him, they are so many tremulations in the ether, and not alive at all. But if the tremulations reach another man alive, he may receive them into his life, and his life may take on a new colour, like a chameleon creeping from a brown rock on to a green leaf. All very well and good. It still doesn't alter the fact that the so-called spirit, the message or teaching of the philosopher or the saint, isn't alive at all, but just a tremulation upon the ether, like a radio message. All this spirit stuff is just tremulations upon the ether. If you, as man alive, quiver from the tremulation of the ether into new life, that is because you are man alive, and you take sustenance and stimulation into your alive man in a myriad ways. But to say that the message, or the spirit which is communicated to you, is more important than your living body, is nonsense. You might as well say that the potato at dinner was more important.

Nothing is important but life. And for myself, I can absolutely see life nowhere but in the living. Life with a capital L is only man alive. Even a cabbage in the rain is cabbage alive. All things that are alive are amazing. And all things that are dead are subsidiary to the living. Better a live dog than a dead lion. But better a live lion than a live dog. *C'est la vie!*

It seems impossible to get a saint, or a philosopher, or a scientist, to stick to this simple truth. They are all, in a sense, renegades. The saint wishes to offer himself up as spiritual food for the multitude. Even Francis of Assisi turns himself into a sort of angel-cake, of which anyone may take a slice. But an angel-cake is rather less than man alive. And poor St Francis might well apologize to his body, when he is dying: 'Oh, pardon me, my body, the wrong I did you through the years!' It was no wafer, for others to eat.

The philosopher, on the other hand, because he can think, decides that nothing but thoughts matter. It is as if a rabbit, because he can make little pills, should decide that nothing but little pills matter. As for the scientist, he has absolutely no use for me so long as I am man alive. To the scientist, I am dead. He puts under the microscope a bit of dead me, and calls it me. He takes me to pieces, and says first one piece, and then another piece, is me. My heart, my liver, my stomach have all been scientifically me, according to the scientist; and nowadays I am either a brain, or nerves, or glands, or something more up-to-date in the tissue line.

Now I absolutely flatly deny that I am a soul, or a body, or a mind, or an intelligence, or a brain, or a nervous system, or a bunch of glands, or any of the rest of these bits of me. The whole is greater than the part. And therefore, I, who am man alive, am greater than my soul, or spirit, or body, or mind, or consciousness, or anything else that is merely a part of me. I am a man, and alive. I am man alive, and as long as I can, I intend to go on being man alive.

For this reason I am a novelist. And being a novelist, I consider myself superior to the saint, the scientist, the philosopher, and the poet, who are all great masters of different bits of man alive, but never get the whole hog.

The novel is the one bright book of life. Books are not life. They are only tremulations on the ether. But the novel as a tremulation can make the whole man alive tremble. Which is more than poetry, philosophy, science, or any other book-tremulation can do.

The novel is the book of life. In this sense, the Bible is a great confused novel. You may say, it is about God. But it is really about man alive. Adam, Eve, Sarai, Abraham, Isaac, Jacob, Samuel, David, Bath-Sheba, Ruth, Esther, Solomon, Job, Isaiah, Jesus, Mark, Judas, Paul, Peter: what is it but man alive, from start to finish? Man alive, not mere bits. Even the Lord is another man alive, in a burning bush, throwing the tablets of stone at Moses's head.

I do hope you begin to get my idea, why the novel is supremely important, as a tremulation on the ether. Plato makes the perfect ideal tremble in me. But that's only a bit of me. Perfection is only a bit, in the strange make-up of man alive. The Sermon on the Mount makes the selfless spirit of me quiver. But that, too, is only a bit of me. The Ten Commandments set the old Adam shivering in me, warning me that I am a thief and a murderer, unless I watch it. But even the old Adam is only a bit of me.

I very much like all these bits of me to be set trembling with life and the wisdom of life. But I do ask that the whole of me shall tremble in its wholeness, some time or other.

And this, of course, must happen in me, living.

But as far as it can happen from a communication, it can only happen when a whole novel communicates itself to me. The Bible—but *all* the Bible—and Homer and Shakespeare: these are the supreme old novels. These are all things to all men. Which means that in their wholeness they affect the whole man alive, which is the man himself, beyond any part of him. They set the whole tree trembling with a new access of life, they do not just stimulate growth in one direction.

I don't want to grow in any one direction any more. And, if I can help it, I don't want to stimulate anybody else into some particular direction. A particular direction ends in a *cul-de-sac*. We're in a *cul-de-sac* at present.

I don't believe in any dazzling revelation, or in any supreme Word. 'The grass withereth, the flower fadeth, but the Word of the Lord shall stand for ever.' That's the kind of stuff we've drugged ourselves with. As a matter of fact, the grass withereth, but comes up all the greener for that reason, after the rains. The flower fadeth, and therefore the bud opens. But the Word of the Lord, being man-uttered and a mere vibration on the ether, becomes staler and staler, more and more boring, till at last we turn a deaf ear and it ceases to exist, far more finally than any withered grass. It is grass that renews its youth like the eagle, not any Word.

We should ask for no absolutes, or absolute. Once and for all and for ever, let us have done with the ugly imperialism of any absolute. There is no absolute good, there is nothing absolutely right. All things flow and change, and even change is not absolute. The whole is a strange assembly of apparently incongruous parts, slipping past one another.

Me, man alive, I am a very curious assembly of incongruous parts. My yea! of today is oddly different from my yea! of yesterday. My tears of tomorrow will have nothing to do with my tears of a year ago. If the one I love remains unchanged and unchanging, I shall cease to love her. It is only because she changes and startles me into change and defies my inertia, and is herself staggered in her inertia by my changing, that I can continue to love her. If she stayed put, I might as well love the pepper-pot.

In all this change, I maintain a certain integrity. But woe betide me if I try to put my finger on it. If I say of myself, I am this, I am that!—then, if I stick to it, I turn into a stupid fixed thing like a lamp-post. I shall never know wherein lies my integrity, my individuality, my me. I *can* never know it. It is useless to talk about my ego. That only means that I have made up an *idea* of myself, and that I am trying to cut myself out to pattern. Which is no good. You can cut your cloth to fit your coat, but you can't clip bits off your living body, to trim it down to your idea. True, you can put yourself into ideal corsets. But even in ideal corsets, fashions change.

Let us learn from the novel. In the novel, the characters can do nothing but *live*. If they keep on being good, according to pattern, or bad, according to pattern, or even volatile, according to pattern, they cease to live, and the novel falls dead. A character in a novel has got to live, or it is nothing.

We, likewise, in life have got to live, or we are nothing.

What we mean by living is, of course, just as indescribable as what we mean by *being*. Men get ideas into their heads, of what they mean by Life, and they proceed to cut life out to pattern. Sometimes they go into the desert to seek God, sometimes they go into the desert to seek cash, sometimes it is wine, woman, and song, and again it is water, political reform, and votes. You never know what it will be next: from killing your neighbour with hideous bombs and gas that tears the lungs, to supporting a Foundlings' Home and preaching infinite Love, and being co-respondent in a divorce.

In all this wild welter, we need some sort of guide. It's no good inventing Thou Shalt Nots!

What then? Turn truly, honourably to the novel, and see wherein you are man alive, and wherein you are dead man in life. You may love a woman as man alive, and you may be making love to a woman as sheer dead man in life. You may eat your dinner as man alive, or as a mere masticating corpse. As man alive you may have a shot at your enemy. But as a ghastly simulacrum of life you may be firing bombs into men who are neither your enemies nor your friends, but just things you are dead to. Which is criminal, when the things happen to be alive.

To be alive, to be man alive, to be whole man alive: that is the point. And at its best, the novel, and the novel supremely, can help you. It can help you not to be dead man in life. So much of a man walks about dead and a carcass in the street and house, today: so much of woman is merely dead. Like a pianoforte with half the notes mute.

But in the novel you can see, plainly, when the man goes dead, the woman goes inert. You can develop an instinct for life, if you will, instead of a theory of right and wrong, good and bad.

In life, there is right and wrong, good and bad, all the time. But what is right in one case is wrong in another. And in the novel you see one man becoming a corpse, because of his so-called goodness, another going dead because of his so-call wickedness. Right and wrong is an instinct: but an instinct of the whole consciousness in a man, bodily, mental, spiritual at once. And only in the novel are *all* things given full play, or at least, they may be given full play, when we realize that life itself, and not inert safety, is the reason for living. For out of the full play of all things emerges the only thing that is anything, the wholeness of a man, the wholeness of a woman, man alive, and live woman.

Edward Morgan Forster (1879-1970) was one of the most distinguished, though not the most prolific, of modern English novelists. His best-known work, A *Passage to India* (1924), was also the last novel he published in his long life, though he continued to write short fiction, essays, biography, and criticism. Cambridge University was probably the main intellectual influence on Forster: he went up to King's College in 1897 and ended his life as an Honorary Fellow of the same college. He was also closely associated with the London Bloomsbury Group (see introductory note on Virginia Woolf, pp. 85-6 above).

  Aspects of the Novel (1927), from which the following extract is taken, is the text of the Clark Lectures which E. M. Forster delivered at Cambridge in the Spring of 1927, and, as he explains in a Prefatory Note, he did not attempt to alter the informal, conversational tone of the lectures for publication. Perhaps for this reason, *Aspects of the Novel* is one of the most entertaining and readable works of modern criticism, without being in the least superficial. Many of Forster's terms and categories, such as the distinction between Flat and Round characters, or between Story and Plot, and the concept of 'rhythm' in fiction, have become part of general critical currency. The prevailing spirit of *Aspects of the Novel* is, however, antitheoretical, lightly mocking the pedantries of scholars and the austere prescriptions of writers like Henry James. Forster's retort to the Jamesian doctrine about narrative method, as interpreted by Percy Lubbock in *The Craft of Fiction* (1921) is: 'For me the whole question of method resolves itself not into formulae but into the power of the writer to bounce the reader into accepting what he says.' Much the same could be said of criticism as Forster practises it. *Aspects of the Novel* is a classic example of a peculiarly English kind of critical discourse at its best: modelled on conversation, carrying its learning very lightly, enthusiastic, personal, provocative—in the best sense of the word, amateur.

  What follows is the fourth chapter (or lecture) from *Aspects of the Novel*, originally entitled 'People (Continued)'. Much of Forster's shorter, occasional literary criticism is collected in *Abinger Harvest* (1936) and *Two Cheers for Democracy* (1951).

CROSS REFERENCES: 4. Henry James
                       7. Virginia Woolf
                    29. Mark Schorer
                    42. Wayne Booth

COMMENTARY: K. W. Gransden, *E. M. Forster* (1962)
E. K. Brown, *Rhythm in the Novel* (Toronto, 1950)

[Flat and round characters and 'point of view']

We now turn from transplantation to acclimatization. We have discussed whether people could be taken out of life and put into a book, and conversely whether they could come out of books and sit down in this room. The answer suggested was in the negative and led to a more vital question: can we, in daily life, understand each other? Today our problems are more academic. We are concerned with the characters in their relation to other aspects of the novel; to a plot, a moral, their fellow characters, atmosphere, etc. They will have to adapt themselves to other requirements of their creator.

It follows that we shall no longer expect them to coincide as a whole with daily life, only to parallel it. When we say that a character in Jane Austen, Miss Bates [in *Emma*] for instance, is 'so like life' we mean that each bit of her coincides with a bit of life, but that she as a whole only parallels the chatty spinster we met at tea. Miss Bates is bound by a hundred threads to Highbury. We cannot tear her away without bringing her mother too, and Jane Fairfax and Frank Churchill, and the whole of Box Hill; whereas we could tear Moll Flanders[a] away, at least for the purposes of experiment. A Jane Austen novel is more complicated than a Defoe, because the characters are interdependent, and there is the additional complication of a plot. The plot in *Emma* is not prominent and Miss Bates contributes little. Still it is there, she is connected with the principals, and the result is a closely woven fabric from which nothing can be removed. Miss Bates and Emma herself are like bushes in a shrubbery—not isolated trees like Moll—and anyone who has tried to thin out a shrubbery knows how wretched the bushes look if they are transplanted elsewhere, and how wretched is the look of the bushes that remain. In most books the characters cannot spread themselves. They must exercise a mutual restraint.

The novelist, we are beginning to see, has a very mixed lot of ingredients to handle. There is the story with its time-sequence of 'and then ... and then ...': there are ninepins about whom he might tell the story, and tell a rattling good one, but no, he prefers to tell his story about human beings; he takes over the life by values as well as the life in time. The characters arrive

---

[a] Forster has discussed Daniel Defoe's *Moll Flanders* (1722) in the preceding section of *Aspects of the Novel.*

137

when evoked, but full of the spirit of mutiny. For they have these numerous parallels with people like ourselves, they try to live their own lives and are consequently often engaged in treason against the main scheme of the book. They 'run away', they 'get out of hand': they are creations inside a creation, and often inharmonious towards it; if they are given complete freedom they kick the book to pieces, and if they are kept too sternly in check, they revenge themselves by dying, and destroy it by intestinal decay.

These trials beset the dramatist also, and he has yet another set of ingredients to cope with—the actors and actresses—and they appear to side sometimes with the characters they represent, sometimes with the play as a whole, and more often to be the mortal enemies of both. The weight they throw is incalculable, and how any work of art survives their arrival I do not understand. Concerned with a lower form of art, we need not worry—but, in passing, is it not extraordinary that plays on the stage are often better than they are in the study, and that the introduction of a bunch of rather ambitious and nervous men and women should add anything to our understanding of Shakespeare and Chekhov?

No, the novelist has difficulties enough, and today we shall examine two of his devices for solving them—instinctive devices, for his methods when working are seldom the same as the methods we use when examining his work. The first device is the use of different kinds of characters. The second is connected with the point of view.

1. We may divide characters into flat and round. Flat characters were called 'humours' in the seventeenth century, and are sometimes called types, and sometimes caricatures. In their purest form, they are constructed round a single idea or quality: when there is more than one factor in them, we get the beginning of the curve towards the round. The really flat character can be expressed in one sentence such as 'I never will desert Mr Micawber.' There is Mrs Micawber—she says she won't desert Mr Micawber; she doesn't, and there she is. Or: 'I must conceal even by subterfuges, the poverty of my master's house.' There is Caleb Balderstone in [Scott's] *The Bride of Lammermoor*. He does not use the actual phrase, but it completely describes him; he has no existence outside it, no pleasures, none of the private lusts and aches that must complicate the most consistent of servitors. Whatever he does, wherever he goes, whatever lies he tells or plates he breaks, it is to conceal the poverty of his master's house. It is not his *idée fixe*, because there is nothing in him into which the idea can be fixed. He is the idea, and such life as he possesses radiates from its edges and from the scintillations it strikes when other elements in the novel impinge. Or take Proust. There are numerous flat characters in Proust, such as the Princess of Parma, or Legrandin. Each can be expressed in a single sentence, the Princess's sentence being, 'I must be particularly careful to be kind.' She does nothing except to be particularly careful, and those of the other characters who are more complex than herself easily see through the kindness, since it is only a byproduct of the carefulness.

One great advantage of flat characters is that they are easily recognized whenever they come in—recognized by the reader's emotional eye, not by the visual eye which merely notes the recurrence of a proper name. In Russian novels, where they so seldom occur, they would be a decided help. It is a convenience for an author when he can strike with his full force at once, and flat characters are very useful to him, since they never need reintroducing, never run away, have not to be watched for development, and provide their own atmosphere—little luminous discs of a pre-arranged size, pushed hither and thither like counters across the void or between the stars; most satisfactory.

A second advantage is that they are easily remembered by the reader afterwards. They remain in his mind as unalterable for the reason that they were not changed by circumstances; they moved through circumstances, which gives them in retrospect a comforting quality, and preserves them when the book that produced them may decay. The Countess in [George Meredith's] *Evan Harrington* furnishes a good example here. Let us compare our memories of her with our memories of Becky Sharp [in Thackeray's *Vanity Fair*]. We do not remember what the Countess did or what she passed through. What is clear is her figure and the formula that surrounds it, namely, 'Proud as we are of dear papa, we must conceal his memory.' All her rich humour proceeds from this. She is a flat character. Becky is round. She, too, is on the make, but she cannot be summed up in a single phrase, and we remember her in connection with the great scenes through which she passed and as modified by those scenes—that is to say, we do not remember her so easily because she waxes and wanes and has facets like a human being. All of us, even the sophisticated, yearn for permanence, and to the unsophisticated permanence is the chief excuse for a work of art. We all want books to endure, to be refuges, and their inhabitants to be always the same, and flat characters tend to justify themselves on this account.

All the same, critics who have their eyes fixed severely upon daily life—as were our eyes last week—have very little patience with such renderings of human nature. Queen Victoria, they argue, cannot be summed up in a single sentence, so what excuse remains for Mrs Micawber? One of our foremost writers, Mr Norman Douglas, is a critic of this type, and the passage from him which I will quote puts the case against flat characters in a forcible fashion. The passage occurs in an open letter to D. H. Lawrence, with whom he is quarrelling: a doughty pair of combatants, the hardness of whose hitting makes the rest of us feel like a lot of ladies up in a pavilion. He complains that Lawrence, in a biography of a mutual friend,[a] has falsified the picture by employing 'the novelist's touch', and he goes on to define what this is:

> It consists, I should say, in a failure to realize the complexities of the ordinary human mind; it selects for literary purposes two or three facets of a man or woman, generally the most spectacular, and therefore useful in-

[a] Maurice Magnus, for whose *Memoirs of the Foreign Legion*, published posthumously in 1925, Lawrence had written an introduction. For a fuller account of this literary quarrel, see Harry T. Moore's biography of Lawrence *The Intelligent Heart* (1955) Pt IV Chap. 2.

gredients of their character and disregards all the others. Whatever fails to fit in with these specially chosen traits is eliminated—must be eliminated, for otherwise the description would not hold water. Such and such are the data: everything incompatible with those data has to go by the board. It follows that the novelist's touch argues, often logically, from a wrong premise: it takes what it likes and leaves the rest. The facts may be correct as far as they go but there are too few of them: what the author says may be true and yet by no means the truth. That is the novelist's touch. It falsifies life.

Well, the novelist's touch as thus defined is, of course, bad in biography, for no human being is simple. But in a novel it has its place: a novel that is at all complex often requires flat people as well as round, and the outcome of their collisions parallels life more accurately than Mr Douglas implies. The case of Dickens is significant. Dickens's people are nearly all flat (Pip and David Copperfield attempt roundness, but so diffidently that they seem more like bubbles than solids). Nearly everyone can be summed up in a sentence, and yet there is this wonderful feeling of human depth. Probably the immense vitality of Dickens causes his characters to vibrate a little, so that they borrow his life and appear to lead one of their own. It is a conjuring trick; at any moment we may look at Mr Pickwick edgeways and find him no thicker than a gramophone record. But we never get the sideway view. Mr Pickwick is far too adroit and well trained. He always has the air of weighing something, and when he is put into the cupboard of the young ladies' school he seems as heavy as Falstaff in the buck-basket at Windsor. Part of the genius of Dickens is that he does use types and caricatures, people whom we recognize the instant they re-enter, and yet achieves effects that are not mechanical and a vision of humanity that is not shallow. Those who dislike Dickens have an excellent case. He ought to be bad. He is actually one of our big writers, and his immense success with types suggest that there may be more in flatness than the severer critics admit.

Or take H. G. Wells. With the possible exceptions of Kipps and the aunt in *Tono Bungay*, all Wells's characters are as flat as a photograph. But the photographs are agitated with such vigour that we forget their complexities lie on the surface and would disappear if it was scratched or curled up. A Wells's character cannot indeed be summed up in a single phrase; he is tethered much more to observation, he does not create types. Nevertheless his people seldom pulsate by their own strength. It is the deft and powerful hands of their maker that shake them and trick the reader into a sense of depth. Good but imperfect novelists, like Wells and Dickens, are very clever at transmitting force. The part of their novel that is alive galvanizes the part that is not, and causes the characters to jump about and speak in a convincing way. They are quite different from the perfect novelist who touches all his material directly, who seems to pass the creative finger down every sentence and into every word. Richardson, Defoe, Jane Austen, are perfect in this particular way; their work may not be great but their hands are always upon it; there is not the tiny interval between the touching of the button and the sound of the bell which occurs in novels where the characters are not under direct control.

For we must admit that flat people are not in themselves as big achievements as round ones, and also that they are best when they are comic. A serious or tragic flat character is apt to be a bore. Each time he enters crying 'Revenge!' or 'My heart bleeds for humanity!' or whatever his formula is, our hearts sink. One of the romances of a popular contemporary writer is constructed round a Sussex farmer who says, 'I'll plough up that bit of gorse.' There is the farmer, there is the gorse; he says he'll plough it up, he does plough it up, but it is not like saying 'I'll never desert Mr Micawber', because we are so bored by his consistency that we do not care whether he succeeds with the gorse or fails. If his formula was analysed and connected up with the rest of the human outfit, we should not be bored any longer, the formula would cease to be the man and become an obsession in the man; that is to say he would have turned from a flat farmer into a round one. It is only round people who are fit to perform tragically for any length of time and can move us to any feelings except humour and appropriateness.

So now let us desert these two-dimensional people, and, by way of transition to the round, let us go to *Mansfield Park*, and look at Lady Bertram, sitting on her sofa with pug. Pug is flat, like most animals in fiction. He is once represented as straying into a rose bed in a cardboard kind of way, but that is all, and during most of the book his mistress seems to be cut out of the same simple material as her dog. Lady Bertram's formula is, 'I am kindly, but must not be fatigued', and she functions out of it. But at the end there is a catastrophe. Her two daughters come to grief—to the worst grief known to Miss Austen's universe, far worse than the Napoleonic wars. Julia elopes; Maria, who is unhappily married, runs off with a lover. What is Lady Bertram's reaction? The sentence describing it is significant:

> Lady Bertram did not think deeply, but, guided by Sir Thomas, she thought justly on all important points, and she saw therefore in all its enormity, what had happened, and neither endeavoured herself, nor required Fanny to advise her, to think little of guilt and infamy.

These are strong words, and they used to worry me because I thought Jane Austen's moral sense was getting out of hand. She may, and of course does, deprecate guilt and infamy herself, she duly causes distress in the minds of Edmund and Fanny, but has she any right to agitate calm, consistent Lady Bertram? Is not it like giving pug three faces and setting him to guard the gates of Hell? Ought not her ladyship to remain on the sofa saying, 'This is a dreadful and sadly exhausting business about Julia and Maria, but where is Fanny gone? I have dropped another stitch'?

I used to think this, through misunderstanding Jane Austen's method— exactly as Scott misunderstood it when he congratulated her for painting on a square of ivory. She is a miniaturist, but never two-dimensional. All her characters are round, or capable of rotundity. Even Miss Bates has a mind, even Elizabeth Eliot a heart, and Lady Bertram's moral fervour ceases to vex us when we realize this: the disc has suddenly extended and become a little globe. When the novel is closed, Lady Bertram goes back to the flat, it is true; the dominant impression she leaves can be summed up in a formula. But that is not how Jane Austen conceived her, and the freshness of her reappearances is due to this. Why do the characters in Jane Austen give us a slightly new pleasure each time they come in, as opposed to the merely repetitive pleasure that is caused by a character in Dickens? Why do they combine so well in a conversation, and draw one another out without seeming to do so, and never perform? The answer to this question can be put in several ways: that, unlike Dickens, she was a real artist, that she never stooped to caricature, etc. But the best reply is that her characters though smaller than his are more highly organized. They function all round, and even if her plot made greater demands on them than it does, they would still be adequate. Suppose that Louisa Musgrove had broken her neck on the Cobb. The description of her death would have been feeble and ladylike—physical violence is quite beyond Miss Austen's powers—but the survivors would have reacted properly as soon as the corpse was carried away, they would have brought into view new sides of their characters, and though *Persuasion* would have been spoiled as a book, we should know more than we do about Captain Wentworth and Anne. All the Jane Austen characters are ready for an extended life, for a life which the scheme of her books seldom requires them to lead, and that is why they lead their actual lives so satisfactorily. Let us return to Lady Bertram and the crucial sentence. See how subtly it modulates from her formula into an area where the formula does not work. 'Lady Bertram did not think deeply.' Exactly: as per formula. 'But guided by Sir Thomas she thought justly on all important points.' Sir Thomas's guidance, which is part of the formula, remains, but it pushes her ladyship towards an independent and undesired morality. 'She saw therefore in all its enormity what had happened.' This is the moral *fortissimo*—very strong but carefully introduced. And then follows a most artful decrescendo, by means of negatives. 'She neither endeavoured herself, nor required Fanny to advise her, to think little of guilt or infamy.' The formula is reappearing, because as a rule she does try to minimize trouble, and does require Fanny to advise her how to do this; indeed Fanny has done nothing else for the last ten years. The words, though they are negatived, remind us of this, her normal state is again in view, and she has in a single sentence been inflated into a round character and collapsed back into a flat one. How Jane Austen can write! In a few words she has extended Lady Bertram, and by so doing she has increased the probability of the elopements of Maria and Julia. I say probability because the elopements belong to the domain of violent physical action, and here, as already indicated, Jane Austen is feeble and ladylike. Except in her schoolgirl novels, she cannot stage a crash. Everything violent has to take place 'off'—Louisa's accident and Marianne Dashwood's putrid throat are the nearest exceptions—and consequently all the comments on the elopement must be sincere and convincing, otherwise we should doubt whether it occurred. Lady Bertram helps us to believe that her daughters have run away, and they have to run away, or there would be no apotheosis for Fanny. It is a little point, and a little sentence, yet it shows us how delicately a great novelist can modulate into the round.

All through her works we find these characters, apparently so simple and flat, never needing reintroduction and yet never out of their depth—Henry Tilney, Mr Woodhouse, Charlotte Lucas. She may label her characters 'Sense', 'Pride', 'Sensibility', 'Prejudice', but they are not tethered to those qualities.

As for the round characters proper, they have already been defined by implication and no more need be said. All I need do is to give some examples of people in books who seem to me round so that the definition can be tested afterwards:

All the principal characters in *War and Peace*, all the Dostoyevsky characters, and some of the Proust—for example, the old family servant, the Duchess of Guermantes, M. de Charlus, and Saint Loup; Madame Bovary—who, like Moll Flanders, has her book to herself, and can expand and secrete unchecked; some people in Thackeray—for instance, Becky and Beatrix; some in Fielding—Parson Adams, Tom Jones; and some in Charlotte Brontë, most particularly Lucy Snowe. (And many more—this is not a catalogue.) The test of a round character is whether it is capable of surprising in a convincing way. If it never surprises, it is flat. If it does not convince, it is a flat pretending to be round. It has the incalculability of life about it—life within the pages of a book. And by using it sometimes alone, more often in combination with the other kind, the novelist achieves his task of acclimatization, and harmonizes the human race with the other aspects of his work.

2. Now for the second device: the point of view from which the story may be told.

To some critics this is the fundamental device.

> The whole intricate question of method, in the craft of fiction (says Mr Percy Lubbock),[a] I take to be governed by the question of the *point of view* —the question of the relation in which the narrator stands to the story.

And his book *The Craft of Fiction* examines various points of view with genius and insight. The novelist, he says, can either describe the characters from outside, as an impartial or partial onlooker; or he can assume omniscience and describe them from within; or he can place himself in the position of one of them and affect to be in the dark as to the motives of the rest; or there are certain intermediate attitudes.

Those who follow him will lay a sure foundation for the aesthetics of fiction—a foundation which I cannot for a moment promise. This is a ramshackly survey and for me the whole intricate question of method resolves itself not into formulae but into the power of the writer to bounce the reader into accepting what he says—a power which Mr Lubbock admits and admires, but locates at the edge of the problem instead of at the centre. I should put it plumb in the centre. Look how Dickens bounces us in *Bleak House*. Chapter I of *Bleak House* is omniscient. Dickens takes us into the Court of Chancery and rapidly explains all the people there. In Chapter 2 he is partially omniscient. We still use his eyes, but for some unexplained reason they begin to grow weak: he can explain Sir Leicester Dedlock to us, part of Lady Dedlock but not all, and nothing of Mr Tulkinghorn. In Chapter 3 he is even more

---

[a] See conclusion of the introductory note on Henry James, p. 44 above.

reprehensible: he goes straight across into the dramatic method and inhabits a young lady, Esther Summerson. 'I have a great deal of difficulty in beginning to write my portion of these pages, for I know I am not clever,' pipes up Esther, and continues in this strain with consistency and competence, so long as she is allowed to hold the pen. At any moment the author of her being may snatch it from her, and run about taking notes himself, leaving her seated goodness knows where, and employed we do not care how. Logically, *Bleak House* is all to pieces, but Dickens bounces us, so that we do not mind the shiftings of the viewpoint.

Critics are more apt to object than readers. Zealous for the novel's eminence they are a little too apt to look out for problems that shall be peculiar to it, and differentiate it from the drama; they feel it ought to have its own technical troubles before it can be accepted as an independent art; and since the problem of a point of view certainly is peculiar to the novel they have rather over-stressed it. I do not myself think it is so important as a proper mixture of characters—a problem which the dramatist is up against also. And the novelist must bounce us; that is imperative.

Let us glance at two other examples of a shifting viewpoint.

The eminent French writer, André Gide, has published a novel called *Les Faux Monnayeurs* [*The Counterfeiters*]: this is a novel which for all its modernity has one aspect in common with *Bleak House*: it is all to pieces logically. Sometimes the author is omniscient: he explains everything, he stands back, '*il juge ses personnages*'; at other times his omniscience is partial; yet again he is dramatic, and causes the story to be told through the diary of one of the characters. There is the same absence of viewpoint, but whereas in Dickens it was instinctive, in Gide it is sophisticated; he expatiates too much about the jolts. The novelist who betrays too much interest in his own method can never be more than interesting; he has given up the creation of character and summoned us to help analyse his own mind, and a heavy drop in the emotional thermometer results. *Les Faux Monnayeurs* is among the more interesting of recent works: not among the vital: and greatly as we shall have to admire it as a fabric we cannot praise it unrestrictedly now.

For our second example we must again glance at *War and Peace*. Here the result is vital: we are bounced up and down Russia—omniscient, semi-omniscient, dramatized here or there as the moment dictates—and at the end we have accepted it all. Mr Lubbock does not, it is true: great as he finds the book, he would find it greater if it had a viewpoint; he feels Tolstoy has not pulled his full weight. I feel that the rules of the game of writing are not like this. A novelist can shift his viewpoint if it comes off, and it came off with Dickens and Tolstoy. Indeed this power to expand and contract perception (of which the shifting viewpoint is a symptom), this right to intermittent knowledge—I find it one of the great advantages of the novel-form, and it has a parallel in our perception of life. We are stupider at some times than others; we can enter into people's minds occasionally but not always, because our own minds get tired; and this intermittence lends in the long run variety and colour to the experiences we receive. A quantity of novelists, English novelists especially, have behaved like this to the people in their books: played fast and loose with them, and I cannot see why they should be censured.

They must be censured if we catch them at it at the time. That is quite true, and out of it arises another question: may the writer take the reader into his confidence about his characters? Answer has already been indicated: better not. It is dangerous, it generally leads to a drop in the temperature, to intellectual and emotional laxity, and worse still to facetiousness, and to a friendly invitation to see how the figures hook up behind. 'Doesn't A look nice—she always was my favourite.' 'Let's think of why B does that—perhaps there's more in him than meets the eye—yes, see—he has a heart of gold—having given you this peep at it I'll pop it back—I don't think he's noticed.' 'And C—he always was the mystery man.' Intimacy is gained but at the expense of illusion and nobility. It is like standing a man a drink so that he may not criticize your opinions. With all respect to Fielding and Thackeray it is devastating, it is bar-parlour chattiness, and nothing has been more harmful to the novels of the past. To take your reader into your confidence about the universe is a different thing. It is not dangerous for a novelist to draw back from his characters, as Hardy and Conrad do, and to generalize about the conditions under which he thinks life is carried on. It is confidences about the individual people that do harm, and beckon the reader away from the people to an examination of the novelist's mind. Not much is ever found in it at such a moment, for it is never in the creative state: the mere process of saying 'come along, let's have a chat' has cooled it down.

12   William Empson

The best introduction to William Empson (b. 1906) is that written by his
former teacher I. A. Richards as a programme note for Empson's lectures
at Yale University in 1940:

> William Empson made his name first with *Seven Types of Ambiguity*
> [1930] a book which came into being more or less in the following
> fashion. He had been a mathematician at Cambridge and switched over
> for his last year to English. As he was at Magdalene, this made me his
> Director of Studies. He seemed to have read more English Literature
> than I had, and to have read it more recently and better, so our roles
> were soon in some danger of being reversed. At about his third visit he
> brought up the games of interpretation which Laura Riding and
> Robert Graves had been playing with the unpunctuated form of 'The
> expense of spirit in a waste of shame'. Taking the sonnet as a conjurer
> takes his hat, he produced an endless swarm of lively rabbits from it
> and ended by 'You could do that with any poetry, couldn't you?'
> This was a godsend to a Director of Studies, so I said, 'You'd better go
> off and do it, hadn't you?' A week later he said he was still slapping
> away at it on his typewriter. Would I mind if he just went on with that?
> Not a bit. The following week there he was with a thick wad of very
> illegible typescript under his arm—the central 30,000 words or so of the
> book. I can't think of any literary criticism written since which seems
> likely to have as persistent and distinctive an influence. If you read
> much of it at once, you will think you are sickening for 'flu'; but read a
> little *with care* and your reading habits may be altered—for the better,
> I believe. (*Furioso*, Spring, 1940. Quoted by Stanley Edgar Hyman,
> *The Armed Vision* (New York, 1948).)

Richards here almost certainly understates his own influence on Empson's
early work—the concept of ambiguity was essentially a refinement of
Richards's 'emotive' language—but scarcely exaggerates the precocious
brilliance of Empson's book or the extent of its influence, which was
particularly felt by the American New Critics, such as Cleanth Brooks.
Empson's virtuoso feats of explication set new standards for the close analysis
of poetry. His approach also tended to reinforce the shift in poetic taste
initiated by Eliot and Pound, away from romantic poetry towards the
metaphysical poetry of the seventeenth century, and to encourage the
antihistoricism inherent in I. A. Richards's criticism. On these grounds,

and perhaps because of his irreverent wit, Empson provoked hostility among more traditional critics, who charged him with many errors of scholarship. Empson dealt with some of these in the footnotes to the revised edition of *Seven Types of Ambiguity* (1947). He never, however, lost the reputation of being a critical *enfant terrible*, a wayward genius as apt to embarrass his admirers as to scandalize his critics. In his second book of criticism, *Some Versions of Pastoral* (1935), he attempted to deal with the meanings of literary works considered as total structures, making use of Freudian and Marxist concepts. In *The Structure of Complex Words* (1951) he returned to close verbal analysis, but with the application of a dauntingly complicated methodology. *Milton's God* (1961) combined astute literary criticism with militant anti-Christian polemic.

William Empson taught in universities in the Far East before and after World War II, and was Professor of English at Sheffield University from 1953 until his retirement in 1971. As well as literary criticism, he has published three volumes of poetry which had considerable influence on the so-called 'Movement' poets in England in the 1950s.

The following extract is taken from the first chapter of *Seven Types of Ambiguity* (1947 edition). Empson is defending his concern with meaning in poetry against 'the objection that the meaning of poetry does not matter, because it is apprehended as Pure Sound, and the objection that what really matters about poetry is the Atmosphere'.

CROSS REFERENCES :   9. I. A. Richards
                     18. John Crowe Ransom
                     23. Cleanth Brooks
                     26. W. K. Wimsatt and Monroe C. Beardsley

COMMENTARY :   Stanley Edgar Hyman, 'William Empson and Categorical Criticism', in *The Armed Vision* (New York, 1948)
                Elder Olson, 'William Empson, Contemporary Criticism and Poetic Diction', in *Critics and Criticism: Ancient and Modern*, ed. R. S. Crane (Chicago, 1952)

[Ambiguity of the first type]

It has been deduced from the belief in Pure Sound that the resultant meaning of the words need not be known, that it is enough to know the meaning of the words in isolation and enough of their syntax to read them aloud rightly. In a degree this is often true, but it is better to regard this state of limited knowledge as a complicated state of indecision which involves much estimating of probabilities, and is less ignorance than an ordered suspension of judgment. Secondly, and more seriously, it has been deduced from this belief that you are liable to destroy the poem if its meaning is discovered, that it is important to preserve one's innocence about the meaning of verses, that one must use sensibility, and as little intelligence as possible. This, also, is often true, but I take a moral line here, and say it is true only of bad poetry. People suspect analysis, often rightly, as the refuge of the emotionally sterile, but that is only to say that analysis is often done badly. In so far as such a destruction occurs because you have used your intelligence it must be accepted, and you may reasonably expect to become interested in another poem, so that the loss is not permanent, because that is the normal process of learning to appreciate poetry.

As for the belief in Atmosphere, about which I shall now make some inadequate remarks, it may be viewed as a third deduction from the belief in Pure Sound. Critics often say or imply casually that some poetic effect conveys a direct 'physical' quality, something mysteriously intimate, something which it is strange a poet could convey, something like a sensation which is not attached to any one of the senses. This may only be a statement of how they themselves applied their conscious attention when reading the poem; thus a musical chord is a direct sensation, but not therefore unanalysable into its separate notes even at the moment of sensing. It can be either felt or thought; the two things are similar but different; and it requires practice to do both at once. Or the statement might, one cannot deny, mean that there has been some confusion of the senses. But it may mean something more important, involving a distinction between 'sensation' and 'feeling'; that what the poet has conveyed is no assembly of grammatical meanings, capable of analysis, but a 'mood', and 'atmosphere', a 'personality', and attitude to life, an undifferentiated mode of being.

Probably it is in this way, as a sort of taste in the head, that one remembers one's own past experiences, including the experience of reading a particular poet. Probably, again, this mode of apprehension is connected with the condition of the whole body, and is as near as one can get to an immediate self-knowledge. You may say, then, that any grammatical analysis of poetry, since it must ignore atmosphere, is trivial; that atmosphere is conveyed in some unknown and fundamental way as a byproduct of meaning; that analysis cannot hope to do anything but ignore it; and that criticism can only state that it is there.

This belief may in part explain the badness of much nineteenth-century poetry, and how it came to be written by critically sensitive people. They admired the poetry of previous generations, very rightly, for the taste it left in the head, and, failing to realize that the process of putting such a taste into a reader's head involves a great deal of work which does not feel like a taste in the head while it is being done, attempting, therefore, to conceive a taste in the head and put it straight on to their paper, they produced tastes in the head which were in fact blurred, complacent, and unpleasing. But to say that the consequences of a critical formula have been unfortunate is not to say that it is untrue or even unusable; it is very necessary for a critic to remember about the atmosphere, chiefly because he must concentrate on the whole of the poem he is talking about rather than on the particular things that he can find to say.

In wishing to apply verbal analysis to poetry the position of the critic is like that of the scientist wishing to apply determinism to the world. It may not be valid everywhere; though it be valid everywhere it may not explain everything; but in so far as he is to do any work he must assume it is valid where he is working, and will explain what he is trying to explain. I assume, therefore, that the 'atmosphere' is the consciousness of what is implied by the meaning, and I believe that this assumption is profitable in many more cases than one would suppose.

I shall try to recommend this opinion by giving what seems to me a striking example; a case, that is, where an affective state is conveyed particularly vividly by devices of particular irrelevance. Macbeth, in these famous lines, may easily seem to be doing something physiological and odd, something outside the normal use of words. It is when he is spurring on his jaded hatred to the murder of Banquo and Fleance.

> Come, seeling Night,
> Skarfe up the tender Eye of pitiful Day
> And with thy bloddie and invisible Hand
> Cancel and teare to pieces that great Bond
> That keepes me pale.
> *Light thickens, and the Crow*
> *Makes Wing to th' Rookie Wood.*
> Good things of Day begin to droope, and drowse,
> While Night's black Agents to their Prey's doe rowse.
> Thou marvell'st at my words, but hold thee still;
> Things bad begun, make strong themselves by ill:
> So prythee go with me.
>
> (III. ii. 50)

The condition of his skin (By the pricking of my thumbs Something wicked this way comes), the sense of being withdrawn far within his own flesh (like an old lecher, a small fire at his heart, all the rest on's body cold), the sense that the affair is prosaic, it need not be mentioned, and yet an occasional squawking of the nerves (Hobbididance croaks in Tom's belly), in short the whole frame of body, as I read the lines, is lit up and imposed upon the reader, from which Macbeth lashes his exhausted energies into a new, into the accustomed, readiness for murder.

I have tried by these almost irrelevant quotations to show how much work the reader of Shakespeare is prepared to do for him, how one is helped by the rest of his work to put a great deal into any part of it, but this seems to explain very little. Various similar sound effects or associations may be noted; there is a suggestion of witches' broth, or curdling blood, about *thickens*, which the vowel sound of *light*, coming next to it, with the movement of stirring treacle, and the cluck of the k-sounds, intensify; a suggestion, too, of harsh, limpid echo, and, under careful feet of poachers, an abrupt crackling of sticks. The vowel sounds at the end make an increasing darkness as the *crow* goes forward. But, after all, one would be very surprised if two people got the same result from putting a sound-effect into words in this way.

It is safer to point out that *rooks* were, in any case, creatures of foreboding:

> Augurs, and understood Relations, have
> By Magot-Pyes, and Choughes, and Rookes, brought forth
> The secret'st man of Blood;
>
> (III. iv. 125)

that Macbeth looked out of the window because Banquo was to be killed soon after dusk, so he wanted to know how the time was going; and that a dramatic situation is always heightened by breaking off the dialogue to look out of the window, especially if some kind of Pathetic Fallacy*a* is to be observed outside. But to notice this particular pathetic fallacy you must withdraw yourself from the apprehension of its effect, and be ready to notice irrelevant points which may act as a clue. I believe it is that the peaceful solitary *crow*, moving towards bed and the other crows, is made unnaturally like Macbeth and a murderer who is coming against them; this is suggested by the next lines, which do not say whether the *crow* is one of the *good things of day* or one of *night's black agents* (it is, at any rate, *black*), by the eerie way that light itself is *thickening*, as a man turns against men, a *crow* against *crows*, perhaps by the portentous way a *crow's* voice will carry at such a time, and by the sharpness of its wings against the even glow of a sky after sundown; but mainly, I think, by the use of the two words *rook* and *crow*.

Rooks live in a crowd and are mainly vegetarian; *crow* may be either another name for a *rook*, especially when seen alone, or it may mean the solitary Carrion crow. This subdued pun is made to imply here that Macbeth, looking out of the window, is trying to see himself as a murderer, and can only see himself as in the position of the *crow*; that his *day* of power, now, is closing; that he has to distinguish himself from the other *rooks* by a difference of name, *rook-crow*, like the kingly title, only; that he is anxious, at bottom, to be at one with the other *rooks*, not to murder them; that he can no longer, or that he may yet, be united with the rookery; and that he is murdering Banquo in a forlorn attempt to obtain peace of mind.

Interest in 'atmospheres' is a critical attitude designed for, and particularly suited to, the poets of the nineteenth century; this may tell us something about them, and in part explain why they are so little ambiguous in the sense with which I am concerned. For a variety of reasons, they found themselves living in an intellectual framework with which it was very difficult to write poetry, in which poetry was rather improper, or was irrelevant to business, especially the business of becoming Fit to Survive, or was an indulgence of one's lower nature in beliefs the scientists knew were untrue. On the other hand, they had a large public which was anxious to escape from this

---

a Description, especially of the natural world, which reflects the internal feelings of the perceiver, by attributing human emotions and properties to non-human objects. The term was coined by John Ruskin in *Modern Painters*, IV, xii.

intellectual framework, on holiday, as they were themselves. Almost all of them, therefore, exploited a sort of tap-root into the world of their childhood, where they were able to conceive things poetically, and whatever they might be writing about they would suck up from this limited and perverted world an unvarying sap which was their poetical inspiration. Mr Harold Nicolson has written excellently about Swinburne's fixation on to the excitements of his early reading and experience, and about the unique position in the life of Tennyson occupied by the moaning of cold wind round a child frightened for its identity upon the fens. Wordsworth frankly had no inspiration other than his use, when a boy, of the mountains as a totem or father-substitute, and Byron only at the end of his life, in the first cantos of *Don Juan* in particular, escaped from the infantile incest-fixation upon his sister which was till then all that he had got to say. As for Keats's desire for death and his mother, it has become a byword among the learned. Shelley, perhaps, does not strike one as keeping so sharp a distinction between the world he considered real and the world from which he wrote poetry, but this did not in his case improve either of them; while Browning and Meredith, who did write from the world they lived in, affect me as novel-writers of merit with no lyrical inspiration at all. Coleridge, it is true, relied on opium rather than the nursery. But of all these men an imposed excitement, a sense of uncaused warmth, achievement, gratification, a sense of hugging to oneself a private dream-world, is the main interest and material.[2]

In that age, too, began the doubt as to whether this man or that was 'grown-up', which has ever since occupied so deeply the minds of those interested in their friends. Macaulay complains somewhere that in his day a man was sure to be accused of a child-mind if no doubt could be cast 'either on the ability of his intelligence or the innocence of his character'; now nobody seems to have said this in the eighteenth century. Before the Romantic Revival the possibilities of not growing up had never been exploited so far as to become a subject for popular anxiety.

Of course, these pat little theories are ridiculously simple; fantasy gratifications and a protective attitude towards one's inner life are in some degree essential for the production of poetry, and I have no wish to pretend the Romantics were not great poets. But I think this will be admitted, that they were making a use of language very different from that of their predecessors; imagine Shakespeare or Pope keeping a tap-root in this way. One might expect, then, that they would not need to use ambiguities of the kind I shall consider to give vivacity to their language, or even ambiguities with which the student of language, as such, is concerned; that the mode of approach to them should be psychological rather than grammatical, and that their distortions of meaning will belong to darker regions of the mind.

This introduction has grown too long and too portentous; it is time I settled down to the little I can do in this chapter, which is to list a few examples of ambiguity of the first type. Many of the preceding paragraphs are designed merely for defence; if it is said that the verbal analyst is a crude irrelevant fellow who should be thinking about the atmosphere, the reply is that though there may be an atmosphere to which analysis is irrelevant, it is not necessarily anything very respectable.

I have already considered the comparison of two things which does not say in virtue of what they are to be compared. Of the same sort, though less common, is the ornamental use of false antithesis, which places words as if in opposition to one another without saying in virtue of what they are to be opposed. Cases in which several ways of opposing them are implied will be found in my later chapters as examples of more advanced ambiguity; but the device may be used to deny such an antithesis altogether. There is a rather trivial example of this in Peacock's *War Song*:

> We there, in strife bewildring,
>   Spilt blood enough to swim in;
> We orphaned many children
>   And widowed many women.
> The eagles and the ravens
>   We glutted with our foemen;
> The heroes and the cravens,
>   The spearmen and the bowmen.

In the last two lines he is not concerned to be thinking, to decide something or convince somebody; he makes a cradle and rocks himself in it; it is the tone of a man imagining himself in a mood wholly alien to him, and looking round with an amused complacent absence of reflection. The lines also give finality in that the impulse is shown to be dying away; some reflection has been implied on the difference between *heroes* and *cravens*, on their equal deaths, and on the relations between *eagles* and *heroes*, *ravens* and *cravens*, but the irrelevant calm of the last line says 'these distinctions may be made at other times, but they are irrelevant to our slaughter and the reaction to it of Nature', he proceeds to another merely technical way of separating the dead into classes, and by the failure of the antithesis shows he is merely thinking of them as a huge pile.

> How loved, how honoured once, avails thee not,
> To whom related, or by whom begot;
> A heap of dust is all remains of thee;
> 'Tis all thou art, and all the proud shall be.
>
> (Pope, *Unfortunate Lady*)

The two parts of the second line make a claim to be alternatives which is not obviously justified, and this I think implies a good deal. If the antithesis is to be serious, *or* must mean 'one of her relations was grand but her father was humble', or the other way about; thus one would take *how* to mean 'whether much or little' (it could mean 'though you were so greatly'), and the last line to contrast her with the *proud*, so as to imply that she is humble (it could unite her with the *proud*, and deduce the death of all of them from the death of one). This obscurity is part of the 'Gothic' atmosphere that Pope wanted: 'her birth was high, but there was a mysterious stain on it'; or 'though you might not think it, her birth was high'; or 'her birth was high, but not higher than births to which I am accustomed'. Here, however, the false antithesis is finding another use, to convey the attitude of Pope to the subject.

> How simple, how irrelevant to the merits of the unfortunate lady, are such relationships; everybody has had both a relation and a father; how little I can admire the arrogance of great families on this point; how little, too, the snobbery of my reader, who is unlikely to belong to a great family; to how many people this subject would be extremely fruitful of antitheses; how little fruitful of antitheses it seems to an independent soul like mine.

What is important about such devices is that they leave it to the reader vaguely to invent something, and make him leave it at the back of his mind.

Not unlike the use of a comparison which does not say in virtue of what the two things are to be compared is the use of a comparative adjective which does not say what its noun is to be compared with; since all adjectives are in a sense comparative, this source of ambiguity is a sufficiently general one. In particular, it is the chief source of euphuistic conceits and the paradoxes cultivated in the 'nineties, which give a noun two contradictory adjectives and leave it to the reader to see how the adjectives are used.[3] Examples of this sort are too well known, and are generally thought too trivial, to be worth quoting. I shall give an example from one of Mr Waley's Chinese translations, to insist upon the profundity of feeling which such a device may enshrine.

> Swiftly the years, beyond recall.
> Solemn the stillness of this spring morning.

The human mind has two main scales on which to measure time. The large one takes the length of a human life as its unit, so that there is nothing to be done about life, it is of an animal dignity and simplicity, and must be regarded from a peaceable and fatalistic point of view. The small one takes as its unit the conscious moment, and it is from this that you consider the neighbouring space, an activity of the will, delicacies of social tone, and your personality. The scales are so far apart as almost to give the effect of defining two dimensions; they do not come into contact because what is too large to be conceived by the one is still too small to be conceived by the other. Thus, taking the units as a century and the quarter of a second, their ratio is ten to the tenth and their mean is the standard working day; or taking the smaller one as five minutes, their mean is the whole of summer. The repose and self-command given by the use of the first are contrasted with the speed at which it shows the years to be passing from you, and therefore with the fear of death; the fever and multiplicity of life, as known by the use of the second, are contrasted with the calm of the external space of which it gives consciousness, with the absolute or extra-temporal value attached to the brief moments of self-knowledge with which it is concerned, and with a sense of security in that it makes death so far off.

Both these time-scales and their contrasts are included by these two lines in a single act of apprehension, because of the words *swift* and *still*. Being contradictory as they stand, they demand to be conceived in different ways; we are enabled, therefore, to meet the open skies with an answering stability of self-knowledge; to meet the brevity of human life with an ironical sense that it is morning and springtime, that there is a whole summer before winter, a whole day before night.

I call *swift* and *still* here ambiguous, though each is meant to be referred to one particular time-scale, because between them they put two time-scales into the reader's mind in a single act of apprehension. But these scales, being both present, are in some degree used for each adjective, so that the words are ambiguous in a more direct sense; the *years* of a man's life seem *swift* even on the small scale, like the mist from the mountains which 'gathers a moment, then scatters'; the *morning* seems *still* even on the large scale, so that this moment is apocalyptic and a type of heaven.

Lacking rhyme, metre, and any overt device such as comparison, these lines are what we should normally call poetry only by virtue of their compactness; two statements are made as if they were connected, and the reader is forced to consider their relations for himself. The reason why these facts should have been selected for a poem is left for him to invent; he will invent a variety of reasons and order them in his own mind. This, I think, is the essential fact about the poetical use of language.

Among metaphors effective from several points of view one may include, by no great extension, those metaphors which are partly recognized as such and partly received simply as words in their acquired sense. All languages are composed of dead metaphors as the soil of corpses, but English is perhaps uniquely full of metaphors of this sort, which are not dead but sleeping, and, while making a direct statement, colour it with an implied comparison. The school rule against mixed metaphor, which in itself is so powerful a weapon, is largely necessary because of the presence of these sleepers, who must be treated with respect; they are harder to use than either plain word or metaphor because if you mix them you must show you are conscious of their meaning, and are not merely being insensitive to the possibilities of the language.

> Beauty is but a flower
> Which wrinkles will devour.
> Brightness falls from the air.
> Queens have died young and fair.
> Dust hath closed Helen's eye.
> I am sick, I must die.
>   Lord, have mercy upon us.
>   (Nash, *Summer's Last Will and Testament.*)

I call it a subdued metaphor here that *devour* should mean 'remove' or 'replace', with no more than an overtone of cruelty and the unnatural. This may seem very different from the less evident subdued metaphor in the derivation of a word like 'apprehension', say, but a reader may ignore the consequences even of so evident a metaphor as *devour*. If you go into the metaphor it may make Time the *edax rerum* [voracious devourer of everything], and wrinkles only time's tooth-marks; more probably it compares long curving wrinkles on the face to rodent ulcers, caterpillars on petals, and the worms that are to gnaw it in the grave. Of these, the caterpillar (from *flower*) are what the comparison insists upon, but the Elizabethan imagination would let slip no chance of airing its miraculous corpse-worm.

On the other hand 'Brightness falls from the air' is an example of ambiguity by vagueness, such as was used to excess by the Pre-Raphaelites. Evidently there are a variety of things the line may be about. The sun and moon pass under the earth after their period of shining, and there are stars falling at odd times; Icarus and the prey of hawks, having soared upwards towards heaven, *fall* exhausted or dead; the glittering turning things the sixteenth century put on the top of a building may have *fallen* too often. In another sense, hawks, lightning, and meteorites *fall* flashing from heaven upon their prey. Taking *brightness* as abstract, not as meaning something bright, it is as a benefit that light *falls*, diffusely reflected, from the sky. In so far as the sky is brighter than the earth (especially at twilight), brightness is natural to it; in so far as the earth may be bright when the clouds are dark, *brightness falls* from the sky to the earth when there is a threat of thunder. 'All is unsafe, even the heavens are not sure of their brightness', or 'the qualities in man that deserve respect are not natural to him but brief gifts from God; they fall like manna, and melt as soon'. One may extract, too, from the oppression in the notion of thunder the idea that now, 'in time of pestilence', the generosity of Nature is mysteriously interrupted; even at the scene of brilliant ecclesiastical festivity for which the poem was written there is a taint of darkness in the very *air*.

It is proper to mention a rather cynical theory that Nash wrote or meant 'hair'; still, though less imaginative, this is very adequate; oddly enough (it is electricity and the mysterious vitality of youth which have *fallen* from the *hair*) carries much the same suggestion as the other version; and gives the relief of a single direct meaning. Elizabethan pronunciation was very little troubled by snobbery, and it is conceivable that Nash meant both words to take effect in some way. Now that all this fuss has been made about aitches it is impossible to imagine what such a line would sound like.

For a final meaning of this line one must consider the line which follows it; there is another case of poetry by juxtaposition. In 'Dust hath closed Helen's eye' one must think of Helen in part as an undecaying corpse or a statue; it is *dust* from outside which settles on her eyelids, and shows that it is long since they have been opened; only in the background, as a truth which could not otherwise be faced, is it suggested that the *dust* is generated from her own corruption. As a result of this ambiguity, the line imposes on *brightness* a further and more terrible comparison; on the one hand, it is the *bright* motes dancing in sunbeams, which *fall* and become dust which is dirty and infectious; on the other, the lightness, gaiety, and activity of humanity, which shall come to *dust* in the grave.

When a word is selected as a 'vivid detail', as particular for general, a reader may suspect alternative reasons why it has been selected; indeed the author might find it hard to say. When there are several such words there may be alternative ways of viewing them in order of importance.

> Pan is our All, by him we breathe, we live,
> We move, we are; ...
> But when he frowns, the sheep, alas,
> The shepherds wither, and the grass.
>
> (Ben Jonson, *Pan's Anniversary*)

Alas, the word explaining which of the items in this list we are to take most seriously, belongs to the *sheep* by proximity and the break in the line, to the *grass* by rhyming with it, and to the *shepherds*, humble though they may be, by the processes of human judgment; so that all three are given due attention, and the balance of the verse is maintained. The Biblical suggestions of *grass* as symbolic of the life of man ('in the mornings it is green and groweth up; in the evening it is cut down, dried up, and withered') add to the solemnity; or from another point of view makes the passage absurdly blasphemous, because Pan here is James I. The grace, the pathos, the 'sheer song' of the couplet is given by an enforced subtlety of intonation, from the difficulty of saying it so as to bring out all the implications.

This last consideration is important, because it gives some hint as to why these devices belong to poetry rather than to prose, or indeed why poetry seems different from prose. A metrical scheme imposes a sort of intensity of interpretation upon the grammar, which makes it fruitful even when there is 'no song'.

> I want to know a butcher paints,
> A baker rhymes for his pursuit,
> Candlestick-maker, much acquaints
> His soul with song, or, haply mute,
> Blows out his brains upon the flute.
>
> (Browning)

'I want to know what the whole class of butchers paints', or 'I want to know that some one butcher paints', or 'I want to know personally a butcher who paints'; any of these may be taken as the meaning, and their resultant is something like, 'I want to know that a member of the class of butchers is moderately likely to be a man who paints, or at any rate that he can do so if he wishes'. The demands of metre allow the poet to say something which is not normal colloquial English, so that the reader thinks of the various colloquial forms which are near to it, and puts them together; weighting their probabilities in proportion to their nearness. It is for such reasons as this that poetry can be more compact, while seeming to be less precise, than prose.

It is for these reasons, too, among others, that an insensitivity in a poet to the contemporary style of speaking, into which he has been trained to concentrate his powers of apprehension, is so disastrous, can be noticed so quickly, and produces that curious thinness or blurring of texture one finds in William Morris. And that is why the practice of putting single words into italics for emphasis (again the Victorians are guilty) is so vulgar; a well-constructed sentence should be able to carry a stress on any of its words and should show in itself how these stresses are to be compounded. Both in prose and poetry, it is the impression that implications of this sort have been handled with more judgment than you yourself realize, that with this language as text innumerable further meanings, which you do not know, could be deduced, that forces you to feel respect for a style.

Notes

1. It was stupid of me to present this example as a sort of test case, with a tidy solution drawn from the names of birds. Obviously the passage is still impressive if you have no opinions at all about the difference between crows and rooks. But it is at least a good example of a heavy Atmosphere, and I don't think my treatment of it was wrong as far as it went.

2. Byron I understand did not meet his half-sister at all till he was grown up. It seems no good trying to improve this paragraph, and I still think that the last sentence summing it up is sufficiently true.

3. Such a trick has usually one meaning which is the answer of the puzzle, but while you are puzzling the words have possible alternative meanings, and even to those who see the answers at once the alternatives are in a way present as being denied. They may appear as the views of commonplace people, who are thereby snubbed; but they can also make a real ambiguity when the denial is not felt to be complete.

13 G. Wilson Knight

George Wilson Knight (b. 1897) was a pioneer in the now familiar method of interpreting Shakespeare's plays by tracing the patterns of repeated metaphors, symbols, and other motifs that are peculiar to each. The systematic tabulation of image-clusters in Shakespeare's plays was first employed and documented by Caroline Spurgeon in her *Sheakespeare's Imagery and What It Tells Us* (Cambridge, 1935) and G. Wilson Knight has acknowledged the value of this work, and Professor Spurgeon's earlier reports on her research, for his own criticism. Knight, however, had started working on these lines quite independently, and there is no doubt that he made better critical use of the method than did Professor Spurgeon. His first books, *The Wheel of Fire* (1930) and *The Imperial Theme* (1931) were brilliant and original essays in interpretation which contributed decisively to the decline of that nineteenth-century tradition of Shakespeare criticism, culminating impressively in A. C. Bradley's *Shakespeare's Tragedies* (1904), which discussed Shakespeare's characters as if they were characters in realistic fiction, if not real people. And the method employed by Knight has been successfully applied by later critics to other kinds of literature, notably the novel.

G. Wilson Knight, Emeritus Professor at the University of Leeds, has had a long and prolific career as a critic, but his later work, somewhat eccentric in its concerns, has had less influence than the earlier. In addition to the titles mentioned above, *The Crown of Life* (1947) on Shakespeare's last plays, and *The Starlit Dome* (1941) on the Romantic poets are perhaps the best known. Professor Knight has also written three studies of Byron, and a book on *Principles of Shakespearian Production* (1936). 'Macbeth and the Metaphysic of Evil' is reprinted from the revised edition of *The Wheel of Fire: Interpretations of Shakespearian Tragedy* (1949).

CROSS REFERENCES: 15. Maud Bodkin
30. Francis Fergusson

COMMENTARY: Arthur M. Eastman, 'G. Wilson Knight',
in *A Short History of Shakespeare Criticism* (New York, 1968)

Macbeth and the metaphysic of evil

Macbeth is Shakespeare's most profound and mature vision of evil. In the ghost and death themes of *Hamlet* we have something of the same quality; in the Brutus-theme of *Julius Caesar* we have an exactly analogous rhythm of spiritual experience; in *Richard III* we have a parallel history of an individual's crime. In *Macbeth* all this, and the many other isolated poetic units of similar quality throughout Shakespeare, receive a final, perfected form. Therefore analysis of *Macbeth* is of profound value: but it is not easy. Much of *Hamlet*, and the *Troilus–Othello–Lear* succession culminating in *Timon of Athens*, can be regarded as representations of the 'hate-theme'. We are there faced by man's aspiring nature, unsatiated of its desire among the frailties and inconsistencies of its world. They point us to good, not evil, and their very gloom of denial is the shadow of a great assertion. They accordingly lend themselves to interpretation in terms of human thought, and their evil can be regarded as a negation of man's positive longing. In *Macbeth* we find not gloom, but blackness: the evil is not relative, but absolute. In point of imaginative profundity *Macbeth* is comparable alone to *Antony and Cleopatra*. There we have a fiery vision of a paradisal consciousness; here the murk and nightmare torment of a conscious hell. This evil, being absolute and therefore alien to man, is in essence shown as inhuman and supernatural, and is most difficult of location within any philosophical scheme. *Macbeth* is fantastical and imaginative beyond other tragedies. Difficulty is increased by that implicit blurring of effects, that palling darkness, that overcasts plot, technique, style. The persons of the play are themselves groping. Yet we are left with an overpowering knowledge of suffocating, conquering evil, and fixed by the basilisk eye of a nameless terror. The nature of this evil will be the subject of my essay.

It is dangerous to abstract the personal history of the protagonist from his environment as a basis for interpretation. The main theme is not primarily differentiated from that of the important subsidiary persons and cannot stand alone. Rather there is a similarity, and the evil in Banquo, Macduff, Malcolm, and the enveloping atmosphere of the play, all form so many steps by which we may approach and understand the titanic evil which grips the two protagonists. The *Macbeth* universe is woven in a texture of a single pattern. The whole play is one swift act of the poet's mind, and as such must be interpreted, since the technique confronts us not with separated integers of 'character' or incident, but with a molten welding of thought with thought, event with event. There is an interpenetrating quality that subdues all to itself. Therefore I shall start by noticing some of the more important elements in this total imaginative effect, and thence I shall pass to the more purely human element. The story and action of the play alone will not carry us far. Here the logic of imaginative correspondence is more significant and more exact than the logic of plot.

Macbeth is a desolate and dark universe where all is befogged, baffled, constricted by the evil. Probably in no play of Shakespeare are so many questions asked. It opens with 'When shall we three meet again?' and 'Where the place?' (I. i. 1 and 6). The second scene starts with, 'What bloody man is that?' (I. ii. 1), and throughout it questions are asked of the Sergeant and Ross. This is followed by:

> FIRST WITCH. Where hast thou been, sister?
> SECOND WITCH. Killing swine.
> FIRST WITCH. Sister, where thou?
>
> (I. iii. 1)

And Banquo's first words on entering are: 'How far is't called to Forres? What are these...?' (I. iii. 39). Questions succeed each other quickly throughout this scene. Amazement and mystery are in the play from the start, and are reflected in continual questions—there are those of Duncan to Malcolm in I. iv, and of Lady Macbeth to the Messenger and then to her lord in I. v. They continue throughout the play. In I. vii they are tense and powerful:

> MACBETH.   ...How now! What news?
> L. MACBETH. He has almost supp'd: why have you left the chamber?
> MACBETH. Hath he asked for me?
> L. MACBETH.   Know you not he has?
>
> (I. vii. 28)

This scene bristles with them. At the climax of the murder they come again, short stabs of fear: 'Didst thou not hear a noise?—Did not you speak? When? —Now.—As I descended?...' (II. ii. 16). Some of the finest and most heart-rending passages are in the form of questions: 'But wherefore could I not pronounce Amen?' and, 'Will all great Neptune's ocean wash this blood clean from my hand?' (II. ii. 32; II. ii. 61). The scene of the murder and that of its discovery form a series of questions. To continue the list in detail would be more tedious than difficult: to quote a few—there are the amazed questions of the guests and Lady Macbeth at the Banquet (III. iii.); Macbeth's continual questioning of the Weird Sisters in the Cauldron scene (IV. i); those of Macduff's son to Lady Macduff (IV. ii); of Macduff to Ross who brings him news of his family's slaughter (IV. iii); of the Doctor to the Gentlewoman (V. i).

These questions are threads in the fabric of mystery and doubt which haunts us in *Macbeth*. All the persons are in doubt, baffled. Duncan is baffled at the treachery of a man he trusted (I. iv. 11). Newcomers strike amaze:

> What a haste looks through his eyes? So should he look
> That seems to speak things strange.
>
> (I. ii. 47)

Surprise is continual. Macbeth does not understand how he can be Thane of Cawdor (I. iii. 108). Lady Macbeth is startled at the news of Duncan's visit (I. v. 32); Duncan at the fact of Macbeth's arrival before himself (I. vi. 20). There is the general amazement at the murder; of Lennox, Ross, and the Old

Man at the strange happenings in earth and heaven on the night of the murder (II. iii. 60-7; II. iv. 1-20). Banquo and Fleance are unsure of the hour (II. i. 1-4). No one is sure of Macduff's mysterious movements. Lady Macbeth is baffled by Macbeth's enigmatic hints as to the 'deed of dreadful note' (III. ii. 44). The two murderers are not certain as to who has wronged them, Macbeth or Banquo (III. i. 76-9); they do not understand the advent of the 'third murderer' (III. iii. 1). Ross and Lady Macduff are at a loss as to Macduff's flight, and warning is brought to Lady Macduff by a mysterious messenger who 'is not to her known' (IV. ii. 63). Malcolm suspects Macduff, and there is a long dialogue due to his 'doubts' (IV. iii); and in the same scene Malcolm recognizes Ross as his countryman yet strangely 'knows him not' (IV. iii. 160). As the atmosphere brightens at the end of the play, the contrast is aptly marked by reference to the stroke of action which will finally dispel the fog of insecurity:

> The time approaches
> That will with due decision make us know
> What we shall say we have and what we owe.
> Thoughts speculative their unsure hopes relate,
> But certain issues strokes must arbitrate.
>
> (v. iv. 17)

This blurring and lack of certainty is increased by the heavy proportion of second-hand or vague knowledge reported during the play's progress. We have the two accounts of the fighting, by the Sergeant and Ross: but the whole matter of the rebellion is vague to us. Later, afer Ross has told Macbeth of his new honours, Angus says that he 'knows not' the exact crimes of the former Thane of Cawdor (I. iii. 111-16). Malcolm has spoken with 'one that saw him die' (I. iv. 4). Lady Macbeth hears amazedly of the Weird Sisters' prophecy by letter (I. v.). Macbeth describes the voice that bade him 'sleep no more' (II. ii. 36) and the dead body of Duncan (II. iii. 118). People are continually receiving the latest news from each other, the climax being Macduff's hearing of his family's slaughter (II. iv; III. vi; IV. iii. 161-239). Rumours are alive throughout:

> MACBETH. How say'st thou that Macduff denies his person
>   At our great bidding?
> L. MACBETH.   Did you send to him, Sir?
> MACBETH. I hear it by the way; but I will send.
>
> (III. iv. 128)

We hear more rumours of Macduff in the dialogue between Lennox and the Lord in III. vi. There is the 'galloping of horses' with the mysterious 'two or three' who bring word of Macduff's flight (IV. i. 141). It is a world of rumours and fears:

> ROSS.   I dare not speak much further;
>   But cruel are the times, when we are traitors
>   And do not know ourselves; when we hold rumour
>   From what we fear, yet know not what we fear,
>   But float upon a wild and violent sea
>   Each way and move.
>
> (IV. ii. 17)

Ross has heard a 'rumour' of a rise in Scotland against Macbeth (IV. iii. 182). In a hushed voice the Gentlewoman describes Lady Macbeth's sleep-walking to the Doctor (V. i.); and the Doctor says he has 'heard something' of Macbeth's 'royal preparation' (V. iii. 57-8). Siward 'learns no other' but that Macbeth is defending his castle (V. iv. 9), and Lady Macbeth, 'as 'tis thought', commits suicide (V. vii. 99). These are but a few random instances: questions, rumours, startling news, and uncertainties are everywhere. From the time when Banquo asks 'How far is't called to Forres?' (I. iii. 39) until Siward's 'What wood is this before us?' (V. iv. 3) we are watching persons lost, mazed.[1] They do not understand themselves even:

> MALCOLM.　　　Why do we hold our tongues
> That most may claim this argument for ours?
>
> (II. iii. 126)

The persons of the drama can say truly, with Ross, 'we ... do not know ourselves' (IV. ii. 19). We too, who read, are in doubt often. Action here is illogical. Why does Macbeth not know of Cawdor's treachery? Why does Lady Macbeth faint? Why do the King's sons flee to different countries when a whole nation is ready in their support? Why does Macduff move so darkly mysterious in the background and leave his family to certain death? Who is the Third Murderer? And, finally, why does Macbeth murder Duncan? All this builds a strong sense of mystery and irrationality within us. We, too, grope in the stifling dark, and suffer from doubt and insecurity.

Darkness permeates the play. The greater part of the action takes place in the murk of night. It is unnecessary to detail more than a few of the numerous references to darkness. Lady Macbeth prays:

> 　　　　　　　　Come, thick night,
> And pall thee in the dunnest smoke of Hell,
> That my keen knife see not the wound it makes,
> Nor Heaven peep through the blanket of the dark
> To cry, Hold! Hold!
>
> (I. v. 51)

And Macbeth:

> 　　　　　　　　Stars, hide your fires.
> Let not light see my black and deep desires;
> The eye wink at the hand; yet let that be,
> Which the eye fears, when it is done, to see.
>
> (I. iv. 50)

During the play 'light thickens' (III. ii. 50), the 'travelling lamp' is 'strangled' (II. iv. 7), there is 'husbandry in heaven' (II. i. 4). This is typical:

> Now spurs the lated traveller apace
> To gain the timely inn.
>
> (III. iii. 6)

Now this world of doubts and darkness gives birth to strange and hideous creatures. Vivid animal disorder-symbolism is recurrent in the play and the animals mentioned are for the most part of fierce, ugly, or ill-omened significance. We hear of 'the Hyrcan tiger' and the 'armed rhinoceros' (III. iv. 101), the 'rugged Russian bear' (II. iv. 100); the wolf, 'whose howl's his watch' (II. i. 54); the raven who croaks the entrance of Duncan under Lady Macbeth's battlements (I. v. 39); the owl, 'fatal bellman who gives the stern'st goodnight' (II. ii. 4). There are 'maggot-pies and choughs and rooks' (III. iv. 125), and

> ...hounds and greyhounds, mongrels, spaniels, curs,
> Shoughs, water-rugs, and demi-wolves...
>
> (III. i. 93)

We have the bat and his 'cloistered flight', the 'shard-borne beetle', the crow making wing to the 'rooky wood'; 'night's black agents' rouse to their preys; Macbeth has 'scotch'd the snake, not killed it'; his mind is full of 'scorpions' (III. ii. 13-53). All this suggests life threatening, ill-omened, hideous: and it culminates in the holocaust of filth prepared by the Weird Sisters in the Cauldron scene. But not only are animals of unpleasant suggestion here present: we have animals, like men, irrational and amazing in their acts. A falcon is attacked and killed by a 'mousing owl', and Duncan's horses eat each other (II. iv. 11-18). There is a prodigious and ghastly tempest, with 'screams of death'; the owl clamoured through the night; the earth itself shook (II. iii. 60-7). We are made aware of a hideous abnormality in this world; and again we feel its irrationality and mystery. In proportion as we let ourselves be receptive to the impact of all these suggestions we shall be strongly aware of the essential fearsomeness of this universe.

We are confronted by mystery, darkness, abnormality, hideousness: and therefore by fear. The word 'fear' is ubiquitous. All may be unified as symbols of this emotion. Fear is predominant. Everyone is afraid. There is scarcely a person in the play who does not feel and voice at some time a sickening, nameless terror. The impact of the play is analogous to nightmare, to which state there are many references:

> Now o'er the one-half world,
> Nature seems dead, and wicked dreams abuse
> The curtain'd sleep...
>
> (II. i. 49)

Banquo cries:

> Merciful powers,
> Restrain in me the cursed thoughts that nature
> Gives way to in repose!
>
> (II. i. 7)

Banquo has dreamed of 'the three weird sisters' (II. i. 20), who are thus associated with a nightmare reality. There are those who cried in their sleep, and said their prayers after (II. ii. 24). Macbeth may 'sleep no more' (II. ii. 44); sleep, balm of hurt minds, 'shall neither night nor day hang upon his penthouse lid' (I. iii. 19)—if we may transfer the reference. He and his wife are condemned to live

> in the affliction of these terrible dreams
That shake us nightly.

(III. ii. 18)

The central act of the play is a hideous murder of sleep. Finally, we have the extreme agony of sleep-consciousness depicted in Lady Macbeth's sleep-walking. Nor are there dreams only: the narrow gulf between nightmare and the abnormal actuality of the *Macbeth* universe—itself of nightmare quality—is bridged by fantasies and ghosts: the dagger of Macbeth's mind, the Ghost of Banquo, the Apparitions, the Vision of Scottish Kings, culminating in the three Weird Sisters. There is no nearer equivalent, in the experience of a normal mind, to the poetic quality of *Macbeth* than the consciousness of nightmare or delirium. That is why life is here a 'tale told by an idiot' (V. v. 27), a 'fitful fever' after which the dead 'sleep well' (III. ii. 23); why the earth itself is 'feverous' (II. iii. 62). The Weird Sisters are nightmare actualized; Macbeth's crime nightmare projected into action. Therefore this world is unknowable, hideous, disorderly, and irrational. The very style of the play has a mesmeric, nightmare quality, for in that dream-consciousness, hateful though it be, there is a nervous tension, a vivid sense of profound significance, an exceptionally rich apprehension of reality electrifying the mind: one is in touch with absolute evil, which, being absolute, has a satanic beauty, a hideous, serpent-like grace and attraction, drawing, paralysing. This quality is in the poetic style: the language is tense, nervous, insubstantial, without anything of the visual clarity of *Othello*, or the massive solemnity of *Timon of Athens*. The poetic effect of the whole, though black with an inhuman abysm of darkness, is yet shot through and streaked with vivid colour, with horrors that hold a mesmeric attraction even while they repel; and things of brightness that intensify the enveloping murk. There is constant reference to blood. Macbeth and Banquo 'bathe in reeking wounds' (I. ii. 40) in the fight reported by the 'bloody' Sergeant; Macbeth's sword 'smoked with bloody execution' (I. ii. 18); there is the blood on Macbeth's hands, and on Lady Macbeth's after she has 'smeared' the sleeping grooms with it (II. ii). There is the description of Duncan's body, 'his silver skin lac'd with his golden blood' (II. iii. 118). There is blood on the face of the Murderer who comes to tell of Banquo's 'trenched gashes' (III. iv. 27); the 'gory locks' (III. iv. 51) of the 'blood-bolter'd' Banquo; the 'bloody child' Apparition; the blood-nightmare of Lady Macbeth's sleep-walking. But though blood-imagery is rich, there is no brilliance in it; rather a sickly smear. Yet there is brilliance in the fire-imagery: the thunder and lightning which accompanies the Weird Sisters; the fire of the cauldron; the green glint of the spectral dagger; the glaring eyes which hold 'no speculation' of Banquo's Ghost, the insubstantial sheen of the three Apparitions, the ghastly pageant of kings unborn.

Macbeth has the poetry of intensity: intense darkness shot with the varied intensity of pure light or pure colour. In the same way the moral darkness is shot with imagery of bright purity and virtue. There is 'the temple-haunting martlet' (I. vi. 4) to contrast with evil creatures. We have the early personation of the sainted Duncan, whose body is 'the Lord's anointed temple' (II. iii. 74), the bright limning of his virtues by Macbeth (I. vii. 16-20), and Macduff (IV.

iii. 108); the latter's lovely words on Malcolm's mother who, 'oftener upon her knees' than on her feet, died every day she lived' (IV. iii. 110); the prayer of Lennox for 'some holy angel' (III. vi. 45) to fly to England's court for saving help; Macbeth's agonized vision of a starry good, of 'Heaven's cherubim' horsed in air, and Pity like a babe; those who pray that God may bless them in their fevered dream; above all, Malcolm's description of England's holy King, health-giver and God-elect who, unlike Macbeth, has power over 'the evil', in whose court Malcolm borrows 'grace' to combat the nightmare evil of his own land:

> MALCOLM.   Comes the King forth, I pray you?
> DOCTOR. Ay, sir; there are a crew of wretched souls
> That stay his cure: their malady convinces
> The great assay of art; but at his touch—
> Such sanctity hath Heaven given his hand—
> They presently amend.
> MALCOLM.   I thank you, doctor.
> MACDUFF. What's the disease he means?
> MALCOLM.   'Tis call'd the evil.
> A most miraculous work in this good king;
> Which often, since my here-remain in England,
> I have seen him do. How he solicits Heaven,
> Himself best knows: but strangely visited people,
> All swoln and ulcerous, pitiful to the eye,
> The mere despair of surgery, he cures,
> Hanging a golden stamp about their necks,
> Put on with holy prayers: and 'tis spoken,
> To the succeeding royalty he leaves
> The healing benediction. With his strange virtue,
> He hath a heavenly gift of prophecy,
> And sundry blessings hang about his throne,
> That speak him full of grace.
>
> (IV. iii. 140)

This description is spoken just before Ross enters with the shattering narration of Macbeth's most dastardly and ruinous crime. The contrast at this instant is vivid and pregnant. The King of England is thus full of supernatural 'grace'. In *Macbeth* this supernatural grace is set beside the supernatural evil. Against such grace Macbeth first struck the blow of evil. Duncan was 'gracious' (III. i. 66); at his death 'renown and grace is dead' (II. iii. 101). By 'the grace of Grace' (V. vii. 101) alone Malcolm will restore health[2] to Scotland. The murk, indeed, thins towards the end. Bright daylight dawns and the green leaves of Birnam come against Macbeth. A world climbs out of its darkness, and in the dawn that panorama below is a thing of nightmare delusion. The 'sovereign flower' (V. ii. 30) is bright-dewed in the bright dawn, and the murk melts into the mists of morning: the Child is crowned, the Tree of Life in his hand.

I have indicated something of the imaginative atmosphere of this play. It is a world shaken by 'fears and scruples' (II. iii. 136). It is a world where 'nothing is but what is not' (I. iii. 141), where 'fair is foul and foul is fair' (I. i. 11). I have emphasized two complementary elements: (i) the doubts, uncertainties, irrationalities; (ii) the horrors, the dark, the abnormalities. These two elements repel respectively the intellect and the heart of man. And, since the contemplating mind is then powerfully unified in its immediate antagonism, our reaction holds the positive and tense fear that succeeds nightmare, wherein there is an experience of something at once insubstantial and unreal to the understanding and appallingly horrible to the feelings: this is the evil of *Macbeth*. In this equal repulsion of the dual attributes of the mind a state of singleness and harmony is induced in the recipient, and it is in respect of this that *Macbeth* forces us to a consciousness more exquisitely unified and sensitive than any of the great tragedies but its polar opposite, *Antony and Cleopatra*. This is how the *Macbeth* universe presents to us an experience of absolute evil. Now, these two peculiarities of the whole play will be found also in the purely human element. The two main characteristics of Macbeth's temptation are (i) ignorance of his own motive, and (ii) horror of the deed to which he is being driven. Fear is the primary emotion of the *Macbeth* universe: fear is at the root of Macbeth's crime. I shall next notice the nature of those human events, actions, experiences to which the atmosphere of unreality and terror bears intimate relation.

The action of the play turns on a deed of disorder. Following the disorderly rebellion which prologues the action we have Macbeth's crime, and the disorder which it creates:

> Confusion now hath made his masterpiece!
> Most sacrilegious murder hath broke ope
> The Lord's anointed temple, and stole thence
> The life o' the building.
>
> (II. iii. 72)

Duncan's murder and its results are felt as events of confusion and disorder, as interruptions of the even tenour of human nature, and are therefore related to the disorder-symbols and instances of unnatural behaviour in man or animal or element throughout the play. The evil of atmospheric effect interpenetrates the evil of individual persons. It has so firm a grip on this world that it fastens not only on the protagonists, but on subsidiary persons too. This point I shall notice before passing to the themes of Macbeth and his wife.

Many minor persons are definitely related to evil: the two—or three—Murderers, the traitors, Cawdor and Macdonald, the drunken porter, doing duty at the gate of Hell. But the major ones too, who are conceived partly as contrasts to Macbeth and his wife, nevertheless succumb to the evil down-pressing on the *Macbeth* universe. Banquo is early involved. Returning with Macbeth from a bloody war, he meets the three Weird Sisters. We may imagine that the latter are related to the bloodshed of battle, and that they have waited until after 'the hurly-burly's done' (I. i. 3) to instigate a continuance of blood-lust in the two generals. We must observe that the two generals' feats of arms are described as acts of unprecedented ferocity:

> Except they meant to bathe in reeking wounds,
> Or memorize another Golgotha,
> I cannot tell.
>
> (I. ii. 40)

This campaign strikes amaze into men. War is here a thing of blood, not romance. Ross addresses Macbeth:

> Nothing afeard of what thyself didst make,
> Strange images of death.
>
> (I. iii. 96)

Macbeth's sword 'smoked with bloody execution' (I. ii. 18). The emphasis is important. The late wine of blood-destruction focuses the inward eyes of these two to the reality of the sisters of blood and evil, and they in turn urge Macbeth to add to those 'strange images of death' the 'great doom's image' (II. iii. 85) of a murdered and sainted king. This knowledge of evil implicit in his meeting with the three Weird Sisters Banquo keeps to himself, and it is a bond of evil between him and Macbeth. It is this that troubles him on the night of the murder, planting a nightmare of unrest in his mind: 'the cursed thoughts that nature gives way to in repose.' He feels the typical *Macbeth* guilt: 'a heavy summons lies like lead' upon him (II. i. 6). He is enmeshed in Macbeth's horror, and, after the coronation, keeps the guilty secret, and lays to his heart a guilty hope. Banquo is thus involved. So also is Macduff. His cruel desertion of his family is emphasized:

> L. MACDUFF. His flight was madness; when our actions do not,
>   Our fears do make us traitors.
> ROSS.   You know not
>   Whether it was his wisdom or his fear.
> L. MACDUFF. Wisdom! to leave his wife, to leave his babes,
>   His mansion and his titles in a place
>   From whence himself does flee?
>
> (IV. ii. 3)

For this, or for some nameless reason, Macduff knows he bears some responsibility for his dear ones' death:

> Sinful Macduff,
> They were all struck for thee! Naught that I am,
> Not for their own demerits, but for mine,
> Fell slaughter on their souls. Heaven rest them now!
>
> (IV. iii. 223)

All the persons seem to share some guilt of the down-pressing enveloping evil. Even Malcolm is forced to repeat crimes on himself. He catalogues every possible sin, and accuses himself of all. Whatever be his reasons, his doing so yet remains part of the integral humanism of this play. The pressure of evil is not relaxed till the end. Not that the persons are 'bad characters'. They are not 'characters' at all, in the proper use of the word. They are but vaguely individualized, and more remarkable for similarity than difference. All the persons are primarily just this: men paralysed by fear and a sense of evil in and outside themselves. They lack will-power: that concept finds no place here. Neither we, nor they, know of what exactly they are guilty: yet they feel guilt.

So, too, with Lady Macbeth. She is not merely a woman of strong will: she is a woman possessed—possessed of evil passion. No 'will-power' on earth would account for her dread invocation:

> Come, you spirits
> That tend on mortal thoughts, unsex me here,
> And fill me from the crown to the toe, top-full
> Of direst cruelty!
>
> (I. v. 41)

This speech, addressed to the 'murdering ministers' who 'in their sightless substances wait on nature's mischief' is demonic in intensity and passion. It is inhuman—as though the woman were controlled by an evil something which masters her, mind and soul. It is mysterious, fearsome, yet fascinating: like all else here, it is a nightmare thing of evil. Whatever it be it leaves her a pure woman, with a woman's frailty, as soon as ever its horrible work is done. She faints at Macbeth's description of Duncan's body. As her husband grows rich in crime, her significance dwindles: she is left shattered, a human wreck who mutters over again in sleep the hideous memories of her former satanic hour of pride. To interpret the figure of Lady Macbeth in terms of 'ambition' and 'will' is, indeed, a futile commentary. The scope and sweep of her evil passion is tremendous, irresistible, ultimate. She is an embodiment—for one mighty hour—of evil absolute and extreme.[3]

The central human theme—the temptation and crime of Macbeth—is, however, more easy of analysis. The crucial speech runs as follows:

> Why do I yield to that suggestion,
> Whose horrid image doth unfix my hair,
> And make my seated heart knock at my ribs
> Against the use of nature? Present fears
> Are less than horrible imaginings.
> My thought whose murder yet is but fantastical
> Shakes so my single state of man that function
> Is smother'd in surmise, and nothing is
> But what is not.
>
> (I. iii. 134)

These lines, spoken when Macbeth first feels the impending evil, expresses again all those elements I have noticed in the mass-effect of the play: questioning doubt, horror, fear of some unknown power; horrible imaginings of the supernatural and 'fantastical'; an abysm of unreality; disorder on the plane of physical life. This speech is a microcosm of the *Macbeth* vision: it contains the germ of the whole. Like a stone in a pond, this original immediate experience of Macbeth sends ripples of itself expanding over the whole play. This is the moment of the birth of evil in Macbeth—he may have had ambitious thoughts before, may even have intended the murder, but now for the first time he feels its oncoming reality. This is the mental experience which he projects into action, thereby plunging his land, too, in fear, horror, darkness, and disorder. In this speech we have a swift interpenetration of idea with idea, from fear and disorder, through sickly imaginings, to abysmal darkness, nothingness. 'Nothing is but what is not': that is the text of the play. Reality and unreality change places. We must see that Macbeth, like the whole universe of this play, is paralysed, mesmerized, as though in a dream. This is not merely 'ambition'—it is fear, a nameless fear which yet fixes itself to a horrid image. He is helpless as a man in a nightmare: and this helplessness is integral to the conception—the will-concept is absent. Macbeth may struggle, but he cannot fight: he can no more resist than a rabbit resists a weasel's teeth fastened in its neck, or a bird the serpent's transfixing eye. Now this evil in Macbeth propels him to an act absolutely evil. For, though no ethical system is ultimate, Macbeth's crime is as near absolute as may be. It is therefore conceived as absolute. Its dastardly nature is emphasized clearly (I. vii. 12-25): Duncan is old, good; he is at once Macbeth's kinsman, king, and guest; he is to be murdered in sleep. No worse act of evil could well be found. So the evil of which Macbeth is at first aware rapidly entraps him in a mesh of events: it makes a tool of Duncan's visit, it dominates Lady Macbeth. It is significant that she, like her husband, is influenced by the Weird Sisters and their prophecy. Eventually Macbeth undertakes the murder, as a grim and hideous duty. He cuts a sorry figure at first, but, once embarked on his allegiant enterprise of evil, his grandeur grows. Throughout he is driven by fear—the fear that paralyses everyone else urges him to an amazing and mysterious action of blood. This action he repeats, again and again.

By his original murder he isolates himself from humanity. He is lonely, endures the uttermost torture of isolation. Yet still a bond unites him to men: that bond he would 'cancel and tear to pieces'—the natural bond of human fellowship and love.[4] He further symbolizes his guilty, pariah soul by murdering Banquo. He fears everyone outside himself but his wife, suspects them. Every act of blood is driven by fear of the horrible disharmony existent between himself and his world. He tries to harmonize the relation by murder. He would let 'the frame of things disjoint, both the worlds suffer' (III. ii. 16) to win back peace. He is living in an unreal world, a fantastic mockery, a ghoulish dream: he strives to make this single nightmare to rule the outward things of his nation. He would make all Scotland a nightmare thing of dripping blood. He knows he cannot return, so determines to go o'er. He seeks out the Weird Sisters a second time. Now he welcomes disorder and confusion, would let them range wide over the earth, since they range unfettered in his own soul:

> ... though the treasure
> Of nature's germens tumble all together,
> Even till destruction sicken; answer me
> To what I ask you.
>
> (IV. i. 58)

So he addresses the Weird Sisters. Castles, palaces, and pyramids—let all fall in general confusion, if only Macbeth be satisfied. He is plunging deeper and deeper into unreality, the severance from mankind and all normal forms of life is now abysmal, deep. Now he is shown Apparitions glassing the future. They promise him success in terms of natural law; no man 'of woman born' shall hurt him, he shall not be vanquished till Birnam Wood come against him. He, based firmly in the unreal, yet thinks to build his future on the laws of reality. He forgets that he is trafficking with things of nightmare fantasy, whose truth is falsehood, falsehood truth. That success they promise is unreal as they themselves. So, once having cancelled the bond of reality he has no home: the unreal he understands not, the real condemns him. In neither can he exist. He asks if Banquo's issue shall reign in Scotland: most horrible thought to him, since, if that be so, it proves that the future takes its natural course irrespective of human acts—that prophecy need not have been interpreted into crime: that he would in truth have been King of Scotland without his own 'stir' (I. iii. 144). Also the very thought of other succeeding and prosperous kings, some of them with 'twofold balls and treble sceptres' (IV. i. 121), is a maddening thing to him who is no real king but only monarch of a nightmare realm. The Weird Sisters who were formerly as the three Parcae, or Fates, fore-telling Macbeth's future, now, at this later stage of his story, become the Erinyes, avengers of murder, symbols of the tormented soul. They delude and madden him with their apparitions and ghosts. Yet he does not give way, and raises our admiration at his undaunted severance from good. He contends for his own individual soul against the universal reality. Nor is his contest unavail-ing. He is fighting himself free from the nightmare fear of his life. He goes on 'till destruction sicken' (IV. i. 60): he actually does 'go o'er', is not lost in the stream of blood he elects to cross. It is true. He wins his battle. He adds crime to crime and emerges at last victorious and fearless:

> I have almost forgot the taste of fears:
> The time has been, my senses would have cool'd
> To hear a night-shriek; and my fell of hair
> Would at a dismal treatise rouse and stir
> As life were in't; I have supp'd full with horrors;
> Direness, familiar to my slaughterous thoughts,
> Cannot once start me.
>
> (v. v. 9)

Again, 'Hang those that talk of fear!' (v. iii. 36) he cries, in an ecstasy of cour-age. He is, at last, 'broad and general as the casing air' (III. iv. 23).

This will appear a strange reversal of the usual commentary; it is, however, true and necessary. While Macbeth lives in conflict with himself there is misery, evil, fear: when, at the end, he and others have openly identified him-self with evil, he faces the world fearless: nor does he appear evil any longer. The worst element of his suffering has been that secrecy and hypocrisy so often referred to throughout the play (I. iv. 12; I. v. 64; III. ii. 34; v. iii. 27). Dark secrecy and night are in Shakespeare ever the badges of crime. But at the end Macbeth has no need of secrecy. He is no longer 'cabin'd, cribb'd, confined, bound in to saucy doubts and fears' (III. iv. 24). He has won through by exces-sive crime to an harmonious and honest relation with his surroundings. He has successfully symbolized the disorder of his lonely guilt-stricken soul by creating disorder in the world, and thus restores balance and harmonious contact. The mighty principle of good planted in the nature of things then asserts itself, condemns him openly, brings him peace. Daylight is brought to Macbeth, as to Scotland, by the accusing armies of Malcolm. He now knows himself to be a tyrant confessed, and wins back that integrity of soul which gives us:

> I have lived long enough: my way of life
> Is fallen into the sere, the yellow leaf ...
>
> (V. iii. 22)

Here he touches a recognition deeper than fear, more potent than nightmare. The delirious dream is over. A clear daylight now disperses the imaginative dark that has eclipsed Scotland. The change is remarkable. There is now movement, surety and purpose, colour: horses 'skirr the country round' (V. iii. 35), banners are hung out on the castle walls (V v. 1), soldiers hew down the bright leaves of Birnam (V. iv. 5). There is, as it were, a paean of triumph as the *Macbeth* universe, having struggled darkly upward, now climbs into radiance. Though they oppose each other in fight, Macbeth and Malcolm share equally in this relief, this awakening from horror. Of a piece with this change is the fulfilment of the Weird Sisters' prophecies. In bright daylight the nightmare reality to which Macbeth has been subdued is insubstantial and transient as sleep-horrors at dawn. Their unreality is emphasized by the very fact that they are nevertheless related to natural phenomena: they are thus parasitic on reality. To these he has trusted, and they fail. But he himself is, at the last, self-reliant and courageous. The words of the Weird Sisters ring true:

> Though his bark cannot be lost
> Yet it shall be tempest-toss'd.
>
> (I. iii. 24)

Each shattering report he receives with redoubled life-zest; and meets the fate marked out by the daylight consciousness of normal man for the nightmare reality of crime. Malcolm may talk of 'this dead butcher and his fiend-like queen' (V. vii. 68). We, who have felt the sickly poise over the abysmal deeps of evil, the hideous reality of the unreal, must couch our judgment in a different phrase.

The consciousness of nightmare is a consciousness of absolute evil, presenting a heightened awareness of positive significance which challenges the goldenest dreams of blissful sleep: it is positive, powerful, autonomous. Whether this be ultimate truth or not, it is what our mental experience knows: and to deny it is to deny the aristocracy of mind. The 'sickly weal' of Scotland is in the throes of this delirious dream, which, while it lasts, has every attribute of reality. Yet this evil is not a native of man's heart: it comes from without. The Weird Sisters are objectively conceived: they are not, as are the dagger and ghost, the subjective effect of evil in the protagonist's mind. They are, within the *Macbeth* universe, independent entities; and the fact that they instigate Macbeth directly and Lady Macbeth indirectly tends to assert the objectivity of evil. This, however, is purely a matter of poetic impact: the word 'absolute' seems a just interpretation of the imaginative reality, in so far as an immediate interpretation only is involved. Its implications in a wider system might not be satisfactory. But, whatever be the evil here, we can say that we understand something of the psychological state which gives these extraneous things of horror their reality and opportunity. And if we are loth to believe in such evil realities, potentially at least alive and powerful, we might call to mind the words of Lafeu in *All's Well that Ends Well*:

They say miracles are past; and we have our philosophical persons, to make modern and familiar things supernatural and causeless. Hence is it that we make trifles of terrors, ensconcing ourselves into seeming knowledge, when we should submit ourselves to an unknown fear.

(II. iii. 1)

A profound commentary on *Macbeth*. But, though the ultimate evil remain a mystery, analysis of the play indicates something of its relation to the mind and the actions of men.

Such analysis must be directed not to the story alone, but to the manifold correspondencies of imaginative quality extending throughout the whole play. The *Macbeth* vision is powerfully superlogical. Yet it is the work of interpretation to give some logical coherence to things imaginative. To do this, it is manifestly not enough to abstract the skeleton of logical sequence which is the story of the play: that is to ignore the very quality which justifies our anxious attention. Rather, relinquishing our horizontal sight of the naked rock-line which is the story, we should, from above, view the whole as panorama, spatialized: and then map out imaginative similarities and differences, hills and vales and streams. Only to such a view does *Macbeth* reveal the full riches of its meaning. Interpretation must thus first receive the quality of the play in the imagination, and then proceed to translate this whole experience into a new logic which will not be confined to those superficialities of cause and effect which we think to trace in our own lives and actions, and try to impose on the persons of literature. In this way, we shall know that *Macbeth* shows us an evil not to be accounted for in terms of 'will' and 'causality'; that it expresses its vision, not to a critical intellect, but to the responsive imagination; and working in terms not of 'character' or any ethical code, but of the abysmal deeps of a spirit-world untuned to human reality, withdraws the veil from the black streams which mill that consciousness of fear symbolized in actions of blood. *Macbeth* is the apocalypse of evil.

ADDITIONAL NOTE (1947)

In *Hamlet* and *Macbeth* supernatural figures are first objective; seen later by the hero alone; and, at the conclusion, clearly do not exist; as though some unrest in the outer universe has been satisfactorily projected and dispelled. Does this help to explain the gathering poetic force of Macbeth's speeches, culminating in the supreme pieces of Act V? Note, too, Macbeth's courage in successfully dismissing the air-drawn dagger and, twice, Banquo's Ghost. Macbeth shows throughout a positive drive. For a further development of this reading, see my *Christ and Nietzsche*.

For a study of the more obvious, countering, positives (e.g. effects of social health, nature, Banquo's descendants and child-images rising to the child-apparitions) see my essay 'The Milk of Concord' in *The Imperial Theme*; and also my analysis of the Apparition scene in *The Shakespearian Tempest*. For Hecate see *The Shakespearian Tempest*, App. B.

Notes

1. Cf. Colin Still's *Shakespeare's Mystery Play: A Study of The Tempest* (Cecil Palmer, 1921; revised and reissued as *The Timeless Theme*, Nicholson and Watson 1936). In his interpretation, the Court Party are related to the maze in ancient ritual; and in my

interpretation of *The Tempest*, I roughly equate the Antonio and Sebastian theme with *Macbeth*.

2. The 'evil' of *Macbeth* is symbolized in a nation's sickness. See v. ii. 27–9; v. iii. 49–56. The spiritual evil of *Macbeth* is directly related to the bodily evil of blood-destruction and sickness in the community.

3. Iago is not absolutely evil in this sense. He is too purely intellectual to antagonize our emotions powerfully.

4. Macbeth prays to night to 'cancel and tear to pieces that great bond which keeps me pale' (III. ii. 49). This is the bond of *nature*, that which binds man to the good which is in him the bond of daylight, reality, life. 'Cancel his bond of life' occurs in *Richard III*, IV. iv. 77.

173

14   C. G. Jung

Carl Gustav Jung (1875-1961) was a pupil and protégé of Freud, but broke
away from his master's teaching in 1913 to develop his own school of
analytical psychology. The main disagreement between the two men was
over the nature of libido, which Jung believed to be more than sexual.
Jung postulated the existence of a *collective* unconscious: i.e., a racial memory
inherited by all members of the human family and connecting modern man
with his primeval roots. The collective unconscious is manifested in the
recurrence of certain images, stories, figures, called 'archetypes'—the 'psychic
residua of numberless experiences of the same type'. Psychological maturity,
or 'individuation' entails the individual's recognition and acceptance of
archetypal elements of his own psyche, for which Jung coined the descriptive
terms 'shadow', 'persona', and 'anima' (a triad that might be compared to
Freud's Id, Ego, and Super-ego). Failure in this regard leads to a neurotic
projection of unacknowledged elements of the psyche on to others.

   Jungian psychology has been in many ways more congenial to the literary
mind than Freud's, though not necessarily more influential. Freud always
regarded himself as an empirical scientist, and science has been
seen as a threat to literary values from the Romantic period onwards. Jung,
much more sympathetic than Freud towards visionary, religious, and even
magical traditions, readily endorsed the claims of literature to embody
knowledge—knowledge of a kind particularly vital to alienated, secularized
modern man; and his assertion that 'it is his art that explains the artist, not
the insufficiencies and conflicts of his personal life' is obviously nearer in
spirit to Eliot's 'Tradition and the Individual Talent' than Freud's 'Creative
Writers and Day-Dreaming'. Jung's theory of the Collective Unconscious
tied in neatly with the anthropological study of primitive myth and ritual,
initiated in England by Sir James Frazer in *The Golden Bough* (1890-1915),
which exerted a strong influence upon modern writers such as T. S. Eliot
and D. H. Lawrence. Out of this fusion of literature, anthropology and
psychology evolved a kind of literary criticism in which the power and
significance of works of literature, or of national literatures, or of the whole
of literature, is explained in terms of the recurrence of certain archetypal
themes, images, and narrative patterns. Jung himself, however, was careful
to point out that this approach was more relevant to some kinds of literature
than to others, and that its emphases were not always relevant to literary
standards of value.

   'Psychology and Literature', first published in 1930, is reprinted here from

Modern Man in Search of a Soul (1933), translated by W. S. Dell and Cary F. Baynes.

CROSS REFERENCES: 3. Sigmund Freud
  15. Maud Bodkin
  31. Northrop Frye
  33. Leslie Fiedler
  40. Claude Lévi-Strauss

COMMENTARY: Joland Jacobi, *The Psychology of C. G. Jung*
  (New Haven, 1962)
  J. Baird, *Call Me Ishmael* (Baltimore, 1956)

Psychology and literature

It is obvious enough that psychology, being the study of psychic processes, can be brought to bear upon the study of literature, for the human psyche is the womb of all the sciences and arts. We may expect psychological research, on the one hand, to explain the formation of a work of art, and on the other to reveal the factors that make a person artistically creative. The psychologist is thus faced with two separate and distinct tasks, and must approach them in radically different ways.

In the case of the work of art we have to deal with a product of complicated psychic activities—but a product that is apparently intentional and consciously shaped. In the case of the artist we must deal with the psychic apparatus itself. In the first instance we must attempt the psychological analysis of a definitely circumscribed and concrete artistic achievement, while in the second we must analyse the living and creative human being as a unique personality. Although these two undertakings are closely related and even interdependent, neither of them can yield the explanations that are sought by the other. It is of course possible to draw inferences about the artist from the work of art, and vice versa, but these inferences are never conclusive. At best they are probable surmises or lucky guesses. A knowledge of Goethe's particular relation to his mother throws some light upon Faust's exclamation: 'The mothers—mothers—how very strange it sounds!' But it does not enable us to see how the attachment to his mother could produce the Faust drama itself, however unmistakably we sense in the man Goethe a deep connection between the two. Nor are we more successful in reasoning in the reverse direction. There is nothing in *The Ring of the Nibelungs* that would enable us to recognize or definitely infer the fact that Wagner occasionally liked to wear womanish clothes, though hidden connections exist between the heroic masculine world of the Nibelungs and a

175

certain pathological effeminacy in the man Wagner.

The present state of development of psychology does not allow us to establish those rigorous causal connections which we expect of a science. It is only in the realm of the psycho-physiological instincts and reflexes that we can confidently operate with the idea of causality. From the point where psychic life begins—that is, at a level of greater complexity—the psychologist must content himself with more or less widely ranging descriptions of happenings and with the vivid portrayal of the warp and weft of the mind in all its amazing intricacy. In doing this, he must refrain from designating any one psychic process, taken by itself, as 'necessary'. Were this not the state of affairs, and could the psychologist be relied upon to uncover the causal connections within a work of art and in the process of artistic creation, he would leave the study of art no ground to stand on and would reduce it to a special branch of his own science. The psychologist, to be sure, may never abandon his claim to investigate and establish causal relations in complicated psychic events. To do so would be to deny psychology the right to exist. Yet he can never make good this claim in the fullest sense, because the creative aspect of life which finds its clearest expression in art baffles all attempts at rational formulation. Any reaction to stimulus may be causally explained; but the creative act, which is the absolute antithesis of mere reaction, will for ever elude the human understanding. It can only be described in its manifestations; it can be obscurely sensed, but never wholly grasped. Psychology and the study of art will always have to turn to one another for help, and the one will not invalidate the other. It is an important principle of psychology that psychic events are derivable. It is a principle in the study of art that a psychic product is something in and for itself—whether the work of art or the artist himself is in question. Both principles are valid in spite of their relativity.

I. The work of art

There is a fundamental difference of approach between the psychologist's examination of a literary work, and that of the literary critic. What is of decisive importance and value for the latter may be quite irrelevant for the former. Literary products of highly dubious merit are often of the greatest interest to the psychologist. For instance, the so-called 'psychological novel' is by no means as rewarding for the psychologist as the literary-minded suppose. Considered as a whole, such a novel explains itself. It has done its own work of psychological interpretation, and the psychologist can at most criticize or enlarge upon this. The important question as to how a particular author came to write a particular novel is of course left unanswered, but I wish to reserve this general problem for the second part of my essay.

The novels which are most fruitful for the psychologist are those in which the author has not already given a psychological interpretation of his characters, and which therefore leave room for analysis and explanation, or even invite it by their mode of presentation. Good examples of this kind of writing are the

novels of Benoît[a], and English fiction in the manner of Rider Haggard, including the vein exploited by Conan Doyle which yields that most cherished article
of mass-production, the detective story. Melville's *Moby Dick*, which I consider
the greatest American novel, also comes within this class of writings. An
exciting narrative that is apparently quite devoid of psychological exposition
is just what interests the psychologist most of all. Such a tale is built upon a
groundwork of implicit psychological assumptions, and, in the measure that the
author is unconscious of them, they reveal themselves, pure and unalloyed, to
the critical discernment. In the psychological novel, on the other hand, the
author himself attempts to reshape his material so as to raise it from the level of
crude contingency to that of psychological exposition and illumination—a
procedure which all too often clouds the psychological significance of the work
or hides it from view. It is precisely to novels of this sort that the layman goes
for 'psychology'; while it is novels of the other kind that challenge the psychologist, for he alone can give them deeper meaning.

I have been speaking in terms of the novel, but I am dealing with a psychological fact which is not restricted to this particular form of literary art. We
meet with it in the works of the poets as well, and are confronted with it when
we compare the first and second parts of the Faust drama. The love-tragedy of
Gretchen explains itself; there is nothing that the psychologist can add to it
that the poet has not already said in better words. The second part, on the
other hand, calls for explanation. The prodigious richness of the imaginative
material has so overtaxed the poet's formative powers that nothing is self-
explanatory and every verse adds to the reader's need of an interpretation. The
two parts of *Faust* illustrate by way of extremes this psychological distinction
between works of literature.

In order to emphasize the distinction, I will call the one mode of artistic
creation *psychological*, and the other *visionary*. The psychological mode deals
with materials drawn from the realm of human consciousness—for instance,
with the lessons of life, with emotional shocks, the experience of passion and
the crises of human destiny in general—all of which go to make up the conscious life of man, and his feeling life in particular. This material is psychically
assimilated by the poet, raised from the commonplace to the level of poetic
experience, and given an expression which forces the reader to greater clarity
and depth of human insight by bringing fully into his consciousness what he
ordinarily evades and overlooks or senses only with a feeling of dull discomfort.
The poet's work is an interpretation and illumination of the contents of consciousness, of the ineluctable experiences of human life with its eternally recurrent sorrow and joy. He leaves nothing over for the psychologist, unless, indeed,
we expect the latter to expound the reasons for which Faust falls in love with
Gretchen, or which drive Gretchen to murder her child! Such themes go to
make up the lot of humankind; they repeat themselves millions of times and
are responsible for the monotony of the police-court and of the penal code. No
obscurity whatever surrounds them, for they fully explain themselves.

[a] Pierre Benoît (b. 1886), French author of novels of adventure, e.g. *Koenigsmark* (1918)
and *L'Atlantide* (1919).

Countless literary works belong to this class: the many novels dealing with love, the environment, the family, crime and society, as well as didactic poetry, the larger number of lyrics, and the drama, both tragic and comic. Whatever its particular form may be, the psychological work of art always takes its materials from the vast realm of conscious human experience—from the vivid foreground of life, we might say. I have called this mode of artistic creation psychological because in its activity it nowhere transcends the bounds of psychological intelligibility. Everything that it embraces—the experiences as well as its artistic expression—belongs to the realm of the understandable. Even the basic experiences themselves, though non-rational, have nothing strange about them; on the contrary, they are that which has been known from the beginning of time—passion and its fated outcome, man's subjection to the turns of destiny, eternal nature with its beauty and its horror.

The profound difference between the first and second parts of *Faust* marks the difference between the psychological and the visionary modes of artistic creation. The latter reverses all the conditions of the former. The experience that furnishes the material for artistic expression is no longer familiar. It is a strange something that derives its existence from the hinterland of man's mind—that suggests the abyss of time separating us from pre-human ages, or evokes a super-human world of contrasting light and darkness. It is a primordial experience which surpasses man's understanding, and to which his is therefore in danger of succumbing. The value and the force of the experience are given by its enormity. It arises from timeless depths; it is foreign and cold, many-sided, demonic, and grotesque. A grimly ridiculous sample of the eternal chaos—a *crimen laesae majestatis humanae* ['treason against humanity'], to use Nietzsche's words—it bursts asunder our human standards of value and of aesthetic form. The disturbing vision of monstrous and meaningless happenings that in every way exceed the grasp of human feeling and comprehension makes quite other demands upon the powers of the artist than do the experiences of the foreground of life. These never rend the curtain that veils the cosmos; they never transcend the bounds of the humanly possible, and for this reason are readily shaped to the demands of art, no matter how great a shock to the individual they may be. But the primordial experiences rend from top to bottom the curtain upon which is painted the picture of an ordered world, and allow a glimpse into the unfathomed abyss of what has not yet become. Is it a vision of other worlds, or of the obscuration of the spirit, or of the beginning of things before the age of man, or of the unborn generations of the future? We cannot say that it is any or none of these.

> Shaping—re-shaping—
> The eternal spirit's eternal pastime.[1]

We find such vision in *The Shepherd of Hermas*[a], in Dante, in the second part of *Faust*, in Nietzsche's Dionysian exuberance, in Wagner's *Nibelungen-*

---

[a] A treatise by Hermas, a Christian writer of the second century, so named because an angel, in the form of a shepherd, was supposed to have dictated part of its contents to the author.

ring in Spitteler's[a] *Olympischer Frühling*, in the poetry of William Blake, in the *Ipnerotomachia* of the Monk Francesco Colonna, and in Jacob Boehme's philosophic and poetic stammerings. In a more restricted and specific way, the primordial experience furnishes material for Rider Haggard in the fiction-cycle that turns upon *She*, and it does the same for Benoît, chiefly in *L'Atlantide*, for Kubin in *Die Andere Seite*, for Meyrink in *Das Grüne Gesicht*—a book whose importance we should not undervalue—for Goetz in *Das Reich ohne Raum*, and for Barlach in *Der Tote Tag*. This list might be greatly extended.

In dealing with the psychological mode of artistic creation, we never need ask ourselves what the material consists of or what it means. But this question forces itself upon us as soon as we come to the visionary mode of creation. We are astonished, taken aback, confused, put on our guard or even disgusted—and we demand commentaries and explanations. We are reminded in nothing of everyday, human life, but rather of dreams, night-time fears and the dark recesses of the mind that we sometimes sense with misgiving. The reading public for the most part repudiates this kind of writing—unless, indeed, it is coarsely sensational—and even the literary critic feels embarrassed by it. It is true that Dante and Wagner have smoothed the approach to it. The visionary experience is cloaked, in Dante's case, by the introduction of historical facts, and, in that of Wagner, by mythological events—so that history and mythology are sometimes taken to be the materials with which these poets worked. But with neither of them does the moving force and the deeper significance lie there. For both it is contained in the visionary experience. Rider Haggard, pardonably enough, is generally held to be a mere inventor of fiction. Yet even with him the story is primarily a means of giving expression to significant material. However much the tale may seem to overgrow the content, the latter outweighs the former in importance.

The obscurity as to the sources of the material in visionary creation is very strange, and the exact opposite of what we find in the psychological mode of creation. We are even led to suspect that this obscurity is not unintentional. We are naturally inclined to suppose—and Freudian psychology encourages us to do so—that some highly personal experience underlies this grotesque darkness. We hope thus to explain these strange glimpses of chaos and to understand why it sometimes seems as though the poet had intentionally concealed his basic experience from us. It is only a step from this way of looking at the matter to the statement that we are here dealing with a pathological and neurotic art— a step which is justified in so far as the material of the visionary creator shows certain traits that we find in the fantasies of the insane. The converse also is true; we often discover in the mental output of psychotic persons a wealth of meaning that we should expect rather from the works of a genius. The psychologist who follows Freud will of course be inclined to take the writings in question as a problem in pathology. On the assumption that an intimate, personal experience underlies what I call the 'primordial vision'—an experience, that is to say, which cannot be accepted by the conscious outlook—he will try to account for the curious images of the vision by calling them cover-figures and

[a] Carl Spitteler (1845–1924), Swiss epic poet, awarded the Nobel Prize for Literature in 1919.

by supposing that they represent an attempted concealment of the basic experience. This, according to his view, might be an experience in love which is morally or aesthetically incompatible with the personality as a whole or at least with certain fictions of the conscious mind. In order that the poet, through his ego, might repress this experience and make it unrecognizable (unconscious), the whole arsenal of a pathological fantasy was brought into action. Moreover, this attempt to replace reality by fiction, being unsatisfactory, must be repeated in a long series of creative embodiments. This would explain the proliferation of imaginative forms, all monstrous, demonic, grotesque, and perverse. On the one hand they are substitutes for the unacceptable experience, and on the other they help to conceal it.

Although a discussion of the poet's personality and psychic disposition belongs strictly to the second part of my essay, I cannot avoid taking up in the present connection this Freudian view of the visionary work of art. For one thing, it has aroused considerable attention. And then it is the only well-known attempt that has been made to give a 'scientific' explanation of the sources of the visionary material or to formulate a theory of the psychic processes that underlie this curious mode of artistic creation. I assume that my own view of the question is not well known or generally understood. With this preliminary remark, I will now try to present it briefly.

If we insist on deriving the vision from a personal experience, we must treat the former as something secondary—as a mere substitute for reality. The result is that we strip the vision of its primordial quality and take it as nothing but a symptom. The pregnant chaos then shrinks to the proportions of a psychic disturbance. With this account of the matter we feel reassured and turn again to our picture of a well-ordered cosmos. Since we are practical and reasonable, we do not expect the cosmos to be perfect; we accept these unavoidable imperfections which we call abnormalities and diseases, and we take it for granted that human nature is not exempt from them. The frightening revelation of abysses that defy the human understanding is dismissed as illusion, and the poet is regarded as a victim and perpetrator of deception. Even to the poet, his primordial experience was 'human—all too human', to such a degree that he could not face its meaning but had to conceal it from himself.

We shall do well, I think, to make fully explicit all the implications of that way of accounting for artistic creation which consists in reducing it to personal factors. We should see clearly where it leads. The truth is that it takes us away from the psychological study of the work of art, and confronts us with the psychic disposition of the poet himself. That the latter presents an important problem is not to be denied, but the work of art is something in its own right, and may not be conjured away. The question of the significance to the poet of his own creative work—of his regarding it as a trifle, as a screen, as a source of suffering or as an achievement—does not concern us at the moment, our task being to interpret the work of art psychologically. For this undertaking it is essential that we give serious consideration to the basic experience that underlies it—namely, to the vision. We must take it at least as seriously as we do the experiences that underlie the psychological mode of artistic creation, and no one doubts that they are both real and serious. It looks, indeed, as if the visionary experience were something quite apart from the ordinary lot of man, and for this reason we have difficulty in believing that it is real. It has about it an unfortunate suggestion of obscure metaphysics and of occultism, so that we feel called upon to intervene in the name of a well-intentioned reasonableness. Our conclusion is that it would be better not to take such things too seriously, lest the world revert again to a benighted superstition. We may, of course, have a predilection for the occult; but ordinarily we dismiss the visionary experience as the outcome of a rich fantasy or of a poetic mood—that is to say, as a kind of poetic licence psychologically understood. Certain of the poets encourage this interpretation in order to put a wholesome distance between themselves and their work. Spitteler, for example, stoutly maintained that it was one and the same whether the poet sang of an Olympian Spring or to the theme: 'May is here!' The truth is that poets are human beings, and that what a poet has to say about his work is often far from being the most illuminating word on the subject. What is required of us, then, is nothing less than to defend the importance of the visionary experience against the poet himself.

It cannot be denied that we catch the reverberations of an initial love-experience in *The Shepherd of Hermas*, in the *Divine Comedy*, and in the *Faust* drama —an experience which is completed and fulfilled by the vision. There is no ground for the assumption that the second part of *Faust* repudiates or conceals the normal, human experience of the first part, nor are we justified in supposing that Goethe was normal at the time when he wrote *Part I*, but in a neurotic state of mind when he composed *Part II*. *Hermas*, Dante and Goethe can be taken as three steps in a sequence covering nearly two thousand years of human development, and in each of them we find the personal love-episode not only connected with the weightier visionary experience, but frankly subordinated to it. On the strength of this evidence which is furnished by the work of art itself and which throws out of court the question of the poet's particular psychic disposition, we must admit that the vision represents a deeper and more impressive experience than human passion. In works of art of this nature—and we must never confuse them with the artist as a person—we cannot doubt that the vision is a genuine, primordial experience, regardless of what reason-mongers may say. The vision is not something derived or secondary, and it is not a symptom of something else. It is true symbolic expression—that is, the expression of something existent in its own right, but imperfectly known. The love-episode is a real experience really suffered, and the same statement applies to the vision. We need not try to determine whether the content of the vision is of a physical, psychic, or metaphysical nature. In itself it has psychic reality, and this is no less real than physical reality. Human passion falls within the sphere of conscious experience, while the subject of the vision lies beyond it. Through our feelings we experience the known, but our intuitions point to things that are unknown and hidden—that by their very nature are secret. If ever they become conscious, they are intentionally kept back and concealed, for which reason they have been regarded from earliest times as mysterious, uncanny and deceptive. They are hidden from the scrutiny of man, and he also hides himself from them out of *deisidaemonia* [fear of demons]. He protects himself with the shield of science and the armour of reason. His enlightenment is born of fear; in the daytime he believes in an ordered cosmos, and he tries to maintain this faith against the fear of chaos that besets him by night. What if there were some living force whose sphere of action lies beyond our world of every day? Are there human needs that are dangerous and unavoidable? Is there something more purposeful than electrons? Do we delude ourselves in thinking that we possess and command our own souls? And is that which science calls the 'psyche' not merely a question-mark arbitrarily confined within the skull, but rather a door that opens upon the human world from a world beyond, now and again allowing strange and unseizable potencies to act upon man and to remove him, as if upon the wings of the night, from the level of common humanity to that of a more than personal vocation? When we consider the visionary mode of artistic creation, it even seems as if the love-episode had served as a mere release—as if the personal experience were nothing but the prelude to the all-important 'divine comedy'.

It is not alone the creator of this kind of art who is in touch with the night-side of life, but the seers, prophets, leaders, and enlighteners also. However dark this nocturnal world may be, it is not wholly unfamiliar. Man has known of it from time immemorial—here, there, and everywhere; for primitive man today it is an unquestionable part of his picture of the cosmos. It is only we who have repudiated it because of our fear of superstition and metaphysics, and because we strive to construct a conscious world that is safe and manageable in that natural law holds in it the place of statute law in a commonwealth. Yet, even in our midst, the poet now and then catches sight of the figures that people the night-world—the spirits, demons, and gods. He knows that purposiveness out-reaching human ends is the life-giving secret for man; he has a presentiment of incomprehensible happenings in the pleroma. In short, he sees something of that psychic world that strikes terror into the savage and the barbarian.

From the very first beginnings of human society onward man's efforts to give his vague intimations a binding form have left their traces. Even in the Rhodesian cliff-drawings of the Old Stone Age there appears, side by side with the most amazingly life-like representations of animals, an abstract pattern—a double cross contained in a circle. This design has turned up in every cultural region, more or less, and we find it today not only in Christian churches, but in Tibetan monasteries as well. It is the so-called sun-wheel, and as it dates from a time when no one had thought of wheels as a mechanical device, it cannot have had its source in any experience of the external world. It is rather a symbol that stands for a psychic happening; it covers an experience of the inner world, and is no doubt as lifelike a representation as the famous rhinoceros with the tick-birds on its back. There has never been a primitive culture that did not possess a system of secret teaching, and in many cultures this system is highly developed. The men's councils and the totem-clans preserve this teaching about hidden things that lie apart from man's daytime existence —things which, from primeval times, have always constituted his most vital experiences. Knowledge about them is handed on to younger men in the rites of initiation. The mysteries of the Graeco-Roman world performed the same office, and the rich mythology of antiquity is a relic of such experiences in the earliest stages of human development.

It is therefore to be expected of the poet that he will resort to mythology in order to give his experience its most fitting expression. It would be a serious mistake to suppose that he works with materials received at second-hand. The primordial experience is the source of his creativeness; it cannot be fathomed, and therefore requires mythological imagery to give it form. In itself it offers no words or images, for it is a vision seen 'as in a glass, darkly'. It is merely a deep presentiment that strives to find expression. It is like a whirlwind that seizes everything within reach and, by carrying it aloft, assumes a visible shape. Since the particular expression can never exhaust the possibilities of the vision, but falls far short of it in richness of content, the poet must have at his disposal a huge store of materials if he is to communicate even a few of his intimations. What is more, he must resort to an imagery that is difficult to handle and full of contradictions in order to express the weird paradoxicality of his vision. Dante's presentiments are clothed in images that run the gamut of Heaven and Hell; Goethe must bring in the Blocksberg and the infernal regions of Greek antiquity; Wagner needs the whole body of Nordic myth; Nietzsche returns to the hieratic style and recreates the legendary seer of prehistoric times; Blake invents for himself indescribable figures, and Spitteler borrows old names for new creatures of the imagination. And no intermediate step is missing in the whole range from the ineffably sublime to the perversely grotesque.

Psychology can do nothing towards the elucidation of this colourful imagery except bring together materials for comparison and offer a terminology for its discussion. According to this terminology, that which appears in the vision is the collective unconscious. We mean by collective unconscious, a certain psychic disposition shaped by the forces of heredity; from it consciousness has developed. In the physical structure of the body we find traces of earlier stages of evolution, and we may expect the human psyche also to conform in its make-up to the law of phylogeny. It is a fact that in eclipses of consciousness—in dreams, narcotic states, and cases of insanity—there come to the surface psychic products or contents that show all the traits of primitive levels of psychic development. The images themselves are sometimes of such a primitive character that we might suppose them derived from ancient, esoteric teaching. Mythological themes clothed in modern dress also frequently appear. What is of particular importance for the study of literature in these manifestations of the collective unconscious is that they are compensatory to the conscious attitude. This is to say that they can bring a one-sided, abnormal, or dangerous state of consciousness into equilibrium in an apparently purposive way. In dreams we can see this process very clearly in its positive aspect. In cases of insanity the compensatory process is often perfectly obvious, but takes a negative form. There are persons, for instance, who have anxiously shut themselves off from all the world only to discover one day that their most intimate secrets are known and talked about by everyone.[2]

If we consider Goethe's *Faust*, and leave aside the possibility that it is compensatory to his own conscious attitude, the question that we must answer is this: In what relation does it stand to the conscious outlook of his time? Great poetry draws its strength from the life of mankind, and we completely miss its meaning if we try to derive it from personal factors. Whenever the collective unconscious becomes a living experience and is brought to bear upon the conscious outlook of an age, this event is a creative act which is of importance to everyone living in that age. A work of art is produced that contains what may truthfully be called a message to generations of men. So *Faust* touches something in the soul of every German. So also Dante's fame is immortal, while *The Shepherd of Hermas* just failed of inclusion in the New Testament canon. Every period has its bias, its particular prejudice and its psychic ailment. An epoch is like an individual; it has its own limitations of conscious outlook, and therefore requires a compensatory adjustment. This is effected by the collective unconscious in that a poet, a seer, or a leader allows himself to be guided by the unexpressed desire of his times and shows the way, by word or deed, to the attainment of that which everyone blindly craves and expects—whether this attainment results in good or evil, the healing of an epoch or its destruction.

It is always dangerous to speak of one's own times, because what is at stake in the present is too vast for comprehension. A few hints must therefore suffice. Francesco Colonna's book [*Hypnerotomachia Polyphili*] is cast in the form of a dream, and is the apotheosis of natural love taken as a human relation; without countenancing a wild indulgence of the senses, he leaves completely aside the Christian sacrament of marriage. The book was written in 1453. Rider Haggard, whose life coincides with the flowering-time of the Victorian era, takes up this subject and deals with it in his own way; he does not cast it in the form of a dream, but allows us to feel the tension of moral conflict. Goethe weaves the theme of Gretchen–Helen–Mater–Gloriosa like a red thread into the colourful tapestry of *Faust*. Nietzsche proclaims the death of God, and Spitteler transforms the waxing and waning of the gods into a myth of the seasons. Whatever his importance, each of these poets speaks with the voice of thousands and ten thousands, foretelling changes in the conscious outlook of his time.

II. The poet

Creativeness, like the freedom of the will, contains a secret. The psychologist can describe both these manifestations as processes, but he can find no solution of the philosophical problems they offer. Creative man is a riddle that we may try to answer in various ways, but always in vain, a truth that has not prevented modern psychology from turning now and again to the question of the artist and his art. Freud thought he had found a key in his procedure of deriving the work of art from the personal experiences of the artist.[3] It is true that certain possibilities lay in this direction, for it was conceivable that a work of art, no less than a neurosis, might be traced back to those knots in psychic life that we call the complexes. It was Freud's great discovery that neuroses have a causal origin in the psychic realm—that they take their rise from emotional states and from real or imagined childhood experiences. Certain of his followers, like Rank and Stekel, have taken up related lines of inquiry and have achieved important results. It is undeniable that the poet's psychic disposition permeates his work root and branch. Nor is there anything new in the statement that personal factors largely influence the poet's choice and use of his materials. Credit, however, must certainly be given to the Freudian school for showing how far-reaching this influence is and in what curious ways it comes to expression.

Freud takes the neurosis as a substitute for a direct means of gratification. He therefore regards it as something inappropriate—a mistake, a dodge, an excuse, a voluntary blindness. To him it is essentially a shortcoming that should never have been. Since a neurosis, to all appearances, is nothing but a disturbance that is all the more irritating because it is without sense or meaning, few people will venture to say a good word for it. And a work of art is brought into questionable proximity with the neurosis when it is taken as something which can be analysed in terms of the poet's repressions. In a sense it finds itself in good company, for religion and philosophy are regarded in the same light by Freudian psychology. No objection can be raised if it is admitted that this approach amounts to nothing more than the elucidation of those personal determinants without which a work of art is unthinkable. But should the claim be made that such an analysis accounts for the work of art itself, then a categorical denial is called for. The personal idiosyncrasies that creep into a work of art are not essential; in fact, the more we have to cope with these peculiarities, the less is it a question of art. What is essential in a work of art is that it should rise far above the realm of personal life and speak from the spirit and heart of the poet as man to the spirit and heart of mankind. The personal aspect is a limitation—and even a sin—in the realm of art. When a form of 'art' is primarily personal it deserves to be treated as if it were a neurosis. There may be some validity in the idea held by the Freudian school that artists without exception are narcissistic—by which is meant that they are undeveloped persons with infantile and auto-erotic traits. The statement is only valid, however, for the artist as a person, and has nothing to do with the man as an artist. In his capacity of artist he is neither auto-erotic, nor hetero-erotic, nor erotic in any sense. He is objective and impersonal—even inhuman—for as an artist he is his work, and not a human being.

Every creative person is a duality or a synthesis of contradictory aptitudes. On the one side he is a human being with a personal life, while on the other side he is an impersonal, creative process. Since as a human being he may be sound or morbid, we must look at his psychic make-up to find the determinants of his personality. But we can only understand him in his capacity of artist by looking at his creative achievement. We should make a sad mistake if we tried to explain the mode of life of an English gentleman, a Prussian officer, or a cardinal in terms of personal factors. The gentleman, the officer, and the cleric function as such in an impersonal role, and their psychic make-up is qualified by a peculiar objectivity. We must grant that the artist does not function in an official capacity—the very opposite is nearer the truth. He nevertheless resembles the types I have named in one respect, for the specifically artistic disposition involves an overweight of collective psychic life as against the personal. Art is a kind of innate drive that seizes a human being and makes him its instrument. The artist is not a person endowed with free will who seeks his own ends, but one who allows art to realize its purposes through him. As a human being he may have moods and a will and personal aims, but as an artist he is 'man' in a higher sense—he is 'collective man'—one who carries and shapes the unconscious, psychic life of mankind. To perform this difficult office it is sometimes necessary for him to sacrifice happiness and everything that makes life worth living for the ordinary human being.

All this being so, it is not strange that the artist is an especially interesting case for the psychologist who uses an analytical method. The artist's life cannot be otherwise than full of conflicts, for two forces are at war within him—on the one hand the common human longing for happiness, satisfaction, and security in life, and on the other a ruthless passion for creation which may go so far as to override every personal desire. The lives of artists are as a rule so highly unsatisfactory—not to say tragic—because of their inferiority on the human and personal side, and not because of a sinister dispensation. There are hardly any exceptions to the rule that a person must pay dearly for the divine gift of the creative fire. It is as though each of us were endowed at birth with a certain capital of energy. The strongest force in our make-up will seize and all but monopolize this energy, leaving so little over that nothing of value can come of it. In this way the creative force can drain the human impulses to such a degree that the personal ego must develop all sorts of bad qualities—ruthlessness, selfishness, and vanity (so-called 'auto-erotism')—and even every kind of vice, in order to maintain the spark of life and to keep itself from being wholly bereft. The auto-erotism of artists resembles that of illegitimate or neglected children who from their tenderest years must protect themselves from the destructive influence of people who have no love to give them—who develop bad qualities for that very purpose and later maintain an invincible egocentrism by remaining all their lives infantile and helpless or by actively offending against the moral code or the law. How can we doubt that it is his art that explains the artist, and not the insufficiencies and conflicts of his personal life? These are nothing but the regrettable results of the fact that he is an artist—that is to say, a man who from his very birth has been called to a greater task than the ordinary mortal. A special ability means a heavy expenditure of energy in a particular direction, with a consequent drain from some other side of life.

It makes no difference whether the poet knows that his work is begotten, grows, and matures with him, or whether he supposes that by taking thought he produces it out of the void. His opinion of the matter does not change the fact that his own work outgrows him as a child its mother. The creative process has feminine quality, and the creative work arises from unconscious depths—we might say, from the realm of the mothers. Whenever the creative force predominates, human life is ruled and moulded by the unconscious as against the active will, and the conscious ego is swept along on a subterranean current, being nothing more than a helpless observer of events. The work in process becomes the poet's fate and determines his psychic development. It is not Goethe who creates *Faust*, but *Faust* which creates Goethe. And what is *Faust* but a symbol? By this I do not mean an allegory that points to something all too familiar, but an expression that stands for something not clearly known and yet profoundly alive. Here it is something that lives in the soul of every German, and that Goethe has helped to bring to birth. Could we conceive of anyone but a German writing *Faust* or *Also sprach Zarathustra*? Both play upon something that reverberates in the German soul—a 'primordial image', as Jacob Burckhardt once called it—the figure of a physician or teacher of mankind. The archetypal image of the wise man, the saviour or redeemer, lies buried and dormant in man's unconscious since the dawn of culture; it is awakened whenever the times are out of joint and a human society is committed to a serious error. When people go astray they feel the need of a guide or teacher or even of the physician. These primordial images are numerous, but do not appear in the dreams of individuals or in works of art until they are called into being by the waywardness of the general outlook. When conscious life is characterized by one-sidedness and by a false attitude, then they are activated—one might say, 'instinctively'—and come to light in the dreams of individuals and the visions of artists and seers, thus restoring the psychic equilibrium of the epoch.

In this way the work of the poet comes to meet the spiritual need of the society in which he lives, and for this reason his work means more to him than his personal fate, whether he is aware of this or not. Being essentially the instrument for his work, he is subordinate to it, and we have no reason for expecting him to interpret it for us. He has done the best that in him lies in giving it form, and he must leave the interpretation to others and to the future. A great work of art is like a dream; for all its apparent obviousness it does not explain itself and is never unequivocal. A dream never says: 'You ought', or: 'This is the truth'. It presents an image in much the same way as nature allows a plant to grow, and we must draw our own conclusions. If a person has a nightmare, it means either that he is too much given to fear, or else that he is too exempt from it; and if he dreams of the old wise man it may mean that he is too pedagogical, as also that he stands in need of a teacher. In a subtle way both meanings come to the same thing, as we perceive when we are able to let the work of art act upon us as it acted upon the artist. To grasp its meaning, we must allow it to shape us as it once shaped him. Then we understand the nature of his experience. We see that he has drawn upon the healing and redeeming forces of the collective psyche that underlies consciousness with its isolation and its painful errors; that he has penetrated to that matrix of life in which all men are embedded, which imparts a common rhythm to all human existence, and allows the individual to communicate his feeling and his striving to mankind as a whole.

The secret of artistic creation and of the effectiveness of art is to be found in a return to the state of *participation mystique*—to that level of experience at which it is man who lives, and not the individual, and at which the weal or woe of the single human being does not count, but only human existence.

This is why every great work of art is objective and impersonal, but none the less profoundly moves us each and all. And this is also why the personal life of the poet cannot be held essential to his art—but at most a help or a hindrance to his creative task. He may go the way of a Philistine, a good citizen, a neurotic, a fool or a criminal. His personal career may be inevitable and interesting, but it does not explain the poet.

Notes

1. *Gestaltung, Umgestaltung,*
    Des ew'gen Sinnes ew'ge Unterhaultung (Goethe).
2. See my article: 'Mind and the Earth', in *Contributions to Analytical Psychology*, Kegan Paul, Trench, Trubner & Co., London, 1928.
3. See Freud's essays on Jensen's *Gradiva* and on Leonardo da Vinci.

15   Maud Bodkin

Maud Bodkin (1875-1967) published *Archetypal Patterns in Poetry: psychological studies of imagination* (Oxford) in 1934, but many years passed before this remarkable work received the recognition it deserved. Preparing his study of modern criticism, *The Armed Vision* (New York, 1948), Stanley Edgar Hyman was able to find only a few reviews and little discussion of Miss Bodkin's book in either England or America. Since then, *Archetypal Patterns in Poetry* has been acknowledged as a classic of modern criticism and a pioneering effort in the application of psycho-analytical ideas to literary criticism. The great influence on Maud Bodkin was Carl Jung (see above, pp. 174-88) with whom she studied for a while in Zurich in the 1920s, though like Jung himself she owed a good deal to Freud.

The task Maud Bodkin set herself is to explain the enduring emotive power of certain works of literature, such as *Hamlet, The Ancient Mariner*, and the *Divine Comedy*, by testing them for the presence of archetypal motifs which express the most profound and universal experiences and concerns of the human race. First, by introspection, she examines the pattern of associations a particular passage of verse evokes in herself; then she looks for a similar pattern in her text, in texts by other writers, and in religious mythology. The extract that follows, taken from a longer discussion of *The Ancient Mariner*, illustrates the method, which, like most critical methods, is theoretically vulnerable but often illuminating and persuasive in practice. A rather sharp comment on Livingston Lowes takes us to the heart of Maud Bodkin's position: Lowes is quoted as denying any 'possible symbolism of wish-fulfilment or conflict or what not' in Coleridge's poem, and Maud Bodkin remarks: 'He does not, apparently, conceive the possibility of conflicts or wish-fulfilments of a character so universal as to echo through poetry from age to age, and to leave in language traces that may, in some sense, be weighed and measured.'

Maud Bodkin taught for several years at a teachers' training college in Cambridge, but retired early to pursue her studies in literature, philosophy, and psychology. In later years her interest turned particularly to the bearing of the theory of archetypes upon religious life and thought. In 1951 she published *Studies of Type Images in Poetry, Religion and Philosophy*.

CROSS REFERENCES :   3. Sigmund Freud
6. T. S. Eliot ('Tradition and the Individual Talent')
14. C. G. Jung
31. Northrop Frye

COMMENTARY: Stanley Edgar Hyman, 'Maud Bodkin and Psychological Criticism' in The Armed Vision (New York, 1948)

[Archetypes in *The Ancient Mariner*]

In this section some study is to be made of the group of stanzas that constitute the climax of the poem's action—the stanzas of the fourth Part that lead up to the blessing of the water snakes, and those of the fifth Part that describe the immediate consequences of that impulse of love.

As before, I would invite the reader to examine his own response to this central passage, which I will not quote at length here, since the poem is so readily accessible. Certain further considerations may be put forward in regard to the attempt to study one's own response to poetry.

When a reader has succeeded in turning the flashlight of attention back upon a moment of vivid emotional apprehension of poetry, inquiring as to its content, the answer to that inquiry is often that nothing is to be discerned there but the words of the poem. Professor Valentine, in his experimental study of 'The Function of Images in the Appreciation of Poetry',[1] found that some of his students, who were quite capable of vivid imagery and accustomed to recognize it, reported that they understood and appreciated various poems, even some of descriptive character, with practically no imagery, other than of the words, present. One such observer noted that certain striking phrases made images 'stir in the depths', but for the most part appreciation took place 'as if by unconscious reference to experience'.[2] Several observers found that the attempt to observe imagery interfered with the enjoyment of the poem, through breaking 'the continuity of poetic experience'.[3] When attention is directed to imagery it seems that something more important is 'displaced'.

My own experience in regard to Coleridge's poem is that at the moment of completest appreciation no imagery, other than the words, is present. I am in some manner aware of a whole of far-reaching significance, concentrated like a force behind any particular stanza or line. It is as the tension of the apprehensive act slackens that I become aware of images, or references to particular past experiences. In speaking of a tissue of interrelated personal and literary reminiscence as found in connection with certain lines of poetry, I was describing what comes into awareness as the grasp of poetic apprehension loosens. Yet when thus discriminated, this material seems to be recognized as having contributed something to the preceding unified experience of meaning—as having operated in the manner of a 'fused' association.[4] The apprehension of the line 'Down dropt the wind...' would have been different for me if some other memory-complex had entered into it than just that one whose constituents I can partly identify as I suffer free associations to arise.[a]

'I cannot think it a personal peculiarity,' writes James Russell Lowell,[5] 'but a matter of universal experience, that more bits of Coleridge have imbedded themselves in my memory than of any other poet who delighted my youth—unless I should except the sonnets of Shakespeare'. This rather naïve confession may illustrate the point that unless we attempt, by the help of comparative psychological study, to measure and allow for our own 'personal equation' in criticism, we are all apt to feel as though our own personal responses were 'matters of universal experience'. It seems as though everyone must experience the grip upon emotion, the sense of penetrating significance, that certain poems or particular passages have for ourselves. Actually, diversity of temperament and of nurture bring it about that very different memory-complexes exert their selective influence in the case of different individuals. We learn that the lines that carry such haunting overtones for ourselves sound quite flatly to another, through the difference, or the lack, of the associations, 'imbedded in the memory' and fused with those particular phrases, images, and rhythms, which give them for us their special significance. Yet amidst the diversity, certain associations may still be reckoned upon as holding good for individuals of widely different nurture and temperament. Those just considered, for instance, of the ship becalmed, and of its homeward flight, would seem to have a universal, 'archetypal' character, amidst whatever minor difference temperament and experience may impose upon the individual response to the lines describing the dropt wind and sails, or the sweet blowing of the breeze.

I will begin the consideration of the stanzas to be examined in this section by some reference to the extremely interesting study which Professor Livingston Lowes has made of *The Ancient Mariner* and its sources, as revealing 'the imaginative energy ... at work'. Professor Lowes shows the relation of certain lines and phrases in the poem to passages in books that Coleridge had read, and thus gives us glimpses of the content of the poet's mind—'the surging chaos of

---

[a] A few pages earlier, Maud Bodkin has described an experimental attempt to identify the emotive power that certain lines of verse have for her by trying, introspectively, to recover the personal associations they evoke: 'When the line, "Down dropt the breeze, the sails dropped down," was used as a starting-point for associations, there came, as immediately linked with it, the lines of Rossetti, from *The Woodspurge*, with its brief characterization of the blankness of "perfect grief":

> The wind flapped loose, the wind was still
> Shaken out from tree and hill:
> I had walked on at the wind's will,—
> I sat now, for the wind was still.

This stanza, when thus recalled in experimenting with *The Ancient Mariner*, appeared to the writer not to have received conscious attention since the distant time when, as girls, she and her sisters were fascinated by Rossetti's poetry. Faint memories were recalled, from nearly the same period, of certain experiences in a little sailing-boat whose response to changes of the wind seemed strangely to magnify one's own awareness of them; also a memory of a remark offered, at that same period of youthful awakening to poetry, by a sister little given to literary confidences, who had noted how vividly the words of Rossetti described what one feels when sails, or other live-seeming things, relapsed to stillness at the falling of the wind.'

the unexpressed', he terms it, 'that suffuses and colours everything which flashes and struggles into utterance'.[6]

Lowes's work presents a striking contrast to that of Fausset,[a] referred to in the last section, in that Lowes, in his detailed study of this suffusing background, makes hardly any reference to emotional forces. He is anxious to keep to evidence which can 'be weighed and tested'; and, on that account perhaps, ventures to call upon the resources of psychology for little but, first, a machinery of associative links—in Coleridge's own phrase 'hooks and eyes of the memory'—equipping the images derived from books he had read; and, secondly, marshalling the flow of these 'hooked atoms', 'a controlling conscious energy' of 'imagination', 'directing intelligence', and 'driving will'.[7] An insight into more than this is implied in certain observations, but in his general theory Lowes seems to take no account of emotional forces as determining either the selection or the fashioning of the material of the poem. Such forces he appears to regard as necessarily personal, not to be discovered, as he says, after the lapse of a hundred and more years. In a note (p. 400) he emphatically repudiates any intention of dealing with the 'possible symbolism of wish-fulfilment or conflict or what not' that might be suspected to underlie the poem. He does not, apparently, conceive the possibility of conflicts or wish-fulfilments of a character so universal as to echo through poetry from age to age, and to leave in language traces that may, in some sense, 'be weighed and tested'.

If, then, we turn to Lowes's study for some suggestion as to what kind of memory-complex in the mind of Coleridge lay behind the lines in which he described the Mariner's despairing vigil on the stagnant tropic seas, we may learn where Coleridge, who at this time had never been to sea, became familiar with such things as he describes.

> The very deep did rot: O Christ!
> That ever this should be!
> Yea, slimy things did crawl with legs
> Upon the slimy sea.
>
> .   .   .   .   .
>
> The many men, so beautiful!
> And they all dead did lie:
> And a thousand thousand slimy things
> Lived on; and so did I.

and again:

> Beyond the shadow of the ship,
> I watched the water-snakes:
> They moved in tracks of shining white,
> And when they reared, the elfish light
> Fell off in hoary flakes.
>
> Within the shadow of the ship
> I watched their rich attire:
> Blue, glossy green, and velvet black,
> They coiled and swam; and every track
> Was a flash of golden fire.

[a] Hugh I'Anson Fausset, *Samuel Taylor Coleridge* (1926).

192

What 'surging chaos of the unexpressed' lay behind these slimy things, and rotting seas, and shining water-snakes?

Lowes tells us of descriptions Coleridge had read of many kinds of 'slime-fish'; of a description, in one of his 'best-loved folios', of 'partie-coloured snakes' seen by Hawkins when he was 'at the Asores many months becalmed' and his men 'could hardly draw a Bucket of Water, cleare of some corruption withall';[8] and again, of a description by Captain Cook of small sea animals swimming during a calm, when 'parts of the sea seemed covered with a kind of slime'—animals that 'emitted the brightest colours of the most precious gems', blue, or red, or green 'with a burnished gloss', and, in the dark, 'a faint appearance of glowing fire'.[9]

Lowes notes the 'hooks', or 'almost chemical affinities of common elements'—here of 'colour and calm and a corrupted sea'—which brought about fusion of the snakes of Hawkins and the animalculae of Cook, and other such memory-fragments—'fortuitously blending images'—in 'the deep well of unconscious cerebration'.[10] He notes, further, the vision and controlling will that imposes form upon the chaos. He has in view such form as appears, for example, in 'the exquisite structural balance' of the two stanzas quoted above, describing the snakes beyond and within the shadow—'stanzas which answer to each other, phrase upon phrase, like an antiphon' (p. 64).

In all this we have no explicit reference to that need for emotional expression which to Fausset, and to the present writer also, appears the supreme shaping force within the poem—and, as I would add, the force also in the mind of the reader, through which the poem is appreciated.

'Few passages,' says Lowes, 'which Coleridge ever read seem to have fecundated his imagination so amazingly as that 257th page of Cook's second volume, which described the "small sea animals swimming about" in "a kind of slime", with "a faint appearance of glowing fire"' (p. 90). Can we at all divine the reason for this powerful influence? Lowes helps us to see the reason—and discerns it himself, one fancies, more clearly—when he is thinking not in terms of psychology but of literary insight. He tells us that Coleridge when reading these descriptions was vigilantly seeking material for those Hymns to the Sun, Moon, and the Elements, which he planned but never executed. His mind was directed 'upon every accident of light, shade and colour through which the very expression on the face of sea, sky, earth, and their fiery exhalations might be seized and held' (p. 76). Lowes quotes the passage from Coleridge's earlier poem, *The Destiny of Nations*, which likens the 'glad noise' of Love's wings fluttering to the fresh breeze breaking up the—

> long and pestful calms
> With slimy shapes and miscreated life
> Poisoning the vast Pacific, . . .

We begin to see what kind of symbolic value the imagination of Coleridge, ever seeking a language for something within, would feel in those shapes, slimy and miscreate in the stagnant water, that yet glowed with gemlike colour and strange fire. Lowes asks, concerning Cook's description:

Would that strong suggestion of a windless sea glowing red in the night be likely to leave his imagination quite unstirred? In the great stanza which leads from the soft ascent of 'the moving Moon' to the luminous shapes whose blue and glossy green derived from those same animalculae, the redness of the protozoa burns ominous in the very sea which before had burnt with their green, and blue, and white:

> Her beams bemocked the sultry main,
> Like April hoar-frost spread;
> But where the ship's huge shadow lay,
> The charmed water burnt alway
> A *still and awful red.*

There is, I suspect, no magic in the poem more potent than this blending of images through which the glowing redness of animalculae once seen in the Pacific has imbued with sombre mystery that still and boding sea (p. 89).

The reader, looking back from this stanza to the suggestion in Cook's page of a windless sea glowing red in the night, may guess from his own response to Coleridge's line what was the emotional symbolism of Cook's description for the imagination of the poet. Here, as always, it is through our sense of the emotional forces stirring in the experience communicated to ourselves that we can discern something of what the forces were that first gripped the significant aspects in the material to the poet's hand, and then held and fashioned this into perfect expressiveness.

I will now attempt, focusing upon that 'great stanza' with its contrast of white moonlight and red shadow, to give something of what I find to be the experience communicated.

In following the description of the Mariner's vigil upon the stagnant sea, it is not till I come to this stanza that I recognize an image detaching itself spontaneously and strongly from the synthetic grasp of the poem's meaning. I live in the Mariner's anguish of repulsion—from the rotting deck where lay the dead, and rotting sea and slimy creatures—with no discernible image at all, other than the voice speaking with inflections of despair, and the faint organic changes that go with such inflections—unless, of course, I demand an image. When I did that on one occasion, there appeared an image of a crowd of people struggling for a bus at a particular London street corner. For a moment I thought the numerical suggestion in the 'thousand thousand slimy things' had broken right away from its context; but then, catching the atmosphere of my street-corner image, I recognized the mood of shrinking disgust that had operated in calling up the picture.

With the transition from the Mariner's utter despair to his yearning vision of the moon in its soft journeying through the sky, there comes a stirring of images which, however, do not emerge spontaneously from out the magic of the charged verse; but when I come to the lines that lead from the white moonlight to the 'huge shadow' of the ship where the water burns red, the emotional stress upon that colour-word has become so intense that an image breaks out from it of a red that burns downward through shadow, as into an abyss. Words, Maupassant has said, have a soul as well as a sense—a soul that a poet may reveal in the word by his placing of it. 'Il faut trouver cette âme qui apparaît au contact d'autres mots....'[11] ['One must find that soul which appears at the contact of other words. ...'] The word 'red' has a soul of terror that has come to it through the history of the race. Dante helped to fashion that soul in the terrible lines that, for one who meets them, even in translation, at the moment of his youth, leave the word 'red' never again quite the same as before Dante touched it:

> ...the city that is named of Dis draws nigh,...
> ...'Master, already I discern its mosques, distinctly there within
> the valley, red as if they had come out of fire.'
> And to me he said: 'The eternal fire, which causes them to glow
> within, shows them red, as thou seest, in this low Hell.'

It is—for me, at least—the same soul that is evoked from the word 'red' in Coleridge's stanza and in Dante's lines; and thus—to my feeling—it is as though the Mariner, his deliverance just begun through the power of the moon's beauty, for the moment falls again to Hell in the red shadow of the ship.

I am not sure how far such an influence as this I recognize of Dante upon the word and image of red, in the stanza of Coleridge, would be accepted by Mr T. S. Eliot as an illustration of what he says concerning a racial or traditional mind, a 'mind of Europe' which to the poet is more important than his private mind. This larger mind, he says, changes, but 'this change is a development which abandons nothing *en route*, which does not superannuate either Shakespeare, or Homer, or the rock drawings of the Magdalenian draughtsman'.[12] One aspect of his 'impersonal theory of poetry is the relation of the poem' to the 'living whole of all the poetry that has ever been written'. Such a relation can clearly not be realized in any individual mind. The 'mind of Europe' is a conception that has meaning only in reference to something approached and realized in different degrees in different minds of individuals, especially through their communication one with another. Through the mystery of communication—operating between the minds of Dante, and Coleridge, and their readers—I, in some degree, realize the presence of a mind in myself beyond my private mind, and it is through this mind that the image of red colour, that had already, we surmise, symbolic value to the artist of the Magdalenian rock drawings, has transmitted its ever-growing significance to Dante and to Coleridge, and on to readers at the present moment.[13]

Let us pass now to the storm—the roaring wind and streaming rain and lightning, by which the stagnant calm and drought is broken, when the Mariner's impulse of love has undone the curse that held both him and Nature transfixed.

> The upper air burst into life!
> And a hundred fire-flags sheen,
> To and fro they were hurried about!
> And to and fro, and in and out,
> The wan stars danced between.

And the coming wind did roar more loud
And the sails did sigh like sedge;
And the rain poured down from one black cloud;
The Moon was at its edge.

The thick black cloud was cleft, and still
The Moon was at its side:
Like waters shot from some high crag,
The lightning fell with never a jag,
A river steep and wide.

Lowes has traced passages in the Voyages known to have been studied by Coleridge, which describe tropical or sub-tropical storms—for instance, a description from Bartram, of torrential rain that obscured every object, 'excepting the continuous streams or rivers of lightning pouring from the clouds'.[14] Such lightning, he remarks, Coleridge had pretty certainly never seen in Devon or Somerset, but he had seen it 'in those ocular spectra of his which kept pace with his reading'.

Lowes traces to passages read by Coleridge not only the lightning, but the more obscure references to 'fire flags' and the 'wan stars' seen through the auroral lights; and we may gratefully acknowledge the interest of the glimpses his researches give of the transmutation into poetry of scattered fragments of traveller's tales. Yet here again, it seems to me we must add to what he tells us insight from our own experience into the emotional forces that are the agents of the transmutation. I would ask the reader who has dwelt upon these storm stanzas of Coleridge, and felt that in his mind they take, as it were, a place shaped and prepared for them, how would he account for such sense of familiarity. In my own mind the streaming rain and lightning of the poem is interrelated with storms felt and seen in dreams. Fading impressions of such rain and lightning recalled on waking have clothed themselves in the flowing words of the poem and become fused with these.

Is it again the racial mind or inheritance, active within the individual sensibility, whether of Coleridge or of his reader, that both assimilates the descriptions of tropical storms, and sees in a heightened pattern those storms of our own country that 'startle', and overpower, and 'send the soul abroad'? It was, I think, of a Sussex storm, 'marching in a dark breastplate and in skirts' of rain, with thunders about it', that Belloc wrote:

No man seeing this creature as it moved solemn and panoplied could have mistaken the memory or the knowledge that stirred within him at the sight. This was that great master, that great friend, that great enemy, that great idol (for it has been all of these things), which, since we have tilled the earth, we have watched, we have welcomed, we have combated, we have unfortunately worshipped.[15]

The thought of the storm image, and the place it has held in the mind, not of Europe only but of a wider, older culture, takes us back to that order of conception, illustrated already in reference to wind and spirit, wherein the two aspects we now distinguish, of outer sense impression and inly felt process, appear undifferentiated. Dr Jung[16] cites from the Vedic Hymns[a] lines where prayers, or ritual fire-boring, are said to lead forth, or release, the flowing streams of Rita; and shows that the ancient idea of Rita represented, in undifferentiated fashion, at once the cycle of nature of which rain and fire are offspring, and also the ritually ordered processes of the inner life, in which pent-up energy can be discharged by fitting ceremonial.

The storm which for the experiencing mind appears not as differentiated physical object but as a phase of its own life, is naturally thought of as let loose by prayer, when prayer transforms the whole current and atmosphere of the inner life. In Coleridge's poem the relief of rain follows the relaxing of the inner tension by the act of love and prayer, as naturally and inevitably as do sleep and healing dreams.

> The silly buckets on the deck,
> That had so long remained,
> I dreamt that they were filled with dew;
> And when I awoke, it rained.
>
> My lips were wet, my throat was cold,
> My garments all were dank;
> Sure I had drunken in my dreams,
> And still my body drank.

We accept the sequence with such feeling as that with which we accept the narration in terms of recognized metaphor, of a psychical sequence of emotional energy-tension and release—as when, for example, we are told by St Augustine in his *Confessions* of the long anxiety and suspense that preceded his conversion, and how, when reflection had 'gathered up and heaped together all my misery in the sight of my heart, a mighty storm arose, bringing a mighty shower of tears'.

Another such psychical sequence, corresponding to that in the story of the Ancient Mariner, may be found set forth in a wealth of detail in the poetry of Emile Verhaeren,[b] as analysed by Charles Baudouin. In Verhaeren's poems the intention of giving expression to states of soul-sickness and recovery, experienced by the poet, is present as it is not in Coleridge's poem. We have metaphor, as against latent emotional symbolism; but a sequence of similar character finds expression, in part through the same imagery.

Thus Baudouin notes that in the poems expressing the 'tortured and tragical phase' of Verhaeren's life there is an obsession by images of reflection in water, especially in foul and stagnant water—the water of meres and marshes. He quotes as an example the lines from *Les rues* in *Les soirs*:

> Une lune souffrante et pâle s'entrevoit
> Et se mire aux égouts, où des clartés pourrissent.
>
> (A suffering and wan moon is glimpsed,
> And is mirrored in the foul ditches wherein radiances rot.)[17]

---

[a] Part of the ancient sacred literature of India.
[b] Belgian poet (1855–1916).

197

And again:

> La lune et tout le grand ciel d'or
> Tombent et roulent vers leur mort....
> Elle le fausse et le salit,
> L'attire à elle au fond du lit
> D'algues et de goëmons flasques.[18]
>
> (The moon and all the great golden firmament
> Fall, and roll towards their death....
> Death violates it and defiles it,
> Drags it to her right down into the bed
> Of algae and of flaccid seaweed.)

The common element in the imagery—of stagnation and corruption, where even radiance is foul—appears in these passages, but with the contrast that in Verhaeren's lines the moon image is caught into the downward movement towards decay and death; while, in the stanzas of the crisis in *The Ancient Mariner*, the movement towards deliverance begins with the vision of the moon's beauty, pure and aloof from the despair of the watcher below.

The shrinking, before the turning-point was reached, in horror and disgust from every surrounding object—the eyelids closed till the balls like pulses beat —in Coleridge's poem, are paralleled by images which Baudouin quotes from the writings of Verhaeren in the crisis of his 'introverted' suffering: for example, the fantasy of self-inflicted blindness, 'the extirpation of the eyes in front of the mirror', in a prose fragment of this period. 'Kindred ideas,' says Baudouin '(a failure of the impetus towards the real world, debility, and withdrawal into the self) are expressed by images of "broken" and "flaccid" things:

> Cassés les mâts d'orgueil, flasques les grandes voiles.[19]
>
> (Broken the masts of pride, flaccid the great sails.)'

And after the crisis, when Verhaeren has turned once more towards the world of men and human interests, the same images stand to him for the sufferings he has left behind:

> Je suis celui des pourritures grandioses
> Qui s'en revient du pays mou des morts.[20]
>
> (I am the one who comes back from the land of widespread corruption,
> The one who comes back from the flaccid realm of the dead.)

In speaking of Verhaeren's deliverance from the state of morbid introversion, Baudouin quotes the saying of Goethe: 'I said to myself that to deliver my mind from this state of gloom in which it was torturing itself, the essential was to turn my attention towards nature, and to share unreservedly in the life of the outer world'. Verhaeren's later poems express vehemently the need to share in the life of the outer world. Baudouin notes how Verhaeren has placed the words 'Admire one another' as an epigraph at the beginning of *La multiple splendeur*; and how he 'carries out his own precept', writing:

> Pour vivre clair, ferme et juste,
> Avec mon cœur, j'admire tout
> Ce qui vibre, travaille et bout
> Dans la tendresse humaine et sur la terre auguste.[21]

> (In order to live serenely and firmly and justly
> With my heart, I admire everything
> Which vibrates and ferments and boils
> In human tenderness and on the august earth.)

and again:

> Si nous admirons vraiment les uns les autres...

> Nous apportons, *ivres du monde et de nous-mêmes*,
> Des cœurs d'hommes nouveaux dans le vieil univers.[22]

> (If we really admire one another...

> We bring, *drunken with the world and with ourselves*,
> The hearts of new men into the ancient universe.)

Thus the sequence of Verhaeren's poems presents the same movement of the spirit that is communicated by Coleridge's story of the paralysing spell undone by the impulse of admiration and love, and of the reawakening of energies within and without.

The wind, that roars in the distance, or breathes magically upon the Mariner as the ship flies homeward, is celebrated in Verhaeren's later verse, with its emotional symbolism made explicit.

> Si j'aime, admire et chante avec folie,
> Le vent,...
> C'est qu'il grandit mon être entier et c'est qu'avant
> De s'infiltrer, par mes poumons et par mes pores
> Jusques au sang dont vit mon corps,
> Avec sa force rude ou sa douceur profonde,
> Immensément, il a étreint le monde.[23]

> (If I love, admire, and fervently sing the praises
> Of the wind,...
> It is because the wind enlarges my whole being, and because,
> Before permeating, through my lungs and through my pores,
> The very blood, which is the life of my body,
> It has with its rugged strength or its consummate tenderness,
> Clasped the world in its titanic embrace.)

From the symbolism made explicit in Verhaeren's poems with the help of Baudouin's commentary, it is but a further step to the generalized exposition of the same psychological sequence by Dr Jung—still in the metaphorical language so inevitable when one speaks of the inner life. In his discussion of Progression and Regression, as 'fundamental concepts of the libido-theory', Jung describes progression as 'the daily advance of the process of psychological adaptation',[24] which, at certain times, fails. Then 'the vital feeling' disappears; there is a damming up of energy—of libido. At such times, in the patients he has studied, neurotic symptoms are observed, and repressed contents appear, of inferior and unadapted character. 'Slime out of the depths' he calls such contents—using the symbolism we have just been studying—but slime that contains not only 'objectionable animal tendencies, but also germs of new possibilities of life'.²⁵

Such an ambivalent character in the slimy things, glowing and miscreate, Coleridge seems to have felt through the travellers' tales, and wrought into expressiveness in his magical picture of the creatures of the calm, which the Mariner first despised and then accepted with love, to his own salvation. Before 'a renewal of life' can come about, Jung urges, there must be an acceptance of the possibilities that lie in the unconscious contents 'activated through regression ... and disfigured by the slime of the deep'.²⁶

The principle which he thus expounds Jung recognizes as reflected in the myth of 'the night journey under the sea'²⁷—the myth of the entrance of the hero into the body of a whale or dragon, and his journey therein towards the East. It is not my intention to examine here in any detail the theory of Dr Jung. I do not wish to venture beyond the range of experience open to the student of literature. But, within that domain, I would select, for comparison with *The Ancient Mariner*, the most familiar example of the night-journey myth—that in the second chapter of the Book of Jonah.

What is perhaps most interesting here is to note the coming together, from different levels of thought, of the wonder-tale and the psalm of spiritual confession, and to observe how easily their rather incongruous coalescence has been accepted by readers content to feel rather than reflect:

> The waters compassed me about, even to the soul: the depth closed me round about, the weeds were wrapped about my head.
>
> I went down to the bottoms of the mountains: the earth with her bars was about me for ever: yet hast thou brought up my life from corruption, O Lord my God.

Here again is the imagery of corruption associated with the descent; imagery too of one transfixed, held motionless as was the Mariner. The weedy bed at the roots of the mountains is little compatible with any literal entry into, and casting forth from, a monster's belly, but the sensibility that seizes the expressive value of the myth is not disturbed by discrepancies discoverable in an attempted matter-of-fact rendering. The earth with her bars, the engulfing seas—like a monster's jaws yawning to receive the victim—or the breathless calm when sea and sky lie like a load on eye and heart, can all alike be made the language of the emotional forces that crave sensuous form for their expression; and, in relation to each symbol, the pattern of deliverance is wrought out in appropriate detail, more or less elaborated, and, as it were, more or less opaque, according as imagination plunges, more or less deeply, and more blindly or with more conscious insight, into its plastic material.

Notes

1. *Brit. J. of Psychol.* xiv, part 2.
2. Ibid., p. 181.
3. Ibid., pp. 183–4.
4. Cf. the use of this term by Professor Valentine and Mr Bullough, as referring to associations 'intimate, unavoidable, permanent'. Op. cit., p. 177.
5. *Complete Writings of James Russell Lowell,* vol. vii, p. 88.
6. *The Road to Xanadu,* by John Livingston Lowes (Constable, 1927), p. 13.
7. Op. cit. See especially pp. 44, 304–5.
8. Quoted op. cit., p. 49.
9. Quoted ibid., p. 46.
10. Op. cit., pp. 56, 58, 65.
11. Quoted by Barfield, who discusses this latent 'soul' in words, *Poetic Diction,* p. 113.
12. *Selected Essays, 1917–32* (Faber & Faber), p. 16.
13. My argument implies an influence of Dante upon Coleridge for which evidence cannot be given—though Lowes, examining the evidence for Dante's influence upon another passage, surmises that, even at the time of writing *The Ancient Mariner,* Coleridge knew Dante, not only in Boyd's translation, but penetrating, perhaps through the help of the Wordsworths, to the true sense of the Italian. By whatever channels it may have passed I think the influence of such lines as those quoted from the *Inferno* would have reached a poet who so far approached the ideal of the European mind as did Coleridge.

In regard to the question of the significance of red, as 'a surrogate for blood', to the artists of the Stone Age, I would refer to the writings of Elliot Smith and others.
14. Quoted op. cit., p. 186.
15. 'The Storm' from *This and That,* Hilaire Belloc.
16. See his discussion of 'the reconciling symbol as the principle of dynamic regulation'. *Psychological Types* (Kegan Paul, 1923), pp. 257 et seq.
17. *Psycho-analysis and Aesthetics* by C. Baudouin, trans. by Eden and Cedar Paul (Allen & Unwin, 1924), p. 115.
18. From *La baie,* in *Les vignes de ma muraille,* quoted ibid., pp. 115–16.
19. From *Les malades,* in *Les soirs,* quoted op. cit., p. 119.
20. From *Celui du rien,* in *Les apparus dans mes chemins,* quoted ibid., p. 162.
21. From *Autour de ma maison,* in *La multiple splendeur,* quoted ibid., p. 258.
22. From *La ferveur,* in *La multiple splendeur,* quoted op. cit., p. 285.
23. From *A la gloire du vent,* in *La multiple splendeur,* quoted ibid., p. 166.
24. *Contributions to Analytical Psychology,* p. 34.
25. Ibid., pp. 39–40.
26. Ibid., p. 38.
27. Ibid., p. 40.

16 Christopher Caudwell

'Christopher Caudwell' was the pen-name of Christopher St John Sprigg (1907-37), a man of remarkable gifts and character who was tragically deprived of the opportunity to fulfil his great promise. Although his background was comfortably middle-class, Caudwell left school at fifteen. He subsequently showed an extraordinary ability to acquire knowledge and skills in many different areas—journalism, aviation, engineering, pure science, and literature. He wrote thrillers and textbooks on aviation as well as poetry and criticism. In 1934 he became interested in Marxism, and in the following year joined the Communist party and settled in a working-class district of London. It was at this time that he wrote *Illusion and Reality: a study of the sources of poetry* (1937), the first and still in many ways the best work of literary theory by an English Marxist critic. Late in 1936 he left England to drive an ambulance to Spain, where he subsequently enlisted on the Republican side in the Civil War. He was killed in action in February 1937. He left behind him many manuscripts, some of which were published posthumously, notably *Studies in a Dying Culture* (1938), essays on Shaw, T. E. Lawrence, D. H. Lawrence, and H. G. Wells. Another work of criticism, *Romance and Realism: A Study in English Bourgeois Literature* was published in 1971.

Illusion and Reality, from which the following extract is taken, falls into two parts. The first is a Marxist account of the historical evolution of poetry from its putative roots in primitive societies, when poetry was a communal art directly linked to production in harvest rituals and the like, to the early, middle, and late bourgeois epochs in which the poet is fatally compromised by the contradictions and injustices of the social and economic system that supports him. The chapter reprinted below (originally entitled 'English Poets II. The Industrial Revolution') is taken from this part of the book. The latter half of *Illusion and Reality* is more concerned with theoretical problems in literary aesthetics, and displays Caudwell's capacity for original thought in these areas as well as his assimilation of the three hundred and fifty books in his bibliography. As Sartre was to do much later in *What is Literature?* (see below, pp. 371-85), Caudwell made a stark distinction between poetry (conceived in terms of modern symbolist poetics) and prose fiction, which is seen as much more directly mimetic of experience and therefore more amenable to Marxist analysis. But unlike Sartre, Caudwell was clearly deeply attached to poetry of the symbolist sort, and this creates an interesting tension in his critical theory, not entirely resolved by the resonant sentence with which he ends his book: 'Thus art is one of the conditions of man's realization of himself, and in its turn one of the realities of man.'

CROSS REFERENCES: 19. Edmund Wilson
28. Jean-Paul Sartre
35. Georg Lukács

COMMENTARY: Stanley Edgar Hyman, 'Christopher Caudwell and
Marxist Criticism' in *The Armed Vision* (New York,
1948)
Samuel Hynes, Introduction to C. Caudwell's *Romance
and Realism: A Study in English Bourgeois Literature*
(1971)

[English poets at the time of the Industrial Revolution]

I

The bourgeois illusion now passes to another stage,[a] that of the Industrial
Revolution, the 'explosive' stage of capitalism. Now the growth of capitalism
transforms all idyllic patriarchal relations—including that of the poet to the
class whose aspirations he voices—into 'callous' cash-nexus.

Of course this does not make the poet regard himself as a shopkeeper and his
poems as cheeses. To suppose this is to overlook the compensatory and dynamic
nature of the connection between illusion and reality. In fact it has the opposite
effect. It has the effect of making the poet increasingly regard himself as a man
removed from society, as an individualist realizing only the instincts of his
heart and not responsible to society's demands—whether expressed in the duties
of a citizen, a fearer of God, or a faithful servant of Mammon. At the same time
his poems come increasingly to seem worthy ends-in-themselves.

This is the final explosive movement of the bourgeois contradiction. The
bourgeois illusion has already swayed from antithesis to antithesis, but as a
result of this last final movement it can only pass, like a whirling piece of metal
thrown off by an exploding flywheel, out of the orbit of the bourgeois categories
of thought altogether.

As a result of the compromise of the eighteenth century, beneath the network
of safeguards and protections which was characteristic of the era of manufacture, bourgeois economy developed to the stage where by the use of the machine,
the steam-engine, and the power-loom it acquired an enormous power of self-
expansion. At the same time the 'factory' broke away from the farm of which

---

[a] Caudwell has been discussing the eighteenth century, when 'bourgeois poetry expresses
the spirit of the petty manufacturing bourgeoisie, beneath the wings of the big landowning capitalists'.

203

it was the handicraft adjunct and challenged it as a mightier and opposed force.

On the one hand organized labour inside the factory progressively increased, on the other hand the individual anarchy of the external market also increased. On the one hand there was an increasingly public form of production, on the other hand an increasingly private form of appropriation. At the one pole was an increasingly landless and toolless proletariat, at the other an increasingly wealthy bourgeoisie. This self-contradiction in capitalist economy provided the terrific momentum of the Industrial Revolution.

The bourgeoisie, who had found its own revolutionary-puritan ideals of liberty 'extreme', and returned to the compromise of mercantilist good taste that seemed eternal reason, now again found its heart had been right, and reason wrong.

This revealed itself first of all as a cleavage between the former landed aristocracy and the industrial bourgeoisie, expressing the rise of the factory to predominance over the farm. The landed aristocracy, and the restrictions it demanded for its growth, was now confronted by industrial capital and its demands. Capital had found an inexhaustible self-expansive power in machinery and outside sources of raw material. So far from any of the earlier forms being of value to it, they were so many restraints. The cost of labour power could safely be left to fall to its real value, for the machine by its competition creates the proletariat it requires to serve it. The real value of labour power in turn depends on the real value of wheat, which is less in the colonies and America than in England because there it embodies less socially necessary labour. The Corn Laws, which safeguard the agricultural capitalist, therefore hamper the industrialist. Their interests—reconciled during the period of wage-labour shortage—are now opposed. All the forms and restraints that oppose this free expansion of the industrial bourgeoisie must be shattered. To accomplish this shattering, the bourgeoisie called to its standard all other classes, precisely as in the time of the Puritan Revolution. It claimed to speak for the people as against the oppressors. It demanded Reform and the Repeal of the Corn Laws. It attacked the Church, either as Puritan (Methodist) or as open sceptic. It attacked all laws as restrictive of equality. It advanced the conception of the naturally good man, born free but everywhere in chains. Such revolts against existing systems of laws, canons, forms, and traditions always appear as a revolt of the heart against reason, a revolt of feeling and the sentiments against sterile formalism and the tyranny of the past. Marlowe, Shelley, Lawrence, and Dali[a] have a certain parallelism here; each expresses this revolt in a manner appropriate to the period.

We cannot understand this final movement of poetry unless we understand that at every step the bourgeois is revolutionary in that he is revolutionizing his own basis. But he revolutionizes it only to make it consistently more bourgeois. In the same way each important bourgeois poet is revolutionary, but he expresses the very movement which brings more violently into the open the contradiction against which his revolutionary poetry is a protest. They are 'mirror revolutionaries'. They attempt to reach an object in a mirror, only to

[a] Salvador Dali, the Spanish surrealist painter.

move farther away from the real object. And what can that object be but the common object of man as producer and as poet—freedom? The poignancy of their tragedy and pessimism derives its bite from this perpetual recession of the desired object as they advance to grasp it. 'La Belle Dame Sans Merci' has them all in thrall. They wake up on the cold hillside.[a]

II

Blake, Byron, Keats, Wordsworth, and Shelley express this ideological revolution, each in their different ways, as a Romantic Revolution.

Byron is an aristocrat—but he is one who is conscious of the break-up of his class as a force, and the necessity to go over to the bourgeoisie. Hence his mixture of cynicism and romanticism.

These deserters are in moments of revolution always useful and always dangerous allies. Too often their desertion of their class and their attachment to another, is not so much a 'comprehension of the historical movement as a whole' as a revolt against the cramping circumstances imposed on them by their own class's dissolution, and in a mood of egoistic anarchy they seize upon the aspirations of the other class as a weapon in their private battle. They are always individualistic, romantic figures with a strong element of the *poseur*. They will the destruction of their own class but not the rise of the other, and this rise, when it becomes evident and demands that they change their merely destructive enmity to the dying class to a constructive loyalty to the new, may, in act if not in word, throw them back into the arms of the enemy. They become counter-revolutionaries. Danton and Trotsky are examples of this type. Byron's death at Missolonghi occurred before any such complete development, but it is significant that he was prepared to fight for liberty in Greece rather than England. In him the revolt of the heart against the reason appears as the revolt of the hero against circumstances, against morals, against all 'pettiness' and convention. This Byronism is very symptomatic, and it is also symptomatic that in Byron it goes with a complete selfishness and carelessness for the sensibilities of others. Milton's Satan has taken on a new guise, one far less noble, petulant even.

Byron is most successful as a mocker—as a Don Juan. On the one hand to be cynical, to mock at the farce of human existence, on the other hand to be sentimental, and complain of the way in which the existing society has tortured one's magnificent capabilities—that is the essence of Byronism. It represents the demoralization in the ranks of the aristocracy as much as a rebellion against the aristocracy. These men are therefore always full of death-thoughts: the death-thoughts of Fascism fighting in the last ditch, the death-thought of Jacobites; the glorification of a heroic death justifying a more dubious life. The same secret death-wishes are shown by these aristocrats if they turn revolutionary, performing deeds of outstanding individual heroism—sometimes unnecessary, sometimes useful, but always romantic and singlehanded. They cannot

---

[a] The allusion is to Keats's ballad, 'La Belle Dame Sans Merci'.

rise beyond the conception of the desperate hero of revolution.

Shelley, however, expresses a far more genuinely dynamic force. He speaks for the bourgeoisie who, at this stage of history, feel themselves the dynamic force of society and therefore voice demands not merely for themselves but for the whole of suffering humanity. It seems to them that if only *they* could realize themselves, that is, bring into being the conditions necessary for their own freedom, this would of itself ensure the freedom of all. Shelley believes that he speaks for all men, for all sufferers, calls them all to a brighter future. The bourgeois trammelled by the restraints of the era of mercantilism is Prometheus, bringer of fire, fit symbol of the machine-wielding capitalist. Free him and the world is free. A Godwinist[a], Shelley believed that man is naturally good —institutions debase him. Shelley is the most revolutionary of the bourgeois poets of this era because *Prometheus Unbound* is not an excursion into the past, but a revolutionary programme for the present. It tallies with Shelley's own intimate participation in the bourgeois–democratic revolutionary movement of his day.

Although Shelley is an atheist, he is not a materialist. He is an idealist. His vocabulary is, for the first time, consciously idealist—that is, full of words like 'brightness', 'truth', 'beauty', 'soul', 'aether', 'wings', 'fainting', 'panting', which stir a whole world of indistinct emotions. Such complexes, because of their numerous emotional associations, appear to make the word indicate one distinct concrete entity, although in fact no such entity exists, but each word denotes a variety of different concepts.

This idealism is a reflection of the revolutionary bourgeois belief that, once the existing social relations that hamper a human being are shattered, the 'natural man will be realized'—his feelings, his emotions, his aspirations, will all be immediately bodied forth as material realities. Shelley does not see that these shattered social relations can only give place to the social relations of the class strong enough to shatter them and that in any case these feelings, aspirations, and emotions are the product of the social relations in which he exists and that to realize them a social act is necessary, which in turn has its effect upon a man's feelings, aspirations, and emotions.

The bourgeois illusion is, in the sphere of poetry, a revolt. In Wordsworth the revolt takes the form of a return to the natural man, just as it does in Shelley. Wordsworth, like Shelley profoundly influenced by French Rousseauism, seeks freedom, beauty—all that is not now in man because of his social relations —in 'Nature'. The French Revolution now intervenes. The bourgeois demand for freedom has now a regressive tinge. It no longer looks forward to freedom by revolt but by return to the natural man.

Wordsworth's 'Nature' is of course a Nature freed of wild beasts and danger by aeons of human work, a Nature in which the poet, enjoying a comfortable income, lives on the products of industrialism even while he enjoys the natural scene 'unspoilt' by industrialism. The very division of industrial capitalism

a William Godwin (1756–1836) was a novelist and political philosopher of anarchical views. His daughter Mary was Shelley's second wife.

from agricultural capitalism has now separated the country from the town. The division of labour involved in industrialism has made it possible for sufficient surplus produce to exist to maintain a poet in austere idleness in Cumberland. But to see the relation between the two, to see that the culture, gift of language and leisure which distinguish a Nature poet from a dumb subhuman are the product of economic activity—to see this would be to pierce the bourgeois illusion and expose the artificiality of 'Nature' poetry. Such poetry can only arise at a time when man by industrialism has mastered Nature—but not himself.

Wordsworth therefore is a pessimist. Unlike Shelley, he revolts regressively —but still in a bourgeois way—by demanding freedom from social relations, the specific social relations of industrialism, while still retaining the products, the freedom, which these relations alone make possible.

With this goes a theory that 'natural', i.e. *conversational* language is better, and therefore more poetic than 'artificial', i.e. *literary* language. He does not see that both are equally artificial—i.e. directed to a social end—and equally natural, i.e. products of man's struggle with Nature. They merely represent different spheres and stages of that struggle and are good or bad not in themselves, but in relation to this struggle. Under the spell of this theory some of Wordsworth's worst poetry is written.

Wordsworth's form of the bourgeois illusion has some kinship with Milton's. Both exalt the natural man, one in the form of Puritan 'Spirit', the other in the more sophisticated form of pantheistic 'Nature'. One appeals to the primal Adam as proof of man's natural innocence, the other to the primal child. In the one case original sin, in the other social relations, account for the fall from grace. Both therefore are at their best when consciously noble and elevated. Milton, reacting against primitive accumulation and its deification of naïve princely desire and will, does not, however—as Wordsworth does—glorify the wild element in man, the natural primitive. Hence he is saved from a technical theory that conduces to 'sinking' in poetry.

Keats is the first great poet to feel the strain of the poet's position in this stage of the bourgeois illusion, as producer for the free market. Wordsworth has a small income; Shelley, although always in want, belongs to a rich family and his want is due simply to carelessness, generosity, and the impracticability which is often the reaction of certain temperaments to a wealthy home. But Keats comes of a small bourgeois family and is always pestered by money problems. The sale of his poems is an important consideration to him.

For Keats therefore freedom does not lie, like Wordsworth, in a return to Nature; his returns to Nature were always accompanied by the uncomfortable worry, where was the money coming from? It could not lie, as with Shelley, in a release from the social relations of this world, for mere formal liberty would still leave the individual with the problem of earning a living. Keats's greater knowledge of bourgeois reality therefore led him to a position which was to set the keynote for future bourgeois poetry: 'revolution' as a flight *from* reality. Keats is the banner-bearer of the Romantic Revival. The poet now escapes upon the 'rapid wings of poesy' to a world of romance, beauty, and sensuous life separate from the poor, harsh, real world of everyday life, which it sweetens and by its own loveliness silently condemns.

This world is the shadowy enchanted world built by Lamia for her lover or by the Moon for Endymion. It is the golden-gated upper world of Hyperion, the word-painted lands of the nightingale, of the Grecian urn, of Baiae's isle. This other world is defiantly counterpoised to the real world.

> 'Beauty is truth, truth beauty'—that is all
> Ye know on earth, and all ye need to know.
> [*Ode on a Grecian Urn*]

And always it is threatened by stern reality in the shape of sages, rival powers or the drab forces of everyday. Isabella's world of love is shattered by the two money-grubbing brothers. Even the wild loveliness of *The Eve of St Agnes* is a mere interlude between storm and storm, a coloured dream snatched from the heart of cold and darkness—the last stanzas proclaim the triumph of decay. 'La Belle Dame Sans Merci' gives her knight only a brief delight before he wakes. The flowering basil sprouts from the rotting head of Isabella's lover, and is watered with her tears.

> The fancy cannot cheat so well
> As she is famed to do, deceiving elf! ...
> Was it a vision or a waking dream?
> Fled is that music—do I wake or sleep?
> [*Ode to a Nightingale*]

Like Cortez, Keats gazes entranced at the New World of poetry, Chapman's realms of gold, summoned into being to redress the balance of the old, but however much voyaged in, it is still only a world of fancy.

A new vocabulary emerges with Keats, the dominating vocabulary of future poetry. Not Wordsworth's—because the appeal is not to the unspoilt simplicity of the country. Not Shelley's—because the appeal is not to the 'ideas' that float on the surface of real material life and can be skimmed off like froth. The country is a part of the real material world, and the froth of these metaphysical worlds is too unsubstantial and therefore is always a reminder of the real world which generated it. A world must be constructed which is more real precisely because it is more unreal and has sufficient inner stiffness to confront the real world with the self-confidence of a successful conjuring trick.

Instead of taking, like Wordsworth and Shelley, what is regarded as the most natural, spiritual, or beautiful part of the real world, a new world is built up out of words, as by a mosaic artist, and these words therefore must have solidity and reality. The Keatsian vocabulary is full of words with a hard material texture, like tesserae, but it is an 'artificial' texture—all crimson, scented, archaic, stiff, jewelled, and anti-contemporary. It is as vivid as missal painting. Increasingly this world is set in the world of feudalism, but it is not a feudal world. It is a bourgeois world—the world of the Gothic cathedrals and all the growing life and vigour of the bourgeois class under late feudalism. Here too poetic revolution has a strong regressive character, just as it had with Wordsworth, but had not with the most genuinely revolutionary poet, Shelley.

The bourgeois, with each fresh demand he makes for individualism, free competition, absence of social relations, and more equality, only brings to birth greater organization, more complex social relations, higher degrees of trustification and combination, more inequality. Yet each of these contradictory movements revolutionizes his basis and creates new productive forces. In the same way the bourgeois revolution, expressed in the poetry of Shelley, Wordsworth, and Keats, although it is contradictory in its movement, yet brings into being vast new technical resources for poetry and revolutionizes the whole apparatus of the art.

The basic movement is in many ways parallel to the movement of primitive accumulation which gave rise to Elizabethan poetry. Hence there was at this era among poets a revival of interest in Shakespeare and the Elizabethans. The insurgent outburst of the genetic individuality which is expressed in Elizabethan poetry had a collective guise, because it was focused on that collective figure, the prince. In romantic poetry it has a more artificial air as an expression of the sentiments and the emotions of the individual figure, the 'independent' bourgeois. Poetry has separated itself from the story, the heart from the intellect, the individual from society; all is more artificial, differentiated, and complex.

The poet now begins to show the marks of commodity-production. We shall analyse this still further when, as in a later date, it sets the whole key for poetry. At present the most important sign is Keats's statement, that he could write for ever, burning his poems afterwards. The poem has become already an end in itself.

But it is more important to note the air of tragedy that from now on looms over all bourgeois poetry that is worth the adjective 'great'. Poetry has become pessimistic and self-lacerating. Byron, Keats, and Shelley die young. And though it is usual to regret that they died with their best works unwritten, the examples of Wordsworth, Swinburne, and Tennyson make fairly clear that this is not the case, that the personal tragedy of their deaths, which in the case of Shelley and Byron at least seemed sought, prevented the tragedy of the bourgeois illusion working itself out impersonally in their poetry. For the contradiction which secures the movement of capitalism was now unfolding so rapidly that it exposed itself in the lifetime of a poet and always in the same way. The ardent hopes, the aspirations, the faiths of the poet's youth melted or else were repeated in the face of a changed reality with a stiffness and sterility that betrayed the lack of conviction and made them a mocking caricature of their youthful sincerity. True, all men grow old and lose their youthful hopes—but not in this way. A middle-aged Sophocles can speak with searching maturity of the tragedy of his life, and at eighty he writes a drama that reflects the open-eyed serenity of wisdom's child grown aged. But mature bourgeois poets are not capable of tragedy or resignation, only of a dull repetition of the faiths of youth—or silence. The movement of history betrays the contradiction for what it is, and yet forces the bourgeois to cling to it. From that moment the lie has entered his soul, and by shutting his eyes to the consciousness of necessity, he has delivered his soul to slavery.

In the French Revolution the bourgeoisie, in the name of liberty, equality, and fraternity, revolted against obsolete social relations. They claimed, like Shelley, to speak in the name of all mankind; but then arose, at first indistinctly, later with continually increasing clarity, the claim of the proletariat also demanding liberty, equality, and fraternity. But to grant these to the proletariat means the abolition of the very conditions which secure the existence of the bourgeois class and the exploitation of the proletariat. Therefore the movement for freedom, which at first speaks largely in the voice of mankind, is always halted at a stage where the bourgeoisie must betray its ideal structure expressed in poetry, forget that it claimed to speak for humanity, and crush the class whose like demands are irreconcilable with its own existence. Once robbed of its mass support, the revolting bourgeoisie can always be beaten back a stage by the forces of reaction. True, these forces have learned 'a sharp lesson' and do not proceed too far against the bourgeoisie who have shown their power. Both ally themselves against the proletariat. Ensues an equilibrium when the bourgeoisie have betrayed their talk of freedom, and compromised their ideal structure, only themselves to have lost part of the ideal fruit of their struggle to the more reactionary forces—feudal forces, if the struggle is against feudalism, landowning, and big financial forces, if the struggle is between agricultural and industrial capitalism.

Such a movement was that from Robespierre to the Directory and the anti-Jacobin movement which as a result of the French Revolution swept Europe everywhere. The whole of the nineteenth century is a record of the same betrayal, which in the life of the poets expresses itself as a betrayal of youthful idealism. 1830, 1848 and, finally, 1871 are the dates which make all bourgeois poets now tread the path of Wordsworth, whose revolutionary fire, as the result of the proletarian content of the final stage of the French Revolution, was suddenly chilled and gave place to common sense, respectability, and piety.

It was Keats who wrote:

> 'None can usurp this height', the shade returned,
> 'Save those to whom the misery of the world
> Is misery and will not let them rest.'
>
> [*The Fall of Hyperion*]

The doom of bourgeois poets in this epoch is precisely that the misery of the world, including their own special misery, will not let them rest, and yet the temper of the time forces them to support the class which causes it. The proletarian revolution has not yet advanced to a stage where 'some bourgeois ideologists, comprehending the historical movement as a whole', can ally themselves with it and really speak for suffering humanity and for a class which is the majority now and the whole world of men tomorrow. They speak only for a class that is creating the world of tomorrow willy-nilly, and at each step draws back and betrays its instinctive aspirations because of its conscious knowledge that this world of tomorrow it is creating, *cannot include itself.*

17　L. C. Knights

Lionel Charles Knights (b. 1906) has been closely associated with the
Cambridge school of criticism led by Dr F. R. Leavis, and was co-editor of the
journal *Scrutiny* which, founded by Dr Leavis and his wife Q. D. Leavis,
exercised very great influence on the teaching and criticism of English
literature both during and after its life-span (1932-53). The *Scrutiny* group
of critics endorsed the revolution in literary taste and critical method initiated
by T. S. Eliot and I. A. Richards, but added to it a particularly rigorous
concern with 'standards'. In their perspective, literary criticism should be
concerned above all with evaluation, with discriminating the truly great
from the ephemeral, the minor, the secondrate; and traditional literary
scholarship, with its tolerance and relativism in judgment, was the great
enemy. Hence the characteristic *Scrutiny* essay was concerned with
'revaluation' (the title of one of Dr Leavis's books). Underlying this often
combative concern with standards was the belief that literature and the study
of it preserved certain life-enhancing values once located in the 'organic
community' of pre-industrial England, but now almost wholly submerged
by mass culture.

L. C. Knights is probably the least polemical and doctrinaire of the
Scrutiny school of critics, but their assumptions and attitudes are clearly
discernible in his 1937 essay, 'Restoration Comedy : the Reality and the Myth'.
His stance is characteristically one of challenge to vested scholarly interests,
and in such comments as, 'the disintegration of the old cultural unity has
plainly resulted in impoverishment [of dramatic speech]', one may clearly
discern a version of the theory of English cultural history developed in
Q. D. Leavis's *Fiction and the Reading Public* (1932) and by F. R. Leavis and
Denys Thompson in *Culture and Environment* (1933). L. C. Knights's first
published work, *Drama and Society in the Age of Jonson*, was indeed directly
concerned with the social context of literature, using a loosely Marxist
framework for the analysis of society. In *Explorations* (1946), a collection of
essays, the main focus of attention is upon the literary texts, and social and
historical comment is subordinated to close analysis.

After teaching at Manchester University, L. C. Knights held Chairs of
English at Sheffield and Bristol Universities. Since 1965 he has been King
Edward VII Professor of English at Cambridge University and Fellow of
Queen's College. His more recent publications, in which a gradual disengage-
ment from the *Scrutiny* 'line' may be observed, include *Some Shakespearian
Themes* (1959) and *Further Explorations* (1965). 'Restoration Comedy : The

Reality and the Myth' was originally published in *Scrutiny* in 1937, and is reprinted here from *Explorations*.

CROSS REFERENCES: 21. D. W. Harding
46. George Steiner

COMMENTARY: F. W. Bateson, 'Second Thoughts: L. C. Knights Restoration Comedy' in *Essays in Critical Dissent* (1972).

Restoration comedy: the reality and the myth

I

Henry James—whose 'social comedy' may be allowed to provide a standard of maturity—once remarked that he found Congreve 'insufferable',[1] and perhaps the first thing to say of Restoration drama—tragedy as well as comedy—is that the bulk of it is insufferably dull. There are long stretches of boredom to be found in the lower ranges of Elizabethan drama, but there is nothing comparable to the unmitigated fatigue that awaits the reader of *Love in a Tub, Sir Martin Mar-all, Mr Limberham, The Relapse,* or *The Mourning Bride.* And who returns to Dryden's heroic plays with renewed zest? The superiority of the common run of plays in the first period to that of the second is, at all events, a commonplace. It should be equally commonplace that the strength of the Elizabethan drama lies partly in the kind and scope—the quality and variety —of the interests that the playwrights were able to enlist, partly in the idiom that they had at their command: the drama drew on a vigorous non-dramatic literature, and literature in general was in close relation with non-literary interests and a rich common language. That is not the whole story, but it is an important part of it, and it seems profitable, in a discussion of Restoration comedy, to keep these facts in mind for comparison. Ever since Collier published *A Short View of the Profaneness and Immorality of the English Stage* [1698] opponents of Restoration comedy have conducted their case almost entirely in moral terms, and it has been easy for recent critics, rightly discarding Lamb's obvious subterfuge[a], to turn the moral argument upside down, to find freedom of manners where Macaulay found licentiousness. 'Morals' are, in the long run, decidedly relevant—but only in the long run: literary criticism has prior claims. If, to start with, we try to see the comedy of manners in relation to its contemporary non-dramatic literature—to take its bearings in the

---

[a] The allusion is to Charles Lamb's essay 'On the Artificial Comedy of the Last Century', in *Essays of Elia* (1820–25), in which he defended his enjoyment of Restoration Comedy on the grounds that it had nothing to do with real life—hence its ostensible immorality was harmless.

general culture of the time—we may at least make possible a free and critical approach.

During the forty years that followed the Restoration, English literature, English culture, was 'upper-class' to an extent that it had never been before, and was not, after Addison, to be again. 'Now if they ask me,' said Dryden, 'whence it is that our conversation is so much refined? I must freely and without flattery, ascribe it to the court', and his insistence, as a writer, on 'the benefit of converse' with his courtly patrons was not merely dedicatory fulsomeness; the influence of the current conception of 'the gentleman' is shown plainly enough by the urbane ease of his critical prefaces; and Dryden's non-dramatic prose is fairly representative of the new age.[2]

It is this that explains why, if one comes to Restoration literature after some familiarity with the Elizabethans, the first impression made by the language is likely to be a sense of what has been lost; the disintegration of the old cultural unity has plainly resulted in impoverishment. The speech of the educated is now remote from the speech of the people (Bunyan's huge sales were, until the eighteenth century, outside 'the circumference of wit'), and idiomatic vigour and evocative power seem to have gone out of the literary medium. But there was gain as well as loss. The common mode of Restoration prose—for there is now a common mode, a norm—was not evolved merely in the interests of good form and polite intercourse; it had behind it a more serious pressure. When, in 1667, Sprat attacked 'this vicious abundance of phrase ... this volubility of tongue, which makes so great a noise in the world', he had in mind the needs of scientific inquiry and rational discussion. 'They have therefore,' he said of the Royal Society,

> been most rigorous in putting in execution the only remedy that can be found for this *extravagance*, and that has been a constant resolution to reject all amplifications, digressions, and swellings of style; to return back to the primitive purity and shortness, when men delivered so many *things* almost in an equal number of *words*. They have exacted from all their members a close, naked, natural way of speaking, positive expressions, clear senses, a native easiness, bringing all things as near the mathematical plainness as they can.[3]

For the first time the English language was made—and to some extent made consciously—an instrument for rational dissection.

> When once the aversion to bear uneasiness taketh place in a man's mind, it doth so check all the passions, that they are dampt into a kind of indifference; they grow faint and languishing, and come to be subordinate to that fundamental maxim, of not purchasing any thing at the price of a difficulty. This made that he had as little eagerness to oblige, as he had to hurt men; the motive of his giving bounties was rather to make men less uneasy to him, than more easy to themselves; and yet no ill-nature all this while. He would slide from an asking face, and could guess very well. It was throwing a man off from his shoulders, that leaned upon them with his whole weight; so that the party was not gladder to receive, than he was to give.

This is from Halifax's *Character of Charles II*, and the even tone, the sinuous ease of movement and the clarity of the analysis mark the passage as unmistakably post-Restoration. Halifax, of course, is in some ways an unusually handsome representative of his age; he is racy (the apt adjective is supplied by his editor, H. C. Foxcroft) as well as polite. But the achievement represented by his style was far from being a merely individual achievement. The shrewd and subtle portrait of Charles II is unlike anything that had appeared in English before his time, and it could only have appeared when it did.

Now an upper-class culture that produced [Dryden's] *Absalom and Achitophel*, [Halifax's] *The Character of a Trimmer*, Dryden's critical prefaces and Locke's *Second Treatise of Government*, may have been limited, but it was not altogether decadent. If the drama is inferior it is not because it represents—by Elizabethan standards—a limited culture, but because it represents contemporary culture so inadequately; it has no significant relation with the best thought of the time. Heroic tragedy is decadent because it is factitious; it substitutes violent emotionalism for emotion, the purple patch for poetry, and its rhetoric, unlike Elizabethan dramatic rhetoric, has no connection with the congenial non-dramatic modes of the age; it is artificial in a completely damaging sense, *and by contemporary standards*. If we look for an early illustration of the bad mid-eighteenth-century conception of poetry as something applied from the outside[4] we find it in Dryden's verse plays, where he adopts canons of style that he would not have dreamed of applying—apart from his Odes—in his non-dramatic verse. Tragedy, he said, 'is naturally pompous and magnificent'. Nothing in English literature is more surprising—if we stop to consider—than the complete discrepancy between the sinewy ease of Dryden's satires and the stiff opaqueness of his dramatic verse; and 'the lofty style', since it cannot modulate, is always coming down with a bump.

> I'm pleased and pained, since first her eyes I saw,
> As I were stung with some tarantula.
> Arms, and the dusty field, I less admire,
> And soften strangely in some new desire;
> Honour burns in me not so fiercely bright,
> But pales as fires when mastered by the light:
> Even while I speak and look, I change yet more,
> And now am nothing that I was before.
> I'm numbed, and fixed, and scarce my eyeballs move;
> I fear it is the lethargy of love![5]

It is only in the easy strength of occasional lines ('A good, luxurious, palatable faith') that we hear his natural voice. In the plays as a whole—each made up of a succession of 'great' moments and heroic postures—the 'nature' that is 'wrought up to a higher pitch'[6] bears little resemblance to the Nature that was to figure so largely in the Augustan code.

This, or a similar account, would probably be accepted by all critics of the Restoration heroic play. What is not commonly recognized (it is, at all events, not said) is that the comedy of manners exhibits a parallel attenuation and enfeeblement of what the age, taken as a whole, had to offer. I am not, for the moment, referring to the moral or social code expressed. The observation to start from is that the prose in which Restoration comedy is written—select

214

which dramatist you like—is poor and inexpressive in comparison with the staple non-dramatic prose.

Congreve is usually accepted as the most brilliant stylist of the five or six comic dramatists who count. But place beside the extract quoted from Halifax a passage or two from *Love for Love* or *The Way of the World* (it makes no difference whether the speaker is Scandal or Mirabell), and Congreve's style shows as nerveless in the comparison:

> A mender of reputations! ay, just as he is a keeper of secrets, another virtue that he sets up for in the same manner. For the rogue will speak aloud in the posture of a whisper; and deny a woman's name, while he gives you the marks of her person: he will forswear receiving a letter from her, and at the same time show you her hand in the superscription; and yet perhaps he has counterfeited the hand too, and sworn to a truth; but he hopes not to be believed; and refuses the reputation of a lady's favour, as a doctor says No to a bishopric, only that it may be granted him. In short, he is a public professor of secrecy, and makes proclamation that he holds private intelligence.

> A. To give t' other his due, he has something of good nature, and does not always want wit.

> B. Not always: but as often as his memory fails him, and his common-place of comparisons. He is a fool with a good memory, and some few scraps of other folks' wit. He is one whose conversation can never be approved, yet it is now and then to be endured. He has indeed one good quality, he is not exceptious; for he so passionately affects the reputation of understanding raillery, that he will construe an affront into a jest; and call downright rudeness and ill language, satire and fire.

This reminds me of Arnold's definition of Macaulayese, 'the external characteristic being a hard metallic movement with nothing of the soft play of life, and the internal characteristic being a perpetual semblance of hitting the right nail on the head without the reality'. Both construction and movement are so far from being expressive *of* anything in particular that the main function of some words is, it seems, to complete an antithesis or to display a riddling wit.[7] The verbal pattern appears at times to be completely unrelated to a mode of perceiving. The passages quoted have an air of preening themselves on their acute discriminations, but the antitheses are mechanical, and the pattern is monotonously repeated: 'She has beauty enough to make any man think she has wit; and complaisance enough not to contradict him who should tell her so'—the common form soon loses the sting of surprise. Burnet can write in an antithetical style which also penetrates:

> And tho' he desired to become absolute, and to overturn both our religion and our laws, yet he would neither run the risk, nor give himself the trouble, which so great a design required. He had an appearance of gentleness in his outward deportment: but he seemed to have no bowels nor tenderness in his nature: and in the end of his life he became cruel.[8]

The nearest approach to subtlety that Congreve's style allows is represented by such things as this:

FAINALL. You are a gallant man, Mirabell; and though you may have cruelty enough not to satisfy a lady's longing, you have too much generosity not to be tender of her honour. Yet you speak with an indifference which seems to be affected, and confesses you are conscious of a negligence.

MIRABELL. You pursue the argument with a distrust that seems to be un-affected, and confess you are conscious of a concern for which the lady is more indebted to you than is your wife.

It isn't, really, very subtle. As for the 'wit', when it isn't merely verbal and obvious ('Fruitful, the head fruitful;—that bodes horns; the fruit of the head is horns', etc.) it is hopelessly dependent on convention.

She that marries a fool, Sir Sampson, forfeits the reputation of her honesty or understanding: and she that marries a very witty man is a slave to the severity and insolent conduct of her husband. I should like a man of wit for a lover, because I would have such a man in my power; but I would no more be his wife than his enemy. For his malice is not a more terrible consequence of his aversion than his jealousy is of his love.

An intelligent husband, you see, must be jealous; take away that entertaining assumption and the point is blunted. Halifax is a witty writer, but his wit springs naturally from the situation he is concerned with and illuminates it: 'A partner in government is so unnatural a thing that it is a squint-eyed allegiance which must be paid to such a double-bottomed monarchy.'[9] Congreve's wit is entirely self-regarding.

If there were space to discuss the manner of Wycherley, Etherege, and Vanbrugh, it is a similar account that would have to be given. I am not suggesting that they write in a completely indistinguishable common mode (though they all have passages that might come from any play); but in essentials—in the way in which they use their similes and antitheses, in the conception of 'style' and 'wit' that they exhibit—they all stand together. Not one of them has achieved a genuinely sensitive and individual mode of expression; and in each the pattern of the prose inhibits any but the narrowest—and the most devastatingly *expected*—response. That, I should claim, is the judgment to which an analysis of their prose inevitably leads. The trouble is not that the Restoration comic writers deal with a limited number of themes, but that they bring to bear a miserably limited set of attitudes. And these, in turn, are factitious to exactly the same degree as the prose is artificial and non-representative of the current non-dramatic medium.

II

Apart from the presentation of incidental and unrelated 'wit' (which soon becomes as tiring as the epigrams of the 'good talker'), Restoration comedy has two main interests—the behaviour of the polite and of pretenders to politeness, and some aspects of sexual relationships. Critics have made out a case for finding in one or other of these themes a unifying principle and a serious base for the comedy of manners. According to Miss Lynch, the 'thoroughly conventionalized social mode' of the courtly circle 'was discovered to have manifestly comic aspects, both when awkwardly misinterpreted, and when completely fulfilled through personalities to which, however, it could not give complete expression',[10] and both these discrepancies were exploited by Etherege and his successors. Bonamy Dobrée, attributing to the comic dramatists 'a deep curiosity, and a desire to try new ways of living', finds that

> the distinguishing characteristic of Restoration comedy down to Congreve is that it is concerned with the attempt to rationalize sexual relationships. It is this that makes it different from any other comedy that has ever been written.... It said in effect, 'Here is life lived upon certain assumptions; see what it becomes'. It also dealt, as no other comedy has ever done, with a subject that arose directly out of this, namely sex-antagonism, a consequence of the experimental freedom allowed to women, which gave matter for some of its most brilliant scenes.[11]

These accounts, as developed, certainly look impressive, and if Restoration comedy really answered to them—if it had something fresh and penetrating to say on sex and social relations—there would be no need to complain, even if one found the 'solutions' distasteful. But Miss Lynch's case, at all events, depends on a vigorous reading into the plays of values which are not there, values which could not possibly be expressed, in fact, in the prose of any of the dramatists. (The candid reader can turn up the passages selected by Miss Lynch in support of her argument, and see if they are not all in the factitious, superficial mode that I have described.)

We may consider, by way of illustration, Etherege's *The Man of Mode*. When the play opens, Dorimant ('the finest of all fine gentlemen in Restoration comedy') is trying to rid himself of an old mistress, Mrs Loveit, before taking up with a new, Bellinda, while Young Bellair, in love with Emilia, is trying to find some way out of marrying Harriet, an heiress whom his father has brought to town for him. The entertainment is made up of these two sets of complications, together with an exhibition of the would-be modishness of Sir Fopling Flutter. Events move fast. After a night spent in various sociabilities Dorimant keeps an appointment with Bellinda at 5 a.m. Letting her out of his lodgings an hour or so later, and swearing to be discreet 'By all the Joys I have had, and those you keep in store', he is surprised by his companions, and in the resulting confusion Bellinda finds herself paying an unwilling visit to Mrs Loveit. Dorimant appears and is rated by the women before he 'flings off'. Meanwhile Young Bellair and Emilia have secretly married. Dorimant, his equanimity recovered, turns up for the exposure, followed by his mistresses. The lovers are forgiven, the mistresses are huddled off the stage, and it is decided that Dorimant, who, the previous day, had ingratiated himself with Harriet's mother, and whose 'soul has quite given up her liberty', shall be allowed to pay court to the heiress.

It seems to me that what the play provides—apart from the briskly handled intrigue—is a demonstration of the physical stamina of Dorimant. But Miss Lynch sees further. For her, Dorimant is 'the fine flowering of Restoration culture'. Illustrating her theory of the double standard, she remarks: 'We laugh at Sir Fopling Flutter because he so clumsily parodies social fashions which

Dorimant interprets with unfailing grace and distinction. We laugh at Dorimant because his assumed affectation admits of so poor and incomplete an expression of an attractive and vigorous personality.'[12] The 'unfailing grace and distinction' are perhaps not much in evidence in Dorimant's spiteful treatment of Mrs Loveit,[13] but even if we ignore those brutish scenes we are forced to ask, How do we know that there *is* this 'attractive and vigorous personality' beneath the conventional forms? Dorimant's intrigues are of no more human significance than those of a barn-yard cock, and as for what Miss Lynch calls 'his really serious affair with Harriet' (I feel this deserves a *sic*), it is purely theatrical, and the 'pangs of love' are expressed in nothing but the conventional formulae: 'She's gone, but she has left a pleasing Image of herself behind that wanders in my Soul.' The answer to the question posed is that Miss Lynch's account is a mere assumption. Nothing that Dorimant actually *says* will warrant it—and nothing in the whole of Restoration comedy—in the words actually spoken—allows us a glimpse of those other 'personalities' to which the conventional social modes 'could not give complete expression'. The 'real values'[14] simply are not there.

A minor point can be made in passing. It is just possible to claim that Restoration comedy contains 'social criticism' in its handling of 'the vulgar'. 'Come Mr Sharper,' says Congreve's Belinda, 'you and I will take a turn, and laugh at the vulgar; both the great vulgar and the small', and Etherege's Lady Townley expresses the common attitude of the polite towards the social nuisances: 'We should love wit, but for variety be able to divert ourselves with the extravagancies of those who want it.' The butts, unfortunately, are only shown as fools by the discrepancy between their ambitions and their achievements, not because their ambitions are puerile. The subject is hardly worth discussing, since it is obviously nothing but an easily satisfied sense of superiority that is diverted by the 'variety' of a constant succession of Dapperwits, Froths, and Fopling Flutters. 'When a humour takes in London,' Tom Brown remarked,

> they ride it to death ere they leave it. The primitive Christians were not persecuted with half that variety as the poor unthinking beaus are tormented with upon the theatre ... A huge great muff, and a gaudy ribbon hanging at a bully's backside, is an excellent jest, and new-invented curses, as, Stap my vitals, damn my diaphragm, slit my wind pipe, sink me ten thousand fathom deep, rig up a new beau, though in the main 'tis but the same everlasting coxcomb.[15]

III

In the matter of sexual relations Restoration comedy is entirely dominated by a narrow set of conventions. The objection that it is only certain characters, not the dramatists themselves, who accept them can be more freely encountered when the assumptions that are expressed most frequently have been briefly illustrated.

The first convention is, of course, that constancy in love, especially in marriage, is a bore. Vanbrugh, who was the most uneasy if not the most honest of the comic dramatists (I think that in *The Provok'd Wife* he shows as unusually honest), unambiguously attributes this attitude to Sir John Brute:

> What cloying meat is love—when matrimony's the sauce to it! Two years marriage has debauch'd my five senses.... No boy was ever so weary of his tutor, no girl of her bib, no nun of doing penance, or old maid of being chaste, as I am of being married. Sure there's a secret curse entail'd upon the very name of wife!

> The woman's well enough; she has no vice that I know of, but she's a wife, and—damn a wife![16]

What Vanbrugh saw as a fit sentiment for Sir John had by that time (1697) served the Restoration stage—without change—for thirty years. In *She Wou'd if She Cou'd* Etherege had exhibited Sir Oliver Cockwood in an identical vein: 'A pox of this tying man and woman together, for better, for worse.' 'To have a mistress love thee entirely' is 'a damn'd trouble'. 'There are sots that would think themselves happy in such a Lady; but to a true bred Gentleman all lawful solace is abomination.'[17] If Sir Oliver is a fool it is only because he is a trifle gross in his expression. 'If you did but know, Madam,' says the polite Freeman, 'what an odious thing it is to be thought to love a Wife in good Company.'[18] And the convention is constantly turning up in Congreve. 'There is no creature perfectly civil but a husband,' explains Mrs Frail, 'for in a little time he grows only rude to his wife, and that is the highest good breeding, for it begets his civility to other people.'[19] 'Marry her! Marry her!' Fainall advises Mirabell, 'Be half as well acquainted with her charms, as you are with her defects, and my life on't, you are your own man again.'[20] And Witwoud: 'A wit should no more be sincere than a woman constant; one argues a decay of parts, as t'other of beauty.'[21] Appetite, it seems (and this is the second assumption), needs perpetually fresh stimulus. This is the faith of Rhodophil in *Marriage à la Mode* and of Constant in *The Provok'd Wife*, as well as of Wycherley's old procuress, Mrs Joyner. 'If our wives would suffer us but now and then to make excursions,' Rhodophil explains to Palamede, 'the benefit of our variety would be theirs; instead of one continued, lazy, tired love, they would, in their turns, have twenty vigorous, fresh, and active lovers.'[22] 'Would anything but a madman complain of uncertainty?' asks Congreve's Angelica, for 'security is an insipid thing, and the overtaking and possessing of a wish, discovers the folly of the chase'.[23] And Fainall, in *The Way of the World*, speaks for a large class when he hints at a liking for sauce—a little gentleman's relish—to his seductions: 'I'd no more play with a man that slighted his ill fortune than I'd make love to a woman who undervalued the loss of her reputation.'[24] Fainall, of course, is what he is, but the attitude that makes sexual pleasure 'the bliss', that makes woman 'delicious'—something to be savoured—as well as 'damned' and 'destructive', demands, for its support, 'the pleasure of a chase'.[25]

> Would you long preserve your lover?
>> Would you still his goddess reign?
> Never let him all discover,
>> Never let him much obtain.[26]

Restoration comedy used to be considered outrageously outspoken, but such stuff as this, far from being 'outspoken', hovers on the outskirts of sexual relations, and sees nothing but the titillation of appetite (''Tis not the success,' Collier observed, 'but the manner of gaining it which is all in all').[27] Sex is a hook baited with tempting morsels;[28] it is a thirst quencher;[29] it is a cordial;[30] it is a dish to feed on;[31] it is a bunch of grapes;[32] it is anything but sex. (This, of course, explains why some people can combine a delighted approval of Restoration comedy with an unbalanced repugnance for such modern literature as deals sincerely and realistically with sexual relationships.)

Now the objection referred to above was that sentiments such as these are not offered for straightforward acceptance. Many of them are attributed to characters plainly marked as Wicked (Maskwell, for example, is the black-a-vised villian of melodrama), or, more frequently, as trivial, and the dramatist can therefore dissociate himself. He may even be engaged in showing his audience the explicit, logical consequences of the half-conscious premises on which they base their own lives, saying, as Mr Dobrée has it, 'Here is life lived upon certain assumptions; see what it becomes.' To this there are several answers. The first is that reflections of the kind that I have quoted are indistinguishable in tone and style from the general epigrammatic stock-in-trade (the audience was not altogether to be blamed if, as Congreve complained, they could not at first 'distinguish betwixt the character of a Witwoud and a Lovewit'); and they are largely 'exhibited', just as all the self-conscious witticisms are exhibited, for the sake of their immediate 'comic' effect. One has only to note the laughter of a contemporary audience at a revival, and the places where the splutters occur, to realize how much of the fun provides a rather gross example of tendency wit.[33] The same attitudes, moreover, are manipulated again and again, turning up with the stale monotony of jokes on postcards, and the play that is made with them demands only the easiest, the most superficial, response. But it is, after all, useless to argue about the degree of detachment, the angle at which these attitudes and assumptions are presented. As soon as one selects a particular comedy for that exercise one realizes that all is equally grist to the mill and that the dramatist (there is no need, here, to make distinctions) has no coherent attitude of his own. A consistent artistic purpose would not be content to express itself in a style that allows so limited, so local an effect.

But it is the triviality that one comes back to. In Dryden's *Marriage à la Mode* the characters accept the usual conventions: constancy is dull, and love only thrives on variety.

PALAMEDE. O, now I have found it! you dislike her for no other reason but because she's your wife.

RHODOPHIL. And is not that enough? All that I know of her perfections now, is only by memory ... At last we arrived at that point, that there was nothing left in us to make us new to one another ...

PALAMEDE. The truth is, your disease is very desperate; but, though you cannot be cured, you may be patched up a little: you must get you a mistress, Rhodophil. That, indeed, is living upon cordials; but, as fast as one fails, you must supply it with another.

The mistress that Rhodophil selects is Melantha, whom Palamede is to marry; Palamede falls in love with Doralice, Rhodophil's wife, and the ensuing complications provide sufficient entertainment (the grotto scene, III, ii, is really funny). Mr Dobrée, however, regards the play as a witty exposure of the impossibility of rationalizing sex relations, as Palamede and Rhodophil attempt to rationalize them. Dryden 'laughs morality back into its rightful place, as the scheme which ultimately makes life most comfortable'.[34] But what Dryden actually does is to *use* the conventions for the amusement they afford, not to examine them. The level at which the play works is fairly indicated by the opening song:

> Why should a foolish marriage vow,
>   Which long ago was made,
> Oblige us to each other now,
>   When passion is decayed?
> We loved, and we loved, as long as we could,
>   'Till our love was loved out in us both;
> But our marriage is dead, when the pleasure is fled:
>   'Twas pleasure first made it an oath.
>
> If I have pleasures for a friend,
>   And further love in store,
> What wrong has he, whose joys did end,
>   And who could give no more?
> 'Tis a madness that he should be jealous of me,
>   Or that I should bar him of another:
> For all we can gain, is to give ourselves pain,
>   When neither can hinder the other.

The lovers make no attempt to 'rationalize sex' for the simple reason that genuine sexual feelings no more enter into the play as a whole than feelings of any kind enter into the song. (The obviously faked emotions of the heroic plot are, after all, relevant—and betraying.) And according to Mr Dobrée, 'In one sense the whole idea of Restoration comedy is summed up in the opening song of *Marriage à la Mode*.'[35]

In a sense, too, Mr Dobrée is right. Restoration comedy nowhere provides us with much more of the essential stuff of human experience than we have there. Even Congreve, by common account the best of the comic writers, is no exception. I have said that his verbal pattern often seems to be quite unrelated to an individual mode of perceiving. At best it registers a very limited mode. Restoration prose is all 'social' in its tone, implications and general tenor, but Congreve's observation is *merely* of the public surface. And Congreve, too, relies on the conventional assumptions. In *The Way of the World*, it is true, they are mainly given to the bad and foolish to express: it is Fainall who discourses on the pleasures of disliking one's wife, and Witwoud who maintains that only old age and ugliness ensure constancy. And Mirabell, who is explicitly opposed to some aspects of contemporary manners, goes through the common forms in a tone of rather weary aloofness: 'I wonder, Fainall, that you who are married, and of consequence should be discreet, will suffer your wife to be of such a party.' But Congreve himself is not above raising a cheap snigger;[36] and, above all, the characters with some life in them have nothing to fall back on—nothing, that is, except the conventional, and conventionally limited, pleasures of sex. Millamant, who says she loathes the country and hates the town, expects to draw vitality from the excitement of incessant solicitation:

> I'll be solicited to the very last, nay, and afterwards ... I should think I was poor and had nothing to bestow, if I were reduced to an inglorious ease, and freed from the agreeable fatigues of solicitation.... Oh, I hate a lover that can dare to think he draws a moment's air, independent of the bounty of his mistress. There is not so impudent a thing in nature, as the saucy look of an assured man, confident of success. The pedantic arrogance of a very husband has not so pragmatical an air.

Everyone seems to have found Millamant intelligent and attractive, but her attitude is not far removed from that expressed in

> Would you long preserve your lover?
> Would you still his goddess reign?

and she shares with characters who are decidedly not attractive a disproportionate belief in 'the pleasure of a chase'. Which is not surprising in view of her other occupations and resources; visiting, writing and receiving letters, tea-parties and small talk make up a round that is never for a moment enlivened by the play of genuine intelligence.[37] And although Congreve recognizes, at times, the triviality of his characters,[38] it is to the world whose confines were the Court, the drawing-room, the play-house and the park—a world completely lacking the real sophistication and self-knowledge that might, in some measure, have redeemed it—that he limits his appeal.

It is, indeed, hard to resist the conclusion that 'society'—the smart town society that sought entertainment at the theatres—was fundamentally bored.[39] In *The Man of Mode* Emilia remarks of Medley, 'I love to hear him talk o' the intrigues, let 'em be never so dull in themselves, he'll make 'em pleasant i' the relation', and the idiotic conversation that follows (II, i), affording us a glimpse of what Miss Lynch calls 'the most brilliant society which Restoration Comedy has to offer',[40] suggests in more than one way how badly society *needed* to be entertained. It is the boredom—the constant need for titillation—that helps to explain not only the heroic 'heightening' of emotion, but the various scenic effects, the devices of staging and costume that became popular at this period. (Charles II 'almost died of laughing' at Nell Gwynn's enormous hat.) The conventions—of sexual pursuit, and so on—were an attempt to make life interesting—an impossible job for those who were aware of so limited a range of human potentialities.

The dominating mood of Restoration comedy is, by common account, a cynical one. But one cannot even say that there is here, in contrast to naïve Romantic fervours, the tough strength of disillusion. If—recognizing that there is a place in the educational process for, say, La Rochefoucauld—one finds the 'cynicism' of the plays distasteful, it is because it is easy and superficial; the attitudes that we are presented with are based on so meagre an amount of observation and experience. Thus, 'Elle retrouvait dans l'adultère toutes les platitudes du mariage' has, superficially, much the same meaning as, 'I find now, by sad experience, that a mistress is much more chargeable than a wife, and after a little time too, grows full as dull and insignificant'. But whereas the first sentence has behind it the whole of *Madame Bovary*, the second comes from *Sir Martin Mar-all*, which (although Dryden shares the honours with the Duke of Newcastle) is perhaps the stupidest play I have ever read, and the context is imbecility.

But the superficiality is betrayed at every turn—by the obvious rhythms of the interspersed songs, as well as by the artificial elegance of the prose. And the cynicism is closely allied with—merges into—sentimentality. One thinks of the sentimentally conceived Fidelia in the resolutely 'tough' *Plain Dealer*; and there is no doubt that the audience was meant to respond sympathetically when, at the end of *Love for Love*, Angelica declared her love for Valentine: 'Had I the world to give you, it could not make me worthy of so generous a passion; here's my hand, my heart was always yours, and struggled very hard to make this utmost trial of your virtue.' There is, of course, a good deal of loose emotion in the heroic plays, written—it is useful to remember—for the same audience:

> I'm numbed, and fixed, and scarce my eyeballs move;
> I fear it is the lethargy of love!
> 'Tis he; I feel him now in every part:
> Like a new lord he vaunts about my heart;
> Surveys, in state, each corner of my breast,
> While poor fierce I, that was, am dispossessed.[41]

> A secret pleasure trickles through my veins:
> It works about the inlets of my soul,
> To feel thy touch, and pity tempts the pass:
> But the tough metal of my heart resists;
> 'Tis warmed with the soft fire, not melted down.[42]

'Feeling', in Dryden's serious plays, is fairly represented by such passages as these, and Dryden, we know, was not alone in admiring the Fletcherian 'pathos'. But it is the lyric verse of the period that provides the strongest confirmatory evidence of the kind of bad taste that is in question. It is not merely that in Etherege, Sedley, and Dorset the feeling comes from much nearer the surface than in the Metaphysicals and the Caroline poets, intellectual 'wit' no longer strengthens and controls the feeling. Conventional attitudes are rigged out in a conventional vocabulary and conventional images. (The stock outfit—the 'fair eyes' that 'wound', the 'pleasing pains', the 'sighs and tears', the 'bleeding hearts' and 'flaming darts'—can be studied in any anthology.[43]) There is, in consequence, a pervasive strain of sentimental vulgarity.

> Farewell, ungrateful traitor!
>   Farewell, my perjured swain!
> Let never injured creature
>   Believe a man again.
> The pleasure of possessing
> Surpasses all expressing,

> But 'tis too short a blessing,
> And love too long a pain.

> .   .   .   .   .

> The passion you pretended,
> Was only to obtain;
> But when the charm is ended,
> The charmer you disdain.
> Your love by ours we measure
> Till we have lost our treasure,
> But dying is a pleasure
> When living is a pain.

This piece of music-hall sentiment comes from Dryden's *The Spanish Friar*, and it does not stand alone. The mode that was to produce, among other things of equal merit, 'When lovely woman stoops to folly', had its origin in the lyrics of the Restoration period. Most of these were written by the group connected with the theatres, and they serve to underline the essential criticism of the plays. The criticism that defenders of Restoration comedy need to answer is not that the comedies are 'immoral', but that they are trivial, gross, and dull.

Notes

1. *Letters*, vol. I, p. 140.
2. On 'the last and greatest advantage of our writing, which proceeds from *conversation*', see in particular the *Defence of the Epilogue*. And the dialogue form in which Dryden cast the *Essay of Dramatic Poesy* was not unrecognizably far from actuality.
3. *The History of the Royal Society of London*: Spingarn, *Critical Essays of the Seventeenth Century*, vol. II, pp. 112 ff.
4. '... enriching every subject (otherwise dry and barren) with a pomp of diction and luxuriant harmony of numbers.' Gray's note to *The Progress of Poesy*, 1754.
5. *The Conquest of Granada*, Part I, III, i.
6. '... the nature of a serious play; this last is indeed the representation of nature, but 'tis nature wrought up to a higher pitch'.—*Of Dramatic Poesy*. The final paragraph of the Preface to *Religio Laici* has some interesting remarks in this connection; e.g. 'The florid, elevated, and figurative way is for the passions.'
7. *The Old Bachelor* shows the riddles in the process of manufacture. BELLMOUR: He is the drum to his own praise—the only implement of a soldier he resembles; like that, being full of blustering noise and emptiness. SHARPER: And like that, of no use but to be beaten, etc.
8. I quote from Professor Nichol Smith's excellent anthology, *Characters from the Histories and Memoirs of the Seventeenth Century* (Clarendon Press), p. 222.
9. Also from *The Character of a Trimmer*: '... the indecent courtship of some silken divines who, one would think, did practise to bow at the altar, only to learn to make the better legs at Court.'
10. K. M. Lynch, *The Social Mode of Restoration Comedy*, p. 216.
11. Bonamy Dobrée, *Restoration Comedy*, pp. 22–3.
12. *The Social Mode of Restoration Comedy*, p. 181.
13. See II, ii and V, i, where Dorimant, trying to force a quarrel with Mrs Loveit, attributes to her a fondness for Sir Fopling. The first of these scenes was too much for Etherege, and he makes Bellinda say:

> He's given me the proof which I desired of his love,
> But 'tis a proof of his ill nature too.
> I wish I had not seen him use her so.

But this is soon forgotten, and we are not, of course, called on to register an unfavourable judgment of Dorimant.

14. 'The love affairs of Courtal and Ariana, Freeman and Gatty [in *She Wou'd if She Cou'd*] are similarly embarrassed by social convention.... The conduct of these polite lovers acquires comic vitality through the continually suggested opposition of artificial and real values.'—Op cit., p. 152.

15. Tom Brown, *Works*, vol. III, *Amusements Comical and Serious*, 'At the Playhouse', p. 39.

16. *The Provok'd Wife*, I, i; II, i.

17. *She Wou'd if She Cou'd*, I, i; III, iii.

18. Ibid., III, iii.

19. *Love for Love*, I, ii.

20. *The Way of the World*, I, ii.

21. Ibid.

22. *Marriage à la Mode*, II, i. Cf. *The Provok'd Wife*, III, i: CONSTANT, 'There's a poor sordid slavery in marriage, that turns the flowing tide of honour, and sinks us to the lowest ebb of infamy. 'Tis a corrupted soil: Ill-nature, sloth, cowardice, and dirt, are all its product.'

23. *Love for Love*, IV, iii.

24. *The Way of the World*, I, i.

25. *The Old Bachelor*, I, i; III, ii ('O thou delicious, damned, dear, destructive woman !'); IV, ii.

26. Ibid., II, ii.

27. *A Short View of the Profaneness and Immorality of the English Stage*, Fifth Edition, 1738, p. 116.

28. ''Tis true you are so eager in pursuit of the temptation, that you save the devil the trouble of leading you into it: nor is it out of discretion that you don't swallow the very hook yourselves have baited, but ... what you meant for a whet turns the edge of your puny stomachs.' *The Old Bachelor*, I, i. 'Strike Heartwell home, before the bait's worn off the hook. Age will come. He nibbled fairly yesterday, and no doubt he will be eager enough today to swallow the temptation.'—Ibid., III, i.

29. 'What was my pleasure is become my duty: and I have as little stomach to her now as if I were her husband.... Pox on't! that a man can't drink without quenching his thirst.' *The Double-Dealer*, III, i.

30. 'You must get you a mistress, Rhodophil. That indeed, is living upon cordials; but as fast as one fails, you must supply it with another.' *Marriage à la Mode*, I, i.

31. 'Because our husbands cannot feed on one dish, therefore we must be starved.' Ibid., III, i.

32. 'The only way to keep us new to one another, is never to enjoy, as they keep grapes, by hanging them upon a line; they must touch nothing, if you would preserve them fresh.' Ibid., V, i.

33. The Freudian 'censor' is at times projected in the form of the stage puritan. The plays written soon after the Commonwealth period appealed to Royalist prejudice by satirizing the 'seemingly precise'; and even later, when 'the bonfires of devotion', 'the bellows of zeal', were forgotten, a good deal of the self-conscious swagger of indecency seems to have been directed against 'our protestant husbands', city merchants, aldermen and the like; the 'daring' effect was intensified by postulating a shockable audience somewhere—not necessarily in the theatre. Not that the really obscene jokes were merely bravado; Collier quite rightly remarked that 'the modern poets seem to use smut as the old ones did Machines, to relieve a fainting situation'. *A Short View*, fifth edition, p. 4.

34. *Restoration Comedy*, p. 133.

35. Ibid., p. 106.

36. Ay there's my grief; that's the sad change of life,
     To lose my title, and yet keep my wife.
       The Way of the World, II, ii.

37. As Lady Brute remarks, 'After all, a woman's life would be a dull business, if it were not for the men ... We shou'd never blame Fate for the shortness of our days; our time would hang wretchedly upon our hands.' *The Provok'd Wife*, III, iii.

38. MIRABELL: You had the leisure to entertain a herd of fools; things who visit you

from their excessive idleness; bestowing on your easiness that time which is the encumbrance of their lives. How can you find delight in such society? *The Way of the World*, II, i.

39. The constitution, habits and demands of the theatre audience are admirably illustrated by Alexander Beljame in that neglected classic of scholarship, *Le Public et les Hommes de Lettres en Angleterre au Dix-Huitième Siècle, 1660–1740*. See also C. V. Deane, *Dramatic Theory and the Rhymed Heroic Play*, chapter i, section 6.

40. *The Social Mode of Restoration Comedy*, p. 177.

41. *The Conquest of Granada*, Part I, III, i.

42. *Don Sebastian*, III, i.

43. See, for example, Aphra Behn's 'Love in fantastic triumph sate', Buckingham's *To his Mistress* ('Phyllis, though your all powerful charms'), Dryden's 'Ask not the cause why sullen spring', and 'Ah, how sweet it is to love', and Sedley's *To Chloris*—all in *The Oxford Book of English Verse*, or Ault's *Seventeenth Century Lyrics*.

18 John Crowe Ransom

John Crowe Ransom (b. 1888) was educated at Vanderbilt (Tennessee) and
Oxford Universities. After service in World War I he returned to teach at
Vanderbilt University, where Cleanth Brooks (see below, pp. 291-304) and Allen
Tate were also educated. All three men are identified with the rise of the New
Criticism in America. They also shared religious, political, and cultural
convictions of a traditional, conservative character, coloured by a special
allegiance to the American South. With a number of other writers, notably
Robert Penn Warren, they formed a recognizable group known as the Southern
Agrarians or Fugitives (after the title of *The Fugitive*, a magazine edited by
Ransom). What exactly was the intellectual connection between the inherently
didactic views of these critics, and the allegedly objective, formalistic principles
and methods of the New Criticism which they promoted, is a difficult question
which perhaps they themselves never quite faced.

As critic, theoretician, poet, teacher, and editor, John Crowe Ransom was
one of the most widely respected and influential American men of letters of his
time. After moving from Vanderbilt to Kenyon College, where he was
Carnegie Professor of Poetry, Ransom edited the *Kenyon Review* from 1939-59,
and made it one of the most successful literary quarterlies of a period especially
rich in such publications.

'Criticism Inc.', first published in the *Virginia Quarterly Review* in 1937, is
not the most substantial essay Ransom ever wrote, but it seems in retrospect
an especially pregnant—and poignant—document in the history of modern
criticism, drawing together in one place all the most characteristic aims,
attitudes, and assumptions of the American New Critics at a moment in time
when they were poised to begin their ultimately successful campaign to direct
the development of English studies in the universities. Ransom holds out the
vision of an 'objective' or (to use his own favourite word) 'ontological' criticism
that will be the product of rigorous, disciplined, collaborative effort in the
elucidation and evaluation of literary texts, including contemporary ones. He
defends this concept of criticism against what he sees as obstructive rival
methods and approaches: dryasdust historical scholarship, impressionistic
appreciation, and various kinds of criticism which focus on the abstracted
content of a work of literature. There is a kind of crusading enthusiasm, an
almost revolutionary élan, in Ransom's appeal to teachers and students to
assert their real interests in the face of obsolete traditions and vested interests,
which one cannot respond to without irony some four decades later, during
which time the New Criticism itself has become in the eyes of some students
and teachers a narrow and irrelevant academic orthodoxy. The very title of

227

Ransom's essay anticipates the now familiar joke that academic literary criticism has become more like an industry than a humane pursuit, though that was clearly the opposite of Ransom's wish and intention.

'Criticism Inc.' was first collected in *The World's Body* (New York, 1938), and is reprinted here from the Louisiana State University Press reprint with a Postscript by the author (Baton Rouge, 1968). In 1941 Ransom published *The New Criticism* (Norfolk, Conn.), a study of Eliot, Richards, and other modern critics. His *Collected Poems* were published in 1963.

CROSS REFERENCES: 23. Cleanth Brooks
24. Yvor Winters
26. W. K. Wimsatt and Monroe C. Beardsley
41. René Wellek

COMMENTARY: John Paul Pritchard, 'John Crowe Ransom', in *Criticism in America* (Norman, Oklahoma, 1956)

Criticism, Inc.

I

It is strange, but nobody seems to have told us what exactly is the proper business of criticism. There are many critics who might tell us, but for the most part they are amateurs. So have the critics nearly always been amateurs; including the best ones. They have not been trained to criticism so much as they have simply undertaken a job for which no specific qualifications were required. It is far too likely that what they call criticism when they produce it is not the real thing.

There are three sorts of trained performers who would appear to have some of the competence that the critic needs. The first is the artist himself. He should know good art when he sees it; but his understanding is intuitive rather than dialectical—he cannot very well explain his theory of the thing. It is true that literary artists, with their command of language, are better critics of their own art than are other artists; probably the best critics of poetry we can now have are the poets. But one can well imagine that any artist's commentary on the art-work is valuable in the degree that he sticks to its technical effects, which he knows minutely, and about which he can certainly talk if he will.

The second is the philosopher, who should know all about the function of the fine arts. But the philosopher is apt to see a lot of wood and no trees, for his theory is very general and his acquaintance with the particular works of art is not persistent and intimate, especially his acquaintance with their technical effects. Or at least I suppose so, for philosophers have not proved that they can write close criticism by writing it; and I have the feeling that even their handsome generalizations are open to suspicion as being grounded more on other generalizations, those which form their prior philosophical stock, than on acute study of particulars.

The third is the university teacher of literature, who is styled professor, and who should be the very professional we need to take charge of the critical activity. He is hardly inferior as critic to the philosopher, and perhaps not on the whole to the poet, but he is a greater disappointment because we have the right to expect more of him. Professors of literature are learned but not critical men. The professional morale of this part of the university staff is evidently low. It is as if, with conscious or unconscious cunning, they had appropriated every avenue of escape from their responsibility which was decent and official; so that it is easy for one of them without public reproach to spend a lifetime in compiling the data of literature and yet rarely or never commit himself to a literary judgment.

Nevertheless it is from the professors of literature, in this country the professors of English for the most part, that I should hope eventually for the erection of intelligent standards of criticism. It is their business.

Criticism must become more scientific, or precise and systematic, and this means that it must be developed by the collective and sustained effort of learned persons—which means that its proper seat is in the universities.

Scientific: but I do not think we need be afraid that criticism, trying to be a sort of science, will inevitably fail and give up in despair, or else fail without realizing it and enjoy some hollow and pretentious career. It will never be a very exact science, or even a nearly exact one. But neither will psychology, if that term continues to refer to psychic rather than physical phenomena; nor will sociology, as Pareto, quite contrary to his intention, appears to have furnished us with evidence for believing; nor even will economics. It does not matter whether we call them sciences or just systematic studies; the total effort of each to be effective must be consolidated and kept going. The studies which I have mentioned have immeasurably improved in understanding since they were taken over by the universities, and the same career looks possible for criticism.

Rather than occasional criticism by amateurs, I should think the whole enterprise might be seriously taken in hand by professionals. Perhaps I use a distasteful figure, but I have the idea that what we need is Criticism, Inc., or Criticism, Ltd.

The principal resistance to such an idea will come from the present incumbents of the professorial chairs. But its adoption must come from them too. The idea of course is not a private one of my own. If it should be adopted before long, the credit would probably belong to Professor Ronald S. Crane[a], of the University of Chicago, more than to any other man. He is the first of the great professors to have advocated it as a major policy for departments of English. It is possible that he will have made some important academic history.

[a] See below, pp. 592–609.

II

Professor Crane published recently a paper of great note in academic circles, on the reform of the courses in English. It appeared in *The English Journal*, under the title: 'History versus Criticism in the University Study of Literature'. He argues there that historical scholarship has been overplayed heavily in English studies, in disregard of the law of diminishing returns, and that the emphasis must now be shifted to the critical.

To me this means, simply: the students of the future must be permitted to study literature, and not merely about literature. But I think this is what the good students have always wanted to do. The wonder is that they have allowed themselves so long to be denied. But they have not always been amiable about it, and the whole affair presents much comic history.

At the University of Chicago, I believe that Professor Crane, with some others, is putting the revolution into effect in his own teaching, though for the time being perhaps with a limited programme, mainly the application of Aristotle's critical views. (My information is not at all exact.) The university is an opulent one, not too old to experience waves of reformational zeal, uninhibited as yet by bad traditions. Its department of English has sponsored plenty of old-line scholarship, but this is not the first time it has gone in for criticism. If the department should now systematically and intelligently build up a general school of literary criticism, I believe it would score a triumph that would be, by academic standards, spectacular. I mean that the alive and brilliant young English scholars all over the country would be saying they wanted to go there to do their work. That would place a new distinction upon the university, and it would eventually and profoundly modify the practices of many other institutions. It would be worth even more than Professor Crane's careful presentation of the theory.

This is not the first time that English professors have tilted against the historians, or 'scholars', in the dull sense which that word has acquired. They did not score heavily, at those other times. Probably they were themselves not too well versed in the historical studies, so that it could be said with honest concern that they scarcely had the credentials to judge of such matters. At the same time they may have been too unproductive critically to offer a glowing alternative.

The most important recent diversion from the orthodox course of literary studies was that undertaken by the New Humanists.[a] I regret to think that it was not the kind of diversion which I am advocating; nor the kind approved by Professor Crane, who comments briefly against it. Unquestionably the Humanists did divert, and the refreshment was grateful to anybody who felt resentful for having his literary predilections ignored under the schedule of

---

[a] Irving Babbitt, W. C. Brownell, and Paul Elmer More were the best known of this school of critics, active in America in the early decades of this century.

230

historical learning. But in the long run the diversion proved to be nearly as unliterary as the round of studies from which it took off at a tangent. No picnic ideas were behind it.

The New Humanists were, and are, moralists; more accurately, historians and advocates of a certain moral system. Criticism is the attempt to define and enjoy the aesthetic or characteristic values of literature, but I suppose the Humanists would shudder at 'aesthetic' as hard as ordinary historical scholars do. Did an official Humanist ever make any official play with the term? I do not remember it. The term 'art' is slightly more ambiguous, and they have availed themselves of that; with centuries of loose usage behind it, art connotes, for those who like, high seriousness, and high seriousness connotes moral self-consciousness, and an inner check, and finally either Plato or Aristotle.

Mr Babbitt consistently played on the terms of classical and romantic. They mean any of several things each, so that unquestionably Mr Babbitt could make war on romanticism for purely moral reasons; and his preoccupation was ethical, not aesthetic. It is perfectly legitimate for the moralist to attack romantic literature if he can make out his case; for example, on the ground that it deals with emotions rather than principles, or the ground that its author discloses himself as flabby, intemperate, escapist, unphilosophical, or simply adolescent. The moral objection is probably valid; a romantic period testifies to a large-scale failure of adaptation, and defence of that failure to adapt, to the social and political environment; unless, if the Humanists will consent, it sometimes testifies to the failure of society and state to sympathize with the needs of the individual. But this is certainly not the charge that Mr T. S. Eliot, a literary critic, brings against romanticism. His, if I am not mistaken, is aesthetic, though he may not ever care to define it very sharply. In other words, the literary critic also has something to say about romanticism, and it might come to something like this: that romantic literature is imperfect in objectivity, or 'aesthetic distance', and that out of this imperfection comes its weakness of structure; that the romantic poet does not quite realize the aesthetic attitude, and is not the pure artist. Or it might come to something else. It would be quite premature to say that when a moralist is obliged to disapprove a work the literary critic must disapprove it too.

Following the excitement produced by the Humanist diversion, there is now one due to the Leftists, or Proletarians, who are also diversionists. Their diversion is likewise moral. It is just as proper for them to ferret out class-consciousness in literature, and to make literature serve the cause of loving-comradeship, as it is for the Humanists to censure romanticism and to use the topic, and the literary exhibit, as the occasion of reviving the Aristotelian moral canon. I mean that these are procedures of the same sort. Debate could never occur between a Humanist and a Leftist on aesthetic grounds, for they are equally intent on ethical values. But the debate on ethical grounds would be very spirited, and it might create such a stir in a department conducting English studies that the conventional scholars there would find themselves slipping, and their pupils deriving from literature new and seductive excitements which would entice them away from their scheduled English exercises.

On the whole, however, the moralists, distinguished as they may be, are like those who have quarrelled with the ordinary historical studies on purer or more aesthetic grounds: they have not occupied in English studies the positions of professional importance. In a department of English, as in any other going business, the proprietary interest becomes vested, and in old and reputable departments the vestees have uniformly been gentlemen who have gone through the historical mill. Their laborious Ph.D.s and historical publications are their patents. Naturally, quite spontaneously, they would tend to perpetuate a system in which the power and the glory belonged to them. But English scholars in this country can rarely have better credentials than those which Professor Crane has earned in his extensive field, the eighteenth century. It is this which makes his disaffection significant.

It is really atrocious policy for a department to abdicate its own self-respecting identity. The department of English is charged with the understanding and the communication of literature, an art, yet it has usually forgotten to inquire into the peculiar constitution and structure of its product. English might almost as well announce that it does not regard itself as entirely autonomous, but as a branch of the department of history, with the option of declaring itself occasionally a branch of the department of ethics. It is true that the historical and the ethical studies will cluster round objects which for some reason are called artistic objects. But the thing itself the professors do not have to contemplate; and only last spring the head of English studies in a graduate school fabulously equipped made the following impromptu disclaimer to a victim who felt aggrieved at having his own studies forced in the usual direction: 'This is a place for exact scholarship, and you want to do criticism. Well, we don't allow criticism here, because that is something which anybody can do.'

But one should never speak impromptu in one's professional capacity. This speech may have betrayed a fluttery private apprehension which should not have been made public: that you can never be critical and be exact at the same time, that history is firmer ground than aesthetics, and that, to tell the truth, criticism is a painful job for the sort of mind that wants to be very sure about things. Not in that temper did Aristotle labour towards a critique in at least one branch of letters; nor in that temper are strong young minds everywhere trying to sharpen their critical apparatus into precision tools, in this decade as never before.

It is not anybody who can do criticism. And for an example, the more eminent (as historical scholar) the professor of English, the less apt he is to be able to write decent criticism, unless it is about another professor's work of historical scholarship, in which case it is not literary criticism. The professor may not be without aesthetic judgments respecting an old work, especially if it is 'in his period', since it must often have been judged by authorities whom he respects. Confronted with a new work, I am afraid it is very rare that he finds anything particular to say. Contemporary criticism is not at all in the hands of those who direct the English studies. Contemporary literature, which is almost obliged to receive critical study if it receives any at all, since it is hardly capable of the usual historical commentary, is barely officialized as a proper field for serious study.

Here is contemporary literature, waiting for its criticism; where are the professors of literature? They are watering their own gardens; elucidating the literary histories of their respective periods. So are their favourite pupils. The persons who save the occasion, and rescue contemporary literature from the humiliation of having to go without a criticism, are the men who had to leave the university before their time because they felt themselves being warped into mere historians; or those who finished the courses and took their punishment but were tough, and did not let it engross them and spoil them. They are home-made critics. Naturally they are not too wise, these amateurs who furnish our reviews and critical studies. But when they distinguish themselves, the universities which they attended can hardly claim more than a trifling share of the honour.

It is not so in economics, chemistry, sociology, theology, and architecture. In these branches it is taken for granted that criticism of the performance is the prerogative of the men who have had formal training in its theory and technique. The historical method is useful, and may be applied readily to any human performance whatever. But the exercise does not become an obsession with the university men working in the other branches; only the literary scholars wish to convert themselves into pure historians. This has gone far to nullify the usefulness of a departmental personnel larger, possibly, than any other, and of the lavish endowment behind it.

III

Presumably the departments of English exist in order to communicate the understanding of the literary art. That will include both criticism and also whatever may be meant by 'appreciation'. This latter term seems to stand for the kind of understanding that is had intuitively, without benefit of instruction, by merely being constrained to spend time in the presence of the literary product. It is true that some of the best work now being done in departments is by the men who do little more than read well aloud, enforcing a private act of appreciation upon the students. One remembers how good a service that may be, thinking perhaps of Professor Copeland of Harvard, or Dean Cross at Greeley Teachers College. And there are men who try to get at the same thing in another way, which they would claim is surer: by requiring a great deal of memory work, in order to enforce familiarity with fine poetry. These might defend their strategy by saying that at any rate the work they required was not as vain as the historical rigmarole which the scholars made their pupils recite, if the objective was really literary understanding and not external information. But it would be a misuse of terms to employ the word instruction for the offices either of the professors who read aloud or of those who require the memory work. The professors so engaged are properly curators, and the museum of which they have the care is furnished with the cherished literary masterpieces, just as another museum might be filled with paintings. They conduct their squads from one work to another, making appropriate pauses or reverent gestures, but their own obvious regard for the masterpieces is somewhat contagious, and contemplation is induced. Naturally they are grateful to the efficient staff of colleagues in the background who have framed the masterpieces, hung them in the proper schools and in the chronological order, and prepared the booklet of information about the artists and the occasions. The colleagues in their turn probably feel quite happy over this division of labour, thinking that they have done the really productive work, and that it is appropriate now if less able men should undertake a little salesmanship.

Behind appreciation, which is private, and criticism, which is public and negotiable, and represents the last stage of English studies, is historical scholarship. It is indispensable. But it is instrumental and cannot be the end itself. In this respect historical studies have the same standing as linguistic studies: language and history are aids.

On behalf of the historical studies. Without them what could we make of Chaucer, for instance? I cite the familiar locus of the 'hard' scholarship, the centre of any programme of advanced studies in English which intends to initiate the student heroically, and once for all, into the historical discipline. Chaucer writes allegories for historians to decipher, he looks out upon institutions and customs unfamiliar to us. Behind him are many writers in various tongues from whom he borrows both forms and materials. His thought bears constant reference to classical and medieval philosophies and sciences which have passed from our effective knowledge. An immense labour of historical adaptation is necessary before our minds are ready to make the aesthetic approach to Chaucer.

Or to any author out of our own age. The mind with which we enter into an old work is not the mind with which we make our living, or enter into a contemporary work. It is under sharp restraints, and it is quite differently furnished. Out of our actual contemporary mind we have to cancel a great deal that has come there under modern conditions but was not in the earlier mind at all. This is a technique on the negative side, a technique of suspension; difficult for practical persons, literal scientists, and aggressive moderns who take pride in the 'truth' or the 'progress' which enlightened man, so well represented in their own instance, has won. Then, on the positive side, we must supply the mind with the precise beliefs and ways of thought it had in that former age, with the specific content in which history instructs us; this is a technique of make-believe. The whole act of historical adaptation, through such techniques, is a marvellous feat of flexibility. Certainly it is a thing hard enough to justify university instruction. But it is not sufficient for an English programme.

The achievement of modern historical scholarship in the field of English literature has been, in the aggregate, prodigious; it should be very proud. A good impression of the volume of historical learning now available for the students of English may be quickly had from inspecting a few chapters of the Cambridge History, with the bibliographies. Or, better, from inspecting one of

a large number of works which have come in since the Cambridge History:
the handbooks, which tell all about the authors, such as Chaucer, Shakespeare,
Milton, and carry voluminous bibliographies; or the period books, which tell
a good deal about whole periods of literature.

There is one sense in which it may be justly said that we can never have too
much scholarship. We cannot have too much of it if the critical intelligence
functions, and has the authority to direct it. There is hardly a critical problem
which does not require some arduous exercises in fact-finding, but each problem is quite specific about the kind of facts it wants. Mountains of facts may
have been found already, but often they have been found for no purpose at all
except the purpose of piling up into a big exhibit, to offer intoxicating delights
to the academic population.

To those who are aesthetically minded among students, the rewards of many
a historical labour will have to be disproportionately slight. The official Chaucer
course is probably over ninety-five per cent historical and linguistic, and less
than five per cent aesthetic or critical. A thing of beauty is a joy forever. But
it is not improved because the student has had to tie his tongue before it. It is
an artistic object, with a heroic human labour behind it, and on these terms it
calls for public discussion. The dialectical possibilities are limitless, and when
we begin to realize them we are engaged in criticism.

IV

What is criticism? Easier to ask, What is criticism not? It is an act now
notoriously arbitrary and undefined. We feel certain that the critical act is
not one of those which the professors of literature habitually perform, and
cause their students to perform. And it is our melancholy impression that it is
not often cleanly performed in those loose compositions, by writers of perfectly
indeterminate qualifications, that appear in print as reviews of books.

Professor Crane excludes from criticism works of historical scholarship and
of Neo-Humanism, but more exclusions are possible than that. I should wish
to exclude:

1. Personal registrations, which are declarations of the effect of the art-work
upon the critic as reader. The first law to be prescribed to criticism, if we may
assume such authority, is that it shall be objective, shall cite the nature of the
object rather than its effects upon the subject. Therefore it is hardly criticism
to assert that the proper literary work is one that we can read twice; or one
that causes in us some remarkable physiological effect, such as oblivion of the
outer world, the flowing of tears, visceral or laryngeal sensations, and such
like; or one that induces perfect illusion, or brings us into a spiritual ecstasy;
or even one that produces a catharsis of our emotions. Aristotle concerned himself with this last in making up his definition of tragedy—though he did not
fail to make some acute analyses of the objective features of the work also. I
have read that some modern Broadway producers of comedy require a reliable
person to seat himself in a trial audience and count the laughs; their method

of testing is not so subtle as Aristotle's, but both are concerned with the effects. Such concern seems to reflect the view that art comes into being because the artist, or the employer behind him, has designs upon the public, whether high moral designs or box-office ones. It is an odious view in either case, because it denies the autonomy of the artist as one who interests himself in the artistic object in his own right, and likewise the autonomy of the work itself as existing for its own sake. (We may define a chemical as something which can effect a certain cure, but that is not its meaning to the chemist; and we may define toys, if we are weary parents, as things which keep our children quiet, but that is not what they are to engineers.) Furthermore, we must regard as uncritical the use of an extensive vocabulary which ascribes to the object properties really discovered in the subject, as: *moving, exciting, entertaining, pitiful; great,* if I am not mistaken, and *admirable,* on a slightly different ground; and, in strictness, *beautiful* itself.

2. Synopsis and paraphrase. The high-school classes and the women's clubs delight in these procedures, which are easiest of all the systematic exercises possible in the discussion of literary objects. I do not mean that the critic never uses them in his analysis of fiction and poetry, but he does not consider plot or story as identical with the real content. Plot is an abstract from content.

3. Historical studies. These have a very wide range, and include studies of the general literary background; author's biography, of course with special reference to autobiographical evidences in the work itself; bibliographical items; the citation of literary originals and analogues, and therefore what, in general, is called comparative literature. Nothing can be more stimulating to critical analysis than comparative literature. But it may be conducted only superficially, if the comparisons are perfunctory and mechanical, or if the scholar is content with merely making the parallel citations.

4. Linguistic studies. Under this head come those studies which define the meaning of unusual words and idioms, including the foreign and archaic ones, and identify the allusions. The total benefit of linguistics for criticism would be the assurance that the latter was based on perfect logical understanding of the content, or 'interpretation'. Acquaintance with all the languages and literatures in the world would not necessarily produce a critic, though it might save one from damaging errors.

5. Moral studies. The moral standard applied is the one appropriate to the reviewer; it may be the Christian ethic, or the Aristotelian one, or the new proletarian gospel. But the moral content is not the whole content, which should never be relinquished.

6. Any other special studies which deal with some abstract or prose content taken out of the work. Nearly all departments of knowledge may conceivably find their own materials in literature, and take them out. Studies have been made of Chaucer's command of medieval sciences, of Spenser's view of the Irish question, of Shakespeare's understanding of the law, of Milton's geography, of Hardy's place-names. The critic may well inform himself of these materials as possessed by the artist, but his business as critic is to discuss the literary assimilation of them.

With or without such useful exercises as these, probably assuming that the intelligent reader has made them for himself, comes the critical act itself.

Mr Austin Warren, whose writings I admire, is evidently devoted to the academic development of the critical project. Yet he must be a fair representative of what a good deal of academic opinion would be when he sees no reason why criticism should set up its own house, and try to dissociate itself from historical and other scholarly studies; why not let all sorts of studies, including the critical ones, flourish together in the same act of sustained attention, or the same scheduled 'course'? But so they are supposed to do at present; and I would only ask him whether he considers that criticism prospers under this arrangement. It has always had the chance to go ahead in the hands of the professors of literature, and it has not gone ahead. A change of policy suggests itself. Strategy requires now, I should think, that criticism receive its own charter of rights and function independently. If he fears for its foundations in scholarship, the scholars will always be on hand to reprove it when it tries to function on an unsound scholarship.

I do not suppose the reviewing of books can be reformed in the sense of being turned into pure criticism. The motives of the reviewers are as much mixed as the performance, and indeed they condition the mixed performance. The reviewer has a job of presentation and interpretation as well as criticism. The most we can ask of him is that he know when the criticism begins, and that he make it as clean and definitive as his business permits. To what authority may he turn?

I know of no authority. But I know of one large class of studies which is certainly critical, and necessary, and I can suggest another sort of study for the critic's consideration if he is really ambitious.

Studies in the technique of the art belong to criticism certainly. They cannot belong anywhere else, because the technique is not peculiar to any prose materials discoverable in the work of art, nor to anything else but the unique form of that art. A very large volume of studies is indicated by this classification. They would be technical studies of poetry, for instance, the art I am specifically discussing, if they treated its metrics; its inversions, solecisms, lapses from the prose norm of language, and from close prose logic; its tropes; its fictions, or inventions, by which it secures 'aesthetic distance' and removes itself from history; or any other devices, on the general understanding that any systematic usage which does not hold good for prose is a poetic device.

A device with a purpose: the superior critic is not content with the compilation of the separate devices; they suggest to him a much more general question. The critic speculates on why poetry, through its devices, is at such pains to dissociate itself from prose at all, and what it is trying to represent that cannot be represented by prose.

I intrude here with an idea of my own, which may serve as a starting-point of discussion. Poetry distinguishes itself from prose on the technical side by the devices which are, precisely, its means of escaping from prose. Something is continually being killed by prose which the poet wants to preserve. But this must be put philosophically. (Philosophy sounds hard, but it deals with natural and fundamental forms of experience.)

The critic should regard the poem as nothing short of a desperate ontological or metaphysical manoeuvre. The poet himself, in the agony of composition, has something like this sense of his labours. The poet perpetuates in his poem an order of existence which in actual life is constantly crumbling beneath his touch. His poem celebrates the object which is real, individual, and qualitatively infinite. He knows that his practical interests will reduce this living object to a mere utility, and that his sciences will disintegrate it for their convenience into their respective abstracts. The poet wishes to defend his object's existence against its enemies, and the critic wishes to know what he is doing, and how. The critic should find in the poem a total poetic or individual object which tends to be universalized, but is not permitted to suffer this fate. His identification of the poetic object is in terms of the universal or commonplace object to which it tends, and of the tissue, or totality of connotation, which holds it secure. How does he make out the universal object? It is the prose object, which any forthright prosy reader can discover to him by an immediate paraphrase; it is a kind of story, character, thing, scene, or moral principle. And where is the tissue that keeps it from coming out of the poetic object? That is, for the laws of the prose logic, its superfluity; and I think I would even say, its irrelevance.

A poet is said to be distinguishable in terms of his style. It is a comprehensive word, and probably means: the general character of his irrelevances, or tissues. All his technical devices contribute to it, elaborating or individualizing the universal, the core-object; likewise all his material detail. For each poem even, ideally, there is distinguishable a logical object or universal, but at the same time a tissue of irrelevance from which it does not really emerge. The critic has to take the poem apart, or analyse it, for the sake of uncovering these features. With all the finesse possible, it is rude and patchy business by comparison with the living integrity of the poem. But without it there could hardly be much understanding of the value of poetry, or of the natural history behind any adult poem.

The language I have used may sound too formidable, but I seem to find that a profound criticism generally works by some such considerations. However the critic may spell them, the two terms are in his mind: the prose core to which he can violently reduce the total object, and the differentia, residue, or tissue, which keeps the object poetical or entire. The character of the poem resides for the good critic in its way of exhibiting the residuary quality. The character of the poet is defined by the kind of prose object to which his interest evidently attaches, plus his way of involving it firmly in the residuary tissue. And doubtless, incidentally, the wise critic can often read behind the poet's public character his private history as a man with a weakness for lapsing into some special form of prosy or scientific bondage.

Similar considerations hold, I think, for the critique of fiction, or of the non-literary arts. I remark this for the benefit of philosophers who believe, with propriety, that the arts are fundamentally one. But I would prefer to leave the documentation to those who are better qualified.

19   Edmund Wilson

Edmund Wilson (b. 1895) graduated from Princeton, where he was a contemporary of F. Scott Fitzgerald, in 1916, and began a career in journalism as reporter for the *New York Evening Sun*. He was managing editor of *Vanity Fair* 1920-1, Associate Editor of the *New Republic* 1926-31, and regular book reviewer for the *New Yorker* 1944-8. Wilson is a rare example of a modern critic who, working successfully in the ephemeral world of literary journalism, has at the same time won the respect and admiration of academic critics, many of whom regard him as the greatest American critic of his generation. Some of Edmund Wilson's books have been deliberately researched and written in time saved from his journalistic work—for example, his study of the Symbolist Movement, *Axel's Castle* (1931), still widely regarded as the best introduction to its subject. But several of Wilson's most interesting and valuable books are collections of his occasional essays and reviews. In a piece entitled 'Thoughts on Being Bibliographed' in the *Princeton University Library Chronicle* (1943), Wilson commented revealingly on his professional life as a literary journalist:

> To write what you are interested in writing and to succeed in getting editors to pay for it, is a feat that may require close calculation and a good deal of ingenuity.... My [strategy] has usually been, first to get books for review ... on subjects in which I happened to be interested; then, later, to use the scattered articles for writing general studies of these subjects; then, finally, to bring out a book in which groups of these essays were revised and combined.

Such books were *The Triple Thinkers* (New York, 1938), *The Wound and the Bow* (Boston, 1941) and *Classics and Commercials* (New York, 1950). In later years Wilson has tended to write books on specific subjects, such as *The Scrolls from the Dead Sea* (New York, 1955), *O Canada: an American's notes on Canadian culture* (New York, 1965), and *Patriotic Gore: studies in the literature of the American Civil War* (New York, 1966).

Edmund Wilson has made extensive and brilliant use of Freudian concepts and methods of analysis: his psycho-analytical interpretations of Henry James's *The Turn of the Screw* in *The Triple Thinkers*, and of the imagination of Charles Dickens in *The Wound and the Bow*, are celebrated examples. He was also, like many critics of his generation, deeply influenced by Marxism. In 1932 he began work on a book about the Russian Revolution published many years later as *To the Finland Station* (New York, 1940). While this work was in progress, however, Wilson became disillusioned with Marxism, particularly as practised and preached under Stalin's dictatorship; and the essay 'Marxism and

Literature', reprinted here from *The Triple Thinkers* (it was first published by the *Atlantic Monthly* in 1937), reflects that disillusionment.

Essentially Edmund Wilson is not a Freudian critic, nor a Marxist critic, nor the exponent of any other methodological or ideological 'ism'. His approach is best described as a kind of empirical, descriptive literary history; and the secret of his immense readability is perhaps his knack of converting whatever he is discussing, however abstract, into narrative. He has, in fact, published two works of prose fiction, *I Thought of Daisy* (New York, 1929) and *Memoirs of Hecate County* (New York, 1946).

CROSS REFERENCES :   16. Christopher Caudwell
                              27. George Orwell
                              28. Jean-Paul Sartre
                              35. Georg Lukács

COMMENTARY :   Sherman Paul, *Edmund Wilson: A Study of Literary Vocation in Our Time* (Urbana, 1965)
Frank Kermode, 'A modest tribute to Edmund Wilson', in *Continuities* (1968)

Marxism and literature

Let us begin with Marx and Engels. What was the role assigned to literature and art in the system of Dialectical Materialism? This role was much less cut-and-dried than is nowadays often supposed. Marx and Engels conceived the forms of human society in any given country and epoch as growing out of the methods of production which prevailed at that place and time; and out of the relations involved in the social forms arose a 'superstructure' of higher activities such as politics, law, religion, philosophy, literature, and art. These activities were not, as is sometimes assumed, wholly explicable in terms of economics. They showed the mould, in ways direct or indirect, of the social configuration below them, but each was working to get away from its roots in the social classes and to constitute a professional group, with its own discipline and its own standards of value, which cut across class lines. These departments 'all react upon one another and upon the economic base. It is not the case that the economic situation is the sole active cause and everything else only a passive effect. But there is a reciprocal interaction within a fundamental economic necessity, which in the last instance always asserts itself' (Engels to Hans Starkenburg, 25 January 1894). So that the art of a great artistic period may reach a point of vitality and vision where it can influence the life of the period down to its very economic foundations. Simply, it must cease to flourish with the social system which made it possible by providing the artist with training and leisure, even though the artist himself may have been working for the destruction of that system.

Marx and Engels, unlike some of their followers, never attempted to furnish social-economic formulas by which the validity of works of art might be tested. They had grown up in the sunset of Goethe before the great age of German literature was over, and they had both set out in their youth to be poets; they responded to imaginative work, first of all, on its artistic merits. They could ridicule a trashy writer like Eugène Sue[a] for what they regarded as his *petit bourgeois* remedies for the miseries of contemporary society (*The Holy Family*); they could become bitter about Ferdinand Freiligrath, who had deserted the Communist League and turned nationalist in 1870 (Marx to Engels, 22 August 1870). And Marx could even make similar jibes at Heine when he thought that the latter had stooped to truckling to the authorities or when he read the expressions of piety in his will (Marx to Engels, 21 December 1866 and 8 May 1856). But Marx's daughter tells us that her father loved Heine 'as much as his work and was very indulgent of his political shortcomings. He used to say that the poets were originals, who must be allowed to go their own way, and that one shouldn't apply to them the same standards as to ordinary people'. It was not characteristic of Marx and Engels to judge literature—that is, literature of power and distinction—in terms of its purely political tendencies. In fact, Engels always warned the socialist novelists against the dangers of *Tendenz-Literatur* [ideologically committed literature] (Engels to Minna Kautsky, 26 November 1885; and to Margaret Harkness, April 1888). In writing to Minna Kautsky about one of her novels, he tells her that the personalities of her hero and heroine had been dissolved in the principles they represent.

> You evidently [he says] felt the need of publicly taking sides in this book, of proclaiming your opinions to the world.... But I believe that the tendency should arise from the situation and the action themselves without being explicitly formulated, and that the poet is not under the obligation to furnish the reader with a ready-made historical solution for the future of the conflict which he describes.

When Ferdinand Lassalle sent Marx and Engels his poetic tragedy, *Franz von Sickingen*, and invited them to criticize it, Marx replied that, 'setting aside any purely critical attitude towards the work', it had on a first reading affected him powerfully—characteristically adding that upon persons of a more emotional nature it would doubtless produce an even stronger effect; and Engels wrote that he had read it twice and had been moved by it so profoundly that he had been obliged to lay it aside in order to arrive at any critical perspective. It was only after pulling themselves together and making some purely literary observations that they were able to proceed to discuss, from their special historical point of view, the period with which the drama dealt and to show how Lassalle's own political position had led him to mistake the role of his hero. Aeschylus Marx loved for his grandeur and for the defiance of Zeus

[a] Marie-Joseph Sue (self-styled 'Eugène') (1804–75) was a French author of popular sensational novels about Parisian low-life.

242

by Prometheus; Goethe they both immensely admired: Engels wrote of him as a 'colossal' and 'universal' genius whose career had been marred by an admixture in his character of the philistine and the courtier (*German Socialism in Verse and Prose*); Shakespeare Marx knew by heart and was extremely fond of quoting, but never—despite the long, learned, and ridiculous essays which have appeared in the Soviet magazine, *International Literature*—attempted to draw from his plays any general social moral. So far, indeed, was Marx from having worked out a systematic explanation of the relation of the arts to social arrangements that he could assert, apropos of Greek art, in his *Introduction to the Critique of Political Economy*, that 'certain periods of highest development of art stand in no direct connection with the general development of society nor with the material basis and the skeleton structure of its organization'.

With Marx and Engels there is not yet any tendency to specialize art as a 'weapon'. They were both too much under the influence of the ideal of the many-sided man of the Renaissance, of the 'complete' man, who, like Leonardo, had been painter, mathematician, and engineer, or, like Machiavelli, poet, historian, and strategist, before the division of labour had had the effect of splitting up human nature and limiting everyone to some single function (Engel's preface to his *Dialectic and Nature*). But with Lenin we come to a Marxist who is specialized himself as an organizer and fighter. Like most Russians, Lenin was sensitive to music; but Gorky tells us that on one occasion, after listening to Beethoven's Appassionata Sonata and exclaiming that he 'would like to listen to it every day: it is marvellous superhuman music—I always think with pride ... what marvellous things human beings can do', he screwed up his eyes and smiled sadly and added:

> But I can't listen to music too often. It affects your nerves, makes you want to say stupid, nice things, and stroke the heads of people who could create such beauty while living in this vile hell. And now you mustn't stroke anyone's head—you might get your hand bitten off.

Yet he was fond of fiction, poetry, and the theatre, and by no means doctrinaire in his tastes. Krupskaya tells how, on a visit to a Youth Commune, he asked the young people, ' "What do you read? Do you read Pushkin?" "Oh, no!" someone blurted out. "He was a bourgeois. Mayakovsky for us."[a] Ilyitch smiled. "I think Pushkin is better." ' Gorky says that one day he found Lenin with *War and Peace* lying on the table: ' "Yes, Tolstoy. I wanted to read over the scene of the hunt, then remembered that I had to write a comrade. Absolutely no time for reading." ... Smiling and screwing up his eyes, he stretched himself deliciously in his armchair and, lowering his voice, added quickly, "What a colossus, eh? What a marvellously developed brain! Here's an artist for you, sir. And do you know something still more amazing? You couldn't find a genuine *muzhik* [peasant] in literature till this count came upon the

---

[a] Vladimir Vladimirovich Mayakovsky (1893–1930), Russian poet, playright, and essayist. He responded enthusiastically to the Revolution in its early years, but committed suicide in 1930. Pushkin (1799–1837) was the greatest of Russian poets.

scene."' In his very acute essays on Tolstoy, he deals with him much as Engels deals with Goethe—with tremendous admiration for Tolstoy's genius, but with an analysis of his non-resistance and mysticism in terms not, it is interesting to note, of the psychology of the landed nobility, but of the patriarchal peasantry with Whom Tolstoy had identified himself. And Lenin's attitude towards Gorky was much like that of Marx towards Heine. He suggests in one of his letters that Gorky would be helpful as a journalist on the side of the Bolsheviks, but adds that he mustn't be bothered if he is busy writing a book.

Trotsky is a literary man as Lenin never was, and he published in 1924 a most remarkable little study called *Literature and Revolution*. In this book he tried to illuminate the problems which were arising for Russian writers with the new society of the Revolution. And he was obliged to come to grips with a question with which Marx and Engels had not been much concerned—the question of what Mr James T. Farrell in his book, *A Note on Literary Criticism*, one of the few sensible recent writings on this subject, calls 'the carry-over value' of literature. Marx had assumed the value of Shakespeare and the Greeks and more or less left it at that. But what, the writers in Russia were now asking, was to be the value of the literature and art of the ages of barbarism and oppression in the dawn of socialist freedom? What in particular was to be the status of the culture of that bourgeois society from which socialism had just emerged and of which it still bore the unforgotten scars? Would there be a new proletarian literature, with new language, new style, new form, to give expression to the emotions and ideas of the new proletarian dictatorship? There had been in Russia a group called the Proletcult, which aimed at monopolizing the control of Soviet literature; but Lenin had discouraged and opposed it, insisting that proletarian culture was not something which could be produced synthetically and by official dictation of policy, but only by natural evolution as a 'development of those reserves of knowledge which society worked for under the oppression of capitalism, of the landlords, of the officials'. Now, in *Literature and Revolution*, Trotsky asserted that 'such terms as "proletarian literature" and "proletarian culture" are dangerous, because they erroneously compress the culture of the future into the narrow limits of the present day'. In a position to observe from his Marxist point of view the effects on a national literature of the dispossession of a dominant class, he was able to see the unexpected ways in which the presentments of life of the novelists, the feelings and images of the poets, the standards themselves of the critics, were turning out to be determined by their attitudes towards the social-economic crises. But he did not believe in a proletarian culture which would displace the bourgeois one. The bourgeois literature of the French Revolution had ripened under the old régime; but the illiterate proletariat and peasantry of Russia had had no chance to produce a culture, nor would there be time for them to do so in the future, because the proletarian dictatorship was not to last: it was to be only a transition phase and to lead the way to 'a culture which is above classes and which will be the first truly human culture'. In the meantime, the new socialist literature would grow directly out of that which had already been produced during the domination of the bourgeoisie. Communism, Trotsky said, had as yet no artistic culture; it had only a political culture.

All this seems to us reasonable enough. But, reasonable and cultured as Trotsky is, ready as he is to admit that 'one cannot always go by the principles of Marxism in deciding whether to accept or reject a work of art', that such a work 'should be judged in the first place by its own law—that is, by the law of art', there is none the less in the whole situation something which is alien to us. We are not accustomed, in our quarter of the world, either to having the government attempt to control literature and art or to having literary and artistic movements try to identify themselves with the government. Yet Russia, since the Revolution, has had a whole series of cultural groups which have attempted to dominate literature either with or without the authority of the government; and Trotsky himself, in his official position, even in combating these tendencies, cannot avoid passing censure and pinning ribbons. Sympathizers with the Soviet régime used to assume that this state of affairs was inseparable from the realization of socialism: that its evils would be easily outgrown and that in any case it was a great thing to have the government take so lively an interest in culture. I believe that this view was mistaken. Under the Tsar, imaginative literature in Russia played a role which was probably different from any role it had ever played in the life of any other nation. Political and social criticism, pursued and driven underground by the censorship, was forced to incorporate itself in the dramatic imagery of fiction. This was certainly one of the principal reasons for the greatness during the nineteenth century of the Russian theatre and novel, for the mastery by the Russian writers—from Pushkin's time to Tolstoy's—of the art of implication. In the 'fifties and 'sixties, the stories of Turgenev, which seem mild enough to us today, were capable of exciting the most passionate controversies—and even, in the case of A *Sportsman's Sketches*, causing the dismissal of the censor who had passed it—because each was regarded as a political message. Ever since the Revolution, literature and politics in Russia have remained inextricable. But after the Revolution the intelligentsia themselves were in power; and it became plain that in the altered situation the identification of literature with politics was liable to terrible abuses. Lenin and Trotsky, Lunacharsky and Gorky, worked sincerely to keep literature free; but they had at the same time, from the years of the Tsardom, a keen sense of the possibility of art as an instrument of propaganda. Lenin took a special interest in the moving pictures from the propaganda point of view; and the first Soviet films, by Eisenstein and Pudovkin, were masterpieces of implication, as the old novels and plays had been. But Lenin died; Trotsky was exiled; Lunacharsky died. The administration of Stalin, unliterary and uncultivated himself, slipped into depending more and more on literature as a means of manipulating a people of whom, before the Revolution, seventy or eighty per cent had been illiterate and who could hardly be expected to be critical of what they read. Gorky seems to have exerted what influence he could in the direction of liberalism: to him was due, no doubt, the liquidation of RAPP, the latest device for the monopoly of culture, and the opening of the Soviet canon to the best

245

contemporary foreign writing and the classics. But though this made possible more freedom of form and a wider range of reading, it could not, under the dictatorship of Stalin, either stimulate or release a living literature. Where no political opposition was possible, there was possible no political criticism; and in Russia political questions involve vitally the fate of society. What reality can there be for the Russians, the most socially-minded writers on earth, in a freedom purely 'aesthetic'? Even the fine melodramatic themes of the post-revolutionary cinema and theatre, with their real emotion and moral conviction, have been replaced by simple trash not very far removed from Hollywood, or by dramatized exemplifications of the latest 'directive' of Stalin which open the night after the speech that has announced the directive. The recent damning of the music of Shostakovich on the ground that the commissars were unable to hum it seems a withdrawal from the liberal position. And it is probable that the death of Gorky, as well as the imprisonment of Bukharin and Radek, have removed the last brakes from a precipitate descent, in the artistic as well as the political field, into a nightmare of informing and repression. The practice of deliberate falsification of social and political history which began at the time of the Stalin–Trotsky crisis and which has now attained proportions so fantastic that the government does not seem to hesitate to pass the sponge every month or so over everything that the people have previously been told and to present them with a new and contradictory version of their history, their duty, and the characters and careers of their leaders—this practice cannot fail in the end to corrupt every department of intellectual life, till the serious, the humane, the clear-seeking must simply, if they can, remain silent.

Thus Marxism in Russia for the moment has run itself into a blind alley—or rather, it has been put down a well. The Soviets seem hardly at the present time to have retained even the Marxist political culture, even in its cruder forms—so that we are relieved from the authority of Russia as we are deprived of her inspiration. To what conclusions shall we come, then, at this time of day, about Marxism and literature—basing our views not even necessarily upon texts from the Marxist Fathers, but upon ordinary common sense? Well, first of all, that we can go even further than Trotsky in one of the dicta I have quoted above and declare that Marxism by itself can tell us nothing whatever about the goodness or badness of a work of art. A man may be an excellent Marxist, but if he lacks imagination and taste he will be unable to make the choice between a good and an inferior book both of which are ideologically unexceptionable. What Marxism *can* do, however, is throw a great deal of light on the origins and social significance of works of art. The study of literature in its relation to society is as old as Herder [1744-1803]—and even Vico [1668-1744]. Coleridge had flashes of insight into the connection between literary and social phenomena, as when he saw the Greek state in the Greek sentence and the individualism of the English in the short separate statements of Chaucer's Prologue. But the great bourgeois master of this kind of criticism was Taine, with his *race* and *moment* and *milieu*; yet Taine, for all his scientific professions, responded artistically to literary art, and responded so vividly that his summings-up of writers and re-creations of periods

246

sometimes rival or surpass their subjects. Marx and Engels further deepened this study of literature in relation to its social background by demonstrating for the first time inescapably the importance of economic systems. But if Marx and Engels and Lenin and Trotsky are worth listening to on the subject of books, it is not merely because they created Marxism, but also because they were capable of literary appreciation.

Yet the man who tries to apply Marxist principles without real understanding of literature is liable to go horribly wrong. For one thing, it is usually true in works of the highest order that the purport is not a simple message, but a complex vision of things, which itself is not explicit but implicit; and the reader who does not grasp them artistically, but is merely looking for simple social morals, is certain to be hopelessly confused. Especially will he be confused if the author *does* draw an explicit moral which is the opposite of or has nothing to do with his real purport. Friedrich Engels, in the letter to Margaret Harkness already referred to above, in warning her that the more the novelist allows his political ideas to 'remain hidden, the better it is for the work of art', says that Balzac, with his reactionary opinions, is worth a thousand of Zola, with all his democratic ones. (Balzac was one of the great literary admirations of both Engels and Marx, the latter of whom had planned to write a book on him.) Engels points out that Balzac himself was, or believed himself to be, a legitimist engaged in deploring the decline of high society; but that actually 'his irony is never more bitter, his satire never more trenchant, than when he is showing us these aristocrats ... for whom he felt so profound a sympathy', and that 'the only men of whom he speaks with undissimulated admiration are his most determined political adversaries, the republican heroes of the Cloître-Saint-Merri, the men who at that period (1830-6) truly represented the popular masses'. Nor does it matter necessarily in a work of art whether the characters are shown engaged in a conflict which illustrates the larger conflicts of society or in one which from that point of view is trivial. In art—it is quite obvious in music, but it is also true in literature—a sort of law of moral interchangeability prevails: we may transpose the actions and the sentiments that move us into terms of whatever we do or are ourselves. Real genius of moral insight is a motor which will start any engine. When Proust, in his wonderful chapter on the death of the novelist Bergotte, speaks of those moral obligations which impose themselves in spite of everything and which seem to come through to humanity from some source outside its wretched self (obligations 'invisible only to fools—and are they really to them?'), he is describing a kind of duty which he felt only in connection with the literary work which he performed in his dark and fetid room; yet he speaks for every moral, aesthetic, or intellectual passion which holds the expediencies of the world in contempt. And the hero of Thornton Wilder's *Heaven's My Destination*, the travelling salesman who tries to save souls in the smoking car and writes Bible texts on hotel blotters, is something more than a symptom of Thornton Wilder's religious tendencies: he is the type of all saints who begin absurdly; and Wilder's story would be as true of the socialist Upton Sinclair as of the Christian George Brush. Nor does it necessarily matter, for the moral effect of a work of literature, whether the forces of bravery or virtue with which we identify ourselves are victorious or vanquished in the end. In Hemingway's story *The Undefeated*, the old bull-fighter who figures as the hero is actually humiliated and killed, but his courage has itself been a victory. It is true, as I. Kashkin, the Soviet critic, has said, that Hemingway has written much about decadence, but in order to write tellingly about death you have to have the principle of life, and those that have it will make it felt in spite of everything.

The Leftist critic with no literary competence is always trying to measure works of literature by tests which have no validity in that field. And one of his favourite occupations is giving specific directions and working out diagrams for the construction of ideal Marxist books. Such formulas are of course perfectly futile. The rules observed in any given school of art become apparent, not before but after, the actual works of art have been produced. As we were reminded by Burton Rascoe at the time of the Humanist controversy, the aesthetic laws involved in Greek tragedy were not formulated by Aristotle until at least half a century after Euripides and Sophocles were dead. And the behaviour of the Marxist critics has been precisely like that of the Humanists.[a] The Humanists knew down to the last comma what they wanted a work of literature to be, but they never—with the possible exception, when pressed, of *The Bridge of San Luis Rey*, about which they had, however, hesitations—were able to find any contemporary work which fitted their specifications. The Marxists did just the same thing. In an article called *The Crisis in Criticism* in the *New Masses* of February 1933, Granville Hicks drew up a list of requirements which the ideal Marxist work of literature must meet. The primary function of such a work, he asserted, must be to 'lead the proletarian reader to recognize his role in the class struggle'—and it must therefore (1) 'directly or indirectly show the effects of the class struggle'; (2) 'the author must be able to make the reader feel that he is participating in the lives described'; and, finally, (3) the author's point of view must 'be that of the vanguard of the proletariat; he should be, or should try to make himself, a member of the proletariat'. This formula, he says, 'gives us ... a standard by which to recognize the perfect Marxian novel'—and adds 'no novel as yet written perfectly conforms to our demands'. But the doctrine of 'socialist realism' promulgated at the Soviet Writers' Congress of August 1934 was only an attempt on a larger scale to legislate masterpieces into existence—a kind of attempt which always indicates sterility on the part of those who engage in it, and which always actually works, if it has any effect at all, to legislate existing good literature *out* of existence and to discourage the production of any more. The prescribers for the literature of the future usually cherish some great figure of the past whom they regard as having fulfilled their conditions and whom they are always bringing forward to demonstrate the inferiority of the literature of the present. As there has never existed a great writer who really had anything in common with these critics' conception of literature,

[a] See John Crowe Ransom's remarks, and note, concerning the New Humanists above, pp. 230–1.

they are obliged to provide imaginary versions of what their ideal great writers are like. The Humanists had Sophocles and Shakespeare; the socialist realists had Tolstoy. Yet it is certain that if Tolstoy had had to live up to the objectives and prohibitions which the socialist realists proposed he could never have written a chapter; and that if Babbitt and More had been able to enforce against Shakespeare their moral and aesthetic injunctions he would never have written a line. The misrepresentation of Sophocles, which has involved even a tampering with his text in the interests not merely of Humanism but of academic classicism in general, has been one of the scandalous absurdities of scholarship. The Communist critical movement in America, which had for its chief spokesman Mr Hicks, tended to identify their ideal with the work of John Dos Passos. In order to make this possible, it was necessary to invent an imaginary Dos Passos. This ideal Dos Passos was a Communist, who wrote stories about the proletariat, at a time when the real Dos Passos was engaged in bringing out a long novel about the effects of the capitalist system on the American middle class and had announced himself—in the *New Republic* in 1930—politically a 'middle-class liberal'. The ideal Dos Passos was something like Gorky without the moustache—Gorky, in the meantime, having himself undergone some transmogrification at the hands of Soviet publicity—and this myth was maintained until the Communist critics were finally compelled to repudiate it, not because they had acquired new light on Dos Passos, the novelist and dramatist, but because of his attitude towards events in Russia.

The object of these formulas for the future, as may be seen from the above quotations from Mr Hicks, is to make of art an effective instrument in the class struggle. And we must deal with the dogma that 'art is a weapon'. It is true that art may be a weapon; but in the case of some of the greatest works of art, some of those which have the longest carry-over value, it is difficult to see that any important part of this value is due to their direct functioning as weapons. The *Divine Comedy*, in its political aspect, is a weapon for Henry of Luxembourg, whom Dante—with his medieval internationalism and his lack of sympathy for the nationalistic instincts which were impelling the Italians of his time to get away from the Austrian emperors—was so passionately eager to impose on his countrymen. Today we may say with Carducci that we would as soon see the crown of his 'good Frederick' rolling in Olona vale : 'Jove perishes; the poet's hymn remains.'[a] And, though Shakespeare's *Henry IV* and *Henry V* are weapons for Elizabethan imperialism, their real centre is not Prince Hal but Falstaff; and Falstaff is the father of *Hamlet* and of all Shakespeare's tragic heroes, who, if they illustrate any social moral—the moral, perhaps, that Renaissance princes, supreme in their little worlds, may go to pieces in all kinds of terrible ways for lack of a larger social organism to restrain them—do so evidently without Shakespeare's being aware of it. If these works may be spoken of as weapons at all, they are weapons in the more general struggle of modern European man emerging from the Middle

[a] The quotation is from a sonnet on Dante by the Italian poet and critic Giosuè Carducci (1835–1907). The 'good Frederick' was the Emperor Frederick Barbarossa.

249

Ages and striving to understand his world and himself—a function for which 'weapon' is hardly the right word. The truth is that there is short-range and long-range literature. Long-range literature attempts to sum up wide areas and long periods of human experience, or to extract from them general laws; short-range literature preaches and pamphleteers with the view to an immediate effect. A good deal of the recent confusion of our writers in the Leftist camp has been due to their not understanding, or being unable to make up their minds, whether they are aiming at long-range or short-range writing.

This brings us to the question of what sort of periods are most favourable for works of art. One finds an assumption on the Left that revolutionary or pre-revolutionary periods are apt to produce new and vital forms of literature. This, of course, is very far from the truth in the case of periods of actual revolution. The more highly developed forms of literature require leisure and a certain amount of stability; and during a period of revolution the writer is usually deprived of both. The literature of the French Revolution consisted of the orations of Danton, the journalism of Camille Desmoulins, and the few political poems that André Chénier had a chance to write before he was guillotined. The literature of the Russian Revolution was the political writing of Lenin and Trotsky, and Alexander Blok's poem, *The Twelve*, almost the last fruit of his genius before it was nipped by the wind of the storm. As for pre-revolutionary periods in which the new forces are fermenting, they *may* be great periods for literature—as the eighteenth century was in France and the nineteenth century in Russia (though here there was a decadence after 1905). But the conditions that make possible the masterpieces are apparently not produced by the impending revolutions, but by the phenomenon of literary technique, already highly developed, in the hands of a writer who has had the support of long-enduring institutions. He may reflect an age of transition, but it will not necessarily be true that his face is set squarely in the direction of the future. The germs of the Renaissance are in Dante and the longing for a better world in Virgil, but neither Dante nor Virgil can in any real sense be described as a revolutionary writer: they sum up or write elegies for ages that are passing. The social organisms that give structure to their thought— the Roman Empire and the Catholic Church—are already showing signs of decay. It is impossible, therefore, to identify the highest creative work in art with the most active moments of creative social change. The writer who is seriously intent on producing long-range works of literature should, from the point of view of his own special personal interests, thank his stars if there is no violent revolution going on in his own country in his time. He may disapprove of the society he is writing about, but if it were disrupted by an actual upheaval he would probably not be able to write.

But what about 'proletarian literature' as an accompaniment of the social revolution? In the earlier days of the Communist régime in Russia, one used to hear about Russian authors who, in the effort to eliminate from their writing any vestige of the bourgeois point of view, had reduced their vocabulary and syntax to what they regarded as an A B C of essentials—with the result of becoming more unintelligible to the proletarian audience at whom they are aiming than if they had been Symbolist poets. (Indeed, the futurist poet Mayakovsky has since that time become a part of the Soviet canon.) Later on, as I have said, Soviet culture followed the road that Trotsky recommended: it began building again on the classics and on the bourgeois culture of other countries and on able revolutionary Russian writers who had learned their trade before the Revolution. 'Soviet publishers'—I quote from the Russian edition of *International Literature*, issue 2 of 1936—

> are bringing out Hemingway and Proust not merely in order to demonstrate 'bourgeois decay'. Every genuine work of art—and such are the productions of Hemingway and Proust—enriches the reader's knowledge of life and heightens his aesthetic sensibility and his emotional culture—in a word, it figures, in the broad sense, as a factor of educational value. Liberated socialist humanity inherits all that is beautiful, elevating, and sustaining in the culture of previous ages.

The truth is that the talk in Soviet Russia about proletarian literature and art has resulted from the persistence of the same situation which led Tolstoy under the old régime to put on the muzhik's blouse and to go in for carpentry, cobbling, and ploughing: the difficulty experienced by an educated minority, who were only about twenty per cent of the people, in getting in touch with the illiterate majority. In America the situation is quite different. The percentage of illiterates in this country is only something like four per cent; and there is relatively little difficulty of communication between different social groups. Our development away from England, and from the old world generally, in this respect—in the direction of the democratization of our idiom— is demonstrated clearly in H. L. Mencken's *The American Language*; and if it is a question of either the use for high literature of the language of the people or the expression of the dignity and importance of the ordinary man, the country which has produced *Leaves of Grass* and *Huckleberry Finn* has certainly nothing to learn from Russia. We had created during our pioneering period a literature of the common man's escape, not only from feudal Europe but also from bourgeois society, many years before the Russian masses were beginning to write their names. There has been a section of our recent American literature of the last fifteen years or so—the period of the boom and the depression—which has dealt with our industrial and rural life from the point of view of the factory hand and the poor farmer under conditions which were forcing him to fight for his life, and this has been called proletarian literature; but it has been accompanied by books on the white-collar worker, the storekeeper, the well-to-do merchant, the scientist, and the millionaire in situations equally disastrous or degrading. And this whole movement of critical and imaginative writing—though with some stimulus, certainly, from Russia— had come quite naturally out of our literature of the past. It is curious to observe that one of the best of the recent strike novels, *The Land of Plenty* by Robert Cantwell, himself a Westerner and a former mill worker, owes a good deal to Henry James.

Yet when all these things have been said, all the questions have not been answered. All that has been said has been said of the past; and Marxism is something new in the world: it is a philosophical system which leads directly to programmes of action. Has there ever appeared before in literature such a phenomenon as M. André Malraux, who alternates between attempts, sometimes brilliant, to write long-range fiction on revolutionary themes, and exploits of aviation for the cause of revolution in Spain? Here creative political action and the more complex kind of imaginative writing have united at least to the extent that they have arisen from the same vision of history and have been included in the career of one man. The Marxist vision of Lenin—Vincent Sheean has said it first—has in its completeness and its compelling force a good deal in common with the vision of Dante; but, partly realized by Lenin during his lifetime and still potent for some years after his death, it was a creation, not of literary art, but of actual social engineering. It is society itself, says Trotsky, which under communism becomes the work of art. The first attempts at this art will be inexpert and they will have refractory material to work with; and the philosophy of the Marxist dialectic involves idealistic and mythological elements which have led too often to social religion rather than to social art. Yet the human imagination has already come to conceive the possibility of re-creating human society; and how can we doubt that, as it acquires the power, it must emerge from what will seem by comparison the revolutionary 'underground' of art as we have always known it up to now and deal with the materials of actual life in ways which we cannot now even foresee? This is to speak in terms of centuries, of ages; but, in practising and prizing literature, we must not be unaware of the first efforts of the human spirit to transcend literature itself.

20 Paul Valéry

Paul Valéry (1871-1945) was born in the South of France, but came as a young man to Paris where he frequented the *salon* of Stephane Mallarmé, *doyen* of the French *Symboliste* poets. Valéry himself carried on the Symbolist poetic in both theory and practice, though perhaps in a more austere, analytical, and detached style than the previous generation of Mallarmé, Verlaine, and Rimbaud. His best-known volumes of poetry were probably *La Jeune Parque* (Paris, 1917) and *Charmes* (Paris, 1922) which included the celebrated 'La Cimitière Marin'. In later life Paul Valéry was a Professor at the Collège de France. He gave many lectures and wrote many essays on the subject of poetry, invariably of a theoretical and introspective kind. As T. S. Eliot remarked: 'He is perpetually engaged in solving an insoluble puzzle—the puzzle of how poetry gets written; and the material upon which he works is his own poetry.'

In the extract from 'Poetry and Abstract Thought' reprinted below, Valéry attempts to identify the special character and value of poetry by distinguishing it as language from other kinds of discourse, lumped together under the heading of prose. The distinction is illustrated and enforced by analogies between prose and walking on the one hand, and between poetry and dancing on the other. Valéry's assertion of a complete discontinuity between poetry and prose is highly debatable on linguistic grounds, and assumes a very narrow concept of poetry (i.e. the modern symbolist lyric). Nevertheless, it is a classic, eloquent statement of the Romantic–Symbolist tradition of thought about literature which underlies so much modern poetry and the criticism of it.

'Poetry and Abstract Thought' was originally delivered as a lecture at Oxford University in 1939. It is reprinted here, in part, from *The Art of Poetry* (1958), translated by Denise Folliot, Volume vii of Valéry's *Collected Works*.

CROSS REFERENCES: 2. W. B. Yeats
                     5. Ezra Pound
                     6. T. S. Eliot
                     9. I. A. Richards
                     47. W. H. Auden

COMMENTARY: T. S. Eliot, Introduction to Valéry's *The Art of Poetry* (1958)
              Frank Kermode, 'Paul Valéry', *Modern Essays* (1971)

[Poetry and abstract thought: dancing and walking]

Let us first see in what may consist that initial and *invariably accidental* shock which will construct the poetic instrument within us, and above all, what are its effects. The problem can be put in this way: Poetry is an art of Language; certain combinations of words can produce an emotion that others do not produce, and which we shall call *poetic*. What kind of emotion is this?

I recognize it in myself by this: that all possible objects of the ordinary world, external or internal, beings, events, feelings, and actions, while keeping their usual appearance, are suddenly placed in an indefinable but wonderfully fitting relationship with the modes of our general sensibility. That is to say that these well-known things and beings—or rather the ideas that represent them—somehow change in value. They attract one another, they are connected in ways quite different from the ordinary; they become (if you will permit the expression) *musicalized*, resonant, and, as it were, harmonically related. The poetic universe, thus defined, offers extensive analogies with what we can postulate of the dream world.

Since the word *dream* has found its way into this talk, I shall say in passing that in modern times, beginning with Romanticism, there has arisen a fairly understandable confusion between the notion of the dream and that of poetry. Neither the dream nor the daydream is necessarily poetic; it may be so: but figures formed *by chance* are only *by chance* harmonious figures.

In any case, our memories of dreams teach us, by frequent and common experience, that our consciousness can be invaded, filled, entirely absorbed by the production of an *existence* in which objects and beings seem the same as those in the waking state; but their meanings, relationships, modes of variation and of substitution are quite different and doubtless represent, like symbols or allegories, the immediate fluctuations of our *general* sensibility uncontrolled by the sensitivities of our *specialized* senses. In very much the same way the *poetic state* takes hold of us, develops, and finally disintegrates.

This is to say that the *state of poetry* is completely irregular, inconstant, involuntary, and fragile, and that we lose it, as we find it, *by accident*. But this state is not enough to make a poet, any more than it is enough to see a treasure in a dream to find it, on waking, sparkling at the foot of one's bed.

A poet's function—do not be startled by this remark—is not to experience the poetic state: that is a private affair. His function is to create it in others. The poet is recognized—or at least everyone recognizes his own poet—by the simple fact that he causes his reader to become 'inspired'. Positively speaking, inspiration is a graceful attribute with which the reader endows his poet: the reader sees in us the transcendent merits of virtues and graces that develop in him. He seeks and finds in us the wondrous cause of his own wonder.

But poetic feeling and the artificial synthesis of this state in some work are two quite distinct things, as different as sensation and action. A sustained action is much more complex than any spontaneous production, particularly when it has to be carried out in a sphere as conventional as that of language. Here you see emerging through my explanations the famous ABSTRACT THOUGHT which custom opposes to POETRY. We shall come back to that in a moment. Meanwhile I should like to tell you a true story, so that you may feel as I felt, and in a curiously clear way, the whole difference that exists between the poetic state or emotion, even creative and original, and the production of a work. It is a rather remarkable observation of myself that I made about a year ago.

I had left my house to relax from some tedious piece of work by walking and by a consequent change of scene. As I went along the street where I live, I was suddenly *gripped* by a rhythm which took possession of me and soon gave me the impression of some force outside myself. It was as though someone else were making use of my *living-machine*. Then another rhythm overtook and combined with the first, and certain strange *transverse* relations were set up between these two principles (I am explaining myself as best I can). They combined the movement of my walking legs and some kind of song I was murmuring, or rather which was being murmured *through me*. This composition became more and more complicated and soon in its complexity went far beyond anything I could reasonably produce with my ordinary, usable rhythmic faculties. The sense of strangeness that I mentioned became almost painful, almost disquieting. I am no musician; I am completely ignorant of musical technique; yet here I was, prey to a development in several parts more complicated than any poet could dream. I argued that there had been an error of person, that this grace had descended on the wrong head, since I could make no use of a gift which for a musician would doubtless have assumed value, form, and duration, while these parts that mingled and separated offered me in vain a composition whose cunningly organized sequence amazed my ignorance and reduced it to despair.

After about twenty minutes the magic suddenly vanished, leaving me on the bank of the Seine, as perplexed as the duck in the fable, that saw a swan emerge from the egg she had hatched. As the swan flew away, my surprise changed to reflection. I knew that walking often induces in me a quickened flow of ideas and that there is a certain reciprocity between my pace and my thoughts—my thoughts modify my pace; my pace provokes my thoughts—which after all is remarkable enough, but is fairly understandable. Our various 'reaction periods' are doubtless synchronized, and it is interesting to have to admit that a reciprocal modification is possible between a form of action which is purely muscular and a varied production of images, judgments, and reasonings.

But in the case I am speaking of, my movement in walking became in my consciousness a very subtle system of rhythms, instead of instigating those images, interior words, and potential actions which one calls *ideas*. As for ideas, they are things of a species familiar to me; they are things that I can note, provoke, and handle.... *But I cannot say the same of my unexpected rhythms.*

What was I to think? I supposed that mental activity while walking must correspond with a general excitement exerting itself in the region of my brain; this excitement satisfied and relieved itself as best it could, and so long as its energy was expended, it mattered little whether this was on ideas, memories, or rhythms unconsciously hummed. On that day, the energy was expended in a rhythmical intuition that developed before the awakening in my consciousness of *the person who knows that he does not know music*. I imagine it is the same as when *the person who knows he cannot fly* has not yet become active in the man who dreams he is flying.

I apologize for this long and true story—as true, that is, as a story of this kind can be. Notice that everything I have said, or tried to say, happened in relation to what we call the *External World*, what we call *Our Body*, and what we call *Our Mind*, and requires a kind of vague collaboration between these three great powers.

Why have I told you this? In order to bring out the profound difference existing between spontaneous production by the mind—or rather by our *sensibility as a whole*—and the fabrication of works. In my story, the substance of a musical composition was freely given to me, but the organization which would have seized, fixed, and reshaped it was lacking. The great painter Degas often repeated to me a very true and simple remark by Mallarmé. Degas occasionally wrote verses, and some of those he left were delightful. But he often found great difficulty in this work accessory to his painting. (He was, by the way, the kind of man who would bring all possible difficulty to any art whatever.) One day he said to Mallarmé: 'Yours is a hellish craft. I can't manage to say what I want, and yet I'm full of ideas....' And Mallarmé answered: 'My dear Degas, one does not make poetry with ideas, but with words.'

Mallarmé was right. But when Degas spoke of ideas, he was, after all, thinking of inner speech or of images, which might have been expressed in *words*. But these words, these secret phrases which he called ideas, all these intentions and perceptions of the mind, do not make verses. There is something else, then, a modification, or a transformation, sudden or not, spontaneous or not, laborious or not, which must necessarily intervene between the thought that produces ideas—that activity and multiplicity of inner questions and solutions—and, on the other hand, that discourse, so different from ordinary speech, which is verse, which is so curiously ordered, which answers no need *unless it be the need it must itself create*, which never speaks but of absent things or of things profoundly and secretly felt: strange discourse, as though made by someone *other* than the speaker and addressed to someone *other* than the listener. In short, it is a *language within a language*.

Let us look into these mysteries.

Poetry is an art of language. But language is a practical creation. It may be observed that in all communication between men, certainty comes only from practical acts and from the verification which practical acts give us. *I ask you for a light. You give me a light:* you have understood me.

But in asking me for a light, you were able to speak those few unimportant words with a certain intonation, a certain tone of voice, a certain inflection, a certain languor or briskness perceptible to me. I have understood your words, since without even thinking I handed you what you asked for—a light. But the matter does not end there. The strange thing: the sound and as it were the features of your little sentence come back to me, echo within me, as though they were pleased to be there; I, too, like to hear myself repeat this little phrase, which has almost lost its meaning, which has stopped being of use, and which can yet go on living, though with quite another life. It has acquired a value; and has acquired it *at the expense of its finite significance.* It has created the need to be heard again.... Here we are on the very threshold of the poetic state. This tiny experience will help us to the discovery of more than one truth.

It has shown us that language can produce effects of two quite different kinds. One of them tends to bring about the complete negation of language itself. I speak to you, and if you have understood my words, those very words are abolished. If you have understood, it means that the words have vanished from your minds and are replaced by their counterpart, by images, relationships, impulses; so that you have within you the means to retransmit these ideas and images in a language that may be very different from the one you received. *Understanding* consists in the more or less rapid replacement of a system of sounds, intervals, and signs by something quite different, which is, in short, a modification or interior reorganization of the person to whom one is speaking. And here is the counterproof of this proposition: the person who does not understand *repeats* the words, or *has them repeated* to him.

Consequently, the perfection of a discourse whose sole aim is comprehension obviously consists in the ease with which the words forming it are transformed into something quite different: the *language* is transformed first into *non-language* and then, if we wish, into a form of language differing from the original form.

In other terms, in practical or abstract uses of language, the form—that is the physical, the concrete part, the very act of speech—does not last; it does not outlive understanding; it dissolves in the light; it has acted; it has done its work; it has brought about understanding; it has lived.

But on the other hand, the moment this concrete form takes on, by an effect of its own, such importance that it asserts itself and makes itself, as it were, respected; and not only remarked and respected, but desired and therefore repeated—then something new happens: we are insensibly transformed and ready to live, breathe, and think in accordance with a rule and under laws which are no longer of the practical order—that is, nothing that may occur in this state will be resolved, finished, or abolished by a specific act. We are entering the poetic universe.

Permit me to support this notion of a *poetic universe* by referring to a similar notion that, being much simpler, is easier to explain: the notion of a *musical universe.* I would ask you to make a small sacrifice: limit yourselves for a moment to your faculty of hearing. One simple sense, like that of hearing, will offer us all we need for our definition and will absolve us from entering into all the difficulties and subtleties to which the conventional structure and historical complexities of ordinary language would lead us. We live by ear in the world of noises. Taken as a whole, it is generally incoherent and irregularly supplied by all the mechanical incidents which the ear may interpret as it can. But the same ear isolates from this chaos a group of noises particularly remarkable and simple—that is, easily recognizable by our sense of hearing and furnishing it with points of reference. These elements have relations with one another which we sense as we do the elements themselves. The interval between two of these privileged noises is as clear to us as each of them. These are the *sounds*, and these units of sonority tend to form clear combinations, successive or simultaneous implications, series, and intersections which one may term *intelligible*: this is why abstract possibilities exist in music. But I must return to my subject.

I will confine myself to saying that the contrast between noise and sound is the contrast between pure and impure, order and disorder; that this differentiation between pure sensations and others has permitted the constitution of music; that it has been possible to control, unify, and codify this constitution, thanks to the intervention of physical science, which knows how to adjust measure to sensation so as to obtain the important result of teaching us to produce this sonorous sensation consistently, and in a continuous and identical fashion, by instruments that are, in reality, *measuring instruments.*

The musician is thus in possession of a perfect system of well-defined means which exactly match sensations with acts. From this it results that music has formed a domain absolutely its own. The world of the art of music, a world of sounds, is distinct from the world of noises. Whereas a *noise* merely rouses in us some isolated event—a dog, a door, a motor car—a *sound evokes, of itself, the musical universe.* If, in this hall where I am speaking to you and where you hear the noise of my voice, a tuning fork or a well-tempered instrument began to vibrate, you would at once, as soon as you were affected by this pure and exceptional noise that cannot be confused with others, have the feeling of a beginning, the beginning of a world; a quite different atmosphere would immediately be created, a new order would arise, and you yourselves would unconsciously *organize* yourselves to receive it. The musical universe, therefore, was within you, with all its associations and proportions—as in a saturated salt solution a crystalline universe awaits the molecular shock of a minute crystal in order *to declare itself.* I dare not say: the crystalline idea of such a system awaits....

And here is the counter proof of our little experiment: if, in a concert hall dominated by a resounding symphony, a chair happens to fall, someone coughs, or a door shuts, we immediately have the impression of a kind of rupture. Something indefinable, something like a spell or a Venetian glass, has been broken or cracked....

The poetic universe is not created so powerfully or so easily. It exists, but the poet is deprived of the immense advantages possessed by the musician. He does not have before him, ready for the uses of beauty, a body of resources expressly made for his art. He has to borrow *language*—the voice of the public, that collection of traditional and irrational terms and rules, oddly created and transformed, oddly codified, and very variedly understood and pronounced. Here there is no physicist who has determined the relations between these elements; no tuning forks, no metronomes, no inventors of scales or theoreticians of harmony. Rather, on the contrary, the phonetic and semantic fluctuations of vocabulary. Nothing pure; but a mixture of completely incoherent auditive and psychic stimuli. Each word is an instantaneous coupling of a *sound* and a *sense* that have no connection with each other. Each sentence is an act so complex that I doubt whether anyone has yet been able to provide a tolerable definition of it. As for the use of the resources of language and the modes of this action, you know what diversity there is, and what confusion sometimes results. A discourse can be logical, packed with sense, but devoid of rhythm and measure. It can be pleasing to the ear, yet completely absurd or insignificant; it can be clear, yet useless; vague, yet delightful. But to grasp its strange multiplicity, which is no more than the multiplicity of life itself, it suffices to name all the sciences which have been created to deal with this diversity, each to study one of its aspects. One can analyse a text in many different ways, for it falls successively under the jurisdiction of phonetics, semantics, syntax, logic, rhetoric, philology, not to mention metrics, prosody, and etymology....

So the poet is at grips with this verbal matter, obliged to speculate on sound and sense at once, and to satisfy not only harmony and musical timing but all the various intellectual and aesthetic conditions, not to mention the conventional rules....

You can see what an effort the poet's undertaking would require if he had *consciously* to solve all these problems....

It is always interesting to try to reconstruct one of our complex activities, one of those complete actions which demand a specialization at once mental, sensuous, and motor, supposing that in order to accomplish this act we were obliged to understand and organize all the functions that we know play their part in it. Even if this attempt, at once imaginative and analytical, is clumsy, it will always teach us something. As for myself, who am, I admit, much more attentive to the formation or fabrication of works than to the works themselves, I have a habit, or obsession, of appreciating works only as actions. In my eyes a poet is a man who, as a result of a certain incident, undergoes a hidden transformation. He leaves his ordinary condition of general disposability, and I see taking shape in him an agent, a living system for producing verses. As among animals one suddenly sees emerging a capable hunter, a nest maker, a bridge builder, a digger of tunnels and galleries, so in a man one sees a composite organization declare itself, bending its functions to a specific piece of work. Think of a very small child: the child we have all been bore many possibilities within him. After a few months of life he has learned, at the same or almost the same time, to speak and to walk. He has acquired two types of action. That is to say that he now possesses two kinds of potentiality from which the accidental circumstances of each moment will draw what they can, in answer to his varying needs and imaginings.

Having learned to use his legs, he will discover that he can not only walk, but run; and not only walk and run, but dance. This is a great event. He has at that moment both invented and discovered a kind of *secondary use* for his limbs, a generalization of his formula of movement. In fact, whereas walking is after all a rather dull and not easily perfectible action, this new form of action, the Dance, admits of an infinite number of creations and variations or *figures*.

But will he not find an analogous development in speech? He will explore the possibilities of his faculty of speech; he will discover that more can be done with it than to ask for jam and deny his little sins. He will grasp the power of reasoning; he will invent stories to amuse himself when he is alone; he will repeat to himself words that he loves for their strangeness and mystery.

So, parallel with *Walking* and *Dancing*, he will acquire and distinguish the divergent types, *Prose and Poetry*.

This parallel has long struck and attracted me; but someone saw it before I did. According to Racan[a], Malherbe made use of it. In my opinion it is more than a simple comparison. I see in it an analogy as substantial and pregnant as those found in physics when one observes the identity of formulas that represent the measurement of seemingly very different phenomena. Here is how our comparison develops.

Walking, like prose, has a definite aim. It is an act directed at something we wish to reach. Actual circumstances, such as the need for some object, the impulse of my desire, the state of my body, my sight, the terrain, etc., which order the manner of walking, prescribe its direction and its speed, and give it a *definite end*. All the characteristics of walking derive from these instantaneous conditions, which combine *in a novel way* each time. There are no movements in walking that are not special adaptations, but, each time, they are abolished and, as it were, absorbed by the accomplishment of the act, by the attainment of the goal.

The dance is quite another matter. It is, of course, a system of actions; but of actions whose end is in themselves. It goes nowhere. If it pursues an object, it is only an ideal object, a state, an enchantment, the phantom of a flower, an extreme of life, a smile—which forms at last on the face of the one who summoned it from empty space.

It is therefore not a question of carrying out a limited operation whose end is situated somewhere in our surroundings, but rather of creating, maintaining, and exalting a certain *state*, by a periodic movement that can be executed on the spot; a movement which is almost entirely dissociated from sight, but which is stimulated and regulated by auditive rhythms.

But please note this very simple observation, that however different the dance may be from walking and utilitarian movements, it uses the same organs, the

---

[a] Honorat de Bueil, Seigneur de Racan (1589–1670) was a disciple and biographer of the French poet François de Malherbe (1555–1628).

same bones, the same muscles, only differently coordinated and aroused.

Here we come again to the contrast between prose and poetry. Prose and poetry use the same words, the same syntax, the same forms, the same sounds or tones, but differently coordinated and differently aroused. Prose and poetry are therefore distinguished by the difference between certain links and associations which form and dissolve in our psychic and nervous organism, whereas the components of these modes of functioning are identical. This is why one should guard against reasoning about poetry as one does about prose. What is true of one very often has no meaning when it is sought in the other. But here is the great and decisive difference. When the man who is walking has reached his goal—as I said—when he has reached the place, book, fruit, the object of his desire (which desire drew him from his repose), this possession at once entirely annuls his whole act; the effect swallows up the cause, the end absorbs the means; and, whatever the act, only the result remains. It is the same with utilitarian language: the language I use to express my design, my desire, my command, my opinion; this language, when it has served its purpose, evaporates almost as it is heard. I have given it forth to perish, to be radically transformed into something else in your mind; and I shall know that I was *understood* by the remarkable fact that my speech no longer exists: it has been completely replaced by its *meaning*—that is, by images, impulses, reactions, or acts that belong to you: in short, by an interior modification in you.

As a result the perfection of this kind of language, whose sole end is to be understood, obviously consists in the ease with which it is transformed into something altogether different.

The poem, on the other hand, does not die for having lived: it is expressly designed to be born again from its ashes and to become endlessly what it has just been. Poetry can be recognized by this property, that it tends to get itself reproduced in its own form: it stimulates us to reconstruct it identically.

That is an admirable and uniquely characteristic property.

21　D. W. Harding

The casual reader of D. W. Harding's criticism might understandably
suppose that he is a teacher of English literature. He is, in fact, Emeritus
Professor of Psychology in the University of London, and social psychology
has always been his professional academic field. He switched from English
to psychology as an undergraduate at Cambridge, and was able to pursue
his interest in literature and literary criticism through his association with
the journal *Scrutiny*, edited at Cambridge by F. R. Leavis and others
(see Introductory Note on L. C. Knights above, pp. 211-12). 'Regulated Hatred:
an aspect of the work of Jane Austen' first appeared in *Scrutiny* in 1940
and is representative of that journal's healthy irreverence for conventional
literary taste and judgment. So far from being a gentle, reassuring writer,
comfortably confirming the values of middle-class gentility, as most admirers of
Jane Austen tended to regard her, she was in fact, Harding argued, in many ways
fiercely hostile to her social environment, and writing was her way of 'finding
some mode of existence for her critical attitudes'. In this latter point, and
in the suggestion that many readers must unconsciously censor the
occasional manifestations of hostility in Jane Austen's work, one may
detect the influence of Harding's professional interest in psychology. The
essay has had a very great influence, not always fully acknowledged, on
subsequent criticism of Jane Austen.

　　D. W. Harding (b. 1906) taught at the London School of Economics,
and at the Universities of Liverpool and Manchester, before taking a
Chair at Bedford College, London. His publications include *Social Psychology
and Individual Values* (1953), *Experience into Words* (1963), and essays
contributed to the *Pelican Guide to English Literature*, vol. v (1957).

CROSS REFERENCES:　　3. Sigmund Freud
　　　　　　　　　　29. Mark Schorer
　　　　　　　　　　42. Wayne Booth

Regulated hatred: an aspect of the work of Jane Austen

I

The impression of Jane Austen which has filtered through to the reading public, down from the first-hand critics, through histories of literature, university courses, literary journalism, and polite allusion, deters many who might be her best readers from bothering with her at all. How can this popular impression be described? In my experience the first idea to be absorbed from the atmosphere surrounding her work was that she offered exceptionally favourable openings to the exponents of urbanity. Gentlemen of an older generation than mine spoke of their intention of rereading her on their deathbeds; Eric Linklater's cultured Prime Minister in *The Impregnable Women* passes from surreptitious to abandoned reading of her novels as a national crisis deepens. With this there also came the impression that she provided a refuge for the sensitive when the contemporary world grew too much for them. So Beatrice Kean Seymour writes (*Jane Austen*): 'In a society which has enthroned the machine-gun and carried it aloft even into the quiet heavens, there will always be men and women—Escapist or not, as you please—who will turn to her novels with an unending sense of relief and thankfulness.'

I was given to understand that her scope was of course extremely restricted, but that within her limits she succeeded admirably in expressing the gentler virtues of a civilized social order. She could do this because she lived at a time when, as a sensitive person of culture, she could still feel that she had a place in society and could address the reading public as sympathetic equals; she might introduce unpleasant people into her stories but she could confidently expose them to a public opinion that condemned them. Chiefly, so I gathered, she was a delicate satirist, revealing with inimitable lightness of touch the comic foibles and amiable weaknesses of the people whom she lived among and liked.

All this was enough to make me quite certain I didn't want to read her. And it is, I believe, a seriously misleading impression. Fragments of the truth have been incorporated in it but they are fitted into a pattern whose total effect is false. And yet the wide currency of this false impression is an indication of Jane Austen's success in an essential part of her complex intention as a writer: her books are, as she meant them to be, read and enjoyed by precisely the sort of people whom she disliked; she is a literary classic of the society which attitudes like hers, held widely enough, would undermine.

In order to enjoy her books without disturbance those who retain the conventional notion of her work must always have had slightly to misread what she wrote at a number of scattered points, points where she took good care (not wittingly perhaps) that the misreading should be the easiest thing in the world. Unexpected astringencies occur which the comfortable reader probably overlooks, or else passes by as slight imperfections, trifling errors of tone brought about by a faulty choice of words. Look at the passage in *Northanger Abbey* where Henry Tilney offers a solemn reprimand of Catherine's fantastic suspicions about his father:

> Dear Miss Morland, consider the dreadful nature of these suspicions you have entertained. What have you been judging from? Remember the country and the age in which we live. Remember that we are English, that we are Christians. Consult your own understanding, your own sense of the probable, your own observation of what is passing around you. Does our education prepare us for such atrocities? Do our laws connive at them? Could they be perpetrated without being known, in a country like this, where social and literary intercourse is on such a footing, and where roads and newspapers lay everything open?

Had the passage really been as I quote it nothing would have been out of tune. But I omitted a clause. The last sentence actually runs: 'Could they be perpetrated without being known, in a country like this, where social and literary intercourse is on such a footing, where every man is surrounded by a neighbourhood of voluntary spies, and where roads and newspapers lay everything open?' 'Where every man is surrounded by a neighbourhood of voluntary spies'—with its touch of paranoia that surprising remark is badly out of tune both with 'Henry's astonishing generosity and nobleness of conduct' and with the accepted idea of Jane Austen.

Yet it comes quite understandably from someone of Jane Austen's sensitive intelligence, living in her world of news and gossip interchanged among and around a large family. She writes to Cassandra (14 September 1804):

> My mother is at this moment reading a letter from my aunt. Yours to Miss Irvine of which she had had the perusal (which by the bye in your place I should not like) has thrown them into a quandary about Charles and his prospects. The case is that my mother had previously told my aunt, without restriction, that ... whereas you had replied to Miss Irvine's inquiries on the subject with less explicitness and more caution. Never mind, let them puzzle on together.

And when Fanny Knight (her niece) writes confidently about her love affair, Jane Austen describes ruses she adopted to avoid having to read the letter to the family, and later implores Fanny to 'write *something* that may do to be read or told' (30 November 1814).

Why is it that, holding the view she did of people's spying, Jane Austen should slip it in among Henry Tilney's eulogies of the age? By doing so she achieves two ends, ends which she may not have consciously aimed at. In such a speech from such a character the remark is unexpected and unbelievable, with the result that it is quite unlikely to be taken in at all by many readers; it slips through their minds without creating a disturbance. It gets said, but with the minimum risk of setting people's backs up. The second end achieved by giving the remark such a context is that of off-setting it at once by more appreciative views of society and so refraining from indulging an exaggerated bitterness. The eulogy of the age is not nullified by the bitter clause, but neither can it wipe out the impression the clause makes on those who attend to it.

One cannot say that here the two attitudes modify one another. The technique is too weak. Jane Austen can bring both attitudes into the picture but she has not at this point made one picture of them. In *Persuasion* she does something of the same kind more delicately. Miss Elliot's chagrin at having failed to marry her cousin is being described in the terms of ordinary satire which invites the reading public to feel superior to Miss Elliot:

> There was not a baronet from A to Z whom her feelings could have so willingly acknowledged as an equal. Yet so miserably had he conducted himself, that though she was at this present time (the summer of 1814) wearing black ribbons for his wife, she could not admit him to be worth thinking of again. The disgrace of his first marriage might, perhaps, as there was no reason to suppose it perpetuated by offspring, have been got over, had he not done worse;

—and then at this point the satire suddenly directs itself against the public instead of Miss Elliot—

> but he had, as by the accustomary intervention of kind friends they had been informed, spoken most disrespectfully of them all. . . .

In *Emma* the same thing is done still more effectively. Again Jane Austen seems to be on perfectly good terms with the public she is addressing and to have no reserve in offering the funniness and virtues of Mr Woodhouse and Miss Bates to be judged by the accepted standards of the public. She invites her readers to be just their natural patronizing selves. But this public that Jane Austen seems on such good terms with has some curious things said about it, not criticisms, but small notes of fact that are usually not made. They almost certainly go unnoticed by many readers, for they involve only the faintest change of tone from something much more usual and acceptable.

When she says that Miss Bates 'enjoyed a most uncommon degree of popularity for a woman neither young, handsome, rich, nor married', this is fairly conventional satire that any reading public would cheerfully admit in its satirist and chuckle over. But the next sentence must have to be mentally re-written by the greater number of Jane Austen's readers. For them it probably runs, 'Miss Bates stood in the very worst predicament in the world for having much of the public favour; and she had no intellectual superiority to make atonement to herself, or compel an outward respect from those who might despise her'. This, I suggest, is how most readers, lulled and disarmed by the amiable context, will soften what in fact reads, '. . . and she had no intellectual superiority to make atonement to herself, or frighten those who might hate her into outward respect'. Jane Austen was herself at this time 'neither young, handsome, rich, nor married', and the passage perhaps hints at the functions which her unquestioned intellectual superiority may have had for her.

This eruption of fear and hatred into the relationships of everyday social life is something that the urbane admirer of Jane Austen finds distasteful; it is not the satire of one who writes securely for the entertainment of her civilized acquaintances. And it has the effect, for the attentive reader, of changing the flavour of the more ordinary satire among which it is embedded.

Emma is especially interesting from this point of view. What is sometimes called its greater 'mellowness' largely consists in saying quietly and undisguisedly things which in the earlier books were put more loudly but in the innocuous form of caricature. Take conversation for instance. Its importance and its high (though by no means supreme) social value are of course implicit in Jane Austen's writings. But one should beware of supposing that a mind like hers therefore found the ordinary social intercourse of the period congenial and satisfying. In *Pride and Prejudice* she offers an entertaining caricature of card-table conversation at Lady Catherine de Bourgh's house.

> Their table was superlatively stupid. Scarcely a syllable was uttered that did not relate to the game, except when Mrs Jenkinson expressed her fears of Miss de Bourgh's being too hot or too cold, or having too much or too little light. A great deal more passed at the other table. Lady Catherine was generally speaking—stating the mistakes of the three others, or relating some anecdote of herself. Mr Collins was employed in agreeing to everything her ladyship said, thanking her for every fish he won, and apologizing if he thought he won too many. Sir William did not say much. He was storing his memory with anecdotes and noble names.

This invites the carefree enjoyment of all her readers. They can all feel superior to Lady Catherine and Mr Collins. But in *Emma* the style changes: the talk at the Coleses' dinner party, a pleasant dinner party which the heroine enjoyed, is described as '...the usual rate of conversation; a few clever things said, a few downright silly, but by much the larger proportion neither the one nor the other—nothing worse than everyday remarks, dull repetitions, old news, and heavy jokes'. 'Nothing worse!'—that phrase is typical. It is not mere sarcasm by any means. Jane Austen genuinely valued the achievements of the civilization she lived within and never lost sight of the fact that there might be something vastly worse than the conversation she referred to. 'Nothing worse' is a positive tribute to the decency, the superficial friendliness, the absence of the grosser forms of insolence and self-display at the dinner party. At least Mrs Elton wasn't there. And yet the effect of the comment, if her readers took it seriously, would be that of a disintegrating attack upon the sort of social intercourse they have established for themselves. It is not the comment of one who would have helped to make her society what it was, or ours what it is.

To speak of this aspect of her work as 'satire' is perhaps misleading. She has none of the underlying didactic intention ordinarily attributed to the satirist. Her object is not missionary; it is the more desperate one of merely finding some mode of existence for her critical attitudes. To her the first necessity was to keep on reasonably good terms with the associates of her everyday life; she had a deep need of their affection and a genuine respect for the ordered, decent civilization that they upheld. And yet she was sensitive to their crudenesses and complacencies and knew that her real existence depended on resisting many of the values they implied. The novels gave her a way out of this dilemma. This, rather than the ambition of entertaining a posterity of urbane gentlemen, was her motive force in writing.

As a novelist, therefore, part of her aim was to find the means for unobtrusive spiritual survival, without open conflict with the friendly people around her whose standards in simpler things she could accept and whose affection she greatly needed. She found, of course, that one of the most useful peculiarities of her society was its willingness to remain blind to the implications of a caricature. She found people eager to laugh at faults they tolerated in themselves and their friends, so long as the faults were exaggerated and the laughter 'good-natured'—so long, that is, as the assault on society could be regarded as a mock assault and not genuinely disruptive. Satire such as this is obviously a means not of admonition but of self-preservation.

Hence one of Jane Austen's most successful methods is to offer her readers every excuse for regarding as rather exaggerated figures of fun people whom she herself detests and fears. Mrs Bennet, according to the Austen tradition, is one of 'our' richly comic characters about whom we can feel superior, condescending, perhaps a trifle sympathetic, and above all heartily amused and free from care. Everything conspires to make this the natural interpretation once you are willing to overlook Jane Austen's bald and brief statement of her own attitude to her: 'She was a woman of mean understanding, little information, and uncertain temper.' How many women among Jane Austen's acquaintance and among her most complacent readers to the present day that phrase must describe! How gladly they enjoy the funny side of the situations Mrs Bennet's unpleasant nature creates, and how easy it is made for them to forget or never observe that Jane Austen, none the less for seeing how funny she is, goes on detesting her. The thesis that the ruling standards of our social group leave a perfectly comfortable niche for detestable people and give them sufficient sanction to persist, would, if it were argued seriously, arouse the most violent opposition, the most determined apologetics for things as they are, and the most reproachful pleas for a sense of proportion.

Caricature served Jane Austen's purpose perfectly. Under her treatment one can never say where caricature leaves off and the claim to serious portraiture begins. Mr Collins is only given a trifle more comic exaggeration than Lady Catherine de Bourgh, and by her standards is a possible human being. Lady Catherine in turn seems acceptable as a portrait if the criterion of verisimilitude is her nephew Mr Darcy. And he, finally, although to some extent a caricature, is near enough natural portraiture to stand beside Elizabeth Bennet, who, like all the heroines, is presented as an undistorted portrait. The simplest comic effects are gained by bringing the caricatures into direct contact with the real people, as in Mr Collins's visit to the Bennets and his proposal to Elizabeth. But at the same time one knows that, though from some points of view caricature, in other directions he does, by easy stages, fit into the real world. He is real enough to Mrs Bennet; and she is real enough to Elizabeth to create a situation of real misery for her when she refuses. Consequently the proposal scene is not only comic fantasy, but it is also, for Elizabeth, a taste of the fantastic nightmare in which economic and social institutions have such power over the values of personal relationships that the comic monster is nearly able to get her.

The implications of her caricatures as criticism of real people in real society is brought out in the way they dovetail into their social setting. The decent, stodgy Charlotte puts up cheerfully with Mr Collins as a husband; and Elizabeth can never quite become reconciled to the idea that her friend is the wife of her comic monster. And that, of course, is precisely the sort of idea that Jane Austen herself could never grow reconciled to. The people she hated were tolerated, accepted, comfortably ensconced in the only human society she knew; they were, for her, society's embarrassing unconscious comment on itself. A recent writer on Jane Austen, Elizabeth Jenkins, puts forward the polite and more comfortable interpretation in supposing Charlotte's marriage to be explained solely by the impossibility of young women's earning their own living at that period. But Charlotte's complaisance goes deeper than that: it is shown as a considered indifference to personal relationships when they conflict with cruder advantages in the wider social world:

> She had always felt that Charlotte's opinion of matrimony was not exactly like her own, but she could not have supposed it possible that, when called into action, she would have sacrificed every better feeling to worldly advantage.

We know too, at the biographical level, that Jane Austen herself, in a precisely similar situation to Charlotte's, spent a night of psychological crisis in deciding to revoke her acceptance of an 'advantageous' proposal made the previous evening. And her letters to Fanny Knight show how deep her convictions went at this point.

It is important to notice that Elizabeth makes no break with her friend on account of the marriage. This was the sort of friend—'a friend disgracing herself and sunk in her esteem'—that went to make up the available social world which one could neither escape materially nor be independent of psychologically. The impossibility of being cut off from objectionable people is suggested more subtly in *Emma*, where Mrs Elton is the high light of the pervasive neglect of spiritual values in social life. One can hardly doubt that Jane Austen's own dealings with society are reflected in the passage where Mr Weston makes the error of inviting Mrs Elton to join the picnic party which he and Emma have planned:

> ...Emma could not but feel some surprise, and a little displeasure, on hearing from Mr Weston that he had been proposing to Mrs Elton, as her brother and sister had failed her, that the two parties should unite, and go together, and that as Mrs Elton had very readily acceded to it, so it was to be, if she had no objection. Now, as her objection was nothing but her very great dislike of Mrs Elton, of which Mr Weston must already be perfectly aware, it was not worth bringing forward: it could not be done without a reproof to him, which would be giving pain to his wife; and she found her-

self, therefore, obliged to consent to an arrangement which she would have done a great deal to avoid; an arrangement which would, probably, expose her even to the degradation of being said to be of Mrs Elton's party! Every feeling was offended; and the forbearance of her outward submission left a heavy arrear due of secret severity in her reflections, on the unmanageable good-will of Mr Weston's temper.

'I am glad you approve of what I have done,' said he, very comfortably. 'But I thought you would. Such schemes as these are nothing without numbers. One cannot have too large a party. A large party secures its own amusement. And she is a good-natured woman after all. One could not leave her out.'

Emma denied none of it aloud, and agreed to none of it in private.

This well illustrates Jane Austen's typical dilemma: of being intensely critical of people to whom she also has strong emotional attachments.

II

The social group having such ambivalence for her, it is not surprising if her conflict should find some outlets not fully within her conscious control. To draw attention to these, however, is not to suggest that they lessen the value of her conscious intention and its achievements.

The chief instance is the fascination she found in the Cinderella theme, the Cinderella theme with the fairy godmother omitted. For in Jane Austen's treatment the natural order of things manages to reassert the heroine's proper pre-eminence without the intervention of any human or quasi-human helper. In this respect she allies the Cinderella theme to another fairy-tale theme which is often introduced—that of the princes brought up by unworthy parents but never losing the delicate sensibilities which are an inborn part of her. This latter theme appears most explicitly in *Mansfield Park*, the unfinished story of *The Watsons*, and, with some softening, in *Pride and Prejudice*. The contrast between Fanny Price's true nature and her squalid home at Portsmouth is the clearest statement of the idea, but in the first four of the finished novels the heroine's final position is, even in the worldly sense, always above her reasonable social expectations by conventional standards, but corresponding to her natural worth.

To leave it at this, however, would be highly misleading. It is the development which occurs in her treatment of the Cinderella theme that most rewards attention. In *Northanger Abbey*, *Sense and Sensibility*, and *Pride and Prejudice* it is handled simply: the heroine is in some degree isolated from those around her by being more sensitive or of finer moral insight or sounder judgment, and her marriage to the handsome prince at the end is in the nature of a reward for being different from the rest and a consolation for the distresses entailed by being different. This is true even of *Northanger Abbey* in spite of the grotesque error of judgment that Catherine Morland is guilty of and has to renounce. For here Jane Austen was interested not so much in the defect in her heroine's judgment as in the absurdly wide currency of the 'gothick' tradition that entrapped her. Catherine throws off her delusion almost as something external to herself. And this is so glaring that Jane Austen seems to have been uncomfortable about it : in describing it she resorts to a rather factitious semi-detachment from her heroine.

> Her mind made up on these several points, and her resolution formed, of always judging and acting in future with the greatest good sense, she had nothing to do but to forgive herself and be happier than ever; and the lenient hand of time did much for her by insensible gradations in the course of another day.

In *Sense and Sensibility* and *Pride and Prejudice* the heroines are still nearer perfection and even the handsome princes have faults to overcome before all is well. Immediately after her final reconciliation with Mr Darcy, Elizabeth Bennet is tempted to laugh at his over-confident direction of his friend Bingley's love affair, '...but she checked herself. She remembered that he had yet to learn to be laughed at, and it was rather too early to begin.'

To put the point in general terms, the heroine of these early novels is herself the criterion of sound judgment and good feeling. She may claim that her values are sanctioned by good breeding and a religious civilization, but in fact none of the people she meets represents those values so effectively as she does herself. She is never in submissive alliance with the representatives of virtue and good feeling in her social world—there is only a selective alliance with certain aspects of their characters. The social world may have material power over her, enough to make her unhappy, but it hasn't the power that comes from having created or moulded her, and it can claim no credit for her being what she is. In this sense the heroine is independent of those about her and isolated from them. She has only to be herself.

The successful handling of this kind of theme and this heroine brought Jane Austen to the point where a development became psychologically possible. The hint of irrationality underlying the earlier themes could be brought nearer the light. She could begin to admit that even a heroine must owe a great deal of her character and values to the social world in which she had been moulded, and, that being so, could hardly be quite so solitary in her excellence as the earlier heroines are. The emphasis hitherto had been almost entirely on the difference between the heroine and the people about her. But this was to slight the reality of her bond with the ordinary 'good' people; there was more to be said for the fundamentals of virtue and seemliness than she had been implying. And so, after the appearance of *Pride and Prejudice*, she wrote to Cassandra, 'Now I will try and write of something else, and it shall be a complete change of subject—ordination...' (29 January 1813).

This sets the tone of *Mansfield Park*, the new novel. Here her emphasis is on the deep importance of the conventional virtues, of civilized seemliness, decorum, and sound religious feeling. These become the worthy objects of the heroine's loyalties; and they so nearly comprise the whole range of her values that Fanny Price is the least interesting of all the heroines. For the first time, Jane Austen sets the heroine in submissive alliance with the conventionally virtuous people of the story, Sir Thomas and Edmund. Mistaken though these pillars of society may in some respects be, the heroine's proper place is at their side; their standards are worthy of a sensitive person's support and complete allegiance.

It is a novel in which Jane Austen pays tribute to the virtuous fundamentals of her upbringing, ranging herself with those whom she considers right on the simpler and more obvious moral issues, and withdrawing her attention—relatively at least—from the finer details of living in which they may disturb her. She allies herself with virtues that are easy to appreciate and reasonably often met with. The result, as one would expect, is a distinct tendency to priggishness. And, of course, the book was greatly liked. 'Mr H[aden] is reading *Mansfield Park* for the first time and prefers it to *P. and P.*' (26 November 1815). 'Mr Cook [himself a clergyman] says "it is the most sensible novel he ever read," and the manner in which I treat the clergy delights them very much' (14 June 1814). Compared with *Mansfield Park*, Jane Austen is afraid that *Emma* will appear 'inferior in good sense' (11 December 1815). It was after reading *Mansfield Park*, moreover, that the pompously self-satisfied Librarian to the Prince Regent offered her, almost avowedly, his own life story as the basis for a novel about an English clergyman. He must have been one of the first of the admirer-victims who have continued to enjoy her work to this day. And her tactful and respectful reply ('The comic part of the character I might be equal to, but not the good, the enthusiastic, the literary') illustrates admirably her capacity for keeping on good terms with people without too great treachery to herself.

The priggishness of *Mansfield Park* is the inevitable result of the curiously abortive attempt at humility that the novel represents. Although it involves the recognition that heroines are not spontaneously generated but owe much of their personality to the established standards of their society, the perfection of the heroine is still not doubted. And so the effort towards humility becomes in effect the exclamation, 'Why, some of the very good people are nearly as good as I am and really do deserve my loyalty!'

There is no external evidence that Jane Austen was other than highly satisfied with *Mansfield Park*, which is, after all, in many ways interesting and successful. But its *reductio ad absurdum* of the Cinderella theme and the foundling princess theme could hardly have been without effect. This, I think, is already visible in the last chapter, which, with its suggestion of a fairy-tale winding up of the various threads of the story, is ironically perfunctory. For instance:

> I purposely abstain from dates on this occasion, that every one may be at liberty to fix their own, aware that the cure of unconquerable passions, and the transfer of unchanging attachments, must vary as to time in different people. I only entreat everybody to believe that exactly at the time when it was quite natural that it should be so, and not a week earlier, Edmund did cease to care about Miss Crawford, and became as anxious to marry Fanny as Fanny herself could desire.

And Sir Thomas's 'high sense of having realized a great acquisition in the promise of Fanny for a daughter, formed just such a contrast with his early opinion on the subject when the poor little girl's coming had first been agitated, as time is for ever producing between the plans and decisions of mortals, for their own instruction and their neighbours' entertainment'.

Whether or not Jane Austen realized what she had been doing, at all events the production of *Mansfield Park* enabled her to go on next to the extraordinary achievement of *Emma*, in which a much more complete humility is combined with the earlier unblinking attention to people as they are. The underlying argument has a different trend. She continues to see that the heroine has derived from the people and conditions around her, but she now keeps clearly in mind the objectionable features of those people; and she faces the far bolder conclusion that even a heroine is likely to have assimilated many of the more unpleasant possibilities of the human being in society. And it is not that society has spoilt an originally perfect girl who now has to recover her pristine good sense, as it was with Catherine Morland, but that the heroine has not yet achieved anything like perfection and is actually going to learn a number of serious lessons from some of the people she lives with.

Consider in the first place the treatment here of the two favourite themes of the earlier novels. The Cinderella theme is now relegated to the sub-heroine, Jane Fairfax. Its working out involves the discomfiture of the heroine, who in this respect is put into the position of one of the ugly sisters. Moreover the Cinderella procedure is shown in the light of a social anomaly, rather a nuisance and requiring the excuse of unusual circumstances.

The associated theme of the child brought up in humble circumstances whose inborn nature fits her for better things is frankly parodied and deflated in the story of Harriet Smith, the illegitimate child whom Emma tries to turn into a snob. In the end, with the insignificant girl cheerfully married to a deserving farmer,

> Harriet's parentage became known. She proved to be the daughter of a tradesman, rich enough to afford her the comfortable maintenance which had ever been hers, and decent enough to have always wished for concealment. Such was the blood of gentility which Emma had formerly been so ready to vouch for!

Thus the structure of the narrative expresses a complete change in Jane Austen's outlook on the heroine in relation to others. And the story no longer progresses towards her vindication or consolation; it consists in her gradual, humbling self-enlightenment. Emma's personality includes some of the tendencies and qualities that Jane Austen most disliked—self-complacency, for instance, malicious enjoyment in prying into embarrassing private affairs, snobbery, and a weakness for meddling in other people's lives. But now, instead of being attributed in exaggerated form to a character distanced into caricature, they occur in the subtle form given them by someone who in many ways has admirably fine standards.

We cannot say that in *Emma* Jane Austen abandons the Cinderella story. She so deliberately inverts it that we ought to regard *Emma* as a bold variant of the theme and a further exploration of its underlying significance for her. In *Persuasion* she goes back to the Cinderella situation in its most direct and simple form, but develops a vitally important aspect of it that she had previously avoided. This is the significance for Cinderella of her idealized dead mother.

Most children are likely to have some conflict of attitude towards their mother, finding her in some respects an ideal object of love and in others an obstacle to their wishes and a bitter disappointment. For a child such as Jane Austen who actually was in many ways more sensitive and able than her mother, one can understand that this conflict may persist in some form for a very long time. Now one of the obvious appeals of the Cinderella story, as of all stories of wicked stepmothers, is that it resolves the ambivalence of the mother by the simple plan of splitting her in two: the ideal mother is dead and can be adored without risk of disturbance; the living mother is completely detestable and can be hated wholeheartedly without self-reproach.[1]

In her early novels Jane Austen consistently avoided dealing with a mother who could be a genuinely intimate friend of her daughter. Lady Susan, of the unfinished novel, is her daughter's enemy. In *Northanger Abbey* the mother is busy with the household and the younger children. In *Sense and Sensibility* she herself has to be guided and kept in hand by her daughter's sounder judgment. In *Pride and Prejudice* she is Mrs Bennet. In *Mansfield Park* she is a slattern whom the heroine only visits once in the course of the novel. In *Emma* the mother is dead and Miss Taylor, her substitute, always remains to some extent the promoted governess. This avoidance may seem strange, but it can be understood as the precaution of a mind which, although in the Cinderella situation, is still too sensitive and honest to offer as a complete portrait the half-truth of the idealized dead mother.

But in *Persuasion* she does approach the problem which is latent here. She puts her heroine in the Cinderella setting, and so heightens her need for affection. And then in Lady Russell she provides a godmother, not fairy but human, with whom Anne Elliot can have much the relationship of a daughter with a greatly loved, but humanly possible, mother. Jane Austen then goes on to face the implications of such a relationship—and there runs through the whole story a lament for seven years' loss of happiness owing to Anne's having yielded to her godmother's persuasion.

The novel opens with her being completely convinced of the wrongness of the advice she received, and yet strongly attached to Lady Russell still and unable to blame her. Her attitude is, and throughout the book remains, curiously unresolved. 'She did not blame Lady Russell, she did not blame herself, for having been guided by her; but she felt that were any young person in similar circumstances to apply to her for counsel, they would never receive any of such certain immediate wretchedness, such uncertain future good.' But for all that the rest of the book shows Anne repeatedly resisting fresh advice from her godmother and being completely vindicated in the upshot.

This might mean that Anne was a repetition of the earlier heroines, detached by her good sense and sound principles from the inferior standards of those about her. That would be true of her relations with her father and eldest sister. But she had no such easy detachment from her godmother. Lady Russell was near enough to the ideal mother to secure Anne's affection, to make her long for the comfort of yielding to her judgment. This satisfaction—the secure submission to a parent who seems completely adequate—was denied Anne by her superior judgment. She was strong enough to retain the insight that separated her from Lady Russell—they never mentioned the episode in the years that followed and neither knew what the other felt about it—but she never came to feel her partial detachment from her as anything but a loss. Nor could she ever regret having yielded to Lady Russell's advice, even though she regretted that the advice had been so mistaken. At the end of the story, reverting to the old dilemma, she tells the lover whom she has now regained:

> I have been thinking over the past, and trying to judge of the right and wrong —I mean with regard to myself; and I must believe that I was right, much as I suffered from it—that I was perfectly right in being guided by the friend whom you will love better than you do now. To me, she was in the place of a parent. Do not mistake me, however. I am not saying that she did not err in her service. It was, perhaps, one of those cases in which advice is good or bad only as the event decides and for myself, I certainly never should, in any circumstances of tolerable similarity, give such advice. But I mean that I was right in submitting to her, and that if I had done otherwise, I should have suffered more in continuing the engagement than I did even in giving it up, because I should have suffered in my conscience.

It is in *Persuasion* that Jane Austen fingers what is probably the tenderest spot for those who identify themselves with Cinderella: she brings the idealized mother back to life and admits that she is no nearer to perfection than the mothers of acute and sensitive children generally are.

This attempt to suggest a slightly different emphasis in the reading of Jane Austen is not offered as a balanced appraisal of her work. It is deliberately lopsided, neglecting the many points at which the established view seems adequate. I have tried to underline one or two features of her work that claim the sort of readers who sometimes miss her—those who would turn to her not for relief and escape but as a formidable ally against things and people which were to her, and still are, hateful.

Notes

1. This is, needless to say, only a very small part of the unconscious significance which such stories may have for a reader. Most obviously it neglects the relationships of the stepmother and the heroine to the father.

22 Lionel Trilling

Lionel Trilling (b. 1905) was born and educated in New York and has taught at Columbia University for most of his professional life. He is the author of two full-length critical studies, *Matthew Arnold* (New York, 1939), and *E. M. Forster* (Norfolk, Con., 1943). The choice of these subjects is perhaps revealing, for Trilling himself is a critic in the Arnoldian tradition of disinterested moral and intellectual inquiry, tempered by a Forsterian awareness of the ironies, pitfalls, and paradoxes in the position of the liberal humanist intellectual. Though, like most American critics of his generation, he was affected by the theory and practice of the New Criticism, the idea of the autonomy of the work of art was never congenial to him. On the contrary, he has always been inclined, by temperament and conviction, to emphasize the ways in which works of literature both affect and reflect the cultural contexts in which they are produced and consumed.

It is arguable that Trilling's greatest critical achievement is to be found in his essays, collected under the following titles: *The Liberal Imagination* (New York, 1950), *The Opposing Self* (1955), *A Gathering of Fugitives* (Boston, 1956), and *Beyond Culture* (New York, 1965). These original, thought-provoking, and eloquent essays cover a wide range of topics, from Jane Austen to the Kinsey Report, but always convey a sense that the cultural history of the last two hundred years has a kind of wholeness and coherence which can be grasped and articulated. Trilling personifies the idea (easier to hold in the 'forties and 'fifties than today) that the intellectual is, by definition, a *literary* intellectual. He is also the author of a small but distinguished body of prose fiction.

'Freud and Literature', as well as being probably the best short introduction to its subject, illustrates Trilling's ability to deal lucidly and gracefully with dauntingly complex material. It was first published in 1941, and is reprinted here from *The Liberal Imagination*.

CROSS REFERENCES: 3. Sigmund Freud
26. W. K. Wimsatt jnr. and Monroe C. Beardsley
('The Intentional Fallacy')
38. Norman O. Brown

275

Freud and literature

The Freudian psychology is the only systematic account of the human mind which, in point of subtlety and complexity, of interest and tragic power, deserves to stand beside the chaotic mass of psychological insights which literature has accumulated through the centuries. To pass from the reading of a great literary work to a treatise of academic psychology is to pass from one order of perception to another, but the human nature of the Freudian psychology is exactly the stuff upon which the poet has always exercised his art. It is therefore not surprising that the psycho-analytical theory has had a great effect upon literature. Yet the relationship is reciprocal, and the effect of Freud upon literature has been no greater than the effect of literature upon Freud. When, on the occasion of the celebration of his seventieth birthday, Freud was greeted as the 'discoverer of the unconscious', he corrected the speaker and disclaimed the title. 'The poets and philosophers before me discovered the unconscious,' he said. 'What I discovered was the scientific method by which the unconscious can be studied.'

A lack of specific evidence prevents us from considering the particular literary 'influences' upon the founder of psycho-analysis; and, besides, when we think of the men who so clearly anticipated many of Freud's own ideas— Schopenhauer and Nietzsche, for example—and then learn that he did not read their works until after he had formulated his own theories, we must see that particular influences cannot be in question here but that what we must deal with is nothing less than a whole *Zeitgeist* [Spirit of the time], a direction of thought. For psycho-analysis is one of the culminations of the Romanticist literature of the nineteenth century. If there is perhaps a contradiction in the idea of a science standing upon the shoulders of a literature which avows itself inimical to science in so many ways, the contradiction will be resolved if we remember that this literature, despite its avowals, was itself scientific in at least the sense of being passionately devoted to a research into the self.

In showing the connection between Freud and this Romanticist tradition, it is difficult to know where to begin, but there might be a certain aptness in starting even back of the tradition, as far back as 1762 with Diderot's *Rameau's Nephew*. At any rate, certain men at the heart of nineteenth-century thought were agreed in finding a peculiar importance in this brilliant little work: Goethe translated it, Marx admired it, Hegel—as Marx reminded Engels in the letter which announced that he was sending the book as a gift—praised and expounded it at length, Shaw was impressed by it, and Freud himself, as we know from a quotation in his *Introductory Lectures,* read it with the pleasure of agreement.

The dialogue takes place between Diderot himself and a nephew of the famous composer. The protagonist, the younger Rameau, is a despised, outcast, shameless fellow; Hegel calls him the 'disintegrated consciousness' and credits him with great wit, for it is he who breaks down all the normal social values and makes new combinations with the pieces. As for Diderot, the deuter-agonist, he is what Hegel calls the 'honest consciousness', and Hegel considers him reasonable, decent, and dull. It is quite clear that the author does not despise his Rameau and does not mean us to. Rameau is lustful and greedy, arrogant yet self-abasing, perceptive yet 'wrong', like a child. Still, Diderot seems actually to be giving the fellow a kind of superiority over himself, as though Rameau represents the elements which, dangerous but wholly neces-sary, lie beneath the reasonable decorum of social life. It would perhaps be pressing too far to find in Rameau Freud's id and in Diderot Freud's ego; yet the connection does suggest itself; and at least we have here the perception which is to be the common characteristic of both Freud and Romanticism, the perception of the hidden element of human nature and of the opposition between the hidden and the visible. We have too the bold perception of just what lies hidden: 'If the little savage (i.e. the child) were left to himself, if he preserved all his foolishness and combined the violent passions of a man of thirty with the lack of reason of a child in the cradle, he'd wring his father's neck and go to bed with his mother.'

From the self-exposure of Rameau to Rousseau's account of his own child-hood [in *Confessions*] is no great step; society might ignore or reject the idea of the 'immorality' which lies concealed in the beginning of the career of the 'good' man, just as it might turn away from Blake struggling to expound a psychology which would include the forces beneath the propriety of social man in general, but the idea of the hidden thing went forward to become one of the dominant notions of the age. The hidden element takes many forms and it is not necessarily 'dark' and 'bad'; for Blake the 'bad' was the good, while for Wordsworth and Burke what was hidden and unconscious was wisdom and power, which work in despite of the conscious intellect.

The mind has become far less simple; the devotion to the various forms of autobiography—itself an important fact in the tradition—provides abundant examples of the change that has taken place. Poets, making poetry by what seems to them almost a freshly discovered faculty, find that this new power may be conspired against by other agencies of the mind and even deprived of its freedom; the names of Wordsworth, Coleridge, and Arnold at once occur to us again, and Freud quotes Schiller on the danger to the poet that lies in the merely analytical reason. And it is not only the poets who are threatened; educated and sensitive people throughout Europe become aware of the depreda-tions that reason might make upon the affective life, as in the classic instance of John Stuart Mill.

We must also take into account the preoccupation—it began in the eighteenth century, or even in the seventeenth—with children, women, peasants, and savages, whose mental life, it is felt, is less overlaid than that of the educated adult male by the proprieties of social habit. With this preoccupation goes a concern with education and personal development, so consonant with the historical and evolutionary bias of the time. And we must certainly note the revolution in morals which took place at the instance (we might almost say) of the *Bildungsroman,a* for in the novels fathered by [Goethe's] *Wilhelm Meister* we get the almost complete identification of author and hero and of the reader with both, and this identification almost inevitably suggests a leniency of moral judgment. The autobiographical novel has a further influence upon the moral sensibility by its exploitation of all the modulations of motive and by its hinting that we may not judge a man by any single moment in his life without taking into account the determining past and the expiating and fulfilling future.

It is difficult to know how to go on, for the further we look the more literary affinities to Freud we find, and even if we limit ourselves to bibliography we can at best be incomplete. Yet we must mention the sexual revolution that was being demanded—by Shelley, for example, by the Schlegel of *Lucinde*, by George Sand, and later and more critically by Ibsen; the belief in the sexual origin of art, baldly stated by Tieck, more subtly by Schopenhauer; the investigation of sexual maladjustment by Stendhal, whose observations on erotic feeling seem to us distinctly Freudian. Again and again we see the effective, utilitarian ego being relegated to an inferior position and a plea being made on behalf of the anarchic and self-indulgent id. We find the energetic exploitation of the idea of the mind as a divisible thing, one part of which can contemplate and mock the other. It is not a far remove from this to Dostoevski's brilliant instances of ambivalent feeling. Novalis brings in the preoccupation with the death wish, and this is linked on the one hand with sleep and on the other hand with the perception of the perverse, self-destroying impulses, which in turn leads us to that fascination by the horrible which we find in Shelley, Poe, and Baudelaire. And always there is the profound interest in the dream—'Our dreams,' said Gerard de Nerval, 'are a second life'—and in the nature of metaphor, which reaches its climax in Rimbaud and the later Symbolists, metaphor becoming less and less communicative as it approaches the relative autonomy of the dream life.

But perhaps we must stop to ask, since these are the components of the *Zeitgeist* from which Freud himself developed, whether it can be said that Freud did indeed produce a wide literary effect. What is it that Freud added that the tendency of literature itself would not have developed without him? If we were looking for a writer who showed the Freudian influence, Proust would perhaps come to mind as readily as anyone else; the very title of his novel, in French more than in English, suggests an enterprise of psycho-analysis and scarcely less so does his method—the investigation of sleep, of sexual deviation, of the way of association, the almost obsessive interest in metaphor; at these and at many other points the 'influence' might be shown. Yet I believe it is true that

a The novel about an individual's development, especially the progress from childhood and youth to maturity.

278

Proust did not read Freud. Or again, exegesis of *The Waste Land* often reads remarkably like the psycho-analytic interpretation of a dream, yet we know that Eliot's methods were prepared for him not by Freud but by other poets.

Nevertheless, it is of course true that Freud's influence on literature has been very great. Much of it is so pervasive that its extent is scarcely to be determined; in one form or another, frequently in perversions or absurd simplifications, it has been infused into our life and become a component of our culture of which it is now hard to be specifically aware. In biography its first effect was sensational but not fortunate. The early Freudian biographers were for the most part Guildensterns who seemed to know the pipes but could not pluck out the heart of the mystery, and the same condemnation applies to the early Freudian critics. But in recent years, with the acclimatization of psycho-analysis and the increased sense of its refinements and complexity, criticism has derived from the Freudian system much that is of great value, most notably the licence and the injunction to read the work of literature with a lively sense of its latent and ambiguous meanings, as if it were, as indeed it is, a being no less alive and contradictory than the man who created it. And this new response to the literary work has had a corrective effect upon our conception of literary biography. The literary critic or biographer who makes use of the Freudian theory is no less threatened by the dangers of theoretical systematization than he was in the early days, but he is likely to be more aware of these dangers; and I think it is true to say that now the motive of his interpretation is not that of exposing the secret shame of the writer and limiting the meaning of his work, but, on the contrary, that of finding grounds for sympathy with the writer and for increasing the possible significances of the work.

The names of the creative writers who have been more or less Freudian in tone or assumption would of course be legion. Only a relatively small number, however, have made serious use of the Freudian ideas. Freud himself seems to have thought this was as it should be : he is said to have expected very little of the works that were sent to him by writers with inscriptions of gratitude for all they had learned from him. The Surrealists have, with a certain inconsistency, depended upon Freud for the 'scientific' sanction of their programme. Kafka, with an apparent awareness of what he was doing, has explored the Freudian conceptions of guilt and punishment, of the dream and of the fear of the father. Thomas Mann, whose tendency, as he himself says, was always in the direction of Freud's interests, has been most susceptible to the Freudian anthropology, finding a special charm in the theories of myths and magical practices. James Joyce, with his interest in the numerous states of receding consciousness, with his use of words as things and of words which point to more than one thing, with his pervading sense of the interrelation and interpenetration of all things, and, not least important, his treatment of familial themes, has perhaps most thoroughly and consciously exploited Freud's ideas.

II

It will be clear enough how much of Freud's thought has significant affinity with the anti-rationalist element of the Romanticist tradition. But we must see with no less distinctness how much of his system is militantly rationalistic. Thomas Mann is at fault when, in his first essay on Freud, he makes it seem that the 'Apollonian', the rationalistic, side of psycho-analysis is, while certainly important and wholly admirable, somehow secondary and even accidental. He gives us a Freud who is committed to the 'night side' of life. Not at all: the rationalistic element of Freud is foremost; before everything else he is positivistic. If the interpreter of dreams came to medical science through Goethe, as he tells us he did, he entered not by way of the *Walpurgisnacht*ᵃ but by the essay which played so important a part in the lives of so many scientists of the nineteenth century, the famous disquisition on Nature.

This correction is needed not only for accuracy but also for any understanding of Freud's attitude to art. And for that understanding we must see how intense is the passion with which Freud believes that positivistic rationalism, in its golden-age pre-Revolutionary purity, is the very form and pattern of intellectual virtue. The aim of psycho-analysis, he says, is the control of the night side of life. It is 'to strengthen the ego, to make it more independent of the super-ego, to widen its field of vision, and so to extend the organization of the id'. 'Where id was',—that is, where all the irrational, non-logical, pleasure-seeking dark forces were—'there shall ego be',—that is, intelligence and control. 'It is', he concludes, with a reminiscence of Faust, 'reclamation work, like the draining of the Zuyder Zee.' This passage is quoted by Mann when, in taking up the subject of Freud a second time, he does indeed speak of Freud's positivistic programme; but even here the bias induced by Mann's artistic interest in the 'night side' prevents him from giving the other aspect of Freud its due emphasis. Freud would never have accepted the role which Mann seems to give him as the legitimizer of the myth and the dark irrational ways of the mind. If Freud discovered the darkness for science he never endorsed it. On the contrary, his rationalism supports all the ideas of the Enlightenment that deny validity to myth or religion; he holds to a simple materialism, to a simple determinism, to a rather limited sort of epistemology. No great scientist of our day has thundered so articulately and so fiercely against all those who would sophisticate with metaphysics the scientific principles that were good enough for the nineteenth century. Conceptualism or pragmatism is anathema to him through the greater part of his intellectual career, and this, when we consider the nature of his own brilliant scientific methods, has surely an element of paradox in it.

From his rationalistic positivism comes much of Freud's strength and what weakness he has. The strength is the fine, clean tenacity of his positive aims, the goal of therapy, the desire to bring to men a decent measure of earthly happiness. But upon the rationalism must also be placed the blame for the often naïve scientific principles which characterize his early thought—they are later much modified—and which consist largely of claiming for his theories a perfect correspondence with an external reality, a position which, for those who admire Freud and especially for those who take seriously his views on art, is troublesome in the extreme.

ᵃ A scene in Goethe's *Faust* which takes place on the traditional 'Witches' Sabbath'.

Now Freud has, I believe, much to tell us about art, but whatever is suggestive in him is not likely to be found in those of his works in which he deals expressly with art itself. Freud is not insensitive to art—on the contrary—nor does he ever intend to speak of it with contempt. Indeed, he speaks of it with a real tenderness and counts it one of the true charms of the good life. Of artists, especially of writers, he speaks with admiration and even a kind of awe, though perhaps what he most appreciates in literature are specific emotional insights and observations; as we have noted, he speaks of literary men, because they have understood the part played in life by the hidden motives, as the precursors and coadjutors of his own science.

And yet eventually Freud speaks of art with what we must indeed call contempt. Art, he tells us, is a 'substitute gratification', and as such is 'an illusion in contrast to reality'. Unlike most illusions, however, art is 'almost always harmless and beneficent' for the reason that 'it does not seek to be anything but an illusion. Save in the case of a few people who are, one might say, obsessed by Art, it never dares make any attack on the realm of reality.' One of its chief functions is to serve as a 'narcotic'. It shares the characteristics of the dream, whose element of distortion Freud calls a 'sort of inner dishonesty'. As for the artist, he is virtually in the same category with the neurotic. 'By such separation of imagination and intellectual capacity', Freud says of the hero of a novel, 'he is destined to be a poet or a neurotic, and he belongs to that race of beings whose realm is not of this world.'

Now there is nothing in the logic of psycho-analytical thought which requires Freud to have these opinions. But there is a great deal in the practice of the psycho-analytical therapy which makes it understandable that Freud, unprotected by an adequate philosophy, should be tempted to take the line he does. The analytical therapy deals with illusion. The patient comes to the physician to be cured, let us say, of a fear of walking in the street. The fear is real enough, there is no illusion on that score, and it produces all the physical symptoms of a more rational fear, the sweating palms, pounding heart, and shortened breath. But the patient knows that there is no cause for the fear, or rather that there is, as he says, no 'real cause' : there are no machine guns, man traps, or tigers in the street. The physician knows, however, that there is indeed a 'real' cause for the fear, though it has nothing at all to do with what is or is not in the street; the cause is within the patient, and the process of the therapy will be to discover, by gradual steps, what this real cause is and so free the patient from its effects.

Now the patient in coming to the physician, and the physician in accepting the patient, make a tacit compact about reality; for their purpose they agree to the limited reality by which we get our living, win our loves, catch our trains and our colds. The therapy will undertake to train the patient in proper ways of coping with this reality. The patient, of course, has been dealing with this reality all along, but in the wrong way. For Freud there are two ways of dealing with external reality. One is practical, effective, positive; this is the way of the conscious self, of the ego which must be made independent of the super-ego and extend its organization over the id, and it is the right way. The antithetical way may be called, for our purpose now, the 'fictional' way. Instead of doing something about, or to, external reality, the individual who uses this way does something to, or about, his affective states. The most common and 'normal' example of this is daydreaming, in which we give ourselves a certain pleasure by imagining our difficulties solved or our desires gratified. Then, too, as Freud discovered, sleeping dreams are, in much more complicated ways, and even though quite unpleasant, at the service of this same 'fictional' activity. And in ways yet more complicated and yet more unpleasant, the actual neurosis from which our patient suffers deals with an external reality which the mind considers still more unpleasant than the painful neurosis itself.

For Freud as psycho-analytic practitioner there are, we may say, the polar extremes of reality and illusion. Reality is an honorific word, and it means what is *there*; illusion is a pejorative word, and it means a response to what is *not there*. The didactic nature of a course of psycho-analysis no doubt requires a certain firm crudeness in making the distinction; it is after all aimed not at theoretical refinement but at practical effectiveness. The polar extremes are practical reality and neurotic illusion, the latter judged by the former. This, no doubt, is as it should be; the patient is not being trained in metaphysics and epistemology.

This practical assumption is not Freud's only view of the mind in its relation to reality. Indeed what may be called the essentially Freudian view assumes that the mind, for good as well as bad, helps create its reality by selection and evaluation. In this view, reality is malleable and subject to creation; it is not static but is rather a series of situations which are dealt with in their own terms. But beside this conception of the mind stands the conception which arises from Freud's therapeutic-practical assumptions; in this view, the mind deals with a reality which is quite fixed and static, a reality that is wholly 'given' and not (to use a phrase of Dewey's) 'taken'. In his epistemological utterances, Freud insists on this second view, although it is not easy to see why he should do so. For the reality to which he wishes to reconcile the neurotic patient is, after all, a 'taken' and not a 'given' reality. It is the reality of social life and of value, conceived and maintained by the human mind and will. Love, morality, honour, esteem—these are the components of a created reality. If we are to call art an illusion then we must call most of the activities and satisfactions of the ego illusions; Freud, of course, has no desire to call them that.

What, then, is the difference between, on the one hand, the dream and the neurosis, and, on the other hand, art? That they have certain common elements is of course clear; that unconscious processes are at work in both would be denied by no poet or critic; they share too, though in different degrees, the element of fantasy. But there is a vital difference between them which Charles Lamb saw so clearly in his defence of the sanity of true genius: 'The ... poet dreams being awake. He is not possessed by his subject but he has dominion over it.'

That is the whole difference: the poet is in command of his fantasy, while it is exactly the mark of the neurotic that he is possessed by his fantasy. And there is a further difference which Lamb states; speaking of the poet's relation to reality (he calls it Nature), he says, 'He is beautifully loyal to that sovereign directress, even when he appears most to betray her'; the illusions of art are made to serve the purpose of a closer and truer relation with reality. Jacques Barzun, in an acute and sympathetic discussion of Freud, puts the matter well: 'A good analogy between art and *dreaming* has led him to a false one between art and *sleeping*. But the difference between a work of art and a dream is precisely this, that the work of art *leads us back to the outer reality by taking account of it.*' Freud's assumption of the almost exclusively hedonistic nature and purpose of art bar him from the perception of this.

Of the distinction that must be made between the artist and the neurotic Freud is of course aware; he tells us that the artist is not like the neurotic in that he knows how to find a way back from the world of imagination and 'once more get a firm foothold in reality'. This however seems to mean no more than that reality is to be dealt with when the artist suspends the practice of his art; and at least once when Freud speaks of art dealing with reality he actually means the rewards that a successful artist can win. He does not deny to art its function and its usefulness; it has a therapeutic effect in releasing mental tension; it serves the cultural purpose of acting as a 'substitute gratification' to reconcile men to the sacrifices they have made for culture's sake; it promotes the social sharing of highly valued emotional experiences; and it recalls men to their cultural ideals. This is not everything that some of us would find that art does, yet even this is a good deal for a 'narcotic' to do.

III

I started by saying that Freud's ideas could tell us something about art, but so far I have done little more than try to show that Freud's very conception of art is inadequate. Perhaps, then, the suggestiveness lies in the application of the analytic method to specific works of art or to the artist himself? I do not think so, and it is only fair to say that Freud himself was aware both of the limits and the limitations of psycho-analysis in art, even though he does not always in practice submit to the former or admit the latter.

Freud has, for example, no desire to encroach upon the artist's autonomy; he does not wish us to read his monograph on Leonardo and then say of the 'Madonna of the Rocks' that it is a fine example of homosexual, autoerotic painting. If he asserts that in investigation the 'psychiatrist cannot yield to the author', he immediately insists that the 'author cannot yield to the psychiatrist', and he warns the latter not to 'coarsen everything' by using for all human manifestations the 'substantially useless and awkward terms' of clinical procedure. He admits, even while asserting that the sense of beauty probably derives from sexual feeling, that psycho-analysis 'has less to say about beauty than about most other things'. He confesses to a theoretical indifference to the form of art and restricts himself to its content. Tone, feeling, style, and the modification that part makes upon part he does not consider.

The layman [he says] may expect perhaps too much from analysis . . . for it must be admitted that it throws no light upon the two problems which probably interest him the most. It can do nothing towards elucidating the nature of the artistic gift, nor can it explain the means by which the artist works—artistic technique.

What, then, does Freud believe that the analytical method can do? Two things: explain the 'inner meanings' of the work of art and explain the temperament of the artist as man.

A famous example of the method is the attempt to solve the 'problem' of *Hamlet* as suggested by Freud and as carried out by Dr Ernest Jones, his early and distinguished follower. Dr Jones's monograph is a work of painstaking scholarship and of really masterly ingenuity. The research undertakes not only the clearing up of the mystery of Hamlet's character, but also the discovery of 'the clue to much of the deeper workings of Shakespeare's mind'. Part of the mystery in question is of course why Hamlet, after he had so definitely resolved to do so, did not avenge upon his hated uncle his father's death. But there is another mystery to the play—what Freud calls 'the mystery of its effect', its magical appeal that draws so much interest towards it. Recalling the many failures to solve the riddle of the play's charm, he wonders if we are to be driven to the conclusion 'that its magical appeal rests solely upon the impressive thoughts in it and the splendour of its language'. Freud believes that we can find a source of power beyond this.

We remember that Freud has told us that the meaning of a dream is its intention, and we may assume that the meaning of a drama is its intention, too. The Jones research undertakes to discover what it was that Shakespeare intended to say about Hamlet. It finds that the intention was wrapped by the author in a dreamlike obscurity because it touched so deeply both his personal life and the moral life of the world; what Shakespeare intended to say is that Hamlet cannot act because he is incapacitated by the guilt he feels at his unconscious attachment to his mother. There is, I think, nothing to be quarrelled with in the statement that there is an Oedipus situation in *Hamlet*; and if psycho-analysis has indeed added a new point of interest to the play, that is to its credit.[1] And, just so, there is no reason to quarrel with Freud's conclusion when he undertakes to give us the meaning of *King Lear* by a tortuous tracing of the mythological implications of the theme of the three caskets, of the relation of the caskets to the Norns, the Fates, and the Graces, of the connection of these triadic females with Lear's daughters, of the transmogrification of the death goddess into the love goddess and the identification of Cordelia with both, all to the conclusion that the meaning of *King Lear* is to be found in the tragic refusal of an old man to 'renounce love, choose death, and make friends with the necessity of dying'. There is something both beautiful and suggestive in this, but it is not *the* meaning of *King Lear* any more than the Oedipus motive is *the* meaning of *Hamlet*.

It is not here a question of the validity of the evidence, though that is of course important. We must rather object to the conclusions of Freud and Dr Jones on the ground that their proponents do not have an adequate conception of what an artistic meaning is. There is no single meaning to any work of art; this is true not merely because it is better that it should be true, that is, because it makes art a richer thing, but because historical and personal experience show it to be true. Changes in historical context and in personal mood change the meaning of a work and indicate to us that artistic understanding is not a question of fact but of value. Even if the author's intention were, as it cannot be, precisely determinable, the meaning of a work cannot lie in the author's intention alone. It must also lie in its effect. We can say of a volcanic eruption on an inhabited island that it 'means terrible suffering', but if the island is un-inhabited or easily evacuated it means something else. In short, the audience partly determines the meaning of the work. But although Freud sees something of this when he says that in addition to the author's intention we must take into account the mystery of *Hamlet's* effect, he nevertheless goes on to speak as if, historically, *Hamlet's* effect had been single and brought about solely by the 'magical' power of the Oedipus motive to which, unconsciously, we so violently respond. Yet there was, we know, a period when *Hamlet* was relatively in eclipse, and it has always been scandalously true of the French, a people not without filial feeling, that they have been somewhat indifferent to the 'magical appeal' of *Hamlet*.

I do not think that anything I have said about the inadequacies of the Freudian method of interpretation limits the number of ways we can deal with a work of art. Bacon remarked that experiment may twist nature on the rack to wring out its secrets, and criticism may use any instruments upon a work of art to find its meanings. The elements of art are not limited to the world of art. They reach into life, and whatever extraneous knowledge of them we gain—for example, by research into the historical context of the work—may quicken our feelings for the work itself and even enter legitimately into those feelings. Then, too, anything we may learn about the artist himself may be enriching and legitimate. But one research into the mind of the artist is simply not practicable, however legitimate it may theoretically be. That is, the investigation of his unconscious intention as it exists apart from the work itself. Criticism understands that the artist's statement of his conscious intention, though it is sometimes useful, cannot finally determine meaning. How much less can we know from his unconscious intention considered as something apart from the whole work? Surely very little that can be called conclusive or scientific. For, as Freud himself points out, we are not in a position to question the artist; we must apply the technique of dream analysis to his symbols, but, as Freud says with some heat, those people do not understand his theory who think that a dream may be interpreted without the dreamer's free association with the multitu-dinous details of his dream.

We have so far ignored the aspect of the method which finds the solution to the 'mystery' of such a play as *Hamlet* in the temperament of Shakespeare him-self and then illuminates the mystery of Shakespeare's temperament by means of the solved mystery of the play. Here it will be amusing to remember that by 1935 Freud had become converted to the theory that it was not Shakespeare of Stratford but the Earl of Oxford who wrote the plays, thus invalidating the important bit of evidence that Shakespeare's father died shortly before the com-position of *Hamlet*. This is destructive enough to Dr Jones's argument, but the evidence from which Dr Jones draws conclusions about literature fails on grounds more relevant to literature itself. For when Dr Jones, by means of his analysis of *Hamlet*, takes us into 'the deeper workings of Shakespeare's mind', he does so with a perfect confidence that he knows what *Hamlet* is and what its relation to Shakespeare is. It is, he tells us, Shakespeare's 'chief masterpiece', so far superior to all his other works that it may be placed on 'an entirely separate level'. And then, having established his ground on an entirely subjective literary judgment, Dr Jones goes on to tell us that *Hamlet* 'probably expresses the core of Shakespeare's philosophy and outlook as no other work of his does'. That is, all the contradictory or complicating or modifying testimony of the other plays is dismissed on the basis of Dr Jones's acceptance of the peculiar position which, he believes, *Hamlet* occupies in the Shakespeare canon. And it is upon this quite inadmissible judgment that Dr Jones bases his argument: 'It may be expected *therefore* that anything which will give us the key to the inner meaning of the play will *necessarily* give us the clue to much of the deeper workings of Shakespeare's mind.' (The italics are mine.)

I should be sorry if it appeared that I am trying to say that psycho-analysis can have nothing to do with literature. I am sure that the opposite is so. For example, the whole notion of rich ambiguity in literature, of the interplay between the apparent meaning and the latent—not 'hidden'—meaning, has been reinforced by the Freudian concepts, perhaps even received its first impetus from them. Of late years, the more perceptive psycho-analysts have surrendered the early pretensions of their teachers to deal 'scientifically' with literature. That is all to the good, and when a study as modest and precise as Dr Franz Alexander's essay on *Henry IV* comes along, an essay which pretends not to 'solve' but only to illuminate the subject, we have something worth having. Dr Alexander undertakes nothing more than to say that in the development of Prince Hal we see the classic struggle of the ego to come to normal adjustment, beginning with the rebellion against the father, going on to the conquest of the super-ego (Hotspur, with his rigid notions of honour and glory), then to the conquests of the *id* (Falstaff, with his anarchic self-indulgence), then to the identification with the father (the crown scene) and the assumption of mature responsibility. An analysis of this sort is not momentous and not exclusive of other meanings; perhaps it does no more than point up and formulate what we all have already seen. It has the tact to *accept* the play and does not, like Dr Jones's study of *Hamlet*, search for a 'hidden motive' and a 'deeper working', which implies that there is a reality to which the play stands in the relation that a dream stands to the wish that generates it and from which it is separable; it is this reality, this 'deeper working', which, according to Dr Jones, produced the play. But *Hamlet* is not merely the product of Shakespeare's thought, it is the very instrument of his thought, and if meaning is intention, Shakespeare did not intend the Oedipus motive or anything less than *Hamlet*; if meaning is effect then it is *Hamlet* which affects us, not the Oedipus motive. *Coriolanus* also deals, and very terribly, with the Oedipus motive, but the effect of the one drama is very different from the effect of the other.

If, then, we can accept neither Freud's conception of the place of art in life nor his application of the analytical method, what is it that he contributes to our understanding of art or to its practice? In my opinion, what he contributes outweighs his errors; it is of the greatest importance, and it lies in no specific statement that he makes about art but is, rather, implicit in his whole conception of the mind.

For, of all mental systems, the Freudian psychology is the one which makes poetry indigenous to the very constitution of the mind. Indeed, the mind, as Freud sees it, is in the greater part of its tendency exactly a poetry-making organ. This puts the case too strongly, no doubt, for it seems to make the working of the unconscious mind equivalent to poetry itself, forgetting that between the unconscious mind and the finished poem there supervene the social intention and the formal control of the conscious mind. Yet the statement has at least the virtue of counterbalancing the belief, so commonly expressed or implied, that the very opposite is true, and that poetry is a kind of beneficent aberration of the mind's right course.

Freud has not merely naturalized poetry; he has discovered its status as a pioneer settler, and he sees it as a method of thought. Often enough he tries to show how, as a method of thought, it is unreliable and ineffective for conquering reality; yet he himself is forced to use it in the very shaping of his own science, as when he speaks of the topography of the mind and tells us with a kind of defiant apology that the metaphors of space relationship which he is using are really most inexact since the mind is not a thing of space at all, but that there is no other way of conceiving the difficult idea except by metaphor. In the eighteenth century Vico spoke of the metaphorical, imagistic language of the early stages of culture; it was left to Freud to discover how, in a scientific age, we still feel and think in figurative formations, and to create, what psychoanalysis is, a science of tropes, of metaphor and its variants, synecdoche and metonymy.

Freud showed, too how the mind, in one of its parts, could work without logic, yet not without that directing purpose, that control of intent from which, perhaps, it might be said, logic springs. For the unconscious mind works without the syntactical conjunctions which are logic's essence. It recognizes no *because*, no *therefore*, no *but*; such ideas as similarity, agreement, and community are expressed in dreams imagistically by compressing the elements into a unity. The unconscious mind in its struggle with the conscious always turns from the general to the concrete and finds the tangible trifle more congenial than the large abstraction. Freud discovered in the very organization of the mind those mechanisms by which art makes its effects, such devices as the condensations of meanings and the displacement of accent.

All this is perhaps obvious enough and, though I should like to develop it in proportion both to its importance and to the space I have given to disagreement with Freud, I will not press it further. For there are two other elements in Freud's thought which, in conclusion, I should like to introduce as of great weight in their bearing on art.

Of these, one is a specific idea which, in the middle of his career (1920), Freud put forward in his essay *Beyond the Pleasure Principle*. The essay itself is a speculative attempt to solve a perplexing problem in clinical analysis, but its relevance to literature is inescapable, as Freud sees well enough, even though his perception of its critical importance is not sufficiently strong to make him revise his earlier views of the nature and function of art. The idea is one which stands beside Aristotle's notion of the catharsis, in part to supplement, in part to modify it.

Freud has come upon certain facts which are not to be reconciled with his earlier theory of the dream. According to this theory, all dreams, even the unpleasant ones, could be understood upon analysis to have the intention of fulfilling the dreamer's wishes. They are in the service of what Freud calls the pleasure principle, which is opposed to the reality principle. It is, of course, this explanation of the dream which had so largely conditioned Freud's theory of art. But now there is thrust upon him the necessity for reconsidering the theory of the dream, for it was found that in cases of war neurosis—what we once called shellshock—the patient, with the utmost anguish, recurred in his dreams to the very situation, distressing as it was, which had precipitated his neurosis. It seemed impossible to interpret these dreams by any assumption of a hedonistic intent. Nor did there seem to be the usual amount of distortion in them: the patient recurred to the terrible initiatory situation with great literalness. And the same pattern of psychic behaviour could be observed in the play of children; there were some games which, far from fulfilling wishes, seemed to concentrate upon the representation of those aspects of the child's life which were most unpleasant and threatening to his happiness.

To explain such mental activities Freud evolved a theory for which he at first refused to claim much but to which, with the years, he attached an increasing importance. He first makes the assumption that there is indeed in the psychic life a repetition-compulsion which goes beyond the pleasure principle. Such a compulsion cannot be meaningless, it must have an intent. And that intent, Freud comes to believe, is exactly and literally the developing fear. 'These dreams,' he says, 'are attempts at restoring control of the stimuli by developing apprehension, the pretermission of which caused the traumatic neurosis.' The dream, that is, is the effort to reconstruct the bad situation in order that the failure to meet it may be recouped; in these dreams there is no obscured intent to evade but only an attempt to meet the situation, to make a new effort of control. And in the play of children it seems to be that 'the child repeats even the unpleasant experiences because through his own activity he gains a far more thorough mastery of the strong impression than was possible by mere passive experience'.

Freud, at this point, can scarcely help being put in mind of tragic drama; nevertheless, he does not wish to believe that this effort to come to mental grips with a situation is involved in the attraction of tragedy. He is, we might say, under the influence of the Aristotelian tragic theory which emphasizes a qualified hedonism through suffering. But the pleasure involved in tragedy is perhaps an ambiguous one; and sometimes we must feel that the famous sense of cathartic resolution is perhaps the result of glossing over terror with beautiful language rather than an evacuation of it. And sometimes the terror even bursts through the language to stand stark and isolated from the play, as does Oedipus's sightless and bleeding face. At any rate, the Aristotelian theory does not deny another function for tragedy (and for comedy, too) which is suggested by Freud's theory of the traumatic neurosis—what might be called the mithridatic function, by which tragedy is used as the homeopathic administration of pain to inure ourselves to the greater pain which life will force upon us. There is in the cathartic theory of tragedy, as it is usually understood, a conception of tragedy's function which is too negative and which inadequately suggests the sense of active mastery which tragedy can give.

In the same essay in which he sets forth the conception of the mind embracing its own pain for some vital purpose, Freud also expresses a provisional assent to the idea (earlier stated, as he reminds us, by Schopenhauer) that there is perhaps a human drive which makes of death the final and desired goal. The death instinct is a conception that is rejected by many of even the most thoroughgoing Freudian theorists (as, in his last book, Freud mildly noted); the late Otto Fenichel in his authoritative work on the neurosis argues cogently against it. Yet even if we reject the theory as not fitting the facts in any operatively useful way, we still cannot miss its grandeur, its ultimate tragic courage in acquiescence to fate. The idea of the reality principle and the idea of the death instinct form the crown of Freud's broader speculation on the life of man. Their quality of grim poetry is characteristic of Freud's system and the ideas it generates for him.

And as much as anything else that Freud gives to literature, this quality of his thought is important. Although the artist is never finally determined in his work by the intellectual systems about him, he cannot avoid their influence; and it can be said of various competing systems that some hold more promise for the artist than others. When, for example, we think of the simple humanitarian optimism which, for two decades, has been so pervasive, we must see that not only has it been politically and philosophically inadequate, but also that it implies, by the smallness of its view of the varieties of human possibility, a kind of check on the creative faculties. In Freud's view of life no such limitation is implied. To be sure, certain elements of his system seem hostile to the usual notions of man's dignity. Like every great critic of human nature—and Freud is that—he finds in human pride the ultimate cause of human wretchedness, and he takes pleasure in knowing that his ideas stand with those of Copernicus and Darwin in making pride more difficult to maintain. Yet the Freudian man is, I venture to think, a creature of far more dignity and far more interest than the man which any other modern system has been able to conceive. Despite popular belief to the contrary, man, as Freud conceives him, is not to be understood by any simple formula (such as sex) but is rather an inextricable tangle of culture and biology. And not being simple, he is not simply good; he has, as Freud says somewhere, a kind of hell within him from which rise everlastingly the impulses which threaten his civilization. He has the faculty of imagining for himself more in the way of pleasure and satisfaction than he can possibly achieve. Everything that he gains he pays for in more than equal coin; compromise and the compounding with defeat constitute his best way of getting through the world. His best qualities are the result of a struggle whose outcome is tragic. Yet he is a creature of love; it is Freud's sharpest criticism of the Adlerian[a] psychology that to aggression it gives everything and to love nothing at all.

One is always aware in reading Freud how little cynicism there is in his thought. His desire for man is only that he should be human, and to this end his science is devoted. No view of life to which the artist responds can insure the quality of his work, but the poetic qualities of Freud's own principles, which are so clearly in the line of the classic tragic realism, suggest that this is a view which does not narrow and simplify the human world for the artist but on the contrary opens and complicates it.

Notes

1. However, A. C. Bradley, in his discussion of Hamlet (*Shakespearean Tragedy*), states clearly the intense sexual disgust which Hamlet feels and which, for Bradley, helps account for his uncertain purpose; and Bradley was anticipated in this view by Löning. It is well known, and Dover Wilson has lately emphasized the point, that to an Elizabethan audience Hamlet's mother was not merely tasteless, as to a modern audience she seems, in hurrying to marry Claudius, but actually adulterous in marrying him at all because he was, as her brother-in-law, within the forbidden degrees.

[a] Alfred Adler was, like Carl Jung, an early disciple of Freud's who broke away from his master to found his own school of psycho-analysis.

23 Cleanth Brooks

Cleanth Brooks (b. 1906) was one of the key figures in the rise of the New Criticism in America in the 'thirties and 'forties, and a leading light of that subgroup within the general movement known as the Fugitives or Southern Agrarians. John Crowe Ransom (see above, pp. 227-39), Allen Tate and Robert Penn Warren were among the other distinguished writers in this group, whose principal organ was the *Southern Review*, edited from 1935-42 by Brooks and Warren. Their poetics derived from Eliot, Richards, Empson and Leavis, but in their right-wing political views and more or less orthodox Christianity they owed a special allegiance to Eliot. The textbook anthologies edited by Brooks and Warren, *Understanding Poetry* (New York, 1938), and *Understanding Fiction* (New York, 1943), were widely adopted in American universities, and in the opinion of many judges were the principal media by which the orthodoxies of the New Criticism were transmitted to a whole generation of American students of literature.

'The Language of Paradox', first published in 1942, subsequently appeared in a slightly revised form as the first chapter of Brooks's best-known work, *The Well-Wrought Urn: studies in the structure of poetry* (New York, 1947) from which it is reprinted here. This essay is entirely characteristic of the New Criticism in seeking a formula or category with which to identify the special character of literary language (compare Brooks's 'paradox' with Richards's 'emotive' and Empson's 'ambiguity')—and not only to identify but also to defend literary language as the medium of a special kind of meaning, or knowledge, not accessible to science and scientific discourse. Also characteristic of the New Criticism is the way Brooks develops his generalizations out of close and subtle analysis of lyric poetry, and his choice of a metaphysical lyric (Donne's *Canonization*) for the most elaborate and exemplary treatment. The approach is antihistorical to the extent that it supposes the existence of some absolute quality in great poetry that transcends the conditions of particular cultural contexts. But of course Brooks is far from being innocent of historical knowledge or the ability to deploy it in criticism; and in his essay 'poetry' is made to stand for a value-saturated past that is contrasted with a debased and alien present. There is a certain connection here with the criticism of Leavis and *Scrutiny*.

Cleanth Brooks was educated at Vanderbilt College and Tulane University in the United States, and later at Oxford. He was Professor of English at Louisiana State University and later at Yale, where he is now Gray Professor of Rhetoric. From 1964 to 1966 he was cultural attaché at the American

Embassy in London. In addition to those already mentioned, his publications include *Literary Criticism: a short history* (New York, 1957), written in collaboration with W. K. Wimsatt, and *William Faulkner: the Yoknapatawpha Country* (1963).

CROSS REFERENCES: 9. I. A. Richards
                         12. William Empson
                         18. John Crowe Ransom
                         20. Paul Valéry

COMMENTARY: Lee T. Lemon, *The Partial Critics* (1965), pp. 139-50.
                     R. S. Crane, 'The critical monism of Cleanth Brooks',
                     in *Critics and Criticism: Ancient and Modern*,
                     ed. R. S. Crane (Chicago, 1957)

The language of paradox

Few of us are prepared to accept the statement that the language of poetry is the language of paradox. Paradox is the language of sophistry, hard, bright, witty; it is hardly the language of the soul. We are willing to allow that paradox is a permissible weapon which a Chesterton may on occasion exploit. We may permit it in epigram, a special subvariety of poetry; and in satire, which though useful, we are hardly willing to allow to be poetry at all. Our prejudices force us to regard paradox as intellectual rather than emotional, clever rather than profound, rational rather than divinely irrational.

Yet there is a sense in which paradox is the language appropriate and inevitable to poetry. It is the scientist whose truth requires a language purged of every trace of paradox; apparently the truth which the poet utters can be approached only in terms of paradox. I overstate the case, to be sure; it is possible that the title of this chapter is itself to be treated as merely a paradox. But there are reasons for thinking that the overstatement which I propose may light up some elements in the nature of poetry which tend to be overlooked.

The case of William Wordsworth, for instance, is instructive on this point. His poetry would not appear to promise many examples of the language of paradox. He usually prefers the direct attack. He insists on simplicity; he distrusts whatever seems sophistical. And yet the typical Wordsworth poem is based upon a paradoxical situation. Consider his celebrated

> It is a beauteous evening, calm and free
> The holy time is quiet as a Nun
> Breathless with adoration....

The poet is filled with worship, but the girl who walks beside him is not worshipping. The implication is that she should respond to the holy time, and become like the evening itself, nunlike; but she seems less worshipful than inanimate nature itself. Yet

> If thou appear untouched by solemn thought,
> Thy nature is not therefore less divine:
> Thou liest in Abraham's bosom all the year;
> And worship'st at the Temple's inner shrine,
> God being with thee when we know it not.

The underlying paradox (of which the enthusiastic reader may well be unconscious) is nevertheless thoroughly necessary, even for that reader. Why does the innocent girl worship more deeply than the self-conscious poet who walks beside her? Because she is filled with an unconscious sympathy for *all* of nature, not merely the grandiose and solemn. One remembers the lines from Wordsworth's friend, Coleridge:

> He prayeth best, who loveth best
> All things both great and small.*a*

Her unconscious sympathy is the unconscious worship. She is in communion with nature 'all the year', and her devotion is continual whereas that of the poet is sporadic and momentary. But we have not done with the paradox yet. It not only underlies the poem, but something of the paradox informs the poem, though, since this is Wordsworth, rather timidly. The comparison of the evening to the nun actually has more than one dimension. The calm of the evening obviously means 'worship', even to the dull-witted and insensitive. It corresponds to the trappings of the nun, visible to everyone. Thus, it suggests not merely holiness, but, in the total poem, even a hint of Pharisaical holiness, with which the girl's careless innocence, itself a symbol of her continual secret worship, stands in contrast.

Or consider Wordsworth's sonnet, *Composed upon Westminster Bridge.* I believe that most readers will agree that it is one of Wordsworth's most successful poems; yet most students have the greatest difficulty in accounting for its goodness. The attempt to account for it on the grounds of nobility of sentiment soon breaks down. On this level, the poem merely says: that the city in the morning light presents a picture which is majestic and touching to all but the most dull of souls; but the poem says very little more about the sight: the city is beautiful in the morning light and it is awfully still. The attempt to make a case for the poem in terms of the brilliance of its images also quickly breaks down: the student searches for graphic details in vain: there are next to no realistic touches. In fact, the poet simply huddles the details together:

> ... silent, bare,
> Ships, towers, domes, theatres, and temples lie
> Open unto the fields ...

We get a blurred impression—points of roofs and pinnacles along the skyline, all twinkling in the morning light. More than that, the sonnet as a whole

a The Rime of the Ancient Mariner.

293

contains some very flat writing and some well-worn comparisons.

The reader may ask: Where, then, does the poem get its power? It gets it, it seems to me, from the paradoxical situation out of which the poem arises. The speaker is honestly surprised, and he manages to get some sense of awed surprise into the poem. It is odd to the poet that the city should be able to 'wear the beauty of the morning' at all. Mount Snowdon, Skiddaw, Mont Blanc—these wear it by natural right, but surely not grimy, feverish London. This is the point of the almost shocked exclamation:

> Never did sun more beautifully steep
> In his first splendour, *valley, rock,* or *hill* ...

The 'smokeless air' reveals a city which the poet did not know existed: man-made London is a part of nature too, is lighted by the sun of nature, and lighted to as beautiful effect.

> The river glideth at his own sweet will ...

A river is the most 'natural' thing that one can imagine; it has the elasticity, the curved line of nature itself. The poet had never been able to regard this one as a real river—now, uncluttered by barges, the river reveals itself as a natural thing, not at all disciplined into a rigid and mechanical pattern: it is like the daffodils, or the mountain brooks, artless, and whimsical, and 'natural' as they. The poem closes, you will remember, as follows:

> Dear God! the very houses seem asleep;
> And all that mighty heart is lying still!

The city, in the poet's insight of the morning, has earned its right to be considered organic, not merely mechanical. That is why the stale metaphor of the sleeping houses is strangely renewed. The most exciting thing that the poet can say about the houses is that they are *asleep*. He has been in the habit of counting them dead—as just mechanical and inanimate; to say they are 'asleep' is to say that they are alive, that they participate in the life of nature. In the same way, the tired old metaphor which sees a great city as a pulsating heart of empire becomes revivified. It is only when the poet sees the city under the semblance of death that he can see it as actually alive—quick with the only life which he can accept, the organic life of 'nature'.

It is not my intention to exaggerate Wordsworth's own consciousness of the paradox involved. In this poem, he prefers, as is usual with him, the frontal attack. But the situation is paradoxical here as in so many of his poems. In his preface to the second edition of the *Lyrical Ballads* Wordsworth stated that his general purpose was 'to choose incidents and situations from common life' but so to treat them that 'ordinary things should be preserved to the mind in an unusual aspect'. Coleridge was to state the purpose for him later, in terms which make even more evident Wordsworth's exploitation of the paradoxical: 'Mr Wordsworth ... was to propose to himself as his object, to give the charm of novelty to things of every day, and to excite a feeling analogous to the supernatural, by awakening the mind's attention from the lethargy of custom,

and directing it to the loveliness and the wonders of the world before us ...'
Wordsworth, in short, was consciously attempting to show his audience that the
common was really uncommon, the prosaic was really poetic.

Coleridge's terms, 'the charm of novelty to things of every day', 'awakening
the mind', suggest the Romantic preoccupation with wonder—the surprise, the
revelation which puts the tarnished familiar world in a new light. This may
well be the *raison d'être* of most Romantic paradoxes; and yet the neo-classic
poets use paradox for much the same reason. Consider Pope's lines from *The
Essay on Man*:

> In doubt his Mind or Body to prefer;
> Born but to die, and reas'ning but to err;
> Alike in ignorance, his Reason such,
> Whether he thinks too little, or too much ...
>
> Created half to rise, and half to fall;
> Great Lord of all things, yet a Prey to all;
> Sole Judge of Truth, in endless Error hurl'd;
> The Glory, Jest, and Riddle of the world!

Here, it is true, the paradoxes insist on the irony, rather than the wonder. But
Pope too might have claimed that he was treating the things of every day, man
himself, and awakening his mind so that he would view himself in a new and
blinding light. Thus, there is a certain awed wonder in Pope just as there is a
certain trace of irony implicit in the Wordsworth sonnets. There is, of course,
no reason why they should not occur together, and they do. Wonder and irony
merge in many of the lyrics of Blake; they merge in Coleridge's *Ancient
Mariner*. The variations in emphasis are numerous. Gray's *Elegy* uses a typical
Wordsworth 'situation' with the rural scene and with peasants contemplated
in the light of their 'betters'. But in the *Elegy* the balance is heavily tilted in
the direction of irony, the revelation an ironic rather than a startling one:

> Can storied urn or animated bust
> Back to its mansion call the fleeting breath?
> Can Honour's voice provoke the silent dust?
> Or Flatt'ry sooth the dull cold ear of Death?

But I am not here interested in enumerating the possible variations; I am
interested rather in our seeing that the paradoxes spring from the very nature
of the poet's language: it is a language in which the connotations play as great
a part as the denotations. And I do not mean that the connotations are important as supplying some sort of frill or trimming, something external to the real
matter in hand. I mean that the poet does not use a notation at all—as the
scientist may properly be said to do so. The poet, within limits, has to make up
his language as he goes.

T. S. Eliot has commented upon 'that perpetual slight alteration of language,
words perpetually juxtaposed in new and sudden combinations', which occurs in
poetry. It *is* perpetual; it cannot be kept out of the poem; it can only be directed
and controlled. The tendency of science is necessarily to stabilize terms, to
freeze them into strict denotations; the poet's tendency is by contrast disruptive.

The terms are continually modifying each other, and thus violating their dictionary meanings. To take a very simple example, consider the adjectives in the first lines of Wordsworth's evening sonnet: *beauteous, calm, free, holy, quiet, breathless*. The juxtapositions are hardly startling; and yet notice this: the evening is like a nun breathless with adoration. The adjective 'breathless' suggests tremendous excitement; and yet the evening is not only quiet but *calm*. There is no final contradiction, to be sure: it is *that* kind of calm and *that* kind of excitement, and the two states may well occur together. But the poet has no one term. Even if he had a polysyllabic technical term, the term would not provide the solution for his problem. He must work by contradiction and qualification.

We may approach the problem in this way: the poet has to work by analogies. All of the subtler states of emotion, as I. A. Richards has pointed out, necessarily demand metaphor for their expression. The poet must work by analogies, but the metaphors do not lie in the same plane or fit neatly edge to edge. There is a continual tilting of the planes; necessary overlappings, discrepancies, contradictions. Even the most direct and simple poet is forced into paradoxes far more often than we think, if we are sufficiently alive to what he is doing.

But in dilating on the difficulties of the poet's task, I do not want to leave the impression that it is a task which necessarily defeats him, or even that with his method he may not win to a fine precision. To use Shakespeare's figure, he can

> ... with assays of bias
> By indirections find directions out.

Shakespeare had in mind the game of lawn bowls in which the bowl is distorted, a distortion which allows the skilful player to bowl a curve. To elaborate the figure, science makes use of the perfect sphere and its attack can be direct. The method of art can, I believe, never be direct—is always indirect. But that does not mean that the master of the game cannot place the bowl where he wants it. The serious difficulties will only occur when he confuses his game with that of science and mistakes the nature of his appropriate instrument. Mr Stuart Chase a few years ago, with a touching naïveté, urged us to take the distortion out of the bowl—to treat language like notation.

I have said that even the apparently simple and straightforward poet is forced into paradoxes by the nature of his instrument. Seeing this, we should not be surprised to find poets who consciously employ it to gain a compression and precision otherwise unobtainable. Such a method, like any other, carries with it its own perils. But the dangers are not overpowering: the poem is not predetermined to a shallow and glittering sophistry. The method is an extension of the normal language of poetry, not a perversion of it.

I should like to refer the reader to a concrete case. Donne's *Canonization* ought to provide a sufficiently extreme instance.[a] The basic metaphor which underlies the poem (and which is reflected in the title) involves a sort of para-

---

[a] The text of Donne's *Canonization* is provided in an appendix to this essay.

dox. For the poet daringly treats profane love as if it were divine love. The canonization is not that of a pair of holy anchorites who have renounced the world and the flesh. The hermitage of each is the other's body; but they do renounce the world, and so their title to sainthood is cunningly argued. The poem then is a parody of Christian sainthood; but it is an intensely serious parody of a sort that modern man, habituated as he is to an easy yes or no, can hardly understand. He refuses to accept the paradox as a serious rhetorical device; and since he is able to accept it only as a cheap trick, he is forced into this dilemma. Either: Donne does not take love seriously; here he is merely sharpening his wit as a sort of mechanical exercise. Or: Donne does not take sainthood seriously; here he is merely indulging in a cynical and bawdy parody.

Neither account is true; a reading of the poem will show that Donne takes both love and religion seriously; it will show, further, that the paradox is here his inevitable instrument. But to see this plainly will require a closer reading than most of us give to poetry.

The poem opens dramatically on a note of exasperation. The 'you' whom the speaker addresses is not identified. We can imagine that it is a person, perhaps a friend, who is objecting to the speaker's love affair. At any rate, the person represents the practical world which regards love as a silly affectation. To use the metaphor on which the poem is built, the friend represents the secular world which the lovers have renounced.

Donne begins to suggest this metaphor in the first stanza by the contemptuous alternatives which he suggests to the friend:

> ... chide my palsie, or my gout,
> My five gray haires, or ruin'd fortune flout....

The implications are: (1) All right, consider my love as an infirmity, as a disease, if you will, but confine yourself to my other infirmities, my palsy, my approaching old age, my ruined fortune. You stand a better chance of curing those; in chiding me for this one, you are simply wasting your time as well as mine. Why don't you pay attention to your own welfare—go on and get wealth and honour for yourself. What should you care if I do give these up in pursuing my love.

The two main categories of secular success are neatly, and contemptuously epitomized in the line:

> Or the Kings reall, or his stamped face ...

Cultivate the court and gaze at the king's face there, or, if you prefer, get into business and look at his face stamped on coins. But let me alone.

This conflict between the 'real' world and the lover absorbed in the world of love runs through the poem; it dominates the second stanza in which the torments of love, so vivid to the lover, affect the real world not at all—

> What merchants ships have my sighs drown'd?

It is touched on in the fourth stanza in the contrast between the word 'Chronicle' which suggests secular history with its pomp and magnificence, the history of kings and princes, and the word 'sonnets' with its suggestions of trivial and precious intricacy. The conflict appears again in the last stanza, only to be resolved when the unworldly lovers, love's saints who have given up the world, paradoxically achieve a more intense world. But here the paradox is still contained in, and supported by, the dominant metaphor: so does the holy anchorite win a better world by giving up this one.

But before going on to discuss this development of the theme, it is important to see what else the second stanza does. For it is in this second stanza and the third, that the poet shifts the tone of the poem, modulating from the note of irritation with which the poem opens into the quite different tone with which it closes.

Donne accomplishes the modulation of tone by what may be called an analysis of love-metaphor. Here, as in many of his poems, he shows that he is thoroughly self-conscious about what he is doing. This second stanza he fills with the conventionalized figures of the Petrarchan tradition: the wind of lovers' sighs, the floods of lovers' tears, etc.—extravagant figures with which the contemptuous secular friend might be expected to tease the lover. The implication is that the poet himself recognizes the absurdity of the Petrarchan love metaphors. But what of it? The very absurdity of the jargon which lovers are expected to talk makes for his argument: their love, however absurd it may appear to the world, does no harm to the world. The practical friend need have no fears: there will still be wars to fight and lawsuits to argue.

The opening of the third stanza suggests that this vein of irony is to be maintained. The poet points out to his friend the infinite fund of such absurdities which can be applied to lovers:

> Call her one, mee another flye,
> We'are Tapers too, and at our owne cost die....

For that matter, the lovers can conjure up for themselves plenty of such fantastic comparisons: *they* know what the world thinks of them. But these figures of the third stanza are no longer the threadbare Petrarchan conventionalities; they have sharpness and bite. The last one, the likening of the lovers to the phoenix, is fully serious, and with it, the tone has shifted from ironic banter into a defiant but controlled tenderness.

The effect of the poet's implied awareness of the lovers' apparent madness is to cleanse and revivify metaphor; to indicate the sense in which the poet accepts it, and thus to prepare us for accepting seriously the fine and seriously intended metaphors which dominate the last two stanzas of the poem.

The opening line of the fourth stanza,

> Wee can dye by it, if not live by love,

achieves an effect of tenderness and deliberate resolution. The lovers are ready to die to the world; they are committed; they are not callow but confident. (The basic metaphor of the saint, one notices, is being carried on; the lovers, in their renunciation of the world, have something of the confident resolution of the saint. By the bye, the word 'legend'—

> ... if unfit for tombes and hearse
> Our legend bee—

in Donne's time meant 'the life of a saint'.) The lovers are willing to forego the ponderous and stately chronicle and to accept the trifling and insubstantial 'sonnet' instead; but then if the urn be well wrought, it provides a finer memorial for one's ashes than does the pompous and grotesque monument. With the finely contemptuous, yet quiet phrase, 'halfe-acre tombes', the world which the lovers reject expands into something gross and vulgar. But the figure works further; the pretty sonnets will not merely hold their ashes as a decent earthly memorial. Their legend, their story, will gain them canonization; and approved as love's saints, other lovers will invoke them.

In the last stanza, the theme receives a final complication. The lovers in rejecting life actually win to the most intense life. This paradox has been hinted at earlier in the phoenix metaphor. Here it receives a powerful dramatization. The lovers in becoming hermits, find that they have not lost the world, but have gained the world in each other, now a more intense, more meaningful world. Donne is not content to treat the lovers' discovery as something which comes to them passively, but rather as something which they actively achieve. They are like the saint, God's athlete:

> Who did the whole worlds soule *contract*, and *drove*
> Into the glasses of your eyes....

The image is that of a violent squeezing as of a powerful hand. And what do the lovers 'drive' into each other's eyes? The 'Countries, Townes', and 'Courts', which they renounced in the first stanza of the poem. The unworldly lovers thus become the most 'worldly' of all.

The tone with which the poem closes is one of triumphant achievement, but the tone is a development contributed to by various earlier elements. One of the more important elements which works towards our acceptance of the final paradox is the figure of the phoenix, which will bear a little further analysis.

The comparison of the lovers to the phoenix is very skilfully related to the two earlier comparisons, that in which the lovers are like burning tapers, and that in which they are like the eagle and the dove. The phoenix comparison gathers up both: the phoenix is a bird, and like the tapers, it burns. We have a selected series of items: the phoenix figure seems to come in a natural stream of association. 'Call us what you will', the lover says, and rattles off in his desperation the first comparisons that occur to him. The comparison to the phoenix seems thus merely another outlandish one, the most outrageous of all. But it is this most fantastic one, stumbled over apparently in his haste, that the poet goes on to develop. It really describes the lovers best and justifies their renunciation. For the phoenix is not two but one, 'we two being one, are it'; and it burns, not like the taper at its own cost, but to live again. Its death is life: 'Wee dye and rise the same ...' The poet literally justifies the fantastic assertion. In the sixteenth and seventeenth centuries to 'die' means to experience the consummation of the act of love. The lovers after the act are the same.

Their love is not exhausted in mere lust. This is their title to canonization. Their love is like the phoenix.

I hope that I do not seem to juggle the meaning of *die*. The meaning that I have cited can be abundantly justified in the literature of the period; Shakespeare uses 'die' in this sense; so does Dryden. Moreover, I do not think that I give it undue emphasis. The word is in a crucial position. On it is pivoted the transition to the next stanza,

> Wee can dye by it, if not live by love,
> And if unfit for tombes ...

Most important of all, the sexual submeaning of 'die' does not contradict the other meanings: the poet is saying: 'Our death is really a more intense life'; 'We can afford to trade life (the world) for death (love), for that death is the consummation of life'; 'After all, one does not expect to live by love, one expects, and wants, to die by it'. But in the total passage he is also saying: 'Because our love is not mundane, we can give up the world'; 'Because our love is not merely lust, we can give up the other lusts, the lust for wealth and power'; 'because', and this is said with an inflection of irony as by one who knows the world too well, 'because our love can outlast its consummation, we are a minor miracle, we are love's saints'. This passage with its ironical tenderness and its realism feeds and supports the brilliant paradox with which the poem closes.

There is one more factor in developing and sustaining the final effect. The poem is an instance of the doctrine which it asserts; it is both the assertion and the realization of the assertion. The poet has actually before our eyes built within the song the 'pretty room' with which he says the lovers can be content. The poem itself is the well-wrought urn which can hold the lovers' ashes and which will not suffer in comparison with the prince's 'halfe-acre tomb'.

And how necessary are the paradoxes? Donne might have said directly, 'Love in a cottage is enough'. *The Canonization* contains this admirable thesis, but it contains a great deal more. He might have been as forthright as a later lyricist who wrote, 'We'll build a sweet little nest,/ Somewhere out in the West,/ And let the rest of the world go by'. He might even have imitated that more metaphysical lyric, which maintains, 'You're the cream in my coffee'. *The Canonization* touches on all these observations, but it goes beyond them, not merely in dignity, but in precision.

I submit that the only way by which the poet could say what *The Canonization* says is by paradox. More direct methods may be tempting, but all of them enfeeble and distort what is to be said. This statement may seem the less surprising when we reflect on how many of the important things which the poet has to say have to be said by means of paradox: most of the language of lovers is such—*The Canonization* is a good example; so is most of the language of religion—'He who would save his life, must lose it'; 'The last shall be first'. Indeed, almost any insight important enough to warrant a great poem apparently has to be stated in such terms. Deprived of the character of paradox with its twin concomitants of irony and wonder, the matter of Donne's poem unravels into 'facts', biological, sociological, and economic. What happens to

Donne's lovers if we consider them 'scientifically', without benefit of the super-naturalism which the poet confers upon them? Well, what happens to Shake-speare's lovers, for Shakespeare uses the basic metaphor of *The Canonization* in his *Romeo and Juliet*? In their first conversation, the lovers play with the analogy between the lover and the pilgrim to the Holy Land. Juliet says:

> For saints have hands, that pilgrims' hands do touch
> And palm to palm is holy palmers' kiss.

Considered scientifically, the lovers become Mr Aldous Huxley's animals, 'quietly sweating, palm to palm'.

For us today, Donne's imagination seems obsessed with the problem of unity; the sense in which the lovers become one—the sense in which the soul is united with God. Frequently, as we have seen, one type of union becomes a metaphor for the other. It may not be too far-fetched to see both as instances of, and metaphors for, the union which the creative imagination itself effects. For that fusion is not logical; it apparently violates science and common sense; it welds together the discordant and the contradictory. Coleridge has of course given us the classic description of its nature and power. It

> reveals itself in the balance or reconcilement of opposite or discordant quali-ties: of sameness, with difference; of the general, with the concrete; the idea, with the image; the individual, with the representative; the sense of novelty and freshness, with old and familiar objects; a more than usual state of emotion, with more than usual order ...[a]

It is a great and illuminating statement, but is a series of paradoxes. Apparently Coleridge could describe the effect of the imagination in no other way.

Shakespeare, in one of his poems, has given a description that oddly parallels that of Coleridge.

> Reason in it selfe confounded,
> Saw Division grow together,
> To themselves yet either neither,
> Simple were so well compounded.

I do not know what his *The Phoenix and the Turtle* celebrates. Perhaps it was written to honour the marriage of Sir John Salisbury and Ursula Stanley; or perhaps the Phoenix is Lucy, Countess of Bedford; or perhaps the poem is merely an essay on Platonic love. But the scholars themselves are so uncertain, that I think we will do little violence to established habits of thinking, if we boldly pre-empt the poem for our own purposes. Certainly the poem is an instance of that magic power which Coleridge sought to describe. I propose that we take it for a moment as a poem about that power;

> So they loved as love in twaine,
> Had the essence but in one,
> Two distincts, Division none,
> Number there in love was slaine.

[a] *Biographia Literaria* (1817), chap. xiv.

> Hearts remote, yet not asunder,
> Distance and no space was seene,
> Twixt this *Turtle* and his Queene;
> But in them it were a wonder....
>
> Propertie was thus appalled,
> That the selfe was not the same;
> Single Natures double name,
> Neither two nor one was called.

Precisely! The nature is single, one, unified. But the name is double, and today with our multiplication of sciences, it is multiple. If the poet is to be true to his poetry, he must call it neither two nor one: the paradox is his only solution. The difficulty has intensified since Shakespeare's day: the timid poet, when confronted with the problem of 'Single Nature's double name', has too often funked it. A history of poetry from Dryden's time to our own might bear as its subtitle 'The Half-Hearted Phoenix'.

In Shakespeare's poem, Reason is 'in it selfe confounded' at the union of the Phoenix and the Turtle; but it recovers to admit its own bankruptcy:

> Love hath Reason, Reason none,
> If what parts, can so remaine....

and it is Reason which goes on to utter the beautiful threnos with which the poem concludes:

> Beautie, Truth, and Raritie,
> Grace in all simplicitie,
> Here enclosde, in cinders lie.
>
> Death is now the *Phoenix* nest,
> And the *Turtles* loyall brest,
> To eternitie doth rest....
>
> Truth may seeme, but cannot be,
> Beautie bragge, but tis not she,
> Truth and Beautie buried be.
>
> To this urne let those repaire,
> That are either true or faire,
> For these dead Birds, sigh a prayer.

Having pre-empted the poem for our own purposes, it may not be too outrageous to go on to make one further observation. The urn to which we are summoned, the urn which holds the ashes of the phoenix, is like the well-wrought urn of Donne's *Canonization* which holds the phoenix-lovers' ashes; it is the poem itself. One is reminded of still another urn, Keats's Grecian urn, which contained for Keats, Truth and Beauty, as Shakespeare's urn encloses 'Beautie, Truth, and Raritie'. But there is a sense in which all such well-wrought urns contain the ashes of a phoenix. The urns are not meant for memorial purposes only, though that often seems to be their chief significance to the professors of literature. The phoenix rises from its ashes; or ought to rise; but it will not arise for all our mere sifting and measuring the ashes, or testing them for their chemical content. We must be prepared to accept the paradox of the imagination itself; else 'Beautie, Truth, and Raritie' remain enclosed in their cinders and we shall end with essential cinders, for all our pains.

Appendix

THE CANONIZATION

For Godsake hold your tongue, and let me love,
 Or chide my palsie, or my gout,
My five gray haires, or ruin'd fortune flout,
 With wealth your state, your minde with Arts improve,
  Take you a course, get you a place,
  Observe his honour, or his grace,
Or the Kings reall, or his stamped face
  Contemplate, what you will, approve,
  So you will let me love.

Alas, alas, who's injur'd by my love?
 What merchants ships have my sighs drown'd?
Who saies my teares have overflow'd his ground?
 When did my colds a forward spring remove?
  When did the heats which my veines fill
  Adde one more to the plaguie Bill?
Soldiers finde warres, and Lawyers finde out still
  Litigious men, which quarrels move,
  Though she and I do love.

Call us what you will, wee are made such by love;
 Call her one, mee another flye,
We'are Tapers too, and at our owne cost die,
 And wee in us finde the Eagle and the Dove.
  The Phoenix ridle hath more wit
  By us, we two being one, are it.
So to one neutrall thing both sexes fit,
  We dye and rise the same, and prove
  Mysterious by this love.

Wee can dye by it, if not live by love,
 And if unfit for tombes and hearse
Our legend bee, it will be fit for verse;
 And if no peece of Chronicle wee prove,
  We'll build in sonnets pretty roomes;
  As well a well wrought urne becomes
The greatest ashes, as halfe-acre tombes,
  And by these hymnes, all shall approve
  Us Canoniz'd for Love:

And thus invoke us; You whom reverend love
 Made one anothers hermitage;
You, to whom love was peace, that now is rage;

Who did the whole worlds soule contract, and drove
   Into the glasses of your eyes
   (So made such mirrors, and such spies,
That they did all to you epitomize,)
   Countries, Townes, Courts: Beg from above
   A patterne of your love!

24 Yvor Winters

Yvor Winters (1900-68) was for most of his life Professor of English at Stanford University, California. He was also a poet who numbered several distinguished younger poets among his students. His critical output was not large: *Primitivism and Decadence* (1937), *Maule's Curse* (1938), *The Anatomy of Nonsense* (1943), and *Edward Arlington Robinson* (1946) are the main titles, and the first three of these were short enough to be collected into a single volume, *In Defence of Reason* (1947). Yvor Winters was notorious for the boldness, not to say eccentricity, of his value-judgments. For example, he ranked Robert Bridges above T. S. Eliot, and Edith Wharton above Henry James. One must suspect that such judgments were often deliberately provocative, designed to express Winters's deep hostility to some of the orthodoxies of modern literary theory and literary taste, and his own conviction that great poetry must retain a strong element of rationality and must have demonstrable moral value. The absurdity of some of Winters's assessments, and the vulnerability of his poetics to logical objections, have been pointed out so many times that it is sometimes difficult to understand why he was always a centre of interest and often admiration. In part, no doubt, the explanation is that, in a period when literary criticism was becoming increasingly and perhaps dangerously 'professional', sophisticated, and specialized, Winters's forthright, fearless criticism was found refreshing and stimulating even by those who did not agree with him. He has often been described as the Dr Johnson of modern criticism, and one imagines that the comparison pleased him.

'Preliminary Problems' was first published in *The Anatomy of Nonsense*, and is reprinted here from *In Defence of Reason*.

CROSS REFERENCES : 6. T. S. Eliot
8. T. E. Hulme
9. I. A. Richards
20. Paul Valéry
47. W. H. Auden

COMMENTARY : Stanley Edgar Hyman, 'Yvor Winters and evaluative criticism', in *The Armed Vision* (New York, 1948)
John Casey, 'Reason defended: Yvor Winters and the nature of criticism', in *The Language of Criticism* (1966)

305

Preliminary problems

First problem

Is it possible to say that Poem A (one of Donne's *Holy Sonnets*, or one of the poems of Jonson or of Shakespeare) is better than Poem B (Collins' *Ode to Evening*) or vice versa?

If not, is it possible to say that either of these is better than Poem C (*The Cremation of Sam Magee*, or something comparable)?

If the answer is no in both cases, then any poem is as good as any other. If this is true, then all poetry is worthless; but this obviously is not true, for it is contrary to all our experience.

If the answer is yes in both cases, then there follows the question of whether the answer implies merely that one poem is better than another for the speaker, or whether it means that one poem is intrinsically better than another. If the former, then we are impressionists, which is to say relativists; and are either mystics of the type of Emerson, or hedonists of the type of [Wallace] Stevens and [John Crowe] Ransom. If the latter, then we assume that constant principles govern the poetic experience, and that the poem (as likewise the judge) must be judged in relationship to those principles. It is important, therefore, to discover the consequences of assuming each of these positions.

If our answer to the first question is no and to the second yes, then we are asserting that we can distinguish between those poems which are of the canon and those which are not, but that within the canon all judgment is impossible. This view, if adopted, will require serious elucidation, for on the face of it, it appears inexplicable. On the other hand, one cannot deny that within the canon judgment will become more difficult, for the nearer two poems may be to the highest degrees of excellence, the harder it will be to choose between them. Two poems, in fact, might be so excellent that there would be small profit in endeavouring to say that one was better, but one could arrive at this conclusion only after a careful examination of both.

Second problem

If we accept the view that one poem can be regarded as better than another, the question then arises whether this judgment is a matter of inexplicable intuition, or whether it is a question of intuition that can be explained, and consequently guided and improved by rational elucidation.

If we accept the view that the judgment in question is inexplicable, then we are again forced to confess ourselves impressionists and relativists, unless we can show that the intuitions of all men agree at all times, or that the intuitions of one man are invariably right and those of all others wrong whenever they differ. We obviously can demonstrate neither of these propositions.

If we start, then, with the proposition that one poem may be intrinsically superior to another, we are forced to account for differences of opinion regarding it. If two critics differ, it is possible that one is right and the other wrong, more likely that both are partly right and partly wrong, but in different respects: neither the native gifts nor the education of any man have ever been wholly adequate to many of the critical problems he will encounter, and no two men are ever the same in these respects or in any others. On the other hand, although the critic should display reasonable humility and caution, it is only fair to add that few men possess either the talent or the education to justify their being taken very seriously, even of those who are nominally professional students of these matters.

But if it is possible by rational elucidation to give a more or less clear account of what one finds in a poem and why one approves or disapproves, then communication between two critics, though no doubt imperfect, becomes possible, and it becomes possible that they may in some measure correct each other's errors and so come more near to a true judgment of the poem.

Third problem

If rational communication about poetry is to take place, it is necessary first to determine what we mean by a poem.

A poem is first of all a statement in words.

But it differs from all such statements of a purely philosophical or theoretical nature, in that it has by intention a controlled content of feeling. In this respect, it does not differ from many works written in prose, however.

A poem differs from a work written in prose by virtue of its being composed in verse. The rhythm of verse permits the expression of more powerful feeling than is possible in prose when such feeling is needed, and it permits at all times the expression of finer shades of feeling.

A poem, then, is a statement in words in which special pains are taken with the expression of feeling. This description is merely intended to distinguish the poem from other kinds of writing; it is not offered as a complete description.

Fourth problem

What, however, are words?

They are audible sounds, or their visual symbols, invented by man to communicate his thoughts and feelings. Each word has a conceptual content, however slight; each word, exclusive, perhaps, of the particles, communicates vague associations of feeling.

The word *fire* communicates a concept; it also connotes very vaguely certain feelings, depending on the context in which we happen to place it—depending, for example, on whether we happen to think of a fire on a hearth, in a furnace, or in a forest. These feelings may be rendered more and more precise as we render the context more and more precise; as we come more and more near to completing and perfecting our poem.

Fifth problem

But if the poem, as compared to prose, pays especial attention to feeling, are we to assume that the rational content of the poem is unimportant to its success?

The rational content cannot be eliminated from words; consequently the rational content cannot be eliminated from poetry. It is there. If it is unsatisfactory in itself, a part of the poem is unsatisfactory; the poem is thus damaged beyond argument. If we deny this, we must surely explain ourselves very fully.

If we admit this, we are faced with another problem: is it conceivable that rational content and feeling-content may both be perfect, and yet that they may be unrelated to each other, or imperfectly related? To me this is inconceivable, because the emotional content of words is generated by our experience with the conceptual content, so that a relationship is necessary.

This fact of the necessity of such relationship may fairly return us for a moment to the original question: whether imperfection of rational content damages the entire poem. If there is a necessary relationship, then feeling must be damaged by way of the relationship.

Sixth problem

If there is a relationship between concept and feeling, what is the nature of that relationship?

To answer this, let us return to the basic unit, the word. The concept represented by the word, motivates the feeling which the word communicates. It is the concept of fire which generates the feelings communicated by the word, though the sound of the word may modify these feelings very subtly, as may other accidental qualities, especially if the word be used skilfully in a given context. The accidental qualities of a word, however, such as its literary history, for example, can only modify, cannot essentially change, for these will be governed ultimately by the concept; that is, *fire* will seldom be used to signify *plum-blossom*, and so will have few opportunities to gather connotations from the concept, *plum-blossom*. The relationship, in the poem, between rational statement and feeling, is thus seen to be that of motive to emotion.

Seventh problem

But has not this reasoning brought us back to the proposition that all poems are equally good? For if each word motivates its own feeling, because of its intrinsic nature, will not any rational statement, since it is composed of words, motivate the feeling exactly proper to it?

This is not true, for a good many reasons, of which I shall enumerate only a few of the more obvious. In making a rational statement, in purely theoretical prose, we find that our statement may be loose or exact, depending upon the relationships of the words to each other. The precision of a word depends to some extent upon its surroundings. This is true likewise with respect to the connotations of words. Two words, each of which has several usably close rational synonyms, may reinforce and clarify each other with respect to their connotations or they may not do so.

Let me illustrate with a simple example from Browning's *Serenade at the Villa*:

> So wore night; the East was grey,
>   White the broad-faced hemlock flowers.

The lines are marred by a crowding of long syllables and difficult consonants, but they have great beauty in spite of the fault. What I wish to point out, for the sake of my argument, is the relationship between the words *wore* and *grey*. The verb *wore* means literally that the night passed, but it carries with it connotations of exhaustion and attrition which belong to the condition of the protagonist; and greyness is a colour which we associate with such a condition. If we change the phrase to read: 'Thus night passed', we shall have the same rational meaning, and a metre quite as respectable, but no trace of the power of the line: the connotation of *wore* will be lost, and the connotation of *grey* will remain merely in a state of ineffective potentiality. The protagonist in seeing his feeling mirrored in the landscape is not guilty of motivating his feeling falsely, for we know his general motive from the poem as a whole; he is expressing a portion of the feeling motivated by the total situation through a more or less common psychological phenomenon. If the poem were such, however, that we did not know why the night *wore* instead of *passed*, we should have just cause for complaint; in fact, most of the strength of the word would probably be lost. The second line contains other fine effects, immediately with reference to the first line, ultimately with reference to the theme; I leave the reader to analyse them for himself, but he will scarcely succeed without the whole poem before him.

Concepts, as represented by particular words, are affected by connotations due to various and curious accidents. A word may gather connotations from its use in folk-poetry, in formal poetry, in vulgar speech, or in technical prose: a single concept might easily be represented by four words with these distinct histories; and any one of the words might prove to be proper in a given poetic context. Words gain connotation from etymological accidents. Something of this may be seen in the English word *outrage*, in which is commonly felt, in all likelihood, something associated with *rage*, although there is no rage whatever in the original word. Similarly the word *urchin*, in modern English, seldom connotes anything related to hedgehogs, or to the familiars of the witches, by whose intervention the word arrived at its modern meaning and feeling. Yet the connotation proper to any stage in the history of such a word might be resuscitated, or a blend of connotations effected, by skilful use. Further, the connotation of a word may be modified very strongly by its function in the metrical structure, a matter which I shall discuss at length in connection with the theories of Ransom.

This is enough to show that exact motivation of feeling by concept is not inherent in any rational statement. Any rational statement will govern the general possibilities of feeling derivable from it, but the task of the poet is to adjust feeling to motive precisely. He has to select words containing not only the right relationships within themselves, but the right relationships to each other. The task is very difficult; and this is no doubt the reason why the great poetry of a great poet is likely to be very small in bulk.

Eighth problem

Is it not possible, however, to escape from this relationship of motive to emotion by confining ourselves very largely to those words which denote emotion: love, envy, anger, and the like?

This is not possible, for these words, like others, represent concepts. If we should confine ourselves strictly to such a vocabulary, we should merely write didactic poetry: poetry about love in general, or about anger in general. The emotion communicated would result from our apprehension of the ideas in question. Such poetry is perfectly legitimate, but it is only one kind of poetry, and it is scarcely the kind which the Romantic theorist is endeavouring to define.

Such poetry has frequently been rendered particular by the use of allegory. The playful allegorizing of minor amoristic themes which one encounters in the Renaissance and which is possibly descended from certain neo-Platonic elements in medieval poetry may serve as illustration. Let us consider these and the subsequent lines by Thomas Lodge:

> Love in my bosom like a bee
>   Doth suck his sweet;
> Now with his wings he plays with me,
>   Now with his feet.

Love itself is a very general idea and might include many kinds of experience; the idea is limited by this allegory to the sentimental and sensual, but we still have an idea, the subdivision of the original idea, and the feeling must be appropriate to the concept. The concept is rendered concrete by the image of Cupid, whose actions, in turn, are rendered visible by comparison to the bee: it is these actions which make the poem a kind of anticipatory meditation on more or less sensual love, a meditation which by its mere tone of expression keeps the subject in its proper place as a very minor one. Sometimes the emphasis is on the mere description of the bee, sometimes on the description of Cupid, sometimes on the lover's feeling; but the feeling motivated in any passage is governed by this emphasis. The elements, once they are united in the poem, are never really separated, of course. In so far as the poet departs from his substantial theme in the direction of mere bees and flowers, he will achieve what Ransom calls irrelevance[a]; but if there is much of this the poem will be weakened. Whether he so departs or not, the relation of motive to emotion must remain the same,

---

[a] See above, p. 238.

within each passage. I have discussed this problem in my essay on Ransom.

A common romantic practice is to use words denoting emotions, but to use them loosely and violently, as if the very carelessness expressed emotion. Another is to make a general statement, but seem to refer it to a particular occasion, which, however, is never indicated: the poet thus seems to avoid the didactic, yet he is not forced to understand the particular motive. Both these faults may be seen in these lines from Shelley:

> Out of the day and night
> A joy has taken flight;
>   Fresh spring, and summer, and winter hoar,
> Move my faint heart with grief, but with delight
>   No more—oh, never more.

The poet's intention is so vague, however, that he achieves nothing but stereotypes of a very crude kind.

The Romantics often tried other devices. For example, it would be possible to write a poem on fear in general, but to avoid in some measure the effect of the purely didactic by illustrating the emotion along the way with various experiences which might motivate fear. There is a danger here, thought it is merely a danger, that the general idea may not dominate the poem, and that the poem may thus fall apart into a group of poems on particular experiences. There is the alternative danger, that the particular quality of the experiences may be so subordinated to the illustrative function of the experiences, that within each illustration there is merely a stereotyped and not a real relationship of motive to feeling: this occurs in Collins' *Ode to Fear*, though a few lines in the Epode come surprisingly to life. But the methods which I have just described really offer no semblance of an escape from the theory of motivation which I am defending.

Another Romantic device, if it is conscious enough to be called a device, is to offer instead of a defensible motive a false one, usually culled from landscape. This kind of writing represents a tacit admission of the principle of motivation which I am defending, but a bad application of the principle. It results in the kind of writing which I have called pseudo-reference in my volume, *Primitivism and Decadence*. One cannot believe, for example, that Wordsworth's passions were charmed away by a look at the daffodils, or that Shelley's were aroused by the sight of the leaves blown about in the autumn wind. A motive is offered, and the poet wants us to accept it, but we recognize it as inadequate. In such a poem there may be fragments of good description, which motivate a feeling more or less purely appropriate to the objects described, and these fragments may sustain our liking for the poem: this happens in Collins' *Ode to Evening*; but one will find also an account of some kind of emotion essentially irrelevant to the objects described, along with the attempt, more or less explicit, to deduce the emotion from the object.

There remains the method of the Post-Romantics, whether French Symbolists or American Experimentalists: the method of trying to extinguish the rational content of language while retaining the content of association. This method I have discussed in *Primitivism and Decadence,* and I shall discuss it again in this book.

Ninth problem

The relationship in the poem of rational meaning to feeling we have seen to be that of motive to emotion; and we have seen that this must be a satisfactory relationship. How do we determine whether such a relationship is satisfactory? We determine it by an act of moral judgment. The question then arises whether moral judgments can be made, whether the concept of morality is or is not an illusion.

If morality can be considered real, if a theory of morality can be said to derive from reality, it is because it guides us towards the greatest happiness which the accidents of life permit: that is, towards the fullest realization of our nature, in the Aristotelian or Thomistic sense. But is there such a thing, abstractly considered, as full realization of our nature?

To avoid discussion of too great length, let us consider the opposite question: is there such a thing as obviously unfulfilled human nature? Obviously there is. We need only turn to the feeble-minded, who cannot think and so cannot perceive or feel with any clarity; or to the insane, who sometimes perceive and feel with great intensity, but whose feelings and perceptions are so improperly motivated that they are classed as illusions. At slightly higher levels, the criminal, the dissolute, the unscrupulously selfish, and various types of neurotics are likely to arouse but little disagreement as examples.

Now if we are able to recognize the fact of insanity—if in fact we are forced to recognize it—that is, the fact of the obvious maladjustment of feeling to motive, we are forced to admit the possibility of more accurate adjustment, and, by necessary sequence, of absolutely accurate adjustment, even though we admit the likelihood that most people will attain to a final adjustment but very seldom indeed. We can guide ourselves towards such an adjustment in life, as in art, by means of theory and the critical examination of special instances; but the final act of judgment is in both life and art a unique act—it is a relationship between two elements, the rational understanding and the feeling, of which only one is classificatory and of which the other has infinite possibilities of variation.

Tenth problem

If the final act of adjustment is a unique act of judgment, can we say that it is more or less right, provided it is demonstrably within the general limits prescribed by the theory of morality which has led to it? The answer to this question is implicit in what has preceded; in fact the answer resembles exactly that reached at the end of the first problem examined. We can say that it is more or less nearly right. If extreme deviation from right judgment is obvious, then there is such a thing as right judgment. The mere fact that life may be conducted in a fairly satisfactory manner, by means of inaccurate judgment within

312

certain limits, and that few people ever bother to refine their judgment beyond the stage which enables them to remain largely within those limits, does not mean that accurate judgment has no reality. Implicit in all that has preceded is the concept that in any moral situation, there is a right judgment as an ultimate possibility; that the human judge, or actor, will approximate it more or less nearly; that the closeness of his approximation will depend upon the accuracy of his rational understanding and of his intuition, and upon the accuracy of their interaction upon each other.

Eleventh problem

Nothing has thus far been said about human action, yet morality is supposed to guide human action. And if art is moral, there should be a relationship between art and human action.

The moral judgment, whether good, bad, or indifferent, is commonly the prelude and instigation to action. Hastily or carefully, intelligently or otherwise, one arrives at some kind of general idea of a situation calling for action, and one's idea motivates one's feeling: the act results. The part played by will, or the lack of it, between judgment and act, the possibility that action may be frustrated by some constitutional or habitual weakness or tendency, such as cowardice or a tendency to anger, in a person of a fine speculative or poetic judgment, are subjects for a treatise on ethics or psychology; a treatise on poetry stops with the consideration of the speculative judgment, which reaches its best form and expression in poetry. In the situations of daily life, one does not, as a rule, write a poem before acting: one makes a more rapid and simple judgment. But if the poem does not individually lead to a particular act, it does not prevent action. It gives us a better way of judging representative acts than we should otherwise have. It is thus a civilizing influence: it trains our power of judgment, and should, I imagine, affect the quality of daily judgments and actions.

Twelfth problem

What, then, is the nature of the critical process?

It will consist (1) of the statement of such historical or biographical knowledge as may be necessary in order to understand the mind and method of the writer; (2) of such analysis of his literary theories as we may need to understand and evaluate what he is doing; (3) of a rational critique of the paraphrasable content (roughly, the motive) of the poem; (4) of a rational critique of the feeling motivated—that is, of the details of style, as seen in language and technique; and (5) of the final act of judgment, a unique act, the general nature of which can be indicated, but which cannot be communicated precisely, since it consists in receiving from the poet his own final and unique judgment of his matter and in judging that judgment. It should be noted that the purpose of the first four processes is to limit as narrowly as possible the region in which the final unique act is to occur.

In the actual writing of criticism, a given task may not require all of these processes, or may not require that all be given equal emphasis; or it may be that in connection with a certain writer, whether because of the nature of the writer or because of the way in which other critics have treated him previously, one or two of these processes must be given so much emphasis that others must be neglected for lack of space. These are practical matters to be settled as the occasions arise.

25 Erich Auerbach

Erich Auerbach (1892-1957) was one of many distinguished German scholars forced into exile by Hitler's régime in Germany. In later life, he was Sterling Professor of Romance Languages at Yale University, but his masterpiece, *Mimesis* 1946), was written during World War II in Istanbul, with very limited research resources. Auerbach has acknowledged that, paradoxically, 'it is quite possible that the book owes its existence to just this lack of a rich and specialized library. If it had been possible for me to acquaint myself with all the work that has been done on so many subjects, I might never have reached the point of writing'. *Mimesis*, as its subtitle declares, undertakes to survey nothing less than the 'representation of reality in Western literature', examining texts by such writers as Tacitus, Petronius, St Augustine, St Francis, Dante, Boccaccio, Rabelais, Montaigne, Saint-Simon, Goethe, Schiller, Balzac, Stendhal, Flaubert, Proust, and Virginia Woolf. Auerbach's method is to take a fairly short passage from his text, and to work outwards from close stylistic analysis to generalizations about literary and cultural history. His ability to respond knowledgeably and sympathetically to so many different cultures and authors is amazing, and it is unlikely that research in the humanities will ever again produce a monument of scholarship so catholic in scope and so unpedantically learned.

'Odysseus' Scar', which makes a fascinating comparison between the literary styles of the Homeric epic and the Old Testament, contains less detailed stylistic analysis than most of the other chapters in *Mimesis*, but as the first chapter of the book it is the best possible introduction to it, vividly conveying the breadth and depth of Auerbach's insights. It is reprinted here from the translation of Willard R. Trask, published in 1953 by Princeton University Press.

CROSS REFERENCES: 32. C. S. Lewis
39. Ian Watt
41. René Wellek
42. Wayne Booth

Odysseus' scar

Readers of the *Odyssey*[a] will remember the well-prepared and touching scene in book 19, when Odysseus has at last come home, the scene in which the old housekeeper Euryclea, who had been his nurse, recognizes him by a scar on his thigh. The stranger has won Penelope's good will; at his request she tells the housekeeper to wash his feet, which, in all old stories, is the first duty of hospitality towards a tired traveller. Euryclea busies herself fetching water and mixing cold with hot, meanwhile speaking sadly of her absent master, who is probably of the same age as the guest, and who perhaps, like the guest, is even now wandering somewhere, a stranger; and she remarks how astonishingly like him the guest looks. Meanwhile Odysseus, remembering his scar, moves back out of the light; he knows that, despite his efforts to hide his identity, Euryclea will now recognize him, but he wants at least to keep Penelope in ignorance. No sooner has the old woman touched the scar than, in her joyous surprise, she lets Odysseus' foot drop into the basin; the water spills over, she is about to cry out her joy; Odysseus restrains her with whispered threats and endearments; she recovers herself and conceals her emotion. Penelope, whose attention Athena's foresight had diverted from the incident, has observed nothing.

All this is scrupulously externalized and narrated in leisurely fashion. The two women express their feelings in copious direct discourse. Feelings though they are, with only a slight admixture of the most general considerations upon human destiny, the syntactical connection between part and part is perfectly clear, no contour is blurred. There is also room and time for orderly, perfectly well-articulated, uniformly illuminated descriptions of implements, ministrations, and gestures; even in the dramatic moment of recognition, Homer does not omit to tell the reader that it is with his right hand that Odysseus takes the old woman by the throat to keep her from speaking, at the same time that he draws her closer to him with his left. Clearly outlined, brightly and uniformly illuminated, men and things stand out in a realm where everything is visible; and not less clear—wholly expressed, orderly even in the ardour—are the feelings and thoughts of the persons involved.

In my account of the incident I have so far passed over a whole series of verses which interrupt it in the middle. There are more than seventy of these verses—while to the incident itself some forty are devoted before the interrup-

[a] Homer's epic poem describes the wanderings and adventures of Odysseus (or Ulysses) trying to return home after the conclusion of the Trojan War, in which he had taken part on the Greek side. During his long absence, Odysseus's wife Penelope has with difficulty resisted the attentions of numerous suitors, and, at the point in the story discussed by Auerbach, the hero has entered his house disguised as a beggar, as part of a plan to revenge himself on these suitors.

tion and some forty after it. The interruption, which comes just at the point when the housekeeper recognizes the scar—that is, at the moment of crisis—describes the origin of the scar, a hunting accident which occurred in Odysseus' boyhood, at a boar hunt, during the time of his visit to his grandfather Autolycus. This first affords an opportunity to inform the reader about Autolycus, his house, the precise degree of the kinship, his character, and, no less exhaustively than touchingly, his behaviour after the birth of his grandson; then follows the visit of Odysseus, now grown to be a youth; the exchange of greetings, the banquet with which he is welcomed, sleep and waking, the early start for the hunt, the tracking of the beast, the struggle, Odysseus' being wounded by the boar's tusk, his recovery, his return to Ithaca, his parents' anxious questions—all is narrated, again with such a complete externalization of all the elements of the story and of their interconnections as to leave nothing in obscurity. Not until then does the narrator return to Penelope's chamber, not until then, the digression having run its course, does Euryclea, who had recognized the scar before the digression began, let Odysseus' foot fall back into the basin.

The first thought of a modern reader—that this is a device to increase suspense—is, if not wholly wrong, at least not the essential explanation of this Homeric procedure. For the element of suspense is very slight in the Homeric poems; nothing in their entire style is calculated to keep the reader or hearer breathless. The digressions are not meant to keep the reader in suspense, but rather to relax the tension. And this frequently occurs, as in the passage before us. The broadly narrated, charming, and subtly fashioned story of the hunt, with all its elegance and self-sufficiency, its wealth of idyllic pictures, seeks to win the reader over wholly to itself as long as he is hearing it, to make him forget what had just taken place during the foot-washing. But an episode that will increase suspense by retarding the action must be so constructed that it will not fill the present entirely, will not put the crisis, whose resolution is being awaited, entirely out of the reader's mind, and thereby destroy the mood of suspense; the crisis and the suspense must continue, must remain vibrant in the background. But Homer—and to this we shall have to return later—knows no background. What he narrates is for the time being only the present, and fills both the stage and the reader's mind completely. So it is with the passage before us. When the young Euryclea (vv. 401 ff.) sets the infant Odysseus on his grandfather Autolycus' lap after the banquet, the aged Euryclea, who a few lines earlier had touched the wanderer's foot, has entirely vanished from the stage and from the reader's mind.

Goethe and Schiller, who, though not referring to this particular episode, exchanged letters in April 1797 on the subject of 'the retarding element' in the Homeric poems in general, put it in direct opposition to the element of suspense —the latter word is not used, but is clearly implied when the 'retarding' procedure is opposed, as something proper to epic, to tragic procedure (letters of 19, 21, and 22 April). The 'retarding element', the 'going back and forth' by means of episodes, seems to me, too, in the Homeric poems, to be opposed to any tensional and suspensive striving towards a goal, and doubtless Schiller is right in regard to Homer when he says that what he gives us is 'simply the quiet existence and operation of things in accordance with their natures'; Homer's goal is 'already present in every point of his progress'. But both Schiller and Goethe raise Homer's procedure to the level of a law for epic poetry in general, and Schiller's words quoted above are meant to be universally binding upon the epic poet, in contradistinction from the tragic. Yet in both modern and ancient times, there are important epic works which are composed throughout with no 'retarding element' in this sense but, on the contrary, with suspense throughout, and which perpetually 'rob us of our emotional freedom'—which power Schiller will grant only to the tragic poet. And besides it seems to me undemonstrable and improbable that this procedure of Homeric poetry was directed by aesthetic considerations or even by an aesthetic feeling of the sort postulated by Goethe and Schiller. The effect, to be sure, is precisely that which they describe, and is, furthermore, the actual source of the conception of epic which they themselves hold, and with them all writers decisively influenced by classical antiquity. But the true cause of the impression of 'retardation' appears to me to lie elsewhere —namely, in the need of the Homeric style to leave nothing which it mentions half in darkness and unexternalized.

The excursus upon the origin of Odysseus' scar is not basically different from the many passages in which a newly introduced character, or even a newly appearing object or implement, though it be in the thick of a battle, is described as to its nature and origin; or in which, upon the appearance of a god, we are told where he last was, what he was doing there, and by what road he reached the scene; indeed, even the Homeric epithets seem to me in the final analysis to be traceable to the same need for an externalization of phenomena in terms perceptible to the senses. Here is the scar, which comes up in the course of the narrative; and Homer's feeling simply will not permit him to see it appear out of the darkness of an unilluminated past; it must be set in full light, and with it a portion of the hero's boyhood—just as, in the *Iliad*, when the first ship is already burning and the Myrmidons finally arm that they may hasten to help, there is still time not only for the wonderful simile of the wolf, not only for the order of the Myrmidon host, but also for a detailed account of the ancestry of several subordinate leaders (16, vv, 155 ff.). To be sure, the aesthetic effect thus produced was soon noticed and thereafter consciously sought; but the more original cause must have lain in the basic impulse of the Homeric style: to represent phenomena in a fully externalized form, visible and palpable in all their parts, and completely fixed in their spatial and temporal relations. Nor do psychological processes receive any other treatment: here too nothing must remain hidden and unexpressed. With the utmost fullness, with an orderliness which even passion does not disturb, Homer's personages vent their inmost hearts in speech; what they do not say to others, they speak in their own minds, so that the reader is informed of it. Much that is terrible takes place in the Homeric poems, but it seldom takes place wordlessly: Polyphemus talks to Odysseus; Odysseus talks to the suitors when he begins to kill them; Hector and Achilles talk at length, before battle and after; and no speech is so filled with anger or scorn that the particles which express logical and grammatical connections are lacking or out of place. This last observation is true, of course, not only of speeches but of the presentation in general. The separate elements of a phenomenon are most clearly placed in relation to one another; a large number of conjunctions, adverbs, particles, and other syntactical tools, all clearly circumscribed and delicately differentiated in meaning, delimit persons, things, and portions of incidents in respect to one another, and at the same time bring them together in a continuous and ever flexible connection; like the separate phenomena themselves, their relationships—their temporal, local, causal, final, consecutive, comparative, concessive, antithetical, and conditional limitations—are brought to light in perfect fullness; so that a continuous rhythmic procession of phenomena passes by, and never is there a form left fragmentary of half-illuminated, never a lacuna, never a gap, never a glimpse of unplumbed depths.

And this procession of phenomena takes place in the foreground—that is, in a local and temporal present which is absolute. One might think that the many interpolations, the frequent moving back and forth, would create a sort of perspective in time and place; but the Homeric style never gives any such impression. The way in which any impression of perspective is avoided can be clearly observed in the procedure for introducing episodes, a syntactical construction with which every reader of Homer is familiar; it is used in the passage we are considering, but can also be found in cases when the episodes are much shorter. To the word scar (v. 393) there is first attached a relative clause ('which once long ago a boar...'), which enlarges into a voluminous syntactical parenthesis; into this an independent sentence unexpectedly intrudes (v. 396: 'A god himself gave him...'), which quietly disentangles itself from syntactical subordination, until, with verse 399, an equally free syntactical treatment of the new content begins a new present which continues unchallenged until, with verse 467 ('The old woman now touched it...'), the scene which had been broken off is resumed. To be sure, in the case of such long episodes as the one we are considering, a purely syntactical connection with the principal theme would hardly have been possible; but a connection with it through perspective would have been all the easier had the content been arranged with that end in view; if, that is, the entire story of the scar had been presented as a recollection which awakens in Odysseus' mind at this particular moment. It would have been perfectly easy to do; the story of the scar had only to be inserted two verses earlier, at the first mention of the word scar, where the motifs 'Odysseus' and 'recollection' were already at hand. But any such subjectivistic-perspectivistic procedure, creating a foreground and background, resulting in the present lying open to the depths of the past, is entirely foreign to the Homeric style; the Homeric style knows only a foreground, only a uniformly illuminated, uniformly objective present. And so the excursus does not begin until two lines later, when Euryclea has discovered the scar—the possibility for a perspectivistic connection no longer exists, and the story of the wound becomes an independent and exclusive present.

The genius of the Homeric style becomes even more apparent when it is compared with an equally ancient and equally epic style from a different world of forms. I shall attempt this comparison with the account of the sacrifice of Isaac, a homogeneous narrative produced by the so-called Elohist. The King James version translates the opening as follows (Genesis 22:1): 'And it came to pass after these things, that God did tempt Abraham, and said to him, Abraham! and he said, Behold, here I am.' Even this opening startles us when we come to it from Homer. Where are the two speakers? We are not told. The reader, however, knows that they are not normally to be found together in one place on earth, that one of them, God, in order to speak to Abraham, must come from somewhere, must enter the earthly realm from some unknown heights or depths. Whence does he come, whence does he call to Abraham? We are not told. He does not come, like Zeus or Poseidon, from the Aethiopians, where he has been enjoying a sacrificial feast. Nor are we told anything of his reasons for tempting Abraham so terribly. He has not, like Zeus, discussed them in set speeches with other gods gathered in council; nor have the deliberations in his own heart been presented to us; unexpected and mysterious, he enters the scene from some unknown height or depth and calls: Abraham! It will at once be said that this is to be explained by the particular concept of God which the Jews held and which was wholly different from that of the Greeks. True enough— but this constitutes no objection. For how is the Jewish concept of God to be explained? Even their earlier God of the desert was not fixed in form and content, and was alone; his lack of form, his lack of local habitation, his singleness, was in the end not only maintained but developed even further in competition with the comparatively far more manifest gods of the surrounding Near Eastern world. The concept of God held by the Jews is less a cause than a symptom of their manner of comprehending and representing things.

This becomes still clearer if we now turn to the other person in the dialogue, to Abraham. Where is he? We do not know. He says, indeed: Here I am—but the Hebrew word means only something like 'behold me', and in any case is not meant to indicate the actual place where Abraham is, but a moral position in respect to God, who has called to him—Here am I awaiting thy command. Where he is actually, whether in Beersheba or elsewhere, whether indoors or in the open air, is not stated; it does not interest the narrator, the reader is not informed; and what Abraham was doing when God called to him is left in the same obscurity. To realize the difference, consider Hermes' visit to Calypso, for example, where command, journey, arrival and reception of the visitor, situation and occupation of the person visited, are set forth in many verses; and even on occasions when gods appear suddenly and briefly, whether to help one of their favourites or to deceive or destroy some mortal whom they hate, their bodily forms, and usually the manner of their coming and going, are given in detail. Here, however, God appears without bodily form (yet he 'appears'), coming from some unspecified place—we only hear his voice, and that utters nothing but a name, a name without an adjective, without a descriptive epithet for the person spoken to, such as is the rule in every Homeric address; and of Abraham too nothing is made perceptible except the words in which he answers God: *Hinne-ni*, Behold me here—with which, to be sure, a most touching gesture expressive of obedience and readiness is suggested, but it is left to the reader to visualize it. Moreover the two speakers are not on the same level: if we conceive of Abraham in the foreground, where it might be possible to picture him as prostrate or kneeling or bowing with outspread arms or gazing upward, God is not there too: Abraham's words and gestures are directed towards the depths of the picture or upward, but in any case the undetermined, dark place from which the voice comes to him is not in the foreground.

After this opening, God gives his command, and the story itself begins: everyone knows it; it unrolls with no episodes in a few independent sentences whose syntactical connection is of the most rudimentary sort. In this atmosphere it is unthinkable that an implement, a landscape through which the travellers passed, the serving-men, or the ass, should be described, that their origin or descent or material or appearance or usefulness should be set forth in terms of praise; they do not even admit an adjective: they are serving-men, ass, wood, and knife, and nothing else, without an epithet; they are there to serve the end which God has commanded; what in other respects they were, are, or will be, remains in darkness. A journey is made, because God has designated the place where the sacrifice is to be performed; but we are told nothing about the journey except that it took three days, and even that we are told in a mysterious way: Abraham and his followers rose 'early in the morning' and 'went unto' the place of which God had told him; on the third day he lifted up his eyes and saw the place from afar. That gesture is the only gesture, is indeed the only occurrence during the whole journey, of which we are told; and though its motivation lies in the fact that the place is elevated, its uniqueness still heightens the impression that the journey took place through a vacuum; it is as if, while he travelled on, Abraham had looked neither to the right nor to the left, had suppressed any sign of life in his followers and himself save only their footfalls.

Thus the journey is like a silent progress through the indeterminate and the contingent, a holding of the breath, a process which has no present, which is inserted, like a blank duration, between what has passed and what lies ahead, and which yet is measured: three days! Three such days positively demand the symbolic interpretation which they later received. They began 'early in the morning'. But at what time on the third day did Abraham lift up his eyes and see his goal? The text says nothing on the subject. Obviously not 'late in the evening', for it seems that there was still time enough to climb the mountain and make the sacrifice. So 'early in the morning' is given, not as an indication of time, but for the sake of its ethical significance; it is intended to express the resolution, the promptness, the punctual obedience of the sorely tried Abraham. Bitter to him is the early morning in which he saddles his ass, calls his serving-men and his son Isaac, and sets out; but he obeys, he walks on until the third day, then lifts up his eyes and sees the place. Whence he comes, we do not know, but the goal is clearly stated: Jeruel in the land of Moriah. What place this is meant to indicate is not clear—'Moriah' especially may be a later correction of some other word. But in any case the goal was given, and in any case it is a matter of some sacred spot which was to receive a particular consecration by being connected with Abraham's sacrifice. Just as little as 'early in the morning' serves as a temporal indication does 'Jeruel in the land of Moriah' serve as a geographical indication; and in both cases alike, the complementary indication is not given, for we know as little of the hour at which Abraham lifted up his eyes as we do of the place from which he set forth—Jeruel is significant not so much as the goal of an earthly journey, in its geographical relation to other places, as through its special election, through its relation to God, who designated it as the scene of the act, and therefore it must be named.

In the narrative itself, a third chief character appears: Isaac. While God and Abraham, the serving-men, the ass, and the implements are simply named, without mention of any qualities or any other sort of definition, Isaac once receives an appositive; God says, 'Take Isaac, thine only son, whom thou lovest.' But this is not a characterization of Isaac as a person, apart from his relation to his father and apart from the story; he may be handsome or ugly, intelligent or stupid, tall or short, pleasant or unpleasant—we are not told. Only what we need to know about him as a personage in the action, here and now, is illuminated, so that it may become apparent how terrible Abraham's temptation is, and that God is fully aware of it. By this example of the contrary, we see the significance of the descriptive adjectives and digressions of the Homeric poems; with their indications of the earlier and as it were absolute existence of the persons described, they prevent the reader from concentrating exclusively on a present crisis; even when the most terrible things are occurring, they prevent the establishment of an overwhelming suspense. But here, in the story of Abraham's sacrifice, the overwhelming suspense is present; what Schiller makes the goal of the tragic poet—to rob us of our emotional freedom, to turn our intellectual and spiritual powers (Schiller says 'our activity') in one direction, to cencentrate them there—is effected in this Biblical narrative, which certainly deserves the epithet epic.

We find the same contrast if we compare the two uses of direct discourse. The personages speak in the Bible story too; but their speech does not serve, as does speech in Homer, to manifest, to externalize thoughts—on the contrary, it serves to indicate thoughts which remain unexpressed. God gives his command in direct discourse, but he leaves his motives and his purpose unexpressed; Abraham, receiving the command, says nothing and does what he has been told to do. The conversation between Abraham and Isaac on the way to the place of sacrifice is only an interruption of the heavy silence and makes it all the more burdensome. The two of them, Isaac carrying the wood and Abraham with fire and a knife, 'went together'. Hesitantly, Isaac ventures to ask about the ram,[a] and Abraham gives the well-known answer. Then the text repeats: 'So they went both of them together.' Everything remains unexpressed.

It would be difficult, then, to imagine styles more contrasted than those of these two equally ancient and equally epic texts. On the one hand, externalized, uniformly illuminated phenomena, at a definite time and in a definite place, connected together without lacunae in a perpetual foreground; thoughts and feeling completely expressed; events taking place in leisurely fashion and with

[a] Actually, Isaac asks, 'Where is the *lamb* for a burnt offering?' [my italics] and Abraham replies, 'My son, God will provide himself a lamb for a burnt offering.' When God withdraws his command that Isaac be sacrificed, the father and son find 'a ram caught in a thicket by his horns' which they offer up instead. (*Genesis* 22. 7–13, King James version.)

very little of suspense. On the other hand, the externalization of only so much of the phenomena as is necessary for the purpose of the narrative, all else left in obscurity; the decisive points of the narrative alone are emphasized, what lies between is nonexistent; time and place are undefined and call for interpretation; thoughts and feeling remain unexpressed, are only suggested by the silence and the fragmentary speeches; the whole, permeated with the most unrelieved suspense and directed towards a single goal (and to that extent far more of a unity), remains mysterious and 'fraught with background'.

I will discuss this term in some detail, lest it be misunderstood. I said above that the Homeric style was 'of the foreground' because, despite much going back and forth, it yet causes what is momentarily being narrated to give the impression that it is the only present, pure and without perspective. A consideration of the Elohistic text teaches us that our term is capable of a broader and deeper application. It shows that even the separate personages can be represented as possessing 'background'; God is always so represented in the Bible, for he is not comprehensible in his presence, as is Zeus; it is always only 'something' of him that appears, he always extends into depths. But even the human beings in the Biblical stories have greater depths of time, fate, and consciousness than do the human beings in Homer; although they are nearly always caught up in an event engaging all their faculties, they are not so entirely immersed in its present that they do not remain continually conscious of what has happened to them earlier and elsewhere; their thoughts and feelings have more layers, are more entangled. Abraham's actions are explained not only by what is happening to him at the moment, nor yet only by his character (as Achilles' actions by his courage and his pride, and Odysseus' by his versatility and foresightedness), but by his previous history; he remembers, he is constantly conscious of, what God has promised him and what God has already accomplished for him—his soul is torn between desperate rebellion and hopeful expectation; his silent obedience is multilayered, has background. Such a problematic psychological situation as this is impossible for any of the Homeric heroes, whose destiny is clearly defined and who wake every morning as if it were the first day of their lives: their emotions, though strong, are simple and find expression instantly.

How fraught with background, in comparison, are characters like Saul and David! How entangled and stratified are such human relations as those between David and Absalom, between David and Joab! Any such 'background' quality of the psychological situation as that which the story of Absalom's death and its sequel (II Samuel 18 and 19, by the so-called Jahvist) rather suggests than expresses, is unthinkable in Homer. Here we are confronted not merely with the psychological processes of characters whose depth of background is veritably abysmal, but with a purely geographical background too. For David is absent from the battlefield; but the influence of his will and his feelings continues to operate, they affect even Joab in his rebellion and disregard for the consequences of his actions; in the magnificent scene with the two messengers, both the physical and psychological background is fully manifest, though the latter is never expressed. With this, compare, for example, how Achilles, who sends

Patroclus first to scout and then into battle, loses almost all 'presentness' so long as he is not physically present. But the most important thing is the 'multi-layeredness' of the individual character; this is hardly to be met with in Homer, or at most in the form of a conscious hesitation between two possible courses of action; otherwise, in Homer, the complexity of the psychological life is shown only in the succession and alternation of emotions; whereas the Jewish writers are able to express the simultaneous existence of various layers of consciousness and the conflict between them.

The Homeric poems, then, though their intellectual, linguistic, and above all syntactical culture appears to be so much more highly developed, are yet comparatively simple in their picture of human beings; and no less so in their relation to the real life which they describe in general. Delight in physical existence is everything to them, and their highest aim is to make that delight perceptible to us. Between battles and passions, adventures and perils, they show us hunts, banquets, palaces and shepherds' cots, athletic contests and washing days—in order that we may see the heroes in their ordinary life, and seeing them so, may take pleasure in their manner of enjoying their savoury present, a present which sends strong roots down into social usages, landscape, and daily life. And thus they bewitch us and ingratiate themselves to us until we live with them in the reality of their lives; so long as we are reading or hearing the poems, it does not matter whether we know that all this is only legend, 'make-believe'. The oft-repeated reproach that Homer is a liar takes nothing from his effectiveness, he does not need to base his story on historical reality, his reality is powerful enough in itself; it ensnares us, weaving its web around us, and that suffices him. And this 'real' world into which we are lured, exists for itself, contains nothing but itself; the Homeric poems conceal nothing, they contain no teaching and no secret second meaning. Homer can be analysed, as we have essayed to do here, but he cannot be interpreted. Later allegorizing trends have tried their arts of interpretation upon him, but to no avail. He resists any such treatment; the interpretations are forced and foreign, they do not crystallize into a unified doctrine. The general considerations which occasionally occur (in our episode, for example, v. 360 : that in misfortune men age quickly) reveal a calm acceptance of the basic facts of human existence, but with no compulsion to brood over them, still less any passionate impulse either to rebel against them or to embrace them in an ecstasy of submission.

It is all very different in the Biblical stories. Their aim is not to bewitch the senses, and if nevertheless they produce lively sensory effects, it is only because the moral, religious, and psychological phenomena which are their sole concern are made concrete in the sensible matter of life. But their religious intent involves an absolute claim to historical truth. The story of Abraham and Isaac is not better established than the story of Odysseus, Penelope, and Euryclea; both are legendary. But the Biblical narrator, the Elohist, had to believe in the objective truth of the story of Abraham's sacrifice—the existence of the sacred ordinances of life rested upon the truth of this and similar stories. He had to believe in it passionately; or else (as many rationalistic interpreters believed and perhaps still believe) he had to be a conscious liar—no harmless liar like Homer, who lied to give pleasure, but a political liar with a definite end in view, lying in the interest of a claim to absolute authority.

To me, the rationalistic interpretation seems psychologically absurd; but even if we take it into consideration, the relation of the Elohist to the truth of his story still remains a far more passionate and definite one than is Homer's relation. The Biblical narrator was obliged to write exactly what his belief in the truth of the tradition (or, from the rationalistic standpoint, his interest in the truth of it) demanded of him—in either case, his freedom in creative or representative imagination was severely limited; his activity was perforce reduced to composing an effective version of the pious tradition. What he produced, then, was not primarily oriented towards 'realism' (if he succeeded in being realistic, it was merely a means, not an end); it was oriented towards truth. Woe to the man who did not believe it! One can perfectly well entertain historical doubts on the subject of the Trojan War or of Odysseus' wanderings, and still, when reading Homer, feel precisely the effects he sought to produce; but without believing in Abraham's sacrifice, it is impossible to put the narrative of it to the use for which it was written. Indeed, we must go even further. The Bible's claim to truth is not only far more urgent than Homer's, it is tyrannical—it excludes all other claims. The world of the Scripture stories is not satisfied with claiming to be a historically true reality—it insists that it is the only real world, is destined for autocracy. All other scenes, issues, and ordinances have no right to appear independently of it, and it is promised that all of them, the history of all mankind, will be given their due place within its frame, will be subordinated to it. The Scripture stories do not, like Homer's, court our favour, they do not flatter us that they may please us and enchant us—they seek to subject us, and if we refuse to be subjected we are rebels.

Let no one object that this goes too far, that not the stories, but the religious doctrine, raises the claim to absolute authority; because the stories are not, like Homer's, simply narrated 'reality'. Doctrine and promise are incarnate in them and inseparable from them; for that very reason they are fraught with 'background' and mysterious, containing a second, concealed meaning. In the story of Isaac, it is not only God's intervention at the beginning and the end, but even the factual and psychological elements which come between, that are mysterious, merely touched upon, fraught with background; and therefore they require subtle investigation and interpretation, they demand them. Since so much in the story is dark and incomplete, and since the reader knows that God is a hidden God, his effort to interpret it constantly finds something new to feed upon. Doctrine and the search for enlightenment are inextricably connected with the physical side of the narrative—the latter being more than simple 'reality'; indeed they are in constant danger of losing their own reality, as very soon happened when interpretation reached such proportions that the real vanished.

If the text of the Biblical narrative, then, is so greatly in need of interpretation on the basis of its own content, its claim to absolute authority forces it still further in the same direction. Far from seeking, like Homer, merely to make us forget our own reality for a few hours, it seeks to overcome our reality: we are to fit our own life into its world, feel ourselves to be elements in its structure of universal history. This becomes increasingly difficult the further our historical environment is removed from that of the Biblical books; and if these nevertheless maintain their claim to absolute authority, it is inevitable that they themselves be adapted through interpretative transformation. This was for a long time comparatively easy; as late as the European Middle Ages it was possible to represent Biblical events as ordinary phenomena of contemporary life, the methods of interpretation themselves forming the basis for such a treatment. But when, through too great a change in environment and through the awakening of a critical consciousness, this becomes impossible, the Biblical claim to absolute authority is jeopardized; the method of interpretation is scorned and rejected, the Biblical stories become ancient legends, and the doctrine they had contained, now dissevered from them, becomes a disembodied image.

As a result of this claim to absolute authority, the method of interpretation spread to traditions other than the Jewish. The Homeric poems present a definite complex of events whose boundaries in space and time are clearly delimited; before it, beside it, and after it, other complexes of events, which do not depend upon it, can be conceived without conflict and without difficulty. The Old Testament, on the other hand, presents universal history: it begins with the beginning of time, with the creation of the world, and will end with the Last Days, the fulfilling of the Covenant, with which the world will come to an end. Everything else that happens in the world can only be conceived as an element in this sequence; into it everything that is known about the world, or at least everything that touches upon the history of the Jews, must be fitted as an ingredient of the divine plan; and as this too became possible only by interpreting the new material as it poured in, the need for interpretation reaches out beyond the original Jewish–Israelitish realm of reality—for example to Assyrian, Babylonian, Persian, and Roman history; interpretation in a determined direction becomes a general method of comprehending reality; the new and strange world which now comes into view and which, in the form in which it presents itself, proves to be wholly unutilizable within the Jewish religious frame, must be so interpreted that it can find a place there. But this process nearly always also reacts upon the frame, which requires enlarging and modifying. The most striking piece of interpretation of this sort occurred in the first century of the Christian era, in consequence of Paul's mission to the Gentiles: Paul and the Church Fathers reinterpreted the entire Jewish tradition as a succession of figures prognosticating the appearance of Christ, and assigned the Roman Empire its proper place in the divine plan of salvation. Thus while, on the one hand, the reality of the Old Testament presents itself as complete truth with a claim to sole authority, on the other hand that very claim forces it to a constant interpretative change in its own content; for millennia it undergoes an incessant and active development with the life of man in Europe.

The claim of the Old Testament stories to represent universal history, their insistent relation—a relation constantly redefined by conflicts—to a single and hidden God, who yet shows himself and who guides universal history by promise and exaction, gives these stories an entirely different perspective from any the Homeric poems can possess. As a composition, the Old Testament is incom-

parably less unified than the Homeric poems, it is more obviously pieced together—but the various components all belong to one concept of universal
history and its interpretation. If certain elements survived which did not immediately fit in, interpretation took care of them; and so the reader is at every
moment aware of the universal religio-historical perspective which gives the
individual stories their general meaning and purpose. The greater the separate-
ness and horizontal disconnection of the stories and groups of stories in relation
to one another, compared with the *Iliad* and the *Odyssey*, the stronger is their
general vertical connection, which holds them all together and which is entirely
lacking in Homer. Each of the great figures of the Old Testament, from Adam
to the prophets, embodies a moment of this vertical connection. God chose and
formed these men to the end of embodying his essence and will—yet choice and
formation do not coincide, for the latter proceeds gradually, historically, during
the earthly life of him upon whom the choice has fallen. How the process is
accomplished, what terrible trials such a formation inflicts, can be seen from
our story of Abraham's sacrifice. Herein lies the reason why the great figures of
the Old Testament are so much more fully developed, so much more fraught
with their own biographical past, so much more distinct as individuals, than are
the Homeric heroes. Achilles and Odysseus are splendidly described in many
well-ordered words, epithets cling to them, their emotions are constantly displayed in their words and deeds—but they have no development, and their life-
histories are clearly set forth once and for all. So little are the Homeric heroes
presented as developing or having developed, that most of them—Nestor, Agamemnon, Achilles—appear to be of an age fixed from the very first. Even
Odysseus, in whose case the long lapse of time and the many events which
occurred offer so much opportunity for biographical development, shows almost
nothing of it. Odysseus on his return is exactly the same as he was when he left
Ithaca two decades earlier. But what a road, what a fate, lie between the Jacob
who cheated his father out of his blessing and the old man whose favourite son
has been torn to pieces by a wild beast!—between David the harp player, perse-
cuted by his lord's jealousy, and the old king, surrounded by violent intrigues,
whom Abishag the Shunnamite warmed in his bed, and he knew her not! The
old man, of whom we know how he has become what he is, is more of an
individual than the young man; for it is only during the course of an eventful
life that men are differentiated into full individuality; and it is this history of a
personality which the Old Testament presents to us as the formation undergone by those whom God has chosen to be examples. Fraught with their development, sometimes even aged to the verge of dissolution, they show a distinct
stamp of individuality entirely foreign to the Homeric heroes. Time can touch
the latter only outwardly, and even that change is brought to our observation
as little as possible; whereas the stern hand of God is ever upon the Old Testament figures; he has not only made them once and for all and chosen them, but
he continues to work upon them, bends them and kneads them, and, without
destroying them in essence, produces from them forms which their youth gave
no grounds for anticipating. The objection that the biographical element of the
Old Testament often springs from the combination of several legendary person-

ages does not apply; for this combination is a part of the development of the text. And how much wider is the pendulum swing of their lives than that of the Homeric heroes! For they are bearers of the divine will, and yet they are fallible, subject to misfortune and humiliation—and in the midst of misfortune and in their humiliation their acts and words reveal the transcendent majesty of God. There is hardly one of them who does not, like Adam, undergo the deepest humiliation—and hardly one who is not deemed worthy of God's personal intervention and personal inspiration. Humiliation and elevation go far deeper and far higher than in Homer, and they belong basically together. The poor beggar Odysseus is only masquerading, but Adam is really cast down, Jacob really a refugee, Joseph really in the pit and then a slave to be bought and sold. But their greatness, rising out of humiliation, is almost superhuman and an image of God's greatness. The reader clearly feels how the extent of the pendulum's swing is connected with the intensity of the personal history—precisely the most extreme circumstances, in which we are immeasurably forsaken and in despair, or immeasurably joyous and exalted, give us, if we survive them, a personal stamp which is recognized as the product of a rich existence, a rich development. And very often, indeed generally, this element of development gives the Old Testament stories a historical character, even when the subject is purely legendary and traditional.

Homer remains within the legendary with all his material, whereas the material of the Old Testament comes closer and closer to history as the narrative proceeds; in the stories of David the historical report predominates. Here too, much that is legendary still remains, as for example the story of David and Goliath; but much—and the most essential—consists in things which the narrators knew from their own experience or from firsthand testimony. Now the difference between legend and history is in most cases easily perceived by a reasonably experienced reader. It is a difficult matter, requiring careful historical and philological training, to distinguish the true from the synthetic or the biased in a historical presentation; but it is easy to separate the historical from the legendary in general. Their structure is different. Even where the legendary does not immediately betray itself by elements of the miraculous, by the repetition of well-known standard motives, typical patterns and themes, through neglect of clear details of time and place, and the like, it is generally quickly recognizable by its composition. It runs far too smoothly. All cross-currents, all friction, all that is casual, secondary to the main events and themes, everything unresolved, truncated, and uncertain, which confuses the clear progress of the action and the simple orientation of the actors, has disappeared. The historical event which we witness, or learn from the testimony of those who witnessed it, runs much more variously, contradictorily, and confusedly; not until it has produced results in a definite domain are we able, with their help, to classify it to a certain extent; and how often the order to which we think we have attained becomes doubtful again, how often we ask ourselves if the data before us have not led us to a far too simple classification of the original events! Legend arranges its material in a simple and straightforward way; it detaches it from its contemporary historical context, so that the latter will not confuse it; it knows only clearly outlined men who act from few and simple motives and the continuity of whose feelings and actions remains uninterrupted. In the legends of martyrs, for example, a stiff-necked and fanatical persecutor stands over against an equally stiff-necked and fanatical victim; and a situation so complicated—that is to say, so real and historical—as that in which the 'persecutor' Pliny finds himself in his celebrated letter to Trajan on the subject of the Christians, is unfit for legend. And that is still a comparatively simple case. Let the reader think of the history which we are ourselves witnessing; anyone who, for example, evaluates the behaviour of individual men and groups of men at the time of the rise of National Socialism in Germany, or the behaviour of individual peoples and states before and during the last war, will feel how difficult it is to represent historical themes in general, and how unfit they are for legend; the historical comprises a great number of contradictory motives in each individual, a hesitation and ambiguous groping on the part of groups; only seldom (as in the last war) does a more or less plain situation, comparatively simple to describe, arise, and even such a situation is subject to division below the surface, is indeed almost constantly in danger of losing its simplicity; and the motives of all the interested parties are so complex that the slogans of propaganda can be composed only through the crudest simplification—with the result that friend and foe alike can often employ the same ones. To write history is so difficult that most historians are forced to make concessions to the technique of legend.

It is clear that a large part of the life of David as given in the Bible contains history and not legend. In Absalom's rebellion, for example, or in the scenes from David's last days, the contradictions and crossing of motives both in individuals and in the general action have become so concrete that it is impossible to doubt the historicity of the information conveyed. Now the men who composed the historical parts are often the same who edited the older legends too; their peculiar religious concept of man in history, which we have attempted to describe above, in no way led them to a legendary simplification of events; and so it is only natural that, in the legendary passages of the Old Testament, historical structure is frequently discernible—of course, not in the sense that the traditions are examined as to their credibility according to the methods of scientific criticism; but simply to the extent that the tendency to a smoothing down and harmonizing of events, to a simplification of motives, to a static definition of characters which avoids conflict, vacillation, and development, such as are natural to legendary structure, does not predominate in the Old Testament world of legend. Abraham, Jacob, or even Moses produces a more concrete, direct, and historical impression than the figures of the Homeric world—not because they are better described in terms of sense (the contrary is the case) but because the confused, contradictory multiplicity of events, the psychological and factual cross-purposes, which true history reveals, have not disappeared in the representation but still remain clearly perceptible. In the stories of David, the legendary, which only later scientific criticism makes recognizable as such, imperceptibly passes into the historical; and even in the legendary, the problem of the classification and interpretation of human history is already passionately apprehended—a problem which later shatters the framework of historical composition and completely overruns it with prophecy; thus the Old Testament, in so far as it is concerned with human events, ranges through all three domains: legend, historical reporting, and interpretative historical theology.

Connected with the matters just discussed is the fact that the Greek text seems more limited and more static in respect to the circle of personages involved in the action and to their political activity. In the recognition scene with which we began, there appears, aside from Odysseus and Penelope, the housekeeper Euryclea, a slave whom Odysseus' father Laertes had bought long before. She, like the swineherd Eumaeus, has spent her life in the service of Laertes's family; like Eumaeus, she is closely connected with their fate, she loves them and shares their interests and feelings. But she has no life of her own, no feelings of her own; she has only the life and feelings of her master. Eumaeus too, though he still remembers that he was born a freeman and indeed of a noble house (he was stolen as a boy), has, not only in fact but also in his own feeling, no longer a life of his own, he is entirely involved in the life of his masters. Yet these two characters are the only ones whom Homer brings to life who do not belong to the ruling class. Thus we become conscious of the fact that in the Homeric poems life is enacted only among the ruling class—others appear only in the role of servants to that class. The ruling class is still so strongly patriarchal, and still itself so involved in the daily activities of domestic life, that one is sometimes likely to forget their rank. But they are unmistakably a sort of feudal aristocracy, whose men divide their lives between war, hunting, marketplace councils, and feasting, while the women supervise the maids in the house. As a social picture, this world is completely stable; wars take place only between different groups of the ruling class; nothing ever pushes up from below. In the early stories of the Old Testament the patriarchal condition is dominant too, but since the people involved are individual nomadic or half-nomadic tribal leaders, the social picture gives a much less stable impression; class distinctions are not felt. As soon as the people completely emerges—that is, after the exodus from Egypt —its activity is always discernible, it is often in ferment, it frequently intervenes in events not only as a whole but also in separate groups and through the medium of separate individuals who come forward; the origins of prophecy seem to lie in the irrepressible politico-religious spontaneity of the people. We receive the impression that the movements emerging from the depths of the people of Israel–Judah must have been of a wholly different nature from those even of the later ancient democracies—of a different nature and far more elemental.

With the more profound historicity and the more profound social activity of the Old Testament text, there is connected yet another important distinction from Homer: namely, that a different conception of the elevated style and of the sublime is to be found here. Homer, of course, is not afraid to let the realism of daily life enter into the sublime and tragic; our episode of the scar is an example, we see how the quietly depicted, domestic scene of the foot-washing is incorporated into the pathetic and sublime action of Odysseus' homecoming. From the rule of the separation of styles which was later almost universally accepted and which specified that the realistic depiction of daily life was incompatible with the sublime and had a place only in comedy or, carefully stylized, in idyll—from any such rule Homer is still far removed. And yet he is closer to it than is the Old Testament. For the great and sublime events in the Homeric poems take place far more exclusively and unmistakably among the members of a ruling class; and these are far more untouched in their heroic elevation than are the Old Testament figures, who can fall much lower in dignity (consider, for example, Adam, Noah, David, Job); and finally, domestic realism, the representation of daily life, remains in Homer in the peaceful realm of the idyllic, whereas, from the very first, in the Old Testament stories, the sublime, tragic, and problematic take shape precisely in the domestic and commonplace: scenes such as those between Cain and Abel, between Noah and his sons, between Abraham, Sarah, and Hagar, between Rebekah, Jacob, and Esau, and so on, are inconceivable in the Homeric style. The entirely different ways of developing conflicts are enough to account for this. In the Old Testament stories the peace of daily life in the house, in the fields, and among the flocks, is undermined by jealousy over election and the promise of a blessing, and complications arise which would be utterly incomprehensible to the Homeric heroes. The latter must have palpable and clearly expressible reasons for their conflicts and enmities, and these work themselves out in free battles; whereas, with the former, the perpetually smouldering jealousy and the connection between the domestic and the spiritual, between the paternal blessing and the divine blessing, lead to daily life being permeated with the stuff of conflict, often with poison. The sublime influence of God here reaches so deeply into the everyday that the two realms of the sublime and the everyday are not only actually unseparated but basically inseparable.

We have compared these two texts, and, with them, the two kinds of style they embody, in order to reach a starting point for an investigation into the literary representation of reality in European culture. The two styles, in their opposition, represent basic types: on the one hand fully externalized description, uniform illumination, uninterrupted connection, free expression, all events in the foreground, displaying unmistakable meanings, few elements of historical development and of psychological perspective; on the other hand, certain parts brought into high relief, others left obscure, abruptness, suggestive influence of the unexpressed, 'background' quality, multiplicity of meanings and the need for interpretation, universal-historical claims, development of the concept of the historically becoming, and preoccupation with the problematic.

Homer's realism is, of course, not to be equated with classical-antique realism in general; for the separation of styles,[a] which did not develop until later, permitted no such leisurely and externalized description of everyday happenings; in tragedy especially there was no room for it; furthermore, Greek culture very soon encountered the phenomena of historical becoming and of the 'multi-

[a] i.e., the classical notion of literary decorum, which prescribed a 'high' style for noble subjects, and a 'low' style for comic and vulgar subjects, with no mixing of different styles in the same work.

layeredness' of the human problem, and dealt with them in its fashion; in Roman realism, finally, new and native concepts are added. We shall go into these later changes in the antique representation of reality when the occasion arises; on the whole, despite them, the basic tendencies of the Homeric style, which we have attempted to work out, remained effective and determinant down into late antiquity.

Since we are using the two styles, the Homeric and the Old Testament, as starting points, we have taken them as finished products, as they appear in the texts; we have disregarded everything that pertains to their origins, and thus have left untouched the question whether their peculiarities were theirs from the beginning or are to be referred wholly or in part to foreign influences. Within the limits of our purpose, a consideration of this question is not necessary; for it is in their full development, which they reached in early times, that the two styles exercised their determining influence upon the representation of reality in European literature.

26 W. K. Wimsatt and Monroe C. Beardsley

The essays on 'The Intentional Fallacy' and 'The Affective Fallacy' by W. K. Wimsatt (b. 1907), in collaboration with Monroe C. Beardsley (b. 1915), are central documents in the development of modern critical theory. As M. H. Abrams suggests (see above, pp. 4-5), all criticism has to deal with the interrelationships between the work of art, its creator, and its audience, but the endeavour of much modern criticism from Eliot and Richards in the twenties to the American New Critics in the forties and fifties, was to achieve an 'objective' criticism in which attention would be focused upon the meaning of the work itself, undistracted by inquiries into its origins in personal experience or effects on particular individuals. The essays of Wimsatt and Beardsley constitute the most uncompromising theoretical statement of this position. Their arguments, especially in 'The Intentional Fallacy' have often been attacked, without being completely disposed of. If absolute objectivity in criticism is impossible to attain, it may still be a useful ideal to aim at; and this, perhaps, when their qualifications are taken into account, is essentially what Wimsatt and Beardsley are saying.

W. K. Wimsatt is Professor of English at Yale University, where he has taught since 1939. 'The Intentional Fallacy' (first published in 1946) and 'The Affective Fallacy' (first published in 1949) are reprinted here from his book *The Verbal Icon: studies in the meaning of poetry* (Lexington, Ky., 1954). His other publications include *The Prose Style of Samuel Johnson* (New Haven, 1941), *Hateful Contraries: studies in literature and criticism* (Lexington, Ky., 1965), and *Literary Criticism: A Short History* (New York, 1957), written in collaboration with Cleanth Brooks. Monroe C. Beardsley has taught philosophy and aesthetics at Yale, Mount Holyoke College, Swarthmore College and Temple University, where he is now Professor of Philosophy. His publications include *Aesthetics: problems in the philosophy of criticism* (New York, 1958), and *Aesthetics from Classical Greece to the Present* (New York, 1966).

CROSS REFERENCES: 6. T. S. Eliot
9. I. A. Richards
18. John Crowe Ransom
24. Yvor Winters
37. Walter J. Ong

COMMENTARY: Frank Cioffi, 'Intention and interpretation in
criticism', *Proceedings of the Aristotelian Society*,
n.s. lxiv (1963), pp. 85-106
Stanley Fish, 'Literature in the reader: affective
stylistics', *New Literary History*, ii (1970), pp. 123-62

The intentional fallacy

I

The claim of the author's 'intention' upon the critic's judgment has been challenged in a number of recent discussions, notably in the debate entitled *The
Personal Heresy* [1939], between Professor Lewis and Tillyard. But it seems
doubtful if this claim and most of its romantic corollaries are as yet subject to
any widespread questioning. The present writers, in a short article entitled
'Intention' for a *Dictionary*[1] of literary criticism, raised the issue but were unable to pursue its implications at any length. We argued that the design or
intention of the author is neither available nor desirable as a standard for judging the success of a work of literary art, and it seems to us that this is a
principle which goes deep into some differences in the history of critical
attitudes. It is a principle which accepted or rejected points to the polar opposites
of classical 'imitation' and romantic expression. It entails many specific truths
about inspiration, authenticity, biography, literary history and scholarship,
and about some trends of contemporary poetry, especially its allusiveness. There
is hardly a problem of literary criticism in which the critic's approach will not
be qualified by his view of 'intention'.

'Intention', as we shall use the term, corresponds to *what he intended* in a
formula which more or less explicitly has had wide acceptance. 'In order to
judge the poet's performance, we must know *what he intended*.' Intention is
design or plan in the author's mind. Intention has obvious affinities for the
author's attitude towards his work, the way he felt, what made him write.

We begin our discussion with a series of propositions summarized and
abstracted to a degree where they seem to us axiomatic.

1. A poem does not come into existence by accident. The words of a poem, as
Professor Stoll has remarked, come out of a head, not out of a hat. Yet to insist
on the designing intellect as a *cause* of a poem is not to grant the design or
intention as a *standard* by which the critic is to judge the worth of the poet's
performance.

2. One must ask how a critic expects to get an answer to the question about
intention. How is he to find out what the poet tried to do? If the poet succeeded
in doing it, then the poem itself shows what he was trying to do. And if the
poet did not succeed, then the poem is not adequate evidence, and the critic

334

must go outside the poem—for evidence of an intention that did not become effective in the poem. 'Only one *caveat* must be borne in mind,' says an eminent intentionalist[2] in a moment when his theory repudiates itself; 'the poet's aim must be judged at the moment of the creative act, that is to say, by the art of the poem itself.'

3. Judging a poem is like judging a pudding or a machine. One demands that it work. It is only because an artifact works that we infer the intention of an artificer. 'A poem should not mean but be.'[a] A poem can *be* only through its *meaning*—since its medium is words—yet it *is*, simply *is*, in the sense that we have no excuse for inquiring what part is intended or meant. Poetry is a feat of style by which a complex of meaning is handled all at once. Poetry succeeds because all or most of what is said or implied is relevant; what is irrelevant has been excluded, like lumps from pudding and 'bugs' from machinery. In this respect poetry differs from practical messages, which are successful if and only if we correctly infer the intention. They are more abstract than poetry.

4. The meaning of a poem may certainly be a personal one, in the sense that a poem expresses a personality or state of soul rather than a physical object like an apple. But even a short lyric poem is dramatic, the response of a speaker (no matter how abstractly conceived) to a situation (no matter how universalized). We ought to impute the thoughts and attitudes of the poem immediately to the dramatic *speaker*, and if to the author at all, only by an act of biographical inference.

5. There is a sense in which an author, by revision, may better achieve his original intention. But it is a very abstract sense. He intended to write a better work, or a better work of a certain kind, and now has done it. But it follows that his former concrete intention was not his intention. 'He's the man we were in search of, that's true,' says Hardy's rustic constable, 'and yet he's not the man we were in search of. For the man we were in search of was not the man we wanted.'

'Is not a critic', asks Professor Stoll, 'a judge, who does not explore his own consciousness, but determines the author's meaning or intention, as if the poem were a will, a contract, or the constitution? The poem is not the critic's own.' He has accurately diagnosed two forms of irresponsibility, one of which he prefers. Our view is yet different. The poem is not the critic's own and not the author's (it is detached from the author at birth and goes about the world beyond his power to intend about it or control it). The poem belongs to the public. It is embodied in language, the peculiar possession of the public, and it is about the human being, an object of public knowledge. What is said about the poem is subject to the same scrutiny as any statement in linguistics or in the general science of psychology.

A critic of our *Dictionary* article, Ananda K. Coomaraswamy, has argued[3] that there are two kinds of inquiry about a work of art: (1) whether the artist achieved his intentions; (2) whether the work of art 'ought ever to have been undertaken at all' and so 'whether it is worth preserving'. Number (2), Coomaraswamy maintains, is not 'criticism of any work of art *qua* work of art', but is rather moral criticism; number (1) is artistic criticism. But we maintain that (2)

---

[a] From Archibald MacLeish's poem *Ars Poetica*.

need not be moral criticism: that there is another way of deciding whether works of art are worth preserving and whether, in a sense, they 'ought' to have been undertaken, and this is the way of objective criticism of works of art as such, the way which enables us to distinguish between a skilful murder and a skilful poem. A skilful murder is an example which Coomaraswamy uses, and in his system the difference between murder and the poem is simply a 'moral' one, not an 'artistic' one, since each if carried out according to plan is 'artistically' successful. We maintain that (2) is an inquiry of more worth than (1), and since (2) and not (1) is capable of distinguishing poetry from murder, the name 'artistic criticism' is properly given to (2).

II

It is not so much a historical statement as a definition to say that the intentional fallacy is a romantic one. When a rhetorician of the first century A.D.[a] writes: 'Sublimity is the echo of a great soul', or when he tells us that 'Homer enters into the sublime actions of his heroes' and 'shares the full inspiration of the combat', we shall not be surprised to find this rhetorician considered as a distant harbinger of romanticism and greeted in the warmest terms by Saintsbury. One may wish to argue whether Longinus should be called romantic, but there can hardly be a doubt that in one important way he is.

Goethe's three questions for 'constructive criticism' are 'What did the author set out to do? Was his plan reasonable and sensible, and how far did he succeed in carrying it out?' If one leaves out the middle question, one has in effect the system of Croce[b]—the culmination and crowning philosophic expression of romanticism. The beautiful is the successful intuition-expression, and the ugly is the unsuccessful; the intuition or private part of art is *the* aesthetic fact, and the medium or public part is not the subject of aesthetic at all.

> The Madonna of Cimabue is still in the Church of Santa Maria Novella; but does she speak to the visitor of today as to the Florentines of the thirteenth century?

> *Historical interpretation* labours ... to reintegrate in us the psychological conditions which have changed in the course of history. It ... enables us to see a work of art (a physical object) as its *author saw it* in the moment of production.[4]

The first italics are Croce's, the second ours. The upshot of Croce's system is an ambiguous emphasis on history. With such passages as a point of departure a critic may write a nice analysis of the meaning or 'spirit' of a play by Shakespeare or Corneille—a process that involves close historical study but remains aesthetic criticism—or he may, with equal plausibility, produce an essay in sociology, biography, or other kinds of non-aesthetic history.

[a] The reference here is to the remarkable Greek treatise *On the sublime* (later referred to by Wimsatt and Beardsley as the *Peri Hypsous*). It is conventionally attributed to 'Longinus', though this derives from an erroneous tradition that the third-century philosopher Cassius Longinus was the author.
[b] Benedetto Croce (1866–1952), Italian philosopher, historian and critic.

I went to the poets; tragic, dithyrambic, and all sorts.... I took them some of the most elaborate passages in their own writings, and asked what was the meaning of them.... Will you believe me?... there is hardly a person present who would not have talked better about their poetry than they did themselves. Then I knew that not by wisdom do poets write poetry, but by a sort of genius and inspiration.[a]

That reiterated mistrust of the poets which we hear from Socrates may have been part of a rigorously ascetic view in which we hardly wish to participate, yet Plato's Socrates saw a truth about the poetic mind which the world no longer commonly sees—so much criticism, and that the most inspirational and most affectionately remembered, has proceeded from the poets themselves.

Certainly the poets have had something to say that the critic and professor could not say; their message has been more exciting: that poetry should come as naturally as leaves to a tree, that poetry is the lava of the imagination, or that it is emotion recollected in tranquillity.[b] But it is necessary that we realize the character and authority of such testimony. There is only a fine shade of difference between such expressions and a kind of earnest advice that authors often give. Thus Edward Young, Carlyle, Walter Pater:

I know two golden rules from *ethics*, which are no less golden in *Composition*, than in life. 1. *Know thyself*; 2dly, *Reverence thyself*.

This is the grand secret for finding readers and retaining them: let him who would move and convince others, be first moved and convinced himself. Horace's rule, *Si vis me flere*[c], is applicable in a wider sense than the literal one. To every poet, to every writer, we might say: Be true, if you would be believed.

Truth! there can be no merit, no craft at all, without that. And further, all beauty is in the long run only *fineness* of truth, or what we call expression, the finer accommodation of speech to that vision within.

And Housman's little handbook to the poetic mind[d] yields this illustration:

Having drunk a pint of beer at luncheon—beer is a sedative to the brain, and my afternoons are the least intellectual portion of my life—I would go out for a walk of two or three hours. As I went along, thinking of nothing in particular, only looking at things around me and following the progress of the seasons, there would flow into my mind, with sudden and unaccountable emotion, sometimes a line or two of verse, sometimes a whole stanza at once.

This is the logical terminus of the series already quoted. Here is a confession of how poems were written which would do as a definition of poetry just as well as 'emotion recollected in tranquillity'—and which the young poet might

[a] Plato, *The Apology*.
[b] The opinions of Keats, Byron, and Wordsworth respectively.
[c] 'If you wish me to weep [you must feel pain yourself].'
[d] *The Name and Nature of Poetry* (Cambridge, 1933).

equally well take to heart as a practical rule. Drink a pint of beer, relax, go walking, think on nothing in particular, look at things, surrender yourself to yourself, search for the truth in your own soul, listen to the sound of your own inside voice, discover and express the *vraie vérité* ['true truth'].

It is probably true that all this is excellent advice for poets. The young imagination fired by Wordsworth and Carlyle is probably closer to the verge of producing a poem than the mind of the student who has been sobered by Aristotle or Richards. The art of inspiring poets, or at least of inciting something like poetry in young persons, has probably gone further in our day than ever before. Books of creative writing such as those issued from the Lincoln School are interesting evidence of what a child can do.[5] All this, however, would appear to belong to an art separate from criticism—to a psychological discipline, a system of self-development, a yoga, which the young poet perhaps does well to notice, but which is something different from the public art of evaluating poems.

Coleridge and Arnold were better critics than most poets have been, and if the critical tendency dried up the poetry in Arnold and perhaps in Coleridge, it is not inconsistent with our argument, which is that judgment of poems is different from the art of producing them. Coleridge has given us the classic 'anodyne' story, and tells what he can about the genesis of a poem[a] which he calls a 'psychological curiosity', but his definitions of poetry and of the poetic quality 'imagination' are to be found elsewhere and in quite other terms.

It would be convenient if the passwords of the intentional school, 'sincerity', 'fidelity', 'spontaneity', 'authenticity', 'genuineness', 'originality', could be equated with terms such as 'integrity', 'relevance', 'unity', 'function', 'maturity', 'subtlety', 'adequacy', and other more precise terms of evaluation—in short, if 'expression' always meant aesthetic achievement. But this is not so.

'Aesthetic' art, says Professor Curt Ducasse, an ingenious theorist of expression, is the conscious objectification of feelings, in which an intrinsic part is the critical moment. The artist corrects the objectification when it is not adequate. But this may mean that the earlier attempt was not successful in objectifying the self, or 'it may also mean that it was a successful objectification of a self which, when it confronted us clearly, we disowned and repudiated in favour of another'.[6] What is the standard by which we disown or accept the self? Professor Ducasse does not say. Whatever it may be, however, this standard is an element in the definition of art which will not reduce to terms of objectification. The evaluation of the work of art remains public; the work is measured against something outside the author.

IV

There is criticism of poetry and there is author psychology, which when applied to the present or future takes the form of inspirational promotion; but author

[a] The fragment 'Kubla Khan' which, according to his own account, Coleridge composed in an opium dream and wrote down immediately on awakening until interrupted by 'a person on business from Porlock'.

psychology can be historical too, and then we have literary biography, a legitimate and attractive study in itself, one approach, as Professor Tillyard would argue, to personality, the poem being only a parallel approach. Certainly it need not be with a derogatory purpose that one points out personal studies, as distinct from poetic studies, in the realm of literary scholarship. Yet there is danger of confusing personal and poetic studies; and there is the fault of writing the personal as if it were poetic.

There is a difference between internal and external evidence for the meaning of a poem. And the paradox is only verbal and superficial that what is (1) internal is also public: it is discovered through the semantics and syntax of a poem, through our habitual knowledge of the language, through grammars, dictionaries, and all the literature which is the source of dictionaries, in general through all that makes a language and culture; while what is (2) external is private or idiosyncratic; not a part of the work as a linguistic fact: it consists of revelations (in journals, for example, or letters or reported conversations) about how or why the poet wrote the poem—to what lady, while sitting on what lawn, or at the death of what friend or brother. There is (3) an intermediate kind of evidence about the character of the author or about private or semi-private meanings attached to words or topics by an author or by a coterie of which he is a member. The meaning of words is the history of words, and the biography of an author, his use of a word, and the associations which the word had for *him*, are part of the word's history and meaning.[7] But the three types of evidence, especially (2) and (3), shade into one another so subtly that it is not always easy to draw a line between examples, and hence arises the difficulty for criticism. The use of biographical evidence need not involve intentionalism, because while it may be evidence of what the author intended, it may also be evidence of the meaning of his words and the dramatic character of his utterance. On the other hand, it may not be all this. And a critic who is concerned with evidence of type (1) and moderately with that of type (3) will in the long run produce a different sort of comment from that of the critic who is concerned with (2) and with (3) where it shades into (2).

The whole glittering parade of Professor Lowes' *Road to Xanadu*, for instance, runs along the border between types (2) and (3) or boldly traverses the romantic region of (2). ' "Kubla Khan",' says Professor Lowes, 'is the fabric of a vision, but every image that rose up in its weaving had passed that way before. And it would seem that there is nothing haphazard or fortuitous in their return.' This is not quite clear—not even when Professor Lowes explains that there were clusters of associations, like hooked atoms, which were drawn into complex relation with other clusters in the deep well of Coleridge's memory, and which then coalesced and issued forth as poems. If there was nothing 'haphazard or fortuitous' in the way the images returned to the surface, that may mean (1) that Coleridge could not produce what he did not have, that he was limited in his creation by what he had read or otherwise experienced, or (2) that having received certain clusters of associations, he was bound to return them in just the way he did, and that the value of the poem may be described in terms of the experiences on which he had to draw. The latter pair of propositions (a sort of

Hartleyan associationism which Coleridge himself repudiated in the *Biographia*)
may not be assented to. There were certainly other combinations, other poems,
worse or better, that might have been written by men who had read Bartram
and Purchas and Bruce and Milton. And this will be true no matter how many
times we are able to add to the brilliant complex of Coleridge's reading. In
certain flourishes (such as the sentence we have quoted) and in chapter headings
like 'The Shaping Spirit', 'The Magical Synthesis', 'Imagination Creatrix', it
may be that Professor Lowes pretends to say more about the actual poems than
he does. There is a certain deceptive variation in these fancy chapter titles; one
expects to pass on to a new stage in the argument, and one finds—more and
more sources, more and more about 'the streamy nature of association'.[8]

'Wohin der Weg?' quotes Professor Lowes for the motto of his book. 'Kein
Weg! Ins Unbetretene.'[a] Precisely because the way is *unbetreten*, we should
say, it leads away from the poem. Bartram's *Travels* contain a good deal of the
history of certain words and of certain romantic Floridian conceptions that
appear in 'Kubla Khan'. And a good deal of that history has passed and was
then passing into the very stuff of our language. Perhaps a person who has read
Bartram appreciates the poem more than one who has not. Or, by looking up the
vocabulary of 'Kubla Khan' in the *Oxford English Dictionary*, or by reading
some of the other books there quoted, a person may know the poem better. But
it would seem to pertain little to the poem to know that *Coleridge* had
read Bartram. There is a gross body of life, of sensory and mental experience,
which lies behind and in some sense causes every poem, but can never be and
need not be known in the verbal and hence intellectual composition which is
the poem. For all the objects of our manifold experience, for every unity, there
is an action of the mind which cuts off roots, melts away context—or indeed
we should never have objects or ideas or anything to talk about.

It is probable that there is nothing in Professor Lowes' vast book which could
detract from anyone's appreciation of either *The Ancient Mariner* or 'Kubla
Khan'. We next present a case where preoccupation with evidence of type (3)
has gone so far as to distort a critic's view of a poem (yet a case not so obvious
as those that abound in our critical journals).

In a well-known poem by John Donne ['A Valediction: forbidding mourning'] appears this quatrain:

> Moving of th' earth brings harmes and feares,
>   Men reckon what it did and meant,
> But trepidation of the spheares,
>   Though greater farre, is innocent.

A recent critic in an elaborate treatment of Donne's learning has written of this
quatrain as follows:

He touches the emotional pulse of the situation by a skilful allusion to the
new and the old astronomy.... Of the new astronomy, the 'moving of the
earth' is the most radical principle; of the old, the 'trepidation of the spheres'
is the motion of the greatest complexity.... The poet must exhort his love to

[a] 'Where is the way?' 'No way! It is untrodden' (Goethe's *Faust*).

340

quietness and calm upon his departure; and for this purpose the figure based upon the latter motion (trepidation), long absorbed into the traditional astronomy, fittingly suggests the tension of the moment without arousing the 'harmes and feares' implicit in the figure of the moving earth.[9]

The argument is plausible and rests on a well substantiated thesis that Donne was deeply interested in the new astronomy and its repercussions in the theological realm. In various works Donne shows his familiarity with Kepler's *De Stella Nova*, with Galileo's *Siderius Nuncius*, with William Gilbert's *De Magnete*, and with Clavius' commentary on the *De Sphaera* of Sacrobosco. He refers to the new science in his Sermon at Paul's Cross and in a letter to Sir Henry Goodyer. In the *First Anniversary* he says the 'new philosophy calls in doubt'. In the *Elegy on Prince Henry* he says that the 'least moving of the centre' makes 'the world to shake'.

It is difficult to answer argument like this, and impossible to answer it with evidence of like nature. There is no reason why Donne might not have written a stanza in which the two kinds of celestial motion stood for two sorts of emotion at parting. And if we become full of astronomical ideas and see Donne only against the background of the new science, we may believe that he did. But the text itself remains to be dealt with, the analysable vehicle of a complicated metaphor. And one may observe: (1) that the movement of the earth according to the Copernican theory is a celestial motion, smooth and regular, and while it might cause religious or philosophic fears, it could not be associated with the crudity and earthiness of the kind of commotion which the speaker in the poem wishes to discourage; (2) that there is another moving of the earth, an earthquake, which has just these qualities and is to be associated with the tear-floods and sigh-tempests of the second stanza of the poem; (3) that 'trepidation' is an appropriate opposite of earthquake, because each is a shaking or vibratory motion; and 'trepidation of the spheres' is 'greater far' than an earthquake, but not much greater (if two such motions can be compared as to greatness) than the annual motion of the earth; (4) that reckoning what it 'did and meant' shows that the event has passed, like an earthquake, not like the incessant celestial movement of the earth. Perhaps a knowledge of Donne's interest in the new science may add another shade of meaning, an overtone to the stanza in question, though to say even this runs against the words. To make the geocentric and heliocentric antithesis the core of the metaphor is to disregard the English language, to prefer private evidence to public, external to internal.

V

If the distinction between kinds of evidence has implications for the historical critic, it has them no less for the contemporary poet and his critic. Or, since every rule for a poet is but another side of a judgment by a critic, and since the past is the realm of the scholar and critic, and the future and present that of the poet and the critical leaders of taste, we may say that the problems arising in literary scholarship from the intentional fallacy are matched by others which arise in the world of progressive experiment.

The question of 'allusiveness', for example, as acutely posed by the poetry of Eliot, is certainly one where a false judgment is likely to involve the intentional fallacy. The frequency and depth of literary allusion in the poetry of Eliot and others has driven so many in pursuit of full meanings to the *Golden Bough* and the Elizabethan drama that it has become a kind of commonplace to suppose that we do not know what a poet means unless we have traced him in his reading—a supposition redolent with intentional implications. The stand taken by F. O Matthiessen is a sound one and partially forestalls the difficulty.

> If one reads these lines with an attentive ear and is sensitive to their sudden shifts in movement, the contrast between the actual Thames and the idealized vision of it during an age before it flowed through a megalopolis is sharply conveyed by that movement itself, whether or not one recognizes the refrain to be from Spenser.

Eliot's allusions work when we know them—and to a great extent even when we do not know them, through their suggestive power.

But sometimes we find allusions supported by notes, and it is a nice question whether the notes function more as guides to send us where we may be educated, or more as indications in themselves about the character of the allusions. 'Nearly everything of importance ... that is apposite to an appreciation of "The Waste Land",' writes Matthiessen of Miss Weston's book [*From Ritual to Romance*], 'has been incorporated into the structure of the poem itself, or into Eliot's notes.' And with such an admission it may begin to appear that it would not much matter if Eliot invented his sources (as Sir Walter Scott invented chapter epigraphs from 'old plays' and 'anonymous' authors, or as Coleridge wrote marginal glosses for *The Ancient Mariner*). Allusions to Dante, Webster, Marvell, or Baudelaire doubtless gain something because these writers existed, but it is doubtful whether the same can be said for an allusion to an obscure Elizabethan:

> The sound of horns and motors, which shall bring
> Sweeney to Mrs Porter in the spring.

'Cf. Day, *Parliament of Bees*:' says Eliot,

> When of a sudden, listening, you shall hear,
> A noise of horns and hunting, which shall bring
> Actaeon to Diana in the spring,
> Where all shall see her naked skin.

The irony is completed by the quotation itself; had Eliot, as is quite conceivable, composed these lines to furnish his own background, there would be no loss of validity. The conviction may grow as one reads Eliot's next note: 'I do not know the origin of the ballad from which these lines are taken: it was reported to me from Sydney, Australia.' The important word in this note—on Mrs Porter and her daughter who washed their feet in soda water—is 'ballad'. And if one should feel from the lines themselves their 'ballad' quality, there would be little need for the note. Ultimately, the inquiry must focus on the integrity of such notes as parts of the poem, for where they constitute special information about the meaning of phrases in the poem, they ought to be subject to the same scrutiny as any of the other words in which it is written. Matthiessen believes the notes were the price Eliot 'had to pay in order to avoid what he would have considered muffling the energy of his poem by extended connecting links in the text itself'. But it may be questioned whether the notes and the need for them are not equally muffling. F. W. Bateson has plausibly argued that Tennyson's 'The Sailor Boy' would be better if half the stanzas were omitted, and the best versions of ballads like 'Sir Patrick Spens' owe their power to the very audacity with which the minstrel has taken for granted the story upon which he comments. What then if a poet finds he cannot take so much for granted in a more recondite context and rather than write informatively, supplies notes? It can be said in favour of this plan that at least the notes do not pretend to be dramatic, as they would if written in verse. On the other hand, the notes may look like unassimilated material lying loose beside the poem, necessary for the meaning of the verbal context, but not integrated, so that the symbol stands incomplete.

We mean to suggest by the above analysis that whereas notes tend to seem to justify themselves as external indexes to the author's *intention*, yet they ought to be judged like any other parts of a composition (verbal arrangement special to a particular context), and when so judged their reality as parts of the poem, or their imaginative integration with the rest of the poem, may come into question. Matthiessen, for instance, sees that Eliot's titles for poems and his epigraphs are informative apparatus, like the notes. But while he is worried by some of the notes and thinks that Eliot 'appears to be mocking himself for writing the note at the same time that he wants to convey something by it', Matthiessen believes that 'the device' of epigraphs 'is not at all open to the objection of not being sufficiently structural'. 'The *intention*', he says, 'is to enable the poet to secure a condensed expression in the poem itself.' 'In each case the epigraph is *designed* to form an integral part of the effect of the poem.' And Eliot himself, in his notes, has justified his poetic practice in terms of intention.

> The Hanged Man, a member of the traditional pack, fits my purpose in two ways: because he is associated in my mind with the Hanged God of Frazer, and because I associate him with the hooded figure in the passage of the disciples to Emmaus in Part V.... The man with Three Staves (an authentic member of the Tarot pack) I associate, quite arbitrarily, with the Fisher King himself.

And perhaps he is to be taken more seriously here, when off guard in a note, than when in his Norton Lectures he comments on the difficulty of saying what a poem means and adds playfully that he thinks of prefixing to a second edition of *Ash Wednesday* some lines from *Don Juan*:

> I don't pretend that I quite understand
> My own meaning when I would be *very* fine;
> But the fact is that I have nothing planned
> Unless it were to be a moment merry.

If Eliot and other contemporary poets have any characteristic fault, it may be in *planning* too much.

Allusiveness in poetry is one of several critical issues by which we have illustrated the more abstract issue of intentionalism, but it may be for today the most important illustration. As a poetic practice allusiveness would appear to be in some recent poems an extreme corollary of the romantic intentionalist assumption, and as a critical issue it challenges and brings to light in a special way the basic premise of intentionalism. The following instance from the poetry of Eliot may serve to epitomize the practical implications of what we have been saying. In Eliot's 'Love Song of J. Alfred Prufrock', towards the end, occurs the line: 'I have heard the mermaids singing, each to each', and this bears a certain resemblance to a line in a Song by John Donne, 'Teach me to heare Mermaides singing', so that for the reader acquainted to a certain degree with Donne's poetry, the critical question arises: Is Eliot's line an allusion to Donne's? Is Prufrock thinking about Donne? Is Eliot thinking about Donne? We suggest that there are two radically different ways of looking for an answer to this question. There is (1) the way of poetic analysis and exegesis, which inquires whether it makes any sense if Eliot-Prufrock is thinking about Donne. In an earlier part of the poem, when Prufrock asks, 'Would it have been worth while, ... To have squeezed the universe into a ball,' his words take half their sadness and irony from certain energetic and passionate lines of Marvell 'To His Coy Mistress'. But the exegetical inquirer may wonder whether mermaids considered as 'strange sights' (to hear them is in Donne's poem analogous to getting with child a mandrake root) have much to do with Prufrock's mermaids, which seem to be symbols of romance and dynamism, and which incidentally have literary authentication, if they need it, in a line of a sonnet by Gérard de Nerval. This method of inquiry may lead to the conclusion that the given resemblance between Eliot and Donne is without significance and is better not thought of, or the method may have the disadvantage of providing no certain conclusion. Nevertheless, we submit that this is the true and objective way of criticism, as contrasted to what the very uncertainty of exegesis might tempt a second kind of critic to undertake: (2) the way of biographical or genetic inquiry, in which, taking advantage of the fact that Eliot is still alive, and in the spirit of a man who would settle a bet, the critic writes to Eliot and asks what he meant, or if he had Donne in mind. We shall not here weigh the probabilities—whether Eliot would answer that he meant nothing at all, had nothing at all in mind—a sufficiently good answer to such a question—or in an unguarded moment might furnish a clear and, within its limit, irrefutable answer. Our point is that such an answer to such an inquiry would have nothing to do with the poem 'Prufrock'; it would not be a critical inquiry. Critical inquiries, unlike bets, are not settled in this way. Critical inquiries are not settled by consulting the oracle.

Notes

1. *Dictionary of World Literature*, Joseph T. Shipley, ed. (New York, 1942), 326–9.
2. J. E. Spingarn, 'The new criticism', in *Criticism in America* (New York, 1924), 24–5.
3. Ananda K. Coomaraswamy, 'Intention', in *American Bookman*, i (1944), 41–8.
4. It is true that Croce himself in his *Ariosto, Shakespeare, and Corneille* (London, 1920), chap. vii, 'The Practical Personality and the Poetical Personality', and in his *Defence of Poetry* (Oxford, 1933), 24, and elsewhere, early and late, has delivered telling attacks on emotive geneticism, but the main drive of the *Aesthetic* is surely towards a kind of cognitive intentionalism.
5. See Hughes Mearns, *Creative Youth* (Garden City, 1925), esp. 10, 27–9. The technique of inspiring poems has apparently been outdone more recently by the study of inspiration in successful poets and other artists. See, for instance, Rosamond E. M. Harding, *An Anatomy of Inspiration* (Cambridge, 1940); Julius Portnoy, *A Psychology of Art Creation* (Philadelphia, 1942); Rudolf Arnheim and others, *Poets at Work* (New York, 1947); Phyllis Bartlett, *Poems in Process* (New York, 1951); Brewster Ghiselin, ed., *The Creative Process: a symposium* (Berkeley and Los Angeles, 1952).
6. Curt Ducasse, *The Philosophy of Art* (New York, 1929), 116.
7. And the history of words *after* a poem is written may contribute meanings which if relevant to the original pattern should not be ruled out by a scruple about intention.
8. Chaps. viii, 'The Pattern', and xvi, 'The Known and Familiar Landscape', will be found of most help to the student of the poem.
9. Charles M. Coffin, *John Donne and the New Philosophy* (New York, 1927), 97–8.

The affective fallacy

I

As the title of this essay invites comparison with that of our first, it may be relevant to assert at this point that we believe ourselves to be exploring two roads which have seemed to offer convenient detours around the acknowledged and usually feared obstacles to objective criticism, both of which, however, have actually led away from criticism and from poetry. The Intentional Fallacy is a confusion between the poem and its origins, a special case of what is known to philosophers as the Genetic Fallacy. It begins by trying to derive the standard of criticism from the psychological *causes* of the poem and ends in biography and relativism. The Affective Fallacy is a confusion between the poem and its *results* (what it *is* and what it *does*), a special case of epistemological scepticism, though usually advanced as if it had far stronger claims than the overall forms of scepticism. It begins by trying to derive the standard of criticism from the psychological effects of the poem and ends in impressionism and relativism. The outcome of either Fallacy, the Intentional or the Affective, is that the poem itself, as an object of specifically critical judgment, tends to disappear.

In the present essay, we would discuss briefly the history and fruits of affective criticism, some of its correlatives in cognitive criticism, and hence certain cognitive characteristics of poetry which have made affective criticism plausible. We would observe also the premises of affective criticism, as they appear today, in certain philosophic and pseudophilosophic disciplines of wide influence. And first and mainly that of 'semantics'.

II

The separation of emotive from referential meaning was urged persuasively about twenty years ago in the earlier works of I. A. Richards. The types of meaning which were defined in his *Practical Criticism* and in the *Meaning of Meaning* of Ogden and Richards created, partly by suggestion, partly with the aid of direct statement, a clean 'antithesis' between 'symbolic[a] and emotive use of language'. In his *Practical Criticism* Richards spoke of 'aesthetic' or 'projectile' words—adjectives by which we project feelings at objects themselves altogether innocent of any qualities corresponding to these feelings. And in his succinct *Science and Poetry*, science is statement, poetry is pseudo statement which plays the important role of making us feel better about things than statements would.[1] After Richards—and under the influence too of Count Korzybski's non-Aristotelian *Science and Sanity*—came the semantic school of Chase, Hayakawa, Walpole, and Lee. Most recently C. L. Stevenson in his *Ethics and Language* has given an account which, as it is more careful and explicit than the others, may be taken as most clearly pleading their cause— and best revealing its weakness.

One of the most emphatic points in Stevenson's system is the distinction between what a word *means* and what it *suggests*. To make the distinction in a given case, one applies what the semiotician calls a 'linguistic rule' ('definition' in traditional terminology), the role of which is to stabilize responses to a word. The word 'athlete' may be said to *mean* one interested in sports, among other things, but merely to suggest a tall young man. The linguistic rule is that 'athletes are necessarily interested in sports, but may or may not be tall'. All this is on the side of what may be called the *descriptive* (or *cognitive*) function of words. For a second and separate main function of words— that is, the *emotive*—there is no linguistic rule to stabilize responses and, therefore, in Stevenson's system, no parallel distinction between meaning and suggestion. Although the term 'quasi-dependent emotive meaning' is recommended by Stevenson for a kind of emotive 'meaning' which is 'conditional to the cognitive *suggestiveness* of a sign', the main drift of his argument is that emotive 'meaning' is something noncorrelative to and independent of descriptive (or cognitive) meaning. Thus, emotive 'meaning' is said to survive sharp changes in descriptive meaning. And words with the same descriptive meaning are said to have quite different emotive 'meanings'. 'Licence' and 'liberty', for example, Stevenson believes to have in some contexts the same descriptive meaning, but opposite emotive 'meanings'. Finally, there are words which he

---

[a] 'Symbolic' here means the referential or scientific use of language. See I. A. Richards, 'The Two Uses of Language', above, pp. 111–14.

believes to have no descriptive meaning, yet a decided emotive 'meaning': these are expletives of various sorts.

But a certain further distinction, and an important one, which does not appear in Stevenson's system—nor in those of his forerunners—is invited by his persistent use of the word 'meaning' for both cognitive and emotive language functions and by the absence from the emotive of his careful distinction between 'meaning' and 'suggestion'. It is a fact worth insisting upon that the term 'emotive meaning', as used by Stevenson, and the more cautious term 'feeling' as used by Richards to refer to one of his four types of 'meaning',[a] do not refer to any such cognitive meaning as that conveyed by the name of an emotion—'anger' or 'love'. Rather, these key terms refer to the *expression* of emotive states which Stevenson and Richards believe to be effected by certain words—for instance 'licence', 'liberty', 'pleasant', 'beautiful', 'ugly'—and hence also to the emotive *response* which these words may evoke in a hearer. As the term 'meaning' has been traditionally and usefully assigned to the cognitive, or descriptive, functions of language, it would have been well if these writers had employed, in such contexts, some less pre-empted term. 'Import' might have been a happy choice. Such differentiation in vocabulary would have had the merit of reflecting a profound difference in linguistic function—all the difference between grounds of emotion and emotions themselves, between what is immediately meant by words and what is evoked by the meaning of words, or what more briefly might be said to be the 'import' of the words themselves.

Without pausing to examine Stevenson's belief that expletives have no descriptive meaning, we are content to observe in passing that these words at any rate have only the vaguest emotive *import*, something raw, unarticulated, imprecise. 'Oh!' (surprise and related feelings), 'Ah!' (regret), 'Ugh!' (distaste). It takes a more descriptive reference to specify the feeling. 'In quiet she reposes. Ah! would that I did too.' But a more central re-emphasis for Stevenson's position—and for that of his forerunners, including Richards—seems required by a fact scarcely mentioned in semantic writings: namely, that a large and obvious area of emotive *import* depends directly upon descriptive meaning (either with or without words of explicit valuation)—as when a person says and is believed: 'General X ordered the execution of 50,000 civilian hostages', or 'General X is guilty of the murder of 50,000 civilian hostages'. And secondly, by the fact that a great deal of emotive *import* which does not depend on descriptive *meaning* does depend on descriptive *suggestion*. Here we have the 'quasi-dependent emotive meaning', of Stevenson's system—a 'meaning' to which surely he assigns too slight a role. This is the kind of emotive import, we should say, which appears when words change in descriptive *meaning* yet preserve a similar emotive 'meaning'—when the Communists take over the term 'democracy' and apply it to something else, preserving, however, the old descriptive *suggestion*, a government of, by, and for the people. It appears in pairs of words like 'liberty' and 'licence', which even if they have the same descriptive meaning (as one may doubt), certainly carry different descriptive sugges-

[a] See above, pp. 115–20.

tions. Or one might cite the word series in Bentham's classic 'Catalogue of Motives': 'humanity, goodwill, partiality', 'frugality, pecuniary interest, avarice'. Or the other standard examples of emotive insinuation: 'Animals sweat, men perspire, women glow.' 'I am firm, thou art obstinate, he is pigheaded.' Or the sentence, 'There should be a revolution every twenty years', to which the experimenter in emotive responses attaches now the name of Karl Marx (and arouses suspicion), now that of Thomas Jefferson (and provokes applause).

The principle applies conspicuously to the numerous examples offered by the school of Hayakawa, Walpole, and Lee. In the interest of brevity, though in what may seem a quixotic defiance of the warnings of this school against un-indexed generalization—according to which semanticist (1) is not semanticist (2) is not semanticist (3), and so forth—we call attention to Irving Lee's *Language Habits in Human Affairs*, particularly Chapters vii and viii. According to Lee, every mistake that anyone ever makes in acting, since in some direct or remote sense it involves language or thought (which is related to language), may be ascribed to 'bad language habits', a kind of magic misuse of words. No distinctions are permitted. Basil Rathbone, handed a scenario entitled *The Monster*, returns it unread, but accepts it later under a different title. The Ephraimite says 'Sibboleth' instead of 'Shibboleth' and is slain. A man says he is offended by four-letter words describing events in a novel, but not by the events. Another man receives an erroneously worded telegram which says that his son is dead. The shock is fatal. One would have thought that with this example Lee's simplifying prejudice might have broken down—that a man who is misinformed that his son is dead may have leave himself to drop dead without being thought a victim of emotive incantation. Or that the title of a scenario is some ground for the inference that it is a Grade-B horror movie; that the use of phonetic principles in choosing a password is reason rather than magic—as 'lollapalooza' and 'lullabye' were used against infiltration tactics on Guadalcanal; that four-letter words may suggest in events certain qualities which a reader finds it distasteful to contemplate. None of these examples (except the utterly anomalous 'Sibboleth') offers any evidence, in short, that what a word *does* to a person is to be ascribed to anything except what it *means*, or if this connection is not apparent, at the most, by what it *suggests*.

A question about the relation of language to objects of emotion is a shadow and index of another question, about the status of emotions themselves. It is a consistent cultural phenomenon that within the same period as the *floruit* of semantics one kind of anthropology has delivered a parallel attack upon the relation of objects themselves to emotions, or more specifically, upon the constancy of their relations through the times and places of human societies. In the classic treatise of Westermarck on *Ethical Relativity* we learn, for example, that the custom of eliminating the aged and unproductive has been practised among certain primitive tribes and nomadic races. Other customs, that of exposing babies, that of suicide, that of showing hospitality to strangers—or the contrary custom of eating them, the reception of the Cyclops rather than that of Alcinous—seem to have enjoyed in some cultures a degree of approval unknown or at least unusual in our own. But even Westermarck has noticed that difference of emotion 'largely originates in different measures of knowledge, based on experience of the consequences of conduct, and in different beliefs'. That is to say, the different emotions, even though they are responses to the same objects or actions, may yet be responses to different qualities or functions —to the edibility of Odysseus rather than to his comeliness or manliness. A converse of this is the fact that for different objects in different cultures there may be on cognitive grounds emotions of similar quality—for the cunning of Odysseus and for the strategy of Montgomery at El Alamein. Were it otherwise, indeed, there would be no way of understanding and describing alien emotions, no basis on which the science of the cultural relativist might proceed.

We shall not pretend to frame any formal discourse upon affective psychology, the laws of emotion. At this point, nevertheless, we venture to rehearse some generalities about objects, emotions, and words. Emotion, it is true, has a well known capacity to fortify opinion, to inflame cognition, and to grow upon itself in surprising proportions to gains of reason. We have mob psychology, psychosis, and neurosis. We have 'free-floating anxiety' and all the vaguely understood and inchoate states of apprehension, depression, or elation, the prevailing complexions of melancholy or cheer. But it is well to remember that these states are indeed inchoate or vague and by that fact may even verge upon the unconscious.[2] We have, again, the popular and self-vindicatory forms of confessing emotion. 'He makes me boil.' 'It burns me up.' Or in the novels of Evelyn Waugh a social event or a person is 'sick-making'. But these locutions involve an extension of the strict operational meaning of *make* or *effect*. A food or a poison causes pain or death, but for an emotion we have a reason or an object, not merely an efficient cause. If objects are ever connected by 'emotional congruity', as in the association psychology which J. S. Mill inherited from the eighteenth century, this can mean only that similar emotions attach to various objects because of similarity in the objects or in their relations. What makes one angry is something false, insulting, or unjust. What makes one afraid is a cyclone, a mob, a holdup man. And in each case the emotion is somewhat different.

The tourist who said a waterfall was pretty provoked the silent disgust of Coleridge, while the other who said it was sublime won his approval. This, as C. S. Lewis so well observes, was not the same as if the tourist had said, 'I feel sick', and Coleridge had thought, 'No, I feel quite well'.

The doctrine of emotive meaning propounded recently by the semanticists has seemed to offer a scientific basis for one kind of affective relativism in poetics—the personal. That is, if a person can correctly say either 'liberty' or 'licence' in a given context independently of the cognitive quality of the context, merely at will or from emotion, it follows that a reader may likely feel either 'hot' or 'cold' and report either 'bad' or 'good' on reading either 'liberty' or 'licence'—either an ode by Keats or a limerick. The sequence of licences is endless. Similarly, the doctrines of one school of anthropology have gone far to fortify another kind of affective relativism, the cultural or historical, the measurement of poetic value by the degree of feeling felt by the readers of a given era. A different psychological criticism, that by author's intention, as we noted in our first essay, is consistent both with piety for the poet and with antiquarian curiosity and has been heavily supported by the historical scholar and biographer. So affective criticism, though in its personal or impressionistic form it meets with strong dislike from scholars, yet in its theoretical or scientific form finds strong support from the same quarter. The historical scholar, if not much interested in his own personal responses or in those of his students, is intensely interested in whatever can be discovered about those of any member of Shakespeare's audience.

III

Plato's feeding and watering of the passions[3] was an early example of affective theory, and Aristotle's countertheory of catharsis was another (with modern intentionalistic analogues in theories of 'relief' and 'sublimation'). There was also the 'transport' of the audience in the *Peri Hypsous* (matching the great soul of the poet), and this had echoes of passion or enthusiasm among eighteenth-century Longinians. We have had more recently the infection theory of Tolstoy (with its intentionalistic analogue in the emotive expressionism of Veron), the *Einfühlung* or empathy of Lipps and related pleasure theories, either more or less tending to the 'objectification' of Santayana: 'Beauty is pleasure regarded as the quality of a thing.' An affinity for these theories is seen in certain theories of the comic during the same era, the relaxation theory of Penjon, the laughter theory of Max Eastman. In their *Foundations of Aesthetics* Ogden, Richards, and Wood listed sixteen types of aesthetic theory, of which at least seven may be described as affective. Among these the theory of Synaesthesis (Beauty is what produces an equilibrium of appetencies) was the one they themselves espoused. This was developed at length by Richards in his *Principles of Literary Criticism*.

The theories just mentioned may be considered as belonging to one branch of affective criticism, and that the main one, the emotive—unless the theory of empathy, with its transport of the self into the object, belongs rather with a parallel and equally ancient affective theory, the imaginative. This is represented by the figure of vividness so often mentioned in the rhetorics—*efficacia*, *enargeia*, or the *phantasiai* in Chapter xv of *Peri Hypsous*. This if we mistake not is the imagination the 'Pleasures' of which are celebrated by Addison in his series of *Spectators*. It is an imagination implicit in the theories of Leibniz and Baumgarten that beauty lies in clear but confused, or sensuous ideas; in the statement of Warton in his *Essay on Pope* that the selection of 'lively pictures ... chiefly constitutes true poetry'. In our time, as the emotive form of psychologistic or affective theory has found its most impressive champion in I. A. Richards, so the imaginative form has in Max Eastman, whose *Literary Mind* and *Enjoyment of Poetry* have much to say about vivid realizations or heightened consciousness.

The theory of intention or author psychology has been the intense conviction of poets themselves, Wordsworth, Keats, Housman, and since the romantic era, of young persons interested in poetry, the introspective amateurs and soul-cultivators. In a parallel way, affective theory has often been less a scientific view of literature than a prerogative—that of the soul adventuring among masterpieces, the contagious teacher, the poetic radiator—a magnetic rhapsode Ion, a Saintsbury, a Quiller-Couch, a William Lyon Phelps. Criticism on this theory has approximated the tone of the Buchmanite confession, the revival meeting. 'To be quite frank', says Anatole France, 'the critic ought to say: "Gentlemen, I am going to speak about myself apropos of Shakespeare, apropos of Racine." ' The sincerity of the critic becomes an issue, as for the intentionalist the sincerity of the poet.

A 'mysterious entity called the Grand Style' is celebrated by Saintsbury—something much like 'the Longinian Sublime'. 'Whenever this perfection of expression acquires such force that it transmutes the subject and transports the hearer or reader, then and there the Grand Style exists, for so long, and in such a degree, as the transmutation of the one and the transportation of the other lasts.' This is the grand style, the emotive style, of nineteenth-century affective criticism. A somewhat less resonant style which has been heard in our columns of Saturday and Sunday reviewing and from our literary explorers is more closely connected with imagism and the kind of vividness sponsored by Eastman. In the *Book-of-the-Month Club News* Dorothy Canfield testifies to the power of a novel: 'To read this book is like living through an experience rather than just reading about it.' A poem, says Hans Zinsser,

> means nothing to me unless it can carry me away with the gentle or passionate pace of its emotion, over obstacles of reality into meadows and coverts of illusion.... The sole criterion for me is whether it can sweep me with it into emotion or illusion of beauty, terror, tranquillity, or even disgust.[4]

It is but a short step to what we may call the physiological form of affective criticism. Beauty, said Burke in the eighteenth century, is something which 'acts by relaxing the solids of the whole system'. More recently, on the side of personal testimony, we have the oft quoted gooseflesh experience in a letter of Emily Dickinson, and the top of her head taken off. We have the bristling of the skin while Housman was shaving, the 'shiver down the spine', the sensation in 'the pit of the stomach'. And if poetry has been discerned by these tests, truth also. 'All scientists,' said D. H. Lawrence to Aldous Huxley, 'are liars.... I don't care about evidence. Evidence doesn't mean anything to me. I don't feel it *here*.' And, reports Huxley, 'he pressed his two hands on his solar plexus'.

An even more advanced grade of affective theory, that of hallucination, would seem to have played some part in the neo-classic conviction about the unities of time and place, was given a modified continuation of existence in phrases of Coleridge about a 'willing suspension of disbelief' and a 'temporary half faith', and may be found today in some textbooks. The hypnotic hypothesis of E. D. Snyder might doubtless be invoked in its support. As this form of affective theory is the least theoretical in detail, has the least content, and makes the least claim on critical intelligence, so it is in its most concrete instances not a theory but a fiction or a fact—of no critical significance. In the eighteenth century Fielding conveys a right view of the hallucinative power of drama in his comic description of Partridge seeing Garrick act the ghost scene in *Hamlet* [in *Tom Jones*]. 'O la! sir. .... If I was frightened, I am not the only person.... You may call me coward if you will; but if that little man there upon the stage is not frightened, I never saw any man frightened in my life.' Partridge is today found perhaps less often among the sophisticates at the theatre than among the myriad audience of movie and radio. It is said, and no doubt reliably, that during World War II Stefan Schnabel played Nazi roles in radio dramas so convincingly that he received numerous letters of complaint, and in particular one from a lady who said that she had reported him to General MacArthur.[5]

IV

A distinction can be made between those who have testified what poetry docs to themselves and those who have coolly investigated what it does to others. The most resolute researches of the latter have led them into the dreary and antiseptic laboratory, to testing with Fechner the effects of triangles and rectangles, to inquiring what kinds of colours are suggested by a line of Keats, or to measuring the motor discharges attendant upon reading it.[6] If animals could read poetry, the affective critic might make discoveries analogous to those of W. B. Cannon about *Bodily Changes in Pain, Hunger, Fear and Rage*—the increased liberation of sugar from the liver, the secretion of adrenalin from the adrenal gland. The affective critic is today actually able, if he wishes, to measure the 'psychogalvanic reflex' of persons subjected to a given moving picture. But, as Herbert J. Muller in his *Science and Criticism* points out: 'Students have sincerely reported an "emotion" at the mention of the word "mother", although a galvanometer indicated no bodily change whatever. They have also reported no emotion at the mention of "prostitute", although the galvanometer gave a definite kick.' Thomas Mann and a friend came out of a movie weeping copiously—but Mann narrates the incident in support of his view that movies are not Art. 'Art is a *cold* sphere.'[7] The gap between various levels of physiological experience and the recognition of value remains wide, in the laboratory or out.

In a similar way, general affective theory at the literary level has, by the very implications of its programme, produced little actual criticism. The author of the ancient *Peri Hypsous* is weakest at the points where he explains that passion and sublimity are the palliatives or excuses (*alexipharmaka*) of bold metaphors, and that passions which verge on transport are the lenitives or remedies (*panakeia*) of such audacities in speech as hyperbole. The literature of catharsis has dealt with the historical and theoretical question whether Aristotle meant a medical or a lustratory metaphor, whether the genitive which follows *katharsis* is of the thing purged or of the object purified. Even the early critical practice of I. A. Richards had little to do with his theory of synaesthesis. His *Practical Criticism* depended mainly on two important constructive principles of criticism which Richards has realized and insisted upon—(1) that rhythm (the vague, if direct, expression of emotion) and poetic form in general are intimately connected with and interpreted by other and more precise parts of poetic meaning,

(2) that poetic meaning is inclusive or multiple and hence sophisticated. The latter quality of poetry may perhaps be the objective correlative of the affective state of synaesthesis, but in applied criticism there would seem to be not much room for synaesthesis or for the touchy little attitudes of which it is composed.

The report of some readers, on the other hand, that a poem or story induces in them vivid images, intense feelings, or heightened consciousness, is neither anything which can be refuted nor anything which it is possible for the objective critic to take into account. The purely affective report is either too physiological or it is too vague. Feelings, as Hegel has conveniently put it, 'remain purely subjective affections of myself, in which the concrete matter vanishes, as though narrowed into a circle of the utmost abstraction'. And the only constant or predictable thing about the vivid images which more eidetic readers experience is precisely their vividness—as may be seen by requiring a class of average pupils to draw illustrations of a short story or by consulting the newest Christmas edition of a childhood classic which one knew with the illustrations of Howard Pyle or N. C. Wyeth. Vividness is not the thing in the work by which the work may be identified, but the result of a cognitive structure, which *is* the thing. 'The story is good', as the student so often says in his papers, 'because it leaves so much to the imagination.' The opaque accumulation of physical detail in some realistic novels has been aptly dubbed by Middleton Murry 'the pictorial fallacy'.

Certain theorists, notably Richards, have anticipated some difficulties of affective criticism by saying that it is not intensity of emotion that characterizes poetry (murder, robbery, fornication, horseracing, war—perhaps even chess—take care of that better), but the subtle quality of patterned emotions which play at the subdued level of disposition or attitude. We have psychological theories of aesthetic distance, detachment, or disinterestedness. A criticism on these principles has already taken important steps towards objectivity. If Eastman's theory of imaginative vividness appears today chiefly in the excited puffs of the newspaper Book Sections, the campaign of the semanticists and the balanced emotions of Richards, instead of producing their own school of affective criticism, have contributed much to recent schools of cognitive analysis, of paradox, ambiguity, irony, and symbol. It is not always true that the emotive and cognitive forms of criticism will sound far different. If the affective critic (avoiding both the physiological and the abstractly psychological form of report) ventures to state with any precision what a line of poetry *does*—as 'it fills us with a mixture of melancholy and reverence for antiquity'—either the statement will be patently abnormal or false, or it will be a description of what the meaning of the line *is*: 'the spectacle of massive antiquity in ruins'. Tennyson's 'Tears, idle tears', as it deals with an emotion which the speaker at first seems not to understand, might be thought to be a specially emotive poem. 'The last stanza,' says Brooks in his recent analysis, 'evokes an intense emotional response from the reader.' But this statement is not really a part of Brooks' criticism of the poem —rather a witness of his fondness for it. 'The second stanza'—Brooks might have said at an earlier point in his analysis—'gives us a momentary vivid realization of past happy experiences, then makes us sad at their loss.' But he says actually:

'The conjunction of the qualities of sadness and freshness is reinforced by the fact that the same basic symbol—the light on the sails of a ship hull down—has been employed to suggest both qualities.' The distinction between these formulations may seem slight, and in the first example which we furnished may be practically unimportant. Yet the difference between translatable emotive formulas and more physiological and psychologically vague ones—cognitively untranslatable—is theoretically of the greatest importance. The distinction even when it is a faint one is at the dividing point between paths which lead to polar opposites in criticism, to classical objectivity and to romantic reader psychology.

The critic whose formulations lean to the emotive and the critic whose formulations lean to the cognitive will in the long run produce a vastly different sort of criticism.

The more specific the account of the emotion induced by a poem, the more nearly it will be an account of the reasons for emotion, the poem itself, and the more reliable it will be as an account of what the poem is likely to induce in other—sufficiently informed—readers. It will in fact supply the kind of information which will enable readers to respond to the poem. It will talk not of tears, prickles, or other physiological symptoms, of feeling angry, joyful, hot, cold, or intense, or of vaguer states of emotional disturbance, but of shades of distinction and relation between objects of emotion. It is precisely here that the discerning literary critic has his insuperable advantage over the subject of the laboratory experiment and over the tabulator of the subject's responses. The critic is not a contributor to statistically countable reports about the poem, but a teacher or explicator of meanings. His readers, if they are alert, will not be content to take what he says as testimony, but will scrutinize it as teaching.

V

Poetry, as Matthew Arnold believed, 'attaches the emotion to the idea; the idea is the fact'. The objective critic, however, must admit that it is not easy to explain how this is done, how poetry makes ideas thick and complicated enough to hold on to emotions. In his essay on 'Hamlet and his Problems' T. S. Eliot finds Hamlet's state of emotion unsatisfactory because it lacks an 'objective correlative', a 'chain of events' which are the 'formula of that *particular* emotion'. The emotion is 'in *excess* of the facts as they appear'. It is 'inexpressible'. Yet Hamlet's emotion must be expressible, we submit, and actually expressed too (by something) in the play; otherwise Eliot would not know it is there—in excess of the facts. That Hamlet himself or Shakespeare may be baffled by the emotion is beside the point. The second chapter of Yvor Winters' *Primitivism and Decadence* has gone much further in clarifying a distinction adumbrated by Eliot. Without embracing the extreme doctrine of Winters, that if a poem cannot be paraphrased it is a poor poem, we may yet with profit reiterate his main thesis: that there is a difference between the motive, as he calls it, or logic of an emotion, and the surface or texture of a poem constructed to describe the emotion, and that both are important to a poem. Winters has shown, we think, how there can be in effect 'fine poems' about nothing. There is rational progression and there is 'qualitative progression',[8] the latter, with several subtly related modes, a characteristic of decadent poetry. Qualitative progression is the succession, the dream float, of images, not substantiated by a plot. 'Moister than an oyster in its clammy cloister, I'm bluer than a wooer who has slipped in a sewer', says Morris Bishop in a recent comic poem:

> Chiller than a killer in a cinema thriller,
> Queerer than a leerer at his leer in a mirror,
> Madder than an adder with a stone in the bladder.
> If you want to know why, I cannot but reply:
> It is really no affair of yours.[9]

The term 'pseudo statement' was for Richards a patronizing term by which he indicated the attractive nullity of poems. For Winters, the kindred term 'pseudo reference' is a name for the more disguised kinds of qualitative progression and is a term of reproach. It seems to us highly significant that for another psychological critic, Max Eastman, so important a part of poetry as metaphor is in effect too pseudo statement. The vivid realization of metaphor comes from its being in some way an obstruction to practical knowledge (like a torn coat sleeve to the act of dressing). Metaphor operates by being abnormal or inept, the wrong way of saying something. Without pressing the point, we should say that an uncomfortable resemblance to this doctrine appears in Ransom's logical structure and local texture of irrelevance.

What Winters has said seems basic. To venture both a slight elaboration of this and a return to the problem of emotive semantics surveyed in our first section: it is a well known but nonetheless important truth that there are two kinds of real objects which have emotive quality, the objects which are the reasons for human emotion, and those which by some kind of association suggest either the reasons or the resulting emotion: the thief, the enemy, or the insult that makes us angry, and the hornet that sounds and stings somewhat like ourselves when angry; the murderer or felon, and the crow that kills small birds and animals or feeds on carrion and is black like the night when crimes are committed by men. The arrangement by which these two kinds of emotive meaning are brought together in a juncture characteristic of poetry is, roughly speaking, the simile, the metaphor, and the various less clearly defined forms of association. We offer the following crude example as a kind of skeleton figure to which we believe all the issues can be attached.

I. X feels as angry as a hornet.
II. X whose lunch has been stolen feels as angry as a hornet.

No. I is, we take it, the qualitative poem, the vehicle of a metaphor, an objective correlative—for nothing. No. II adds the tenor of the metaphor, the motive for feeling angry, and hence makes the feeling itself more specific. The total statement has a more complex and testable structure. The element of aptitude, or ineptitude, is more susceptible of discussion. 'Light thickens, and the crow makes wing to the rooky wood' might be a line from a poem about nothing, but initially owed much of its power, and we daresay still does, to the fact that it is spoken by a tormented murderer who, as night draws on, has sent his agents out to perform a further 'deed of dreadful note'.

These distinctions bear a close relation to the difference between historical statement which may be a reason for emotion because it is believed (Macbeth has killed the king) and fictitious or poetic statement, where a large component of suggestion (and hence metaphor) has usually appeared. The first of course seldom occurs pure, at least not for the public eye. The coroner or the intelligence officer may content himself with it. Not the chronicler, the bard, or the newspaperman. To these we owe more or less direct words of value and emotion (the murder, the atrocity, the wholesale butchery) and all the repertoire of suggestive meanings which here and there in history—with somewhat to start upon—a Caesar or a Macbeth—have created out of a mere case of factual reason for intense emotion a specified, figuratively fortified, and permanent object of less intense but far richer emotion. With a decline of heroes and of faith in external order, we have had during the last century a great flowering of poetry which has tried the utmost to do without any hero or action or fiction of these—the qualitative poetry of Winters' analysis. It is true that any hero and action when they become fictitious take the first step towards the simply qualitative, and all poetry, so far as separate from history, tends to be formula of emotion. The hero and action are taken as symbolic. A graded series from fact to quality might include: (1) the historic Macbeth, (2) Macbeth as Renaissance tragic protagonist, (3) a *Macbeth* written by Eliot, (4) a *Macbeth* written by Pound. As Winters has explained, 'the prince is briefly introduced in the footnotes' of *The Waste Land*; 'it is to be doubted that Mr Pound could manage such an introduction'. Yet in no one of these four pages has anything like a pure emotive poetry been produced. The semantic analysis which we have offered in our first section would say that even in the last stages a poetry of pure emotion is an illusion. What we have is poetry where kings are only symbols or even a poetry of hornets and crows, rather than of human deeds. Yet a poetry about things. How these things are joined in patterns and with what names of emotion remains always the critical question. 'The *Romance of the Rose* could not, without loss,' observes C. S. Lewis, 'be rewritten as The *Romance of the Onion.*'

Poetry is characteristically a discourse about both emotions and objects, or about the emotive quality of objects. The emotions correlative to the objects of poetry become a part of the matter dealt with—not communicated to the reader like an infection or disease, not inflicted mechanically like a bullet or knife wound, not administered like a poison, not simply expressed as by expletives or grimaces or rhythms, but presented in their objects and contemplated as a pattern of knowledge. Poetry is a way of fixing emotions or making them more permanently perceptible when objects have undergone a functional change from culture to culture, or when as simple facts of history they have lost emotive value with the loss of immediacy. Though the reasons for emotion in poetry may not be so simple as Ruskin's 'noble grounds for the noble emotions', yet a great deal of constancy for poetic objects of emotion—if we will look for constancy—may be traced through the drift of human history. The murder of Duncan by Macbeth, whether as history of the eleventh century or chronicle of the sixteenth, has not tended to become the subject of a Christmas carol. In Shakespeare's play it is an act difficult to duplicate in all its immediate adjuncts of treachery, deliberation, and horror of conscience. Set in its galaxy of symbols—the hoarse raven, the thickening light, and the crow making wing, the babe plucked from the breast, the dagger in the air, the ghost, the bloody hands —this ancient murder has become an object of strongly fixed emotive value. The corpse of Polyneices, a far more ancient object and partially concealed from us by the difficulties of the Greek, shows a similar pertinacity in remaining among the understandable motives of higher duty. Funeral customs have changed, but not the intelligibility of the web of issues, religious, political, and private, woven about the corpse 'unburied, unhonoured, all unhallowed'. Again, certain objects partly obscured in one age wax into appreciation in another, and partly through the efforts of the poet. It is not true that they suddenly arrive out of nothing. The pathos of Shylock, for example, is not a creation of our time, though a smugly modern humanitarianism, because it has slogans, may suppose that this was not felt by Shakespeare or Southampton—and may not perceive its own debt to Shakespeare. 'Poets,' says Shelley, 'are the unacknowledged legislators of the world.' And it may be granted at least that poets have been leading expositors of the laws of feeling.[10]

To the relativist historian of literature falls the uncomfortable task of establishing as discrete cultural moments the past when the poem was written and first appreciated, and the present into which the poem with its clear and nicely interrelated meanings, its completeness, balance, and tension has survived. A structure of emotive objects so complex and so reliable as to have been taken for great poetry by any past age will never, it seems safe to say, so wane with the waning of human culture as not to be recoverable at least by a willing student. And on the same grounds a confidence seems indicated for the objective discrimination of all future poetic phenomena, though the premises or materials of which such poems will be constructed cannot be prescribed or foreseen. If the exegesis of some poems depends upon the understanding of obsolete or exotic customs, the poems themselves are the most precise emotive report on the customs. In the poet's finely contrived objects of emotion and in other works of art the historian finds his most reliable evidence about the emotions of antiquity —and the anthropologist, about those of contemporary primitivism. To appreciate courtly love we turn to Chrétien de Troyes and Marie de France. Certain attitudes of late fourteenth-century England, towards knighthood, towards monasticism, towards the bourgeoisie, are nowhere more precisely illustrated than in the prologue to *The Canterbury Tales*. The field worker among the Zunis or the Navahos finds no informant so informative as the poet or the member of the tribe who can quote its myths.[11] In short, though cultures have changed, poems remain and explain.

Notes

1. Richards has recently reiterated these views in the context of a more complicated account of language that seems to look in the direction of Charles Morris. See his 'Emotive language still', *Yale Review*, xxxix (1949), 108–18.

2. 'If feeling be regarded as conscious, it is unquestionable that it involves in some measure an intellectual process'. F. Paulhan, *The Laws of Feeling* (London, 1930), 153.

3. Strictly, a theory not of poetry but of morals, as, to take a curious modern instance, Lucie Guillet's *La Poéticothérapie, Efficacités du Fluide Poétique* (Paris, 1946) is a theory not of poetry but of healing. Aristotle's catharsis is a true theory of poetry, that is, part of a definition of poetry.

4. *As I Remember Him*, quoted by J. Donald Adams, 'Speaking of Books', in *New York Times Book Review*, 20 April 1947, p. 2. Mr. Adams's weekly department has been a happy hunting ground for such specimens.

5. *New Yorker*, xix (11 December 1943), 28.

6. 'The final averages showed that the combined finger movements for the Byron experiments were eighteen metres longer than they were for Keats', R. C. Givler, *The Psycho-Physiological Effect of the Elements of Speech in Relation to Poetry* (Princeton, 1915), 62.

7. 'Ueber den Film', in *Die Forderung des Tages* (Berlin, 1930), 387.

8. The term, as Winters indicates, is borrowed from Kenneth Burke's *Counter-Statement*.

9. *New Yorker*, xxiii (31 May 1947), 33.

10. Cp. Paulhan, *The Laws of Feeling*, 105, 110.

11. 'The anthropologist', says Bronislaw Malinowski, 'has the myth-maker at his elbow', *Myth in Primitive Psychology* (New York, 1926), 17.

27 George Orwell

George Orwell (1903-50), whose real name was Eric Blair, was born in India, the son of a British civil servant. He was educated in England at a prep school and then at Eton. Instead of proceeding to a university, Orwell served in the Indian Imperial Police in Burma from 1922 to 1928, an experience that provided the material for the first of his novels, *Burmese Days* (1934). For a couple of years, Orwell deliberately allowed himself to sink to the lowest strata of society, subsisting as a tramp and casual labourer, and recorded his experiences in *Down and Out in London and Paris* (1933). In 1937 he published *The Road to Wigan Pier*, a semi-autobiographical, semi-documentary study of the effects of economic depression in northern England. In the same year he went to Spain to fight on the Republican side in the Spanish Civil War, and was wounded at the front. As *Homage to Catalonia* (1938) makes clear, however, the traumatic episode of this experience for Orwell was the Communist purge of rival political elements on the Republican side. From this one may date the hardening of Orwell's distrust of all political parties, institutions, slogans, and his insistence that Stalinist Communism was a totalitarian system as odious as Nazism. In the 'thirties and during World War II this was an unpopular viewpoint in intellectual and literary circles. With the onset of the Cold War, however, the ideas Orwell expressed fictionally in *Animal Farm* (1945) and *1984* (1949), became highly topical, and brought him worldwide fame, which he did not live long to enjoy.

Throughout most of his literary career Orwell made little money from his novels, and relied upon reviewing and journalism for financial support. Most of this prose (splendidly edited by Sonia Orwell and Ian Angus in *The Collected Essays, Journalism and Letters of George Orwell*, 4 vols, 1964) was ephemeral, but it includes several long essays—on Dickens, on Shakespeare, on Swift and on literature between the wars ('Inside the Whale')—which are rare examples, for their time, of essays which manage to do justice to their subjects and communicate to the 'common reader' at the same time. Orwell's essays on 'Boys' Weeklies', on the comic postcard artist Donald McGill, and on the thriller ('From Raffles to Miss Blandish') were pioneering studies in the criticism of popular art.

'Politics and the English Language' is a characteristic production in both its strengths and its limitations. The theory of language which underlies it—the notion, for instance, that one can 'think' prior to language—is vulnerable, but this does not disqualify Orwell's pragmatic critique of linguistic usage that is either deliberately or carelessly destructive of meaning. The link Orwell makes between the corruption of language and political oppression is deeply characteristic of the man, and foreshadows the invention of 'Newspeak' in 1984. 'Politics and the English Language' was first published in 1946, and is reprinted here from *The Collected Essays, Journalism and Letters*.

CROSS REFERENCES: 28. Jean-Paul Sartre
47. W. H. Auden

COMMENTARY: Raymond Williams, *George Orwell* (1971)
Brian Wicker, 'An analysis of Newspeak',
Blackfriars xliii (1962), 272-85.

Politics and the English language

Most people who bother with the matter at all would admit that the English language is in a bad way, but it is generally assumed that we cannot by conscious action do anything about it. Our civilization is decadent, and our language —so the argument runs—must inevitably share in the general collapse. It follows that any struggle against the abuse of language is a sentimental archaism, like preferring candles to electric light or hansom cabs to aeroplanes. Underneath this lies the half-conscious belief that language is a natural growth and not an instrument which we shape for our own purposes.

Now, it is clear that the decline of a language must ultimately have political and economic causes: it is not due simply to the bad influence of this or that individual writer. But an effect can become a cause, reinforcing the original cause and producing the same effect in an intensified form, and so on indefinitely. A man may take to drink because he feels himself to be a failure, and then fail all the more completely because he drinks. It is rather the same thing that is happening to the English language. It becomes ugly and inaccurate because our thoughts are foolish, but the slovenliness of our language makes it easier for us to have foolish thoughts. The point is that the process is reversible. Modern English, especially written English, is full of bad habits which spread by imitation and which can be avoided if one is willing to take the necessary trouble. If one gets rid of these habits one can think more clearly, and to think clearly is a necessary first step towards political regeneration: so that the fight against bad English is not frivolous and is not the exclusive concern of professional writers. I will come back to this presently, and I hope that by that time the meaning of what I have said here will have become clearer. Meanwhile, here are five specimens of the English language as it is now habitually written.

These five passages have not been picked out because they are especially bad— I could have quoted far worse if I had chosen—but because they illustrate various of the mental vices from which we now suffer. They are a little below the average, but are fairly representative samples. I number them so I can refer back to them when necessary:

1. I am not, indeed, sure whether it is not true to say that the Milton who once seemed not unlike a seventeenth-century Shelley had not become, out of an experience ever more bitter in each year, more alien [*sic*] to the founder of that Jesuit sect which nothing could induce him to tolerate.

Professor Harold Laski (Essay in *Freedom of Expression*).

2. Above all, we cannot play ducks and drakes with a native battery of idioms which prescribes such egregious collocations of vocables as the Basic*a* *put up with* for *tolerate* or *put at a loss* for *bewilder*.

Professor Lancelot Hogben (*Interglossa*).

3. On the one side we have the free personality: by definition it is not neurotic, for it has neither conflict nor dream. Its desires, such as they are, are transparent, for they are just what institutional approval keeps in the forefront of consciousness; another institutional pattern would alter their number and intensity; there is little in them that is natural, irreducible, or culturally dangerous. But *on the other side*, the social bond itself is nothing but the mutual reflection of these self-secure integrities. Recall the definition of love. Is not this the very picture of a small academic? Where is there a place in this hall of mirrors for either personality or fraternity?

Essay on psychology in *Politics* (New York).

4. All the 'best people' from the gentlemen's clubs, and all the frantic Fascist captains, united in common hatred of Socialism and bestial horror of the rising tide of the mass revolutionary movements, have turned to acts of provocation, to foul incendiarism, to medieval legends of poisoned wells, to legalize their own destruction of proletarian organizations, and rouse the agitated petty-bourgeoisie to chauvinistic fervour on behalf of the fight against the revolutionary way out of the crisis.

Communist pamphlet.

5. If a new spirit *is* to be infused into this old country, there is one thorny and contentious reform which must be tackled, and that is the humanization and galvanization of the B.B.C. Timidity here will bespeak canker and atrophy of the soul. The heart of Britain may be sound and of strong beat, for instance, but the British lion's roar at present is like that of Bottom in Shakespeare's *Midsummer Night's Dream*—as gentle as any sucking dove. A virile new Britain cannot continue indefinitely to be traduced in the eyes, or rather ears, of the world by the effete languors of Langham Place, brazenly masquerading as 'standard English'. When the Voice of Britain is heard at nine o'clock, better far and infinitely less ludicrous to hear aitches honestly dropped than the present priggish, inflated, inhibited, school-ma'amish arch braying of blameless, bashful, mewing maidens!

Letter in *Tribune*.

Each of these passages has faults of its own, but, quite apart from avoidable ugliness, two qualities are common to all of them. The first is staleness of

a Basic English, a form of English with a vocabulary of only 850 words, was invented by C. K. Ogden, and intended as a medium of international communication.

imagery: the other is lack of precision. The writer either has a meaning and cannot express it, or he inadvertently says something else, or he is almost indifferent as to whether his words mean anything or not. This mixture of vagueness and sheer incompetence is the most marked characteristic of modern English prose, and especially of any kind of political writing. As soon as certain topics are raised, the concrete melts into the abstract and no one seems able to think of turns of speech that are not hackneyed: prose consists less and less of *words* chosen for the sake of their meaning, and more of *phrases* tacked together like the sections of a prefabricated hen-house. I list below, with notes and examples, various of the tricks by means of which the work of prose construction is habitually dodged:

Dying metaphors. A newly invented metaphor assists thought by evoking a visual image, while on the other hand a metaphor which is technically 'dead' (e.g. *iron resolution*) has in effect reverted to being an ordinary word and can generally be used without loss of vividness. But in between these two classes there is a huge dump of worn-out metaphors which have lost all evocative power and are merely used because they save people the trouble of inventing phrases for themselves. Examples are: *Ring the changes on, take up the cudgels for, toe the line, ride roughshod over, stand shoulder to shoulder with, play into the hands of, no axe to grind, grist to the mill, fishing in troubled waters, rift within the lute, on the order of the day, Achilles' heel, swan song, hotbed.* Many of these are used without knowledge of their meaning (what is a 'rift', for instance?), and incompatible metaphors are frequently mixed, a sure sign that the writer is not interested in what he is saying. Some metaphors now current have been twisted out of their original meaning without those who use them even being aware of the fact. For example, *toe the line* is sometimes written *tow the line.* Another example is *the hammer and the anvil,* now always used with the implication that the anvil gets the worst of it. In real life it is always the anvil that breaks the hammer, never the other way about: a writer who stopped to think what he was saying would be aware of this, and would avoid perverting the original phrase.

Operators, or verbal false limbs. These save the trouble of picking out appropriate verbs and nouns, and at the same time pad each sentence with extra syllables which give it an appearance of symmetry. Characteristic phrases are: *render inoperative, militate against, prove unacceptable, make contact with, be subjected to, give rise to, give grounds for, have the effect of, play a leading part (role) in, make itself felt, take effect, exhibit a tendency to, serve the purpose of,* etc. etc. The keynote is the elimination of simple verbs. Instead of being a single word, such as *break, stop, spoil, mend, kill,* a verb becomes a *phrase,* made up of a noun or adjective tacked on to some general-purposes verb such as *prove, serve, form, play, render.* In addition, the passive voice is wherever possible used in preference to the active, and noun constructions are used instead of gerunds (*by examination of* instead of *by examining*). The range of verbs is further cut down by means of the *-ize* and *de-* formations, and banal statements are given an appearance of profundity by means of the *not un-* formation. Simple conjunctions and prepositions are replaced by such phrases as *with respect to, having regard to, the fact that, by dint of, in view of, in the interests of, on the hypothesis that*; and the ends of sentences are saved from anticlimax by such resounding commonplaces as *greatly to be desired, cannot be left out of account, a development to be expected in the near future, deserving of serious consideration, brought to a satisfactory conclusion,* and so on and so forth.

Pretentious diction. Words like *phenomenon, element, individual* (as noun), *objective, categorical, effective, virtual, basic, primary, promote, constitute, exhibit, exploit, utilize, eliminate, liquidate,* are used to dress up simple statements and give an air of scientific impartiality to biased judgments. Adjectives like *epoch-making, epic, historic, unforgettable, triumphant, age-old, inevitable, inexorable, veritable,* are used to dignify the sordid processes of international politics, while writing that aims at glorifying war usually takes on an archaic colour, its characteristic words being: *realm, throne, chariot, mailed fist, trident, sword, shield, buckler, banner, jackboot, clarion.* Foreign words and expressions such as *cul de sac, ancien régime, deus ex machina, mutatis mutandis, status quo, Gleichschaltung, Weltanschauung,* are used to give an air of culture and elegance. Except for the useful abbreviations *i.e., e.g.,* and *etc.,* there is no real need for any of the hundreds of foreign phrases now current in English. Bad writers, and especially scientific, political, and sociological writers, are nearly always haunted by the notion that Latin or Greek words are grander than Saxon ones, and unnecessary words like *expedite, ameliorate, predict, extraneous, deracinated, clandestine, sub-aqueous* and hundreds of others constantly gain ground from their Anglo-Saxon opposite numbers.[1] The jargon peculiar to Marxist writing (*hyena, hangman, cannibal, petty bourgeois, these gentry, lackey, flunkey, mad dog, White Guard,* etc.) consists largely of words and phrases translated from Russian, German, or French; but the normal way of coining a new word is to use a Latin or Greek root with the appropriate affix and, where necessary, the *-ize* formation. It is often easier to make up words of this kind (*deregionalize, impermissible, extramarital, non-fragmentary* and so forth) than to think up the English words that will cover one's meaning. The result, in general, is an increase in slovenliness and vagueness.

Meaningless words. In certain kinds of writing, particularly in art criticism and literary criticism, it is normal to come across long passages which are almost completely lacking in meaning.[2] Words like *romantic, plastic, values, human, dead, sentimental, natural, vitality,* as used in art criticism, are strictly meaningless, in the sense that they not only do not point to any discoverable object, but are hardly even expected to do so by the reader. When one critic writes, 'The outstanding features of Mr X's work is its living quality', while another writes, 'The immediately striking thing about Mr X's work is its peculiar deadness', the reader accepts this as a simple difference of opinion. If words like *black* and *white* were involved, instead of the jargon words *dead* and *living,* he would see at once that language was being used in an improper way. Many political words are similarly abused. The word *Fascism* has now no meaning except in so far as it signifies 'something not desirable'. The words *democracy, socialism, freedom, patriotic, realistic, justice,* have each of them several different meanings which cannot be reconciled with one another. In the case of a word like *democracy,* not only is there no agreed definition, but the attempt to make one is resisted from all sides. It is almost universally felt that when we call a country democratic we are praising it: consequently the defenders of every kind of régime claim that it is a democracy, and fear that they might have to stop using the word if it were tied down to any one meaning. Words of this kind are often used in a consciously dishonest way. That is, the person who uses them has his own private definition, but allows his hearer to think he means something quite different. Statements like *Marshall Pétain was a true patriot, The Soviet press is the freest in the world, The Catholic Church is opposed to persecution,* are almost always made with intent to deceive. Other words used in variable meanings, in most cases more or less dishonestly, are: *class, totalitarian, science, progressive, reactionary, bourgeois, equality.*

Now that I have made this catalogue of swindles and perversions, let me give another example of the kind of writing that they lead to. This time it must of its nature be an imaginary one. I am going to translate a passage of good English into modern English of the worst sort. Here is a well-known verse from *Ecclesiastes*:

I returned, and saw under the sun, that the race is not to the swift, nor the battle to the strong, neither yet bread to the wise, nor yet riches to men of understanding, nor yet favour to men of skill; but time and chance happeneth to them all.

Here it is in modern English:

Objective consideration of contemporary phenomena compels the conclusion that success or failure in competitive activities exhibits no tendency to be commensurate with innate capacity, but that a considerable element of the unpredictable must invariably be taken into account.

This is a parody, but not a very gross one. Exhibit 3, above, for instance, contains several patches of the same kind of English. It will be seen that I have not made a full translation. The beginning and ending of the sentence follow the original meaning fairly closely, but in the middle the concrete illustrations— race, battle, bread—dissolve into the vague phrase 'success or failure in competitive activities'. This had to be so, because no modern writer of the kind I am discussing—no one capable of using phrases like 'objective consideration of contemporary phenomena'—would ever tabulate his thoughts in that precise and detailed way. The whole tendency of modern prose is away from concreteness. Now analyse these two sentences a little more closely. The first contains 49 words but only 60 syllables, and all its words are those of everyday life. The second contains 38 words of 90 syllables: 18 of its words are from Latin roots, and one from Greek. The first sentence contains six vivid images, and only one phrase ('time and chance') that could be called vague. The second contains not a single fresh, arresting phrase, and in spite of its 90 syllables it gives only a shortened version of the meaning contained in the first. Yet without a doubt it is the second kind of sentence that is gaining ground in modern English. I do not want to exaggerate. This kind of writing is not yet universal, and outcrops of simplicity will occur here and there in the worst-written page. Still, if you or I were told to write a few lines on the uncertainty of human fortunes, we should probably come much nearer to my imaginary sentence than to the one from *Ecclesiastes.*

As I have tried to show, modern writing at its worst does not consist in picking out words for the sake of their meaning and inventing images in order to make the meaning clearer. It consists in gumming together long strips of words which have already been set in order by someone else, and making the results presentable by sheer humbug. The attraction of this way of writing is that it is easy. It is easier—even quicker, once you have the habit—to say *In my opinion it is a not unjustifiable assumption that* than to say *I think*. If you use ready-made phrases, you not only don't have to hunt about for words; you also don't have to bother with the rhythms of your sentences, since these phrases are generally so arranged as to be more or less euphonious. When you are composing in a hurry—when you are dictating to a stenographer, for instance, or making a public speech—it is natural to fall into a pretentious, latinized style. Tags like *a consideration which we should do well to bear in mind* or *a conclusion to which all of us would readily assent* will save many a sentence from coming down with a bump. By using stale metaphors, similes, and idioms, you save much mental effort, at the cost of leaving your meaning vague, not only for your reader but for yourself. This is the significance of mixed metaphors. The sole aim of a metaphor is to call up a visual image. When these images clash —as in *The Fascist octopus has sung its swan song, the jackboot is thrown into the melting pot*—it can be taken as certain that the writer is not seeing a mental image of the objects he is naming; in other words he is not really thinking. Look again at the examples I gave at the beginning of this essay. Professor Laski (1) uses five negatives in 53 words. One of these is superfluous, making nonsense of the whole passage, and in addition there is the slip *alien* for akin, making further nonsense, and several avoidable pieces of clumsiness which increase the general vagueness. Professor Hogben (2) plays ducks and drakes with a battery which is able to write prescriptions, and, while disapproving of the everyday phrase *put up with*, is unwilling to look *egregious* up in the dictionary and see what it means. (3), if one takes an uncharitable attitude towards it, is simply meaningless: probably one could work out its intended meaning by reading the whole of the article in which it occurs. In (4) the writer knows more or less what he wants to say, but an accumulation of stale phrases chokes him like tea-leaves blocking a sink. In (5) words and meaning have almost parted company. People who write in this manner usually have a general emotional meaning—they dislike one thing and want to express solidarity with another—but they are not interested in the detail of what they are saying. A scrupulous writer, in every sentence that he writes, will ask himself at least four questions, thus: What am I trying to say? What words will express it? What image or idiom will make it clearer? Is this image fresh enough to have an effect? And he will probably ask himself two more: Could I put it more shortly? Have I said anything that is avoidably ugly? But you are not obliged to go to all this trouble. You can shirk it by simply throwing your mind open and letting the ready-made phrases come crowding in. They will construct your sentences for you—even think your thoughts for you, to a certain extent—and at need they will perform the important service of partially concealing your meaning even from yourself. It is at this point that the special connection between politics and the debasement of language becomes clear.

In our time it is broadly true that political writing is bad writing. Where it is not true, it will generally be found that the writer is some kind of rebel, expressing his private opinions, and not a 'party line'. Orthodoxy, of whatever colour, seems to demand a lifeless, imitative style. The political dialects to be found in pamphlets, leading articles, manifestos, White Papers and the speeches of Under-Secretaries do, of course, vary from party to party, but they are all alike in that one almost never finds in them a fresh, vivid, home-made turn of speech. When one watches some tired hack on the platform mechanically repeating the familiar phrases—*bestial atrocities, iron heel, bloodstained tyranny, free peoples of the world, stand shoulder to shoulder*—one often has a curious feeling that one is not watching a live human being but some kind of dummy: a feeling which suddenly becomes stronger at moments when the light catches the speaker's spectacles and turns them into blank discs which seem to have no eyes behind them. And this is not altogether fanciful. A speaker who uses that kind of phraseology has gone some distance towards turning himself into a machine. The appropriate noises are coming out of his larynx, but his brain is not involved as it would be if he were choosing words for himself. If the speech he is making is one that he is accustomed to make over and over again, he may be almost unconscious of what he is saying, as one is when one utters the responses in church. And this reduced state of consciousness, if not indispensable, is at any rate favourable to political conformity.

In our time, political speech and writing are largely the defence of the indefensible. Things like the continuance of British rule in India, the Russian purges and deportations, the dropping of the atom bombs on Japan, can indeed be defended, but only by arguments which are too brutal for most people to face, and which do not square with the professed aims of political parties. Thus political language has to consist largely of euphemism, question-begging and sheer cloudy vagueness. Defenceless villages are bombarded from the air, the inhabitants driven out into the countryside, the cattle machine-gunned, the huts set on fire with incendiary bullets: this is called *pacification*. Millions of peasants are robbed of their farms and sent trudging along the roads with no more than they can carry: this is called *transfer of population* or *rectification of frontiers*. People are imprisoned for years without trial, or shot in the back of the neck or sent to die of scurvy in Arctic lumber camps: this is called *elimination of unreliable elements*. Such phraseology is needed if one wants to name things without calling up mental pictures of them. Consider for instance some comfortable English professor defending Russian totalitarianism. He cannot say outright, 'I believe in killing off your opponents when you can get good results by doing so'. Probably, therefore, he will say something like this:

> While freely conceding that the Soviet régime exhibits certain features which the humanitarian may be inclined to deplore, we must, I think, agree that a certain curtailment of the right to political opposition is an unavoidable concomitant of transitional periods, and that the rigours which the Russian people have been called upon to undergo have been amply justified in the sphere of concrete achievement.

The inflated style is itself a kind of euphemism. A mass of Latin words falls upon the facts like soft snow, blurring the outlines and covering up all the details. The great enemy of clear language is insincerity. When there is a gap between one's real and one's declared aims, one turns as it were instinctively to long words and exhausted idioms, like a cuttlefish squirting out ink. In our age there is no such thing as 'keeping out of politics'. All issues are political issues, and politics itself is a mass of lies, evasions, folly, hatred, and schizophrenia. When the general atmosphere is bad, language must suffer. I should expect to find—this is a guess which I have not sufficient knowledge to verify—that the German, Russian, and Italian languages have all deteriorated in the last ten or fifteen years, as a result of dictatorship.

But if thought corrupts language, language can also corrupt thought. A bad usage can spread by tradition and imitation, even among people who should and do know better. The debased language that I have been discussing is in some ways very convenient. Phrases like *a not unjustifiable assumption, leaves much to be desired, would serve no good purpose, a consideration which we should do well to bear in mind*, are a continuous temptation, a packet of aspirins always at one's elbow. Look back through this essay, and for certain you will find that I have again and again committed the very faults I am protesting against. By this morning's post I have received a pamphlet dealing with conditions in Germany. The author tells me that he 'felt impelled' to write it. I open it at random, and here is almost the first sentence that I see: '(The Allies) have an opportunity not only of achieving a radical transformation of Germany's social and political structure in such a way as to avoid a nationalistic reaction in Germany itself, but at the same time of laying the foundations of a co-operative and unified Europe.' You see, he 'feels impelled' to write—feels, presumably, that he has something new to say—and yet his words, like cavalry horses answering the bugle, group themselves automatically into the familiar dreary pattern. This invasion of one's mind by ready-made phrases (*lay the foundations, achieve a radical transformation*) can only be prevented if one is constantly on guard against them, and every such phrase anaesthetizes a portion of one's brain.

I said earlier that the decadence of our language is probably curable. Those who deny this would argue, if they produced an argument at all, that language merely reflects existing social conditions, and that we cannot influence its development by any direct tinkering with words and constructions. So far as the general tone or spirit of a language goes, this may be true, but it is not true in detail. Silly words and expressions have often disappeared, not through any evolutionary process but owing to the conscious action of a minority. Two recent examples were *explore every avenue* and *leave no stone unturned*, which were killed by the jeers of a few journalists. There is a long list of fly-blown metaphors which could similarly be got rid of if enough people would interest themselves in the job; and it should also be possible to laugh the *not un-* formation out of existence,[3] to reduce the amount of Latin and Greek in the average sentence, to drive out foreign phrases and strayed scientific words, and, in general, to make pretentiousness unfashionable. But all these are minor points. The defence of the English language implies more than this, and perhaps it is best to start by saying what it does *not* imply.

To begin with, it has nothing to do with archaism, with the salvaging of obsolete words and turns of speech, or with the setting-up of a 'standard English' which must never be departed from. On the contrary, it is especially concerned with the scrapping of every word or idiom which has outworn its usefulness. It has nothing to do with correct grammar and syntax, which are of no importance so long as one makes one's meaning clear or with the avoidance of Americanisms, or with having what is called a 'good prose style'. On the other hand it is not concerned with fake simplicity and the attempt to make written English colloquial. Nor does it even imply in every case preferring the Saxon word to the Latin one, though it does imply using the fewest and shortest words that will cover one's meaning. What is above all needed is to let the meaning choose the word, and not the other way about. In prose, the worst thing one can do with words is to surrender to them. When you think of a concrete object, you think wordlessly, and then, if you want to describe the thing you have been visualizing, you probably hunt about till you find the exact words that seem to fit it. When you think of something abstract you are more inclined to use words from the start, and unless you make a conscious effort to prevent it, the existing dialect will come rushing in and do the job for you, at the expense of blurring or even changing your meaning. Probably it is better to put off using words as long as possible and get one's meaning as clear as one can through pictures or sensations. Afterwards one can choose—not simply *accept*—the phrases that will best cover the meaning, and then switch round and decide what impression one's words are likely to make on another person. This last effort of the mind cuts out all stale or mixed images, all prefabricated phrases, needless repetitions, and humbug and vagueness generally. But one can often be in doubt about the effect of a word or a phrase, and one needs rules that one can rely on when instinct fails. I think the following rules will cover most cases:

i. Never use a metaphor, simile, or other figure of speech which you are used to seeing in print.
ii. Never use a long word where a short one will do.
iii. If it is possible to cut a word out, always cut it out.
iv. Never use the passive where you can use the active.

v. Never use a foreign phrase, a scientific word, or a jargon word if you can think of an everyday English equivalent.

vi. Break any of these rules sooner than say anything outright barbarous.

These rules sound elementary, and so they are, but they demand a deep change of attitude in anyone who has grown used to writing in the style now fashionable. One could keep all of them and still write bad English, but one could not write the kind of stuff that I quoted in those five speciments at the beginning of this article.

I have not here been considering the literary use of language, but merely language as an instrument for expressing and not for concealing or preventing thought. Stuart Chase and others have come near to claiming that all abstract words are meaningless, and have used this as a pretext for advocating a kind of political quietism. Since you don't know what Fascism is, how can you struggle against Fascism? One need not swallow such absurdities as this, but one ought to recognize that the present political chaos is connected with the decay of language, and that one can probably bring about some improvement by starting at the verbal end. If you simplify your English, you are freed from the worst follies of orthodoxy. You cannot speak any of the necessary dialects, and when you make a stupid remark its stupidity will be obvious, even to yourself. Political language—and with variations this is true of all political parties, from Conservatives to Anarchists—is designed to make lies sound truthful and murder respectable, and to give an appearance of solidity to pure wind. One cannot change this all in a moment, but one can at least change one's own habits, and from time to time one can even, if one jeers loudly enough, send some worn-out and useless phrase—some *jackboot, Achilles' heel, hotbed, melting pot, acid test, veritable inferno* or other lump of verbal refuse—into the dustbin where it belongs.

Notes

1. An interesting illustration of this is the way in which the English flower names which were in use till very recently are being ousted by Greek ones, *snapdragon* becoming *antirrhinum, forget-me-not* becoming *myosotis*, etc. It is hard to see any practical reason for this change of fashion: it is probably due to an instinctive turning-away from the more homely word and a vague feeling that the Greek word is scientific.

2. Example: 'Comfort's catholicity of perception and image, strangely Whitmanesque in range, almost the exact opposite in aesthetic compulsion, continues to evoke that trembling atmospheric accumulative hinting at a cruel, an inexorably serene timelessness.... Wrey Gardiner scores by aiming at simple bullseyes with precision. Only they are not so simple, and through this contented sadness runs more than the surface bitter-sweet of resignation.' (*Poetry Quarterly*.)

3. One can cure oneself of the *not un-* formation by memorizing this sentence: A *not unblack dog was chasing a not unsmall rabbit across a not ungreen field.*

28   Jean-Paul Sartre

Jean-Paul Sartre (b. 1905) is one of the great Frenchmen of the twentieth
century, renowned inside and outside his own country as philosopher, novelist,
dramatist and political journalist. His first novel, La Nausée (1938), attracted
little attention on its first appearance, but has since become a modern classic. It
was in World War II, during the Nazi occupation of France that Sartre (himself
a member of the Resistance) became well known as the author of plays, like
Les Mouches [The Flies] (1942), which gave subtly disguised encouragement
to his oppressed countrymen. In 1943 Sartre published his great philosophical
treatise, L'Etre et le Néant [Being and Nothingness]. The atheistic existentialism
expounded in this book, affirming that the individual is, paradoxically, both
autonomous and responsible, made Sartre the most influential French
intellectual in the immediate postwar period. Although his relationship with
the official Communist Party has been stormy and contentious, he has always
been a man of the far Left, and a spirited apologist for the idea of an
ideologically committed or engagé literature. In 1947 Sartre published a series
of essays expounding this theory of literature in the magazine Les Temps
Modernes which he himself had founded two years previously, and these essays
were subsequently collected into a volume entitled Qu'est que c'est la Littérature?
[What is Literature?] (Paris, 1947). 'Why write?' is the second chapter of this
book, and is reprinted here from the translation of Bernard Frechtman (1949).

In the first chapter, 'What is Writing?', Sartre skilfully, if somewhat
speciously, excludes poetry from the scope of his discussion by classing poetry
with painting, sculpture, and music on the grounds that it treats words as
things: 'For the word, which tears the writer of prose away from himself and
throws him into the midst of the world, sends back to the poet his own image,
like a mirror.' It is essentially the distinction made by Valéry (see above,
pp. 253-61), but with the priorities reversed. In the second chapter, 'Why
Write?' Sartre develops a phenomenological view of the work of literature as
existing by virtue of a collaboration between writer and reader. It is a subtle,
profound, and eloquent argument, which applies to more than Sartre's category
of engagé writing.

Jean-Paul Sartre was offered the Nobel Prize for Literature in 1964, but
declined it on ideological grounds. Among his more recent writings, his
psychological study of Jean Genet, Saint Genet (Paris, 1963), and his short,
scintillating volume of autobiography Les Mots [Words] (Paris, 1963), are of
special interest to students of literature.

CROSS REFERENCES: 20. Paul Valéry
                  27. George Orwell
                  29. Mark Schorer
                  42. Wayne Booth
                  43. Raymond Williams

COMMENTARY: Benjamin Suhl, *Jean-Paul Sartre: the philosopher as a literary critic* (1970)

Why write?

Each one has his reasons: for one, art is a flight; for another, a means of conquering. But one can flee into a hermitage, into madness, into death. One can conquer by arms. Why does it have to be *writing*, why does one have to manage his escapes and conquests by *writing*? Because, behind the various aims of authors, there is a deeper and more immediate choice which is common to all of us. We shall try to elucidate this choice, and we shall see whether it is not in the name of this very choice of writing that the engagement of writers must be required.

Each of our perceptions is accompanied by the consciousness that human reality is a 'revealer', that is, it is through human reality that 'there is' being, or, to put it differently, that man is the means by which things are manifested. It is our presence in the world which multiplies relations. It is we who set up a relationship between this tree and that bit of sky. Thanks to us, that star which has been dead for millennia, that quarter moon, and that dark river are disclosed in the unity of a landscape. It is the speed of our auto and our airplane which organizes the great masses of the earth. With each of our acts, the world reveals to us a new face. But, if we know that we are directors of being, we also know that we are not its producers. If we turn away from this landscape, it will sink back into its dark permanence. At least, it will sink back; there is no one mad enough to think that it is going to be annihilated. It is we who shall be annihilated, and the earth will remain in its lethargy until another consciousness comes along to awaken it. Thus, to our inner certainty of being 'revealers' is added that of being inessential in relation to the thing revealed.

One of the chief motives of artistic creation is certainly the need of feeling that we are essential in relationship to the world. If I fix on canvas or in writing a certain aspect of the fields or the sea or a look on someone's face which I have disclosed, I am conscious of having produced them by condensing relationships, by introducing order where there was none, by imposing the unity of mind on the diversity of things. That is, I feel myself essential in relation to my creation. But this time it is the created object which escapes me; I can not reveal and

371

produce at the same time. The creation becomes inessential in relation to the creative activity. First of all, even if it appears to others as definitive, the created object always seems to us in a state of suspension; we can always change this line, that shade, that word. Thus, it never *forces itself*. A novice painter asked his teacher, 'When should I consider my painting finished?' And the teacher answered, 'When you can look at it in amazement and say to yourself "*I'm* the one who did *that!*"'

Which amounts to saying 'never'. For it is virtually considering one's work with someone else's eyes and revealing what one has created. But it is self-evident that we are proportionally less conscious of the thing produced and more conscious of our productive activity. When it is a matter of poetry or carpentry, we work according to traditional norms, with tools whose usage is codified; it is Heidegger's famous 'they'[a] who are working with our hands. In this case, the result can seem to us sufficiently strange to preserve its objectivity in our eyes. But if we ourselves produce the rules of production, the measures, the criteria, and if our creative drive comes from the very depths of our heart, then we never find anything but ourselves in our work. It is we who have invented the laws by which we judge it. It is our history, our love, our gaiety that we recognize in it. Even if we should regard it without touching it any further, we never *receive* from it that gaiety or love. We put them into it. The results which we have obtained on canvas or paper never seem to us *objective*. We are too familiar with the processes of which they are the effects. These processes remain a subjective discovery; they are ourselves, our inspiration, our ruse, and when we seek to *perceive* our work, we create it again, we repeat mentally the operations which produced it; each of its aspects appears as a result. Thus, in the perception, the object is given as the essential thing and the subject as the inessential. The latter seeks essentiality in the creation and obtains it, but then it is the object which becomes the inessential.

The dialectic is nowhere more apparent than in the art of writing, for the literary object is a peculiar top which exists only in movement. To make it come into view a concrete act called reading is necessary, and it lasts only as long as this act can last. Beyond that, there are only black marks on paper. Now, the writer can not read what he writes, whereas the shoemaker can put on the shoes he has just made if they are his size, and the architect can live in the house he has built. In reading, one foresees; one waits. He foresees the end of the sentence, the following sentence, the next page. He waits for them to confirm or disappoint his foresights. The reading is composed of a host of hypotheses, of dreams followed by awakenings, of hopes and deceptions. Readers are

[a] Martin Heidegger (b. 1889), German existentialist philosopher who greatly influenced Sartre. John Passmore summarizes this aspect of his thought as follows: 'Indeed, in its most characteristic, "everyday" form, Human Existence consists not in being oneself—revealing one's own *Existenz*—but in being "They" (or as the German illuminatingly has it, *Man*). In our everyday "average" life we act as "the others" act, not because we have *deliberately chosen* to conform to "the tasks, the rules, the standards, the urgency" of others, but simply because "acting as They do" is the typical mode of behaviour of Human Existence. "Acting as They do", however, although "everyday" is none the less "inauthentic".' *A Hundred Years of Philosophy* (Penguin edn, 1968).

always ahead of the sentence they are reading in a merely probable future which partly collapses and partly comes together in proportion as they progress, which withdraws from one page to the next and forms the moving horizon of the literary object. Without waiting, without a future, without ignorance, there is no objectivity.

Now the operation of writing involves an implicit quasi-reading which makes real reading impossible. When the words form under his pen, the author doubtless sees them, but he does not see them as the reader does, since he knows them before writing them down. The function of his gaze is not to reveal, by stroking them, the sleeping words which are waiting to be read, but to control the sketching of the signs. In short, it is a purely regulating mission, and the view before him reveals nothing except for slight slips of pen. The writer neither foresees nor conjectures; he *projects*. It often happens that he awaits, as they say, the inspiration. But one does not wait for himself the way he waits for others. If he hesitates, he knows that the future is not made, that he himself is going to make it, and if he still does not know what is going to happen to his hero, that simply means that he has not thought about it, that he has not decided upon anything. The future is then a blank page, whereas the future of the reader is two hundred pages filled with words which separate him from the end. Thus, the writer meets everywhere only *his* knowledge, *his* will, *his* plans, in short, himself. He touches only his own subjectivity; the object he creates is out of reach; he does not create it *for himself*. If he re-reads himself, it is already too late. The sentence will never quite be a thing in his eyes. He goes to the very limits of the subjective but without crossing it. He appreciates the effect of a touch, of an epigram, of a well-placed adjective, but it is the effect they will have on others. He can judge it, not feel it. Proust never discovered the homosexuality of Charlus, since he had decided upon it even before starting on his book. And if a day comes when the book takes on for its author a semblance of objectivity, it is that years have passed, that he has forgotten it, that its spirit is quite foreign to him, and doubtless he is no longer capable of writing it. This was the case with Rousseau when he re-read the *Social Contract* at the end of his life.

Thus, it is not true that one writes for himself. That would be the worst blow. In projecting his emotions on paper, one barely manages to give them a languishing extension. The creative act is only an incomplete and abstract moment in the production of a work. If the author existed alone he would be able to write as much as he liked; the work as *object* would never see the light of day and he would either have to put down his pen or despair. But the operation of writing implies that of reading as its dialectical correlative and these two connected acts necessitate two distinct agents. It is the conjoint effort of author and reader which brings upon the scene that concrete and imaginary object which is the work of the mind. There is no art except for and by others.

Reading seems, in fact, to be the synthesis of perception and creation.[1] It supposes the essentiality of both the subject and the object. The object is essential because it is strictly transcendent, because it imposes its own structures, and because one must wait for it and observe it; but the subject is also essential because it is required not only to disclose the object (that is, to make *there be* an object) but also so that this object might *be* (that is, to produce it). In a word, the reader is conscious of disclosing in creating, of creating by disclosing. In reality, it is not necessary to believe that reading is a mechanical operation and that signs make an impression upon him as light does on a photographic plate. If he is inattentive, tired, stupid, or thoughtless, most of the relations will escape him. He will never manage to 'catch on' to the object (in the sense in which we see that fire 'catches' or 'doesn't catch'). He will draw some phrases out of the shadow, but they will seem to appear as random strokes. If he is at his best, he will project beyond the words a synthetic form, each phrase of which will be no more than a partial function: the 'theme', the 'subject', or the 'meaning'. Thus, from the very beginning, the meaning is no longer contained in the words, since it is he, on the contrary, who allows the signification of each of them to be understood; and the literary object, though realized *through* language, is never given *in* language. On the contrary, it is by nature a silence and an opponent of the word. In addition, the hundred thousand words aligned in a book can be read one by one so that the meaning of the work does not emerge. Nothing is accomplished if the reader does not put himself from the very beginning and almost without a guide at the height of this silence; if, in short, he does not invent it and does not then place there, and hold on to, the words and sentences which he awakens. And if I am told that it would be more fitting to call this operation a re-invention or a discovery, I shall answer that, first, such a re-invention would be as new and as original an act as the first invention. And, especially, when an object has never existed before, there can be no question of re-inventing it or discovering it. For if the silence about which I am speaking is really the goal at which the author is aiming, he has, at least, never been familiar with it; his silence is subjective and anterior to language. It is the absence of words, the undifferentiated and lived silence of inspiration, which the word will then particularize, whereas the silence produced by the reader is an object. And at the very interior of this object there are more silences—which the author does not tell. It is a question of silences which are so particular that they could not retain any meaning outside of the object which the reading causes to appear. However, it is these which give it its density and its particular face.

To say that they are unexpressed is hardly the word; for they are precisely the inexpressible. And that is why one does not come upon them at any definite moment in the reading; they are everywhere and nowhere. The quality of the marvellous in [Alain-Fournier's] *The Wanderer* (*Le Grande Meaulnes*), the grandiosity of *Armance*[a], the degree of realism and truth of Kafka's mythology, these are never given. The reader must invent them all in a continual exceeding of the written thing. To be sure, the author guides him, but all he does is guide him. The landmarks he sets up are separated by the void. The reader must unite them; he must go beyond them. In short, reading is directed creation.

On the one hand, the literary object has no other substance than the reader's subjectivity; Raskolnikov's[b] waiting is *my* waiting which I lend him. Without

[a] *Armance* (1827) was the first of Stendhal's novels to be published.
[b] Chief character of Dotoyevsky's *Crime and Punishment* (1866).

this impatience of the reader he would remain only a collection of signs. His hatred of the police magistrate who questions him is my hatred which has been solicited and wheedled out of me by signs, and the police magistrate himself would not exist without the hatred I have for him via Raskolnikov. That is what animates him, it is his very flesh.

But on the other hand, the words are there like traps to arouse our feelings and to reflect them towards us. Each word is a path of transcendence; it shapes our feelings, names them, and attributes them to an imaginary personage who takes it upon himself to live them for us and who has no other substance than these borrowed passions; he confers objects, perspectives, and a horizon upon them.

Thus, for the reader, all is to do and all is already done; the work exists only at the exact level of his capacities; while he reads and creates, he knows that he can always go further in his reading, can always create more profoundly, and thus the work seems to him as inexhaustible and opaque as things. We would readily reconcile that 'rational intuition' which Kant reserved to divine Reason with this absolute production of qualities, which, to the extent that they emanate from our subjectivity, congeal before our eyes into impermeable objectivities.

Since the creation can find its fulfilment only in reading, since the artist must entrust to another the job of carrying out what he has begun, since it is only through the consciousness of the reader that he can regard himself as essential to his work, all literary work is an appeal. To write is to make an appeal to the reader that he lead into objective existence the revelation which I have undertaken by means of language. And if it should be asked *to what* the writer is appealing, the answer is simple. As the sufficient reason for the appearance of the aesthetic object is never found either in the book (where we find merely solicitations to produce the object) or in the author's mind, and as his subjectivity, which he cannot get away from, cannot give a reason for the act of leading into objectivity, the appearance of the work of art is a new event which cannot *be explained* by anterior data. And since this directed creation is an absolute beginning, it is therefore brought about by the freedom of the reader, and by what is purest in that freedom. Thus, the writer appeals to the reader's freedom to collaborate in the production of his work.

It will doubtless be said that all tools address themselves to our freedom since they are the instruments of a possible action, and that the work of art is not unique in that. And it is true that the tool is the congealed outlines of an operation. But it remains on the level of the hypothetical imperative. I may use a hammer to nail up a case or to hit my neighbour over the head. In so far as I consider it in itself, it is not an appeal to my freedom; it does not put me face to face with it; rather, it aims at using it by substituting a set succession of traditional procedures for the free invention of means. The book does not serve my freedom; it requires it. Indeed, one cannot address himself to freedom as such by means of constraint, fascination, or entreaties. There is only one way of attaining it; first, by recognizing it, then, having confidence in it, and finally, requiring of it an act, an act in its own name, that is, in the name of the confidence that one brings to it.

Thus, the book is not, like the tool, a means for any end whatever; the end to which it offers itself is the reader's freedom. And the Kantian expression 'finality without end' seems to me quite inappropriate for designating the work of art. In fact, it implies that the aesthetic object presents only the appearance of a finality and is limited to soliciting the free and ordered play of the imagination. It forgets that the imagination of the spectator has not only a regulating function, but a constitutive one. It does not play; it is called upon to recompose the beautiful object beyond the traces left by the artist. The imagination can not revel in itself any more than can the other functions of the mind; it is always on the outside, always engaged in an enterprise. There would be finality without end if some object offered such a set ordering that it would lead us to suppose that it has one even though we can not ascribe one to it. By defining the beautiful in this way one can—and this is Kant's aim—liken the beauty of art to natural beauty, since a flower, for example, presents so much symmetry, such harmonious colours, and such regular curves, that one is immediately tempted to seek a finalist explanation for all these properties and to see them as just so many means at the disposal of an unknown end. But that is exactly the error. The beauty of nature is in no way comparable to that of art. The work of art *does not have* an end; there we agree with Kant. But the reason is that it is an end. The Kantian formula does not account for the appeal which resounds at the basis of each painting, each statue, each book. Kant believes that the work of art first exists as fact and that it is then seen. Whereas, it exists only if one *looks* at it and if it is first pure appeal, pure exigence to exist. It is not an instrument whose existence is manifest and whose end is undetermined. It presents itself as a task to be discharged; from the very beginning it places itself on the level of the categorical imperative. You are perfectly free to leave that book on the table. But if you open it, you assume responsibility for it. For freedom is not experienced by its enjoying its free subjective functioning, but in a creative act required by an imperative. This absolute end, this imperative which is transcendent yet acquiesced in, which freedom itself adopts as its own, is what we call a value. The work of art is a value because it is an appeal.

If I appeal to my reader so that we may carry the enterprise which I have begun to a successful conclusion, it is self-evident that I consider him as a pure freedom, as an unconditioned activity; thus, in no case can I address myself to his passivity, that is, try to *affect* him, to communicate to him, from the very first, emotions of fear, desire, or anger. There are, doubtless, authors who concern themselves solely with arousing these emotions because they are foreseeable, manageable, and because they have at their disposal sure-fire means for provoking them. But it is also true that they are reproached for this kind of thing, as Euripides has been since antiquity because he had children appear on the stage. Freedom is alienated in the state of passion; it is abruptly engaged in partial enterprises; it loses sight of its task which is to produce an absolute end. And the book is no longer anything but a means for feeding hate or desire. The writer should not seek to *overwhelm*; otherwise he is in contradiction with himself; if he wishes to *make demands* he must propose only the task to be fulfilled.

Hence, the character of pure presentation which appears essential to the work of art. The reader must be able to make a certain aesthetic withdrawal. This is what Gautier foolishly confused with 'art for art's sake' and the Parnassians with the imperturbability of the artist. It is simply a matter of precaution, and Genet more justly calls it the author's politeness towards the reader. But that does not mean that the writer makes an appeal to some sort of abstract and conceptual freedom. One certainly creates the aesthetic object with feelings; if it is touching, it appears through our tears; if it is comic, it will be recognized by laughter. However, these feelings are of a particular kind. They have their origin in freedom; they are loaned. The belief which I accord the tale is freely assented to. It is a Passion, in the Christian sense of the word, that is, a freedom which resolutely puts itself into a state of passivity to obtain a certain transcendent effect by this sacrifice. The reader renders himself credulous; he descends into credulity which, though it ends by enclosing him like a dream, is at every moment conscious of being free. An effort is sometimes made to force the writer into this dilemma: 'Either one believes in your story, and it is intolerable, or one does not believe in it, and it is ridiculous.' But the argument is absurd because the characteristic of aesthetic consciousness is to be a belief by means of engagement, by oath, a belief sustained by fidelity to one's self and to the author, a perpetually renewed choice to believe. I can awaken at every moment, and I know it; but I do not want to; reading is a free dream. So that all feelings which are exacted on the basis of this imaginary belief are like particular modulations of my freedom. Far from absorbing or masking it, they are so many different ways it has chosen to reveal itself to itself. Raskolnikov, as I have said, would only be a shadow, without the mixture of repulsion and friendship which I feel for him and which makes him live. But, by a reversal which is the characteristic of the imaginary object, it is not his behaviour which excites my indignation or esteem, but my indignation and esteem which give consistency and objectivity to his behaviour. Thus, the reader's feelings are never dominated by the object, and as no external reality can condition them, they have their permanent source in freedom; that is, they are all generous— for I call a feeling generous which has its origin and its end in freedom. Thus, reading is an exercise in generosity, and what the writer requires of the reader is not the application of an abstract freedom but the gift of his whole person, with his passions, his prepossessions, his sympathies, his sexual temperament, and his scale of values. Only this person will give himself generously; freedom goes through and through him and comes to transform the darkest masses of his sensibility. And as activity has rendered itself passive in order for it better to create the object, vice-versa, passivity becomes an act; the man who is reading has raised himself to the highest degree. That is why we see people who are known for their toughness shed tears at the recital of imaginary misfortunes; for the moment they have become what they would have been if they had not spent their lives hiding their freedom from themselves.

Thus, the author writes in order to address himself to the freedom of readers, and he requires it in order to make his work exist. But he does not stop there; he also requires that they return this confidence which he has given them, that they recognize his creative freedom, and that they in turn solicit it by a symmetrical and inverse appeal. Here there appears the other dialectical paradox of reading; the more we experience our freedom, the more we recognize that of the other; the more he demands of us, the more we demand of him.

When I am enchanted with a landscape, I know very well that it is not I who create it, but I also know that without me the relations which are established before my eyes among the trees, the foliage, the earth, and the grass would not exist at all. I know that I can give no reason for the appearance of finality which I discover in the assortment of hues and in the harmony of the forms and movements created by the wind. Yet, it exists; there it is before my eyes, and I can make *there be* being only if being already *is*. But even if I believe in God, I can not establish any passage, unless it be purely verbal, between the divine, universal solicitude and the particular spectacle which I am considering. To say that He made the landscape in order to charm me or that He made me the kind of person who is pleased by it is to take a question for an answer. Is the marriage of this blue and that green deliberate? How can I know? The idea of a universal providence is no guarantee of any particular intention, especially in the case under consideration, since the green of the grass is explained by biological laws, specific constants, and geographical determinism, while the reason for the blue of the water is accounted for by the depth of the river, the nature of the soil and the swiftness of the current. The assorting of the shades, if it is willed, can only be something *thrown into the bargain*; it is the meeting of two causal series, that is to say, at first sight, a fact of chance. At best, the finality remains problematic. All the relations we establish remain hypotheses; no end is proposed to us in the manner of an imperative, since none is expressly revealed as having been willed by a creator. Thus, our freedom is never *called forth* by natural beauty. Or rather, there is an appearance of order in the ensemble of the foliage, the forms, and the movements, hence, the illusion of a calling forth which seems to solicit this freedom and which appears immediately when one regards it. Hardly have we begun to run our eyes over this argument, than the call disappears; we remain alone, free to tie up one colour with another or with a third, to set up a relationship between the tree and the water or the tree and the sky, or the tree, the water, and the sky. My freedom becomes caprice. To the extent that I establish new relationships, I remove myself further from the illusory objectivity which solicits me. I *muse* about certain motifs which are vaguely outlined by the things; the natural reality is no longer anything but a pretext for musing. Or, in that case, because I have deeply regretted that this arrangement which was momentarily perceived was not offered to me by somebody and consequently is not *real*, the result is that I fix my dream, that I transpose it to canvas or in writing. Thus, I interpose myself between the finality without end which appears in the natural spectacles and the gaze of other men. I transmit it to them. It becomes human by this transmission. Art here is a ceremony of the *gift* and the gift alone brings about the metamorphosis. It is something like the transmission of titles and powers in the matriarchate where the mother does not possess the names, but is the indispensable intermediary between uncle and nephew. Since I have captured this illusion in flight, since I lay it out for other men and have disengaged it and rethought it for them, they can consider it with confidence. It has become intentional. As for me, I remain, to be sure, at the border of the subjective and the objective without ever being able to contemplate the objective *ordonnance* which I transmit.

The reader, on the contrary, progresses in security. However far he may go, the author has gone farther. Whatever connections he may establish among the different parts of the book—among the chapters or the words—he has a guarantee, namely, that they have been expressly willed. As Descartes says, he can even pretend that there is a secret order among parts which seem to have no connection. The creator has preceded him along the way, and the most beautiful disorders are effects of art, that is, again order. Reading is induction, interpolation, extrapolation, and the basis of these activities rests on the reader's will, as for a long time it was believed that that of scientific induction rested on the divine will. A gentle force accompanies us and supports us from the first page to the last. That does not mean that we fathom the artist's intentions easily. They constitute, as we have said, the object of conjectures, and there is an *experience* of the reader; but these conjunctures are supported by the great certainty we have that the beauties which appear in the book are never accidental. In nature, the tree and the sky harmonize only by chance; if, on the contrary, in the novel, the protagonists find themselves in a *certain* tower, in a *certain* prison, if they stroll in a *certain* garden, it is a matter both of the restitution of independent causal series (the character had a certain state of mind which was due to a succession of psychological and social events; on the other hand, he betook himself to a determined place and the layout of the city required him to cross a certain park) and of the expression of a deeper finality, for the park came into existence only *in order to* harmonize with a certain state of mind, to express it by means of things or to put it into relief by a vivid contrast, and the state of mind itself was conceived in connection with the landscape. Here it is causality which is appearance and which might be called 'causality without cause', and it is the finality which is the profound reality. But if I can thus in all confidence put the order of ends under the order of causes, it is because by opening the book I am asserting that the object has its source in human freedom.

If I were to suspect the artist of having written out of passion and in passion, my confidence would immediately vanish, for it would serve no purpose to have supported the order of causes by the order of ends. The latter would be supported in its turn by a psychic causality and the work of art would end by re-entering the chain of determinism. Certainly I do not deny when I am reading that the author may be impassioned, nor even that he might have conceived the first plan of his work under the sway of passion. But his decision to write supposes that he withdraws somewhat from his feelings, in short, that he has transformed his emotions into free emotions as I do mine while reading him; that is, that he is in an attitude of generosity.

Thus, reading is a pact of generosity between author and reader. Each one trusts the other; each one counts on the other, demands of the other as much as he demands of himself. For this confidence is itself generosity. Nothing can force the author to believe that his reader will use his freedom; nothing can force the reader to believe that the author has used his. Both of them make a free decision. There is then established a dialectical going-and-coming; when I read, I make demands; if my demands are met, what I am then reading provokes me to demand more of the author, which means to demand of the author that he demand more of me. And, vice-versa, the author's demand is that I carry my demands to the highest pitch. Thus, my freedom, by revealing itself, reveals the freedom of the other.

It matters little whether the aesthetic object is the product of 'realistic' art (or supposedly such) or 'formal' art. At any rate, the natural relations are inverted; that tree on the first plane of the Cézanne painting first appears as the product of a causal chain. But the causality is an illusion; it will doubtless remain as a proposition as long as we look at the painting, but it will be supported by a deep finality; if the tree is placed in such a way, it is because the rest of the painting *requires* that this form and those colours be placed on the first plane. Thus, through the phenomenal causality, our gaze attains finality as the deep structure of the object, and, beyond finality, it attains human freedom as its source and original basis. Vermeer's realism is carried so far that at first it might be thought to be photographic. But if one considers the splendour of his texture, the pink and velvety glory of his little brick walls, the blue thickness of a branch of woodbine, the glazed darkness of his vestibules, the orange-coloured flesh of his faces which are as polished as the stone of holy-water basins, one suddenly feels, in the pleasure that he experiences, that the finality is not so much in the forms or colours as in his material imagination. It is the very substance and temper of the things which here give the forms their reason for being. With this realist we are perhaps closest to absolute creation, since it is in the very passivity of the matter that we meet the unfathomable freedom of man.

The work is never limited to the painted, sculpted, or narrated object. Just as one perceives things only against the background of the world, so the objects represented by art appear against the background of the universe. On the background of the adventures of Fabrice[a] are the Italy of 1820, Austria, France, the sky and stars which the Abbé Blanis consults, and finally the whole earth. If the painter presents us with a field or a vase of flowers, his paintings are windows which are open on the whole world. We follow the red path which is buried among the wheat much farther than Van Gogh has painted it, among other wheat fields, under other clouds, to the river which empties into the sea, and we extend to infinity, to the other end of the world, the deep finality which supports the existence of the field and the earth. So that, through the various objects which it produces or reproduces, the creative act aims at a total renewal of the world. Each painting, each book, is a recovery of the totality of being. Each of them presents this totality to the freedom of the spectator. For this is quite the final goal of art: to recover this world by giving it to be seen as it is, but as if it had its source in human freedom. But, since what the author creates takes on objective reality only in the eyes of the spectator, this recovery is consecrated by the ceremony of the spectacle—and particularly of reading. We are

[a] Fabrice del Dongo is the hero of Stendhal's novel *La Chartreuse de Parme* (1839).

already in a better position to answer the question we raised a while ago: the writer chooses to appeal to the freedom of other men so that, by the reciprocal implications of their demands, they may re-adapt the totality of being to man and may again enclose the universe within man.

If we wish to go still further, we must bear in mind that the writer, like all other artists, aims at giving his reader a certain feeling that is customarily called aesthetic pleasure, and which I would very much rather call aesthetic joy, and that this feeling, when it appears, is a sign that the work is achieved. It is therefore fitting to examine it in the light of the preceding considerations. In effect, this joy, which is denied to the creator, in so far as he creates, becomes one with the aesthetic consciousness of the spectator, that is, in the case under consideration, of the reader. It is a complex feeling but one whose structures and condition are inseparable from one another. It is identical, at first, with the recognition of a transcendent and absolute end which, for a moment, suspends the utilitarian round of ends–means and means–ends[2], that is, of an appeal or, what amounts to the same thing, of a value. And the positional consciousness which I take of this value is necessarily accompanied by the non-positional consciousness of my freedom, since my freedom is manifested to itself by a transcendent exigency. The recognition of freedom by itself is joy, but this structure of non-ethical consciousness implies another: since, in effect, reading is creation, my freedom does not only appear to itself as pure autonomy but as creative activity, that is, it is not limited to giving itself its own law but perceives itself as being constitutive of the object. It is on this level that the phenomenon specifically is manifested, that is, a creation wherein the created object is given *as object* to its creator. It is the sole case in which the creator gets any enjoyment out of the object he creates. And the word enjoyment which is applied to the positional consciousness of the work read indicates sufficiently that we are in the presence of an essential structure of aesthetic joy. The positional enjoyment is accompanied by the non-positional consciousness of being essential in relation to an object perceived as essential. I shall call this aspect of aesthetic consciousness the feeling of security; it is this which stamps the strongest aesthetic emotions with a sovereign calm. It has its origin in the authentication of a strict harmony between subjectivity and objectivity. As, on the other hand, the aesthetic object is properly the world in so far as it is aimed at through the imaginary, aesthetic joy accompanies the positional consciousness that the world is a value, that is, a task proposed to human freedom. I shall call this the aesthetic modification of the human project, for, as usual, the world appears as the horizon of our situation, as the infinite distance which separates us from ourselves, as the synthetic totality of the given, as the undifferentiated ensemble of obstacles and implements—but never as a demand addressed to our freedom. Thus, aesthetic joy proceeds to this level of the consciousness which I take of recovering and internalizing that which is non-ego par excellence, since I transform the given into an imperative and the fact into a value. The world is *my task*, that is, the essential and freely accepted function of my freedom is to make that unique and absolute object which is the universe come into being in an unconditioned movement. And, thirdly, the preceding structures imply a pact between human freedoms, for, on the one hand, reading is a confident and exacting recognition of the freedom of the writer, and, on the other hand, aesthetic pleasure, as it is itself experienced in the form of a value, involves an absolute exigence in regard to others; every man, in so far as he is a freedom, feels the same pleasure in reading the same work. Thus, all mankind is present in its highest freedom; it sustains the being of a world which is both *its* world and the 'external' world. In aesthetic joy the positional consciousness is an *image-making* consciousness of the world in its totality both as being and having to be, both as totally ours and totally foreign, and the more ours as it is the more foreign. The non-positional consciousness *really* envelops the harmonious totality of human freedoms in so far as it makes the object of a universal confidence and exigency.

To write is thus both to disclose the world and to offer it as a task to the generosity of the reader. It is to have recourse to the consciousness of others in order to make one's self be recognized as *essential* to the totality of being; it is to wish to live this essentiality by means of interposed persons; but, on the other hand, as the real world is revealed only by action, as one can feel himself in it only by exceeding it in order to change it, the novelist's universe would lack thickness if it were not discovered in a movement to transcend it. It has often been observed that an object in a story does not derive its density of exist-ence from the number and length of the descriptions devoted to it, but from the complexity of its connections with the different characters. The more often the characters handle it, take it up, and put it down, in short, go beyond it to-wards their own ends, the more real will it appear. Thus, of the world of the novel, that is, the totality of men and things, we may say that in order for it to offer its maximum density the disclosure-creation by which the reader discovers it must also be an imaginary engagement in the action; in other words, the more disposed one is to change it, the more alive it will be. The error of realism has been to believe that the real reveals itself to contemplation, and that con-sequently one could draw an impartial picture of it. How could that be possible, since the very perception is partial, since by itself the naming is already a modification of the object? And how could the writer, who wants himself to be essential to this universe, want to be essential to the injustice which this universe comprehends? Yet, he must be; but if he accepts being the creator of injustices, it is in a movement which goes beyond them towards their abolition. As for me who read, if I create and keep alive an unjust world, I can not help making myself responsible for it. And the author's whole art is bent on obliging me to *create* what he *discloses*, therefore to compromise myself. So both of us bear the responsibility for the universe. And precisely because this universe is supported by the joint effort of our two freedoms, and because the author, with me as medium, has attempted to integrate it into the human, it must appear truly *in itself*, in its very marrow, as being shot through and through with a freedom which has taken human freedom as its end, and if it is not really the city of ends that it ought to be, it must at least be a stage along the way; in a word, it must be a becoming and it must always be considered and presented not as a crushing mass which weighs us down, but from the point of view of its going beyond towards that city of ends. However bad and hopeless the humanity which it paints may be, the work must have an air of generosity. Not, of course, that this generosity is to be expressed by means of edifying discourses and virtuous characters; it must not even be premeditated, and it is quite true that fine sentiments do not make fine books. But it must be the very warp and woof of the book, the stuff out of which the people and things are cut; whatever the subject, a sort of essential lightness must appear everywhere and remind us that the work is never a natural datum, but an *exigence* and a *gift*. And if I am given this world with its injustices, it is not so that I might contemplate them coldly, but that I might animate them with my indignation, that I might disclose them and create them with their nature as injustices, that is, as abuses to be suppressed. Thus, the writer's universe will only reveal itself in all its depth to the examination, the admiration, and the indignation of the reader; and the generous love is a promise to maintain, and the generous indignation is a promise to change, and the admiration a promise to imitate; although literature is one thing and morality a quite different one, at the heart of the aesthetic imperative we discern the moral imperative. For, since the one who writes recognizes, by the very fact that he takes the trouble to write, the freedom of his readers, and since the one who reads, by the mere fact of his opening the book, recognizes the freedom of the writer, the work of art, from whichever side you approach it, is an act of confidence in the freedom of men. And since readers, like the author, recognize this freedom only to demand that it manifest itself, the work can be defined as an imaginary presentation of the world in so far as it demands human freedom. The result of which is that there is no 'gloomy literature', since, however dark may be the colours in which one paints the world, he paints it only so that free men may feel their freedom as they face it. Thus, there are only good and bad novels. The bad novel aims to please by flattering, whereas the good one is an exigence and an act of faith. But above all, the unique point of view from which the author can present the world to those freedoms whose concurrence he wishes to bring about is that of a world to be impregnated always with more freedom. It would be inconceivable that this unleashing of generosity provoked by the writer could be used to authorize an injustice, and that the reader could enjoy his freedom while reading a work which approves or accepts or simply abstains from condemning the subjection of man by man. One can imagine a good novel being written by an American Negro even if hatred of the whites were spread all over it, because it is the freedom of his race that he demands through this hatred. And, as he invites me to assume the attitude of generosity, the moment I feel myself a pure freedom I can not bear to identify myself with a race of oppressors. Thus, I require of all freedoms that they demand the liberation of coloured people against the white race and against myself in so far as I am a part of it, but nobody can suppose for a moment that it is possible to write a good novel in praise of anti-Semitism.[3] For, the moment I feel that my freedom is indissolubly linked with that of all other men, it can not be demanded of me that I use it to approve the enslavement of a part of these men. Thus, whether he is an essayist, a pamphleteer, a satirist, or a novelist, whether he speaks only of individual passions or

383

whether he attacks the social order, the writer, a free man addressing free men, has only one subject—freedom.

Hence, any attempt to enslave his readers threatens him in his very art. A blacksmith can be affected by fascism in his life as a man, but not necessarily in his craft; a writer will be affected in both, and even more in his craft than in his life. I have seen writers, who before the war, called for fascism with all their hearts, smitten with sterility at the very moment when the Nazis were loading them with honours. I am thinking of Drieu la Rochelle in particular; he was mistaken, but he was sincere. He proved it. He had agreed to direct a Nazi-inspired review. The first few months he reprimanded, rebuked, and lectured his countrymen. No one answered him because no one was free to do so. He became irritated; he no longer *felt* his readers. He became more insistent, but no sign appeared to prove that he had been understood. No sign of hatred, nor of anger either; nothing. He seemed disoriented, the victim of a growing distress. He complained bitterly to the Germans. His articles had been superb; they became shrill. The moment arrived when he struck his breast; no echo, except among the bought journalists whom he despised. He handed in his resignation, withdrew it, again spoke, still in the desert. Finally, he kept still, gagged by the silence of others. He had demanded the enslavement of others, but in his crazy mind he must have imagined that it was voluntary, that it was still free. It came; the man in him congratulated himself mightily, but the writer could not bear it. While this was going on, others, who, happily, were in the majority, understood that the freedom of writing implies the freedom of the citizen. One does not write for slaves. The art of prose is bound up with the only régime in which prose has meaning, democracy. When one is threatened, the other is too. And it is not enough to defend them with the pen. A day comes when the pen is forced to stop, and the writer must then take up arms. Thus, however you might have come to it, whatever the opinions you might have professed, literature throws you into battle. Writing is a certain way of wanting freedom; once you have begun, you are engaged, willy-nilly.

Engaged in what? Defending freedom? That's easy to say. Is it a matter of acting as guardian of ideal values like Benda's clerk before the betrayal,[4] or is it concrete, everyday freedom which must be protected by our taking sides in political and social struggles? The question is tied up with another one, one very simple in appearance but which nobody ever asks himself: 'For whom does one write?'

Notes

1. The same is true in different degrees regarding the spectator's attitude before other works of art (paintings, symphonies, statues, etc.).

2. In *practical life* a means may be taken for an end as soon as one searches for it, and each end is revealed as a means of attaining another end.

3. This last remark may arouse some readers. If so, I'd like to know a single good novel whose express purpose was to serve oppression, a single good novel which has been written against Jews, Negroes, workers, or colonial people. 'But if there isn't any, that's no reason why someone may not write one some day.' But you then admit that you are an abstract

theoretician. You, not I. For it is in the name of your abstract conception of art that you assert the possibility of a fact which has never come into being, whereas I limit myself to proposing an explanation for a recognized fact.

4. The reference here is to Benda's *La Trahison des clercs*, translated into English as *The Treason of the Intellectuals.*—Translator's note.

29 Mark Schorer

Mark Schorer (b. 1908) is Professor of English at the University of California, Berkeley, where he has taught since 1945. He himself was educated at the University of Wisconsin and at Harvard, where he also taught for a time. He has published several novels and a collection of short stories as well as the works of literary criticism for which he is best known: *William Blake: the politics of vision* (New York, 1954), *Sinclair Lewis: an American life* (New York, 1961) and many essays, some of which were collected in *The World We Imagine* (New York, 1968).

First published in *The Hudson Review* in 1948, 'Technique as Discovery' must be among the most frequently cited and reprinted of all modern critical essays—and for good reasons. It both marked and contributed to an important stage in the development of Anglo-American criticism, namely, the application to prose fiction of principles and methods already established in the criticism of poetry and drama. Succinctly summarizing, at the outset of his essay, the principles of the New Criticism, which all derive from the central doctrine of the inseparability of form and content, Schorer noted that the implications of these principles for the criticism of fiction had been largely ignored or denied. As the final section of his essay makes clear, Schorer was writing with certain topical literary issues in mind; and his criticism of earlier English novelists, such as Wells and Lawrence, might now be judged somewhat inflexible and prescriptive. Schorer himself has certainly become one of the most sympathetic critics of D. H. Lawrence in recent years. Debate over specific value judgments does not, however, affect the fundamental importance of Schorer's general insistence in 'Technique as Discovery', that 'the difference between content, or experience, and achieved content, or art is technique', and that the technique of the novel is a verbal one. In a complementary essay, 'Fiction and the Analogical Matrix' (*Kenyon Review*, 1949), Schorer further explored the significance of the language novelists use, by investigating the submerged patterns of imagery and symbolism that can be found beneath the surface of even the most realistic and literal-minded novelist. This kind of analysis—which clearly derives from much earlier work on poetry and poetic drama, such as Wilson Knight's (see above, pp. 158-73)—has since become one of the most widely used (and abused) methods in criticism of the novel.

CROSS REFERENCES: 7. Virginia Woolf
11. E. M. Forster
39. Ian Watt
42. Wayne Booth

Technique as discovery

I

Modern criticism, through its exacting scrutiny of literary texts, has demonstrated with finality that in art beauty and truth are indivisible and one. The Keatsian overtones of these terms are mitigated and an old dilemma solved if for beauty we substitute form, and for truth, content. We may, without risk of loss, narrow them even more, and speak of technique and subject matter. Modern criticism has shown us that to speak of content as such is not to speak of art at all, but of experience; and that it is only when we speak of the *achieved* content, the form, the work of art as a work of art, that we speak as critics. The difference between content, or experience, and achieved content, or art, is technique.

When we speak of technique, then, we speak of nearly everything. For technique is the means by which the writer's experience, which is his subject matter, compels him to attend to it; technique is the only means he has of discovering, exploring, developing his subject, of conveying its meaning, and, finally, of evaluating it. And surely it follows that certain techniques are sharper tools than others, and will discover more; that the writer capable of the most exacting technical scrutiny of his subject matter will produce works with the most satisfying content, works with thickness and resonance; works which reverberate, works with maximum meaning.

We are no longer able to regard as seriously intended criticism of poetry which does not assume these generalizations; but the case for fiction has not yet been established. The novel is still read as though its content has some value in itelf, as though the subject matter of fiction has greater or lesser value in itself, and as though technique were not a primary but a supplementary element, capable perhaps of not unattractive embellishments upon the surface of the subject, but hardly of its essence. Or technique is thought of in blunter terms than those which one associates with poetry, as such relatively obvious matters as the arrangement of events to create plot; or, within plot, of suspense and climax; or as the means of revealing character motivation, relationship, and development; or as the use of point of view,[a] but point of view as some nearly arbitrary device for the heightening of dramatic interest through the narrowing or broadening of perspective upon the material, rather than as a means towards the positive definition of theme. As for the resources of language, these, somehow, we almost never think of as a part of the technique of fiction—language as used to create a certain texture and tone which in themselves state and define themes and meanings; or language, the counters of our ordinary speech, as forced, through conscious manipulation, into all those larger meanings which

[a] Cf. E. M. Forster, p. 143 above.

our ordinary speech almost never intends. Technique in fiction, all this is a way of saying, we somehow continue to regard as merely a means to organizing material which is 'given' rather than as the means of exploring and defining the values in an area of experience which, for the first time *then*, are being given.

Is fiction still regarded in this odd, divided way because it is really less tractable before the critical suppositions which now seem inevitable to poetry? Let us look at some examples: two well-known novels of the past, both by writers who may be described as 'primitive', although their relative innocence of technique is of a different sort—Defoe's *Moll Flanders* and Emily Brontë's *Wuthering Heights*; and three well-known novels of this century—*Tono Bungay*, by a writer who claimed to eschew technique; *Sons and Lovers*, by a novelist who, because his ideal of subject matter ('the poetry of the immediate present') led him at last into the fallacy of spontaneous and unchangeable composition, in effect eschewed technique; and *A Portrait of the Artist as a Young Man*, by a novelist whose practice made claims for the supremacy of technique beyond those made by anyone in the past or by anyone else in this century.

Technique in fiction is, of course, all those obvious forms of it which are usually taken to be the whole of it, and many others; but for present purposes, let it be thought of in two respects particularly: the uses to which language, as language, is put to express the quality of the experience in question; and the uses of point of view not only as a mode of dramatic delimitation, but more particularly, of thematic definition. Technique is really what T. S. Eliot means by 'convention': any selection, structure, or distortion, any form or rhythm imposed upon the world of action; by means of which, it should be added, our apprehension of the world of action is enriched or renewed. In this sense, everything is technique which is not the lump of experience itself, and one cannot properly say that a writer has no technique, or that he eschews technique, for, being a writer, he cannot do so. We can speak of good and bad technique, of adequate and inadequate, of technique which serves the novel's purpose, or disserves.

II

In the prefatory remarks to *Moll Flanders*, Defoe tells us that he is not writing fiction at all, but editing the journals of a woman of notorious character, and rather to instruct us in the necessities and the joys of virtue than to please us. We do not, of course, take these professions seriously, since nothing in the conduct of the narrative indicates that virtue is either more necessary or more enjoyable than vice. On the contrary, we discover that Moll turns virtuous only after a life of vice has enabled her to do so with security; yet it is precisely for this reason that Defoe's profession of didactic purpose has interest. For the actual morality which the novel enforces is the morality of any commercial culture, the belief that virtue pays—in worldly goods. It is a morality somewhat less than skin deep, having no relation to motives arising from a sense of good and evil, least of all, of evil-*in*-good, but exclusively from the presence or absence of food, drink, linen, damask, silver, and timepieces. It is the morality of measurement, and without in the least intending it, *Moll Flanders* is our classic revelation of the mercantile mind: the morality of measurement, which Defoe has completely neglected to measure. He fails not only to evaluate this material in his announced way, but to evaluate it at all. His announced purpose is, we admit, a pious humbug, and he meant us to read the book as a series of scandalous events; and thanks to his inexhaustible pleasure in excess and exaggeration, this element in the book continues to amuse us. Long before the book has been finished, however, this element has also become an absurdity; but not half the absurdity as that which Defoe did not intend at all—the notion that Moll could live a rich and full life of crime, and yet, repenting, emerge spotless in the end. The point is, of course, that she has no moral being, nor has the book any moral life. Everything is external. Everything can be weighed, measured, handled, paid for in gold, or expiated by a prison term. To this, the whole texture of the novel testifies—the bolts of goods, the inventories, the itemized accounts, the landlady's bills, the lists, the ledgers—all this, which taken together comprises what we call Defoe's method of circumstantial realism.

He did not come upon that method by any deliberation; it represents precisely his own world of value, the importance of external circumstance to Defoe. The point of view of Moll is indistinguishable from the point of view of her creator. We discover the meaning of the novel (at unnecessary length, without economy, without emphasis, with almost none of the distortions or the advantages of art) in spite of Defoe, not because of him. Thus the book is not the true chronicle of a disreputable female, but the true allegory of an impoverished soul, the author's; not an anatomy of the criminal class, but of the middle class. And we read it as an unintended comic revelation of self and of a social mode. Because he had no adequate resources of technique to separate himself from his material, thereby to discover and to define the meanings of his material, his contribution is not to fiction but to the history of fiction, and to social history.

The situation in *Wuthering Heights* is at once somewhat the same and yet very different. Here, too, the whole novel turns upon itself, but this time to its estimable advantage; here, too, is a revelation of what is perhaps the author's secret world of value, but this time, through what may be an accident of technique, the revelation is meaningfully accomplished. Emily Brontë may merely have stumbled upon the perspectives which define the form and the theme of her book. Whether she knew from the outset, or even at the end, what she was doing, we may doubt; but what she did and did superbly we can see.

We can assume, without at all becoming involved in the author's life but merely from the tone of somnambulistic excess which is generated by the writing itself, that this world of monstrous passion, of dark and gigantic emotional and nervous energy, is for the author, or was in the first place, a world of ideal value; and that the book sets out to persuade us of the moral magnificence of such unmoral passion. We are, I think, expected, in the first place, to take at their own valuation these demonic beings, Heathcliff and Cathy: as special creatures, set apart from the cloddish world about them by their heightened capacity for feeling, set apart, even, from the ordinary objects of human passion as, in their transcendent, sexless relationship, they identify themselves with an uncompromising landscape and cosmic force. Yet this is absurd, as much of the detail that surrounds it ('Other dogs lurked in other recesses') is absurd. The novelist Emily Brontë had to discover these absurdities to the girl Emily; her technique had to evaluate them for what they were, so that we are persuaded that it is not Emily who is mistaken in her estimate of her characters, but they who are mistaken in their estimate of themselves. The theme of the moral magnificence of unmoral passion is an impossible theme to sustain, and what interests us is that it was device—and this time, mere, mechanical device—which taught Emily Brontë—the needs of her temperament to the contrary, all personal longing and reverie to the contrary, perhaps—that this was indeed not at all what her material must mean as art. Technique objectifies.

To lay before us the full character of this passion, to show us how it first comes into being and then comes to dominate the world about it and the life that follows upon it, Emily Brontë gives her material a broad scope in time, lets it, in fact, cut across three generations. And to manage material which is so extensive, she must find a means of narration, points of view, which can encompass that material, and, in her somewhat crude concept of motive, justify its telling. So she chooses a foppish traveller who stumbles into this world of passionate violence, a traveller representing the thin and conventional emotional life of the far world of fashion, who wishes to hear the tale; and for her teller she chooses, almost inevitably, the old family retainer who knows everything, a character as conventional as the other, but this one representing not the conventions of fashion, but the conventions of the humblest moralism.

What has happened is, first, that she has chosen as her narrative perspective those very elements, conventional emotion and conventional morality, which her hero and heroine are meant to transcend with such spectacular magnificence; and second, that she has permitted this perspective to operate throughout a long period of time. And these two elements compel the novelist to see what her unmoral passions come to. Moral magnificence? Not at all; rather, a devastating spectacle of human waste; ashes. For the time of the novel is carried on long enough to show Heathcliff at last an emptied man, burned out by his fever ragings, exhausted and will-less, his passion meaningless at last. And it goes even a little further, to Lockwood, the fop, in the graveyard, sententiously contemplating headstones. Thus in the end the triumph is all on the side of the cloddish world, which survives.

Perhaps not all on that side. For, like Densher at the end of [Henry James's] *The Wings of the Dove*, we say, and surely Hareton and the second Cathy say, 'We shall never be again as we were!' But there is more point in observing that a certain body of materials, a girl's romantic daydreams, have, through the most conventional devices of fiction, been pushed beyond their inception in fancy to their meanings, their conception as a written book—that they, that is, are not at all as they were.

Technique alone objectifies the materials of art; hence technique alone evaluates those materials. This is the axiom which demonstrates itself so devastatingly whenever a writer declares under the urgent sense of the importance of his materials—whether these are autobiography, or social ideas, or personal passions —whenever such a writer declares that he cannot linger with technical refinements. That art will not tolerate such a writer H. G. Wells handsomely proves. His enormous literary energy included no respect for the techniques of his medium, and his medium takes its revenge upon his bumptiousness.

> I have never taken any very great pains about writing. I am outside the hierarchy of conscious and deliberate writers altogether. I am the absolute antithesis of Mr James Joyce.... Long ago, living in close conversational proximity to Henry James, Joseph Conrad, and Mr Ford Madox Hueffer, I escaped from under their immense artistic preoccupations by calling myself a journalist.

Precisely. And he escaped—he disappeared—from literature into the annals of an era.

Yet what confidence!

> Literature (Wells said) is not jewelry, it has quite other aims than perfection, and the more one thinks of 'how it is done' the less one gets it done. These critical indulgences lead along a fatal path, away from every natural interest towards a preposterous emptiness of technical effort, a monstrous egotism of artistry, of which the later work of Henry James is the monumental warning. 'It', the subject, the thing or the thought, has long since disappeared in these amazing works; nothing remains but the way it has been manipulated.

Seldom has a literary theorist been so totally wrong; for what we learn as James grows for us and Wells disappears is that without what he calls 'manipulation', there is no 'it', no 'subject' in art. There is again only social history.

The virtue of the modern novelist—from James and Conrad down—is not only that he pays so much attention to his medium, but that, when he pays most, he discovers through it a new subject matter, and a greater one. Under the 'immense artistic preoccupations' of James and Conrad and Joyce, the form of the novel changed, and with the technical change, analogous changes took place in substance, in point of view, in the whole conception of fiction. And the final lesson of the modern novel is that technique is not the secondary thing that it seemed to Wells, some external machination, a mechanical affair, but a deep and primary operation; not only that technique *contains* intellectual and moral implications, but that it *discovers* them. For a writer like Wells, who wished to give us the intellectual and the moral history of our times, the lesson is a hard one; it tells us that the order of intellect and the order of morality do not exist at all, in art, except as they are organized in the order of art.

Wells' ambitions were very large. 'Before we have done, we will have all life within the scope of the novel.' But that is where life already is, within the scope of the novel; where it needs to be brought is into novels. In Wells we have all the important topics in life, but no good novels. He was not asking too much of art, or asking that it include more than it happily can; he was not asking anything of it—as art, which is all that it can give, and that is everything.

A novel like *Tono Bungay*, generally thought to be Wells' best, is therefore instructive. 'I want to tell—*myself*,' says George, the hero, 'and my impressions of the thing as a whole'—the thing as a whole being the collapse of traditional British institutions in the twentieth century. George 'tells himself' in terms of three stages in his life which have rough equivalents in modern British social history, and this is, to be sure, a plan, a framework; but it is the framework of Wells' abstract thinking, not of his craftsmanship, and the primary demand which one makes of such a book as this—that means be discovered whereby the dimensions of the hero contain the experiences he recounts—is never met. The novelist flounders through a series of literary imitations—from an early Dickensian episode, through a kind of Shavian interlude, through a Conradian episode, to a Jules Verne vision at the end. The significant failure is in that end, and in the way that it defeats not only the entire social analysis of the bulk of the novel, but Wells' own ends as a thinker. For at last George finds a purpose in science. 'I decided that in power and knowledge lay the salvation of my life; the secret that would fill my need; that to these things I would give myself.'

But science, power, and knowledge are summed up at last in a destroyer. As far as one can tell Wells intends no irony, although he may here have come upon the essence of the major irony in modern history. The novel ends in a kind of meditative rhapsody which denies every value that the book had been aiming towards. For of all the kinds of social waste which Wells has been describing, this is the most inclusive, the final waste. Thus he gives us in the end not a novel, but a hypothesis; not an individual destiny, but a theory of the future; and not his theory of the future, but a nihilistic version quite opposite from everything that he meant to represent. With a minimum of attention to the virtues of technique, Wells might still not have written a good novel; but he would at any rate have established a point of view and a tone which would have told us what he meant.

To say what one means in art is never easy, and the more intimately one is implicated in one's material, the more difficult it is. If, besides, one commits fiction to a therapeutic function which is to be operative not on the audience but on the author, declaring, as D. H. Lawrence did, that 'One sheds one's sicknesses in books, repeats and presents again one's emotions to be master of them', the difficulty is vast. It is an acceptable theory only with the qualification that technique, which objectifies, is under no other circumstances so imperative. For merely to repeat one's emotions, merely to look into one's heart and write, is also merely to repeat the round of emotional bondage. If our books are to be exercises in self-analysis, then technique must—and alone can—take the place of the absent analyst.

Lawrence, in the relatively late Introduction to his *Collected Poems*, made that distinction of the amateur between his 'real' poems and his 'composed' poems, between the poems which expressed his demon directly and created their own form 'willy-nilly', and the poems which, through the hocus-pocus of technique, he spuriously put together and could, if necessary, revise. His belief in a 'poetry of the immediate present', poetry in which nothing is fixed, static, or final, where all is shimmeriness and impermanence and vitalistic essence, arose from this mistaken notion of technique. And from this notion, an unsympathetic critic like D. S. Savage can construct a case which shows Lawrence driven 'concurrently to the dissolution of personality and the dissolution of art'. The argument suggests that Lawrence's early, crucial novel, *Sons and Lovers*, is another example of meanings confused by an impatience with technical resources.

The novel has two themes: the crippling effects of a mother's love on the emotional development of her son; and the 'split' between kinds of love, physical and spiritual, which the son develops, the kinds represented by two young women, Clara and Miriam. The two themes should, of course, work together, the second being, actually, the result of the first: this 'split' is the 'crippling'. So one would expect to see the novel developed, and so Lawrence, in his famous letter to Edward Garnett, where he says that Paul is left at the end with the 'drift towards death', apparently thought he had developed it. Yet in the last few sentences of the novel, Paul rejects his desire for extinction and turns towards 'the faintly humming, glowing town', to life—as nothing in his previous history persuades us that he could unfalteringly do.

The discrepancy suggests that the book may reveal certain confusions between intention and performance.

One of these is the contradiction between Lawrence's explicit characterizations of the mother and father and his tonal evaluations of them. It is a problem not only of style (of the contradiction between expressed moral epithets and the more general texture of the prose which applies to them) but of point of view. Morel and Lawrence are never separated, which is a way of saying that Lawrence maintains for himself in this book the confused attitude of his character. The mother is a 'proud, *honourable* soul', but the father has a 'small, *mean* head'. This is the sustained contrast: the epithets are characteristic of the whole, and they represent half of Lawrence's feelings. But what is the other half? Which of these characters is given his real sympathy—the hard, self-righteous, aggressive, demanding mother who comes through to us, or the simple, direct, gentle, downright, fumbling, ruined father? There are two attitudes here. Lawrence (and Morel) loves his mother, but he also hates her for compelling his love; and he hates his father with the true Freudian jealousy, but he also loves him for what he is in himself, and he sympathizes more deeply with him because his wholeness has been destroyed by the mother's domination, just as his, Lawrence–Morel's, has been.

This is a psychological tension which disrupts the form of the novel and obscures its meaning, because neither the contradiction in style nor the confusion in point of view is made to right itself. Lawrence is merely repeating his emotions, and he avoids an austerer technical scrutiny of his material because it would compel him to master them. He would not let the artist be stronger than the man.

The result is that, at the same time that the book condemns the mother, it justifies her; at the same time that it shows Paul's failure, it offers rationalizations which place the failure elsewhere. The handling of the girl, Miriam, if viewed closely, is pathetic in what it signifies for Lawrence, both as man and artist. For Miriam is made the mother's scapegoat, and in a different way from the way that she was in life. The central section of the novel is shot through with alternate statements as to the source of the difficulty: Paul is unable to love Miriam wholly, and Miriam can love only his spirit. These contradictions appear sometimes within single paragraphs, and the point of view is never adequately objectified and sustained to tell us which is true. The material is never seen as material; the writer is caught in it exactly as firmly as he was caught in his experience of it. 'That's how women are with me,' said Paul. 'They want me like mad, but they don't want to belong to me.' So he might have said, and believed it; but at the end of the novel, Lawrence is still saying that, and himself believing it.

For the full history of this technical failure, one must read *Sons and Lovers* carefully and then learn the history of the manuscript from the book called *D. H. Lawrence: A Personal Record*, by one E. T., who was Miriam in life. The basic situation is clear enough. The first theme—the crippling effects of the mother's love—is developed right through to the end; and then suddenly, in the last few sentences, turns on itself, and Paul gives himself to life, not death. But all the way through, the insidious rationalizations of the second theme have crept in to destroy the artistic coherence of the work. A 'split' would occur in Paul; but as the split is treated, it is superimposed upon rather than developed in support of the first theme. It is a rationalization made from it. If Miriam is made to insist on spiritual love, the meaning and the power of theme one are reduced; yet Paul's weakness is disguised. Lawrence could not separate the investigating analyst, who must be objective, from Lawrence, the subject of the book; and the sickness was not healed, the emotion not mastered, the novel not perfected. All this, and the character of a whole career, would have been altered if Lawrence had allowed his technique to discover the full meaning of his subject.

A Portrait of the Artist as a Young Man, like *Tono Bungay* and *Sons and Lovers*, is autobiographical, but unlike these it analyses its material rigorously, and it defines the value and the quality of its experience not by appended comment or moral epithet, but by the texture of the style. The theme of *A Portrait*, a young artist's alienation from his environment, is explored and evaluated through three different styles and methods as Stephen Dedalus moves from childhood through boyhood into maturity. The opening pages are written in something like the Ulyssesean stream of consciousness, as the environment impinges directly on the consciousness of the infant and the child, a strange, opening world which the mind does not yet subject to questioning, selection, or judgment. But this style changes very soon, as the boy begins to explore his surroundings; and as his sensuous experience of the world is enlarged, it takes on heavier and heavier rhythms and a fuller and fuller body of sensuous detail, until it reaches a crescendo of romantic opulence in the emotional climaxes which mark Stephen's rejection of domestic and religious values.

Then gradually the style subsides into the austere intellectuality of the final sections, as he defines to himself the outlines of the artistic task which is to usurp his maturity.

A highly self-conscious use of style and method defines the quality of experience in each of these sections, and, it is worth pointing out in connection with the third and concluding section, the style and method evaluate the experience. What has happened to Stephen is, of course, a progressive alienation from the life around him as he progressed in his initiation into it, and by the end of the novel, the alienation is complete. The final portion of the novel, fascinating as it may be for the developing aesthetic creed of Stephen–Joyce, is peculiarly bare. The life experience was not bare, as we know from *Stephen Hero*; but Joyce is forcing technique to comment. In essence, Stephen's alienation is a denial of the human environment; it is a loss; and the austere discourse of the final section, abstract and almost wholly without sensuous detail or rhythm, tells us of that loss. It is a loss so great that the texture of the notation-like prose here suggests that the end is really an illusion, that when Stephen tells us and himself that he is going forth to forge in the smithy of his soul the uncreated conscience of his race, we are to infer from the very quality of the icy, abstract void he now inhabits, the implausibility of his aim. For *Ulysses* does not create the conscience of the race; it creates our consciousness.

In the very last two or three paragraphs of the novel, the style changes once more, reverts from the bare, notative kind to the romantic prose of Stephen's adolescence. 'Away! Away! The spell of arms and voices: the white arms of roads, their promise of close embraces and the black arms of tall ships that stand against the moon, their tale of distant nations. They are held out to say: We are alone—come.' Might one not say that the austere ambition is founded on adolescent longing? That the excessive intellectual severity of one style is the counterpart of the excessive lyric relaxation of the other? And that the final passage of *A Portrait* punctuates the illusory nature of the whole ambition?

For *Ulysses* does not create a conscience. Stephen, in *Ulysses*, is a little older, and gripped now by guilt, but he is still the cold young man divorced from the human no less than the institutional environment. The environment of urban life finds a separate embodiment in the character of Bloom, and Bloom is as lost as Stephen, though touchingly groping for moorings. Each of the two is weakened by his inability to reach out, or to do more than reach out to the other. Here, then, is the theme again, more fully stated, as it were in counterpoint.

But if Stephen is not much older, Joyce is. He is older as an artist not only because he can create and lavish his godlike pity on a Leopold Bloom, but also because he knows now what both Stephen and Bloom mean, and *how much*, through the most brilliant technical operation ever made in fiction, they can be made to mean. Thus *Ulysses*, through the imaginative force which its techniques direct, is like a pattern of concentric circles, with the immediate human situation at its centre, this passing on and out to the whole dilemma of modern life, this passing on and out beyond that to a vision of the cosmos, and this to the mythical limits of our experience. If we read *Ulysses* with more satisfaction than any other novel of this century, it is because its author held an attitude towards technique and the technical scrutiny of subject matter which enabled him to order, within a single work and with superb coherence, the greatest amount of our experience.

IV

In the United States during the last twenty-five years, we have had many big novels but few good ones. A writer like James T. Farrell[a] apparently assumes that by endless redundancy in the description of the surface of American life, he will somehow write a book with the scope of *Ulysses*. Thomas Wolfe apparently assumed that by the mere disgorging of the raw material of his experience he would give us at last our epic. But except in a physical sense, these men have hardly written novels at all.

The books of Thomas Wolfe were, of course, journals, and the primary role of his publisher in transforming these journals into the semblance of novels is notorious. For the crucial act of the artist, the unique act which is composition, a sympathetic editorial blue pencil and scissors were substituted. The result has excited many people, especially the young, and the ostensibly critical have observed the prodigal talent with the wish that it might have been controlled. Talent there was, if one means by talent inexhaustible verbal energy, excessive response to personal experience, and a great capacity for auditory imitativeness, yet all of this has nothing to do with the novelistic quality of the written result; for until the talent is controlled, the material organized, the content achieved, there is simply the man and his life. It remains to be demonstrated that Wolfe's conversations were any less interesting as novels than his books, which is to say that his books are without interest as novels. As with Lawrence, our response to the books is determined, not by their qualities as novels, but by our response to him and his qualities as a temperament.

This is another way of saying that Thomas Wolfe never really knew what he was writing *about*. *Of Time and the River* is merely a euphemism for 'Of a Man and his Ego'. It is possible that had his conception of himself and of art included an adequate respect for technique and the capacity to pursue it, Wolfe would have written a great novel on his true subject—the dilemma of romantic genius; it was his true subject, but it remains his undiscovered subject, it is the subject which *we* must dig out for him, because he himself had neither the lamp nor the pick to find it in and mine it out of the labyrinths of his experience. Like Emily Brontë, Wolfe needed a point of view beyond his own which would separate his material and its effect.

With Farrell, the situation is opposite. He knows quite well what his subject is and what he wishes to tell us about it, but he hardly needs the novel to do so. It is significant that in sheer clumsiness of style no living writer exceeds him, for his prose is asked to perform no service beyond communication of the most rudimentary kind of fact. For his ambitions the style of the newspaper and the

---

[a] Best known for his *Studs Lonigan* trilogy (1923–35).

lens of the documentary camera would be quite adequate, yet consider the diminution which Leopold Bloom, for example, would suffer, if he were to be viewed from these, the technical perspectives of James Farrell. Under the eye of this technique, the material does not yield up enough; indeed, it shrinks.

More and more writers in this century have felt that naturalism as a method imposes on them strictures which prevent them from exploring through all the resources of technique the full amplifications of their subjects, and that thus it seriously limits the possible breadth of aesthetic meaning and response. James Farrell is almost unique in the complacency with which he submits to the blunt techniques of naturalism; and his fiction is correspondingly repetitive and flat.

That naturalism had a sociological and disciplinary value in the nineteenth century is obvious; it enabled the novel to grasp materials and make analyses which had eluded it in the past, and to grasp them boldly; but even then it did not tell us enough of what, in Virginia Woolf's phrase, is 'really real', nor did it provide the means to the maximum of reality coherently contained. Even the Flaubertian ideal of objectivity seems, today, an unnecessarily limited view of objectivity, for as almost every good writer of this century shows us, it is quite as possible to be objective about subjective states as it is to be objective about the circumstantial surfaces of life. Dublin, in *Ulysses*, is a moral setting: not only a city portrayed in the naturalistic fashion of Dickens' London, but also a map of the modern psyche with its oblique and baffled purposes. The second level of reality in no way invalidates the first, and a writer like Joyce shows us that, if the artist truly respects his medium, he can be objective about both at once. What we need in fiction is a devoted fidelity to every technique which will help us to discover and to evaluate our subject matter, and more than that, to discover the amplification of meaning of which our subject matter is capable.

Most modern novelists have felt this demand upon them. André Gide allowed one of his artist-heroes[a] to make an observation which considerably resembles an observation we have quoted from Wells. 'My novel hasn't got a subject... Let's say, if you prefer it, it hasn't got *one* subject ... "A slice of life," the naturalist school said. The great effect of that school is that it always cuts its slice in the same direction, lengthwise. Why not in breadth? Or in depth? As for me I should like not to cut at all. Please understand; I should like to put everything into my novel.' Wells, with his equally large blob of potential material, did not know how to cut it to the novel's taste; Gide cut, of course— in every possible direction. Gide and others. And those 'cuts' are all the new techniques which modern fiction has given us. None, perhaps, is more important than that inheritance from French symbolism which [Aldous] Huxley, in the glittering wake of Gide, called 'the musicalization of fiction'. Conrad anticipated both when he wrote that the novel 'must strenuously aspire to the plasticity of sculpture, to the colour of painting, and to the magic suggestiveness of music—which is the art of arts', and when he said of that early but wonderful piece of symbolist fiction, *Heart of Darkness*, 'It was like another art altogether. That sombre theme had to be given a sinister resonance, a tonality

[a] Edouard, in *The Counterfeiters* (1927).

of its own, a continued vibration that, I hoped, would hang in the air and dwell on the ear after the last note had been struck.'

The analogy with music, except as a metaphor, is inexact, and except as it points to techniques which fiction can employ as fiction, not very useful to our sense of craftsmanship. It has had an approximate exactness in only one work, Joyce's final effort, an effort unique in literary history, *Finnegans Wake*, and here, of course, those readers willing to make the effort Joyce demands, discovering an inexhaustible wealth and scope, are most forcibly reminded of the primary importance of technique to subject, and of their indivisibility.

The techniques of naturalism inevitably curtail subject and often leave it in its original area, that of undefined social experience. Those of our writers who, stemming from this tradition, yet, at their best, achieve a novelistic definition of social experience—writers like the occasional Sherwood Anderson, William Carlos Williams, the occasional Erskine Caldwell, Nathanael West, and Ira Wolfert in *Tucker's People*—have done so by pressing naturalism far beyond itself, into positively Gothic distortions. The structural machinations of Dos Passos and the lyrical interruptions of Steinbeck are the desperate manoeuvres of men committed to a method of whose limitations they despair. They are our symbolists *manqué*, who end as allegorists.

Our most accomplished novelists leave no such impressions of desperate and intentional struggle, yet their precise technique and their determination to make their prose work in the service of their subjects have been the measure of their accomplishment. Hemingway's *The Sun Also Rises* and [Glenway] Wescott's *The Pilgrim Hawk* are consummate works of art not because they may be measured by some external, neoclassic notion of form, but because their forms are so exactly equivalent with their subjects, and because the evaluation of their subjects exists in their styles.

Hemingway has recently said that his contribution to younger writers lay in a certain necessary purification of the language; but the claim has doubtful value. The contribution of his prose was to his subject, and the terseness of style for which his early work is justly celebrated is no more valuable, as an end in itself, than the baroque involutedness of Faulkner's prose, or the cold elegance of Wescott's. Hemingway's early subject, the exhaustion of value, was perfectly investigated and invested by his bare style, and in story after story, no meaning at all is to be inferred from the fiction except as the style itself suggests that there is no meaning in life. This style, more than that, was the perfect technical substitute for the conventional commentators; it expresses and it measures that peculiar morality of the stiff lip which Hemingway borrowed from athletes. It is an instructive lesson, furthermore, to observe how the style breaks down when Hemingway moves into the less congenial subject matter of social affirmation: how the style breaks down, the effect of verbal economy as mute suffering is lost, the personality of the writer, no longer protected by the objectification of an adequate technique, begins its offensive intrusion, and the entire structural integrity slackens. Inversely, in the stories and early novels, the technique was the perfect embodiment of the subject and it gave that subject its astonishing largeness of effect and of meaning.

One should correct Buffon[a] and say that style is the subject. In Wescott's *Pilgrim Hawk*—a novel which bewildered its many friendly critics by the apparent absence of subject—the subject, the story, is again in the style itself. This novel, which is a triumph of the sustained point of view, is only bewildering if we try to make a story out of the narrator's observations upon others; but if we read his observations as oblique and unrecognized observations upon himself the story emerges with perfect coherence, and it reverberates with meaning, is as suited to continuing reflection as the greatest lyrics.

The rewards of such respect for the medium as the early Hemingway and the occasional Wescott have shown may be observed in every good writer we have. The involutions of Faulkner's style are the perfect equivalent of his uninvolved structures, and the two together are the perfect representation of the moral labyrinths he explores, and of the ruined world which his novels repeatedly invoke and in which these labyrinths exist. The cultivated sensuousity of Katherine Anne Porter's style—as of Eudora Welty's and Jean Stafford's—has charm in itself, of course, but no more than with these others does it have aesthetic value in itself; its values lie in the subtle means by which sensuous details become symbols, and in the way the symbols provide a network which is the story, and which at the same time provides the writer and us with a refined moral insight by means of which to test it. When we put such writers against a writer like William Saroyan, whose respect is reserved for his own temperament, we are appalled by the stylistic irresponsibility we find in him, and by the almost total absence of theme, or defined subject matter, and the abundance of unwarranted feeling. Such a writer inevitably becomes a sentimentalist because he has no means by which to measure his emotion. Technique, at last, is measure.

These writers, from Defoe to Porter, are of unequal and very different talent, and technique and talent are, of course, after a point, two different things. What Joyce gives us in one direction, Lawrence, for all his imperfections as a technician, gives us in another, even though it is not usually the direction of art. Only in some of his stories and in a few of his poems, where the demands of technique are less sustained and the subject matter is not autobiographical, Lawrence, in a different way from Joyce, comes to the same aesthetic fulfilment. Emily Brontë, with what was perhaps her intuitive grasp of the need to establish a tension between her subject matter and her perspective upon it, achieves a similar fulfilment; and, curiously, in the same way and certainly by intuition alone, Hemingway's early work makes a moving splendour from nothingness.

And yet, whatever one must allow to talent and forgive in technique, one risks no generalization in saying that modern fiction at its best has been peculiarly conscious of itself and of its tools. The technique of modern fiction, at once greedy and fastidious, achieves as its subject matter not some singleness, some topic or thesis, but the whole of the modern consciousness. It discovers the complexity of the modern spirit, the difficulty of personal morality, and the fact of evil—all the untractable elements under the surface which a technique of the

[a] Georges Louis De Buffon (1707–88), who said, 'Le style est l'homme même' ['Style is the man himself'].

surface alone cannot approach. It shows us—in Conrad's words, from *Victory*—
that we all live in an 'age in which we are camped like bewildered travellers
in a garish, unrestful hotel', and while it puts its hard light on our environment,
it penetrates, with its sharp weapons, the depths of our bewilderment. These
are not two things, but only an adequate technique can show them as one. In a
realist like Farrell, we have the environment only, which we know from the
newspapers; in a subjectivist like Wolfe, we have the bewilderment only, which
we record in our diaries and letters. But the true novelist gives them to us together, and thereby increases the effect of each, and reveals each in its full
significance.

Elizabeth Bowen, writing of Lawrence, said of modern fiction, 'We want the
naturalistic surface, but with a kind of internal burning. In Lawrence every bush
burns.' But the bush burns brighter in some places than in others, and it burns
brightest when a passionate private vision finds its objective in exacting technical search. If the vision finds no such objectification, as in Wolfe and Saroyan,
there is a burning without a bush. In our committed realists, who deny the
resources of art for the sake of life, whose technique forgives both innocence
and slovenliness—in Defoe and Wells and Farrell—there is a bush but it does
not burn. There, at first glance, the bush is only a bush; and then, when we
look again, we see that, really, the thing is dead.

30 Francis Fergusson

Francis Fergusson (b. 1904) was born in New Mexico, but took his B.A. at Oxford University. He was Assistant Director of the Laboratory Theatre in New York, and dramatic critic of the *Bookman* before he turned to academic teaching and research in the fields of comparative literature and drama at Bennington College, Princeton and Rutger's University. He has been University Professor of Comparative Literature at Rutger's since 1952.

Fergusson is an eclectic critic who combines practical experience of the theatre with concepts derived from academic scholars and critics of various persuasions to produce original insights of his own. It is clear that the research of the Cambridge school of cultural anthropologists, Frazer, Cornford, and Harrison, and the associated work of classicist Gilbert Murray into the ritual origins of drama, have had a particularly significant influence upon Fergusson's thought. His *The Idea of a Theatre* (Princeton, 1949) from which the following extract is taken, holds up as supreme achievements of dramatic art the plays of Sophocles and Shakespeare, 'both of which were developed in theatres which focused, at the centre of the life of the community, the complementary insights of the whole culture'. The quotation is from Fergusson's Introduction, and he continues: 'We do not have such a theatre, nor do we see how to get it. But we need the "Idea of a Theatre" both to understand the masterpieces of drama at its best, and to get our bearings in our own time.'

Francis Fergusson's subsequent publications include *Dante's Drama of the Mind* (Princeton, 1952) and *The Human Image in Dramatic Literature* (Garden City, N.Y., 1957).

CROSS REFERENCES: 13. G. Wilson Knight
15. Maud Bodkin
40. Claude Lévi-Strauss

Oedipus Rex:
the tragic rhythm of action

...quel secondo regno
dove l'umano spirito si purga.
—*Purgatoria*, CANTO I[a]

I suppose there can be little doubt that *Oedipus Rex* is a crucial instance of drama, if not *the* play which best exemplifies this art in its essential nature and its completeness. It owes its position partly to the fact that Aristotle founded his definitions upon it. But since the time of Aristotle it has been imitated, re-written, and discussed by many different generations, not only of dramatists, but also of moralists, psychologists, historians, and other students of human nature and destiny.

Though the play is thus generally recognized as an archetype, there has been little agreement about its meaning or its form. It seems to beget, in every period, a different interpretation and a different dramaturgy. From the seventeenth century until the end of the eighteenth, a Neoclassic and rationalistic interpre-tation of *Oedipus*, of Greek tragedy, and of Aristotle, was generally accepted; and upon this interpretation was based the dramaturgy of Corneille and Racine. Nietzsche, under the inspiration of Wagner's *Tristan und Isolde*, developed a totally different view of it, and thence a different theory of drama.[b] These two views of Greek tragedy, Racine's and Nietzsche's, still provide indispensable per-spectives upon *Oedipus*. They show a great deal about modern principles of dramatic composition; and they show, when compared, how central and how essential Sophocles' drama is. In the two essays following, the attempt is made to develop the analogies, the similarities and differences, between these three conceptions of drama.

In our day a conception of *Oedipus* seems to be developing which is neither that of Racine nor that of Nietzsche. This view is based upon the studies which the Cambridge School, Frazer, Cornford, Harrison, Murray, made of the ritual origins of Greek tragedy. It also owes a great deal to the current interest in myth as a way of ordering human experience. *Oedipus*, we now see, is both myth and ritual. It assumes and employs these two ancient ways of understanding and representing human experience, which are prior to the arts and sciences and philosophies of modern times. To understand it (it now appears) we must en-

---

[a] '... that second realm where the human spirit is purged.'
[b] In *The Birth of Tragedy* (1872).

deavour to recapture the habit of significant make-believe, of the direct perception of action, which underlies Sophocles' theatre.

If *Oedipus* is to be understood in this way, then we shall have to revise our ideas of Sophocles' dramaturgy. The notion of Aristotle's theory of drama, and hence of Greek dramaturgy, which still prevails (in spite of such studies as Butcher's of the *Poetics*) is largely coloured by Neoclassic taste and rationalistic habits of mind. If we are to take it that Sophocles was imitating action before theory, instead of after it, like Racine, then both the elements and the form of his composition appear in a new light.

In the present essay the attempt is made to draw the deductions, for Sophocles' theatre and dramaturgy, which the present view of *Oedipus* implies. We shall find that the various traditional views of this play are not so much wrong as partial.

Oedipus, myth and play

When Sophocles came to write his play he had the myth of Oedipus to start with. Laius and Jocasta, King and Queen of Thebes, are told by the oracle that their son will grow up to kill his father and marry his mother. The infant, his feet pierced, is left on Mount Kitharon to die. But a shepherd finds him and takes care of him; at last gives him to another shepherd, who takes him to Corinth, and there the King and Queen bring him up as their own son. But Oedipus—'Clubfoot'—is plagued in his turn by the oracle; he hears that he is fated to kill his father and marry his mother; and to escape that fate he leaves Corinth never to return. On his journey he meets an old man with his servants; gets into a dispute with him, and kills him and all his followers. He comes to Thebes at the time when the Sphinx is preying upon that City; solves the riddle which the Sphinx propounds, and saves the City. He marries the widowed Queen, Jocasta; has several children by her; rules prosperously for many years. But, when Thebes is suffering under a plague and a drought, the oracle reports that the gods are angry because Laius' slayer is unpunished. Oedipus, as King, undertakes to find him; discovers that he is himself the culprit and that Jocasta is his own mother. He blinds himself and goes into exile. From this time forth he becomes a sort of sacred relic, like the bones of a saint; perilous, but 'good medicine' for the community that possesses him. He dies, at last, at Athens, in a grove sacred to the Eumenides, female spirits of fertility and night.

It is obvious, even from this sketch, that the myth, which covers several generations, has as much narrative material as *Gone with the Wind.[a]* We do not know what versions of the story Sophocles used. It is the way of myths that they generate whole progenies of elaborations and varying versions. They are so suggestive, seem to say so much, yet so mysteriously, that the mind cannot rest content with any single form, but must add, or interpret, or simplify—reduce to terms which the reason can accept. Mr William Troy suggests that

[a] Bestselling romantic novel (also a famous motion-picture) about the American Civil War, by Margaret Mitchell. First published in 1936.

'what is possibly most in order at the moment is a thoroughgoing refurbishment of the medieval fourfold method of interpretation, which was first developed, it will be recalled, for just such a purpose—to make at least partially available to the reason that complex of human problems which are embedded, deep and imponderable, in the Myth.'[1] It appears that Sophocles, in his play, succeeded in preserving the suggestive mystery of the Oedipus myth, while presenting it in a wonderfully unified dramatic form; and this drama has all the dimensions which the fourfold method was intended to explore.

Everyone knows that when Sophocles planned the plot of the play itself, he started almost at the end of the story, when the plague descends upon the City of Thebes which Oedipus and Jocasta had been ruling with great success for a number of years. The action of the play takes less than a day, and consists of Oedipus' quest for Laius' slayer—his consulting the Oracle of Apollo, his examination of the Prophet, Tiresias, and of a series of witnesses, ending with the old Shepherd who gave him to the King and Queen of Corinth. The play ends when Oedipus is unmistakably revealed as himself the culprit.

At this literal level, the play is intelligible as a murder mystery. Oedipus takes the role of District Attorney; and when he at last convicts himself, we have a twist, a *coup de théâtre*, of unparalleled excitement. But no one who sees or reads the play can rest content with its literal coherence. Questions as to its meaning arise at once: Is Oedipus really guilty, or simply a victim of the gods, of his famous complex, of fate, of original sin? How much did he know, all along? How much did Jocasta know? The first, and most deeply instinctive effort of the mind, when confronted with this play, is to endeavour to reduce its meanings to some set of rational categories.

The critics of the Age of Reason tried to understand it as a fable of the enlightened moral will, in accordance with the philosophy of that time. Voltaire's version of the play, following Corneille, and his comments upon it, may be taken as typical. He sees it as essentially a struggle between a strong and righteous Oedipus, and the malicious and very human gods, aided and abetted by the corrupt priest Tiresias; he makes it an antireligious tract, with an unmistakable moral to satisfy the needs of the discursive intellect. In order to make Oedipus 'sympathetic' to his audience, he elides, as much as possible, the incest motif; and he adds an irrelevant love story. He was aware that his version and interpretation were not those of Sophocles but, with the complacent provinciality of his period, he attributes the difference to the darkness of the age in which *Sophocles* lived.

Other attempts to rationalize *Oedipus Rex* are subtler than Voltaire's, and take us further towards an understanding of the play. Freud's reduction of the play to the concepts of his psychology reveals a great deal, opens up perspectives which we are still exploring. If one reads *Oedipus* in the light of Fustel de Coulanges' *The Ancient City*, one may see it as the expression of the ancient patriarchal religion of the Greeks. And other interpretations of the play, theological, philosophical, historical, are available, none of them wrong, but all partial, all reductions of Sophocles' masterpiece to an alien set of categories. For the peculiar virtue of Sophocles' presentation of the myth is that it preserves the ultimate mystery by focusing upon the tragic human at a level beneath, or prior to any rationalization whatever. The plot is so arranged that we see the action, as it were, illumined from many sides at once.

By starting the play at the end of the story, and showing onstage only the last crucial episode in Oedipus' life, the past and present action of the protagonist are revealed together; and, in each other's light, are at last felt as one. Oedipus' quest for the slayer of Laius becomes a quest for the hidden reality of his own past; and as that slowly comes into focus, like repressed material under psycho-analysis—with sensory and emotional immediacy, yet in the light of acceptance and understanding—his immediate quest also reaches its end: he comes to see himself (the Saviour of the City) and the guilty one, the plague of Thebes, at once and at one.

This presentation of the myth of Oedipus constitutes, in one sense, an 'interpretation' of it. What Sophocles saw as the essence of Oedipus' nature and destiny, is not what Seneca or Dryden or Cocteau saw; and one may grant that even Sophocles did not exhaust the possibilities in the materials of the myth. But Sophocles' version of the myth does not constitute a 'reduction' in the same sense as the rest.

I have said that the action which Sophocles shows is a quest, the quest for Laius' slayer; and that as Oedipus' past is unrolled before us his whole life is seen as a kind of quest for his true nature and destiny. But since the object of this quest is not clear until the end, the seeking action takes many forms, as its object appears in different lights. The object, indeed, the final perception, the 'truth', looks so different at the end from what it did at the beginning that Oedipus' action itself may seem not a quest, but its opposite, a flight. Thus it would be hard to say, simply, that Oedipus either succeeds or fails. He succeeds; but his success is his undoing. He fails to find what, in one way, he sought; yet from another point of view his search is brilliantly successful. The same ambiguities surround his effort to discover who and what he is. He seems to find that he is nothing; yet thereby finds himself. And what of his relation to the gods? His quest may be regarded as a heroic attempt to escape their decrees, or as an attempt, based upon some deep natural faith, to discover what their wishes are, and what true obedience would be. In one sense Oedipus suffers forces he can neither control nor understand, the puppet of fate; yet at the same time he wills and intelligently intends his every move.

The meaning, or spiritual content of the play, is not to be sought by trying to resolve such ambiguities as these. The spiritual content of the play is the tragic action which Sophocles directly presents; and this action is in its essence *zweideutig* [ambiguous]: triumph and destruction, darkness and enlightenment, mourning and rejoicing, at any moment we care to consider it. But this action has also a shape: a beginning, middle, and end, in time. It starts with the reasoned purpose of finding Laius' slayer. But this aim meets unforeseen difficulties, evidences which do not fit, and therefore shake the purpose as it was first understood; and so the characters suffer the piteous and terrible sense of the mystery of the human situation. From this suffering or passion, with its shifting visions, a new perception of the situation emerges; and on that basis

the purpose of the action is redefined, and a new movement starts. This movement, or *tragic rhythm of action*, constitutes the shape of the play as a whole;
it is also the shape of each episode, each discussion between principals with
the chorus following. Mr Kenneth Burke has studied the tragic rhythm in his
Philosophy of Literary Form, and also in *A Grammar of Motives*, where he
gives the three moments traditional designations which are very suggestive:
Poiema, Pathema, Mathema. They may also be called, for convenience, Purpose,
Passion (or Suffering) and Perception. It is this tragic rhythm of action which
is the substance or spiritual content of the play, and the clue to its extraordinarily comprehensive form.

In order to illustrate these points in more detail, it is convenient to examine
the scene between Oedipus and Tiresias with the chorus following it. This
episode, being early in the play (the first big agon), presents, as it were, a preview of the whole action and constitutes a clear and complete example of action
in the tragic rhythm.

Hero and scapegoat: the agon between Oedipus and Tiresias

The scene between Oedipus and Tiresias comes after the opening sections of
the play. We have seen the citizens of Thebes beseeching their King to find
some way to lift the plague which is on the City. We have had Oedipus' entrance (majestic, but for his tell-tale limp) to reassure them, and we have heard
the report which Creon brings from the Delphic Oracle: that the cause of the
plague is the unpunished murder of Laius, the former king. Oedipus offers
rewards to anyone who will reveal the culprit, and he threatens with dire
punishment anyone who conceals or protects him. In the meantime, he decides,
with the enthusiastic assent of the chorus, to summon Tiresias as the first
witness.

Tiresias is that suffering seer whom Sophocles uses in *Antigone* also to reveal
a truth which other mortals find it hard and uncomfortable to see. He is
physically blind, but Oedipus and chorus alike assume that if anyone can see
who the culprit is, it is Tiresias, with his uncanny inner vision of the future.
As Tiresias enters, led by a boy, the chorus greets him in these words:[2]

CHORUS. But the man to convict him is here. Look: they are bringing the
one human being in whom the truth is native, the godlike seer.

Oedipus is, at this point in the play, at the opposite pole of experience from
Tiresias: he is hero, monarch, helmsman of the state; solver of the Sphinx's
riddle, the triumphant being. He explains his purpose in the following proud
clear terms:

OEDIPUS. O Tiresias, you know all things: what may be told, and the unspeakable: things of earth and things of heaven. You understand the City
(though you do not see it) in its present mortal illness—from which to save
us and protect us, we find, Lord, none but you. For you must know, in case
you haven't heard it from the messengers, that Apollo, when we asked him,
told us there was only one way with this plague: to discover Laius' slayers,

and put them to death or send them into exile. Therefore you must not jealously withhold your omens, whether of birds or other visionary way, but save yourself and the City—save me, save all of us—from the defilement of the dead. In your hand we are. There is no handsomer work for a man, than to bring, with what he has, what help he can.

This speech is the prologue of the scene, and the basis of the agon or struggle which follows. This struggle in effect analyses Oedipus' purpose; places it in a wider context, reveals it as faulty and dubious. At the end of the scene Oedipus loses his original purpose altogether, and suffers a wave of rage and fear, which will have to be rationalized in its turn before he can 'pull himself together' and act again with a clear purpose.

In the first part of the struggle, Oedipus takes the initiative, while Tiresias, on the defensive, tries to avoid replying:

TIRESIAS. Oh, oh. How terrible to know, when nothing can come of knowing! Indeed, I had lost the vision of these things, or I should never have come.
OEDIPUS. What things? ... In what discouragement have you come to us here!
TIR. Let me go home. I shall endure this most easily, and so will you, if you do as I say.
OED. But what you ask is not right. To refuse your word is disloyalty to the City that has fed you.
TIR. But I see that your demands are exorbitant, and lest I too suffer such a—
OED. For the sake of the gods, if you know, don't run away! Speak to us, we are your suppliants here.
TIR. None of you understands. But I—I never will tell my misery. Or yours.
OED. What are you saying? You know, but tell us nothing? You intend treachery to us, and death to the City?
TIR. I intend to grieve neither myself nor you. Why then do you try to know? You will never learn from me.
OED. Ah, evil old man! You would anger a stone! You will say *nothing*? Stand futile, speechless before us?
TIR. You curse my temper, but you don't see the one that dwells in you; no, you must blame me.
OED. And who would *not* lose his temper, if he heard you utter your scorn of the City?
TIR. It will come. Silent though I be.
OED. Since it will come, it is your duty to inform me.
TIR. I shall say no more. Now, if you like, rage to your bitter heart's content.
OED. Very well: in my 'rage' I shall hold back nothing which I now begin to see. I think you planned that deed, even performed it, though not with your own hands. If you could see, I should say that the work was yours alone.

In the last speech quoted, Oedipus changes his tack, specifying his purpose differently; he accuses Tiresias, and that makes Tiresias attack. In the next part of the fight the opponents trade blow for blow:

TIR. You would? I charge you, abide by the decree you uttered: from this day forth, speak neither to these present, nor to me, unclean as you are, polluter of the earth!

407

OED. You have the impudence to speak out words like these! And now how do you expect to escape?

TIR. I have escaped. The truth strengthens and sustains me.

OED. Who taught you the truth? Not your prophet's art.

TIR. You did; you force me against my will to speak.

OED. Speak what? Speak again, that I may understand better.

TIR. *Didn't* you understand? Or are you goading me?

OED. I can't really grasp it: speak again.

TIR. I say you are the murderer of the man whose murderer you seek.

OED. You won't be glad to have uttered that curse twice.

TIR. Must I say more, so you may rage the more?

OED. As much as you like—all is senseless.

TIR. I say you do not know your own wretchedness, nor see in what shame you live with those you love.

OED. Do you think you can say that forever with impunity?

TIR. If the truth has power.

OED. It has, with all but you: helpless is truth with you: for you are blind, in eye, in ear, in mind.

TIR. You are the impotent one: you utter slanders which every man here will apply to you.

OED. You have your being only in the night; you couldn't hurt me or any man who sees the sun.

TIR. No. Your doom is not to fall by me. Apollo suffices for that, he will bring it about.

OED. Are these inventions yours, or Creon's?

TIR. Your wretchedness is not Creon's, it is yours.

OED. O wealth, and power, and skill—which skill, in emulous life, brings low—what envy eyes you! if for this kingly power which the City gave into my hands, unsought—if for *this* the faithful Creon, my friend from the first, has stalked me in secret, yearning to supplant me! if he has bribed this juggling wizard, this deceitful beggar, who discerns his profit only, blind in his own art!

Tell me now, tell me where you have proved a true diviner? Why, when the song-singing sphinx was near, did you not speak the deliverance to the people? Her riddles were not for any comer to solve, but for the mantic art, and you were apparently instructed neither by birds nor by any sign from the gods. Yet when I came, I Oedipus, all innocent, I stopped her song. No birds taught me, by my own wit I found the answer. And it is I whom you wish to banish, thinking that you will then stand close to Creon's throne.

You and your ally will weep, I think, for this attempt; and in fact. if you didn't seem to be an old man, you would already have learned, in pain, of your presumption.

In this part the beliefs, the visions, and hence the purposes of the antagonists are directly contrasted. Because both identify themselves so completely with their visions and purposes, the fight descends from the level of dialectic to a level below the rational altogether: it becomes cruelly *ad hominem*. We are made to see the absurd incommensurability of the very beings of Oedipus and Tiresias; they shrink from one another as from the uncanny. At the end of the round, it is Oedipus who has received the deeper wound; and his great speech, 'O wealth and power', is a far more lyric utterance than the ordered exposition with which he began.

The end of this part of the fight is marked by the intervention of the chorus, which endeavours to recall the antagonists to the most general version of purpose which they supposedly share: the discovery of the truth and the service of the gods:

CHORUS. To us it appears that this man's words were uttered in anger, and yours too, Oedipus. No need for that: consider how best to discharge the mandate of the god.

The last part of the struggle shows Tiresias presenting his whole vision, and Oedipus, on the defensive, shaken to the depths:

TIR. Although you rule, we have equally the right to reply; in that I too have power. Indeed, I live to serve, not you, but Apollo; and I shall not be enrolled under Creon, either. Therefore I say, since you have insulted even my blindness, that though you have eyesight, you do not see what misery you are in, nor where you are living, nor with whom. Do you know whence you came? No, nor that you are the enemy of your own family, the living and the dead. The double prayer of mother and father shall from this land hound you in horror—who now see clearly, but then in darkness.
 Where then will your cry be bounded? What part of Kitharon not echo it quickly back, when you shall come to understand that marriage, to which you sailed on so fair a wind, homelessly home? And many other evils which you do not see will bring you to yourself at last, your children's equal.
 Scorn Creon, therefore, and my words: you will be struck down more terribly than any mortal.
OED. Can I really hear such things from him? Are you not gone? To death? To punishment? Not fled from this house?
TIR. I should never have come if you hadn't called me.
OED. I didn't know how mad you would sound, or it would have been a long time before I asked you here to my house.
TIR. This is what I am; foolish, as it seems to you; but wise, to the parents who gave you birth.
OED. To whom? Wait: *who* gave me birth?
TIR. This day shall give you birth, and death.
OED. In what dark riddles you always speak.
TIR. Aren't you the best diviner of riddles?
OED. Very well: mock that gift, which, you will find, is mine.
TIR. That very gift was your undoing.
OED. But if I saved the City, what does it matter?
TIR. So be it. I am going. Come, boy, lead me.
OED. Take him away. Your presence impedes and trips me; once you are gone, you can do no harm.
TIR. I shall go when I have done my errand without fear of your frowns, for they can't hurt me. I tell you, then, that the man whom you have long been seeking, with threats and proclamations, Laius' slayer, is here. He is thought to be an alien, but will appear a native Theban, and this circumstance will not please him. Blind, who once could see; destitute, who once was rich, leaning on a staff, he will make his way through a strange land. He will be revealed as brother and father of his own children; of the woman who bore him, both son and husband; sharer of his father's bed; his father's killer.
 Go in and ponder this. If you find it wrong, say then I do not understand the prophetic vision.

409

Oedipus rushes off-stage, his clear purpose gone, his being shaken with fear and anger. Tiresias departs, led by his boy. The chorus is left to move and chant, suffering the mixed and ambivalent feelings, the suggestive but mysterious images, which the passion in which the agon eventuated produces in them.

CHORUS

Strophe I. Who is it that the god's voice from the Rock of
 Delphi says
 Accomplished the unspeakable with murderous hands?
 Time now that windswift
 Stronger than horses
 His feet take flight.
 In panoply of fire and lightning
 Now springs upon him the son of Zeus
 Whom the dread follow,
 The Fates unappeasable.
Antistrophe I. New word, like light, from snowy Parnassus:
 Over all the earth trail the unseen one.
 For in rough wood,
 In cave or rocks,
 Like bull bereft—stampeded, futile
 He goes, seeking with futile foot to
 Flee the ultimate
 Doom, which ever
 Lives and flies over him.
Strophe II. In awe now, and soul's disorder, I neither accept
 The augur's wisdom, nor deny: I know not what to say.
 I hover in hope, see neither present nor future.
 Between the House of Laius
 And Oedipus, I do not hear, have never heard, of any feud:
 I cannot confirm the public charge against him, to help
 Avenge the dark murder.
Antistrophe II. Zeus and Apollo are wise, and all that is mortal
 They know: but whether that human seer knows more than I
 There is no way of telling surely, though in wisdom
 A man may excel.
 Ah, never could I, till I see that word confirmed, consent to blame him!
 Before all eyes the winged songstress, once, assailed him;
 Wise showed he in that test, and to the City, tender; in my heart
 I will call him evil never.

The chorus is considered in more detail below. At this point I merely wish to point out that Oedipus and Tiresias show, in their agon, the 'purpose' part of the tragic rhythm; that this turns to 'passion', and that the chorus presents the passion and also the new perception which follows. This new perception is that of Oedipus as the possible culprit. But his outlines are vague; perhaps the vision itself is illusory, a bad dream. The chorus has not yet reached the end of its quest; that will come only when Oedipus, in the flesh before them, is unmistakably seen as the guilty one. We have reached merely a provisional resting-place, the end of the first figure in which the tragic rhythm is presented. But this figure is a reduced version of the shape of the play as a whole, and the fleeting and unwelcome image of Oedipus as guilty corresponds to the final perception or epiphany, the full-stop, with which the play ends.

Oedipus: ritual and play

The Cambridge School of Classical Anthropologists has shown in great detail that the form of Greek tragedy follows the form of a very ancient ritual, that of the *Enniautos-Daimon*, or seasonal god.[3] This was one of the most influential discoveries of the last few generations, and it gives us new insights into *Oedipus* which I think are not yet completely explored. The clue to Sophocles' dramatizing of the myth of Oedipus is to be found in this ancient ritual, which had a similar form and meaning—that is, it also moved in the 'tragic rhythm'.

Experts in classical anthropology, like experts in other fields, dispute innumerable questions of fact and of interpretation which the layman can only pass over in respectful silence. One of the thornier questions seems to be whether myth or ritual came first. Is the ancient ceremony merely an enactment of the Ur-Myth of the year-god—Attis, or Adonis, or Osiris, or the 'Fisher-King'—in any case that Hero–King–Father–High Priest who fights with his rival, is slain and dismembered, then rises anew with the spring season? Or did the innumerable myths of the kind arise to 'explain' a ritual which was perhaps mimed or danced or sung to celebrate the annual change of season?

For the purpose of understanding the form and meanings of *Oedipus*, it is not necessary to worry about the answer to this question of historic fact. The figure of Oedipus himself fulfils all the requirements of the scapegoat, the dismembered king or god-figure. The situation in which Thebes is presented at the beginning of the play—in peril of its life; its crops, its herds, its women mysteriously infertile, signs of a mortal disease of the City, and the disfavour of the gods—is like the withering which winter brings, and calls, in the same way, for struggle, dismemberment, death, and renewal. And this tragic sequence is the substance of the play. It is enough to know that myth and ritual are close together in their genesis, two direct imitations of the perennial experience of the race.

But when one considers *Oedipus* as a ritual one understands it in ways which one cannot by thinking of it merely as a dramatization of a story, even that story. Harrison has shown that the Festival of Dionysos, based ultimately upon the yearly vegetation ceremonies, included *rites de passage*, like that celebrating the assumption of adulthood—celebrations of the mystery of individual growth and development. At the same time, it was a prayer for the welfare of the whole City; and this welfare was understood not only as material prosperity, but also as the natural order of the family, the ancestors, the present members, and the generations still to come, and, by the same token, obedience to the gods who were jealous, each in his own province, of this natural and divinely sanctioned order and proportion.

We must suppose that Sophocles' audience (the whole population of the City) came early, prepared to spend the day in the bleachers. At their feet was the semicircular dancing-ground for the chorus, and the thrones for the priests, and the altar. Behind that was the raised platform for the principal actors, backed

411

by the all-purpose, emblematic façade, which would presently be taken to represent Oedipus' palace in Thebes. The actors were not professionals in our sense, but citizens selected for a religious office, and Sophocles himself had trained them and the chorus.

This crowd must have had as much appetite for thrills and diversion as the crowds who assemble in our day for football games and musical comedies, and Sophocles certainly holds the attention with an exciting show. At the same time his audience must have been alert for the fine points of poetry and dramaturgy, for *Oedipus* is being offered in competition with other plays on the same bill. But the element which distinguishes this theatre, giving it its unique directness and depth, is the *ritual expectancy* which Sophocles assumed in his audience. The nearest thing we have to this ritual sense of theatre is, I suppose, to be found at an Easter performance of the *Mattias Passion*. We also can observe something similar in the dances and ritual mummery of the Pueblo Indians. Sophocles' audience must have been prepared, like the Indians standing around their plaza, to consider the playing, the make-believe it was about to see—the choral invocations, with dancing and chanting; the reasoned discourses and the terrible combats of the protagonists; the mourning, the rejoicing, and the contemplation of the final stage-picture or epiphany—as imitating and celebrating the mystery of human nature and destiny. And this mystery was at once that of individual growth and development, and that of the precarious life of the human City.

I have indicated how Sophocles presents the life of the mythic Oedipus in the tragic rhythm, the mysterious quest of life. Oedipus is shown seeking his own true being; but at the same time and by the same token, the welfare of the City. When one considers the ritual form of the whole play, it becomes evident that it presents the tragic but perennial, even normal, quest of the whole City for its wellbeing. In this larger action, Oedipus is only the protagonist, the first and most important champion. This tragic quest is realized by all the characters in their various ways; but in the development of the action as a whole it is the chorus alone that plays a part as important as that of Oedipus; its counterpart, in fact. The chorus holds the balance between Oedipus and his antagonists, marks the progress of their struggles, and restates the main theme, and its new variation, after each dialogue or agon. The ancient ritual was probably performed by a chorus alone without individual developments and variations, and the chorus, in *Oedipus*, is still the element that throws most light on the ritual form of the play as a whole.

The chorus consists of twelve or fifteen 'Elders of Thebes'. This group is not intended to represent literally all of the citizens either of Thebes or of Athens. The play opens with a large delegation of Theban citizens before Oedipus' palace, and the chorus proper does not enter until after the prologue. Nor does the chorus speak directly for the Athenian audience; we are asked throughout to make-believe that the theatre is the agora at Thebes; and at the same time Sophocles' audience is witnessing a ritual. It would, I think, be more accurate to say that the chorus represents the point of view and the faith of Thebes as a whole, and, by analogy, of the Athenian audience. Their errand before

Oedipus' palace is like that of Sophocles' audience in the theatre: they are watching a sacred combat, in the issue of which they have an all-important and official stake. Thus they represent the audience and the citizens in a particular way—not as a mob formed in response to some momentary feeling, but rather as an organ of a highly self-conscious community: something closer to the 'conscience of the race' than to the overheated affectivity of a mob.

According to Aristotle, a Sophoclean chorus is a character that takes an important role in the action of the play, instead of merely making incidental music between the scenes, as in the plays of Euripides. The chorus may be described as a group personality, like an old Parliament. It has its own traditions, habits of thought and feeling, and mode of being. It exists, in a sense, as a living entity, but not with the sharp actuality of an individual. It perceives; but its perception is at once wider and vaguer than that of a single man. It shares, in its way, the seeking action of the play as a whole; but it cannot act in all the modes; it depends upon the chief agonists to invent and try out the detail of policy, just as a rather helpless but critical Parliament depends upon the Prime Minister to act but, in its less specific form of life, survives his destruction.

When the chorus enters after the prologue, with its questions, its invocation of the various gods, and its focus upon the hidden and jeopardized welfare of the City—Athens or Thebes—the list of essential *dramatis personae*, as well as the elements needed to celebrate the ritual, is complete, and the main action can begin. It is the function of the chorus to mark the stages of this action, and to perform the suffering and perceiving part of the tragic rhythm. The protagonist and his antagonists develop the 'purpose' with which the tragic sequence begins; the chorus, with its less than individual being, broods over the agons, marks their stages with a word (like that of the chorus leader in the middle of the Tiresias scene), and (expressing its emotions and visions in song and dance) suffers the results, and the new perception at the end of the fight.

The choral odes are lyrics but they are not to be understood as poetry, the art of words, only, for they are intended also to be danced and sung. And though each chorus has its own shape, like that of a discrete lyric—its beginning, middle, and end—it represents also one passion or pathos in the changing action of the whole. This passion, like the other moments in the tragic rhythm, is felt at so general or, rather, so deep a level that it seems to contain both the mob ferocity that Nietzsche felt in it and, at the other extreme, the patience of prayer. It is informed by faith in the unseen order of nature and the gods, and moves through a sequence of modes of suffering. This may be illustrated from the chorus I have quoted at the end of the Tiresias scene.

It begins (close to the savage emotion of the end of the fight) with images suggesting that cruel 'Bacchic frenzy' which is supposed to be the common root of tragedy and of the 'old' comedy: 'In panoply of fire and lightning/The son of Zeus now springs upon him.' In the first antistrophe these images come together more clearly as we relish the chase; and the fleeing culprit, as we imagine him, begins to resemble Oedipus, who is lame, and always associated with the rough wilderness of Kitharon. But in the second strophe, as though appalled by its ambivalent feelings and the imagined possibilities, the chorus sinks back into a more dark and patient posture of suffering, 'in awe', 'hovering in hope'. In the second antistrophe this is developed into something like the orthodox Christian attitude of prayer, based on faith, and assuming the possibility of a hitherto unimaginable truth and answer: 'Zeus and Apollo are wise', etc. The whole chorus then ends with a new vision of Oedipus, of the culprit, and of the direction in which the welfare of the City is to be sought. This vision is still coloured by the chorus's human love of Oedipus as Hero, for the chorus has still its own purgation to complete, cannot as yet accept completely either the suffering in store for it, or Oedipus as scapegoat. But it marks the end of the first complete 'purpose passion perception' unit, and lays the basis for the new purpose which will begin the next unit.

It is also to be noted that the chorus changes the scene which we, as audience, are to imagine. During the agon between Oedipus and Tiresias, our attention is fixed upon their clash, and the scene is literal, close, and immediate: before Oedipus' palace. When the fighters depart and the choral music starts, the focus suddenly widens, as though we had been removed to a distance. We become aware of the interested City around the bright arena; and beyond that, still more dimly, of Nature, sacred to the hidden gods. Mr Burke has expounded the fertile notion that human action may be understood in terms of the scene in which it occurs, and vice-versa: the scene is defined by the mode of action. The chorus's action is not limited by the sharp, rationalized purposes of the protagonist; its mode of action, more patient, less sharply realized, is cognate with a wider, if less accurate, awareness of the scene of human life. But the chorus's action, as I have remarked, is not that of passion itself (Nietzsche's cosmic void of night) but suffering informed by the faith of the tribe in a human and a divinely sanctioned natural order: 'If such deeds as these are honoured', the chorus asks after Jocasta's impiety, 'why should I dance and sing?' (lines 894, 895). Thus it is one of the most important functions of the chorus to reveal, in its widest and most mysterious extent, the theatre of human life which the play, and indeed the whole Festival of Dionysos, assumed. Even when the chorus does not speak, but only watches, it maintains this theme and this perspective— ready to take the whole stage when the fighters depart.

If one thinks of the movement of the play, it appears that the tragic rhythm analyses human action temporally into successive modes, as a crystal analyses a white beam of light spatially into the coloured bands of the spectrum. The chorus, always present, represents one of these modes, and at the recurrent moments when reasoned purpose is gone, it takes the stage with its faith-informed passion, moving through an ordered succession of modes of suffering, to a new perception of the immediate situation.

Sophocles and Euripides, the rationalist

Oedipus Rex is a changing image of human life and action which could have been formed only in the mirror of the tragic theatre of the Festival of Dionysos. The perspectives of the myth, of the rituals, and of the traditional *hodos*, the way of life of the City—'habits of thought and feelings' which constitute the traditional wisdom of the race—were all required to make this play possible. That is why we have to try to regain these perspectives if we are to understand the written play which has come down to us: the analysis of the play leads to an analysis of the theatre in which it was formed.

But though the theatre was there, everyone could not use it to the full: Sophocles was required. This becomes clear if one considers the very different use which Euripides, Sophocles' contemporary, makes of the tragic theatre and its ritual forms.

Professor Gilbert Murray has explained in detail how the tragic form is derived from the ritual form; and he has demonstrated the ritual forms which are preserved in each of the extant Greek tragedies. In general, the ritual had its agon, or sacred combat, between the old King, or god or hero, and the new, corresponding to the agons in the tragedies, and the clear 'purpose' moment of the tragic rhythm. It had its *Sparagmos*, in which the royal victim was literally or symbolically torn asunder, followed by the lamentation and/or rejoicing of the chorus: elements which correspond to the moments of 'passion'. The ritual had its messenger, its recognition scene, and its epiphany; various plot devices for representing the moment of 'perception' which follows the 'pathos'. Professor Murray, in a word, studies the art of tragedy in the light of ritual forms, and thus, throws a really new light upon Aristotle's *Poetics*. The parts of the ritual would appear to correspond to parts of the plot, like recognitions and scenes of suffering, which Aristotle mentions, but, in the text which has come down to us, fails to expound completely. In this view, both the ritual and the more highly elaborated and individualized art of tragedy would be 'imitating' action in the tragic rhythm; the parts of the ritual, and the parts of the plot, would both be devices for showing forth the three moments of this rhythm.

Professor Murray, however, does not make precisely these deductions. Unlike Aristotle, he takes the plays of Euripides, rather than Sophocles' *Oedipus*, as the patterns of the tragic form. That is because his attitude to the ritual forms is like Euripides' own: he responds to their purely theatrical effectiveness, but has no interest or belief in the prerational image of human nature and destiny which the ritual conveyed; which Sophocles felt as still alive and significant for his generation, and presented once more in *Oedipus*. Professor Murray shows that Euripides restored the literal ritual much more accurately than Sophocles— his epiphanies, for example, are usually the bodily showing-forth of a very human god, who cynically expounds his cruel part in the proceedings; while the 'epiphany' in *Oedipus*, the final tableau of the blind old man with his incestuous brood, merely conveys the moral truth which underlay the action, and implies the anagoge: human dependence upon a mysterious and divine order of nature. Perhaps these distinctions may be summarized as follows: Professor Murray is interested in the ritual forms in abstraction from all content; Sophocles saw also the spiritual content of the old forms: understood them at a level deeper than the literal, as imitations of an action still 'true' to life in his sophisticated age.

Though Euripides and Sophocles wrote at the same time and for the same theatre, one cannot understand either the form or the meaning of Euripides' plays on the basis of Sophocles' dramaturgy. The beautiful lyrics sung by Euripides' choruses are, as I have said, incidental music rather than organic parts of the action; they are not based upon the feeling that all have a stake in the common way of life and therefore in the issue of the present action. Euripides' individualistic heroes find no light in their suffering, and bring no renewal to the moral life of the community: they are at war with the very clear, human, and malicious gods, and what they suffer, they suffer unjustly and to no good end. Where Sophocles' celebrated irony seems to envisage the *condition humaine* itself—the plight of the psyche in a world which is ultimately mysterious to it —Euripides' ironies are all aimed at the incredible 'gods' and at the superstitions of those who believe in them. In short, if these two writers both used the tragic theatre, they did so in very different ways.

Verral's *Euripides the Rationalist* shows very clearly what the basis of Euripides' dramaturgy is. His use of myth and ritual is like that which Cocteau or, still more exactly, Sartre makes of them—for parody or satirical exposition, but without any belief in their meaning. If Euripides presents the plight of Electra in realistic detail, it is because he wants us to feel the suffering of the individual without benefit of any objective moral or cosmic order—with an almost sensational immediacy: he does not see the myth, as a whole, as significant as such. If he brings Apollo, in the flesh, before us, it is not because he 'believes' in Apollo, but because he disbelieves in him, and wishes to reveal this figment of the Greek imagination as, literally, incredible. He depends as much as Sophocles upon the common heritage of ritual and myth: but he 'reduces' its form and images to the uses of parody and metaphorical illustration, in the manner of Ovid and of the French Neoclassic tradition. And the human action he reveals is the extremely modern one of the psyche caught in the categories its reason invents, responding with unmitigated sharpness to the feeling of the moment, but cut off from the deepest level of experience, where the mysterious world is yet felt as real and prior to our inventions, demands, and criticisms.

Though Sophocles was not using the myths and ritual forms of the tragic theatre for parody and to satirize their tradition, it does not appear that he had any more naïve belief in their literal validity than Euripides did. He would not, for his purpose, have had to ask himself whether the myth of Oedipus conveyed any historic facts. He would not have had to believe that the performance of *Oedipus*, or even the Festival of Dionysos itself, would assure the Athenians a good crop of children and olives. On the contrary he must have felt that the tragic rhythm of action which he discerned in the myth, which he felt as underlying the forms of the ritual, and which he realized in so many ways in his play, was a deeper version of human life than any particular manifestation of it, or any conceptual understanding of it, whether scientific and rationalistic, or theological; yet potentially including them all. If one takes Mr Troy's suggestion, one might say, using the medieval notion of fourfold symbolism, that Sophocles might well have taken myth and ritual as literally 'fictions', yet still have accepted their deeper meanings—trope, allegory, and anagoge—as valid.

416

Oedipus: the imitation of an action

The general notion we used to compare the forms of spiritual content of tragedy and of ancient ritual was the 'imitation of action'. Ritual imitates action in one way, tragedy in another; and Sophocles' use of ritual forms indicates that he sensed the tragic rhythm common to both.

But the language, plot, characters of the play may also be understood in more detail and in relation to each other as imitations, in their various media, of the one action. I have already quoted Coleridge on the unity of action: 'not properly a rule', he calls it, 'but in itself the great end, not only of the drama, but of the epic, lyric, even to the candle-flame cone of an epigram—not only of poetry, but of poesy in general, as the proper generic term inclusive of all the fine arts, as its species'.[4] Probably the influence of Coleridge partly accounts for the revival of this notion of action which underlies the recent studies of poetry which I have mentioned. Mr Burke's phrase, 'language as symbolic action', expresses the idea, and so does his dictum: 'The poet spontaneously knows that "beauty *is* as beauty *does*" (that the "state" must be embodied in an "actualization").' (*Four Tropes*.)

This idea of action, and of the play as the imitation of an action, is ultimately derived from the *Poetics*. This derivation is explained in the Appendix. At this point I wish to show how the complex form of *Oedipus*—its plot, characters, and discourse—may be understood as the imitation of a certain action.

The action of the play is the quest for Laius' slayer. That is the over-all aim which informs it—'to find the culprit in order to purify human life', as it may be put. Sophocles must have seen this seeking action as the real life of the Oedipus myth, discerning it through the personages and events as one discerns 'life in a plant through the green leaves'. Moreover, he must have seen this particular action as a type, or crucial instance, of human life in general; and hence he was able to present it in the form of the ancient ritual which also presents and celebrates the perennial mystery of human life and action. Thus by 'action' I do not mean the events of the story but the focus or aim of psychic life from which the events, in that situation, result.

If Sophocles was imitating action in this sense, one may schematically imagine his work of composition in three stages, three mimetic acts: 1. He makes the plot: i.e. arranges the events of the story in such a way as to reveal the seeking action from which they come. 2. He develops the characters of the story as individualized forms of 'quest'. 3. He expresses or realizes their actions by means of the words they utter in the various situations of the plot. This scheme, of course, has nothing to do with the temporal order which the poet may really have followed in elaborating his composition, nor to the order we follow in becoming acquainted with it; we start with the words, the 'green leaves'. The scheme refers to the 'hierarchy of actualizations' which we may eventually learn to see in the completed work.

1. The first act of imitation consists in making the plot or arrangement of incidents. Aristotle says that the tragic poet is primarily a maker of plots, for the plot is the 'soul of a tragedy', its formal cause. The arrangement which

Sophocles made of the events of the story—starting near the end, and rehearsing the past in relation to what is happening now—already to some degree actualizes the tragic quest he wishes to show, even before we sense the characters as individuals or hear them speak and sing.

(The reader must be warned that this conception of the plot is rather unfamiliar to us. Usually we do not distinguish between the plot as the form of the play and the plot as producing a certain effect upon the audience—excitement, 'interest', suspense, and the like. Aristotle also uses 'plot' in this second sense. The mimicry of art has a further purpose, or final—as distinguished from its formal—cause, i.e. to reach the audience. Thinking of the Athenian theatre, he describes the plot as intended to show the 'universal', or to rouse and purge the emotions of pity and terror. These two meanings of the word—the form of the action, and the device for reaching the audience—are also further explained in the Appendix. At this point I am using the word *plot* in the first sense: as the form, the actualization, of the tragic action.)

2. The characters, or agents, are the second actualization of the action. According to Aristotle, 'the agents are imitated mainly with a view to the action'—i.e. the soul of the tragedy is there already in the order of events, the tragic rhythm of the life of Oedipus and Thebes; but this action may be more sharply realized and more elaborately shown forth by developing individual variations upon it. It was with this principle in mind that Ibsen wrote to his publisher, after two years of work on *The Wild Duck*, that the play was nearly complete, and he could now proceed to 'the more energetic individuation of the characters'.

If one considers the Oedipus–Tiresias scene which I have quoted, one can see how the characters serve to realize the action of the whole. They reveal, at any moment, a 'spectrum of action' like that which the tragic rhythm spread before us in temporal succession, at the same time offering concrete instances of almost photographic sharpness. Thus Tiresias 'suffers' in the darkness of his blindness while Oedipus pursues his reasoned 'purpose'; and then Tiresias effectuates his 'purpose' of serving his mantic vision of the truth, while Oedipus 'suffers' a blinding passion of fear and anger. The agents also serve to move the action ahead, develop it in time, through their conflicts. The chorus meanwhile, in some respects between, in others deeper than, the antagonists, represents the interests of that resolution, that final chord of feeling, in which the end of the action, seen ironically and sympathetically as one, will be realized.

3. The third actualization is in the words of the play. The seeking action which is the substance of the play is imitated first in the plot, second in the characters, and third in the words, concepts, and forms of discourse wherein the characters 'actualize' their psychic life in its shifting forms, in response to the everchanging situations of the play. If one thinks of plotting, characterization, and poetry as successive 'acts of imitation' by the author, one may also say that they constitute, in the completed work, a hierarchy of forms; and that the words of the play are its 'highest individuation'. They are the 'green leaves' which we actually perceive; the product and the sign of the one 'life of the plant' which, by an imaginative effort, one may divine behind them all.

At this point one encounters again Mr Burke's theory of 'language as symbolic action', and the many contemporary studies of the arts of poetry which have been made from this point of view. It would be appropriate to offer a detailed study of Sophocles' language, using the modern tools of analysis, to substantiate my main point. But this would require the kind of knowledge of Greek which a Jebb spent his life to acquire; and I must be content to try to show, in very general terms, that the varied forms of the poetry of *Oedipus* can only be understood on a histrionic basis: i.e. as coming out of a direct sense of the tragic rhythm of *action*.

In the Oedipus-Tiresias scene, there is a 'spectrum of the forms of discourse' corresponding to the 'spectrum of action' which I have described. It extends from Oedipus' opening speech—a reasoned exposition not, of course, without feeling but based essentially upon clear ideas and a logical order—to the choral chant, based upon sensuous imagery and the 'logic of feeling'. Thus it employs, in the beginning, the principle of composition which Mr Burke calls 'syllogistic progression', and, at the other end of the spectrum, Mr Burke's 'progression by association and contrast'. When the Neoclassic and rationalistic critics of the seventeenth century read *Oedipus*, they saw only the order of reason; they did not know what to make of the chorus. Hence Racine's drama of 'Action as Rational': a drama of static situations, of clear concepts and merely illustrative images. Nietzsche, on the other hand, saw only the passion of the chorus; for his insight was based on *Tristan*, which is composed essentially in sensuous images, and moves by association and contrast according to the logic of feeling: the drama which takes 'action as passion'. Neither point of view enables one to see how the scene, as a whole, hangs together.

If the speeches of the characters and the songs of the chorus are only the foliage of the plant, this is as much as to say that the life and meaning of the whole is never literally and completely present in any one formulation. It takes *all* of the elements—the shifting situation, the changing and developing characters, and their reasoned or lyric utterances, to indicate, in the round, the action Sophocles wishes to convey. Because this action takes the form of reason as well as passion, and of contemplation by way of symbols; because it is essentially moving (in the tragic rhythm); and because it is shared in different ways by all the characters, the play has neither literal unity nor the rational unity of the truly abstract idea, or 'univocal concept'. Its parts and its moments are one only 'by analogy'; and just as the Saints warn us that we must believe in order to understand, so we must 'make believe', by a sympathetic and imitative act of the histrionic sensibility, in order to get what Sophocles intended by his play.

It is the histrionic basis of Sophocles' art which makes it mysterious to us, with our demands for conceptual clarity, or for the luxury of yielding to a stream of feeling and subjective imagery. But it is this also which makes it so crucial an instance of the art of the theatre in its completeness, as though the author understood 'song, spectacle, thought, and diction' in their primitive and subtle roots. And it is the histrionic basis of drama which 'undercuts theology and science'.

Notes

1. 'Myth, method and the future', by William Troy, *Chimera*, Spring, 1946.

2. I am responsible for the English of this scene. The reader is referred to *Oedipus Rex*, translated by Dudley Fitts and Robert Fitzgerald (New York, 1949), a very handsome version of the whole play.

3. See especially Jane Ellen Harrison's *Ancient Art and Ritual*, and her *Themis* which contains an 'Excursus on the ritual forms preserved in Greek Tragedy' by Professor Gilbert Murray.

4. The essay on *Othello*.

31   Northrop Frye

Northrop Frye (b. 1912) was born in Canada and studied at Toronto University and Merton College, Oxford, moving into the field of literature after beginning as a student of theology. His first major publication was *Fearful Symmetry: a study of William Blake* (1947), but it was the *Anatomy of Criticism* (1957) that firmly established him as one of the most brilliant, original and influential of modern critics.

Frye's general position is simply described. Like many modern critics from I. A. Richards onwards, he is impatient with the confusions and contradictions of most extant literary criticism, and believes that it should acquire something of the methodological discipline and coherence of the sciences. This, in his view, can only be attained by assuming a total coherence in criticism based on a hypothesis about literature itself, and the primary source of this coherence, Frye argues, is the recurrence, with various degrees of 'displacement', of certain archetypes in literature of all periods and cultures. This theory is expounded with characteristic lucidity, economy and wit in 'The Archetypes of Literature' (1951), much of which was later incorporated into the *Anatomy*. 'Literature as Context: Milton's *Lycidas*' (1959) is a virtuoso demonstration of Frye's method applied to a single text.

Frye's work has aroused considerable controversy. In particular, his scorn for value judgments, which he consigns to the 'history of taste' has aroused deep hostility among those critics for whom evaluation has always been the *raison d'être* of literary studies. In fact Frye's difference with such critics is not as irreconcilable as it might seem, for he has simply transferred the concept of value from the individual work to the collective work, the 'total order of words' that is literature. Few critics have in fact made such large claims for literature as Frye: 'Literature imitates the total dream of man...,' he writes in the *Anatomy*, 'Poetry unites total ritual, or unlimited social action, with total dream, or unlimited individual thought.'

Other objections to Frye's criticism are that it is excessively schematic, that it neglects the historical, particular, verbally unique aspects of literary artefacts, and that archetypal criticism, so far from being scientific, is neither verifiable nor falsifiable. Frye is well able to defend himself against such charges, and has observed reasonably enough that, 'Many who consider the structure of my view of literature repellent find useful parenthetic insights in me, but the insights would not be there unless the structure were there too.' He is certainly one of the most stimulating, cultured and witty of contemporary literary critics.

Northrop Frye is University Professor at the University of Toronto, and has been Visiting Professor at several other North American universities. 'The

Archetypes of Literature' and 'Literature as Context: Milton's *Lycidas*' are reprinted here from *Fables of Identity: studies in poetic mythology* (New York, 1963). Other publications of Northrop Frye include *The Well-Tempered Critic* (Bloomington, Indiana, 1963), *T. S. Eliot* (1963), *A Natural Perspective: the development of Shakespearian comedy and romance* (New York, 1965), and, most recently, *The Stubborn Structure: essays on criticism and society* (1970).

CROSS REFERENCES: 6. T. S. Eliot
                          14. C. G. Jung
                          15. Maud Bodkin
                          33. Leslie Fiedler
                          40. Claude Lévi-Strauss
                          41. René Wellek

COMMENTARY: *Northrop Frye in Modern Criticism*, ed. Murray Krieger (New York, 1966)

The archetypes of literature

I

Every organized body of knowledge can be learned progressively; and experience shows that there is also something progressive about the learning of literature. Our opening sentence has already got us into a semantic difficulty. Physics is an organized body of knowledge about nature, and a student of it says that he is learning physics, not that he is learning nature. Art, like nature, is the subject of a systematic study, and has to be distinguished from the study itself, which is criticism. It is therefore impossible to 'learn literature': one learns about it in a certain way, but what one learns, transitively, is the criticism of literature. Similarly, the difficulty often felt in 'teaching literature' arises from the fact that it cannot be done: the criticism of literature is all that can be directly taught. So while no one expects literature itself to behave like a science, there is surely no reason why criticism, as a systematic and organized study, should not be, at least partly, a science. Not a 'pure' or 'exact' science, perhaps, but these phrases form part of a nineteenth-century cosmology which is no longer with us. Criticism deals with the arts and may well be something of an art itself, but it does not follow that it must be unsystematic. If it is to be related to the sciences too, it does not follow that it must be deprived of the graces of culture.

Certainly criticism as we find it in learned journals and scholarly monographs has every characteristic of a science. Evidence is examined scientifically; previous authorities are used scientifically; fields are investigated scientifically; texts are edited scientifically. Prosody is scientific in structure; so is phonetics; so is philology. And yet in studying this kind of critical science the student becomes aware of a centrifugal movement carrying him away from literature. He finds that literature is the central division of the 'humanities', flanked on one side by history and on the other by philosophy. Criticism so far ranks only as a subdivision of literature; and hence, for the systematic mental organization of the subject, the student has to turn to the conceptual framework of the historian for events, and to that of the philosopher for ideas. Even the more centrally placed critical sciences, such as textual editing, seem to be part of a 'background' that recedes into history or some other non-literary field. The thought suggests itself that the ancillary critical disciplines may be related to a central expanding pattern of systematic comprehension which has not yet been established, but which, if it were established, would prevent them from being centrifugal. If such a pattern exists, then criticism would be to art what philosophy is to wisdom and history to action.

Most of the central area of criticism is at present, and doubtless always will be, the area of commentary. But the commentators have little sense, unlike the researchers, of being contained within some sort of scientific discipline: they are chiefly engaged, in the words of the gospel hymn, in brightening the corner where they are. If we attempt to get a more comprehensive idea of what criticism is about, we find ourselves wandering over quaking bogs of generalities, judicious pronouncements of value, reflective comments, perorations to works of research, and other consequences of taking the large view. But this part of the critical field is so full of pseudo-propositions, sonorous nonsense that contains no truth and no falsehood, that it obviously exists only because criticism, like nature, prefers a waste space to an empty one.

The term 'pseudo-proposition' may imply some sort of logical positivist attitude on my own part. But I would not confuse the significant proposition with the factual one; nor should I consider it advisable to muddle the study of literature with a schizophrenic dichotomy between subjective–emotional and objective–descriptive aspects of meaning, considering that in order to produce any literary meaning at all one has to ignore this dichotomy. I say only that the principles by which one can distinguish a significant from a meaningless statement in criticism are not clearly defined. Our first step, therefore, is to recognize and get rid of meaningless criticism: that is, talking about literature in a way that cannot help to build up a systematic structure of knowledge. Casual value-judgments belong not to criticism but to the history of taste, and reflect, at best, only the social and psychological compulsions which prompted their utterance. All judgments in which the values are not based on literary experience but are sentimental or derived from religious or political prejudice may be regarded as casual. Sentimental judgments are usually based either on non-existent categories or antitheses ('Shakespeare studied life, Milton books') or on a visceral reaction to the writer's personality. The literary chit-chat which makes the reputations of poets boom and crash in an imaginary stock exchange is pseudo-criticism. That wealthy investor Mr Eliot, after dumping Milton on the Market, is now buying him again; Donne has probably reached his peak and will begin to taper off; Tennyson may be in for a slight flutter but the Shelley stocks are still bearish. This sort of thing cannot be part of any systematic study, for a systematic study can only progress: whatever dithers or vacillates or reacts is merely leisure-class conversation.

We next meet a more serious group of critics who say: the foreground of criticism is the impact of literature on the reader. Let us, then, keep the study of literature centripetal, and base the learning process on a structural analysis of the literary work itself. The texture of any great work of art is complex and ambiguous, and in unravelling the complexities we may take in as much history and philosophy as we please, if the subject of our study remains at the centre. If it does not, we may find that in our anxiety to write about literature we have forgotten how to read it.

The only weakness in this approach[a] is that it is conceived primarily as the antithesis of centrifugal or 'background' criticism, and so lands us in a somewhat unreal dilemma, like the conflict of internal and external relations in philosophy. Antitheses are usually resolved, not by picking one side and refuting the other, or by making eclectic choices between them, but by trying to get past the antithetical way of stating the problem. It is right that the first effort of critical apprehension should take the form of a rhetorical or structural analysis of a work of art. But a purely structural approach has the same limitation in criticism that it has in biology. In itself it is simply a discrete series of analyses based on the mere existence of the literary structure, without developing any explanation of how the structure came to be what it was and what its nearest relatives are. Structural analysis brings rhetoric back to criticism, but we need a new poetics as well, and the attempt to construct a new poetics out of rhetoric alone can hardly avoid a mere complication of rhetorical terms into a sterile jargon. I suggest that what is at present missing from literary criticism is a co-ordinating principle, a central hypothesis which, like the theory of evolution in biology, will see the phenomena it deals with as part of a whole. Such a principle, though it would retain the centripetal perspective of structural analysis, would try to give the same perspective to other kinds of criticism too.

The first postulate of this hypothesis is the same as that of any science: the assumption of total coherence. The assumption refers to the science, not to what it deals with. A belief in an order of nature is an inference from the intelligibility of the natural sciences; and if the natural sciences ever completely demonstrated the order of nature they would presumably exhaust their subject. Criticism, as a science, is totally intelligible; literature, as the subject of a science, is, so far as we know, an inexhaustible source of new critical discoveries, and would be even if new works of literature ceased to be written. If so, then the search for a limiting principle in literature in order to discourage the development of criticism is mistaken. The assertion that the critic should not look for more in a poem than the poet may safely be assumed to have been conscious of putting there is a common form of what may be called the fallacy of premature teleology. It corresponds to the assertion that a natural phenomenon is as it is because Providence in its inscrutable wisdom made it so.

[a] Frye is evidently thinking of the New Criticism—for example John Crowe Ransom (pp. 227–39 above) and Cleanth Brooks (pp. 291–304 above).

Simple as the assumption appears, it takes a long time for a science to discover that it is in fact a totally intelligible body of knowledge. Until it makes this discovery it has not been born as an individual science, but remains an embryo within the body of some other subject. The birth of physics from 'natural philosophy' and of sociology from 'moral philosophy' will illustrate the process. It is also very approximately true that the modern sciences have developed in the order of their closeness to mathematics. Thus physics and astronomy assumed their modern form in the Renaissance, chemistry in the eighteenth century, biology in the nineteenth and the social sciences in the twentieth. If systematic criticism, then, is developing only in our day, the fact is at least not an anachronism.

We are now looking for classifying principles lying in an area between two points that we have fixed. The first of these is the preliminary effort of criticism, the structural analysis of the work of art. The second is the assumption that there is such a subject as criticism, and that it makes, or could make, complete sense. We may next proceed inductively from structural analysis, associating the data we collect and trying to see larger patterns in them. Or we may proceed deductively, with the consequences that follow from postulating the unity of criticism. It is clear, of course, that neither procedure will work indefinitely without correction from the other. Pure induction will get us lost in haphazard guessing; pure deduction will lead to inflexible and over-simplified pigeon-holing. Let us now attempt a few tentative steps in each direction, beginning with the inductive one.

II

The unity of a work of art, the basis of structural analysis, has not been produced solely by the unconditioned will of the artist, for the artist is only its efficient cause: it has form, and consequently a formal cause. The fact that revision is possible, that the poet makes changes not because he likes them better but because they are better, means that poems, like poets, are born and not made. The poet's task is to deliver the poem in as uninjured a state as possible, and if the poem is alive, it is equally anxious to be rid of him, and screams to be cut loose from his private memories and associations, his desire for self-expression, and all the other navel-strings and feeding tubes of his ego. The critic takes over where the poet leaves off, and criticism can hardly do without a kind of literary psychology connecting the poet with the poem. Part of this may be a psychological study of the poet, though this is useful chiefly in analysing the failures of his expression, the things in him which are still attached to his work. More important is the fact that every poet has his private mythology, his own spectroscopic band or peculiar formation of symbols, of much of which he is quite unconscious. In works with characters of their own, such as dramas and novels, the same psychological analysis may be extended to the interplay of characters, though of course literary psychology would analyse the behaviour of such characters only in relation to literary convention.

There is still before us the problem of the formal cause of the poem, a problem deeply involved with the question of genres. We cannot say much about genres, for criticism does not know much about them. A good many critical efforts to grapple with such words as 'novel' or 'epic' are chiefly interesting as examples of the psychology of rumour. Two conceptions of the genre, however, are obviously fallacious, and as they are opposite extremes, the truth must lie somewhere between them. One is the pseudo-Platonic conception of genres as existing prior to and independently of creation, which confuses them with mere conventions of form like the sonnet. The other is that pseudo-biological conception of them as evolving species which turns up in so many surveys of the 'development' of this or that form.

We next inquire for the origin of the genre, and turn first of all to the social conditions and cultural demands which produced it—in other words to the material cause of the work of art. This leads us into literary history, which differs from ordinary history in that its containing categories, 'Gothic', 'Baroque', 'Romantic', and the like are cultural categories, of little use to the ordinary historian. Most literary history does not get as far as these categories, but even so we know more about it than about most kinds of critical scholarship. The historian treats literature and philosophy historically; the philosopher treats history and literature philosophically; and the so-called history of ideas approach marks the beginning of an attempt to treat history and philosophy from the point of view of an autonomous criticism.

But still we feel that there is something missing. We say that every poet has his own peculiar formation of images. But when so many poets use so many of the same images, surely there are much bigger critical problems involved than biographical ones. As Mr Auden's brilliant essay *The Enchafèd Flood* shows, an important symbol like the sea cannot remain within the poetry of Shelley or Keats or Coleridge: it is bound to expand over many poets into an archetypal symbol of literature. And if the genre has a historical origin, why does the genre of drama emerge from medieval religion in a way so strikingly similar to the way it emerged from Greek religion centuries before? This is a problem of structure rather than origin, and suggests that there may be archetypes of genres as well as of images.

It is clear that criticism cannot be systematic unless there is a quality in literature which enables it to be so, an order of words corresponding to the order of nature in the natural sciences. An archetype should be not only a unifying category of criticism, but itself a part of a total form, and it leads us at once to the question of what sort of total form criticism can see in literature. Our survey of critical techniques has taken us as far as literary history. Total literary history moves from the primitive to the sophisticated, and here we glimpse the possibility of seeing literature as a complication of a relatively restricted and simple group of formulas that can be studied in primitive culture. If so, then the search for archetypes is a kind of literary anthropology, concerned with the way that literature is informed by pre-literary categories such as ritual, myth and folk tale. We next realize that the relation between these categories and literature is by no means purely one of descent, as we find them reappearing in the greatest classics—in fact there seems to be a general tendency on the part of great classics to revert to them. This coincides with a feeling that we have all had: that the study of mediocre works of art, however energetic, obstinately remains a random and peripheral form of critical experience, whereas the profound masterpiece seems to draw us to a point at which we can see an enormous number of converging patterns of significance. Here we begin to wonder if we cannot see literature, not only as complicating itself in time, but as spread out in conceptual space from some unseen centre.

This inductive movement towards the archetype is a process of backing up, as it were, from structural analysis, as we back up from a painting if we want to see composition instead of brushwork. In the foreground of the grave-digger scene in *Hamlet*, for instance, is an intricate verbal texture, ranging from the puns of the first clown to the *danse macabre* of the Yorick soliloquy, which we study in the printed text. One step back, and we are in the Wilson Knight and Spurgeon group of critics, listening to the steady rain of images of corruption and decay.[a] Here, too, as the sense of the place of this scene in the whole play begins to dawn on us, we are in the network of psychological relationships which were the main interest of Bradley. But after all, we say, we are forgetting the genre: *Hamlet* is a play, and an Elizabethan play. So we take another step back into the Stoll and Shaw group and see the scene conventionally as part of its dramatic context. One step more, and we can begin to glimpse the archetype of the scene, as the hero's *Liebestod*[b] and first unequivocal declaration of his love, his struggle with Laertes and the sealing of his own fate, and the sudden sobering of his mood that marks the transition to the final scene, all take shape around a leap into and return from the grave that has so weirdly yawned open on the stage.

At each stage of understanding this scene we are dependent on a certain kind of scholarly organization. We need first an editor to clean up the text for us, then the rhetorician and philologist, then the literary psychologist. We cannot study the genre without the help of the literary social historian, the literary philosopher and the student of the 'history of ideas', and for the archetype we need a literary anthropologist. But now that we have got our central pattern of criticism established, all these interests are seen as converging on literary criticism instead of receding from it into psychology and history and the rest. In particular, the literary anthropologist who chases the source of the Hamlet legend from the pre-Shakespeare play to Saxo,[c] and from Saxo to nature-myths, is not running away from Shakespeare: he is drawing closer to the archetypal form which Shakespeare recreated. A minor result of our new perspective is that contradictions among critics, and assertions that this and not that critical approach is the right one, show a remarkable tendency to dissolve into unreality. Let us now see what we can get from the deductive end.

[a] Cf. pp. 158–73 above.

[b] This German word, for which there is no satisfactory English equivalent, means something like, 'the convergence of love and death'. It is particularly associated with Wagnerian opera.

[c] Saxo Grammaticus, the thirteenth-century Danish historian whose Latin history of the Danes, *Gesta Danorum*, contains the original story of Hamlet.

Some arts move in time, like music; others are presented in space, like painting. In both cases the organizing principle is recurrence, which is called rhythm when it is temporal and pattern when it is spatial. Thus we speak of the rhythm of music and the pattern of painting; but later, to show off our sophistication, we may begin to speak of the rhythm of painting and the pattern of music. In other words, all arts may be conceived both temporally and spatially. The score of a musical composition may be studied all at once; a picture may be seen as the track of an intricate dance of the eye. Literature seems to be intermediate between music and painting: its words form rhythms which approach a musical sequence of sounds at one of its boundaries, and form patterns which approach the hieroglyphic or pictorial image at the other. The attempts to get as near to these boundaries as possible form the main body of what is called experimental writing. We may call the rhythm of literature the narrative, and the pattern, the simultaneous mental grasp of the verbal structure, the meaning or significance. We hear or listen to a narrative, but when we grasp a writer's total pattern we 'see' what he means.

The criticism of literature is much more hampered by the representational fallacy than even the criticism of painting. That is why we are apt to think of narrative as a sequential representation of events in an outside 'life', and of meaning as a reflection of some external 'idea'. Properly used as critical terms, an author's narrative is his linear movement; his meaning is the integrity of his completed form. Similarly an image is not merely a verbal replica of an external object, but any unit of a verbal structure seen as part of a total pattern or rhythm. Even the letters an author spells his words with form part of his imagery, though only in special cases (such as alliteration) would they call for critical notice. Narrative and meaning thus become respectively, to borrow musical terms, the melodic and harmonic contexts of the imagery.

Rhythm, or recurrent movement, is deeply founded on the natural cycle, and everything in nature that we think of as having some analogy with works of art, like the flower or the bird's song, grows out of a profound synchronization between an organism and the rhythms of its environment, especially that of the solar year. With animals some expressions of synchronization, like the mating dances of birds, could almost be called rituals. But in human life a ritual seems to be something of a voluntary effort (hence the magical element in it) to re-capture a lost rapport with the natural cycle. A farmer must harvest his crop at a certain time of year, but because this is involuntary, harvesting itself is not precisely a ritual. It is the deliberate expression of a will to synchronize human and natural energies at that time which produces the harvest songs, harvest sacrifices and harvest folk customs that we call rituals. In ritual, then, we may find the origin of narrative, a ritual being a temporal sequence of acts in which the conscious meaning or significance is latent: it can be seen by an observer, but is largely concealed from the participators themselves. The pull of ritual is towards pure narrative, which, if there could be such a thing, would be auto-matic and unconscious repetition. We should notice too the regular tendency of ritual to become encyclopedic. All the important recurrences in nature, the day, the phases of the moon, the seasons and solstices of the year, the crises of existence from birth to death, get rituals attached to them, and most of the higher religions are equipped with a definitive total body of rituals suggestive, if we may put it so, of the entire range of potentially significant actions in human life.

Patterns of imagery, on the other hand, or fragments of significance, are oracular in origin, and derive from the epiphanic moment, the flash of instantaneous comprehension with no direct reference to time, the importance of which is indicated by Cassirer in *Myth and Language*. By the time we get them, in the form of proverbs, riddles, commandments and etiological folk tales, there is already a considerable element of narrative in them. They too are encyclopedic in tendency, building up a total structure of significance, or doctrine, from random and empiric fragments. And just as pure narrative would be unconscious act, so pure significance would be an incommunicable state of consciousness, for communication begins by constructing narrative.

The myth is the central informing power that gives archetypal significance to the ritual and archetypal narrative to the oracle. Hence the myth *is* the archetype, though it might be convenient to say myth only when referring to narrative, and archetype when speaking of significance. In the solar cycle of the day, the seasonal cycle of the year, and the organic cycle of human life, there is a single pattern of significance, out of which myth constructs a central narrative around a figure who is partly the sun, partly vegetative fertility and partly a god or archetypal human being. The crucial importance of this myth has been forced on literary critics by Jung and Frazer[a] in particular, but the several books now available on it are not always systematic in their approach, for which reason I supply the following table of its phases:

1. The dawn, spring and birth phase. Myths of the birth of the hero, of revival and resurrection, of creation and (because the four phases are a cycle) of the defeat of the powers of darkness, winter and death. Subordinate characters: the father and the mother. The archetype of romance and of most dithyrambic and rhapsodic poetry.

2. The zenith, summer, and marriage or triumph phase. Myths of apotheosis, of the sacred marriage, and of entering into Paradise. Subordinate characters: the companion and the bride. The archetype of comedy, pastoral and idyll.

3. The sunset, autumn and death phase. Myths of fall, of the dying god, of violent death and sacrifice, and of the isolation of the hero. Subordinate characters: the traitor and the siren. The archetype of tragedy and elegy.

4. The darkness, winter and dissolution phase. Myths of the triumph of these powers; myths of floods and the return of chaos, of the defeat of the hero, and Götterdämmerung myths. Subordinate characters: the ogre and the witch. The archetype of satire (see, for instance, the conclusion of *The Dunciad*).

The quest of the hero also tends to assimilate the oracular and random verbal

[a] Sir James Frazer, author of *The Golden Bough* (1890–1915), a large-scale comparative study of primitive religions.

structures, as we can see when we watch the chaos of local legends that results from prophetic epiphanies consolidating into a narrative mythology of departmental gods. In most of the higher religions this in turn has become the same central quest-myth that emerges from ritual, as the Messiah myth became the narrative structure of the oracles of Judaism. A local flood may beget a folk tale by accident, but a comparison of flood stories will show how quickly such tales become examples of the myth of dissolution. Finally, the tendency of both ritual and epiphany to become encyclopedic is realized in the definitive body of myth which constitutes the sacred scriptures of religions. These sacred scriptures are consequently the first documents that the literary critic has to study to gain a comprehensive view of his subject. After he has understood their structure, then he can descend from archetypes to genres, and see how the drama emerges from the ritual side of myth and lyric from the epiphanic or fragmented side, while the epic carries on the central encyclopedic structure.

Some words of caution and encouragement are necessary before literary criticism has clearly staked out its boundaries in these fields. It is part of the critic's business to show how all literary genres are derived from the quest-myth, but the derivation is a logical one within the science of criticism: the quest-myth will constitute the first chapter of whatever future handbooks of criticism may be written that will be based on enough organized critical knowledge to call themselves 'introductions' or 'outlines' and still be able to live up to their titles. It is only when we try to expound the derivation chronologically that we find ourselves writing pseudo-prehistorical fictions and theories of mythological contract. Again, because psychology and anthropology are more highly developed sciences, the critic who deals with this kind of material is bound to appear, for some time, a dilettante of those subjects. These two phases of criticism are largely undeveloped in comparison with literary history and rhetoric, the reason being the later development of the sciences they are related to. But the fascination which [Frazer's] *The Golden Bough* and Jung's book on libido symbols[a] have for literary critics is not based on dilettantism, but on the fact that these books are primarily studies in literary criticism, and very important ones.

In any case the critic who is studying the principles of literary form has a quite different interest from the psychologist's concern with states of mind or the anthropologist's with social institutions. For instance: the mental response to narrative is mainly passive; to significance mainly active. From this fact Ruth Benedict's *Pattern of Culture* develops a distinction between 'Apollonian' cultures based on obedience to ritual and 'Dionysiac' ones based on a tense exposure of the prophetic mind to epiphany. The critic would tend rather to note how popular literature which appeals to the inertia of the untrained mind puts a heavy emphasis on narrative values, whereas a sophisticated attempt to disrupt the connection between the poet and his environment produces the Rimbaud type of *illumination*, Joyce's solitary epiphanies, and Baudelaire's conception of

---

[a] *Wandlungen und Symbole der Libido* (Leipzig, 1912), published in English under the title *Psychology of the Unconscious* (New York, 1916). *Symbols of Transformation*, vol. v of the *Collected Works* (1956), is a translation of the revised 1952 text of this work.

nature as a source of oracles. Also how literature, as it develops from the primitive to the self-conscious, shows a gradual shift of the poet's attention from narrative to significant values, this shift of attention being the basis of Schiller's distinction between naïve and sentimental poetry.[a]

The relation of criticism to religion, when they deal with the same documents, is more complicated. In criticism, as in history, the divine is always treated as a human artifact. God for the critic, whether he finds him in *Paradise Lost* or the Bible, is a character in a human story; and for the critic all epiphanies are explained, not in terms of the riddle of a possessing god or devil, but as mental phenomena closely associated in their origin with dreams. This once established, it is then necessary to say that nothing in criticism or art compels the critic to take the attitude of ordinary waking consciousness towards the dream or the god. Art deals not with the real but with the conceivable; and criticism, though it will eventually have to have some theory of conceivability, can never be justified in trying to develop, much less assume, any theory of actuality. It is necessary to understand this before our next and final point can be made.

We have identified the central myth of literature, in its narrative aspect, with the quest-myth. Now if we wish to see this central myth as a pattern of meaning also, we have to start with the workings of the subconscious where the epiphany originates, in other words in the dream. The human cycle of waking and dreaming corresponds closely to the natural cycle of light and darkness, and it is perhaps in this correspondence that all imaginative life begins. The correspondence is largely an antithesis: it is in daylight that man is really in the power of darkness, a prey to frustration and weakness; it is in the darkness of nature that the 'libido' or conquering heroic self awakes. Hence art, which Plato called a dream for awakened minds, seems to have as its final cause the resolution of the antithesis, the mingling of the sun and the hero, the realizing of a world in which the inner desire and the outward circumstance coincide. This is the same goal, of course, that the attempt to combine human and natural power in ritual has. The social function of the arts, therefore, seems to be closely connected with visualizing the goal of work in human life. So in terms of significance, the central myth of art must be the vision of the end of social effort, the innocent world of fulfilled desires, the free human society. Once this is understood, the integral place of criticism among the other social sciences, in interpreting and systematizing the vision of the artist, will be easier to see. It is at this point that we can see how religious conceptions of the final cause of human effort are as relevant as any others to criticism.

The importance of the god or hero in the myth lies in the fact that such characters, who are conceived in human likeness and yet have more power over nature, gradually build up the vision of an omnipotent personal community beyond an indifferent nature. It is this community which the hero regularly enters in his apotheosis. The world of this apotheosis thus begins to pull away from the rotary cycle of the quest in which all triumph is temporary. Hence if

[a] In Friedrich Schiller's essay *Über naïve and sentimentalische Dichtung* (1795), 'naïve' denotes ancient or classical poetry, and 'sentimental' modern, romantic poetry.

we look at the quest-myth as a pattern of imagery, we see the hero's quest first of all in terms of its fulfilment. This gives us our central pattern of archetypal images, the vision of innocence which sees the world in terms of total human intelligibility. It corresponds to, and is usually found in the form of, the vision of the unfallen world or heaven in religion. We may call it the comic vision of life, in contrast to the tragic vision, which sees the quest only in the form of its ordained cycle.

We conclude with a second table of contents, in which we shall attempt to set forth the central pattern of the comic and tragic visions. One essential principle of archetypal criticism is that the individual and the universal forms of an image are identical, the reasons being too complicated for us just now. We proceed according to the general plan of the game of Twenty Questions, or, if we prefer, of the Great Chain of Being:

1. In the comic vision the *human* world is a community, or a hero who represents the wish-fulfilment of the reader. The archetype of images of symposium, communion, order, friendship and love. In the tragic vision the human world is a tyranny or anarchy, or an individual or isolated man, the leader with his back to his followers, the bullying giant of romance, the deserted or betrayed hero. Marriage or some equivalent consummation belongs to the comic vision; the harlot, witch and other varieties of Jung's 'terrible mother' belongs to the tragic one. All divine, heroic, angelic or other superhuman communities follow the human pattern.

2. In the comic vision the *animal* world is a community of domesticated animals, usually a flock of sheep, or a lamb, or one of the gentler birds, usually a dove. The archetype of pastoral images. In the tragic vision the animal world is seen in terms of beasts and birds of prey, wolves, vultures, serpents, dragons and the like.

3. In the comic vision the *vegetable* world is a garden, grove or park, or a tree of life, or a rose or lotus. The archetype of Arcadian images, such as that of Marvell's green world or of Shakespeare's forest comedies. In the tragic vision it is a sinister forest like the one in *Comus* or at the opening of the *Inferno*, or a heath or wilderness, or a tree of death.

4. In the comic vision the *mineral* world is a city, or one building or temple, or one stone, normally a glowing precious stone—in fact the whole comic series, especially the tree, can be conceived as luminous or fiery. The archetype of geometrical images, the 'starlit dome' belongs here. In the tragic vision the mineral world is seen in terms of deserts, rocks, and ruins, or of sinister geometrical images like the cross.

5. In the comic vision the *unformed* world is a river, traditionally fourfold, which influenced the Renaissance image of the temperate body with its four humours. In the tragic vision this world usually becomes the sea, as the narrative myth of dissolution is so often a flood myth. The combination of the sea and beast images gives us the leviathan and similar water-monsters.

Obvious as this table looks, a great variety of poetic images and forms will be found to fit it. Yeats's 'Sailing to Byzantium', to take a famous example of the comic vision at random, has the city, the tree, the bird, the community of sages, the geometrical gyre, and the detachment from the cyclic world. It is, of course, only the general comic or tragic context that determines the interpretation of any symbol: this is obvious with relatively neutral archetypes like the island, which may be Prospero's island or Circe's.

Our tables are, of course, not only elementary but grossly over-simplified, just as our inductive approach to the archetype was a mere hunch. The important point is not the deficiencies of either procedure, taken by itself, but the fact that, somewhere and somehow, the two are clearly going to meet in the middle. And if they do meet, the ground plan of a systematic and comprehensive development of criticism has been established.

Literature as context: Milton's *Lycidas*

I should like to begin with a brief discussion of a familiar poem, Milton's *Lycidas*, in the hope that some of the inferences drawn from the analysis will be relevant to the theme of this conference.[a] *Lycidas*, then, is an elegy in the pastoral convention, written to commemorate a young man named Edward King who was drowned at sea. The origins of the pastoral are partly classical, the tradition that runs through Theocritus and Virgil, and partly Biblical, the imagery of the twenty-third Psalm, of Christ as the Good Shepherd, of the metaphors of 'pastor' and 'flock' in the Church. The chief connecting link between the traditions in Milton's day was the Fourth or Messianic Eclogue of Virgil.[b] Hence it is common enough to have pastoral images echoing both traditions at once, and not surprising to find that *Lycidas* is a Christian poem as well as a humanistic one.

In the classical pastoral elegy the subject of the elegy is not treated as an individual but as a representative of a dying spirit of nature. The pastoral elegy seems to have some relation to the ritual of the Adonis lament, and the dead poet Bion, in Moschus's poem, is celebrated with much the same kind of imagery as Bion himself uses in his lament for Adonis.[c] The phrase 'dying god',

---

[a] The Second Congress of the International Comparative Literature Association, University of North Carolina, 1958, at which this paper was originally delivered.

[b] Virgil's Fourth Eclogue, written in 40 B.C., acclaims the birth of a child destined to bring back the Golden Age, and was interpreted by patristic and medieval Christian writers as a prophecy of the birth of Christ.

[c] Bion of Smyrna and Moschus of Syracuse were bucolic poets of the second century B.C.

433

for such a figure in later pastoral, is not an anachronism: Virgil says of Daphnis, for example, in the Fifth Eclogue: *'deus, deus ille, Menalca'* ['a god, he is a god, Menalca']. Besides, Milton and his learned contemporaries, Selden, for example, or Henry Reynolds, knew at least as much about the symbolism of the 'dying god' as any modern student could get out of *The Golden Bough*, which depends mainly on the same classical sources that were available to them. The notion that twentieth-century poets differ from their predecessors in their understanding or use of myth will not bear much scrutiny. So King is given the pastoral name of Lycidas, which is equivalent to Adonis, and is associated with the cyclical rhythms of nature. Of these three are of particular importance: the daily cycle of the sun across the sky, the yearly cycle of the seasons, and the cycle of water, flowing from wells and fountains through rivers to the sea. Sunset, winter, and the sea are emblems of Lycidas' death; sunrise and spring, of his resurrection. The poem begins in the morning, 'Under the opening eyelids of the morn', and ends with the sun, like Lycidas himself, dropping into the western ocean, yet due to rise again as Lycidas is to do. The imagery of the opening lines, 'Shatter your leaves before the mellowing year', suggests the frosts of autumn killing the flowers, and in the great roll-call of flowers towards the end, most of them early blooming flowers like the 'rathe primrose', the spring returns. Again, the opening invocation is to the 'Sisters of the sacred well', and the water imagery carries through a great variety of Greek, Italian, and English rivers to the sea in which the dead body of Lycidas lies.

Lycidas, then, is the 'archetype' of Edward King. By an archetype I mean a literary symbol, or cluster of symbols, which are used recurrently throughout literature, and thereby become conventional. A poetic use of a flower, by itself, is not necessarily an archetype. But in a poem about the death of a young man it is conventional to associate him with a red or purple flower, usually a spring flower like the hyacinth. The historical origin of the convention may be lost in ritual, but it is a constantly latent one, not only in literature but in life, as the symbolism of the scarlet poppies in World War I shows. Hence in *Lycidas* the 'sanguine flower inscrib'd with woe' is an archetype, a symbol that recurs regularly in many poems of its kind. Similarly Lycidas himself is not only the literary form of Edward King, but a conventional or recurring form, of the same family as Shelley's Adonais, the Daphnis of Theocritus and Virgil, and Milton's own Damon. King was also a clergyman and, for Milton's purposes, a poet, so, having selected the conventional archetype of King as drowned young man, Milton has then to select the conventional archetypes of King as poet and of King as priest. These are, respectively, Orpheus and Peter.

Both Orpheus and Peter have attributes that link them in imagery with Lycidas. Orpheus was also an 'enchanting son' or spirit of nature; he died young, in much the same role as Adonis, and was flung into the water. Peter would have drowned too without the help of Christ; hence Peter is not named directly, but only as 'The Pilot of the Galilean Lake', just as Christ is not named directly, but only as 'Him that walked the waves'. When Orpheus was torn to pieces by the Maenads, his head went floating 'Down the swift Hebrus to the Lesbian shore'. The theme of salvation out of water is connected with the image of the dolphin, a conventional type of Christ, and dolphins are called upon to 'waft the hapless youth' just before the peroration begins.

The body of the poem is arranged in the form ABACA, a main theme repeated twice with two intervening episodes, as in the musical rondo. The main theme is the drowning of Lycidas in the prime of his life; the two episodes, presided over by the figures of Orpheus and Peter, deal with the theme of premature death as it relates to poetry and to the priesthood respectively. In both the same type of image appears: the mechanical instrument of execution that brings about a sudden death, represented by the 'abhorred shears' in the meditation on fame and the 'grim two-handed engine' in the meditation on the corruption of the Church. The most difficult part of the construction is the managing of the transitions from these episodes back to the main theme. The poet does this by alluding to his great forerunners in the pastoral convention, Theocritus of Sicily, Virgil of Mantua, and the legendary Arcadians who preceded both:

> O fountain Arethuse, and thou honour'd flood,
> Smooth-sliding Mincius, crown'd with vocal reeds...

and later:

> Return, Alpheus, the dread voice is past
> That shrunk thy streams: return, Sicilian Muse.

The allusion has the effect of reminding the reader that this is, after all, a pastoral. But Milton also alludes to the myth of Arethusa and Alpheus, the Arcadian water-spirits who plunged underground and reappeared in Sicily, and this myth not only outlines the history of the pastoral convention, but unites the water imagery with the theme of disappearance and revival.

In pastoral elegy the poet who laments the death is often so closely associated with the dead man as to make him a kind of double or shadow of himself. Similarly Milton represents himself as intimately involved with the death of Lycidas. The theme of premature death is skilfully associated in the opening lines with the conventional apology for a 'harsh and crude' poem; the poet hopes for a similar elegy when he dies, and at the end he accepts the responsibilities of survival and turns 'Tomorrow to fresh woods, and pastures new', bringing the elegy to a full rich *tierce de Picardie* or major chord. By appearing himself at the beginning and end of the poem, Milton presents the poem as, in a sense, contained within the mind of the poet.

Apart from the historical convention of the pastoral, however, there is also the conventional framework of ideas or assumptions which forms the background of the poem. I call it a framework of ideas, and it may also be that, but in poetry it is rather a framework of images. It consists of four levels of existence. First is the order revealed by Christianity, the order of grace and salvation and of eternal life. Second is the order of human nature, the order represented by the Garden of Eden in the Bible and the Golden Age in classical myth, and which man in his fallen state can, up to a point, regain through education, obedience to law, and the habit of virtue. Third is the order of

435

physical nature, the world of animals and plants which is morally neutral but theologically 'fallen'. Fourth is the disorder of the unnatural, the sin and death and corruption that entered the world with the Fall.

Lycidas has his connections with all of these orders. In the first place, all the images of death and resurrection are included in and identified with the body of Christ. Christ is the sun of righteousness, the tree of life, the water of life, the dying god who rose again, the saviour from the sea. On this level Lycidas enters the Christian heaven and is greeted by the 'Saints above' 'In solemn troops, and sweet societies', where the language echoes the Book of Revelation. But simultaneously Lycidas achieves another apotheosis as the Genius of the shore, corresponding to the Attendant Spirit in *Comus*, whose habitation is said to be a world above our own, identified, not with the Christian heaven, but with Spenser's Gardens of Adonis. The third level of physical nature is the world of ordinary experience, where death is simply a loss, and those who mourn the death have to turn to pick up their tasks again. On this level Lycidas is merely absent, 'to our moist vows denied', represented only by the empty bier with its flowers. It is on this level too that the poem is contained within the mind of the surviving poet, as on the Christian level it is contained within the body of Christ. Finally, the world of death and corruption holds the drowned corpse of Lycidas, which will soon come to the surface and 'welter to the parching wind'. This last is an unpleasant and distressing image, and Milton touches it very lightly, picking it up again in an appropriate context:

> But swoln with wind and the rank mist they draw,
> Rot inwardly . . .

In the writing of *Lycidas* there are four creative principles of particular importance. To say that there are four does not mean, of course, that they are separable. One is convention, the reshaping of the poetic material which is appropriate to this subject. Another is genre, the choosing of the appropriate form. A third is archetype, the use of appropriate, and therefore recurrently employed, images and symbols. The fourth, for which there is no name, is the fact that the forms of literature are autonomous: that is, they do not exist outside literature. Milton is not writing an obituary: he does not start with Edward King and his life and times, but with the conventions and archetypes that poetry requires for such a theme.

Of the critical principles illustrated by this analysis, one will be no surprise to the present audience. *Lycidas* owes quite as much to Hebrew, Greek, Latin, and Italian traditions as it does to English. Even the diction, of which I have no space to speak, shows strong Italian influence. Milton was of course a learned poet, but there is no poet whose literary influences are entirely confined to his own language. Thus every problem in literary criticism is a problem in comparative literature, or simply of literature itself.

The next principle is that the provisional hypothesis which we must adopt for the study of every poem is that that poem is a unity. If, after careful and repeated testing, we are forced to conclude that it is not a unity, then we must abandon the hypothesis and look for the reasons why it is not. A good deal of

436

bad criticism of *Lycidas* has resulted from not making enough initial effort to understand the unity of the poem. To talk of 'digressions' in *Lycidas* is a typical consequence of a mistaken critical method, of backing into the poem the wrong way round. If, instead of starting with the poem, we start with a handful of peripheral facts about the poem, Milton's casual knowledge of King, his ambitions as a poet, his bitterness against the episcopacy, then of course the poem will break down into pieces corresponding precisely to those fragments of knowledge. *Lycidas* illustrates, on a small scale, what has happened on a much bigger scale in, for example, the criticism of Homer. Critics knowing something about the fragmentary nature of heroic lays and ballads approached the *Iliad* and the *Odyssey* with this knowledge in mind, and the poems obediently split up into the pieces that they wished to isolate. Other critics came along and treated the poems as imaginative unities, and today everyone knows that the second group were more convincing.

The same thing happens when our approach to 'sources' becomes fragmented or piecemeal. *Lycidas* is a dense mass of echoes from previous literature, chiefly pastoral literature. Reading through Virgil's Eclogues with *Lycidas* in mind, we can see that Milton had not simply read or studied these poems: he possessed them; they were part of the material he was shaping. The passage about the hungry sheep reminds us of at least three other passages: one in Dante's *Paradiso*, one in the Book of Ezekiel, and one near the beginning of Hesiod's *Theogony*. There are also echoes of Mantuan and Spenser, of the Gospel of John, and it is quite possible that there are even more striking parallels with poems that Milton had not read. In such cases there is not *a* source at all, no one place that the passage 'comes from', or, as we say with such stupefying presumption, that the poet 'had in mind'. There are only archetypes, or recurring themes of literary expression, which *Lycidas* has recreated, and therefore re-echoed, yet once more.

The next principle is that the important problems of literary criticism lie within the study of literature. We notice that a law of diminishing returns sets in as soon as we move away from the poem itself. If we ask, who is Lycidas? the answer is that he is a member of the same family as Theocritus' Daphnis, Bion's Adonis, the Old Testament Abel, and so on. The answer goes on building up a wider comprehension of literature and a deeper knowledge of its structural principles and recurring themes. But if we ask, who was Edward King? What was his relation to Milton? How good a poet was he? we find ourselves moving dimly in the intense inane. The same is true of minor points. If we ask, why is the image of the two-handed engine in *Lycidas*? we can give an answer, along the lines suggested above, that illustrates how carefully the poem has been constructed. If we ask, what is the two-handed engine? there are forty-odd answers, none of them completely satisfactory; yet the fact that they are not wholly satisfactory hardly seems to be important.

Another form of the same kind of fallacy is the confusion between personal sincerity and literary sincerity. If we start with the facts that *Lycidas* is highly conventional and that Milton knew King only slightly, we may see in *Lycidas* an 'artificial' poem without 'real feeling' in it. This red herring, though more common among third-rate romantics, was dragged across the study of *Lycidas* by Samuel Johnson.[a] Johnson knew better, but he happened to feel perverse about this particular poem, and so deliberately raised false issues. It would not have occurred to him, for example, to question the conventional use of Horace in the satires of Pope, or of Juvenal in his own. Personal sincerity has no place in literature, because personal sincerity as such is inarticulate. One may burst into tears at the news of a friend's death, but one can never spontaneously burst into song, however doleful a lay. *Lycidas* is a passionately sincere poem, because Milton was deeply interested in the structure and symbolism of funeral elegies, and had been practising since adolescence on every fresh corpse in sight, from the university beadle to the fair infant dying of a cough.

If we ask what inspires a poet, there are always two answers. An occasion, an experience, an event, may inspire the impulse to write. But the impulse to write can only come from previous contact with literature, and the formal inspiration, the poetic structure that crystallizes around the new event, can only be derived from other poems. Hence while every new poem is a new and unique creation, it is also a reshaping of familiar conventions of literature, otherwise it would not be recognizable as literature at all. Literature often gives us the illusion of turning from books to life, from second-hand to direct experience, and thereby discovering new literary principles in the world outside. But this is never quite what happens. No matter how tightly Wordsworth may close the barren leaves of art and let nature be his teacher, his literary forms will be as conventional as ever, although they may echo an unaccustomed set of conventions, such as the ballad or the broadside. The pretence of personal sincerity is itself a literary convention, and Wordsworth makes many of the flat simple statements which represent, in literature, the inarticulateness of personal sincerity:

> No motion has she now, no force:
> She neither hears nor sees.

But as soon as a death becomes a poetic image, that image is assimilated to other poetic images of death in nature, and hence Lucy inevitably becomes a Proserpine figure, just as King becomes an Adonis:

> Rolled round in earth's diurnal course
> With rocks, and stones, and trees.

In Whitman we have an even more extreme example than Wordsworth of a cult of personal statement and an avoidance of learned conventions. It is therefore instructive to see what happens in *When Lilacs Last in Dooryard Bloomed*. The dead man is not called by a pastoral name, but neither is he called by his historical name. He is in a coffin which is carried the length and breadth of the land; he is identified with a 'powerful western fallen star'; he is the

[a] In his *Life of Milton* Dr Johnson criticized *Lycidas* in these terms: 'It is not to be considered as the effusion of real passion; for passion runs not after remote allusions and obscure opinions ... where there is leisure for fiction there is little grief.'

beloved comrade of the poet, who throws the purple flower of the lilac on his coffin; a singing bird laments the death, just as the woods and caves do in *Lycidas*. Convention, genre, archetype, and the autonomy of forms are all illustrated as clearly in Whitman as they are in Milton.

Lycidas is an occasional poem, called forth by a specific event. It seems, therefore, to be a poem with a strong external reference. Critics who cannot approach a poem except as a personal statement of the poet's thus feel that if it says little about King, it must say a good deal about Milton. So, they reason, *Lycidas* is really autobiographical, concerned with Milton's own pre-occupations, including his fear of death. There can be no objection to this unless Milton's conventional involving himself with the poem is misinterpreted as a personal intrusion into it.

For Milton was even by seventeenth-century standards an unusually professional and impersonal poet. Of all Milton's poems, the one obvious failure is the poem called *The Passion*, and if we look at the imagery of that poem we can see why. It is the only poem of Milton's in which he is preoccupied with himself in the process of writing it. 'My muse', 'my song', 'my harp', 'my roving verse', 'my Phoebus', and so on for eight stanzas until Milton abandons the poem in disgust. It is not a coincidence that Milton's one self-conscious poem should be the one that never gets off the ground. There is nothing like this in *Lycidas*: the 'I' of that poem is a professional poet in his conventional shepherd disguise, and to think of him as a personal 'I' is to bring *Lycidas* down to the level of *The Passion*, to make it a poem that has to be studied primarily as a biographical document rather than for its own sake. Such an approach to *Lycidas* is apt to look most plausible to those who dislike Milton, and want to see him cut down to size.

One more critical principle, and the one that I have written this paper to enunciate, seems to me to follow inevitably from the previous ones. Every poem must be examined as a unity, but no poem is an isolatable unity. Every poem is inherently connected with other poems of its kind, whether explicitly, as *Lycidas* is with Theocritus and Virgil, or implicitly, as Whitman is with the same tradition, or by anticipation, as *Lycidas* is with later pastoral elegies. And, of course, the kinds or genres of literature are not separable either, like the orders of pre-Darwinian biology. Everyone who has seriously studied literature knows that he is not simply moving from poem to poem, or from one aesthetic experience to another: he is also entering into a coherent and progressive discipline. For literature is not simply an aggregate of books and poems and plays: it is an order of words. And our total literary experience, at any given time, is not a discrete series of memories or impressions of what we have read, but an imaginatively coherent body of experience.

It is literature as an order of words, therefore, which forms the primary context of any given work of literary art. All other contexts—the place of *Lycidas* in Milton's development; its place in the history of English poetry; its place in seventeenth-century thought or history—are secondary and derivative contexts. Within the total literary order certain structural and generic principles, certain configurations of narrative and imagery, certain conventions and devices and *topoi*, occur over and over again. In every new work of literature some of these principles are reshaped.

Lycidas, we found, is informed by such a recurring structural principle. The short, simple, and accurate name for this principle is myth. The Adonis myth[a] is what makes *Lycidas* both distinctive and traditional. Of course if we think of the Adonis myth as some kind of Platonic idea existing by itself, we shall not get far with it as a critical conception. But it is only incompetence that tries to reduce or assimilate a poem to a myth. The Adonis myth in *Lycidas* is the structure of *Lycidas*. It is in *Lycidas* in much the same way that the sonata form is in the first movement of a Mozart symphony. It is the connecting link between what makes *Lycidas* the poem it is and what unites it to other forms of poetic experience. If we attend only to the uniqueness of *Lycidas*, and analyse the ambiguities and subtleties of its diction, our method, however useful in itself, soon reaches a point of no return to the poem. If we attend only to the conventional element, our method will turn it into a scissors-and-paste collection of allusive tags. One method reduces the poem to a jangle of echoes of itself, the other to a jangle of echoes from other poets. If we have a unifying principle that holds these two tendencies together from the start, neither will get out of hand.

Myths, it is true, turn up in other disciplines, in anthropology, in psychology, in comparative religion. But the primary business of the critic is with myth as the shaping principle of a work of literature. Thus for him myth becomes much the same thing as Aristotle's *mythos*, narrative or plot, the moving formal cause which is what Aristotle called the 'soul' of the work and assimilates all details in the realizing of its unity.

In its simplest English meaning a myth is a story about a god, and Lycidas is, poetically speaking, a god or spirit of nature, who eventually becomes a saint in heaven, which is as near as one can get to godhead in ordinary Christianity. The reason for treating Lycidas mythically, in this sense, is conventional, but the convention is not arbitrary or accidental. It arises from the metaphorical nature of poetic speech. We are not told simply that Lycidas has left the woods and caves, but that the woods and caves and all their echoes mourn his loss. This is the language of that curious identification of subject and object, of personality and thing, which the poet has in common with the lunatic and the lover. It is the language of metaphor, recognized by Aristotle as the distinctive language of poetry. And, as we can see in such phrases as sun-god and tree-god, the language of metaphor is interdependent with the language of myth.

I have said that all problems of criticism are problems of comparative literature. But where there is comparison there must be some standard by which we can distinguish what is actually comparable from what is merely analogous. The scientists discovered long ago that to make valid comparisons you have to know what your real categories are. If you're studying natural history, for instance,

---

[a] Adonis, a beautiful youth, was beloved by Aphrodite. He died of a wound inflicted by a boar, but the grief of the goddess was so great that he was released from the underworld for six months in every year. Adonis's death and return to life was associated with the cycle of the seasons in ancient religion and ritual.

no matter how fascinated you may be by anything that has eight legs, you can't just lump together an octopus and a spider and a string quartet. In science the difference between a scientific and a pseudo-scientific procedure can usually be spotted fairly soon. I wonder if literary criticism has any standards of this kind. It seems to me that a critic practically has to maintain that the Earl of Oxford wrote the plays of Shakespeare before he can be clearly recognized as making pseudo-critical statements. I have read some critics on Milton who appeared to be confusing Milton with their phallic fathers, if that is the right phrase. I should call them pseudo-critics; others call them neoclassicists. How is one to know? There is such a variety of even legitimate critics. There are critics who can find things in the Public Records Office, and there are critics who, like myself, could not find the Public Records Office. Not all critical statements or procedures can be equally valid.

The first step, I think, is to recognize the dependence of value judgments on scholarship. Scholarship, or the knowledge of literature, constantly expands and increases; value judgments are produced by a skill based on the knowledge we already have. Thus scholarship has both priority to value judgments and the power of veto over them. The second step is to recognize the dependence of scholarship on a coordinated view of literature. A good deal of critical taxonomy lies ahead of us. We need to know much more than we do about the structural principles of literature, about myth and metaphor, conventions and genres, before we can distinguish with any authority a real from an imaginary line of influence, an illuminating from a misleading analogy, a poet's original source from his last resource. The basis of this central critical activity that gives direction to scholarship is the simple fact that every poem is a member of the class of things called poems. Some poems, including *Lycidas*, proclaim that they are conventional, in other words that their primary context is in literature. Other poems leave this inference to the critic, with an appealing if often misplaced confidence.

32 C. S. Lewis

Clive Staples Lewis (1896-1963) was born in Belfast. His education at Oxford was interrupted by service in World War I, in which he was wounded. Subsequently he taught English as a Fellow of Magdalen until 1954, when he was appointed to the newly-created Chair of Medieval and Renaissance English Literature at Cambridge. *De Descriptione Temporum* ['Concerning the Description of Periods'] was his Inaugural Lecture in this position.

C. S. Lewis was a prolific and versatile author who enjoyed considerable success as a writer of science-fiction stories (e.g. *Out of the Silent Planet*, 1938), and works of popular theology (e.g. *The Screwtape Letters*, 1942), and children's books, as well as literary criticism. The criticism itself shows a remarkable range of interest and expertise, but Lewis was probably best known and admired for his work on medieval literature, especially his masterly book on the literature of Courtly Love, *The Allegory of Love: a study in medieval tradition* (Oxford, 1936). Other publications included *The Personal Heresy: a controversy* (with E. M. W. Tillyard, 1939), *A Preface to Paradise Lost* (1941), *English Literature in the Sixteenth Century, excluding Drama* (Oxford, 1954), *An Experiment in Criticism* (Cambridge, 1961) and *They Asked for a Paper: papers and addresses* (1962). from which *De Descriptione Temporum* is reprinted here.

C. S. Lewis in many ways represented the 'Oxford' tradition of literary criticism at its best: relaxed, knowledgeable, enthusiastic, conservative. Certainly he stood for principles and practice antithetical to those of the *Scrutiny* group at Cambridge. Lewis was a convinced Christian who, with certain associates (notably Charles Williams and Dorothy L. Sayers) formed a kind of High Anglican school of literary intellectuals based on Oxford that was particularly influential in the 1940s. It is clear that he regarded the study of literature as primarily a historical one, and its justification as the conservation of the past. *De Descriptione Temporum* expresses eloquently, learnedly and wittily this conception of the subject and Lewis's doubts about its viability in the future.

CROSS REFERENCES: 25. Erich Auerbach
41. René Wellek
44. R. S. Crane
50. Frank Kermode

COMMENTARY: *Light on C. S. Lewis*, ed. Jocelyn Gibbs (1965)

De descriptione temporum

Speaking from a newly founded Chair, I find myself freed from one embarrassment only to fall into another. I have no great predecessors to overshadow me; on the other hand, I must try (as the theatrical people say) 'to create the part'. The responsibility is heavy. If I miscarry, the University might come to regret not only my election—an error which, at worst, can be left to the great healer—but even, which matters very much more, the foundation of the Chair itself. That is why I have thought it best to take the bull by the horns and devote this lecture to explaining as clearly as I can the way in which I approach my work; my interpretation of the commission you have given me.

What most attracted me in that commission was the combination 'Medieval and Renaissance'. I thought that by this formula the University was giving official sanction to a change which has been coming over historical opinion within my own lifetime. It is temperately summed up by Professor Seznec in the words: 'As the Middle Ages and the Renaissance come to be better known, the traditional antithesis between them grows less marked.'[1] Some scholars might go further than Professor Seznec, but very few, I believe, would now oppose him. If we are sometimes unconscious of the change, that is not because we have not shared it but because it has been gradual and imperceptible. We recognize it most clearly if we are suddenly brought face to face with the old view in its full vigour. A good experiment is to re-read the first chapter of J. M. Berdan's *Early Tudor Poetry*.[2] It is still in many ways a useful book; but it is now difficult to read that chapter without a smile. We begin with twenty-nine pages (and they contain several misstatements) of unrelieved gloom about grossness, superstition, and cruelty to children, and on the twenty-ninth comes the sentence, 'The first rift in this darkness is the Copernican doctrine'; as if a new hypothesis in astronomy would naturally make a man stop hitting his daughter about the head. No scholar could now write quite like that. But the old picture, done in far cruder colours, has survived among the weaker brethren, if not (let us hope) at Cambridge, yet certainly in that Western darkness from which you have so lately bidden me emerge.[a] Only last summer a young gentleman whom I had the honour of examining described Thomas Wyatt as 'the first man who scrambled ashore out of the great, dark surging sea of the Middle Ages'.[3] This was interesting because it showed how a stereotyped image can obliterate a man's own experience. Nearly all the medieval texts which the syllabus had required him to study had in reality led him into formal gardens where every passion was subdued to a ceremonial and every problem of conduct was dovetailed into a complex and rigid moral theology.

[a] i.e. the University of Oxford, where C. S. Lewis had taught prior to his appointment to the Chair at Cambridge.

From the formula 'Medieval and Renaissance', then, I inferred that the University was encouraging my own belief that the barrier between those two ages has been greatly exaggerated, if indeed it was not largely a figment of Humanist propaganda. At the very least, I was ready to welcome any increased flexibility in our conception of history. All lines of demarcation between what we call 'periods' should be subject to constant revision. Would that we could dispense with them altogether! As a great Cambridge historian[4] has said: 'Unlike dates, periods are not facts. They are retrospective conceptions that we form about past events, useful to focus discussion, but very often leading historical thought astray.' The actual temporal process, as we meet it in our lives (and we meet it, in a strict sense, nowhere else) has no divisions, except perhaps those 'blessed barriers between day and day', our sleeps. Change is never complete, and change never ceases. Nothing is ever quite finished with; it may always begin over again. (This is one of the sides of life that [Samuel] Richardson hits off with wearying accuracy.) And nothing is quite new; it was always somehow anticipated or prepared for. A seamless, formless continuity-in-mutability is the mode of our life. But unhappily we cannot as historians dispense with periods. We cannot use for literary history the technique of Mrs Woolf's *The Waves*. We cannot hold together huge masses of particulars without putting into them some kind of structure. Still less can we arrange a term's work or draw up a lecture list. Thus we are driven back upon periods. All divisions will falsify our material to some extent; the best one can hope is to choose those which will falsify it least. But because we must divide, to reduce the emphasis on any one traditional division must, in the long run, mean an increase of emphasis on some other division. And that is the subject I want to discuss. If we do not put the Great Divide between the Middle Ages and the Renaissance, where should we put it? I ask this question with the full consciousness that, in the reality studied, there is no Great Divide. There is nothing in history that quite corresponds to a coastline or a watershed in geography. If, in spite of this, I still think my question worth asking, that is certainly not because I claim for my answer more than a methodological value, or even much of that. Least of all would I wish it to be any less subject than others to continual attack and speedy revision. But I believe that the discussion is as good a way as any other of explaining how I look at the work you have given me. When I have finished it, I shall at least have laid the cards on the table and you will know the worst.

The meaning of my title will now have become plain. It is a chapter-heading borrowed from Isidore.[5] In that chapter Isidore[a] is engaged in dividing history, as he knew it, into its periods; or, as he calls them, *aetates*. I shall be doing the same. Assuming that we do not put our great frontier between the Middle Ages and the Renaissance, I shall consider the rival claims of certain other divisions which have been, or might be, made. But, first, a word of warning. I am not, even on the most Lilliputian scale, emulating Professor Toynbee or

---

[a] Saint Isidore (560-636) was Bishop of Seville, Spain, and the author of an encyclopaedia.

Spengler.[a] About everything that could be called 'the philosophy of history' I am a desperate sceptic. I know nothing of the future, not even whether there will be any future. I don't know whether past history has been necessary or contingent. I don't know whether the human tragi-comedy is now in Act I or Act V; whether our present disorders are those of infancy or of old age. I am merely considering how we should arrange or schematize those facts—ludicrously few in comparison with the totality—which survive to us (often by accident) from the past. I am less like a botanist in a forest than a woman arranging a few cut flowers for the drawing-room. So, in some degree, are the greatest historians. We can't get into the real forest of the past; that is part of what the word *past* means.

The first division that naturally occurs to us is that between Antiquity and the Dark Ages—the fall of the Empire, the barbarian invasions, the christening of Europe. And of course no possible revolution in historical thought will ever make this anything less than a massive and multiple change. Do not imagine that I mean to belittle it. Yet I must observe that three things have happened since, say, Gibbon's[b] time, which make it a shade less catastrophic for us than it was for him.

1. The partial loss of ancient learning and its recovery at the Renaissance were for him both unique events. History furnished no rivals to such a death and such a re-birth. But we have lived to see the second death of ancient learning. In our time something which was once the possession of all educated men has shrunk to being the technical accomplishment of a few specialists. If we say that this is not total death, it may be replied that there was no total death in the Dark Ages either. It could even be argued that Latin, surviving as the language of Dark Age culture, and preserving the disciplines of Law and Rhetoric, gave to some parts of the classical heritage a far more living and integral status in the life of those ages than the academic studies of the specialists can claim in our own. As for the area and the *tempo* of the two deaths, if one were looking for a man who could not read Virgil though his father could, he might be found more easily in the twentieth century than in the fifth.

2. To Gibbon the literary change from Virgil to *Beowulf* or the *Hildebrand*,[c] if he had read them, would have seemed greater than it can to us. We can now see quite clearly that these barbarian poems were not really a novelty comparable to, say, *The Waste Land* or Mr [David] Jones's *Anathemata*. They were rather an unconscious return to the spirit of the earliest classical poetry. The audience of Homer, and the audience of *Hildebrand*, once they had learned one another's language and metre, would have found one another's poetry perfectly intelligible. Nothing new had come into the world.

3. The christening of Europe seemed to all our ancestors, whether they welcomed it themselves as Christians, or, like Gibbon, deplored it as humanistic

---

[a] Arnold J. Toynbee, author of A *Study of History* (1934–54), and Oswald Spengler, German author of *The Decline of the West* (1918).

[b] Edward Gibbon (1737–94), author of *History of the Decline and Fall of the Roman Empire*.

[c] A German alliterative poem of about the year 800. Only a fragment of it has survived.

445

unbelievers, a unique, irreversible event. But we have seen the opposite process. Of course the un-christening of Europe in our time is not quite complete; neither was her christening in the Dark Ages. But roughly speaking we may say that whereas all history was for our ancestors divided into two periods, the pre-Christian and the Christian, and two only, for us it falls into three—the pre-Christian, the Christian, and what may reasonably be called the post-Christian. This surely must make a momentous difference. I am not here considering either the christening or the un-christening from a theological point of view. I am considering them simply as cultural changes.[6] When I do that, it appears to me that the second change is even more radical than the first. Christians and Pagans had much more in common with each other than either has with a post-Christian. The gap between those who worship different gods is not so wide as that between those who worship and those who do not. The Pagan and Christian ages alike are ages of what Pausanias would call the δρωμενον,[7] the externalized and enacted idea; the sacrifice, the games, the triumph, the ritual drama, the Mass, the tournament, the masque, the pageant, the epithalamium, and with them ritual and symbolic costumes, *trabea* and laticlave, crown of wild olive, royal crown, coronet, judge's robes, knight's spurs, herald's tabard, coat-armour, priestly vestment, religious habit—for every rank, trade, or occasion its visible sign. But even if we look away from that into the temper of men's minds, I seem to see the same. Surely the gap between Professor Ryle[a] and Thomas Browne is far wider than that between Gregory the Great and Virgil? Surely Seneca and Dr Johnson are closer together than Burton and Freud?

You see already the lines along which my thought is working; and indeed it is no part of my aim to save a surprise for the end of the lecture. If I have ventured, a little, to modify our view of the transition from 'the Antique' to 'the Dark', it is only because I believe we have since witnessed a change even more profound.

The next frontier which has been drawn, though not till recently, is that between the Dark and the Middle Ages. We draw it somewhere about the early twelfth century. This frontier clearly cannot compete with its predecessor in the religious field; nor can it boast such drastic redistribution of populations. But it nearly makes up for these deficiencies in other ways. The change from Ancient to Dark had, after all, consisted mainly in losses. Not entirely. The Dark Ages were not so unfruitful in progress as we sometimes think. They saw the triumph of the *codex* or hinged book over the roll or *volumen*—a technical improvement almost as important for the history of learning as the invention of printing. All exact scholarship depends on it. And if—here I speak under correction—they also invented the stirrup, they did something almost as important for the art of war as the inventor of Tanks. But in the main, they were a period of retrogression: worse houses, worse drains, fewer baths, worse roads, less security. (We notice in *Beowulf* that an old sword is expected to be better than a new one.) With the Middle Ages we reach a

[a] Gilbert Ryle, author of *The Concept of Mind* (1949), one of the most influential works of modern British linguistic philosophy.

period of widespread and brilliant improvement. The text of Aristotle is recovered. Its rapid assimilation by Albertus Magnus and Thomas Aquinas opens up a new world of thought. In architecture new solutions of technical problems lead the way to new aesthetic effects. In literature the old alliterative and assonantal metres give place to that rhymed and syllabic verse which was to carry the main burden of European poetry for centuries. At the same time the poets explore a whole new range of sentiment. I am so far from underrating this particular revolution that I have before now been accused of exaggerating it. But 'great' and 'small' are terms of comparison. I would think this change in literature the greatest if I did not know of a greater. It does not seem to me that the work of the Troubadours and Chrestien and the rest was really as great a novelty as the poetry of the twentieth century. A man bred on the *Chanson de Roland* might have been puzzled by the *Lancelot* [of Chrétien de Troyes]. He would have wondered why the author spent so much time on the sentiments and so (comparatively) little on the actions. But he would have known that this was what the author had done. He would, in one important sense, have known what the poem was 'about'. If he had misunderstood the intention, he would at least have understood the words. That is why I do not think the change from 'Dark' to 'Middle' can, on the literary side, be judged equal to the change which has taken place in my own lifetime. And of course in religion it does not even begin to compete.

A third possible frontier remains to be considered. We might draw our line somewhere towards the end of the seventeenth century, with the general acceptance of Copernicanism, the dominance of Descartes, and (in England) the foundation of the Royal Society. Indeed, if we were considering the history of thought (in the narrower sense of the word) I believe this is where I would draw my line. But if we are considering the history of our culture in general, it is a different matter. Certainly the sciences then began to advance with a firmer and more rapid tread. To that advance nearly all the later, and (in my mind) vaster, changes can be traced. But the effects were delayed. The sciences long remained like a lion-cub whose gambols delighted its master in private; it had not yet tasted man's blood. All through the eighteenth century the tone of the common mind remained ethical, rhetorical, juristic, rather than scientific, so that Johnson[8] could truly say, 'the knowledge of external nature, and the sciences which that knowledge requires or includes, are not the great or the frequent business of the human mind'. It is easy to see why. Science was not the business of Man because Man had not yet become the business of science. It dealt chiefly with the inanimate; and it threw off few technological by-products. When Watt makes his engine, when Darwin starts monkeying with the ancestry of Man, and Freud with his soul, and the economists with all that is his, then indeed the lion will have got out of its cage. Its liberated presence in our midst will become one of the most important factors in everyone's daily life. But not yet; not even in the seventeenth century.

It is by these steps that I have come to regard as the greatest of all divisions in the history of the West that which divides the present from, say, the age of Jane Austen and Scott. The dating of such things must of course be rather hazy and indefinite. No one could point to a year or a decade in which the change indisputably began, and it has probably not yet reached its peak. But somewhere between us and the Waverley Novels, somewhere between us and *Persuasion*, the chasm runs. Of course, I had no sooner reached this result than I asked myself whether it might not be an illusion of perspective. The distance between the telegraph post I am touching and the next telegraph post looks longer than the sum of the distances between all the other posts. Could this be an illusion of the same sort? We cannot pace the periods as we could pace the posts. I can only set out the grounds on which, after frequent reconsideration, I have found myself forced to reaffirm my conclusion.

1. I begin with what I regard as the weakest; the change, between Scott's age and ours, in political order. On this count my proposed frontier would have serious rivals. The change is perhaps less than that between Antiquity and the Dark Ages. Yet it is very great; and I think it extends to all nations, those we call democracies as well as dictatorships. If I wished to satirize the present political order I should borrow for it the name which *Punch* invented during the first German War: *Govertisement*. This is a portmanteau word and means 'government by advertisement'. But my intention is not satiric; I am trying to be objective. The change is this. In all previous ages that I can think of the principal aim of rulers, except at rare and short intervals, was to keep their subjects quiet, to forestall or extinguish widespread excitement and persuade people to attend quietly to their several occupations. And on the whole their subjects agreed with them. They even prayed (in words that sound curiously old-fashioned) to be able to live 'a peaceable life in all godliness and honesty' and 'pass their time in rest and quietness'. But now the organization of mass excitement seems to be almost the normal organ of political power. We live in an age of 'appeals', 'drives', and 'campaigns'. Our rulers have become like school-masters and are always demanding 'keenness'. And you notice that I am guilty of a slight archaism in calling them 'rulers'. 'Leaders' is the modern word. I have suggested elsewhere that this is a deeply significant change of vocabulary. Our demand upon them has changed no less than theirs on us. For of a ruler one asks justice, incorruption, diligence, perhaps clemency; of a leader, dash, initiative, and (I suppose) what people call 'magnetism' or 'personality'.

On the political side, then, this proposed frontier has respectable, but hardly compulsive, qualifications.

2. In the arts I think it towers above every possible rival. I do not think that any previous age produced work which was, in its own time, as shatteringly and bewilderingly new as that of the Cubists, the Dadaists, the Surrealists, and Picasso has been in ours. And I am quite sure that this is true of the art I love best, that is, of poetry. This question has often been debated with some heat, but the heat was, I think, occasioned by the suspicion (not always ill-grounded) that those who asserted the unprecedented novelty of modern poetry intended thereby to discredit it. But nothing is farther from my purpose than to make any judgment of value, whether favourable or the reverse. And if once we can eliminate that critical issue and concentrate on the historical fact, then I do not see how anyone can doubt that modern poetry is not only a greater novelty

than any other 'new poetry' but new in a new way, almost in a new dimension. To say that all new poetry was once as difficult as ours is false; to say that any was is an equivocation. Some earlier poetry was difficult, but not in the same way. Alexandrian poetry was difficult because it presupposed a learned reader; as you became learned you found the answers to the puzzles. Skaldic*a* poetry was unintelligible if you did not know the *kenningar*, but intelligible if you did. And—this is the real point—all Alexandrian men of letters and all skalds would have agreed about the answers. I believe the same to be true of the dark conceits in Donne; there was one correct interpretation of each and Donne could have told it to you. Of course you might misunderstand what Wordsworth was 'up to' in *Lyrical Ballads*; but everyone understood what he said. I do not see in any of these the slightest parallel to the state of affairs disclosed by a recent symposium on Mr Eliot's *Cooking Egg*.[9] Here we find seven adults (two of them Cambridge men) whose lives have been specially devoted to the study of poetry discussing a very short poem which has been before the world for thirty-odd years; and there is not the slightest agreement among them as to what, in any sense of the word, it means. I am not in the least concerned to decide whether this state of affairs is a good thing, or a bad thing.[10] I merely assert that it is a new thing. In the whole history of the West, from Homer— I might almost say from the *Epic of Gilgamesh*b—there has been no bend or break in the development of poetry comparable to this. On this score my proposed division has no rival to fear.

3. Thirdly, there is the great religious change which I have had to mention before: the un-christening. Of course there were lots of sceptics in Jane Austen's time and long before, as there are lots of Christians now. But the presumption has changed. In her days some kind and degree of religious belief and practice were the norm: now, though I would gladly believe that both kind and degree have improved, they are the exception. I have already argued that this change surpasses that which Europe underwent at its conversion. It is hard to have patience with those Jeremiahs, in Press or pulpit, who warn us that we are 'relapsing into Paganism'. It might be rather fun if we were. It would be pleasant to see some future Prime Minister trying to kill a large and lively milk-white bull in Westminster Hall. But we shan't. What lurks behind such idle prophecies, if they are anything but careless language, is the false idea that the historical process allows mere reversal: that Europe can come out of Christianity 'by the same door as in she went' and find herself back where she was. It is not what happens. A post-Christian man is not a Pagan; you might as well think that a married woman recovers her virginity by divorce. The post-Christian is cut off from the Christian past and therefore doubly from the Pagan past.

4. Lastly, I play my trump card. Between Jane Austen and us, but not between her and Shakespeare, Chaucer, Alfred, Virgil, Homer, or the Pharaohs, comes the birth of the machines. This lifts us at once into a region of change far above

a The ancient Scandinavian poetry to which Anglo-Saxon poetry (e.g. *Beowulf*) is related. 'Skald' means poet. *Kenningar* are formulaic figurative phrases characteristic of this poetry.

b An ancient Babylonian epic.

all that we have hitherto considered. For this is parallel to the great changes by which we divide epochs of pre-history. This is on a level with the change from stone to bronze, or from a pastoral to an agricultural economy. It alters Man's place in nature. The theme has been celebrated till we are all sick of it, so I will here say nothing about its economic and social consequences, immeasurable though they are. What concerns us more is its psychological effect. How has it come about that we use the highly emotive word 'stagnation', with all its malodorous and malarial overtones, for what other ages would have called 'permanence'? Why does the word 'primitive' at once suggest to us clumsiness, inefficiency, barbarity? When our ancestors talked of the primitive church or the primitive purity of our constitution they meant nothing of that sort. (The only pejorative sense which Johnson gives to *Primitive* in his Dictionary is, significantly, 'Formal; affectedly solemn; imitating the supposed gravity of old times'.) Why does 'latest' in advertisements mean 'best'? Well, let us admit that these semantic developments owe something to the nineteenth-century belief in spontaneous progress which itself owes something either to Darwin's theorem of biological evolution or to that myth of universal evolutionism which is really so different from it, and earlier. For the two great imaginative expressions of the myth, as distinct from the theorem—Keats's *Hyperion* and Wagner's *Ring* —are pre-Darwinian. Let us give these their due. But I submit that what has imposed this climate of opinion so firmly on the human mind is a new archetypal image. It is the image of old machines being superseded by new and better ones. For in the world of machines the new most often really is better and the primitive really is the clumsy. And this image, potent in all our minds, reigns almost without rival in the minds of the uneducated. For to them, after their marriage and the births of their children, the very milestones of life are technical advances. From the old push-bike to the motor-bike and thence to the little car; from gramophone to radio and from radio to television; from the range to the stove; these are the very stages of their pilgrimage. But whether from this cause or from some other, assuredly that approach to life which has left these footprints on our language is the thing that separates us most sharply from our ancestors and whose absence would strike us as most alien if we could return to their world. Conversely, our assumption that everything is provisional and soon to be superseded, that the attainment of goods we have never yet had, rather than the defence and conservation of those we have already, is the cardinal business of life, would most shock and bewilder them if they could visit ours.

I thus claim for my chosen division of periods that on the first count it comes well up to scratch; on the second and third it arguably surpasses all; and on the fourth it quite clearly surpasses them without any dispute. I conclude that it really is the greatest change in the history of Western Man.

At any rate, this conviction determines my whole approach to my work from this Chair. I am not preparing an excuse in advance lest I should hereafter catch myself lecturing either on the *Epic of Gilgamesh* or on the Waverley Novels. The field 'Medieval and Renaissance' is already far too wide for my powers. But you see how to me the appointed area must primarily appear as a specimen of something far larger, something which had already begun when the *Iliad* was composed and was still almost unimpaired when Waterloo was fought. Of course within that immense period there are all sorts of differences. There are lots of convenient differences between the area I am to deal with and other areas; there are important differences within the chosen area. And yet—despite all this—that whole thing, from its Greek or pre-Greek beginnings down to the day before yesterday, seen from the vast distance at which we stand today, reveals a homogeneity that is certainly important and perhaps more important than its interior diversities. That is why I shall be unable to talk to you about my particular region without constantly treating things which neither began with the Middle Ages nor ended with the end of the Renaissance. In that way I shall be forced to present to you a great deal of what can only be described as Old European, or Old Western, Culture. If one were giving a lecture on Warwickshire to an audience of Martians (no offence : Martians may be delightful creatures) one might loyally chose all one's *data* from that county : but much of what you told them would not really be Warwickshire lore but 'common tellurian'.

The prospect of my becoming, in such halting fashion as I can, the spokesman of Old Western Culture, alarms me. It may alarm you. I will close with one reassurance and one claim.

First, for the reassurance. I do not think you need fear that the study of a dead period, however prolonged and however sympathetic, need prove an indulgence in nostalgia or an enslavement to the past. In the individual life, as the psychologists have taught us, it is not the remembered but the forgotten past that enslaves us. I think the same is true of society. To study the past does indeed liberate us from the present, from the idols of our own market-place. But I think it liberates us from the past too. I think no class of men are less enslaved to the past than historians. The unhistorical are usually, without knowing it, enslaved to a fairly recent past. Dante read Virgil. Certain other medieval authors[11] evolved the legend of Virgil as a great magician. It was the more recent past, the whole quality of mind evolved during a few preceding centuries, which impelled them to do so. Dante was freer; he also knew more of the past. And you will be no freer by coming to misinterpret Old Western Culture as quickly and deeply as those medievals misinterpreted Classical Antiquity; or even as the Romantics misinterpreted the Middle Ages.[12] Such misinterpretation has already begun. To arrest its growth while arrest is still possible, is surely a proper task for a university.

And now for the claim : which sounds arrogant but, I hope, is not really so. I have said that the vast change which separates you from Old Western has been gradual and is not even now complete. Wide as the chasm is, those who are native to different sides of it can still meet; are meeting in this room. This is quite normal at times of great change. The correspondence of Henry More[13] and Descartes is an amusing example; one would think the two men were writing in different centuries. And here comes the rub. I myself belong far more to that Old Western order than to yours. I am going to claim that this, which in one way is a disqualification for my task, is yet in another a qualification. The disqualification is obvious. You don't want to be lectured on Neanderthal Man by a Neanderthaler, still less on dinosaurs by a dinosaur. And yet, is that the whole story? If a live dinosaur dragged its slow length into the laboratory, would we not all look back as we fled? What a chance to know at last how it really moved and looked, and smelled and what noises it made! And if the Neanderthaler could talk, then though his lecturing technique might leave much to be desired, should we not almost certainly learn from him some things about him which the best modern anthropologist could never have told us? He would tell us without knowing he was telling. One thing I know: I would give a great deal to hear any ancient Athenian, even a stupid one, talking about Greek tragedy. He would know in his bones so much that we seek in vain. At any moment some chance phrase might, unknown to him, show us where modern scholarship had been on the wrong track for years. Ladies and gentlemen, I stand before you somewhat as that Athenian might stand. I read as a native texts that you must read as foreigners. You see why I said that the claim was not really arrogant; who can be proud of speaking fluently his mother tongue or knowing his way about his father's house? It is my settled conviction that in order to read Old Western literature aright you must suspend most of the responses and unlearn most of the habits you have acquired in reading modern literature. And because this is the judgment of a native, I claim that, even if the defence of my conviction is weak, the fact of my conviction is a historical *datum* to which you should give full weight. That way, where I fail as a critic, I may yet be useful as a specimen. I would even dare to go further. Speaking not only for myself but for all other Old Western men whom you may meet, I would say, use your specimens while you can. There are not going to be many more dinosaurs.

Notes

1. J. Seznec, *La Survivance des dieux antiques* (London, 1940), trans. B. F. Sessions (Kingsport, Tennessee, 1953), p. 3.
2. New York, 1920.
3. A delicious passage in Comparetti, *Vergil in the Middle Ages*, trans. E. F. M. Benecke (London, 1895), p. 241, contrasts the Middle Ages with 'more normal periods of history'.
4. G. M. Trevelyan, *English Social History* (London, 1944), p. 92.
5. *Etymologiarum*, ed. W. M. Lindsay, 2 vols (Oxford, 1911), V, xxxix.
6. It is not certain that either process, seen (if we could see it) *sub specie aeternitatis*, would be more important than it appears to the historian of culture. The amount of Christian (that is, of penitent and regenerate) life in an age, as distinct from 'Christian Civilization', is not to be judged by mortals.
7. *De Descriptione Graec.* II, xxxvii.
8. *Life of Milton.*
9. *Essays in Criticism*, iii, 3 (July 1953).
10. In music we have pieces which demand more talent in the performer than in the composer. Why should there not come a period when the art of writing poetry stands lower than the art of reading it? Of course rival readings would then cease to be 'right' or 'wrong' and become more and less brilliant 'performances'.
11. On their identity see Comparetti, *Virgilio nel Medio Evo*, ed. G. Pasquali (Firenze, 1943), p. xxii. I owe this reference to Mr G. C. Hardie.
12. As my examples show, such misinterpretations may themselves produce results

which may have imaginative value. If there had been no Romantic distortion of the Middle Ages, we should have no *Eve of St Agnes*. There is room both for an appreciation of the imagined past and an awareness of its difference from the real past; but if we want only the former, why come to a university? (The subject deserves much fuller treatment than I can give it here.)

13. A *Collection of several Philosophical Writings* (Cambridge, 1662).

33   Leslie A. Fiedler

Leslie A. Fiedler (b. 1917) is a prolific writer on many different subjects, but is probably best known as the author of *Love and Death in the American Novel* (New York, 1960), a brilliant, controversial work which Fiedler himself has invited his readers to regard 'not as a conventional scholarly book—or an eccentric one—but a kind of gothic novel (complete with touches of black humour) whose subject is the American experience as recorded in our classic fiction' (preface to the second edition of 1966). Fiedler is one of those critics of American literature and culture who have evidently been inspired by D. H. Lawrence's *Studies in Classic American Literature* (see above, pp. 122-7). Like Lawrence, Fiedler emphasizes, instead of apologizing for, the non-European qualities of American literature, and writes about it in a free-wheeling, provocative, speculative, idiomatic style, drawing eclectically on psychology, anthropology, mythology, and history for illumination. One should not, of course, press the parallel too far : Fiedler writes from within the American experience, and accepts—indeed, celebrates—the mass culture of modern urbanized America which Lawrence would certainly have rejected fiercely. Yet when Fiedler observes of comic books, 'In a society which thinks of itself as "scientific"—and of the Marvellous as childish—such a literature must seem primarily children's literature', one cannot help being reminded of Lawrence's warning against thinking 'of the old-fashioned American classics as children's books'.

Fiedler's irreverent attitude towards 'Establishment' culture and traditional aesthetic values makes him an uninhibited and illuminating critic of popular art and the mass media. 'The Middle Against Both Ends', first published in *Encounter* in 1955, is an early example of this kind of criticism, and it is interesting to compare it with Richard Hoggart's contemporaneous discussion of British working-class women's magazines in *The Uses of Literacy* (1957)—Hoggart being attentive, and indeed sympathetic, to his materials, but without finding it necessary to suspend, or abandon, conventional literary-critical criteria (see below, pp. 488-96). The apocalyptic note Fiedler sounds in his essay on comic books—that traditional literary culture, now defended by the liberal bourgeoisie, is dying, and that there is an alliance between the most advanced high art and the most popular low art to hasten its end—has become more and more strident in his subsequent critical writings (see, for example, Frank Kermode's discussion of his essay, 'The New Mutants' below, pp. 671-3). These include : *An End to Innocence: essays in culture and politics* (Boston, 1955), *No! In Thunder* (Boston, 1960), *Waiting for the End* (New York, 1964), and *The Return of the Vanishing American* (1968). Leslie Fiedler is also the author of several works of

454

fiction and of an autobiographical book, *Being Busted* (New York, 1969). After being Professor of English at Montana State University for many years, Leslie Fiedler moved to the University of Buffalo; but he is a widely travelled man who has taught or lectured at more than a hundred different colleges and universities in America and around the world.

CROSS REFERENCES: 10. D. H. Lawrence
14. C. G. Jung
49. Susan Sontag
50. Frank Kermode

The middle against both ends

I am surely one of the few people pretending to intellectual respectability who can boast that he has read more comic books than attacks on comic books. I do not mean that I have consulted or studied the comics—I have read them, often with some pleasure. Nephews and nieces, my own children, and the children of neighbours, have brought them to me to share their enjoyment. An old lady on a ferry boat in Puget Sound once dropped two in my lap in wordless sympathy; I was wearing, at the time, a sailor's uniform.

I have somewhat more difficulty in getting through the books that attack them. I am put off, to begin with, by inaccuracies of fact. When Mr Geoffrey Wagner in his *Parade of Pleasure* calls Superboy 'Superman's brother' (he is, of course, Superman himself as a child), I am made suspicious. Actually, Mr Wagner's book is one of the least painful on the subject; confused, to be sure, but quite lively and not in the least smug; though it propounds the preposterous theory that the whole of 'popular literature' is a conspiracy on the part of the 'plutos' to corrupt an innocent American people. Such easy melodrama can only satisfy someone prepared to believe, as Mr Wagner apparently does, that the young girls of Harlem are being led astray by the *double-entendres* of blues records!

Mr Wagner's notions are at least more varied and subtle than Mr Gershon Legman's, who cries out in his *Love and Death* that it is simply our sexual frustrations which breed a popular literature dedicated to violence. But Mr Legman's theory explains too much: not only comic books but Hemingway, war, Luce, Faulkner, the status of women—and, I should suppose, Mr Legman's own shrill hyperboles. At that, Mr Legman seems more to the point in his search for some deeply underlying cause than Frederic Wertham, in *Seduction of the Innocent*, with his contention that the pulps and comics in themselves are schools for murder. That the undefined aggressiveness of disturbed children can be given a shape by comic books, I do not doubt; and one could make a good case for the contention that such literature standardizes crime woefully or inhibits imagination in violence, but I find it hard to consider so obvious a symptom a prime cause of anything. Perhaps I am a little sensitive on this score, having heard the charge this week that the recent suicide of one of our college freshmen was caused by his having read (in a course of which I am in charge), Goethe, Dostoievsky, and *Death of a Salesman*. Damn it, he *had* read them, and he *did* kill himself!

In none of the books on comics I have looked into, and in none of the reports of ladies' clubs, protests of legislators, or statements of moral indignation by pastors, have I come on any real attempt to understand comic books: to define the form, midway between icon and story; to distinguish the subtypes—animal, adolescent, crime, western, etc.; or even to separate out, from the deadpan varieties, tongue-in-cheek sports like *Pogo*, frank satire like *Mad*, or semi-surrealist variations like *Plastic Man*. It would not take someone with the talents of an Aristotle, but merely with his method to ask the rewarding questions about this kind of literature that he asked once about an equally popular and bloody genre: what are its causes and its natural form?

A cursory examination would show that the super-hero comic (*Superman*, *Captain Marvel*, *Wonder Woman*, etc.) is the final form; it is statistically the most popular with the most avid readers, as well as providing the only new legendary material invented along with the form rather than adapted to it.

Next, one would have to abstract the most general pattern of the myth of the super-hero and deduce its significance: the urban setting, the threatened universal catastrophe, the hero who never uses arms, who returns to weakness and obscurity, who must keep his identity secret, who is impotent, etc. Not until then could one ask with any hope of an answer: what end do the comics serve? Why have they gained an immense body of readers precisely in the past fifteen or twenty years? Why must they be disguised as children's literature though read by men and women of all ages? And having answered these, one could pose the most dangerous question of all: why the constant virulent attacks on the comics, and, indeed, on the whole of popular culture of which they are especially flagrant examples?

Strategically, if not logically, the last question should be asked first. Why the attacks? Such assaults by scientists and laymen are as characteristic of our age as puritanic diatribes against the stage of the Elizabethan Era, and pious protests against novel reading in the later eighteenth century. I suspect that a study of such conventional reactions reveals at least as much about the nature of a period as an examination of the forms to which they respond. The most fascinating and suspicious aspect of the opposition to popular narrative is its unanimity; everyone from the members of the Montana State Legislature to the ladies of the Parent Teachers Association of Boston, Massachusetts, from British M.P.s to the wilder post-Freudians of two continents agree on this, though they may agree on nothing else. What they have in common is, I am afraid, the sense that they are all, according to their lights, righteous. And their protests represent only one more example (though an unlikely one) of the notorious failure of righteousness in matters involving art.

Just what is it with which vulgar literature is charged by various guardians of morality or sanity? With everything: encouraging crime, destroying literacy, expressing sexual frustration, unleashing sadism, spreading anti-democratic ideas, and, of course, corrupting youth. To understand the grounds of such charges, their justification and their bias, we must understand something of the nature of the subart with which we are dealing.

Perhaps it is most illuminating to begin by saying that it is a peculiarly American phenomenon, an unexpected byproduct of an attempt, not only to extend literacy universally, but to delegate taste to majority suffrage. I do not mean, of course, that it is found only in the United States, but that wherever it is found, it comes first from us, and is still to be discovered in fully developed form only among us. Our experience along these lines is, in this sense, a preview for the rest of the world of what must follow the inevitable dissolution of the older aristocratic cultures.

One has only to examine certain Continental imitations of picture magazines like *Look* or *Life* or Disney-inspired cartoon books to be aware at once of the debt to American examples and of the failure of the imitations. For a true 'popular literature' demands a more than ordinary slickness, the sort of high finish possible only to a machine-produced commodity in an economy of maximum prosperity. Contemporary popular culture, which is a function of an industrialized society, is distinguished from older folk art by its refusal to be shabby or secondrate in appearance, by a refusal to know its place. It is a product of the same impulse which has made available the sort of ready-made clothing which aims at destroying the possibility of knowing a lady by her dress.

Yet the articles of popular culture are made, not to be treasured, but to be thrown away; a paperback book is like a disposable diaper or a paper milk-container. For all its competent finish, it cannot be preserved on dusty shelves like the calf-bound volumes of another day; indeed, its very mode of existence challenges the concept of a library, private or public. The sort of conspicuous waste once reserved for an élite is now available to anyone; and this is inconceivable without an absurdly high standard of living, just as it is unimaginable without a degree of mechanical efficiency that permits industry to replace nature, and invents—among other disposable synthetics—one for literature.

Just as the production of popular narrative demands industrial conditions most favourably developed in the United States, its distribution requires the peculiar conditions of our market places: the mass or democratized market. Subbooks and subarts are not distributed primarily through the traditional institutions: museums, libraries, and schools, which remain firmly in the hands of those who deplore mass culture. It is in drugstores and supermarkets and airline terminals that this kind of literature mingles without condescension with chocolate bars and soapflakes. We have reached the end of a long process, begun, let us say, with Samuel Richardson, in which the work of art has approached closer and closer to the status of a commodity. Even the comic book is a last descendant of *Pamela*, the final consequence of letting the tastes (or more precisely, the buying power) of a class unpledged to maintaining the traditional genres determine literary success or failure.

Those who cry out now that the work of a Mickey Spillane or *The Adventures of Superman* travesty the novel, forget that the novel was long accused of travestying literature. What seems to offend us most is not the further downgrading of literary standards so much as the fact that the medium, the very notion and shape of a book, is being parodied by the comics. Jazz or the movies, which are also popular urban arts, depending for the distribution and acceptance on developments in technology (for jazz, the phonograph), really upset us much less.

It is the final, though camouflaged, rejection of literacy implicit in these new forms which is the most legitimate source of distress; but all arts so universally consumed have been for illiterates, even stained glass windows and the plays of Shakespeare. What is new in our present situation, and hence especially upsetting, is that this is the first art for *post*literates, i.e. for those who have refused the benefit for which they were presumed to have sighed in their long exclusion. Besides, modern popular narrative is disconcertingly not oral; it will not surrender the benefits of the printing press as a machine, however indifferent it may be to that press as the perpetuator of techniques devised first for the pen or quill. Everything that the press can provide—except matter to be really read—is demanded: picture, typography, even in many cases the illusion of reading along with the relaxed pleasure of illiteracy. Yet the new popular forms remain somehow prose narrative or pictographic substitutes for the novel; even the cognate form of the movies is notoriously more like a novel than a play in its handling of time, space, and narrative progression.

From the folk literature of the past, which ever since the triumph of the machine we have been trying sentimentally to recapture, popular literature differs in its rejection of the picturesque. Rooted in prose rather than verse, secular rather than religious in origin, defining itself against the city rather than the world of outdoor nature, a byproduct of the factory rather than agriculture, presentday popular literature defeats romantic expectations of peasants in their embroidered blouses chanting or plucking balalaikas for the approval of their betters. The haters of our own popular art love to condescend to the folk; and on records or in fashionable night clubs in recent years, we have had entertainers who have earned enviable livings producing commercial imitations of folk songs. But contemporary vulgar culture is brutal and disturbing: the quasi-spontaneous expression of the uprooted and culturally dispossessed inhabitants of anonymous cities, contriving mythologies which reduce to manageable form the threat of science, the horror of unlimited war, the general spread of corruption in a world where the social bases of old loyalties and heroisms have long been destroyed. That such an art is exploited for profit in a commercial society, mass produced by nameless collaborators, standardized and debased, is of secondary importance. It is the patented nightmare of us all, a packaged way of coming to terms with one's environment sold for a dime to all those who have rejected the unasked-for gift of literacy.

Thought of in this light, the comic books with their legends of the eternally threatened metropolis eternally protected by immaculate and modest heroes (who shrink back after each exploit into the image of the crippled newsboy, the

458

impotent and cowardly reporter) are seen as inheritors, for all their superficial differences, of the *inner* impulses of traditional folk art. Their gross drawing, their poverty of language cannot disguise their heritage of aboriginal violence, their exploitation of an ancient conflict of black magic and white. Beneath their journalistic commentary on A-bomb and Communism, they touch archetypal material: those shared figures of our lower minds more like the patterns of dream than fact. In a world where men threaten to dissolve into their most superficial and mechanical techniques, to become their borrowed newspaper platitudes, they remain close to the impulsive, subliminal life. They are our not quite machine-subdued Grimm, though the Black Forest has become, as it must, the City; the Wizard, the Scientist; and Simple Hans, Captain Marvel. In a society which thinks of itself as 'scientific'—and of the Marvellous as childish— such a literature must seem primarily children's literature, though, of course, it is read by people of all ages.

We are now in a position to begin to answer the question: what do the righteous really have against comic books? In some parts of the world, simply the fact that they are American is sufficient, and certain homegrown self-contemners follow this line even in the United States. But it is really a minor argument, lent a certain temporary importance by passing political exigencies. To declare oneself against 'the Americanization of culture' is meaningless unless one is set resolutely against industrialization and mass education.

More to the point is the attack on mass culture for its betrayal of literacy itself. In a very few cases, this charge is made seriously and with full realization of its import; but most often it amounts to nothing but an accusation of 'bad grammar' or 'slang' on the part of some school marm to whom the spread of 'different than' seems to threaten the future of civilized discourse. What should set us on guard in this case is that it is not the fully literate, the intellectuals and serious writers, who lead the attack, but the insecure semiliterate. In America, there is something a little absurd about the indignant delegation from the Parent Teachers Association (themselves clutching the latest issue of *Life*) crying out in defence of literature. Asked for suggestions, such critics are likely to propose the *Readers' Digest* as required reading in high school—or to urge more comic-book versions of the 'classics': emasculated Melville, expurgated Hawthorne, or a child's version of something 'uplifting' like *The Fall of the House of Usher*. In other countries, corresponding counterparts are not hard to find.

As a matter of fact, this charge is scarcely ever urged with much conviction. It is really the portrayal of crime and horror (and less usually sex) that the enlightened censors deplore. It has been charged against vulgar art that it is sadistic, fetishistic, brutal, full of terror; that it pictures women with exaggeratedly full breasts and rumps, portrays death on the printed page, is often covertly homosexual, etc., etc. About these charges, there are two obvious things to say. First, by and large, they are true. Second, they are also true about much of the most serious art of our time, especially that produced in America.

There is no count of sadism and brutality which could not be equally proved against Hemingway or Faulkner or Paul Bowles—or, for that matter, Edgar

Allan Poe. There are certain more literate critics who are victims of their own confusion in this regard, and who will condemn a Class B movie for its images of flagellation or bloodshed only to praise in the next breath such an orgy of highminded sadism as *Le Salaire de la Peur* [The Wages of Fear]. The politics of the French picture may be preferable, or its photography; but this cannot redeem the scene in which a mud- and oil-soaked truckdriver crawls from a pit of sludge to reveal the protruding white bones of a multiple fracture of the thigh. This is as much horror-pornography as *Scarface* or *Little Caesar*. You cannot condemn *Superman* for the exploitation of violence, and praise the existentialist–homosexual–sadist shockers of Paul Bowles. It is possible to murmur by way of explanation something vague about art or catharsis; but no one is ready to advocate the suppression of anything merely because it is aesthetically bad. In this age of conflicting standards, we would all soon suppress each other.

An occasional Savonarola is, of course, ready to make the total rejection; and secretly or openly, the run-of-the-mill condemner of mass culture does condemn, on precisely the same grounds, most contemporary literature of distinction. Historically, one can make quite a convincing case to prove that our highest and lowest arts come from a common antibourgeois source. Edgar Allan Poe, who lived the image of the dandy that has been haunting high art ever since, also, one remembers, invented the popular detective story; and there is a direct line from Hemingway to O'Hara to Dashiell Hammett to Raymond Chandler to Mickey Spillane.

Of both lines of descent from Poe, one can say that they tell a black and distressing truth (we are creatures of dark impulse in a threatened and guilty world), and that they challenge the more genteel versions of 'good taste'. Behind the opposition to vulgar literature, there is at work the same fear of the archetypal and the unconscious itself that motivated similar attacks on Elizabethan drama and on the eighteenth-century novel. We always judge Gosson[a] a fool in terms of Shakespeare; but this is not the point—he was just as wrong in his attack on the worst-written, the most outrageously bloody and bawdy plays of his time. I should hate my argument to be understood as a defence of what is banal and mechanical and dull (there is, of course, a great deal!) in mass culture; it is merely a counterattack against those who are aiming through that banality and dullness at what moves all literature of worth. Anyone at all sensitive to the life of the imagination would surely prefer his kids to read the coarsest fables of Black and White contending for the City of Man, rather than have them spell out, 'Oh, see, Jane. Funny, funny Jane', or read to themselves hygienic accounts of the operation of supermarkets or manureless farms. Yet most schoolboard members are on the side of mental hygiene; and it is they who lead the charge against mass culture.

---

[a] Stephen Gosson (1554–1624) wrote an attack on contemporary poets and dramatists from the Puritan point of view in his *School of Abuse* (1579). This work partly provoked Sir Philip Sidney into writing his celebrated *Apology for Poetry*.

Anyone old enough to have seen, say, *Rain*[a] is on guard against those who in the guise of wanting to destroy savagery and ignorance wage war on spontaneity and richness. But we are likely to think of such possibilities purely in sexual terms; the new righteous themselves have been touched lightly by Freud and are firm believers in frankness and 'sex education'. But in the very midst of their self-congratulation at their emancipation, they have become victims of a new and ferocious prudery. One who would be ashamed to lecture his masturbating son on the dangers of insanity, is quite prepared (especially if he has been reading Wertham) to predict the electric chair for the young scoundrel caught with a bootlegged comic. Superman is our Sadie Thompson. We live in an age when the child who is exposed to the 'facts of life' is protected from 'the facts of death'. In the United States, for instance, a certain Doctor Spock has produced an enlightened guide to childcare for modern mothers—a paperback book which sold, I would guess, millions of copies. Tell the child all about sex, the good doctor advises, but on the subject of death—hush!

By more 'advanced' consultants, the taboo is advanced further towards absurdity: no bloodsoaked Grimm, no terrifying Andersen, no childhood verses about cradles that fall—for fear breeds insecurity; insecurity, aggression; aggression, war. There is even a 'happy', that is to say, expurgated, Mother Goose in which the three blind mice have become 'kind mice'—and the farmer's wife no longer hacks off their tails, but 'cuts them some cheese with a carving knife'. Everywhere the fear of fear is endemic, the fear of the very names of fear; those who have most ardently desired to end warfare and personal cruelty in the world around them, and are therefore most frustrated by their persistence, conspire to stamp out violence on the nursery bookshelf. This much they can do anyhow. If they can't hold up the weather, at least they can break the bloody glass.[b]

This same fear of the instinctual and the dark, this denial of death and guilt by the enlightened genteel, motivates their distrust of serious literature, too. Faulkner is snubbed and the comic books are banned, not in the interests of the classics or even of Robert Louis Stevenson, as the attackers claim, but in the name of a literature of the middle ground which finds its fictitious vision of a kindly and congenial world attacked from above and below. I speak now not of the few intellectual converts to the cause of censorship, but of the main body of genteel book-banners, whose idol is Lloyd Douglas or even A. J. Cronin. When a critic such as Mr Wagner is led to applaud what he sees as a 'trend' towards making doctors, lawyers, etc., the heroes of certain magazine stories, he has fallen into the trap of regarding middling fiction as a transmission belt from the vulgar to the high. There is no question, however, of a slow climb

---

[a] A film (also a stage-play) based on a story with a Far Eastern setting by W. Somerset Maugham, 'Miss Thompson'. It concerns a repressed, and repressive, Christian missionary whose flaws are exposed through his involvement with a prostitute, Sadie Thompson.
[b] An allusion to Louis MacNeice's poem, 'Bagpipe Music':
>The glass is falling hour by hour, the glass will fall for ever,
>But if you break the bloody glass you won't hold up the weather.

from the level of literature which celebrates newspaper reporters, newsboys, radio commentators (who are also super-heroes in tight-fitting uniforms with insignia), through one which centres around prosperous professionals, to the heights of serious literature, whose protagonists are suicides full of incestuous longings, lady lushes with clipped hair, bootleggers, gangsters, and broken-down pugs. To try to state the progression is to reveal its absurdity.

The conception of such a 'trend' is nothing more than the standard attitude of a standard kind of literature, the literature of slick-paper ladies' magazines, which prefers the stereotype to the archetype, loves poetic justice, sentiment-ality, and gentility, and is peopled by characters who bathe frequently, live in the suburbs, and are professionals. Such literature circles mindlessly inside the trap of its two themes: unconsummated adultery and the consummated pure romance. There can be little doubt about which kind of persons and which sort of fables best typify our plight, which tell the truth—or better, a truth—in the language of those to whom they speak.

In the last phrase, there is a rub. The notion that there is more than one language of art, or rather, that there is something not quite art, which performs art's function for most men in our society, is disquieting enough for anyone, and completely unacceptable to the sentimental egalitarian, who had dreamed of universal literacy leading directly to a universal culture. It is here that we begin to see that there is a politics as well as a pathology involved in the bour-geois hostility to popular culture. I do not refer only to the explicit political ideas embodied in the comics or in the literature of the cultural élite; but cer-tainly each of these arts has a characteristic attitude: populist–authoritarian on the one hand and aristocratic–authoritarian on the other.

It is notorious how few of the eminent novelists or poets of our time have shared the political ideals we would agree are the most noble available to us. The flirtations of Yeats and Lawrence with fascism, Pound's weird amalgam of Confucianism, Jeffersonianism, and social credit, the modified Dixiecrat prin-ciples of Faulkner—all make the point with terrible reiteration. Between the best art and poetry of our age and the critical liberal reader there can be no bond of shared belief; at best we have the ironic confrontation of the sceptical mind and the believing imagination. It is this division which has, I suppose, led us to define more and more narrowly the 'aesthetic experience', to attempt to isolate a quality of seeing and saying that has a moral value quite independent of *what* is seen or heard.

> Time that with this strange excuse
> Pardoned Kipling and his views,
> And will pardon Paul Claudel,
> Pardons him for writing well.[a]

But the genteel middling mind which turns to art for entertainment and uplift, finds this point of view reprehensible; and cries out in rage against those who give Ezra Pound a prize and who claim that 'to permit other considera-tions than that of poetic achievement to sway the decision would ... deny the

[a] W. H. Auden, 'In Memory of W. B. Yeats'.

validity of that objective perception of value on which any civilized society must rest'. We live in the midst of a strange two-front class war: the readers of the slicks battling the subscribers to the 'little reviews' and the consumers of pulps; the sentimental-egalitarian conscience against the ironical-aristocratic sensibility on the one hand and the brutal-populist mentality on the other. The joke, of course, is that it is the 'democratic' centre which calls here and now for the suppression of its rivals; while the élite advocate a condescending tolerance, and the vulgar ask only to be let alone.

It is disconcerting to find cultural repression flourishing at the point where middling culture meets a kindly, if not vigorously thought-out, liberalism. The sort of right-thinking citizen who subsidizes trips to America for Japanese girls scarred by the Hiroshima bombing, and deplores McCarthy in the public press, also deplores, and would censor, the comics. In one sense, this is fair enough; for beneath the veneer of slogans that 'crime doesn't pay' and the superficial praise of law and order, the comics do reflect that dark populist faith which Senator McCarthy has exploited. There is a kind of 'black socialism' of the American masses which underlies formal allegiances to one party or another: the sense that there is always a conspiracy at the centres of political and financial power; the notion that the official defenders of the commonwealth are 'bought' more often than not; an impatience with moral scruples and a distrust of intelligence, especially in the expert and scientist; a willingness to identify the enemy, the dark projection of everything most feared in the self, on to some journalistically defined political opponent of the moment.

This is not quite the 'fascism' it is sometimes called. There is, for instance, no European anti-Semitism involved, despite the conventional hooked nose of the scientist-villain. (The inventors and chief producers of comic books have been, as it happens, Jews.) There is also no adulation of a dictator-figure on the model of Hitler or Stalin; though one of the archetypes of the Deliverer in the comics is called Superman, he is quite unlike the Nietzschean figure—it is the image of Cincinnatus which persists in him, an archetype that has possessed the American imagination since the time of Washington: the leader who enlists for the duration and retires unrewarded to obscurity.

It would be absurd to ask the consumer of such art to admire in the place of images that project his own impotence and longing for civil peace some hero of middling culture—say, the good boy of Arthur Miller's *Death of a Salesman*, who, because he has studied hard in school, has become a lawyer who argues cases before the Supreme Court and has friends who own their own tennis courts. As absurd as to ask the general populace to worship Stephen Dedalus or Captain Ahab! But the high-minded petty-bourgeois cannot understand or forgive the rejection of his own dream, which he considers as nothing less than the final dream of humanity. The very existence of a kind of art depending on allegiances and values other than his challenges an article of his political faith; and when such an art is 'popular', that is, more read, more liked, more bought than his own, he feels his *raison d'être*, his basic self-defence, imperilled. The failure of the petty-bourgeoisie to achieve cultural hegemony threatens their

463

dream of a truly classless society; for they believe, with some justification, that such a society can afford only a single culture. And they see, in the persistence of a high art and a low art on either side of their average own, symptoms of the re-emergence of classes in a quarter where no one had troubled to stand guard.

The problem posed by popular culture is finally, then, a problem of class distinction in a democratic society. What is at stake is the refusal of cultural equality by a large part of the population. It is misleading to think of popular culture as the product of a conspiracy of profiteers against the rest of us. This venerable notion of an eternally oppressed and deprived but innocent people is precisely what the rise of mass culture challenges. Much of what upper-class egalitarians dreamed for him, the ordinary man does not want—especially literacy. The situation is bewildering and complex, for the people have not rejected completely the notion of cultural equality; rather, they desire its symbol but not its fact. At the very moment when half of the population of the United States reads no *hard-covered* book in a year, more than half of all high-school graduates are entering universities and colleges; in twenty-five years almost all Americans will at least begin a higher education. It is clear that what is demanded is a B.A. for everyone, with the stipulation that no one be forced to read to get it. And this the colleges, with 'objective tests' and 'audio-visual aids', are doing their reluctant best to satisfy.

One of the more exasperating aspects of the cultural defeat of the egalitarians is that it followed a seeming victory. For a while (in the Anglo-Saxon world at least) it appeared as if the spread of literacy, the rise of the bourgeoisie, and the emergence of the novel as a reigning form would succeed in destroying both traditional folk art and an aristocratic literature still pledged to epic, ode, and verse tragedy. But the novel itself (in the hands of Lawrence, Proust, Kafka, etc.) soon passed beyond the comprehension of those for whom it was originally contrived; and the retrograde derivations from it—various steps in a retreat towards wordless narrative: digests, pulp fiction, movies, picture magazines— revealed that middling literature was not in fact the legitimate heir of either folk art or high art, much less the successor of both, but a *tertium quid* of uncertain status and value.

The middlebrow reacts with equal fury to an art that baffles his understanding and to one which refuses to aspire to his level. The first reminds him that he has not yet, after all *arrived* (and, indeed, may never make it); the second suggests to him a condition to which he might easily relapse, one perhaps that might have made him happier with less effort (and here exacerbated puritanism is joined to baffled egalitarianism), even suggests what his state may appear like to those a notch above. Since he cannot, on his own terms, explain to himself why anyone should choose any level but the highest (that is, his own), the failure of the vulgar seems to him the product of mere ignorance and laziness—a crime! And the rejection by the advanced artist of his canons strikes him as a finicking excess, a pointless and unforgiveable snobbism. Both, that is, suggest the intolerable notion of a hierarchy of taste, a hierarchy of values, the possibility of cultural classes in a democratic state; and before this, puzzled and enraged, he can only call a cop. The fear of the vulgar is the obverse of the fear of excellence, and both are aspects of the fear of difference: symptoms of a drive for conformity on the level of the timid, sentimental, mindless–bodiless genteel.

34 Alain Robbe-Grillet

Alain Robbe-Grillet (b. 1922) is a graduate of the Institute Nationale Agronomique, Paris, and was for some years a professional agronomist (i.e. concerned with the economics of agriculture). This scientific education may partly explain Robbe-Grillet's literary theories and the character of the novels he began to produce in the nineteen-fifties, such as Le Voyeur (Paris, 1955) and La Jalousie (Paris, 1957). For his aim appears to be the achievement of a 'scientific' objectivity or neutrality in the imitation of reality by disinfecting literary language of all those figures of speech which—covertly or explicity—attribute human meanings to the inanimate world of things, What is to take the place of this fraudulently humanizing language is the language of factual description and measurement. Whether this enterprise is in fact, given the nature of language, feasible, or, given the limited interest of mere facts, desirable, are questions which have been hotly debated. It is not too difficult to argue that Robbe-Grillet succeeds as a novelist by violating the consistency of his own theory; and it seems evident from 'A Future for the Novel', that this theory was a lever which Robbe-Grillet used to break into the French literary world, creating space for new ideas and techniques. He was successful to the extent that his own fiction, and that of writers associated with him, such as Nathalie Sarraute and Michel Butor, was recognized as constituting a *nouveau roman* or 'new novel', challenging the reputations and influence of Sartre, Camus, and other French writers of the preceding generation. The *nouveaux romanciers* have been widely read and eagerly discussed in France : outside, interest has been confined to a fairly small minority of readers, many of them academics more interested in the aesthetic theories behind the novels than in the novels themselves. Robbe-Grillet has perhaps made his greatest impact internationally with the film he made with the director Alain Resnais, *L'Année Dernière à Marienbad* [Last Year in Marienbad], which appeared in 1961 and was one of the seminal films of the decade.

'A Future for the Novel', first published in 1956, is reprinted here from *For a New Novel* (New York, 1965), a translation by Richard Howard of Robbe-Grillet's collection of essays, *Pour un nouveau roman* (Paris, 1963).

CROSS REFERENCES : 28. Jean-Paul Sartre
42. Wayne Booth
43. Raymond Williams
49. Susan Sontag
50. Frank Kermode

COMMENTARY: John Sturrock, *The French New Novel: Claude Simon, Michel Butor, Alain Robbe-Grillet* (1969)

A future for the novel

It seems hardly reasonable at first glance to suppose that an entirely *new* literature might one day—now, for instance—be possible. The many attempts made these last thirty years to drag fiction out of its ruts have resulted, at best, in no more than isolated works. And—we are often told—none of these works, whatever its interest, has gained the adherence of a public comparable to that of the bourgeois novel. The only conception of the novel to have currency today is, in fact, that of Balzac.

Or that of Mme de La Fayette.[a] Already sacrosanct in her day, psychological analysis constituted the basis of all prose: it governed the conception of the book, the description of its characters, the development of its plot. A 'good' novel, ever since, has remained the study of a passion—or of a conflict of passions, or of an absence of passion—in a given milieu. Most of our contemporary novelists of the traditional sort—those, that is, who manage to gain the approval of their readers—could insert long passages from *The Princess of Clèves* or [Balzac's] *Père Goriot* into their own books without awakening the suspicions of the enormous public which devours whatever they turn out. They would merely need to change a phrase here and there, simplify certain constructions, afford an occasional glimpse of their own 'manner' by means of a word, a daring image, the rhythm of a sentence.... But all acknowledge, without seeing anything peculiar about it, that their preoccupations as writers date back several centuries.

What is so surprising about this, after all? The raw material—the French language—has undergone only very slight modifications for three hundred years; and if society has been gradually transformed, if industrial techniques have made considerable progress, our intellectual civilization has remained much the same. We live by essentially the same habits and the same prohibitions—moral, alimentary, religious, sexual, hygienic, etc. And of course there is always the human 'heart', which as everyone knows is eternal. There's nothing new under the sun, it's all been said before, we've come on the scene too late, etc., etc.

The risk of such rebuffs is merely increased if one dares claim that this new literature is not only possible in the future, but is already being written, and that it will represent—in its fulfilment—a revolution more complete than those which in the past produced such movements as romanticism or naturalism.

[a] Madame de la Fayette (1633–93) was the author of *La Princesse de Clèves* (1678), one of the earliest works of fiction that may be described as a 'novel' in the modern sense.

There is, of course, something ridiculous about such a promise as 'Now things are going to be different!' How will they be different? In what direction will they change? And, especially, why are they going to change now?

The art of the novel, however, has fallen into such a state of stagnation—a lassitude acknowledged and discussed by the whole of critical opinion—that it is hard to imagine such an art can survive for long without some radical change. To many, the solution seems simple enough: such a change being impossible, the art of the novel is dying. This is far from certain. History will reveal, in a few decades, whether the various fits and starts which have been recorded are signs of a death agony or of a rebirth.

In any case, we must make no mistake as to the difficulties such a revolution will encounter. They are considerable. The entire caste system of our literary life (from publisher to the humblest reader, including bookseller and critic) has no choice but to oppose the unknown form which is attempting to establish itself. The minds best disposed to the idea of a necessary transformation, those most willing to countenance and even to welcome the values of experiment, remain, none the less, the heirs of a tradition. A new form will always seem more or less an absence of any form at all, since it is unconsciously judged by reference to the consecrated forms. In one of the most celebrated French reference works, we may read in the article on Schoenberg: 'Author of audacious works, written without regard for any rules whatever'! This brief judgment is to be found under the heading *Music*, evidently written by a specialist.

The stammering newborn work will always be regarded as a monster, even by those who find experiment fascinating. There will be some curiosity, of course, some gestures of interest, always some provision for the future. And some praise; though what is sincere will always be addressed to the vestiges of the familiar, to all those bonds from which the new work has not yet broken free and which desperately seek to imprison it in the past.

For if the norms of the past serve to measure the present, they also serve to construct it. The writer himself, despite his desire for independence, is situated within an intellectual culture and a literature which can only be those of the past. It is impossible for him to escape altogether from this tradition of which he is the product. Sometimes the very elements he has tried hardest to oppose seem, on the contrary, to flourish more vigorously than ever in the very work by which he hoped to destroy them; and he will be congratulated, of course, with relief for having cultivated them so zealously.

Hence it will be the specialists in the novel (novelists or critics or over-assiduous readers) who have the hardest time dragging themselves out of its rut.

Even the least conditioned observer is unable to see the world around him through entirely unprejudiced eyes. Not, of course, that I have in mind the naïve concern for objectivity which the analysts of the (subjective) soul find it so easy to smile at. Objectivity in the ordinary sense of the word—total impersonality of observation—is all too obviously an illusion. But *freedom* of obser-

468

vation should be possible, and yet it is not. At every moment, a continuous fringe of culture (psychology, ethics, metaphysics, etc.) is added to things, giving them a less alien aspect, one that is more comprehensible, more reassuring. Sometimes the camouflage is complete: gesture vanishes from our mind, supplanted by the emotions which supposedly produced it, and we remember a landscape as *austere* or *calm* without being able to evoke a single outline, a single determining element. Even if we immediately think, 'That's literary', we don't try to react against the thought. We accept the fact that what is *literary* (the word has become pejorative) functions like a grid or screen set with bits of different coloured glass that fracture our field of vision into tiny assimilable facets.

And if something resists this systematic appropriation of the visual, if an element of the world breaks the glass, without finding any place in the interpretative screen, we can always make use of our convenient category of 'the absurd' in order to absorb this awkward residue.

But the world is neither significant nor absurd. It *is*, quite simply. That, in any case, is the most remarkable thing about it. And suddenly the obviousness of this strikes us with irresistible force. All at once the whole splendid construction collapses; opening our eyes unexpectedly, we have experienced, once too often, the shock of this stubborn reality we were pretending to have mastered. Around us, defying the noisy pack of our animistic or protective adjectives, things *are there*. Their surfaces are distinct and smooth, *intact*, neither suspiciously brilliant nor transparent. All our literature has not yet succeeded in eroding their smallest corner, in flattening their slightest curve.

The countless movie versions of novels that encumber our screens provide an occasion for repeating this curious experiment as often as we like. The cinema, another heir of the psychological and naturalistic tradition, generally has as its sole purpose the transposition of a story into images: it aims exclusively at imposing on the spectator, through the intermediary of some well-chosen scenes, the same meaning the written sentences communicated in their own fashion to the reader. But at any given moment the filmed narrative can drag us out of our interior comfort and into this proffered world with a violence not to be found in the corresponding text, whether novel or scenario.

Anyone can perceive the nature of the change that has occurred. In the initial novel, the objects and gestures forming the very fabric of the plot disappeared completely, leaving behind only their *significations*: the empty chair became only absence or expectation, the hand on a shoulder became a sign of friendliness, the bars on the window became only the impossibility of leaving.... But in the cinema, one *sees* the chair, the movement of the hand, the shape of the bars. What they signify remains obvious, but instead of monopolizing our attention, it becomes something added, even something in excess, because what affects us, what persists in our memory, what appears as essential and irreducible to vague intellectual concepts are the gestures themselves, the objects, the movements, and the outlines, to which the image has suddenly (and unintentionally) restored their *reality*.

469

It may seem peculiar that such fragments of crude reality, which the filmed narrative cannot help presenting, strike us so vividly, whereas identical scenes in real life do not suffice to free us of our blindness. As a matter of fact, it is as if the very conventions of the photographic medium (the two dimensions, the black-and-white images, the frame of the screen, the difference of scale between scenes) help free us from our own conventions. The slightly 'unaccustomed' aspect of this reproduced world reveals, at the same time, the un-accustomed character of the world that surrounds us: it, too, is unaccustomed in so far as it refuses to conform to our habits of apprehension and to our classification.

Instead of this universe of 'signification' (psychological, social, functional), we must try, then, to construct a world both more solid and more immediate. Let it be first of all by their *presence* that objects and gestures establish themselves, and let this presence continue to prevail over whatever explanatory theory that may try to enclose them in a system of references, whether emotional, socio-logical, Freudian, or metaphysical.

In this future universe of the novel, gestures and objects will be *there* before being *something*; and they will still be there afterwards, hard, unalterable, eternally present, mocking their own 'meaning', that meaning which vainly tries to reduce them to the role of precarious tools, of a temporary and shame-ful fabric woven exclusively—and deliberately—by the superior human truth expressed in it, only to cast out this awkward auxiliary into immediate oblivion and darkness.

Henceforth, on the contrary, objects will gradually lose their instability and their secrets, will renounce their pseudo-mystery, that suspect interiority which Roland Barthes[a] has called 'the romantic heart of things'. No longer will objects be merely the vague reflection of the hero's vague soul, the image of his tor-ments, the shadow of his desires. Or rather, if objects still afford a momentary prop to human passions, they will do so only provisionally, and will accept the tyranny of significations only in appearance—derisively, one might say—the better to show how alien they remain to man.

As for the novel's characters, they may themselves suggest many possible interpretations; they may, according to the preoccupations of each reader, accommodate all kinds of comment—psychological, psychiatric, religious, or pol-itical—yet their indifference to these 'potentialities' will soon be apparent. Whereas the traditional hero is constantly solicited, caught up, destroyed by these interpretations of the author's, ceaselessly projected into an immaterial and unstable *elsewhere*, always more remote and blurred, the future hero will remain on the contrary, *there*. It is the commentaries that will be left else-where; in the face of his irrefutable presence, they will seem useless, super-fluous, even improper.

Exhibit X in any detective story gives us, paradoxically, a clear image of this

---

[a] See below, pp. 646–51.

situation. The evidence gathered by the inspectors—an object left at the scene of the crime, a movement captured in a photograph, a sentence overheard by a witness—seem chiefly, at first, to require an explanation, to exist only in relation to their role in a context which overpowers them. And already the theories begin to take shape: the presiding magistrate attempts to establish a logical and necessary link between things; it appears that everything will be resolved in a banal bundle of causes and consequences, intentions and coincidences....

But the story begins to proliferate in a disturbing way: the witnesses contradict one another, the defendant offers several alibis, new evidence appears that had not been taken into account.... And we keep going back to the recorded evidence: the exact position of a piece of furniture, the shape and frequency of a fingerprint, the word scribbled in a message. We have the mounting sense that nothing else is *true*. Though they may conceal a mystery, or betray it, these elements which make a mockery of systems have only one serious, obvious quality, which is to *be there*.

The same is true of the world around us. We had thought to control it by assigning it a meaning, and the entire art of the novel, in particular, seemed dedicated to this enterprise. But this was merely an illusory simplification; and far from becoming clearer and closer because of it, the world has only, little by little, lost all its life. Since it is chiefly in its presence that the world's reality resides, our task is now to create a literature which takes that presence into account.

All this might seem very theoretical, very illusory, if something were not actually changing—changing totally, definitively—in our relations with the universe. Which is why we glimpse an answer to the old ironic question, 'Why now?' There is today, in fact, a new element that separates us radically this time from Balzac as from Gide or from Mme de La Fayette: it is the destitution of the old myths of 'depth'.

We know that the whole literature of the novel was based on these myths, and on them alone. The writer's traditional role consisted in excavating Nature, in burrowing deeper and deeper to reach some ever more intimate strata, in finally unearthing some fragment of a disconcerting secret. Having descended into the abyss of human passions, he would send to the seemingly tranquil world (the world on the surface) triumphant messages describing the mysteries he had actually touched with his own hands. And the sacred vertigo the reader suffered then, far from causing him anguish or nausea, reassured him as to his power of domination over the world. There were chasms, certainly, but thanks to such valiant speleologists, their depths could be sounded.

It is not surprising, given these conditions, that the literary phenomenon par excellence should have resided in the total and unique adjective, which attempted to unite all the inner qualities, the entire hidden soul of things. Thus the word functioned as a trap in which the writer captured the universe in order to hand it over to society.

The revolution which has occurred is in kind: not only do we no longer consider the world as our own, our private property, designed according to our needs and readily domesticated, but we no longer even believe in its 'depth'. While essentialist conceptions of man met their destruction, the notion of 'condition' henceforth replacing that of 'nature', the *surface* of things has ceased to be for us the mask of their heart, a sentiment that led to every kind of metaphysical transcendence.

Thus it is the entire literary language that must change, that is changing already. From day to day, we witness the growing repugnance felt by people of greater awareness for words of a visceral, analogical, or incantatory character. On the other hand, the visual or descriptive adjective, the word that contents itself with measuring, locating, limiting, defining, indicates a difficult but most likely direction for a new art of the novel.

35   Georg Lukács

Not the least achievement of the Hungarian Marxist critic Georg Lukács
(1885-1971) was to survive into old age the almost continuous experience of
being an intellectual in situations of extreme political danger. Born in
Budapest, Lukács was educated at various German universities and
experimented with various philosophies until 1917, when the Russian
Revolution fired his enthusiasm and led him to adopt Marxism. His brilliant
theoretical work *History and Class Consciousness* (1923), however, offended
the rapidly hardening Marxist–Leninist orthodoxy of Moscow, and Lukács
was subsequently obliged to repudiate some of the ideas expressed in that work
as the price for remaining within the Communist party. During the Stalinist
era, much of which Lukács spent inside Russia, the writings he produced were
undeviatingly orthodox and often propagandist. From 1933 to 1944 Lukács
worked at the Philosophical Institute of the Moscow Academy of Sciences,
returning in 1944 to teach at the University of Budapest. In 1956 he joined
the shortlived government of Imre Nagy established by the uprising of
October–November, but managed to survive the re-imposition of Russian
control with nothing worse than a brief period of exile and an official ban on
the publication of his work. He was readmitted to the party in 1967, and was
subsequently allowed to express his opinions openly.

Lukács is a complex and controversial figure. His style of thought, and the
contexts in which he had to operate, are so different from anything in
English or American experience that we almost certainly have a distorted
view of him. In particular, it is extremely difficult to assess the significance of
the political and ideological bias in his work. This was undoubtedly in part a
necessary accommodation to the brutal facts of life in totalitarian states, as
Lukács himself plainly hinted in his later years; but it is probably a mistake
to explain away too much in this fashion.

'The Ideology of Modernism' is a fairly representative case of the problems
Lukács poses. This was one of three essays collected under the title, *The
Meaning of Contemporary Realism*, which had first been given as lectures
in 1955, before the intellectual climate of Eastern Europe was totally
transformed by Khrushchev's attack on Stalin at the Twentieth Party Congress
of 1956, and by the Hungarian uprising which followed. In his Prefaces
of 1957 and 1962, Lukács attempted tortuously to relate his essays to these
momentous events, but in the opinion of one commentator (George
Lichtheim) the book remains 'an exercise in Cold War polemics pure and
simple'. Certainly the attack on modernism will seem to many Western

readers rigidly dogmatic and at times insensitive, but possibly Lukács's Eastern European readers would have been more struck by his easy and often appreciative familiarity with modern bourgeois literature.

Lukács probably first attracted widespread attention among English and American critics when his book *The Historical Novel*, written in Russia in the 'thirties, was translated into English and published in 1962. Other works by Lukács available in English include: *Studies in European Realism* (1950) and *Goethe and his Age* (1968). 'The Ideology of Modernism' is reprinted (in part) from *The Meaning of Contemporary Realism* (1963), translated by John and Necke Mander.

CROSS REFERENCES: 16. Christopher Caudwell
19. Edmund Wilson
43. Raymond Williams
50. Frank Kermode

COMMENTARY: George Lichtheim, *Lukács* (1971)
George Steiner, 'Georg Lukács and his Devil's Pact' in *Language and Silence* (1967)

The ideology of modernism

It is in no way surprising that the most influential contemporary school of writing should still be committed to the dogmas of 'modernist' anti-realism. It is here that we must begin our investigation if we are to chart the possibilities of a bourgeois realism. We must compare the two main trends in contemporary bourgeois literature, and look at the answers they give to the major ideological and artistic questions of our time.

We shall concentrate on the underlying ideological basis of these trends. What must be avoided at all costs is the approach generally adopted by bourgeois-modernist critics themselves: that exaggerated concern with formal criteria, with questions of style and literary technique. This approach may appear to distinguish sharply between 'modern' and 'traditional' writing (i.e. contemporary writers who adhere to the styles of the last century). In fact it fails to locate the decisive formal problems and turns a blind eye to their inherent dialectic. We are presented with a false polarization which, by exaggerating the importance of stylistic differences, conceals the opposing principles actually underlying and determining contrasting styles.

To take an example: the *monologue intérieur*. Compare, for instance, Bloom's monologue in the lavatory or Molly's monologue in bed, at the beginning and at the end of *Ulysses*, with Goethe's early-morning monologue as conceived by Thomas Mann in his *Lotte in Weimar*. Plainly, the same stylistic technique is being employed. And certain of Thomas Mann's remarks about Joyce and his methods would appear to confirm this.

Yet it is not easy to think of any two novels more basically dissimilar than *Ulysses* and *Lotte in Weimar*. This is true even of the superficially rather similar scenes I have indicated. I am not referring to the—to my mind—striking difference in intellectual quality. I refer to the fact that with Joyce the stream-of-consciousness technique is no mere stylistic device; it is itself the formative principle governing the narrative pattern and the presentation of character. Technique here is something absolute; it is part and parcel of the aesthetic ambition informing *Ulysses*. With Thomas Mann, on the other hand, the *monologue intérieur* is simply a technical device, allowing the author to explore aspects of Goethe's world which would not have been otherwise available. Goethe's experience is not presented as confined to momentary sense-impressions. The artist reaches down to the core of Goethe's personality, to the complexity of his relations with his own past, present, and even future experience. The stream of association is only apparently free. The monologue is composed with the utmost artistic rigour: it is a carefully plotted sequence gradually piercing to the core of Goethe's personality. Every person or event, emerging momentarily from the stream and vanishing again, is given a specific weight, a definite position, in the pattern of the whole. However unconventional the presentation, the compositional principle is that of the traditional epic; in the way the pace is controlled, and the transitions and climaxes are organized, the ancient rules of epic narration are faithfully observed.

It would be absurd, in view of Joyce's artistic ambitions and his manifest abilities, to qualify the exaggerated attention he gives to the detailed recording of sense-data, and his comparative neglect of ideas and emotions, as artistic failure. All this was in conformity with Joyce's artistic intentions; and, by use of such techniques, he may be said to have achieved them satisfactorily. But between Joyce's intentions and those of Thomas Mann there is a total opposition. The perpetually oscillating patterns of sense- and memory-data, their powerfully charged—but aimless and directionless—fields of force, give rise to an epic structure which is *static*, reflecting a belief in the basically static character of events.

These opposed views of the world—dynamic and developmental on the one hand, static and sensational on the other—are of crucial importance in examining the two schools of literature I have mentioned. I shall return to the opposition later. Here, I want only to point out that an exclusive emphasis on formal matters can lead to serious misunderstanding of the character of an artist's work.

What determines the style of a given work of art? How does the intention determine the form? (We are concerned here, of course, with the intention realized in the work; it need not coincide with the writer's conscious intention.) The distinctions that concern us are not those between stylistic 'techniques' in the formalistic sense. It is the view of the world, the ideology or *weltanschauung* underlying a writer's work, that counts. And it is the writer's attempt to reproduce this view of the world which constitutes his 'intention' and is the formative principle underlying the style of a given piece of writing. Looked at in

475

this way, style ceases to be a formalistic category. Rather, it is rooted in content; it is the specific form of a specific content.

Content determines form. But there is no content of which Man himself is not the focal point. However various the *données* of literature (a particular experience, a didactic purpose), the basic question is, and will remain: what is Man?

Here is a point of division: if we put the question in abstract, philosophical terms, leaving aside all formal considerations, we arrive—for the realist school— at the traditional Aristotelian dictum (which was also reached by other than purely aesthetic considerations): Man is *zoon politikon*, a social animal. The Aristotelian dictum is applicable to all great realistic literature. Achilles and Werther, Oedipus and Tom Jones, Antigone and Anna Karenina: their individual existence—their *Sein an sich* [Being-in-itself], in the Hegelian terminology; their 'ontological being', as a more fashionable terminology has it— cannot be distinguished from their social and historical environment. Their human significance, their specific individuality cannot be separated from the context in which they were created.

The ontological view governing the image of man in the work of leading modernist writers is the exact opposite of this. Man, for these writers, is by nature solitary, asocial, unable to enter into relationships with other human beings. Thomas Wolfe once wrote: 'My view of the world is based on the firm conviction that solitariness is by no means a rare condition, something peculiar to myself or to a few specially solitary human beings, but the inescapable, central fact of human existence.' Man, thus imagined, may establish contact with other individuals, but only in a superficial, accidental manner; only, ontologically speaking, by retrospective reflection. For 'the others', too, are basically solitary, beyond significant human relationship.

This basic solitariness of man must not be confused with that individual solitariness to be found in the literature of traditional realism. In the latter case, we are dealing with a particular situation in which a human being may be placed, due either to his character or to the circumstances of his life. Solitariness may be objectively conditioned, as with Sophocles' Philoctetes, put ashore on the bleak island of Lemnos. Or it may be subjective, the product of inner necessity, as with Tolstoy's Ivan Ilyitsch or Flaubert's Frédéric Moreau in the *Education Sentimentale*. But it is always merely a fragment, a phase, a climax or anti-climax, in the life of the community as a whole. The fate of such individuals is characteristic of certain human types in specific social or historical circumstances. Beside and beyond their solitariness, the common life, the strife and togetherness of other human beings, goes on as before. In a word, their solitariness is a specific social fate, not a universal *condition humaine*.

The latter, of course, is characteristic of the theory and practice of modernism. I would like, in the present study, to spare the reader tedious excursions into philosophy. But I cannot refrain from drawing the reader's attention to Heidegger's[a] description of human existence as a 'thrownness-into-being' (*Geworfenheit*

---

[a] See note on p. 372 above.

ins Dascin). A more graphic evocation of the ontological solitariness of the individual would be hard to imagine. Man is 'thrown-into-being'. This implies, not merely that man is constitutionally unable to establish relationships with things or persons outside himself, but also that it is impossible to determine theoretically the origin and goal of human existence.

Man, thus conceived, is an ahistorical being. (The fact that Heidegger does admit a form of 'authentic' historicity in his system is not really relevant. I have shown elsewhere that Heidegger tends to belittle historicity as 'vulgar'; and his 'authentic' historicity is not distinguishable from ahistoricity). This negation of history takes two different forms in modernist literature. First, the hero is strictly confined within the limits of his own experience. There is not for him—and apparently not for his creator—any pre-existent reality beyond his own self, acting upon him or being acted upon by him. Secondly, the hero himself is without personal history. He is 'thrown-into-the-world': meaninglessly, unfathomably. He does not develop through contact with the world; he neither forms nor is formed by it. The only 'development' in this literature is the gradual revelation of the human condition. Man is now what he has always been and always will be. The narrator, the examining subject, is in motion; the examined reality is static.

Of course, dogmas of this kind are only really viable in philosophical abstraction, and then only with a measure of sophistry. A gifted writer, however extreme his theoretical modernism, will in practice have to compromise with the demands of historicity and of social environment. Joyce uses Dublin, Kafka and Musil[a] the Hapsburg Monarchy, as the locus of their masterpieces. But the locus they lovingly depict is little more than a backcloth; it is not basic to their artistic intention.

This view of human existence has specific literary consequences. Particularly in one category, of primary theoretical and practical importance, to which we must now give our attention: that of *potentiality*. Philosophy distinguishes between *abstract* and *concrete* (in Hegel, 'real') *potentiality*. These two categories, their interrelation and opposition, are rooted in life itself. *Potentiality*—seen abstractly or subjectively—is richer than actual life. Innumerable possibilities for man's development are imaginable, only a small percentage of which will be realized. Modern subjectivism, taking these imagined possibilities for actual complexity of life, oscillates between melancholy and fascination. When the world declines to realize these possibilities, this melancholy becomes tinged with contempt. Hofmannsthal's[b] Sobeide expressed the reaction of the generation first exposed to this experience:

> The burden of those endlessly pored-over
> And now forever perished possibilities...

How far were those possibilities ever concrete or 'real'? Plainly, they existed

---

[a] Robert Musil (1880–1942), Austrian novelist, author of *The Man Without Qualities* (3 vols. 1930–42).

[b] Hugo von Hofmannsthal (1874–1929), Austrian poet.

only in the imagination of the subject, as dreams or day-dreams. Faulkner, in whose work this subjective potentiality plays an important part, was evidently aware that reality must thereby be subjectivized and made to appear arbitrary. Consider this comment of his: 'They were all talking simultaneously, getting flushed and excited, quarrelling, making the unreal into a possibility, then into a probability, then into an irrefutable fact, as human beings do when they put their wishes into words.' The possibilities in a man's mind, the particular pattern, intensity and suggestiveness they assume, will of course be characteristic of that individual. In practice, their number will border on the infinite, even with the most unimaginative individual. It is thus a hopeless undertaking to define the contours of individuality, let alone to come to grips with a man's actual fate, by means of potentiality. The *abstract* character of potentiality is clear from the fact that it cannot determine development—subjective mental states, however permanent or profound, cannot here be decisive. Rather, the development of personality is determined by inherited gifts and qualities; by the factors, external or internal, which further or inhibit their growth.

But in life potentiality can, of course, become reality. Situations arise in which a man is confronted with a choice; and in the act of choice a man's character may reveal itself in a light that surprises even himself. In literature—and particularly in dramatic literature—the denouement often consists in the realization of just such potentiality, which circumstances have kept from coming to the fore. These potentialities are, then, 'real' or concrete potentialities. The fate of the character depends upon the potentiality in question, even if it should condemn him to a tragic end. In advance, while still a subjective potentiality in the character's mind, there is no way of distinguishing it from the innumerable abstract potentialities in his mind. It may even be buried away so completely that, before the moment of decision, it has never entered his mind even as an abstract potentiality. The subject, after taking his decision, may be unconscious of his own motives. Thus Richard Dudgeon, Shaw's Devil's Disciple, having sacrificed himself as Pastor Andersen, confesses: 'I have often asked myself for the motive, but I find no good reason to explain why I acted as I did.'

Yet it is a decision which has altered the direction of his life. Of course, this is an extreme case. But the qualitative leap of the denouement, cancelling and at the same time renewing the continuity of individual consciousness, can never be predicted. The concrete potentiality cannot be isolated from the myriad abstract potentialities. Only actual decision reveals the distinction.

The literature of realism, aiming at a truthful reflection of reality, must demonstrate both the concrete and abstract potentialities of human beings in extreme situations of this kind. A character's concrete potentiality once revealed, his abstract potentialities will appear essentially inauthentic. [Alberto] Moravia, for instance, in his novel *The Indifferent Ones*, describes the young son of a decadent bourgeois family, Michel, who makes up his mind to kill his sister's seducer. While Michel, having made his decision, is planning the murder, a large number of abstract—but highly suggestive—possibilities are laid before us. Unfortunately for Michel the murder is actually carried out; and, from the sordid details of the action, Michel's character emerges as what it is—representative of that background from which, in subjective fantasy, he had imagined he could escape.

Abstract potentiality belongs wholly to the realm of subjectivity; whereas concrete potentiality is concerned with the dialectic between the individual's subjectivity and objective reality. The literary presentation of the latter thus implies a description of actual persons inhabiting a palpable, identifiable world. Only in the interaction of character and environment can the concrete potentiality of a particular individual be singled out from the 'bad infinity' of purely abstract potentialities, and emerge as the determining potentiality of just this individual at just this phase of his development. This principle alone enables the artist to distinguish concrete potentiality from a myriad abstractions.

But the ontology on which the image of man in modernist literature is based invalidates this principle. If the 'human condition'—man as a solitary being, incapable of meaningful relationships—is identified with reality itself, the distinction between abstract and concrete potentiality becomes null and void. The categories tend to merge. Thus Cesare Pavese notes with John Dos Passos, and his German contemporary, Alfred Döblin,[a] a sharp oscillation between 'superficial *verisme*' and 'abstract Expressionist schematism'. Criticizing Dos Passos, Pavese writes that fictional characters 'ought to be created by deliberate selection and description of individual features'—implying that Dos Passos' characterizations are transferable from one individual to another. He describes the artistic consequences: by exalting man's subjectivity, at the expense of the objective reality of his environment, man's subjectivity itself is impoverished.

The problem, once again, is ideological. This is not to say that the ideology underlying modernist writings is identical in all cases. On the contrary: the ideology exists in extremely various, even contradictory forms. The rejection of narrative objectivity, the surrender to subjectivity, may take the form of Joyce's stream of consciousness, or of Musil's 'active passivity', his 'existence without quality', or of Gide's[b] '*action gratuite*', where abstract potentiality achieves pseudo-realization. As individual character manifests itself in life's moments of decision, so too in literature. If the distinction between abstract and concrete potentiality vanishes, if man's inwardness is identified with an abstract subjectivity, human personality must necessarily disintegrate.

T. S. Eliot described this phenomenon, this mode of portraying human personality, as

> Shape without form, shade without colour,
> Paralysed force, gesture without motion.
> ['The Hollow Men']

The disintegration of personality is matched by a disintegration of the outer world. In one sense, this is simply a further consequence of our argument. For

[a] Caesae Pavese (1908–57) was a distinguished Italian novelist, essayist and literary journalist. John Dos Passos (b. 1896) the American novelist, is best known for his *Manhattan Transfer* (1925) and the trilogy U.S.A. (1930–6). Alfred Döblin (1878–1957) was a German expressionist novelist, influenced by James Joyce.

[b] André Gide (1869–1951 was one of the most distinguished of modern French writers and intellectuals. He was awarded the Nobel Prize in 1947, mainly for his novels.

the identification of abstract and concrete human potentiality rests on the assumption that the objective world is inherently inexplicable. Certain leading modernist writers, attempting a theoretical apology, have admitted this quite frankly. Often this theoretical impossibility of understanding reality is the point of departure, rather than the exaltation of subjectivity. But in any case the connection between the two is plain. The German poet Gottfried Benn[a], for instance, informs us that 'there is no outer reality, there is only human consciousness, constantly building, modifying, rebuilding new worlds out of its own creativity'. Musil, as always, gives a moral twist to this line of thought. Ulrich, the hero of his *The Man without Qualities*, when asked what he would do if he were in God's place, replies: 'I should be compelled to abolish reality.' Subjective existence 'without qualities' is the complement of the negation of outward reality.

The negation of outward reality is not always demanded with such theoretical rigour. But it is present in almost all modernist literature. In conversation, Musil once gave as the period of his great novel, 'between 1912 and 1914'. But he was quick to modify this statement by adding: 'I have not, I must insist, written a historical novel. I am not concerned with actual events.... Events, anyhow, are interchangeable. I am interested in what is typical, in what one might call the ghostly aspect of reality.' The word 'ghostly' is interesting. It points to a major tendency in modernist literature: the attenuation of actuality. In Kafka, the descriptive detail is of an extraordinary immediacy and authenticity. But Kafka's artistic ingenuity is really directed towards substituting his *angst*-ridden vision of the world for objective reality. The realistic detail is the expression of a ghostly un-reality, of a nightmare world, whose function is to evoke *angst*. The same phenomenon can be seen in writers who attempt to combine Kafka's techniques with a critique of society—like the German writer, Wolfgang Koeppen, in his satirical novel about Bonn, *Das Treibhaus* ['The Hothouse']. A similar attenuation of reality underlies Joyce's stream of consciousness. It is, of course, intensified where the stream of consciousness is itself the medium through which reality is presented. And it is carried *ad absurdum* where the stream of consciousness is that of an abnormal subject or of an idiot—consider the first part of Faulkner's *Sound and Fury* or, a still more extreme case, Beckett's *Molloy*.

Attenuation of reality and dissolution of personality are thus interdependent: the stronger the one, the stronger the other. Underlying both is the lack of a consistent view of human nature. Man is reduced to a sequence of unrelated experiential fragments; he is as inexplicable to others as to himself. In Eliot's *Cocktail Party* the psychiatrist, who voices the opinions of the author, describes the phenomenon:

> Ah, but we die to each other daily
> What we know of other people
> Is only our memory of the moments

[a] Gottfried Benn (1886–1956), German Expressionist poet.

During which we knew them. And they have changed since then.
To pretend that they and we are the same
Is a useful and convenient social convention
Which must sometimes be broken. We must also remember
That at every meeting we are meeting a stranger.

The dissolution of personality, originally the unconscious product of the identification of concrete and abstract potentiality, is elevated to a deliberate principle in the light of consciousness. It is no accident that Gottfried Benn called one of his theoretical tracts '*Doppelleben*' ['Double-life']. For Benn, this dissolution of personality took the form of a schizophrenic dichotomy. According to him, there was in man's personality no coherent pattern of motivation or behaviour. Man's animal nature is opposed to his denaturized, sublimated thought-processes. The unity of thought and action is 'backwoods philosophy'; thought and being are 'quite separate entities'. Man must be either a moral or a thinking being—he cannot be both at once.

These are not, I think, purely private, eccentric speculations. Of course, they are derived from Benn's specific experience. But there is an inner connection between these ideas and a certain tradition of bourgeois thought. It is more than a hundred years since Kierkegaard first attacked the Hegelian view that the inner and outer world form an objective dialectical unity, that they are indissolubly married in spite of their apparent opposition. Kierkegaard denied any such unity. According to Kierkegaard, the individual exists within an opaque, impenetrable 'incognito'.

This philosophy attained remarkable popularity after the Second World War —proof that even the most abstruse theories may reflect social reality. Men like Martin Heidegger, Ernst Jünger, the lawyer Carl Schmitt, Gottfried Benn and others passionately embraced this doctrine of the eternal incognito which implies that a man's external deeds are no guide to his motives. In this case, the deeds obscured behind the mysterious incognito were, needless to say, these intellectuals' participation in Nazism : Heidegger, as Rector of Freiburg University, had glorified Hitler's seizure of power at his Inauguration; Carl Schmitt had put his great legal gifts at Hitler's disposal. The facts were too well known to be simply denied. But, if this impenetrable incognito were the true '*condition humaine*', might not—concealed within their incognito—Heidegger or Schmitt have been secret opponents of Hitler all the time, only supporting him in the world of appearances? Ernst von Salomon's cynical frankness about his opportunism in *The Questionnaire* (keeping his reservations to himself or declaring them only in the presence of intimate friends) may be read as an ironic commentary on this ideology of the incognito as we find it, say, in the writings of Ernst Jünger.

This digression may serve to show, taking an extreme example, what the social implications of such an ontology may be. In the literary field, this particular ideology was of cardinal importance; by destroying the complex tissue of man's relations with his environment, it furthered the dissolution of personality. For it is just the opposition between a man and his environment that determines the development of his personality. There is no great hero of fiction—

from Homer's Achilles to Mann's Adrian Leverkühn[a] or Sholochov's Grigory Melyekov[b]—whose personality is not the product of such an opposition. I have shown how disastrous the denial of the distinction between abstract and concrete potentiality must be for the presentation of character. The destruction of the complex tissue of man's interaction with his environment likewise saps the vitality of this opposition. Certainly, some writers who adhere to this ideology have attempted, not unsuccessfully, to portray this opposition in concrete terms. But the underlying ideology deprives these contradictions of their dynamic, developmental significance. The contradictions coexist, unresolved, contributing to the further dissolution of the personality in question.

It is to the credit of Robert Musil that he was quite conscious of the implications of his method. Of his hero Ulrich he remarked: 'One is faced with a simple choice: either one must run with the pack (when in Rome, do as the Romans do); or one becomes a neurotic.' Musil here introduces the problem, central to all modernist literature, of the significance of psychopathology.

This problem was first widely discussed in the Naturalist period. More than fifty years ago, that doyen of Berlin dramatic critics, Alfred Kerr, was writing: 'Morbidity is the legitimate poetry of Naturalism. For what is poetic in everyday life? Neurotic aberration, escape from life's dreary routine. Only in this way can a character be translated to a rarer clime and yet retain an air of reality.' Interesting, here, is the notion that the poetic necessity of the pathological derives from the prosaic quality of life under capitalism. I would maintain —we shall return to this point—that in modern writing there is a continuity from Naturalism to the Modernism of our day—a continuity restricted, admittedly, to underlying ideological principles. What at first was no more than dim anticipation of approaching catastrophe developed, after 1914, into an all-pervading obsession. And I would suggest that the ever-increasing part played by psychopathology was one of the main features of the continuity. At each period—depending on the prevailing social and historical conditions—psychopathology was given a new emphasis, a different significance, and artistic function. Kerr's description suggests that in naturalism the interest in psychopathology sprang from an aesthetic need; it was an attempt to escape from the dreariness of life under capitalism. The quotation from Musil shows that some years later the opposition acquired a moral slant. The obsession with morbidity had ceased to have a merely decorative function, bringing colour into the greyness of reality, and become a moral protest against capitalism.

With Musil—and with many other modernist writers—psychopathology became the goal, the *terminus ad quem* [destination], of their artistic intention. But there is a double difficulty inherent in their intention, which follows from its underlying ideology. There is, first, a lack of definition. The protest expressed by this flight into psychopathology is an abstract gesture; its rejection of reality is wholesale and summary, containing no concrete criticism. It is a gesture, moreover, that is destined to lead nowhere; it is an escape into nothingness.

[a] In *Doktor Faustus* (1947).
[b] In *And Quiet Flows the Don* (1934).

Thus the propagators of this ideology are mistaken in thinking that such a protest could ever be fruitful in literature. In any protest against particular social conditions, these conditions themselves must have the central place. The bourgeois protest against feudal society, the proletarian against bourgeois society, made their point of departure a criticism of the old order. In both cases the protest—reaching out beyond the point of departure—was based on a concrete *terminus ad quem*: the establishment of a new order. However indefinite the structure and content of this new order, the will towards its more exact definition was not lacking.

How different the protest of writers like Musil! The *terminus a quo* [starting-point] (the corrupt society of our time) is inevitably the main source of energy, since the *terminus ad quem* (the escape into psychopathology) is a mere abstraction. The rejection of modern reality is purely subjective. Considered in terms of man's relation with his environment, it lacks both content and direction. And this lack is exaggerated still further by the character of the *terminus ad quem*. For the protest is an empty gesture, expressing nausea, or discomfort, or longing. Its content—or rather lack of content—derives from the fact that such a view of life cannot impart a sense of direction. These writers are not wholly wrong in believing that psychopathology is their surest refuge; it is the ideological complement of their historical position.

This obsession with the pathological is not only to be found in literature. Freudian psycho-analysis is its most obvious expression. The treatment of the subject is only superficially different from that in modern literature. As everybody knows, Freud's starting-point was 'everyday life'. In order to explain 'slips' and day-dreams, however, he had to have recourse to psychopathology. In his lectures, speaking of resistance and repression, he says: 'Our interest in the general psychology of symptom-formation increases as we understand to what extent the study of pathological conditions can shed light on the workings of the normal mind.' Freud believed he had found the key to the understanding of the normal personality in the psychology of the abnormal. This belief is still more evident in the typology of Kretschmer, which also assumes that psychological abnormalities can explain normal psychology. It is only when we compare Freud's psychology with that of Pavlov, who takes the Hippocratic view that mental abnormality is a deviation from a norm, that we see it in its true light.

Clearly, this is not strictly a scientific or literary-critical problem. It is an ideological problem, deriving from the ontological dogma of the solitariness of man. The literature of realism, based on the Aristotelean concept of man as *zoon politikon*, is entitled to develop a new typology for each new phase in the evolution of a society. It displays the contradictions within society and within the individual in the context of a dialectical unity. Here, individuals embodying violent and extraordinary passions are still within the range of a socially normal typology (Shakespeare, Balzac, Stendhal). For, in this literature, the average man is simply a dimmer reflection of the contradictions always existing in man and society; eccentricity is a socially-conditioned distortion. Obviously, the passions of the great heroes must not be confused with 'eccentricity' in the colloquial sense: Christian Buddenbrook[a] is an 'eccentric'; Adrian Leverkühn is not.

The ontology of *Geworfenheit* makes a true typology impossible; it is replaced by an abstract polarity of the eccentric and the socially average. We have seen why this polarity—which in traditional realism serves to increase our understanding of social normality—leads in modernism to a fascination with morbid eccentricity. Eccentricity becomes the necessary complement of the average; and this polarity is held to exhaust human potentiality. The implications of this ideology are shown in another remark of Musil's: 'If humanity dreamt collectively, it would dream Moosbrugger.' Moosbrugger, you will remember, was a mentally-retarded sexual pervert with homicidal tendencies.

What served, with Musil, as the ideological basis of a new typology—escape into neurosis as a protest against the evils of society—becomes with other modernist writers an immutable *condition humaine*. Musil's statement loses its conditional 'if' and becomes a simple description of reality. Lack of objectivity in the description of the outer world finds its complement in the reduction of reality to a nightmare. Beckett's *Molloy* is perhaps the *ne plus ultra* [extreme point] of this development, although Joyce's vision of reality as an incoherent stream of consciousness had already assumed in Faulkner a nightmare quality. In Beckett's novel we have the same vision twice over. He presents us with an image of the utmost human degradation—an idiot's vegetative existence. Then, as help is imminent from a mysterious unspecified source, the rescuer himself sinks into idiocy. The story is told through the parallel streams of consciousness of the idiot and of his rescuer.

Along with the adoption of perversity and idiocy as types of the *condition humaine*, we find what amounts to frank glorification. Take Montherlant's *Pasiphae*, where sexual perversity—the heroine's infatuation with a bull—is presented as a triumphant return to nature, as the liberation of impulse from the slavery of convention. The chorus—i.e. the author—puts the following question (which, though rhetorical, clearly expects an affirmative reply): 'Si l'absence de pensée et l'absence de morale ne contribuent pas beaucoup à la dignité des bêtes, des plantes et des eaux...?' ['If the absence of thought, and the absence of morality, do not contribute much to the dignity of animals, plants and water...?'] Montherlant expresses as plainly as Musil, though with different moral and emotional emphasis, the hidden—one might say repressed—social character of the protest underlying this obsession with psychopathology, its perverted Rousseauism, its anarchism. There are many illustrations of this in modernist writing. A poem of Benn's will serve to make the point:

> O that we were our primal ancestors,
> Small lumps of plasma in hot, sultry swamps;
> Life, death, conception, parturition
> Emerging from those juices soundlessly.

---

[a] *Buddenbrooks* (1901) was Thomas Mann's first novel.

> A frond of seaweed or a dune of sand,
> Formed by the wind and heavy at the base;
> A dragonfly or gull's wing—already, these
> Would signify excessive suffering.

This is not overtly perverse in the manner of Beckett or Montherlant. Yet, in his primitivism, Benn is at one with them. The opposition of man as animal to man as social being (for instance, Heidegger's devaluation of the social as '*das Man*', Klages' assertion of the incompatibility of *Geist* and *Seele* ['Spirit and Soul'], or Rosenberg's[a] racial mythology) leads straight to a glorification of the abnormal and to an undisguised anti-humanism.

A typology limited in this way to the *homme moyen sensuel* [average sensual man] and the idiot also opens the door to 'experimental' stylistic distortion. Distortion becomes as inseparable a part of the portrayal of reality as the recourse to the pathological. But literature must have a concept of the normal if it is to 'place' distortion correctly: that is to say, to see it *as* distortion. With such a typology this placing is impossible, since the normal is no longer a proper object of literary interest. Life under capitalism is, often rightly, presented as a distortion (a petrification or paralysis) of the human substance. But to present psychopathology as a way of escape from this distortion is itself a distortion. We are invited to measure one type of distortion against another and arrive, necessarily, at universal distortion. There is no principle to set against the general pattern, no standard by which the petty-bourgeois and the pathological can be seen in their social context. And these tendencies, far from being relativized with time, become ever more absolute. Distortion becomes the normal condition of human existence; the proper study, the formative principle, of art and literature.

I have demonstrated some of the literary implications of this ideology. Let us now pursue the argument further. It is clear, I think, that modernism must deprive literature of a sense of *perspective*. This would not be surprising; rigorous modernists such as Kafka, Benn, and Musil have always indignantly refused to provide their readers with any such thing. I will return to the ideological implications of the idea of perspective later. Let me say here that, in any work of art, perspective is of overriding importance. It determines the course and content; it draws together the threads of the narration; it enables the artist to choose between the important and the superficial, the crucial and the episodic. The direction in which characters develop is determined by perspective, only those features being described which are material to their development. The more lucid the perspective—as in Molière or the Greeks—the more economical and striking the selection.

Modernism drops this selective principle. It asserts that it can dispense with it, or can replace it with its dogma of the *condition humaine*. A naturalistic style is bound to result. This state of affairs—which to my mind characterizes all modernist art of the past fifty years—is disguised by critics who systematic-

---

[a] Alfred Rosenberg (1893–1946), German Nazi ideologist whose book *The Myth of the Twentieth Century* (1930) provided a spurious philosophical basis for Hitler's racial policies.

485

ally glorify the modernist movement. By concentrating on formal criteria, by isolating technique from content and exaggerating its importance, the critics refrain from judgment on the social or artistic significance of subject-matter. They are unable, in consequence, to make the aesthetic distinction between *realism* and *naturalism*. This distinction depends on the presence or absence in a work of art of a 'hierarchy of significance' in the situations and characters presented. Compared with this, formal categories are of secondary importance. That is why it is possible to speak of the basically *naturalistic* character of modernist literature—and to see here the literary expression of an ideological continuity. This is not to deny that variations in style reflect changes in society. But the particular form this principle of naturalistic arbitrariness, this lack of hierarchic structure, may take is not decisive. We encounter it in the all-determining 'social conditions' of Naturalism, in Symbolism's impressionist methods and its cultivation of the exotic, in the fragmentation of objective reality in Futurism and Constructivism and the German *Neue Sachlichkeit* [New Objectivity], or, again, in Surrealism's stream of consciousness.

These schools have in common a basically static approach to reality. This is closely related to their lack of perspective. Characteristically, Gottfried Benn actually incorporated this in his artistic programme. One of his volumes bears the title, *Static Poems*. The denial of history, of development, and thus of perspective, becomes the mark of true insight into the nature of reality.

> The wise man is ignorant
> of change and development
> his children and children's children
> are no part of his world.

The rejection of any concept of the future is for Benn the criterion of wisdom. But even those modernist writers who are less extreme in their rejection of history tend to present social and historical phenomena as static. It is, then, of small importance whether this condition is 'external', or only a transitional stage punctuated by sudden catastrophes (even in early Naturalism the static presentation was often broken up by these catastrophes, without altering its basic character). Musil, for instance, writes in his essay, *The Writer in our Age*: 'One knows just as little about the present. Partly, this is because we are, as always, too close to the present. But it is also because the present into which we were plunged some two decades ago is of a particularly all-embracing and inescapable character.' Whether or not Musil knew of Heidegger's philosophy, the idea of *Geworfenheit* is clearly at work here. And the following reveals plainly how, for Musil, this static state was upset by the catastrophe of 1914: 'All of a sudden, the world was full of violence.... In European civilization, there was a sudden rift....' In short: this static apprehension of reality in modernist literature is no passing fashion; it is rooted in the ideology of modernism.

To establish the basic distinction between modernism and that realism which, from Homer to Thomas Mann and Gorky, has assumed change and development to be the proper subject of literature, we must go deeper into the underlying ideological problem. In *The House of the Dead* Dostoievsky gave an interesting account of the convict's attitude to work. He described how the prisoners, in spite of brutal discipline, loafed about, working badly or merely going through the motions of work until a new overseer arrived and allotted them a new project, after which they were allowed to go home. 'The work was hard,' Dostoievsky continues, 'but, Christ, with what energy they threw themselves into it! Gone was all their former indolence and pretended incompetence.' Later in the book Dostoievsky sums up his experiences: 'If a man loses hope and has no aim in view, sheer boredom can turn him into a beast....' I have said that the problem of perspective in literature is directly related to the principle of selection. Let me go further: underlying the problem is a profound ethical complex, reflected in the composition of the work itself. Every human action is based on a presupposition of its inherent meaningfulness, at least to the subject. Absence of meaning makes a mockery of action and reduces art to naturalistic description.

Clearly, there can be no literature without at least the appearance of change or development. This conclusion should not be interpreted in a narrowly metaphysical sense. We have already diagnosed the obsession with psychopathology in modernist literature as a desire to escape from the reality of capitalism. But this implies the absolute primacy of the *terminus a quo*, the condition from which it is desired to escape. Any movement towards a *terminus ad quem* is condemned to impotence. As the ideology of most modernist writers asserts the unalterability of outward reality (even if this is reduced to a mere state of consciousness) human activity is, *a priori*, rendered impotent and robbed of meaning.

The apprehension of reality to which this leads is most consistently and convincingly realized in the work of Kafka. Kafka remarks of Josef K., as he is being led to execution: 'He thought of flies, their tiny limbs breaking as they struggle away from the fly-paper.' This mood of total impotence, of paralysis in the face of the unintelligible power of circumstances, informs all his work. Though the action of *The Castle* takes a different, even an opposite, direction to that of *The Trial*, this view of the world, from the perspective of a trapped and struggling fly, is all-pervasive. This experience, this vision of a world dominated by *angst* and of man at the mercy of incomprehensible terrors, makes Kafka's work the very type of modernist art. Techniques, elsewhere of merely formal significance, are used here to evoke a primitive awe in the presence of an utterly strange and hostile reality. Kafka's *angst* is the experience *par excellence* of modernism.

36   Richard Hoggart

Richard Hoggart (b. 1918) was born into a working-class family in Leeds, Yorkshire, and was orphaned early in childhood. Scholarships took him eventually to Leeds University, where he read English and graduated just before World War II. After service in the Army, Richard Hoggart was extra-mural tutor at Hull University for some years, and subsequently Senior Lecturer at Leicester University. Since 1962 he has been Professor of English and Director of the Centre for Contemporary Cultural Studies at Birmingham University. In 1970 he was seconded for three years to be Assistant Director-General (for Social Sciences, Human Sciences, and Culture) of UNESCO in Paris. He has served on many committees concerned with education, broadcasting, the youth services, and the arts.

Richard Hoggart's first full-length work of criticism was a study of *Auden* (1951), but he has been best known as a critic and commentator in the field of cultural studies since the publication of *The Uses of Literacy: Aspects of working-class life with special reference to publications and entertainments* (1957), undoubtedly one of the key books of its decade in England. The first part of this work is a finely written evocation, combining autobiographical reminiscence with descriptive analysis of cultural documents, of traditional urban working-class life in England, before and just after World War II—a way of life that, as Hoggart wrote, was already beginning to change under the pressures of postwar affluence and social mobility. The second part of the book is concerned with the kind of art and entertainment purveyed to the working class under the new conditions. Hoggart's general conclusion was that 'the working classes have tended to lose, culturally, much that was valuable and to gain less than their new situation should have allowed'. This is perhaps evident from the extract from Part One of *The Uses of Literacy* reprinted below, in which Hoggart, without being either sentimental or patronizing, found in the more traditional magazines designed for the working-class woman, certain values that were missing from the glossier products which were competing with them and that (true to his final prediction) have since supplanted them.

The effectiveness of *The Uses of Literacy* depends very much on Richard Hoggart's own experience, eloquence, and intuition. As Director of the Centre for Contemporary Cultural Studies he has been concerned with the problems and possibilities of extending the study of popular art and related cultural phenomena in a more systematic way, collaborating with other disciplines, such as sociology, anthropology, and social psychology. Some of his recent papers in this area are included in a collection of his occasional essays, *Speaking to Each Other*: vol. 1. *About Society*: vol. 2. *About Literature* (1970).

CROSS REFERENCES : 33. Leslie Fiedler
43. Raymond Williams

COMMENTARY : Jean Claude Passeron, 'A Preface to *The Uses of Literacy*', *Working Papers in Cultural Studies*, Spring 1971

The 'real' world of people: illustrations from popular art —*Peg's Paper*

This overriding interest in the close detail of the human condition is the first pointer to an understanding of working-class art. To begin with, working-class art is essentially a 'showing' (rather than an 'exploration'), a presentation of what is known already. It starts from the assumption that human life is fascinating in itself. It has to deal with recognizable human life, and has to begin with the photographic, however fantastic it may become; it has to be underpinned by a few simple but firm moral rules.

Here is the source of the attraction, the closely, minutely domestic attraction, of *Thomson's Weekly News*. It is this, more than a vicarious snobbery, which makes radio serials with middle-class settings popular with working-class people, since these serials reflect daily the minutiae of everyday life. It is this which helps to ensure that the news-presentation of most popular newspapers belongs to the realms of imaginative or fictional writing of a low order. Those special favourites of working-class people, the Sunday gossip-with-sensation papers, the papers for the free day, assiduously collect from throughout the British Isles all the suitable material they can find, for the benefit of almost the whole of the adult working-class population. It is true that their interest, whether in news-reporting or in fiction, is often increased by the 'ooh-aah' element—a very 'ordinary' girl is knocked down by a man who proves to be a film-star; an attractive young widow proves to have disposed of two husbands with arsenic and popped them under the cellar-flagstones—and it is easy to think that most popular literature is of the 'ooh-aah' kind. One should think first of the photographically detailed aspect; the staple fare is not something which suggests an escape from ordinary life, but rather it assumes that ordinary life is intrinsically interesting. The emphasis is initially on the human and detailed, with or without the 'pepping-up' which crime or sex or splendour gives. De Rougemont[a]

[a] Denis de Rougemont, *Passion and Society* (1940).

489

speaks of millions (though he has in mind particularly the middle classes) who 'breathe in ... a romantic atmosphere in the haze of which passion seems to be the supreme test'. As we shall see, there is much in working-class literature too which gives support to this view; but it is not the first thing to say about the more genuinely working-class publications which persist. For them passion is no more interesting than steady home life.

Some BBC programmes underline the point. Notice how popular the 'homely' programmes are, not simply such programmes as *Family Favourites* ('for Good Neighbours') nor simply the family serials and feature-programmes such as *Mrs Dale's Diary, The Archers, The Huggetts, The Davisons, The Grove Family, The Hargreaves*; but the really ordinary homely programmes, often composed, rather like the more old-fashioned papers, of a number of items linked only by the fact that they all deal with the ordinary lives of ordinary people. I have in mind programmes like Wilfred Pickles's *Have a Go* and Richard Dimbleby's *Down Your Way*. They have no particular shape; they do not set out to be 'art' or entertainment in the music-hall sense; they simply 'present the people to the people' and are enjoyed for that. So are the programmes which still make use of the music-hall 'comic's' tradition of handling working-class life, programmes like Norman Evans's *Over the Garden Wall* and Al Read's superb sketches. It is not necessary, for success, that the programmes should be a form of professional art; if it is really homely and ordinary it will be interesting and popular.

I have suggested that it is commonly thought that some magazines—for example, those predominantly read by working-class women and usually spoken of as 'Peg's Paper[a] and all that'—provide little other than undiluted fantasy and sensation. This is not true; in some ways the more genuinely working-class magazines are preferable to those in the newer style. They are in some ways crude, but often more than that; they still have a felt sense of the texture of life in the group they cater for. I shall refer to them as 'the older magazines' because they carry on the *Peg's Paper* tradition, and reflect the older forms of working-class life: in fact, most of them, under their present titles, are between ten and twenty years old.

Almost all are produced by the three large commercial organizations: Amalgamated Press, the Newnes Group, and Thomson and Leng. But the authors and illustrators seem to have a close knowledge of the lives and attitudes of their audience. One wonders whether the publishers take in much of their material piecemeal from outside, rather as the stocking-makers of Nottingham once did. Most of the material is conventional—that is, it mirrors the attitudes of the readers; but those attitudes are by no means as ridiculous as one might at first be tempted to think. In comparison with these papers, some of those more recently in the front are as a smart young son with a quick brain and a bundle of up-to-date opinions beside his sentimental, superstitious, and old-fashioned mother.

---

[a] *Peg's Paper*, one of the first cheap magazines aimed at teenage girls and young women, enjoyed great popularity in the early years of this century. It consisted mainly of fiction.

These older magazines can often be recognized by their paper, a roughly textured newsprint which tends to have a smell—strongly evocative to me now, because it is also that of the old boys' magazines and comics—of something slightly damp and fungoid. They can be recognized also by their inner lay-out, in which only a few kinds of type are likely to be used; by their covers, which are usually 'flat' and boldly coloured in a limited range—almost entirely of black with strong shades of blue, red, and yellow, with few intermediates. They usually sell at threepence each, and have such titles as *Secrets, Red Star Weekly, Lucky Star* (which now incorporates *Peg's Paper*), *The Miracle, The Oracle, Glamour, Red Letter,* and *Silver Star.* They are apparently designed for adolescent girls and young married women in particular; thus, two in three of the readers of *Red Letter* are under thirty-five. There is some provision for older readers. The number of their readers varies between one-third and three-quarters of a million each, with most of them above the half-million. There will be much overlapping, but the total number of readers remains considerable, and they are almost entirely from the working-classes.

In composition they are all much alike. There are many advertisements, scattered throughout in penny packets, on the back cover and over large parts of the last couple of text-pages; there are usually no advertisements on the front cover pages and first text-pages. After the coloured cover, the inner cover page is generally given to some regular editorial feature; or the main serial, or the week's 'dramatic long complete novel', begins there. The advertisements, regularly recurring throughout the whole group of magazines, cover a narrow range of goods. Some cosmetics still use an aristocratic appeal, with photographs of titled ladies dressed for a ball. The same ailments appear so often in the advertisements for proprietary remedies that a hasty generalizer might conclude from them that the British working-classes are congenitally both constipated and 'nervy'. There are many announcements of cures for disabilities which are likely to make a girl a 'wallflower'. The 'scientists tell us' approach is there, but so still is its forerunner, the 'gypsy told me' approach. Thus, there are occasionally esoteric Indian remedies in this manner—'Mrs Johnson learned this secret many years ago from her Indian nurse in Bombay. Since then, many thousands have had cause to be glad that they reposed confidence in her system.' For married women there are washing-powder advertisements, and those for headache powders or California Syrup of Figs for children. But, in general, the assumption is that the married women readers are young enough to want to keep up with the unmarried by the use of cosmetics and hair-shampoos. Mail-order firms advertise fancy wedge-shoes, nylon underwear for—I suppose—the young women, and corsets for the older. For all groups, but especially, it appears, for the youngish married women with little money to spare, there are large advertisements (much the biggest in these magazines) inviting them to become agents for one of the great Clothing or General Credit Clubs, which proliferate, chiefly from the Manchester area, and usually give their agents two shillings in the pound, a fat catalogue, and free notepaper.

Stories make up the body of the text pages, but interspersed are the regular and occasional features. There are no politics, no social questions, nothing about the arts. This is neither the world of the popular newspapers which still purport to be alive to events, nor that of those women's magazines which have an occasional flutter with 'culture'. There are beauty hints, often over the signature of a well-known film-star: and some very homely home hints; there is a half-page of advice from an 'aunt' or a nurse on personal problems—the kind of thing laughed at as 'Aunt Maggie's advice'; in fact, it is usually very sensible. I do not mean, though this is true, that there is never a breath which is not firmly moral. But the general run of the advice is practical and sound, and when a problem arises whose answer is beyond the competence of the journalist, the inquirer is told to go to a doctor or to one of the advisory associations. There is a fortune-teller's section, based on the stars or birthday dates.

The stories divide easily into serials, the long complete story of the week, and the short stories (probably only one page in length). The long stories and the serials often have startling surprises, as a young man proves to be really wealthy or a girl finds she wins a beauty competition, even though she has always thought of herself as a plain Jane. This is particularly the case with the serials, which must be 'dramatic' and mount their accumulated series of suspended shocks as week follows week. So they tend to deal in what are called wild passions and in murder. There are handsome men on the loose, usually called Rafe. But much more interesting, because much more obviously feared, are the 'fascinating bitches', the Jezebels, as most advance trailers dub them. These are the women who set up in provincial towns and fail to report that they have a 'dreadful past' or that a 'dreadful secret' lies in their previous home a hundred miles away; or they get rid of pretty young girls by whom the man they are after is really attracted, by tipping them overboard from a rowing-boat, trussed in a cabin-trunk; or they convert an electric kettle into a lethal weapon: 'She did not look evil—yet her presence was like a curse'—'She was a woman fashioned by the Devil himself into the mould of the fairest of angels.'

The strong case against this kind of literature is well known, and I do not mean to take that case lightly. It applies, one should remember, to popular literature for all classes. When one has said that some of these stories supply the thrill of the wicked or evil, can one go further? Can one distinguish them from the general run of this kind of popular writing? Denis de Rougemont points out that this type of story, especially when it is written for the middle classes, usually manages to have things both ways, that though the villains never triumph in fact, they do triumph emotionally; that where, for instance, adulterous love is the subject, these stories imply an emotional betrayal. They 'hold the chains of love to be indefeasible and [imply] the superiority from a "spiritual" standpoint of mistress over wife'. 'Therefore,' M. de Rougemont continues, 'the institution of marriage comes off rather badly, but that does not matter ... since the middle-class (especially on the Continent) is well aware that this institution is no longer grounded in morality or religion, but rests securely upon financial foundations.' M. de Rougemont also emphasizes the fascination of the love/death theme, of an adulterous love-relationship which can find some sort of resolution only in death.

There seems to me a difference between this and most of the 'thrilling' stories in these 'older' magazines. There seems to be little emotional betrayal of the explicit assumptions here; the thrill comes because the villain is striking—'making passes at'—some things still felt underneath to be important, at a sense of the goodness of home and married life, above individual relations of passion. Thus there is no use of the love/death theme, since that would be to kill altogether the positive and actual home/marriage theme. The villain, inviting an adulterous relationship, seems to be found interesting less because he offers a vicarious enjoyment of a relationship which, though forbidden, is desired, as because he makes a shocking attack on what is felt to count greatly. He is a kind of bogy-man rather than a disguised hero. He does not usually triumph emotionally in the way he does in that more sophisticated literature which I take M. de Rougemont to be describing; this is, in fact, an extremely uncomplicated kind of literature.

These stories differ yet more obviously from many later versions of the sex-and-violence tale, from the kind of tale which is serialized in some of the Sunday papers. In those the author tries—while the rape or violence is being committed—to give a mild thrill and then laps the whole in hollow moral triteness. They are even further from the two-shilling sex-and-violence novelettes. They have no sexual excitement at all, and no description aiming to arouse it; and this, I think, is not only because women are not usually as responsive as men to that kind of stimulus, but because the stories belong to different worlds. These stories from the working-class women's magazines belong neither to the middle-class world, nor to that of the more modern Sunday papers, nor to that of the later novelettes, nor, even less, to an environment in which illicit relations can be spoken of as 'good fun', as 'smart' or 'progressive'. If a girl does lose her virginity here, or a wife commit adultery, you hear, 'And so that night I fell,' or 'I committed the great sin': and though a startled thrill is evident there, you feel that the sense of a fall and a sin is real also.

The strongest impression, after one has read a lot of these stories, is of their extraordinary fidelity to the detail of the readers' lives. The short stories take up as much space as the serial or long story, and they seem to be mainly faithful transcripts of minor incidents, amusing or worrying, from ordinary life. The serials may erupt into the startlingly posh world of what are still called 'the stately homes of England', or present a Rajah or a Sheik: but often the world is that the readers live in, with a considerable accuracy in its particulars. A fair proportion of the crime is of that world too—the distress when Mrs Thompson is suspected of shoplifting, and so on. I open *Silver Star*: on the inner front cover the complete long novel, *Letters of Shame*, begins:

> As Stella Kaye unlatched the gate of number 15, the front door opened and her mother beckoned agitatedly.
> 'Whatever's made you so late?' she whispered. 'Did you remember the sausages? Oh, good girl!'
> Stella looked at her mother's flushed face and best flowered apron.
> Visitors! Just when she was bursting to spring her news on them all! It would have to keep.

A typical copy of *Secrets* has as its week's verse, 'Mother's Night Out', about the weekly visit by Father and Mother to the pictures: 'It's Monday night and at No. 3, Mother and Dad are hurrying tea. In fact, poor Dad has scarcely done before Mother's urging, "Fred, come on!"'

A short story at the back of the *Oracle*, 'Hero's Homecoming', opens: 'Most of the women who dealt at the little general store on the corner of Roper's Road were rather tired of hearing about Mrs Bolsom's boy, but they couldn't very well tell her so because she was so obliging and so handy to run to at times of emergency.' A typical *Lucky Star* one-page story starts: 'Lilian West glanced at the clock on the kitchen wall. "My goodness," she thought. "How quickly I get through the housework these days!"' It goes on to tell how, after deciding to leave her married children alone so as not to be thought a nuisance, she found fresh happiness in realizing how much she was still needed. 'Mary was an ordinary girl doing an ordinary job in a factory', another story begins, and incidentally epitomizes the points of departure for almost all of them.

The illustrations help to create the same atmosphere. Some of the newer magazines specialize in photographic illustrations of the candid camera kind. The 'older' ones still use black-and-white drawings in an unsophisticated style. There exist, particularly in more modern publications, black-and-white line drawings which are very sophisticated: compared with them the cartoons still to be found in some provincial newspapers, drawn by a local man, belong to thirty years ago. So it is with most of the drawings here (the main illustration to the serial or the long complete novel is sometimes an exception); they are not smart in their manner, and their detail is almost entirely romanticized. The girls are usually pretty (unless the burden is that even a plain girl can find a good husband), but they are pretty in an unglamorous way, in the way working-class girls are often very pretty. They wear blouses and jumpers with skirts, or their one dance-dress. The factory chimney can be seen sticking up in one corner and the street of houses with intermittent lamp-posts stretches behind; there are the buses and the bikes and the local dance-halls and the cinemas.

Such a nearness to the detail of the lives of readers might be simply the prelude to an excursion into the wish-fulfilment story about the surprising things that can happen to someone from that world. Sometimes this is so, and there is occasionally a stepping-up of the social level inside the stories, so that people can feel how nice it would be to be a member of the villa or good-class housing groups. But often what happens is what might happen to anyone, and the environment is that of most readers.

If we look more closely at the stories we are reminded at once of the case against 'stock responses'[a]: every reaction has its fixed counter for presentation. I run through the account of a trial: the mouths are 'set', the faces 'tense with excitement'; tremors run down spines; the hero exhibits 'iron control' and faces his captors with a 'stony look'; his watching girl-friend is the victim of an 'agonized heart' as 'suspense thickens in the air'. But what does this indicate? That the writers use cliché, and that the audience seems to want cliché, that they are not exploring experience, realizing experience through language? That

[a] L. A. Richards' phrase, in *Practical Criticism* (see above, p 115, n.).

is true. But these are first, I repeat, statements; picture presentations of the known. A reader of them is hardly likely to tackle anything that could be called serious literature; but there are worse diets, especially today. If we regard them as faithful but dramatized presentations of a life whose form and values are known, we might find it more useful to ask what are the values they embody. There is no virtue in merely laughing at them: we need to appreciate first that they may in all their triteness speak for a solid and relevant way of life. So may the tritest of Christmas and birthday card verses; that is why those cards are chosen with great care, usually for the 'luvliness' and 'rightness' of their verse. The world these stories present is a limited and simple one, based on a few accepted and long-held values. It is often a childish and garish world, and the springs of the emotions work in great gushings. But they do work; it is not a corrupt or a pretentious world. It uses boldly words which serious writers for more sophisticated audiences understandably find difficulty in using today, and which many other writers are too knowing to be caught using. It uses, as I noted in another connection, words like 'sin', 'shame', 'guilt', 'evil', with every appearance of meaningfulness. It accepts completely, has as its main point of reference, the notion that marriage and a home, founded on love, fidelity, and cheerfulness, are the right purpose of a woman's life. If a girl 'sins' the suggestion is—and this reinforces what I said earlier about the ethical emphasis in working-class beliefs—not that the girl has 'sinned against herself', as another range of writers would put it, or that she has fallen short in some relationship other than the human and social, but that she has spoiled her chances of a decent home and family. One of the commoner endings to this kind of serial is for the girl either to find again the man responsible, and marry him, or to find another man who, though he knows all, is prepared to marry her and be a father to the child, loving them both. One can appreciate the force of the mistrust of 'the other woman', the Jezebel, the home-breaker, the woman who sets out to wreck an existing marriage or one just about to start. Even the man with a roving eye gets short shrift if he goes in for marriage-breaking; before that he comes under dispensations more indulgent than those accorded to women on the loose.

It is against this ground-pattern that the thrills throw their bold reliefs, and to which they are indissolubly bound. I do not think that the thrills tempt the readers to imitate them, or much to dream of them in a sickly way. They bear the same relation to their lives as the kite to the solid flat common from which it is flown. The ground-pattern of ordinary life weaves its strands in and out through the serials and the short stories, in all the magazines. It is the pattern of the main assumptions:

Don't spoil today because some friend has left you; you cannot say of ALL
God has bereft you. Life is too brief for anger or for sorrow...

or:

Happiness is made up
Of a million tiny things
That often pass unnoticed...

In its outlook, this is still substantially the world of Mrs Henry Wood (*East Lynne; Danesbury House; Mrs Haliburton's Troubles*), of Florence L. Barclay (one million copies of *The Rosary* sold), of Marie Corelli (*The Sorrows of Satan*—a 'classic' to my aunts), of Silas K. Hocking (*Ivy; Her Benny; His Father*), of Annie S. Swan (*A Divided House*), of Ruth Lamb (*A Wilful Ward; Not Quite a Lady; Only a Girl Wife; Thoughtful Joe and How He Gained His Name*), and of a great number of others, often published by the Religious Tract Society and given as prizes in the upper classes of Sunday schools. It is being ousted now by the world of the newer kind of magazine. I wonder, incidentally, whether it is resisting longer in Scotland: a very plain but attractive threepenny weekly, *People's Friend*, is still published there; a similar magazine, the *Weekly Telegraph* from Sheffield, died only a few years ago, I believe. Some of the 'older' magazines are trying to preserve themselves by producing the glamour of the newer magazines, often linked to an inflated form of the older thrills. Tense and gripping new serials are announced on the placards, with large illustrations compounded of the old-style ordinariness and the new-style close-up.

But a few of the newer kind of magazines continue to increase their already phenomenal circulations. In many ways they embody the same attitudes as the 'older' magazines, though they aim at too large an audience to be able to identify themselves with one social class. They are considerably smarter in presentation and presumably can provide more specialized articles on home problems than the 'older' magazines. There are crudities in the 'older' magazines whose removal ought not to be regretted. I have not stressed these qualities because I have been concerned to show the better links with working-class life. But the smartness of the newer magazines often extends, it seems to me, to their attitudes, and the change is not always for the good. The smartness easily becomes a slickness; there is an emphasis on money-prestige (figures of salaries or winnings are given in brackets after the names of people in the news), much 'fascinated' attention is given to public personalities such as the gay wives of industrial magnates, or radio and film-stars; there is a kittenish domesticity and a manner predominantly arch or whimsical.

The 'glossies' are aiming, successfully, to attract the younger women who want to be smart and up to date, who do not like to seem old-fashioned. The 'older' magazines would perhaps like to catch up with the 'glossies', but that would be very costly; and there is still presumably a large enough audience for them to be profitably produced in much their old form. When that ceases to be the case they will, I suppose, either make really radical changes in the direction indicated by the 'glossies', or die.

37 Walter J. Ong

Walter J. Ong, S.J. (b. 1912) is a Jesuit priest and Professor of English at St Louis University. His distinguished scholarly career was founded on a study of the Huguenot rhetorician and educationalist Peter Ramus, *Ramus, Method and the Decay of Dialogue* (Cambridge, Mass., 1958). In Ong's view, Ramus was a crucially important figure in the transformation of scholastic logic at the time of the Renaissance, from a method of inquiry and exposition based on oral disputation, to one based on the model of the visualized spatial diagram. Ong's specialized research seems to have influenced and been itself reinforced by the more speculative and global theorizing of his friend, colleague, and co-religionist, Marshall McLuhan (see below, pp. 610-20) who argued in *The Gütenberg Galaxy* (1962) that after the invention of the printing press western society increasingly neglected oral–aural methods of communication, with a consequent impoverishment of human perception and sympathies—a condition which may be alleviated by modern developments in communications technology. In numerous essays, some of which are collected in *The Barbarian Within* (New York, 1962) and *In The Human Grain* (1967), Fr. Ong has continued to explore the implications of these ideas for education, literary criticism, cultural history, and religion. Teilhard de Chardin, Jesuit author of *The Phenomenon of Man* (Paris, 1955) was another friend whose mystical evolutionary thought has influenced Ong profoundly, and made him (rather rarely among modern literary intellectuals) a generally optimistic commentator.

Fr. Ong has been visiting professor at many of America's great universities. His Terry lectures at Yale University were published in 1968 under the title *The Presence of the Word*. In 'A Dialogue of Aural and Objective Correlatives', first published in 1958, he opposes to the notion (implied by most of the New Critics and their masters) that the poem has some kind of objective, spatially defined existence, the idea of the poem as an utterance, as the expression of a personal interiority. Ong's aim, however, is not to dismiss the effort at objectivity in criticism, but to suggest that it may not be absolutely attainable or desirable. The essay is reprinted here from *The Barbarian Within*.

CROSS REFERENCES: 6. T. S. Eliot
        9. I. A. Richards
        26. W. K. Wimsatt and Monroe C. Beardsley
        45. Marshall McLuhan

COMMENTARY: Frank Kermode, 'Father Ong', in *Modern Essays* (1971)

A dialectic of aural
and objective correlatives

Soun ys noght but eyr ybroken[a]

The eagle to Chaucer in *The House of Fame*

I

The likening of a poem to a monument or to some sort of object is as old at least as Horace's 'Exegi monumentum aere perennius'.[b] Nevertheless, a certain fixation upon the analogy between a poem and an object is characteristic of the present English-speaking world. Here a great deal of criticism feeds on this analogy, which is featured not only in titles such as Cleanth Brooks's *The Well Wrought Urn* or William K. Wimsatt's *The Verbal Icon*[c] but also in the substructure of much of our most active critical thinking and writing. In his 'Science and Poetry', I. A. Richards deals with a poem as the 'skeleton' of a 'body of experience', as a 'structure' by which the 'impulses' making up the experience are 'adjusted' to one another. In their highly influential *Theory of Literature*, René Wellek and Austin Warren answer their own capital question regarding the mode of existence of the literary work by explaining it as a 'structure' of norms or 'stratified system' of norms. T. S. Eliot's great critical essay, 'Tradition and the Individual Talent',[d] underwrites the poem as a 'monument', and treats of tradition with no discernible explicit attention to the radically acoustic quality of the dialogue between man and man in which all verbal expression has its being. Accordance with tradition is for Mr Eliot a matter not of harmony or counterpoint, but of objects which 'fit' in with one another. The creative process is envisioned as outside the world of voice, in terms of chemicals (objects) 'working' on one another. Despite his own recent disavowal, Mr Eliot's 'objective correlative'[e] is deservedly famous, for it provides

---

[a] 'Sound is nothing but broken air.'
[b] I have completed a monument more lasting than brass.'
[c] See pp. 291–304 and 333–58.
[d] See pp. 71–7 above.
[e] In his 1919 essay on *Hamlet*, T. S. Eliot declared: 'The only way of expressing emotion in the form of art is by finding an "objective correlative"; in other words, a set of objects, a situation, a chain of events which shall be the formula of that *particular* emotion; such that when the external facts, which terminate in sensory experience, are given, the emotion is immediately evoked.' The term 'objective correlative' passed

498

support for a whole state of mind fixed on a world of space and surfaces. It is noteworthy that by the time of *The Confidential Clerk*, the symbol for artistic performance is even more committed to the visual and tactile. Sir Claude Mul-hammer, the unsuccessful artist—poet in the larger sense—is presented as a spoiled potter.

This tactile and visualist bias is shared by poets themselves when they speak of their own achievement. Archibald MacLeish, always a sensitive register of contemporary critical and literary trends, in his *Ars Poetica* compares a poem to a whole series of nonvocal, visually and tactually apprehended 'objects':

> A poem should be palpable and mute
> As globed fruit
> As old medallions to the thumb
> Dumb
> Silent as the sleeve-worn stone
> Of casement ledges where the moss has grown—
> A poem should be wordless
> As the flight of birds.

This has, of course, a certain validity. It suggests earlier Imagist preoccupations with poetry which is 'hard' and 'clear'—made up, that is, of images (with a bias towards visual images) rather than of words. It likewise suggests still earlier Platonic and Aristotelian theories of poetry such as the 'kodachrome theory' espoused by Sir Philip Sidney (poetry makes the grass greener and the roses redder). But it is a far cry from Sidney's and others' notion of a poem as a *speaking* picture.

II

Many of the critics just cited as preoccupied with objects, structures, skeletons, and stratified systems have pressed the point that poetry belongs primarily to the world of voice and sound, but in doing so have based their explanations perhaps too innocently on spatial analogies. To consider the work of literature in its primary oral and aural existence, we must enter more profoundly into this world of sound as such, the I–thou world where, through the mysterious interior resonance which sound best of all provides, persons commune with persons, reaching one another's interiors in a way in which one can never reach the interior of an 'object'. Here, instead of reducing words to objects, runes, or even icons, we take them simply as what they are even more basically, as utter-ances, that is to say, as cries. All verbalization, including all literature, is radically a cry, a sound emitted from the interior of a person, a modification of one's exhalation of breath which retains the intimate connection with life which we find in breath itself, and which registers in the etymology of the word 'spirit', that is, breath. 'Whoever loses his breath loses also his speech', and, we might add, his life as well. The cry which strikes our ear, even the

into the common currency of critical discussion, and was no doubt in Eliot's mind when he alluded late in life to 'a few notorious phrases [of his own] which have had a truly embarrassing success in the world' (*The Frontiers of Criticism*, 1957).

animal cry, is consequently a sign of an interior condition, indeed of that special interior focus or pitch of being which we call life, an invasion of all the atmosphere which surrounds a being by that being's interior state, and in the case of man, it is an invasion of his own interior self-consciousness. Not that man's interior through this invasion entirely exteriorizes itself, loses its interiority. Quite the contrary, it keeps this interiority and self-possession in the cry and advertises to all that is outside and around it that this *interior* is here, and, refusing to renounce itself, is manifesting itself. Precisely because he does not renounce his own interior self, the cry of the wounded, suffering man invades his surroundings and makes its terrible demands on those persons who hear it. For this invasion, under one aspect a raid or sally into others' interiors, is also a strangely magnetic action, which involves not so much one's going out to others as one's drawing other interiors into the ambit of one's being. The voice of the agonizing man, we say, 'captivates' others' attention, their very selves, 'involving' them, as we have recently learned to put it, by pulling them into his own interior and forcing them to share the state which exists there.

There is, indeed, no way for a cry completely to exteriorize itself. A mark made by our hand will remain when we are gone. But when the interior—even the physical, corporeal interior, as well as the spiritual interior of consciousness —from which a cry is emitted ceases to function as an interior, the cry itself has perished. To apprehend what a person has produced in space—a bit of writing, a picture—is not at all to be sure that he is alive. To hear his voice (provided it is not *reproduced* from a frozen spatial design on a phonograph disc or tape) is to be *sure.*

'Soun ys noght but eyr ybroken', says the loquacious and pedantic eagle who soars through Chaucer's dream in *The House of Fame.* The frightened, airborne Chaucer had not only his heart in his mouth as he heard this, but his tongue in his cheek as he reported it. He sensed that this simple reduction of sound to 'broken' air and thus to spatial components was psychologically unreal, much too facile. Today we have the same awareness as Chaucer, set in a more complex context. We know that we can study sound in measurable wave lengths, on graphs, and on oscillographs, calibrating it in a thousand different ways. But we also know that this spatial reduction of sound, which externalizes it completely and enables us to handle it scientifically and with impeccable accuracy, has one supreme disadvantage. Through such study we know everything— except sound itself. To find what the sound *is*, we must make it really exist: we must hear it. As soon as we hear it, all its mysterious quality—the thing which makes it really different from a measurement or a graph—asserts itself once more. And this is precisely what makes it *sound.*

In its ineluctable interiority, related to this irreducible and elusive and interior economy of the sound world, all verbal expression, and in particular all true literature, remains forever something mysterious. Like the self or person, the word refuses to submit completely to any of those norms of clarity or explicitness (which means 'unfoldedness') such as we derive through considering knowledge and communication by analogy with sight. It refuses to be completely exposed (as a surface) or explicated (unfolded) or explained (laid out flat) or defined (marked with boundary lines) or to be entirely clear (separated from its ground or background) and distinct (pricked out).

What I am trying to say here is not properly conveyed by stating simply that utterance, and in particular the true literary work, has 'depth'. For depth is a concept which can be resolved, ultimately if circuitously, in terms of surfaces. Interiority cannot be. For I mean by interiority here precisely the opposite of surface, that which does not have surface at all, and can never have.

Language retains this interiority because it, and the concepts which are born with it, remain always the medium wherein persons discover and renew their discovery that they are persons, that is, discover and renew their own proper interiority and selves. Persons who do not (in one way or another) learn to talk remain imbeciles, unable to enter fully into themselves. The pitch of utterance which bears towards the interior of the speaker—and by the same token towards the interior of the bearer, who repeats in his own interior the words of the speaker and thereby understands them—can never be done away with, despite the fact that the same utterance must always have some reference, at least oblique, to exterior reality as well. Because of this double reference of language, to person and to object, 'I do not understand *you*' can be tantamount to 'I do not understand the *things* you are trying to say'.

But if all language faces some towards the interior, and the interior of both speaker and hearer, of all the forms of language literature has in a sense most interiority because, more than other forms of expression, it exists within the medium of words themselves and does not seek escape from this medium. In some sense, most, if not all, other forms of expression do ambition such escape. Typically, scientific expression does. It hedges words about with definitions and restrictions of all sorts in order to keep them to a certain extent from leading their own uninhibited life in the mysterious interior world of communication between persons wherein they came into being. It drives towards complete explanation. It bends words to extrinsic ends at the expense of intrinsic in the sense that it tries to keep their reference to 'objective' reality under a kind of surface control. Science relies heavily on diagrams or on diagram-type concepts. And, in so far as it is quasi-scientific, so does my present discussion here.

And yet science works its designs on language here with only partial success, for two reasons. First, the scientific policing of terminology is itself a linguistic activity, not a technique of object-manipulation, and hence itself exhibits a certain mysterious interiority. At any moment in its development, even science, not to mention philosophy, is only arrested dialogue.

Secondly, as its source for its own proper terms science can avail itself only of a stock of words or morphemes which have come into being in a curiously nonscientific way. Science must establish itself within an already going language grown into being through nonscientifically controlled etymologies. Thus scientific conceptualization and expression is tempered everywhere with nonscientific relicts, and always will be. In the last analysis, all science must in some fashion be perpetuated by explanation in nonscientific terms, for otherwise no one could be inducted from the world of ordinary human speech into the world of scientific meanings but would have to be born into this latter world.

This is to say that, basically, science can invent no entirely new words, only new combinations of those words or morphemes which it has inherited from history, that is, from the interior world in which person has communed with person over the eons in the age-old dialogue which is central to the story of mankind and which is carried on in the curious interiority of the world of sound. Still, because this world in which it operates is interior and hence mysterious and unexplained, science and philosophy itself must seek in some way to exteriorize it. For this is the business of science and, in a somewhat different way, of philosophy, to explain, to 'open up' or to 'open out', to explicate and unfold the mysteries, that they may remain mysteries no longer— to some extent, for in part they will always so remain.

III

Although it is not to be equated with science, criticism is in some degree explanation, and has something of this same scientific bent. Unless it is to be itself a poem, criticism of a poem must involve some elucidation. Its ultimate object may be to introduce the reader more fully into the mystery which is the poem, but its technique will be to some extent to 'clear up' certain things.

It should be owned that criticism, more than science, does acquiesce somewhat explicitly to the mysteriousness of language. A look at its very meaning, supported by its own complex etymology, makes this fact clear. For criticism means radically judgment, which in turn means not explaining or diagramming but *saying* yes or no. The critic, as a sayer of yes or no, is a denizen of the sound-world. The notion of judgment, the action of the saying yes or no, simply cannot be reduced in terms of spatial analogy. Thus the fact that criticism or judgment, which is a notion certainly applicable in one way or another in all sciences, attaches itself most conspicuously to operations on literature—or to works of art, which, as will be seen, are in their own way 'words', too— bears stubborn witness to the fact that literature moves certainly in the realm of the word. More than that, it bears witness to the fact that literature (and art) exists in a particular relationship to the interior of man, to that 'selfless self of self, most strange, most still', as Gerard Manley Hopkins describes it, which lies forever folded in its own mysterious decision expressed by the word—'fast furled, and all foredrawn to No or Yes'.

Such considerations or perspectives must, I believe, temper our critical ambitions to reduce the work of literature—most typically the poem—to some sort of object. For, although, as Eliot justly maintains in his essay mentioned earlier, works of literature are 'not the expression of personality but an escape from personality', and in this are unlike ordinary dialogue, they are nevertheless not quite an escape to an object, a thing adequately conceivable, even analogously, in terms of surfaces and visual or tactile perceptions. Works of literature consist in words, and, as we have suggested, words themselves retain in themselves ineluctably something of the interiority of their birth within that interior which is a person. As cries, they go 'out', but they are not extensions of, or projections of interiority. In this sense Camus's and Sartre's view of man as an interior

502

exteriorizing itself is quite inadequate to the totality of the human situation. We are more accurate if we keep our metaphors closer to the world of sound and think of speech and of works of literature as 'amplifications' or, better, as intensifications of an interior. All words projected from a speaker remain, as has been seen, somehow interior to him, being an invitation to another person, another interior, to share the speaker's interior, an invitation to enter in, not to regard from the outside. The Hegelian master-slave dialectic manifests a brilliant partial insight, but it does not cover the whole of the person-to-person relationship revealed by voice considered as voice.

In so far as all works of art are in some measure utterances, expressions emanating from the human psyche, they, too, partake of this interiority. Even the works of pottery in *The Confidential Clerk*, to resume Sir Claude's musings, in this sense consist in words, resonant with human life, for Sir Claude goes on to identify his experience of pottery as a mode of communication between persons:

> But when I am alone, and look at one thing long enough,
> I sometimes have that sense of identification
> With the maker of which I spoke—an agonizing ecstasy
> Which makes life bearable ...

IV

The piece of pottery serves to join the often otherwise unknown artist and observer—uniting those into whom the word enters, or who enter into it. But if a piece of pottery or any other object of art can be said to consist in a word or words, works of literature can be said to do so even more. They consist not only in words, they consist of words. For this reason they remain most mysterious among all works of art—more mysterious, even, than music, which, divorced from words, is pure voice, but voice with a human point of reference missing.

It is a commonplace that Aristotle once observed that music is the most 'imitative' of arts. This implies that, in so far as art is imitation, music is the most consummate art—a paradoxical notion if our idea of imitation is formed chiefly by reference, even analogous reference, to the world of sight and space. For what construct existing outside itself does a work of Beethoven or Bartok 'imitate'? However, Aristotle's remark need not be interpreted in terms of such constructs. It seems to contain in germ an idea which can be developed in another way, although from Aristotle's point in intellectual history this development could not yet be explicitly realized, especially since he appears to have conceived of music regularly in conjunction with voice. The idea is this: Among the arts, music enjoys a kind of primacy in so far as the sound world has a primacy over the space world in artistic creation because all art must always in some fashion be more voice than 'object'. Pure music, that is, melodic or harmonic sound without words, although it is defective in not being a human voice, still has a certain primacy even over the human voice because of its existence totally within sound. Music is sound exploited as pure sound, symbolizing directly no 'object' at all. Music suggests what voice might do in the way of pure communication of interior to interior, of person to person, of knowledge to

503

knowledge, and love to love, if only voice did not find itself involved also in representing objects and hence involved in the tangle of explanation in which the human voice operates and which is half its excuse for being.

But by the same token, because music is not directly involved with the opacity of objects—except in so far as it is assimilable to an object itself, and this it is only at the very minimum, being pure sound, 'noght but eyr ybroken' —music manages to shirk half of the twofold responsibility of the human voice, which in giving utterance to the human word looks inward and outward simultaneously. In its purer forms music, while it is not inward in the sense of being purely subjective, nevertheless is inward in that, while it speaks, it says nothing—that is, *nothing*. Pure music shrugs off all effort at *representation*. It is pure presentation. But because of this calculated irresponsibility, to which it owes its bewitching beauty, music bears within itself the germ of its own disintegration. Unconcerned about symbolizing an object despite the fact that it is a denizen of the sound world, the realm of voice, and that it capitalizes on this situation, music utters a 'word' which actually falls short of being a voice. For the human voice, interior though it be, achieves its inward perfection only by bearing outward too. In being a voice about nothing outside, music amplifies only a fictional interior. In being about no object, in the last analysis it also is the voice of no person. For this reason, the more music becomes pure music, the more it risks being identified with mathematics, as the history of the arts in antiquity and the Middle Ages shows, and thus being viewed not really as sound at all. By carrying the artistic process to one of its extremes, music thus reveals the impossible tensions under which all art works and which all art must strive ceaselessly to resolve with never the hope of complete success. These tensions manifest themselves most spectacularly in the realm of sound, for all art, as voice or word, exists with special reference to this realm.

V

If it is desirable that criticism go beyond its admittedly healthy interest in the art 'object' or the 'objective correlative' by giving more explicit attention to the oral–aural commitments of all art, and particularly of literature, one can suggest that the perspectives open to the phenomenological and existential outlooks ought at this point to be exploited to a greater extent by American and British critics. Now is the time to infuse into criticism awareness such as those of Louis Lavelle, Martin Buber, and Gabriel Marcel, which make it feasible to deal to a greater extent with language as sound, with correlatives which are not merely 'objective', or, for that matter, merely 'subjective' either, but which transcend this objective–subjective classification (itself a derivative from an unreflective visualist notion of reality). We need the Kierkegaardian sense of dialectic, as well as an awareness of the existential implications of dialogue— that is, of all expression viewed for what it basically is, an exchange between an 'I' and a 'thou'—such as registers variously in the works of post-Hegelians like Jaspers or Camus. (In [Camus's] *The Fall*, only one person's speech is recorded, but the direct partner to the dialogue becomes the 'I' who is the reader, and the person speaking, it is to be noted, is a judge—one who decides, says yes or no —who is a penitent judge, aware that he is one himself made to be judged.) If it is not too much to expect that these typical Continental developments take root in our still basically Anglo-Saxon critical soil, certain problems of criticism, hitherto highly intractable, can be dealt with much more satisfactorily.

There is first of all the problem of the 'boundaries' of a literary work. Any criticism which insists that each work be regarded as a whole, somewhat in the sense in which an object is felt to be a whole, and that the value of any items in the work depends on the interior organization of the work, will feel the work as having definite boundaries. It will be disconcerting to find, for example, in the influential textbook, *Understanding Poetry*, of Cleanth Brooks and Robert Penn Warren, where works do have definite boundaries, the admission that 'it is sometimes said that a poet's work is really one long poem of which the individual poems are but parts'. Messrs Brooks and Warren do not undertake to refute this view. But it is a puzzling view if we wish with Brooks and Warren to take each poem individually as a discrete object existing in its own right, a unique 'well wrought urn'—unless we are willing to recall that the well wrought urn, too, as a 'word', is like the individual poem, a moment in an age-old conversation in which what goes on within the artist's psyche and registers in his work echoes the whole evolution of the cosmos. From this latter point of view the single poem is discrete somewhat in the abstract way in which a moment in a dialogue is discrete—only somewhat more than nonpoetic moments in a dialogue, at least in that it provides a unit for pause and meditation. It communicates a unique something which cannot be quite laid hold of outside the poem. But, while standing by itself more than a riposte in a conversation might do, this something does not stand entirely by itself. Each literary work marks a definite advance over what has gone before and is big with promise for the future, and this precisely because it is not a mere object, but something said, a 'word', a moment in an age-old exchange of talk. Thinking and speaking of a literary work as a moment in a dialogue engenders an awareness of its 'open' or unbounded historical potential, and of its unlikeness to a discrete 'object'. It appears as something like a Sartrean *pour-soi* as well as an *en-soi*.[a]

A second area or problem of criticism which can be dealt with in terms of oral and aural performance is that of the literary genre. Just as a poem or other work of art as word resists complete framing as an 'object' thought of as clearly and distinctly outlined in space, so it resists complete framing in terms of types and genres. For these represent an attempt to define, to delimit, to mark off, and in this way conceal a visualist approach to knowledge, feeling, and communication which is—I must repeat—a necessary and inevitable approach for purposes of explanation, but which can never be entirely satisfactory in the case of works which are, again, not objects but moments in a dialogue. Awareness of this state of affairs enables us to explain in some sort an annoying fact that we all know, namely, that, in a very real sense, among all the diverse works of a writer as, for example, Jonathan Swift (to take one who used a great variety of

[a] In Sartre's ontology, Consciousness is Being-for-itself (*pour-soi*) and objective appearance is Being-in-itself (*en-soi*).

genres), whether these be lyric poems or prose travel fiction or literary hoaxes of the Bickerstaff sort or satirical pamphlets or sermons—in all these diverse works, there is a certain unity greater than that found in the genres to which these various works belong. The basis for this unity is that they are all the utterances, the word, of one man.

Thirdly, explicit attention to the mysterious oral–aural nature of the work of literature enables us to account more fully for the function of the critic—and even for the fact that criticism is constantly worrying over the function of the critic. For, once we recognize explicitly the fact that all poetry and all literature is, from one point of view, a moment in a dialogue, the role of the critic becomes both clearer and more complicated. If the art 'object' which is 'made' of words were really that—an 'object'—alone, one could talk about it without becoming involved in it in the way in which, despite everything, the critic is constantly becoming involved. However, since it is not simply an object, but also something that someone (a historical person, speaking in a certain place at a certain historical time and after certain historical literary events) utters after and because others have uttered something else, and since the work of the critics is also something that someone utters after and because others have uttered something else (this something else being both the work of art and its antecedents, as well as other criticism), the lines of literature and of criticism are necessarily interwoven. They are interwoven as words are interwoven, each belonging to a certain moment in the totality of activity emanating from human life in history. Seen this way, criticism is perhaps somewhat less the poor relation of literature than it is sometimes made out to be. It is part of the total dialogue in which all literature exists.

The art 'object', literary or other, precisely in so far as it is an 'object', invites being treated with words. For, in spite of everything, words are more intelligible, more alive, and in this sense more real than what we perceive in space, even analogously. We use words to process, understand, and assimilate spatial conceptions. We learn *from* sight, but we think *in* words, mental and vocal. We explain diagrams *in* words. The art 'object', in so far as it is an object with at least an oblique spatial reference and not a word, has somehow divorced itself from the flow of conversation and understanding in which human life moves. It must be returned to this flow, related somehow to the continuum of actuality, that is to say, to what concrete, existent persons are actually saying and thinking. Undertaking to talk about the art object, the critic undertakes to effect this relationship or reintegration. But in doing so, he must somehow violate the work of art in its effort to subsist alone. For by talking about it he advertises the fact that it does not really and wholly and entirely exist alone.

Moreover, the critic is likely to violate the work of art in another and opposite way. For, in so far as he does more than merely initiate into the experience of a given work of art, help create a climate of empathy—and few if any critical works can pretend to do merely this—in so far, that is, as he seeks not merely to induct the reader into the experience but also to 'elucidate', to 'explicate', to 'clarify' the work of art, the critic is actually taking the work in quite the opposite way, not as an object to be reintegrated in the mysterious world of words, but as a mysterious 'word' which must be made tractable by explanation of at least a quasi-scientific, objective sort. One does not elucidate or clarify a work of art in so far as it is an object, but rather in so far as it is a word. For we do not elucidate or explicate an object—a quartz crystal, for example, or a fish. We elucidate or explicate words or remarks (which may, indeed, be 'about' objects). But if to 'elucidate' or 'explicate' a poem or a painting is thus to regard it as a word, it is at the same time to ambition moving it in some sort out of the world of resonance and voice into space. For in so far as one aims to 'elucidate', to 'explicate', to 'clarify', one aims to process one's knowledge through considering it by analogy with a space-and-light world of vision, not a world of sound. Concepts of this sort—elucidate, explicate, clarify—are all based on this visualist analogy.

Thus, between Scylla and Charybdis, the critic is caught in the dialectic of object and word in which the work of art has its being. He can take the work as an object and attempt in some sort to verbalize it—or if it is a piece of literature already, to verbalize it still more—or he can take it as a word and attempt to objectify it, to exploit its likeness to 'things'. Generally he does partly the one and partly the other. In either case he advertises its limitations—or, we might say, the limitations of all human perception and intellectual activity, or for that matter, of all finitude, or finiteness. For in this universe of ours all objects are in some sense words, and all our words invite manoeuvring as objects. Like the poet himself, the critic can encode the object in words or decode the word into a quasi object. He cannot do both at once. To gain ground in one sector is to relinquish it in another. And yet the overall loss is never so great as the gain. For the critic can overcome the impasse in which he finds himself at least to the extent that he realizes that it is an impasse. The mind cannot get outside its limitations absolutely. But it can get outside them to this extent: it can recognize its limitations as limitations. Combined with an awareness that indefinite progress in both empathic criticism and explicatory criticism is possible, we must cultivate an awareness of the limitations within which both types of criticism must ineluctably operate and we must develop techniques of talking about these limitations.

Finally a more explicit recognition of the oral–aural world in which literary works, and in their own way other works of art, have their being makes it possible to deal more directly with the all-important problem of history and artistic tradition. Philosophies or world views which consider all human knowledge, wittingly or unwittingly, by analogy with sight-knowledge (abetted more or less by tactile perception of spatial relations) to the exclusion of sound-knowledge, have no place for history, and are helpless to deal with evolution, cosmic, organic, or intellectual. For history they tend to substitute cyclicism. It is a commonplace that the early Hebraeo-Christian tradition, which has been the great well-spring of mankind's genuine historical awareness, as the late Erich Auerbach has so masterfully shown in the first chapter of his book, *Mimesis*,[a] is a heritage rooted in an oral–aural notion of knowledge, not in the more visualist Hellenic notion.

[a] See above, pp. 315–32.

The growth in the reflexiveness of human thought and in explicit and deliberate attention to the individual, unique in his interiority, which, despite many spectacular and disheartening setbacks, is the dominant pattern in the intellectual history of man over the ages, is another manifestation, at a higher level or pitch, of this same interiorizing economy which marks, so it seems, cosmic developments taken in their larger phases. It is this increase in interiority which makes history possible and which governs artistic tradition. Only when mankind has become pretty thoroughly reflexive, not only individually but socially on a large scale, does history as a subject take form and begin to dominate in a specific way man's outlook on the world. At this same stage, art and literature become intensely conscious of their past, not as outside the artist and his works, but as in them, and the age-old dialectic is intensified between tradition, claiming more and more attention as historical lore deepens, and the individual, courted with growing fervour as philosophies of personalism come into being.

So far, no way of philosophizing about history has arisen to compete with that which sees the movements of history as analogous to those of dialogue—to what happens when one inviolable interiority or human person sets about communicating with another. In the primacy of this analogue for the handling of history, a late-comer in the evolution of the cosmos, the interiorizing momentum which seems to dominate large-scale developments asserts a kind of ultimate claim. If literary history is to be more than a sheer enumeration of befores and afters, more than, quite literally, a surface treatment proceeding by likening works of art to discrete objects apprehended by sight rather than, in a mysterious way, to persons themselves (for voice is an intensification of person), it will have to avail itself of this notion of dialogue more explicitly, although not quite in the Hegelian, much less in the Marxian way—for Hegel's dialectic is too little vocal in preoccupation, deflecting attention from the word as word to a visualist analogue of the word, the *idea*, the that-which-is-seen, reflected in an equally visualist (thesis–antithesis–synthesis) reduction of dialogue itself.

If it is difficult to consider literature under a definitive aural aspect, and if any such consideration must necessarily involve visualist references and analogies (as this present discussion, and this very sentence, certainly does), nevertheless it should be less difficult in this age than it has been in the past. It should even come rather naturally to us in an age dominated by figures such as Proust, whose work seeks to perpetuate in the hollows of the mind all the reverberations of the past; Joyce, whose work seeks to condense all the past, present, and future into the fathomless, echoing interior of one night's monologue; Faulkner, whose North Mississippi county resounds with the voices of four or five continents; and Pound, who presents in the *Cantos* an attempt at something like 'pure' poetry which nevertheless consists in an echo and amplification of snatches of conversation salvaged from all over this world's history —snatches, that is, of what registered in the interiors of men and women since these interiors began that communication with one another within which we still live our conscious lives.

38 Norman O. Brown

Norman O. Brown's study of Swift, 'The Excremental Vision', is taken from his book *Life Against Death: the psychoanalytical meaning of history* (1959). As its subtitle implies, this book is not primarily a work of literary criticism, but a commentary on and a development of the ideas of Sigmund Freud (see above, pp. 35-42), especially his later work such as *Civilization and its Discontents* (1930). Freud had argued that 'civilization' was based on the repression and sublimation of erotic energy, and implied that although this process involved some loss, it was desirable, or at least inevitable. Brown, however, argues that since civilization is self-evidently neurotic and on the verge of self-destruction, man should abandon civilized values and seek the 'resurrection of the body'— a manoeuvre that might be described as turning the weapons of Nietzsche upon Freud. In Brown's view, psycho-analysis should be, not a therapy for returning deviants to a normative state of resigned frustration but a method for probing 'the universal neurosis of mankind'.

If the cultural and prophetic aspects of this position are contentious, it undoubtedly has (as 'The Excremental Vision' shows) great advantages for the psycho-analytical interpretation of literature, encouraging the critic to explain, rather than explain away, the products of a great writer's imagination.

Norman O. Brown (b. 1913) was educated at the Universities of Oxford, Chicago, and Wisconsin. Since 1946 he has been Professor of Classics at Wesleyan University. In 1966 he published *Love's Body* (New York), an extension, unconventional in form, of the ideas expressed in *Life Against Death*.

CROSS REFERENCES: 3. Freud
22. Lionel Trilling
44. R. S. Crane.

The excremental vision

Any reader of Jonathan Swift knows that in his analysis of human nature there is an emphasis on, and attitude towards, the anal function that is unique in Western literature. In mere quantity of scatological imagery he may be equalled by Rabelais and Aristophanes; but whereas for Rabelais and Aristophanes the anal function is a part of the total human being which they make us love because it is part of life, for Swift it becomes the decisive weapon in his assault on the pretensions, the pride, even the self-respect of mankind. The most scandalous pieces of Swiftian scatology are three of his later poems—*The Lady's Dressing Room, Strephon and Chloe, Cassinus and Peter*—which were all variations on the theme:

Oh ! *Caelia, Caelia, Caelia* ——.

Aldous Huxley explicates, saying, 'The monosyllabic verb, which the modesties of 1929 will not allow me to reprint, rhymes with "wits" and "fits".'[1] But even more disturbing, because more comprehensively metaphysical, is Swift's vision of man as Yahoo, and Yahoo as excrementally filthy beyond all other animals, in the fourth part of *Gulliver's Travels*. Nor is the anal theme a new feature in Swift's mature or later period; it is already adumbrated in A *Tale of a Tub*, that intoxicated overflow of youthful genius and fountainhead of the entire Swiftian apocalypse. The understanding of Swift therefore begins with the recognition that Swift's anatomy of human nature, in its entirety and at the most profound and profoundly disturbing level, can be called 'The Excremental Vision'.

'The Excremental Vision' is the title of a chapter in Middleton Murry's book (1954) on Jonathan Swift.[2] The credit for recognizing the central importance of the excremental theme in Swift belongs to Aldous Huxley. In an essay in *Do What You Will* (1929) he says, 'Swift's greatness lies in the intensity, the almost insane violence of that "hatred of the bowels" which is the essence of his misanthropy and which underlies the whole of his work.'[3] Murry deserves credit for his arresting phrase, which redirects criticism to the central problem in Swift. Aldous Huxley's essay had no effect on Quintana's book *The Mind and Art of Jonathan Swift* (1936), which perfectly illustrates the poverty of criticism designed to domesticate and housebreak this tiger of English literature. Quintana buries what he calls the 'noxious compositions' in a general discussion of Swift's last phase as a writer, saying, 'From scatology one turns with relief to the capital verses entitled *Helter Skelter, or The Hue and Cry after the Attorney's going to ride the Circuit*, which exhibits Swift's complete mastery of vigorous rhythm.' The excremental theme in the fourth part of *Gulliver's Travels* is dismissed as bad art (criticism here, as so often, functioning as a mask for moral prejudice): 'The sensationalism into which Swift falls while developing the theme of bestiality.... Had part IV been toned down, *Gulliver's Travels* would have been a finer work of art.'[4] It is reassuring to know that English literature is expounded at our leading universities by men who, like Bowdler, know how to improve the classics. The history of Swiftian criticism, like the history of psychoanalysis, shows that repression weighs more heavily on anality than on genitality. Psycho-analytical theorems on the genital function have become legitimate hypotheses in circles which will not listen to what Freud has to say about anality, or to what Swift had to say (and who yet write books on *The Mind and Art of Jonathan Swift*).

Even Huxley and Murry, though they face the problem, prove incapable of seeing what there is to see. After admitting into consciousness the unpleasant facts which previous criticism had repressed, they proceed to protect themselves and us against the disturbing impact of the excremental vision by systematic distortion, denunciation, and depreciation. It is a perfect example, in the field of literary criticism, of Freud's notion that the first way in which consciousness becomes conscious of a repressed idea is by emphatically denying it.[5] The basic device for repudiating the excremental vision is, of course, denunciation. Huxley adopts a stance of intellectual superiority—'the absurdity, the childish silliness, of this refusal to accept the universe as it is given'.[6] Murry, echoing that paradoxically conservative philosopher of sexuality, D. H. Lawrence, adopts a stance of moral superiority—'so perverse, so unnatural, so mentally diseased, so humanly *wrong*'.[7] The transparently emotional character of their reaction to Swift is then masked as a psycho-analytical diagnosis; the excremental vision is a product of insanity. Huxley speaks of the 'obsessive preoccupation with the visceral and excrementitious subject', 'to the verge of insanity', and suggests a connection between it and the 'temperamental coldness' of Swift's relations to Stella and Vanessa, implying a disturbance in the genital function.[8]

Murry's attempt to transform Huxley's suggestions into a full-dress biography is a case study in perverted argumentation. The texts of the 'noxious compositions' and the fourth part of *Gulliver* are crudely distorted, as we shall see later, so as to transform Swift's misanthropy into misogyny; then the entire excremental vision can be explained away as an attempt to justify his genital failure (with Varina, Vanessa, and Stella) by indicting the filthiness of the female sex. It is falsely insinuated that the excremental vision is restricted to Swift's latest phase. This insinuation not only has the advantage of suggesting that there is a Swiftian vision which is not excremental (on this point Huxley is more tough-minded than Murry); it has the further advantage of linking the excremental vision with Swift's final mental breakdown. The fact that the mental breakdown came ten years later (1742) will not stop anyone ignorant of psychopathology and determined to lobotomize Swift's scatology; the chronological gap is filled by an enthusiastic vision of Swift's mental breakdown as God's punishment for the scatology. The fact that the excremental theme is already prominent in the fourth part of *Gulliver* (1723) is explained away by a little psycho-analytical jargon buttressed by a little flight of historical imagination: 'Evidently the whole complex was working in Swift's mind when he wrote the fourth part of *Gulliver*.... Its emergence at that moment may have been the outcome of a deep emotional upheaval caused by the death of Vanessa.' The prominence of the same complex in the *Letter of Advice to a Young Poet* (1721), two years before the death of Vanessa, is ignored. Murry's amateur diagnosis finds the origin of the entire complex in Swift's rejection by Varina (1696). It is therefore essential to his thesis to regard A *Tale of a Tub* (1696-1698) as uninfected by the complex. Murry sustains this interpretation by averting his eyes from the prominence of anality in the *Tale* and by interpreting the whole book as wonderful tomfoolery which is not to be taken seriously—that is, by a notion of comedy which denies meaning to wit.[9]

If the duty of criticism towards Jonathan Swift is to judge him insane, criticism should be turned over to the psycho-analysts. They have risen to the occasion and have shown that they can be counted on to issue a medical certificate of insanity against genius. Their general verdict is substantially the same as that of Huxley and Murry, with the addition of some handsome new terminology. Thus Ferenczi (1926):

> From the psycho-analytical standpoint one would describe his neurotic behaviour as an inhibition of normal potency, with a lack of courage in relation to women of good character and perhaps with a lasting aggressive tendency towards women of a lower type. This insight into Swift's life surely justifies us who come after him in treating the fantasies in *Gulliver's Travels* exactly as we do the free associations of neurotic patients in analysis, especially when interpreting their dreams.[10]

Karpman (1942):

> It is submitted on the basis of such a study of *Gulliver's Travels* that Swift was a neurotic who exhibited psycho-sexual infantilism, with a particular showing of coprophilia, associated with misogyny, misanthropy, mysophilia and mysophobia.[11]

Greenacre (1955):

> One gets the impression that the anal fixation was intense and binding, and the genital demands so impaired or limited at best that there was a total retreat from genital sexuality in his early adult life, probably beginning with the unhappy relationship with Jane Waring, the first of the goddesses.[12]

In developing their diagnosis, the psycho-analysts, as might be expected, trace the origin of Swift's neurosis to his earliest childhood. If the psycho-analytical theory of the neuroses is correct, we must abandon Murry's attempt to isolate the excremental vision as a late excrescence; we must also abandon Murry's thesis (interconnected with his attempt to salvage part of Swift for respectability) that until he was rejected by her, Swift's love for Varina (Jane Waring) was 'the healthy natural love of a naturally passionate, and naturally generous nature'.[13] We shall have to return to Huxley's more tough-minded literary judgment that Swift *is* the excremental vision, and to his more tough-minded psychological judgment that Swift's sexuality was structurally abnormal from the start. And the biographical evidence, most carefully analysed by Greenacre, supplies more than enough confirmation. Swift lost his father before he was born; was kidnapped from his mother by his nurse at the age of one; was returned to his mother only three years later, only to be abandoned by his mother one month after his return to her at the psycho-analytically crucial Oedipal period.[14] By psycho-analytical standards such a succession of infantile traumata must establish more than a predisposition to lifelong neurosis.

The case, then, would appear to be closed. The psycho-analytical experts concur with the critics that Swift was mad and that his works should be read only as documents in a case history. Not just the fourth part of *Gulliver* and the 'noxious compositions' but all of Swift. For if we cry 'insane' to the objectionable parts of Swift, in all honesty we must hand the case over to the psychoanalysts. But after psycho-analytical scrutiny, there is nothing left of Swift that is not objectionable. We must not underestimate the ability of psycho-analysis to uncover the real meaning of symbols. For example, a psycho-analytical comment on Gulliver as a little man in a little boat on the island of Brobdingnag says that 'the common symbolism of the man in the boat as the clitoris suggests the identification with the female phallus thought to be characteristic of the male transvestite'. Similarly, psycho-analysis leaves the Dean's character without a shred of integrity.

> Swift showed marked anal characteristics (his extreme personal immaculateness, secretiveness, intense ambition, pleasure in less obvious dirt [sc. satire], stubborn vengefulness in righteous causes) which indicate clearly that early control of the excretory function was achieved under great stress and perhaps too early.[15]

At this point common humanity revolts. If personal immaculateness, ambition, and the championship of righteous causes are neurotic traits, who shall 'scape whipping? And certainly no genius will escape if this kind of psychoanalysis is turned loose on literary texts. Common humanity makes us turn in revulsion against Huxley, Murry, and the psycho-analysts. By what right do they issue certificates of lunacy? By virtue of their own pre-eminent sanity? Judged for sanity and truthfulness, *Gulliver's Travels* will not suffer in comparison with the works of Murry and Huxley. Only Swift could do justice to the irony of Huxley condemning Swift for misanthropic distortion in a volume of essays devoted to destroying the integrity not only of Swift, but also of St Francis and Pascal. Nor is the sanity of psycho-analysts—and their interpretations of what a man in a boat signifies—utterly beyond question. Only Swift could do justice to the irony of psycho-analysts, whose capacity for finding the anus in the most unlikely places is notorious, condemning Swift for obsessive preoccupation with anality. Fortunately Swift is not himself speechless in the face of these accusations of insanity:

> He gave the little Wealth he had
> To build a House for Fools and Mad.[16]

In Dr Swift's mental hospital there is a room for Huxley and Murry; their religious eccentricities are prefigured under the name of Jack, the prototype of religious enthusiasm in A *Tale of a Tub*. For Huxley, as for Jack, it later came to pass that 'it was for certain reported that he had run out of his Wits. In a short time after, he appeared abroad, and confirmed the Report by falling into the oddest Whimsies that ever a sick Brain conceived'.[17] Swift has also prepared a room for the psycho-analysts with their anal complex; for are they not prophetically announced as those 'certain Fortune-tellers in Northern America, who have a Way of reading a Man's Destiny, by peeping in his Breech'?[18]

The argument thus ends in a bedlamite babel filling the air with mutual accusations of madness. If we resist the temptation to stop our ears and run away, if we retain a psychiatric interest and a clinical detachment, we can only conclude that the accusations are all justified; they are all mad. And the crux of their madness is their proud insistence that everybody except themselves—Huxley, Murry, the psycho-analysts—are mad. We can only save ourselves

513

from their madness by admitting that we are all mad. Psycho-analysis deserves the severest strictures, because it should have helped mankind to develop this kind of consciousness and this kind of humility. Freud saw psycho-analysis as the third great wound, comparable to the Newtonian and Darwinian revolutions, inflicted by science on human narcissism.[19] The Epigoni of Freud have set themselves up as a proud elect exempt from the general damnation. As we have argued elsewhere, the proper aim of psycho-analysis is the diagnosis of the universal neurosis of mankind, in which psycho-analysis is itself a symptom and a stage, like any other phase in the intellectual history of mankind.

If we reorient phycho-analysis in this direction, then a different method for the application of psycho-analysis to Swift (or any other literary figure) is in order. We no longer try to explain away Swift's literary achievements as mere epiphenomena on his individual neurosis. Rather we seek to appreciate his insight into the universal neurosis of mankind. Then psycho-analysis becomes a method not for explaining away but for explicating Swift. We are not disturbed by the fact that Swift had his individual version of the universal human neurosis; we are not even disturbed by the thought that his individual neurosis may have been abnormally acute, or by the thought that his abnormality may be inseparable from his art.

Intense suffering may be necessary, though not sufficient, for the production of genius; and psycho-analysis has never thought through its position towards the age-old tradition of an affinity between genius and madness. Perhaps there is that 'necessity of doctors and nurses *who themselves are sick*' of which Nietzsche spoke.[20] Psycho-analysis is then not less necessary for the study of Swift, but more so, though in a different way. It is necessary in order to sustain the requisite posture of humility—about ourselves, about mankind, and towards genius. It is also necessary in order to take seriously the Swiftian exploration of the universal neurosis of mankind. The thesis of this chapter is that if we are willing to listen to Swift we will find startling anticipations of Freudian theorems about anality, about sublimation, and about the universal neurosis of mankind. To anticipate objections, let me say that Swiftian psycho-analysis differs from the Freudian in that the vehicle for the exploration of the unconscious is not psycho-analysis but wit. But Freud himself recognized, in *Wit and the Unconscious*, that wit has its own way of exploring the universal neurosis of mankind.

Psycho-analysis is apparently necessary in order to explicate the 'noxious compositions'; at least the unpsycho-analysed neurotic appears to be incapable of correctly stating what these poems are about. These are the poems which provoke Murry to ecstasies of revulsion—'nonsensical and intolerable', 'so perverse, so unnatural, so mentally diseased, so humanly *wrong*'. What Murry is denouncing is the proposition that woman is abominable because she is guilty of physical evacuation. We need not consider whether the proposition deserves such denunciation, for the simple reason that it comes from Murry's imagination, not Swift's. Murry, like Strephon and the other unfortunate men in the poems, loses his wits when he discovers that Caelia ——, and thus unconsciously bears witness to the truth of Swift's psychological insight. Any mind that is at all open to the antiseptic wisdom of psycho-analysis will find nothing extra-

514

ordinary about the poems, except perhaps the fact that they were written in the first half of the eighteenth century. For their real theme—quite obvious on a dispassionate reading—is the conflict between our animal body, appropriately epitomized in the anal function, and our pretentious sublimations, more specifically the pretensions of sublimated or romantic-Platonic love. In every case it is a 'goddess', 'so divine a Creature', 'heavenly Chloe', who is exposed; or rather what is exposed is the illusion in the head of the adoring male, the illusion that the goddess is all head and wings, with no bottom to betray her sublunary infirmities.

The peculiar Swiftian twist to the theme that Caelia —— is the notion that there is some absolute contradiction between the state of being in love and an awareness of the excremental function of the beloved. Before we dismiss this idea as the fantasy of a diseased mind, we had better remember that Freud said the same thing. In an essay written in 1912 surveying the disorder in the sexual life of man, he finally concludes that the deepest trouble is an unresolved ambivalence in the human attitude towards anality:[21]

> We know that at its beginning the sexual instinct is divided into a large number of components—or rather it develops from them—not all of which can be carried on into its final form; some have to be surpassed or turned to other uses before the final form results. Above all, the coprophilic elements in the instinct have proved incompatible with our aesthetic ideas, probably since the time when man developed an upright posture and so removed his organ of smell from the ground; further, a considerable proportion of the sadistic elements belonging to the erotic instinct have to be abandoned. All such developmental processes, however, relate only to the upper layers of the complicated structure. The fundamental processes which promote erotic excitation remain always the same. Excremental things are all too intimately and inseparably bound up with sexual things; the position of the genital organs—*inter urinas et faeces*—remains the decisive and unchangeable factor. The genitals themselves have not undergone the development of the rest of the human form in the direction of beauty; they have retained their animal cast; and so even today love, too, is in essence as animal as it ever was.

Again, in *Civilization and Its Discontents*, Freud pursues the thought that the deepest cause of sexual repression is an organic factor, a disbalance in the human organism between higher and lower functions:[22]

> The whole of sexuality and not merely anal erotism is threatened with falling a victim to the organic repression consequent upon man's adoption of the erect posture and the lowering in value of the sense of smell; so that since that time the sexual function has been associated with a resistance not susceptible of further explanation, which puts obstacles in the way of full satisfaction and forces it away from its sexual aim towards sublimations and displacements of libido.... All neurotics, and many others too, take exception to the fact that '*inter urinas et faeces nascimur.*'... Thus we should find, as the deepest root of the sexual repression that marches with culture, the organic defence of the new form of life that began with the erect posture.

Those who, like Middleton Murry, anathematize Swift's excremental vision

515

as unchristian might ponder the quotation from St Augustine[a] that Freud uses in both these passages.

That Swift's thought is running parallel with Freud's is demonstrated by the fact that a fuller explication of the poems would have to use the terms 'repression' and 'sublimation'. It is of course not ignorance but repression of the anal factor that creates the romantic illusions of Strephon and Cassinus and makes the breakthrough of the truth so traumatic. And Swift's ultimate horror in these poems is at the thought that sublimation—that is to say, all civilized behaviour—is a lie and cannot survive confrontation with the truth. In the first of his treatments of the theme (*The Lady's Dressing Room*, 1730) he reasons with Strephon that sublimation is still possible:

> Should I the Queen of Love refuse,
> Because she rose from stinking Ooze?

Strephon should reconcile himself to—

> Such Order from Confusion sprung,
> Such gaudy Tulips rais'd from Dung.

But in *Strephon and Chloe* (1731) sublimation and awareness of the excremental function are presented as mutually exclusive, and the conclusion is drawn that sublimation must be cultivated at all costs, even at the cost of repression:

> Authorities both old and recent
> Direct that Women must be decent:
> And, from the Spouse each Blemish hide
> More than from all the World beside...
> On Sense and Wit your Passion found,
> By Decency cemented round.

In *Cassinus and Peter*, the last of these poems, even this solution is exploded. The life of civilized sublimation, epitomized in the word 'wit', is shattered because the excremental vision cannot be repressed. The poem tells of two undergraduates—

> Two College Sophs of *Cambridge* growth
> Both special Wits, and Lovers both—

and Cassinus explains the trauma which is killing him:

> Nor wonder how I lost my Wits;
> Oh! *Caelia, Caelia Caelia* sh—.

That blessed race of horses, the Houyhnhnms, are free from the illusions of romantic-Platonic love, or rather they are free from love.

> Courtship, Love, Presents, Joyntures, Settlements, have no place in their thoughts; or Terms whereby to express them in their Language. The young Couple meet and are joined, merely because it is the Determination of their Parents and Friends: it is what they see done every Day; and they look upon it as one of the necessary Actions in a reasonable Being.[23]

[a] i.e. *inter urinas et faeces nascimur*—'we are born between urine and faeces'.

If the Houyhnhnms represent a critique of the genital function and genital institutions of mankind, the Yahoos represent a critique of the anal function.

The Yahoos represent the raw core of human bestiality; but the essence of Swift's vision and Gulliver's redemption is the recognition that the civilized man of Western Europe not only remains Yahoo but is worse than Yahoo—'a sort of Animals to whose Share, by what Accident he could not conjecture, some small Pittance of *Reason* had fallen, whereof we made no other use than by its Assistance to aggravate our *natural* Corruptions, and to acquire new ones which Nature had not given us'. And the essence of the Yahoo is filthiness, a filthiness distinguishing them not from Western European man but from all other animals: 'Another Thing he wondered at in the *Yahoos*, was their strange Disposition to Nastiness and Dirt; whereas there appears to be a natural Love of Cleanliness in all other Animals.' The Yahoo is physically endowed with a very rank smell—'the Stink was somewhat between a *Weasel* and a *Fox*'—which, heightened at mating time, is a positive attraction to the male of the species. The recognition of the rank odour of humanity stays with Gulliver after his return to England: 'During the first Year I could not endure my Wife or Children in my Presence, the very Smell of them was intolerable'; when he walked the street, he kept his nose 'well stopt with Rue, Lavender, or Tobacco-leaves'. The Yahoo eating habits are equally filthy: 'There was nothing that rendered the *Yahoos* more odious, than their undistinguishing Appetite to devour everything that came in their Way, whether Herbs, Roots, Berries, corrupted Flesh of Animals, or all mingled together.'

But above all the Yahoos are distinguished from other animals by their attitude towards their own excrement. Excrement to the Yahoos is no mere waste product but a magic instrument for self-expression and aggression. This attitude begins in infancy: 'While I held the odious Vermin in my Hands, it voided its filthy Excrements of a yellow liquid Substance, all over my Cloaths.' It continues in adulthood. 'Several of this cursed Brood getting hold of the Branches behind, leaped up into the Tree, from whence they began to discharge their Excrements on my Head.' It is part of the Yahoo ritual symbolizing the renewal of society: when the old leader of the herd is discarded, 'his Successor, at the Head of all the *Yahoos* in that District, Young and Old, Male and Female, come in a Body, and discharge their Excrements upon him from Head to Foot'. Consequently, in the Yahoo system of social infeudation, 'this *Leader* had usually a Favourite as *like himself* as he could get, whose Employment was to *lick his Master's Feet and Posteriors, and drive the Female* Yahoos *to his Kennel'*. This recognition that the human animal is distinguished from others as the distinctively excremental animal stays with Gulliver after his return to England, so that he finds relief from the oppressive smell of mankind in the company of his groom: 'For I feel my Spirits revived by the Smell he contracts in the Stable.' Swift does not, as Huxley says he does, hate the bowels, but only the human use of the bowels.[24]

This demonic presentation of the excremental nature of humanity is the great stumbling block in *Gulliver's Travels*—an aesthetic lapse, crude sensationalism, says Quintana; a false libel on humanity, says Middleton Murry, 'for even if we carry the process of stripping the human to the limit of imaginative possibility, we do not arrive at the Yahoo. We might arrive at his cruelty and malice; we should never arrive at his nastiness and filth. That is a gratuitous degredation of humanity; not a salutary, but a shocking one'.[25] But if we measure Swift's correctness not by the conventional and complacent prejudices in favour of human pride which are back of Quintana's and Murry's strictures, but by the ruthless wisdom of psycho-analysis, then it is quite obvious that the excremental vision of the Yahoo is substantially identical with the psycho-analytical doctrine of the extensive role of anal erotism in the formation of human culture.

According to Freudian theory the human infant passes through a stage—the anal stage—as a result of which the libido, the life energy of the body, gets concentrated in the anal zone. This infantile stage of anal erotism takes the essential form of attaching symbolic meaning to the anal product. As a result of these symbolic equations the anal product acquires for the child the significance of being his own child or creation, which he may use either to obtain narcissistic pleasure in play, or to obtain love from another (faeces as gift), or to assert independence from another (faeces as property), or to commit aggression against another (faeces as weapon). Thus some of the most important categories of social behaviour (play, gift, property, weapon) originate in the anal stage of infantile sexuality and—what is more important—never lose their connection with it. When infantile sexuality comes to its catastrophic end, non-bodily cultural objects inherit the symbolism originally attached to the anal product, but only as second-best substitutes for the original (sublimation). Sublimations are thus symbols of symbols. The category of property is not simply transferred from faeces to money; on the contrary, money is faeces, because the anal erotism continues in the unconscious. The anal erotism has not been renounced or abandoned but repressed.[26]

One of the central ambiguities in psycho-analytical theory is the question of whether the pregenital infantile organizations of the libido, including the anal organization, are biologically determined. We have elsewhere taken the position that they are not biologically determined but are constructed by the human ego, or rather that they represent that distortion of the human body which *is* the human ego. If so, then psycho-analysis concurs with Swift's thesis that anal erotism—in Swift's language, 'a strange Disposition to Nastiness and Dirt'—is a specifically human privilege; on the other hand, psycho-analysis would differ from Swift's implication that the strange Disposition to Nastiness and Dirt is biologically given. It comes to the same thing to say that Swift errs in giving the Yahoos no 'Pittance of Reason' and in assigning to Reason only the transformation of the Yahoo into the civilized man of Western Europe. If anal organization is constructed by the human ego, then the strange Disposition to Nastiness and Dirt is a primal or infantile manifestation of human Reason. Swift also anticipates Freud in emphasizing the connection between anal erotism and human aggression. The Yahoos' filthiness is manifested primarily in excremental aggression: psycho-analytical theory stresses the interconnection between anal organization and human aggression to the point of labelling this phase of infantile sexuality the anal-sadistic phase. Defiance, mastery, will to power are attributes of human reason first developed in the symbolic manipulation of excrement and perpetuated in the symbolic manipulation of symbolic substitutes for excrement.

The psycho-analytical theory of anal erotism depends on the psycho-analytical theory of sublimation. If money, etc., are not faeces, there is not much reason for hypothesizing a strange human fascination with excrement. By the same token it is hard to see how Swift could have come by his anticipation of the doctrine of anal erotism if he did not also anticipate the doctrine of sublimation. But Swift did anticipate the doctrine of sublimation. Full credit for perceiving this goes to William Empson. Referring to A *Tale of a Tub* and its appendix, *The Mechanical Operation of the Spirit*, Empson writes: [27]

> It is the same machinery, in the fearful case of Swift, that betrays not consciousness of the audience but a doubt of which he may himself have been unconscious. 'Everything spiritual and vulnerable has a gross and revolting parody, very similar to it, with the same name. Only unremitting judgment can distinguish between them'; he set out to simplify the work of judgment by giving a complete set of obscene puns for it. The conscious aim was the defence of the Established Church against the reformers' Inner Light; only the psycho-analyst can wholly applaud the result. Mixed with his statement, part of what he satirized by pretending (too convincingly) to believe, the source of his horror, was 'everything spiritual is really material; Hobbes and the scientists have proved this; all religion is really a perversion of sexuality'.

The source of Swift's horror, according to Empson, is the discovery of that relation between higher and lower, spiritual and physical, which psycho-analysis calls sublimation. Swift hit upon the doctrine of sublimation as a new method for the psychological analysis of religion, specifically religious enthusiasm. His new method sees religious enthusiasm as the effect of what he calls the 'Mechanical Operation of the Spirit'. At the outset he distinguishes his psychology of religion from traditional naturalistic psychology, which treats religious enthusiasm as 'the Product of Natural Causes, the effect of strong Imagination, Spleen, violent Anger, Fear, Grief, Pain, and the like'. If you want a distinctive label for Swift's new psychology of religion, it can only be called psycho-analysis. The first step is to define religious enthusiasm as 'a lifting up of the Soul or its Faculties above Matter'. Swift then proceeds to the fundamental proposition that 'the Corruption of the Senses is the Generation of the Spirit'. By corruption of the senses Swift means repression, as is quite clear from his explanation.[28]

> Because the Senses in Men are so many Avenues to the Fort of Reason, which in this Operation is wholly block'd up. All Endeavours must be therefore used, either to divert, bind up, stupify, fluster, and amuse the Senses, or else to justle them out of their Stations; and while they are either absent, or otherwise employ'd or engaged in a Civil War against each other, the Spirit enters and performs its Part.

The doctrine that repression is the cause of sublimation is vividly implied in the analogy which Swift sets up for the 'Mechanical Operation of the Spirit': [29]

Among our Ancestors, the Scythians, there was a Nation, call'd Longheads, which at first began by a Custom among Midwives and Nurses, of molding, and squeezing, and bracing up the Heads of Infants; by which means, Nature shut out at one Passage, was forc'd to seek another, and finding room above, shot upwards, in the Form of a Sugar-Loaf.

Swift affirms not only that the spirit is generated by repression of bodily sensuousness, but also, as is implied by the analogy of the Scythian Longheads, that the basic structure of sublimation is, to use the psycho-analytical formula, displacement from below upward. Displacement from below upward, conferring on the upper region of the body a symbolic identity with the lower region of the body, is Swift's explanation for the Puritan cult of large ears: the ear is a symbolic penis. According to psycho-analysis, displacement of the genital function to another organ is the basic pattern in conversion hysteria. 'Conversion hysteria genitalizes those parts of the body at which the symptoms are manifested'; maidenly blushing, for example, is a mild case of conversion hysteria— that is, a mild erection of the entire head.[30] According to Swift's analysis of the Puritans, 'The Proportion of largeness, was not only lookt upon as an Ornament of the Outward Man, but as a Type of Grace in the Inward. Besides, it is held by Naturalists, that if there be a Protuberancy of Part in the *Superiour* Region of the Body, as in the Ears and Nose, there must be a Parity also in the *Inferior.*' Hence, says Swift, the devouter Sisters 'lookt upon all such extraordinary Dilatations of that Member, as Protrusions of Zeal, or spiritual Excrescencies' and also 'in hopes of conceiving a suitable Offspring by such a Prospect'.[31] By this road Swift arrives at Freud's theorem on the identity of what is highest and lowest in human nature. In Freud's language: 'Thus it is that what belongs to the lowest depths in the minds of each one of us is changed, through this formation of the ideal, into what we value highest in the human soul.'[32] In Swift's language:[33]

Whereas the mind of Man, when he gives the Spur and Bridle to his Thoughts, doth never stop, but naturally sallies out into both extreams of High and Low, of Good and Evil; His first Flight of Fancy, commonly transports Him to Ideas of what is most Perfect, finished and exalted; till having soared out of his own Reach and Sight, not well perceiving how near the Frontiers of Height and Depth, border upon each other; With the same Course and Wing, he falls down plum into the lowest Bottom of Things; like one who travels the *East* into the *West*; or like a strait Line drawn by its own Length into a Circle.

Such is the demonic energy with which Swift pursues his vision that twice, once in A *Tale of a Tub* and once in *The Mechanical Operation of the Spirit*, he arrives at the notion of the unity of those opposites of all opposites, God and the Devil. Men,

pretending ... to extend the Dominion of one Invisible Power, and contract that of the other, have discovered a gross Ignorance in the Natures of Good and Evil, and most horribly confounded the Frontiers of both. After Men have lifted up the Throne of their Divinity to the *Coelum Empyraeum;* ... after they have sunk their *Principle* of *Evil* to the lowest Centre ... I laugh

520

aloud, to see these Reasoners, at the same time, engaged in wise Dispute, about certain walks and Purlieus, whether they are in the Verge of God or the Devil, seriously debating, whether such and such Influences come into Men's Minds, from above or below, or whether certain Passions and Affections are guided by the Evil Spirit or the Good.... Thus do Men establish a Fellowship of Christ with Belial, and such is the Analogy they make between *cloven Tongues*, and *cloven Feet*.[34]

Empson has shown how and by what law of irony the partially disclaimed thought is Swift's own thought.

As we have argued elsewhere, psycho-analysis finds far-reaching resemblances between a sublimation and a neurotic symptom. Both presuppose repression; both involve a displacement resulting from the repression of libido from the primary erogenous zones. Thus the psycho-analytic theory of sublimation leads on to the theory of the universal neurosis of mankind. In the words of Freud:[35]

The neuroses exhibit on the one hand striking and far-reaching points of agreement with ... art, religion and philosophy. But on the other hand they seem like distortions of them. It might be maintained that a case of hysteria is a caricature of a work of art, that an obsessional neurosis is a caricature of religion and that a paranoic delusion is a caricature of a philosophical system.

Swift develops his doctrine of the universal neurosis of mankind in the 'Digression concerning the Original, the Use and Improvement of Madness in a Commonwealth', in A *Tale of a Tub*. Here Swift attributes to Madness 'the greatest Actions that have been performed in the World, under the Influence of Single Men; which are, *the Establishment of New Empires by Conquest: the Advance and Progress of New Schemes in Philosophy; and the contriving, as well as the propagating of New Religion'*. Psycho-analysis must regret the omission of art, but applaud the addition of politics, to Freud's original list; Freud himself added politics in his later writings. And Swift deduces the universal neurosis of mankind from his notion of sublimation; in his words:

For the *upper Region* of Man, is furnished like the *middle Region* of the Air; The Materials are formed from Causes of the widest Difference, yet produce at last the same Substance and Effect. Mists arise from the Earth, Steams from Dunghils, Exhalations from the Sea, and Smoak from Fire; yet all Clouds are the same in Composition, as well as Consequences: and the Fumes issuing from a Jakes, will furnish as comely and useful a Vapour, as Incense from an Altar. Thus far, I suppose, will easily be granted me; and then it will follow, that as the Face of Nature never produces Rain, but when it is overcast and disturbed, so Human Understanding, seated in the Brain, must be troubled and overspread by vapours, ascending from the lower Faculties, to water the Invention, and render it fruitful.

After a witty review of kings, philosophers, and religious fanatics Swift concludes: 'If the *Moderns* mean by *Madness*, only a Disturbance or Transposition of the Brain, by force of certain *Vapours* issuing up from the lower Faculties; then has this *Madness* been the Parent of all these mighty Revolutions, that have happened in *Empire*, in *Philosophy*, and in *Religion*.' And Swift Ends the

Digression on Madness with a humility and consistency psycho-analysis has never known, by applying his own doctrine to himself:[36]

> Even I myself, the Author of these momentous Truths, am a Person, whose Imaginations are hard-mouthed, and exceedingly disposed to run away with his *Reason*, which I have observed from long Experience to be a very light Rider, and easily shook off; upon which account, my Friends will never trust me alone, without a solemn Promise, to vent my Speculations in this, or the like manner, for the universal Benefit of Human kind.

Swift, as we have seen, sees in sublimation, or at least certain kinds of sublimation, a displacement upward of the genital function. So much was implied in his attribution of genital significance to the Puritans' large ears. He makes a similar, only more elaborately obscene, derivation of the nasal twang of Puritan preachers. He also speaks of 'certain Sanguine Brethren of the first Class', that 'in the Height and *Orgasmus* of their Spiritual exercise it has been frequent with them *****; immediately after which they found the *Spirit* to relax and flag of a sudden with the Nerves, and they were forced to hasten to a Conclusion'. Swift explains all these phenomena with his notion of sublimation:[37]

> The Seed or Principle, which has ever put Men upon *Visions* in Things *Invisible*, is of a corporeal Nature. . . . The Spinal Marrow, being nothing else but a Continuation of the Brain, must needs create a very free Communication between the Superior Faculties and those below: And thus the *Thorn in the Flesh* serves for a *Spur* to the *Spirit*.

Not only the genital function but also the anal function is displaced upward, according to Swift. The general theorem is already stated in the comparison of the upper Region of Man to the middle Region of the Air, in which 'the Fumes issuing from a Jakes, will furnish as comely and useful a Vapour, as Incense from an Altar'.[38] The idea is developed in the image of religious enthusiasts as Aeolists, or worshippers of wind. Swift is here punning on the word 'spirit', and as Empson says, 'The language plays into his hands here, because the spiritual words are all derived from physical metaphors'.[39] Psycho-analysis, of course, must regard language as a repository of the psychic history of mankind, and the exploration of words, by wit or poetry or scientific etymology, as one of the avenues into the unconscious.[40] At any rate, Swift's wit, pursuing his 'Physicological Scheme' for satirical anatomy, 'dissecting the Carcass of Human Nature',[41] asks where all this windy preaching comes from, and his answer gives all the emphasis of obscenity to the anal factor:[42]

> At other times were to be seen several Hundreds link'd together in a circular Chain, with every Man a Pair of Bellows applied to his Neighbour's Breech, by which they blew up each other to the Shape and Size of a *Tun*; and for that Reason, with great Propriety of Speech, did usually call their Bodies, their *Vessels*. When by these and the like Performances, they were grown sufficiently replete, they would immediately depart, and disembogue for the Public Good, a plentiful Share of their Acquirements into their Disciples Chaps.

Another method of inspiration involves a Barrel instead of a Bellows:

> Into this *Barrel*, upon Solemn Days, the Priest enters; where, having before

duly prepared himself by the methods already described, a secret Funnel is also convey'd from his Posteriors, to the Bottom of the Barrel, which admits of new Supplies of Inspiration from a *Northern* Chink or Crany. Whereupon, you behold him swell immediately to the Shape and Size of his *Vessel*. In this posture he disembogues whole Tempests upon his Auditory, as the Spirit from beneath gives his Utterance; which issuing *ex adytis*, and *penetralibus*, is not performed without much Pain and Gripings.

Nor is Swift's vision of sublimated anality limited to religious preaching or *A Tale of a Tub*. In *Strephon and Chloe* the malicious gossip of women is so explained:

> You'd think she utter'd from behind
> Or at her Mouth were breaking Wind.

And more generally, as Greenacre observes, there is throughout Swift 'a kind of linking of the written or printed word with the excretory functions'.[43] When Swift writes in a letter to Arbuthnot, 'Let my anger break out at the end of my pen',[44] the psycho-analytically uninitiated may doubt the psycho-analytical interpretation. But Swift makes references to literary polemics (his own literary form) as dirt-throwing (compare the Yahoos). More generally he meditates that 'mortal man is a broomstick', which 'raiseth a mighty Dust where there was none before; sharing deeply all the while in the very same Pollutions he pretends to sweep away'.[45] In the *Letter of Advice to a Young Poet*, he advocates the concentration of writers in a Grub Street, so that the whole town be saved from becoming a sewer: 'When writers of all sizes, like freemen of cities, are at liberty to throw out their filth and excrementitious productions, in every street as they please, what can the consequence be, but that the town must be poisoned and become such another jakes, as by report of great travellers, Edinburgh is at night.'[46] This train of thought is so characteristically Swift's that in the *Memoirs of Martinus Scriblerus*, now thought to have been written by Pope after talks with Arbuthnot and Swift, the story of Scriblerus' birth must be an inspiration of Swift's:

> Nor was the birth of this great man unattended with prodigies: he himself has often told me, that on the night before he was born, Mrs Scriblerus dreamed she was brought to bed of a huge ink-horn, out of which issued several large streams of ink, as it had been a fountain. This dream was by her husband thought to signify that the child should prove a very voluminous writer.[47]

Even the uninitiated will recognize the fantasy, discovered by psycho-analysis, of anal birth.

It would be wearisome to rehearse the parallels to Swift in psycho-analytical literature. The psycho-analysts, alas, think they can dispense with wit in the exploration of the unconscious. Fenichel in his encyclopedia of psycho-analytical orthodoxy refers to the 'anal-erotic nature of speech' without intending to be funny.[48] Perhaps it will suffice to quote from Ferenczi's essay on the proverb 'Silence is golden' (for Ferenczi the proverb itself is one more piece of evidence on the anal character of speech):[49]

That there are certain connections between anal erotism and speech I had already learnt from Professor Freud, who told me of a stammerer all whose singularities of speech were to be traced to anal fantasies. Jones too has repeatedly indicated in his writings the displacement of libido from anal activities to phonation. Finally I too, in an earlier article ('On Obscene Words') was able to indicate the connection between musical voice-culture and anal erotism.

Altogether Ernest Jones' essay on 'Anal-Erotic Character Traits'[50] leaves us with the impression that there is no aspect of higher culture uncontaminated by connections with anality. And Swift leaves us with the same impression. Swift even anticipates the psycho-analytical theorem that an anal sublimation can be decomposed into simple anality. He tells the story of a furious conqueror who left off his conquering career when 'the *Vapour* or *Spirit*, which animated the Hero's Brain, being in perpetual Circulation, seized upon that Region of the Human Body, so renown'd for furnishing the *Zibeta Occidentalis*[a], and gathering there into a Tumor, left the rest of the World for that Time in Peace'.[51]

The anal character of civilization is a topic which requires sociological and historical as well as psychological treatment. Swift turns to the sociology and history of anality in a poem called *A Panegyrick on the Dean*. The poem is written as if by Lady Acheson, the lady of the house at Market Hill where Swift stayed in 1729-30. In the form of ironic praise, it describes Swift's various roles at Market Hill, as Dean, as conversationalist with the ladies, as Butler fetching a bottle from the cellar, as Dairymaid churning Butter. But the Dean's greatest achievement at Market Hill was the construction of 'Two Temples of magnifick Size,' where—

> In sep'rate Cells the He's and She's
> Here pay their vows with *bended Knees*,

to the 'gentle Goddess *Cloacine*'. As he built the two out-houses, Swift seems to have meditated on the question of why we are ashamed of and repress the anal function :

> Thee bounteous Goddess *Cloacine*,
> To Temples why do we confine?

The answer he proposes is that shame and repression of anality did not exist in the age of innocence (here again we see how far wrong Huxley's notion of Swift's 'hatred of the bowels' is) :

> When *Saturn* ruled the Skies alone
> That *golden* Age, to *Gold* unknown;
> This earthly Globe to thee assign'd
> Receiv'd the Gifts of all Mankind.

After the fall—the usurpation of Jove—came '*Gluttony* with greasy Paws', with her offspring 'lolling *Sloth*', '*Pale Dropsy*', 'lordly *Gout*', 'wheezing *Asthma*', 'voluptuous *Ease*, the Child of *Wealth*'—

---

[a] Literally, 'Western Civet'. Civet is a substance, used in perfumery, which is extracted from a gland in the anal pouch of the oriental species of the civet cat. *Zibeta Occidentalis* is therefore a Swiftian periphrasis for human faeces.

> This bloated Harpy sprung from Hell
> Confin'd Thee Goddess to a Cell.

The corruption of the human body corrupted the anal function and alienated the natural Cloacine:

> ... unsav'ry Vapours rose,
> Offensive to thy nicer Nose.

The correlative doctrine in psycho-analysis is of course the equation of money and faeces. Swift is carried by the logic of the myth (myth, like wit, reaches into the unconscious) to make the same equation: the age of innocence, 'the *golden* Age, to *Gold* unknown', had another kind of gold. The golden age still survives among the Swains of Northern Ireland—

> Whose Off'rings plac't in golden Ranks,
> Adorn our Chrystal River's Banks.

But the perspectives now opening up are too vast for Swift, or for us:

> But, stop ambitious Muse, in time;
> Nor dwell on Subjects too sublime.

Notes

The following abbreviations are used for Freud's works:

CP *Collected Papers*, ed. J. Riviere and J. Strachey (London & New York, 1924-50).
Civ *Civilization and Its Discontents*, tr. J. Riviere (1930).
EI *The Ego and the Id*, tr. J. Riviere (1927).
GI *A General Introduction to Psychoanalysis*, tr. J. Riviere (New York, 1953).

1. Huxley, *Do What You Will* (1931), p. 94.
2. Murry, *Jonathan Swift* (1954), pp. 432–48.
3. Huxley, op. cit., p. 99.
4. Quintana, *The Mind and Art of Jonathan Swift* (1936), pp. 327, 360.
5. CP v, 182.
6. Huxley, op. cit., p. 101.
7. Murry, op. cit., p. 440; Lawrence, *Sex, Literature and Censorship* (New York, 1953), p. 60.
8. Huxley, op. cit., pp. 94, 104.
9. Murry, op. cit., pp. 78–82, 86, 346–55, 432–48.
10. Ferenczi, *Final Contributions to the Problems and Methods of Psycho-analysis* (1955), p. 59.
11. Karpman, 'Neurotic Traits of Jonathan Swift', *Psychoanalytic Review*, xxix (1942), p. 132.
12. Greenacre, 'The Mutual Adventures of Jonathan Swift and Lemuel Gulliver', *Psychoanalytic Quarterly*, xxiv (1955), p. 60.
13. Murry, op. cit., p. 60.
14. Greenacre, op. cit., pp. 21–2.
15. Greenacre, op. cit., pp. 41, 56.
16. Swift, *Verses on the Death of Dr. Swift*, vss. 479–80.
17. Swift, *A Tale of a Tub*, in *Prose Works of Jonathan Swift* (Oxford, 1939), i, 88.
18. Swift, *A Discourse Concerning the Mechanical Operation of the Spirit, Etc.*, in *Prose Works of Jonathan Swift* (Oxford, 1939), i, 186.
19. CP iv, 351–5.

20. Nietzsche, *The Philosophy of Nietzsche*, p. 752.
21. CP iv, 215.
22. *Civ.* 78n.
23. Swift, *Gulliver's Travels*, in *Prose Works of Jonathan Swift* (Oxford, 1941), xi, 253.
24. *Gulliver's Travels*, pp. 243, 245–7, 250, 272–4.
25. Murry, op. cit., p. 352; Quintana, op. cit., p. 327.
26. CP ii, 45–50, 164–71; Jones, *Papers on Psycho-Analysis* (1918), pp. 664–88; Abraham, *Selected Papers on Psychoanalysis* (New York, 1953), pp. 370–92.
27. Empson, *Some Versions of Pastoral* (1935), p. 60.
28. Swift, *Mechanical Operation of the Spirit*, pp. 174–6.
29. Swift, *Mechanical Operation of the Spirit*, p. 175.
30. Ferenczi, *Further Contributions*, p. 90; Ferenczi, *Thalassa* (New York, 1938), p. 14.
31. Swift, *Tale of a Tub*, p. 129.
32. EI 48.
33. Swift, *A Tale of a Tub*, p. 99.
34. Swift, *Mechanical Operation of the Spirit*, pp. 179–80. Cf. Swift, *A Tale of a Tub*, pp. 99–100.
35. Works (T & T), xiii, 73.
36. Swift, *A Tale of a Tub*, pp. 102–3, 107–8, 114.
37. Swift, *Mechanical Operation of the Spirit*, pp. 184–5, 188–9.
38. Swift, *A Tale of a Tub*, p. 102.
39. Empson, op. cit., p. 60.
40. GI 166, 174–75; CP iv, 184–91.
41. Swift, *A Tale of a Tub*, pp. 37, 77.
42. Swift, *A Tale of a Tub*, pp. 96, 98.
43. Greenacre, op. cit., p. 56.
44. Cf. Greenacre, op. cit., p. 56.
45. Swift, *A Tale of a Tub*, pp. 5, 63, 116; Swift, *A Meditation upon a Broomstick*, in *Prose Works of Jonathan Swift* (Oxford, 1939), i, 239–40.
46. Swift, *Letter of Advice to a Young Poet*, in *Prose Works of Jonathan Swift* (London, 1907), xi, 108.
47. Pope, *Works*, x, 281.
48. Fenichel, *The Psychoanalytic Theory of Neurosis* (New York, 1945), p. 312.
49. Ferenczi, *Further Contributions*, p. 251.
50. See above, note 26.
51. Swift, *A Tale of a Tub*, p. 104.

39   Ian Watt

Ian Watt (b. 1917) is probably best known as the author of *The Rise of the Novel: studies in Defoe, Richardson and Fielding* (1957), a book which is not only essential reading for students of the eighteenth-century novel, but also an important statement about the generic character of the novel form. According to Watt, it was the novel's formal realism that made it truly 'novel' (in relation to earlier narrative literature) and this in turn was a reflection of vast changes in society, economics, religion and philosophy in the seventeenth and eighteenth centuries. The essay on Henry James's *The Ambassadors* reprinted here contrasts with *The Rise of the Novel* in both scope and method: instead of the broad-ranging discussion of literature and its contexts, we have a close scrutiny of a single paragraph. Yet the results are no less illuminating. Ian Watt's article has the further interest and value of beginning with an excellent concise account of modern stylistic criticism, and the differences between the English and Continental traditions in this field.

Ian Watt was educated at Cambridge University. His research on the eighteenth-century novel was interrupted by World War II, most of which he spent as a prisoner of war in the Far East. Since the War he has taught at Cambridge, Berkeley, and East Anglia and is now Professor of English at Stanford University, California. 'The First Paragraph of *The Ambassadors*: an explication' was originally a conference paper, and when first published in *Essays in Criticism* in 1960 carried the following note by the author:

A paper given at the Ninth Annual Conference of Non-Professorial University Teachers of English at Oxford on 5 April 1959. I am very grateful for the many criticisms and suggestions made in the course of the subsequent discussion: in preparing the paper for publication I have taken as much account of them as was possible, short of drastic expansion or alteration. I also acknowledge my debt to Dorothea Krook, Frederick C. Crews, and Henry Nash Smith.

For a synopsis of *The Ambassadors* see the introductory note on Henry James, pp. 43-4 above.

CROSS REFERENCES: 4. Henry James
                     9. I. A. Richards
                     11. E. M. Forster
                     25. Erich Auerbach
                     29. Mark Schorer
                     42. Wayne Booth

COMMENTARY :   David Lodge, 'Strether by the River', in *Language of Fiction* (1966)
Ian Watt, 'Serious reflections on *The Rise of the Novel*', *Novel* i (1968), 205-18

The first paragraph of *The Ambassadors*: an explication

When I was asked if I would do a piece of explication at this conference, I was deep in Henry James, and beginning *The Ambassadors*: so the passage chose itself; but just what was explication, and how did one do it to prose? I take it that whereas explanation, from *explanare*, suggests a mere making plain by spreading out, explication, from *explicare*, implies a progressive unfolding of a series of literary implications, and thus partakes of our modern preference for multiplicity in method and meaning: explanation assumes an ultimate simplicity, explication assumes complexity.

Historically, the most systematic tradition of explication is presumably that which developed out of medieval textual exegesis and became the chief method of literary instruction in French secondary and higher education in the late nineteenth century. *Explication de texte* in France reflects the rationalism of nineteenth-century Positivist scholarship. At its worst the routine application of the method resembles a sort of bayonet drill in which the exposed body of literature is riddled with etymologies and dates before being despatched in a harrowingly insensitive *résumé*. At its best, however, *explication de texte* can be solidly illuminating, and it then serves to remind us that a piece of literature is not necessarily violated if we give systematic attention to such matters as its author, its historical setting, and the formal properties of its language.

Practical Criticism, on the other hand, as it was developed at Cambridge by I. A. Richards,[a] continues the tradition of the British Empiricists. Inductive rather than deductive, it makes a point of excluding linguistic and historical considerations, so as to derive—in appearance at least—all the literary values of a work empirically from the words on the page. In the last thirty years the emphasis of Practical Criticism on the autonomy of the text has revolutionized the approach to literary studies, and has proved itself a technique of supreme value for teaching and examining students; I myself certainly believe that its use should be expanded rather than curtailed. Yet, at least in the form in which

[a] See above, p. 105.

I picked it up as a student and have later attempted to pass it on as a teacher, both its pedagogical effects and its basic methodological assumptions seem to me to be open to serious question. For many reasons. Its air of objectivity confers a spurious authority on a process that is often only a rationalization of an un-examined judgment, and that must always be to some extent subjective; its exclusion of historical factors seems to authorize a more general anti-historicism; and—though this objection is perhaps less generally accepted—it contains an inherent critical bias in the assumption that the part is a complete enough reflection of the literary whole to be profitably appreciated and discussed in isolation from its context. How far this is true, or how far it can be made to appear so by a well-primed practitioner, is a matter of opinion; but it is surely demonstrable that Practical Criticism tends to find the most merit in the kind of writing which has virtues that are in some way separable from their larger context; it favours kinds of writing that are richly concrete in themselves, stylistically brilliant, or composed in relatively small units. It is therefore better suited to verse than to prose; and better suited to certain kinds of either than to others where different and less concentrated merits are appropriate, as in the novel.

As for its pedagogical effects—and here again I have mainly my own past experience in mind—Practical Criticism surely tends to sensitize us towards objects only within a certain range of magnitude: below that threshold it becomes subjective and impressionist, paying very little attention to the humble facts of the grammar and syntax of the words on the page; while, at the other extreme, it often ignores the larger meaning, and the literary and historical contexts of that meaning.

As a practical matter these restrictions may all be necessary for the pupil and salutary for the teacher; and I mention them mainly to justify my present attempt to develop the empirical and inductive methods of Practical Criticism in such a way as to deal with those elements in a literary text whose vibrations are so high or so low that we Ricardian dogs have not yet been trained to bark at them.

It is mainly in these penumbral areas, of course, that the French *explication de texte* habitually operates; but its analysis of grammar and of the literary and historical background are usually a disconnected series of discrete demonstrations which stop short of the unifying critical synthesis that one hopes for. Until fairly recently the same could have been said, and perhaps with greater emphasis, about the German tradition of literary scholarship, with its almost entirely independent pursuit of philology and philosophy. More recent trends in *Stilforschung* [style studies] however—of which Wolfgang Clemen's *The Development of Shakespeare's Imagery* (Bonn, 1936) was an early example—come closer to, and indeed partly reflect, the more empirical Anglo-American models of literary criticism; while, even more promising perhaps for the study of prose, though seemingly quite independent of the influence of Practical Criticism, is the development, mainly from Romance philology, of what has come to be called 'stylistics'.

For my purposes, however, it remains not so much a method as a small group of isolated, though spectacular, individual triumphs. I yield to no one in my admiration for Leo Spitzer's *Linguistics and Literary History* (Baltimore, 1948), or for the continual excitement and illumination offered in Erich Auerbach's *Mimesis*[a] (1946: trans. Willard Trask, 1953); their achievements, however, strike me mainly as tributes to the historical imagination and philosophical understanding of the German mind at its best; I find their brilliant commentaries on words or phrases or passages essentially subjective; and if I am tempted to emulate the *bravura* with which they take off from the word on the page to leap into the farthest empyreans of *Kulturgeschichte* [cultural history], I soon discover that the Cambridge east winds have condemned me to less giddy modes of critical transport.

Yet what other models are there to help one to analyse a paragraph of Jamesian prose? Some of the historical studies of prose style could, conceivably, be applied; but I am fearful of ending up with the proposition that James was a Ciceronian—with Senecan elements, of course, like everyone else. As for the new linguistics, the promises as regards literary analysis seem greater than the present rewards: the most practical consequence of my exposure to Charles Fries's *The Structure of English: An Introduction to the Construction of English Sentences* (1952), for example, was to deprive me of the innocent pleasure that comes from imagining you know the names of things. Structural linguistics in general is mainly (and rightly) concerned with problems of definition and description at a considerably more basic level of linguistic usage than the analysis of the literary effect of Henry James's grammatical particularities seems to require.

Perhaps the most promising signs of the gaps being filled have come from what are—in that particular area—amateurs: from Francis Berry's *Poet's Grammar* (1958), or Donald Davie's *Articulate Energy* (1955). But they don't help much with prose, of course, and they aren't basically concerned with grammatical structure in the ordinary sense; although Davie's notion that the principle of continuity in poetry is, after all, primarily grammatical and rational, at least lessens the separation between the stylistic domains of poetry and prose, and suggests some ways of studying how syntax channels expressive force.

Virtually helpless,[1] then, I must face the James passage alone as far as any fully developed and acceptable technique for explicating prose is concerned; but there seem to be good reasons why practical criticism should be supplemented by some of the approaches of French and German scholarship, and by whatever else will lead one from the words on the page to matters as low as syntax and as high as ideas, or the total literary structure.

I

Strether's first question, when he reached the hotel, was about his friend; yet on his learning that Waymarsh was apparently not to arrive till evening he was not wholly disconcerted. A telegram from him bespeaking a room 'only if not noisy', reply paid, was produced for the inquirer at the office,

[a] See above, pp. 315-32.

5 so that the understanding they should meet at Chester rather than at
Liverpool remained to that extent sound. The same secret principle, however, that had prompted Strether not absolutely to desire Waymarsh's
presence at the dock, that had led him thus to postpone for a few hours
his enjoyment of it, now operated to make him feel he could still wait with-
10 out disappointment. They would dine together at the worst, and, with all
respect to dear old Waymarsh—if not even, for that matter, to himself—
there was little fear that in the sequel they shouldn't see enough of each
other. The principle I have just mentioned as operating had been, with the
most newly disembarked of the two men, wholly instinctive—the fruit of
15 a sharp sense that, delightful as it would be to find himself looking, after
so much separation, into his comrade's face, his business would be a trifle
bungled should he simply arrange for this countenance to present itself to
the nearing steamer as the first 'note' of Europe. Mixed with everything
was the apprehension, already, on Strether's part, that it would, at best,
20 throughout, prove the note of Europe in quite a sufficient degree.[2]

It seems a fairly ordinary sort of prose, but for its faint air of elaborate portent; and on second reading its general quality reminds one of what Strether is
later to observe—approvingly—in Maria Gostrey: an effect of 'expensive, subdued suitability'. There's certainly nothing particularly striking in the diction
or syntax; none of the immediate drama or rich description that we often get
at the beginning of novels; and certainly none of the sensuous concreteness that,
until recently, was regarded as a chief criterion of good prose in our long post-
imagistic phase: if anything, the passage is conspicuously un-sensuous and un-
concrete, a little dull perhaps, and certainly not easy reading.

The difficulty isn't one of particularly long or complicated sentences: actually
they're of fairly usual length: I make it an average of 41 words; a little, but
not very much, longer than James's average of 35 (in Book 2, ch. 2. of *The
Ambassadors*, according to R. W. Short's count, in his very useful article 'The
Sentence Structure of Henry James', *American Literature*, xviii, March 1946,
71-88).[3] The main cause of difficulty seems rather to come from what may be
called the delayed specification of referents: 'Strether' and 'the hotel' and 'his
friend' are mentioned before we are told who or where they are. But this
difficulty is so intimately connected with James's general narrative technique
that it may be better to begin with purely verbal idiosyncrasies, which are more
easily isolated. The most distinctive ones in the passage seem to be these: a
preference for non-transitive verbs; many abstract nouns; much use of 'that'; a
certain amount of elegant variation to avoid piling up personal pronouns and
adjectives such as 'he', 'his', and 'him'; and the presence of a great many
negatives and near-negatives.

By the preference for non-transitive verbs I mean three related habits: a
great reliance on copulatives—'Strether's first question *was* about his friend';
'*was* apparently not to arrive': a frequent use of the passive voice—'*was* not
wholly *disconcerted*'; 'a telegram ... *was produced*'; 'his business *would be* a
trifle *bungled*'; and the employment of many intransitive verbs—'the under-

standing ... remained ... sound'; 'the ... principle ... operated to'. My count of all the verbs in the indicative would give a total of 14 passive, copulative, or intransitive uses as opposed to only 6 transitive ones: and there are in addition frequent infinitive, participial, or gerundial uses of transitive verbs, in all of which the active nature of the subjective-verb-and-object sequence is considerably abated—'on his learning'; 'bespeaking a room'; 'not absolutely to desire'; 'led him thus to postpone'.

This relative infrequency of transitive verbal usages in the passage is associated with the even more pronounced tendency towards using abstract nouns as subjects of main or subordinate clauses: 'question'; 'understanding'; 'the same secret principle'; 'the principle'; 'his business'. If one takes only the main clauses, there are four such abstract nouns as subjects, while only three main clauses have concrete and particular subjects ('he', or 'they').[4]

I detail these features only to establish that in this passage, at least, there is a clear quantitative basis for the common enough view that James's late prose style is characteristically abstract: more explicitly, that the main grammatical subjects are very often nouns for mental ideas, 'question', 'principle', etc.; and that the verbs—because they are mainly used either non-transitively, or in infinitive, participial and gerundial forms—tend to express states of being rather that particular finite actions affecting objects.

The main use of abstractions is to deal at the same time with many objects or events rather than single and particular ones: and we use verbs that denote states of being rather than actions for exactly the same reason—their much more general applicability. But in this passage, of course, James isn't in the ordinary sense making abstract or general statements; it's narrative, not expository prose; what need exploring, therefore, are the particular literary imperatives which impose on his style so many of the verbal and syntactical qualities of abstract and general discourse; of expository rather than narrative prose.

Consider the first sentence. The obvious narrative way of making things particular and concrete would presumably be 'When Strether reached the hotel, he first asked "Has Mr Waymarsh arrived yet?" ' Why does James say it the way he does? One effect is surely that, instead of a sheer stated event, we get a very special view of it; the mere fact that actuality has been digested into reported speech—the question 'was about his friend'—involves a narrator to do the job, to interpret the action, and also a presumed audience that he does it for: and by implication, the heat of the action itself must have cooled off somewhat for the translation and analysis of the events into this form of statement to have had time to occur. Lastly, making the subject of the sentence 'question' rather than 'he', has the effect of subordinating the particular actor, and therefore the particular act, to a much more general perspective: mental rather than physical, and subjective rather than objective; 'question' is a word which involves analysis of a physical event into terms of meaning and intention: it involves, in fact, both Strether's mind and the narrator's. The narrator's because he interprets Strether's act: if James had sought the most concrete method of taking us into Strether's mind—' "Has Mr Waymarsh come yet?" I at once asked'—he would have obviated the need for the implied external categorizer of Strether's action. But James disliked the 'mere platitude of statement' involved in first-person narrative; partly, presumably, because it would merge Strether's consciousness into the narrative, and not isolate it for the reader's inspection. For such isolation, a more expository method is needed: no confusion of subject and object, as in first-person narration, but a narrator forcing the reader to pay attention to James's primary objective—Strether's mental and subjective state.

The 'multidimensional' quality of the narrative, with its continual implication of a community of three minds—Strether's, James's, and the reader's—isn't signalled very obviously until the fourth sentence—'The principle I have just mentioned as operating ...'; but it's already been established tacitly in every detail of diction and structure, and it remains pervasive. One reason for the special demand James's fictional prose makes on our attention is surely that there are always at least three levels of development—all of them subjective: the characters' awareness of events; the narrator's seeing of them; and our own trailing perception of the relation between these two.

The primary location of the narrative in a mental rather than a physical continuum gives the narrative a great freedom from the restrictions of particular time and place. Materially, we are, of course, in Chester, at the hotel—characteristically 'the hotel' because a fully particularized specification—'The Pied Bull Inn' say—would be an irrelevant brute fact which would distract attention from the mental train of thought we are invited to partake in. But actually we don't have any pressing sense of time and place: we feel ourselves to be spectators, rather specifically, of Strether's thought processes, which easily and imperceptibly range forwards and backwards both in time and space. Sentence three, for example, begins in the past, at the Liverpool dock; sentence four looks forward to the reunion later that day, and to its many sequels: such transitions of time and place are much easier to effect when the main subjects of the sentences are abstract: a 'principle' exists independently of its context.

The multiplicity of relations—between narrator and object, and between the ideas in Strether's mind—held in even suspension throughout the narrative, is presumably the main explanation for the number of 'thats' in the passage, as well as of the several examples of elegant variation. There are 9 'thats'—only two of them demonstrative and the rest relative pronouns (or conjunctions or particles if you prefer those terms); actually there were no less than three more of them in the first edition, which James removed from the somewhat more colloquial and informal New York edition; while there are several other 'thats' implied—in 'the principle [that] I have just mentioned', for instance.

The number of 'thats' follows from two habits already noted in the passage. 'That' characteristically introduces relative clauses dealing not with persons but with objects, including abstractions; and it is also used to introduce reported speech—'on his learning that Waymarsh'—not 'Mr Waymarsh isn't here'. Both functions are combined in the third sentence where we get a triple definition of a timeless idea based on the report of three chronologically separate events: 'the same secret principle, however, that had prompted Strether not absolutely to desire Waymarsh's presence at the dock, that had led him thus to postpone for a few hours his enjoyment of it, now operated to make him feel that he could still wait without disappointment'.

Reported rather than direct speech also increases the pressure towards elegant variation: the use, for example, in sentence 1 of 'his friend', where in direct speech it would be 'Mr Waymarsh' (and the reply—'He hasn't come yet'). In the second sentence—'a telegram ... was produced for the inquirer'—'inquirer' is needed because 'him' has already been used for Waymarsh just above; of course, 'the inquirer' is logical enough after the subject of the first sentence has been an abstract noun—'question'; and the epithet also gives James an opportunity for underlining the ironic distance and detachment with which we are invited to view his dedicated 'inquirer', Strether. Later, when Strether is 'the most newly disembarked of the two men', we see how both elegant variation and the grammatical subordination of physical events are related to the general Jamesian tendency to present characters and actions on a plane of abstract categorization; the mere statement, 'Mr Waymarsh had already been in England for (so many) months', would itself go far to destroy the primarily mental continuum in which the paragraph as a whole exists.

The last general stylistic feature of the passage to be listed above was the use of negative forms. There are 6 'noes' or 'nots' in the first 4 sentences; four implied negatives—'postpone'; 'without disappointment'; 'at the worst'; 'there was little fear': and two qualifications that modify positiveness of affirmation —'not wholly', and 'to that extent'. This abundance of negatives has no doubt several functions: it enacts Strether's tendency to hesitation and qualification; it puts the reader into the right judicial frame of mind; and it has the further effect of subordinating concrete events to their mental reflection; 'Waymarsh was not to arrive', for example, is not a concrete statement of a physical event: it is subjective—because it implies an expectation in Strether's mind (which was not fulfilled); and it has an abstract quality—because while Waymarsh's arriving would be particular and physical, his *not* arriving is an idea, a non-action. More generally, James's great use of negatives or near-negatives may also, perhaps, be regarded as part of his subjective and abstractive tendency: there are no negatives in nature but only in the human consciousness.

II

The most obvious grammatical features of what Richard Chase has called Henry James's 'infinitely syntactical language' (*The American Novel and its Tradition*, 1957) can, then, be shown to reflect the essential imperatives of his narrative point of view; and they could therefore lead into a discussion of the philosophical qualities of his mind, as they are discussed, for example, by Dorothea Krook in her notable article 'The Method of the Later Works of Henry James' (*London Magazine*, i, 1954, 55-70); our passage surely exemplifies James's power 'to generalize to the furthest limit the particulars of experience', and with it the characteristic way in which both his 'perceptions of the world itself and his perceptions of the logic of his perceptions of the world ... happen simultaneously, are the parts of a single comprehensive experience'.

Another aspect of the connection between James's metaphysic and his method as a novelist has inspired a stimulating stylistic study—Carlo Izzo's 'Henry James, Scrittore Sintattico' (*Studi Americani*, ii, 1956, 127-42). The connection between thought and style finds its historical perspective in John Henry Raleigh's illuminating study 'Henry James: the poetics of empiricism' (*PMLA*, lxvi, 1951, 107-23), which establishes connections between Lockean epistemology and James's extreme, almost anarchic, individualism; while this epistemological preoccupation, which is central to Quentin Anderson's view of how James worked out his father's cosmology in fictional terms (*The American Henry James*, 1957), also leads towards another large general question, the concern with 'point of view',[a] which became a crucial problem in the history and criticism of fiction under the influence of the sceptical relativism of the late nineteenth century.

In James's case, the problem is fairly complicated. He may be classed as an 'Impressionist', concerned, that is, to show not so much the events themselves, but the impressions which they make on the characters. But James's continual need to generalize and place and order, combined with his absolute demand for a point of view that would be plastic enough to allow him freedom for the formal 'architectonics' of the novelist's craft, eventually involved him in a very idiosyncratic kind of multiple Impressionism: idiosyncratic because the dual presence of Strether's consciousness and of that of the narrator, who translates what he sees there into more general terms, makes the narrative point of view both intensely individual and yet ultimately social.

Another possible direction of investigation would be to show that the abstractness and indirection of James's style are essentially the result of this characteristic multiplicity of his vision. There is, for example, the story reported by Edith Wharton that after his first stroke James told Lady Prothero that 'in the very act of falling ... he heard in the room a voice which was distinctly, it seemed, not his own, saying: "So here it is at last, the distinguishing thing."' James, apparently, could not but see even his own most fateful personal experience, except as evoked by some other observer's voice in terms of the long historical and literary tradition of death. Carlo Izzo regards this tendency as typical of the Alexandrian style, where there is a marked disparity between the rich inheritance of the means of literary expression, and the meaner creative world which it is used to express; but the defence of the Jamesian habit of mind must surely be that what the human vision shares with that of animals is presumably the perception of concrete images, not the power to conceive universals: such was Aristotle's notion of man's distinguishing capacity. The universals in the present context are presumably the awareness that behind every petty individual circumstance there ramifies an endless network of general moral, social, and historical relations. Henry James's style can therefore be seen as a supremely civilized effort to relate every event and every moment of life to the full complexity of its circumambient conditions.

---

[a] i.e., the 'point of view' from which a story is narrated. Cf. E. M. Forster, p. 143 above.

535

Obviously James's multiple awareness can go too far; and in the later novels it often poses the special problem that we do not quite know whether the awareness implied in a given passage is the narrator's or that of his character. Most simply, a pronoun referring to the subject of a preceding clause is always liable to give trouble if one hasn't been very much aware of what the grammatical subject of that preceding clause was; in the last sentence of the paragraph, for example, 'the apprehension, already, on Strether's part, that ... it would, at best, ... prove the "note" of Europe', 'it' refers to Waymarsh's countenance: but this isn't at first obvious; which is no doubt why, in his revision of the periodical version for the English edition James replaced 'it' by 'he'—simpler, grammatically, but losing some of the ironic visual precision of the original. More seriously, because the narrator's consciousness and Strether's are both present, we often don't know whose mental operations and evaluative judgments are involved in particular cases. We pass, for instance, from the objective analysis of sentence 3 where the analytic terminology of 'the same secret principle' must be the responsibility of the narrator, to what must be a verbatim quotation of Strether's mind in sentence 4: 'with all respect to dear old Waymarsh' is obviously Strether's licensed familiarity.

But although the various difficulties of tense, voice, and reference require a vigilance of attention in the reader which some have found too much to give, they are not in themselves very considerable: and what perhaps is much more in need of attention is how the difficulties arising from the multiplicity of points of view don't by any means prevent James from ordering all the elements of his narrative style into an amazingly precise means of expression: and it is this positive, and in the present case, as it seems to me, triumphant, mastery of the difficulties which I want next to consider.

Our passage is not, I think, James either at his most memorable or at his most idiosyncratic: *The Ambassadors* is written with considerable sobriety and has, for example, little of the vivid and direct style of the early part of *The Wings of the Dove*, or of the happy symbolic complexities of *The Golden Bowl*. Still, the passage is fairly typical of the later James; and I think it can be proved that all or at least nearly all the idiosyncrasies of diction or syntax in the present passage are fully justified by the particular emphases they create.

The most flagrant eccentricity of diction is presumably that where James writes 'the most newly disembarked of the two men' (lines 16-17). 'Most' may very well be a mere slip; and it must certainly seem indefensible to anyone who takes it as an absolute rule that the comparative must always be used when only two items are involved.[5] But a defence is at least possible. 'Most newly disembarked' means something rather different from 'more newly disembarked'. James, it may be surmised, did not want to compare the recency of the two men's arrival, but to inform us that Strether's arrival was 'very' or as we might say, 'most' recent; the use of the superlative also had the advantage of suggesting the long and fateful tradition of transatlantic disembarcations in general.

The reasons for the other main syntactical idiosyncrasies in the passage are much clearer. In the first part of the opening sentence, for example, the separa-

536

tion of subject—'question'—from verb—'was'—by the longish temporal clause 'when he reached the hotel', is no doubt a dislocation of normal sentence structure; but, of course, 'Strether' must be the first word of the novel: while, even more important, the delayed placing of the temporal clause, forces a pause after 'question' and thus gives it a very significant resonance. Similarly with the last sentence; it has several peculiarities, of which the placing of 'throughout' seems the most obvious. The sentence has three parts: the first and last are comparatively straightforward, but the middle is a massed block of portentous qualifications: 'Mixed with everything was the apprehension— already, on Strether's part, that he would, at best, throughout—prove the note of Europe in quite a sufficient degree.' The echoing doom started by the connotation of 'apprehension'—reverberates through 'already' ('much more to come later') 'on Strether's part' ('even he knows') and 'at best' ('the worst has been envisaged, too'); but it is the final collapse of the terse rhythm of the parenthesis that isolates the rather awkwardly placed 'throughout', and thus enables James to sound the fine full fatal note; there is no limit to the poignant eloquence of 'throughout'. It was this effect, of course, which dictated the preceding inversion which places 'apprehension' not at the start of the sentence, but in the middle where, largely freed from its syntactical nexus, it may be directly exposed to its salvos of qualification.

The mockingly fateful emphasis on 'throughout' tells us, if nothing had before, that James's tone is in the last analysis ironic, comic, or better, as I shall try to suggest, humorous. The general reasons for this have already been suggested. To use Maynard Mack's distinction (in his Preface to *Joseph Andrews*, Rinehart editions, New York, 1948), 'the comic artist subordinates the presentation of life as experience, where the relationship between ourselves and the characters experiencing it is a primary one, to the presentation of life as a spectacle, where the primary relation is between himself and us as onlookers'. In the James passage, the primacy of the relation between the narrator and the reader has already been noted, as has its connection with the abstraction of the diction, which brings home the distance between the narrator and Strether. Of course, the application of abstract diction to particular persons always tends towards irony,[6] because it imposes a dual way of looking at them: few of us can survive being presented as general representatives of humanity.

The paragraph, of course, is based on one of the classic contradictions in psychological comedy—Strether's reluctance to admit to himself that he has very mixed feelings about his friend: and James develops this with the narrative equivalent of *commedia dell'arte* technique: virtuoso feats of ironic balance, comic exaggeration, and deceptive hesitation conduct us on a complicated progress towards the foreordained illumination.

In structure, to begin with, the six sentences form three groups of two: each pair of them gives one aspect of Strether's delay; and they are arranged in an ascending order of complication so that the fifth sentence—72 words—is almost twice as long as any other, and is succeeded by the final sentence, the punch line, which is noticeably the shortest—26 words. The development of the ideas is as controlled as the sentence structure. Strether is obviously a man with an enormous sense of responsibility about personal relationships; so his first question is about his friend. That loyal *empressement* [assiduity], however, is immediately checked by the balanced twin negatives that follow: 'on his learning that Waymarsh *was not* to arrive till evening, he *was not* wholly disconcerted': one of the diagnostic elements of irony, surely, is hyperbole qualified with mock-scrupulousness, such as we get in 'not wholly disconcerted'. Why there are limits to Lambert Strether's consternation is to transpire in the next sentence; Waymarsh's telegram bespeaking a room 'only if not noisy' is a laconic suggestion of that inarticulate worthy's habitually gloomy expectations —from his past experiences of the indignities of European hotel noise we adumbrate the notion that the cost of their friendly *rencontre* may be his sleeping in the street. In the second part of the sentence we have another similar, though more muted, hint: 'the understanding that they should meet in Chester rather than at Liverpool remained to that extent sound'; 'to that extent', no doubt, but to *any other?*—echo seems to answer 'No'.

In the second group of sentences we are getting into Strether's mind, and we have been prepared to relish the irony of its ambivalences. The negatived hyperbole of 'not absolutely to desire', turns out to mean 'postpone'; and, of course, a voluntarily postponed 'enjoyment' itself denotes a very modified rapture, although Strether's own consciousness of the problem is apparently no further advanced than that 'he could still wait without disappointment'. Comically loyal to what he would like to feel, therefore, we have him putting in the consoling reflection that 'they would dine together at the worst'; and the ambiguity of 'at the worst' is followed by the equally dubious thought: 'there was little fear that in the sequel they shouldn't see enough of each other'. That they should, in fact, see too much of each other; but social decorum and Strether's own loyalties demand that the outrage of the open statement be veiled in the obscurity of formal negation.

By the time we arrive at the climactic pair of sentences, we have been told enough for more ambitious effects to be possible. The twice-mentioned 'secret principle', it appears, is actually wholly 'instinctive' (line 14); but in other ways Strether is almost ludicrously self-conscious. The qualified hyperbole of 'his business would be a trifle bungled', underlined as it is by the alliteration, prepares us for a half-realized image which amusingly defines Strether's sense of his role: he sees himself, it appears, as the stage-manager of an enterprise in which his solemn obligations as an implicated friend are counterbalanced by his equally ceremonious sense that due decorums must also be attended to when he comes face to face with another friend of long ago—no less a person than Europe. It is, of course, silly of him, as James makes him acknowledge in the characteristic italicizing of 'the "note" of Europe';[7] but still, he does have a comically ponderous sense of protocol which leads him to feel that 'his business would be a trifle bungled' should he simply arrange for this countenance to present itself to the nearing steamer as the first 'note' of Europe. The steamer, one imagines, would not have turned hard astern at the proximity of Waymarsh's sacred rage; but Strether's fitness for ambassadorial functions is defined by his thinking in terms of 'arranging' for a certain countenance at the docks to give just the right symbolic greeting.

Strether's notion of what Europe demands also shows us the force of his aesthetic sense. But in the last sentence the metaphor, though it remains equally self-conscious, changes its mode of operation from the dramatic, aesthetic, and diplomatic, to something more scientific: for, although ten years ago I should not have failed to point out, and my readers would not, I suppose, have failed to applaud, the ambiguity of 'prove', it now seems to me that we must choose between its two possible meanings. James may be using 'prove' to mean that Waymarsh's face will 'turn out to be' the 'note of Europe' for Strether. But 'prove' in this sense is intransitive, and 'to be' would have to be supplied; it therefore seems more likely that James is using 'prove' in the older sense of 'to test': Waymarsh is indeed suited to the role of being the sourly acid test of the siren songs of Europe 'in quite a sufficient degree', as Strether puts it with solemn but arch under-statement.

The basic development structure of the passage, then, is one of progressive and yet artfully delayed clarification; and this pattern is also typical of James's general novelistic method. The reasons for this are suggested in the Preface to *The Princess Casamassima*, where James deals with the problem of maintaining a balance between the intelligence a character must have to be interesting, and the bewilderment which is nevertheless an essential condition of the novel's having surprise, development, and tension: 'It seems probable that if we were never bewildered there would never be a story to tell about us.'

In the first paragraph of *The Ambassadors* James apprises us both of his hero's supreme qualities and of his associated limitations. Strether's delicate critical intelligence is often blinkered by a highly vulnerable mixture of moral generosity towards others combined with an obsessive sense of personal inadequacy; we see the tension in relation to Waymarsh, as later we are to see it in relation to all his other friends; and we understand, long before Strether, how deeply it bewilders him; most poignantly about the true nature of Chad, Madame de Vionnet—and himself.

This counterpoint of intelligence and bewilderment is, of course, another reason for the split narrative point of view we've already noted: we and the narrator are inside Strether's mind, and yet we are also outside it, knowing more about Strether than he knows about himself. This is the classic posture of irony. Yet I think that to insist too exclusively on the ironic function of James's narrative point of view would be mistaken.

Irony has lately been enshrined as the supreme deity in the critical pantheon: but, I wonder, is there really anything so wonderful about being distant and objective? Who wants to see life only or mainly in intellectual terms? In art as in life we no doubt can have need of intellectual distance as well as of emotional commitment; but the uninvolvement of the artist surely doesn't go very far without the total involvement of the person; or, at least, without a deeper human involvement than irony customarily establishes. One could, I suppose, call the aesthetically perfect balance between distance and involvement, open or positive irony: but I'm not sure that humour isn't a better word, especially when the final balance is tipped in favour of involvement, of ultimate commitment to the characters; and I hope that our next critical movement will be the New Gelastics.[a]

At all events, although the first paragraph alone doesn't allow the point to be established fully here, it seems to me that James's attitude to Strether is better described as humorous than ironical; we must learn like Maria Gostrey, to see him 'at last all comically, all tragically'. James's later novels in general are most intellectual; but they are also, surely, his most compassionate: and in this particular paragraph Strether's dilemma is developed in such a way that we feel for him even more than we smile at him. This balance of intention, I think, probably explains why James keeps his irony so quiet in tone: we must be aware of Strether's 'secret' ambivalence towards Waymarsh, but not to the point that his unawareness of it would verge on fatuity; and our controlling sympathy for the causes of Strether's ambivalence turns what might have been irony into something closer to what Constance Rourke characterizes as James's typical 'low-keyed humor of defeat' (*American Humor*, 1931).

That James's final attitude is humorous rather than ironic is further suggested by the likeness of the basic structural technique of the paragraph to that of the funny story—the incremental involvement in an endemic human perplexity which can only be resolved by laughter's final acceptance of contradiction and absurdity. We don't, in the end, see Strether's probing hesitations mainly as an ironic indication by James of mankind's general muddlement; we find it, increasingly, a touching example of how, despite all their inevitable incongruities and shortcomings, human ties remain only, but still, human.

Here it is perhaps James's very slowness and deliberation throughout the narrative which gives us our best supporting evidence: greater love hath no man than hearing his friend out patiently.

III

The function of an introductory paragraph in a novel is presumably to introduce: and this paragraph surely has the distinction of being a supremely complex and inclusive introduction to a novel. It introduces the hero, of course, and one of his companions; also the time; the place; something of what's gone before. But James has carefully avoided giving us the usual retrospective beginning, that pile of details which he scornfully termed a 'mere seated mass of information'. All the details are scrupulously presented as reflections from the novel's essential centre—the narrator's patterning of the ideas going forwards and backwards in Strether's mind. Of course, this initially makes the novel more difficult, because what we probably think of as primary—event and its setting—is subordinated to what James thinks is—the mental drama of the hero's consciousness, which, of course, is not told but shown: scenically dramatized. At the same time, by selecting thoughts and events which are representative of the book as a whole, and narrating them with an abstractness which suggests their larger import, James introduces the most general themes of the novel.

[a] Gelastics: remedies operating by causing laughter (*Shorter Oxford English Dictionary*).

540

James, we saw, carefully arranged to make 'Strether's first question', the first three words; and, of course, throughout the novel, Strether is to go on asking questions—and getting increasingly dusty answers. This, it may be added, is stressed by the apparent aposiopesis[a]: for a 'first' question when no second is mentioned, is surely an intimation that more are—in a way unknown to us or to Strether—yet to come. The later dislocations of normal word-order already noted above emphasize other major themes; the 'secret principle' in Strether's mind, and the antithesis Waymarsh–Europe, for instance.

The extent to which these processes were conscious on James's part cannot, of course, be resolved; but it is significant that the meeting with Maria Gostrey was interposed before the meeting with Waymarsh, which James had originally planned as his beginning in the long (20,000) word scenario of the plot which he had prepared for *Harper's*. The unexpected meeting had many advantages; not least that James could repeat the first paragraph's pattern of delayed clarification in the structure of the first chapter as a whole. On Strether's mind we get a momentously clear judgment at the end of the second paragraph: 'there was detachment in his zeal, and curiosity in his indifference'; but then the meeting with Maria Gostrey, and its gay opportunities for a much fuller presentation of Strether's mind, intervene before Waymarsh himself finally appears at the end of the chapter; only then is the joke behind Strether's uneasy hesitations in the first paragraph brought to its hilariously blunt climax: 'It was already upon him even at that distance—Mr Waymarsh was for *his* part joyless.'

One way of evaluating James's achievement in this paragraph, I suppose, would be to compare the openings of James's other novels, and with those of previous writers: but it would take too long to do more than sketch the possibilities of this approach. James's early openings certainly have some of the banality of the 'mere seated mass of information': in *Roderick Hudson* (1876), for example: 'Rowland Mallet had made his arrangements to sail for Europe on the 5th of September, and having in the interval a fortnight to spare, he determined to spend it with his cousin Cecilia, the widow of a nephew of his father....' Later, James showed a much more comprehensive notion of what the introductory paragraph should attempt: even in the relatively simple and concrete opening of *The Wings of the Dove* (1902): 'She waited, Kate Croy, for her father to come in, but he kept her unconscionably, and there were moments at which she showed herself, in the glass over the mantle, a face positively pale with irritation that had brought her to the point of going away without sight of him....' 'She waited, Kate Croy'—an odd parenthetic apposition artfully contrived to prefigure her role throughout the novel—to wait.

One could, I suppose, find this sort of symbolic prefiguring in the work of earlier novelists; but never, I imagine, in association with all the other levels of introductory function that James manages to combine in a single paragraph. Jane Austen has her famous thematic irony in the opening of *Pride and Prejudice* (1813): 'It is a truth universally acknowledged, that a single man in

[a] A technical term in classical and neoclassical rhetoric, denoting the omission of something for a particular effect.

possession of a good fortune must be in want of a wife'; but pride and prejudice must come later. Dickens can hurl us overpoweringly into *Bleak House* (1852-3), into its time and place and general theme; but characters and opening action have to wait:

> London. Michaelmas Term lately over, and the Lord Chancellor sitting in Lincoln's Inn Hall. Implacable November weather. As much mud in the streets, as if the waters had but newly retired from the face of the earth, and it would not be wonderful to meet a Megalosaurus, forty feet long or so, waddling like an elephantine lizard up Holborn-Hill. Smoke lowering down from chimney-pots....

In Dickens, characteristically, we get a loud note that sets the tone, rather than a polyphonic series of chords that contain all the later melodic developments, as in James. And either the Dickens method, or the 'mere seated mass of information', seem to be commonest kinds of opening in nineteenth-century novels. For openings that suggest something of James's ambitious attempt to achieve a prologue that is a synchronic introduction of all the main aspects of the narrative, I think that Conrad is his closest rival. But Conrad, whether in expository or dramatic vein, tends to an arresting initial vigour that has dangers which James's more muted tones avoid. In *An Outcast of the Islands* (1896), for example:

> When he stepped off the straight and narrow path of his peculiar honesty, it was with an inward assertion of unflinching resolve to fall back again into the monotonous but safe stride of virtue as soon as his little excursion into the wayside quagmires had produced the desired effect. It was going to be a short episode—a sentence in brackets, so to speak, in the flowing tale of his life....

Conrad's sardonic force has enormous immediate impact; but it surely gives too much away: the character, Willems, has been dissected so vigorously that it takes great effort for Conrad—and the reader—to revivify him later. The danger lurks even in the masterly combination of physical notation and symbolic evaluation at the beginning of *Lord Jim* (1900): 'He was an inch, perhaps two, under six feet ...': the heroic proportion is for ever missed, by an inch, perhaps two; which is perhaps too much, to begin with.

It is not for me to assess how far I have succeeded in carrying out the general intentions with which I began, or how far similar methods of analysis would be applicable to other kinds of prose. As regards the explication of the passage itself, the main argument must by now be sufficiently clear, although a full demonstration would require a much wider sampling both of other novels and of other passages in *The Ambassadors*.[8] The most obvious and demonstrable features of James's prose style, its vocabulary and syntax, are direct reflections of his attitude to life and his conception of the novel; and these features, like the relation of the paragraph to the rest of the novel, and to other novels, make clear that the notorious idiosyncrasies of Jamesian prose are directly related to the imperatives which led him to develop a narrative texture as richly complicated and as highly organized as that of poetry.

No wonder James scorned translation and rejoiced, as he so engagingly confessed to his French translator, Auguste Monod, that his later works were 'locked fast in the golden cage of the *intraduisible*'. Translation could hardly do justice to a paragraph in which so many levels of meaning and implication are kept in continuous operation; in which the usual introductory exposition of time, place, character, and previous action, are rendered through an immediate immersion of the processes of the hero's mind as he's involved in perplexities which are characteristic of the novel as a whole and which are articulated in a mode of comic development which is essentially that, not only of the following chapter, but of the total structure. To have done all that is to have gone far towards demonstrating the contention which James announced at the end of the Preface to *The Ambassadors*, that 'the Novel remains still, under the right persuasion, the most independent, most elastic, most prodigious of literary forms'; and the variety and complexity of the functions carried out in the book's quite short first paragraph also suggest that, contrary to some notions, the demonstration is, as James claimed, made with 'a splendid particular economy'.

Notes

1. This was before the appearance of the English Institute's symposium *Style in Prose Fiction* (1959), which offers, besides two general surveys and a valuable bibliography of the field, stylistic studies of six novelists, including one by Charles R. Crow, of 'The Style of Henry James: *The Wings of the Dove*.'

2. Henry James, *The Ambassadors* (Revised Collected Edition, Macmillan; London, 1923). Since there are a few variants that have a bearing on the argument, it seems desirable to give a collation of the main editions; P is the periodical publication (*The North American Review*, clxxvi, 1903); 1A the first American edition (Harper and Brothers, New York, 1903); 1E the first English edition (Methuen and Co., London, 1903); N.Y., the 'New York Edition', New York and London, 1907–9 (the London Macmillan edition used the sheets of the American edition); CR the 'Collected Revised Edition', London and New York, 1921–31 (which uses the text of the New York Edition). It should perhaps be explained that the most widely used editions in England and America make misleading claims about their text: the 'Everyman' edition claims to use the text of the revised Collected Edition, but actually follows the first English edition in the last variant; while the 'Anchor' edition, claiming to be 'a faithful copy of the text of the Methuen first edition', actually follows the first American edition, including the famous misplaced chapters.

l. 4. *reply paid* NY, CR; *with the answer paid* P, 1A, 1E.
l. 4. *inquirer* P, 1A, 1E, CR; *enquirer* NY.
l. 5. *understanding they* NY, CR; *understanding that they* P, 1A, 1E.
l. 9. *feel he* NY, CR; *feel that he* P, 1A. 1E.
l. 12. *shouldn't* CR; *shouldn't* NY; *should not* P, 1A, 1E.
l. 14. *newly disembarked*, all eds. except P: *newly-disembarked*.
l. 17. *arrange for this countenance to present* NY, CR; *arrange that this countenance should present* P, 1A, 1E.
l. 18. *'note' of Europe* CR; *'note', for him, of Europe*, P, 1A, 1E; *'note', of Europe*, NY.
l. 19. *that it would* P, 1A, NY, CR; *that he would*, 1E.

3. I am also indebted to the same author's 'Henry James's world of images', PMLA lxviii, Dec., 1953, 943–60.

4. Sentences one and four are compound or multiple, but in my count I haven't included the second clause in the latter—'there was little fear'; though if we can talk of the clause having a subject it's an abstract one—'fear'.

5. Though consider *Rasselas*, ch. xxviii: 'Both conditions may be bad, but they cannot both be worst.'

6. As I have argued in 'The ironic tradition in Augustan prose from Swift to Johnson', *Restoration and Augustan Prose* (Los Angeles, 1957).

7. See George Knox, 'James's rhetoric of quotes', *College English*, xvii, 1956, 293–7.

8. A similar analysis of eight other paragraphs selected at fifty-page intervals revealed that, as would be expected, there is much variation: the tendency to use non-transitive verbs, and abstract nouns as subjects, for instance, seems to be strong throughout the novel, though especially so in analytic rather than narrative passages; but the frequent use of 'that' and of negative forms of statement does not recur significantly.

40   Claude Lévi-Strauss

Claude Lévi-Strauss (b. 1908) is not a literary critic, but a social anthropologist.
He is represented in this Reader partly because his work on myth and
mythologies impinges on literary studies, but more importantly because his
intellectual aims and methods have been found capable of wider application
in the field of literary criticism. The general term for these aims and methods
is 'structuralism'—one that derives from modern linguistics as variously
practised by Saussure, Jakobson, and Chomsky. Structural linguistics goes
beyond the description of any particular language to pursue the 'deep
structures' that are common to all languages, and in the first example given
by Lévi-Strauss in the extract printed below, the social anthropologist tries
to analyse the various manifestations of the incest taboo in the same way.
Structuralism, therefore, is concerned to discover *universal* truths about
the human mind, and this entails working at a very high level of generality—
at the level, sometimes, of algebra.

All this may seem very remote from the concerns of literary criticism,
particularly of criticism in the Anglo-American tradition, focused on the
individual text and the individual author. Lévi-Strauss's second example,
however, in which he pursues the incest theme into mythology and succeeds
in uncovering a remarkable structural relationship between South American
folklore, the Oedipus myth and the Grail legend, indicates the possibilities
of the structuralist method for ordering and interpreting larger masses of
literary materials. To date these possibilities have been pursued mainly in
France; though Northrop Frye, in Canada, might fairly be said to have
independently evolved and practised his own form of structuralist literary
criticism.

Claude Lévi-Strauss was born in Belgium and educated at the University
of Paris. He taught at the University of Sâo Paulo, Brazil, from 1935 to
1939, during which period he did field work among the South American
Indians. He was appointed to the Chair of Social Anthropology at the
Collège de France, Paris, in 1958. The extract which follows is from his
inaugural lecture, given on 5 January 1960, and published in an English
translation by Sherry Ortner Paul and Robert A. Paul as *The Scope of
Anthropology* in 1967. Other works by Claude Lévi-Strauss include:
Tristes Tropiques (Paris 1955) [*World on the Wane*, 1961]; *Anthropologie
Structurale* (Paris, 1958) [*Structural Anthropology*, New York 1963];
and *La Pensée Sauvage* (Paris, 1962) [*The Savage Mind*, 1966].

CROSS REFERENCES: 15. Maud Bodkin
30. Francis Fergusson
31. Northrop Frye
48. Roland Barthes

COMMENTARY: Edmund Leach, *Lévi-Strauss* (1970)
George Steiner, 'Orpheus and his myths: Claude
Lévi-Strauss', in *Language and Silence* (1967)

[Incest and myth]

I shall attempt to show by two examples how social anthropology now
endeavours to justify its programme.

We know how incest prohibitions function in primitive societies. By casting
sisters and daughters out of the consanguineal group, so to speak, and by
assigning them to husbands who belong to other groups, the prohibition of
incest creates bonds of alliance between these biological groups, the first such
bonds which one can call social. The incest prohibition is thus the basis of
human society: in a sense it is the society.

We did not proceed inductively to justify this interpretation. How could we
have done, with phenomena which are universally correlated, but among which
different societies have posited all sorts of curious connections? Moreover, this
is not a matter of facts but of meanings. The question we asked ourselves was
that of the *meaning* of the incest prohibition (the eighteenth century would
have said 'its spirit'), not the meaning of its *results*, real or imaginary. It was
necessary, then, to establish the systematic nature of each kinship terminology
and its corresponding set of marriage rules. And this was made possible only
by the additional effort of elaborating the system of these systems and of
putting them into transformational relationship. From then on what had been
merely a huge and disordered scene became organized in grammatical terms
involving a coercive charter for all conceivable ways of setting up and maintaining a reciprocity system.

This is where we are now. How then should we proceed to answer the next
question: that of the universality of these rules in the totality of human
societies, including contemporary ones? Even if we do not define the incest
prohibition in Australian or Amerindian terms, does the form it takes among
us still have the same function? It could be that we remain attached to it for
very different reasons, such as the relatively recent discovery of the harmful
consequences of consanguineal unions. It could also be—as Durkheim thought
—that the institution no longer plays a positive role among us and that it
survives only as a vestige of obsolete beliefs, anchored in popular lore. Or, is it
not rather the case that our society, a particular instance in a much vaster

family of societies, depends, like all others, for its coherence and its very existence on a network—grown infinitely unstable and complicated among us —of ties between consanguineal families? If so, do we have to admit that the network is homogeneous in all its parts, or must we recognize therein types of structures differing according to environment or region and variable as a function of local historical traditions?

These problems are essential for anthropology, since the response to them will determine the innermost nature of the social fact and its degree of plasticity. Now, it is impossible to settle this once and for all by using methods borrowed from the logic of John Stuart Mill. We cannot vary the complex relationships—on the technical, economic, professional, political, religious, and *biological* planes—which a contemporary society presupposes. We cannot interrupt and re-establish them at will in the hope of discovering which ones are indispensable to the existence of the society as such, and which ones it could do without if it had to.

However, we could choose the most complex and least stable of those matrimonial systems whose reciprocity function is best established. We could then construct models of them in the laboratory to determine how they would function if they involved increasing numbers of individuals; we could also distort our models in the hope of obtaining others of the same type but even more complex and unstable; and we could compare the reciprocity cycles thus obtained with the simplest cycles it is possible to observe in the field among contemporary societies, e.g. in regions characterized by small isolates. Through a series of trips from laboratory to field and field to laboratory, we would try gradually to fill in the gap between two series—one known, the other unknown—by the insertion of a series of intermediary forms. In the end, we would have done nothing but elaborate a language whose only virtues, as in the case of any language, would reside in its coherence and its ability to account, in terms of a very small number of rules, for phenomena thought to be very different until that moment. In the absence of an inaccessible factual truth, we would have arrived at a truth of reason.

The second example relates to problems of the same type approached on another level: it will still be concerned with the incest prohibition, but no longer in the form of a system of rules—rather, in the form of a theme for mythical thought.

The Iroquois and Algonquin Indians tell the story of a young girl subjected to the amorous leanings of a nocturnal visitor whom she believes to be her brother. Everything seems to point to the guilty one: physical appearance, clothing, and the scratched cheek which bears witness to the heroine's virtue. Formally accused by her, the brother reveals that he has a counterpart or, more exactly, a double, for the tie between them is so strong that any accident befalling the one is automatically transmitted to the other. To convince his incredulous sister, the young man kills his double before her, but at the same time he condemns himself, since their destinies are linked.

Of course, the mother of the victim will want to avenge her son. As it happens she is a powerful sorceress, the mistress of the owls. There is only one way of misleading her: that the sister marry her brother, the latter passing for the double he has killed. Incest is so inconceivable that the old woman never suspects the hoax. The owls are not fooled and denounce the guilty ones, but they succeed in escaping.

The Western listener easily perceives in this myth a theme established by the Oedipus legend: the very precautions taken to avoid incest in fact make it inevitable; in both cases a sensational turn of events arises from the fact that two characters, originally introduced as distinct, are identified with each other. Is this simply a coincidence—different causes explaining the fact that the same motifs are arbitrarily found together—or does the analogy have deeper foundations? In making the comparison, have we not put our finger on a fragment of a meaningful whole?

If so, the incest between brother and sister of the Iroquois myth would constitute a permutation of the Oedipal incest between mother and son. The contingency which rendered the former inevitable—the double personality of the hero—would be a permutation of the double identity of Oedipus—supposed dead and nevertheless living, condemned child and triumphant hero. To complete the demonstration, it would be necessary to discover in the American myth a transformation of the sphinx episode, which is the only element of the Oedipus legend still lacking.

Now, in this particular case (and hence we have chosen it in preference to others), the proof would be truly decisive, since, as Boas was the first to point out, riddles or puzzles, along with proverbs, are rather rare among the North American Indians. If puzzles were to be found in the semantic framework of the American myth, it would not be the effect of chance, but a proof of necessity.

In the whole of North America only two puzzle situations are found whose origins are unquestionably indigenous: (1) among the Pueblo Indians of the south-western United States we have a family of ceremonial clowns who set riddles to the spectators and whom myths describe as having been born of an incestuous union; and (2) precisely among the Algonquin themselves (remember that the sorceress in the myth summarized here is a mistress of owls), there are myths in which owls, or sometimes the ancestor of owls, set riddles to the hero which he must answer under pain of death. Consequently, in America too, riddles present a double Oedipal character: by way of incest, on the one hand, and by way of the owl, in which we are led to see a transposed form of the sphinx, on the other.

The correlation between riddle and incest thus seems to obtain among peoples separated by history, geography, language, and culture. In order to set up the comparison, let us construct a model of the riddle, expressing as best we can its constant properties throughout the various mythologies. Let us define it, from this point of view, *as a question to which one postulates that there is no answer.* Without considering here all the possible transformations of this statement, let us simply, by way of an experiment, invert its terms. This produces *an answer for which there is no question.*

This is, apparently, a formula completely devoid of sense. And yet, it is

☙

immediately obvious that there are myths, or fragments of myths, which derive their dramatic power from this structure—a symmetrical inversion of the other. Time is too limited for me to recount the American examples, I will therefore restrict myself to reminding you of the death of the Buddha, rendered inevitable because a disciple fails to ask the expected question. Closer to home, there are the old myths refurbished in the Holy Grail cycle,[a] in which the action depends on the timidity of the hero. In the presence of the magic vessel he dare not ask, 'What is it good for?'

Are these myths independent, or must they be considered in turn as a species of a vaster genus, of which Oedipal myths constitute only another species? Repeating the procedure we have described, we will see if, and to what extent, the characteristic elements of one group can be reduced to permutations (which will here be inversions) of the characteristic elements of the other. And that indeed is what takes place: from a hero who misuses sexual intercourse (since he carries it as far as incest), we pass on to a chaste man who abstains from it; a shrewd person who knows all the answers gives way to an innocent who is not even aware of the need to ask questions. In the American variants of this second type, and in the Holy Grail cycle, the problem to be resolved is that of the '*gaste pays*', that is to say, the cancelled summer. Now, all the American myths of the first or 'Oedipal' type refer to an eternal winter which the hero dispels when he solves the puzzles, thereby bringing on the summer. Simplifying a great deal, Perceval thus appears as an inverted Oedipus—a hypothesis we would not have dared to consider had we been called upon to compare a Greek with a Celtic source, but which is forced upon us in a North American context, where the two types are present in the same population.

However, we have not reached the end of our demonstration. As soon as we have verified that, in a semantic system, chastity is related to 'the answer without a question' as incest is related to 'the question without an answer', we must also admit that the two socio-biological statements are themselves in a homologous relation to the two grammatical statements. Between the puzzle solution and incest there exists a relationship, not external and of fact, but internal and of reason, and that indeed is why civilizations as different as those of classical antiquity and indigenous America can independently associate the two. Like the solved puzzle, incest brings together elements doomed to remain separate: the son marries the mother, the brother marries the sister, *in the same way in which the answer succeeds, against all expectations, in getting back to its question.*

In the legend of Oedipus, then, marriage with Jocasta does not arbitrarily follow hard upon victory over the sphinx. Besides the fact that myths of the Oedipal type (which this argument defines fairly precisely) always assimilate the discovery of incest to the solution of a living puzzle personified by the hero, their various episodes are repeated on different levels and in different languages and provide the same demonstration which one finds in an inverted form in the

[a] The Holy Grail was, in medieval legend, the cup used by Christ at the Last Supper, in which Joseph of Arimathea received the Saviour's blood at the Crucifixion. Many of the stories about King Arthur and the Knights of the Round Table are concerned with the quest for this precious object.

old myths of the Holy Grail. The audacious union of masked words or of consanguines unknown to themselves engenders decay and fermentation, the unchaining of natural forces—one thinks of the Theban plague—just as impotence in sexual matters (and in the ability to initiate a proposed dialogue) dries up animal and vegetable fertility.

In the face of the two possibilities which might seduce the imagination—an eternal summer or a winter just as eternal, the former licentious to the point of corruption, the latter pure to the point of sterility—man must resign himself to choosing equilibrium and the periodicity of the seasonal rhythm. In the natural order, the latter fulfils the same function which is fulfilled in society by the exchange of women in marriage and the exchange of words in conversation, when these are practised with the frank intention of communicating, that is to say, without trickery or perversity, and above all, without hidden motives.

41   René Wellek

René Wellek (b. 1903) was born in Vienna, and emigrated to the United States after taking his Ph.D. at the University of Prague. He has taught at the universities of Princeton, Prague, London, and Iowa, and is now Sterling Professor of Comparative Literature at Yale. Professor Wellek's many publications include: *The Rise of English Literary History* (Chapel Hill, N.C., 1941), *Theory of Literature*, with Austin Warren (New York, 1949), *A History of Modern Criticism 1750-1950*, 2 vols, (New Haven, 1955), and *Concepts of Criticism* (New Haven, 1963), a collection of occasional essays from which 'Literary Theory, Criticism and History', first published in the *Sewanee Review* in 1960, is reprinted here.

As these titles suggest, René Wellek has always been interested in the study of literature as itself an object of study. He has been concerned to describe, order, and relate the different contexts, methods, and aims which may be involved in literary criticism and scholarship, always with a view to establishing common principles upon which literary criticism may proceed as a useful, responsible, and intellectually coherent enterprise. *Theory of Literature* described the achievements, problems, and possibilities of literary studies at a point in time when the New Criticism had firmly established itself in America, and it reflected the orthodoxies of that criticism without being narrowly bound by them. In 'Literary Theory, Criticism and History', written a decade later, Wellek discusses the revival of what had always been the main objection to the New Criticism—that it was antihistorical. Wellek's argument is that literary theory, literary criticism, and literary history are three distinct, though interdependent forms of inquiry which do not necessarily compete with each other; but his pluralism does not extend to conceding that all value judgments are relative, for this would condemn criticism to change without progress. Wellek's unhesitating, unapologetic commitment to the life of the mind, and his cosmopolitan range of reference, no doubt reflect his Central European cultural background.

CROSS REFERENCES: 18. John Crowe Ransom
25. Erich Auerbach
31. Northrop Frye
32. C. S. Lewis

Literary theory, criticism, and history

In *Theory of Literature*[1] I tried to maintain the distinctions between certain main branches of literary study. 'There is, first,' I said, 'the distinction between a view of literature as a simultaneous order and a view of literature which sees it primarily as a series of works arranged in a chronological order and as integral parts of the historical process. There is, then, the further distinction between the study of the principles and criteria of literature and the study of the concrete literary works of art, whether we study them in isolation or in chronological series.'

'Literary theory' is the study of the principles of literature, its categories, criteria, and the like, while the studies of concrete works of art are either 'literary criticism' (primarily static in approach) or 'literary history'. Of course, 'literary criticism' is frequently used in such a way as to include literary theory.[2] I pleaded for the necessity of a collaboration among the three disciplines: 'They implicate each other so thoroughly as to make inconceivable literary theory without criticism or history, or criticism without theory or history, or history without theory and criticism', and I concluded somewhat naïvely that 'these distinctions are fairly obvious and rather widely accepted' (pp. 30-1).

Since these pages were written many attempts have been made either to obliterate these distinctions or to make more or less totalitarian claims for some of these disciplines: either to say, e.g. that there is only history or only criticism or only theory or, at least, to reduce the triad to a duo, to say that there is only theory and history or only criticism and history. Much of this debate is purely verbal: a further example of the incredible confusion of tongues, the veritable Tower of Babel which seems to me one of the most ominous features of our civilization. It is not worth trying to disentangle these confusions if they do not point to actual issues. Terminological disagreements are inevitable, especially if we take into consideration the different associations and scope of such terms in the main European languages. For instance, the term *Literaturwissenschaft* has preserved in German its ancient meaning of systematic knowledge. But I would try to defend the English term 'literary theory' as preferable to 'science of literature', because 'science' in English has become limited to natural science and suggests an emulation of the methods and claims of the natural sciences which seems, for literary studies, both unwise and misleading. 'Literary scholarship' as a possible translation or alternative to 'Literaturwissenschaft' seems also inadvisable, as it seems to exclude criticism, evaluation, speculation. A 'scholar' has ceased to be so broad and wise a man as Emerson wanted the American scholar to be. Again, 'literary theory' is preferable to 'poetics', as, in English, the term 'poetry' is still usually restricted to verse and has not assumed the wide meaning of German *Dichtung*. 'Poetics' seems to exclude the theory of such forms as the novel or the essay and it has also the handicap of suggesting prescriptive poetics: a set of principles obligatory for practising poets.

I do not want to trace at length the history of the term 'criticism' here, as it is properly the topic of the second essay. In English, the term criticism is often used to include literary theory and poetics. This usage is rare in German where the term *Literaturkritik* is usually understood in the very narrow sense of day-by-day reviewing. It might be interesting to show how this restriction has come about. In Germany, Lessing, certainly, and the Schlegels thought of themselves as literary critics, but apparently the overwhelming prestige of German philosophy, particularly the Hegelian system, combined with the establishment of a specialized literary historiography led to a sharp distinction between philosophical aesthetics and poetics on the one hand and scholarship on the other, while 'criticism' taken over by politically oriented journalism during the 'thirties of the nineteenth century became degraded to something purely practical, serving temporal ends. The critic becomes a middleman, a secretary, even a servant, of the public. In Germany, the late Werner Milch, in an essay 'Literaturkritik und Literaturgeschichte'[3] has tried to rescue the term by an argument in favour of 'literary criticism' as a specific art-form, a literary genre. Its distinguishing characteristic is that in criticism everything must be related to *us*, while in literary history, literature is conceived as involved in a period, judged only relatively to the period. The only criterion of criticism is personal feeling, experience, the magic German word: *Erlebnis*. But Milch hardly touches on the distinction between literary criticism and theory. He rejects a general 'science of literature', as all knowledge about literature has its place in history, and poetics cannot be divorced from historical relations.

I recognize that Milch's discussion raises interesting historical questions about the forms in which the insights of criticism have been conveyed, and that there is a real issue in the debate whether criticism is an art or a science (in the old, wide sense). I shall be content to say here that criticism has been conveyed in the most different art-forms, even in poems, such as those of Horace, Vida, and Pope, or in brief aphorisms, such as those by Friedrich Schlegel, or in abstractly, prosaically, even badly written treatises. The history of the 'literary review' (*Rezension*) as a genre raises historical and social questions, but it seems to me a mistake to identify 'criticism' with this one limited form. There still remains the problem of the relation between criticism and art. A feeling for art will enter into criticism: many critical forms require artistic skills of composition and style; imagination has its share in all knowledge and science. Still, I do not believe that the critic is an artist or that criticism is an art (in the strict modern sense). Its aim is intellectual cognition. It does not create a fictional imaginative world such as the world of music or poetry. Criticism is conceptual knowledge, or aims at such knowledge. It must ultimately aim at systematic knowledge about literature, at literary theory.

This point of view has recently been eloquently argued by Northrop Frye[a] in the 'Polemical Introduction' to his *Anatomy of Criticism*,[4] a work of literary theory which has been praised as the greatest book of criticism since Matthew Arnold. Frye, convincingly, rejects the view that literary theory and criticism are a kind of parasite on literature, that the critic is an artist *manqué* and postulates that 'criticism is a structure of thought and knowledge existing in its own right' (p. 5). I agree with his general enterprise, his belief in the necessity of a theory of literature. I want to argue here only against his attempt to erect literary theory into the uniquely worthwhile discipline and to expel criticism (in our sense of criticism of concrete works) from literary study. Frye makes a sharp distinction between, on the one hand, both 'literary theory' and 'genuine criticism', which progresses towards making the whole of literature intelligible, and, on the other hand, a kind of criticism which belongs only to the history of taste. Obviously Frye has little use for the 'public critic'—Sainte-Beuve, Hazlitt, Arnold, etc.—who represents the reading public and merely registers its prejudices. Frye laughs at 'the literary chit-chat which makes the reputations of poets boom and crash in an imaginary stock exchange. That wealthy investor, Mr Eliot, after dumping Milton on the market, is now buying him again; Donne has probably reached his peak and will begin to taper off; Tennyson may be in for a slight flutter but the Shelley stocks are still bearish' (p. 18). Frye is obviously right in ridiculing the 'whirligig of taste'; but he must be wrong in drawing the conclusion that 'as the history of taste has no organic connection with criticism, it can be easily separated'.

In my own *History of Modern Criticism* I have discovered that it cannot be done.[5] Frye's view that 'the study of literature can never be founded on value judgements', that the theory of literature is not directly concerned with value judgments, seems to me quite mistaken. He himself concedes that the 'critic will find soon, and constantly, that Milton is a more rewarding and suggestive poet to work with than Blackmore' (p. 25). Whatever his impatience with arbitrary literary opinions may be or with the game of rankings, I cannot see how such a divorce as he seems to advocate is feasible in practice. Literary theories, principles, criteria cannot be arrived at *in vacuo*: every critic in history has developed his theory in contact (as has Frye himself) with concrete works of art which he has had to select, interpret, analyse and, after all, to judge. The literary opinions, rankings, and judgments of a critic are buttressed, confirmed, developed by his theories, and the theories are drawn from, supported, illustrated, made concrete and plausible by works of art. The relegation, in Frye's *Anatomy of Criticism*, of concrete criticisms, judgments, evaluations to an arbitrary, irrational, and meaningless 'history of taste' seems to me as indefensible as the recent attempts to doubt the whole enterprise of literary theory and to absorb all literary study into history.

In the 'forties, during the heyday of the New Criticism[b], historical scholarship was on the defensive. Much was done to reassert the rights of criticism and

---

[a] See above, pp. 421–41.

[b] See the introductory notes on John Crowe Ransom (pp. 227–8 above) and Cleanth Brooks (pp. 291–2 above).

literary theory and to minimize the former overwhelming emphasis on biography and historical background. In the colleges a textbook, Brooks and Warren's *Understanding Poetry*[6] (1938), was the signal for the change. I believe my own *Theory of Literature* (1949) was widely understood as an attack on 'extrinsic' methods, as a repudiation of 'literary history', though the book actually contains a final chapter on 'Literary History' which emphatically argues against the neglect of this discipline and provides a theory of a new, less external literary history. But in recent years the situation has become reversed, and criticism, literary theory, the whole task of interpreting and evaluating literature as a simultaneous order has been doubted and rejected. The New Criticism, and actually any criticism, is today on the defensive. One type of discussion moves on an empirical level as a wrangle about the interpretation of specific passages or poems. The theoretical issue is there put often in very sweeping and vague terms. A straw man is set up: the New Critic, who supposedly denies that a work of art can be illuminated by historical knowledge at all. It is then easy to show that poems have been misunderstood because the meaning of an obsolete word was missed or a historical or biographical allusion ignored or misread. But I do not believe that there ever was a single reputable 'New' critic who has taken the position imputed to him. The New Critics, it seems to me rightly, have argued that a literary work of art is a verbal structure of a certain coherence and wholeness, and that literary study had often become completely irrelevant to this total meaning, that it had moved all too often into external information about biography, social conditions, historical backgrounds, etc. But this argument of the New Critics did not mean and could not be conceived to mean a denial of the relevance of historical information for the business of poetic interpretation. Words have their history; genres and devices descend from a tradition; poems often refer to contemporary realities. Cleanth Brooks—surely a New Critic who has focused on the close reading of poetry—has, in a whole series of essays (mainly on seventeenth-century poems), shown very precisely some of the ways in which historical information may be necessary for the understanding of specific poems. In a discussion of Marvell's 'Horatian Ode',[7] Brooks constantly appeals to the historical situation for his interpretation, though he is rightly very careful to distinguish between the exact meaning of the poem and the presumed attitude of Marvell towards Cromwell and Charles I. He argues 'that the critic needs the help of the historian—all the help he can get', but insists that 'the poem has to be read as a poem—that what it "says" is a question for the critic to answer, and that no amount of historical evidence as such can finally determine what the poem says' (p. 155). This seems a conciliatory, sensible attitude which holds firmly to the critical point of view and still admits the auxiliary value of historical information, and does not of course deny the separate enterprise of literary history.

Usually, however, the defenders of the historical point of view are dissatisfied with such a concession. They remind us loudly that a literary work can be interpreted only in the light of history and that ignorance of history distorts a reading of the work. Thus Rosemond Tuve, in three very learned books,[8] has kept up a running battle against the modern readers of the metaphysical poets and of Milton. But the issues debated by her are far from clear-cut conflicts between historical scholarship and modern criticism. For instance, in her attack on Empson's[a] reading of Herbert's 'Sacrifice',[9] she clearly has the upper hand not because she is a historian and Empson is a critic but because Empson is an arbitrary, wilful, fantastic reader of poetry who is unwilling or unable to look at his text as a whole but runs after all sorts of speculations and associations. 'All the Freudian stuff,' says Empson disarmingly, 'what fun!' He takes the line of Christ complaining, 'Man stole the fruit, but I must climb the tree', to mean that Christ is 'doing the stealing, that so far from sinless he is Prometheus and the criminal', that 'Christ is climbing upwards, like Jack on the Beanstalk, and taking his people with him back to Heaven'. Christ is 'evidently smaller than Man or at any rate than Eve, who could pluck the fruit without climbing... the son stealing from his father's orchard is a symbol of incest', etc. (p. 294). Miss Tuve seems right in insisting that 'I must climb the tree' means only 'I must ascend the cross', and that 'must' does not imply Christ's littleness or boyishness but refers to the command of God. Miss Tuve appeals, plausibly, to the concept of *figura*, of typology: Adam was considered as the type of Christ. Christ was the second Adam, the cross the other tree. Miss Tuve accumulates, in *A Reading of George Herbert*, a mass of learning to show that there are liturgical phrases, Middle English and Latin poems, devotional treatises, etc., which anticipate the general situation of Herbert's poem, and that even many details of the complaint of Christ can be found long before Herbert in texts Herbert probably had never seen as well as in texts he might have known or knew for certain as an Anglican priest. All this is useful and even impressive as a study of sources and conventions, but it surely does not prove what she apparently hopes to prove: that Herbert's poem is somehow unoriginal, that Empson is mistaken in speaking of 'Herbert's method' and its 'uniqueness'. Empson in his sly rejoinder[10] quite rightly argues that no amount of background study can solve the problem of poetic value. What is at issue is not a conflict between history and criticism but empirical questions about the correctness or incorrectness of certain interpretations. I think one must grant that Empson laid himself wide open to the charge of misreading but then one must say in his defence that nobody, literally nobody, had yet commented on that poem in any detail and that Empson's method, atomistic, associative, arbitrary as it is, is at least an ingenious attempt to come to grips with the problem of meaning. 'Close reading' has led to pedantries and aberrations, as have all the other methods of scholarship; but it is surely here to stay, as any branch of knowledge can advance and has advanced only by a careful, minute inspection of its objects, by putting things under the microscope even though general readers or even students and teachers may be often bored by the procedure.

But these debates, like the debate between the Chicago critics and the New Critics or between the Chicago critics and the mythographs,[b] concern rather

---

[a] William Empson—see above, pp. 146–57.

[b] For a note on the Chicago school of critics, see the Introductory Note on R. S. Crane, p. 592 below. By 'mythographs' Wellek presumably means critics, such as Maud Bodkin and Francis Fergusson in this Reader, who have used concepts and methods drawn from anthropology and Jungian psychology.

specific problems of interpretation than our wider debate about the relationship of theory, criticism, and history. Far greater and more difficult issues are raised by those who have genuinely embraced the creed of 'historicism', which after a long career in Germany and Italy, after its theoretical formulations by Dilthey, Windelband, Rickert, Max Weber, Troeltsch, Meinecke, and Croce, has finally reached the United States and has been embraced by literary scholars almost as a new religion. To give a characteristic recent example, Roy Harvey Pearce, in an article, 'Historicism Once More',[11]—strangely enough lauded and endorsed by J. C. Ransom—preaches a new historicism and concludes by quoting a poem by Robert Penn Warren with this climactic line, 'The World is real. It is there' (*Promises* 2).

Warren, hardly an enemy of the New Criticism, is quoted as the key witness for 'historicism', though his fine poem has nothing whatever to do with historicism and merely conveys, powerfully and movingly, a feeling for the reality of the past which might conceivably rather be called 'existential'. It asserts the kind of realization and wonder which Carlyle insisted upon in many of his later writings after he had repudiated his early adherence to German historicism. To quote Carlyle's examples: Dr Johnson actually told a street-walker, 'No, no, my girl, it won't do'; Charles I actually stayed the night in a hayloft with a peasant in 1651; King Lackland 'was verily there', at St Edmundsbury, and left '*tredecim sterlingii*, if nothing more, and did live and look in one way or the other, and a whole world was living and looking at him'.[12] But such wonder, appropriate to the poet or Carlyle, is only the beginning of historicism as a method or a philosophy. Pearce's historicism is a confused mixture of existentialism and historicism, a string of bombastic assertions about humanity, the possibility of literature, and so on, with the constant polemical refrain that 'criticism is a form of historical study' (p. 568). It is not worth trying to disentangle the hopeless muddles of Pearce's amazing stew of existence, eschatology, history, the 'creative ground of all values', the whole weird mixture of Rudolph Bultmann, Américo Castro, Kenneth Burke, and Walter J. Ong, S.J., all quoted on one page. It is better to turn to a knowledgeable and sophisticated upholder of the historistic creed such as my late colleague and friend, Erich Auerbach.[a]

In a review of my *History of Modern Criticism*[13] from which certain formulations passed, without explicit reference to my work, into the introduction of his posthumous book, *Literatursprache und Publikum in der lateinischen Spätantike und im Mittelalter* [*Literary Language and the Public in the late Classical and Middle Ages*],[14] and into his English article 'Vico's Contribution to Literary Criticism',[15] Auerbach states most clearly the historistic creed:

> Our historistic way of feeling and judging is so deeply rooted in us that we have ceased to be aware of it. We enjoy the art, the poetry and the music of many different peoples and periods with equal preparedness for understanding.... The variety of periods and civilizations no longer frightens us.... It is true that perspectivistic understanding fails as soon as political interests are at stake; but otherwise, especially in aesthetic matters, our historistic capacity of adaptation to the most various forms of beauty is almost bound-

[a] See above, pp. 315–32.

less.... But the tendency to forget or to ignore historical perspectivism is widespread, and it is, especially among literary critics, connected with the prevailing antipathy to philology of the nineteenth-century type, this philology being considered as the embodiment and the result of historicism. Thus, many believe that historicism leads to antiquarian pedantry, to the over-evaluation of biographical detail, to complete indifference to the values of the work of art; therefore to a complete lack of categories with which to judge, and finally to arbitrary eclecticism. [But] it is wrong to believe that historical relativism or perspectivism makes us incapable of evaluating and judging the work of art, that it leads to arbitrary eclecticism, and that we need, for judgment, fixed and absolute categories. Historicism is not eclecticism.... Each historian (we may also call him, with Vico's terminology, 'philologist') has to undertake this task for himself, since historical relativism has a twofold aspect: it concerns the understanding historian as well as the phenomena to be understood. This is an extreme relativism; but we should not fear it.... The historian does not become incapable of judging; he learns what judging means. Indeed, he will soon cease to judge by abstract and unhistorical categories; he even will cease to search for such categories of judgment. That general human quality, common to the most perfect works of the particular periods, which alone may provide for such categories, can be grasped only in its particular forms, or else as a dialectical process in history; its abstract essence cannot be expressed in exact significant terms. It is from the material itself that he will learn to extract the categories or concepts which he needs for describing and distinguishing the different phenomena. These concepts are not absolute; they are elastic and provisional, changeable with changing history. But they will be sufficient to enable us to discover what the different phenomena mean within their own period, and what they mean within the three thousand years of conscious literary human life we know of; and finally, what they mean to us, here and now. That is judgment enough; it may lead also to some understanding of what is common to all of these phenomena, but it would be difficult to express it otherwise than as a dialectical process in history....

This is an excellent statement, moderately phrased, concrete in its proposals, supported by the authority of a scholar who knew the relevant German tradition and had the experience of working within it. It contains, no doubt, a measure of truth which we all have to recognize, but still it rouses ultimate, insuperable misgivings, a final dissatisfaction with the 'extreme relativism' accepted here so resignedly and even complacently. Let me try to sort out some of the problems raised and marshal some answers to this influential point of view. Let me begin at the most abstract level: the assertion of the inevitable conditioning of the historian's own point of view, the recognition of one's own limited place in space and time, the relativism elaborated and emphasized by the 'sociology of knowledge', particularly by Karl Mannheim in *Ideologie und Utopie*.[16] This kind of relativism was and is extremely valuable as a method of investigating the hidden assumptions and biases of the investigator himself. But it surely can serve only as a general warning, as a kind of *memento mori*. As Isaiah Berlin observes, in a similar context:

Such charges [of subjectiveness or relativity] resemble suggestions, sometimes casually advanced, that life is a dream. We protest that 'everything' cannot be a dream, for then, with nothing to contrast with dreams, the notion of a 'dream' loses all specific reference.... If everything is subjective or relative, nothing can be judged to be more so than anything else. If words like 'subjective' and 'relative', 'prejudiced' and 'biased', are terms not of comparison and contrast—do not imply the possibility of their own opposites, of 'objective' (or at least 'less subjective') or 'unbiased' (or at least 'less biased'), what meaning have they for us?[17]

The mere recognition of what A. O. Lovejoy has called, with a barbarous word formed on the analogy of the 'egocentric predicament', the 'presenticentric predicament'[18] does not get us anywhere: it merely raises the problem of all knowing; it leads only to universal scepticism, to theoretical paralysis. Actually the case of knowledge and even of historical knowledge is not that desperate. There are universal propositions in logic and mathematics such as two plus two equal four, there are universally valid ethical precepts, such, for instance, as that which condemns the massacre of innocent people, and there are many neutral true propositions concerning history and human affairs. There is a difference between the psychology of the investigator, his presumed bias, ideology, perspective, and the logical structure of his propositions. The genesis of a theory does not necessarily invalidate its truth. Men can correct their biases, criticize their presuppositions, rise above their temporal and local limitations, aim at objectivity, arrive at some knowledge and truth. The world may be dark and mysterious, but it is surely not completely unintelligible.

But the problems of literary study need not actually be approached in terms of this very general debate about the relativity of all knowledge or even the special difficulties of all historical knowledge. Literary study differs from historical study in having to deal not with documents but with monuments. A historian has to reconstruct a long-past event on the basis of eye-witness accounts, the literary student, on the other hand, has direct access to his object: the work of art. It is open to inspection whether it was written yesterday or three thousand years ago, while the battle of Marathon and even the battle of the Bulge have passed irrevocably. Only peripherally, in questions which have to do with biography or, say, the reconstruction of the Elizabethan playhouse, does the literary student have to rely on documents. He can examine his object, the work itself; he must understand, interpret, and evaluate it; he must, in short, be a critic in order to be a historian. The political or economic or social historian, no doubt, also selects his facts for their interest or importance, but the literary student is confronted with a special problem of value; his object, the work of art, is not only value-impregnated, but is itself a structure of values. Many attempts have been made to escape the inevitable consequences of this insight, to avoid the necessity not only of selection but of judgment, but all have failed and must, I think, fail unless we want to reduce literary study to a mere listing of books, to annals or a chronicle. There is nothing which can obviate the necessity of critical judgment, the need of aesthetic standards, just as there is nothing which can obviate the need of ethical or logical standards.

One widely used escape door leads nowhere: the assertion that we need not judge, but that we simply need adopt the criteria of the past: that we must reconstruct and apply the values of the period we are studying. I shall not merely argue that these standards cannot be reconstructed with certainty, that we are confronted with insurmountable difficulties if we want to be sure what Shakespeare intended by his plays and how he conceived them or what the Elizabethan audience understood by them. There are different schools of scholarship which try to get at this past meaning by different routes: E. E. Stoll believes in reconstructing stage conventions; Miss Tuve appeals to rhetorical training, or liturgical and iconographic traditions; others swear by the authority of the NED; still others, like J. Dover Wilson, think that 'the door to Shakespeare's workshop stands ajar' when they discover inconsistencies in punctuation or line arrangements from bibliographical evidence. Actually, in reconstructing the critical judgment of the past we appeal only to one criterion: that of contemporary success. But if we examine any literary history in the light of the actual opinions of the past we shall see that we do not admit and cannot admit the standards of the past. When we properly know the views of Englishmen about their contemporary literature, e.g. late in the eighteenth century, we may be in for some suprises: David Hume, for instance, thought Wilkie's *Epigoniad* comparable to Homer; Nathan Drake thought Cumberland's *Calvary* greater than Milton's *Paradise Lost*. Obviously, accepting contemporary evaluation requires our discriminating between a welter of opinions: who valued whom and why and when? Professor Geoffrey Barraclough, in a similar argument against historians who recommend that we should study 'the things that were important *then* rather than the things that are important *now*', advises them to look, for instance, at thirteenth-century chronicles: 'a dreary recital of miracles, tempests, comets, pestilences, calamities, and other wonderful things',[19] Clearly the standards of contemporaries cannot be binding on us, even if we could reconstruct them and find a common lowest denominator among their diversities. Nor can we simply divest ourselves of our individuality or the lessons we have learned from history. Asking us to interpret *Hamlet* only in terms of what the very hypothetical views of Shakespeare or his audience were is asking us to forget three hundred years of history. It prohibits us to use the insights of a Goethe or Coleridge, it impoverishes a work which has attracted and accumulated meanings in the course of history. But again this history itself, however instructive, cannot be binding on us: its authority is open to the same objections as the authority of the author's contemporaries. There is simply no way of avoiding judgment by us, by myself. Even the 'verdict of the ages' is only the accumulated judgment of other readers, critics, viewers, and even professors. The only truthful and right thing to do is to make this judgment as objective as possible, to do what every scientist and scholar does: to isolate his object, in our case, the literary work of art, to contemplate it intently, to analyse, to interpret, and finally to evaluate it by criteria derived from, verified by, buttressed by, as wide a knowledge, as close an observation, as keen a sensibility, as honest a judgment as we can command.

The old absolutism is untenable: the assumption of one eternal, narrowly defined standard had to be abandoned under the impact of our experience of the wide variety of art, but on the other hand, complete relativism is equally untenable; it leads to paralysing scepticism, to an anarchy of values, to the acceptance of the old vicious maxim: *de gestibus non est disputandum.* ['there is no arguing about tastes']. The kind of period relativism recommended as a solution by Auerbach is no way out: it would split up the concept of art and poetry into innumerable fragments. Relativism in the sense of a denial of all objectivity is refuted by many arguments: by the parallel to ethics and science, by recognition that there are aesthetic as well as ethical imperatives and scientific truths. Our whole society is based on the assumption that we know what is just, and our science on the assumption that we know what is true. Our teaching of literature is actually also based on aesthetic imperatives, even if we feel less definitely bound by them and seem much more hesitant to bring these assumptions out into the open. The disaster of the 'humanities' as far as they are concerned with the arts and literature is due to their timidity in making the very same claims which are made in regard to law and truth. Actually we do make these claims when we teach *Hamlet* or *Paradise Lost* rather than Grace Metalious or, to name contemporaries of Shakespeare and Milton, Henry Glapthorne or Richard Blackmore. But we do so shamefully, apologetically, hesitatingly. There is, contrary to frequent assertions, a very wide agreement on the great classics: the main canon of literature. There is an insuperable gulf between really great art and very bad art: between say 'Lycidas' and a poem on the leading page of the *New York Times*, between Tolstoy's *Master and Man* and a story in *True Confessions*. Relativists always shirk the issue of thoroughly bad poetry. They like to move in the region of near-great art, where disputes among critics are most frequent, as works are valued for very different reasons. The more complex a work of art, the more diverse the structure of values it embodies, and hence the more difficult its interpretation, the greater the danger of ignoring one or the other aspect. But this does not mean that all interpretations are equally right, that there is no possibility of differentiating between them. There are utterly fantastic interpretations, partial, distorted interpretations. We may argue about Bradley's or Dover Wilson's or even Ernest Jones' interpretation of Hamlet: but we know that Hamlet was no woman in disguise. The concept of adequacy of interpretation leads clearly to the concept of the correctness of judgment. Evaluation grows out of understanding; correct evaluation out of correct understanding. There is a hierarchy of viewpoints implied in the very concept of adequacy of interpretation. Just as there is correct interpretation, at least as an ideal, so there is correct judgment, good judgment. Auerbach's relativistic argument that nowadays we enjoy the art of all ages and peoples: neolithic cave-paintings, Chinese landscapes, Negro masks, Gregorian chants, etc., should and can be turned against the relativists. It shows that there is a common feature in all art which we recognize today more clearly than in earlier ages. There is a common humanity which makes every art remote in time and place, and originally serving functions quite different from aesthetic contemplation, accessible and enjoyable to us. We have risen above the limitations of tradition Western taste—the parochialism and relativism of such taste—into a realm if not of absolute then of universal art. There is such a realm, and the various historical manifestations are often far less historically limited in character than is assumed by historians interested mainly in making art serve a temporary social purpose and illuminate social history. Some Chinese or ancient Greek love lyrics on basic simple themes are hardly dateable in space or time except for their language. Even Auerbach, in spite of his radical relativism, has to admit 'some understanding of what is common to all of these phenomena' and grants that we do not adopt relativism when our political (that is ethical, vital) interests are at stake. Logic, ethics and, I believe, aesthetics cry aloud against a complete historicism which, one should emphasize, in men such as Auerbach, is still shored up by an inherited ideal of humanism and buttressed methodologically by an unconsciously held conceptual framework of grammatical, stylistic and *geistesgeschichtlich* [history-of-ideas] categories. In such radical versions as, e.g. George Boas' *A Primer for Critics*,[20] Bernard Heyl's *New Bearings in Esthetics and Art Criticism*,[21] or Wayne Shumaker's *Elements of Critical Theory*,[22] the theory leads to a dehumanization of the arts, to a paralysis of criticism, to a surrender of our primary concern for truth. The only way out is a carefully defined and refined absolutism, a recognition that 'the Absolute is in the relative, though not finally and fully in it'. This was the formula of Ernst Troeltsch, who struggled more than any other historian with the problem of historicism and came to the conclusion that 'historicism' must be superseded.[23]

We must return to the task of building a literary theory, a system of principles, a theory of values which will necessarily draw on the criticism of concrete works of art and will constantly invoke the assistance of literary history. But the three disciplines are and will remain distinct: history cannot absorb or replace theory, while theory should not even dream of absorbing history. André Malraux has spoken eloquently of the imaginary museum, the museum without walls, drawing on a world-wide acquaintance with the plastic arts. Surely in literature we are confronted with the same task as that of the art critic, or at least an analogous task: we can more directly and easily assemble our museum in a library but we are still faced with the walls and barriers of languages and historical forms of languages. Much of our work aims at breaking down these barriers, at demolishing these walls by translations, philological study, editing, comparative literature, or simply imaginative sympathy. Ultimately literature, like the plastic arts, like Malraux's voices of silence, is a chorus of voices—articulate throughout the ages—which asserts man's defiance of time and destiny, his victory over impermanence, relativity, and history.

Notes

1. René Wellek and Austin Warren, *Theory of Literature* (New York, 1949).
2. I have used the term thus widely in my *History of Modern Criticism* (New Haven, 1955).
3. *Germanisch-romanische Monatsschrift*, xviii, 1930, 1–15, reprinted in *Kleine Schriften zur Literatur- und Geistesgeschichte* (Heidelberg, 1957), pp. 9–24.
4. Princeton, 1957.
5. In his very generous review, Mr Frye apparently wished I had done so, cf. *Virginia Quarterly*, xxxii, 1956, 310–15.

6. Cleanth Brooks, Jr. and R. P. Warren, *Understanding Poetry; an Anthology for College Students* (New York, 1938).

7. 'Literary Criticism', in *English Institute Essays, 1946* (New York, 1947), pp. 127–58.

8. *Elizabethan and Metaphysical Imagery* (Chicago, 1947); *A Reading of George Herbert* (Chicago, 1952); *Images and Themes in Five Poems by Milton* (Cambridge, Mass., 1957).

9. In William Empson, *Seven Types of Ambiguity* (London, 1930), pp. 286 ff.

10. *Kenyon Review*, xii, 1950, 735–8.

11. Ibid., xx, 1958, 554–91.

12. Carlyle, *Works*, Centenary edn. (London, 1898–9), *Essays*, iii, 54–6; *Past and Present*, p. 46.

13. *Romanische Forschungen*, lxii, 1956, 387–97.

14. Bern, 1958.

15. *Studia philologica et letteraria in honorem L. Spitzer*, ed. A. G. Hatcher and K. L. Selig (Bern, 1958), pp. 31–7.

16. Bonn, 1929, Eng. trans. London, 1936.

17. *Historical Inevitability* (Oxford, 1954), p. 61.

18. A. O. Lovejoy, 'Present standpoints and past history', *Journal of Philosophy*, xxxvi, 1939, 477–89.

19. *History in a Changing World* (Norman, Oklahoma, 1956), p. 22.

20. Baltimore, 1937 (renamed *Wingless Pegasus: A Handbook for Critics*, Baltimore, 1950).

21. New Haven, 1943.

22. Berkeley, 1952.

23. Cf. 'Historiography' in Hastings' *Encylopaedia of Religion and Ethics*, vi (Edinburgh, 1913), 722.

42   Wayne Booth

At the end of his book *The Rhetoric of Fiction* (1961), from which the following
extract is taken, Wayne Booth (b. 1921) sums up his position thus:

> Nothing the writer does can be finally understood in isolation from his effort
> to make it all accessible to someone else—his peers, himself as imagined
> reader, his audience. The novel comes into existence *as* something
> communicable, and the means of communication are not shameful
> intrusions unless they are made with shameful ineptitude.

In other words, the art of fiction is essentially persuasive or rhetorical—
rhetorical in Booth's terms being a matter not only of verbal style but also of
broader narrative strategies, especially the choice and manipulation of 'point of
view'. And if this is granted, it follows that there is no inherent virtue in
suppressing the rhetorical possibilities of the novel form, and no inherent
wickedness in exploiting them.

In this way Wayne Booth challenged a certain body of critical opinion which,
deriving from the precept and practice of Flaubert, James, and other modern
masters of fiction, had hardened into a kind of orthodoxy by the 'forties and
'fifties of this century; an orthodoxy that not only prescribed impersonal,
indirect narration for modern fiction, but retrospectively condemned such
novelists as Dickens and George Eliot for their authorial omniscience and
intrusiveness. Part of Booth's argument is that absolute 'objectivity' in literature
is unattainable, and that the literary qualities that we may legitimately denote
by the word are not necessarily to be associated with any particular narrative
technique. This is the area explored in the following extract which, under the
title, 'General Rules II: "All Authors Should Be Objective"', constitutes
Chapter iii of *The Rhetoric of Fiction*.

It is arguable that in the course of his book, Professor Booth evinces a
prejudice (against the ironic and ambiguous qualities of modern fiction) as
extreme and unnecessary as the one he himself exposes. Without doubt,
however, he has made all readers more aware of the complex varieties of
narrative technique and greatly extended the available terms for describing
them.

Wayne Booth was Professor of English at Earlham College, Indiana, when he
published *The Rhetoric of Fiction*, but has since returned to the University of
Chicago, where he himself was educated. *The Rhetoric of Fiction* is dedicated to
R. S. Crane, leader of the Chicago Aristotelian school of criticism (see below,
pp. 592-3) to which Booth is clearly indebted.

CROSS REFERENCES: 4. Henry James
11. E. M. Forster
29. Mark Schorer
34. Alain Robbe-Grillet

COMMENTARY: David Lodge, 'The rhetoric of Wayne Booth',
Critical Survey, iii (1966), 4-6
Wayne Booth, '*The Rhetoric of Fiction* and the Poetics
of Fictions', *Novel*, i (1968), 105-17

['Objectivity' in fiction]

'A novelist's characters must be with him as he lies down to sleep, and as he wakes from his dreams. He must learn to hate them and to love them.' TROLLOPE

'The less one feels a thing, the more likely one is to express it as it really is.' FLAUBERT

'An ecstatically happy prose writer ... can't be moderate or temperate or brief. ...He can't be detached.... In the wake of anything as large and consuming as happiness, he necessarily forfeits the much smaller but, for a writer, always rather exquisite pleasure of appearing on the page serenely sitting on a fence.' The narrator of J. D. Salinger's *Seymour: An Introduction*

'M. de Maupassant is remarkably objective and impersonal, but he would go too far if he were to entertain the belief that he has kept himself out of his books. They speak of him eloquently, even if it only be to tell us how easy ... he has found this impersonality.' HENRY JAMES

'Now you are, through Maury, expressing your views, of course; but you would do so differently if you were deliberately stating them as your views.' MAXWELL PERKINS, in a letter to F. Scott Fitzgerald

A surprising number of writers, even those who have thought of their writing as 'self-expression', have sought a freedom from the tyranny of subjectivity, echoing Goethe's claim that 'Every healthy effort ... is directed from the inward to the outward world'.[1] From time to time others have risen to defend commitment, engagement, involvement. But, at least until recently, the predominant demand in this century has been for some sort of objectivity.

Like all such terms, however, *objectivity* is many things. Underlying it and its many synonyms—impersonality, detachment, disinterestedness, neutrality, etc.—we can distinguish at least three separate qualities: neutrality, impartiality, and *impassibilité*.

Neutrality and the author's 'second self'

Objectivity in the author can mean, first, an attitude of neutrality towards all values, an attempt at disinterested reporting of all things good and evil. Like many literary enthusiasms, the passion for neutrality was imported into fiction from the other arts relatively late. Keats was saying in 1818 the kind of thing that novelists began to say only with Flaubert.

> The poetical character ... has no character.... It lives in gusto, be it foul or fair, high or low, rich or poor, mean or elevated. It has as much delight in conceiving an Iago as an Imogen. What shocks the virtuous philosopher, delights the camelion Poet. It does not harm from its relish of the dark side of things any more than from its taste for the bright one; because they both end in speculation.[2]

Three decades later Flaubert recommended a similar neutrality to the novelist who would be a poet. For him the model is the attitude of the scientist. Once we have spent enough time, he says, in 'treating the human soul with the impartiality which physical scientists show in studying matter, we will have taken an immense step forward'.[3] Art must achieve 'by a pitiless method, the precision of the physical sciences'.[4]

It should be unnecessary here to show that no author can ever attain to this kind of objectivity. Most of us today would, like Sartre, renounce the analogy with science even if we could admit that science is objective in this sense. What is more, we all know by now that a careful reading of any statement in defence of the artist's neutrality will reveal commitment; there is always some deeper value in relation to which neutrality is taken to be good. Chekhov, for example, begins bravely enough in defence of neutrality, but he cannot write three sentences without committing himself.

> I am afraid of those who look for a tendency between the lines, and who are determined to regard me either as a liberal or as a conservative. I am not a liberal, not a conservative, not a believer in gradual progress, not a monk, not an indifferentist. I should like to be a free artist and nothing more.... I have no preference either for gendarmes, or for butchers, or for scientists, or for writers, or for the younger generation. I regard trade-marks and labels as a superstition.[5]

Freedom and art are good, then, and superstition bad? Soon he is carried away to a direct repudiation of the plea for 'indifference' with which he began. 'My holy of holies is the human body, health, intelligence, talent, inspiration, love, and the most absolute freedom—freedom from violence and lying, whatever forms they may take' (p. 63). Again and again he betrays in this way the most passionate kind of commitment to what he often calls objectivity.

> The artist should be, not the judge of his characters and their conversations, but only an unbiased witness. I once overheard a desultory conversation about pessimism between two Russians; nothing was solved,—and my business is to report the conversation exactly as I heard it, and let the jury,—that is, the readers, estimate its value. My business is merely to be talented, i.e., to be able ... to illuminate the characters and speak their language (pp. 58-9).

But 'illuminate' according to what lights? 'A writer must be as objective as a chemist; he must abandon the subjective line; he must know that dung-heaps play a very respectable part in a landscape, and that evil passions are as inherent in life as good ones' (pp. 275-6). We have learned by now to ask of such statements: Is it *good* to be faithful to what is 'inherent'? Is it good to include every part of the 'landscape'? If so, why? According to what scale of values? To repudiate one scale is necessarily to imply another.

It would be a serious mistake, however, to dismiss talk about the author's neutrality simply because of this elementary and understandable confusion between neutrality towards *some* values and neutrality towards *all*. Cleansed of the polemical excesses, the attack on subjectivity can be seen to rest on several important insights.

To succeed in writing some kinds of works, some novelists find it necessary to repudiate all intellectual or political causes. Chekhov does not want himself, *as artist*, to be either liberal or conservative. Flaubert, writing in 1853, claims that even the artist who recognizes the demand to be a 'triple-thinker', even the artist who recognizes the need for ideas in abundance, 'must have neither religion, nor country, nor social conviction'.[6]

Unlike the claim to complete neutrality, this claim will never be refuted, and it will not suffer from shifts in literary theory or philosophical fashion. Like its opposite, the existentialist claim of Sartre and others that the artist should be totally *engagé*, its validity depends on the kind of novel the author is writing. Some great artists have been committed to the causes of their times, and some have not. Some works seem to be harmed by their burden of commitment (many of Sartre's own works, for example, in spite of their freedom from authorial comment) and some seem to be able to absorb a great deal of commitment (*The Divine Comedy, Four Quartets, Gulliver's Travels,* [Arthur Koestler's] *Darkness at Noon,* [Ignazio Silone's] *Bread and Wine*). One can always find examples to prove either side of the case; the test is whether the particular ends of the artist enable him to do something with his commitment, not whether he has it or not.

Everyone is against everyone else's prejudices and in favour of his own commitment to the truth. All of us would like the novelist somehow to operate on the level of our own passion for truth and right, a passion which by definition is not in the least prejudiced. The argument in favour of neutrality is thus useful in so far as it warns the novelist that he can seldom afford to pour his untransformed biases into his work. The deeper he sees into permanency, the more likely he is to earn the discerning reader's concurrence. The author as he writes should be like the ideal reader described by Hume in 'The Standard of Taste', who, in order to reduce the distortions produced by prejudice, considers himself as 'man in general' and forgets, if possible, his 'individual being' and his 'peculiar circumstances'.

To put it in this way, however, is to understate the importance of the author's individuality. As he writes, he creates not simply an ideal, impersonal 'man in general' but an implied version of 'himself' that is different from the implied authors we meet in other men's works. To some novelists it has seemed, indeed,

567

that they were discovering or creating themselves as they wrote. As Jessamyn West says, it is sometimes 'only by writing the story that the novelist can discover—not his story—but its writer, the official scribe, so to speak, for that narrative'.[7] Whether we call this implied author an 'official scribe', or adopt the term recently revived by Kathleen Tillotson—the author's 'second self'[8]— it is clear that the picture the reader gets of this presence is one of the author's most important effects. However impersonal he may try to be, his reader will inevitably construct a picture of the official scribe who writes in this manner— and of course that official scribe will never be neutral towards all values. Our reactions to his various commitments, secret or overt, will help to determine our response to the work. The reader's role in this relationship I must save for chapter v. Our present problem is the intricate relationship of the so-called real author with his various official versions of himself.

We must say various versions, for regardless of how sincere an author may try to be, his different works will imply different versions, different ideal combinations of norms. Just as one's personal letters imply different versions of oneself, depending on the differing relationships with each correspondent and the purpose of each letter, so the writer sets himself out with a different air depending on the needs of particular works.

These differences are most evident when the second self is given an overt, speaking role in the story. When Fielding comments, he gives us explicit evidence of a modifying process from work to work; no single version of Fielding emerges from reading the satirical Jonathan Wild, the two great 'comic epics in prose', Joseph Andrews and Tom Jones, and that troublesome hybrid, Amelia. There are many similarities among them, of course; all of the implied authors value benevolence and generosity; all of them deplore self-seeking brutality. In these and many other respects they are indistinguishable from most implied authors of most significant works until our own century. But when we descend from this level of generality to look at the particular ordering of values in each novel, we find great variety. The author of Jonathan Wild is by implication very much concerned with public affairs and with the effects of unchecked ambition on the 'great men' who attain to power in the world. If we had only this novel by Fielding, we would infer from it that in his real life he was much more single-mindedly engrossed in his role as magistrate and reformer of public manners than is suggested by the implied author of Joseph Andrews and Tom Jones—to say nothing of Shamela (what would we infer about Fielding if he had never written anything but Shamela!). On the other hand, the author who greets us on page one of Amelia has none of that air of facetiousness combined with grand insouciance that we meet from the beginning in Joseph Andrews and Tom Jones. Suppose that Fielding had never written anything but Amelia, filled as it is with the kind of commentary we find at the beginning:

> The various accidents which befell a very worthy couple after their uniting in the state of matrimony will be the subject of the following history. The distresses which they waded through were some of them so exquisite, and the incidents which produced these so extraordinary, that they seemed to

require not only the utmost malice, but the utmost invention, which superstition hath ever attributed to Fortune: though whether any such being interfered in the case, or, indeed, whether there be any such being in the universe, is a matter which I by no means presume to determine in the affirmative.

Could we ever infer from this the Fielding of the earlier works? Though the author of *Amelia* can still indulge in occasional jests and ironies, his general air of sententious solemnity is strictly in keeping with the very special effects proper to the work as a whole. Our picture of him is built, of course, only partly by the narrator's explicit commentary; it is even more derived from the kind of tale he chooses to tell. But the commentary makes explicit for us a relationship which is present in all fiction, but which, in fiction without commentary, may be overlooked.

It is a curious fact that we have no terms either for this created 'second self' or for our relationship with him. None of our terms for various aspects of the narrator is quite accurate. 'Persona', 'mask', and 'narrator' are sometimes used, but they more commonly refer to the speaker in the work who is after all only one of the elements created by the implied author and who may be separated from him by large ironies. 'Narrator' is usually taken to mean the 'I' of a work, but the 'I' is seldom if ever identical with the implied image of the artist.

'Theme', 'meaning', 'symbolic significance', 'theology', or even 'ontology'— all these have been used to describe the norms which the reader must apprehend in each work if he is to grasp it adequately. Such terms are useful for some purposes, but they can be misleading because they almost inevitably come to seem like purposes for which the works exist. Though the old-style effort to find the theme or moral has been generally repudiated, the new-style search for the 'meaning' which the work 'communicates' or 'symbolizes' can yield the same kinds of misreading. It is true that both types of search, however clumsily pursued, express a basic need: the reader's need to know where, in the world of values, he stands—that is, to know where the author *wants* him to stand. But most works worth reading have so many possible 'themes', so many possible mythological or metaphorical or symbolic analogues, that to find any one of them, and to announce it as what the work is *for*, is to do at best a very small part of the critical task. Our sense of the implied author includes not only the extractable meanings but also the moral and emotional content of each bit of action and suffering of all of the characters. It includes, in short, the intuitive apprehension of a completed artistic whole; the chief value to which *this* implied author is committed, regardless of what party his creator belongs to in real life, is that which is expressed by the total form.

Three other terms are sometimes used to name the core of norms and choices which I am calling the implied author. 'Style' is sometimes broadly used to cover whatever it is that gives us a sense, from word to word and line to line, that the author sees more deeply and judges more profoundly than his presented characters. But, though style is one of our main sources of insight into the author's norms, in carrying such strong overtones of the merely verbal the word *style* excludes our sense of the author's skill in his choice of character and episode and scene and idea. 'Tone' is similarly used to refer to the implicit evaluation which the author manages to convey behind his explicit presentation,[9] but it almost inevitably suggests again something limited to the merely verbal; some aspects of the implied author may be inferred through tonal variations, but his major qualities will depend also on the hard facts of action and character in the tale that is told.

Similarly, 'technique' has at times been expanded to cover all discernible signs of the author's artistry. If everyone used 'technique' as Mark Schorer does,[10] covering with it almost the entire range of choices made by the author, then it might very well serve our purposes. But it is usually taken for a much narrower matter, and consequently it will not do. We can be satisfied only with a term that is as broad as the work itself but still capable of calling attention to that work as the product of a choosing, evaluating person rather than as a self-existing thing. The 'implied author' chooses, consciously or unconsciously, what we read; we infer him as an ideal, literary, created version of the real man; he is the sum of his own choices.

It is only by distinguishing between the author and his implied image that we can avoid pointless and unverifiable talk about such qualities as 'sincerity' or 'seriousness' in the author. Because Ford Madox Ford thinks of Fielding and Defoe and Thackeray as the unmediated authors of their novels, he must end by condemning them as insincere, since there is every reason to believe that they write 'passages of virtuous aspirations that were in no way any aspirations of theirs'.[11] Presumably he is relying on external evidences of Fielding's lack of virtuous aspirations. But we have only the work as evidence for the only kind of sincerity that concerns us: Is the implied author in harmony with himself—that is, are his other choices in harmony with his explicit narrative character? If a narrator who by every trustworthy sign is presented to us as a reliable spokesman for the author professes to believe in values which are never realized in the structure as a whole, we can then talk of an insincere work. A great work establishes the 'sincerity' of its implied author, regardless of how grossly the man who created that author may belie in his *other* forms of conduct the values embodied in his work. For all we know, the only sincere moments of his life may have been lived as he wrote his novel.

What is more, in this distinction between author and implied author we find a middle position between the technical irrelevance of talk about the artist's objectivity and the harmful error of pretending that an author can allow direct intrusions of his own immediate problems and desires. The great defenders of objectivity were working on an important matter and they knew it. Flaubert is right in saying that Shakespeare does not barge clumsily into his works. We are never plagued with his undigested personal problems. Flaubert is also right in rebuking Louise Colet for writing 'La Servante' as a personal attack on Musset, with the personal passion destroying the aesthetic value of the poem (9-10 January 1854). And he is surely right when he forces the hero of the youthful version of *The Sentimental Education* (1845) to choose between the merely confessional statement and the truly rendered work of art.

But is he right when he claims that we do not know what Shakespeare loved or hated?[12] Perhaps—if he means only that we cannot easily tell from the plays whether the man Shakespeare preferred blondes to brunettes or whether he disliked bastards, Jews, or Moors. But the statement is most definitely mistaken if it means that the implied author of Shakespeare's plays is neutral towards all values. We do know what *this* Shakespeare loved and hated; it is hard to see how he could have written his plays at all if he had refused to take a strong line on at least one or two of the seven deadly sins. I return in chapter v to the question of beliefs in literature, and I try there to list a few of the values to which Shakespeare is definitely and obviously committed. They are for the most part not personal, idiosyncratic; Shakespeare is thus not recognizably subjective. But they are unmistakable violations of true neutrality; the implied Shakespeare is thoroughly engaged with life, and he does not conceal his judgment on the selfish, the foolish, and the cruel.

Even if all this were denied, it is difficult to see why there should be any necessary connection between neutrality and an absence of commentary. An author might very well use comments to warn the reader against judging. But if I am right in claiming that neutrality is impossible, even the most nearly neutral comment will reveal some sort of commitment.

> Once upon a time there lived in Berlin, Germany, a man called Albinus. He was rich, respectable, happy; one day he abandoned his wife for the sake of a youthful mistress; he loved; was not loved; and his life ended in disaster.
> This is the whole of the story and we might have left it at that had there not been profit and pleasure in the telling; and although there is plenty of space on a gravestone to contain, bound in moss, the abridged version of a man's life, detail is always welcome.[13]

Nabokov may here have purged his narrator's voice of all commitments save one, but that one is all-powerful: he believes in the ironic interest—and as it later turns out, the poignancy—of a man's fated self-destruction. Maintaining the same detached tone, this author can intrude whenever he pleases without violating our conviction that he is as objective as it is humanly possible to be. Describing the villain, he can call him both a 'dangerous man' and 'a very fine artist indeed' without reducing our confidence in his open-mindedness. But he is not neutral towards all values, and he does not pretend to be.

Impartiality and 'unfair' emphasis

The author's objectivity has also sometimes meant an attitude of impartiality towards his characters. Much of what Flaubert and Chekhov wrote about objectivity is really a plea to the artist not to load the dice, not to take sides unjustly against or for particular characters. Chekhov writes to a friend, 'I do not venture to ask you to love the gynaecologist and the professor, but I venture to remind you of the justice which for an objective writer is more precious than the air he breathes' (*Letters on the Short Story*, p. 78). Sometimes this impartiality is made to sound like universal love or pity or toleration: 'There is no one to blame, and should the guilt be traceable, that is the affair of the health officers and not of the artist.... She [your character] may act in any way she pleases, but the author should be kindly to the fingertips' (pp. 81, 82). Indeed, a very great deal of modern fiction has been written on the assumption, itself a basic commitment to a value, that to understand all is to forgive all. But this assumption is very different from the neutrality described in the first section. Writers who are successful in getting their readers to reserve judgment are not impartial about whether judgment should be reserved. As H. W. Leggett said, almost three decades ago, in a forgotten little classic on the role of what he calls the author's and reader's 'code', modern fiction often presents occasions to the reader to 'observe and refrain from judging ... and a part at least of the reader's satisfaction is due to his consciousness of his own broadmindedness'.[14]

In practice, no author ever manages to create a work which shows complete impartiality, whether impartial scorn, like Flaubert in *Bouvard et Pécuchet* attempting to 'attack everything', or impartial forgiveness. Flaubert could sometimes write as if he thought Shakespeare and the Greeks were impartial in a sense they would have been astonished by. 'The magnificent William sides with no one', and he refused to 'declaim against usury' in *The Merchant of Venice*.[15] But Shakespeare never pretends that Goneril and Regan stand equal with Cordelia before the bar of justice, even though they are judged by the same standard. And in *The Merchant of Venice* he is so far from impartiality that he can really be accused of employing a double standard at Shylock's expense, at least in the latter part of the play. Certainly he does not work according to any abstract notion of impartial treatment for all characters. Similarly, the Greek dramatists never pretended that there was no basic distinction between men like Oedipus and Orestes on the one hand, and the fools and knaves on the other. Though they did not deal in 'blacks and whites', as the popular attack on melodrama goes, they did not reduce all human worth to a grey blur.

Even among characters of equal moral, intellectual, or aesthetic worth, all authors inevitably take sides. A given work will be 'about' a character or set of characters. It cannot possibly give equal emphasis to all, regardless of what its author believes about the desirability of fairness. *Hamlet* is not fair to Claudius. No matter how hard G. Wilson Knight labours to convince us that we have misjudged Claudius,[16] and no matter how willing we are to admit that Claudius' story is potentially as interesting as Hamlet's, *this* is Hamlet's story, and it cannot do justice to the king. *Othello* is not fair to Cassio; *King Lear* is not just to the Duke of Cornwall; *Madame Bovary* is unfair to almost everyone but Emma; and *A Portrait of the Artist as a Young Man* positively maligns everyone but Stephen.

But who cares? The novelist who chooses to tell *this* story cannot at the same time tell *that* story; in centring our interest, sympathy, or affection on one character, he inevitably excludes from our interest, sympathy, or affection some other character. Art imitates life in this respect as in so many others; just as in real life I am inevitably unfair to everyone but myself or, at best, my immediate loved ones, so in literature complete impartiality is impossible. Is *Ulysses* fair to the bourgeois Irish characters that throng about Bloom and Stephen and Molly? We can thank our stars that it is not.

It is true, nevertheless, that some works are marred by an impression that the author has weighed his characters on dishonest scales. But this impression depends not on whether the author explicitly passes judgment but on whether the judgment he passes seems defensible in the light of the dramatized facts. A clear illustration can be seen in *Lady Chatterley's Lover*. Lawrence can talk as passionately as the next man about the dangers of partiality: 'Morality in the novel is the trembling instability of the balance. When the novelist puts his thumb in the scale, to pull down the balance to his own predilection, that is immorality.

'The modern novel tends to become more and more immoral, as the novelist tends to press his thumb heavier and heavier in the pan: either on the side of love, pure love: or on the side of licentious "freedom".'[17] What he hates, he tells us again and again, is the novel that is merely a 'treatise'. Though he is more aware than many have been that every novel implies 'some theory of being, some metaphysic', he demands that 'the metaphysic must always sub-serve the artistic purpose beyond the artist's conscious aim'.[18]

Though critics of *Lady Chatterley's Lover* are agreed on little else, they seem to agree that the novelist has in this work pressed his thumb very heavily indeed in the pan containing his prophetic vision of a love that is neither 'love, pure love' nor 'licentious freedom', a love that can save us from the destructive forces of civilization. Critics who approve of the position praise the book— but in terms that make clear its courageous exposition of the truth. Critics who think the thesis exaggerated or false may admit to Lawrence's gift but deplore the injustices he commits in defence of his lovers. But everyone seems to deal with the book in terms of its thesis.[19] Even the critics who feel, with Mark Schorer, that Lawrence managed to make 'the preacher' and 'the poet' coincide 'formally' cannot discuss the book without spending most of their energies on the preachments.[20]

Significantly enough the question of Lawrence's impartiality seems com-pletely unrelated to his choice of technical devices. Whether we accept or reject Lawrence's vision of a new salvation, our decision is not based on whether he uses this or that form of authorial preachment; objections against Lawrence's bias have more often dealt with his portrayal of Mellors, the gamekeeper, than with the fact that he allows authorial commentary of various kinds. When Mellors presents at great length his belief that 'if men could fuck with warm hearts, and the women take it warm-heartedly everything would come all right' (chap. xiv), the panacea may strike us as inadequate to the point of comedy or as an inspiring portrait of a brave new world acomin', but we will receive little help in our choice by asking whether the beliefs are given in dramatic form. Those of us who reject this side of the book do so finally on the grounds that what Mellors says implies for us a version of D. H. Lawrence that we cannot admire; there is an unbridgeable disparity between the implied author's proffered salvation and our own views.[21]

What we object to, then, is the Lawrence implied by some of the drama, not necessarily the Lawrence given in the commentary. The little disquisition in chapter nine on the powers and limitations of fiction, which a critic has deplored as evidence of 'unsteadiness of control in points of view',[22] really shows Lawrence in very attractive form. Since we recognize the validity of the author's attack on the conventional fiction that appeals only to the vices of the public, the fiction that is humiliating because it glorifies the most corrupt feelings under the guise of 'purity', we grant to the author the superiority of his effort to use the novel to 'reveal the most secret places of life'. Lawrence's essential integrity seems to us beyond question after such a passage—at least until we encounter another long-winded outburst by Mellors.

In short, whatever unfairness there is in this book lies at the core of the novel; so long as Lawrence is determined to damn everyone who does not follow Mellors' way, to labour for surface impartiality would be pointless. If we finish the book with a sense of embarrassment at its special pleading, if we read Mellors' final pseudobiblical talk of 'the peace that comes of fucking' and of his 'Pentecost, the forked flame between me and you', with regrets rather than conviction, it is ultimately because no literary technique can conceal from us the confused and pretentious little author who is implied in too many parts of the book. Even our memory of the very different author implied by the better novels—Women in Love, say—is not enough to redeem the bad portions of this one.

'Impassibilité'

The author's objectivity can mean, finally, what Flaubert called impassibilité, an unmoved or unimpassioned feeling towards the characters and events of one's story. Although Flaubert did not maintain the distinction clearly, this quality is distinct from neutrality of judgment about values; an author could be committed to one or another value and still not feel with or against any of his characters. At the same time, it is clearly distinct from impartiality, since the artist could feel a lively hate or love or pity for all of his characters impartially. There seems to be a genuine temperamental difference among authors in the amount of detachment of this kind they find congenial[23]—somewhat like the difference between actors who 'feel' their roles and actors like the heroine of Somerset Maugham's Theatre, who finds that as soon as she feels a role her power to perform effectively is destroyed. Trollope in his Autobiography describes himself as wandering alone in the woods, crying at the grief of his characters and 'laughing at their absurdities, and thoroughly enjoying their joy'. It was perhaps natural that authors like Flaubert should have reacted to a similarly impassioned approach in some of the French romantics by pretending to an equally impassioned rejection of passion.

But this hardly suggests that there is any natural connection between the author's impassibilité and any one kind of rhetoric or any particular level of achievement. Authors at either extreme of the scale of emotional involvement might write works which were full of highly personal commentary, stories that were altogether 'told', or works that were strictly dramatic, strictly 'shown'.

One sign that there is no connection between the author's feelings and any necessary technique or achieved quality of his work is the fact that we can never securely infer, without external evidence, whether an author has *felt* his work or written with cold detachment. Did Fielding hate Jonathan Wild or weep for Amelia? Was he personally amused when Parson Adams, on his way to London to sell sermons which Fielding and the reader know to be unmarketable, discovers that he has left them at home?

Saintsbury praised Fielding for his 'detachment' in *Jonathan Wild*, presumably because the narrator is maintained throughout as a character who differs obviously and markedly from any real Fielding we could possibly imagine. But is there any reason to suppose that Fielding was less detached from his materials when dealing with the lovable fool Adams than when portraying Wild? We too easily fall into the habit of talking as if the narrator who says, 'O my good readers!' were Fielding, forgetting that for all we know he may have worked as deliberately and with as much detachment in creating the wise, urbane narrator of *Joseph Andrews* and *Tom Jones* as he did in creating the cynical narrator of *Jonathan Wild*. What was said above about the relation between the author's own values and the values supported by his second self applies here in precisely the same sense. A great artist can create an implied author who is either detached or involved, depending on the needs of the work in hand.

We see, then, that none of the three major claims to objectivity in the author has any necessary bearing on technical decisions. Though it may be important at a given moment in the history of an art or in the development of a writer to stress the dangers of a misguided commitment, partiality, or emotional involvement, the tendency to connect the author's objectivity with a required impersonality of technique is quite indefensible.

Subjectivism encouraged by impersonal techniques

Impersonal narration may, in fact, encourage the very subjectivism that it is supposed to cure. The effort to avoid signs of explicit evaluation can be peculiarly dangerous for the author who is fighting to keep himself out of his works. Although it is true that commentary can be a medium for meretricious subjective outpourings, the effort to construct such commentary can, in some authors, create precisely the right kind of wall between the author's weaker self and the self he must create if his book is to succeed. The art of constructing reliable narrators is largely that of mastering all of oneself in order to project the *persona*, the second self, that really belongs in the book. And, in laying his cards on the table, an author can discover in himself, and at least then find some chance of combating, the two extremes of subjectivism that have marred some impersonal fiction.

Indiscriminate sympathy or compassion. By giving the impression that judgment is withheld, an author can hide from himself that he is sentimentally involved with his characters, and that he is asking for his reader's sympathies without providing adequate reasons. The older technique of reliable narration, as Q. D. Leavis says, forced the author and reader to remain somewhat distant from even the most sympathetic character. But she finds that often in the modern best seller 'the author has poured his own day-dreams, hot and hot, into dramatic form, without bringing them to any such touchstone as the "good sense, but not common-sense" of a cultivated society: the author is himself—or more usually herself—identified with the leading character, and the reader is invited to share the debauch'.[24]

Such sentimentality was of course possible in older forms of fiction. 'Our hero' could often get away with murder, while his enemies were condemned for minor infractions of the moral code. But the modern author can reject the charge of sentimentality by saying, in effect, 'Who, me? Not at all. It is the reader's fault if he feels any excessive or unjustified compassion. I didn't say a word. I'm as tight-lipped and unemotional as the next man.' Such effects are most evident, perhaps, in the worst of the tough-guy school of detective fiction. Mickey Spillane's Mike Hammer can, in effect, do no wrong—for those who can stomach him at all. But many of Spillane's readers would drop him immediately if he intruded to make explicit the vicious morality on which enjoyment of the books is based: 'You may notice, reader, that when Mike Hammer beats up an Anglo-Saxon American he is less brutal than when he beats up a Jew, and that when he beats up a Negro he is most brutal of all. In this way our hero discriminates his punishment according to the racial worth of his victims.' It is wise of Spillane to avoid making such things explicit.

If, as Chekhov said, 'Subjectivity is an awful thing—even for the reason that it betrays the poor writer hand over fist', we can now see that the kind of subjectivity he deplored is not by any means prevented by the standard devices of so-called objectivity. In what is perhaps a different sense of the word, we can see that even the most rigorously impersonal techniques can *betray* the poor writer hand over fist. Betrayal for betrayal, there is probably less danger for author and reader in a literature that lays its cards on the table, in a literature that betrays to the poor writer just how poor a thing he has created.

Indiscriminate irony. We have no word like sentimentality to cover the opposite fault of the author who allows an all-pervasive, 'unearned' irony to substitute for an honest discrimination among his materials. The fault is always hard to prove, but most of us have, I suspect, encountered novelists who people their novels with very short heroes because they themselves want to appear tall. The author who maintains his invulnerability by suggesting irony at all points but never holding himself responsible for definition of its limits can be as irresponsible as the writer of best sellers based on naïve identification.[25]

Henry James talks of Flaubert's 'two refuges' from the need to look at humanity squarely. One was the exotic, as in *Salammbo* and *The Temptation of Saint Anthony*, the 'getting away from the human' altogether. The other was irony, which enabled him to deal with the human without having to commit himself about it directly. But, James asks, 'when all was said and done was he absolutely and exclusively condemned to irony?' Might he 'not after all have fought out his case a little more on the spot?' Coming from James, this is a powerful question. One cannot help feeling, as one reads many of the 'objective' yet corrosive portraits that have been given us since James, that the author is using irony to protect himself rather than to reveal his subject. If the author's characters reveal themselves as fools and knaves when we cast a cold eye upon them, how about the author himself? How would he look if his true opinions were served up cold? Or does he have no opinions?

Like the female novelist satirized by Randall Jarrell, these novelists can show us 'the price of every sin and the value of none'.

> Her books were a systematic, detailed, and conclusive condemnation of mankind for being stupid and bad; yet if mankind had been clever and good, what would have become of Gertrude? ... When she met someone who was either good or clever, she looked at him in uneasy antagonism. Yet she need not have been afraid. Clever people always came to seem to her, after a time, bad; good people always came to seem to her, after a time, stupid. She was always able to fail the clever for being bad, the good for being stupid; and if somebody was both clever and good, Gertrude stopped grading. If a voice had said to her, 'Hast thou considered my servant Gottfried Rosenbaum, that there is none like him in Benton, a kind and clever man,' she would have answered: 'I can't *stand* that Gottfried Rosenbaum.'[26]

Subjectivism of these two kinds can ruin a novel; the weaker the novel, on the whole, the more likely we are to be able to make simple and accurate inferences about the real author's problems based on our experience of the implied author. There is this much truth to the demand for objectivity in the author: signs of the real author's untransformed loves and hates are almost always fatal. But clear recognition of this truth cannot lead us to doctrines about technique, and it should not lead us to demand of the author that he eliminate love and hate, and the judgments on which they are based, from his novels. The emotions and judgments of the implied author are, as I hope to show, the very stuff out of which great fiction is made.[27]

Notes

1. 'Conversations with Eckerman', 29 January 1826, trans. John Oxenford, as reprinted in *Criticism: The Major Texts*, ed. Walter Jackson Bate (New York, 1952), p. 403.

2. Letter to Richard Woodhouse, 27 October 1818, *The Poetical Works and Other Writings of John Keats*, ed. H. Buxton Forman (New York, 1939), vii, 129.

3. *Correspondence*, (12 October 1853) (Paris, 1926–33), iii, 367–8. For some of the citations from Flaubert in what follows I am indebted to the excellent monograph by Marianne Bonwit, *Gustave Flaubert et le principe d'impassibilité* (Berkeley, Calif., 1950). My distinction among the three forms of objectivity in the author is derived in part from her discussion.

4. Ibid., (12 December 1857), iv, 243.

5. *Letters on the Short Story, the Drama and other Literary Topics*, selected and edited by Louis S. Friedland (New York, 1924), p. 63.

6. Corr. (26–27 April 1853), iii, 183: '... ne doit avoir ni religion, ni patrie, ni même aucune conviction sociale...' ['have neither religion nor fatherland nor any social conviction'].

7. 'The slave cast out', in *The Living Novel*, ed. Granville Hicks (New York, 1957), p. 202. Miss West continues: 'Writing is a way of playing parts, of trying on masks, of assuming roles, not for fun but out of desperate need, not for the self's sake but for the writing's sake. "To make any work of art," says Elizabeth Sewell, "is to make, or rather to unmake and remake one's self." '

8. In her inaugural lecture at the University of London, published as *The Tale and the Teller* (London, 1959). 'Writing on George Eliot in 1877, Dowden said that the form

that most persists in the mind after reading her novels is not any of the characters, but "one who, if not the real George Eliot, is that second self who writes her books, and lives and speaks through them". The "second self," he goes on, is "more substantial than any mere human personality" and has "fewer reserves": while "behind it, lurks well pleased the veritable historical self secure from impertinent observation and criticism" ' (p. 22).

9. e.g., Fred B. Millett, *Reading Fiction* (New York, 1950): 'This tone, the general feeling which suffuses and surrounds the work, arises ultimately out of the writer's attitude toward his subject.... *The subject derives its meaning from the view of life which the author has taken*' (p. 11).

10. 'When we speak of technique, then, we speak of nearly everything. For technique is the means by which the writer's experience, which is his subject matter, compels him to attend to it; technique is the only means he has of discovering, exploring, developing his subject, of conveying its meaning, and finally of evaluating it.... Technique in fiction is, of course, all those obvious forms of it which are usually taken to be the whole of it, and many others' ('Technique as Discovery', *Hudson Review*, i, Spring, 1948, 67–68). [See above, pp. 387–400].

11. *The English Novel* (London, 1930), p. 58. See Geoffrey Tillotson, *Thackeray the Novelist* (Cambridge, 1954), esp. chap. iv, 'The Content of the Authorial "I"' (pp. 55–70), for a convincing argument that the 'I' of Thackeray's works should be carefully distinguished from Thackeray himself.

12. 'Qu'est qui me dira, en effet ce que Shakespeare a aimé ce qu'il a haï, ce qu'il a senti?' (*Corr.*, i, 386). ['Who will tell me, in fact, what Shakespeare loved, what he hated and what he felt?']

13. Vladimir Nabokov, *Laughter in the Dark* (New York, 1938), p. 1.

14. W. Leggett, *The Idea in Fiction* (London, 1934), p. 16.

15. *Corr.* (2 November 1852), iii, 47; (9 December 1852), 60–2.

16. *The Wheel of Fire* (rev. edn.; London, 1949), pp. 32–8.

17. 'Morality and the novel' (1925), reprinted in *Phoenix* (London, 1936), pp. 528–9. [See above, pp. 127–31].

18. 'Study of Thomas Hardy', in *Phoenix* (London, 1936), as quoted by Allott, *Novelists on the Novel* (New York, 1959), p. 104.

19. Stanley Kauffman, ' "Lady Chatterley" at last', *The New Republic*, 25 May 1959, p. 16; Paul Lauter, 'Lady C. with Love and Money', *The New Leader*, 21 September 1959: 'Lawrence refines the gamekeeper with each revision of the novel, perhaps to make him more acceptable to Connie (and to the reader) as a lover. His finish in the final version, however, is partly a concession to the very society to which he stands opposed.... What does make Mellors eligible for salvation? Why cannot Michaelis or Tommy Dukes then enter?' (p. 24).

20. See Schorer's Introduction to the Grove Press reprint (New York, 1959), esp. pp. 21 ff.

21. See, for example, Colin Welch's attack on the book in 'Black magic, white lies', *Encounter*, xvi, February 1961, 75–9: 'What it preaches is this: that mankind can only be regenerated by freeing itself from the tyranny of the intellect and the soul, from the tyranny of Jesus Christ, and by prostrating itself before its own phallus ...' (p. 79). Whether one accepts Welch's charges or the defence of Lawrence by Rebecca West and Richard Hoggart in the following issue of *Encounter*, it is clear that what is in dispute is Lawrence's success in winning us to accept his basic vision; no tinkering with the proportions of telling and showing will make much difference here.

22. Kauffmann, op. cit., p. 16.

23. See Chekhov, *Letters*, pp. 97–8.

24. *Fiction and the Reading Public* (London, 1932), p. 236. See also Roger Vailland, 'La loi du romancier', *L'Express* (Paris), 12 July 1957, pp. 13, 15. Vailland found that he was ready to write 'de vrais romans' only when he had ceased to be the hero of his own daydreams. 'J'en étais complètement absent; je m'en suis brusquement aperçu; preuve était donc faite que mon rêve ne constituait pas un moyen détourné de me rapprocher de la bergère [the heroine of the daydream]' (p. 14).

['I was completely absent from it; I suddenly noticed it; the proof was thus given that my dream was not a roundabout way to bring me close to my shepherdess.']

25. See May Sarton, 'The shield of irony', *The Nation*, 14 April 1956, pp. 314–16.

26. *Pictures from an Institution* (New York, 1954), p. 134.

27. Mauriac discusses this complex problem brilliantly in *Le Romancier et ses personages* (Paris, 1933), esp. pp. 142–3 : "Derrière le roman le plus objectif, s'il s'agit d'une belle œuvre, d'une grande œuvre, se dissimule toujours ce drame vécu du romancier, cette lutte individuelle avec ses démons et avec ses sphinx. Mais peut-être est-ce précisément la réussite du génie que rien de ce drame personnel ne se trahisse au dehors. Le mot fameux de Flaubert : "Mme Bovary, c'est moi-meme," est très compréhensible,—il faut seulement prendre le temps d'y réfléchir, tant à première vue l'auteur d'un pareil livre y paraît être peu mêlé. C'est que *Madame Bovary* est un chef-d'œuvre,—c'est-à-dire une œuvre qui forme bloc et qui s'impose comme un tout, comme un monde séparé de celui qui l'a créé. C'est dans la mesure où notre œuvre est imparfaite qu'à travers les fissures se trahit l'âme tourmenté de son misérable auteur.'

['Behind the most objective novel, if it is a work of beauty, a great work, is always concealed the lived drama of the novelist, that individual struggle with his demons and his sphinx. But perhaps it is precisely the achievement of the genius that nothing of this personal drama is overtly betrayed. The famous saying of Flaubert, "Madame Bovary is me" is very comprehensible—only one must take time to think about it, so little, at first sight, does the author of such a book seem to be involved in it. *Madame Bovary* is a masterpiece—that is to say, a work which forms a whole and imposes itself as a whole, as a world separate from that of its creator. It is to the extent that our work is imperfect that through its cracks is revealed the tormented soul of its miserable author.']

43   Raymond Williams

Raymond Williams (b. 1921) was born and brought up in the Welsh border country, where his father was a railway signalman. From Abergavenny Grammar School he won a scholarship to Trinity College, Cambridge, and after service in World War II he became a tutor in adult education at Oxford University. In 1961 he was elected Fellow of Jesus College, Cambridge, where he is now University Reader in Drama. Raymond Williams has not concealed the fact that his personal experience of moving, via education, up through the English class system, has shaped his intellectual commitment to the idea of a common culture; and he has dealt with this experience directly in two novels, *Border Country* (1960) and *Second Generation* (1964). He has also been one of the leading theoreticians of the British New Left after World War II, editing *May Day Manifesto* in 1968. By his own account Marx and F. R. Leavis were the major intellectual influences upon Williams, and he has combined and modified them in a way which many postwar British literary intellectuals have found deeply appealing. Williams's insistence that all significant human activity is communal is clearly Marxist in derivation, but by seeking, in life and art, a reconciliation of the claims of the individual and society, rather than a subordination of one to another, he retains some of the values of liberal humanism. Like Leavis's, Williams's critical approach to literature assumes a close connection between art and life, and fans out into a general concern with the quality of both in modern industrial societies. Whereas Leavis and *Scrutiny* espoused an élitist concept of culture, however, and were invariably hostile and negative in dealing with the mass media, Williams has been more patiently objective in analysing such phenomena and more concerned to look for points of possible growth and benevolent change in contemporary culture. In this respect his work has often been linked with that of Richard Hoggart, author of *The Uses of Literacy* (1957) (see above, pp. 488-96.) In the Foreword to *Culture and Society 1780-1950* (1958), Williams wrote: 'We live in an expanding culture, yet we spend much of our energy regretting the fact, rather than seeking to understand its nature and conditions.' Williams sought that understanding in *Culture and Society* by a historical analysis of the 'cultural debate' in the nineteenth and twentieth centuries, and more speculatively in *The Long Revolution* (1961). These books, which work on the frontiers of literature, sociology, history, and philosophy, are probably his best known works. He is also the author of *Drama From Ibsen to Eliot* (1952), *Modern Tragedy* (1965) and *The English Novel From Dickens to Lawrence* (1970).

'Realism and the Contemporary English Novel' is chapter 7 of *The Long Revolution*, and is reprinted here from the Pelican edition of 1965, to which Williams added the footnotes.

CROSS REFERENCES :   7. Virgina Woolf
                                   10. D. H. Lawrence
                                   25. Erich Auerbach
                                   35. Georg Lukács
                                   42. Wayne Booth

COMMENTARY :   E. P. Thompson, 'The Long Revolution', *New Left Review*, May-June, pp. 24-33, July-August pp. 34-9 (1961)

Realism and the contemporary novel

The centenary of 'realism' as an English critical term occurred but was not celebrated in 1956. Its history, in this hundred years, has been so vast, so complicated, and so bitter that any celebration would in fact have turned into a brawl. Yet realism is not an object, to be identified, pinned down, and appropriated. It is, rather, a way of describing certain methods and attitudes, and the descriptions, quite naturally, have varied, in the ordinary exchange and development of experience. Recently, I have been reconsidering these descriptions, as a possible way of defining and generalizing certain personal observations on the methods and substance of contemporary fiction. I now propose to set down: first, the existing variations in 'realism' as a descriptive term; second, my own view of the ways in which the modern novel has developed; third, a possible new meaning of realism.

There has, from the beginning, been a simple technical use of 'realism', to describe the precision and vividness of a rendering in art of some observed detail. In fact, as we shall see, this apparently simple use involves all the later complexities, but it seemed, initially, sufficiently accurate to distinguish one technique from others: realism as opposed to idealization or caricature. But, also from the beginning, this technical sense was flanked by a reference to content: certain kinds of subject were seen as realism, again by contrast with different kinds. The most ordinary definition was in terms of an ordinary, contemporary, everyday reality, as opposed to traditionally heroic, romantic, or legendary subjects. In the period since the Renaissance, the advocacy and support of this 'ordinary, everyday, contemporary reality' have been normally associated with the rising middle class, the bourgeoisie. Such material was called 'domestic' and 'bourgeois' before it was called 'realistic', and the connections are clear. In literature the domestic drama and, above all, the novel, both developing in early eighteenth-century England with the rise of an independent middle class, have been the main vehicles of this new consciousness. Yet, when the 'realist' description arrived, a further development was taking place, both in content and in attitudes to it. A common adjective used with 'realism' was 'startling', and, within the mainstream of 'ordinary, contemporary, everyday reality' a particular current of attention to the unpleasant, the exposed, the sordid could be distinguished. Realism thus appeared as in part a revolt against the ordinary bourgeois view of the world; the realists were making a further selection of ordinary material which the majority of bourgeois artists preferred to ignore. Thus 'realism', as a watchword, passed over to the progressive and revolutionary movements.

This history is paralleled in the development of 'naturalism', which again had a simple technical sense, to describe a particular method of art, but which underwent the characteristic broadening to 'ordinary, everyday reality' and then, in particular relation to Zola, became the banner of a revolutionary school—what the *Daily News* in 1881 called 'that unnecessarily faithful portrayal of offensive incidents'.

Thus, entwined with technical descriptions, there were in the nineteenth-century meanings doctrinal affiliations. The most positive was Strindberg's definition of naturalism as the exclusion of God: naturalism as opposed to supernaturalism, according to the philosophical precedents. Already, however, before the end of the century, and with increasing clarity in our own, 'realism' and 'naturalism' were separated: naturalism in art was reserved to the simple technical reference, while realism, though retaining elements of this, was used to describe subjects and attitudes to subjects.

The main twentieth-century development has been curious. In the West, alongside the received uses, a use of 'realism' in the sense of 'fidelity to psychological reality' has been widely evident, the point being made that we can be convinced of the reality of an experience, of its essential realism, by many different kinds of artistic method, and with no necessary restriction of subject-matter to the ordinary, the contemporary, and the everyday. In the Soviet Union, on the other hand, the earlier definitions of realism have been maintained and extended, and the elements of 'socialist realism', as defined, may enable us to see the tradition more clearly. There are four of these elements: *narodnost, tipichnost, ideinost,* and *partiinost. Narodnost* is in effect technical, though also an expression of spirit: the requirement of popular simplicity and traditional clarity, as opposed to the difficulties of 'formalism'. *Ideinost* and *partiinost* refer to the ideological content and partisan affiliations of such realism, and just as *narodnost* is a restatement of an ordinary technical meaning of realism, so *ideinost* and *partiinost* are developments of the ideological and revolutionary attitudes already described. There is a perfectly simple sense in which 'socialist realism' can be distinguished from 'bourgeois realism', in relation to these changes in ideology and affiliation. Much Western popular literature is in fact 'bourgeois realism', with its own versions of *ideinost* and *partiinost*, and with its ordinary adherence to *narodnost*. It is in relation to the fourth element, *tipichnost*, that the problem broadens.

Engels defined 'realism' as 'typical characters in typical situations', which would pass in a quite ordinary sense, but which in this case has behind it the body of Marxist thinking. *Tipichnost* is a development of this definition, which radically affects the whole question of realism. For the 'typical', Soviet theorists tell us, 'must not be confused with that which is frequently encountered'; the truly typical is based on 'comprehension of the laws and perspectives of future social development'. Without now considering the application of this, in the particular case of Soviet literature (the critical touchstone, here, is the excellence of Scholokhov, in *Tikhii Don* and *Virgin Soil Upturned*, as against the *external* pattern of Alexei Tolstoy's *Road to Calvary*), we can see that the concept of *tipichnost* alters 'realism' from its sense of the direct reproduction of observed reality: 'realism' becomes, instead, a principled and organized selection. If 'typical' is understood as the most deeply characteristic human experience, in an individual or in a society (and clearly Marxists think of it as this, in relation to their own deepest beliefs), then it is clearly not far from the developed sense of the 'convincingly real' criterion, now commonplace in the West in relation to works of many kinds, both realist and non-realist in technique. And it is not our business to pick from the complex story the one use that we favour, the one true 'realism'. Rather, we must receive the actual meanings, distinguish and clarify them, and see which, if any, may be useful in describing our actual responses to literature.

The major tradition of European fiction, in the nineteenth century, is commonly described as a tradition of 'realism', and it is equally assumed that, in the West at any rate, this particular tradition has ended. The realistic novel, it was said recently, went out with the hansom cab. Yet it is not at all easy, at first sight, to see what in practice this means. For clearly, in the overwhelming majority of modern novels, including those novels we continue to regard as literature, the ordinary criteria of realism still hold. It is not only that there is still a concentration on contemporary themes; in many ways elements of ordinary everyday experience are more evident in the modern novel than in the nineteenth-century novel, through the disappearance of certain taboos. Certainly nobody will complain of the modern novel that it lacks those startling or offensive elements which it was one of the purposes of the term 'realism' to describe. Most description is still realistic, in the sense that describing the object as it actually appears is a principle few novelists would dissent from. What we usually say is that the realistic novel has been replaced by the 'psychological novel', and it is obviously true that the direct study of certain states of consciousness, certain newly apprehended psychological states, has been a primary modern feature. Yet realism as an intention, in the description of these states, has not been widely abandoned. Is it merely that 'everyday, ordinary reality' is now differently conceived, and that new techniques have been developed to describe this new kind of reality, but still with wholly realistic intentions? The questions are obviously very difficult, but one way of approaching an answer to them may be to take this ordinary belief that we have abandoned (developed beyond) the realistic novel, and to set beside it my own feeling that there is a formal gap in modern fiction, which makes it incapable of expressing one kind of experience, a kind of experience which I find particularly important and for which, in my mind, the word 'realism' keeps suggesting itself.

Now the novel is not so much a literary form as a whole literature in itself. Within its wide boundaries, there is room for almost every kind of contemporary writing. Great harm is done to the tradition of fiction, and to the necessary critical discussion of it, if 'the novel' is equated with any one kind of prose work. It was such a wrong equation which made Tolstoy say of *War and Peace*: 'it is not a novel'. A form which in fact includes *Middlemarch* and *Auto da Fé*, *Wuthering Heights* and *Huckleberry Finn*, *The Rainbow* and *The Magic Mountain*, is indeed, as I have said, more like a whole literature. In drawing attention to what seems to me now a formal gap, I of course do not mean that this whole vast form should be directed to filling it. But because it is like a whole literature, any formal gap in the novel seems particularly important.

When I think of the realist tradition in fiction, I think of the kind of novel which creates and judges the quality of a whole way of life in terms of the qualities of persons. The balance involved in this achievement is perhaps the most important thing about it. It looks at first sight so general a thing, the sort of thing most novels do. It is what *War and Peace* does; what *Middlemarch* does; what *The Rainbow* does. Yet the distinction of this kind is that it offers a valuing of a whole way of life, a society that is larger than any of the individuals composing it, and at the same time valuing creations of human beings who, while belonging to and affected by and helping to define this way of life, are also, in their own terms, absolute ends in themselves. Neither element, neither the society nor the individual, is there as a priority. The society is not a background against which the personal relationships are studied, nor are the individuals merely illustrations of aspects of the way of life. Every aspect of personal life is radically affected by the quality of the general life, yet the general life is seen at its most important in completely personal terms. We attend with our whole senses to every aspect of the general life, yet the centre of value is always in the individual human person—not any one isolated person, but the many persons who are the reality of the general life. Tolstoy and George Eliot, in particular, often said, in much these terms, that it was this view they were trying to realize.

Within this realist tradition, there are of course wide variations of degree of success, but such a viewpoint, a particular apprehension of a relation between individuals and society, may be seen as a mode. It must be remembered that this viewpoint was itself the product of maturity; the history of the novel from the eighteenth century is essentially an exploration towards this position, with many preliminary failures. The eighteenth-century novel is formally most like our own, under comparable pressures and uncertainties, and it was in the deepening understanding of the relations between individuals and societies that the form actually matured. When it is put to me that the realist tradition has broken down, it is this mature viewpoint that I see as having been lost, under new pressures of particular experience. I do not mean that it is, or should be, tied to any particular style. The kind of realistic (or as we now say, naturalistic) description that 'went out with the hansom cab' is in no way essential to it; it was even, perhaps, in writers like Bennett, a substitute for it. Such a vision is not realized by detailed stocktaking descriptions of shops or back-parlours or station waiting-rooms. These may be used, as elements of the action, but they are not this essential realism. If they are put in, for the sake of description as such, they may in fact destroy the balance that is the essence of this method; they may, for example, transfer attention from the people to the things. It was actually this very feeling, that in this kind of fully-furnished novel everything was present but actual individual life, that led, in the 1920s, to the disrepute of 'realism'. The extreme reaction was in Virginia Woolf's *The Waves*, where all the furniture, and even the physical bodies, have gone out of the window, and we are left with voices and feelings, voices in the air—an equally damaging unbalance, as we can now see. It may indeed be possible to write the history of the modern novel in terms of a polarization of styles, object-realist and subject-impressionist, but the more essential polarization, which has mainly occurred since 1900, is the division of the realist novel, which had created the substance and quality of a way of life in terms of the substance and qualities of persons, into two separate traditions, the 'social' novel and the 'personal' novel. In the social novel there may be accurate observation and description of the general life, the aggregation; in the personal novel there may be accurate observation and description of persons, the units. But each lacks a dimension, for the way of life is neither aggregation nor unit, but a whole indivisible process.

We now commonly make this distinction between 'social' and 'personal' novels; indeed in one way we take this distinction of interest for granted. By looking at some examples, the substantial issue may be made clear. There are now two main kinds of 'social' novel. There is, first, the descriptive social novel, the documentary. This creates, as priority, a general way of life, a particular social or working community. Within this, of course, are characters, sometimes quite carefully drawn. But what we say about such novels is that if we want to know about life in a mining town, or in a university, or on a merchant ship, or on a patrol in Burma, this is the book. In fact, many novels of this kind are valuable; the good documentary is usually interesting. It is right that novels of this kind should go on being written, and with the greatest possible variety of setting. Yet the dimension that we miss is obvious: the characters are miners, dons, soldiers first; illustrations of the way of life. It is not the emphasis I have been trying to describe, in which the persons are of absolute interest in themselves, and are yet seen as parts of a whole way of living. Of all current kinds of novel, this kind, at its best, is *apparently* nearest to what I am calling the realist novel, but the crucial distinction is quite apparent in reading: the social-descriptive function is in fact the shaping priority.

A very lively kind of social novel, quite different from this, is now significantly popular. The tenor, here, is not description, but the finding and materialization of a *formula* about society. A particular pattern is abstracted, from the sum of social experience, and a society is created from this pattern. The simplest examples are in the field of the future-story, where the 'future' device (usually only a device, for nearly always it is obviously contemporary society that is being written about; indeed this is becoming the main way of writing about social experience) removes the ordinary tension between the selected pattern and normal observation. *Brave New World, Nineteen Eighty-Four, Fahrenheit 451,* are powerful social fiction, in which a pattern taken from contemporary society is materialized, as a whole, in another time or place. Other examples are Golding's *Lord of the Flies* and *The Inheritors,* and nearly all serious 'science fiction'. Most of these are written to resemble realistic novels, and operate in the same essential terms. Most of them contain, fundamentally, a conception of the relation between individuals and society; ordinarily a virtuous individual, or small personal group, against a vile society. The action, normally, is a release of tensions in this personal–social complex, but I say release, and not working-out, because ordinarily the device subtly alters the tensions, places them in a pre-selected light, so that it is not so much that they are explored but indulged. The experience of isolation, of alienation, and of self-exile is an important part of the contemporary structure of feeling, and any contemporary realist novel would have come to real terms with it. (It is ironic, incidentally, that it was come to terms with, and worked to a resolution very different from the contemporary formula of 'exile versus masses; stalemate', at several points in the realist tradition, notably in *Crime and Punishment* and, through Bezukhov, in *War and Peace*.) Our formula novels are lively, because they are about lively social feelings, but the obvious dimension they lack is that of a substantial society and correspondingly substantial persons.[1] For the common life is an abstraction, and the personal lives are defined by their function in the formula.

The 'realist' novel divided into the 'social' and the 'personal', and the 'social novel', in our time, has further divided into social documentary and social formula. It is true that examples of these kinds can be found from earlier periods, but they were never, as now, the modes. The same point holds for the 'personal novel', and its corresponding division into documentary and formula. Some of the best novels of our time are those which describe, carefully and subtly, selected personal relationships. These are often very like *parts* of the realist novel as described, and there is a certain continuity of method and substance. Forster's *A Passage to India* is a good example, with traces of the older balance still clearly visible, yet belonging, in a high place, in this divided kind, because of elements in the Indian society of the novel which romanticize the actual society to the needs of certain of the characters. This is quite common in this form: a society, a general way of living, is apparently there, but is in fact often a highly personalized landscape, to clarify or frame an individual portrait, rather than a country within which the individuals are actually contained. Graham Greene's social settings are obvious examples: his Brighton, West Africa, Mexico and Indo-China have major elements in common which relate not to their actual ways of life but to the needs of his characters and of his own emotional pattern. When this is frankly and absolutely done, as in Kafka, there is at least no confusion; but ordinarily, with a surface of realism, there is merely the familiar unbalance. There is a lack of dimension similar to that in the social descriptive novel, but in a different direction. There the characters were aspects of the society; here the society is an aspect of the characters. The balance we remember is that in which both the general way of life and the individual persons are seen as there and absolute.

Of course, in many personal novels, often very good in their own terms, the general way of life does not appear even in this partial guise, but as a simple backcloth, of shopping and the outbreak of war and buses and odd minor characters from another social class. Society is outside the people, though at times, even violently, it breaks in on them. Now of course, where there is deliberate selection, deliberate concentration, such personal novels are valuable, since there is a vast field of significant experience, of a directly personal kind, which can be excitingly explored. But it seems to me that for every case of conscious selection (as in Proust, say, where the concentration is entirely justified and yet produces, obliquely, a master-portrait of a general way of life) there are perhaps a thousand cases where the restriction is simply a failure of consciousness, a failure to realize the extent to which the substance of a general way of life actively affects the closest personal experience. Of course if, to these writers, society has become the dull abstract thing of the social novel at its worst, it is not surprising that they do not see why it should concern them. They insist on the people as people first, and not as social units, and they are quite right to do so. What is missing, however, is that element of common substance which again and again the great realists seemed able to apprehend. Within the small group, personality is valued, but outside the group it is nothing. We are people, one sometimes hears between the lines; to *us* these things are important; but the strange case of the Virginia Woolf 'charwoman' or 'village woman', with the sudden icy drop in the normally warm sensibility, symbolizes a common limitation. And this is not only social exclusiveness or snobbery, though it can be diagnosed in such ways, but also a failure to realize the nature of the general social element in *our own* lives. We are people (such novels say), people, just like that; the rest is the world or society or politics or something, dull things that are written about in the newspapers. But in fact we are people and people within a society: that whole view was at the centre of the realist novel.

In spite of its limitations, the personal-descriptive novel is often a substantial achievement, but the tendencies evident in it seem increasingly to be breaking it down into the other personal kind, the novel of the personal formula. Here, as in the novel of social formula, a particular pattern is abstracted from the sum of experience, and not now societies, but human individuals, are created from the pattern. This has been the method of powerful and in its own terms valid fiction, but it seems to me to be rapidly creating a new mode, the fiction of special pleading. We can say of novels in this class that they take only one person seriously, but then ordinarily very seriously indeed. Joyce's *Portrait of the Artist* is not only this, but contains it as a main emphasis. And to mention this remarkable work is to acknowledge the actual gain in intensity, the real development of fictional method, which this emphasis embodied. A world is actualized on one man's senses: not narrated, or held at arm's length, but taken as it is lived. Joyce showed the magnificent advantages of this method when in *Ulysses* he actualized a world not through one person but through three; there are three ways of seeing, three worlds, of Stephen, Bloom, and Molly, yet the three worlds, as in fact, compose one world, the whole world of the novel. *Ulysses* does not maintain this balance throughout; it is mainly in the first third of the book that the essential composition is done, with the last section as a coda. Yet here was the realist tradition in a new form, altered in technique but continuous in experience.

Since *Ulysses*, this achievement has been diluted, as the technique has also been diluted. Cary's *The Horse's Mouth* is an interesting example, for in it one way of seeing has been isolated, and the world fitted to that. This analysis is also the key to the popular new kind of novel represented by Amis's *That Uncertain Feeling* and Wain's *Living in the Present*. The paradox of these novels is that on the one hand they seem the most real kind of contemporary writing—they were welcomed because they recorded so many actual feelings—and yet on the other hand their final version of reality is parodic and farcical. This illustrates the general dilemma: these writers start with real personal feelings, but to sustain and substantiate them, in their given form, the world of action in which they operate has to be pressed, as it were inevitably, towards caricature. (This was also the process of Dickens, at the limits of what he could openly see or state, and caricature and sentimentality are in this sense opposite sides of the same coin, used to avoid the real negotiation.)[2] To set these feelings in our actual world, rather than in this world farcically transformed at crisis, would be in fact to question the feelings, to go on from them to a very difficult questioning of reality. Instead of this real tension, what we get is a fantasy release: swearing on the telephone, giving a mock-lecture, finding a type-figure on which aggression can be concentrated. Because these are our liveliest writers, they illustrate our contemporary difficulty most clearly. The gap between our feelings and our social observation is dangerously wide.

The fiction of special pleading can be seen in its clearest form in those many contemporary novels which, taking one person's feelings and needs as absolute, create other persons in these sole terms. This flourishes in the significantly popular first-person narrative, which is normally used simply for this end. *Huckleberry Finn*, in its middle sections, creates a general reality within which the personal narrative gains breadth. Salinger's *Catcher in the Rye* has a saving irony, yet lacks this other dimension, a limitation increasingly obvious as the novel proceeds. Braine's *Room at the Top* breaks down altogether, because there is no other reality to refer to; we are left with the familiar interaction of crudity and self-pity, a negative moral gesture at best. Compare, for example, Carson McCullers' *Member of the Wedding*, which has its realist dimension, and in which the reality of personal feeling, growing into fantasy, interacts at the necessary tension with the world in which the feelings must be lived out. Or again, on the opposite side, there is Sagan's *Bonjour Tristesse*, where the persons are presented almost objectively, but are then made to act in accordance with the fantasy of the central character. A comparison of McCullers and Sagan is the comparison of realism and its breakdown. And it is the breakdown, unfortunately, of which we have most examples; the first-person narrative, on which so much technical brilliance has been lavished, is now ordinarily the mechanism of rationalizing this breakdown. The fiction of special pleading extends, however, into novels still formally resembling the realist kind. In [Elizabeth] Bowen's *Heat of the Day*, for example, the persons exist primarily as elements in the central character's emotional landscape, and are never seen or valued in any other terms, though there is no first-person narrative, and there is even some careful descriptive realism, to make the special pleading less stark. As it is now developing, the personal novel ends by denying the majority of persons. The reality of society is excluded, and this leads, inevitably, in the end, to the exclusion of all but a very few individual people. It is not surprising, in these circumstances, that so much of the personal feeling described should be in fact the experience of breakdown.

I offer this fourfold classification—social description, social formula, personal description, personal formula—as a way of beginning a general analysis of the contemporary novel, and of defining, by contrast, the realist tradition which, in various ways, these kinds have replaced. The question now is whether these kinds correspond to some altered reality, leaving the older tradition as really irrelevant as the hansom cab, or whether they are in fact the symptoms of some very deep crisis in experience, which throws up these talented works yet persists, unexplored, and leaves us essentially dissatisfied. I would certainly not say that the abandonment of the realist balance is in some way wilful; that these writers are deliberately turning away from a great tradition, with the perversity that many puzzled readers assign to them. The crisis, as I see it, is too deep for any simple, blaming explanation. But what then is the crisis, in its general nature?

There are certain immediate clarifying factors. The realist novel needs, obviously, a genuine community: a community of persons linked not merely by one kind of relationship—work or friendship or family—but many, interlocking kinds. It is obviously difficult, in the twentieth century, to find a community of this sort. Where *Middlemarch* is a complex of personal, family and working relationships, and draws its whole strength from their interaction in an indivisible process, the links between persons in most contemporary novels are relatively single, temporary, discontinuous. And this was a change in society, at least in that part of society most nearly available to most novelists, before it was a change in literary form. Again, related to this, but affected by other powerful factors, the characteristic experience of our century is that of asserting and preserving an individuality (again like much eighteenth-century experience), as compared with the characteristic nineteenth-century experience of finding a place and making a settlement. The ordinary Victorian novel ends, as every parodist knows, with a series of settlements, of new engagements and formal relationships, whereas the ordinary twentieth-century novel ends with a man going away on his own, having extricated himself from a dominating situation, and found himself in so doing. Again, this actually happened, before it became a common literary pattern. In a time of great change, this kind of extrication and discovery was a necessary and valuable movement; the recorded individual histories amount to a common history. And while old establishments linger, and new establishments of a dominating kind are continually instituted, the breakaway has continually to be made, the personal assertion given form and substance, even to the point where it threatens to become the whole content of our literature. Since I know the pressures, I admit the responses, but my case is that we are reaching deadlock, and that to explore a new definition of realism may be the way to break out of the deadlock and find a creative direction.

The contemporary novel has both reflected and illuminated the crisis of our society, and of course we could fall back on the argument that only a different society could resolve our literary problems. Yet literature is committed to the detail of known experience, and any valuable social change would be the same kind of practical and responsible discipline. We begin by identifying our actual situation, and the critical point, as I see it, is precisely that separation of the individual and society into absolutes, which we have seen reflected in form. The truly creative effort of our time is the struggle for relationships, of a whole kind, and it is possible to see this as both personal and social: the practical learning of *extending* relationships. Realism, as embodied in its great tradition, is a touchstone in this, for it shows, in detail, that vital interpenetration, idea into feeling, person into community, change into settlement, which we need, as growing points, in our own divided time. In the highest realism, society is seen in fundamentally personal terms, and persons, through relationships, in fundamentally social terms. The integration is controlling, yet of course it is not to be achieved by an act of will. If it comes at all, it is a creative discovery, and can perhaps only be recorded within the structures and substance of the realist novel.

Yet, since it is discovery, and not recovery, since nostalgia and imitation are not only irrelevant but hindering, any new realism will be different from the tradition, and will comprehend the discoveries in personal realism which are the main twentieth-century achievement. The point can be put theoretically, in relation to modern discoveries in perception and communication. The old, naïve realism is in any case dead, for it depended on a theory of natural seeing which is now impossible. When we thought we had only to open our eyes to see a common world, we could suppose that realism was a simple recording process, from which any deviation was voluntary. We know now that we literally create the world we see, and that this human creation—a discovery of how we can live in the material world we inhabit—is necessarily dynamic and active; the old static realism of the passive observer is merely a hardened convention. When it was first discovered that man lives through his perceptual world, which is a human interpretation of the material world outside him, this was thought to be a basis for the rejection of realism; only a personal vision was possible. But art is more than perception; it is a particular kind of active response, and a part of all human communication. Reality, in our terms, is that which human beings make common, by work or language. Thus, in the very acts of perception and communication, this practical interaction of what is personally seen, interpreted and organized and what can be socially recognized, known and formed is richly and subtly manifested. It is very difficult to grasp this fundamental interaction, but here, undoubtedly, is the clue we seek, not only in our thinking about personal vision and social communication, but also in our thinking about the individual and society. The individual inherits an evolved brain, which gives him his common human basis. He learns to see, through this inheritance, and through the forms which his culture teaches. But, since the learning is active, and since the world he is watching is changing and being changed, new acts of perception, interpretation, and organization are not only possible but deeply necessary. This is human growth, in personal terms, but the essential growth is in the interaction which then can occur, in the individual's effort to communicate what he has learned, to match it with known reality and by work and language to make a new reality. Reality is continually established, by common effort, and art is one of the highest forms of this process. Yet the tension can be great, in the necessarily difficult struggle to establish reality, and many kinds of failure and breakdown are possible. It seems to me that in a period of exceptional growth, as ours has been and will continue to be, the tension will be exceptionally high, and certain kinds of failure and breakdown may become characteristic. The recording of creative effort, to explore such breakdowns, is not always easy to distinguish from the simple, often rawly exciting exploitation of breakdown. Or else there is a turning away, into known forms, which remind us of previously learned realities and seek, by this reminder, to establish probability of a kind. Thus the tension can either be lowered, as in the ordinary social novel, or played on, as in the ordinary personal novel. Either result is a departure from realism, in the sense that I am offering. For realism is precisely this living tension, achieved in a communicable form. Whether this is seen as a problem of the individual in society, or as a problem of the offered description and the known description, the creative challenge is similar. The achievement of realism is a continual achievement of balance, and the ordinary absence of balance, in the forms of the contemporary novel, can be seen as both a warning and a challenge. It is certain that any effort to achieve a contemporary balance will be complex and difficult, but the effort is necessary, a new realism is necessary, if we are to remain creative.

Notes

1. Irving Howe thought I was asking for something which by definition this form could not offer. I see his point, but I do not find it easy to accept that kind of formalist approach; surely the form itself and what 'by definition' it 'cannot do', must submit to be criticised from a general position in experience. I agree with Mr Howe so often that I am sorry to have to insist.

2. As it stands, this is too limiting on Dickens. I have discussed the significance of his way of seeing people, as a literary method necessarily correspondent to a particular and critical vision of life and society, in 'Social criticism in Dickens', *Critical Quarterly*, Autumn 1964.

44   R. S. Crane

In 1935 R. S. Crane (1886-1967) published an essay, 'History versus Criticism in the University Study of Literature', which was enthusiastically welcomed by John Crowe Ransom in his article 'Criticism Inc.' (see above, pp. 227-39). Ransom clearly saw Crane as potentially a valuable ally of the American New Critics in their efforts, over the next two decades, to direct English Studies away from traditional literary scholarship towards evaluative and analytical criticism. Crane and his associates at the University of Chicago, however, had ideas of their own about the way criticism should develop. As Crane himself commented much later, they soon began to have misgivings about two aspects of the New Criticism:

> One was the fact that, despite the great flourishing of practical criticism, there were few signs that this was moving beyond the rather narrow set of ideas and interests which the critics of the thirties had derived from Eliot, Hulme and Richards, or had taken over from the psycho-analysis, analytical psychology and cultural anthropology of the first years of the century.... The other thing was the striking effect of unscholarly improvisation that characterized much of the literary theorizing of the period from Richards on —as if none of the essential problems of literature had ever been discussed before or any important light thrown on them in more than a score of centuries during which literature had been an object of critical attention.

This quotation comes from R. S. Crane's Preface to the abridged 1957 edition of *Critics and Criticism: ancient and modern* (Chicago, 1952), which he edited. This large collection of essays by Crane, Richard McKeon, Elder Olson, and others, was a kind of counterblast to R. D. Stallman's Neocritical anthology, *Critiques and Essays in Criticism 1920-1948* (New York, 1949). The Chicago critics attacked the narrowness of the New Critics' criteria, and advocated a more pluralistic and inductive approach to literary criticism. They suggested that the *Poetics* of Aristotle might be developed into, or serve as the model for, an inclusive critical system; hence these critics are usually referred to as the 'Chicago neo-Aristotelians'.

'The Houyhnhnms, the Yahoos, and the History of Ideas' does not explicitly invoke the *Poetics*, but it does exemplify the Aristotelian virtues of lucidity, logic, and scrupulous attention to evidence in critical discourse which Crane and his associates admired and emulated. It also makes clear that Crane's position was quite different from Ransom's in 'Criticism Inc.'—Crane being unsympathetic not to the historical approach to literature as such, but to interpretation based on dubious, inexact, and over-confident historical hypotheses.

R. S. Crane taught at the University of Chicago from 1924 until his death, though he was visiting professor at many other American universities. He was Emeritus Professor at Chicago from 1951. His Alexander Lectures at the University of Toronto were published as *The Languages of Criticism and the Structure of Poetry* (Toronto, 1953), 'The Houyhnhnms, the Yahoos, and the History of Ideas' is reprinted here from *The Idea of the Humanities and other essays critical and historical* (Chicago, 1967). It was first published in *Reason and the Imagination: Essays in the History of Ideas, 1600-1800* (1962) ed. Joseph Mazzeo, and was originally a paper read to the Annual Conference of Non-Professorial University Teachers of English at Oxford, 1959.

CROSS REFERENCES: 18. John Crowe Ransom
                     32. C. S. Lewis
                     38. Norman O. Brown

COMMENTARY: W. K. Wimsatt, Jnr., 'The Chicago critics: The fallacy of the neoclassic species', in *The Verbal Icon* (Lexington, Ky., 1954)
               Wayne Booth, Introduction to *The Idea of the Humanities and other essays critical and historical* by R. S. Crane (Chicago, 1967)

The Houyhnhnms, the Yahoos, and the history of ideas

I shall be concerned in this essay with two ways of using the history of ideas—or, in the case of the first of them, as I shall argue, misusing it—in the historical interpretation of literary works. The particular issue I have in mind is forced on one in an unusually clearcut manner, I think, by what has been said of the 'Voyage to the Country of the Houyhnhnms' in the criticism of the past few decades; and for this reason, and also because I wish to add a theory of my own about Swift's satirical argument in that work to the theories now current, I base the discussion that follows almost exclusively on it.

With a very few exceptions (the latest being George Sherburn)[1] since the 1920s, and especially since the later 1930s, writers on the fourth Voyage have been mainly dominated by a single preoccupation.[2] They have sought to correct the misunderstanding of Swift's purpose in the Voyage which had vitiated, in their opinion, most earlier criticism of it and, in particular, to defend Swift from the charge of all-out misanthropy that had been levelled against him so often in the past—by Thackeray,[a] for example, but many others also—on the strength of Gulliver's wholesale identification of men with the Yahoos and his unqualified worship of the Houyhnhnms.

It is easy to see what this task would require them to do. It would require them to show that what Gulliver is made to say about human nature in the Voyage, which is certainly misanthropic enough, and what Swift wanted his readers to believe about human nature are, in certain crucial respects at any rate, two different and incompatible things. It would require them, that is, to draw a clear line between what is both Swift and Gulliver and what is only Gulliver in a text in which Gulliver alone is allowed to speak to us.

The resulting new interpretations have differed considerably in emphasis and detail from critic to critic, but they have been generally in accord on the following propositions: The attitudes of Swift and his hero do indeed coincide up to a certain point, it being true for Swift no less than for Gulliver that men in the mass are terrifyingly close to the Yahoos in disposition and behaviour, and true for both of them also that the Houyhnhnms are in some of their qualities—their abhorrence of falsehood, for instance—proper models for human emulation. That, however, is about as far as the agreement goes: it is to Gulliver alone and not to Swift that we must impute the radical pessimism of the final chapters—it is he and not Swift who reduces men literally to Yahoos; it is he and not Swift who despairs of men because they cannot or will not lead the wholly rational life of the Houyhnhnms. Gulliver, in other words, is only in part a reliable spokesman for his creator's satire; he is also, and decisively at the end, one of the targets of that satire—a character designed to convince us, through his obviously infatuated actions, of the absurdity both of any view of man's nature that denies the capacity of at least some men for rational and virtuous conduct, however limited this capacity may be, and of any view of the best existence for man that makes it consist in taking 'reason alone' as a guide. What, in short, Swift offers us, as the ultimate moral of the Voyage, is a compromise between these extremist opinions of Gulliver: human nature, he is saying, is bad enough, but it is not altogether hopeless; reason is a good thing, but a life of pure reason is no desirable end for man.

Now it is evident that however appealing this interpretation may be to those who want to think well of Swift and to rescue him from his nineteenth-century maligners, it is not a merely obvious exegesis of the 'Voyage to the Country of the Houyhnhnms', or one that most common readers, past or present, have spontaneously arrived at. It is not an exegesis, either, that goes at all comfortably with that famous letter of Swift's in 1725 in which he told Pope that his chief aim was 'to vex the world rather than divert it' and that he never would have peace of mind until 'all honest men' were of his opinion. For there is nothing particularly vexing in the at least partly reassuring moral now being

[a] In his *The English Humourists of the Eighteenth Century*, William Makepeace Thackeray described Swift in Book Four of *Gulliver's Travels* as 'a monster gibbering shrieks, and gnashing imprecations against mankind'.

attributed to the Voyage or anything which 'honest men' in 1726 would have had much hesitation in accepting. And again, although we must surely agree that there is a significant difference between Gulliver and Swift, why must we suppose that the difference has to be one of basic doctrine? Why could it not be simply the difference between a person who has just discovered a deeply disturbing truth about man and is consequently, like Socrates' prisoner in the myth of the cave,[a] considerably upset and one who, like Socrates himself, has known this truth all along and can therefore write of his hero's discovery of it calmly and with humour?

I introduce these points here not as decisive objections to the new interpretation but rather as signs that it is not the kind of interpretation which (in Johnson's phrase), upon its first production, must be acknowledged to be just. Confirmatory arguments are plainly needed; and a consideration of the arguments that have in fact been offered in support of it will bring us rather quickly to the special problem I wish to discuss.

A good deal has been made, to begin with, of what are thought to be clear indications in the Voyage itself that Swift wanted his readers to take a much more critical view than Gulliver does of 'the virtues and ideas of those exalted Houyhnhms' and a much less negative view of human possibilities. If he had designed the Houyhnhnms to be for us what they are for Gulliver, namely, the 'perfection of nature' and hence an acceptable standard for judging of man, he would surely, it is argued, have endowed them with more humanly engaging qualities than they have; he would surely not have created them as the 'remote, unsympathetic, and in the end profoundly unsatisfying' creatures so many of his readers nowadays find them to be. We must therefore see in Gulliver's worship of the rational horses a plain evidence of the extremist error into which he has fallen. And similarly, if Swift had expected us to go the whole way with Gulliver in his identification of men with the Yahoos, he would hardly have depicted the human characters in his story—especially the admirable Portuguese captain, Don Pedro de Mendez, and his crew—in the conspicuously favourable light in which they appear to us. They are bound to strike us as notable exceptions to the despairing estimate of 'human kind' to which Gulliver has been led by his Houyhnhnm master; and we can only conclude that Gulliver's failure to look upon them as other than Yahoos, whom at best he can only 'tolerate', is meant as still another sign to us of the false extremism of his attitude.

All this looks at first sight convincing—until we begin to think of other possible intentions that Swift might have had in the Voyage with which these signs would be equally compatible. Suppose that his primary purpose was indeed to 'vex the world' by administering as severe a shock as he could to the cherished belief that man is par excellence a 'rational creature', and suppose that he chose to do this, in part at least, by forcing his readers to dwell on the unbridgeable gap between what is involved in being a truly 'rational creature' and what not only the worse but also the better sort of men actually are. It is plain what he

[a] Plato, *Republic* Book VII. Socrates here compares man's apprehension of reality to a prisoner who perceives only shadows cast upon the wall of his cave.

would have had to do in working out such a design. He would have had to give to his wholly rational beings precisely those 'unhuman' characteristics that have been noted, to their disadvantage, in the Houyhnhnms; to have made them creatures such as we would normally like or sympathize with would have been to destroy their value as a transcendent standard of comparison. And it would have been no less essential to introduce characters, like Don Pedro, or, for that matter, Gulliver himself, who, in terms of ordinary human judgments, would impress us as unmistakably good; otherwise he would have exempted too many of his readers from the shock to their pride in being men which, on this hypothesis, he was trying to produce. He would have had to do, in short, all those things in the Voyage that have been taken as indications of a purpose very different from the one I am now supposing, and much less misanthropic. Clearly, then, some other kind of proof is needed than these ambiguous internal signs before the current view of Swift's meaning can be thought of as more than one possibility among other competing ones.

A good many defenders of this view, especially during the past decade, have attempted to supply such proof by relating the Voyage to its presumed background in the intellectual and religious concerns of Swift and his age; and it is their manner of doing this—of using hypotheses based on the history of ideas in the determination of their author's meaning—that I want to examine in what immediately follows.

They have been fairly well agreed on these three points: in the first place, that Swift's main design in the Voyage was to uphold what they describe as the traditional and orthodox conception of human nature, classical and Christian alike, that 'recognizes in man an inseparable complex of good and evil', reason and passion, spiritual soul and animal body; secondly, that he conceived the Houyhnhnms and the Yahoos, primarily at least, as allegorical embodiments of these two parts of man's constitution taken in abstraction the one from the other; and thirdly, that he developed his defence of the orthodox view by directing his satire against those contemporary doctrines, on the one hand, that tended to exalt the Houyhnhnm side of man in forgetfulness of how Yahoo-like man really is, and those doctrines, on the other hand, that tended to see man only as a Yahoo in forgetfulness of his Houyhnhnm possibilities, limited though these are. All this has been more or less common doctrine among critics of the Voyage at least since Ernest Bernbaum in 1920; there has been rather less agreement on the identity of the contemporary movements of ideas which Swift had in view as objects of attack. It was usual in the earlier phases of the discussion to say simply, as Bernbaum does, that he was thinking, at the one extreme, of the 'sentimental optimism' of writers like Shaftesbury and, at the other, of the pessimism or cynicism of writers like Hobbes and Mandeville. Since then, however, other identifications have been added to the list, as relevant especially to his conception of the Houyhnhnms; we have been told, thus, that he 'obviously' intended to embody in the principles and mode of life of these creatures, along with certain admittedly admirable qualities, the rationalistic errors of the neo-Stoics, the Cartesians, and the deists—some or all of these, depending upon the critic.

596

Now if we could feel sure that what was in Swift's mind when he conceived the fourth Voyage is even approximately represented by these statements, we should have little reason for not going along with the interpretation of his design they have been used to support. For if he was indeed engaged in vindicating the 'Christian humanist' view of human nature against those contemporary extremists who made either too much or too little of man's capacity for reason and virtue, the current view of Gulliver as partly a vehicle and partly an object of the satire is surely correct. Everything depends, therefore, on how much relevance to what he was trying to do in the Voyage this particular historical hypothesis can be shown to have.

Its proponents have offered it as relevant beyond reasonable doubt; which suggests to me that some special assumptions about the application of intellectual history to the exegesis of literary works must be involved here. For they would find it difficult, I think, to justify their confidence in terms merely of the ordinary canons of proof in this as well as other historical fields.

They can indeed show that the hypothesis is a possible one, in the sense that it is consistent with some of the things we know about Swift apart from the Voyage. We know that he was a humanistically educated Anglican divine, with traditionalist inclinations in many matters; that he looked upon man's nature as deeply corrupted by the Fall but thought that self-love and the passions could be made, with the help of religion, to yield a positive though limited kind of virtue; that he held reason in high esteem as a God-given possession of man but distrusted any exclusive reliance on it in practice or belief, ridiculing the Stoics and Cartesians and making war on the deists; and that he tended, especially in his political writings, to find the useful truth in a medium between extremes. A man of whom these things can be said might very well have conceived the 'Voyage to the Country of the Houyhnhnms' in the terms in which, on the present theory, Swift is supposed to have conceived it. And beyond this, it is possible to point to various characteristics in the Voyage itself which, *if* the hypothesis is correct, can be interpreted as likely consequences of it. If Swift had in fact intended to symbolize, in the sustained opposition of Houyhnhnms and Yahoos, the deep division and conflict within man between his rational and his animal natures, he would undoubtedly have depicted these two sets of creatures, in essentials at least, much as they are depicted in the text (although this would hardly account for his choice of horses as symbols of rationality). So too with the supposition that we were meant to see in the Houyhnhnms, among other things, a powerful reminder of how inadequate and dangerous, for weak and sinful human nature, is any such one-sided exaltation of reason as was being inculcated at the time by the deists, the neo-Stoics, and the Cartesians: it would not be surprising, if that were actually Swift's intention, to find Gulliver saying of 'those exalted quadrupeds', as he does, that they consider 'reason alone sufficient to govern a rational creature', that they neither affirm nor deny anything of which they are not certain, and that they keep their passions under firm control, practise 'universal friendship and benevolence', and are immune to fear of death and grief for the death of others.

Now all this is to the good, to the extent at least that without such considerations as these about both Swift and the fourth Voyage there would be no reason for entertaining the hypothesis at all. But can we say anything more than this —so long, that is, as we judge the question by the ordinary standards of historical criticism? In other words, do the considerations I have just summarized tend in any decisive way to establish the hypothesis as fact? The answer must surely be that they do not, and for the simple reason that they are all merely positive and favouring considerations, such as can almost always be adduced in support of almost any hypothesis in scholarship or common life, however irrelevant or false it may turn out to be. It is a basic maxim of scholarly criticism, therefore, that the probability of a given hypothesis is proportionate not to our ability to substantiate it by confirmatory evidence (although there obviously must be confirmatory evidence) but to our inability—after serious trial—to rule it out in favour of some other hypothesis that would explain more completely and simply the particulars it is concerned with. We have to start, in short, with the assumption that our hypothesis may very well be false and then permit ourselves to look upon it as fact only when, having impartially considered all the counter-possibilities we can think of, we find disbelief in it more difficult to maintain than belief. This is a rule which few of us consistently live up to (otherwise we would not publish as much as we do); but there are varying degrees of departure from it; and I can see few signs that its requirements are even approximated in the current historical discussions of the fourth Voyage. It would be a different matter if these critics had been able to show statements by Swift himself about *Gulliver's Travels* that defy reasonable interpretation except as references to the particular issues and doctrines which the hypothesis supposes were in his mind when he wrote the Voyage. But they have not succeeded in doing this; and they have given no attention at all to the possibility that there were other traditions of thought about human nature in Swift's time (I can thing of one such, as will appear later) with which he can be shown to have been familiar—traditions which they ought to have considered and then, if possible, excluded as irrelevant before their hypothesis can be said, on ordinary scholarly grounds, to be confirmed.

What then are the special assumptions about interpretative method on which, in view of all this, their confidence must be presumed to rest? Their problem has naturally led them, as it would any historian, to make propositions about Swift's thought apart from *Gulliver* and about the thought of Swift's age: what is distinctive is the character of these propositions and the use they are put to in the interpretation of the Voyage. In the eyes of the ordinary historian of ideas inquiring into the intellectual antecedents and constituents of this work, the thought of Swift as expressed in his other writings is simply an aggregate of particular statements and arguments, some of which may well turn out to be relevant to an understanding of its meaning; for any of them, however, this is merely a possibility to be tested, not a presumption to be argued from. It is the same, too, with the thought of Swift's age: this, again, in the eyes of the ordinary historian, is nothing more determinate than the sum of things that were being written in the later seventeenth and early eighteenth centuries, from varying points of view and in varying traditions of analysis, on the general theme of human nature. Some of these, once more, may well be relevant to the argument developed in the Voyage, but the historian can know what they are only after an unprejudiced inquiry that presupposes no prior limitation of the ideas Swift might have been influenced by or have felt impelled to attack in constructing it. For the ordinary historian, in short, the fact that the 'Voyage to the Country of the Houyhnhnms' was written by Swift at a particular moment in the general history of thought about man has only this methodological significance: that it defines the region in which he may most hopefully look for the intellectual stimuli and materials that helped to shape the Voyage; it gives him, so to speak, his working reading list; it can never tell him—only an independent analysis of the Voyage can do that—how to use the list.

That the critics we are concerned with have taken a different view of the matter from this is suggested by the title of the book in which the current historical theory of Swift's intentions in the Voyage is argued most fully and ingeniously—Kathleen Williams' *Jonathan Swift and the Age of Compromise*. For to think of a period in intellectual history in this way—as the age of something or other, where the something or other is designated by an abstract term like 'compromise'—is obviously no longer to consider it as an indefinite aggregate of happenings; it is to consider it rather as a definite system of happenings something like the plot of a novel in which a great many diverse characters and episodes are unified, more or less completely, by a principal action or theme. It is to assume, moreover, not only that the historian can determine what was the central problem, the basic conflict or tension, the dominant world view of a century or generation, either in general or in some particular department of thought, but that he can legitimately use his formula for this as a confirmatory premise in arguing the meanings and causes of individual works produced in that age. It is to suppose that there is a kind of probative force in his preferred formula for the period which can confer *a priori* a privileged if not unique relevance upon one particular hypothesis about a given work of that period as against other hypotheses that are less easily brought under the terms of the formula, so that little more is required by way of further proof than a demonstration, which is never hard to give, that the work makes sense when it is 'read' as the hypothesis dictates.

These are, I think, the basic assumptions which underlie most of the recent historical discussions of the fourth Voyage and which go far towards explaining the confidence their authors have felt in the correctness of their conclusions. It would be hard, otherwise, to understand why they should think it important to introduce propositions about what was central and unifying in the moral thought of Swift's age; the reason must be that they have hoped, by so doing, to establish some kind of antecedent limitation on the intentions he could be expected to have had in writing the Voyage. And that, indeed, is the almost unavoidable effect of the argument for any reader who closes his mind, momentarily, to the nature of the pre-suppositions on which it rests. For suppose we agree with these critics that the dominant and most significant issue in the moral speculation of the later seventeenth and early eighteenth centuries was a conflict between the three fundamentally different views of man's nature represented by the orthodox 'classical-Christian' dualism in the middle and, at opposite extremes, the newer doctrines of the rationalists and benevolists on the one side and of the materialists and cynics on the other. Since this is presented as an exhaustive scheme of classification, it will be easy for us to believe that the view of man asserted in the Voyage must have been one of these three. And then suppose we agree to think of Swift as a man predisposed by his humanist education and his convictions as an Anglican divine to adhere to the traditional and compromising view as against either of the modern extremists. It will be difficult for us now to avoid believing that the 'Voyage to the Country of the Houyhnhnms' was therefore more probably than not an assertion of this middle view against its contemporary enemies, and it will be harder than it would be without such an argument from the age to the author to the work, to resist any interpretations of its details that may be necessary to make them accord with that theory of Swift's intentions.

This is likely to be our reaction, at any rate, until we reflect on the peculiar character of the argument we have been persuaded to go along with. There are many arguments like it in the writings of modern critics and historians of ideas in other fields (those who have interpreted Shakespeare in the light of 'the Elizabethan world picture', for instance); but they all betray, I think, a fundamental confusion in method. The objection is not that they rest on a false conception of historical periods. There is nothing intrinsically illegitimate in the mode of historical writing that organizes the intellectual happenings of different ages in terms of their controlling 'climates of opinion', dominant tendencies, or ruling oppositions of attitude or belief; and the results of such synthesizing efforts are sometimes—as in A. O. Lovejoy, for example—illuminating in a high degree. The objection is rather to the further assumption, clearly implicit in these arguments, that the unifying principles of histories of this type have something like the force of empirically established universal laws, and can therefore be used as guarantees of the probable correctness of any interpretations of individual writings that bring the writings into harmony with their requirements. That this is sheer illusion can be easily seen if we consider what these principles really amount to. Some of them amount simply to assertions that there was a tendency among the writers of a particular time to concentrate on such and such problems and to solve them in such and such ways. There is no implication here that this trend affected all writers or any individual writer at all times: whether a given work of the age did or did not conform to the trend remains therefore an open question, to be answered only by independent inquiry unbiased by the merely statistical probabilities affirmed in the historian's generalization. But there are also principles of a rather different sort, among which we must include, I think, the formula of Swift's critics for the dominant conflict about human nature in his time. These are best described as dialectical constructs, since they organize the doctrinal facts they refer to by imposing on them abstract schemes of logical relationships among ideas which may or may not be identical with any of the various classifications and oppositions of doctrines influential at the time. Thus our critics' characterization of Swift's age and of Swift himself as a part of that age derives its apparent exhaustiveness from a pattern of general terms—

the concept of 'Christian humanism' and the two contraries of this—which these critics clearly owe to the ethical and historical speculations of Irving Babbitt and his school.[a] Now it may be that this scheme represents accurately enough the distinctions Swift had in mind when he conceived the fourth Voyage; but that would be something of a coincidence, and it is just as reasonable to suppose that he may have been thinking quite outside the particular framework of notions which this retrospective scheme provides. We must conclude, then, that this whole way of using the history of ideas in literary interpretation is misconceived. From the generalizations and schematisms of the synthesizing historians we can very often get suggestions for new working hypotheses with which to approach the exegesis of individual works. What we cannot get from them is any assurance whatever that any of these hypotheses are more likely to be correct than any others that we have hit upon without their aid.

I should now like to invite the reader's criticism, in the light of what I have been saying, on another view of the intellectual background and import of the fourth Voyage (or a considerable part of it at least) which I shall attempt to argue on the basis merely of ordinary historical evidence, independently of any general postulates about Swift or his age.

II

Whatever else may be true of the Voyage, it will doubtless be agreed that one question is kept uppermost in it from the beginning, for both Gulliver and the reader. This is the question of what sort of animal man, as a species, really is; and the point of departure in the argument is the answer to this question which Gulliver brings with him into Houyhnhnmland and which is also, we are reminded more than once, the answer which men in general tend, complacently, to give to it. Neither he nor they have any doubt that only man, among 'sensitive' creatures, can be properly called 'rational'; all the rest—whether wild or tame, detestable or, like that 'most comely and generous' animal, the horse, the reverse of that—being merely 'brutes', not 'endued with reason'. The central issue, in other words, is primarily one of definition: is man, or is he not, correctly defined as a 'rational creature'? It is significant that Gulliver's misanthropy at the end is not the result of any increase in his knowledge of human beings in the concrete over what he has had before; it is he after all who expounds to his Houyhnhnm master all those melancholy facts about men's 'actions and passions' that play so large a part in their conversations; he has known these facts all along, and has still been able to call himself a 'lover of mankind'. The thing that changes his love into antipathy is the recognition that is now forced upon him that these facts are wholly incompatible with the formula for man's nature which he has hitherto taken for granted—are compatible, indeed, only with a formula, infinitely more humiliating to human pride, which pushes man nearly if not quite over to the opposite pole of the animal world.

What brings about the recognition is, in the first place, the deeply disturbing

[a] Cf. J. C. Ransom's comments on this school of critics, pp. 230–31 above.

spectacle of the Houyhnhnms and the Yahoos. I can find nothing in the text that forces us to look on these two sets of strange creatures in any other light than that in which Gulliver sees them—not, that is, as personified abstractions, but simply as two concrete species of animals: existent species for Gulliver, hypothetical species for us. The contrast he draws between them involves the same pair of antithetical terms (the one positive, the other privative) that he has been accustomed to use in contrasting men and the other animals. The essential character of the Houyhnhnms, he tells us, is that they are creatures 'wholly governed by reason'; the essential character of the Yahoos is that 'they are the most unteachable of brutes', without 'the least tincture of reason'. The world of animals in Houyhnhnmland, in other words, is divided by the same basic difference as the world of animals in Europe. Only, of course—and it is the shock of this that prepares Gulliver for his ultimate abandonment of the definition of man he has started with—it is a world in which the normal distribution of species between 'rational creatures' and irrational 'brutes' is sharply inverted, with horses, which he cannot help admiring, in the natural place of men, and manlike creatures, which he cannot help abhorring, in the natural place of horses.

This is enough in itself to cause Gulliver to view his original formula for his own species, as he says, 'in a very different light'. But he is pushed much further in the same misanthropic direction by the questions and comments of his Houyhnhnm master, acting as a kind of Socrates. What thus develops is partly a reduction to absurdity of man's 'pretensions to the character of a rational creature' and partly a demonstration of the complete parity in essential nature between men and the Houyhnhnmland Yahoos. There is of course one difference—unlike the Yahoos, men are after all possessed of at least a 'small proportion', a 'small pittance' of reason, some in greater degree than others. But I can see no clear signs in the text that this qualification is intended to set men apart as a third, or intermediate, species for either Gulliver or the reader. For what is basic in the new definition of man as a merely more 'civilized' variety of Yahoo is the fundamentally irrational 'disposition' which motivates his habitual behaviour; and in relation to that his 'capacity for reason' is only an acquired attribute which he is always in danger of losing and of which, as Gulliver says, he makes no other use, generally speaking, than 'to improve and multiply those vices' whereof his 'brethren [in Houyhnhnmland] had only the share that nature allotted them'.

It is clear what a satisfactory historical explanation of this line of argument in the Voyage would have to do. It would have to account for Swift's patent assumption that there would be a high degree of satirical force, for readers in 1726, in a fable which began with the notion that man is pre-eminently a 'rational creature' and then proceeded to turn this notion violently upside down, and which, in doing so, based itself on a division of animal species into the extremes of 'rational creatures' and irrational 'brutes' and on the paradoxical identification of the former with horses and of the latter with beings closely resembling men. Was there perhaps a body of teaching, not so far brought into the discussion of the Voyage but widely familiar at the time, that could have supplied Swift with the particular scheme of ideas he was exploiting here? I suggest that there was, and also that there is nothing strange in the fact that it has been hitherto overlooked by Swift's critics. For one principal medium through which these ideas could have come to Swift and his readers—the only one, in fact, I know of that could have given all of them—was a body of writings, mainly in Latin, which students of literature in our day quite naturally shy away from reading: namely, the old-fashioned textbooks in logic that still dominated the teaching of that subject in British universities during the later seventeenth and early eighteenth centuries.[3]

It is impossible not to be impressed, in the first place, by the prominence in these textbooks of the particular definition of man which the Voyage sought to discredit. *Homo est animal rationale* ['man is a rational animal'] : no one could study elementary logic anywhere in the British Isles in the generation before *Gulliver* without encountering this formula or variations of it (*Nullus homo est irrationalis* ['No man is irrational']) in his manuals and the lectures he heard. It appears as the standard example of essential definition in the great majority of logics in use during these years at Oxford, Cambridge, and Dublin; and in most of those in which it occurs, it is given without comment or explanation as the obviously correct formula for man's distinctive nature, as if no one would ever question that man is, uniquely and above all, a rational creature. It is frequently brought in many times over, in various contexts, in individual textbooks: I have counted a dozen or so occurrences of it in Milton's *Art of Logic*, and many times that number in the *Institutionum logicarum ... libri duo* of Franco Burgersdijck (or Burgersdicius), which was one of the most widely used, and also one of the longest lived, of all these writings—it appeared in 1626 and was still prescribed at Dublin when Edmund Burke went there as a Junior Freshman in 1744.[4] I shall have some more to say of Burgersdicius, or 'Burgy' as Burke called him, presently; but it is worth noting that he provides us, in one passage, with the very question on which much of the fourth Voyage was to turn and with the answer Swift was *not* to give to it: 'Quaerenti enim, Quale animal est homo? appositè respondetur, Rationale.' ['To the question "What kind of animal is man?" the correct answer is, "Rational".']

Not only, however, was the definition omnipresent in these books, but there is some evidence that it was thought of, in Swift's time, as the special property of the academic logicians. Locke, for instance, calls it in his *Essay* 'the ordinary Definition of the Schools', the 'sacred Definition of *Animal Rationale*' of 'the learned Divine and Lawyer'; it goes, he implies, with 'this whole *Mystery* of *Genera* and *Species*, which make a noise in the Schools, and are, with Justice, so little regarded out of them' (III. iii. 10; vi. 26; iii. 9). And there are other later testimonies to the same effect; among them these opening lines of an anonymous poem of the period after *Gulliver*, once ascribed to Swift—'The Logicians Refuted':

> Logicians have but ill defin'd
> As rational, the human kind;
> Reason, they say, belongs to man,
> But let them prove it if they can.

> Wise Aristotle and Smiglesius,
> By ratiocinations specious,
> Have strove to prove with great precision,
> With definition and division,
> *Homo est ratione preditum;* [man is endowed with reason]
> But for my soul I cannot credit 'em.[5]

But the logicians had more to offer Swift than the great authority which they undoubtedly conferred on the definition 'rational animal'. They could have suggested to him also the basic principle on which the inverted animal world of Houyhnhnmland was constructed, and consequently the disjunction that operated as major premise in his argument about man. Whoever it was, among the Greeks, that first divided the genus 'animal' by the differentiae 'rational' and 'irrational', there is much evidence that this antithesis had become a commonplace in the Greco-Roman schools long before it was taken up by the writer who did more than anyone else to determine the context in which the definition *animal rationale* was chiefly familiar to Englishmen of Swift's time. This writer was the Neoplatonist Porphyry of the third century, whose little treatise, the *Isagoge,* or introduction to the categories of Aristotle, became, as is well known, one of the great sources of logical theorizing and teaching from the time of Boethius until well beyond the end of the seventeenth century. There is no point in going into the details of Porphyry's doctrine: what is important for our purpose here is the new sanction he gave to the older division of animal species through his incorporation of it into the general scheme of differentiae for the category of substance which was later known as the *arbor porphyriana* or Porphyry's tree, especially in the diagrams of it that became a regular feature of the more elementary textbooks. Here it is, set forth discursively, in the crabbed prose of Burgersdicius (I quote the English version of 1697, but the Latin is no better). In seeking the definition of man, he writes, we must first observe that

> Man is a Substance; but because an Angel is also a Substance; *That it may appear how Man differs from an Angel,* Substance ought to be divided into Corporeal and Incorporeal. A Man is a *Body,* an Angel *without a Body:* But a Stone also is a *Body:* That therefore a Man may be distinguished from a Stone, divide Bodily or Corporeal Substance into Animate and Inanimate, that is, *with or without a Soul.* Man is a Corporeal Substance Animate, Stone Inanimate. But Plants are also *Animate:* Let us divide therefore again Corporeal Substance Animate into *Feeling and void of Feeling.* Man feels, a Plant not: But a Horse *also feels,* and likewise other Beasts. Divide we therefore Animate Corporeal Feeling Substance into Rational and Irrational. Here therefore *are we to stand,* since it appears that every, and only Man is Rationale.[6]

And there was, finally, one other thing in these logics that could have helped to shape Swift's invention in the fourth Voyage. In opposing man as the only species of 'rational animal' to the brutes, Porphyry obviously needed a specific instance, parallel to man, of an 'irrational' creature; and the instance he chose—there were earlier precedents for the choice[7]—was the horse. The proportion 'rational' is to 'irrational' as man is to horse occurs more than once in the *Isagoge*; and the juxtaposition, in the same context, of *homo* and *equus* was a frequently recurring cliché in his seventeenth-century followers, as in the passage in Burgersdicius just quoted: other species of brutes were occasionally mentioned, but none of them nearly so often. And anyone who studied these books could hardly fail to remember a further point—that the distinguishing 'property' of this favourite brute was invariably given as whinnying (*facultas hinniendi*); *equus*, it was said again and again, *est animal hinnibile*.

To most Englishmen of Swift's time who had read logic in their youth—and this would include nearly all generally educated men—these commonplaces of Porphyry's tree, as I call them for short, were as familiar as the Freudian commonplaces are to generally educated people today, and they were accepted, for the most part, in an even less questioning spirit, so that it might well have occurred to a clever satirist then, that he could produce a fine shock to his readers' complacency as human beings by inventing a world in which horses appeared where the logicians had put men and men where they had put horses, and by elaborating, through this, an argument designed to shift the position of man as a species from the *animal rationale* branch of the tree, where he had always been proudly placed, as far as possible over towards the *animal irrationale* branch, with its enormously less flattering connotations. But have we any warrant for thinking that this, or something like it, was what Swift actually had in mind? It is clearly possible to describe the Voyage as, in considerable part at least, an anti-Porphyrian satire[8] in the genre of the poem I quoted from earlier, 'The Logicians Refuted'. But is there any evidence that Swift planned it as such?

That the Porphyrian commonplaces had been known to him in their full extent from his days at Trinity College in the early 1680s we can hardly doubt in view of the kind of education in logic he was exposed to there. Among the books which all Junior Freshmen at Dublin in those years were required to study or hear lectures on, we know of three in which the Porphyrian apparatus and examples had a prominent place: the *Isagoge* itself (which was prescribed by the statutes of the College to be read twice over during the year), the older logic of Burgersdicius, and the newer *Institutio logicae* of Narcissus Marsh. It is true that Swift, according to his own later statement, detested this part of the curriculum, and it is true that on one examination in the 'philosophy' course (specifically Physica), in his last year, his mark was *Male* [Bad] (he had a *Bene* [Good] in Greek and Latin). But this was an examination in a more advanced part of the Aristotelian system, and it is likely that he had fared better in the earlier examination in logic, since he had evidently been allowed to proceed with his class. It is possible, moreover, to infer from his occasional use of logical terms in his later writings that, abhorrent as the subject was to him, the time he had been compelled to spend on it as a Junior Freshman was not a total loss. He at least remembered enough of it to allude familiarly in different places to such things as a 'long sorites', 'the first proposition of a hypothetical syllogism', and the fallacy of two middle terms in a single syllogism;[9] and if this was possible, there is good reason to suppose that he had not forgotten the much simpler Porphyrian points about genera, species, and definition, 'rational' versus 'irrational' animals, men and horses which he had been introduced to at the same time.

The crucial question, however, is whether he had these notions of the logicians actively in mind when, in the 1720s, he conceived and wrote the 'Voyage to the Country of the Houyhnhnms'. And here it will be well to take a fresh look at the two much-quoted letters about *Gulliver's Travels* which he sent to Pope in 1725, just after that work was completed. In the first of these, that of 29 September, after having told Pope that his chief aim is 'to vex the world rather than divert it' and that he hates and detests 'that animal called man', he goes on to remark: 'I have got materials towards a treatise proving the falsity of that definition *animal rationale*, and to show it should be only *rationis capax* [capable of reason]. Upon this great foundation of misanthropy, though not in Timon's manner, the whole building of my Travels is erected; and I never will have peace of mind till all honest men are of my opinion.' In the second letter, that of 26 November, he desires that Pope and 'all my friends' will 'take a special care that my disaffection to the world may not be imputed to my age, for I have credible witnesses ... that it has never varied from the twenty-first to the f——ty-eighth year of my life'. He then adds a passage which has been read as a retraction of the judgment on humanity expressed in the first letter, although the final sentence makes clear, I think, that it was not so intended:

> I tell you after all, that I do not hate mankind; it is *vous autres* [Pope and Bolingbroke] who hate them, because you would have them reasonable animals, and are angry for being disappointed. I have always rejected that definition, and made another of my own. I am no more angry with —— than I am with the kite that last week flew away with one of my chickens; and yet I was glad when one of my servants shot him two days after.

The casual references in both letters to 'that definition' *animal rationale* and 'reasonable animals'—which Swift tells Pope he has 'always rejected' have usually been interpreted by his modern critics as allusions to such contemporary philosophical or theological heresies (from Swift's point of view) as the 'optimism' of Shaftesbury or the 'rationalism' of Descartes and the deists. It is surely, however, a much less far-fetched conjecture, especially in view of the familiar textbook Latin of the first letter, to see in 'that definition' nothing other or more than the 'sacred definition' of the logicians which had been inflicted on him, by thoroughly orthodox tutors, in his undergraduate days at Dublin.

I find this explanation, at any rate, much harder to disbelieve than any other that has been proposed; and all the more so because of another passage in the first letter which is almost certainly reminiscent of the Trinity logic course in the early 1680s. It is the famous sentence—just before the allusion to 'that definition *animal rationale*' and leading on to it—in which Swift says: 'But principally I hate and detest that animal called man, although I heartily love John, Peter, Thomas, and so forth.' Now to anyone at all widely read in the logic textbooks of Swift's time two things about this sentence are immediately evident: first, that the distinction it turns on is the distinction to be found in nearly all these books between a species of animals and individual members of that species; and second, that the names 'John, Peter, Thomas, and so forth' are wholly in line with one of the two main traditions of names for individuals of the species man that had persisted side by side in innumerable manuals of logic since the Middle Ages: not, of course, the older tradition of classical names—Socrates, Plato, Alexander, Caesar—but the newer tradition (which I have noted first in Occam, although it doubtless antedates him) that drew upon the list of apostles—Peter, John, Paul, James, Thomas, in roughly that descending order of preference. (Other non-classical names, like Stephen, Catharine, Charles, Richard, also appear, but much less frequently.)

We can go further than this, however. For although all three of Swift's names occur separately in various texts (Thomas least often), the combination 'John, Peter, Thomas, and so forth' was an extremely unusual one. I have met with it, in fact, in only one book before 1725; and I have examined nearly all the logics, both Latin and English, down to that date for which I can find any evidence that they had even a minor circulation in Britain. The exception, however, is a book which Swift could hardly have escaped knowing as an undergraduate, since it was composed expressly for the use of Trinity College students by the then Provost and had just recently come 'on the course' when he entered the College in 1682—namely, the *Institutio logicae*, already referred to, of Narcissus Marsh (Dublin, 1679: reissued Dublin, 1681). Early in the book Marsh gives a full-page diagram of Porphyry's tree, with its inevitable opposition of *animal—rationale—homo* and *animal—irrationale—brutum*; and here, as *individua* under *homo*, we find 'Joannes, Petrus, Thomas, &c.' And a little later in the book the same names are repeated in the same order as individual specimens of *homo* in Marsh's analytical table for the category *substantia*.

Was this combination of names, then, Marsh's invention? There is one further circumstance which suggests that it may well have been. We know from his own testimony,[10] as well as from internal evidence, that the source on which he based the greater part of his Dublin logic of 1679 was his own revision, published at Oxford in 1678, of the *Manuductio ad logicam* of the early seventeenth-century Jesuit logician Philippe Du Trieu. Now of the two passages in the Dublin book that contain Swift's three names, the first—the diagram of Porphyry's tree—has no counterpart in the Oxford book of 1678, although it has in Du Trieu's original text, where the names are 'Petrus' and 'Joannes'. It seems likely, then, that Marsh first thought of the combination 'John, Peter, Thomas, and so forth' when he revised his earlier revision of Du Trieu for his Trinity students in 1679; and this is borne out by what he did at the same time with the other passage—the table of substance. This he retained almost exactly as it had been in Du Trieu except for the names under *homo*: here, where in 1678 he had reprinted Du Trieu's 'Stephanus, Johannes, Catharina, &c.', he now wrote 'Johannes, Petrus, Thomas, &c.' Which would seem to imply a certain sense of private property in these particular names in this particular combination.

It is somewhat hard, then, not to conclude that Swift was remembering Marsh's logic as he composed the sentence, in his letter to Pope, about 'John, Peter, Thomas, and so forth'. But if that is true, can there be much doubt, in view of the Porphyrian context in which these names appear in Marsh, about what tradition of ideas was in his mind when he went on to remark, immediately afterwards, that 'the great foundation of misanthropy' on which 'the

607

whole building of his *Travels* rested was his proof—against Marsh and the other logicians he had been made to study at Trinity—of 'the falsity of that definition *animal rationale*'?[11]

Notes

1. See his 'Errors concerning the Houyhnhnms', MP, lvi, 1958, 92–7. To this may now be added Edward Rosenheim, Jr.'s 'The Fifth Voyage of Lemuel Gulliver: a footnote', MP, lx, 1962, 103–19, and his *Swift and the Satirist's Art* (Chicago, 1963), *passim*.

2. The list of writings that reflect this preoccupation is now a fairly long one; in the present essay I have had in view chiefly the following: Ernest Bernbaum, 'The significance of "Gulliver's Travels"', in his edition of that work (New York, 1920); T. O. Wedel, 'On the philosophical background of *Gulliver's Travels*', SP, xxiii 1926, 434–50; John F. Ross, 'The Final Comedy of Lemuel Gulliver', in *Studies in the Comic* (University of California Publications in English, vol. viii, no. 2, 1941), pp. 175–96; Robert B. Heilman, Introduction to his edition of *Gulliver's Travels* (New York, 1950), especially pp. xii-xxii; Ernest Tuveson, 'Swift: the Dean as satirist', *University of Toronto Quarterly*, xxii, 1953, 368–75; Roland M. Frye, 'Swift's Yahoo and the Christian symbols for Sin', *JHI*, xv, 1953, 201–15; W. A. Murray's supplementary note to Frye, ibid., pp. 596–601; Samuel H. Monk, 'The Pride of Lemuel Gulliver', *Sewanee Review*, lxiii, 1955, 48–71; Irvin Ehrenpreis, 'The origins of *Gulliver's Travels*', PMLA, lxxii, 1957, 880–99 (reprinted with some revisions in his *The Personality of Jonathan Swift* [London, 1958]); Kathleen Williams, *Jonathan Swift and the Age of Compromise* (Lawrence, Kansas, 1958); Calhoun Winton, 'Conversion on the road to Houyhnhnmland', *Sewanee Review*, lxviii, 1960, 20–33; Martin Kallich, 'Three ways of looking at a horse: Jonathan Swift's 'Voyage to the Houyhnhnms' Again', *Criticism*, ii, 1960, 107–24.

3. There are useful descriptions of many, though by no means all, of these in Wilbur Samuel Howell, *Logic and Rhetoric in England, 1500–1700* (Princeton, 1956).

4. *The Correspondence of Edmund Burke*, edited by Thomas W. Copeland, I (Cambridge and Chicago, 1958), iv, 7–9, 21, 28.

5. *The Busy Body*, no. 5, 18 October 1759. Both the ascription to Swift, which occurs in a note prefixed to this first known printing of the poem, and the later ascription to Goldsmith seem to me highly dubious.

6. *Monitio logica: or, An Abstract and Translation of Burgersdicius His logick* (London, 1697), pp. 13–14 (second pagination).

7. e.g., Quintilian, *Institutio oratoria*, VII. iii, 3, 24. For the contrast of man and horse in Porphyry see especially Migne, PL, lxiv, col. 128 (Boethius' translation): 'Differentia est quod est aptum natum dividere ea quae sub eodem genere sunt: rationale enim et irrational, hominem et equum quae sub eodem genere sunt animali dividunt.'

8. Since this essay was first printed, my colleague Edward Rosenheim has pointed out (MP, lx, 109–10; cf. his *Swift and the Satirist's Art*, p. 100 n.) that this description of the fourth Voyage as an 'anti-Porphyrian satire' needs some clarification. How, he asks, 'are our own opinions changed by Swift's discrediting the definition of man to be found in such texts on logic as that of Narcissus Marsh? Is the reader's scepticism being chiefly directed against the texts themselves? (Crane's phrase, "anti-Porphyrian satire" suggests that he may think so.) Or, on the other hand, is the satire directed against the substance of the proposition itself without particular concern for the contexts in which it has appeared?'
My phrase, I must acknowledge, clearly invites the construction Rosenheim puts on it. It does seem to imply that just as the targets of Swift's satire in Part III of *Gulliver* were the experimenters and projectors of the Royal Society, so, in much the same sense, his targets in Part IV were the academic logicians of the Porphyrian school. My actual view of the relation between the Voyage and these logicians, however, is quite different from this and much closer to the view Rosenheim himself expounds in the latter part of his essay. Like him, I regard the fourth Voyage, not as an attack on either logicians or **logic** (low as was his opinion of this subject), but as a satirical 'homily' directed against a much more nearly universal object—namely, that form of human pride which the late Arthur O. Lovejoy once called 'the generic pride of man as such' (*Essays in the History*

of *Ideas*, p. 63), the pride that springs from the imagined superiority of man as a species over all other living creatures in some major aspect of his nature.

For Swift in the fourth Voyage, the chief foundation of this pride was the almost universally prevalent conviction, which the academic logicians in the tradition of Porphyry and his Greek and Roman predecessors did so much to keep alive, that the essence of man—and hence of all men—is contained in 'that definition *animal rationale*'. He had only to prove the falsity of this, and he had knocked out one of the great supports—perhaps the greatest support—of man's pretension to unique eminence in the animate world. This—I think Rosenheim would agree with me—was the major task he set himself in contriving his fable of Gulliver among the Houyhnhnms and the Yahoos, to the end of shocking his readers into that attitude of philosophic misanthropy ('not in Timon's manner') which consisted in thinking less exaltedly of themselves and expecting less of virtue and sense from their fellow creatures.

9. See John M. Bullitt, *Jonathan Swift and the Anatomy of Satire* (Cambridge, Mass., 1953), p. 73. Cf. also Swift, 'A Preface to the B——p of S——m's Introduction', in *Works*, edited by Temple Scott, iii, 150.

10. See his preface 'Ad lectorem' in the 1681 issue (it is missing from some copies but can be found in the Cambridge University Library copy and in that belonging to Archbishop Marsh's Library, Dublin); also the entry for 20 December 1690, in his manuscript diary. I owe this latter reference to Mary Pollard, of Archbishop Marsh's Library. For the rather complicated bibliographical history of Marsh's *Institutio logicae* (the title was altered to *Institutiones logicae* in the reissue of 1681), see her article, 'The printing of the Provost's Logic and the supply of text-books in the late seventeenth century', in *Friends of the Library of Trinity College, Dublin: Annual Bulletin*, 1959–61.

11. I have discussed some further aspects of the subject in a brief article, 'The Rationale of the Fourth Voyage', in *Gulliver's Travels: an annotated text with critical essays*, edited by Robert A. Greenberg (New York, 1961), pp. 300–7, and in a review of two papers on Swift and the deists, in *PQ*, xl, 1961, 427–30.

45   Marshall McLuhan

Marshall McLuhan (b. 1911) was born and brought up in Canada. He studied at Manitoba University and subsequently at Cambridge, England, where he experienced the teaching of Dr F. R. Leavis. McLuhan's own early criticism (mainly periodical essays written while he was teaching at St Louis University) was somewhat Leavisian in character, defending and interpreting the work of certain modern writers as preservers of important cultural values in the hostile environment of mass society. In the 1940s, however, McLuhan moved towards a more objective, more analytical engagement with mass culture, of which the first result was his study of modern advertising, *The Mechanical Bride: folklore of industrial man* (New York, 1951). This pioneering study was almost entirely ignored until *The Gütenberg Galaxy: the making of typographical man* (1962) made McLuhan a figure of international fame and controversy. He is now Director of the Centre for Culture and Technology at the University of Toronto.

The *Gütenberg Galaxy* is based on the assumption that the nature and development of human knowledge are best understood by studying our modes of perception and communication, which are subject to change. In the words of McLuhan's most celebrated aphorism, 'the medium is the message'. In primitive, preliterate societies (so the theory goes) communication is basically oral–aural, but involves *all* the senses in person-to-person encounters. The next phase of cultural development is that of script, which depersonalizes communication to some extent, but not entirely. It is the printing press (invention of Gütenberg) which divorces communication from all senses except the visual. In the Gütenberg era, knowledge is acquired in silence and solitude as the mind follows the linear, logical connections of the printed text. The human family and the Gestalt of the human person are fragmented into various specialized functions, with consequent alienation and angst. The Gütenberg era, however, is already being superseded by electric and electronic media, especially television, which operate in a way analogous to primitive oral–aural communication, converting the world into a 'global village'.

McLuhan's subsequent publications, which include *Understanding Media* (New York, 1964), and *The Medium is the Massage* (New York, 1967), are all extensions or explorations of the ideas expounded in *The Gütenberg Galaxy*. With that book, McLuhan transformed himself from a literary critic into a cultural historian and utopian prophet, but much of his illustration and inspiration is drawn from imaginative literature—Blake and Joyce being especially important influences.

The weaknesses of McLuhan's argument as regards both evidence and logic have been pointed out often enough, and his characteristic defensive gambit—

to suggest that his critics, by their objections, merely demonstrate their Gütenberg conditioning—is not entirely satisfactory. But he has probably done more than any other single man to make us conscious of the various media of communication *as* media, instead of merely attending to the information they carry. He has done this partly by synthesizing and expressing with epigrammatic force a great deal of specialized scholarship in a wide range of different fields. The extract from *The Gütenberg Galaxy* reprinted below, which is mainly about Pope's *The Dunciad*, illustrates McLuhan's ability to startle the reader into viewing a familiar object from an unfamiliar angle.

CROSS REFERENCES :   37. Walter J. Ong
38. Norman O. Brown
44. R. S. Crane.

COMMENTARY :   Jonathan Miller, *McLuhan* (1971)
George Steiner, 'On reading Marshall McLuhan', in *Language and Silence* (1967)

[*The Dunciad* and the Gütenberg galaxy]

The Gütenberg galaxy was theoretically dissolved in 1905 with the discovery of curved space, but in practice it had been invaded by the telegraph two generations before that

Whittaker[a] notes (p. 98) that the space of Newton and Gassendi was 'so far as geometry was concerned, the space of Euclid: it was infinite, homogeneous, and completely featureless, one point being just like another...' Much earlier our concern had been to explain why this fiction of homogeneity and uniform continuity had derived from phonetic writing, especially in print form. Whittaker says that from a physics point of view the Newtonian space was 'mere emptiness into which things could be put'. But even for Newton, the gravitational field seemed incompatible with this neutral space. 'As a matter of fact, the successors of Newton felt this difficulty; and, having started with a space that was in itself simply nonentity having no property except a capacity for being occupied, they proceeded to fill it several times over with ethers

---

[a] Edmund Whittaker, *Space and Spirit* (Hinsdale, Ill., 1948).

designed to provide electric, magnetic, and gravitational forces, and to account for the propagation of light' (pp. 98-9).

Perhaps no more striking evidence of the merely visual and uniform character of space was given than in the famous phrase of Pascal: 'Le silence éternel des espaces infinis m'effraie' ['The eternal silence of infinite space terrifies me']. Some meditation on why silent space should be so terrifying yields much insight into the cultural revolution going on in human sensibilities by the visual stress of the printed book.

But the absurdity of speaking of space as a neutral container will never trouble a culture which has separated its visual awareness from the other senses. Yet, says Whittaker, 'in Einstein's conception, space is no longer the stage in which the drama of physics is performed: it is itself one of the performers; for gravitation, which is a physical property, is entirely controlled by curvature, which is a geometrical property of space' (p. 100).

With this recognition of curved space in 1905 the Gütenberg galaxy was officially dissolved. With the end of lineal specialisms and fixed points of view, compartmentalized knowledge became as unacceptable as it had always been irrelevant. But the effect of such a segregated way of thinking has been to make science a departmental affair, having no influence on eye and thought except indirectly through its applications. In recent years this isolationist attitude has weakened. And it has been the effort of this book to explain how the illusion of segregation of knowledge had become possible by the isolation of the visual sense by means of alphabet and typography. Perhaps it cannot be said too often. This illusion may have been a good or a bad thing. But there can only be disaster arising from unawareness of the causalities and effects inherent in our own technologies.

In the later seventeenth century there is a considerable amount of alarm and revulsion expressed concerning the growing quantity of printed books. The first hopes for a great reform of human manners by means of the book had met disappointment, and in 1680 Leibnitz was writing:

> I fear we shall remain for a long time in our present confusion and indigence through our own fault. I even fear that after uselessly exhausting curiosity without obtaining from our investigations any considerable gain for our happiness, people may be disgusted with the sciences, and that a fatal despair may cause them to fall back into barbarism. To which result that horrible mass of books which keeps on growing might contribute very much. For in the end the disorder will become nearly insurmountable; the indefinite multitude of authors will shortly expose them all to the danger of general oblivion; the hope of glory animating many people at work in studies will suddenly cease; it will be perhaps as disgraceful to be an author as it was formerly honourable. At best, one may amuse himself with little books of the hour which will run their course in a few years and will serve to divert a reader from boredom for a few moments, but which will have been written without any design to promote our knowledge or to deserve the appreciation of posterity. I shall be told that since so many people write it is impossible for all their works to be preserved. I admit that, and I do not entirely disapprove those little books in fashion which are like the flowers of a springtime or like the fruits of an autumn, scarcely surviving a year. If they are

well made, they have the effect of a useful conversation, not simply pleasing and keeping the idle out of mischief but helping to shape the mind and language. Often their aim is to induce something good in men of our time, which is also the end I seek by publishing this little work ...[1]

Leibnitz here envisages the book as the natural successor, as well as executioner, of scholastic philosophy, which might yet return. The book as a spur to fame and as the engine of immortality now seems to him in the utmost danger from 'the indefinite multitude of authors'. For the general run of books he sees the function of serving as a furtherer of conversation 'keeping the idle out of mischief' and 'helping to shape the mind and language'. It is clear that the book was yet far from having become the main mode of politics and society. It was still a surface fact which had only begun to obscure the traditional lineaments of Western society. With regard to the continuing threat of scholastic renewal there is the ever-present literary or visual complaint about oral scholasticism that it is words, words, words. Leibnitz, writing on the 'Art of Discovery', says:

Among the Scholastics there was a certain Jean Suisset called the Calculator, whose works I have not yet been able to find and I have seen only those of a few disciples of his. This Suisset began to use Mathematics in scholastic arguments, but few people imitated him because they would have to give up the method of disputation for that of book-keeping and reasoning, and a stroke of the pen would have spared much clamor.[2]

Pope's *Dunciad* indicts the printed book as the agent of a primitivistic and Romantic revival. Sheer visual quantity evokes the magical resonance of the tribal horde. The box office looms as a return to the echo chamber of bardic incantation

In 1683-4 there appeared in London by Joseph Moxon, *Mechanick Exercises on the Whole Art of Printing*. The editors point out (p. vii) that 'it put in writing a knowledge that was wholly traditional', and that Moxon's book 'was by forty years the earliest manual of printing in any language'. Like Gibbon in his retrospect of Rome, Moxon seems to have been animated by a sense of print as having reached a terminus. A similar sentiment inspires *The Tale of a Tub* and *The Battle of the Books* by Dean Swift. But it is to *The Dunciad* that we must turn for the epic of the printed word and its benefits to mankind. For here is the explicit study of plunging of the human mind into the sludge of an unconscious engendered by the book. It has been obscured to posterity, in keeping with the prophecy at the end of Book IV, just why literature should be charged with stupefying mankind, and mesmerically ushering the polite world back into primitivism, the Africa within, and above all, the unconscious. The simple key to this operation is that which we have had in hand throughout this book—the increasing separation of the visual faculty from the interplay with the other senses leads to the rejection from consciousness of most of our experience, and the consequent hypertrophy of the unconscious. This ever-enlarging domain Pope calls the world 'of Chaos and old Night'. It is the tribal, non-literate world celebrated by Mircea Eliade in *The Sacred and the Profane*.

Martinus Scriblerus*a* in his notes to *The Dunciad* reflects on how much more difficult it is to write an epic about the numerous scribblers and industrious hacks of the press than about a Charlemagne, a Brute, or a Godfrey. He then mentions the need for a satirist 'to dissuade the dull and punish the wicked', and looks at the general situation that has brought on the crisis:

> We shall next declare the occasion and the cause which moved our Poet to this particular work. He lived in those days when (after providence had per-mitted the Invention of Printing as a scourge for the Sins of the learned) Paper also became so cheap, and printers so numerous, that a deluge of authors cover'd the land: Whereby not only the peace of the honest unwrit-ing subject was daily molested, but unmerciful demands were made of his applause, yea of his money, by such as would neither earn the one, or deserve the other; At the same time, the Liberty of the Press was so unlimited, that it grew dangerous to refuse them either: For they would forthwith publish slanders unpunish'd, the authors being anonymous; nay the immediate pub-lishers thereof lay sculking under the wings of an Act of Parliament, assuredly intended for better purposes.[3]

Next he turns (p. 50) from the general economic causes to the private moral motivation of authors inspired by 'Dulness and Poverty; the one born with them, the other contracted by neglect of their proper talents ...' In a word, the attack is on applied knowledge as it manifests itself in 'Industry' and 'Plodding'. For authors inspired by self-opinion and the craving for self-expression are driven into 'setting up this sad and sorry merchandise'.

By means of the agglomerate action of many such victims of applied know-ledge—that is, self-opinionated authors endowed with Industry and Plodding—there is now the restoration of the reign of Chaos and old Night and 'the removal of the imperial seat of Dulness their daughter from the City to the Polite world'. As the book market expands, the division between intellect and commerce ends. The book trade takes over the functions of wit and spirit and government.

That is the meaning of the opening lines of the first editions of the poem:

> Books and the man I sing, the first who brings
> The Smithfield Muses to the ears of Kings.

It seemed quite unnatural to the 'polite world' of the time that decision-making and kingly rule should be accessible to popular authors. We no longer consider it odd or revolting to be ruled by people for whom the book of the month might appear quite respectable fare. Smithfield, where Bartholomew Fair was kept, was still a place for book-peddling. But in later editions Pope changed the opening:

*a*The Scriblerus Club, formed about 1713, included Pope, Swift, Arbuthnot and Gay. They collaborated in the composition of *The Memoirs of Martin Scriblerus*, a satire on 'false tastes in learning', and Pope used the name as a pseudonym in writing notes to *The Dunciad*.

> The mighty Mother, and her Son, who brings
> The Smithfield Muses to the ear of Kings.

He has encountered the public, the collective unconscious, and dubbed it 'the mighty Mother', in accordance with the occultism of his time. It is Joyce's 'Lead kindly Fowl' (foule, owl, crowd), which we have seen earlier.

As the book market enlarged and the gathering and reporting of news improved, the nature of authorship and public underwent the great changes that we accept as normal today. The book had retained from manuscript times some of its private and conversational character, as Leibnitz indicated in his evaluation. But the book was beginning to be merged in the newspaper as the work of Addison and Steele reminds us. Improved printing technology carried this process all the way by the end of the eighteenth century and the arrival of the steam press.

Yet Dudek in *Literature and the Press* (p. 46) considers that even after steam-power had been applied to printing:

> English newspapers in the first quarter of the century, however, were by no means designed to appeal to the whole population. By modern standards they would be considered too dull to interest more than a small minority of serious readers.... Early nineteenth century newspapers were run largely for the genteel. Their style was stiff and formal, ranging between Addisonian gracefulness and Johnsonian elevation. The contents consisted of small advertisements, of local affairs and national politics, especially of commercial news and long transcriptions of parliamentary reports.... the best current literature was noticed in the newspapers.... 'In those days', Charles Lamb recalled, 'every morning paper, as an essential retainer to its establishment, kept an author, who was bound to furnish daily a quantum of witty paragraphs....' And since the divorce between the language of journalism (journalese) and the literary use of language had not yet been brought about, we find in the eighteenth and early nineteenth century that some of the principal men of letters contributed to the newspapers or made a living by writing.

But Pope peopled his *Dunciad* with these very figures, for his perceptions and criticisms were not personal or based on a private point of view. Rather he was concerned with a total change. It is significant that this change is not specified until the fourth book of *The Dunciad*, which came out in 1742. It is after introducing the famous classics master, Dr Busby of Westminster School, that we hear the ancient and especially Ciceronian theme concerning the excellence of man (IV, ll, 147-50):

> The pale Boy-Senator yet tingling stands,
> And holds his breeches close with both his hands.
>   Then thus. 'Since Man from beast by Words is known,
> Words are Man's province, Words we teach alone.'

Earlier we had noted the meaning of this theme for Cicero who regarded eloquence as an inclusive wisdom harmonizing our faculties, unifying all knowledge. Pope is here quite explicit in citing the destruction of this unity as deriving from word specialism and denudation. The theme of the denudation of consciousness we have followed continuously throughout the Renaissance. It is also the theme of Pope's *Dunciad*. The Boy-Senator continues:

> When Reason doubtful, like the Samian letter,
> Points him two ways, the narrower is the better.
> Plac'd at the door of Learning, youth to guide,
> We never suffer it to stand too wide.
> To ask, to guess, to know, as they commence,
> As Fancy opens the quick springs of Sense,
> We ply the Memory, we load the brain,
> Bind rebel Wit, and double chain on chain,
> Confine the thought, to exercise the breath;
> And keep them in the pale of Words till death.
> Whate'er the talents, or howe'er design'd,
> We hang one jingling padlock on the mind:
> A Poet the first day, he dips his quill;
> And what the last? a very Poet still.
> Pity! the charm works only in our wall,
> Lost, lost too soon in yonder House or Hall.

Pope has not received his due as a serious analyst of the intellectual *malaise* of Europe. He continues Shakespeare's argument in *Lear* and Donne's in the *Anatomy of the World*:

> 'Tis all in pieces, all coherence gone,
> All just supply and all relation.

It is the division of sense and the separation of words from their functions that Pope decries exactly as does Shakespeare in *King Lear*. Art and science had been separated as visual quantification and homogenization penetrated to every domain and the mechanization of language and literature proceeded:

> Beneath her foot-stool *Science* groans in Chains,
> And Wit dreads Exile, Penalties and Pains.
> There foam'd rebellious *Logic* gagg'd and bound,
> There, stript fair *Rhet'ric* languish'd on the ground.[4]

The new collective unconscious Pope saw as the accumulating backwash of private self-expression

Pope had a very simple scheme for his first three books. Book I deals with authors, their egotism and desire for self-expression and eternal fame. Book II turns to the book sellers who provide the conduits to swell the tides of public confession. Book III concerns the collective unconscious, the growing backwash from the tidal wave of self-expression. It is Pope's simple theme that the fogs of Dulness and new tribalism are fed by the printing press. Wit, the quick interplay among our senses and faculties, is thus steadily anaesthetized by the encroaching unconscious. Anybody who tried to get Pope's meaning by considering the content of the writers he presents would miss the needed clues. Pope is offering a formal causality, not an efficient causality, as an explanation of the

616

metamorphosis from within. The entire matter is thus to be found in a single couplet (I, ll. 89-90):

> Now night descending, the proud scene was o'er,
> But liv'd, in Settle's numbers, one day more.

Print, with its uniformity, repeatability, and limitless extent, does give reincarnate life and fame to anything at all. The kind of limp life so conferred by dull heads upon dull themes formalistically penetrates all existence. Since readers are as vain as authors, they crave to view their own conglomerate visage and, therefore, demand the dullest wits to exert themselves in ever greater degree as the collective audience increases. The 'human interest' newspaper is the ultimate mode of this collective dynamic:

> Now May'rs and Shrieves all hush'd and satiate lay,
> Yet eat, in dreams, the custard of the day;
> While pensive Poets painful vigils keep,
> Sleepless themselves to give their readers sleep.[5]

Of course, Pope does not mean that the readers will be bored by the products of sleepless poets or news writers. Quite the contrary. They will be thrilled, as by seeing their own image in the press. The readers' sleep is of the spirit. In their wits they are not pained but impaired.

Pope is telling the English world what Cervantes had told the Spanish world and Rabelais the French world concerning print. It is a delirium. It is a transforming and metamorphosing drug that has the power of imposing its assumptions upon every level of consciousness. But for us in the 1960s, print has much of the quaint receding character of the movie and the railway train. In recognizing its hidden powers at this late date we can learn to stress the positive virtues of print but we can gain insight into the much more potent and recent forms of radio and television also.

In his analysis of books, authors, and markets, Pope, like Harold Innis in *The Bias of Communication*, assumes that the entire operation of print in our lives is not only unconscious but that for this very reason it immeasurably enlarges the domain of the unconscious. Pope placed an owl at the beginning of *The Dunciad*, and Innis entitled the opening chapter of *The Bias of Communication*, 'Minerva's Owl': 'Minerva's Owl begins its flight only in the gathering dusk ...'

Aubrey Williams has a fine treatment[6] of the second *Dunciad* of 1729 in which he quotes Pope's own words to Swift:

The Dunciad is going to be printed in all pomp... It will be attended with *Proeme, Prolegomena, Testimonia Scriptorum, Index Authorum,* and Notes *Variorum.* As to the latter, I desire you to read over the text, and make a few in any way you like best, whether dry raillery, upon the style and way of commenting of trivial critics; or humorous, upon the authors in the poem; or historical, of persons, places, times; or explanatory; or collecting the parallel passages of the ancients.

Instead, that is, of a mere individual book attack on Dulness, Pope has provided

617

a collective newspaper format and much 'human interest' for the poem. He can thus render the plodding industry of Baconian applied knowledge and group toil with a dramatic quality that renders, yet irradiates, the very Dulness he decries. Williams[a] points out (p. 60) that the reason why 'the new material attached to the poem has never been adequately defined is due, I think, to the assumptions most critics and editors have made: that the notes are to be taken at the level of history, and that their main purpose is to continue the personal satire in a prose commentary'.

The last book of The Dunciad proclaims the metamorphic power of mechanically applied knowledge as a stupendous parody of the Eucharist

The entire fourth book of *The Dunciad* has to do with the theme of *The Gütenberg Galaxy*, the translation or reduction of diverse modes into a single mode of homogenized things. Right off, (ll. 44-5) this theme is rendered in terms of the new Italian opera.

> When lo' a Harlot form soft sliding by,
> With mincing step, small voice, and languid eye;

In the new chromatics, Pope finds (ll. 57-60) the all-reducing and homogenizing power that the book exercises on the human spirit:

> Wake the dull Church, and lull the ranting Stage;
> One Trill shall harmonize joy, grief, and rage,
> To the same notes thy sons shall hum, or snore,
> And all thy yawning daughters cry, *encore*.

Reduction and metamorphosis by homogenization and fragmentation are the persistent themes of the fourth book (ll. 453-6):

> O! would the Sons of Men once think their Eyes
> And Reason giv'n them but to study *Flies*!
> See Nature in some partial narrow shape,
> And let the Author of the Whole escape:

But these were the means by which, as Yeats tells us:

> Locke sank into a swoon;
> The Garden died;
> God took the spinning jenny
> Out of his side.

The popular mesmerism achieved by uniformity and repeatability, taught men the miracles of the division of labour and the creation of world markets. It is these miracles that Pope anticipates in *The Dunciad*, for their transforming power had long affected the mind. The mind now afflicted with the desire and power to climb by sheer sequential additive toil:

[a] Aubrey Williams, *Pope's Dunciad* (Baton Rouge, La., 1955).

> Why all your Toils? Your Sons have learn'd to sing.
> How quick Ambition hastes to ridicule!
> The Sire is made a Peer, the Son a Fool.

Then follows a decisive passage of explicit comment (ll. 549-57) on the Gütenberg miracles of applied knowledge and human transformation:

> On some, a Priest succinct in amice white
> Attends; all flesh is nothing in his sight!
> Beeves, at his touch, at once to jelly turn,
> And the huge Boar is shrunk into an Urn:
> The board with specious miracles he loads,
> Turns Hares to Larks, and Pigeons into Toads.
> Another (for in all what one can shine?)
> Explains the *Seve* and *Verdeur* of the Vine.
> What cannot copious Sacrifice attone?

Pope deliberately makes the miracles of applied knowledge a parody of the Eucharist. It is the same transforming and reducing power of applied knowledge which has confounded and confused all the arts and sciences, for, says Pope, the new *translatio studii* or transmission of studies and disciplines by the printed book has not been so much a transmission as a complete transformation of the disciplines and of the human mind as well. Studies have been translated exactly as was Bottom the Weaver.

How closely Pope's progress of Dulness over the earth conforms to the concept of *translatio studii* can be seen easily if lines 65-112 of Dunciad III are compared to this statement of the historic theme by an English humanist of the fourteenth century, Richard de Bury: 'Admirable Minerva seems to bend her course to all the nations of the earth, and reacheth from end to end mightily, that she may reveal herself to all mankind. We see that she has already visited the Indians, the Babylonians, the Egyptians and Greeks, the Arabs and the Romans. Now she has passed by Paris, and now has happily come to Britain, the most noble of islands, nay, rather a microcosm in itself, that she may show herself a debtor both to the Greeks and to the Barbarians.'[7]

And Pope in making Dulness the goddess of the unconscious is contrasting her with Minerva, goddess of alert intellect and wit. It is not Minerva but her obverse complement, the owl, that the printed book has conferred on Western man. 'However ill-fitting their heroic garb,' Williams remarks (p. 59), 'one at last finds the dunces invested with uncivilizing powers of epic proportions.'

Supported by the Gütenberg technology, the power of the dunces to shape and befog the human intellect is unlimited. Pope's efforts to clarify this basic point have been in vain. His intense concern with the *pattern* of action in his armed horde of nobodies has been mistaken for personal spite. Pope was entirely concerned with the *formalistic pattern* and penetrative and configuring power of the new technology. His readers have been befogged by 'content' obsession and the practical benefits of applied knowledge. He says in a note to Book III, l. 337:

> Do not gentle reader, rest too secure in thy contempt of the Instruments for such a revolution in learning, or despise such weak agents as have been

described in our poem, but remember what the *Dutch* stories somewhere relate, that a great part of their Provinces was once overflow'd, by a small opening made in one of their dykes by a single *Water-Rat*.

But the new mechanical instrument and its mesmerized and homogenized servants, the dunces, are irresistible:

> In vain, in vain,—The all-composing Hour
> Resistless falls: The Muse obeys the Pow'r.
> She comes! she comes! the sable Throne behold
> Of *Night* Primaeval, and of *Chaos* old!
> Before her, *Fancy's* gilded clouds decay,
> And all its varying Rain-bows die away.
> *Wit* shoots in vain its momentary fires,
> The meteor drops, and in a flash expires.
> As one by one, at dread Medea's strain,
> The sick'ning stars fade off th'ethereal plain;
> As Argus' eyes by Hermes' wand opprest,
> Clos'd one by one to everlasting rest;
> Thus at her felt approach, and secret might,
> *Art* after *Art* goes out, and all is Night.
> See skulking *Truth* to her old Cavern fled,
> While the Great Mother bids Britannia sleep,
> And pours her Spirit o'er the Land and Deep.
> She comes! she comes! The Gloom rolls on,
> Mountains of Casuistry heap'd o'er her head!
> *Philosophy*, that lean'd on Heav'n before,
> Shrinks to her second cause, and is no more.
> *Physic* of *Metaphysic* begs defence,
> And *Metaphysic* calls for aid on *Sense*!
> See *Mystery* to *Mathematics* fly!
> In vain! they gaze, turn giddy, rave, and die.
> *Religion* blushing veils her sacred fires,
> And unawares *Morality* expires.
> Nor *public* Flame, nor *private*, dares to shine;
> Nor *human* Spark is left, nor Glimpse *divine*!
> Lo! thy dread Empire, CHAOS! is restor'd;
> Light dies before thy uncreating word:
> Thy hand, great Anarch! lets the curtain fall;
> And Universal Darkness buries All.[8]

This is the Night from which Joyce invites the Finnegans to Wake.

Notes

1. *Selections*, ed. Philip P. Wiener, pp. 29–30.
2. Ibid., p. 52.
3. *The Dunciad* (B), ed. James Sutherland, p. 49.
4. Ibid., IV, ll. 21–4.
5. Ibid., IV, ll. 91–4.
6. *Pope's Dunciad*, p. 60.
7. Ibid., p. 47.
8. *Dunciad* (B), IV, II. 627–56. [This quotation is, intentionally or unintentionally, a garbled version of Sutherland's text and variants.]

46   George Steiner

George Steiner (b. 1929) was born in Paris and had a cosmopolitan education
in France, America, and England. After holding a Rhodes Scholarship at
Oxford, he joined the editorial staff of the *Economist*. In 1956 he was elected
a member of the Institute for Advanced Study at Princeton where he wrote
Tolstoy or Dostoevsky: An Essay in the Old Criticism (New York, 1959) and
began his comparative survey of tragedy, *The Death of Tragedy* (1961).
Steiner's subsequent publications have been mainly in the form of occasional
essays and review articles, many of which were collected in *Language and
Silence* (1967). This volume reflects the impressive range of Steiner's interests
and linguistic competence, including essays on Homer, Schoenberg, Lévi-Strauss,
Marshall McLuhan, Georg Lukács, pornography, language, literary education,
and many other topics. In an age of specialisms and nationalisms, George
Steiner has striven commendably to view the art and intellectual endeavour
of Western civilization as a single entity—one which he sees as now
threatened with extinction by various kinds of political, social and linguistic
barbarism. In particular he has been preoccupied, not to say obsessed, with
the fate of the Jews under Hitler's Nazi regime, and with the problems of
coming to terms with that holocaust both as a cultural historian and as a
human being. Steiner's cosmopolitan and apocalyptic perspective gives a
special interest to his appraisal of the intensely (some might say narrowly)
English temperament and achievement of Dr F. R. Leavis. The essay was
originally published in *Encounter* in 1962, marking the retirement of
Dr Leavis as a teacher at Cambridge, and is reprinted here from the abridged
Penguin edition of *Language and Silence* (1969). A Fellow of Churchill
College, Cambridge, since 1961, Steiner is familiar with Dr Leavis's academic
milieu. In the same period, however, he has travelled extensively, and has
held visiting professorships at Princeton, Harvard, and New York universities.
In addition to the publications mentioned above, George Steiner is editor of
The Penguin Book of Modern Verse Translation (1966) and the author of
three novels published together under the title *Anno Domini* (1964).

CROSS REFERENCES :   17. L. C. Knights
                     21. D. W. Harding
                     41. René Wellek

F. R. Leavis

No ceremony. Only a don, spare of voice and stature, but unforgettable in his intensity, leaving a lectern in a Cambridge hall and brushing out the door with a step characteristically sinuous, lithe, and unheeding.

Yet when Dr Leavis quits Mill Lane for the last time, an era will have ended in the history of English sensibility. No less, perhaps, than that of Wittgenstein or R. H. Tawney, Leavis's retirement, the cessation of his teaching at Cambridge, marks an intricate, controversial chapter in the history of feeling.

That a literary critic should have done so much to re-shape the tenor of spirit in his time, that he should have enforced on the development of literary taste much of his own unrelenting, abstract gait—the man walks in the outward guise of his thought—is, of itself, an arresting fact. In the vulgate sense literary criticism is not that important. Most critics feed upon the substance of literature; they are outriders, hangers-on, or shadows to lions. Writers write books; critics write about books in an eternity of second-hand. The distinction is immense. Where criticism endures, it does so either because it is a counterpart to creation, because the poetic force of a Coleridge and a T. S. Eliot gives to their judgment the authority of private experience, or because it marks a signal moment in the history of ideas. The vitalizing power of the *Poetics* is historical; it depends only in minor part on our awareness of the works Aristotle is actually citing. The great mass of criticism is ephemeral, bordering on journalism or straightforward literary history, on a spurt of personal impression scarcely sustained, or on the drab caution of tradition, erudite assent. Very few critics survive in their own right. Those that do—and how many can one add to Dr Johnson, Lessing, Sainte-Beuve, and Belinsky[a]?—make of criticism an act of pivotal social intelligence. They work outward from the particular literary instance to the far reaches of moral and political argument.

This has been radically the case with Leavis. Writing of *Ulysses*, Ezra Pound declared: 'We are governed by words, the laws are graven in words, and literature is the sole means of keeping these words living and accurate.' Leavis would add that only criticism can see to it that literature does the job. Behind this vision of criticism as 'the central humanity', as the exhibitor and guardian of values which are no less moral and social than they are technical, lies a complex, articulate theory of the critical process.

To Leavis, the critic is the complete reader: 'the ideal critic is the ideal reader.' He realizes to the full the experience given in the words of the poet or the novelist. He aims at complete responsiveness, at a kind of poised vulner-

---

[a] Gotthold Lessing (1729–81) was the chief figure of the German Enlightenment, and author of *Laokoon* (1766). Charles Augustin Sainte-Beuve (1804–69) was a prolific French critic and literary historian. Vissarian Grigoryevich Belinsky (1810–48) was the founder of modern Russian literary criticism and the champion of Dostoievsky and Turgenev.

ability and consciousness in the encounter with the text. He proceeds with an attention which is close and stringent, yet also provisional, and at all times susceptible to revaluation. Judgment arises from response; it does not initiate it:

> The critic's aim is, first, to realize as sensitively and completely as possible this or that which claims his attention; and a certain valuing is implicit in the realizing. As he matures in experience of the new thing he asks, explicitly and implicitly: 'Where does this come? How does it stand in relation to ...?' How relatively important does it seem?' and the organization into which it settles as a constituent in becoming 'placed' is an organization of similarly 'placed' things, things that have found their bearings with regard to one another, and not a theoretical system or a system determined by abstract considerations.*a*

The critical judgment (the 'placing') is put forward with an attendant query: 'This is so, isn't it?' And what the critic hopes for is qualified assent, a 'Yes, but ...' which will compel him to re-examine or refine his own response and lead to fruitful dialogue. This notion of dialogue is central to Leavis. No less than the artist—indeed, more so—the critic is in need of a public. Without it the act of ideal reading, the attempt to recreate the work of art in the critical sensibility is doomed to becoming arbitrary impression or mere dictate. There must exist or be trained within the community a body of readers seeking to achieve in vital concert a mature response to literature. Only then can the critic work with that measure of consent which makes disagreement creative. Language itself is a supreme act of community. The poem has its particular existence in a 'third realm', at a complex, unstable distance between the poet's private use of words and the shape of these same words in current speech. To be realized critically the work of literature must find its complete reader; but that reader (the critic) can only quicken and verify his response if a comparable effort at insight is occurring somewhere around him.

Such effort bears directly on the fortunes of society. The commanding axiom in Leavis's life-work is the conviction that there is a close relation between a man's capacity to respond to art and his general fitness for humane existence. That capacity can be woken and richened by the critic. Literacy of feeling is a pre-condition to sane judgment in human affairs: 'thinking about political and social matters ought to be done by minds of some literary education, and done in an intellectual climate informed by a vital literary culture'. Where a society does not have within it a significant contemporary literature and the parallel exercise of critical challenge, 'the "mind" (and mind includes memory) is not fully alive'. In short, Leavis's conception of literary criticism is, above all else, a plea for a live, humane social order.

Hence the tremendous importance he ascribes to the idea of a university. Like Newman (who is one of the really distinctive influences on his style and manner), Leavis regards the ideal university as the root and mould of those energies of spirit which can keep the body-politic functioning in a sane, creative way.

---

a The quotation is from 'Criticism and Philosophy', an essay in which Dr Leavis replied to certain criticisms of his book *Revaluation* (1936) by René Wellek. 'Criticism and Philosophy' is reprinted in Leavis's *The Common Pursuit* (1952).

All his criticism has sprung from the context of teaching. The words which come at the close of the preface to *Revaluation* are meant literally: 'The debt that I wish to acknowledge is to those with whom I have, during the past dozen years, discussed literature as a "teacher": if I have learnt anything about the methods of profitable discussion I have learnt it in collaboration with them.' If he execrates the 'academic mind', losing no occasion to pour upon it the vials of his prophetic scorn, it is because Leavis believes that Oxford and Cambridge, in their present guise, have largely betrayed the true, indispensable functions of teaching. But he has dwelt inside their walls in angry devotion.

Much of the finest in Leavis's performance is unrecapturable, being the sum of a generation of actual teaching, of unstinting commitment to the art of broken discourse between tutor and pupil. Yet his impact extends formidably beyond Downing [College]. He has made a banal academic title inseparably a part of his own name; the Muses have conferred only two doctorates, his and Dr Johnson's. Like certain writers of narrow, characteristic force, Leavis has set aside from the currency of language a number of words and turns of phrase for his singular purpose. Strong use has made these words nearly his property; *ils portent la griffe du maître* [they bear the stamp of the master]: 'discrimination ... centrality ... poise ... responsibility ... tactics ... enforcement ... realization ... presentment ... vitalizing ... performance ... assent ... robustness. ...' 'Close, delicate wholeness'; 'pressure of intelligence'; 'concrete realization'; 'achieved actuality'—are phrases which carry Leavis's signature as indelibly as 'high seriousness' bears that of Matthew Arnold.

The list is worth examining. It does not rely on jargon, on the shimmering technical obscurities which mar so much of American New Criticism. It is a spiky, grey, abstract parlance, heavy with exact intent. A style which tells us that Tennyson's verse 'doesn't offer, characteristically, any very interesting local life for inspection', or that 'Shakespeare's marvellous faculty of intense local realization is a faculty of realizing the whole locally' can be parodied with fearful ease. But what matters is to understand why Leavis 'writes badly', why he insists on presenting his case in a grim suet of prose.

His refusal of elegance is the expression of a deep, underlying Puritanism. Leavis detests the kind of 'fine' writing which by flash of phrase or lyric surge of argument obscures thinness of meaning or unsoundness of logic. He distrusts as spurious frivolity all that would embroider on the naked march of thought. His manner is so easy to parody precisely because there lies behind it so unswerving a preoccupation with the matter in hand, so constant a refusal to be distracted by grace of touch. It has a kind of noble ugliness and points a finger of Puritan scorn at the false glitter of Pater.

But the source of Leavis's style, of that bleak, hectoring yet ultimately hypnotizing tone, may lie even deeper. One striking fact distinguishes him from all other major critics. So far as I am aware, he has never wished or striven to be a writer—a poet, novelist, or playwright. In the criticism of Dryden, Coleridge, and Arnold, there is an immediate neighbourhood of art. In Edmund Wilson there lurks a disappointed novelist. Sainte-Beuve yielded to his critical genius with rage in heart, having failed to match the fiction and lyric verse of his romantic peers. John Crowe Ransom, R. P. Blackmur, Allen Tate, are poets who turned to criticism either in defence or elaboration of their own view of poetry, or when the vein of invention had run dry. In most great critics (perhaps even in Johnson) there is a writer *manqué*.[1]

This has two effects. It can make of criticism a minor art, an attempt to achieve, by force of style, something like the novel or drama which the critic has failed to produce successfully. Dryden's *Essay of Dramatic Poesy*, Sainte-Beuve's critical portraits, Edmund Wilson's *To the Finland Station*, have in them strong relics of poetic form. Blackmur's critical essays are often poems arrested. This can produce a grace of persuasion to which Leavis hardly comes near. But he would not wish to. For it can also entail a subtle disloyalty to the critical purpose. Where it becomes a substitute for 'creative writing', where it shows the scars of lost dreams, criticism tends towards rhetoric, self-revelation, shapely aphorism. It loses its grip on the objects before it turns into an unsteady mirror held up by the critic to his own ambitions or humility.

Leavis conveys persistently the absolute conviction that criticism is a central, life-giving pursuit. It need offer no apology for not being something else. Though in a manner radically different from that of the poet, it creates possibilities of apprehension and a consensus of perceived values without which poetry could not be sustained. To see Dr Leavis at his lectern, compact and indrawn as if wary of some inner challenge, yet richly communicative to his listeners, is to observe a man doing precisely the job he wishes to do. And it is a job he regards as immensely important.

What has he made of it?

Unlike Coleridge or Hegel, Leavis has not initiated a formal theory of art; he has not sought to redefine the epistemology of aesthetic judgment. He regards the generalizing, abstract mode of philosophy as sharply distinct from the specific re-creative perception which is the job of the literary critic; philosophic training might lead to

> blunting of edge, blurring of focus and muddled misdirection of attention: consequences of queering one discipline with the habits of another. The business of the literary critic is to attain a peculiar completeness of response and to observe a peculiarly strict relevance in developing his response into commentary; he must be on his guard against abstracting improperly from what is in front of him and against any premature or irrelevant generalizing of it or from it. ... There is, I hope, a chance that I may in this way have advanced theory, even if I haven't done the theorizing. I know that the cogency and precision I have aimed at are limited; but I believe that any approach involves limitations, and that it is by recognizing them and working within them that one may hope to get something done.[a]

The 'general ideas' behind Leavis's criticism are derived, in large part, from T. S. Eliot, D. H. Lawrence, I. A. Richards, and William Empson. By the time he began his own revaluation of the history of English poetry, Eliot, Ezra Pound, and Robert Graves had already proclaimed the quality of the new. The attitudes which inspired *The Oxford Book of English Verse* to give Donne only

[a] The quotation is from 'Criticism and Philosophy' (see note on p. 623 above).

as much space as Bulwer Lytton and less than a third as much as Herrick, or which made of Bridges a major figure who had, in munificence of heart, been patron to the eccentric thwarted talent of Hopkins, were already under critical fire. After *Prufrock* and the first Pound and Eliot essays, it was becoming increasingly difficult to regard Tennyson or Swinburne as the sole or pre-eminent forces directing English poetry. A colder air was blowing.

Leavis's reorientation of critical focus—his stress on that lineage of intelligence and realized form which goes from Shakespeare and the Metaphysicals to Pope, Blake, Hopkins, and Eliot—is rooted in the change of sensibility occurring in the 1920s and the early '30s. What he has done is to give that change its most precise and cogent critical justification. His mastery lies not in the general devising, but in the particular instance.

Here there is much that will live among the classic pages of criticism. Wherever one turns in the impressive array of Leavis's writings, one is arrested by the exhilarating presence of an intelligence superbly exact, and having within reach formidable resources of historical and textual knowledge. That intelligence is brought into close, subtle commerce with the poem in an act of total awareness which is, in the best instances, near to art. Leavis is difficult to quote from because the progress of response is so continuous and dense-woven. Yet certain moments do stand out for sheer brilliance and propriety of gathered insight.

The reading of Hopkins's *Spelt from Sibyl's Leaves* (from *New Bearings in English Poetry*) is unusual in that it shows Leavis recreating the sense and impact of the poem not only by responsive judgment, but by a kind of lyric counterpart:

> The trees are no longer the beautiful, refreshing things of daylight; they have turned fantastically strange, hard and cruel, 'beak-leaved' suggesting the cold, hard light, steely like the gleam of polished tools, against which they appear as a kind of damascene-work ('damask') on a blade. Then follows the anguished surrender to the realization:
>
>   '... Our tale, O oúr oracle ! / Lét life, wáned, ah lét life wind
> Off hér one skéined stained véined variety / upon áll on twó spools;
>   pàrt, pen, páck
> Now her áll in twó flocks, twó folds—black, white; / right,
>   wrong ...'
>
> The run of alliterations, rimes and assonances suggests the irresistible poignancy of the realization. The poem ends with a terrible effect as of unsheathed nerves grinding upon one another. The grinding might at first be taken to be merely that of 'right' against 'wrong', the inner conflict of spirit and flesh, and the pain that which the believer knows he must face, the simple pain of renunciation. Yet we are aware of a more subtle anguish and a more desperate plight.

Criticism is, necessarily, comparison. But only a great critic is able to make of the act of preference, of the 'placing' of one writer above another, an exercise of equal illumination. The sustained, gradually deepening comparison of Pope and Dryden in *Revaluation* is one of Leavis's master strokes. Setting the *Dunciad* beside *Mac Flecknoe*, Leavis notes that above every line of Pope we can imagine a tensely flexible and complex curve, representing the modulation, emphasis, and changing tone and tempo of the voice in reading; the curve varying from line to line and the lines playing subtly against one another. The verse of *Mac Flecknoe*, in the comparison, is both slack and monotonous; again and again there are awkward runs and turns, unconvinced and unconvincing, requiring the injected rhetorical conviction of the declaimer to carry them off.

Yet at once, the qualifying mechanism of Leavis's approach intrudes. The comparison 'is unfair: Dryden's effects are all for the public ear'. Read in a spirit appropriate to their intent, Dryden's satiric poems were 'magnificently effective'. But the spirit which Pope demands is something different; behind his immediate effects lies an organization finer, more inward than that required or exhibited by Dryden. Indeed, it is his limitations which make of Dryden the 'great representative poet of the later seventeenth century'. He belongs entirely to the community of reigning taste. There is between him and the sensibility of the time none of the distance, critical or nostalgic, that forces upon Marvell or Pope a greater delicacy of organization: 'Dryden is the voice of his age.' The whole analysis is masterly; it shows how Leavis reads with what Klee would have called 'the thinking eye'.

That eye is at work again, though narrowed, in Leavis's examination of Milton's style: 'He exhibits a feeling *for* words rather than a capacity for feeling *through* words ... habituation could not sensitize a medium so cut off from speech—speech that belongs to the emotional and sensory texture of actual living and is in resonance with the nervous system.' I believe that Leavis is wrong, that Milton (like Joyce) built of language a realness no less coherent or filled with the roughage of experience than is common speech—but the cogency and challenge of Leavis's case are obvious.

No single passage illustrates more compactly the peculiar genius of Leavis's criticism than the close of his essay on Swift:

> It is not merely that he had an Augustan contempt for metaphysics; he shared the shallowest complacencies of Augustan common sense: his irony might destroy these, but there is no conscious criticism.
> He was, in various ways, curiously unaware—the reverse of clairvoyant. He is distinguished by the intensity of his feelings, not by insight into them, and he certainly does not impress us as a mind in possession of its experience.
> We shall not find Swift remarkable for intelligence if we think of Blake.

The judgment is formidable for comprehensiveness, for coolness and finality of tone, for sheer implication of evidence marshalled and weighed. The 'mind in possession of its experience'—here a purely critical note—takes on pertinent, sombre precision if we recall that Swift's intellect fell into the literal possession of madness. But there is more: the power of the verdict is gathered in the final touch, in the evocation of Blake, placed so designedly as the last word. The *rapprochement* of Blake and Swift is of itself superb criticism. Here it sets a seal of relative dimension, of comparable but unequal greatness. Only those who have themselves wrestled with the task of trying to say something fresh or perceptive about established classics, will fully realize how much there is of preliminary response, of close, unbroken thought, behind Leavis's concise assurance.

Undoubtedly, Leavis's principal achievement is his critique of the English novel. *The Great Tradition* is one of those very rare books of literary comment (one thinks of Johnson's *Lives of the Poets* or Arnold's *Essays in Criticism*) that have reshaped the inner landscape of taste. Anyone dealing seriously with the development of English fiction must start, even if in disagreement, from Leavis's proposals. Whereas much of what Leavis argued about poetry, moreover, was already being said around him, his treatment of the novel has only one precedent—the essays and prefaces of Henry James. Like James, but with a more deliberate intent of order and completeness, Leavis has brought to bear on the novel that closeness of reading and expectation of form reserved previously for the study of poetry or poetic drama.

Now every book reviewer or undergraduate is able to mouth insights about the 'stature' of Jane Austen, the 'mature art' of George Eliot, or the 'creative wealth' of intelligence in *The Portrait of a Lady*. Today it would see ludicrous or wilfully eccentric to deny that *The Secret Sharer* or *Women in Love* are works of consummate art and classics of imagined life. But the very triumph of it should not make us forget the novelty, the unflinching audacity of Leavis's revaluation. Even where we challenge his list for ranking or omission, our sense of the novel as form, of its responsibility to moral perception and 'vivid essential record', is that defined by Leavis's treatment. The assertion that after the decline of the epic and of verse drama the prose novel has concentrated the major energies in western literature—an assertion put forward provisionally by Flaubert, Turgenev, and James—is now a commonplace. It was not so when Leavis first focused on a chapter in *Middlemarch* or a paragraph in *Nostromo* the same kind of total apprehension exhibited in relation to Shakespeare or Donne. The mere suggestion (at present nearly a cliché) that there is in *Heart of Darkness* a realization of evil comparable to the study of diminishing moral awareness in, say, *Macbeth*, has behind it a revolution in criticism. More than any man except James, Leavis has caused that revolution.

Only in part by his actual writings; the impact has been that of a *persona*. Like Péguy,[a] Leavis has stood out against the climate of the age in a stance of harried isolation, partially real, partially strategic. I remember waiting for those grey, austerely wrapped numbers of *Scrutiny* as one waits for a bottle flung into the sea. Inevitably, by their grey garb, by the angular tightness of print and page, they conveyed the image of a prophet, surrounded by a tiny, imperilled guard of the elect, expounding and disseminating his acrid truths by bent of will and privation. As a schoolboy, I sent in my subscription with a feeling of embarrassed awe, with a sense of conspiratorial urgency, as if there was food and fuel to be bought so as to keep going an enterprise of eminent danger. In a time of fantastic intellectual cheapness, of unctuous pseudo-culture and sheer indifference to values—in the century of the book club, the digest and the

[a] Charles Péguy (1873–1914) was a French writer isolated in his lifetime by his unconventional religious and political views.

hundred great ideas on the instalment plan—Leavis's 'necessary attitude of absolute intransigence' has had an exemplary, moving force. But he has sustained that attitude at a cruel psychological cost.

He has had to define, and in significant measure, create for himself 'the Enemy'. Like a fabled, heraldic monster, the Enemy has many heads. They include the Sunday papers and the *Guardian* and all dons who write for them; the *Times Literary Supplement*, Mr Pryce-Jones and his father (who enters the myth of vituperation in an obscure, recurrent fashion); the Third Programme 'intellectuals' and the *entourage* of the *New Statesman*; the British Council and *Encounter*; Mr John Hayward, Professor C. S. Lewis, Lord David Cecil, and all who divide the study and teaching of literature with the pursuit of elegance or science fiction; and, of late, pre-eminent among hydra-heads, C. P. Snow. The Enemy represents cosiness, frivolity, mundane cliques, the uses of culture for mutual adulation or warmth. He incarnates 'the currency values of Metropolitan literary society and the associated University milieu'. The Enemy creates philosophic giants such as Mr Colin Wilson in a Sunday morning only to trample on them when the wind turns. He propagates the notion that Virginia Woolf was a major intellect or that the life-blood of English thought pulses in the Athenaeum, in the still waters of All Souls or in Printing House Square. The Enemy is the Establishment of the mind. His brow is middle and his tone is suave.

Behind this contrived dragon there *is* a certain complex reality. Being geographically compact, English intellectual life is sharply susceptible to the pressures of club and cabal; the artifice of renown can be swiftly conjured or revoked. In small ponds sharks can be made to pass for momentary leviathans. It is also true that there is between the universities and the world of press, magazine and radio an alliance of brisk vulgarization. An unusual number of academics have a flair for showmanship; too often, ideas which are, in fact, intricate, provisional and raw to the throat, are thrown to the public as if they were bouquets. Watching some of the more brilliant performers at work, one would scarcely suppose that thought and scholarship are a rare, lonely, often self-consuming exercise of the spirit when it is at full, painful stretch. Above all, there is in the English intellectual and artistic establishment a dangerous bias towards personal charm, towards understatement and amateur grace. The judgments of critics and Fellowship electors are too often shadowed by the complex, hardly indefinable yet deep-rooted criteria of social acceptance. The 'good chap', the man one would care to dine with, glides smoothly to the top. The awkward, spiky, passionate genius—whether he be a great historian of politics, the inventor of the jet or the author of *The Rainbow*—fits ill into the soft grooves of the great common room. The corridors of power or official sponsorship are closed to his obtrusive, tactless intensity.

Unquestionably, Leavis has suffered under the bland claw of coterie culture. And he may be right in his fierce, nonconformist belief that the possibilities of a genuinely educated community—a community able to judge and echo what is radical and serious in art—are being constantly eroded by the 'near-culture' of the Brains Trust and the Sunday review. At a time when he was already being widely recognized (particularly in America) as the most compelling voice in the teaching of literature, Leavis found among his own university colleagues little but hostility or amused distaste. Like Péguy's *Cahiers de la quinzaine*, which alone match it in sustained integrity and wealth of provocation, *Scrutiny* was made possible by an utter expense of private energy. Unable to pay its contributors, receiving no official support, it was passed under silence by those (i.e. the British Council) who were seeking to define to the world what was most vital in English culture. The first, and so far the only, gathering from its pages was made in America, on a purely private basis, by Eric Bentley.[a]

Yet between these facts and the legend of self and society in which Leavis has encased his spirit there is a wide, tragic gap. As if out of some essential solitude, he has conjured up a detailed melodrama of persecution and neglect, of conspiracy and betrayal. Though surrounded by disciples who ape even what is most ephemeral in his mannerisms, though approached from many lands by those who hear and acclaim him, Leavis clings tenaciously to the mask of the pariah. He alludes to his endurance at Cambridge as a stroke of occult good fortune, as an oversight by the Enemy. He has in the past refused invitations from America lest dark malignity achieve its ends during his absence. Though a number of distinguished critics have been among his students and sought to carry on his own vision (Turnell, D. A. Traversi, Marius Bewley, L. C. Knights), there is hardly one with whom Leavis has not broken. Though he claims that he invites no more than qualified, challenging assent, Leavis has come to demand, perhaps unconsciously, complete loyalty to his creed. The merest doubt or deviation is heresy, and is soon followed by excommunication from the kirk. Thus, although he is one of the greatest teachers of the age, he leaves behind few representatives of what is most vital in his manner. There are those who can mimic his lashing tone, his outward austerities and turns of phrase. But like the rows of students who snicker, in drilled fidelity, at every rasping mention of 'Sunday papers', Leavis's immediate followers do him little honour. They merely bark and fang on the heels of his greatness.

But it is not the personal commitment to artificial or obsolete polemics, it is not the charring expense of nerve or intellect that matter. These are sad, demeaning aspects; but they are, in the last analysis, private to Dr Leavis. What needs alertness is the measure in which Leavis's melodramatic image of his own life and role has bent or corroded his critical judgment. It is this which gives his assault on C. P. Snow what relevance it has.

The Richmond Lecture[b] was an ignoble performance.[2] In it, Leavis yielded entirely to a streak of obsessed cruelty. Over and over, he proclaimed to his audience that Snow was ignorant, that he knew nothing of literature or history and not much, one gathered, of science. Such an attempt to prove by mere rep-

---

[a] *The Importance of Scrutiny* (New York, 1948). Since this essay was written A *Selection from 'Scrutiny'*, compiled by F. R. Leavis, has been published (Cambridge, 1968).

[b] Dr Leavis's Richmond Lecture *Two Cultures? The significance of C. P. Snow* (Cambridge, 1962) was an attack upon Lord (then Sir Charles) Snow and his Rede Lecture of 1959, *The Two Cultures and the Scientific Revolution*. It provoked a great deal of controversy and public discussion.

etition is characteristically totalitarian. Though he is personally ignorant of America, Leavis threw out shop-worn clichés about the 'emptiness' of American life, about the inhumanity of technological values. One realized, with a painful start, how much of Leavis's arsenal of insight dates back to the mythologies and tactics of the 1930s. Whereas Snow is wholly of the present, responsive in every way to what is new and jarring in our novel condition, Leavis has sought to bring time to a halt in a pastoral, Augustan dream of order.

Leavis accused Snow of using clichés; his own performance was nothing else. Banality followed on banality in dull virulence. He did not even attempt to engage seriously what is crucial in Snow's argument—the sense of a realignment in international affairs, the redefinition of literacy to include the syntax of number. Snow is, indeed, trying to be a 'new kind of man', if only in that he wishes to be equally and vitally at home in England, Russia, or the United States. Now it could be argued, in a close, discriminating way, that this 'new ubiquity' of the imagination jeopardizes those values of narrow, rooted inwardness for which Leavis stands. Though a rearguard action, such counter-statement to Snow would be stimulating. But none was forthcoming; instead of argument came stale insult. On the one hand was 'Snow', on the other side were a set of approved clichés—'life', 'humane values', 'vital intelligence'. What has been advertised as a responsible examination of the concept of 'the two cultures' dissolved—as so much else in Leavis's recent work has done—into a ceremonial dance before the dark god, D. H. Lawrence.

Leavis's relation to Lawrence has become obsessive. It has passed from rational exposition into a weird self-identification. Lawrence is not only the 'greatest English writer of the twentieth century', but a master of life, a prophet by whose teaching alone our society may recapture humane poise and creative fire. That there is much in Lawrence which is monotonous and hysterical, that very few of his works are unflawed by hectoring idiosyncrasies, that there was little in his genius either of laughter or tolerance—these are considerations Leavis can scarcely allow. In a dualistic image, as artificial and shallow as all Manicheism, Leavis opposes Lawrence to all that is inhuman, frivolous, insensitive or modish in our culture. To query Lawrence, or to propose as Snow has done by his work and example that there are crises of spirit and political fact more actual or different than those dreamt of in *Women in Love*, is to query 'life'. Yet nothing could be less humane or more devoid of the tact of living encounter than was Leavis's harangue. Hearing it, one was brought up against the stubborn fact that a critic, however great, is barred from certain generosities of imagination to which an artist has title.

The Richmond Lecture and much else that is indefensible in Leavis's late pronouncements may soon be forgotten. But even at its prime, Leavis's criticism exhibits certain grave limitations and quirks. If the scope of his radical accomplishments is to be defined, these too must be noted.

There are the overestimates (particularly in Leavis's early criticism) of such minor talents as Ronald Bottrall or the novelist, L. H. Myers. There is the lack of any confrontation, large or sustained, with the poetry of Yeats, a body of work, one would have thought, no less in need of close valuation than that of

Eliot or Pound. Like the Augustan critics, Leavis has been most at ease with the poetry in which the pulse of argument and systematic intelligence beats strong. Hence his decisive reading of *Mauberley* but his disinclination to allow for the occasions of pure lyric force, of articulate image, in the parched chaos of Pound's *Cantos*.

With respect to the novel, one's sense of omission is more acute. The case of Dickens is notorious:

> The genius was that of a great entertainer, and he had for the most part no profounder responsibility as a creative artist than this description suggests. ... The adult mind doesn't as a rule find in Dickens a challenge to an unusual and sustained seriousness. I can think of only one of his books in which his distinctive creative genius is controlled throughout to a unifying and organizing significance, and that is *Hard Times*.

The limitation proposed here has always seemed to me restrictive of Leavis, not of Dickens. And the preference of *Hard Times* over such manifestly ampler achievements as *Bleak House* or *Great Expectations* is illuminating. In the main, Dickens is working outside the criteria of organizing awareness and 'significance' exhibited in *The Wings of the Dove* or *Nostromo*. But there is another vein of utter seriousness, of seriousness of committed feeling, of vehement imaginative enactment. It is this which Dickens possesses and that makes of him, after Shakespeare, the principal creator of remembered life in English literature.[3]

Equally suggestive of a limitation in allowed criteria has been Leavis's neglect of Joyce. He has observed in *Ulysses* set pieces of sensuous realization, but has nowhere done justice either to the architectural genius of the book, or to its enrichment and renovation of the language. Leavis has taken over D. H. Lawrence's scorn and misapprehension of Joyce's achievement. By Leavis's own requirements of seriousness and vitalizing moral poise, much in *Dubliners* and *A Portrait of the Artist* should rank high in the tradition. But he has read in the obscuring light of a false distinction. The choice is not Lawrence or Joyce. Both are indispensable; and it is Joyce who has done as much as any writer in our age to keep English confident and creative.

Closely related to this imperception of Joyce is Leavis's failure to extend the reach of his criticism to two other novelists, both of them masters of poetic structure and vision. The one is Melville; a lineage of the English novel which can find a central place for James and an important preliminary role for Hawthorne, but which tells us nothing of *Moby Dick* or *Benito Cereno* (a tale to match the finest in Conrad), is necessarily incomplete. Only a full response to Dickens, Melville, and Joyce, moreover, makes possible a just approach to the novelist whom I take to be, after Hardy and Lawrence, the eminent master of modern English fiction—John Cowper Powys. If neither *The Glastonbury Romance* nor *Wolf Solent* (the one English novel to rival Tolstoy) can find a place in the Great Tradition, it is precisely because their distinctive virtues— lyric, philosophical, stylistic, religious—lie outside the central but narrowing grasp of Leavis's sensibility.

One other great domain lies outside it. Leavis has refused to concern himself, on any but a perfunctory scale, with foreign literature. There is in this refusal a proud scruple. If criticism presumes complete response to a text, complete possession, how can a critic hope to deal maturely with anything but his own language? There is, unquestionably, a stringent honesty in this position. But it can be carried too far. How, for example, could most critics refer to landmarks as dominant, as unavoidable as the Bible, Homer, Dante, or Goethe, if they did not rely, in one or the other instance, on the crutch of translation? And is it not the duty of a critic to avail himself, in some imperfect measure at least, of another language—if only to experience the defining contours of his own?

Leavis's austere concentration may, indeed, have a deeper root. The vision of a nonconformist, morally literate England, of an England in the style of Bunyan, Cobbett, and D. H. Lawrence, informs his critical thought. 'Englishness' is in Leavis's interior vocabulary a notion of tremendous positive force; it connotes a specific tone and natural excellence: 'in *Rasselas* we have something deeply English that relates Johnson and Jane Austen to Crabbe'. Much of the argument against Joyce is conducted in terms of the native as against the eccentric and uprooted. Joyce's experiments with language reflects a 'cosmopolitan' sophistication. The veritable genius of English lies nearer home:

> This strength of English belongs to the very spirit of the language—the spirit that was formed when the English people who formed it were predominantly rural.... And how much richer the *life* was in the old, predominantly rural order than in the modern suburban world.... When one adds that speech in the old order was a popularly cultivated art, that people talked (so making Shakespeare possible) instead of reading or listening to the wireless, it becomes plain that the promise of regeneration by American slang, popular city-idiom, or the invention of *transition*-cosmopolitans is a flimsy consolation for our loss.

Written in 1933, this passage has a curious ring; it belongs to that complex of agrarian autonomism, of *la terre et ses morts* [the land and its dead], which ranges from Péguy and Barrès to Allen Tate and the southern Fugitives in America. Behind it shimmers an historical vision (largely fanciful) of an older order, rural, customary, moralistic. It is the vision of men who fought the First World War—as Leavis did, a Milton in his pocket—only to observe what had been striven for at inhuman cost decline into the cheap chaos of the 1920s.

Leavis's 'critical nationalism', which contrasts so sharply with the far-ranging humanism of an Edmund Wilson, is an instrument of great discrimination and power. But it has limiting consequences. The wide, subtle plurality of modern culture, the interplay of languages and national styles, may be regrettable— but it is a fact. To 'place' Henry James without close reference to Flaubert and Turgenev; to exalt the treatment of politics in *Nostromo* and *Middlemarch* without an attendant awareness of [Dostoievsky's] *The Possessed*; to discern the realization of social nuance in Jane Austen without allowing the presence of Proust in the critical context; all this is to proceed in an artifice of isolation. Is it possible to discuss comprehensively the nature of prose fiction without introducing, at signal stages of the argument, the realization that Kafka has altered, lastingly, the relations between observed and imagined truth? Could Leavis advance as far as he does in support of Lawrence, of Lawrence's treatment of social feeling, if he set *Women in Love* next to *The Brothers Karamazov*?

This resolute provincialism has its counterpart in Leavis's treatment of time. There is scarcely anything written during the past twenty years that he has found worthy of serious examination. He has abdicated from one of the commanding functions of criticism, which is to perceive and welcome the new. One has the impression that he cannot forgive Auden for the fact that English verse should have a history after Eliot even as he cannot forgive Snow for suggesting that the English novel should have a future beyond Lawrence. To use an epithet which he himself applies to Johnson, Leavis's criticism has, since 1945, rarely been 'life-giving'. Dealing with contemporary literature it has pleaded not from love but from scorn.

These are, obviously, major reservations. They accumulate towards the image of a career divided midway by some essential constriction of mood and purpose. Much in the late Leavis exhibits a quality of inhumane unreality (the Richmond Lecture being merely a flagrant instance). The depth of insight is increasingly marred by waspish contempt. There has been no criticism since Rymer's[a] less magnanimous.

It is this which makes any 'placing' of Leavis's work difficult and premature. Great critics are rarer than great poets or novelists (though their gift is more distant from the springs of life). In English, Johnson and Coleridge and Matthew Arnold are of the first order. In the excellence of both Dryden and Saintsbury there is an unsteadiness of focus, a touch of the amateur. Among moderns, T. S. Eliot and Edmund Wilson are of this rare company. What of Leavis? One's instinct calls for immediate assent. There is in the sum of his labours a power, a cogency that looms large above what has been polemic and harshly arrogant in the circumstance. If some doubt persists, it is simply because criticism must be, by Leavis's own definition, both central and humane. In his achievement the centrality is manifest; the humanity has often been tragically absent.

[a] *Thomas Rymer* (1641–1713), a Restoration writer and critic best known for his severe criticisms of the Elizabethan and Jacobean dramatists, including Shakespeare.

Notes

1. This is very obviously true of the past. It may no longer be so.... Distinctions between literary genres are losing their relevance. Increasingly, the 'act of writing' supersedes, in its problematic, self-conscious character, the particular form chosen. The role of the essay and of fact/fiction in present literature suggests that the whole distinction between creation and criticism, between analytic statement and poetic invention needs rethinking. Both may be, as Roland Barthes says, part of a linguistic totality more significant, more comprehensive than either.

2. Looking back, one is struck by the underlying political, social significance of the affair. The controversy between Leavis and Snow is, essentially, a controversy over the future shape of life in England. It sets the vision or reactionary utopia of a small, economically reduced but autonomous and humanistically literate England against that of a nation renewed, energized, rationalized according to technological and mass consumer principles. It is, thus, a debate over the relationship of England both to its own past and to

the essentially American present. England's future, the kind of society in which Leavis's and Snow's children will grow up and live—or from which they will emigrate—hinges on the alternative chosen. Can England, a small, crowded island, blessed neither by climate nor natural elbow-room for waste, 'go modern' without sacrificing irreplaceable amenities of tolerance and humane leisure? But can any of the latter survive effectively if it diminishes too sharply, if it folds inward into a kind of 'post-Habsburg' provincialism? These are, I think, the questions underlying the Leavis/Snow debate, and they give to it a dignity far exceeding the obsessive, injurious form of the Richmond Lecture.

3. Dr Leavis is, reportedly, at work on a full-scale critical study of Dickens's major novels. A number of essays which may be part of this study have already appeared in print. Such a book will not only be of very great interest in itself, but as constituting one of the rare instances in which Dr Leavis has 'revalued' one of his own, and most influential, dismissals. [This book, Dickens the Novelist, by F. R. and Q. D. Leavis, appeared in 1970.]

47 W. H. Auden

Wystan Hugh Auden (b. 1907) is generally recognized as the most
distinguished of the English poets who emerged in the 'thirties. Auden's poetry
in that decade reflected his involvement (on the left wing side) in political and
economic issues, his extensive travels, and the intellectual influences of Marx
and Freud. In 1939 he emigrated to the United States and his intellectual
development subsequently took a religious turn. In recent years he has lived
partly in America and partly in Austria. The standard editions of his poems are
Collected Shorter Poems 1927-57 (1966) and *Collected Longer Poems* (1968),
though many of his readers have regretted the revisions and omissions in these
volumes.

Since 1940 Auden has lectured and taught at many universities, especially in
the United States. In 1960-1 he was Professor of Poetry at Oxford. As a literary
critic, however, Auden has not acquired academic habits. In the Foreword to
his most recent collection of occasional criticism, *The Dyer's Hand* (1963), he
wrote: 'A poem must be a closed system, but there is something, in my opinion,
lifeless, even false, about systematic criticism. In going over my critical pieces, I
have reduced them, when possible, to sets of notes, because, as a reader, I prefer
a critic's notebooks to his treatises.' Recently Auden has published his
commonplace book, *A Certain World* (1971), in lieu of an autobiography.
'Writing' is reprinted from *The Dyer's Hand*.

CROSS REFERENCES: 2. W. B. Yeats
6. T. S. Eliot
20. Paul Valéry
28. Jean-Paul Sartre

COMMENTARY: *Auden: A Collection of Critical Essays*, ed. Monroe
K. Spears (Englewood Cliffs, N.J., 1964)

Writing

It is the author's aim to say once and emphatically, 'He said.'

H. D. THOREAU

The art of literature, vocal or written, is to adjust the language so that it
embodies what it indicates.

A. N. WHITEHEAD

All those whose success in life depends neither upon a job which satisfies some specific and unchanging social need, like a farmer's, nor, like a surgeon's, upon some craft which he can be taught by others and improve by practice, but upon 'inspiration', the lucky hazard of ideas, live by their wits, a phrase which carries a slightly pejorative meaning. Every 'original' genius, be he an artist or a scientist, has something a bit shady about him, like a gambler or a medium.

Literary gatherings, cocktail parties, and the like, are a social nightmare because writers have no 'shop' to talk. Lawyers and doctors can entertain each other with stories about interesting cases, about experiences, that is to say, related to their professional interests but yet impersonal and outside themselves. Writers have no impersonal professional interests. The literary equivalent of talking shop would be writers reciting their own work at each other, an unpopular procedure for which only very young writers have the nerve.

No poet or novelist wishes he were the only one who ever lived, but most of them wish they were the only one alive, and quite a number fondly believe their wish has been granted.

In theory, the author of a good book should remain anonymous, for it is to his work, not to himself, that admiration is due. In practice, this seems to be impossible. However, the praise and public attention that writers sometimes receive does not seem to be as fatal to them as one might expect. Just as a good man forgets his deed the moment he has done it, a genuine writer forgets a work as soon as he has completed it and starts to think about the next one; if he thinks about his past work at all, he is more likely to remember its faults than its virtues. Fame often makes a writer vain, but seldom makes him proud.

Writers can be guilty of every kind of human conceit but one, the conceit of the social worker: 'We are all here on earth to help others; what on earth the others are here for, I don't know.'

When a successful author analyses the reasons for his success, he generally underestimates the talent he was born with, and overestimates his skill in employing it.

Every writer would rather be rich than poor, but no genuine writer cares about popularity as such. He needs approval of his work by others in order to be reassured that the vision of life he believes he has had is a true vision and not a self-delusion, but he can only be reassured by those whose judgment he respects. It would only be necessary for a writer to secure universal popularity if imagination and intelligence were equally distributed among all men.

When some obvious booby tells me he has liked a poem of mine, I feel as if I had picked his pocket.

Writers, poets especially, have an odd relation to the public because their medium, language, is not, like the paint of the painter or the notes of the composer, reserved for their use but is the common property of the linguistic group to which they belong. Lots of people are willing to admit that they don't understand painting or music, but very few indeed who have been to school and learned to read advertisements will admit that they don't understand English. As Karl Kraus said: 'The public doesn't understand German, and in Journalese I can't tell them so.'

How happy the lot of the mathematician! He is judged solely by his peers, and the standard is so high that no colleague or rival can ever win a reputation he does not deserve. No cashier writes a letter to the press complaining about the incomprehensibility of Modern Mathematics and comparing it unfavourably with the good old days when mathematicians were content to paper irregularly shaped rooms and fill bathtubs without closing the waste pipe.

To say that a work is inspired means that, in the judgment of its author or his readers, it is better than they could reasonably hope it would be, and nothing else.

All works of art are commissioned in the sense that no artist can create one by a simple act of will but must wait until what he believes to be a good idea for a work 'comes' to him. Among those works which are failures because their initial conceptions were false or inadequate, the number of self-commissioned works may well be greater than the number commissioned by patrons.

The degree of excitement which a writer feels during the process of composition is as much an indication of the value of the final result as the excitement felt by a worshipper is an indication of the value of his devotions, that is to say, very little indication.

The Oracle claimed to make prophecies and give good advice about the future; it never pretended to be giving poetry readings.

If poems could be created in a trance without the conscious participation of the poet, the writing of poetry would be so boring or even unpleasant an operation that only a substantial reward in money or social prestige could induce a man to be a poet. From the manuscript evidence, it now appears that Coleridge's account of the composition of 'Kubla Khan' was a fib.[a]

It is true that, when he is writing a poem, it seems to a poet as if there were two people involved, his conscious self and a Muse whom he has to woo or an Angel with whom he has to wrestle, but, as in an ordinary wooing or wrestling match, his role is as important as Hers. The Muse, like Beatrice in *Much Ado*, is a spirited girl who has as little use for an abject suitor as she has for a vulgar brute. She appreciates chivalry and good manners, but she despises those who will not stand up to her and takes a cruel delight in telling them nonsense and lies which the poor little things obediently write down as 'inspired' truth.

> When I was writing the chorus in G Minor, I suddenly dipped my pen into the medicine bottle instead of the ink; I made a blot, and when I dried it with sand (blotting paper had not been invented then) it took the form of a natural, which instantly gave me the idea of the effect which the change from G minor to G major would make, and to this blot all the effect—if any— is due. (Rossini to Louis Engel)

Such an act of judgment, distinguishing between Chance and Providence, deserves, surely, to be called an inspiration.

To keep his errors down to a minimum, the internal Censor to whom a poet submits his work in progress should be a Censorate. It should include, for instance, a sensitive only child, a practical housewife, a logician, a monk, an

[a] See note, p. 338 above.

irreverent buffoon, and even perhaps, hated by all the others and returning their dislike, a brutal, foul-mouthed drill sergeant who considers all poetry rubbish.

In the course of many centuries a few laboursaving devices have been introduced into the mental kitchen—alcohol, coffee, tobacco, Benzedrine, etc.—but these are very crude, constantly breaking down, and liable to injure the cook. Literary composition in the twentieth century A.D. is pretty much what it was in the twentieth century B.C.: nearly everything has still to be done by hand.

Most people enjoy the sight of their own handwriting as they enjoy the smell of their own farts. Much as I loathe the typewriter, I must admit that it is a help in self-criticism. Typescript is so impersonal and hideous to look at that, if I type out a poem, I immediately see defects which I missed when I looked through it in manuscript. When it comes to a poem by somebody else, the severest test I know of is to write it out in longhand. The physical tedium of doing this ensures that the slightest defect will reveal itself; the hand is constantly looking for an excuse to stop.

'Most artists are sincere and most art is bad, though some insincere (sincerely insincere) works can be quite good' (Stravinsky). Sincerity is like sleep. Normally, one should assume that, of course, one will be sincere, and not give the question a second thought. Most writers, however, suffer occasionally from bouts of insincerity as men do from bouts of insomnia. The remedy in both cases is often quite simple: in the case of the latter, to change one's diet, in the case of the former, to change one's company.

The schoolmasters of literature frown on affectations of style as silly and unhealthy. Instead of frowning, they ought to laugh indulgently. Shakespeare makes fun of the Euphuists[a] in *Love's Labour's Lost* and in *Hamlet*, but he owed them a great deal and he knew it. Nothing, on the face of it, could have been more futile than the attempt of Spenser, [Gabriel] Harvey, and others to be good little humanists and write English verse in classical metres, yet, but for their folly, many of Campion's most beautiful songs and the choruses in *Samson Agonistes* would never have been written. In literature, as in life, affectation, passionately adopted and loyally persevered in, is one of the chief forms of self-discipline by which mankind has raised itself by its own bootstraps.

A mannered style, that of Góngora[b] or Henry James, for example, is like eccentric clothing: very few writers can carry it off, but one is enchanted by the rare exception who can.

When a reviewer describes a book as 'sincere', one knows immediately that it is (a) insincere (insincerely insincere) and (b) badly written. Sincerity in the proper sense of the word, meaning authenticity, is, however, or ought to be, a writer's chief preoccupation. No writer can ever judge exactly how good or bad a work of his may be, but he can always know, not immediately perhaps, but

[a] Imitators of the elaborately patterned and allusive prose style used by John Lyly (1554–1606) in his romance *Euphues* (1578–80).

[b] The Spanish poet Don Luis de Gongora y Argote (1561–1627) used a mannered style comparable to Lyly's 'euphuism'.

certainly in a short while, whether something he has written is authentic—in his handwriting—or a forgery.

The most painful of all experiences to a poet is to find that a poem of his which he knows to be a forgery has pleased the public and got into the anthologies. For all he knows or cares, the poem may be quite good, but that is not the point; *he* should not have written it.

The work of a young writer—[Goethe's] *Werther* is the classic example— is sometimes a therapeutic act. He finds himself obsessed by certain ways of feeling and thinking of which his instinct tells him he must be rid before he can discover his authentic interests and sympathies, and the only way by which he can be rid of them forever is by surrendering to them. Once he has done this, he has developed the necessary antibodies which will make him immune for the rest of his life. As a rule, the disease is some spiritual malaise of his generation. If so, he may, as Goethe did, find himself in an embarrassing situation. What he wrote in order to exorcise certain feelings is enthusiastically welcomed by his contemporaries because it expresses just what they feel but, unlike him, they are perfectly happy to feel in this way; for the moment they regard him as their spokesman. Time passes. Having gotten the poison out of his system, the writer turns to his true interests which are not, and never were, those of his early admirers, who now pursue him with cries of 'Traitor!'

> The intellect of man is forced to choose
> Perfection of the life or of the work. (Yeats)

This is untrue; perfection is possible in neither. All one can say is that a writer who, like all men, has his personal weaknesses and limitations, should be aware of them and try his best to keep them out of his work. For every writer, there are certain subjects which, because of defects in his character and his talent, he should never touch.

What makes it difficult for a poet not to tell lies is that, in poetry, all facts and all beliefs cease to be true or false and become interesting possibilities. The reader does not have to share the beliefs expressed in a poem in order to enjoy it. Knowing this, a poet is constantly tempted to make use of an idea or a belief, not because he believes it to be true, but because he sees it has interesting poetic possibilities. It may not, perhaps, be absolutely necessary that he *believe* it, but it is certainly necessary that his emotions be deeply involved, and this they can never be unless, as a man, he takes it more seriously than as a mere poetic convenience.

The integrity of a writer is more threatened by appeals to his social conscience, his political or religious convictions, than by appeals to his cupidity. It is morally less confusing to be goosed by a travelling salesman than by a bishop.

Some writers confuse authenticity, which they ought always to aim at, with originality, which they should never bother about. There is a certain kind of person who is so dominated by the desire to be loved for himself alone that he has constantly to test those around him by tiresome behaviour; what he says and does must be admired, not because it is intrinsically admirable, but because it is *his* remark, *his* act. Does not this explain a good deal of avant-garde art?

Slavery is so intolerable a condition that the slave can hardly escape deluding himself into thinking that he is choosing to obey his master's commands when, in fact, he is obliged to. Most slaves of habit suffer from this delusion and so do some writers, enslaved by an all too 'personal' style.

'Let me think: was I the same when I got up this morning? ... But if I'm not the same, the next question is "Who in the world am I?" ... I'm sure I'm not Ada ... for her hair goes in such long ringlets and mine doesn't go in ringlets at all; and I'm sure I can't be Mabel, for I know all sorts of things, and she, oh! she knows such a very little! Besides *she's* she and *I'm* I and— oh dear, how puzzling it all is! I'll try if I know all the things I used to know....' Her eyes filled with tears ... : 'I must be Mabel after all, and I shall have to go and live in that poky little house, and have next to no toys to play with, and oh!—ever so many lessons to learn! No, I've made up my mind about it: if I'm Mabel, I'll stay down here!'

(*Alice in Wonderland*)

At the next peg the Queen turned again and this time she said: 'Speak in French when you can't think of the English for a thing—turn your toes out as you walk—and remember who you are.'

(*Through the Looking Glass*)

Most writers, except the supreme masters who transcend all systems of classification are either Alices or Mabels. For example:

Alice	*Mabel*
Montaigne	Pascal
Marvell	Donne
Burns	Shelley
Jane Austen	Dickens
Turgenev	Dostoievsky
Valéry	Gide
Virginia Woolf	Joyce
E. M. Forster	Lawrence
Robert Graves	Yeats

'Orthodoxy,' said a real Alice of a bishop, 'is reticence.'

Except when used as historical labels, the terms *classical* and *romantic* are misleading terms for two poetic parties, the Aristocratic and the Democratic, which have always existed and to one of which every writer belongs, though he may switch his party allegiance or, on some specific issue, refuse to obey his Party Whip.

The Aristocratic Principle as regards subject matter:
  No subject matter shall be treated by poets which poetry cannot digest. It defends poetry against didacticism and journalism.
The Democratic Principle as regards subject matter:
  No subject matter shall be excluded by poets which poetry is capable of digesting. It defends poetry against limited or stale conceptions of what is 'poetic'.
The Aristocratic Principle as regards treatment:

No irrelevant aspects of a given subject shall be expressed in a poem which treats it. It defends poetry against barbaric vagueness.
The Democratic Principle as regards treatment:
No relevant aspect of a given subject shall remain unexpressed in a poem which treats it. It defends poetry against decadent triviality.

Every work of a writer should be a first step, but this will be a false step unless, whether or not he realize it at the time, it is also a further step. When a writer is dead, one ought to be able to see that his various works, taken together, make one consistent *oeuvre*.

It takes little talent to see clearly what lies under one's nose, a good deal of it to know in which direction to point that organ.

The greatest writer cannot see through a brick wall but, unlike the rest of us, he does not build one.

Only a minor talent can be a perfect gentleman; a major talent is always more than a bit of a cad. Hence the importance of minor writers—as teachers of good manners. Now and again, an exquisite minor work can make a master feel thoroughly ashamed of himself.

The poet is the father of his poem; its mother is a language: one could list poems as race horses are listed—*out of L by P*.

A poet has to woo, not only his own Muse but also Dame Philology, and, for the beginner, the latter is the more important. As a rule, the sign that a beginner has a genuine original talent is that he is more interested in playing with words than in saying something original; his attitude is that of the old lady, quoted by E. M. Forster—'How can I know what I think till I see what I say?' It is only later, when he has wooed and won Dame Philology, that he can give his entire devotion to his Muse.

Rhymes, metres, stanza forms, etc., are like servants. If the master is fair enough to win their affection and firm enough to command their respect, the result is an orderly happy household. If he is too tyrannical, they give notice; if he lacks authority, they become slovenly, impertinent, drunk, and dishonest.

The poet who writes 'free' verse is like Robinson Crusoe on his desert island: he must do all his cooking, laundry, and darning for himself. In a few exceptional cases, this manly independence produces something original and impressive, but more often the result is squalor—dirty sheets on the unmade bed and empty bottles on the unswept floor.

There are some poets, Kipling for example, whose relation to language reminds one of a drill sergeant: the words are taught to wash behind their ears, stand properly at attention, and execute complicated manoeuvres, but at the cost of never being allowed to think for themselves. There are others, Swinburne, for example, who remind one more of Svengali[a]: under their hypnotic suggestion, an extraordinary performance is put on, not by raw recruits, but by feeble-minded schoolchildren.

Due to the Curse of Babel, poetry is the most provincial of the arts, but today, when civilization is becoming monotonously same all the world over,

[a] The evil genius of George du Maurier's popular novel *Trilby* (1894).

one feels inclined to regard this as a blessing rather than a curse: in poetry, at least, there cannot be an 'International Style'.

'My language is the universal whore whom I have to make into a virgin' (Karl Kraus). It is both the glory and the shame of poetry that its medium is not its private property, that a poet cannot invent his words and that words are products, not of nature, but of a human society which uses them for a thousand different purposes. In modern societies where language is continually being debased and reduced to nonspeech, the poet is in constant danger of having his ear corrupted, a danger to which the painter and the composer, whose media are their private property, are not exposed. On the other hand he is more protected than they from another modern peril, that of solipsist subjectivity; however esoteric a poem may be, the fact that all its words have meanings which can be looked up in a dictionary makes it testify to the existence of other people. Even the language of *Finnegans Wake* was not created by Joyce *ex nihilo*; a purely private verbal world is not possible.

The difference between verse and prose is self-evident, but it is a sheer waste of time to look for a definition of the difference between poetry and prose. Frost's definition of poetry as the untranslatable element in language looks plausible at first sight but, on closer examination, will not quite do. In the first place, even in the most rarefied poetry, there are some elements which are translatable. The sound of the words, their rhythmical relations, and all meanings and association of meanings which depend upon sound, like rhymes and puns, are, of course, untranslatable, but poetry is not, like music, pure sound. Any elements in a poem which are not based on verbal experience are, to some degree, translatable into another tongue, for example, images, similes, and metaphors which are drawn from sensory experience. Moreover, because one characteristic that all men, whatever their culture, have in common is uniqueness—every man is a member of a class of one—the unique perspective on the world which every genuine poet has survives translation. If one takes a poem by Goethe and a poem by Hölderlin and makes literal prose cribs of them, every reader will recognize that the two poems were written by two different people. In the second place, if speech can never become music, neither can it ever become algebra. Even in the most 'prosy' language, in informative and technical prose, there is a personal element because language is a personal creation. *Ne pas se pencher au dehors* has a different feeling tone from *Nichthinauslehnen.*[a] A purely poetic language would be unlearnable, a purely prosaic not worth learning.

Valéry bases his definitions of poetry and prose on the difference between the gratuitous and the useful, play and work, and uses as an analogy the difference between dancing and walking. But this will not do either. A commuter may walk to his suburban station every morning, but at the same time he may enjoy the walk for its own sake; the fact that his walk is necessary does not exclude the possibility of its also being a form of play. Vice versa, a dance does not cease to be play if it is also believed to have a useful purpose like promoting a good harvest.

[a] 'Do not lean out', in French and German respectively.

If French poets have been more prone than English to fall into the heresy of thinking that poetry ought to be as much like music as possible, one reason may be that, in traditional French verse, sound effects have always played a much more important role than they have in English verse. The English-speaking peoples have always felt that the difference between poetic speech and the conversational speech of everyday should be kept small, and, whenever English poets have felt that the gap between poetic and ordinary speech was growing too wide, there has been a stylistic revolution to bring them closer again. In English verse, even in Shakespeare's grandest rhetorical passages, the ear is always aware of its relation to everyday speech. A good actor must—alas, today he too seldom does—make the audience hear Shakespeare's lines as verse not prose, but if he tries to make the verse sound like a different language, he will make himself ridiculous.

But French poetry, both in the way it is written and the way it is recited, has emphasized and gloried in the difference between itself and ordinary speech; in French drama, verse and prose *are* different languages. Valéry quotes a contemporary description of Rachel's[a] powers of declamation; in reciting she could and did use a range of two octaves, from F below Middle C to F in alt; an actress who tried to do the same with Shakespeare as Rachel did with Racine would be laughed off the stage.

One can read Shakespeare to oneself without even mentally *hearing* the lines and be very moved; indeed, one may easily find a performance disappointing because almost anyone with an understanding of English verse can speak it better than the average actor and actress. But to read Racine to oneself, even, I fancy, if one is a Frenchman, is like reading the score of an opera when one can hardly play or sing; one can no more get an adequate notion of *Phèdre* without having heard a great performance, than one can of *Tristan und Isolde* if one has never heard a great Isolde like Leider or Flagstad.

(Monsieur St John Perse tells me that, when it comes to everyday speech, it is French which is the more monotonous and English which has the wider range of vocal inflection.)

I must confess that French classical tragedy strikes me as being opera for the unmusical. When I read the *Hippolytus*, I can recognize, despite all differences, a kinship between the world of Euripides and the world of Shakespeare, but the world of Racine, like the world of opera, seems to be another planet altogether. Euripides' Aphrodite is as concerned with fish and fowl as she is with human beings; Racine's Venus is not only unconcerned with animals, she takes no interest in the Lower Orders. It is impossible to imagine any of Racine's characters sneezing or wanting to go to the bathroom, for in his world there is neither weather nor nature. In consequence, the passions by which his characters are consumed can only exist, as it were, on stage, the creation of the magnificent speech and the grand gestures of the actors and actresses who endow them with flesh and blood. This is also the case in opera, but no speaking voice, however magnificent, can hope to compete, in expressiveness through sound, with a great singing voice backed by an orchestra.

[a] Elisa Rachel (1821–58), French actress celebrated for her performances in tragic roles.

'Whenever people talk to me about the weather, I always feel certain that they mean something else' (Oscar Wilde). The only kind of speech which approximates to the symbolist's poetic ideal is polite tea table conversation, in which the meaning of the banalities uttered depends almost entirely upon vocal inflections.

Owing to its superior power as a mnemonic, verse is superior to prose as a medium for didactic instruction. Those who condemn didacticism must disapprove *a fortiori* of didactic prose; in verse, as the Alka-Seltzer advertisements testify, the didactic message loses half its immodesty. Verse is also certainly the equal of prose as a medium for the lucid exposition of ideas; in skilful hands, the form of the verse can parallel and reinforce the steps of the logic. Indeed, contrary to what most people who have inherited the romantic conception of poetry believe, the danger of argument in verse—Pope's *Essay on Man* is an example—is that the verse may make the ideas too clear and distinct, more Cartesian than they really are.

On the other hand, verse is unsuited to controversy, to proving some truth or belief which is not universally accepted, because its formal nature cannot but convey a certain scepticism about its conclusions.

> Thirty days hath September,
> April, June, and November

is valid because nobody doubts its truth. Were there, however, a party who passionately denied it, the lines would be powerless to convince him because, formally, it would make no difference if the lines ran:

> Thirty days hath September,
> August, May, and December.

Poetry is not magic. In so far as poetry, or any other of the arts, can be said to have an ulterior purpose, it is, by telling the truth, to disenchant and disintoxicate.

'The unacknowledged legislators of the world'[a] describes the secret police, not the poets.

Catharsis is properly effected, not by works of art, but by religious rites. It is also effected, usually improperly, by bull-fights, professional football matches, bad movies, military bands, and monster rallies at which ten thousand girl guides form themselves into a model of the national flag.

The condition of mankind is, and always has been, so miserable and depraved that, if anyone were to say to the poet: 'For God's sake stop singing and do something useful like putting on the kettle or fetching bandages', what just reason could he give for refusing? But nobody says this. The self-appointed unqualified nurse says: 'You are to sing the patient a song which will make him believe that I, and I alone, can cure him. If you can't or won't, I shall confiscate your passport and send you to the mines.' And the poor patient in his delirium cries: 'Please sing me a song which will give me sweet dreams instead of nightmares. If you succeed, I will give you a penthouse in New York or a ranch in Arizona.'

[a] Shelley's description of poets in his *Defence of Poetry*.

48 Roland Barthes

Roland Barthes (b. 1915) studied French literature and classics at the
University of Paris, and taught French at universities in Romania and Egypt
before joining the Centre National de la Recherche Scientifique to work in
the fields of sociology and linguistics. In 1947 Barthes began to publish a
number of articles on literary criticism which formed the basis of his first
book of criticism, *Le Degré zéro de l'écriture* (Paris, 1953) [*Writing Degree
Zero* (1967)]. His subsequent publications include books and articles on
Racine, the French 'new novel' and semiology—the theory of signs, verbal
and non-verbal, which is Barthes's specialism in his present position as
Director of Studies at the Ecole Pratique des Hautes Etudes in Paris. (See
Elements de Semiologie (Paris, 1964) [*Elements of Semiology* (1967)].
Semiology, in Barthes's terms, is a development of the linguistics of Saussure
and Jakobson, which also influenced the social anthropologist Lévi-Strauss.
Barthes, therefore, belongs to that inter-disciplinary intellectual movement,
especially associated with France, known as 'structuralism' (see introductory
note on Lévi-Strauss above, p. 545).

'Criticism as Language' was originally published in the second of two special
issues of *The Times Literary Supplement* (1963) in which distinguished
English, American, and Continental critics were invited to state their intellectual credos. The essays were later collected into a volume, *The Critical
Moment* (1964). It is not necessary, however, to read Barthes's essay in this
context to recognize the ways in which it affronts the orthodox assumptions
behind most Anglo-American criticism. The majority of English and
American critics, whether primarily interested in evaluation or in interpretation, would think of themselves as pursuing the truth about the works of
art with which they are concerned, even if they do not expect to arrive at it
in an absolute and final sense. Barthes's brusque denial that criticism is
concerned with 'truth' in any sense, his brilliant logical demonstration that
criticism consists not in *discovering* something previously unperceived in the
work, but in *covering*, or fitting together, the language of the artist with the
language of the critic, and his assertion that criticism, like logic, is ultimately
tautological—these are all arguments profoundly disconcerting to the
orthodox assumptions of literary criticism, in France as elsewhere.

CROSS REFERENCES: 6. T. S. Eliot ('The Function of Criticism')
                    18. John Crowe Ransom
                    26. W. K. Wimsatt Jnr. and Monroe C. Beardsley

41. René Wellek
49. Susan Sontag

COMMENTARY: Gabriel Josipovici, 'Structures of truth: the premises of the French new criticism' in *The Word In the Desert (Critical Quarterly* 10th Anniversary No.) (1968), ed. C. B. Cox and A. E. Dyson

Criticism as language

It is always possible to promulgate certain major critical principles in the light of contemporary ideology, especially in France, where theoretical formulations carry great weight, no doubt because they give the practising critic the assurance that he is, at one and the same time, taking part in a fight, making history and exemplifying a philosophical system. We can say that, during the last fifteen years French criticism has developed, with various degrees of success, with four great 'philosophies'. There is, first of all, Existentialism, or what is generally so called, although the appropriateness of the term is debatable; it has produced Sartre's critical works, his studies of Baudelaire and Flaubert, his shorter articles on Proust, Mauriac, Giraudoux, and Ponge, and above all his outstanding book on Genet. Next Marxism; it is well known by now (the matter was thrashed out long ago) that orthodox Marxism has proved critically sterile through offering a purely mechanical explanation of works of literature and providing slogans rather than criteria of value. It follows that the most fruitful criticism has to be looked for, as it were, on the frontiers of Marxism, not at its recognized centre. The work of Lucien Goldmann on Racine, Pascal, the 'New Novel', the avant-garde theatre, and Malraux owes a large and explicit debt to Lukács, and it would be difficult to imagine a more flexible and ingenious form of criticism based on political and social history. Then there is psychoanalysis; at the moment, the best representative of Freudian psycho-analytical criticism is Charles Mauron, who has written on Racine and Mallarmé. But here again, 'marginal' activities have proved more fruitful. Gaston Bachelard, starting from an analysis of substances rather than of works and tracing the dynamic distortions of imagery in a great many poets, founded a whole critical school which is, indeed, so prolific that present-day French criticism in its most flourishing aspect can be said to be Bachelardian in inspiration (G. Poulet, J. Starobinski, J.-P. Richard). Lastly, there is structuralism (which, if reduced to extremely simple, perhaps excessively simple, terms, might be called formalism): the movement has been important, one might almost say fashionable, in France since Claude Lévi-Strauss brought it into the social sciences and philosophical reflection. So far, it has produced very few critical works, but such works are in preparation and they will no doubt show the influence of the linguistic model worked out by de Saussure and elaborated by Roman Jakobson (who, in his earlier years, belonged to a literary critical movement, the Russian formalist school). It would seem possible, for instance, to develop a variety of literary criticism on the basis of the two rhetorical categories established by Jakobson, metaphor and metonymy.

As can be seen, this French criticism is both 'national' (it owes little or nothing to Anglo-American, Spitzerian or Crocian[a] criticism) and up to date or— if the expression seems preferable—'unfaithful to the past' (since it belongs entirely to an aspect of contemporary ideology, it can hardly consider itself as being indebted to any critical tradition, whether founded by Sainte-Beuve, Taine, or Lanson). However, the last-named type of criticism raises a particular problem in this connection. Lanson[b] was the prototype of the French teacher of literature and, during the last fifty years, his work, method, and mentality, as transmitted by innumerable disciples, have continued to govern academic criticism. Since the principles, or at least the declared principles, of this kind of criticism are accuracy and objectivity in the establishment of facts, it might be thought that there would be no incompatibility between Lansonianism and the various forms of ideological criticism, which are all interpretative. But although most presentday French critics (I am thinking of those who deal with structure, not those concerned with current reviewing) are themselves teachers, there is a certain amount of tension between interpretative and positivistic (academic) criticism. The reason is that Lansonianism is itself an ideology; it is not simply content to demand the application of the objective rules of all scientific research, it also implies certain general convictions about man, history, literature, and the relationship between the author and his work. For instance, Lansonian psychology is quite out of date, since it consists fundamentally of a kind of analogical determinism, according to which the details of a given work must resemble the details of the author's life, the characters the innermost being of the author, and so on. This makes it a very peculiar ideology because, since it was invented, psychology has, among other things, imagined the opposite relationship of negation between the work and the author. Of course, it is inevitable that an ideology should be based on philosophical postulates; the argument against Lansonianism is not that it has assumptions, but that instead of admitting them, it drapes them in a moral cloak of rigorous and objective investigation; it is as if ideology were being smuggled surreptitiously into the scientific approach.

Since these different ideological principles can coexist *simultaneously* (and for my part, I can, in a certain sense, accept both *simultaneously*), we have to conclude that the ideological choice is not the essence of criticism nor 'truth' its ultimate test. Criticism is something other than making correct statements

[a] Leo Spitzer was one of the most distinguished practitioners of the stylistic criticism that developed out of Romance philology, especially in pre-Nazi Germany. His work is comparable with that of Erich Auerbach, see above, pp. 315–32). The Italian philosopher, historian, and aesthetician Benedetto Croce is especially associated with an extreme version of the romantic-expressionist theory of art.

[b] Gustave Lanson (1857–1934) was a French academic literary historian whose *Histoire de la litterature française* (1894) became a standard textbook.

in the light of 'true' principles. It follows that the major sin in criticism is not to have an ideology but to keep quiet about it. There is a name for this kind of guilty silence; it is self-deception or bad faith. How can anyone believe that a given work is an *object* independent of the psyche and personal history of the critic studying it, with regards to which he enjoys a sort of extraterritorial status? It would be a very remarkable thing if the profound relationship that most critics postulate between the author they are dealing with and his works were non-existent in the case of their own works and their own situation in time. It is inconceivable that the creative laws governing the writer should not also be valid for the critic. All criticism must include (although it may do so in the most indirect and discreet way) an implicit comment on itself; all criticism is criticism both of the work under consideration and of the critic; to quote Claudel's pun, it is knowledge (connaissance) of the other and co-birth (co-naissance) of oneself to the world. Or, to express the same thing in still another way, criticism is not in any sense a table of results or a body of judgments; it is essentially an activity, that is to say a series of intellectual acts inextricably involved with the historical and subjective (the two terms are synonymous) existence of the person who carries them out and has to assume responsibility for them. It is pointless to ask whether or not an activity is 'true'; the imperatives governing it are quite different.

Whatever the complexities of literary theory, a novelist or a poet is supposed to speak about objects and phenomena which, whether imaginary or not, are external and anterior to language. The world exists and the writer uses language; such is the definition of literature. The object of criticism is very different; it deals not with 'the world', but with the linguistic formulations made by others; it is a comment on a comment, a secondary language or *meta-language* (as the logicians would say), applied to a primary language (or language-as-object). It follows that critical activity must take two kinds of relationships into account: the relationship between the critical language and the language of the author under consideration and the relationship between the latter (language-as-object) and the world. Criticism is defined by the interaction of these two languages and so bears a close resemblance to another intellectual activity, logic, which is also entirely founded on the distinction between language-as-object and meta-language.

Consequently, if criticism is only a meta-language, its task is not to discover forms of 'truth' but forms of 'validity'. In itself, a language cannot be true or false; it is either valid or non-valid. It is valid when it consists of a coherent system of signs. The rules governing the language of literature are not concerned with the correspondence between that language and reality (whatever the claims made by schools of realism), but only with its being in line with the system of signs that the author has decided on (of course, in this connection great stress must be laid on the term *system*). It is not the business of criticism to decide whether Proust told 'the truth'—whether, for instance, Baron de Charlus was really Montesquiou or Françoise, Céleste or even, more generally, whether the society Proust describes is an adequate representation of the historical conditions in which the aristocracy was finally eliminated at the end of the nineteenth century—its function is purely to evolve its own language and to make it as coherent and logical, that is as systematic, as possible, so that it can render an account of, or better still 'integrate' (in the mathematical sense) the greatest possible quantity of Proust's language just as a logical equation tests the validity of a piece of reasoning, without taking sides about the 'truth' of the arguments used. We might say that the task of criticism (and this is the only guarantee of its universality) is purely formal; it does not consist in 'discovering' in the work or the author under consideration something 'hidden' or 'profound' or 'secret' which has so far escaped notice (through what miracle? Are we more perceptive than our predecessors?) but only in *fitting together*—as a skilled cabinet maker, by a process of 'intelligent' fumbling, interlocks two parts of a complicated piece of furniture—the language of the day (Existentialism, Marxism, or psycho-analysis) and the language of the author, that is, the formal system of logical rules that he evolved in the conditions of his time. The 'proof' of a given form of criticism is not 'alethiological' in nature (i.e. is not concerned with the truth), since critical writing, like logical writing, can never be other than tautology; in the last resort, it consists in the delayed statement (but the delay, through being fully accepted, is itself significant) that 'Racine is Racine', 'Proust is Proust'. If there is such a thing as a critical proof, it lies not in the ability to *discover* the work under consideration but, on the contrary, to *cover* it as completely as possible with one's own language.

In this respect too, then, criticism is an essentially formal activity, not in the aesthetic, but in the logical sense of the term. It might be said that the only means by which criticism can avoid the self-deception or bad faith referred to earlier is to set itself the moral aim not of deciphering the meaning of the work under consideration, but of reconstituting the rules and compulsions which governed the elaboration of that sense; provided always it is also agreed that a work of literature is a very special semantic system, the aim of which is to put 'meaning' into the world, but not 'a meaning'. A work of literature, at least of the kind that is normally considered by the critics (and this itself may be a possible definition of 'good' literature), is neither ever quite meaningless (mysterious or 'inspired') nor ever quite clear; it is, so to speak, *suspended* meaning; it offers itself to the reader as a declared system of significance, but as a signified object it eludes his grasp. This kind of *dis-appointment* or *deception* (de-capio: un-take) inherent in the meaning explains how it is that a work of literature has such power to ask questions of the world (by undermining the definite meanings that seem to be the apanage of beliefs, ideologies, and common sense) without, however, supplying any answers (no great work is 'dogmatic'): it also explains how a work can go on being reinterpreted indefinitely, since there is no reason why critics should ever stop discussing Racine or Shakespeare (except through an act of abandonment which would itself be a kind of language). Literature, since it consists at one and the same time of the insistent offering of a meaning and the persistent elusiveness of that meaning, is definitely no more than a language, that is, a system of signs: its being lies not in the message but in the system. This being so, the critic is not called upon to reconstitute the message of the work, but only its system, just as the business of the linguist is not to decipher the meaning of a sentence but to determine the formal structure which permits the transmission of its meaning.

It is precisely through the admission, on the part of criticism, that it is only a language (or, more accurately, a meta-language) that it can, paradoxically yet genuinely, be objective and subjective, historical and existential, totalitarian and liberal. The language that a critic chooses to speak is not a gift from heaven; it is one of the range of languages offered by his situation in time and, object-ively, it is the latest stage of a certain historical development of knowledge, ideas, and intellectual passions; it is a *necessity*. On the other hand, each critic chooses this necessary language, in accordance with a certain existential pattern, as the *means of exercising* an intellectual function which is his, and his alone, putting into the operation his 'deepest self', that is, his preferences, pleasures, resistances, and obsessions. In this way the critical work contains within itself a dialogue between two historical situations and two subjectivities, those of the author and those of the critic. But this dialogue shows a complete egotistical bias towards the present; criticism is neither a 'tribute' to the truth of the past nor to the truth of 'the other'; it is the ordering of that which is intelligible in our own time.

49 Susan Sontag

Susan Sontag (b. 1934) was born in Arizona, but is especially associated
with the New York intellectual and artistic 'scene'. She published a novel
called *The Benefactor* in 1964, and in the same year became something of a
celebrity when her essay 'Notes on Camp' was published in *Partisan Review*
and, by a familiar process, picked up and exploited by the mass media. 'Camp'
as defined by Miss Sontag was not so much a kind of art as a kind of artistic
consumption, which converted conventionally 'bad' art (like *Batman*) into
a source of refined pleasure by ignoring its intentions and relishing its style;
but it had affiliations with pop art, happenings, underground movies, and
other manifestations of the avant-garde. The 1960s saw a remarkable
burgeoning of the avant-garde in America, and Miss Sontag was one of its
most subtle and influential apologists, announcing the death of traditional
élitist literary culture with all the skill and authority of someone well educated
in that culture. 'Against Interpretation' is in fact less novel than it seems at
first sight: the links with the aesthetics of Symbolism are clear. First published
in the *Evergreen Review* in 1964, it was the title essay of her first collection
of essays, published in America in 1697. Since then Miss Sontag has published
a second collection of essays, *Styles of Radical Will* (New York, 1969) and a
novel, *Death Kit* (1968).

CROSS REFERENCES: 20. Paul Valéry
33. Leslie Fiedler
34. Alain Robbe-Grillet
48. Roland Barthes
50. Frank Kermode

Against interpretation

Content is a glimpse of something, an encounter like a flash. It's very tiny—
very tiny, content.

WILLEM DE KOONING,[a] in an interview

It is only shallow people who do not judge by appearances. The mystery of the
world is the visible, not the invisible.

OSCAR WILDE, in a letter

[a] American abstract expressionist painter.

I

The earliest experience of art must have been that it was incantatory, magical; art was an instrument of ritual (cf. the paintings in the caves at Lascaux, Altamira, Niaux, La Pasiega, etc.). The earliest *theory* of art, that of the Greek philosophers, proposed that art was mimesis, imitation of reality.

It is at this point that the peculiar question of the *value* of art arose. For the mimetic theory, by its very terms, challenges art to justify itself.

Plato, who proposed the theory, seems to have done so in order to rule that the value of art is dubious. Since he considered ordinary material things as themselves mimetic objects, imitations of transcendent forms or structures, even the best painting of a bed would be only an 'imitation of an imitation'. For Plato, art is neither particularly useful (the painting of a bed is no good to sleep on), nor, in the strict sense, true. And Aristotle's arguments in defence of art do not really challenge Plato's view that all art is an elaborate *trompe l'oeil*, and therefore a lie. But he does dispute Plato's idea that art is useless. Lie or no, art has a certain value according to Aristotle because it is a form of therapy. Art is useful, after all, Aristotle counters, medicinally useful in that it arouses and purges dangerous emotions.

In Plato and Aristotle, the mimetic theory of art goes hand in hand with the assumption that art is always figurative. But advocates of the mimetic theory need not close their eyes to decorative and abstract art. The fallacy that art is necessarily a 'realism' can be modified or scrapped without ever moving outside the problems delimited by the mimetic theory.

The fact is, all Western consciousness of and reflection upon art have remained within the confines staked out by the Greek theory of art as mimesis or representation. It is through this theory that art as such—above and beyond given works of art—becomes problematic, in need of defence. And it is the defence of art which gives birth to the odd vision by which something we have learned to call 'form' is separated off from something we have learned to call 'content', and to the well-intentioned move which makes content essential and form accessory.

Even in modern times, when most artists and critics have discarded the theory of art as representation of an outer reality in favour of the theory of art as subjective expression, the main feature of the mimetic theory persists. Whether we conceive of the work of art on the model of a picture (art as a picture of reality) or on the model of a statement (art as the statement of the artist), content still comes first. The content may have changed. It may now be less figurative, less lucidly realistic. But it is still assumed that a work of art *is* its content. Or, as it's usually put today, that a work of art by definition *says* something. ('What X is saying is ...', 'What X is trying to say is ...', 'What X said is ...' etc., etc.)

None of us can ever retrieve that innocence before all theory when art knew no need to justify itself, when one did not ask of a work of art what it *said* because one knew (or thought one knew) what it *did*. From now to the end of consciousness, we are stuck with the task of defending art. We can only quarrel with one or another means of defence. Indeed, we have an obligation to overthrow any means of defending and justifying art which becomes particularly obtuse or onerous or insensitive to contemporary needs and practice.

This is the case, today, with the very idea of content itself. Whatever it may have been in the past, the idea of content is today mainly a hindrance, a nuisance, a subtle or not so subtle philistinism.

Though the actual developments in many arts may seem to be leading us away from the idea that a work of art is primarily its content, the idea still exerts an extraordinary hegemony. I want to suggest that this is because the idea is now perpetuated in the guise of a certain way of encountering works of art thoroughly ingrained among most people who take any of the arts seriously. What the overemphasis on the idea of content entails is the perennial, never consummated project of *interpretation*. And, conversely, it is the habit of approaching works of art in order to *interpret* them that sustains the fancy that there is such a thing as the content of a work of art.

Of course, I don't mean interpretation in the broadest sense, the sense in which Nietzsche (rightly) says, 'There are no facts, only interpretations'. By interpretation, I mean here a conscious act of the mind which illustrates a certain code, certain 'rules' of interpretation.

Directed to art, interpretation means plucking a set of elements (the X, the Y, the Z, and so forth) from the whole work. The task of interpretation is virtually one of translation. The interpreter says, Look, don't you see that X is really—or, really means—A? That Y is really B? That Z is really C?

What situation could prompt this curious project for transforming a text? History gives us the materials for an answer. Interpretation first appears in the culture of late classical antiquity, when the power and credibility of myth had been broken by the 'realistic' view of the world introduced by scientific enlightenment. Once the question that haunts post-mythic consciousness—that of the *seemliness* of religious symbols—had been asked, the ancient texts were, in their pristine form, no longer acceptable. Then interpretation was summoned, to reconcile the ancient texts to 'modern' demands. Thus, the Stoics, to accord with their view that the gods had to be moral, allegorized away the rude features of Zeus and his boisterous clan in Homer's epics. What Homer really designated by the adultery of Zeus with Leto, they explained, was the union between power and wisdom. In the same vein, Philo of Alexandria interpreted the literal historical narratives of the Hebrew Bible as spiritual paradigms. The story of the exodus from Egypt, the wandering in the desert for forty years, and the entry into the promised land, said Philo, was really an allegory of the individual soul's emancipation, tribulations, and final deliverance. Interpretation thus presupposes a discrepancy between the clear meaning of the text and the demands of (later) readers. It seeks to resolve that discrepancy. The situation is that for some reason a text has become unacceptable; yet it cannot be discarded. Interpretation is a radical strategy for conserving an old text, which is thought too precious to repudiate, by revamping it. The interpreter, without actually erasing or rewriting the text, *is* altering it. But he can't admit to doing this. He claims to be only making it intelligible, by disclosing its true meaning. However far the interpreters alter the text (another notorious example is the Rabbinic and Christian 'spiritual' interpretations of the clearly erotic Song of Songs), they must claim to be reading off a sense that is already there.

Interpretation in our own time, however, is even more complex. For the contemporary zeal for the project of interpretation is often prompted not by piety towards the troublesome text (which may conceal an aggression), but by an open aggressiveness, an overt contempt for appearances. The old style of interpretation was insistent, but respectful; it erected another meaning on top of the literal one. The modern style of interpretation excavates, and as it excavates, destroys; it digs 'behind' the text, to find a sub-text which is the true one. The most celebrated and influential modern doctrines, those of Marx and Freud, actually amount to elaborate systems of hermeneutics[a], aggressive and impious theories of interpretation. All observable phenomena are bracketed, in Freud's phrase, as *manifest content*. This manifest content must be probed and pushed aside to find the true meaning—the *latent content*—beneath. For Marx, social events like revolutions and wars; for Freud, the events of individual lives (like neurotic symptoms and slips of the tongue) as well as texts (like a dream or a work of art)—all are treated as occasions for interpretation. According to Marx and Freud, these events only *seem* to be intelligible. Actually, they have no meaning without interpretation. To understand *is* to interpret. And to interpret is to restate the phenomenon, in effect to find an equivalent for it.

Thus, interpretation is not (as most people assume) an absolute value, a gesture of mind situated in some timeless realm of capabilities. Interpretation must itself be evaluated, with a historical view of human consciousness. In some cultural contexts, interpretation is a liberating act. It is a means of revising, of transvaluing, of escaping the dead past. In other cultural contexts, it is reactionary, impertinent, cowardly, stifling.

IV

Today is such a time, when the project of interpretation is largely reactionary, stifling. Like the fumes of the automobile and of heavy industry which befoul the urban atmosphere, the effusion of interpretations of art today poisons our sensibilities. In a culture whose already classical dilemma is the hypertrophy of the intellect at the expense of energy and sensual capability, interpretation is the revenge of the intellect upon art.

[a] The art or science of interpretation, especially of scripture.

Even more. It is the revenge of the intellect upon the world. To interpret is to impoverish, to deplete the world—in order to set up a shadow world of 'meanings'. It is to turn *the* world into *this* world. ('This world'! As if there were any other.)

The world, our world, is depleted, impoverished enough. Away with all duplicates of it, until we again experience more immediately what we have.

V

In most modern instances, interpretation amounts to the philistine refusal to leave the work of art alone. Real art has the capacity to make us nervous. By reducing the work of art to its content and then interpreting *that*, one tames the work of art. Interpretation makes art manageable, comfortable.

This philistinism of interpretation is more rife in literature than in any other art. For decades now, literary critics have understood it to be their task to translate the elements of the poem or play or novel or story into something else. Sometimes a writer will be so uneasy before the naked power of his art that he will install within the work itself—albeit with a little shyness, a touch of the good taste of irony—the clear and explicit interpretation of it. Thomas Mann is an example of such an over-co-operative author. In the case of more stubborn authors, the critic is only too happy to perform the job.

The work of Kafka, for example, has been subjected to a mass ravishment by no less than three armies of interpreters. Those who read Kafka as a social allegory see case studies of the frustrations and insanity of modern bureaucracy and its ultimate issuance in the totalitarian state. Those who read Kafka as a psycho-analytic allegory see desperate revelations of Kafka's fear of his father, his castration anxieties, his sense of his own impotence, his thraldom to his dreams. Those who read Kafka as a religious allegory explain that K. in *The Castle* is trying to gain access to heaven, that Joseph K. in *The Trial* is being judged by the inexorable and mysterious justice of God.... Another *oeuvre* that has attracted interpreters like leeches is that of Samuel Beckett. Beckett's delicate dramas of the withdrawn consciousness—pared down to essentials, cut off, often represented as physically immobilized—are read as a statement about man's alienation from meaning or from God, or as an allegory of psycho-pathology.

Proust, Joyce, Faulkner, Rilke, Lawrence, Gide ... one could go on citing author after author; the list is endless of those around whom thick encrustations of interpretation have taken hold. But it should be noted that interpretation is not simply the compliment that mediocrity pays to genius. It is, indeed, *the* modern way of understanding something, and is applied to works of every quality. Thus, in the notes that Elia Kazan published on his production of *A Streetcar Named Desire*, it becomes clear that, in order to direct the play, Kazan had to discover that Stanley Kowalski represented the sensual and vengeful barbarism that was engulfing our culture, while Blanche Du Bois was Western civilization, poetry, delicate apparel, dim lighting, refined feelings and all, though a little the worse for wear to be sure. Tennessee Williams's forceful psychological melodrama now became intelligible: it was *about* something, about the decline of Western civilization. Apparently, were it to go on being a play about a handsome brute named Stanley Kowalski and a faded mangy belle named Blanche Du Bois, it would not be manageable.

VI

It doesn't matter whether artists intend, or don't intend, for their work to be interpreted. Perhaps Tennessee Williams thinks *Streetcar* is about what Kazan thinks it to be about. It may be that Cocteau in *The Blood of a Poet* and in *Orpheus* wanted the elaborate readings which have been given these films, in terms of Freudian symbolism and social critique. But the merit of these works certainly lies elsewhere than in their 'meanings'. Indeed, it is precisely to the extent that Williams's plays and Cocteau's films do suggest these portentous meanings that they are defective, false, contrived, lacking in conviction.

From interviews, it appears that Resnais and Robbe-Grillet consciously designed *Last Year at Marienbad* to accommodate a multiplicity of equally plausible interpretations. But the temptation to interpret *Marienbad* should be resisted. What matters in *Marienbad* is the pure, untranslatable, sensuous immediacy of some of its images, and its rigorous if narrow solutions to certain problems of cinematic form.

Again, Ingmar Bergman may have meant the tank rumbling down the empty night street in *The Silence* as a phallic symbol. But if he did, it was a foolish thought. ('Never trust the teller, trust the tale,' said Lawrence.)[a] Taken as a brute object, as an immediate sensory equivalent for the mysterious abrupt armoured happenings going on inside the hotel, that sequence with the tank is the most striking moment in the film. Those who reach for a Freudian interpretation of the tank are only expressing their lack of response to what is there on the screen.

It is always the case that interpretation of this type indicates a dissatisfaction (conscious or unconscious) with the work, a wish to replace it by something else.

Interpretation, based on the highly dubious theory that a work of art is composed of items of content, violates art. It makes art into an article for use, for arrangement into a mental scheme of categories.

VII

Interpretation does not, of course, always prevail. In fact, a great deal of today's art may be understood as motivated by a flight from interpretation. To avoid interpretation, art may become parody. Or it may become abstract. Or it may become ('merely') decorative. Or it may become non-art.

The flight from interpretation seems particularly a feature of modern painting. Abstract painting is the attempt to have, in the ordinary sense, no content; since there is no content, there can be no interpretation. Pop Art works by the

[a] Lawrence actually said: 'Never trust the *artist*.' See p. 123 above.

opposite means to the same result; using a content so blatant, so 'what it is', it, too, ends by being uninterpretable.

A good deal of modern poetry as well, starting from the great experiments of French poetry (including the movement that is misleadingly called Symbolism) to put silence into poems and to reinstate the *magic* of the word, has escaped from the rough grip of interpretation. The most recent revolution in contemporary taste in poetry—the revolution that has deposed Eliot and elevated Pound—represents a turning away from content in poetry in the old sense, an impatience with what made modern poetry prey to the zeal of interpreters.

I am speaking mainly of the situation in America, of course. Interpretation runs rampant here in those arts with a feeble and negligible avant-garde: fiction and the drama. Most American novelists and playwrights are really either journalists or gentlemen sociologists and psychologists. They are writing the literary equivalent of programme music. And so rudimentary, uninspired, and stagnant has been the sense of what might be done with *form* in fiction and drama that even when the content isn't simply information, news, it is still peculiarly visible, handier, more exposed. To the extent that novels and plays (in America), unlike poetry and painting and music, don't reflect any interesting concern with changes in their form, these arts remain prone to assault by interpretation.

But programmatic avant-gardism—which has meant, mostly, experiments with form at the expense of content—is not the only defence against the infestation of art by interpretations. At least, I hope not. For this would be to commit art to being perpetually on the run. (It also perpetuates the very distinction between form and content which is, ultimately, an illusion.) Ideally, it is possible to elude the interpreters in another way, by making works of art whose surface is so unified and clean, whose momentum is so rapid, whose address is so direct that the work can be ... just what it is. Is this possible now? It does happen in films, I believe. This is why cinema is the most alive, the most exciting, the most important of all art forms right now. Perhaps the way one tells how alive a particular art form is, is by the latitude it gives for making mistakes in it, and still being good. For example, a few of the films of Bergman—though crammed with lame messages about the modern spirit, thereby inviting interpretations—still triumph over the pretentious intentions of their director. In *Winter Light* and *The Silence*, the beauty and visual sophistication of the images subvert before our eyes the callow pseudo-intellectuality of the story and some of the dialogue. (The most remarkable instance of this sort of discrepancy is the work of D. W. Griffith.) In good films, there is always a directness that entirely frees us from the itch to interpret. Many old Hollywood films, like those of Cukor, Walsh, Hawks, and countless other directors, have this liberating anti-symbolic quality, no less than the best work of the new European directors, like Truffaut's *Shoot the Piano Player* and *Jules and Jim*, Godard's *Breathless* and *Vivre Sa Vie*, Antonioni's *L'Avventura*, and Olmi's *The Fiancés*.

The fact that films have not been overrun by interpreters is in part due simply to the newness of cinema as an art. It also owes to the happy accident that films for such a long time were just movies; in other words, that they were understood to be part of mass, as opposed to high, culture, and were left alone by most people with minds. Then, too, there is always something other than content in the cinema to grab hold of, for those who want to analyse. For the cinema, unlike the novel, possesses a vocabulary of forms—the explicit, complex, and discussable technology of camera movements, cutting, and composition of the frame that goes into the making of a film.

VIII

What kind of criticism, of commentary on the arts, is desirable today? For I am not saying that works of art are ineffable, that they cannot be described or paraphrased. They can be. The question is how. What would criticism look like that would serve the work of art, not usurp its place?

What is needed, first, is more attention to form in art. If excessive stress on *content* provokes the arrogance of interpretation, more extended and more thorough descriptions of *form* would silence. What is needed is a vocabulary—a descriptive, rather than prescriptive, vocabulary—for forms.[1] The best criticism, and it is uncommon, is of this sort that dissolves considerations of content into those of form. On film, drama, and painting respectively, I can think of Erwin Panofsky's essay, 'Style and Medium in the Motion Pictures', Northrop Frye's essay, 'A Conspectus of Dramatic Genres', Pierre Francastel's essay, 'The Destruction of a Plastic Space'. Roland Barthes's book *On Racine* and his two essays on Robbe-Grillet are examples of formal analysis applied to the work of a single author. (The best essays in Erich Auerbach's *Mimesis*, like 'The Scar of Odysseus',[a] are also of this type.) An example of formal analysis applied simultaneously to genre and author is Walter Benjamin's essay, 'The Story Teller: reflections on the works of Nicolai Leskov'.

Equally valuable would be acts of criticism which would supply a really accurate, sharp, loving description of the appearance of a work of art. This seems even harder to do than formal analysis. Some of Manny Farber's film criticism, Dorothy Van Ghent's essay, 'The Dickens World: a view from Todgers'', Randall Jarrell's essay on Walt Whitman are among the rare examples of what I mean. These are essays which reveal the sensuous surface of art without mucking about in it.

IX

Transparence is the highest, most liberating value in art—and in criticism—today. Transparence means experiencing the luminousness of the thing in itself, of things being what they are. This is the greatness of, for example, the films of Bresson and Ozu and Renoir's *The Rules of the Game*.

Once upon a time (say, for Dante), it must have been a revolutionary and creative move to design works of art so that they might be experienced on several levels. Now it is not. It reinforces the principle of redundancy that is the principal affliction of modern life.

[a] See above, pp. 315-32.

Once upon a time (a time when high art was scarce), it must have been a revolutionary and creative move to interpret works of art. Now it is not. What we decidedly do not need now is further to assimilate Art into Thought, or (worse yet) Art into Culture.

Interpretation takes the sensory experience of the work of art for granted, and proceeds from there. This cannot be taken for granted, now. Think of the sheer multiplication of works of art available, to every one of us, superadded to the conflicting tastes and odours and the sights of the urban environment that bombard our senses. Ours is a culture based on excess, on overproduction; the result is a steady loss of sharpness in our sensory experience. All the conditions of modern life—its material plentitude, its sheer crowdedness—conjoin to dull our sensory faculties. And it is in the light of the condition of our senses, our capabilities (rather than those of another age), that the task of the critic must be assessed.

What is important now is to recover our senses. We must learn to *see* more, to *hear* more, to *feel* more.

Our task is not to find the maximum amount of content in a work of art, much less to squeeze more content out of the work than is already there. Our task is to cut back content so that we can *see* the thing at all.

The aim of all commentary on art now should be to make works of art—and, by analogy, our own experience—more, rather than less, real to us. The function of criticism should be to show *how it is what it is*, even *that it is what it is*, rather than to show *what it means*.

X

In place of a hermeneutics we need an erotics of art.

Notes

1. One of the difficulties is that our idea of form is spatial (the Greek metaphors for form are all derived from notions of space). This is why we have a more ready vocabulary of forms for the spatial than for the temporal arts. The exception among the temporal arts, of course, is the drama; perhaps this is because the drama is a narrative (i.e. temporal) form that extends itself visually and pictorially, upon a stage. . . . What we don't have yet is a poetics of the novel, any clear notion of the forms of narration. Perhaps film criticism will be the occasion of a breakthrough here, since films are primarily a visual form, yet they are also a subdivision of literature.

50   Frank Kermode

Frank Kermode (b. 1919) is one of the most versatile of modern literary critics. His publications cover a wide range of literature, from *Shakespeare, Spenser, Donne* (1971) to *Romantic Image* (1957) and *Wallace Stevens* (1960). *The Sense of An Ending* (1966), described as 'an attempt to relate the theory of literary fictions to a more general theory of fiction, using the fictions of apocalypse as a model', took him even farther afield, into theology, medieval history, sociology, philosophy, and even physics. A university teacher who has held chairs at the Universities of Manchester, Bristol, and London (where he is now Lord Northcliffe Professor of English Literature), Frank Kermode is also a prolific reviewer, broadcaster, and literary journalist. He is a brilliant exponent of the occasional literary essay, and his work in this genre has been collected in *Puzzles and Epiphanies* (1962) and *Continuities* (1968). A paperback volume *Modern Essays* (1971) combines essays taken from both these collections with some others.

'Objects, Jokes and Art' is a good example of Kermode's ability to assimilate, connect, and communicate in a crisp, epigrammatic style, information and ideas from a host of different specialisms, literary and non-literary, adding original insights of his own. It is the second of three related essays on the idea of the Modern in the arts. In the first of these, 'Discrimination of Modernisms', Kermode proposed a distinction between 'paleo-modernism' (i.e. the art of Joyce, Stravinsky, Picasso, Eliot, etc., experimental but still continuous with tradition) and 'neo-modernism'—the anti-art of the contemporary avant-garde which, inspired by Dadaism and Surrealism, attempts a total break with tradition. This second phase is the subject of 'Objects, Jokes and Art', which first appeared in *Encounter* (1966) and is reprinted here from *Continuities*.

CROSS REFERENCES: 33. Leslie Fiedler
34. Alain Robbe-Grillet
35. Georg Lukács
43. Raymond Williams
49. Susan Sontag

Objects, jokes, and art

Do we have a 'rage for order'? It has long been thought so, and the arts have long been thought ways of appeasing it. But there is a difference between 'order' and 'an order'; and what looked like the first can become simply the second: the conventional literary epic, or pastoral poetry, or the heroic couplet, or history-painting, or sonata form. In the older modernism, order grew mysterious. Following the organicist view of the Romantics, and the sophisticated gloss put on it by the Symbolists, poets treated it as the property of works purged of personality and emotion, new shapes out there and independent, perceptible by an *élite* which had transcended bourgeois literacy and could operate a logic of imagination divinely void of intellect. Thus the highly original forms of Mallarmé and, later, Eliot, have only a tenuous relation to more vulgar notions of form; and in the novel, for instance, the kind of extreme deviation from prevailing norms which had formerly occurred only now and again became a regular feature. The great experimental novels of early modernism—Kafka, Proust, Joyce, Musil[a], for instance—are all characterized by a kind of formal desperation.

Yet such forms continue to assume that there was an inescapable relationship between art and order. Admittedly, when the forms of the past grew 'rigid and a bit absurd' you undertook a new research and produced modern forms. They might indeed be extremely researched, as Wallace Stevens suggests when he says we can't have the old 'romantic tenements' and that what will now suffice may be much less palpable: merely, perhaps

> a woman dancing, a woman
> Combing. The poem of the act of the mind—

but the act of the mind is still a form-creating act, and the form it creates provides satisfactions of the rage for order that cannot be had in life not so organized, so that art is different from life at least in this respect. And this view of the matter is still in many ways standard. Its various implications— 'autonomy', anti-didacticism, everything that attracts, both for the arts and the criticism that attends them, the epithet 'formalist'—are, whether we like it or not, still in the minds of most of us when we consider a work of art. The first thing we think about is that this is a poem or a painting, and if it were not we should find another way of speaking than the one we choose. 'Art is not life and cannot be/A midwife to society', as Mr Auden pedagogically explained. It may be somewhat illiberal, even untruthful, and reactionary by its very nature, as Mr Trilling thinks; he is supported in his opinion by the theorist of the

[a] See note, p. 477 above.

formal *nouveau roman*,[1] and also, as we will see, by the Apollinaire[a] of the New York renaissance, Harold Rosenberg.

The fact that we have inherited the set of aesthetic assumptions I have very roughly sketched above makes it all the more difficult for most of us to understand the new men, who claim to be destroying the barrier between life and art, asserting their indifference to the question 'Is this a picture?' and professing contempt for ideas of order, especially when they can be associated with the art of the past. Nevertheless we shall certainly understand the older modernism better if we come to terms with the newer.

There seems to be much agreement that the new rejection of order and the past is not quite the same thing as older rejections of one's elders and their assumptions. It is also agreed that this neo-modernist anti-traditionalism and anti-formalism, though anticipated by Apollinaire, begins with Dada[b]. Whether for the reason that its programme was literally impossible, or because their nihilism lacked ruthlessness, it is undoubtedly true, as Harold Rosenberg has observed, that Dada had many of the characteristics of a new art movement, and that its devotees treated it as such, so in some measure defeating its theoretical anti-art programme. Raoul Haussmann only recently attacked the 'Neo-Dadaists' because what they were doing was ignorantly imitative, but also it wasn't 'art'. If what we want is to understand anti-art I suppose our best plan is to follow the signs back to Duchamp, whose importance in this context is that he expressly and intelligently sought ways of 'no longer thinking the thing in question is a picture'.

The point is simply this: whereas such a poem as The Waste Land draws upon a tradition which imposes the necessity of form, though it may have none that can be apprehended without a disciplined act of faith, a new modernism prefers and professes to do without the tradition and the illusion. At this point there begin to proliferate those manifold theoretical difficulties associated with neo-modernist art. They are usually discussed in terms of the visual arts and music, probably because they are palpably even greater in the case of literature. Duchamp could pick something up and sign it, as he did with his 'ready-mades'[c], and this raises problems, but at least it does not move from 'the plane of the feasible'.[2] In poetry one can of course use chunks of economic history and the collage of allusion, but usually for some formal irony, or to get a special effect by juxtaposition; simply to sign a passage ready-made by somebody else is not to change it but to plagiarize it. It would not matter if the borrowed passage were in most ways as commonplace as a mass-produced artefact; it would only be a more obvious case of plagiarism. A legal argument about a

[a] Guillaume Apollinaire (1890–1918), poet and publicist of the avant-garde in Paris in the first two decades of this century.

[b] Dadaism was a nihilistic artistic movement, international in character, which originated in Zurich in 1916. It was dedicated to defying all traditional notions of form, meaning and taste in the arts. The sound of the word 'Dada' was intended to suggest these attitudes. 'Happenings' and random poetry were among the innovations sponsored by the Dadaists.

[c] The ready-mades of the artist Marcel Duchamp were manufactured objects, such as a hat-rack or a ceramic urinal, which he converted into 'works of art' by selecting, signing, and exhibiting them.

Duchamp ready-made might be interesting, but one would not expect a plausible defence in a case on literary ready-mades. The closest poetry can get is to cultivate impersonality and objectivity—Williams's wheel-barrow and Robbe-Grillet's out-there coffee-pot[a]. The things made are not wheel-barrows and coffee-pots; but similar theoretical assumptions are involved.

Duchamp used to speak of 'Dada blankness'—a way of making or naming things which has no relation to humanity or nature, no 'responsibility'; 'alien objects of the outer world,' as Lawrence D. Steefel puts it, 'are reduced to instruments of the artist's transcendence to them.'[3] Blankness and indifference, like the 'impersonality' of Eliot, become, from one angle, a kind of egoism, indeed dehumanisation has always been, from this angle, the apotheosis of the *culte du moi* [cult of myself]. Dada, at its most apocalyptic, had it both ways, and proclaimed that after the present phase of quasi-Oriental 'indifference' there was to follow an era of purged personality, 'the cleanliness of the individual' (according to [Tristan] Tzara). The extreme and, on the face of it, paradoxical individualism of, say, Eliot, Lewis, and Pound, is the parallel case.

There is, in short, a family resemblance between the modernisms. 'Indifference' and the abrogation of 'responsibility' are the wilder cousins of the more literary 'impersonality' and 'objectivity'. The palaeo-modernist[b] conspiracy which made a cult of occult forms is not unrelated to the extremist denial that there are any. These are the self-reconciling opposites of modernism.

Duchamp, like some of the older poets, is a man whose intelligence has been dedicated to anti-intellectualist ends. The paradoxical pursuit of randomness in the arts—a consequence of doctrinaire anti-formalism—is now carried on with every resource of ingenuity by very intelligent men. To early modernists the subjection of personality and the attack on false orders were one and the same process; the logicians of neo-modernism have not only accepted the position but developed it into an attack on order, perhaps not successfully, but with energy. Viewed in this light, the new theory bristles with paradoxes as, for instance, in [Robert] Rauschenberg's remark: 'I consider myself successful only when I do something that resembles the lack of order I sense.'

The theoretical situation is in detail puzzling, but it must be admitted that in its practical and personal manifestations it is often pleasing, and indeed funny. For this reason Calvin Tomkins's book, which is not only a set of 'profiles' but an intelligent presentation of ideas, is as amusing as it is informative.[4] His four subjects are Duchamp, Cage, Tinguely, and Rauschenberg. They are all, as he says, very different—Duchamp more detached, Tinguely more destructive, Cage more programmatic, and Rauschenberg more anti-art than the others—but they have many interests in common. For instance, all of them say that *art is much less interesting than life,* and not generically different from it. All seek impersonality (though strong personalities are vividly present in their work) and therefore *experiment with chance.* All *accept that art is characteristically impermanent,* being made up of things with transcendence. And *all* rejoice to *work*

[a] See above, pp. 469–70.
[b] See introductory note.

on the borders of farce. They make random and unpredictable things in a world consisting of random and unpredictable things, an activity that is anyway absurd; the purposeless is pursued with fanatic purpose, and this is farcical in itself. One difference between a Tinguely machine and a Heath Robinson is that Tinguely takes it past the drawing-board stage, but another is that Robinson aimed to amuse, whereas Tinguely, though he doesn't mind amusing, has no affective purpose at all; and there is a somewhat similar distinction to be drawn between a Hoffnung concert and a Cage recital.*a*

These propositions and attitudes are characteristic of neo-modernism, and the literary man should learn what he can from them. The view that art is not distinct from life, to which (in Cage's words) it is 'inferior in complexity and unpredictability', is of course 'anti-formalist'. In the past we have simply been wrong in supposing that order is a differentia of art; hence the new doctrine, propounded by Cage and given an elaborate philosophical defence in Morse Peckham's recent book, *Man's Rage for Chaos*, that 'a work of art is what the perceiver observes in what has been culturally established as a perceiver's space. This can be anything. . . .' In Cage's 4′ 33″ the pianist sits before a closed piano for four minutes and thirty-three seconds, and the only sound is what floats in randomly from outside—bird song, buses—or what the spectators make themselves. So long as there is a concert-situation there is a concert, although the content of the concert is random and minimal. This is a logical step forward from Satie's musical collage, and is perhaps more like Kurt Schwitters simply planting bits of things before the observer in a 'perceiver's space'. It pushes the protest against 'retinal' art, and its musical equivalent, to the point where it is a protest against the seriousness of palaeo-modernist protest, and where the difference between art and joke is as obscure as that between art and non-art. A point to remember, though, is that the development can be seen as following from palaeo-modernist premises without any violent revolutionary stage.

I myself believe that there is a difference between art and joke, while admitting that it has sometimes been a difficult one to establish; and I would want to call 4′ 3″ and Tinguely's famous self-destroying machine ('Homage to New York') jokes, if only because however satisfying they may be, they do not seem sufficient in respect of the needs which what is called art has usually sufficed. But this is to use very inadequate criteria; and having supposed vaguely that neo-modernism was heavily dependent on the extension of modernist *theory*, I was glad to find a philosopher, Arthur Danto,[5] saying this very thing in a sharper way. Danto says the difficulties begin when one forsakes the old mimetic assumptions and says, for example, that a painting of a table is as real as a table. If this seems hard to take when the painting is Post-Impressionist, it becomes easier when the objects painted are strictly inimitable—the numeral 3, for example. Any copy of that simply *is* the numeral 3. What kind of mistake would you be making if you tried to sleep in Rauschenberg's famous *Bed*, which is a bed? You cannot mistake reality for reality. Danto suggests that we use *is*

---

a Heath Robinson was a *Punch* artist who specialized in drawing fanciful machines. Gerald Hoffnung was another *Punch* cartoonist who delighted in organizing musical events of a humorous nature.

in two distinct senses. We say a spot of white paint 'is' Icarus, and also that 'this is a bed'. These two usages are presumably both present when we say that *Bed* is a bed; but if it has paint on it and is in a 'perceiver's space' then the Icarus *is* is dominant.

Actually for Danto the physical location is less important than a sort of intellectual or theoretical space—call it the atmosphere of intellectual assumptions breathed alike by the artist and the game spectator. 'To see something as art requires something the eye cannot descry—an atmosphere of artistic theory, a knowledge of art: an artworld.' But it all comes to the same thing. If Brillo made their boxes out of plywood they would still not be Warhols, and if Andy Warhol made his out of cardboard they would not be Brillo boxes. Provided the 'space' and the aesthetic convention were right he could simply sign a real Brillo box ready-made. We know what it is by where it is, and by our being induced to make the necessary theoretical dispositions (or not, as the case may be). As Jasper Johns puts it, 'What makes an object into art is its introduction into the art context.' Examination question: what is a signed Warhol Brillo box, found among a stack of Brillo boxes in a supermarket? Assuming, of course, that the customer knows the name, and what Mr Warhol does for a living. Another related question is, 'What makes an object into a joke?'

The theory so far is, then, that art is whatever you provide when the place in which you provide it is associated with the idea, and contains people who are prepared to accept this and perhaps other assumptions. Mr Peckham would argue that our failure to have noticed this earlier resulted from persistent brainwashing of the kind that stuck us with the notion that we have a 'rage for order'—that we seek the consolations of form amid natural chaos inhospitable to humans. This in his view is entirely false. We have, on the contrary, a natural rage for *chaos*, and that is why, truth prevailing, the concept of form is dead. With it, of course, dies the notion that the artist has to do with establishing and controlling a formal order in his work (what Keats in ignorance called 'information') and, also, the notion that this order has a high degree of permanence. Of course these notions have at one time or another been challenged before, though perhaps not in their totality. Artists have always known that there was an element of luck in good work ('grace', if you like) and that they rarely knew what they meant till they'd seen what they said; and there are milder traces of a doctrine of impermanence in palaeo-modernism, even in poetry, where Stevens articulates it clearly. But once again neo-modernism presses the point, and gives it practical application.

The most notable instance of this seems to be the neo-modernist *interest in chance*, a long way on from what Pope called 'a grace beyond the reach of art'. Although 'indeterminacy' has affected literature, it has had more importance so far in music and painting, and these are the areas of theoretical inquiry. There is obviously room for teleological differences between artists who employ random methods. Duchamp argued that 'your chance is not the same as my chance', and when he wrote random music insisted on regarding it as personal to himself and also funny. His dislike of order (perhaps as betraying him) emerges in his publishing the notes on *La Mariée mise à nu par ses célibataires, même* ['The Bride Stripped Bare by her Bachelors, Even'] in random order, so anticipating the cut-up-fold-in [William] Burroughs techniques as he had anticipated the methods of aleatory music. Duchamp, incidentally, for all that he anticipated so many innovations, was always aware of a tradition, which he saw himself at the end of; he is a very sophisticated figure, and his critical superiority over some of his imitators is demonstrated by his immediate dismissal of the idea that there could be any relation at all between indeterminacy in the arts and indeterminacy in physics—this covert bid for prestige promotes nothing but confusion, of which (*pace* Peckham) there is quite enough already.

The layman who wants to know what Cage is up to has to confront the whole problem of chance. Without being at all solemn, Cage employs his considerable intellectual resources on constantly changing experiments of which the object is to ensure that his art shall be 'purposeless play'. Not for the first time in musical history, harmony (ideologically associated with ideas of order) had to go; it is replaced by 'duration', as percussion replaces melody. Music now deals in every kind of natural sound (the extreme naturalism of Cage is attributed by Tomkins to the influence of [Ananda K.] Coomaraswamy) but every other kind of sound too, except what might be made by conventional instruments. The piano has bolts between the strings to make it simply percussive. As to indeterminacy, Cage achieves it by many methods, including the use of the Chinese I Ching, coin-tossing, and yarrow-sticks. In one piece every note required 18 tosses of the coin.[6] He has now found speedier methods, using, like Rossini before him, the imperfections in paper as a suggestion for notes.

On this view of the matter there can be no question of judging a particular work. 'There are no catastrophes,' he says. But audiences can of course be affected in different ways, and Cage has experienced wildly various reactions from his auditors. Certainly he sometimes makes it seem that aleatory art is, in a manner as yet unexplored, close to humour, as in the view of some tragedy is close to farce. Tomkins quotes Virgil Thomson's account of a concert given in New York's Town Hall in 1958, which was

> a jolly good row and a good show. What with the same man playing two tubas at once, a trombone player using only his instrument's mouthpiece, a violinist sawing away across his knees, and the soloist David Tudor crawling around on the floor and thumping the piano from below, for all the world like a 1905 motorist, the Town Hall spectacle, as you can imagine, was one of cartoon comedy ... it is doubtful whether any orchestra ever before had so much fun or gave such joyful hilarity to its listeners.

This is very sympathetic, but Cage believes that 'everything is music', and if, out of all the possibilities, he often chooses what makes for hilarity, this is evidence that such an assumption tends to confuse art and joke. There is a current of apocalypticism in all neo-modernism, and it is no bad thing that the Last Days should occasionally be good for a giggle, as they are in Beckett and in Tinguely. 'When seeing a Tinguely mechanism for the first time,' says Mr Tomkins, 'most people burst out laughing.' Peter Selz, the Curator of Painting and Sculpture at the Museum of Modern Art, was delighted with the famous

Homage, which destroyed itself successfully, though not quite in the manner planned by the artist, before a distinguished audience. 'Art hasn't been fun for a long time,' he said. Duchamp congratulated Tinguely on being funny, and said that humour was a thing of great dignity.

It is, no doubt, part of the picture that all this would have been less funny had it gone according to plan. The humour is a matter of chance, of 'aleation'. Aleation in the arts, I suggested, pushes into absurdity a theory based on observation, that chance or grace plays a role in composition. In so far as palaeo-modernism pretended to be classical, it played this down; but between it and neo-modernism stands surrealism, and other manifestations of irrationalism. On the new theory, which has a wild logic, you leave everything to chance, and the result will make its mark either as very natural or as providing the material from which the spectators in the right place will make whatever they need for their own satisfaction. Anything random has some kind of an order, for ex-ample a bag of marbles emptied on to a table. Or, as Monroe Beardsley puts it in that interesting section of his *Aesthetics* from which I have already bor-rowed, 'they are in an order but not in order'. The difference between aleatory art and the art which appealed to 'the logic of imagination' (if for a moment we imagine them both as doctrinally pure) is simply this: the first in theory seeks only to produce an order (and in this it cannot fail) whereas the palaeo-modernists had not reduced grace to chance, and sought to make order.

So far as I can see this would be disastrous to aleatory art were it absolutely true, because the reason why we speak of 'an order' as against 'order' is that we drop the article as a sign of our wish to dignify what interests us more. We have discovered, in the process of getting by amid what Cage thinks of as the wonder-ful complexities of life, that order is more *useful* than an order: for example, the telephone book would be harder to use if the names were printed haphaz-ardly. In a way, the alphabetical arrangement is perfectly arbitrary, but it happens to be something that the people who compose it and the people who use it agree upon. It might, of course, be said to give a very imperfect impression of the chaos and absurdity of metropolitan life, or life at large, and the con-solation of knowing you can find your way about in it is in some ways on some very strict views perhaps somewhat fraudulent. It is not quite 'order', anyway, though it is not merely *an* order. And this in-between order is what most of us mean when we talk about 'order' in aesthetic contexts. One can avoid a divorce between art and life without going to the extremes recommended by Cage. When Cage grew interested in mushrooms he quickly discovered that some knowledge of their botanical classifications was a necessary modification to the practice of eating them at random.[7] Also, that when somebody arranged a hap-pening in his honour, which required that he should be physically assaulted, he had to say that whereas his view was still that 'anything goes', this was so only on condition that one could manage to be free without being foolish. The implied criteria can only derive from the sort of education which distinguishes between an order and order. Order turns out to be more comfortable and useful. If our orientation towards it is not biological, then it is cultural or educational; and the reason why an order posing as order sometimes seems funny is that it is always presupposing orderly criteria by which its randomness can be meas-ured; so, having reduced tradition to absurdity, one makes allusions to tradition by which the absurdity can be enjoyed as such. Thus silent music and Void or all-black painting presuppose music which employs conventional sounds and paintings with colour and shapes. They are piquant allusions to what funda-mentally interests us more than they do, and they could not exist without it.[8]

Aleatory art is accordingly, for all its novelty, an extension of past art, indeed the hypertrophy of one aspect of that art. Virgil Thomson, who has been very sympathetic to Cage, allows that his random music is not really a matter of pure chance but a game of which the rules are established by Cage himself. No matter how much he tries to eliminate his own choices, it is always a Cage-game, and it involves calculation and personal choice. Admirers of William Burroughs' *Nova Express* admit that the randomness of the composition pays off only when the text looks as if it had been composed straightforwardly, with calculated inspiration. The argument is too obvious to labour. Even Du-champ didn't pick up *anything* and sign it. What seems clear is that a gross overdevelopment of the aleatory element in art tends to make it approximate to humour; thus the seventeenth-century conceit, over-extended, became a joke, and Jan Kott can turn *King Lear* into an absurd farce. The transformation would be impossible without the theory and practice of predecessors. Its nihilism is meaningless without an assumption of the plenitude of the past. Thus neo-modernists tend to make the mistake they often scold other people for, which is to attribute too much importance to the art of the period between the Renais-sance and Modernism. By constantly alluding to this as a norm they despise, they are stealthy classicists, as the palaeo-modernists, who constantly alluded to Byzantine and archaic art, were stealthy romantics.

The point that in theory there is nothing very new about the New, that it is in this respect little more than a reverie concerning the more important and self-conscious theoretical developments of an earlier modernism, was made by Harold Rosenberg himself, when he observed that an Oldenburg plastic pie is not so much art, and not so much a pie, as 'a demonstration model in an un-spoken lecture on the history of illusionism', adding that this kind of thing represents the union of many different tendencies in the art of the past half-century. As to why modernism should tend in this way towards pure farce, he cites Marx's observation that farce is the final form of action in a situation which has become untenable. Like Beckett's hero we can't and must go on, so that going on is bound to look absurd, a very old-fashioned thing to be doing in a situation you have shown to be absolutely new. On rather similar grounds he attacks the fashionable 'aesthetics of impermanence', saying that the time-philosophy involved is evidently wrong, and that 'art cannot transform the conditions of its existence'.

Such comment amounts to a radical criticism of the theoretical bases of extreme neo-modernism, and it prepares one for the impact of one of Rosenberg's best essays, so far uncollected, which appeared five years ago in *Partisan Review* under the title 'Literary Form and Social Hallucination'. When the subject is literary, this critic seems to see with great clarity truths which become obscure when the topic is painting. He argues that the form of a literary work militates against its ability to 'tell the truth'; that part of its function is in fact to 'tease us out of thought' (an argument employed, though with differences, by Iris Murdoch). From the political point of view this makes form suspect, anti-liberal; for by inducing us to descend into 'outlived areas of the psyche' it takes our eye off the actual demands and complexities of the world, arms us against the fact. It could perhaps be said that here the criticism is of Form when it ought to be of forms; that the constant researches of the arts into form have as a principal motive the fear that obsolescent *fictions of form* will cause them to be untruthful, or at any rate less truthful than they might be. Thus it is in the popular arts, where the question of fidelity to the world as the clerisy understands it does not arise, that conventions have the longest life. While the highbrows are pondering the *nouveau roman*, the great mass of fiction, which satisfies readers who would never dream of asking that it do more than a token amount of truth-telling, continues to use the old stereotypes.[9] It would probably not occur to the readers of such fiction that truth required the abolition of form. and if it did they might think the point too obvious to mention. Fiction, they know, is different from fact because it is made up. Yet it is precisely this point that, as Rosenberg sees, we need to be reminded of. Theoretical contempt for form in the arts is a fraud.

> Formlessness is simply another look and a temporary one at that. In time, organization begins to show through the most chaotic surface ... the subversion of literary form cannot be established except by literary means, that is, through an effort essentially formal.

This must be true, despite all the recent anti-formalist researches, aleatory, schismatic, and destructive. In neo-, as in palaeo-modernism, research into form is the true means of discovery, even when form is denied existence. So it becomes a real question whether it helps to introduce indeterminacy into the research, even if it is agreed that this is possible to any significant degree (and it is not). With Danto's remarks in mind we can at least ask ourselves whether dependence on an erroneous or distorted theory cannot be in some measure incapacitating. We need not expect a simple answer, since a great deal that is done in the arts is founded on theoretical positions which are later found to be leaky. We should need to reflect that there is a certain prestige to be had in minorities by professing to concur with what appear to be revolutionary advances in thinking about the arts, so that to find an audience claiming proficiency in a 'new' language is at present by no means difficult.

This is not a problem one can discuss now. What one can do is to say of the theoretical bases of neo-modernism, in so far as they show themselves in relation to form, chance, humour, that they are not 'revolutionary'. They are marginal developments of older modernism. It can be added that disparagement and nihilist rejection of the past are founded partly on ignorance and partly on a development of the earlier modernist doctrine which spoke of retrieving rather than of abolishing tradition, just as the abolition of form is a programme founded on the palaeo-modernist programme to give form a new researched look. A certain extremism is characteristic of both phases. Early modernism tended towards fascism, later modernism towards anarchism. What Cyril Connolly[a] calls the evolution of sensibility is a matter of changing theory, Romantic egotism becoming 'impersonality' and this later turning into 'indifference'. In the same way chance replaces the quasi-fortuitous collocation of images characteristic of earlier modernism. The anti-humanism—if Mr Connolly will allow the expression—the anti-humanism of early modernism (anti-intellectualist, authoritarian, eugenicist) gives way to the anti-humanism (hipsterish, free-sexed, anti-intellectualist) of later modernism. As to the past, history continues to be the means by which we recognize what is new as well as what is not. What subverts form is 'an effort essentially formal'; and the sense of standing at an end of time, which is so often invoked as an explanation of difference, is in fact evidence of similarity. The earlier humanism went in a good deal for the capitalization of what Mr Rosenburg calls 'outlived areas of the psyche', and so does the new modernism. For a 'movement' united by a detestation of logic, Modernism has generated an immense amount of theory; this was admittedly much more coherently expressed in the earlier phase. Later it has been scrambled by the babble of smaller voices, and in some aspects has been heavily overdeveloped, as I have tried to show. In both periods there was a natural tendency (inescapable from the Modern at any period and easier to justify half a century back) to exaggerate the differences between what one was doing and what had been done by the old guard, and this has helped to conceal the truth that there has been only one Modernist Revolution, and that it happened a long time ago. So far as I can see there has been little radical change in modernist thinking since then. More muddle, certainly, and almost certainly more jokes, but no revolution, and much less talent.

That is why, on the one hand, one cannot accept Cyril Connolly's assurance that it is virtually all over, and on the other Leslie Fiedler's claim that we have a new art which reflects a social revolution so radical that he can call it a 'mutation' and its proponents 'The New Mutants' (*Partisan Review*, Autumn 1965). Henceforth, he thinks, literature and criticism will forget their traditional observance of the past, and observe the future instead. Pop fiction demonstrates 'a growing sense of the irrelevance of the past' and Pop writers ('post-Modernists') are catching on. The new subject will be 'the end of man' and the transformation of the human life into something else (curious echoes of Mr Connolly, who also thinks of modern writers as post-Modernist in sensibility, and anti-humanist). Mr Fiedler explains that he means by humanism the cult of reason, from Socrates to Freud. This is what is being annihilated, and the Berkeley students were protesting against universities as the transmitters and continuators of the unwanted rationalist tradition. The protest systematically *anti-s* everything: a Teach-in is an *anti*-class, banners inscribed FUCK are *anti*-language, and so on. Actually a teach-in is only an especially interesting class, because the teachers are volunteers and just as engaged with the subject as you

[a] This and other references to Cyril Connolly are to the latter's *The Modern Movement: 100 key books from England, France and America (1880–1950)*, (1965).

are. There is the oddity that this class really works as a 'dialogue' and goes on and on. The banners are no more anti-language than collage is anti-painting; and the absolutely blank banners which succeeded the 'dirty' ones were certainly a very good joke in the new manner, like Rauschenberg erasing a De Kooning, or a Klein Void.

Fiedler's observations on the new life-style of his 'mutants' are more interesting. He stresses a post-Humanist contempt for ideology; a post-Humanist sexuality which has discounted masculinity and developed characteristic patterns of homosexuality, usurpation of female attitudes, polymorphous perversity; and a new range of post-Humanist stimulants (LSD, airplane glue, etc.). This amounts, he argues, to 'a radical metamorphosis of the Western male', a real revolt, unlike our ritual contentions with father. These young people have made the breakthrough into new psychic possibilities, and recognize in Burroughs the laureate of their conquest.[10]

Whether this is nonsense, and whether it is dangerous, is not in my brief. I will only say that the whole argument about 'mutation' is supererogatory; the phenomena should be explained more economically. If the prole has replaced the shepherd, the savage, and the child as pastoral hero, it isn't surprising that those who seek to imitate him should imitate his indifference to ideology and history and sexual orthodoxies. This is not the first recorded instance of libertinage among the well-heeled. Drugs and four-letter words are not new, even among poets, even among the young. The display may seem unusually ostentatious, but it is worth remembering that Fiedler's prime example derives from that highly abnormal institution, the University of California, the unbelievably well-endowed organ of the educational aspirations of a state which is not only very rich but is famous for the unique predominance of the young in its population. In so far as the protest was 'pure' protest, protesting against nothing whatever, it was surely luxurious attitudinizing on a familiar undergraduate model but hypertrophied by sociological causes well within the purview of old-style analysis. A thirst for the unique and unprecedented can lead to the exaggeration of triviality or to claims which the record refutes. Thus Fiedler finds in Ken Kesey's (very good) novel *One Flew Over the Cuckoo's Nest* evidence that for the mutants the schizophrenic has replaced the sage as culture hero, whereas by narrating this madhouse fiction from the point of view of an inmate of limited and varying perceptiveness Kesey is using a now time-honoured technique. So with his sociological observations. Even the male behaviour to be observed after midnight on 32nd and 43rd Streets hardly needs to be explained in terms of 'mutation'. To treat such symptoms as unique, as signs that the Last Days are at hand, is to fall headlong into a very naïve—and historically very well-known—apocalyptism.

It is the constant presence of more or less subtle varieties of apocalyptism that makes possible the repetitive claims for uniqueness and privilege in modernist theorising about the arts. So far as I can see these claims are unjustified. The price to be paid for old-style talk about 'evolving sensibility' is new-style talk about 'mutation'. It is only rarely that one can say there is nothing to worry about, but in this limited respect there appears not to be. Mr

Fiedler professes alarm at the prospect of being a stranded humanist, wandering among unreadable books in a totally new world. But when sensibility has evolved that far there will be no language and no concept of form, so no books. Its possessors will be idiots. However, it will take more than jokes, dice, random shuffling, and smoking pot to achieve this, and in fact very few people seem to be trying. Neo-modernists have examined, in many different ways (many more than I have talked about), various implications in traditional modernism. As a consequence we have, not unusually, some good things, many trivial things, many jokes, much nonsense. Among other things they enable us to see more clearly that certain aspects of earlier modernism really were so revolutionary that we ought not to expect—even with everything so speeded up—to have the pains and pleasures of another comparable movement quite so soon. And by exaggerating and drawing, the neo-modernist does help us to understand rather better what the Modern now is, and has been during this century.

On the whole one has to say that the older modernists understood all this better. Eliot in his last book, tired and unadventurous as it is, said it once again, and said it right: [11]

> A new kind of writing appears, to be greeted at first with disdain and derision; we hear that the tradition has been flouted, and that chaos has come. After a time it appears that the new way of writing is not destructive but re-creative. It is not that we have repudiated the past, as the obstinate enemies —and also the stupidest supporters—of any new movement like to believe; but that we have enlarged our conception of the past; and that in the light of what is new we see the past in a new pattern.

This does not allow for the possibility that chaos and destruction could be introduced into the programme, except by its 'stupidest supporters'; but it does seem to make sense in terms of a quest for 'what will suffice'. In the end what Simone Weil called 'decreation' (easy to confuse with destruction) is the true modernist process in respect of form and the past. Or if it is not we really shall destroy ourselves at some farcical apocalypse.

Notes

1. Robbe-Grillet's collection of essays, *Pour un nouveau roman*, published in 1963, has now been translated, together with the short pieces called *Instances* of the same year, by Barbara Wright (*Snapshots & Towards a New Novel*, Calder).
Robbe-Grillet comes out strongly for the view that art is gratuitous, and from the revolutionary point of view 'useless, if not frankly reactionary'; the fact that it will be on the good side at the barricades must not be allowed to interfere with our freedom to pursue 'art for art's sake'. This book, obviously one of the really important contributions to the theory of the novel, deserves much more discussion than it has yet had in England or the U.S., and the translation is welcome. Incidentally, there is some justice in his claim that it is other people who have *theories* of the novel; his is an anti-theory, so to speak, and for all his 'formalism' that is modern enough.
I should also mention here Anthony Cronin's A *Question of Modernity* (Secker & Warburg) which is somewhat commonplace in the title essay, and often simply bad-tempered, but as to the matter of art and life there are some fine things, including a brilliant long essay on *Ulysses* and one about the novel which is full of original ideas.
2. The phrase is Beckett's. His 'Three Dialogues with George Duthuit' (on Tal Coat,

Masson, and Bram von Velde) have just been published, together with the early Proust essay, by John Calder. They are excellent examples of Beckett's philosophico-farcical manner in the discussion of the arts.

3. 'The Art of Marcel Duchamp', *Art Journal*, xxii, Winter 1962–3.

4. *The Bride and the Bachelors* (London, Weidenfeld; New York, Viking).

5. 'The artworld', *Journal of Philosophy*, lxi, 1964, 571.

6. The process is described at length in Cage's *Silence* (Wesleyan University Press, 1961) pp. 60–1. This beautiful and very pleasant book contains material of great interest to anybody concerned with avant-gardism.

7. See *Silence*, pp. 261–2 for a gastronomic misadventure.

8. The *ought* concealed in Cage's *is* is just that this should not be so, because such an interest is a vestige of the false fictions of order that should die with old technologies. Thus: 'let sounds be themselves rather than vehicles for man-made theories in expressions of human sentiments' (*Silence*, p. 10). And the interest of an all-white painting lies in its shadows, the random change of light upon it.

9. It is obviously in order to meet this situation head-on that Robbe-Grillet makes his fantastic claim to have at last found a novel-form acceptable to the man-in-the-street.

10. It may be worth pointing out that Burroughs himself is far from thinking that drugs will bring this about. His recent *Paris Review* interviewer (Fall '65) asked: 'The visions of drugs and the visions of art don't mix?' and he said, 'Never.... They are absolutely contraindicated for creative work, and I include in the lot alcohol, morphine, barbiturates, tranquillizers....'

11. To *Criticise the Critics* (London, Faber; New York, Farrar, Straus).

Index

(Note: The names of writers represented in the Reader, are printed in caps and small caps, and the page numbers of the contributions in italics. Subject entries are printed in BLOCK CAPITALS. The titles of poems, plays, novels, etc., will be found under the name of the appropriate author.)

675

Index

IMITATION, 5-11, 417-18, 553
IMPERSONALITY, 72-6, 107, 185-7, 565, 574-577, 637
Innis, Harold, 617
INTENTION, 55-6, 70, 108, 116-17, 123, 186-187, 284-5, 334-44, 393
Isidore, St., 444
Izzo, Carlo, 535

Jacobi, Joland, 175
Jakobson, Roman, 545, 646, 648
JAMES, HENRY, 64, 85, 136, 143n., 212, 240, 251, 305, 391, 564-5, 576, 628, 633, 639; *The Ambassadors*, 43-56, 527-44; *Golden Bowl*, 536; *Princess Casamassima*, 539; *Roderick Hudson*, 541
Jammes, Francis, 67 & n.
Jarrell, Randall, 577, 659
Jaspers, Karl, 504
Jebb, Sir Richard, 419
Jeffares, Norman A., 27
Jefferson, Thomas, 348
Jeffrey, 22-3, 26n.
Jenkins, Elizabeth, 268
Johnson, Samuel, 1, 14-16, 23, 25n., 123n., 305, 438 & n., 446, 450, 544n., 557, 595, 622, 624-5, 628, 634; *Rasselas*, 633
Johnston, J. K., 86
Jones, Alun Richard, 92
Jones, David; *Anathemata*, 445
Jones, Ernest, 284-6, 524, 561
Jonson, Ben, 12, 211, 306; *Pan's Anniversary*, 156
Josipovici, Gabriel, 647
Joyce, James, 57, 66-7, 85, 391, 399, 430n., 479n., 480, 484, 508, 610, 615, 622, 627, 633, 641, 656, 661-2, 673; *A Portrait*, 388, 394-5, 572, 587-8, 632; *Dubliners*, 632; *Finnegans Wake*, 398, 620, 643; *Stephen Hero*, 395; *Ulysses*, 89-90, 395-6, 397, 474-5, 477, 572, 587-8, 632
JUNG, CARL GUSTAV, 35, 109, 122, 174-88, 189, 197, 199-200, 290n., 422, 429, 455, 556
Junger, Ernest, 481
Juvenal, 438

Kafka, Franz, 279, 374, 464, 477, 480, 485, 586, 633, 662; *The Castle*, 487, 656; *The Trial*, 487, 656
Kames, Lord, 10, 23, 24n.
Kant, Immanuel, 3, 21, 375-6
Karpman, B., 512, 525n.
Kashkin, I., 248
Kauffman, Stanley, 577n.
Kautsky, Minna, 242
Kazan, Elia, 656
Keast, W. R., 25n.
Keats, John, 20, 95, 99, 113, 151, 207-9, 337n., 349-50, 352, 358n., 426, 565, 577n., 666; *Eve of St Agnes*, 208, 453n.; *Grecian Urn*, 208, 302; *Hyperion*, 210, 450; *La Belle Dame Sans Merci*, 205 & n., 207; *Nightingale*, 75, 207
Keble, John, 23, 25n.
Kenner, Hugh, 58
Ker, W. P., 24n., 83

KERMODE, FRANK, 241, 253, 442, 454-5, 466, 474, 497, 652, 661-74
Kerr, Alfred, 482
Kesey, Ken, 672
Keynes, Maynard, 85
Kierkegaard, Soren, 481, 564
Kipling, Rudyard, 462, 642
KNIGHT, G. WILSON, 158-173, 386, 401, 427, 572
KNIGHTS, L. C., 211-26, 262, 621, 630
Knox, George, 544n.
Koeppen, Wolfgang, 480
Koestler, Arthur, 567
Korzybski, Count, 346
Kott, Jean, 669
Kraus, Karl, 637, 643
Krieger, Murray, 422
Krook, Dorothea, 534

La Fayette, Mme de., 471; *La Princesse de Clèves*, 467 & n.
Laforgue, Jules, 67
Lamartine, Alphonse de, 95
Lamb, Charles, 212, 282-3, 496
La Rochefoucauld, Francois, 222
La Rochelle, Drieu, 384
Laski, Harold, 361, 365
Lassalle, Ferdinand, 242
Lauter, Paul, 578n.
LAWRENCE, D. H., 85, 111, 121-35, 139 & n., 174, 204, 351, 386, 392, 396, 399-400, 454-455, 462, 464, 511, 581-2, 625, 631, 633, 641, 656-7; *Lady Chatterley*, 573-4; *Rainbow*, 584, 629; *Sons and Lovers*, 393-4; *Women in Love*, 574, 628, 634
Lawrence, T. E., 202
Leach, Edmund, 546
Leavis, F. R., 70, 121, 211, 262, 291, 580, 610, 621-35
Leavis, Q. D., 211, 575, 635n.
Lee, Irving, 346, 348
Leggett, H. W., 572, 578n.
Legman, Gershon, 455
Leibnitz, Gottfried Wilhelm, 350, 612-13, 615
Lemon, Lee T., 290
Lenin, Vladimir Ilyich, 243-5, 247, 250, 252
Leonardo, da Vinci, 283
Lesage, René, 53 & n.
Lessing, Gotthold, 9-10, 24n., 553, 622 & n.
LÉVI-STRAUSS, CLAUDE, 175, 401, 422, 545-50, 621, 646
LEWIS, C. S., 22n., 315, 334, 349, 356, 442-53, 551, 593, 629
Lewis, Sinclair, 386
Lewis, Wyndham, 57, 66-7, 664
Lichtheim, George, 473-4
Lindsay, W. M., 452n.
Linklater, Eric, 263
L'Isle-Adam, Villiers de, 33 & n.
Locke, John, 16, 214, 603, 618
Lodge, David, 528, 565
Lodge, Thomas, 310
Longinus, 336 & n., 350-2
Lovejoy, A. O., 559, 563n., 600, 608n.
Lowell, James Russell, 191, 201n.